W9-ALW-882

The Oxford Companion to Shakespeare

The Oxford Companion to SHAKESPEARE

General Editor
Michael Dobson

Associate General Editor
Stanley Wells

UNIVERSITY PRESS

OXFORD
UNIVERSITY PRESS

Great Clarendon Street, Oxford OX2 6DP

Oxford University Press is a department of the University of Oxford.
It furthers the University's objective of excellence in research, scholarship,
and education by publishing worldwide in

Oxford New York
Athens Auckland Bangkok Bogotá Buenos Aires Cape Town
Chennai Dar es Salaam Delhi Florence Hong Kong Istanbul Karachi
Kolcutta Kuala Lumpur Madrid Melbourne Mexico City Mumbai Nairobi
Paris São Paulo Singapore Taipei Tokyo Toronto Warsaw

with associated companies in Berlin Ibadan

Oxford is a registered trade mark of Oxford University Press
in the UK and in certain other countries

Published in the United States
by Oxford University Press Inc., New York

First published 2001

British Library Cataloguing in Publication Data
Data available

Library of Congress Cataloging in Publication Data
Data available

ISBN 0-19-811735-3

1 3 5 7 9 10 8 6 4 2

Typeset in Adobe Garamond
by Alliance Phototypesetters, Pondicherry, India
Printed by Giunti Industrie Grafiche
Prato, Italy

Contents

Preface vii
Acknowledgements viii
Contributors ix
Thematic listing of entries xi
List of plays xxviii
Note to the reader xxix
THE OXFORD COMPANION TO SHAKESPEARE 1
The British Isles and France in the English Histories and *Macbeth* 530
The royal family in Shakespeare's English Histories 532
Shakespeare's life, works, and reception: a partial chronology 533
Further reading 537
Picture acknowledgements 541

Preface

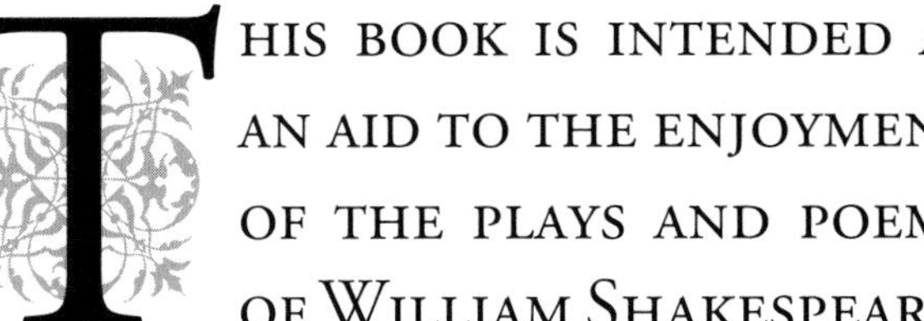

THIS BOOK IS INTENDED AS AN AID TO THE ENJOYMENT OF THE PLAYS AND POEMS OF WILLIAM SHAKESPEARE, a writer, actor, and man of the theatre who lived from 1564 to 1616. In pursuit of this objective, it hopes to contribute to a better understanding of the place occupied by his writings both in the Elizabethan and Jacobean era in which they were composed and in the many subsequent periods in which they have been read, performed, and reinterpreted. In so far as the two aims are separable, *The Oxford Companion to Shakespeare* is designed primarily to inform readers about Shakespeare's works, times, lives, and afterlives rather than to interpret them, so we have preferred to balance its composition in favour of short, informative entries as against chapter-length meditations on large topics. A map of the coverage which these entries offer of the many different fields of knowledge which the word 'Shakespeare' has come to include—biography, theatre history, printing and publishing, criticism, translation, and so on—is provided by the Thematic Listing of Entries.

Shakespeare and his canon have come to be so central to anglophone culture over the last four centuries that the category of knowledge about them might easily be extended indefinitely in almost any direction, and any readers hoping, for example, that this book will describe the whole of Western cultural history prior to Shakespeare as a background to his achievement and the whole of literary history since as an index to his influence are bound to be disappointed. Nor does it offer a glossary to all the now unfamiliar words in Shakespeare's vocabulary, nor a family tree of his entire clan (although it does offer entries on all of Shakespeare's characters, with the exception of those who, like Hamlet and Othello, are both eponymous and fictitious, who are covered as part of the entries describing the plays to which they give their names). With a mere half-million words at our disposal we have of course had to be selective, and we hope that readers will concur in the often difficult decisions we have had to make about the relative space to be apportioned between, for example, the literary sources, the original performances, and the subsequent worldwide reception of Shakespeare's plays. Selective as it is, however, we hope that this volume reflects something of the breadth of present-day Shakespearian studies, a diversity of opinions as well as scope which we have not attempted to iron out. Our wide range of contributors, who are in no way answerable for one another's views, can be identified by initials appended to each entry. Cross-references are marked by an asterisk, but, since there are separate entries on all Shakespeare's works and all his characters, we have generally refrained from asterisking their titles and names except under special circumstances.

As an Oxford Companion, this book is appropriately geared to the Oxford Shakespeare, specifically the modern-spelling edition of the Complete Works published under the general editorship of Stanley Wells and Gary Taylor in 1986 (and subsequently used as the basis of the Norton Shakespeare, published under the editorship of Stephen Greenblatt in 1997). All scene and line references are to this text of Shakespeare's works, and accounts of the dating and of the textual histories of individual works are in broad conformity with its complementary volume *William Shakespeare: A Textual Companion* (Wells, Taylor, et al., 1987). The Oxford edition is notable for, among many other things, a scrupulous return, as far as is possible, to the texts of Shakespeare's plays as they were produced in Shakespeare's theatre: in place of the standardized titles of some of the history plays imposed after Shakespeare's death by the editors of the First Folio, for example, it returns to the titles under which Shakespeare composed them. Wherever these titles might be unfamiliar, we have added the Folio titles in brackets, and have of course supplied appropriate cross-references: hence a reader looking up *Henry VIII* will be referred to the entry describing the play under its original name, *All Is True*, and references to the third of Shakespeare's plays to be set in the reign of Henry VI call it *Richard, Duke of York (3 Henry VI)*. The Oxford edition is notable, too, for the consistency with which it modernizes Shakespeare's spellings, including those of foreign names, so that readers looking up the characters 'Iachimo' and 'Petruchio' will be referred to Giacomo and Petruccio, the forms also used here in the entries describing *Cymbeline* and *The Taming of the Shrew* respectively. In outlining the stage histories of such roles, however, we have retained the names by which different performers actually knew them: hence in describing the plot of *Cymbeline* we have called the play's heroine Innogen (as did Shakespeare, despite the Folio's posthumous printing error to the contrary), but in summarizing the career of one of her most notable impersonators, the Victorian actress Ellen

Terry, we have called her Imogen (as did Terry and her contemporaries).

Entries on individual plays supply an account of their place in the chronology of Shakespeare's works, a brief discussion of their early texts and their provenance, a short account of their literary and dramatic sources and how they treat them, and a scene-by-scene synopsis. (These synopses are designed solely to aid readers in finding scenes in the play, rather than as attempts to provide narrative equivalents for the play's own effects; as an antidote to the potentially misleading impressions such plot summaries can give, each is followed by a very short account of the play's most distinctive artistic features. Any scene-by-scene synopsis of *Hamlet*, for example, is liable to make the play seem a good deal more busy and plot-centred than it ever does in performance, and it seems only fair to record that it is in fact as notable for meditative soliloquies as it is for crowded action.) The synopsis is followed by summaries of the play's critical reception, its performance history, and its fortunes in the cinema and on television, and then by a very short and selective reading list including recent important single-play editions. With limited space at our disposal, we have had to be especially selective in discussing the stage histories of these endlessly revived plays, and given that this is an Oxford Companion to Shakespeare—published in the city through which Shakespeare himself passed between the town of his birth and the city of his career—we hope we may be forgiven for betraying some small bias in favour of the theatres found at the two destinations between which Shakespeare commuted, London and Stratford-upon-Avon.

Michael Dobson
Stanley Wells
April 2001

Acknowledgements

No book this size can come into being without a good deal of help. I am very happy to acknowledge various kinds of assistance from the following: the University of Illinois at Chicago Center for the Humanities; the University of Surrey Roehampton; Professor Lois Potter; Professor Marcia Pointon; Dr José Roberto O'Shea and Dr Márcia A. P. Martins (who helped Margarida Rauen with the Brazilian entry); Alison Jones, Joanna Harris, and Wendy Tuckey at OUP; Edwin and Jackie Pritchard, patient copy-editors. At Roehampton Anne Button provided tireless administrative assistance, helped for one short but crucial period by Mauritza Roach. To venture beyond the category of help, Stanley Wells has been a wonderful Associate General Editor, and working with him has been, as always, an inspiration and a pleasure. The support of Nicola Watson, including her expertise in the matter of food and drink, has been invaluable. It seems only appropriate, in a book about a writer who found it necessary to flee to London to get some writing done after the birth of his own twins, that I should conclude by acknowledging the crucial role that has been played by Elizabeth and Rosalind, who made the completion of this book both necessary and at times almost impossible, and who continually remind me that whatever great things Shakespeare achieved he may have missed out on some greater ones.

Michael Dobson

Contributors

AB	Anne Button, University of Surrey Roehampton
ABr	Alan Brissenden, University of Adelaide
AC	Alice Clark, Université de Nantes
AD	Anthony Davies, Victoria College, Jersey
AL	Ania Loomba, University of Illinois at Urbana
ALP	A. Luis Pujante, Universidad de Murcia
AM	Andrew Murphy, St Andrews University
AMM	Alfredo Michel Modenessi, Universidad Nacional Autónoma de México
AO	Arkady Ostrovsky, *Financial Times*
BE	Barbara Everett, Somerville College, Oxford
BEn	Balz Engler, University of Basel
BK	Bernice Kliman, Nassau Community College, New York
BR	Bradley Ryner, University of Maryland
BS	Boika Sokolova, Royal Holloway and Bedford New College, University of London
CB	Chris Baldick, Goldsmiths College, University of London
CC	Charity Charity, J. Walter Thompson Advertising
CMSA	Catherine Alexander, Shakespeare Birthplace Trust
CS	Cathy Shrank, University of Aberdeen
CT	Catherine Tite, University of Manchester
DB	Douglas Bruster, University of Texas at Austin
DK	Dennis Kennedy, Trinity College, Dublin
DL	Douglas Lanier, University of New Hampshire
DP	Diane Purkiss, Keble College, Oxford
ER	Eric Rasmussen, University of Nevada
GE	Gabriel Egan, Globe Education, Shakespeare's Globe
GI	Grace Ioppolo, Reading University
GTW	George T. Wright, University of Minnesota
HG	Hugh Grady, Beaver College
HQX	Qixin He, Beijing Foreign Studies University
HS	Hannah Scolnikov, Tel Aviv University
HV	Helen Vendler, Harvard University
IBC	Irena Cholij, *New Grove Dictionary of Music*
IM	Irene Makaryk, University of Ottawa
I-SE	Inga-Stina Ewbank, University of Leeds
ISG	Isabelle Schwartz-Gastine, Université de Caen
JB	Jeremy Barlow, MA, ARCM, ARAM
JBn	Jerry Brotton, Royal Holloway and Bedford New College, University of London
JBt	Jonathan Bate, University of Liverpool
JC	Jean Chothia, Selwyn College, Cambridge
JH	Jonathan Hope, Middlesex University
JKS	Jane Kingsley-Smith, University of Hull
JL	Jerzy Limon, University of Gdańsk
JM	Jean Marsden, University of Connecticut
J-MM	Jean-Marie Maguin, Université de Montpellier
JS	James Shapiro, Columbia University
KC	Kate Chedgzoy, University of Newcastle
KN	Kate Newman, Courtauld Institute
KP	Kenneth Parker, University of East London
KS	Kay Stanton, California State University, Fullerton
MB	Michael Bristol, McGill University
MD	Michael Dobson, University of Surrey Roehampton
MG	Margreta de Grazia, University of Pennsylvania
MH	Michael Holroyd
MHn	Mark Houlahan, University of Waikato
MJ	Michael Jamieson, University of Sussex
MLW	Marcus Walsh, University of Birmingham
MM	Mairi MacDonald, Shakespeare Birthplace Trust
MN	Michael Neill, University of Auckland
MO	Martin Orkin, University of Haifa
MP	Maurice Pope
MR	Margarida Gandara Rauen, Faculdade de Artes de Parana, Curitiba
MS	Marvin Spevack, University of Münster
MTB	Mark Thornton Burnett, Queen's University, Belfast
MW	Martin Wiggins, Shakespeare Institute, University of Birmingham
NJW	Nicola Watson, The Open University
OB	Odette Blumenfeld, Al Cusa University, Tasi
PH	Park Honan, University of Leeds
PHm	Peter Hulme, University of Essex
PK	Panos Karagiorgos, Ionian University, Corfu
PME	Paul Edmondson, Shakespeare Institute, University of Birmingham
PP	Paola Pugliatti, University of Florence
RAF	R. A. Foakes, University of California, Los Angeles
RB	Robert Bearman, Shakespeare Birthplace Trust
RD	Rafiq Darragi, University of Tunis
RF	Richard Foulkes, University of Leicester

CONTRIBUTORS

RG Rex Gibson, Cambridge Institute of Education
RJ Richard Johns, Courtauld Institute
RLS Robert Smallwood, Shakespeare Birthplace Trust
RM Robert Maslen, Glasgow University
RS Robert Shaughnessy, University of Surrey Roehampton
RSB Simon Blatherwick, Museum of London
RW René Weis, University College, London
RWFM Randall Martin, University of New Brunswick
SLB Susan Brock, Shakespeare Birthplace Trust
SM Sonia Massai, St Mary's, Strawberry Hill, University of Surrey
SO Stephen Orgel, Stanford University
SS Steve Sohmer, Lincoln College, Oxford
SW Stanley Wells, Shakespeare Birthplace Trust and University of Birmingham
TH Ton Hoenselaars, Rijksuniversiteit, Utrecht
TK Tetsuo Kishi, Kyoto University
TM Tom Matheson, Shakespeare Institute, University of Birmingham
VS Vivian Salmon, Keble College, Oxford
WH Werner Habicht, Universität Würzburg
WR Wolfgang Riehle, Karl-Franzens Universität, Graz
YH Younglim Han, Chungwoon University, Korea
ZM Zoltan Markus, New York University
ZS Zdeněk Stříbrný, Charles University, Prague

Thematic listing of entries

Longer, more discursive entries are listed first within each sub-heading.

BIOGRAPHY

biographies of Shakespeare

Shakespeare and his family

Shakespeare, William
Stratford-upon-Avon
education

Arden, Mary
arms, Shakespeare's coat of
Bagley, Edward
Belott-Mountjoy suit
Bernard, Sir John
crabtree, Shakespeare's
epitaph, Shakespeare's
grave, Shakespeare's
Hall, Elizabeth
Hall, John
Hart, William
highways subscription
Impresa
'lost years'
Quiney, Thomas
Shakeshaft, William
Shakespeare, Agnes/Anne
Shakespeare, Anne
Shakespeare as a surname
Shakespeare, Edmund
Shakespeare, Gilbert
Shakespeare, Hamnet
Shakespeare, Henry
Shakespeare, Joan (i and ii)
Shakespeare, John
Shakespeare, Judith
Shakespeare, Margaret
Shakespeare, Richard
Shakespeare, Susanna
signatures
Welcombe enclosure
will, Shakespeare's
Willobie his Avisa

Stratford acquaintances and contemporaries

Addenbrooke, John
Aspinall, Alexander
Bretchgirdle, John
Clopton family
Collins, Francis
Combe family
Cottom, John
Greene, John and Thomas
Hamlett, Katherine
Harvard, John
Hathaway, Anne
Hunt, Simon
Jenkins, Thomas
Johnson, Robert
Lambert, Edmund
Lane, John
Lucy, Sir Thomas
Nash, Anthony and John
Nash, Thomas
Quiney, Richard
Reynolds, William
Roche, Walter
Rogers, Philip
Russell, Thomas
Sadler, Hamnet and Judith
Shaw, July
Sturley (Strelly), Abraham
Tyler, Richard
Underhill, William
Walker, William
Whately, Anne
Whittington, Thomas

Stratford places, buildings, and residences

Stratford-upon-Avon

Anne Hathaway's Cottage
Arden
Asbies
Aston Cantlow
Barton-on-the-Heath
Bidford
Birthplace
Budbrooke
Chapel Lane Cottage
Charlecote
Clifford Chambers
Clopton
Davenport, James
Dowdall, John
Dursley
fires in Stratford-upon-Avon
Fulbrook
grammar school
Greene, Joseph
Guild Chapel
Hall's Croft
Hampton Lucy
Henley Street
Holy Trinity Church
Ingon
Jordan, John
Kenilworth
Luddington
Lyance
Maidenhead Inn (Woolshop)
Mary Arden's House
New Place
Old Stratford
Payton, Mr
Rowington
Shakespeare's grave
Snitterfield
Stratford-upon-Avon, Elizabethan, and the theatre
Temple Grafton
Ward, John
Warwick
Welcombe
Wilmcote
Wincot
Wroxall

London acquaintances and contemporaries, excluding literary and theatrical

Andrewes, Robert
Atkinson, William
Belott-Mountjoy suit
Clayton, John
'Dark Lady'
Dethick, Sir William
'Fair Youth'
Gardiner, William
'Hughes, William'
Jackson, John
Mr W.H.
Pembroke, Henry Herbert, 2nd Earl of
Pembroke, Mary Herbert, Countess of
Pembroke, Philip Herbert, 4th Earl of
Pembroke, William Herbert, 3rd Earl of
'Rival Poet'
Savage, Thomas
School of Night
Southampton, Henry Wriothesley, 3rd Earl of
Walker, Henry
Witter, John

London residences and haunts, excluding theatres

Belott-Mountjoy suit
Blackfriars Gatehouse
Mermaid Tavern

Portraits and sculptures, including spurious, before 1700

portraits

Ashbourne (Kingston) Portrait
Burdett-Coutts Portrait
Chandos Portrait
death mask
Droeshout engraving
Ely Palace Portrait
Faithorne, William, engraving
Felton portrait
Flower portrait
Hilliard miniature
Janssen bust
Kneller, Sir Godfrey
Soest portrait
Zuccaro, Federico

THE SHAKESPEARE LEGEND

Authorship controversy, hoaxes, and aspects of bardolatry

authorship controversy

advertising
Bacon, Delia
Baconian theory
Bard
bardolatry
birthday celebrations
Chalmers, George
Chetwood, William Rufus
Defoe theory
Derby theory
Elizabeth theory
Fenton, Richard
forgery
Gastrell, Francis
James I theory
Jubilee
King James' Bible
Lefranc, Abel
Marlovian theory
monuments
mulberry tree
Oxford theory
poems on Shakespeare
popular culture
portraits
Rutland theory
Salom, Jaime
schools, Shakespeare in (British)
Shakespeare, William, as a literary character
Shakespeare Tercentenary Festival
Shakespeariana
statuary

SHAKESPEARE'S WORKS

Comedies

All's Well That Ends Well
As You Like It
The Comedy of Errors
Cymbeline
Love's Labour's Lost
Measure for Measure
The Merchant of Venice
The Merry Wives of Windsor
A Midsummer Night's Dream
Much Ado About Nothing
Pericles
The Taming of the Shrew
The Tempest
Twelfth Night
The Two Gentlemen of Verona
The Two Noble Kinsmen
The Winter's Tale

Histories

All Is True (*Henry VIII*)
The First Part of the Contention (*2 Henry VI*)
1 Henry IV
2 Henry IV
Henry V
1 Henry VI
King John
Richard Duke of York (*3 Henry VI*)
Richard II
Richard III

Tragedies

Antony and Cleopatra
Coriolanus
Hamlet
Julius Caesar
King Lear
Macbeth
Othello
Romeo and Juliet
Timon of Athens
Titus Andronicus
Troilus and Cressida

Lost plays

Cardenio
Love's Labour's Won

Collaborative works and their co-authors

All Is True (*Henry VIII*)
Cardenio
Chettle, Henry
Dekker, Thomas
Fletcher, John
1 Henry VI
Heywood, Thomas
Macbeth
Middleton, Thomas
Munday, Anthony
Nashe, Thomas
Pericles
Sir Thomas More
Timon of Athens
The Two Noble Kinsmen
Wilkins, George

Apocryphal plays

apocrypha
Arden of Feversham
The Birth of Merlin
Duke Humfrey
Edmund Ironside
Edward III
Edward IV
Fair Em
Hoffman
Locrine
The London Prodigal
The Merry Devil of Edmonton
Moseley, Humphrey
Mucedorus
The Puritan
The Second Maiden's Tragedy
Sir John Oldcastle (*Part One*)
The Taming of a Shrew
Thomas, Lord Cromwell
The Troublesome Reign of King John
The Yorkshire Tragedy

Principal characters in the plays

(Information on characters who have their names in the titles can be found in entries on individual plays. Modern equivalents of foreign names have been used, as in the Oxford Complete Works modern spelling edition.)

***All Is True* (*Henry VIII*)**
Abergavennny, Lord
Boleyn, Anne
Brandon
Buckingham, Duke of
Butts, Doctor
Caputius, Lord
Campeius, Cardinal
Cromwell, Thomas
Cranmer, Archbishop of Canterbury
Denny, Sir Anthony
Ely, Bishop of
Gardiner
Griffith
Guildford, Sir Henry
Henry VIII
Katherine, Queen
Lincoln, Bishop of
London, Lord Mayor of
Lord Chamberlain
Lord Chancellor
Lovell, Sir Thomas
Norfolk, Duke of
Old Lady, an
Page, Gardiner's
Patience
Porter, a
Sands, Lord
Suffolk, Duke of
Surrey, Earl of
Surveyor, Buckingham's
Vaux, Sir Nicholas
Wolsey, Cardinal

All's Well That Ends Well

Austringer, an
Bertram
Diana
Florence, Duke of
France, King of
Helen
Lafeu
Lavatch
Lord Dumain, First and Second
Mariana
Paroles
Reynaldo
Roussillon, Dowager Countess of
Widow Capilet

Antony and Cleopatra

Agrippa
Alexas
Ambassador, an
Antony, Mark
Caesar, Octavius
Camidius
Charmian
Cleopatra
Clown, a
Decretas
Demetrius
Diomed
Dolabella
Enobarbus
Eros
Gallus
Iras
Maecenas
Mardian
Menas
Menecrates
Octavia
Philo
Pompey, Sextus
Proculeius
Scarus
Seleucus
Silius
Soothsayer, a
Taurus
Thidias
Varrus
Ventidius

As You Like It

Adam
Amiens
Audrey
Celia
Charles
Corin
Denis
Frederick, Duke
Hymen
Jaques
Jaques (de Bois)
Le Beau
Martext, Sir Oliver
Oliver
Orlando
Pages, Two
Phoebe
Rosalind
Senior, Duke
Silvius
Touchstone
William

The Comedy of Errors

Adriana
Angelo
Antipholus of Ephesus
Antipholus of Syracuse
Balthasar
Dromio of Ephesus
Dromio of Syracuse
Egeon
Emilia
Jailer, a
Luciana
Nell
Pinch, Doctor
Solinus, Duke of Ephesus

Coriolanus

Adrian
Aediles
Aufidius, Tullus
Brutus, Junius
Cominius
Conspirators
Herald, a
Lartius, Titus
Martius, Caius (afterwards Coriolanus)
Martius, Young
Menenius Agrippa
Nicanor
Valeria
Virgilia
Volumnia

Cymbeline

Arviragus
Belarius
Captain, a Roman
Captains, two British
Cloten
Cornelius
Cymbeline, King
Filario
Ghosts of Posthumus's brothers
Ghost of Posthumus's mother
Ghost of Sicilius Leonatus
Giacomo
Guiderius
Helen
Innogen
Jailers, two
Jupiter
Lord, a Briton
Lords, two
Lucius, Caius
Pisanio
Posthumus Leonatus
Queen
Senators, two Roman
Soothsayer, a
Tribunes, Roman

The First Part of the Contention (2 Henry VI)

Asnath
Beadle
Beaufort, Cardinal
Bolingbroke, Roger
Buckingham, Duke of
Butcher, Dick the
Cade, Jack
Captain of a ship
Clerk of Chatham, the
Clifford, Old Lord
Clifford, Young
Edward, Earl of March
Gloucester, Humphrey, Duke of
Gloucester, Duchess of
Gough, Matthew
Henry VI, King
Herald, a
Horner, Thomas
Hume, Sir John
Iden, Alexander
Jordan, Margery
Margaret, Queen
Master of a ship
Master's mate
Mayor of Saint Albans
Murderers, two
Richard, Crookback
Salisbury, Earl of
Saye, Lord
Scales, Lord
Simpcox, Simon
Simpcox's wife
Somerset, Duke of
Southwell, John
Stafford, Sir Humphrey
Stafford's brother
Stanley, Sir John
Suffolk, Marquis, later Duke of
Thump, Peter
Vaux
Warwick, Earl of
Weaver, Smith the
Whitmore, Walter
York, Duke of

Hamlet

Ambassadors from England
Barnardo
Captain, a
Claudius, King
Clowns, two
Cornelius
Fortinbras
Francisco
Gertrude, Queen
Ghost of Hamlet (late king)
Guildenstern
Hamlet
Horatio
Laertes
Marcellus
Ophelia
Osric
Players

Polonius
Priest, a
Reynaldo
Rosencrantz
Valtemand

1 Henry IV

Blunt, Sir Walter
Carriers, two
Chamberlain
Douglas, Earl of
Francis
Gadshill
Glyndŵr, Owain
Harry, Prince
Harvey
Henry IV, King
Hotspur
John of Lancaster, Prince
Michael, Sir
Mortimer, Lord Edmund
Mortimer, Lady
Northumberland, Earl of
Oldcastle, Sir John
Percy, Lady
Poins
Quickly, Mistress
Russell
Travellers
Vernon, Sir Richard
Westmorland, Earl of
Worcester, Earl of
York, Archbishop (Scrope) of

2 Henry IV

Bardolph
Bardolph, Lord
Blunt, Sir John
Bullcalf
Clarence, Thomas, Duke of
Coleville, Sir John
Davy
Epilogue
Falstaff, Sir John
Fang
Feeble
Gloucester, Humphrey, Duke of
Gower
Harcourt
Harry, Prince
Hastings, Lord
Henry IV, King
John of Lancaster, Prince
Lord Chief Justice
Mouldy
Mowbray, Lord Thomas
Northumberland, Lady
Northumberland, Lord
Page, Falstaff's
Peto
Pistol
Poins
Porter, a
Quickly, Mistress
Rumour
Shadow, Simon
Shallow, Robert
Silence
Snare
Surrey, Earl of
Tearsheet, Doll
Travers
Wart, Thomas
Warwick, Earl of
Westmorland, Earl of
York, Archbishop (Scrope) of

Henry V

Alice
Ambassadors, French
Bardolph
Bates, John
Berri, Duke of
Bourbon, Duke of
Boy, a
Burgundy, Duke of
Cambridge, Earl of
Canterbury, Archbishop of
Catherine
Charles VI of France, King
Clarence, Duke of
Constable of France
Court, Alexander
Dauphin, the
Ely, Bishop of
Erpingham, Sir Thomas
Exeter, Duke of
Fluellen, Captain
Gloucester, Duke of
Governor of Harfleur
Gower, Captain
Grandpré, Lord
Grey, Sir Thomas
Harry, King (Henry V)
Herald, a
Hostess (formerly Mistress Quickly)
Isabel, Queen
Jamy, Captain
Macmorris, Captain
Montjoy
Nim
Orléans, Duke of
Pistol
Rambures, Lord
Salisbury, Earl of
Scrope, Lord Henry
Warwick, Earl of
Westmorland, Earl of
Williams, Michael
York, Duke of

1 Henry VI

Alençon, Duke of
Auvergne, Countess of
Basset
Bastard of Orléans
Bedford, Duke of
Burgundy, Duke of
Charles, Dauphin of France
Exeter, Duke of
Fastolf, Sir John
Gargrave, Sir Thomas
Glasdale, Sir William
Gloucester, Duke of
Henry VI, King
Joan la Pucelle
Lucy, Sir William
Margaret of Anjou
Master Gunner of Orléans/his son
Mayor of London
Mortimer, Edmund
Plantagenet, Richard (later Duke of York)
René, Duke of Anjou, King of Naples
Salisbury, Earl of
Shepherd, a
Somerset, Duke of
Suffolk, Earl of
Talbot, Lord
Vernon
Warwick, Earl of
Winchester, Bishop of (later Cardinal)
Woodville

Julius Caesar

Antony
Artemidorus
Brutus
Caesar, Julius
Calpurnia
Casca
Cassius
Cato, young
Cicero
Cinna the conspirator
Cinna the poet
Claudio
Clitus
Dardanius
Decius
Flavius
Ghost of Caesar
Lepidus
Ligarius
Lucillius
Lucius
Messala
Metellus
Murellus
Octavius
Pindarus
Poet, a
Popilius
Portia
Publius
Soothsayer, a
Strato
Titinius
Trebonius
Varrus
Volumnius

King John

Arthur
Austria, Duke of
Bastard, Phillip the
Bigot, Lord
Blanche, Lady

Châtillon
Citizen of Angers
Constance, Lady
Eleanor, Queen
Essex, Earl of
Falconbridge, Lady
Falconbridge, Robert
Gurney, James
Henry, Prince
Hubert
John, King
Louis the Dauphin
Melun, Count
Pandolf, Cardinal
Pembroke, Earl of
Peter of Pomfret
Phillip, King of France
Salisbury, Earl of

King Lear

Albany, Duke of
Burgundy, Duke of
Cordelia
Cornwall, Duke of
Curan
Edgar
Edmond
Fool, Lear's
France, King of
Gloucester, Earl of
Goneril
Herald, a
Kent, Earl of
Lear, King
Oswald
Regan
Servant, Cornwall's

Love's Labour's Lost

Armado, Don Adriano de
Biron
Boyet
Catherine
Costard
Dull, Anthony
Dumaine
France, Princess of
Holofernes
Jaquenetta
Longueville
Lords, two
Maria
Mercadé
Mote
Nathaniel, Sir
Navarre, King of, Ferdinand
Rosaline

Macbeth

Angus
Apparitions, three
Banquo
Caithness
Doctor of Physic, a
Doctor, an English
Donalbain
Duncan, King of Scotland
Fleance
Hecate
Lennox
Macbeth
Macbeth, Lady
Macduff
Macduff, Lady
Malcolm
Menteith
Murderers, three
Porter, a
Ross
Seyton
Siward
Siward, Young
Witches, three

Measure for Measure

Abhorson
Angelo
Barnardine
Claudio
Elbow
Escalus
Francesca
Friar Peter
Froth
Isabella
Juliet
Lucio
Mariana
Overdone, Mistress
Pompey
Provost, a
Varrius
Vincentio, Duke of Vienna

The Merchant of Venice

Antonio
Aragon, Prince of
Balthasar
Bassanio
Gobbo
Graziano
Jessica
Lancelot
Leonardo
Lorenzo
Morocco, Prince of
Nerissa
Portia
Salerio
Shylock
Solanio
Stefano
Tubal
Venice, Duke of

The Merry Wives of Windsor

Bardolph
Caius, Doctor
Evans, Sir Hugh
Falstaff, Sir John
Fenton, Master
Ford, Master Frank
Ford, Mistress Alice
Host of the Garter Inn
John
Nim
Page, Anne
Page, Master George
Page, Mistress Margaret
Page, William
Pistol
Quickly, Mistress
Robert
Robin
Rugby, John
Shallow, Robert
Simple, Peter
Slender, Master Abraham

A Midsummer Night's Dream

Bottom, Nick
Cobweb
Demetrius
Egeus
Fairy
Flute, Francis
Goodfellow, Robin
Helena
Hermia
Hippolyta
Lysander
Mote
Mustardseed
Oberon
Peaseblossom
Philostrate
Quince, Peter
Snout, Tom
Snug
Starveling, Robin
Theseus
Titania

Much Ado About Nothing

Antonio
Balthasar
Beatrice
Benedick
Borachio
Boy, a
Claudio
Conrad
Dogberry
Friar Francis
Hero
John, Don
Leonato
Margaret
Pedro, Don
Sexton, a
Ursula
Verges

Othello

Bianca
Brabanzio
Cassio
Clown, a
Desdemona
Emilia
Graziano
Herald, a
Iago
Lodovico
Montano
Othello

Roderigo
Senators
Venice, Duke of

Pericles
Aeschines
Antiochus
Antiochus's daughter
Bawd, a
Boult
Cerimon
Cleon
Diana
Dioniza
Fishermen, three
Gower, John
Helicanus
Knights, five
Leonine
Lychorida
Lysimachus
Marina
Marshal, a
Pander, a
Pericles
Philemon
Simonides, King
Thaisa
Thaliart

Richard Duke of York (3 Henry VI)
Bona, Lady
Bourbon, Lord
Clarence, George, Duke of
Clifford, Lord
Edward, Earl of March (later Edward IV)
Edward, Prince
Exeter, Duke of
Gloucester, Richard, Duke of
Gray, Lady
Hastings, Lord
Henry VI, King
Huntsman, a
Lieutenant of the Tower
Louis, King
Margaret, Queen
Mayor of Coventry
Mayor of York
Montague, Marquis of
Montgomery, Sir John
Mortimer, Sir John and Sir Hugh
Norfolk, Duke of
Nothumberland, Earl of
Oxford, Earl of
Pembroke, Earl of
Rivers, Earl
Rutland, Earl of
Soldier who has killed his father, a
Soldier who has killed his son, a
Somerset, Duke of
Somerville
Stafford, Lord
Stanley, Sir William
Tutor, Rutland's
Warwick, Earl of
York, Duke of (Richard Plantagenet)

Richard II
Aumerle, Duke of
Bagot
Berkeley, Lord
Bolingbroke, Harry
Bushy
Captain of the Welsh army
Carlisle, Bishop of
Exton, Sir Piers
Fitzwalter, Lord
Gaunt, John of
Gloucester, Duchess of
Green
Lord Marshal
Mowbray, Thomas
Northumberland, Earl of
Percy, Harry
Queen
Richard II, King
Ross, Lord
Salisbury, Earl of
Scrope, Sir Stephen
Surrey, Duke of
Westminster, Abbot of
Willoughby, Lord
York, Duchess of
York, Duke of

Richard III
Anne, Lady
Blunt, Sir James
Brackenbury, Sir Robert
Buckingham, Duke of
Cardinal
Catesby, Sir William
Christopher, Sir
Clarence, George, Duke of
Clarence's daughter
Clarence's son
Dorset, Marquis of
Edward IV, King
Edward, Prince
Elizabeth, Queen
Ely, Bishop of
Gray, Lord
Hastings, Lord
Herbert, Sir Walter
Margaret, Queen
Mayor of London, Lord
Murderers
Norfolk, Duke of
Oxford, Earl of
Page, a
Priest, a
Ratcliffe, Sir Richard
Richard, Duke of Gloucester (later Richard III)
Richmond, Earl of (later Henry VII)
Rivers, Earl
Stanley, Lord
Tyrrel, Sir James
Vaughan, Sir Thomas
York, Duchess of
York, Richard, Duke of

Romeo and Juliet
Abraham
Apothecary, an
Balthasar
Benvolio
Capulet
Capulet's cousin
Capulet's wife
Chorus
Escalus, Prince of Verona
Friar John
Friar Laurence
Gregory
Juliet
Mercutio
Montague
Montague's wife
Nurse, Juliet's
Page, Mercutio's
Page, Paris's
Paris, County
Peter
Petruccio
Romeo
Samson
Tybalt

The Taming of the Shrew
Baptista Minola
Bartholomew
Bianca
Biondello
Curtis
Gremio
Grumio
Haberdasher, a
Hortensio
Hostess, a
Huntsmen, two
Joseph
Katherine
Lord, a
Lucentio
Nathaniel
Pedant, a
Peter
Petruccio
Philip
Players
Sly, Christopher
Tailor, a
Tranio
Vincentio
Widow, a

The Tempest
Adrian
Alonso
Antonio
Ariel
Boatswain
Caliban
Ceres
Ferdinand
Francisco
Gonzalo
Iris
Juno

Master of a ship
Miranda
Prospero
Sebastian
Stefano
Trinculo

Timon of Athens
Alcibiades
Apemantus
Caphis
Flaminius
Flavius
Fool, a
Hortensius' servant
Isidore's servant
Lucilius
Lucius
Lucius' servant
Lucullus
Lucullus' servant
Page, a
Painter, a
Philotus's servant
Phrynia
Poet, a
Sempronius
Servilius
Timandra
Timon
Titus' servant
Varro's servants
Ventidius

Titus Andronicus
Aaron
Aemilius
Alarbus
Bassianus
Caius
Captain, a
Chiron
Clown, a
Demetrius
Lavinia
Lucius
Lucius, Young
Marcus Andronicus
Martius
Mutius
Nurse, a
Publius
Quintus
Saturnius
Sempronius
Tamora
Titus Andronicus
Valentine

Troilus and Cressida
Achilles
Aeneas
Agamemnon
Ajax
Alexander
Andromache
Antenor
Calchas
Cassandra
Cressida
Deiphobus
Diomedes
Hector
Helen
Helenus
Margareton
Menelaus
Nestor
Pandarus
Paris
Patroclus
Priam
Thersites
Troilus
Ulysses

Twelfth Night
Aguecheek, Sir Andrew
Antonio
Belch, Sir Toby
Captain, a
Curio
Fabian
Feste
Malvolio
Maria
Olivia
Orsino
Priest, a
Sebastian
Valentine
Viola

The Two Gentlemen of Verona
Antonio
Eglamour, Sir
Host, a
Julia
Lance
Lucetta
Milan, Duke of
Panthino
Proteus
Silvia
Speed
Thurio
Valentine

The Two Noble Kinsmen
Arcite
Artesius
Emilia
Gerald
Hippolyta
Hymen
Jailer, a
Jailer's daughter
Palamon
Pirithous
Theseus
Valerius

The Winter's Tale
Antigonus
Archidamus
Autolycus
Camillo
Cleomenes
Clown, a
Dion
Dorcas
Emilia
Florizel
Hermione
Jailer, a
Leontes
Mamillius
Mariner, a
Mopsa
Paulina
Perdita
Polixenes
Shepherd, Old

Songs and song-fragments in the plays, and composers of early settings

songs in the plays

ballad
broadside ballad
Johnson, Robert
Morley, Thomas
music
Wilson, John

All Is True (Henry VIII)
'Orpheus with his lute'

Antony and Cleopatra
'Come, thou monarch of the vine'

As You Like It
'Blow, blow, thou winter wind'
'It was a lover and his lass'
'Under the greenwood tree'
'Wedding is great Juno's crown'
'What shall he have that killed the deer?'

Cymbeline
'Fear no more the heat o' the sun'
'Hark, hark, the lark'

Hamlet
'And will a not come again'
'For Bonny and sweet Robin is all my joy'
'How should I your true love know'
'In youth when I did love'
'They bore him barefaced on the bier'
'Tomorrow is Saint Valentine's day'

2 Henry IV
'A cup of wine that's brisk and fine'
'And Robin Hood, Scarlet and John'

'Be merry, be merry, my wife has all'
'Carman's Whistle'
'Do me right, and dub me knight'
'Do nothing but eat and make good cheer'
Fill the cup and let it come'
'When Arthur first in court'

Henry v
'And sword and shield | In bloody field'
'Calin o custure me'
'If wishes would prevail with me'

King Lear
'Child Rowland to the dark tower came'
'Come o'er the bourn, Bessy, to me'
'He that has and a little tiny wit'
'Then they for sudden joy did weep'

Love's Labour's Lost
'King Cophetua and the Beggar Maid'
'When daisies pied'
'When icicles hang by the wall'

Measure for Measure
'Take, O take those lips away'

The Merchant of Venice
'Tell me, where is Fancy bred?'

The Merry Wives of Windsor
'To shallow rivers, to whose falls'
Fie on sinful fantasy'
'Fortune my foe'
'Greensleeves'

A Midsummer Night's Dream
'The ousel cock so black of hue'
'You spotted snakes'

Much Ado About Nothing
'Pardon, goddess of the night'
'Sigh no more, ladies'
'The god of love that sits above'

Othello
'And let me the cannikin clink'
'King Stephen was and a worthy peer'
Willow song ('The poor soul sat sighing by a sycamore tree')

Romeo and Juliet
'An old hare hoar'
'Heart's Ease'
'Hunt's up, the'
'My heart is full of woe'
'When griping grief the heart doth wound'

The Taming of the Shrew
'It was the Friar of orders grey'
'Where is the life that late I led?'

The Tempest
'Come unto these yellow sands'
Flout 'em and cout 'em'
'Full fathom five'
'Honour, riches, marriage, blessing'
'I shall no more to sea'
'No more dams I'll make for fish'
'The master, the swabber, the bosun and I'
'Where the bee sucks'
'While you here do snoring lie'

Troilus and Cressida
'Love, love, nothing but love'

Twelfth Night
'Come away, come away, death'
'Farewell, dear heart, for I must needs be gone'
'Hey Robin, jolly Robin, tell me how thy Lady does'
'Hold thy peace'
'O mistress mine'
'O' the twelfth day of December'
'Peg a Ramsay'
'There dwelt a man in Babylon'
'Three merry men be we'
'When that I was and a little tiny boy'

The Two Gentlemen of Verona
'Light o' love'
'Who is Silvia?'

The Two Noble Kinsmen
'Roses, their sharp spines being gone'
'Urns and odours, bring away'

The Winter's Tale
'But shall I go mourn for that'
'Get you hence, for I must go'
'Jog on, jog on'
'Lawn as white as driven snow'
'When daffodils begin to peer'
'Whoop, do me no harm, good man'
'Will you buy any tape'

Locations in the plays

Ardenne
Athens
Berkeley Castle
Bosworth Field
Dover
Dunsinane
Elsinore
Florence
Gloucestershire
Illyria
Kent
Leicester Abbey
Mantua
Milan
Milford Haven
Muscovy
Naples
Normandy
Padua
Rome
Shrewsbury
Sicilia
Sutton Cop Hill
Venice
Verona
Vienna
Windsor

Poems

lyric poetry, Shakespeare's

Epitaph on Elias James
Epitaphs on John Combe
A Lover's Complaint
'On Ben Jonson'
'The Phoenix and Turtle'
The Rape of Lucrece
Sonnets
Venus and Adonis

Attributed poems

Belvedere, or The Garden of the Muses
'Crabbed age and youth'
England's Helicon
England's Parnassus
'A Funeral Elegy'
The Passionate Pilgrim
'Shall I die'
Sonnets to Sundry Notes of Music
'Upon the King'

Literary features and terms

Genres, forms and modes

dramatic poetry, Shakespeare's
lyric poetry, Shakespeare's

city comedy
comedy
doggerel
epyllion
history
Jacobean tragedy

last plays
lyric
masque
pastoral
'Problem Plays'
prose
revenge tragedy
rhyme royal
romance
romances
sonnet
Tetralogy, First
Tetralogy, Second
tragedy
tragicomedy

Dramatic terms

anagnorisis
anticlimax
deus ex machina
dramatis personae
dumb shows
epilogue
induction
'mutes'
prologue
shared lines
soliloquy

Figures of speech

anadiplosis
anaphora
antithesis
aporia
blazon
chiasmus
conceit
euphuism
hyperbole
imagery
litotes
meiosis
metaphor
metonymy
onomatopoeia
oxymoron
paradox
parison
pathetic fallacy
prolepsis
prosopopoeia
puns
rhetoric
simile
stichomythia
synecdoche

Metrical terms

alexandrine
anapaest
anaptyxis
blank verse
brokenbacked line
caesura
couplet
dactyl
dimeter
elision
end-stopped
enjambment
epic caesura
feminine endings
foot
headless line
heroic couplets
iambic
long lines
metre
pauses
pentameter
Pyrrhic foot
short lines
spondee
squinting line
synaeresis
syncope
tetrameter
trimeter
trochee
weak endings

Linguistic features

English, Elizabethan

alliteration
anacoluthon
dialects
Dogberryism
foreign words
hendiadys
pronunciation
spelling
vocabulary

Other literary terms

allusion
anachronism
dramatic irony
irony
rhyme

Elizabethan and Jacobean literary context

Sources and influences

sources

Apuleius, Lucius
Ariosto, Ludovico
Bandello, Matteo
Belleforest, Francois de
Bible
Boccaccio, Giovanni
Brooke, Arthur
Castiglione, Baldassare
Caxton, William
Cervantes Saavedra, Miguel de
Chaucer, Geoffrey
Cinthio
commedia dell'arte
Du Bellay, Joachim
Elyot, Sir Thomas
Euripides
Fabyan, Robert
Famous Victories of Henry v
'Felix and Philiomena'
Florio, Giovanni (John)
Foxe, John
Froissart, Jean
Gamelyn, Tale of
Gascoigne, George
Geoffrey of Monmouth
Giovanni (Florentino), Ser
Giulio Romano
Gl'Ingannati
Gonzaga, Curzio
Gower, John
Grafton, Richard
Greek drama
Greene, Robert
Hakluyt, Richard
Hall, Joseph
Halle, Edward
Harington, Sir John
Harrison, William
Harsnett, Samuel
Hayward, Sir John
Henryson, Robert
Holinshed, Raphael
Homer
Huon de Bordeaux
interludes
Jodelle, Etienne
Jonson, Ben
Jourdan, Sylvester
King Leir
Knolles, Richard
Kyd, Thomas
Legh, Gerard
'Li Tre Saltiri'
Livy
Lodge, Thomas
Lucan
Lucian
Lydgate, John
Lyly, John
Machiavelli, Niccolo
Mantuanus, Baptista Spagnolo
Marlowe, Christopher
masque
Masque of the Inner Temple and Gray's Inn
Menander
miracle plays
The Mirror for Magistrates
Molyneux, Emerie
Monarcho
Montaigne, Michel de
Montemayor, Jorge de
morality plays
Mouffet, Thomas
mystery plays
oral traditions
Ovid
Painter, William
Petrarch, Francesco
Plautus
Pleiade
Pliny
Plutarch
Puttenham, George and Richard
Rare Triumphs of Love and Fortune

revenge tragedy
Rich, Barnabe
Ronsard, Pierre de
Rowley, Samuel
Saxo Grammaticus
Scot, Reginald
Segar, Sir William
Seneca, Lucius Annaeus
Sidney, Sir Philip
Sir Clyomon and Clamydes
Speed, John
Spenser, Edmund
Strachey, William
Terence
Thomas of Woodstock
Topsell, John
Tottell, Richard
The True Tragedy of Richard III
Twine, Laurence
ur-*Hamlet*
Virgil
'War of the Theatres'
Warner, William
Whetstone, George

Shakespeare's literary contemporaries

Armin, Robert
Ayrer, Jakob
Bacon, Francis
Barnes, Barnabe
Barnfield, Richard
Beaumont, Francis
Brooke, Arthur
Campion, Thomas
Cervantes Saavedra, Miguel de
Chapman, George
Chester, Robert
Chettle, Henry
Cinthio
Coryat, Thomas
Cotgrave, Randle
Daniel, Samuel
Davenport, Robert
Day, John
Dekker, Thomas
Deloney, Thomas
Donne, John
Dorset, Thomas Sackville, 1st Earl of
Drayton, Michael
Drummond, William
Fletcher, John
Florio, Giovanni (John)
Foxe, John
Gascoigne, George
Gonzaga, Curzio
Gosson, Stephen
Grafton, Richard
Greene, Robert
Greville, Fulke
Grimestone, Edward
Hakluyt, Richard
Hall, Joseph
Harington, Sir John
Harrison, William
Harvey, Gabriel
Hayward, Sir John
Heywood, Thomas
Holinshed, Raphael
Jodelle, Etienne
Jonson, Benjamin
Knolles, Richard
Kyd, Thomas
Lanier, Emilia
Lodge, Thomas
Lyly, John
Markham, Gervase
Marlowe, Christopher
Massinger, Philip
Middleton, Thomas
Milton, John
Mouffet, Thomas
Mulcaster, Richard
Munday, Anthony
Nashe, Thomas
Norton, Thomas
Painter, William
Peacham, Henry
Peele, George
Pembroke, Mary Herbert, Countess of
Pleiade
Porter, Henry
Puttenham, George and Richard
Raleigh, Sir Walter
Rich, Barnabe
Ronsard, Pierre de
Rowley, Samuel
Rowley, William
Scot, Reginald
Segar, Sir William
Sidney, Sir Philip
Spenser, Edmund
Stubbes, Phillip
Topsell, John
Tottel, Richard
Turner, William
Twine, Laurence
University Wits
Warner, William
Webster, John
Whetstone, George
Wilkins, George
Wither, George
(See also **Criticism and allusions before 1660**, below.)

Theatrical context to 1660

The playgoing experience

acting, Elizabethan
acting profession, Elizabethan and Jacobean

act and scene divisions
audiences
groundlings
intervals
jigs
performance times, lengths
revivals
Roxana title page
soundings (of trumpets)
The Wits, title page

Theatre hierarchy, management, and records

acting profession, Elizabethan and Jacobean
companies, playing

apprentices
book-keeper
boy actors
doubling
gatherers
Henslowe, Philip
hired men
housekeepers
Langley, Francis
parts
pay
playbook
plots
prompt-book
rehearsal
repertory system
sharer
stage-hand
stage-keeper
tireman

The theatre building

flags
galleries
Gentlemen's Rooms
groundlings
heavens
Lords Room
orchestra
pit
shadow
yard

The stage space, mechanics, and properties

'above'
apron stage
back-cloths
costume
curtains
descent
discovery space
flats/shutters
flying
footlights
forestage
furniture
Hell
'inner stage'
lighting
locality boards
machines
multiple setting
music room
perspective
properties
proscenium
scenery
stage decoration

stage doors
stage furniture
throne or state
tiring house
trap doors
upper stage

Theatre companies and patronage

acting profession, Elizabethan and Jacobean
companies, playing

Admiral's Men
Chamberlain's Men/King's Men
Chapel Royal
children's companies
Derby's (Strange's) Men
livery
patronage
Pembroke's Men
protection of players
provincial companies, tours
Stratford-upon-Avon, Elizabethan, and the theatre

Theatres

theatres, Elizabethan and Jacobean

Blackfriars
Curtain Theatre
Fortune Theatre
Globe Theatre
Hotel de Bourgogne
London
Palladio, Andrea
Porter's Hall
Red Lion
Rose Theatre
Swan Theatre
Theatre, The

Inns

inns

State regulation and court performances

An Act to restrain abuses of players (1606)
Buck, Sir George
censorship
Chamber Accounts
court performances
Cromwell, Oliver
Elizabeth I
Greenwich Palace
Hampton Court
Herbert, Sir Henry
James I
Lent
Lord Chamberlain
Master of the Revels
plague regulations
Privy Council
revels office and accounts
Tilney, Sir Edmund
Whitehall

Anti-theatrical debate

anti-theatrical polemic
Heywood, Thomas
religion
Stubbes, Philip

Other entertainments

animal shows
civic entertainments
masques
pageants
university performances

Theatre personnel to 1660

acting, Elizabethan
acting profession, Elizabethan and Jacobean
companies, playing

Allen, Giles
Alleyn, Edward
Armin, Robert
Beeston, Christopher
Benfield, Robert
Brayne, John
Bryan, George
Burbage, Cuthbert
Burbage, James
Burbage, Richard
Cholmeley, Richard
Condell, Henry
Cooke, Alexander
Cowley, Richard
Cox, Robert
Crosse, Samuel
Davenant, Sir William
Ecclestone, William
Field, Nathan
Gilburne, Samuel
Gough, Robert
Heminges, John
Henslowe, Philip
Hunnis, William
Jones, Inigo
Jonson, Ben
Kempe, William
Keysar, Robert
Lowin, John
Ostler, William
Phillips, Augustine
Pope, Thomas
Rice, John
Robinson, Richard
Shank, John
Sharpham, Edward
Sincler (Sinklo), John
Sly, William
Spencer, Gabriel
Street, Peter
Swanston, Eliard
Tarlton, Richard
Tawyer, William
Taylor, Joseph
Tooley, Nicholas
Underwood, John
Williams, John

Historical, social, and cultural context

art
astrology
calendar
childbirth and child-rearing
crime and punishment
death
Dutch wars
education
enclosure
fairies
food and drink
fools
ghosts
Gowrie conspiracy
Gunpowder Plot
heraldry
hunting and sports
Jews
law
marriage
medicine
monsters
Moors
nationalism
patronage
plagues
prostitution
reading and the book trade
religion
science
service
sexuality
tobacco
travel, trade, and colonialism
vagrancy
war
witchcraft

Elizabethan London

(See also **Theatre buildings**.)

London

Bankside
Barbican
City
Clink
Counter
Dulwich
Finsbury
Greenwich Palace
Guilds
Hampton Court
Hollar, Wenceslaus
Holywell
Inns of Court
Liberties
Merchant Taylors' School
Mermaid Tavern
Moorfields
Southwark
St Mary Overies
Stow, John
Westminster
Whitehall
Winchester House

Prominent contemporaries

Bales, Peter
Bracciano, Orsini, Duke of
Buckingham, George Villiers, Duke of
Carey, Elizabeth
Cecil, Robert
Cecil, William, Lord Burghley
Cobham, William Brooke, 7th Lord
Essex, Robert Devereux, 2nd Earl of
Garnet, Henry
Gates, Sir Thomas
Gerard, John
Hollar, Wenceslaus
Hooker, Richard
Hunsdon, George Carey, 2nd Lord
Hunsdon, Henry Carey, 1st Lord
Jones, Inigo
Leicester, Robert Dudley, Earl of
Lopez, Roderigo
Pembroke, Henry Herbert, 2nd Earl of
Pembroke, Mary Herbert, Countess of
Pembroke, Philip Herbert, 4th Earl of
Pembroke, William Herbert, 3rd Earl of
Southampton, Henry Wriothesley, 3rd Earl of
Stanley, Sir Thomas
Vernon, Elizabeth

The monarchy

Anne of Denmark
Charles I
Elector Palatine
Elizabeth I
Elizabeth of Bohemia
Henri IV of France
Henrietta Maria
Henry Frederick, Prince of Wales
James I

Elizabethan music and dance

music
songs in the plays

alarums
bagpipe
ballad
Bergomask (bergamasca)
brawl (branle)
broadside ballad
broken music (consort)
Byrd, William
canaries
cinquepace (sinkapace)
cittern
coranto
cornet
dance in the plays
dirge
divisions
Dowland, John
drums
dump
Edwardes, Richard
excursions
fanfare
fiddle
fife
flourish
flute
freemen's songs
galliard
gavotte
harp
hautboy
hay (hey)
horn
hornpipe
jigs
Johnson, Robert
Jones, Robert
lute
madrigal
marches
measure
Morley, Thomas
morris dance
music of the spheres
organ
passamezzo
pavan
proportion
psaltery
rebec
recorder
regal
retreat
roundel
sackbut
sennet
strain
tabor
trumpet
tucket
ventage
viol
virginal
volta, la
Weelkes, Thomas
Wilson, John

Elizabethan and Jacobean printing, publishing, and manuscripts

printing and publishing
reading and the book trade

act and scene divisions
anonymous publications
assembled texts
blocking entry
'book'
bookkeeper
cancel
capitalization
cases
cast-off copy
collaboration
colophon
compositors
copy
copyright
Crane, Ralph
deletion
derelict plays
Dering manuscript
device
Douai promptbooks and manuscripts
dramatis personae
emendation
entrances and exits
F
Folios
forme
foul case
foul papers
galley
handwriting
imprint
interpolations
italics
Jaggard, William and Isaac
Longleat manuscript
manuscript plays
mislineation
misprints
Moseley, Humphrey
Northumberland manuscript
Octavo
'plots'
proofreading
punctuation
Q
Quartos
reported text
revision
Roberts, James
shorthand
Sir Thomas More
speech-prefixes
stage directions
Stationers' Company and Register
title pages
transcripts

The editing of Shakespeare since 1700

Aspects of editing

authenticity
bibliography
canon
chronology
computers
concordances
copyright
disintegration

editing
electronic media
emendation
facsimile editions
metrical tests
parallel texts
textual criticism

Editions and editors in English

Restoration and eighteenth-century editors and editions

Bell, John
Capell, Edward
Dodd's Beauties of Shakespeare
Hanmer, Sir Thomas
Johnson, Samuel
Malone, Edmond
Pope, Alexander
Reed, Isaac
Rowe, Nicholas
Steevens, George
Theobald, Lewis
Warburton, William

Nineteenth-century editors and editions

Boswell, James, jr
Clark, William George
Clarke, Charles Cowden
Dyce, Alexander
Family Shakespeare
Fleay, Frederick Gard
Furness, Horace Howard
Furnivall, Frederick James
Globe Shakespeare
Halliwell-Phillipps, James Orchard
Henry Irving Shakespeare
'Leopold' Shakespeare
New Variorum
Pitt Press Shakespeare
Rochfort-Smith, Teena
Rolfe's Shakespeare
Temple Shakespeare
Variorum Shakespeare
Wright, W. Aldis

Editors and editions since 1900

Alexander, Peter
Arden Shakespeare
Bevington Shakespeare
Boas, Frederick S.
Bowers, Fredson
Cambridge Shakespeare
Cambridge Shakespeare, New
Challis Shakespeare
Folger Shakespeare
Folio Society Shakespeare
Greg, Walter Wilson
Halliday, F. E.
Harrison, George Bagshawe
Hinman, Charlton
Kittredge, G. L.
Mack, Maynard
Muir, Kenneth
New Shakespeare
New Temple Shakespeare
New Variorum
Nicoll, Allardyce
Norton Shakespeare
Old-spelling Shakespeare
Oxford Shakespeare
Pelican Shakespeare
Penguin Shakespeare
Players' Shakespeare
Riverside Shakespeare
Signet Shakespeare
Sisson, C. J.
strip-cartoon Shakespeare
Tudor Shakespeare
Wilson, John Dover
Yale Shakespeare

Theatrical history of the plays

Shakespeare in the theatre, 1660–1800

Restoration and eighteenth-century Shakespearian production

Stage personnel, 1660–1800

Baddeley, Sophia
Barry, Ann
Barry, Elizabeth
Barry, Spranger
Beeston, William
Behn, Aphra
Betterton, Mary
Betterton, Thomas
Booth, Barton
Bowman, John
Bracegirdle, Anne
Cibber, Colley
Cibber, Susannah Maria
Cibber, Theophilus
Clive, Catherine
Colman, George, the Elder
Cooke, George Frederick
Crowne, John
Cumberland, Richard
Dance, James
Dogget, Thomas
Downes, John
Durfey, Thomas
Fleetwood, Charles
Foote, Samuel
Garrick, David
Harris, Henry
Henderson, John
Howard, James
Hughes, Margaret
Hull, Thomas
Johnson, Charles
Jordan, Dorothea
Kemble, Charles
Kemble, John Philip
Killigrew, Thomas
King, Thomas
Kynaston, Edward
Lacy, John
Loutherbourg, Philip Jacques de
Macklin, Charles
Mohun, Michael
Nokes, James
Palmer, John
Pope, Elizabeth
Powell, William
Pritchard, Hannah
Quin, James
Rich, John
Robinson, Mary 'Perdita'
Schroder, Friedrich Ludwig
Sheridan, Thomas
Siddons, Sarah
Verbruggen, Susannah
Woffington, Margaret 'Peg'
Woodward, Henry
Yates, Mary Ann

Restoration and eighteenth-century theatres and companies

Comedie Française
Covent Garden Theatre
Drury Lane Theatre
Duke's Company
Goodman's Fields Theatre
Her Majesty's Theatre
Lincoln's Inn Fields
Smock Alley

Adaptations and adaptors, 1640–1850

(See also the accounts of the stage history of each play, particularly for adaptations which do not significantly alter the titles of the plays they rewrite.)
adaptation
burlesques and travesties of Shakespeare's plays

All for Love
Der Bestrafte Brudermord
Betterton, Thomas
Bottom the Weaver
The Bouncing Knight
The History and Fall of Caius Marius
Capell, Edward
Catharine and Petruchio
The Cobbler of Preston
Colman, George, the elder
The Comical Gallant
Conspiracy Discovered
Cox, Robert
Crowne, John
Cumberland, Richard
A Cure for a Scold
Cymbeline, a tragedy, altered from Shakespeare
Davenant, Sir William
Dennis, John
Dorastus and Fawnia
Droll
Dryden, John

Duffett, Thomas
Durfey, Thomas
The Fairies
The Fairy Queen
A Fairy Tale
Garrick, David
The Grave-Makers
Hauptmann, Gerhart
Hawkins, William
The History of King Lear
The Ingratitude of a Commonwealth
The Jew of Venice
Johnson, Charles
Kemble, John Philip
King Henry the Fifth: or, the Conquest of France by the English
Kirkman, Francis
Lacy, John
The Law against Lovers
Lillo, George
Love in a Forest
The Modern Receipt
Reynolds, Frederick
The Rivals
The Shipwreck
Tate, Nahum
Theobald, Lewis

Shakespeare in the theatre 1800–1900

burlesques and travesties of Shakespeare's plays
nineteenth-century Shakespearian production
recitations and one-person shows

Stage personnel, 1800–1900

Aldridge, Ira
Anderson, Mary
Barrett, Lawrence
Barrymore family
Benson, Frank
Bernhardt, Sarah
Betty, William Henry West
Bjoernson, Bjoernstjerne
Booth, Edwin
Booth, Junius Brutus
Calvert, Charles
Cooke, George F.
Cushman, Charlotte
Daly, Augustin
Drew family
Elliston, Robert William
Faucit, Helena Saville
Fechter, Charles Albert
Fiske, Minnie Maddern
Forbes-Robertson, Sir Johnston
Forrest, Edwin
Greet, Sir Philip Barling Ben
Hackett family
Harvey, Sir Martin
Irving, Sir Henry
Kean, Charles
Kean, Edmund
Kemble, Frances Anne
Langtry, Lily
Macready, William Charles
Mansfield, Richard
Mantell, R. B.
Mathews, Charles James
McCullough, John Edward
Modjeska, Helena
Neilson, Adelaide
Neilson, Julia
O'Neill, Eliza
Phelps, Samuel
Planche, James Robinson
Poel, William
Rehan, Ada
Ristori, Adelaide
Rossi, Ernesto
Salvini
Savits, Jocza
Sothern, Edward Hugh
Sullivan, Barry
Terry, Ellen
Tree, Beerbohm
Vestris, Elizabeth
Ward, Genevieve
Young, Charles Mayne

Nineteenth-century theatres and companies

Comédie Française
Covent Garden Theatre
Drury Lane Theatre
Her Majesty's Theatre
Lyceum Theatre
Odeon, Theatre de l'
Old Vic
Sadler's Wells
Shakespeare Memorial Theatre

Shakespeare in the theatre, 1900–

twentieth-century Shakespearean production
modern dress

Stage personnel, 1900–

Anderson, Dame Judith
Artaud, Antonin
Ashcroft, Dame Peggy
Atkins, Robert
Audley, Maxine
Badel, Alan
Barrault, Jean-Louis
Barton, John
Baylis, Lilian Mary
Benthall, Michael
Bergman, Ingmar
Bloom, Claire
Bogdanov, Michael
Branagh, Kenneth
Braunschweig, Stephane
Brecht, Bertolt
Bridges-Adams
Brook, Peter
Burton, Richard
Byam Shaw, Glen
Calhern, Louis
Calvert, Louis
Chereau, Patrice
Ciulei, Liviu
Colicos, John
Copeau, Jacques
Craig, Gordon
Deguchi, Norio
Dench, Dame Judi
Devine, George
Evans, Dame Edith
Evans, Maurice
Finney, Albert
Fluchere, Henri
Fukuda, Tsuneari
Gambon, Sir Michael
Gielgud, Sir John
Godfrey, Derek
Goodbody, Buzz
Goring, Marius
Granville-Barker, Harley
Gray, Terence
Guinness, Sir Alec
Guthrie, Sir Tyrone
Hall, Sir Peter
Hands, Terry
Hardy, Robert
Helpmann, Robert
Holm, Sir Ian
Hordern, Sir Michael
Houseman, John
Howard, Alan
Hunt, Hugh
Hutt, William
Jackson, Sir Barry
Jacobi, Sir Derek
Jefford, Barbara
Jones, James Earl
Kingsley, Ben
Komisarjevsky, Theodore
Kortner, Fritz
Krauss, Werner
Langham, Michael
Laughton, Charles
Leigh, Vivien
Lepage, Robert
Llorca, Denis
Marlowe, Julia
McCarthy, Lillah
McKellen, Sir Ian
Miller, Jonathan
Mirren, Helen
Mnouchkine, Ariane
Monck, Nugent
'Motley'
Neville, John
Ninagawa, Yukio
Noble, Adrian
Nunn, Trevor
Okhlopkov, Nikolai
Olivier, Lord
Pasco, Richard
Pennington, Michael
Planchon, Roger
Plummer, Christopher
Porter, Eric
Quayle, Sir Anthony
Rain, Douglas (Ontario)
Redgrave, Sir Michael
Redgrave, Vanessa
Reinhardt, Max
Richardson, Ian

Richardson, Sir Ralph
Richardson, Tony
Rigg, Dame Diana
Robeson, Paul
Schell, Maximilian
Scofield, Paul
Seale, Douglas
Shaw, Glen Byam
Sher, Sir Antony
Sinden, Sir Donald
Sjoberg, Ald
Smith, Dame Maggie
Speaight, Robert
Stanislavsky, Konstantin
Stein, Peter
Stephens, Sir Robert
Stewart, Patrick
Strehler, Giorgio
Suzman, Janet
Suzuki, Tadashi
Thorndike, Dame Sybil
Tutin, Dorothy
Tynan, Kenneth
Valk, Frederick
Vanbrugh, Violet
Vilar, Jean
Visconti, Luchino
Vitez, Antoine
Warner, David
Warner, Deborah
Webster, Margaret
Welles, Orson
Williams, Clifford
Williams, Harcourt
Williamson, Nicol
Wolfit, Sir Donald
Wood, John
Worth, Irene
Zadek, Peter

Twentieth-century theatres and companies

Barbican Theatre
Birmingham Repertory Theatre
Cheek by Jowl
Chichester Festival Theatre
Comédie Française
English Shakespeare Company
English Stage Company
Glasgow Citizens'
Globe reconstructions
Her Majesty's Theatre
National Theatre (Royal National Theatre)
New York Shakespeare Festival
Old Vic
Odeon, Theatre de l'
Open Air Theatre, Regent's Park
Royal Shakespeare Company
Royal Shakespeare Theatre

Stage adaptations and burlesques, 1900–

(See also **Shakespeare on film** and **Shakespeare's literary influence.**)

Brecht, Bertolt
burlesques and travesties of Shakespeare's plays
Lepage, Robert
Macbett
Marowitz, Charles
Muller, Heiner
musicals
opera
A Place Calling Itself Rome
Return to the Forbidden Planet
Verdi, Giuseppe
The Wars of the Roses
West Side Story
Your Own Thing

Critical history of the works

critical history
scholarship

Critical schools and periods

Christian criticism
cultural materialism
feminist criticism
formalism
humanism
Jungian criticism
Marxist criticism
modernist criticism
moralist criticism
neoclassicism
New Criticism
new historicism
performance criticism
postmodernism
psychoanalytic criticism
Romanticism
structuralism and poststructuralism

Criticism and allusions before 1660

Addenbrooke, John
Aubrey, John
Barksted, William
Barnfield, Richard
Basse, William
Beaumont, Francis
Belott-Mountjoy suit
Boaden, James
Bolton, Edmund
Camden, William
Carew, Richard
Chamberlain, John
Chettle, Henry
Combe family
Cope, Sir Walter
Corbet, Richard
Covell, William
Davenant, William
Davies, John
Digges, Leonard
Dugdale, Sir William
Forman, Simon
Freeman, Thomas
Fuller, Thomas
Gesta Grayorum
Greene, Robert
Harvey, Gabriel
Harvey, Sir William
Holland, Hugh
Howes, Edmund
Impresa
James, Richard
Jonson, Ben
Keeling, Captain William
Knight, Charles
Lambarde, William
M., I. (Mabbe, James?)
Manningham, John
Markham, Gervase
Meres, Francis
Parnassus plays
Phillips, Augustine
Pimlico
Platter, Thomas
Pudsey, Edward
Quiney, Richard
Ratsey, Gamaliel
Renoldes, William
Richardson, Nicholas
Taylor, John
Webster, John
Weever, John
Wayte, William
Willobie his Avisa
Wotton, Henry

Criticism and scholarship, 1660–1800

Addison, Joseph
Ayscough, Samuel
Bishop, Sir William
Capell, Edward
Chalmers, Alexander
Collier, Jeremy
Davies, Richard
Dennis, John
Dodd's Beauties of Shakespeare
Dryden, John
Farmer, Richard
Gentleman, Francis
George III
Gildon, Charles
Griffith, Elizabeth
Hanmer, Sir Thomas
Hawkins, William
Johnson, Samuel
Kames, Henry Home, Lord
Kenrick, William
Langbaine, Gerard
Lennox, Charlotte
Lessing, G. E.
Mackenzie, Henry
Malone, Edmond
Montagu, Elizabeth
Morgann, Maurice
Newcastle, Margaret Cavendish, Duchess of
Oldys, William
Pepys, Samuel
Pope, Alexander
Reed, Isaac
Richardson, William

Rowe, Nicholas
Rymer, Thomas
Steevens, George
Theobald, Lewis
Thirlby, Styan
Tyrwhitt, Thomas
Warburton, William
Wharton, Joseph
Wood, Anthony
Wright, James

Criticism and scholarship, 1800–1900

Abbott, E. A.
Arnold, Matthew
Bagehot, Walter
Bartlett, John
Boswell, James, jr.
Bradley, A. C.
Brandes, Georg
Carlyle, Thomas
Clark, William George
Clarke, Charles Cowden
Clarke, Mary Cowden
Coleridge, Samuel Taylor
Cornwall, Barry (Procter, Bryan Waller)
Creizenach, Wilhelm
Cunningham, Peter
Davies, Thomas
De Quincey, Thomas
Delius, Nikolaus
Douce, Francis
Dowden, Edward
Drake, Nathan
Dyce, Alexander
Elze, Karl
Fleay, Frederick Gard
Furness, Horace Howard
Furnivall, Frederick James
Gaedertz, Karl Theodor
Gautier, Theophile
Genest, John
Gervinus, Georg Gottfried
Gollancz, Israel
Hales, John
Halliwell-Phillipps, James Orchard
Hazlitt, William
Herrera Bustamante, Manuel
Hudson, Henry Norman
Hunt, Leigh
Lamb, Charles and Mary
Lee, Sidney
Mallarmé, Stéphane
Matthews, James Brander
Moulton, Richard Green
Nerval, Gerard de
Pater, Walter
Poe, Edgar Allan
Rochfort-Smith, Teena
Saintsbury, George
Sand, George
Schlegel, August Wilhelm
Simpson, Richard
Stopes, Charlotte Carmichael
Taine, Hippolyte
Tyler, Thomas
Watkins-Lloyd, W.
Wright, W. Aldis
Ulrici, Hermann

Criticism and scholarship, 1900–

Adams, J. C.
Adams, Joseph Quincy
Alexander, Peter
Archer, William
Baldwin, Thomas Whitfield
Beerbohm, Max
Bentley, Gerald Eades
Bian Zhilin
Boas, Frederick S.
Bowers, Fredson
Bradbrook, Muriel
Brooke, C. F. Tucker
Bullough, Geoffrey
Chambers, Edmund Kerchever
Clemen, Wolfgang
Croce, Benedetto
Eliot, Thomas Stearns
Ellis-Fermor, Una
Empson, William
Freud, Sigmund
Fripp, Edgar Innes
Frye, Northrop
Greg, Walter Wilson
Gundolf, Friedrich
Halliday, F. E.
Harbage, Alfred
Harris, Frank
Harrison, George Bagshawe
Hinman, Charlton
Hotson, Leslie
Hughes, Ted
Jones, Ernest
Kittredge, G. L.
Knight, George Wilson
Knights, L. C.
Kott, Jan
Leavis, F. R.
Legouis, Emile
Mack, Maynard
McKerrow, Ronald Brunlees
McManaway, James Gilmer
Morozov, Mikhail
Muir, Kenneth
Murry, Middleton
Nicoll, Allardyce
Pollard, Alfred William
Quiller-Couch, Sir Arthur
Raleigh, Sir Walter
Rowse, A. L.
Schoenbaum, Samuel
Schucking, Levin Ludwig
Sissons, C. J.
Smidt, Kristin
Spielmann, Marion Harry
Sprague, Arthur Colby
Stoll, Elmer Edgar
Spurgeon, Caroline
Tillyard, Eustace M. W.
Wallace, Charles William
Whiter, Walter
Wilson, John Dover
Yates, Frances, Dame

Periodicals

journals

Cahiers Elisabethains
Etudes Anglaises
Hamlet Studies
Notes and Queries
Shakespeare Jahrbuch
Shakespeare Newsletter
Shakespeare Quarterly
Shakespeare Studies
Shakespeare Survey
Shakespeare Yearbook

Institutions

Birmingham Shakespeare Memorial Library
Bodleian Library
Bodmer Library
British Council
British Library
Cambridge University
Folger Shakespeare Library
Huntington Library
International Shakespeare Conference
Oxford English Dictionary
schools, Shakespeare in (British)
Shakespeare Birthplace Trust
Shakespeare Institute
Theatre Museum
World Shakespeare Congress

Societies and Clubs

British Empire Shakespeare Society
Deutsche Shakespeare-Gesellschaft
International Shakespeare Association
Malone Society
New Shakespeare Society
New York Shakespeare Society
Oxford University Dramatic Society
Shakespeare Association
Shakespeare Association of America
Shakespeare Club
Shakespeare Ladies' Club
Shakespeare Society of China
Societé Française Shakespeare
Yale Elizabethan Club

Shakespeare's Literary Influence

Authors pervasively influenced by, and works inspired by or derived from, Shakespeare and his works

fiction

poems on Shakespeare
popular culture
Shakespeare, William, as a literary character

Auden, W. H.
Austen, Jane
Baring, Maurice
Beckett, Samuel
Bond, Edward
Borges, Jorge Luis
Brecht, Bertolt
Burgess, Anthony
Byron, George Gordon, Lord
Cayatte, Andre
Cesaire, Aime
Chekhov, Anton
Clarke, Mary Cowden
Dickens, Charles
Dostoievsky, Fyodor
Dryden, John
Dumas, Alexandre
Emerson, Ralph Waldo
Falstaff's Wedding
Fletcher, John
Forbidden Planet
Freud, Sigmund
Goethe, Johann Wolfgang von
Gothic literature
Gray, Thomas
Harlequin Student
Harlequin's Invasion
Hauptmann, Gerhart
Heine, Heinrich
Herder, Johann Gottfried
Hughes, Ted
Hugo, Victor Marie
Ibsen, Henrik
Irving, Washington
James, Henry
Jameson, Anna Brownwell
Joyce, James
Judith Shakespeare: A Romance
Keats, John
Laforgue, Jules
Lamb, Charles and Mary
Lessing, Gotthold Ephraim
Lewis, Matthew 'Monk'
Ludwig, Otto
Macbett
Mallarmé, Stéphane
Melville, Herman
Milton, John
Mortimer, Sir John
Muller, Heiner
Murdoch, Iris
No Bed for Bacon
Nye, Robert
Oehlenschlager, Adam
Poe, Edgar Allan
Pushkin, Alexander
Queen Margaret, or Shakespeare Goes to the Falklands
Richardson, Samuel
Romanoff and Juliet
Salom, Jaime
Schiller, Friedrich
Scott, Sir Walter
Shakespeare Wallah
Shaw, George Bernard
Soyinka, Wole
Sterne, Laurence
Stoppard, Sir Tom
Strindberg, August
Swinburne, Algernon Charles
Tamayo y Baus, Manuel
Tennyson, Alfred, Lord
Tolstoy, Leo
Turgenev, Ivan
Twain, Mark
Vigny, Alfred de
Voltaire
Wesker, Arnold
West Side Story
Wilde, Oscar
Woolf, Virginia
Wordsworth, William
Yeats, William Butler

Shakespeare on film and television

(See entries on individual plays for information on screen versions.)
popular culture
Shakespeare on sound film
silent films
television
United States of America

Branagh, Kenneth
Forbidden Planet
Hall, Sir Peter
Kozintsev, Grigori
Kurosawa, Akira
Miller, Jonathan
musicals
Noble, Adrian
Nunn, Trevor
Olivier, Lord
Reinhardt, Max
Shakespeare: The Animated Tales
Shakespeare Wallah
West Side Story
Zeffirelli, Franco

Radio and recordings

Marlowe Society
radio, British
recordings
Rylands, George (Dadie)
Shakespeare Recording Society

Music and dance since 1660

ballet
music
opera

Arne, Thomas Augustine
Bach, Carl Philip Emmanuel
Beethoven, Ludwig van
Berlioz, Hector
Birtwistle, Sir Harrison
Bishop, Sir Henry Rowley
Boyce, William
Britten, Benjamin
Dibdin, Charles
Elgar, Edward
Ellington, Duke
Faure, Gabriel
Haydn, Franz Josef
Holst, Gustav
jazz
Lampe, John Frederick
Leveridge, Richard
Linley, Thomas, jr.
Locke, Matthew
Mendelssohn, Felix
Milhaud, Darius
Mozart, Wolfgang Amadeus
musicals
Nicolai, Otto
Parry, Sir Hubert
pop music
Porter, Cole
Prokofiev, Serge
Purcell, Henry
Reynolds, Frederick
Scarlatti, Domenico
Schubert, Franz
Sibelius, Jan
Smetana, Bedrich
Strauss, Richard
Sullivan, Sir Arthur
Tchaikovsky, Pyotr
Tippett, Sir Michael
Vaughan-Williams, Ralph
Verdi, Giuseppe
Wagner, Richard
Walton, William
West Side Story
Woolfenden, Guy
Your Own Thing

Shakespeare and the visual arts since 1660

painting

advertising
Barry, Sir James
Blake, William
Boydell, John
Bunbury, Henry William
Cattermole, Charles
ceramics
Cruikshank, George
Dadd, Richard
Delacroix, Eugene
Fairholt, Frederick William
Fuseli, Henry
Gower memorial
Hayman, Francis
Hogarth, William
illustrations
monuments
National Portrait Gallery
Northcote, James
Paton, Sir (Joseph) Noel
Picasso, Pablo
Pre-Raphaelite Brotherhood
Romney, George
Roubiliac, Louis Francois
RSC Collection and Gallery

Rysbrack, Michael
Scheemakers, Peter
Shakespeare Gallery
Shakespeariana
statuary
Wright, Joseph (of Derby)
Zoffany, Johann

SHAKESPEARE AROUND THE GLOBE

Countries and regions

Arab world
Australia
Austria
Bohemia and the former Czechoslovakia
Brazil
Bulgaria
Canada
Caribbean, The
China
East Africa
France
Germany
Greece
Hungary
India
Ireland
Israel
Italy
Japan
Korea
Latin America
Low Countries
New Zealand
Poland
Portugal
Romania
Russia and the former USSR
Scandinavia
Scotland
Southern Africa
Spain
Switzerland
United States of America
Wales
West Africa

Translators and translations

translation

Astrana Marín, Luis
Beyer, Sille
Clark, Jaime
Conejero, Manuel Angel
Cruz, Ramón de la
Eschenburg, Johann Joachim
Foersom, Peter
Fukuda, Tsuneari
Geijer, Erik Gustaf
Gide, André
Hagberg, Karl August
Hallstrom, Per
Hugo, Francois Victor
Instituto Shakespeare
Kinoshita, Junji
Lembcke, Edvard
Letourneur, Pierre
Liang Shiqui
Macpherson, Guillermo
Moratín, Leondro Fernández de
Nyerere, Julius
Odashima, Yushi
Oehlenschlager, Adam
Oliva, Salvador
Pasternak, Boris
Pujante, Angel-Luis
Rothe, Hans
Sagarra, Josep Maria de
Schiller, Friedrich
Schlegel, August Wilhelm
Simrock, Karl Joseph
Tieck, Johann Ludwig
Tsubouchi, Shoyo
Valverde, José María
Voss, Johann Heinrich
Wieland, Christoph Martin
Zhu Shenghao

List of plays in alphabetical order

All Is True (*Henry* VIII)
All's Well That Ends Well
Antony and Cleopatra
As You Like It
[*Cardenio*]
The Comedy of Errors
Coriolanus
Cymbeline, King of Britain
The First Part of the Contention (2 *Henry* VI)
Hamlet, Prince of Denmark
1 Henry IV
2 Henry IV
Henry V
1 Henry VI
Julius Caesar
King John
King Lear
Love's Labour's Lost
[*Love's Labour's Won*]
Macbeth
Measure for Measure
The Merchant of Venice
The Merry Wives of Windsor
A Midsummer Night's Dream
Much Ado About Nothing
Othello
Pericles
Richard Duke of York (*3 Henry* VI)
Richard II
Richard III
Romeo and Juliet
Sir Thomas More
The Taming of the Shrew
The Tempest
Timon of Athens
Titus Andronicus
Troilus and Cressida
Twelfth Night; or, What You Will
The Two Gentlemen of Verona

Note to the reader

This book is designed to be easy to use, but the following notes may be helpful to the reader.

ALPHABETICAL ARRANGEMENT: Entries are arranged in letter-by-letter alphabetical order of their headwords, which are shown in bold type.

NAMES OF PLAYS AND CHARACTERS: *The Oxford Companion to Shakespeare* follows the Oxford Shakespeare (1986), edited by Stanley Wells and Gary Taylor, in returning to the titles of the plays Shakespeare used when he composed them, rather than the titles that appeared in the First Folio, and which have since become standard. For example, the play known as *Henry VIII* appears under its original name of *All Is True*. Signpost entries direct the reader from the standard title to the entry under the original title. The Companion also follows the Oxford Shakespeare in its modernization of Shakespeare's spellings of names, for example, a reader looking up Iachimo will be redirected to Giacomo.

CROSS REFERENCES: An asterisk (*) in front of a word in the text signals a cross reference to a related entry that may be of interest. Also, 'see' or 'see also' followed by a headword in small capitals is used to indicate a cross reference when the precise form of a headword does not appear in the text. Entries are marked as cross references the first time they appear in an individual entry only. To avoid cluttering the text, the names of plays and poems by Shakespeare, and of the characters that appear in the plays, are not marked as cross references, although there are entries on all of these.

THEMATIC LISTING OF ENTRIES: This is a list of entries under major topics, which appears at the front of the book (see pp. xi–xxviii), and offers another means of accessing the material in the Companion. It allows the reader to see all the entries relating to a particular subject—such as songs in the plays or extant portraits of Shakespeare—at a glance.

CONTRIBUTORS' INITIALS: These are given at the end of each entry, and a key to these initials appears on pp. ix–x.

Aaron, a *Moor and Tamora's lover, is ultimately sentenced to be buried and starved, *Titus Andronicus* 5.3. *AB*

Abbess. She reveals herself to be Emilia, mother of the Antipholus twins, at the end of *The Comedy of Errors.* *AB*

Abbott, E(dwin) A(bbott) (1838–1926), English headmaster and grammarian, who addressed the first meeting of the New Shakespeare Society (13 March 1874). His *A Shakespearian Grammar: An Attempt to Illustrate Some of the Differences between Elizabethan and Modern English* (1869, repr. 1966) is an important attempt to describe Elizabethan syntax and idiom. *TM*

Abergavenny, Lord. He complains about Wolsey's pride and is imprisoned alongside Buckingham in *All Is True* (*Henry VIII*) 1.1. The historical figure was George Neville, 3rd Baron Abergavenny (*c.*1461–1535). *AB*

Abhorson, an executioner, defends his profession in *Measure for Measure* 4.2 and attempts to rouse drunken Barnadine for execution, 4.3. *AB*

'above'. About half of Shakespeare's plays need an elevated playing space which is often signalled by a stage direction of the kind 'enter above', and most of these use this location just once or twice. An actor appearing 'above' is usually to be thought of as appearing at a window, or upon the walls of a castle or fortified town. Contemporary accounts and drawings (most clearly the de Witt drawing of the *Swan) indicate a balcony set in the back wall of the stage which could be used as a spectating position but also would be ideal to provide the occasional 'above' acting space. *GE*

Hosley, Richard, 'The Gallery over the Stage in the Public Playhouse of Shakespeare's Time', *Shakespeare Quarterly*, 8 (1957)

Abraham (Abram), Montague's servant, participates in a fight in *Romeo and Juliet* 1.1. *AB*

Abram. See ABRAHAM.

academic drama. See UNIVERSITY PERFORMANCES.

Achilles, the treacherous champion of the Greek army (he appears in a more sympathetic light in *Homer's *Iliad*), instructs his followers to kill the unarmed Hector, *Troilus and Cressida* 5.9. *AB*

act and scene divisions. Of the original quartos of Shakespeare's plays, none is divided into numbered scenes (although in Q1 *Romeo and Juliet* a printer's ornament occasionally appears where new scenes begin) and only *Othello* (1622) is divided into acts. In the First Folio, nineteen of the plays are divided into acts and scenes, and another ten are divided into acts. Nicholas Rowe's edition (1709) was the first to divide all of the plays into numbered acts and scenes.

Division into scenes was a structural element of early English plays—a new scene began whenever the stage was clear and the action not continuous—but division into acts was a later convention, perhaps adopted from classical drama. Although very few plays written for the adult dramatic companies before 1607 are divided into acts, nearly every one of the extant printed plays written for those companies thereafter is divided into five acts. Gary Taylor has suggested that the transition to act-intervals occurred when the adult companies moved from outdoor to indoor theatres (the King's Men acquired the Blackfriars playhouse in August of 1608). Pauses between acts would not only have been better facilitated in indoor theatres, but might also have been required so that candles could be trimmed. Shakespeare's later plays were thus apparently written for a different convention from his early and middle ones. *ER*

Greg, W. W., 'Act Divisions in Shakespeare', *Review of English Studies*, 4 (1928)
Taylor, Gary, 'The Structure of Performance: Act-Intervals in the London Theatres, 1576–1642', in *Shakespeare Reshaped 1606–1623* (1993)

acting, Elizabethan. The Elizabethan word for what we call acting was 'playing', and the word 'acting' was reserved for the gesticulations of an orator. We have little direct evidence about the style of Elizabethan acting, although a few general principles can be derived from the conditions of performance. The relative shortness of rehearsal periods and the large number of plays in the repertory at any one time suggest that an actor was not likely to think of his character as having a unique and complex human psychology in the way which, in our time, the *Stanislavskian technique encourages. Likewise, the distribution of parts as individual rolls of paper giving only the particular speeches needed for one character suggests that what we think of as dramatic interaction was less important than the individual's interpretation of his speeches. Modern ensemble acting requires lengthy rehearsals which were unknown on the early modern stage. But this should not be taken as evidence that the acting was mere declamation without emotion. When the King's Men played *Othello* at Oxford in 1610 an eyewitness was moved to report that Desdemona 'killed by her husband, in her death moved us especially when, as she lay in her bed, her face alone implored the pity of the audience'. Likewise Simon Forman's records of performances of *Cymbeline, The Winter's Tale, Macbeth*, and a play about Richard II clearly express his enjoyment of the intensity of the emotional experience, and hence the quality of the acting. The mere fact that boys played great tragic roles such as a Cleopatra, Desdemona, Hermione, and Lady Macbeth indicates that a degree of unrealistic formalism (symbolic gestures and convention) must have been used, but scholars do not agree about precisely how 'naturalistic' or 'formalistic' the acting usually was, or whether perhaps some mixed style was used.

There was hardly a professional acting tradition in existence in 1576 when James Burbage built the Theatre, and until the early 1600s most actors were men who had taken up this career having first trained in something else. Once the profession was established the system of apprenticeship must have helped systematize an actor's training, although without a governing guild practice might have varied greatly from one master to another. Acting was taught as part of a standard grammar-school education and of course actors had to be literate, so despite the apparent low status of the profession actors were amongst the better-educated Elizabethans. Scholars have looked to the education system, and especially the instruction in oratory, for evidence of the acting style of the period; educational policy at least is well documented. Bernard Beckerman thought that the styles and conventional gestures of the Elizabethan orator and actor were essentially the same but found manuals of oratory rather vague: a number of gestures were offered to accompany a particular emotion and the individual orator was left to choose whichever best suited the occasion.

Another source of information about acting styles is the drama itself, and the most overused piece of evidence is Hamlet's advice to the players (3.2.1–45) which includes 'Speak the speech . . . trippingly on the tongue', 'do not saw the air too much with your hand', and avoid imitating those who have 'strutted and bellowed' on the stage. This does not tell us much, and indeed the conscious contradiction of the general and transcendent ('hold as 'twere the mirror up to nature, to show virtue her own feature, scorn her own image') and the particular and contingent ('[show] the very age and body of the time his form and pressure') makes this if anything an evasion of detailed instruction in acting style. Commentators have relied heavily upon Hamlet's advice because we have no direct description of Elizabethan acting.

Despite the lack of direct evidence, certain trends which impinged upon acting can be traced across the period. The drama of the 1570s used strong rhyme and rhythm (especially the 'galloping' fourteen-syllable line) which gave an actor little scope for personal interpretation, whereas Marlowe's looser verse style and increasingly subtle characterization gave the Admiral's Men new opportunities for virtuoso acting. Stable long-term residences at the Rose and the Globe after 1594 allowed a star system to develop with Edward Alleyn for the Admiral's and Richard Burbage for the Chamberlain's Men being the most highly praised actors of their time. T. W. Baldwin developed a complex model of the character types ('lines') which were the special skills of particular actors of the period but other scholars feel that flexibility, not specialization, was the most valued attribute in an actor. Whether Shakespeare ever got the performances he wanted is uncertain. Shakespeare's characters use acting as a metaphor for public behaviour of all kinds but, as M. C. Bradbrook noted, the descriptions ('strutting player', 'frets', 'wooden dialogue') are seldom complimentary.

The differences in conditions at different venues appear to have had an effect on the acting. Indoor theatres were smaller than the open-air amphitheatres and had less extraneous noise, so actors could afford to soften their voices and make smaller physical gestures. Players at the northern playhouses, especially the Fortune and Red Bull, were more commonly attacked for exaggerated acting once the private theatres had developed their own subtle style. Also, an actor in an amphitheatre is effectively surrounded on all sides by spectators and may choose to keep moving so that everyone has a chance to see him. The indoor theatres, however, had a greater mass of spectators directly in front of the stage and this probably encouraged playing 'out front' rather than 'in the round' as we would now call it. Adjusting between the two modes must have been fairly easy for the actors, however, as on tour they were unlikely to find many venues which provided the 'in-the-round' experience of the London amphitheatres. *GE*

Baldwin, T. W., *The Organization and Personnel of the Shakespearean Company* (1927)

Beckerman, Bernard, *Shakespeare at the Globe, 1599–1609* (1962)

Bradbrook, M. C., *Elizabethan Stage Conditions: A Study of their Place in the Interpretation of Shakespeare's Plays* (1932)

Gurr, Andrew, 'Playing in Amphitheatres and Playing in Hall Theatres', in A. L. Magnusson and C. E. McGee (eds.), *The Elizabethan Theatre XIII: Papers Given at the 13th International Conference on Elizabethan Theatre Held at the University of Waterloo, Ontario, in July 1989* (1994)

Harbage, Alfred, 'Elizabethan Acting', *Publications of the Modern Language Association of America*, 54 (1939)

Salgado, Gamini (ed.), *Eyewitnesses of Shakespeare: First Hand Accounts of Performances 1590–1890* (1975)

acting profession, Elizabethan and Jacobean. The Elizabethan word for an actor was 'player' and there were three classes: the sharer, the hired man, and the apprentice. The nucleus of the company was the sharers, typically between four and ten men, who were named on the patent which gave them the authority to perform and which identified their aristocratic patron. The sharers owned the capital of the company, its playbooks and costumes, in common and shared the profits earned. All other actors were the employees of the sharers. The sharers were not necessarily the finest actors but they would have to bring a significant contribution to the company in the form either of capital or, as in the case of Shakespeare, writing ability. The sharing took place after the rent on the venue—often simply consisting of the takings from the galleries—had been paid and the hired men had received their wages. There was no guild system in place to regulate the industry, so an apprentice was in the unusual position of being legally apprenticed in the secondary trade practised by the individual sharer who was his master.

The sharers of London companies selected a new play by audition reading and, if purchased, they would rehearse it in the morning while playing items from the current repertory in the afternoon. The inconclusive evidence from Henslowe's account book suggests that at least two weeks were allowed for rehearsal of a new play, including time needed for the player to privately 'study' (memorize) his part. With no cheap mechanical means of reproducing an entire play, players were issued with rolls of paper containing only their own lines plus their cues. This practice and the short rehearsal periods suggests that acting skill was largely considered to reside in expressing the meanings and emotions in one's part rather than reacting to the speeches of others.

The majority of players were hired men, and amongst these there was not a strict distinction between what we now call 'front of house' and 'stage' work: an entrance-fee gatherer or costumer might well be expected to take a minor role at need, and those providing musical accompaniment might have to portray onstage musicians. Fee-gathering was the only job open to women as well as men; apart from ambiguous evidence concerning Middleton and Dekker's *The Roaring Girl* (1611) there is nothing to suggest that women ever acted. Usually the apprentices played the female roles in the drama but because of the anomalous lack of a guild governing the acting profession we do not know the precise extent of an apprentice's responsibilities, or if indeed any standard arrangements existed other than the customary provision of board, keep, and training.

There is little evidence that players were typecast although a dramatist attached to a company, as Shakespeare was, would have thought about his human resources during composition. However, there was a distinct position of 'clown' or 'fool' in each of the major companies and Richard Tarlton of the Queen's Men and William Kempe and later Robert Armin of the Chamberlain's Men had roles written to suit their abilities and did not perform in plays which lacked a 'clown' or 'fool' character. The emergence of actor 'stars' in the early 1590s appears to be related to the increasingly long residences at London playhouses which allowed audiences to follow the particular development of an individual's career. Star actors could expect to take just one of the major roles in a play, but other actors, and especially hired men, would be expected to 'double' as needed. *GE*

Bentley, Gerald Eades, *The Profession of Player in Shakespeare's Time, 1590–1642* (1984)
Ingram, William, *The Business of Playing: The Beginnings of the Adult Professional Theater in Elizabethan England* (1992)

act-intervals. See ACT AND SCENE DIVISIONS.

Act to Restrain Abuses of Players (1606), a parliamentary bill introducing a fine of £10 for each occasion upon which an actor 'jestingly or profanely' spoke the name of God or Jesus Christ. Plays written after this date have little or no such profanity, and plays already written show alteration of the offending phrases when revived, although the original unexpurgated text could safely be printed. Words such as 'zounds' (a contraction of 'God's wounds') could be replaced by 'why' or 'come', and exclamations such as 'O God!' softened to 'O heaven!' *GE*

Taylor, Gary, 'Swounds Revisited: Theatrical, Editorial, and Literary Expurgation', in Gary Taylor and John Jowett (eds.), *Shakespeare Reshaped 1606–1623* (1993)

'A cup of wine that's brisk and fine', sung by Silence in *2 Henry IV*, 5.3.46; the original tune is unknown. *JB*

Adam, Oliver's servant in *As You Like It*, helps Orlando escape into the forest of Ardenne. *AB*

Adams, J(ohn) C(ranford) (1903–86), American scholar, author of *The Globe Playhouse: Its Design and Equipment* (1942, 2nd edn. 1961), giving considerable prominence to the *inner* and the *upper* areas of the stage, now largely superseded. He was responsible for a reconstruction of the Globe for the Hofstra College Shakespeare Festival. *TM*

Adams, Joseph Quincy (1881–1946), American scholar, first director of the Folger Shakespeare Library (1934) and an editor of the New Variorum edition of Shakespeare. He was author of *A Life of William Shakespeare* (1916) and, using Revels records, *Shakespearean Playhouses: A History of English Theatres from the Beginnings to the Restoration* (1917). *TM*

adaptation. The practice of rewriting plays to fit them for conditions of performance different from those for which they were originally composed, in ways which go beyond cutting and the transposition of occasional scenes. Even leaving aside the questions as to whether Shakespeare's use of dramatic sources itself constitutes adaptation (e.g. whether *King Lear* can be regarded as an adaptation of *The True Chronicle History of King Leir*), or whether his own *revisions to plays such as *Hamlet* and *King Lear* might be classed as such, the altering of Shakespeare's scripts for later revivals certainly dates to before the publication of the First *Folio, which prints *Macbeth* in a form revised by Thomas *Middleton.

The adaptation of Shakespeare was at its most widespread, however, between the Restoration in 1660 and the middle of the 18th century (see RESTORATION AND EIGHTEENTH-CENTURY SHAKESPEARIAN PRODUCTION), when drastic changes in the design of playhouses (with the inception of elaborate changeable scenery), in the composition of theatre companies (with the advent of the professional actress), and in literary language and tastes (with the vogue for French neoclassicism, and its patriotic aftermath) motivated many playwrights and actor-managers to stage Shakespearian plays in heavily rewritten forms. The pioneer of adaptation was Sir William *Davenant, whose *The Law against Lovers* (1662) transplants Beatrice and Benedick into a sanitized *Measure for Measure* cast largely in rhyming couplets: this was followed by his immensely popular semi-operatic versions of *Macbeth* (1664) and *The Tempest* (1667), the latter co-written with one of his most successful followers in this vein, John *Dryden, who went on to write his own *Antony and Cleopatra* play *All for Love* (1677) and alter *Troilus and Cressida* (1679). Other major adaptors include Nahum *Tate (most famous for giving *King Lear* back the happy ending it had enjoyed in its sources, in 1681), Colley *Cibber, and David *Garrick.

An increasing veneration for Shakespeare's original texts had brought the practice of adaptation into disrepute in England by the middle of the 19th century, and while certain less canonical plays have regularly been retouched for performance since (notably the Henry VI plays, condensed at different times by both John *Barton and Adrian *Noble for the *Royal Shakespeare Company alone), full-scale adaptation has in modern times been more frequently associated with the work of translators fitting Shakespeare's plays to performance traditions far removed from his own, and with the transformation of his plays into *ballets, *operas, and *films.

Although many adaptations of Shakespeare may now seem objectionable, or at best merely quaint (simplifying his language, plotting, characterization, and morality alike), some constitute intelligent and engaged contemporary critical responses to his plays, and a few more recent playwrights have continued to use the medium as a form of practical Shakespeare criticism, notably Charles *Marowitz. *MD*

Clark, Sandra (ed.), *Shakespeare Made Fit: Restoration Adaptations of Shakespeare* (1997)
Marsden, Jean, *The Re-Imagined Text: Shakespeare, Adaptation, and Eighteenth-Century Literary Theory* (1995)
Sorelius, Gunnar, *'The Giant Race before the Flood': Pre-Restoration Drama on the Stage and in the Criticism of the Restoration* (1966)
Spencer, Christopher (ed.), *Five Restoration Adaptations of Shakespeare* (1965)

Addenbrooke, John, a 'gentleman' whom Shakespeare sued in the Stratford court of record for a debt of £6 in 1608. The case dragged on from 17 August 1608 to 7 June 1609. Addenbrooke was arrested but freed when Thomas Hornby, a blacksmith, stood surety for him. A jury awarded Shakespeare his debt and 24*s.* in costs which he tried to recover from Hornby as Addenbrooke could not be found. *SW*

Addison, Joseph (1672–1719), poet, playwright, and essayist, most famous as an author, with Sir Richard Steele, of the *Spectator* papers. In *Spectator* 40 he voiced one of the first attacks on Nahum Tate's adaptation of *King Lear*, in particular its addition of a happy ending and use of poetic justice. *JM*

Admiral's Men, the players of Charles Howard, second Lord Effingham—made Lord Admiral in 1585 and Earl of Nottingham in 1597—who were the main rivals of Shakespeare's company. Also known as the Lord Howard's Men (1576–85), the Earl of Nottingham's Men (1597–1603), Prince Henry's Men (1603–12), and Elector Palatine's Men (1613–24), their greatest asset in the 1590s and 1600s was the actor Edward Alleyn, whose uncle Philip Henslowe owned the Rose and Fortune playhouses used by the company. *GE*

Adonis. See VENUS AND ADONIS.

Adrian. (1) A Volscian who hears from the Roman Nicanor that Coriolanus has been banished from *Rome, *Coriolanus* 4.3. **(2)** A lord shipwrecked with Alonso on Prospero's island in *The Tempest.* *AB*

Adriana, wife to Antipholus of Ephesus in *The Comedy of Errors*, is unable to distinguish between him and his twin. *AB*

advertising. The use of Shakespeare in advertising can be traced back to the adoption of an image based on the *Chandos portrait as the publisher Jacob Tonson's trademark in 1710. More recently, some of the more famous characters from Shakespeare's plays have provided manufacturers with richly associative brand names (the tobacco sector alone has given us Hamlet cigars, Romeo Y Julietta panatellas, and Falstaff cigars). Shakespeare's characters also supply television commercials with conveniently familiar dramatic situations which can be rapidly established and then usually debased, for comic effect. Thus King Lear, ready to divide his kingdom, overlooks his two daughters who speak of love and loyalty for a third who offers a supply of ice-cold drinks (Coca-Cola, USA, 1997). Romeo woos Juliet, but only after her rumbling stomach has been prevented from joining in the dialogue (Shreddies Cereals, UK, 2000). Hamlet, about to meditate on Yorick's skull, drops it, improvises a football pass, and is endorsed as a lager drinker who 'gets it right' (Carling Black Label, UK, 1986). True Shakespearian dialogue is rarely used, but longer speeches may be quoted for effect; John of Gaunt's major speech from *Richard II* has been both used to convince consumers as to the Englishness of a certain tea (Typhoo, UK, 1994) and counterposed against images of dropped litter, to urge the use of refuse bins (Central Office of Information, UK, 1983.) Although *The Merchant of Venice* and *Timon of Athens* show that Shakespeare held much mercantile practice in low esteem, the epilogue to *As You Like It* suggests he took a more tolerant view of the advertising, such as it was, of his own day. *CC*

aediles, assistants to the tribunes Brutus and Sicinius, appear in *Coriolanus,* speaking at 3.1 and 3.3. *AB*

Aegeon. See EGEON.

Aemilia. See EMILIA.

Aemilius, a messenger in *Titus Andronicus* 4.4 and 5.1, presents Lucius as emperor, 5.3. *AB*

Aeneas, a Trojan commander in *Troilus and Cressida* (drawn from *Homer and *Virgil), gives Troilus the news that Cressida must be given to the Greeks, 4.3. *AB*

Aeschines, a lord of Tyre, appears with Helicanus, *Pericles* 3 and 8. *AB*

Aeschylus. See CRITICAL HISTORY; GREEK DRAMA.

Africa. See EAST AFRICA; SOUTHERN AFRICA; WEST AFRICA.

Agamemnon, leader of the Greek army (based on the character in *Homer's *Iliad*) presides over meetings of his commanders in *Troilus and Cressida.* *AB*

Agrippa, friend to Caesar in *Antony and Cleopatra,* suggests Antony should marry Octavia and hears Enobarbus' description of Cleopatra, 2.2. *AB*

Seven characters in search of seven cars
Prince Hal first! He's got flair! So give him the Corsair. Not just for its flair. But for its princely comfort and royal quality. Cleopatra of course will just have to have a Mk III Zodiac, for the speed, status and luxury that befit a queen. Now! For Romeo-and-Juliet! Only the Capri, that rich jewel of a car. Benedick prefers something smart and snappy—the Anglia. Bravo! For Prospero, the tempestuous magician, something magical. Like the Cortina, which pulls so many big-car qualities out of its small-car costs. What about Falstaff, the mountainous Falstaff. Choose him a car that makes molehills out of mountains. The Zephyr 4. Or the Zephyr 6 if he needs to make even faster escapes. Shylock has an embarrassment of choice. *Every* Ford car with its outstanding quality, proven reliability and unbeatable value for money, gives him his pound of flesh.
FORD–the dramatic choice

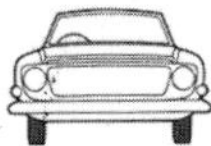

A classic Shakespearian advertisement, devised by Ford in honour of Shakespeare's 400th birthday in 1964. As ever, Shakespeare means authenticity and quality, though the idea of Prospero driving a Ford Cortina may rather strain the point.

Aguecheek, Sir Andrew, Sir Toby Belch's drinking companion in *Twelfth Night.* *AB*

Ajax, a Greek commander (based on the character in *Homer's *Iliad*), fights Hector, *Troilus and Cressida* 4.7. When the fight is abandoned, he invites Hector to dine at the Greek camp. *AB*

Alarbus, Tamora's eldest son in *Titus Andronicus,* is sacrificed to avenge the deaths of Titus' sons, 1.1. *AB*

alarums, a battle call or signal, usually for *drum(s), but exceptionally for *trumpet; it occurs more than 80 times in stage directions and texts of Shakespeare's plays. *JB*

Albany, Duke of. Husband of Goneril in *King Lear,* he moves from unease with Goneril, Regan, and Cornwall to defiance. *AB*

Albret, Charles d'. See CONSTABLE OF FRANCE.

alchemy. See SCOT, REGINALD.

Alcibiades, exiled and disaffected, leads an army against his native Athens in *Timon of Athens.* *AB*

Aldridge, Ira (1807–67), African-American actor who, following the closure of the African

Theatre in New York where he had played Romeo, moved to England where he appeared as Othello at the Royal Coburg in 1825. Though he added Lear, Macbeth, Richard III, and Aaron (in a drastically adapted version of *Titus Andronicus*) to his repertoire, it was with Othello that he was most closely identified in a career which was spent touring all over Europe. When he made his overdue West End debut at the Lyceum in 1858, Aldridge was praised for the originality of his interpretation in which Othello's softer elements were to the fore. *RF*

Marshall, Herbert, and Stock, Mildred, *Ira Aldridge: The Negro Tragedian* (1958)

Alençon, Duke of. He gives militant advice to Charles the Dauphin, *1 Henry VI* 5.2 and 5.7. *AB*

Alexander, servant to Cressida in *Troilus and Cressida*, describes Hector and Ajax to her, 1.2. *AB*

'Alexander'. See NATHANIEL, SIR.

Alexander, Peter (1894–1969), Scottish editor, biographer, and textual and literary critic. His *Shakespeare's Henry VI and Richard III* (1929) argues that the *First Part of the Contention* and *The True Tragedy of Richard III* (both 1594) are not independent source plays but pirated 'bad' quartos of the second and third parts of Shakespeare's *Henry VI*. This radical revision of the early canon is reflected in Alexander's later *Shakespeare's Life and Art* (1939), *A Shakespeare Primer* (1951), and *Shakespeare* (1964). His one-volume modernized edition of *The Complete Works* (1951) was adopted as a standard text by the BBC and many academic institutions. *TM*

alexandrine, the twelve-syllable line of classical French verse; or an English six-stress line (hexameter); sometimes found as a variant line in Shakespeare's dramatic verse, also as the line of *Biron's sonnet in *Love's Labour's Lost* (4.2.106–19). *CB*

Alexas is one of Cleopatra's attendants. His treachery and execution are related in *Antony and Cleopatra* 4.6. *AB*

Alice, Catherine's gentlewoman in *Henry V*, teaches her English, 3.4, and interprets for King Harry and Catherine, 5.2. *AB*

'Aliena'. See CELIA.

Allde, Edward. See PRINTING AND PUBLISHING.

Allen, Giles (d. 1608), owner of the site upon which the Theatre was built. On 13 April 1576 Allen leased a plot of land in Shoreditch to James Burbage who, with his brother-in-law John Brayne, built the Theatre on it. Allen and the Burbages failed to reach agreement on renewal of the lease in 1597, and December/January 1598–9 the Burbages removed their playhouse to re-erect it as the Bankside Globe. Allen's ensuing legal battles with the Burbages provide much of our knowledge about the Theatre and the Globe. *GE*

Berry, Herbert, *Shakespeare's Playhouses* (1987)

Alleyn, Edward (1566–1626), actor (Worcester's Men 1583, Admiral's/Prince Henry's 1589–97 and 1600–6) and housekeeper. The 17-year-old Alleyn was named as one of Worcester's Men in a licence of 14 January 1583 and he was already a renowned actor when, on 22 October 1592, he married Joan Woodward, the stepdaughter of Philip Henslowe, at whose Rose playhouse he had led Lord Strange's Men from February to June that year. We know of Alleyn's personal life through charming letters which passed between him and Joan while he led Lord Strange's Men on tour in 1593, and we hear of his ever-rising professional fame through glowing reports by Thomas Nashe, amongst others. Contemporary allusions suggest that Alleyn was an unusually large man—which undoubtedly helped his celebrated presentation of Marlowe's anti-hero Tamburlaine—and a surviving portrait and signet ring confirm that he was about 6 feet (2 m) tall, well above the period's average. To augment his bulk Alleyn apparently developed a powerful style of large gestures and loud speaking which others mocked as 'stalking' or 'strutting' and 'roaring'. Alleyn took the lead roles in Marlowe's *The Jew of Malta* and *Doctor Faustus*, Greene's *Orlando furioso*, and also Sebastian in the anonymous *Frederick and Basilea*, Muly Mahamet in Peele's *The Battle of Alcazar*, and Tamar Cam in the anonymous *1 Tamar Cam*. After three more years at the Rose (1594–7) Alleyn retired but he returned to the stage when Henslowe's Fortune opened in 1600 and continued until some time before 30 April 1606 when the Prince's Men were issued a patent which lacks his name. In early May 1608 Alleyn performed in an entertainment for James I at Salisbury House on the Strand and received £20. On 13 September 1619 Alleyn founded the College of God's Gift at Dulwich which received Alleyn's and Henslowe's papers, most importantly the latter's *Diary*, upon which much of our knowledge of the theatre is based. Joan Alleyn died on 28 June 1623 and on 3 December that year Alleyn married Constance, the eldest daughter of John Donne, the Dean of St Paul's. *GE*

Cerasano, S. P., 'Tamburlaine and Edward Alleyn's Ring', *Shakespeare Survey*, 47 (1994)

All for Love. See ANTONY AND CLEOPATRA.

All Is True (Henry VIII) *(see page 6)*

alliteration, repetition of similar sounds (usually initial consonants) within any sequence of words:

> Borne on the bier with white and bristly beard
> (Sonnet 12)

Alliteration may also link the initial stressed consonant of a word with that of a stressed syllable *within* a word: 'Beated and chopp'd with *t*ann'd an*t*iqui*t*y' (Sonnet 62, l. 10); 'When I did *s*peak of some di*st*ressful *st*roke' (*Othello* 1.3.157). *CB*

All's Well That Ends Well *(see page 10)*

allusion, a passing or indirect reference to something (e.g. a written work, a legend, a historical figure) assumed to be understood by the audience or reader, as with the reference to the mythical Phoenix in Sonnet 19. *CB*

Alonso is the King of Naples in *The Tempest.* His son Ferdinand and Prospero's daughter (Miranda) become betrothed, reconciling him to Prospero. *AB*

ambassadors. (1) French ambassadors bring 'treasure' (actually tennis balls) on behalf of the Dauphin to King Harry, *Henry V* 1.2.245–57. **(2)** Ambassadors from England announce the deaths of Rosencrantz and Guildenstern, *Hamlet* 5.2.321–6. **(3)** Antony uses his schoolmaster (see 3.11.71–2) as an ambassador, *Antony and Cleopatra* 3.12 and 3.13 (he was first named as Euphronius by *Capell, following Shakespeare's source *Plutarch). *AB*

America. See UNITED STATES OF AMERICA; LATIN AMERICA.

Amiens, one of Duke Senior's attendants in *As You Like It*, sings in 2.5 and 2.7. *AB*

Amyot, Jacques. See PLUTARCH.

anachronism, the introduction of anything not belonging to the supposed time of a play's action: most famously the clock in *Julius Caesar* (2.1.192). The term may also be applied to modern-dress productions of Shakespearian plays. *CB*

anacoluthon, a change of grammatical construction in mid-sentence, leaving the initial utterance unfinished:

> Today as I came by I callèd there—
> But I shall grieve you to report the rest
> (*Richard II* 2.2.94–5)

CB

anadiplosis, a rhetorical figure in which clauses, lines, or sentences are linked by repetition of the final word or phrase of the first in the initial word or phrase of the second:

> My brain I'll prove the female to my soul,
> My soul the father . . .
> (*Richard II* 5.5.6–7)

CB

(cont. on page 9)

All Is True (Henry VIII)

During a performance of this play on 29 June 1613 the cannon fired to salute the King's entry in 1.4 set alight the Globe theatre's thatch, and the whole building was destroyed. According to one letter about the disaster, this was at most the play's fourth performance, and stylistic examination confirms that this must have been a new play in 1613.

Text: Three out of five surviving accounts of the fire refer to the play by what was clearly its original title, *All Is True* (a ballad on the subject even has the allusive refrain 'All this is true'), while the other two cite only its subject matter, calling it 'the play of Henry 8'. A decade later the compilers of the First Folio adopted the latter procedure (as they did with the other English histories), publishing the play's only authoritative text as *The Famous History of the Life of King Henry the Eight* (abbreviated to *The Life of King Henry the Eight* for the running title: the *Oxford edition, 1986, was the first to restore the title by which Shakespeare knew the play). The text (to judge, in part, from its unusual number of brackets) was probably set from a scribal transcript of authorial papers, possibly annotated for theatrical use.

Although there is no external evidence to confirm what many students of the play's versification have believed since the mid-19th century, *All Is True* was probably written in collaboration with John *Fletcher, as were two other plays from this final phase of Shakespeare's career, *The Two Noble Kinsmen* (1613–14) and the lost *Cardenio* (1613). Based on a variety of linguistic and stylistic criteria (particularly the frequency and nature of rare vocabulary, usage of colloquialisms in verse passages, and the use of certain grammatical constructions), the Prologue, 1.3–4, 3.1, 5.2–4, and the Epilogue are most commonly attributed to Fletcher, who may also have revised Shakespeare's 2.1–2, much of 3.2, and all of 4.1–2.

Sources: The playwrights' principal sources for their account of the middle years of Henry's reign—from the Field of the Cloth of Gold (1520) to the christening of Princess Elizabeth (1533)—were the chronicles of Raphael *Holinshed and Edward *Halle. *Foxe's *Book of Martyrs* (1563) supplied material for Cranmer's scenes in Act 5, and Samuel Rowley's earlier play on Henry's reign, *When You See Me, You Know Me* (*c*.1603–5), may have influenced the depiction of Wolsey's fall. The dramatists' principal alterations to their material consist in the compression of events, and the sometimes cosmetic alteration of their sequence. Despite the impression given by the play, Queen Catherine was still alive when Princess Elizabeth was born (hence the Catholic view that she was illegitimate), and despite the impression of an achieved harmony at the play's close, Cranmer's troubles with the Council, dramatized in 5.1–2, still lay seven years ahead when she was christened.

Synopsis: A prologue promises a serious play which will depict the abrupt falls of great men. **1.1** The Duke of Norfolk tells the Duke of Buckingham about the spectacular recent meeting in France between King Henry VIII, his French counterpart, and their respective courts, arranged by Cardinal Wolsey. As Buckingham marvels at Wolsey's influence, Lord Abergavenny joins the conversation, and the three lament the Cardinal's power, noting that the spurious peace he negotiated with France has already been broken. When Wolsey enters he and Buckingham exchange disdainful stares before the Cardinal, questioning his secretary about a pending interview with Buckingham's Surveyor, leaves, confident the Duke will soon be humbled. As Buckingham informs Norfolk of his intention to denounce Wolsey, officials arrest him for high treason.

1.2 Queen Katherine, seconded by Norfolk, speaks against Wolsey's special taxations: surprised by what he hears, the King orders them to be repealed and their defaulters pardoned, a decision Wolsey quietly instructs his secretary to credit to his own intercession. Despite the Queen's scepticism, the allegations made at Wolsey's instigation by the surveyor are sufficient to persuade the King of Buckingham's treason. **1.3** The Lord Chamberlain, Lord Sands, and Sir

Thomas Lovell deplore the influence of French fashions before leaving for a lavish supper at Wolsey's palace. **1.4** During Wolsey's feast, the King and his party arrive disguised as shepherds and choose dancing partners: the King takes Anne Boleyn, in whose company he withdraws after his identity is revealed.

2.1 Two gentlemen discuss Buckingham, just condemned to death: under guard, Buckingham speaks to his sympathizers, forgiving his enemies and comparing his downfall to that of his father, also unjustly condemned on a corrupted servant's evidence. The gentlemen lament his fate and speak of a rumour that Wolsey has incited the King to initiate divorce proceedings against Katherine, to be heard before the newly arrived Cardinal Campeius. **2.2** The Lord Chamberlain, Norfolk, and the Duke of Suffolk deplore Wolsey's machinations against the Queen. The pensive King dismisses Norfolk and Suffolk but welcomes Campeius and Wolsey, and confers with Wolsey's secretary Gardiner: meanwhile Wolsey assures Campeius of Gardiner's complete obedience. The King sends Gardiner to Katherine: their case will be heard at Blackfriars. **2.3** In conversation with an old lady, Anne Boleyn pities Katherine the sorrows of queenship, and is ribaldly accused of hypocrisy, especially when the Lord Chamberlain arrives to tell Anne that the King has made her Marchioness of Pembroke. **2.4** After ceremonious preliminaries, the divorce hearing begins with Katherine pleading eloquently for the validity of her marriage and her own status as a loyal wife: she denies the authority and impartiality of the court, which has her enemy Wolsey as one judge, appeals to the Pope, and walks out. The King explains his grounds for seeking the divorce: since Katherine was formerly married to his elder brother, his conscience tells him their marriage is incestuous, although if the court decrees otherwise he will accept its decision. Prevaricating, Campeius adjourns the case, and the King places his hopes instead in his adviser Thomas Cranmer.

3.1 Katherine, among her women, listens to a song before Wolsey and Campeius arrive to urge her to accept the divorce: angrily insisting that they speak English rather than Latin, she defends her position with spirit before subsiding into a more biddable despair. **3.2** Norfolk, Suffolk, Lord Surrey, and the Lord Chamberlain muster their opposition to the now vulnerable Wolsey: the King has intercepted letters to Rome in which the Cardinal, opposing the King's wish to marry Anne Boleyn, advised the Pope to refuse the divorce, and with Cranmer's support he has secretly married Anne already. They watch as a discontented Wolsey is called to the King, who has been reading an inventory of the Cardinal's personal wealth accidentally enclosed with some state papers. Sarcastically praising Wolsey's selfless devotion to duty, the King leaves with his nobles, giving Wolsey two papers to read as he goes—the inventory and the letter to the Pope. The nobles return in triumph to announce the Cardinal's arrest for high treason and the confiscation of his property. Left alone, Wolsey bids farewell to his glory, before a commiserating Thomas Cromwell confirms his utter defeat: Sir Thomas More will replace Wolsey as Chancellor, Cranmer is Archbishop of Canterbury, and Anne Boleyn will shortly be crowned. The humbled Wolsey, weeping at Cromwell's loyalty, urges him to forsake him and serve the King faithfully.

4.1 The two gentlemen watch Anne Boleyn's coronation procession, after which a third describes the ceremony itself, and reports the enmity between Cranmer and Gardiner, now Bishop of Winchester. **4.2** The ailing Katherine hears of Wolsey's death from her usher Griffith, who speaks of Wolsey's virtues and assures her that he died a penitent. Falling asleep, Katherine has a vision of six white-robed figures who hold a garland over her head: both Griffith and her woman Patience are sure she is near death. Caputius, ambassador from her nephew the Holy Roman Emperor, arrives, and Katherine gives him a letter to the King asking him to look after their daughter and her attendants, before she is carried away to bed.

5.1 Gardiner, in response to Lovell's news that Anne is in labour, says he would be glad if she, Cranmer, and Cromwell were dead: he has moved the Council against Cranmer, whom they will interrogate next morning. The King speaks privately with Cranmer, whom he warns against his enemies' malice and to whom he gives a ring as a sign of his protection. The Old Lady announces the birth of a daughter. **5.2** Cranmer is kept waiting outside the council chamber: seeing this, Doctor Butts places the King where he can secretly watch the Council's proceedings. The Lord Chancellor, seconded by Gardiner, accuses Cranmer of spreading heresies, and though defended by Cromwell the Archbishop is sentenced to the Tower. Cranmer's enemies are discomfited when he produces the King's ring, and more so when the King enters, reprimanding Gardiner, whom he forces to embrace Cranmer, and further showing his support for the Archbishop by inviting him to be his daughter's godfather. **5.3** A porter and his man are unable to control the mob trying to see the state christening, and are rebuked by the Lord Chamberlain. **5.4** At the grandly ceremonial baptism of Princess Elizabeth, Cranmer is inspired to prophesy that both her reign and that of her successor will be golden ages. An epilogue hopes the play may at least have pleased female spectators by its depiction of a good woman.

Artistic features: As its title suggests, *All Is True* is unusually interested in historical verisimilitude, although the history it narrates between its elaborate recreations of Tudor royal pageantry (described in the longest and most detailed stage directions in the canon) is one which counsels against putting any faith in specious appearances. Compared to the earlier histories it is episodic, resembling an anthology of morality plays in its successive depictions of the falls of Buckingham, Wolsey, and Katherine (each given memorable rhetorical set pieces rather than sustained characterization), and its version of history has a strong tinge of the non-realistic late romances. The wronged Katherine's self-defence at her trial is reminiscent of Hermione's in *The Winter's Tale*, and her husband too will perhaps ultimately be redeemed, according to Cranmer's concluding prophecy, by his infant daughter.

Critical history: Despite the perennial presence of its great speeches in anthologies of Shakespeare's beauties (most famously Wolsey's farewell to his greatness), the play was long dismissed by literary critics as a mere theatrical showpiece, notable for what *Johnson called its 'pomp', interesting primarily as a specimen of how far Shakespeare was prepared to depart from his historical sources in the interests of flattering King James's views of kingship and of the dynasty which had preceded his own accession. *Gervinus, writing from outside the British engagement with this crucial passage of royal history, was one of the few 19th-century commentators to praise Shakespeare's portrayal of Henry. Much commentary on *All Is True* remains inextricably bound up with the interpretation of the history it depicts, its significance to Shakespeare's Jacobean audience, and, to a lesser degree, how far the authors intended that responses to the play should be coloured by a knowledge of the events it chooses not to dramatize (such as the imminent judicial murder of Anne Boleyn). To E. M. W. *Tillyard and others, the play upheld the 'Tudor Myth', showing the King's gradual accession to maturity (and, by extension, that of his kingdom), which is signalled by his break from Wolsey and Rome and ultimately rewarded by the birth of the destined Protestant national heroine Elizabeth. More recent critics, when not sidetracked by the issue of the play's authorship, have found the play at best sceptical about Tudor politics, if not nostalgically Catholic in its sympathies, preferring to focus on the unusually sympathetic depiction of Queen Katherine (the only Catholic character granted a heavenly vision in all of English Renaissance drama), and the downplaying, compared to other contemporary plays about the Tudors, of Reformation doctrine.

Stage history: The play enjoys the unusual distinction in the canon of being less popular on stage now than at any time in its history. Sir Henry *Wotton, reporting the Globe fire, admittedly, feared that its detailed representation of state ceremonies might be 'sufficient in truth within a while to make greatness very familiar, if not ridiculous', but it was still in the King's Company's repertoire in 1628 (when Charles I's favourite George Villiers, Duke of Buckingham, commissioned a private performance at the rebuilt Globe), and after the Restoration it established itself as a regularly revived 'stock' play from 1664 onwards. Thomas *Betterton played the King, coached (according to a memoir of 1708) by Sir William *Davenant, who had his view of the role from *Lowin, said to have been instructed in it by Shakespeare himself. During the 18th century the play was performed often, especially whenever public interest in royal pageantry was piqued by a real-life coronation, at ever-increasing expense: *Garrick's production (much revived between 1742 and 1768, with Garrick as Henry) employed 140 actors for the coronation procession in 4.1. These spectacular interludes necessitated ever-greater cuts to the text as later generations of actor-managers, more usually casting themselves as Wolsey, sought to outdo their predecessors. *Kemble played the Cardinal in his own redaction, with his sister Sarah *Siddons as a much admired Queen, from 1788 to 1816: he was succeeded by Macready from 1823, and by the time Samuel Phelps first played Wolsey at Sadler's Wells in 1845 the play was finishing at his final exit, though Phelps later restored Act 4. The vogue for spectacle reached a climax with Charles *Kean's production, which achieved a record 100 performances at the Princess's in 1855 and was repeated three years later (with the young Ellen *Terry as one of Katherine's visionary angels): this featured numbers of grandly robed aldermen heading for Elizabeth's christening in state barges, in front of a moving diorama of all London. Irving's popular 1892 production at the Lyceum, with himself as Wolsey, also cut most of Acts 4 and 5, and Beerbohm Tree's in 1910 (which subsequently toured the United States) ended with Anne's coronation.

In the 20th-century theatre the play, apparently inseparable from pictorial traditions of staging which now seemed quaintly or offensively Victorian, fell into some disfavour, though still revived at intervals for major actors to measure themselves against the starring roles: Sybil *Thorndike played Katherine (Old Vic, 1918, Empire theatre, 1925), Charles *Laughton played Henry (Sadler's Wells, 1933, directed by Tyrone Guthrie, with Flora *Robson as Katherine), and John *Gielgud Wolsey (Old Vic, 1958). Guthrie revived the play twice more, the last time in 1953, when the onlookers at Anne's coronation held anachronistic newspapers above their heads against rain in an allusion to the recent coronation of Elizabeth II. There were two notable attempts to rebel against the dominant, Holbein-based way of designing the play, one at the Cambridge Festival Theatre in 1931, when Terence *Gray caused an uproar by using a modernist aluminium set and Lewis Carroll-influenced costumes based on playing cards (further defying expectations by having the baby doll Elizabeth thrown into the audience in 5.4), and one at Stratford in 1984, when Howard Davies offered a professedly Brechtian production full of deliberate anachronisms associating Henry's regime with Stalin's. The play's last major 20th-century revival, though, directed by Greg Doran for the RSC at the Swan in 1997, returned opulently to Tudor dress, with Jane Lapotaire as a traditionally poignant Katherine. *MD*

On the screen: Two silent versions were made, a British film featuring Sir Herbert Beerbohm Tree (1911) and an American one from Vitagraph (1912). The only sound film is BBC TV's *Henry the Eighth* (1979). *AD*

Recent major editions

R. A. Foakes (Arden, 1958); Jay L. Halio (Oxford, 1999); A. R. Humphreys (Penguin, 1971)

Some representative criticism

Hoy, Cyrus, 'The Shares of Fletcher and his Collaborators in the Beaumont and Fletcher Canon (VII)', *Studies in Bibliography* 15 (1962)

Jackson, MacD. P., *Studies in Attribution: Middleton and Shakespeare* (1979)
Rackin, Phyllis, *Stages of History: Shakespeare's English Chronicles* (1990)
Tillyard, E. M. W., 'Why did Shakespeare write *Henry VIII*?', *Critical Quarterly* 3 (1961)
Woolf, D. R., *The Idea of History in Early Stuart England* (1990)

anagnorisis (Greek, 'recognition'), the turning point in a drama at which the protagonist discovers the true state of affairs to which he or she had been blind—as with Othello's recognition that Desdemona had not betrayed him. *CB*

anapaest, a metrical unit ('foot') comprising two unstressed syllables followed by one stressed syllable, rarely found as the basis of full lines:

> With a hey, and a ho, and a hey-nonny-no
> (*As You Like It* 5.3.16)

CB

anaphora, repetition of the same word or phrase at the start of successive clauses or lines:

> This blessèd plot, this earth, this realm, this England
> (*Richard II* 2.1.50)

CB

anaptyxis, insertion of an extra vowel, usually before a medial *r* or *l* and after the word's principal accent. This occurs sometimes in words like *ang-ry, Hen-ry, monst-rous, child-ren, fiddler, wrast-ler,* and even *Eng-land* (*Hamlet* 4.3.46). Cf. Lady Macbeth's 'The raven himself is hoarse | That croaks the fatal *ent-rance* of Duncan | Under my battlements' (1.5.38–40). *CB*

Anatomy of Abuses, The. See Stubbes, Philip.

Anderson, Dame Judith (1898–1992), American actress, who arrived in the USA from Australia in 1918. Throughout her career she specialized in operatic, *grande dame* roles, and came to be regarded as the last of the grand-style tragedy queens. Her Shakespearian roles included Gertrude (in John *Gielgud's *Hamlet* in New York, 1936), Hamlet (in which she toured, remarkably, at the age of 71), and—famously and self-definingly—Lady Macbeth, first opposite *Olivier in London in 1937, and later opposite Maurice Evans in New York (1941, and again on film in 1960). Her last role was in an American daytime soap opera called *Santa Barbara* (1984). *MD*

Anderson, Mary (1858–1940), American actress, who made her debut in 1875 at Louisville, aged 16, as Juliet, a role to which her natural gifts of stature, face, and voice were well suited, as they were to Rosalind, Hermione, and Perdita. Within this limited range Mary Anderson adorned the stage on both sides of the Atlantic. Her *Romeo and Juliet* at the Lyceum (1884), with William Terriss as Romeo and designs by Lewis Wingfield, enhanced her reputation at home as much as in London and she was fêted during her 1885–6 US tour, but later resentment at her European pretensions contributed to her breakdown (1889) and subsequent retirement to Broadway, England, where she wrote several volumes of memoirs. *RF*

'And let me the cannikin clink', sung by Iago in *Othello* 2.3.63; the original tune is unknown. *JB*

Andrewes, Robert, a scrivener who drew up and witnessed the documents for Shakespeare's purchase of the *Blackfriars Gatehouse in 1613. Another possible though faint Shakespearian connection is his preparing the will of Marie James, mother of the brewer Elias James, whose epitaph Shakespeare may have written. *SW*

'And Robin Hood, Scarlet and John', snatch of a *broadside ballad sung by Silence in *2 Henry IV* 5.3.104; also alluded to by Falstaff in *The Merry Wives of Windsor* 1.1.158. The original tune is unknown. *JB*

Andromache, Hector's wife in *Troilus and Cressida,* tries to dissuade him from going into battle, 5.3. *AB*

Andronicus, Marcus, a Roman tribune in *Titus Andronicus* who helps his brother Titus take revenge. *AB*

Andronicus, Titus. See Titus Andronicus.

'And sword and shield | In bloody field', fragment sung by Pistol in *Henry V* 3.2.9; the original tune is unknown. *JB*

'And will a not come again', sung by Ophelia in *Hamlet* 4.5.188. A tune with 17th-century origins (a variant of 'The merry, merry milkmaids') was apparently sung to the words at Drury Lane in the late 18th century. *JB*

Angelica. See nurses.

Angelo. (1) A goldsmith in *The Comedy of Errors,* he has Antipholus of Ephesus arrested, 4.1. **(2)** Given absolute power by the resigning Duke Vincentio, he threatens Isabella's brother with execution if she refuses to have sex with him in *Measure for Measure.* *AB*

Angers, Citizen of. See Citizen of Angers.

Angus, a thane, announces Cawdor's lost thaneship in *Macbeth* 1.2.107–14 and marches against Macbeth in Act 5. *AB*

The American actress Mary Anderson (1859–1940), the first to double the roles of Hermione and Perdita in *The Winter's Tale*.

animal shows. Baiting of bulls and bears using dogs was already a popular entertainment on Bankside when the first playhouses were constructed. Like open-air playhouses, baiting rings were wooden structures, approximately round, and scholars have conjectured that a travelling players' booth placed within a baiting ring gave the design for the playhouses. However, baiting rings do not elevate the lowest auditorium gallery—which is essential in a playhouse else the yardlings obscure the view—because the baiting ring yard is necessarily free of spectators. Also, the barriers needed to contain animals make for poor sightlines. Philip Henslowe, joint Master and Keeper of the King's Bears with Edward Alleyn from 1604, built the first combined playhouse and baiting ring, the Hope, in 1614. *GE*

Brownstein, Oscar, 'Why Didn't Burbage Lease the Beargarden? A Conjecture in Comparative Architecture', in Herbert Berry (ed.), *The First Public Playhouse: The Theatre in Shoreditch 1576–1598* (1979)

Animated Tales, The. See Shakespeare: The Animated Tales.

Anjou, Margaret of. See Margaret.

(*cont. on page 13*)

All's Well That Ends Well

Ambivalent and autumnal in mood, *All's Well That Ends Well* clearly belongs to the period of the *problem comedies (of which it is perhaps the most accomplished and the most elusive), although its precise date, in the absence of any external evidence or clear topical references, is harder to fix. In vocabulary it is closely linked to *Measure for Measure*, *Troilus and Cressida*, and *Othello*, and it is most likely to have been written just after them, probably around 1604–5.

Text: The play's only substantive text is that printed in the First Folio, apparently (to judge from its inconsistent speech prefixes, idiosyncratic punctuation, and *mute characters) from Shakespeare's own *foul papers. This was probably the first play the Folio's compositors set from such copy, which may help to explain its high percentage of misprints, errors, and cruces. Some details—such as the play's division into five acts, its specification of *cornets in stage directions, and its use of the initials 'G' and 'E' in speech prefixes for the respective Dumaine brothers (possibly indications that these roles once belonged to King's Company actors Gough and Ecclestone)—suggest that this authorial manuscript may have been used as a *promptbook for a conjectural revival around 1610–11.

Source: The main plot of the play is from *Boccaccio, the novella of Beltramo de Rossiglione and Giglietta de Narbone recounted on the third day of the *Decameron*, which Shakespeare probably read in English in William *Painter's *Palace of Pleasure* (1566–7). Shakespeare's additions are, principally, the comic roles of Paroles and Lavatch.

Synopsis: **1.1** The widowed Countess of Roussillon takes leave of her son Bertram, who has been summoned to court by the terminally ill King of France, of whom he is a ward: with him goes the Countess's old friend Lord Lafeu. The Countess's own ward, Helen, weeping orphaned daughter of the physician Gérard de Narbonne, confesses in soliloquy that her tears are inspired not by her father's death but by Bertram's departure, lamenting that the difference between their ranks renders her secret desire for him hopeless. She is interrupted by the self-styled captain Paroles, Bertram's companion, who engages in a bantering dialogue about virginity before following the Count: alone again, Helen hints that she may use the King's illness as a means towards furthering her pursuit of Bertram. **1.2** The King, declining to aid Florence in its campaign against Siena, nevertheless agrees that French noblemen may volunteer on either side. Presented with Bertram by Lafeu, he waxes nostalgic about the Count's late father, laments his own sickness, and asks wistfully after the dead Gérard de Narbonne. **1.3** The Countess is asked for permission to marry by her misogynistic servant Lavatch, whom she sends to fetch Helen, reported to have been overheard sighing for Bertram. Alone with Helen, the Countess exacts a confession of love from her, and gives her approval for Helen's plan to visit Paris in the hopes of curing the King by means of one of her late father's prescriptions.

2.1 The King bids farewell to the two Lords Dumaine, off to the Italian wars, as does Bertram, who longs to follow them despite the King's commands to the contrary. Lafeu introduces Helen to the King, and she succeeds in persuading him to try her father's remedy: he agrees that if it succeeds he will grant her any husband in his power. **2.2** The Countess sends Lavatch to court with a letter for Helen. **2.3** The fully restored King calls together all his lords for Helen to make her choice of bridegroom: she picks Bertram, who indignantly resists the idea of marrying a poor physician's daughter. The King compels him, however, to go through an immediate wedding ceremony: meanwhile Lafeu scoffs at Paroles's pretensions to courage and social status. Returning from his enforced wedding, Bertram tells Paroles he means to send Helen back to Roussillon without consummating the marriage and run away to the wars. **2.4** Paroles tells a grieved but compliant Helen that Bertram must depart at once on unspecified business and wishes her to return home. **2.5** Lafeu warns Bertram, in vain, against placing any faith in Paroles. Bertram takes a cold farewell from Helen, before he and Paroles leave for Italy.

3.1 The Lords Dumaine are welcomed to the battlefront by the Duke of Florence. **3.2** The Countess, delighted by the news of Bertram's marriage to Helen, is shocked to learn that he has run off, never intending to consummate it. Helen arrives with the Lords Dumaine, who confirm that Bertram has joined the Duke of Florence's army: in a letter he vows that he will never be Helen's husband until she can show him the ring from his finger (which he never means to take off) and a child of hers to which he is father (which he never means to beget). Alone, Helen resolves to steal away, so that Bertram may be willing to return home from the perils of combat. **3.3** The Duke of Florence makes Bertram general of his cavalry. **3.4** The Countess receives a letter from Helen explaining that she has gone away on a pilgrimage so that Bertram may come home: she dispatches this news towards Bertram, hoping that both he and Helen may return to Roussillon. **3.5** A Florentine widow, her daughter Diana, and their neighbour Mariana are looking out for the army: Mariana warns Diana against Paroles, who has been soliciting on Bertram's behalf, before an incognito Helen arrives as a pilgrim, and, accepting a lodging at the Widow's guesthouse, learns of Bertram's pursuit of Diana. They watch the troops pass—and see Paroles's affected vexation about the capture of a drum—and agree, at Helen's insistence, to speak further. **3.6** The Lords Dumaine persuade Bertram to expose Paroles's cowardice by encouraging his boasted solo attempt to recapture the drum, offering to capture Paroles disguised as enemy soldiers and allow Bertram to overhear his interrogation. **3.7** Helen, her identity revealed, persuades the Widow to allow Diana to pretend to accept Bertram's advances so that she can be replaced at a clandestine rendezvous by Helen.

4.1 The Lords Dumaine and others lie in wait for a frightened Paroles: simulating an absurd foreign language, they ambush him and lead him off to be questioned. **4.2** Bertram ardently woos Diana, who, following Helen's instructions, persuades him to give her his ring before inviting him to her darkened chamber, for an hour only, at midnight. **4.3** The Lords Dumaine reflect on Bertram's vices and virtues, on his reported seduction of Diana, and on the reported death of Helen: an exhilarated and unrepentant Bertram arrives to witness Paroles's interrogation before setting off for France, the wars being over. The blindfolded Paroles, questioned through a supposed interpreter, invents scandalous gossip about the Lords Dumaine as well as revealing military secrets, and denounces Bertram as an immature seducer. Finally unmuffled and confronted by his comrades, who leave in contempt, Paroles resolves henceforth to make a shameless living as a laughing stock. **4.4** Helen, the Widow, and Diana set off for Marseille to see the King on their way to Roussillon. **4.5** Awaiting Bertram's arrival, Lafeu and the Countess plan that the forgiven Bertram should marry Lafeu's daughter, a scheme the King has already approved.

5.1 Hearing that the King has left Marseille for Roussillon, Helen and her two companions proceed thither. **5.2** Paroles begs to be received by Lafeu, who has already heard of his exposure and agrees to employ him as a fool. **5.3** The Countess, Lafeu, and the King, though lamenting the supposedly dead Helen, receive a pardoned Bertram, who claims that he disdained Helen only because already in love with Lafeu's daughter, for whom, with the King's approval, he produces an engagement ring. The ring, however, is one given him in the dark by Helen in Florence, and is recognized by the King as one he himself gave her. Bertram's denials that he took it from Helen are in vain, and he is arrested under suspicion of having killed her. A letter arrives from Diana, revealing that Bertram promised to marry her on Helen's death: she and the Widow are admitted and confront Bertram, confounding his insistence that Diana was a common prostitute by producing the ancestral ring he gave her. Diana's claim that it was she who gave Bertram Helen's ring, though, brings her evidence into question, and Paroles's comically equivocal testimony clarifies nothing. Finally, a riddling Diana sends the Widow to fetch the pregnant Helen, whom Bertram, the conditions of his earlier letter now conclusively fulfilled, has to accept as his wife. The King, after promising to reward Diana with any husband she chooses, speaks an epilogue.

Artistic features: The play highlights the folk-tale origins of its story by casting dialogue in rhyme at crucial points of the narrative: these include Helen's last soliloquy in 1.1, her interview with the King in 2.1, her choice of husband in 2.3, and the epistolary sonnet in 3.4 by which she announces her departure as a pilgrim, as well as Diana's riddles and Bertram's final capitulation in 5.3. Since this folk tale, however, is depicted as taking place in a realistic world (in which even the clown Lavatch is a bitter and unhappy cynic), the play is most remarkable for its irony, holding us at a reflective distance from its driven and unconfiding heroine and its caddish hero alike. Shakespeare multiplies the story's ironies and parallelisms by his pointed juxtaposition of the gulling of Paroles (who believes himself to be committing treason when he is merely destroying his credit with his comrades) with the bed-trick used against Bertram (who believes himself to be committing adultery when he is really condemning himself to his arranged marriage).

Critical history: Before the mid-20th century, *All's Well That Ends Well* characteristically received only qualified or grudging praise from literary critics, when it enjoyed their attention at all. Throughout its critical history the play's inversions of the normal patterns of romantic comedy—its sympathy with an older generation who are usually right to circumscribe the freedom of the younger, the relentless pursuit by the play's heroine of a love she knows to be unrequited, and the general atmosphere of disenchantment, loss, and mourning within which her plot unfolds—have made readers happier with Shakespeare's more festive comedies uncomfortable, while the play's closeness to a single narrative source has allowed some to dismiss it as a hasty piece of professional scriptwriting, some of whose faults (such as the indelicacy or improbability of the bed-trick) can be blamed on Boccaccio. Charlotte *Lennox was among the first to make the comparison between play and source, in 1753, generally to the play's disadvantage, and her dislike of Bertram in particular was memorably seconded by Samuel *Johnson (1765): 'a man noble without generosity, and young without truth; who marries *Helen* as a coward, and leaves her as a profligate: when she is dead by his unkindness, sneaks home to a second marriage, is accused by a woman whom he has wronged, defends himself by falsehood, and is dimissed to happiness.' *Coleridge, more sympathetic to Bertram's plight, defended him by attacking Helen instead ('it must be confessed that her character is not very delicate, and it required all Shakespeare's consummate skill to interest us for her', *Table Talk*, 1835, although elsewhere he describes her as 'Shakespeare's loveliest character'), and for most of the next century discussions of the play continued to centre on whether its hero (hapless victim or bounder) or its heroine (virtuous exemplar of self-help or rapist upstart) was less objectionable. George Bernard *Shaw, for example, who praised the play as a prefiguration of Ibsen, sided with Helen, Frank *Harris with Bertram. Only since the 1930s have what once seemed the play's moral failures or equivocations been revalued as successful dramatizations of an ethically complex world, its interest in expiation, pilgrimage, and forgiveness (particularly its plays on the word 'grace') often linked with the (similarly revalued) late romances. Enthusiastic supporters have included George Wilson *Knight and E. M. W. *Tillyard, although it is notable that the first monograph devoted solely to this play (by J. G. Price) only appeared in 1968, and is called *The Unfortunate Comedy.*

Stage history: Price's book is largely concerned with the fortunes of the play on the English stage down to the 1960s, which had amply earned it this title. No performances are recorded before a revival at Goodman's Fields in 1741: over the next 60 years it had only 51 London performances and for the whole of the 19th century only seventeen. Early comment on the play is largely confined to the much loved role of Paroles, played successively by Theophilus *Cibber, Charles *Macklin, and, especially, Henry *Woodward: the nature of the play's 18th-century appeal is suggested by Frederick Pilon's unpublished adaptation of 1785, which concentrated almost entirely on Paroles's gulling, cutting most of the first three acts. In 1794 John Philip *Kemble became the first major actor to bother with the role of Bertram, in an adaptation of his own which offered an idealized Helen, played by Mrs *Jordan, as its sentimental focus: this achieved only one performance, and when revived by Samuel *Phelps in 1852 (in a cut form which politely eliminated the bed-trick) it proved equally unpopular. Meanwhile a musical version by Frederick *Reynolds (1832) had equally failed to reconcile playgoers to what now seemed an unacceptably indecent plot-line, and the play was not performed professionally again until Frank *Benson cast himself as Paroles in a Stratford revival in 1916.

The play's unfamiliarity and unpopularity freed 20th-century directors to take unusual liberties with its text, and even purists sought to justify their revivals by highlighting topical parallels. William *Poel's production in 1920, taking a hint from Shaw, presented Helen as a proto-suffragette, while Barry *Jackson's Birmingham Repertory Theatre production seven years later was in modern dress, with Laurence *Olivier as a would-be sophisticated jazz-age Paroles. Robert *Atkins produced the play three times (1921, 1932, 1940), to little avail, and it was only when Tyrone *Guthrie turned his attentions to it during the opening season of the Stratford, Ontario, festival in 1953 that *All's Well That Ends Well* began to receive good notices again. Guthrie's production (of a heavily cut and altered text which omitted Lavatch altogether), repeated in Stratford in 1959 (with Edith *Evans as the Countess), was given an Edwardian setting, except for the comically elaborated war scenes, which were set as if among General Montgomery's Desert Rats. Michael *Benthall's 1953 production for the Old Vic was if anything even more drastically cut and pasted, adding music and comic business in the interests of light-heartedness, so that Paroles, played by Michael *Hordern, once more became the centre of the play.

A return to Shakespeare's text was marked in John Houseman's production at Stratford, Connecticut, in 1959, and emulated in John *Barton's successful 1967 production for the Royal Shakespeare Company (with Ian *Richardson as a redeemable Bertram). The play was at last fully vindicated by two widely praised revivals a decade later, David Jones's at Stratford, Ontario, in 1977 (with Margaret Tyzack as the Countess), and, especially, Trevor *Nunn's for the RSC in 1981 (with Peggy *Ashcroft as the Countess, Harriet Walter as Helen, and Robert Eddison as Lafeu), a production which followed Guthrie in setting the play in Edwardian dress but which played it more consistently as a moving Chekovian tragicomedy. *MD*

On the screen: Four television films have been based on the play between 1968 and 1985, three adapted from stage productions. Only Elija Moshinsky's BBC TV version (1980) was initially designed for television. *AD*

Recent major editions

Russell Fraser (New Cambridge, 1985); G. K. Hunter (Arden, 1959); Susan Snyder (Oxford, 1993)

Some representative criticism

Arthos, J., 'The Comedy of Generation', *Essays in Criticism*, 5 (1955)

Cole, H. G., *The 'All's Well' Story from Boccaccio to Shakespeare* (1981)

Price, J. G., *The Unfortunate Comedy* (1968)

Smallwood, R. L., 'The Design of *All's Well That Ends Well*', *Shakespeare Survey*, 25 (1972)

Styan, J. L., *Shakespeare in Performance: All's Well That Ends Well* (1984)

Tillyard, E. M. W., *Shakespeare's Problem Plays* (1949)

Anjou, René, Duke of. See René, Duke of Anjou, King of Naples.

Anne, Lady. She curses Richard and any future wife of his but is wooed and won by him, *Richard III* 1.2 (based on Anne Neville (1456–85), daughter of Warwick 'the Kingmaker').

AB

Anne of Denmark, Queen of England and Scotland (1574–1619), consort of James I and VI. Independent and literate, she studied Italian with John *Florio, who dedicated both his Montaigne translation and his dictionary to her. For the first decade of the reign, she was the principal patron of the court masque, and *Jonson essentially reinvented the form to her taste. It is probably in deference to her that the references to drunkenness as a Danish national trait in *Hamlet* 1.4 are omitted from Q2 (1604).

SO

Anne Hathaway's Cottage (Hewland) is a timber-framed and thatched building in Shottery, a hamlet within the parish of Stratford-upon-Avon but just over a mile (1.5 km) from the town centre. It is known to have been held by the Hathaway family from at least 1543, as part of copyhold property granted then to John Hathaway. Hewland was the name attached to land belonging to one of two messuages included in this grant, and has come to be taken as the original name for Anne Hathaway's Cottage itself. John's holdings subsequently passed to Richard Hathaway, probably his son, whose daughter Anne married William Shakespeare in November 1582. Richard died in September 1581, when his property passed to his widow Joan, probably his second wife. She lived until 1599.

The term 'cottage' hardly does justice to the Hathaway family home, which, by the standards of the day, was a substantial residence of a well-to-do yeoman farmer. It appears to have been built in two stages. The lower part, adjoining the road, has been conclusively dated to the 1460s and consisted of a cross-passage, where the visitor enters today, with a hall to the left and kitchen to the right. The hall, when originally built, would probably have been open to the roof. On the first floor, above the cross-passage, is a space of matching size where the early construction of this part of the house is clearly visible. The evidence for this is a cruck, a pair of large and matching curved timbers reaching from the ground to the apex of the roof, a characteristic of medieval timber-framed buildings. On either side are bedchambers, the one to the west created when a floor was inserted into the open hall. The chimney stack, which runs up through this part of the house, probably dates from the time of this alteration: outside, it bears a plaque, with the date 1697 and the initials I.H. (for John Hathaway): this would seem rather late for the alterations to the hall and may simply record repairs or rebuilding of the exterior stonework.

In 1610, Richard's son and heir Bartholomew Hathaway acquired the freehold of the family's property and it may have been he who added a taller section to the house at the orchard end. This is now divided into three small rooms on the ground floor, with two bedchambers above. Ownership descended in the male line of the Hathaway family until the death, in 1746, of John Hathaway. It then passed, through his sister Susanna, to his nephew John Hathaway Taylor, whose son William Taylor lived there until his death in 1846. Financial problems had led to the division of the house into two cottages by 1836 and to its sale two years later, but Taylor had remained in occupation as tenant of one half. His daughter Mary, the wife of George Baker, was still living there in 1892 (in one of three cottages into which the house had been further divided), when the Shakespeare Birthplace Trust purchased the property. Mary Baker, who died in 1899, was appointed first custodian. Subsequent changes have primarily affected the building's setting, notably the redesign of the garden in the 1920s under the supervision of Ellen Ann Wilmot.

The earliest published attribution of the house as the home of Anne Hathaway, together with the first known drawing, is to be found in Samuel Ireland's *Picturesque Views on the Warwickshire Avon* of 1795, although it is clear from his account that the tradition was well established, perhaps reaching back to the time of the Shakespeare Jubilee of 1769. Nicholas Rowe had been the first to record a local tradition that Anne's maiden name was Hathaway, but it was not until the middle of the century that her name had first been linked to the Shottery family of that name. It is worth noting, in this instance, that the discovery, over 50 years later, of the documents recording Shakespeare's marriage confirmed rather than disproved this tradition.

RB

Halliwell-Phillipps, J. O., *Outlines of the Life of Shakespeare* (6th edn. 1886)

Schoenbaum, Samuel, *Shakespeare's Lives* (1991)

Styles, Philip, 'Stratford-upon-Avon', in *Victoria History of the County of Warwick*, vol. iii (1945)

Anne Page. See Page, Anne.

'An old hare hoar', sung by Mercutio in *Romeo and Juliet* 2.3.125; the original tune is unknown.

JB

anonymous publications. The earliest *quarto texts of Shakespeare's plays—*Titus Andronicus* (1594), *The First Part of the Contention* (*2 Henry VI*) (1594), *Richard Duke of York* (*3 Henry VI*) (1595), *Romeo and Juliet* (1597), *Richard II* (1597), *Richard III* (1597)—were printed without naming the dramatist on the *title page. Shakespeare's name first appeared on the 1598 quarto of *Love's Labour's Lost*, although in the same year *1 Henry IV* was published anonymously, as was *Henry V* in 1600. Later quartos prominently advertised their texts as 'Written by William Shakespeare'. The dramatist received top billing in the largest type-font on the title page of *King Lear* (1608), and the publisher of *Othello* (1622) wrote that 'the author's name is sufficient to vent his work'.

ER

Antenor, based on the character from *Homer's *Iliad*, is exchanged for Cressida in *Troilus and Cressida*, Act 4.

AB

Anthony, Mark. See Antony and Cleopatra; Julius Caesar.

anticlimax, a deflating descent into banality, usually knowingly—as distinct from inadvertent bathos:

> And then he drew a dial from his poke,
> And looking on it with lack-lustre eye
> Says very wisely, 'It is ten o'clock.'
> (*As You Like It* 2.7.20–2)

CB

Antigonus, husband of Paulina in *The Winter's Tale*, is killed by a bear as he attempts to abandon baby Perdita.

AB

Antiochus is King of Antioch. His incest with his daughter is discovered by Pericles, *Pericles* 1.1.

AB

Antiochus' Daughter. See Antiochus.

Antipholus of Ephesus, long estranged from his family, is eventually reunited with his parents and twin of the same name (who has come to Ephesus from Syracuse to seek him) in *The Comedy of Errors*.

AB

Antipholus of Syracuse. See Antipholus of Ephesus.

anti-theatrical polemic. The first important attack on the theatre was Stephen Gosson's rather mild *The School of Abuse* (1579), followed by the stronger *Plays Confuted in Five Actions* (1582). The former was dedicated, without authority, to Philip Sidney, whose *Defence of Poetry* partly answers it. In January 1583 the bear-baiting stadium at Paris Garden collapsed killing many in the lowest gallery and Puritan preachers hailed this as God's judgement. Later the same year Philip Stubbes, in his *Anatomy of Abuses* (1583), complained that 'the running to Theaters and Curtains, daily and hourly, time and tide, to see plays and interludes' was bound to 'insinuate foolery, and renew the remembrance of heathen idolatory' and to 'induce whoredom and uncleanness'. Two aspects of playing were subject to criticism in these attacks. The subject matter was likely to incite irreligious sensual pleasure via spectacles of 'wrath, cruelty, incest, injury [and] murder' in the tragedies and

The substantial farmhouse owned by the Hathaways of Shottery, originally known as 'Hewland' but now almost universally famous as Anne Hathaway's Cottage.

'love, cozenage, flattery, bawdry [and] sly conveyance of whoredom' in the comedies, as Gosson put it. Furthermore, acting itself was suspect because commoners feigned the actions of monarchs and men the actions of women, which might suggest that God-given social and sexual distinctions were matters merely of conduct rather than being.

In a sermon at Paul's Cross delivered on 3 November 1577, Thomas White broke off his attack on Sunday pleasures in general to focus on playing: 'behold the sumptuous Theatre houses, a continual monument of London's prodigality and folly.' White welcomed the cessation of playing due to the plague and saw a spiritual as well as a practical causal connection: 'the cause of plagues is sin, if you look to it well, and the cause of sin are plays; therefore the cause of plagues are plays.' Puritanism had initially been a movement to expunge remaining elements of Catholicism from the Church of England, but the reform movement fragmented and there was no simple Puritan objection to the stage. John *Milton was a Puritan playgoer and many reformist aristocrats patronized playing companies. Dramatists often represented Puritans as anti-sensual hypocrites (Zeal-of-the-Land Busy in Jonson's *Bartholomew Fair* is a fine example) but historians no longer see the court as essentially pro-theatre and the city authorities (dominated by Puritans) as essentially anti-theatre. Rather, the theatre industry was one of the sites upon which was played out the larger political conflict between court and city. The longest anti-theatrical polemic was William Prynne's *Histrio-mastix: The Players' Scourge* of 1633 which specifically laments the folio format, once reserved for Bibles and other high-quality work, being used for play anthologies such as 'Ben Johnsons, Shackspeers and others'. Prynne was imprisoned and his ears were removed because his condemnation of women acting was taken to be a direct reference to Queen *Henrietta Maria's participation in a masque, but his book was influential in the suppression of playing in 1642. *GE*

antithesis, an effect of contrast produced by framing opposed terms in parallel syntactical constructions: 'Before, a joy proposed; behind, a dream' (Sonnet 129). *CB*

Antium, Citizen of. See CITIZEN OF ANTIUM.

Antoine, Théâtre, founded by the naturalist director André Antoine (1858–1948) in 1897 on a Parisian 'Boulevard' and still operating independently. Its innovative electrical fittings allowed for safe, complete darkness on stage and in the auditorium. Antoine staged his first memorable Shakespearian drama, *King Lear* (1904), in Loti and Vedel's integral translation. *ISG*

Antonio. (1) He is the father of Proteus in *The Two Gentlemen of Verona.* (2) Having failed to repay a debt to Shylock, he narrowly escapes having to give him a pound of his flesh in *The Merchant of Venice.* (3) He is Leonato's brother in *Much Ado About Nothing.* (4) He lends Sebastian his purse and is dismayed when 'Cesario'—whom he believes to be Sebastian—disavows him when he is arrested in *Twelfth Night.* (5) Having usurped his brother Prospero's dukedom of *Milan many years before the action of the play, he is shipwrecked on Prospero's island in *The Tempest.* *AB*

Antony, Mark (Marcus Antonius). See ANTONY AND CLEOPATRA; JULIUS CAESAR.

Antony and Cleopatra *(see page 15)*

Apemantus, 'a churlish philosopher' in *Timon of Athens,* anticipates Timon's misanthropy with his own, but is reviled by Timon in the woods, 4.3. *AB*

apocrypha, a term, borrowed from biblical studies, used to denote works which have at one

(cont. on page 19)

Antony and Cleopatra

Extravagantly fluid in language and structure alike, *Antony and Cleopatra* marks a major stylistic departure from its immediate predecessors *King Lear* and *Macbeth*, although external evidence suggests that it cannot have been written much later. Echoes of its phraseology have been detected in Samuel *Daniel's revision of his play on the same subject, *Cleopatra*, published in 1607, and in Barnabe Barnes's play *The Devil's Charter*, acted by the King's Men in February 1607, so in all probability *Antony and Cleopatra* enjoyed its first performances late in 1606. It was entered in the *Stationers' Register on 20 May 1608.

Text: Despite this entry, the play was not printed until the publication of the First Folio in 1623, which provides the only authoritative text. It seems to have been printed from a good transcript of Shakespeare's own *foul papers, though not a *promptbook: although the spelling suggests the work of a scribe, some of the text's minor errors (such as mistaken speech prefixes) are characteristically authorial, and others (such as entry directions for characters who play no part in the subsequent action) would have been eliminated if the manuscript had been used in the theatre.

Source: Although possibly influenced in minor respects by the earlier version of Daniel's *Cleopatra* (1594), and drawing some historical details from Appian's *Civil Wars*, the play is primarily a dramatization of the latter part of *Plutarch's life of Marcus Antonius, as it appeared in Sir Thomas North's translation of *Lives of the Noble Grecians and Romans* (1579). (This was also a source for *Julius Caesar*, to which *Antony and Cleopatra* can be regarded as a sequel.) Shakespeare, though, greatly compresses Plutarch's narrative: the events dramatized here took place over an entire decade, and began only two years after the battle of Philippi with which *Julius Caesar* concludes (though this play makes that remembered victory seem a comparatively remote event in Antony's youth). Most crucially, Shakespeare has Antony's involvement with Cleopatra pre-date the death of his wife Fulvia, although historically it began after Antony had already married her successor Octavia. (This makes the relationship between the lovers at once more adulterous and, after a fashion, more faithful.) Shakespeare seems to have had a similar eye for telling details of human behaviour to Plutarch's, from whom he takes many minor incidents almost verbatim. He develops, though, the roles of Cleopatra's women Charmian and Iras and, especially, the almost choric figure of Antony's lieutenant Enobarbus, who is at times allowed to speak words taken directly from Plutarch's third-person narration—most famously, the set-piece description of Cleopatra on her barge in 2.2, a stunningly effective but very faithful versification of North's prose.

Synopsis: 1.1 In Alexandria Antony, teased by Cleopatra, declines to hear a messenger sent from his fellow triumvir Octavius Caesar. 1.2 While Antony's second-in-command Enobarbus makes arrangements for yet another feast, Cleopatra's attendants Charmian, Iras, and Alexas talk with a soothsayer, who prophesies that Charmian will outlive Cleopatra but that the most fortunate part of their lives is already over. From the messenger, Antony learns of his wife Fulvia's reverses in the civil war she and his brother have been waging against Caesar, and of Parthian advances in the Middle East; from another he learns of Fulvia's subsequent death. Aware that he has been neglecting his political and military interests, Antony passes on this news to Enobarbus, announcing that they must leave for Rome. 1.3 Antony breaks the news of Fulvia's death and his immediate departure to a contrary but ultimately compliant Cleopatra. 1.4 In Rome Caesar tells Lepidus, the third triumvir, of Antony's idleness in Egypt, the more regrettable since they are now threatened by seaborne rebels Pompey (son of Julius Caesar's old adversary Pompey the Great), Menecrates, and Menas. 1.5 In Alexandria Cleopatra, daydreaming of the absent Antony, receives a letter from him; Charmian taunts her with her former passion for Julius Caesar.

2.1 Menas tells Pompey and Menecrates that Caesar and Lepidus have assembled an army; Varrius brings the unwelcome news that Antony is on his way to Rome to join them.

2.2 In Rome, at a formal meeting between the triumvirs, Antony denies responsibility for Fulvia's conduct, and defends himself against charges of denying Caesar military aid: Enobarbus impertinently suggests that the triumvirs should simply postpone this feud until they have defeated Pompey together. Agrippa, one of Caesar's subordinates, proposes that the alliance between Antony and Caesar should be reaffirmed by a marriage between Antony and Caesar's sister Octavia, to which Antony and Caesar agree. Left among Caesar's staff, Enobarbus boasts of Antony's Alexandrian hedonism, describes Cleopatra's appearance when she sailed down the River Cydnus on a barge to meet Antony for the first time, and declares that marriage to Octavia will not be sufficient to keep Antony away from the Egyptian Queen. 2.3 Antony bids a formal goodnight to Caesar and Octavia, promising that he will behave honourably, but after the Soothsayer urges him to stay away from Caesar—in whose presence, he observes, Antony's luck fails—he resolves to return to the pleasures of Egypt. He sends Ventidius to Parthia. 2.4 Lepidus parts from two of Caesar's subordinates, all of them on their way to confront Pompey. 2.5 Cleopatra's nostalgic reveries about her past games with Antony are interrupted by a messenger who brings the news of his marriage; enraged, she strikes him repeatedly, but finally subsides into lovelorn grief. 2.6 Parleying before their armies, Pompey accepts the triumvirs' terms for peace, and the leaders repair to a feast on Pompey's barge. Menas and Enobarbus reflect on Pompey's unwise submission, and Enobarbus, reporting Antony's marriage, again predicts that Antony will return to Cleopatra. 2.7 At the feast, Menas urges Pompey to cut the barge's cable and assassinate the triumvirs; wishing that Menas had done this first on his own initiative, Pompey nonetheless refuses his suggestion. Lepidus is carried off drunk before the party disperses.

3.1 Victorious Roman forces, led by Ventidius, parade the corpse of the Parthian Prince Pacorus: Ventidius, however, declines to pursue his advantage against the Parthians, aware that too much success on his part would make his superior Antony dangerously envious. 3.2 Agrippa and Enobarbus ridicule the absent Lepidus, before Antony and Octavia, leaving for Athens, bid Caesar farewell. 3.3 Cleopatra interrogates the still-frightened messenger, who humours her by dispraising Octavia. 3.4 Antony, angry with Caesar for launching new hostilities against Pompey, allows Octavia to leave for Rome as a mediator, though continuing to gather his forces against her brother. 3.5 Enobarbus and his comrade Eros have heard that Caesar has defeated and killed Pompey and deposed Lepidus, taking over his third of the empire. 3.6 In Rome Caesar reports that Antony, now back in Alexandria with Cleopatra, has held a public ceremony granting the kingdoms of the eastern empire to her and to their children: when Octavia arrives he tells her bluntly of Antony's return to Cleopatra and of their preparations for war. 3.7 Near Actium, Enobarbus urges Cleopatra in vain to absent herself from Antony's military campaign, since her presence affects his judgement: despite repeated advice to the contrary from their soldiers, Antony and Cleopatra resolve to fight Caesar by sea. 3.8 Caesar orders his army to avoid battle until after the naval engagement. 3.9 Antony disposes his land forces. 3.10 The armies cross the stage and the noise of a sea-fight is heard. A horrified Enobarbus has seen the Egyptian flagship flee, taking the rest of Cleopatra's navy with it: Scarus, another soldier, reports that this happened just as Antony might have achieved victory, but that when Cleopatra fled he followed; Camidius, another of Antony's disgusted commanders, deserts. 3.11 In shame and despair Antony urges his attendants to leave his service; when Cleopatra arrives he rages at her, but when she cries he asserts that one of her tears is worth more than all they have lost. 3.12 Caesar receives Antony's schoolmaster, sent with terms for peace: continuing queenship for Cleopatra, and a private life in either Alexandria or Athens for Antony. Caesar offers to grant Cleopatra's request only on condition that she expel or kill Antony, and sends Thidias further to woo Cleopatra from Antony. 3.13 Antony, receiving Caesar's answer, challenges him to single combat. Cleopatra receives Thidias and his proposals kindly; when Antony finds him kissing Cleopatra's hand he has him whipped, railing at Cleopatra until, reassured of her fidelity, he rallies and decides to feast all his captains once more. Enobarbus, convinced of his folly, resolves to defect.

4.1 Caesar scoffs at Antony's challenge and prepares for one last battle. 4.2 Antony takes leave of each of his tearful followers, belatedly telling them he still hopes for victory. 4.3 His sentries hear supernatural music, which they are convinced is the sound of the god Hercules abandoning Antony. 4.4 Cleopatra helps Antony to arm, and he departs for battle in high spirits. 4.5 A soldier tells Antony Enobarbus has joined Caesar: magnanimously, Antony sends Enobarbus' treasure after him. 4.6 Caesar orders that defectors should be placed in the front rank against their former commander. Enobarbus, learning of Antony's generosity, feels he will die of shame. 4.7–9 Antony, Scarus, and others pursue Caesar's retreating forces before returning in triumph to Cleopatra at the end of the day's fighting. 4.10 Caesar's sentries overhear Enobarbus lamenting his disloyalty and dying of grief. 4.11–13 The second day's battle takes place mainly by sea: watching from the shore, Antony sees the Egyptian fleet surrender and, despairing, orders his army to disperse. When Cleopatra appears he drives her away with threats, claiming she has betrayed him to Caesar, and he resolves to kill both her and himself. 4.14 As Cleopatra and her attendants retreat to her monument, she instructs the eunuch Mardian to tell Antony she has committed suicide and to report his reaction. 4.15 Antony is telling Eros all is lost when Mardian brings his message. Antony instructs Eros to help him unarm and, reconciled to Cleopatra, whom he longs to join in death, orders Eros to kill him with his own sword. Eros, however, kills himself instead, and the wound Antony then inflicts upon himself is not immediately fatal. The guards who arrive also refuse to kill him: when news comes that Cleopatra is not really dead, the dying Antony is carried off towards her monument. 4.16 Cleopatra,

Charmian, and Iras hoist Antony up into the monument: dying, after a final kiss, he urges her to seek safety with Caesar and to trust none of Caesar's followers except Proculeius. Cleopatra's response, though, suggests that she too intends suicide, and she confirms this in the passionate lament that follows his death.

5.1 Among his followers Caesar learns of Antony's death: pointing out that the news makes him weep, he insists that only necessity, not ambition, prompted this war against his old ally. A messenger from Cleopatra asks his intentions: Caesar replies that he means her only kindness, but he tells Proculeius to flatter Cleopatra only to dissuade her from suicide, so that she may be carried in triumph to Rome. **5.2** At the monument, while Proculeius gives Cleopatra promises of gentle treatment from Caesar, his soldiers ambush and disarm her, narrowly preventing her from stabbing herself. She speaks elegiacally of Antony to another of Caesar's followers, Dolabella, who just has time to warn her that Caesar really means to lead her captive through Rome before Caesar himself arrives. Submitting an inventory of her possessions to her conqueror, Cleopatra is apparently embarrassed when her treasurer Seleucus informs Caesar that she has declared less than half of her wealth, but Caesar leaves still professing friendship. Dolabella hurries back to tell her she and her children will be sent away within three days: horrified at the idea of being exhibited in Rome, Cleopatra and her attendants prepare to die. A rustic, who engages the Queen in quibbling banter, brings asps concealed in a basket of figs. Iras and Charmian dress Cleopatra in the same royal robes she wore on the Cydnus: she kisses them farewell, Iras dying before the Queen, who applies an asp to her breast and arm, and herself dies, anticipating a reunion in the afterlife with Antony. Charmian adjusts Cleopatra's crown and puts an asp to her own arm as Caesar's guards enter, too late. Caesar himself arrives with his train and deduces the cause of their deaths, conceding that Cleopatra shall be buried with Antony.

Artistic features: One of Shakespeare's longest plays (at over 3,000 lines), *Antony and Cleopatra* has an unusually large number of scenes, some very short. Its action flows rapidly all around a Mediterranean world which in its concluding movement inexorably contracts to the monument, where most of the last act after Antony's death is given over to Cleopatra's self-transfiguring suicide. Despite its profusion of character and incident, the play is remarkable for the degree to which its poetry—dense in metaphor, unprecedentedly free in versification—defies its onstage drama, with key events (including most of Antony and Cleopatra's time together, and the decisive battle of Actium) evoked in language rather than shown on stage. The lovers' glamorous past seems as significant as the coldly rational present (personified by the efficient Octavius Caesar) in which they are being defeated: during the last act Cleopatra's poetic invocation of a heroic Antony seeks to upstage and eclipse the flawed failure whom the action of the play has in fact shown. In so far as she succeeds, *Antony and Cleopatra* anticipates the late romances by moving from tragedy back into something closer to Shakespearian comedy, its final death coming at the hands of a rural clown and serving as the means to a transcendent (albeit posthumous) marriage ('Husband, I come', 5.2.282).

Critical history: Although its influence on Daniel and Rich shows that it impressed contemporaries, *Antony and Cleopatra* was long neglected after its author's death. John Dryden's much tidier, domesticated, neoclassical play on the same subject, *All for Love; or, The World Well Lost* (1676, professedly 'written in imitation of Shakespeare's style'), with its mild, would-be virtuous Cleopatra and simpler conflict between love and honour, made more sense to later 17th-century sensibilities. To Charles *Gildon (1710) Shakespeare's play was 'full of scenes strangely broken', and Samuel *Johnson (1765) felt that its events were 'produced without any art of connection or care to disposition' (a fault Henry Brooke attempted to mend in his unacted adaptation, printed in 1778). It was not until the Romantic age that the play's exoticism and excess, and what then seemed its disdain for theatrical practicality, came to be valued, with S. T. *Coleridge declaring it Shakespeare's 'most wonderful' play. Subsequent 19th-century critics largely concentrated on the character of Cleopatra, to whom even those who regarded the play as a simple moral warning against dissipation responded vigorously. Anna Brownell Jameson called Cleopatra 'one brilliant impersonation of classical elegance, Oriental voluptuousness, and gipsy sorcery' (1832), and the serpent of old Nile predictably fascinated the self-consciously decadent writers (and painters, such as John Collier) of a later generation, A. C. *Swinburne enthusing that 'here only once and for all [Shakespeare] has given us the perfect and the everlasting woman' (1880). A. C. *Bradley, though an admirer of the play, excluded it from his category of Shakespeare's 'great' tragedies, sensing that it belonged to some less affective genre ('It is better for the world's sake, not less for [Antony and Cleopatra's] own, that they should fail and die . . . the fact that we mourn so little saddens us,' 1909), but over the following century it was this very avoidance of heroic, operatic emotion, and the play's apparent preference for language over character, which endeared it to modern criticism, and its highly patterned poetry lent it perfectly to the studies in Shakespeare's imagery pioneered by Caroline *Spurgeon. In later 20th-century criticism the play has been of particular importance to *feminist critics interested in Shakespeare's representations of sexual difference, and to postcolonial commentators more concerned with its images of empire and of race.

Stage history: Although early allusions allow us to infer that the play was performed in 1606–7, no records exist of any further performances before 1759, when David *Garrick and Edward *Capell prepared it for the proscenium stage by a great deal of transposition and cutting. Despite Garrick's efforts as Antony, and heavy expenditure on sets and costumes, this achieved only four performances: contemporaries

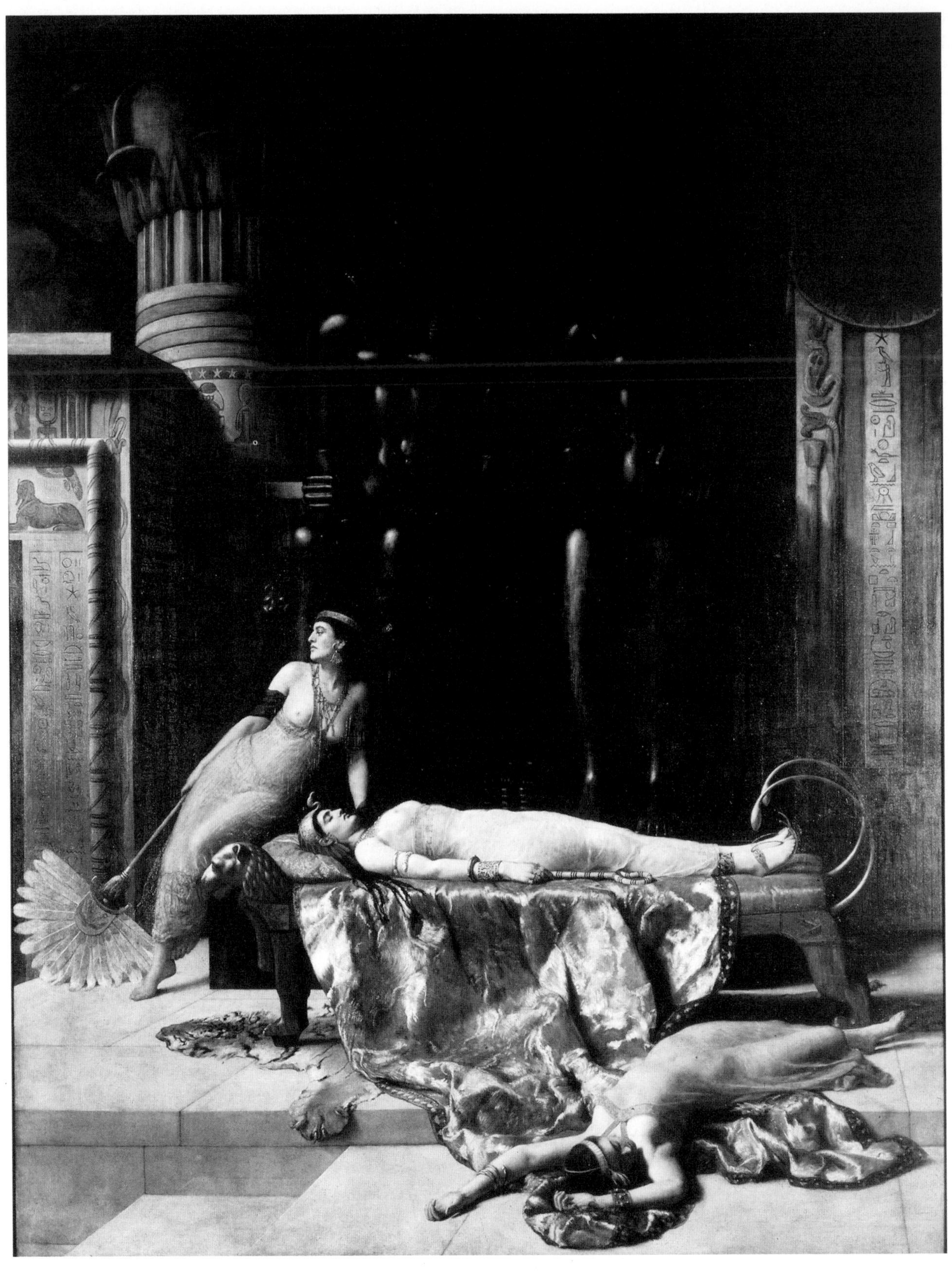

A characteristically voluptuous late Victorian rendition of 5.2, *The Death of Cleopatra*, by the painter John Collier (1850–1934).

preferred Dryden's *All for Love*. The next two attempts to revive the play (by *Kemble in 1813, and *Macready in 1833) attempted, as the preface to Kemble's adaptation put it, 'to blend the regular play of Dryden with the wild tragedy of Shakespeare', but this hybrid failed to please. Samuel Phelps returned to a cut version of Shakespeare only at Sadler's Wells in 1849, and although this was not a commercial success the spectacular potential of the play's subject matter attracted further 19th-century producers, in both London and New York, despite the difficulties presented by its profusion of scenes. These included Charles *Calvert in 1867, F. B. Chatterton in 1873, Rose Eytinge (who played Cleopatra) on Broadway in 1877, and even Lily Langtry, who cast herself as Cleopatra at the Princess's in 1890. Although Beerbohm *Tree staged a predictably lavish version in 1907, this approach to the play had already been superseded in Frank *Benson's much sparer production (with himself as Antony) at Stratford, seconded by Robert *Atkins's revolutionary, almost bare-stage production at the Old Vic in 1922, in which Edith *Evans played her first Cleopatra.

Throughout the play's stage history, productions in which both central performances have been equally praised have been rare: for many Vivien *Leigh's Cleopatra (1951) outshone Olivier's Antony, and Michael *Redgrave's Antony (1953) overpowered Peggy *Ashcroft's Cleopatra, felt by some to be 'too English' (a complaint still often raised against British actresses by critics with a more exotic, Orientalist view of the role). In the later 20th century, many directors tried to solve this problem by scaling down both performances and the entire play: Trevor *Nunn's much-praised RSC production of 1972, with Janet *Suzman as Cleopatra, used a comparatively simple set, and Peter *Brook's of 1978 (his last work for the company), with Glenda Jackson as Cleopatra, a stylized setting framed by glass panels. (Peter *Hall, however, successfully bucked this trend at the National Theatre in 1987, casting Judi *Dench and Anthony Hopkins in a satisfactorily lavish production in the Olivier auditorium). It is interesting in this respect that one of the most admired productions of the period was Adrian *Noble's (1981), in the tiny Other Place in Stratford (with Michael *Gambon as Antony), where Helen Mirren was a concentrated, intelligent Cleopatra, while when Mirren repeated the role in 1998 at the National, in a production by Matthew Warchus which aimed at spectacle, the effort was a critical disaster. *MD*

On the screen: A five-minute version (now lost) was made by George Méliès in 1899, the same year as Beerbohm Tree's *King John*. Between 1951 and 1980 five versions were made, including a British film with Robert Speaight as Antony, a TV adaptation as part of the *The Spread of the Eagle* series (1963), the Charlton Heston film (1972), Trevor Nunn's much acclaimed TV film of his RSC production (1972), and the Jonathan Miller BBC TV production (1980). *AD*

Recent major editions

Michael Neill (Oxford, 1994); John Wilders (New Arden, 1997); J. Dover Wilson (New Cambridge, 1950)

Some representative criticism

Bradley, A. C., 'Shakespeare's *Antony and Cleopatra*', in *Oxford Lectures on Poetry* (1909)
Charney, Maurice, *Shakespeare's Roman Plays* (1961)
Daiches, David, 'Imagery and Meaning in *Antony and Cleopatra*', in *Modern Literary Essays* (1968)
Kahn, Coppélia, *Roman Shakespeare* (1997)
Spencer, T. J. B., 'Shakespeare and the Elizabethan Romans', *Shakespeare Survey*, 10 (1958)

time or another been attributed to Shakespeare but are not currently regarded as part of the *canon. *Pericles*, *The Two Noble Kinsmen*, and the small Shakespearian portion of *Sir Thomas More*, though excluded from the First Folio, are no longer regarded as apocryphal, but seven plays which the Third Folio (1664), following the example of their Jacobean quartos, did attribute to Shakespeare are no longer considered to be by Shakespeare, namely **Locrine*, *The *London Prodigal*, *The *Puritan*, **Sir John Oldcastle*, **Thomas, Lord Cromwell*, and *A *Yorkshire Tragedy*. Other apocryphal plays attributed to Shakespeare by 17th-century printers or booksellers are *The *Troublesome Reign of King John*, *The *Birth of Merlin*, **Arden of Faversham*, **Fair Em*, and **Mucedorus*. The apocrypha also include some plays never attributed to Shakespeare in his own time at all, but claimed as his by modern scholars on internal evidence alone. These include *Edmund Ironside*, and the apocryphal play with the strongest claim to be considered genuine, **Edward III*. *MD*

Maxwell, B., *Studies in the Shakespeare Apocrypha* (1956)
Schoenbaum, Samuel, *Internal Evidence and Elizabethan Dramatic Authorship* (1966)
Tucker Brooke, C. F. (ed.), *The Shakespeare Apocrypha* (1908)

Apology for Actors, An. See Heywood, Thomas.

aporia, a rhetorical figure in which the speaker hesitates between alternatives. Hamlet's 'To be or not to be' soliloquy is the most celebrated extended example. *CB*

Apothecary He sells poison to Romeo, *Romeo and Juliet* 5.1. *AB*

apparitions, three. In turn they tell Macbeth to 'beware Macduff', that 'none of woman born' shall harm him, and that he 'shall never vanquished be' until Birnam Wood comes to Dunsinane, *Macbeth* 4.1. *AB*

apprentices. See boy actors.

apron stage, the technical name for the part of the modern stage projecting in front of the curtain, but used anachronistically to refer to the entire stage of Shakespeare's time which projected into the audience (seated at the indoor theatres and standing at the open-air theatres) who thus surrounded it on three sides. Also known as the thrust stage and to be contrasted with the proscenium arch stage. *GE*

Apuleius, Lucius (b. *c.*AD 123), Roman writer and rhetorician, educated at Carthage and Athens, who travelled in the East before returning to Africa to marry a rich widow. *The Golden Ass*, translated into English by William Adlington in 1566, with reprints in 1571, 1582, and 1596, is the only surviving Latin novel. Recycling Greek and Roman narratives, including the Ovidian tale of Midas' transformation into an ass, it tells how one Lucius, in this asinine shape, attracts the attention of a powerful woman, but is finally restored to human form by Isis. This precursor of *A Midsummer Night's Dream* may also have influenced *Venus and Adonis*, *Macbeth*, and *Cymbeline*. *JKS*

Starnes, D. T., 'Shakespeare and Apuleius', *PMLA* 60 (1945)

Arab world. The first translator of Shakespeare in the Arab world was the Egyptian writer Najib El Haddad (1867–99) and the first Shakespearian play ever performed in Egypt was *Othello* (produced by Suleimen Effendi Kerdahy in November 1887).

Several prestigious Arab poets and writers felt the need to translate or adapt Shakespeare such as Tanyus Abduh (*Hamlet*, 1902), Khalil Mutran (*Othello*, 1912, *Macbeth*, *Hamlet*, and *The Merchant of Venice*), Muhammad Hamdi (*Julius Caesar*, 1912), Sami Al-Juraidini (*Julius Caesar*, 1912), Muhammad Lutfi Jum'a (*Hamlet*), Muhammad Al-Siba'i (*Coriolanus*), Mahmood Ahmed Al-'Aqqad (*Julius Caesar*), Muhammad Awad Ibraheem (*Antony and Cleopatra*, *As You Like It*), Jabra Ibraheem Jabra (most of Shakespeare's works, including the Sonnets), Ali Al-Ra'i, Muhammad Teymour, Mahmood Teymour, Iz Al-Deen Isma'il, Lewis Awad, Abdel Oadir Al-Out, etc.

Because they had to comply with the prevailing taste of the public, the early translators did not hesitate to change the titles of some plays and even to give Arabic names to popular dramatis personae: Utail or Atta'Ullah for Othello, Ghalban for Caliban, Ya'qub for Iago, etc. Given the operatic trend in that period, not a single play, including *Hamlet*, was ever performed without songs. The Egyptian actor and producer Cheik Salama El Higazy, whose company had staged successfully a musical comedy with a happy ending adapted from *Romeo and Juliet* under the title *The Martyrs of Love* in 1906, gave up the songs when he produced *Hamlet* the following year, but the public was so much disappointed that he thought fit to ask his friend, the great poet Ahmed Shawky, for some songs. The success of the Shakespearian play, in which the hero does not die on stage, lasted until 1914.

Hamlet inspired many Arab playwrights such as Alfred Farag (*Sulaiman Al-Halabv* and *Ali Janah Al-Tabrizi Wa-Tabia Ghufa*); Salah Abdul Sabour (*Leila and Majnoun*); Mamdouh Adwan (*Hamlet Yastaghs Mutaakhar*). Great actors including Youssef Wahby, Abdelaziz Khalil, Aly El Kassar, and George Abyadh staged it not only in Egypt but also in many Arab countries. It was Suleimen Effendi Kerdahy who performed *Hamlet* for the first time in 1909 in Tunis, along with *Othello* and *Romeo and Juliet*, before he died a few weeks later. In Algeria, *Hamlet* was played by the great actor Muhi'l-Din in 1953.

Most of the translators used literary Arabic prose; however, there were a few attempts of verse translations by Muhammad Iffat (*Macbeth*, 1911; *The Tempest*, 1909) but without much success. Other translators, like Ahmed Zaky Abu Shady (*The Tempest*, 1930), Muhammad Ferid Abu Hadid (*Macbeth*. 1934), and Aly Ahmad Bakathir (*Romeo and Juliet*, 1936), adopted the Shakespearian blank verse.

Aziz Abadah's *Qaysar* is almost a faithful adaptation of *Julius Caesar*. Though inspired by Garnier's work, Shawky's *Masr'a Cleopatra* (*The Death of Cleopatra*, 1929) evokes the Shakespearian play in so far as the two heroines experience through death the same catharsis, heralding the same message of love and freedom. More recent works are Saad Al-Khadim's *Dr Othello* and Abdul Karim Barsheed's *Othello Wal-Kail Wal-Baroud* (1965).

Shakespeare's sonnets and poems, known to the Arab world through F. T. Palgrave's popular anthology, *The Golden Treasury of the Best Songs and Lyrical Poems in the English Language* (1861), influenced several Arab poets, such as Abderrahman Chokry, Al Aqqad (Egypt), Abul Kacem Echebbi (Tunisia), and Nazek Al-Malayika (Iraq).

After the Second World War, the Arab League decided, in collaboration with UNESCO, and the supervision of the great Egyptian writer Taha Hussain, to have all Shakespeare's work translated and printed. As shown through the growing number of Shakespearian scholars (Aly Ahmed Bakathir, Jabra Ibrahim Jabra, Ramsees Awad, etc.) and the repertory of talented men of the theatre, Yusuf Idris, Alfred Farag, Mahmoud Dyab, Khaled Galal (Egypt), Nidal Ashkar (Lebanon), Saadallah Wannous (Syria), Muhammad Kooka (Tunisia), Farid Al Zahirl (Yemen), Shakespeare is considered in the Arab world as a playwright who still commands theatrical authority. *RD*

Aragon, Catherine of. See KATHERINE.

Aragon, Prince of. One of Portia's unsuccessful suitors in *The Merchant of Venice* 2.9. *AB*

Arc, Joan of. See JOAN LA PUCELLE.

archbishops. See CANTERBURY, ARCHBISHOP OF; YORK, ARCHBISHOP OF.

Archer, William (1856–1924), Scottish dramatic critic, best known for his promotion, with G. B. Shaw, of Ibsen's works, but also author of 'What We Know of the Elizabethan Stage' in the *Quarterly Review* (1908) and *The Old Drama and the New* (1923), vindicating contemporary drama against its predecessors, exempting only Shakespeare. *TM*

Archidamus comments on the hospitality of Leontes and praises his son Mamillius, *The Winter's Tale* 1.1. *AB*

Arcite, Palamon's rival for Emilia in *The Two Noble Kinsmen*, dies when thrown by his horse, 5.6. *AB*

Arden, forest of, an extensive area of woodland north of Stratford, largely cleared by Shakespeare's time, which has the name of Shakespeare's mother's family. The name derives from *Ardenna silva*, the Latin name for the Ardennes; and in *Britannia* (Latin version 1586, English 1610) William Camden writes of 'Arden; which word the Gauls and Britons heretofore seem to have used for a wood, since two great forests, the one in *Gallia Belgica*, the other amongst us in Warwickshire, are both called by one and the same name of Arden'; Camden opines, correctly, that 'woodland' and 'arden' 'are words importing the same thing'.

The forest of Arden—or Ardenne, as the Oxford edition has it—in *As You Like It* derives from Thomas *Lodge's *Rosalynde*, which has a clearly French setting; it begins 'There dwelled adjoining to the city of Bordeaux a knight of most honourable parentage.' Lodge uses the spelling 'Arden', which is also found in the Folio text of *As You Like It*. Much of Shakespeare's play too is localized in France, and Arden is clearly distinguished from England when Charles the wrestler says (in the Folio spelling) that the old Duke 'is already in the Forrest of *Arden*, and a many merry men with him; and there they liue like the old *Robin Hood* of *England*' (1.1.109–11). Nevertheless Shakespeare seems to have conflated the two forests in his imagination; the flora and fauna of the play are not compatible with any single location. The idea that Shakespeare alludes to his mother's name seems purely sentimental. *SW*

Arden, Mary (d. 1608). Shakespeare's mother, wife of John *Shakespeare, was the youngest of the eight daughters of a prosperous farmer, Robert Arden, by his first wife, whose name is unknown. Mary's date of birth, too, is unknown; her father married his second wife, Agnes Hill, who brought with her two sons and two daughters, in 1548, and Mary was unmarried on 24 November 1556 when her father, who died soon afterwards, made his will, naming her as one of his two executors and leaving her 'all my land in Wilmcote called *Asbies and the crop upon the ground sown and tilled as it is' along with 10 marks. She probably married in 1557; her first child, Joan, was christened on 15 September 1558, her last, Edmund, on 3 May 1580. The story of her marriage, in so far as it is known, is chronicled in the entry for her husband. She made her mark on a deed of 1579; this does not necessarily imply that she could not read, or even write. *SW*

Ardenne. See ARDEN, FOREST OF.

Arden of Faversham, anonymous domestic tragedy, written in 1592 and first attributed to

Shakespeare in mid-17th-century printers' catalogues (see APOCRYPHA). Edward Jacob published it in 1770 as 'the earliest dramatic work of Shakespeare now remaining'. Thomas *Kyd has since been suggested as a possible author.

Based on an actual murder committed in Kent in 1551, *Arden of Faversham* provides a vivid account of the social and economic conflicts that marked the rise of the middle classes in the early modern period. Arden's murderers include his wife's upstart lover Mosbie, Arden's servant Michael, a victim of the law of primogeniture, and Master Greene, who is left destitute after Arden's unlawful enclosure of the lands of the abbey of Faversham. *SM*

Arden Shakespeare. The first volume in the Arden Shakespeare, *Hamlet*, edited by Edward Dowden, appeared in 1899, and although the quality of the volumes that followed was variable, the series at once set a new standard for editions of individual works by printing a textual collation and extensive explanatory notes on the same pages as the text. The spaciousness of a handsome edition that included also a critical introduction and had room for appendices and passages from sources guaranteed its success. The first general editor, W. J. Craig (1899–1906), was succeeded by R. H. Case in 1909, who remained in charge until the completion of the series in 1924. A second series intended to replace the by now outmoded older volumes was launched under the general editorship of Una Ellis-Fermor with the publication of Kenneth Muir's editions of *Macbeth* and *King Lear* in 1951–2. These two were 'based on' the earlier Ardens, and at first an attempt was made to use the stereotype plates from the old edition, but this idea had to be quickly abandoned, and the revision of the Arden became to all intents and purposes a new edition, though it retained the general appearance of Arden 1, only changing the colour of the covers from red to blue. Arden 2, later guided by Harold Brooks, Harold Jenkins, and Brian Morris, was edited by a more distinguished cast of scholars than the first, and rapidly gained recognition as the foremost critical edition of Shakespeare's works in its time, providing a very full apparatus and commentary, and reconsidering the nature of all the textual problems. However, the earlier volumes in this series also began to look textually and critically obsolescent by 1982, when Harold Jenkins's massive edition of *Hamlet* appeared, and a third Arden series began to appear in 1995, general editors Richard Proudfoot, Ann Thompson, and David Scott Kastan. Arden 3 includes illustrations, takes note of the many advances in textual scholarship that occurred in the 1980s and 1990s, and has a greater concern with performance on stage and screen than does Arden 2. *RAF*

Argentina. See LATIN AMERICA.

Ariel. The characterization of Ariel, the 'airy spirit' (sometimes classified among Shakespeare's *fairies) who serves Prospero in *The Tempest*, is enigmatic. Performers, literary critics, and, conspicuously, painters have sought to interpret his relationship with Prospero. It might be easier to see the ugly and earth-bound *Caliban as his slave, who in Prospero's words is 'a born devil', than the 'dainty' Ariel, whom Prospero claims to love 'dearly': yet they are both held to servitude with similar threats of torture. Performers have had to decide how far Ariel is in sympathy with Prospero's revenge, of which he seems to be the primary, if not sole, instrument. These performers have been both male and female: we are never told why Ariel is dressed as a sea-nymph in Act 1 (even though he is invisible as such to everyone except Prospero), a harpy thereafter, and finally Ceres, the goddess of agriculture and fertility, in the *masque of Act 4. Ariel was almost invariably a female role from the Restoration onwards, until the (male) dancer Leslie French played it at the Old Vic in 1930. Post-war Ariels in major productions have nearly all been male. *AB*

Ariosto, Lodovico (1474–1533), Italian poet and dramatist, central figure of the Italian Renaissance, whose work exerted a powerful influence upon English Renaissance literature. His prose comedy *I suppositi* (1509) was translated by George Gascoigne as *Supposes* in 1573 and provided the sub-plot of *The Taming of the Shrew*. But it was Ariosto's epic poem *Orlando furioso*, published in Italian (1516, 1532), and translated into English by Sir John Harington (1591), that secured his fame. Robert Greene dramatized part of it in a play of the same title (1591). Edmund Spenser used the epic as a model for *The Faerie Queene*. *Orlando*'s influence upon Shakespeare is suggested by the name of *As You Like It*'s male protagonist and by the story of Hero and Claudio in *Much Ado About Nothing*. *JKS*

Aristophanes. See CRITICAL HISTORY; GREEK DRAMA.

Armado, Don Adriano de. A Spanish 'braggart' who loves Jaquenetta in *Love's Labour's Lost*, he presents 'The Nine Worthies', 5.2, in which he plays Hector. *AB*

Armin, Robert (*c*.1568–1615), comic actor in the Chamberlain's/King's Men. William *Kempe left the Chamberlain's Men in 1599 and was replaced by Armin, a successful writer and comedian first heard of as apprenticed to the goldsmith John Lonyson in 1581. During his apprenticeship Armin wrote a number of popular ballads and after completing his term he joined Chandos's Men. A collection of tales called *Fool upon Fool* was published in 1600 by the author 'Clonnico de Curtanio Snuffe' (Snuff, the clown at the Curtain) and was reprinted in 1605 under the authorship 'Clonnico del Mondo Snuffe' (Snuff, the clown at the Globe) and finally under Armin's name as *A Nest of Ninnies* in 1608. Armin's association with the Curtain may well indicate that he was already a member of the Chamberlain's Men before Kempe's departure, which might then have been hastened by the availability of a suitable internal replacement.

Armin took over Kempe's existing roles while Shakespeare adjusted his comic output to suit the new star's less physical, more cerebral, style of wit. Roles in the style included Touchstone in *As You Like It*, Feste in *Twelfth Night*, Lavatch in *All's Well That Ends Well*, Thersites in *Troilus and Cressida*, and the Fool in *King Lear*. Although small in stature Armin was dependent less on the comedy of physical deformity than his predecessors *Tarlton and Kempe and although he continued their tradition of singing, he was not a dancer of vigorous jigs. A successful dramatist in his own right, Armin had more reason than Kempe to share Hamlet's, and presumably Shakespeare's, annoyance at clowns who unbalance the performance by straying from the text. The title page of Armin's *Two Maids of More-Clacke* (printed in 1609) has a woodcut which may well represent Armin himself in costume. *GE*

Wiles, David, *Shakespeare's Clown: Actor and Text in the Elizabethan Playhouse* (1987)

arms, Shakespeare's coat of. In 1596 John Shakespeare, or perhaps William acting for his father, applied to the College of Heralds for a coat of arms, conferring upon him and his descendants the status of gentleman. Two surviving drafts of a document prepared by William Dethick, Garter king-of-arms, dated 20 October grant the request. A note indicates that John had initiated a similar application 20 years before, that he was a justice of the peace in Stratford and had served as bailiff, that he had 'lands and tenements of good wealth and substance, £500', and that he had married 'a daughter and heir of Arden, a gentleman of worship'. Now he was granted the right to a shield depicting a spear, and, as his 'crest or cognizance', a falcon, 'his wings displayed', standing on a wreath and supporting a spear set upon a helmet. The spear alludes to the family name; the falcon, punningly 'shaking' its wings, may indicate an interest in falconry. The inscription 'Non sans droit'—'not without right'—is presumably a motto. The shield and crest are displayed on William Shakespeare's monument and on Susanna Hall's seal.

In 1599 John applied to combine his arms with those of the Ardens. Three years later his right to the arms was questioned on the grounds that they were not distinct enough from those of Lord Mauley, and that the Shakespeares were unworthy: a note 'Shakespeare the player by

THE
History of the two Maids of More-clacke,
VVith the life and simple maner of IOHN
in the Hospitall.
Played by the Children of the Kings
Maiesties Reuels.
VVritten by ROBERT ARMIN, seruant to the Kings
most excellent Maiestie.

LONDON,
[Pr]inted by N.O. for Thomas Archer, and is to be sold at his
shop in Popes head Pallace, 1609.

The comic actor, singer, and writer Robert Armin, the original Touchstone, Feste, and Lear's Fool. This title page illustration shows him dressed as 'John of the Hospital' in his own play *The History of the Two Maids of More-Clacke* (1609).

Garter' seems to suggest that an actor could not deserve the distinction, but a reply denies the former charge and reaffirms John Shakespeare's claims. *SW*

Schoenbaum, S., *William Shakespeare: A Documentary Life* (1975; compact edn. 1977)
Scott-Giles, C. W., *Shakespeare's Heraldry* (1950)

Arne, Thomas Augustine (1710–78), English composer. As the most important English theatrical composer during the mid-18th century, Arne composed music for a number of Shakespearian productions at a time when Shakespeare's 'originals' (rather than the adaptations of the previous 70 years) were being restored to the theatre. He is best remembered for his 'Where the bee sucks' (1746) and a wonderfully spirited setting of 'Sigh no more ladies' (1748; pub. 1749). *IBC*

Arnold, Matthew (1822–88), English poet and critic. His preface to *Poems* (1853) uses Shakespeare as a touchstone for both ancient Greeks and modern Germans. Shakespeare's 'self-schooled' genius is remote and inscrutable, concealed behind his work. His sonnet 'Others abide our question. Thou art free' (1849) emphasizes this objectivity. *TM*

Arragon, Prince of. See ARAGON, PRINCE OF.

art. The comparative paucity of references to the visual arts in Shakespeare's works—largely confined to figurative tapestries (such as those which decorate Innogen's bedchamber, *Cymbeline* 2.4.68–76) and to portraits (most famously those of King Hamlet and Claudius, *Hamlet* 3.4.52–66)—accurately reflects the poverty and inaccessibility of the visual arts in Shakespeare's England. The only contemporary painter named in the canon, 'that rare Italian master Giulio Romano' (*The Winter's Tale* 5.2.96), is cited as a sculptor (on the authority of the Italian art historian Giorgio Vasari, probably at second or third hand; it is profoundly unlikely that Shakespeare had seen any of *Giulio Romano's work, whether on canvas or in stone), while the painting of the siege of Troy in Lucrece's room (*The Rape of Lucrece* 1366–463) owes far more to literary sources than to visual ones. Although there was a strong native tradition of ornament (exemplified not only in textiles but in book design, the page borders in the Folio providing a good example), and although Nicholas *Hilliard was producing exquisite portrait miniatures, England lagged well behind continental Europe in book illustration, in genre painting, in still life, and in landscape. Woodcuts were comparatively crude, and their exponents were more accustomed to providing them for emblem books than to tackling more naturalistic subjects. It is not surprising, then, that the first works of art on Shakespearian subjects are *portraits of Shakespeare himself, with the *painting of scenes from the plays (and of actors in them) not gathering momentum until the 18th century. *MD*

Artaud, Antonin (1896–1948), French director and dramatic theorist, who turned to Elizabethan drama to promote a theatre without scenery but with a multi-levelled stage. A solo staged reading of *Richard II* in 1934 illustrated his *Theatre of Cruelty* (1932). *The Theatre and its Double* (1938) and his conception of acting as 'affective athletism' influenced many theatre directors including Roger Blin, Jean-Louis Barrault, and Peter Brook. *ISG*

Artemidorus vainly attempts to give Caesar a paper (read out, 2.3) warning him about his enemies, *Julius Caesar* 3.1. *AB*

Artesius, a silent attendant, appears in *The Two Noble Kinsmen* 1.1. *AB*

Arthur, Prince. He contests the throne of his uncle (King John) and dies in an attempt to escape his custody, *King John* 4.3. *AB*

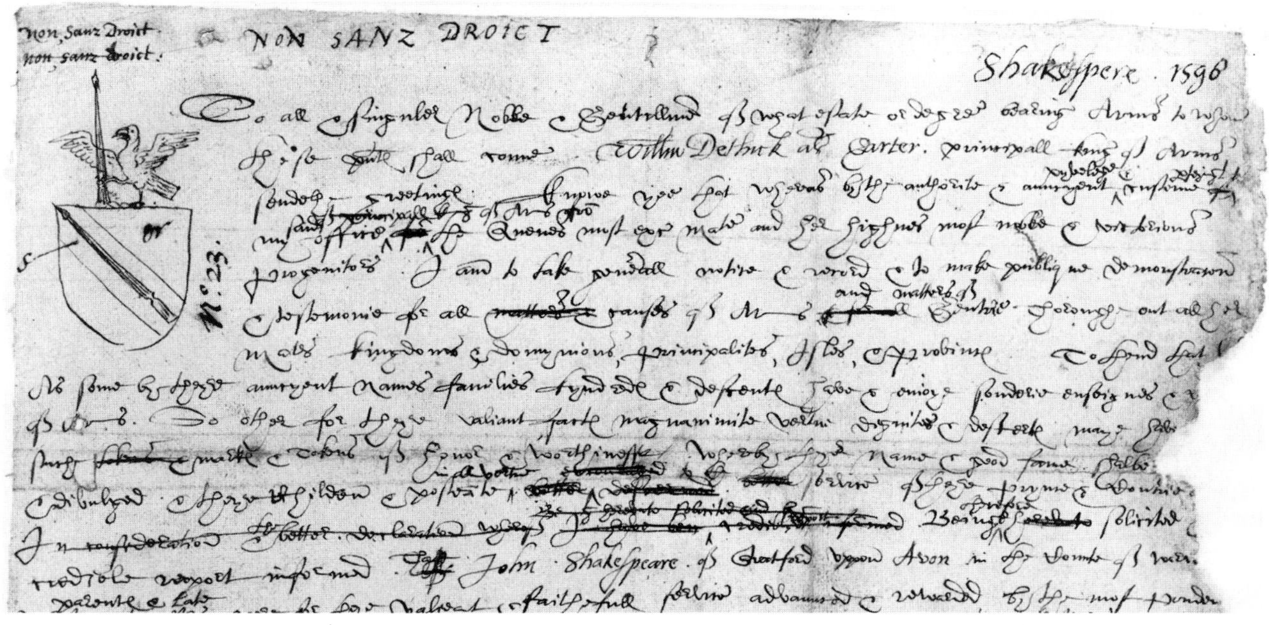

The Shakespeare coat of arms, as granted by Garter King-of-Arms, 20 October 1596.

Arviragus, stolen by Belarius along with his brother Guiderius, is reunited with the King his father, *Cymbeline* 5.6. *AB*

Asbies (Asbyes), the name of the area of land in *Wilmcote that Robert *Arden left in 1556 to his youngest daughter Mary, Shakespeare's mother, possibly in anticipation of her marriage, which took place the following year. The fact that Robert Arden's will does not mention a house suggests that this was the 70 acres (28 ha) of arable land and 16 acres (6.5 ha) of meadow and pasture that John and Mary Shakespeare leased to Thomas Webbe and Humphrey Hooper in 1578, but it could be the estate mortgaged to Edmund *Lambert in the same year. No house of this name is known, though in 1794 John *Jordan attached it to the property known until 2000 as *Mary Arden's House. *SW*

Ashbourne (Kingston) portrait, three-quarter length, oil, *Folger Collection. This portrait of *c.*1611 first emerged in 1847, when it was bought by the Revd Clement Kingston of Ashbourne, Derbyshire, after whom the image is named. Upon its discovery, the portrait was identified as a likely representation of Shakespeare. Restoration work undertaken in 1979, however, revealed a coat of arms and the motto 'honore et amore' beneath heavy layers of patina. Both the motto and heraldic insignia were later discovered to have been those of Sir Hugh Hammersley, a prominent public figure during the first half of the 17th century, a finding which undermined the earlier identification of the sitter. *CT*

Ashcroft, Dame Peggy (1907–91), British actress. She made her mark as *Desdemona to Paul Robeson's Othello in London in 1930 and two years later first acted Juliet as a guest of Oxford undergraduates directed by John *Gielgud, with whom she was often to collaborate. At the *Old Vic in 1932–3 she played a range of Shakespeare's young heroines (roles to which she returned) and was Juliet in the West End when Gielgud and Laurence *Olivier exchanged roles as Mercutio and Romeo. At this time she was admired as a fresh, lyrical actress though sometimes criticized for a too English gentility. In 1950 at Stratford she was Beatrice to Gielgud's Benedick—a pinnacle of high comedy playing. That year she was Viola in *Twelfth Night* when the Old Vic reopened after bomb damage. At Stratford in her fifties she gave the illusion of young ardour as Rosalind and Imogen; she also rose to the challenge of Cleopatra. She was a valued member of Peter *Hall's ensemble at the Royal Shakespeare Theatre; in *The *Wars of the Roses* she took Margaret from young princess to vituperative queen. In Trevor *Nunn's autumnal *All's Well That Ends Well* (1981) her old Countess had a valedictory quality. A committed socialist, she passionately believed in state support for the theatre. *MJ*

Billington, Michael, *Peggy Ashcroft* (1988)

Ashland. See UNITED STATES OF AMERICA.

Asnath. See BOLINGBROKE, ROGER.

Aspinall, Alexander, master of Stratford grammar school from 1582 until he died in 1624, and the subject of a 'posy' ascribed to Shakespeare in a manuscript miscellany compiled by Sir Francis Fane (1611–80):

> The gift is small,
> The will is all,
> Alexander Aspinall.

Fane added the note 'Shakespeare upon a pair of gloves that master sent to his mistress' and it has been conjectured that Aspinall bought the gloves from John Shakespeare for his betrothed before his marriage in 1594; *Fripp proposed him (on no evidence) as a model for Holofernes in *Love's Labour's Lost.* A Lancashire man, he graduated BA from Brasenose College, Oxford, in 1575 and took his MA in 1578. He became a leading and respected townsman, and many of his pupils also went to Oxford. The posy resembles *Pericles* 14, 17: 'Yet my good will is great, though the gift small.' *SW*

Aspley, William. See COLOPHON; FOLIOS; PRINTING AND PUBLISHING.

assembled texts. A theory first proposed by Edmond *Malone held that if *manuscript playbooks were not available for all of the plays in the First *Folio, certain play texts may have been assembled for the printer by combining actors' individual parts with the *'plot' of the play. Proponents of this theory have argued that the massed entrance directions in *The Two Gentlemen of Verona, The Merry Wives of Windsor,* and *The Winter's Tale,* which list all of the characters who appear in a scene in a single opening direction regardless of whether they enter at the beginning or later, would be characteristic of the 'plot' but not of a playbook; others have suggested that massed entries may represent a *neoclassical convention imposed

Dame Peggy Ashcroft in her last Shakespearian role, the Countess in *All's Well That Ends Well* (RSC, directed by Trevor Nunn, 1981), with Geoffrey Hutchings as Lavatch.

upon the texts by the scribe Ralph *Crane in the course of preparing *transcripts. *ER*

Aston Cantlow, a parish which included Wilmcote, home of Shakespeare's mother Mary *Arden. Presumably she married John Shakespeare in its church, but there are no registers for this period. *SW*

Astrana Marín, Luis (1889–1960), Spanish scholar and translator of Shakespeare, of whom he also wrote a biography (1930). He was the first to translate Shakespeare's complete works into Spanish (1929), though in prose. Astrana's understanding of Shakespeare's language has sometimes been found wanting, and his unremittingly high-sounding and verbose Spanish now sounds old-fashioned. Until recently, Astrana's were the most widely distributed translations of Shakespeare both in Spain and in Spanish-speaking countries. *ALP*

Astringer, Gentle. See Austringer, Gentleman.

astrology, a pseudo-science arising in Mesopotamia in the 3rd millennium BC and elaborated over many centuries, which pretends to predict terrestrial events through a minute analysis of the positions of celestial objects. During the Renaissance natural astrology (astronomy) and judicial astrology (astromancy) enjoyed equal footing, and leading scientists such as Tycho Brahe, Johannes Kepler, Thomas Digges, and John Dee moved easily between them. Professional astrologers found followers in all classes. Dee was patronized by Queen Elizabeth and luminaries including Leicester, Pembroke, Oxford, Ralegh, and John Cheke. Even Francis Bacon could not entirely free himself from the grasp of the ubiquitous superstition. The religious community was, generally, antagonistic to astromancy. Luther and Calvin were outspoken opponents, but Cardinal Wolsey and Philip Melanchthon were lifelong adherents. In 16th-century intellectual circles, attacks by the humanists Pietro Pomponazzi and Pico della Mirandola challenged the standing of astromancy, as did the Copernican heliocentric solar system which deprived mankind of its position as the focus of the universe. During Shakespeare's working lifetime the legitimacy of judicial astrology was hotly debated; John Chamber's *Treatise against* (1601) was answered by Christopher Heydon's *Defence* (1603). The fatal blow would be Sir Isaac Newton's *Principia mathematica* (1687), which provided a purely mechanistic explanation of planetary movement.

The lover of Shakespeare's Sonnets imputes to the stars an influence over human destiny, but doubts that persons can interpret their stars correctly (Sonnet 14). This may be a précis of the poet's own view. Shakespeare ascribes a belief in judicial astrology to various characters in his plays set in ancient times: Gloucester and Kent in *The History of King Lear* 2.96–104 and 17.33–6, Aaron in *Titus Andronicus* 4.2.32–3, Octavius in *Antony and Cleopatra* 5.1.46–8. Among his medieval and Renaissance characters, Shakespeare seems to associate these beliefs with light-mindedness, e.g. King Richard in *Richard II* 4.1.21–2, Henry VI in *Richard Duke of York* (*3 Henry VI*) 4.6.21–2, Malvolio in *Twelfth Night* 2.5.140. By contrast, Shakespeare's pragmatists—Cassius in *Julius Caesar* 1.2.139–40, Warwick in *Richard Duke of York* (*3 Henry VI*) 4.6.26–9, Helena in *All's Well That Ends Well* 1.1.186–215—either exploit another's credulous faith in astrology or deplore the practice as 'the excellent foppery of the world' (Edmund in *The History of King Lear* 2.105–17). A London astrologer, Simon *Forman, left the

(cont. on page 28)

As You Like It

One of the best loved of Shakespeare's mature comedies, *As You Like It* was entered in the Stationers' Register in 1600: the fact that it is not mentioned in Francis *Meres's list of Shakespeare's works in September 1598, coupled with its high proportion of prose and the precise frequency with which its verse uses colloquial contractions, has inclined most scholars to date the play in 1599–1600, just after *Henry v* (with which it shares some unusual vocabulary) and *Julius Caesar.* Although it may pre-date the play, the publication of 'It was a lover and his lass' (sung in 5.3) in Thomas *Morley's *First Book of Airs* in 1600 would appear to support this dating.

Text: Despite the *Stationers' Register entry of 1600 the play was not printed until the First Folio appeared in 1623. The Folio supplies a generally reliable text which, lacking distinctively authorial spellings and errors, was probably set from a *promptbook, or perhaps a literary transcript of *foul papers.

Sources: The main plot of *As You Like It* derives from Thomas *Lodge's *Rosalynde* (1590), a prose tale interspersed with poems which had already reached its fourth edition in 1598, although Shakespeare makes some telling alterations to this well-known pastoral romance. The play, for example, makes Lodge's rival dukes into brothers (so that their antagonism parallels that between the hero and his eldest brother), and has the usurper spontaneously repent so as to permit the concluding restoration of the exiled court (enabled in *Rosalynde* only by a bloody battle in which the usurper dies). Shakespeare, moreover, changes all the characters' names except those of Phoebe and the (respelled) Rosalind, sometimes allusively: Lodge's Rosader becomes Orlando—named after the hero of *Ariosto's *Orlando furioso,* dramatized by *Greene in around 1591, who runs mad after learning from inscriptions on trees that his beloved has married a shepherd—and his brother becomes Oliver, after Orlando's legendary comrade. Shakespeare adds the characters of Touchstone, Le Beau, Amiens, Jaques, William, Sir Oliver Martext, and the old shepherd Corin, whose name may derive from the anonymous play *Sir Clyomon and Clamydes* (pub. 1599).

Synopsis: **1.1** Orlando laments to the old servant Adam that since the death of his father Sir Roland de Bois his elder brother Oliver has denied him the education and treatment due to his rank, and on Oliver's arrival Orlando confronts him to demand his patrimony. Dismissing him, Oliver summons Charles the wrestler, and after Charles has recounted the (stale) news that the Duke has been driven into exile in the forest of Ardenne (spelt *'Arden' in the Folio text) by his younger brother Frederick, who retains the Duke's daughter Rosalind at court to keep his own daughter company, Oliver maligns Orlando, instructing Charles to be sure to kill him in the following day's wrestling tournament. Alone, Oliver reflects briefly on his rancorous envy of his deservedly admired younger brother, before leaving to encourage Orlando to enter the wrestling. **1.2** At court, Celia, the usurping Duke's daughter, attempts to cheer up Rosalind; they are joined first by the jester Touchstone and then by the courtier Le Beau, who brings news of the wrestling. Frederick and his court arrive to watch Charles wrestle against Orlando, whom the two princesses endeavour in vain to dissuade from the contest: cheered on by Rosalind and Celia, Orlando defeats Charles, but when Frederick learns who his father was he leaves in an ill temper without rewarding him. Instead the cousins congratulate him, and Rosalind gives him her necklace, Orlando finding himself comically tongue-tied with love. Le Beau warns him to flee from Frederick's displeasure. **1.3** Rosalind has just confided her own love for Orlando to Celia when the angry Frederick banishes her from his court. After his departure Celia proposes they both flee to Ardenne together in peasant disguise, and Rosalind, agreeing, decides to dress as a man and call herself Ganymede, while Celia will become Aliena. They leave to enlist Touchstone and make plans for their flight.

2.1 In the forest of Ardenne the exiled Duke Senior speaks to his followers about the moral lessons which console him for the discomforts of their bucolic existence: they leave in search of their melancholy comrade Jaques, last seen pronouncing a sententious lament over a wounded deer. **2.2** Duke Frederick interrogates his courtiers about the disappearance of Celia, feared to have fled with Rosalind in pursuit of Orlando, and has Oliver summoned to court to assist in the manhunt. **2.3** The returning Orlando is warned to flee his murderous brother by Adam, who offers to accompany him as his servant. **2.4** Rosalind and Celia, in their respective disguises, arrive wearily in Ardenne with Touchstone, and overhear the young shepherd Silvius bemoaning his love for Phoebe to his older colleague Corin: questioned, Corin tells Rosalind that his master's cottage, pastures, and flocks are now for sale, and Rosalind and Celia resolve to buy them. **2.5** Amiens sings 'Under the greenwood tree' to some of Duke Senior's lords: they are joined by Jaques, who contributes a satirical verse of his own. **2.6** Adam is fainting with hunger: Orlando promises to fetch him food. **2.7** Duke Senior and his lords, about to eat, are joined by Jaques, who describes meeting Touchstone and speaks of his own ambition to be a satirical jester: they are interrupted when Orlando arrives, sword drawn, to demand food, a demand which is graciously met. Apologizing for his rudeness, Orlando goes to fetch Adam, while Jaques reflects that all the world's a stage. Feeding Adam while Amiens sings 'Blow, blow, thou winter wind', Orlando is warmly welcomed by the Duke, who loved his father.

3.1 An angry Frederick sends Oliver to fetch the missing Orlando, confiscating his lands until his brother is delivered. **3.2** Orlando pins a love poem about Rosalind on a tree before leaving to pin up many more. Corin and Touchstone engage in a comic debate about the relative merits of country and court life before Rosalind arrives, reading another unsigned poem in her own praise, which is mocked by Touchstone. Celia arrives reading yet another such verse: alone with Rosalind, she teases her cousin before finally letting her know that the poet is Orlando, who is also in the forest. They watch as Orlando arrives engaged in a prickly conversation with Jaques: when these two part by mutual consent, Rosalind accosts Orlando in her guise as Ganymede, questions him about his love poems, and proposes to cure him of his love by posing as a realistically contrary Rosalind during daily counselling sessions. **3.3** Touchstone is persuaded to postpone his marriage to Audrey, the ignorant goatherd he lusts after, by Jaques, who feels Touchstone deserves a better priest than Sir Oliver Martext. **3.4** Rosalind is distressed that Orlando is late for his appointment with Ganymede: Celia says he is not to be trusted. Corin arrives, promising to take them to see Silvius trying to woo the disdainful shepherdess Phoebe. **3.5** Seeing Phoebe's scorn for Silvius, Rosalind steps forward and accuses her of ingratitude before she, Celia, and Corin leave. Phoebe, falling in love at first sight with Ganymede, says she will give Silvius an angry letter to deliver to him.

4.1 Rosalind scoffs at Jaques, who leaves on the arrival of Orlando: Rosalind rebukes Orlando for his tardiness, and parries his clichéd declarations of love for Rosalind with a more realistic account of the relations between husbands and wives. Nonetheless, she has Celia act as priest for a mock-betrothal ceremony, and allows Orlando to leave only after exacting solemn promises of a punctual return: alone with Celia she confesses the depth of her love. **4.2** Jaques has some of the Duke's lords, who have been hunting, sing a jovial song about cuckoldry, 'What shall he have that killed the deer?' **4.3** Once more waiting for Orlando, Rosalind and Celia receive Phoebe's letter, delivered by Silvius: instead of a challenge, as Silvius believes, it is a love poem to Ganymede, and Rosalind sends Silvius away with a scornful reply. Oliver now enters, bearing a bloody cloth for Ganymede, whom he recognizes by his description. He relates how Orlando, finding him asleep and at the mercy of a waiting lioness, overcame his righteous indignation against his treacherous brother and killed the lioness, incurring a wound to his arm in the process. Waking in the midst of this, Oliver explains, he has been entirely converted from his former wickedness, and has been sent by his reconciled brother Orlando—who back among the exiled court briefly fainted from loss of blood—to carry the bloody cloth to Ganymede as an apology for his absence. Receiving it, Rosalind faints, nearly betraying her male disguise.

5.1 Audrey and Touchstone meet her rustic suitor William, whom Touchstone, flaunting his superior vocabulary, dismisses. **5.2** Oliver tells Orlando that he and Aliena have fallen instantaneously in love and that he means to marry her immediately, leaving the family estate to Orlando while he remains in Ardenne as a shepherd: Orlando consents to this and urges Oliver to prepare to marry her before Duke Senior and his lords the following day. Rosalind arrives, and after Oliver's departure she promises Orlando that he will be able to marry Rosalind at the same time that his envied brother marries Celia, claiming she will be able to effect this by magic. Phoebe and Silvius arrive, and Rosalind promises that if she ever marries a woman it will be Phoebe: she assures Silvius that he too will be married, and instructs him, Orlando, and Phoebe to meet her the following day in their best clothes, ready for marriage. **5.3** Touchstone and Audrey, too, will be married the next day: in the meantime two pages sing them 'It was a lover and his lass'. **5.4** Before Duke Senior, his followers, Oliver, and Celia, Rosalind, still disguised as Ganymede, has the participants in the multiple wedding ceremony she purports to have devised recap what they have promised: Duke Senior to give Rosalind in marriage to Orlando if she can be produced, Orlando to marry Rosalind, Phoebe to marry Ganymede or, if she chooses not to, to accept Silvius as her husband, Silvius to marry Phoebe. Rosalind and Celia then leave: meanwhile Touchstone and Audrey arrive, and with Jaques' encouragement Touchstone recounts the comically elaborate rules by which courtiers challenge one another but avoid fighting. To the accompaniment of music, Rosalind and Celia enter dressed in their own clothes, conducted by Hymen, god of marriage: Rosalind presents herself to her father and to Orlando, Phoebe renounces her claim to Ganymede, and Hymen blesses the four couples with the song 'Wedding is great Juno's crown'. The festivities are interrupted by the arrival of Jaques de Bois, Sir Rowland's second son, who brings the news that Frederick, leading an expeditionary force against Duke Senior, has undergone a religious conversion and become a hermit, returning all the banished lords' sequestered lands and restoring the dukedom to Duke Senior. Only Jaques declines to return home with them, leaving to join Frederick. After a rustic dance, Rosalind is left to speak a flirtatious epilogue, conjuring women to like as much of the play as pleases them for the sake of the love they bear to men, and vice versa.

Artistic features: *As You Like It* casts some of its most important passages in prose (including the wonderfully inconclusive set-piece debate between court and country in 3.2, Rosalind's dialogues on love with Orlando in 3.2, 4.1, and 5.2, and her epilogue), and, in keeping with its engagement with the pastoral tradition, is correspondingly relaxed about its own (or Lodge's) plot: once most of the cast have got into the forest Shakespeare seems simply to let them pass the time meeting one another and talking until Rosalind feels that the time has come to relinquish her disguise.

Critical history: The earliest critical responses to this play are two adaptations, Charles Johnson's **Love in a Forest* (1723) and John Carrington's unacted *The *Modern Receipt; or, The Cure for Love* (1735), both of which share with later 18th-century commentators a sense that the play could use some tidying up. However, although Dr *Johnson (in sympathy with Jaques) felt that Shakespeare had rushed his happy ending and should have shown the sketchily reported dialogue between Frederick and the hermit, most were prepared to forgive its looseness of construction, accepting that it was in keeping with the play's pastoral nature that it should concentrate on character and sentiment at the expense of plot. What the 18th century had forgiven, the Romantics worshipped, finding in Duke Senior's celebration of the moral lessons of Nature a statement of Shakespeare's own imputed views on the wisdom to be found outside a corrupted urban society, and finding the play's preference for reflection over action equally sympathetic: *Schlegel, influentially, saw the play as a manifesto for the view that 'nothing is wanted to call forth the poetry which has its dwelling in nature and the human mind but to throw off all artificial constraint, and restore both to their native liberty' (1811).

Nineteenth-century criticism in general concentrated on the play's characters, with Rosalind often idealized as the perfect, morally superior heroine. A well-established tradition of valuing Shakespeare's depiction of the relationship between Rosalind and Celia as literature's prime celebration of female bonding found its fullest expression in Mary Cowden Clarke's 'Rosalind and Celia: The Friends' in *Girlhood of Shakespeare's Heroines* (1850–2). Victorian and Edwardian comments on the play's pastoralism stressed the forest's kinship with the *Arden of Warwickshire rather than the French Ardenne, seeing Shakespeare's woodland as a place where native common sense triumphed over the foreign affectations represented by Phoebe: according to Frederick Boas, for example, the play replaced 'the artificial atmosphere of the Renaissance pastoral' with 'the open-air freshness, the breeze and blue of the old English ballad-poetry' (1896).

The 20th century saw a renewed and usually more complicated interest in the play's dealings with the literary conventions of its time, with scholars reading it not only against Lodge's *Rosalynde* (dismissed as 'worthless' by George *Steevens in 1770, but studied with increasing respect thereafter) but alongside the versions of pastoral offered by *Sidney, *Spenser, *Greene, and others. Such critics, unusually, tended to concur in seeing the play as simultaneously a celebration and a debunking of the pastoral convention as Shakespeare had found it (although attempts to find topical references in the play, whether to Sir John *Harington or to riots against *enclosure, commanded less agreement). Two further influential lines of enquiry combined with this one later in the century: one, following Northrop *Frye and C. L. Barber, has pursued the play's interest in patterns of seasonal renewal and fertility, while another has been more interested in its sexual politics, particularly the issues raised by Rosalind's successful disguise as Ganymede.

Stage history: The play's early history is haunted by two ill-substantiated rumours: one, not recorded before 1865, that the play was acted for James I at Wilton House in Wiltshire in 1603, and the other, reported by *Capell in 1779, that Shakespeare himself played the role of Adam. Whether or not there is any truth in these, there are no records of any performances of the play before Johnson's *Love in a Forest* appeared at Drury Lane in 1723 (though most have assumed that the play was first acted at the Globe soon after its opening in 1599). It did not appear in unadapted form until 1740, when it was revived at Covent Garden with Hannah *Pritchard as Rosalind, Kitty Clive as Celia, and the songs set by Thomas *Arne: this sparkling production immediately established *As You Like It* as one of the most popular plays of the century, and since then few major actresses have not attempted the role of Rosalind. Peg *Woffington was the first to compete with Pritchard, at Drury Lane (for six nights in 1741 both Theatres Royal competed with their rival productions), and indeed made her final stage appearance in the role, collapsing with a stroke in the middle of the epilogue in 1757. Even Sarah *Siddons played Rosalind in 1785 and 1786, but her gravity of demeanour suited her badly to the part (generally played at the time with tomboyish extroversion): far more successful was Dorothea *Jordan, whose roguish performance helped to assure that from 1787 to her departure in 1814 the play was acted at Drury Lane more frequently than any other in the Shakespeare canon. Nineteenth-century Rosalinds, increasingly performing on lavishly decorated sets and in carefully specified period costumes (a trend initiated by *Macready's 1842 production, with its French 15th-century designs), tended to be more ladylike, even in disguise: Helen *Faucit, who shed tears of joy in her love scenes with Orlando, was especially praised for always being 'the Duke's daughter' even at her most playful

moments. The decorously cut and decorative productions in which a succession of such Rosalinds predominated—from Faucit to Ada *Rehan, Mary *Anderson, and Lily Brayton—perhaps reached their apogee in 1908, when Richard Flanagan's Manchester production filled the forest with real deer, which unfortunately terrified the Orlando, Harcourt *Williams.

In the 20th century this Merrie English tradition was gradually supplanted—most notably by Nigel Playfair's controversially stylized production at Stratford in 1919—and a less jolly side to the play has sometimes been found by directors embarrassed by deer except as potential archetypal symbols. Despite a continuing succession of joyously sunny Rosalinds—from Peggy *Ashcroft (Old Vic, 1932) through Edith *Evans (Old Vic, 1936, in Watteau-style costumes, with Michael Redgrave as Orlando) to Vanessa *Redgrave (RSC, 1961)—the play has often belonged more to Jaques than to Touchstone on the modern stage, with Duke Senior's remarks on the joys of exile rendered ironic by uncomfortably snowbound Ardens. Notably tense readings of the play include Adrian *Noble's (RSC, 1985, with Fiona Shaw as a memorably cut-glass Celia) and Michael Grandage's (Sheffield and on tour, 2000, with Nicholas le Prevost a commanding Jaques). This continuing disagreement as to whether the play works best as 'hard' or 'soft' pastoral has been compounded by discussions as to whether it is best played by mixed or same-sex companies: Ben *Greet directed an all-male production in 1920 (appropriately, at the Central YMCA in London), Clifford *Williams another for the National Theatre in 1967, and *Cheek by Jowl's exuberant all-male version of 1991–2, which toured extensively around the world, was the most successful and talked-about Shakespeare production of its time. *MD*

On the screen: The Paul Czinner film (1936) with Olivier as Orlando was the first sound cinema adaptation of the play. An acclaimed BBC TV production (1953) included Margaret Leighton and Michael Hordern. Michael Elliott's RSC theatre production with Vanessa Redgrave (Rosalind) was directed for BBC TV by Ronald Eyre (1963). Cedric Messina's 1978 BBC TV production is memorable for Helen Mirren's Rosalind and Richard Pasco's Jaques. Christine Edzard's *As You Like It* (1992), while refreshing and daring in its approach, sets the play amidst urban dereliction which runs against the grain of the play's language. *AD*

Major editions

Alan Brissenden (Oxford, 1993); Agnes Latham (Arden, 1975); Arthur Quiller-Couch and John Dover Wilson (New Cambridge, 1926)

Some representative criticism

Barber, C. L., *Shakespeare's Festive Comedy* (1959)

Barton, Anne, '*As You Like It* and *Twelfth Night*: Shakespeare's Sense of an Ending', in Malcolm Bradbury and David Palmer (eds.), *Shakespearian Comedy* (1972)

Jenkins, Harold, '*As You Like It*', *Shakespeare Survey*, 8 (1955)

McFarland, Thomas, *Shakespeare's Pastoral Comedy* (1972)

---

most detailed eyewitness accounts of performances of Shakespeare's plays during the playwright's lifetime. *SS*

Rowse, A. L., *Sex and Society in Shakespeare's Age: Simon Forman, the Astrologer* (1974)

Thomas, Sir Keith, *Religion and the Decline of Magic* (1973)

As You Like It *(see page 25)*

Athenian, Old. He is the father of the woman that Lucilius wishes to marry, *Timon of Athens* 1.1. *AB*

Athens, the ancient capital of Greece, provides settings for both *A Midsummer Night's Dream* and *Timon of Athens*. *AB*

Atkins, Robert (1886–1972), British actor and director. A robust player, he devoted his long life to keeping Shakespeare on the stage. He acted with Beerbohm *Tree but his Shakespearian affinities were with Frank *Benson, Ben *Greet, and William *Poel. Before war service in 1916 he played leading parts under Greet in the first regular Shakespeare seasons at the *Old Vic. He so impressed the formidable manager Lilian Baylis that she appointed him her director and from 1920 to 1925 he staged all but one of the 36 plays in the First Folio, acting in many of them. He then ran the Open Air Theatre in Regent's Park, where his own parts included Bottom, Sir Toby Belch, Falstaff, and *Caliban (played, after *Granville-Barker, as 'a missing link'). In 1938 he directed *Henry V* at a boxing ring in Blackfriars in an approximation of Elizabethan stage conditions. From 1944 to 1945 he was director of productions at Stratford-upon-Avon, staging sixteen plays and acting in some of them. He then returned to his activities at Regent's Park and to touring in Shakespeare. His simple, ungimmicky productions were admired by Arthur Colby Sprague whose essay on Atkins is appended to the autobiography. *MJ*

Robert Atkins: An Unfinished Autobiography, ed. George Rowell (1994).

Atkinson, William (b. 1571), witness to Shakespeare's purchase of the *Blackfriars Gatehouse in 1613. Like John *Heminges and Henry *Condell, he lived in the London parish of St Mary Aldermanbury, and as clerk of the Brewers' Company probably knew Shakespeare's trustees in the purchase, William Johnson, host of the Mermaid Tavern, and John Jackson, who drank there. *SW*

Aubrey, John (1626–97), antiquary and compiler of over 400 biographical sketches known as the *Brief Lives*. Educated at Trinity College, Oxford, Aubrey carefully enquired into Shakespeare's life and left brief and hectic jottings about it, amidst a chaos of manuscripts first edited by Andrew Clark in 1898. Aubrey is exceedingly important among Shakespeare's early biographers. Free of moral bias, he is sometimes inaccurate, but he recorded what he heard. Thus he wrote of the poet's relations with John and Jane Davenant, Oxford tavern-keepers, after consulting several of their children (he knew Jane, Robert, and Sir William). Stratford 'neighbours' had told him of Shakespeare's early feats as the son of a 'Butcher'. They were doubtless wrong; but around 1681 Aubrey sought out a more likely authority, namely William Beeston (a son of Christopher, the poet's colleague in the Chamberlain's Servants), who is the source for the remark that Shakespeare knew Latin 'pretty well' for he had been a 'schoolmaster in the country'. Aubrey twice states that Shakespeare visited Stratford 'once a year', and discusses his appearance, personality, and it seems his circumspect behaviour ('not a company keeper') in notes which deserve one's caution and high respect alike. *PH*

Chambers, E. K., *William Shakespeare: A Study of Facts and Problems* (1930)

Auden, W(ystan) H(ugh) (1907–73), English poet and critic. Auden's attention to Shakespeare is continuous. He lectured on Shakespeare in New York in 1946 and in Oxford in

1957 (collected as part of *The Dyer's Hand*, 1962). His long semi-dramatized poem *The Sea and the Mirror* (1944) is subtitled 'A Commentary on Shakespeare's *The Tempest*'. His introduction to the Sonnets (Signet, 1964) spurns biographical speculation, concentrating on formal and technical questions and the 'mystical' Vision of Eros. *Love's Labour's Lost*, adapted (with Chester Kallman) as an opera libretto from Shakespeare's play, was premièred, with music by Nicolas Nabokov, in Brussels, 1973. *TM*

audiences. The minimum price of admission at open-air playhouses (for example the Theatre and the Globe) was traditionally a penny—about 10% of an artisan's daily pay—while at the indoor playhouses (for example the Blackfriars) it was sixpence. Thus the wealthy might attend either type of venue but the average worker was likely to visit only the open-air playhouses. Women of all social classes attended the playhouses and although their presence at the open-air theatres was criticized as dangerous folly, if not flagrant prostitution, their numbers rose steadily in line with the increased respectability of the industry in the reigns of James and Charles. Pickpockets and prostitutes naturally found the open-air playhouses, with their crowds and bustle, more productive than the sedentary indoor playhouses.

The different types of theatre accommodated different tastes: the indoor theatres providing masque-like spectacles and subtle music while the open-air playhouses had jigs and explosive sound effects. However, each had elements of the other's specialism and the King's Men showed the same plays at the Blackfriars and the Globe at least until the 1620s. When the Queen's Men left the Red Bull to open Christopher Beeston's new Cockpit in Drury Lane in late 1616, rioting apprentices vented frustration at their elitist move up market by attacking the Cockpit and Beeston's adjoining home. The ultimate triumph of the indoor playhouses—no open-air amphitheatres were built in the Restoration—marks the disappearance of the truly popular (in the sense of appealing to all classes) theatrical tradition. *GE*

Cook, Ann Jennalie, *The Privileged Playgoers of Shakespeare's London* (1981)
Gurr, Andrew, *Playgoing in Shakespeare's London* (1987)
Harbage, Alfred, *Shakespeare and the Rival Traditions* (1952)
Harbage, Alfred, *Shakespeare's Audience* (1941)

Audley, Maxine (1923–92), British actress. When in 1951 this dark and voluptuous player acted Charmian in *Antony and Cleopatra* she was obviously capable of taking the lead. Her effective Shakespearian roles included Goneril in *King Lear*, Emilia in *Othello*, and Lady Macbeth. Her most memorable performance was as the Empress Tamora in Peter *Brook's great *Titus Andronicus* in 1955–7. *MJ*

Audrey, a goatherd, is wooed and won by Touchstone in *As You Like It*. *AB*

Aufidius, Tullus. Coriolanus' adversary, he allies with Coriolanus, 4.5, but joins the conspirators who kill him, 5.6. *AB*

Augustus Caesar. See CAESAR, OCTAVIUS.

Aumerle, Duke of. One of Richard's supporters, his father the Duke of York denounces him to King Henry in *Richard II* 5.3 (based on Edward Plantagenet, 1373–1415). See also YORK, DUKE OF. *AB*

Austen, Jane (1775–1817), English novelist. Although some commentators have found structural resemblances between *Pride and Prejudice* and *Much Ado About Nothing*, Austen's engagement with Shakespeare is most visible in *Mansfield Park* (1814), which takes its three daughters from *King Lear* and elements of its love plot from *All's Well That Ends Well* (hence its hero's surname, Bertram). Henry Crawford reveals his insincerity by the skill with which he reads aloud from *Henry VIII* in his attempt to court Fanny Price, though Austen clearly endorses his identification of Shakespeare as 'part of an Englishman's constitution'. *NJW*

Australia. Although Shakespeare was inevitably part of the cultural baggage brought to Australia by its British colonizers in 1788, the first evidence of performance is a playbill dated 8 April 1800 for 'the favorite play Henry the Fourth' at Robert Sidaway's theatre; it is not known if the play was performed. The authorities closed the four-year-old theatre the same year, considering drama unsuitable for a convict settlement, but on 26 December 1833 *Richard III* in *Cibber's version with John Meredith as Richard inaugurated professional Shakespeare in the colony. Conrad Knowles was the country's first Hamlet and played eight other Shakespearian roles before dying in 1844; his protégée Eliza Winstanley was Australia's first significant Shakespearian actress. The gold rush which began in 1851 attracted American and British actors including G. V. Brooke, who appeared in 73 plays between 1855 and 1861, 23 by Shakespeare. Barry Sullivan, Charles and Ellen Kean, James Anderson, and Walter Montgomery were all acclaimed, but Shakespeare's popularity declined until George Rignold's spectacular *Henry V* (1876) and Essie Jenyns, the first Australian-born Shakespearian star, played Juliet and the heroines of the comedies (1885–8). Shakespeare societies, established in cities and towns including Melbourne (1884), Adelaide (1885), and Wagga Wagga (1895), helped move Shakespeare away from popular theatre into the lecture hall.

During the early 20th century lavish imported productions retarded development of an Australian Shakespearian tradition, and the first Shakespearian company, established in 1920 by *Irving idolater Allan Wilkie, continued in the English mould; however Wilkie's frequently simple staging allowed a more fluent performance style. Touring Australia and New Zealand for a decade, he aimed to present all the plays and, astonishingly, achieved 27. The dearth of commercial productions between 1930 and 1960 led to the growth of amateur companies, stimulated by visits from the *Old Vic with the *Oliviers (1948) and expatriate Robert Helpmann and Katharine Hepburn (1955) and the Stratford Memorial Theatre led by Anthony Quayle (1949, 1953). Such visits reinforced belief that English Shakespeare was the best and only model, and underpinned the John Alden company which, beginning as amateur in 1948, toured professionally but intermittently 1952–61. By then Hugh Hunt had directed *Twelfth Night* and *Hamlet* for the Australian Elizabethan Theatre Trust, a funding body formed in 1954, and the Young Elizabethan Players were touring schools with Shakespearian adaptations.

In 1970 John Bell, who had played Hamlet at 22, returned to Sydney after five years acting with the Royal Shakespeare Company and the Bristol Old Vic; with Ken Horler he formed the Nimrod Theatre Company, producing new plays and the classics, especially Shakespeare, with a radical disregard for tradition. Jim Sharman produced an irreverent *As You Like It* with Australian accents in 1971 at Sydney's Old Tote Theatre and Bell's 1973 *Hamlet* was spoken with 'normal' voices; at an exciting time politically and theatrically for Australia the plays were becoming more accessible to a public wider than the middle- and upper-class theatre-going audience.

The Bell Shakespeare Company was formed in 1990, John Bell as artistic director saying, 'We want to evolve a way of playing Shakespeare that makes sense to Australians young and old, and to encourage actors of varied ethnic backgrounds to join our troupe so that we may truly reflect the face of Australian society.' By 2000 the company had produced fifteen plays and toured to all Australian states. Until the 1980s Shakespeare was a compulsory study in state education systems, and Wilkie, Alden, and Bell all played to large school audiences.

Subsidized companies, founded mostly in the capital cities in the 1960s, usually staged an annual Shakespeare production, some, such as Sharman's *A Midsummer Night's Dream* (Adelaide, 1983), thrillingly innovative. Independent outdoor productions drew huge crowds—Glenn Elston's energetic *A Midsummer Night's Dream* (1987) in Melbourne's Royal Botanic Gardens ran for twelve weeks, went on tour, and was revived four times. An Aboriginal interpretation of the same play for the 1997 Sydney Festival of the Dreaming was the first staging of a classic play by an all-indigenous cast.

The taste for Shakespeare was further boosted by films and television, particularly the anomalously titled *William Shakespeare's Romeo+Juliet* (1996) directed by Baz Luhrmann, whose 1993 production of Benjamin Britten's *A Midsummer Night's Dream* for the Australian Opera was a 1994 Edinburgh Festival hit. Ballets of that play were created by Barry Moreland (Perth, 1990) and Harold Collins (Brisbane, 1991), two of several choreographers to produce Shakespearian works. Arts festivals, particularly those held in Perth since 1953 and Adelaide since 1960, have brought productions from many countries, outstandingly from Georgia, Poland, Britain, China, and Japan. The first Australian Shakespeare Festival was held in Bowral in 1997.

As well as those mentioned, Australia has given many notable Shakespearian actors and directors to the world, among them Oscar Asche (1871–1936), Judith *Anderson (1898–1992), Coral Browne (1913–91), Leo McKern (b. 1920), Keith Michell (b. 1928), Patricia Conolly (b. 1933), Geoffrey Rush (b. 1951), Gale Edwards (b. 1955), and Neil Armfield (b. 1955).

Printed reviews, essential resources for performance history, have contributed to the rich store of Australian writing on Shakespeare since the early 19th century. William à Beckett's *Lectures on the Poets and Poetry of Great Britain* (1839) included Shakespeare, F. W. Haddon's *The Hamlet Controversy: Was Hamlet Mad?* (1867) reprinted comments aroused by the performances of Montgomery and Anderson, and editions of the plays range from Rignold's acting versions (1876–9) to the Bell Shakespeare, begun in 1994. The academic Shakespearian tradition stemming principally from Sydney University's Mungo McCallum (*Shakespeare's Roman Plays and their Background*, 1910) prospered and from the 1920s onward books, articles, and editions by Australian scholars were being published at home and abroad in increasing numbers. The Australian and New Zealand Shakespeare Association, formed at Monash University, Melbourne, in 1990, held its first international conference in Adelaide in 1992.

In no way considered the 'national poet' as he could be as late as 1900, Shakespeare continues potently in Australian culture generally. In 1891 a horse called Malvolio won the nation's premier sporting event, the Melbourne Cup; in 1999 a horse named Classic Romeo was racing in Queensland. *ABr*

Golder, John, and Madelaine, Richard (eds.), *O Brave New World: Two Centuries of Shakespeare on the Australian Stage* (2000)

Rickard, John, 'Shakespeare', in Philip Parsons (ed.), *Companion to Theatre in Australia* (1995)

'Shakespeare in Australia', in William H. Wilde, Joy Hooton, and Barry Andrews (eds.), *The Oxford Companion to Australian Literature* (1985)

Austria is usually mentioned in a negative context in Shakespeare's plays, and Vienna is the morally perverted setting for the action in *Measure for Measure*. In the city of Graz, as early as 1608, an English play 'about the Jew' was performed; however, this was possibly *The Jew of Malta* rather than *The Merchant of Venice*. In the late 18th century, *Mozart saw Shakespearian characters performed by Emanuel Schikaneder in the popular Viennese tradition. When he attempted to revolutionize the opera, Mozart expressly referred to *Hamlet*. Franz *Schubert wrote three lieder with texts adapted from *The Two Gentlemen of Verona*, *Antony and Cleopatra*, and *Cymbeline* (1826).

During the first decades of the 20th century there was another remarkable period of Shakespearian activity. After Sigmund *Freud had started interpreting Shakespearian characters using his own psychoanalytical theory, Hugo von Hofmannsthal wrote his tragedy *Elektra* (1904, used as an opera libretto by Richard Strauss), in which the protagonist in certain respects both resembles Hamlet and contrasts with him. The great language critic Karl Kraus adapted some Shakespearian plays and made a rather free German translation of the Sonnets (1932). Shakespeare was first performed at the annual Salzburg Festival in 1927, when Max Reinhardt delighted the audience with his wonderfully poetic *A Midsummer Night's Dream*. A considerable number of Shakespearian highlights were presented in the history of this festival. In 1992 and the two following years, the productions of the Roman plays, two directed by Peter Stein and one by Deborah Warner, were spectacular, albeit controversially received, Salzburg events.

From the major Viennese and other Austrian theatres the renowned Vienna Burgtheater with its important contributions to theatre history must be singled out. Since the 1960s it has been particularly active in the field of Shakespeare reception. A memorable achievement was, for example, Leopold Lindtberg's staging of the histories in 1964. In 1985/6 Klaus Maria Brandauer played Hamlet over 100 times. Under Claus Peymann's direction there were a number of much discussed modern productions at the Burgtheater, such as Peter *Zadek's *Merchant of Venice* (1988), in which Shylock's behaviour was an intentional response to the profiteering Christians who despised him. The great Austrian actor and director Fritz *Kortner had already taken a similar approach in a moving Austro-German TV production in 1968. George Tabori has become well known for his innovative theatrical work on Shakespeare, for example, with his version of *King Lear*, based on the text by Erich Fried, the most prominent Austrian Shakespeare translator. It was performed at the Bregenz Festspiele in 1988 by six women, as this production centred entirely on the tragedy's often neglected sexual aspects.

There are interesting Shakespearian echoes in Ingeborg Bachmann's fine poem 'Böhmen liegt am Meer' (Bohemia on the Sea, 1964), and in Thomas Bernhard's play *Minetti* (1977). In Gerhard Rühm's *Ophelia und die Wörter* (Ophelia and the Words, 1969) her acting 'partners' are her own words rather than dramatic persons. Gertrud Fussenegger has written short stories about Ophelia, Jessica, and a fictive sister of Juliet (*Shakespeares Töchter* (Shakespeare's Daughters), 1999). *WR*

Austria, Duke of (Limoges). He first supports and then deserts Arthur, and is killed by the Bastard, *King John* 3.2. *AB*

Austringer, Gentleman. He takes a petition from Helen to give to the King of France, *All's Well That Ends Well* 5.1. An austringer (sometimes spelt 'astringer') is a falconer. See HUNTING AND SPORTS. *AB*

authenticity. In the 17th century, the term 'authenticity' applied primarily to abstract principles (reasons, rules, doctrines) that were undeniable, approved by all. By the end of the 18th century, the word had come to be applied to concrete terms. Shakespearian scholars, beginning with Edmond *Malone, have since engaged in a Grail quest for Shakespeare's authentic texts, authentic *signatures, and authentic *portraits. *ER*

de Grazia, Margreta, *Shakespeare Verbatim: The Reproduction of Authenticity and the 1790 Apparatus* (1991)

Orgel, Stephen, 'The Authentic Shakespeare', *Representations*, 21 (1988)

Authorship Controversy, a term used to describe the various attempts which have been made to persuade the world that Shakespeare's works were not written by Shakespeare.

This curious and seemingly unstoppable phenomenon, Shakespearian scholarship's distorted shadow, began in obscurity with the Warwickshire cleric James Wilmot in 1785 (see BACONIAN THEORY), and approached its classic form in Joseph Hart's little-read *The Romance of Yachting* (1848, see below), but it only becomes fully visible with the publication of Delia *Bacon's article 'William Shakespeare and his Plays; an Inquiry Concerning Them' in *Putnam's Magazine* (1856). Delia Bacon darkly attributes the Shakespeare canon to her namesake Sir Francis, or perhaps to an occult committee dominated by him. Since then other champions have credited the plays to *Bacon alone, to Christopher *Marlowe, to the 5th Earl of *Rutland, to the 6th Earl of *Derby, to the

17th Earl of *Oxford, and even to Queen *Elizabeth I, among many others. The controversy has itself become an object of scholarly attention, as generations of Shakespearian critics have wondered why it should be so much easier to get into print with bizarre untruths about Shakespeare than with anything else on the subject. Many commentators have paid reluctant tribute to the sheer determination and ingenuity which 'anti-Stratfordian' writers have displayed—indeed, have invariably had to display, since any theory suggesting that the theatre professional William Shakespeare did not write the Shakespeare canon somehow has to explain why so many of his contemporaries said that he did (from *Heminges, *Condell, *Jonson, and the other contributors to the Folio through Francis *Meres and the Master of the Revels to the parish authorities of *Holy Trinity in Stratford, to name only a few), and why none of the rest said that he did not. Most observers, however, have been more impressed by the anti-Stratfordians' dogged immunity to documentary evidence, not only that which confirms that Shakespeare wrote his own plays, but that which establishes that several of the alternative candidates were long dead before he had finished doing so. 'One thought perhaps offers a crumb of redeeming comfort,' observed the controversy's most thorough historian, Samuel *Schoenbaum, 'the energy absorbed by the mania might otherwise have gone into politics.' Schoenbaum's account (which provides a valuable survey of earlier literature) has been supplemented since by more philosophical accounts of the origin and development of the phenomenon.

By the middle of the 19th century, the Authorship Controversy was an accident waiting to happen. In the wake of *Romanticism, especially its German variants, such transcendent, quasi-religious claims were being made for the supreme poetic triumph of the Complete Works that it was becoming well-nigh impossible to imagine how any mere human being could have written them at all. At the same time the popular understanding of what levels of cultural literacy might have been achieved in 16th-century Stratford was still heavily influenced by a British tradition of *bardolatry (best exemplified by David *Garrick's Shakespeare *Jubilee) which had its own nationalist reasons for representing Shakespeare as an uninstructed son of the English soil, a thoroughly native genius who had out-written the world without any help from foreign or classical literary models. These two notions—that the Shakespeare canon represented the highest achievement of human culture, while William Shakespeare was a completely uneducated rustic—combined to persuade Delia Bacon and her successors that the Folio's title page and preliminaries could only be part of a fabulously elaborate charade orchestrated by some more elevated personage, and they accordingly misread the distinctive literary traces of Shakespeare's solid Elizabethan grammar-school *education visible throughout the volume as evidence that the 'real' author had attended Oxford or Cambridge. This misapprehension was reinforced by the 19th century's deepening sense that there was an absolute boundary between Poetry (a disinterested manifestation of high culture) and the live theatre (a mercenary form of vulgar entertainment). At a time when the theatrical dimension of the works was especially ill understood (the plays heavily cut and altered to fit the contemporary stage, and read by critics after Charles *Lamb as sublime poems rather than as practical scripts), it became possible, perversely, for the fact that William Shakespeare had been a known professional actor and man of the theatre to be cited as evidence that he could not have written the plays rather than as corroboration that he did.

As this factor and the privileged birth of the principal claimants suggest, the Authorship Controversy, consciously or not, is very largely about class. The social assumptions behind Bacon's view that the plays are too lofty to have been written by a middle-class Warwickshire thespian are shared, for example, by Colonel Joseph C. Hart, who anticipated the controversy proper in his *The Romance of Yachting* (1848). Apparently ignorant of any editions prior to 1709, Hart claimed that Nicholas *Rowe and Thomas *Betterton had cynically misattributed the plays, really written by teams of unnamed 'university men', to Shakespeare, who had in fact contributed only their more obscene passages. These are often just the passages which Alexander *Pope's edition had identified a century earlier as vulgar un-Shakespearian interpolations by 'the players', and Hart is typical of many anti-Stratfordians since in hereby unselfconsciously reproducing the snobbish and anachronistic judgements of *neoclassical criticism, only with Shakespeare himself placed outside the pale of respectable authorship rather than just certain unacceptably 'low' aspects of his writings.

It is worth noting that the controversy also has a national dimension: both Hart and Delia Bacon were Americans, and blue-blooded candidates for the authorship continue to find their most eager (and munificent) supporters in the United States—a country whose citizens, long emancipated from the British monarchy and aristocracy, apparently find it easier to entertain romantic fantasies about their unacknowledged talents than do the British themselves. Members of other nationalities, too, have enjoyed the sense that they know the 'real' Shakespeare better than do his compatriots: during the early 20th century German conspiracy theorists particularly favoured the Earl of Rutland, for example, though their French counterparts preferred the Earl of Derby, and in Austria Sigmund *Freud, in a classic instance of the fantasies about secret aristocratic origins which he had identified in children, placed his faith in the Earl of Oxford. *MD*

Bate, Jonathan, *The Genius of Shakespeare* (1997)
Garber, Marjorie, *Shakespeare's Ghost Writers* (1987)
Matus, Irvin Leigh, *Shakespeare, in Fact* (1999)
Schoenbaum, Samuel, *Shakespeare's Lives* (1970, rev. edn. 1991)

Autolycus, a singing pedlar, deceives and robs the rustics in Acts 4 and 5 of *The Winter's Tale*. *AB*

Auvergne, Countess of. She attempts to take Talbot prisoner but has to beg forgiveness when his soldiers arrive, *1 Henry VI* 2.4. *AB*

Ayrer, Jakob (1543–1605), popular German playwright who worked in Nuremberg, writing carnival plays and musical dramas. The latter were influenced by the English companies who toured Germany in the 1590s. Two of his plays are thought to share their sources with Shakespeare's *Much Ado About Nothing* and *The Tempest*. *RM*

Ayscough, Samuel (1745–1804), an assistant librarian at the British Museum, whose *Index to the Remarkable Passages and Words Made Use of by Shakespeare* (1790) was the first *concordance, listing words alphabetically and locating them by play, act, scene, page, column, and line number, keyed to his own edition of Shakespeare. *CMSA*

WILLIAM SHAKESPEARE, HIS METHOD OF WORK

Max Beerbohm's wry *reductio ad absurdum* of the Baconian theory, 'William Shakespeare, his method of work', from *The Poets' Corner*, 1904.

Babion. The 'He-babion' and 'She-babion' (sometimes spelled 'bavian': baboon) are among the rustic dancers who perform in *The Two Noble Kinsmen* 3.5. *AB*

Bach, Carl Philip Emanuel (1714–88), German composer, the most famous son of Johann Sebastian Bach. Although he did not set any Shakespeare texts himself, the sixth sonata of his *Achtzehn Probestücke in sechs Sonaten* (W63/6) was adapted by Heinrich Wilhelm von Gerstenberg in 1767 as a song with the words 'To be or not to be'. Consequently it became known as Bach's 'Hamlet' Fantasia. *IBC*

Bacon, Delia (1811–59), American writer and conspiracy theorist, who became convinced in the late 1840s that Shakespeare's plays had been written by Sir Francis *Bacon. With some encouragement from *Emerson she sailed to England in 1853, and with his help published 'William Shakespeare and his Plays: An Inquiry Concerning Them' in *Putnam's Magazine* in 1856, the article credited (if that is the word) with initiating the *Authorship Controversy. The well-nigh incomprehensible (and largely unread) *The Philosophy of the Plays of Shakspere Unfolded* (which never mentions Bacon by name) followed in 1857. After an aborted attempt to dig up Shakespeare's grave in Stratford Bacon became wholly mad, and died in an institution in 1859. *MD*

Bacon, Francis (1561–1627), the greatest English philosopher of early modern times. Some people (not many) think him to have written the works of Shakespeare (see Bacon, Delia; Baconian theory). The son of an eminent statesman, Bacon began his career as an ambitious young lawyer, using every available means to get government office and often in debt. He was involved in the prosecution of the Earl of *Essex after his abortive rebellion (1601), and his *Declaration of the Practices and Treasons . . . Committed by . . . Essex* (1601) refers to the production of Shakespeare's *Richard II* staged on the day before the rising. His fortunes improved after 1606, when he married a rich man's daughter. He eventually rose to become Lord Chancellor (1618), but was dismissed from office three years later for taking bribes, and died as he began, in debt. In the 1590s he contributed speeches to entertainments at the Inns of Court; later he wrote a *History of Henry VII* (1622) and an account of an imaginary intellectual society (*The New Atlantis*, 1627). But his chief literary achievement was the *Essays*, first published in 1597, and revised and expanded in two later editions (1612 and 1625). These offer shiftily sophisticated commentaries on ideas (Truth, Revenge, Love, Superstition), institutions (Marriage, Kingdoms, Ceremonies), activities, and people, involved, for the most part, in what preoccupied Bacon obsessively: the struggle for wealth and power. His great project as a philosopher was to write a complete account of the state of knowledge in his time, which he called the *Instauratio magna* (The Great Renewal). One part of this he finished was the introduction, *Of the Advancement of Learning* (1605), which was mainly concerned with the problem of getting it done. *RM*

Jardine, Lisa, and Stewart, Alan, *Hostage to Fortune: The Troubled Life of Francis Bacon* (1998)

Bacon, Mathias See Blackfriars Gatehouse.

Baconian theory, a term for the notion that Shakespeare's works were really written by Sir Francis *Bacon, the first phase of the *Authorship Controversy.

Although first espoused in print by Delia *Bacon in 1856—closely and more comprehensibly followed in 1857 by Dr William Henry Smith, author of *Bacon and Shakespeare: An Inquiry Touching Players, Playhouses, and Play-Writers in the Days of Elizabeth*—this idea had independently occurred in 1785 to the Revd James Wilmot, rector of *Barton-on-the-Heath, near Stratford, but at the age of 80 Wilmot, perhaps renouncing the heresy, had all his papers on the subject destroyed, and we know of his speculations only from an Ipswich antiquary who had visited him in 1805.

Smith claimed that Shakespeare's works were too refined to have been written by a mere actor from Warwickshire, and on the basis of alleged verbal parallels between the Shakespeare canon and the published writings of Bacon (such as the supposed resemblance between 'Nor are those empty hearted, whose low sound | Reverbs no hollowness' and 'For the sound will be greater or less, as the barrel is more empty or more full') he attributed them to Sir Francis, who had elaborately concealed his authorship due to the social stigma attached to writing for the stage.

This hypothesis found particular favour among readers keener to find occult Neoplatonic allegory than drama in the plays, such as the American judge Nathaniel Holmes (who published *The Authorship of Shakespeare* in 1866), and it was later offered dubious support by the American spiritualist Ignatius Donnelly, whose *The Great Cryptogram: Francis Bacon's Cipher in the So-Called Shakespeare Plays* (1888) purports to find clues to Bacon's authorship concealed in the Folio in a complex (and wholly inconsistent) mathematical code. Later Baconians elaborated even on Donnelly's version of the theory: Dr Orville Ward Owen, for example, devised a vast 'decoding' machine, by which, according to the five volumes of *Sir Francis Bacon's Cipher Story* (1893–5), he was able to discover that the Shakespeare canon contained Bacon's autobiography and revealed that he was really the son of Elizabeth I by the Earl of Leicester.

Baconianism had its heyday in the last decade of the 19th century and the first of the 20th (enlisting Mark *Twain among its disciples, whose erratic and intemperate *Is Shakespeare Dead?* appeared in 1909), but although there is still a Bacon Society (founded in 1886) it has since lost ground among Shakespearian conspiracy theorists, most of whom now prefer to attribute the canon to other aristocrats, or to Elizabeth herself. *MD*

Harbage, Alfred, 'Shakespeare as Culture Hero', in *Conceptions of Shakespeare* (1966)
Schoenbaum, Samuel, *Shakespeare's Lives* (1970)

Baddeley, Sophia (?1745–86), a fashionable and popular English actress, who played Ophelia, Cordelia, and Imogen early in her career at Drury Lane and was later successful as Olivia. She sang in *Judith* (Arne) at the 1769 Stratford *Jubilee and in Garrick's subsequent Drury Lane show. An engraving of her as Joan la Pucelle accompanies *1 Henry VI* in *Bell's Shakespeare (1776). *CMSA*

Badel, Alan (1923–82), British actor. A player of great flair, he appeared in 1950 at Stratford-upon-Avon as Claudio in *Measure for Measure* and as Lear's Fool. He vividly proved his versatility the next season as Ariel and as a doddering Justice Shallow. At the *Old Vic he was Romeo to Claire *Bloom's Juliet. He returned to Stratford in 1956 to play Berowne, Lucio in *Measure for Measure*, and a mercurial Hamlet. In 1970 he acted Othello at Oxford. *MJ*

'bad' quartos. See QUARTOS.

Bagehot, Walter (1826–77), English economist and constitutional theorist. His essay 'Shakespeare' (*Prospective Review*, 1853), revised as 'Shakespeare: The Individual' and retitled as 'Shakespeare the Man' in Hutton's 1879 edition, displays limited biographical knowledge, but derives a sympathetic and sentimental picture of Shakespeare's character from a reading of the plays. *TM*

Bagley, Edward (fl. 1647–75), citizen and pewterer of London, kinsman, executor, and residuary legatee of Shakespeare's granddaughter Elizabeth Bernard (Hall). He acquired property that had belonged to Shakespeare, including *New Place, which he sold to Sir Edward Walker in 1675. He sold the *Blackfriars Gatehouse in 1667 to Sir Heneage Fetherston, having bought it probably in 1647. *SW*

Bagot, one of Richard's supporters, accuses Aumerle of Gloucester's death before Bolingbroke, *Richard II* 4.1. *AB*

bagpipe, found throughout much of England as well as in Scotland during Shakespeare's time (e.g. the 'Lincolnshire bagpipe' in *1 Henry IV* 1.2.76). Its status had been higher in medieval England. *JB*

Baldwin, Thomas Whitfield (1890–1984), American scholar of copious and exhaustive learning. His *Organization and Personnel of the Shakespearian Company* (1927), *William Shakespeare's Five-Act Structure* (1947), and *Smalle Latine and Lesse Greeke* (2 vols., 1947) are important works of research and scholarship, revealing Shakespeare's complex inheritance from classical and Elizabethan culture. *TM*

Bales, Peter (1547–?1610), a calligraphist, who was employed in connection with state service and intercepted letters. Bale's *The Writing Schoolmaster* (1590) contains a section on shorthand, expanded in 1597 and published as *The Art of Brachygraphy*. However, the system seems too cumbersome to have been much use recording plays in performance. *CS*

ballad, a narrative strophic song, often traditional. Shakespeare frequently quotes from, or alludes to, ballads and *broadside ballads, e.g. *'king Cophetua and the Beggar Maid'. *JB*

ballet. Dancing contributes essentially to at least twelve of Shakespeare's plays, but late 17th-century semi-operas like *The *Fairy Queen* (1692), which translated *A Midsummer Night's Dream* into a spectacle with dances, set a pattern for versions of certain plays which persisted into the 20th century. The earliest complete Shakespearian ballets, however, derived from the tragedies—Eusebio Luzzi's *Romeo and Juliet* (Venice, 1785), Charles Le Picq's *Macbeth* (London, 1785), Francesco Clerico's *Hamlet* (Venice, 1788), Salvatore Viganò's *Coriolanus* (Milan, 1804) and *Othello* (1818), and Vincenzo Galeotti's *Romeo and Juliet* (Copenhagen, 1811). Louis Henry's *Hamlet* (Paris, 1816) had a happy ending.

The Romantic movement, the development of dancing on pointe in the early 19th century, and the consequent domination of the ballerina did not favour Shakespearian ballets, although the greatest Romantic ballet, *Giselle* (Paris, 1841), has been likened to *Hamlet* in its histrionic demands. Not until Marius Petipa's one-act *A Midsummer Night's Dream* to Mendelssohn's overture (St Petersburg, 1876) was a significant dancework based on one of the comedies. The letter scenes in *Twelfth Night* gave Antony Tudor the basis for his first ballet, *Cross-Garter'd* (London, 1931); Andrée Howard set a one-act *Twelfth Night* to Grieg (London, 1942); Boris Eifman used Donizetti for his near-farcical version (Leningrad, 1984). Vladimir Bourmeister's full-length *Merry Wives of Windsor* (Moscow, 1942) followed its source closely. *The Taming of the Shrew* has been choreographed by Maurice Béjart (Paris, 1954), Kai Tai Chan (Sydney, 1986), who set the story in China and Australia, and pre-eminently by John Cranko, whose 1969 version for the Stuttgart Ballet quickly entered the international repertoire. John Neumeier turned, unusually, to *As You Like It* for his *Mozart und Theme aus 'Wie es euch gefällt'* (Salzburg, 1988), but *The Tempest* inspired Glen Tetley (Schwetzingen, 1979) and Rudolf Nureyev (Paris, 1984) among others.

The overwhelmingly favourite comedy for choreographers is *A Midsummer Night's Dream.* Mikhail Fokine revised Petipa (St Petersburg, 1906), George Balanchine chose it for his first wholly original full-length ballet (New York, 1962), and Frederick Ashton created a one-act masterpiece, *The Dream*, for the Royal Ballet's Shakespeare quatercentenary programme (London, 1964). Swiss choreographer Heinz Spoerli developed four related versions (1976–94). Others using the play include Neumeier (Hamburg, 1977), Pierre Lacotte (Rome, 1988), László Seregi (Budapest, 1989), Harold Collins (Brisbane, 1990), Bruce Wells (Detroit, 1993), and Veronica Paeper (Cape Town, 1993).

The tragedies have attracted choreographers since the 18th century, and José Limón's *The Moor's Pavane* (New London, Conn., 1949), an elegant interpretation of *Othello* for four dancers, was probably the most performed Shakespearian ballet of the 20th century. Other notable *Othello* ballets are those by Erika Hanka (Vienna, 1955), Tatjana Gsovsky (Berlin, 1956), Jiri Nemecek (Prague, 1959), Vakhtang Chaboukian (Tbilisi 1957), Garth Welch (Sydney, 1968), Neumeier (Hamburg, 1985), and Dmitri Bryantsev (Moscow, 1994). The Kerala Kalamandalam Dance Troupe's *Kathakali King Lear* (Kerala, 1989) and the ever-imaginative Béjart's *King Lear-Prospero* (Lausanne, 1994) are two of very few *King Lear* ballets. The influential modernist Pina Bausch worked on a *Macbeth* project (1979, 1985), one of several, particularly Central European, choreographers to draw on the Scottish play. The most significant *Hamlet* ballet remains Robert *Helpmann's one-act representation of images in the dying prince's mind (London, 1942); Bronislava Nijinska's version with herself as the hero (Paris, 1934) failed, but those of later choreographers including Victor Gsovsky (Munich, 1950), Konstantin Sergeyev (Leningrad, 1970), Chaboukiani (Tbilisi, 1971), Neumeier (New York, 1976), Jonathan Taylor (Dunedin, 1992), and Barry Moreland (Perth, W. Australia, 1993) won praise.

Of all the plays, *Romeo and Juliet* has inspired by far the most ballets. Most have used Sergei Prokofiev's score, commissioned for Moscow's Bolshoi Theatre in 1935 but rejected as 'undanceable'; the first ballet to Prokofiev was by Czechoslovakian Vana Psota (Brno, 1938). The first Russian version was Leonid Lavrovsky's (Leningrad, 1940). Others using the same music include Ashton (Copenhagen, 1955), Cranko (Venice, 1958), Kenneth Macmillan (London, 1965), Nureyev (London, 1977), and Seregi (Budapest, 1985). Antony Tudor took music by

Delius (New York, 1943), Béjart (Brussels, 1966) and others *Berlioz, a few *Tchaikovsky. Jerome Robbins's integral choreogaphy for his and Leonard Bernstein's *West Side Story* (New York, 1957) profoundly influenced dance in musical theatre, and deconstructionist Angelin Preljocaj (Lyon, 1990) set the story in a modern police state. Most late 20th-century ballet companies, large or small, had in their repertoire a *Romeo and Juliet* production, from a pas de deux to a full-length work. *ABr*

Bremser, Martha (ed.), *International Dictionary of Ballet* (1993)
Brissenden, Alan, *Shakespeare and the Dance* (1981)
Cohen, Selma Jeanne (ed.), *International Encyclopedia of Dance* (1998)
Koegler, Horst, *The Concise Oxford Dictionary of Ballet* (2nd edn. 1977)

Balthasar. (1) Invited to the house of Antipholus of Ephesus, he advises him against breaking in, *The Comedy of Errors* 3.1. (2) He is Romeo's servant in *Romeo and Juliet.* (3) He is one of Portia's servants in *The Merchant of Venice.* (4) Don Pedro's attendant, he sings *'Sigh no more' in *Much Ado About Nothing* 2.3. *AB*

'Balthasar'. See PORTIA.

Bandello, Matteo (?1480–1562), Italian courtier, priest, soldier, and writer. Between 1554 and 1573 Bandello published his *Novelle*, a collection of 214 prose romances. Through this edition and the translations that followed, notably the *Histoires tragiques* (1559–1582) by Boiastuau and Belleforest, and *Certain Tragical Discourses* (1567) by Geoffrey Fenton, the *Novelle* became a popular resource for English dramatists. The stories of *Romeo and Juliet*, *Much Ado About Nothing*, and *Twelfth Night* are all found here. Although it is doubtful that Shakespeare used the Italian original, a few minor details in *Much Ado* and *Twelfth Night* allow for this possibility. *JKS*

banditti (thieves) are 'charmed' from their profession by Timon, *Timon of Athens* 4.3. *AB*

Bankside, an area of land, now located within the London Borough of Southwark, which takes its name from the medieval embankment built along the front of the River Thames. Bankside extends from the Thames in the north to Park Street in the south and from Bankend in the east to Paris Garden in the west. The land was situated within the Liberty of the Clink, in the manor of the bishops of Winchester, although the bishops had alienated most of the land by the 15th century. After the 16th-century Henrician dissolution, monastic land remained at Liberty outside of the jurisdiction of city authorities, although two of Bankside's attractions (*prostitution and commercial fishponds) had already become established by the 14th century. The district also became known as 'the Stews', from the stewponds (fishponds) and stewhouses (brothels): the word apparently derives from the French *estui*, meaning a case or sheath or a tub for keeping fish in a boat.

Topographically, Bankside is a low-lying area which was subject to flooding by the Thames. The nature of the ground meant not only that fishponds were easy to establish but also that the Surrey and Kent Sewer Commissioners maintained a vigilant watch on the sewers and ditches in the area. The records of the Sewer Commissioners often provide valuable evidence about property ownership on Bankside.

Proximity to the Thames meant that Bankside was within easy access for inhabitants of the city who could cross the river either by foot on London Bridge or by using transport provided by the Thames watermen. Close to the city, but outside the jurisdiction of the city authorities and the Surrey justices, Bankside developed as an area of ill-regarded activities, with the construction of animal-baiting pits and playhouses. However, indirect attempts to regulate activities on Bankside included an edict from the city which banned boatmen from taking anybody to Bankside between sunset and sunrise and forbade them from tying up within 20 fathoms (36 m) of the shore. *RSB*

Carlin, M., *Medieval Southwark* (1996)
Johnson, D., *Southwark and the City* (1969)
Mullaney, Steven, *The Place of the Stage: License, Play and Power in Renaissance England* (1988)
Survey of London, XXII, *Bankside (The Parishes of St. Saviour and Christchurch Southwark)* (1950)

Banquo, Macbeth's comrade-in-arms, hailed by the witches as the founder of a line of kings. Killed by his colleague's three murderers, 3.3, his *ghost terrifies Macbeth at a feast, *Macbeth* 3.4. *AB*

'Baptista'. See PLAYERS.

Baptista Minola, the father of Katherine and Bianca in *The Taming of the Shrew.* *AB*

Barber, Samuel. See OPERA.

Barbican. Named after a former fortress on London's city wall, and briefly the location of a theatre for apprentice actors in the late 17th century, this is now the site of the Barbican Centre, opened in 1982, the London home of the *Royal Shakespeare Company, the London Symphony Orchestra, and the Guildhall drama school, among much else. The area where this ambitious but little-loved development now stands was heavily damaged by bombing in the Second World War, although Shakespeare's sometime lodgings with the *Mountjoy family in nearby Silver Street had vanished long before. Surviving within the Barbican complex is the church of St Giles Cripplegate, built *c.*1545–50, which holds monuments to John Speed and John *Milton. *RSB*

Pevsner, N., *London*, i: *The Cities of London and Westminster*, rev. B. Cherry (3rd edn. 1989)

Barbican theatre. See BARBICAN; ROYAL SHAKESPEARE COMPANY.

Bardolph, a tapster (barman) in *The Merry Wives of Windsor* and one of Falstaff's companions in *2 Henry IV* (and in most editions of *1 Henry IV*, see HARVEY), becomes a soldier in *Henry V*, and is condemned to hang for theft, 3.6. *AB*

Bard, sometimes extended to 'the Bard of Avon', a widespread nickname for Shakespeare, once reverent but now usually used at least half-facetiously. Identifying Shakespeare as the chronicler of his tribe's golden age—implicitly, an English *Homer—the term was first commonly applied to Shakespeare around the time of David *Garrick, one of whose songs at the *Jubilee in 1769 proclaimed that 'The bard of all bards was a Warwickshire bard.' *MD*

bardolatry, a term for the uncritical, quasi-religious worship of Shakespeare's genius, particularly in its *Romantic and 19th-century variants. The term was first coined by the agnostic George Bernard *Shaw in 1901, and owes something to Ben *Jonson's remark that he loved Shakespeare and honoured his memory 'on this side idolatry, as much as any' (in *Discoveries*, *c.*1630). David *Garrick made no such qualification in 1769, when he adapted a phrase from *Romeo and Juliet* in his *Jubilee ode—''Tis he, 'tis he, | "The god of our idolatry!" '—and Shaw's distaste for this attitude to Shakespeare is anticipated by William Cowper's attack on Garrick's whole festival as blasphemous in his poem *The Task* (1785). *MD*

Babcock, R. W., *The Genesis of Shakespeare Idolatry, 1766–1799* (1931)
Dávidházi, Peter, *The Romantic Cult of Shakespeare: Literary Reception in Anthropological Perspective* (1998)
Holderness, Graham, 'Bardolatry', in *The Shakespeare Myth* (1988).

Bardolph, Lord. One of the rebels against Henry, he is mentioned as having been defeated, *2 Henry IV* 4.3.97–9. *AB*

Baring, Maurice (1874–1945), English novelist, essayist, poet, and playwright, credited with helping to introduce Chekhov into Britain. His *Unreliable History* (1934) includes travesties of, among others, Shakespeare with a rehearsal of *Macbeth* at the Globe theatre and a letter from Goneril to her sister Regan: 'I have writ my sister'. *TM*

Barksted, William (*c.*1590–1616), actor and playwright. Barksted was called a 'fine Comedian' for his performances with the Children of the Queen's Revels and other Jacobean troupes.

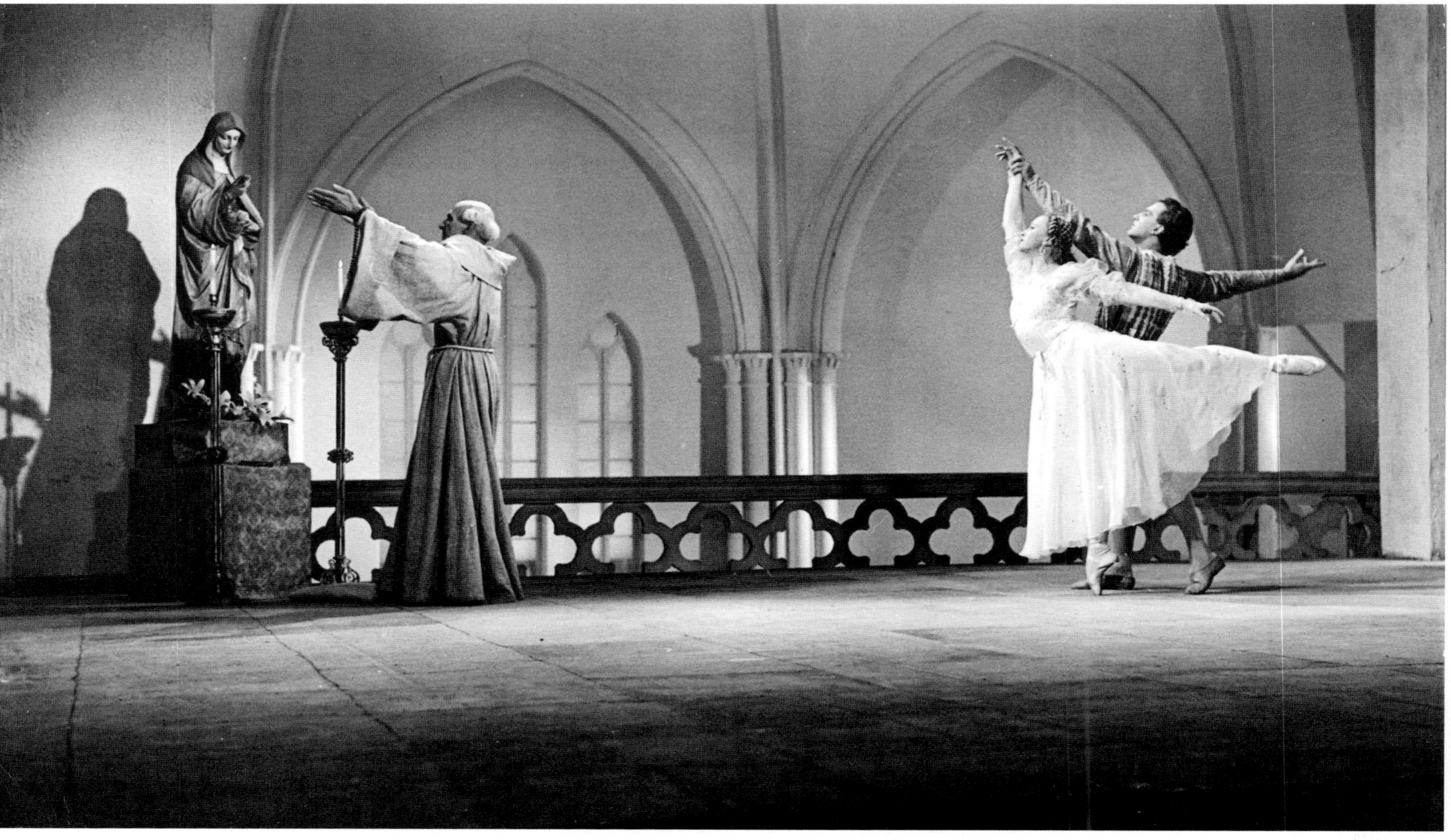

The marriage of Romeo and Juliet: the Bolshoi Ballet, 1946, dancing to the Prokofiev score they had earlier rejected as 'undanceable'. Alexei Bulgakov as Friar Laurence, Galina Ulanova as Juliet, Mikhail Gabovich as Romeo.

In his poem *Myrra, the Mother of Adonis* (1607), he urges that Shakespeare's 'art and wit' deserve the 'laurel', significant praise from a rival actor. *PH*

Barnadine, a murderer who comically refuses to be executed and is ultimately pardoned by Duke Vincentio, *Measure for Measure* 5.1.479–84. *AB*

Barnardo (Bernardo), a sentinel, describes the *ghost of Hamlet's father to Horatio, *Hamlet* 1.1.33–7. *AB*

Barnes, Barnabe (1571–1609), sonneteer. He was famous as a braggart and composer of flamboyant and often intensely erotic verse, and is one of several candidates for the role of the rival poet mentioned in Shakespeare's Sonnets. Born the son of the Bishop of Nottingham, he first went to Oxford, then accompanied the Earl of Essex on his expedition to Normandy in 1591. His brief military career formed the basis of his bragging, according to Thomas *Nashe. In 1593 he published a celebrated collection of poems, *Parthenophil and Parthenophe*, which proclaims its debt to *Sidney's *Astrophil and Stella* (1591). The collection begins as a sequence of sonnets interspersed with madrigals, followed by a variety of experiments in different verse forms: sestinas, elegies, odes, pastoral lyrics, and others. The sonnets are characterized by their vigorous articulation of male sexual fantasies, frustrations, and emotional crises—what Barnes aptly calls his 'sorrow's outrage'. In one notorious sonnet Barnes wishes to become the wine his mistress drinks so that he may 'pass by Pleasure's part' when she urinates; in another he castigates his thighs for failing to become vines encircling the elms of his mistress's legs. The sequence closes with an elaborate erotic wish-fulfilment fantasy involving Parthenophil, Parthenophe, and an obliging goat. The poems also parade Barnes's learning, particularly in the fields of law and astronomy. Shakespeare's sonnets echo them often. Barnes published *A Divine Century of Spiritual Sonnets* in 1595, as if in atonement for his earlier collection. But this does not seem to have marked a transformation in his personality: in 1598 he was accused of trying to murder a man with a poisoned lemon. *RM*

Doyno, Victor A. (ed.), *Parthenophil and Parthenophe* (1971)
Eccles, Mark, 'Barnabe Barnes', in C. J. Sisson (ed.), *Thomas Lodge and Other Elizabethans* (1933)
Roche, Thomas P., *Petrarch and the English Sonnet Sequences* (1989)

Barnfield, Richard (1574–1627), poet. He published homoerotic verse in two collections, *The Affectionate Shepherd* (1594) and *Cynthia* (1595), the second of which may have provided hints for both the structure and the content of Shakespeare's sonnet sequence. His *Lady Pecunia* (1598) contained the first printed tribute to Shakespeare in verse. *RM*

Barrault, Jean-Louis (1910–94), French actor-director of great fame. Starting in 1942 he played Hamlet in a series of memorable productions, some of which he directed. His versions of *Henry VI* and *Richard III* drew upon post-war absurdism, and *Julius Caesar* in 1960 was icily beautiful, designed by Balthus after the paintings of Andrea Mantegna. *DK*

Barrett, Lawrence (1838–91), American actor, whose association with Edwin Booth stretched (with breaks) from 1863 to 1891 and included alternating Othello and Iago and playing his acclaimed Cassius to Booth's Brutus. His Hamlet was said to be imitative of Booth's; he was admired as Shylock and Leontes. He toured with his own company across America. *RF*

Barry, Ann (1734–1801), sensitive English tragedian, who began her career in York, coming to prominence in Dublin playing Cordelia to Spranger Barry's Lear. She accompanied him to London in 1767, married him, and scored particular success as Juliet to his Romeo, Desdemona, and later as Rosalind, Beatrice, and Viola. *CMSA*

Barry, Elizabeth (*c.*1658–1713), usually credited as the first great English actress. She worked with Davenant, played opposite Betterton, including Cordelia, for the Duke's Company, and was particularly successful in history and tragedy (although not as Lady Macbeth). The frontispiece of Rowe's 1709 Shakespeare shows her as Gertrude. *CMSA*

Barry, James (1741–1808), Irish history painter, active in England. Propelled to fame for his decoration of the Great Room at the Society for the Encouragement of Arts, Sciences, and Manufacture, Barry held ambitious views on history painting which he put forward in a pamphlet entitled *An Enquiry into the Real and Imaginary Obstacles to the Acquisition of the Arts in England*, of 1775. The paintings for the Great Room, however, failed to bring the artist financial success. The artist executed three works for the *Shakespeare Gallery; his *King Lear Weeping over the Dead Body of Cordelia* (1786–8, Tate Gallery), exhibited at the opening show held by the Gallery in 1789, was noted as a work which displayed cerebral intensity. John Williams (writing under the pseudonym Anthony Pasquin) criticized Barry's work, claiming, 'Mr Barry is intellectually superior to his Brethren, . . . however, he is not practically so—he appears to me, like Caesar's mother, to conceive too powerfully for the ordinary methods of deliverance.' Williams's comment reflects the artist's reception in the popular press generally. *CT*

Barry, Spranger (?1717–1777), actor and manager, who came to prominence as Othello in Dublin and then in his 1746 Drury Lane, London, debut. As famed for his looks as his technique, the alternate playing of Hamlet and Macbeth with *Garrick developed into professional rivalry culminating in the 1750 'Battle of the Romeos' when Barry moved to Covent Garden. *CMSA*

Barrymore family. The founding parents of what has become known as America's theatrical 'royal family' were Georgiana Drew (1856–93), daughter of John and Louisa Lane-Drew, and Maurice Barrymore (1847–1905), who had begun his career at the Theatre Royal, Windsor, in 1872. Maurice Barrymore was blessed with the natural talents of physique, voice, charm, intelligence, and magnetism which all aspiring actors crave, but dissipated them apparently almost wilfully. His most successful role was Orlando opposite the exacting Helena Modjeska. All three of the Barrymores' children pursued acting careers: Lionel (1878–1954), Ethel (1879–1959), and John (1882–1942). Following the failure of his Macbeth in 1921, Lionel devoted himself to films as he had done in the early years of his career. In contrast Ethel was—until her mid-sixties—a stage actress, dominating Broadway for 40 years, principally in contemporary plays, though she triumphed when she applied her natural beauty, grace, and intelligence to Shakespearian roles (Juliet, 1922; Ophelia and Portia, both 1925).

For much of his career (until 1925) John Barrymore combined stage and film work, achieving acclaim in the two Shakespearian roles which he essayed: Richard III (New York, 1920) and Hamlet (New York 1922, tour 1923–4, London 1925). Inspiration for his Richard III came from a red tarantula—with a grey bald spot on its back—which Barrymore saw in the Bronx zoo. As Richard, Barrymore glided swiftly across the stage like some unearthly arachnid. His preparations were intense. He corresponded voluminously with the British Museum about his sword and armour, making 40 trips to an elderly German armourer in Newark for fittings. For six weeks he worked on his voice with his coach Mrs Carrington, who suggested that he throw the 'Was ever woman in this humour wooed?' speech right out into the auditorium. Barrymore's efforts were rewarded as he transformed himself into Shakespeare's 'Crookback'.

Hamlet did not necessitate such a thorough physical transformation, but Barrymore worked as hard to create his sane and human Prince, whose strangeness he made plausible. He disregarded tradition and convention, notably in the closet scene which he invested heavily with Freudian/Oedipal emotion. Barrymore achieved 101 consecutive Broadway performances—one more than Edwin Booth—but

R. Pyle Pinx.[t] Wm. Elliott Sculp.

Mr. Barry and Miss Nossiter,

in the Characters of Romeo and Juliet.

Act 2d. Scene 2d.

Published according to Act of Parliament May 9th 1759

following his well-received appearance in London he forsook the stage for the screen. In 1933 he began tests for a film of *Hamlet* in Technicolor, but his memory kept failing him and the project was abandoned. He appeared as Mercutio in MGM's film *Romeo and Juliet* (1936). Subsequent generations have upheld the Barrymore acting (if not Shakespearian) tradition, most recently Drew Barrymore (b. 1975). *RF*

Morrison, Michael A., *John Barrymore, Shakespearean Actor* (1998)
Peters, M., *The House of Barrymore* (1990)

Bartholomew, a page, acts as Sly's wife in the Induction to *The Taming of the Shrew.* *AB*

Bartlett, John (1820–1905), American publisher, author of *A New and Complete Concordance or Verbal Index to Words, Phrases, and Passages in the Dramatic Works of Shakespeare with a Supplementary Concordance to the Poems* (1894). 'Bartlett' was an essential tool of reference until the appearance of computer-based concordances in the 1960s. *TM*

Barton, John (b. 1928), British director, whose career has been almost entirely with the *Royal Shakespeare Company. Joining Peter *Hall at Stratford in 1960, he contributed much to philosophy and style in the early years, particularly in the realms of verse-speaking, vocal training, and directorial interpretation. Chiefly interested in making Shakespeare understandable for contemporary audiences, Barton has never been a purist: he adapted the English histories into a seven-part cycle called *The Wars of the Roses,* directed by Hall in 1963–4, slashing large sections of text of the *Henry VI* plays and adding some 1,000 lines of pseudo-Elizabethan verse to fill the gaps. He also wrote a successful platform piece for RSC actors, *The Hollow Crown* (1961). His own directing has been consistently intelligent and accessible. *Troilus and Cressida* (1968) made the Trojan War into an erotic experience; *Twelfth Night* (1969) stressed melancholy and fear; *Richard II* (1973) underlined the doubled identity of Richard and Bolingbroke by placing two huge escalators on stage and alternating the actors Richard Pasco and Ian Richardson in the roles. Barton was the only member of the original team still closely associated with the RSC at the end of the century, 40 years after its founding. A great teacher, his TV series *Playing Shakespeare* (published as a book in 1984) summarized his approach and had a large influence on a new generation of actors. *DK*

Greenwald, Michael L., *Directions by Indirections: John Barton of the Royal Shakespeare Company* (1985)

Spranger Barry as Romeo to Miss Nossiter's Juliet. 'Had I been Juliet to Barry's Romeo,' one woman in his audience is said to have remarked of the balcony scene in 1750, 'so tender, so eloquent and so seductive was he, I should certainly have gone down to him.'

John Barrymore (1882–1942), perhaps the greatest of the Barrymore dynasty, as a brooding, romantic Hamlet, 1923.

Barton-on-the-Heath, a village 15 miles (24 km) south of Stratford, home of Edmund *Lambert, who married Shakespeare's aunt Joan (Arden) in or before 1550. Shakespeare may allude to it in *The Taming of the Shrew* when Christopher Sly describes himself as 'old Sly's son of Burton Heath' (Induction 2.17). *SW*

Bassanio borrows money from Shylock on Antonio's security in order to finance his courtship of *Portia in *The Merchant of Venice.* *AB*

Basse, William (*c.*1583–*c.*1653), poet. Basse's elegiac sonnet 'On Mr. Wm. Shakespeare' circulated extensively in manuscript and was first printed in 1633; Ben Jonson replies to it in his own elegy on Shakespeare (1623). Basse assigns Shakespeare to one grave's 'bed' with Chaucer, Spenser, and Beaumont. Jonson pointedly divides him from those three (he is 'without a tomb'). *PH*

Basset, a Lancastrian, is challenged to a duel by Vernon (a Yorkist), *1 Henry VI* 3.8. The King refuses to let them fight, 4.1. The incident is not recorded by *Holinshed. *AB*

Bassianus, Saturninus' brother, betrothed to Lavinia, is murdered by Tamora's sons in *Titus Andronicus* 2.3. *AB*

Bassus, Publius Ventidius. See VENTIDIUS.

Bastard. See MARGARETON.

Bastard, Philip the. He disclaims his right to the Falconbridge inheritance and is knighted 'Sir Richard and Plantagenet', *King John* 1.1: he goes on to give commentaries on the events of the play. *AB*

Bastard of Orléans. One of Talbot's French adversaries, he presents Joan la Pucelle to Charles the Dauphin, *1 Henry VI* 1.3. *AB*

Bates, John. A soldier in *Henry V*, Bates talks to the disguised King Harry, 4.1. *AB*

Battey, George M. See DEFOE THEORY.

Bavian. See BABION.

Bawd. Wife of a pander, she presents Marina to Lysimachus in a brothel, *Pericles* 19. *AB*

Baylis, Lilian (1874–1937), British theatre manager. The legendary Lady of the *Old Vic on the Waterloo Road was the niece of the philanthropist Emma Cons, who in 1880 transformed a run-down playhouse in the slums of Lambeth into the Royal Victoria Coffee and Music Hall which offered edifying temperance entertainment to the locals. Lilian, largely uneducated but with some training as a singer and a deep Christian faith, took over in 1912. Under her dynamic, frugal management the Shakespeare seasons began in 1914 and by the time of Baylis's death in 1937 the Vic had become the leading British theatre for Shakespeare (with opera and ballet established at Sadler's Wells). Baylis, who at first nights proudly wore her robes as an honorary MA of Oxford, was created a Companion of Honour in 1929. *MJ*

Findlater, Richard, *Lilian Baylis: The Lady of the Old Vic* (1975)

BBC. See RADIO, BRITISH; TELEVISION.

BBC Shakespeare. See TELEVISION.

Beadle. He whips the supposed 'cripple' Simpcox to make him jump over a stool, *The First Part of the Contention* (*2 Henry VI*) 2.1.155. *AB*

beadles. They arrest Mistress Quickly and Doll Tearsheet, *2 Henry IV* 5.4. *AB*

Bear. It chases Antigonus off the stage, *The Winter's Tale* 3.3.57, giving rise to Shakespeare's most famous stage direction: '*Exit, pursued by a bear.*' The clown describes in comic terms the bear's slaughter of Antigonus, 3.3.92–9. *AB*

bear-baiting. See ANIMAL SHOWS.

Beargarden. See ANIMAL SHOWS; FLAGS; HENSLOWE, PHILIP.

bear gardens. See ANIMAL SHOWS.

Beatrice. See MUCH ADO ABOUT NOTHING.

Beauchamp, Richard. See WARWICK, EARL OF.

Beaufort, Cardinal. In *1 Henry VI* (called the Bishop of Winchester) he is accused by Gloucester of having murdered Henry V (1.4.34); he crowns Henry VI in Paris (4.1); and first appears as a cardinal in 5.1. In *The First Part of the Contention* (*2 Henry VI*) he helps to secure the disgrace of the Duchess of Gloucester and Gloucester's arrest and murder, but dies himself, guilt-stricken, 3.3. He is based on Henry Beaufort (d. 1447). *AB*

Beaufort, Edmund. See SOMERSET, DUKE OF.

Beaufort, Henry. See BEAUFORT, CARDINAL; SOMERSET, DUKE OF.

Beaufort, John. See SOMERSET, DUKE OF.

Beaufort, Thomas. See EXETER, DUKE OF.

Beaumont, Francis (*c.*1585–1616), poet and playwright. With John Fletcher he formed the most celebrated play-writing partnership in English theatrical history. A member of the landed gentry, he entered the Inner Temple in 1600 to study law, but started writing plays instead in the mid-1600s. His erotic narrative poem *Salmacis and Hermaphroditus* (1602), modelled on Marlowe's *Hero and Leander* (1598) and Shakespeare's *Venus and Adonis* (1593), takes its satirical tone from the poetry of John Marston, especially in the passage where Jupiter becomes entangled with the corrupt Olympian legal system. Marston also influenced his first play, a city comedy called *The Woman Hater* (1607). The other play he wrote as sole author, *The Knight of the Burning Pestle* (acted 1607; pub. 1613), is an outstanding example of early modern metatheatre—theatre that comments on theatrical practices. In it a grocer and his wife step out of the audience to hijack the performance of a comedy, installing their apprentice Rafe as the hero of the dramatized chivalric romance they would rather see, and thereby poking fun at the social ambitions of the Jacobean mercantile classes. After teaming up with Fletcher in about 1607, Beaumont wrote many more serious adaptations of romance for the stage, which both fed upon and fed into the late works of Shakespeare. His fine verse epistle to Ben Jonson, published in *Comedies and Tragedies Written by Francis Beaumont and John Fletcher* (1647), celebrates Shakespeare's natural talent in terms that anticipate Jonson's famous tribute to Shakespeare in the First Folio (1623). He retired from writing for the stage in 1613 after marrying an heiress. *RM*

Bliss, Lee, *Francis Beaumont* (1987)
Clark, Sandra, *The Plays of Beaumont and Fletcher: Sexual Themes and Dramatic Representation* (1994)

Beckett, Samuel (1906–89), Irish writer whose poems, prose, plays, and even films are permeated with literary reference, sometimes ironic or parodistic, to the work of his classical predecessors. Beckett the minimalist found in Shakespeare's prodigality a vividness of stage and verbal imagery; a bleak and unrelenting tragic vision; and an associative richness and precision of language that is repeatedly drawn upon in poems such as *Echo's Bones* (1935); prose fictions, including *Murphy* (1937), *Company* (1980), *Ill Seen Ill Said* (1981), and *Worstward Ho* (1983); the plays *Endgame* (1958) and *Come and Go* (1967); and even the film *Ghost Trio* (1976). *TM*

Bedford, Duke of. See JOHN OF LANCASTER, LORD.

Beerbohm, Sir Max (1872–1956), English satirical writer and artist. A cartoon ('William Shakespeare, his method of work' in *Poets' Corner*, 1904) shows Shakespeare as complicit plagiarist (see page 32). Stanley Wells discusses his theatre reviews in *Shakespeare Survey*, 29 (1976), while Craig Brown (*Daily Telegraph*, 12 June 1999) complains of their absence from print. *TM*

Beeston, Christopher (*c.*1580–*c.*1639), actor (Chamberlain's Men 1598, Worcester's/Queen Anne's Men 1602–19, Prince Charles's Men 1619–22, Lady Elizabeth's Men 1622–5, Queen Henrietta's Men 1625–37) and theatre entrepreneur. Beeston first enters the theatrical record in the cast list (contained in the 1616 Folio) for performances in 1598 of Jonson's *Every Man in his Humour*. By 1602 he was with Worcester's Men, who became Queen Anne's Men in the new reign, and in 1605 Augustine Phillips described Beeston as 'my servant' in his will. As a member of Queen Anne's Men Beeston formed a lifelong friendship with Thomas Heywood to whose *Apology for Actors* (1612) he contributed verses. Beeston took over as manager of the Queen's Men from Thomas Greene when the latter died in 1612 and in 1617 he built the Cockpit in Drury Lane, possibly designed by Inigo Jones as an adaptation of an existing circular auditorium. Beeston's plan to move the Queen's Men from their home, the open-air Red Bull, to the new expensive (and hence exclusive) playhouse was thwarted when city apprentices attacked the Cockpit during their common Shrove Tuesday rioting. Beeston repaired the Cockpit and, appropriately, renamed it the Phoenix.

After he built the Cockpit/Phoenix, Beeston was always a member of the playing company which occupied it: Queen Anne's (1617–19), Prince Charles's (1619–22), Lady Elizabeth's (1622–5), Queen Henrietta's (1625–37), and finally Beeston's Boys (1637–9). However, his role appears to have become solely managerial and he was repeatedly criticized for sharp business practices. On 10 August 1639 Beeston's son William is described as 'governor' of Beeston's

Boys at the Cockpit, which must mean he had died. His will indicates large debts owed by him and to him 'which no-one but my wife understands, where or how to receive pay or take in', for which reason he made her executrix. *GE*

Beeston, William (*c.*1606–1682), an actor and manager who supplied *Aubrey with material for his *Brief Life* of Shakespeare ('in his younger years a schoolmaster in the country'), possibly gleaned from his father Christopher *Beeston who acted with Shakespeare in *Every Man in his Humour* for the Chamberlain's Men. *CMSA*

Beethoven, Ludwig van (1770–1827), German composer. His Piano Sonatas Op. 31 No. 2 ('Tempest') and Op. 57 ('Appassionata') were both inspired by *The Tempest*, while his String Quartet Op. 18 No. 2 was apparently inspired by the vault scene in *Romeo and Juliet*. His *Coriolan* Overture, Op. 62, however, was written for H. J. von Collin's tragedy *Coriolan* and not Shakespeare's play. *IBC*

Behn, Aphra (?1640–1689), a writer and dramatist who used Shakespeare to defend herself against charges of being uneducated ('Epistle to the Reader' of *The Dutch Lover*), and who defended Shakespeare's use of 'obscene' language in *Othello* (preface to *The Lucky Chance*). *Othello* is considered influential in the creation of her noble African hero *Oroonoko* (1688). *CMSA*

Belarius, banished by Cymbeline, has kidnapped his sons and brought them up in a Welsh cave, having taken the name 'Morgan' (*Cymbeline* 3.3.106). He reveals his identity and restores the princes, 5.6. *AB*

Belch, Sir Toby. Olivia's kinsman, he marries Maria in 'recompense' for helping him deceive Malvolio, *Twelfth Night* 5.1.361. *AB*

Belgium. See Low Countries.

Bell, John (1745–1831), English publisher. In 1773–4, Bell published the first 'acting edition' of Shakespeare's works, 'As they are now performed at the Theatres Royal in London. Regulated from the Prompt Books of each House.' Dedicated to David *Garrick, the edition provides a record of Shakespeare's plays as staged in the later 18th century, including adaptations such as Nahum *Tate's *King Lear*, with its notorious happy ending, and Garrick's *Romeo and Juliet* with its addition of a scene between Romeo and Juliet in the tomb. The edition also contains an introduction and notes 'both critical and illustrative' by Francis *Gentleman. Along with omitting the lines cut from performances, the edition strove, as Gentleman notes in his introduction, to remove 'glaring indecencies' from Shakespeare's text and thus to make it more acceptable to a refined audience. Gentleman's notes refer both to the plays themselves and to contemporary productions, in particular to Garrick's performances. Known for hiring some of the best artists of the day to illustrate his publications, Bell provided each volume with fine engravings, including frontispieces of contemporary actors and actresses. He later published additional multi-volume sets such as 'Bell's British Theatre', an acting edition of non-Shakespearian drama, and 'Bell's British Poets'. *JM*

Belleforest, François de (1530–83), French poet, translator, and historiographer. Belleforest succeeded Pierre Boiastuau as author of the *Histoires tragiques*. Published in seven volumes from 1559 to 1582, this collection of prose tales was repeatedly plundered by English dramatists. Here, Shakespeare may have found the plots for *Much Ado About Nothing*, *Twelfth Night*, *All's Well That Ends Well*, and *Hamlet*. The *Histoires* was based on Bandello's *Novelle* but included tales from other sources, notably the legend of Amleth. Belleforest translated this well-known story from the Danish history of Saxo Grammaticus. His translation was probably the main source for Shakespeare's tragedy and may have suggested Hamlet's excessive melancholy. *JKS*

Bell Inn. See inns.

Bell Savage Inn. See inns.

Belott–Mountjoy suit. In spring 1612, Shakespeare gave evidence in a lawsuit brought by Stephen Belott against Christopher Mountjoy, a maker of tires, or tiaras—jewelled headdresses for ladies. Belott, his former apprentice, had married Mountjoy's daughter Mary on 19 November 1604. Some years later Belott quarrelled with his father-in-law and brought the lawsuit alleging that Mountjoy had broken promises to pay a marriage portion of £60 and to leave his daughter £200 in his will. A former servant testified that Mountjoy had asked 'one Mr Shakespeare that lay in the house' to act as a go-between in the marriage negotiations, and Shakespeare was required to testify. His depositions, though not specially revealing, are the most substantial and accurate reports of words that he actually spoke (see also Greene, John and Thomas).

On 11 May 1612 he is described as 'William Shakespeare of Stratford-upon-Avon ... of the age of 48 years or thereabouts'. He testified that he had known Mountjoy and Belott 'for the space of ten years or thereabouts'. If accurate, this means that he had lodged in the house (not necessarily continuously) for at least two years before the marriage. He had known Belott 'when he was servant' to Mountjoy, and regarded him as 'a very good and industrious servant'. Mountjoy had shown Belott 'great good will and affection' and had 'made a motion' to him of marriage with his daughter. Mrs Mountjoy 'did solicit and entreat' Shakespeare to 'move and persuade' Belott 'to effect the said marriage', and Shakespeare had complied. Mountjoy had promised to give Belott a 'portion', but Shakespeare could not remember exactly what, nor when it was to be paid, nor did he know that Mountjoy had promised to leave Belott £200. But he affirmed that Belott had been living in the house and that they 'had amongst themselves many conferences [conversations] about their marriage which afterwards was consummated and solemnized'. He knew nothing about 'what implements and necessaries of household stuff' Mountjoy gave Belott on his marriage. Other witnesses confirmed that the Mountjoys had asked Shakespeare to persuade Belott to marry their daughter, and one of them said Shakespeare had told him that Mountjoy had promised 'about the sum of fifty pounds in money and certain household stuff'. There appears to have been an intention to call Shakespeare at a second hearing, in June, but no deposition is known. The case was referred to the overseers and elders of the French Church in London; they awarded Belott 20 nobles which Mountjoy, who appears to have been leading a dissolute life, had not paid a year later.

Shakespeare's inability to remember the financial settlement has been used as evidence that he was suffering from a general failure of memory; but he had had much to think about in the meantime. *SW*

Chambers, E. K., *William Shakespeare: A Study of Facts and Problems* (2 vols., 1930)
Schoenbaum, S., *William Shakespeare: A Documentary Life* (1975, compact edn. 1977)
Wallace, C. W., 'Shakespeare and his London Associates ...', *Nebraska University Studies*, 10 (1910)

Belvedere; or, The Garden of the Muses, a dictionary of quotations, published, like **England's Helicon*, under the auspices of John Bodenham, and edited by 'A.M.' (probably Anthony Munday). It contains over 200 extracts from Shakespeare including at least 92 from *Lucrece*, 47 from *Richard II*, and 35 from *Venus and Adonis*. *SW*

'Be merry, be merry, my wife has all', Shrovetide carol fragment sung by Silence in *2 Henry IV* 5.3.33; the original tune is unknown. *JB*

Benedick. See Much Ado About Nothing.

Benfield, Robert (*c.*1583–1649), actor (Lady Elizabeth's Men *c.*1613, King's Men *c.*1615–42). When William Ostler died in 1614 his part as Antonio in Webster's *The Duchess of Malfi* appears to have been taken by Robert Benfield, who came to the King's Men from Lady Elizabeth's Men. On 23 April 1615 Benfield married Mary Bugge, probably a relative of the

Dr John Bugges to whom Richard Benfield (kinsman to 'Robert Benefeild') left £15 in his will. Robert Benfield is named in the actor lists of Beaumont and Fletcher's *The Coxcomb* and *The Honest Man's Fortune* for performances probably by the Lady Elizabeth's Men in 1613, as recorded in the 1679 folio of their plays, and he is named as an actor in the 1623 Folio of Shakespeare's plays. The 1679 Beaumont and Fletcher folio also lists Benfield as a player in *The Mad Lover, The Knight of Malta, The Humorous Lieutenant, The Custom of the Country, The Island Princess, Women Pleased, The Little French Lawyer, The False One, The Double Marriage, The Pilgrim, The Prophetess, The Spanish Curate, The Maid in the Mill, The Lovers' Progress,* and *A Wife for a Month*, all performed by the King's Men between 1616 and 1624. In 1619 the renewed patent of the King's Men names Benfield as a sharer. As a result of the sharers' dispute of 1635 he, along with Eliard Swanston and Thomas Pollard, became a housekeeper in the Globe and the Blackfriars. *GE*

Benson, Sir Frank (1858–1939), English actor who helped to found the Oxford University Dramatic Society. He showed an early disposition towards management and Shakespeare by mounting *Romeo and Juliet* at the Imperial theatre in 1882. Having played Paris with *Irving at the Lyceum, in 1883 he acquired control of a touring company which he expanded to fulfil his mission of taking Shakespeare's plays across the country and beyond.

Though he acknowledged his debt to the Duke of Saxe-Meiningen's Shakespeare productions—the influence was particularly evident in the forum scene of *Julius Caesar*—the prevailing style of Benson's productions was captured by Max *Beerbohm, who likened his *Henry V* (Lyceum, 1900) to 'a branch of university cricket'. In the title role Benson was forthrightly heroic, but he achieved greater subtlety as the 'poet-king' Richard II.

Benson, loyally supported by his wife Constance, had up to four companies touring at once and also performed overseas, but his spiritual home was Stratford-upon-Avon, where he ran the annual festival(s) from 1886 to 1919. In 1916 he was knighted on the stage of Drury Lane at the conclusion of a special, tercentenary performance of *Julius Caesar*. Of his four ventures in filming Shakespeare only *Richard III* survives and is included in the BFI video *Silent Shakespeare* (1999). *RF*

Trewin, J. C., *Benson and the Bensonians* (1960)

Benson, John. See Sonnets; 'Phoenix and Turtle, The'.

Benthall, Michael (1917–78), British director. The lifelong partner of the dancer-actor Robert *Helpmann (with whom he devised a *ballet *Hamlet* in 1942), he won admiration in the austere post-war years for his visually opulent Shakespearian productions in collaboration with painterly designers like Leslie Hurry and Loudon Sainthill. His Stratford successes (some starring Helpmann) included a Victorian *Hamlet* and a baroque *Tempest.* He was director of the *Old Vic from 1953 to 1962 where within five years all the First Folio plays were staged with performers of great achievement or extraordinary promise. By the 1960s his approach had come to seem old-fashioned and his achievement has been much underrated. *MJ*

Bentley, Gerald Eades (1901–94), American academic, author of *The Jacobean and Caroline Stage* (7 vols., 1941–68), an indispensable reference guide to the authors, plays, actors, and theatres of Shakespeare's later career, his contemporaries, and successors; see also *Shakespeare and Jonson* (2 vols., 1945, 1965); and *Shakespeare: A Biographical Handbook* (1961). *TM*

Benvolio is Montague's nephew and Romeo's friend in *Romeo and Juliet.* *AB*

Bergman, Ingmar (b. 1918), Swedish director. Renowned as a film-maker, Bergman has reserved Shakespeare for his stage work, though *Hamlet* is intertextually woven into *Fanny and Alexander* (1982). After directing *Macbeth* twice in the 1940s, he returned to Shakespeare late in his career at the Royal Dramatic Theatre, focusing (as in his films) on psycho-sexual and familial relationships, isolating Cordelia in *King Lear* (1984) and Ophelia in *Hamlet* (1986) as silent, ever-present observers. His *Winter's Tale* (1994), framed as a play-within-the-play, became a parable about the theatre and the death and resurrection of love. *I-SE*

Törnqvist, E., *Between Stage and Screen: Ingmar Bergman Directs* (1995)

bergomask (bergamasca), a dance, perhaps originating in Bergamo (Italy). Its context in *A Midsummer Night's Dream* 5.1.355, together with the simple chord sequence and tune found in musical examples, suggests a rustic, comic character. People from Bergamo were stereotyped as idiotic and clownish by Italians. *JB*

Berkeley, Lord. At the behest of York he asks Bolingbroke why he has returned to England, *Richard II* 2.3.74–80. *AB*

Berkeley Castle in Gloucestershire is mentioned in *Richard II*: the Duke of York orders his men to be mustered there, 2.2.118–19. Hotspur has trouble recalling it as the place where he first gave allegiance to Bolingbroke, *1 Henry IV* 1.3.242–6. *AB*

Berliner Ensemble. See Brecht, Bertolt.

Berlioz, Hector (1803–69), French composer. The 'first thunderbolt' (as he described it) in

Berlioz's compositional career was the simultaneous discovery of Shakespeare and the English actress Harriet Smithson (whom he later married), who played Ophelia to Charles Kemble's Hamlet (Odéon theatre, Paris, 11 September 1827). (The 'second thunderbolt' was the discovery of Beethoven in 1828.) Thereafter Berlioz read Shakespeare avidly and Shakespeare's influence is felt in many of his works.

Berlioz's only Shakespearian opera as such is *Béatrice et Bénédict* (1860–2), a two-act *opéra comique* based on *Much Ado About Nothing*, written for the Stadttheater in Baden-Baden. However, his operatic masterpiece *Les Troyens* (1856–8) not only includes a love duet taken from the *Merchant of Venice* (5.1.1–24) but was described by the composer as 'Virgil Shakespearianized'. Berlioz also considered writing operas on *Antony and Cleopatra*, *Hamlet*, *A Midsummer Night's Dream*, and *Romeo and Juliet*, though none came to fruition. Nevertheless, Shakespeare's plays are at the heart of his dramatic symphony *Roméo et Juliette* (1839), the *Roi Lear* overture (1831), and his fantasy on *The Tempest* (1830). This last work was included in *Lélio, ou Le Retour à la vie* (original title *Le Retour à la vie*), a lyric monodrama in six sections (composed as a sequel to his *Symphonie fantastique*) whose text contains many references to Shakespeare and Shakespearian characters. Berlioz was particularly inspired by *Hamlet*: he apparently identified Lélio (in the aforementioned work) with Hamlet; he composed a *Marche funèbre pour la dernière scène d'Hamlet* and the song *La Mort d'Ophélie* (both *c.*1848); and his autograph score of *Huit Scènes de Faust* (1828–9) contains quotations from *Hamlet* and *Romeo and Juliet*. *IBC*

Bernard, Elizabeth. See Bagley, Edward; Shakespeare, William.

Bernard (Barnard), Sir John (1605–74), second husband of Shakespeare's granddaughter Elizabeth *Hall, whom he married on 3 June 1649, after the death of her first husband Thomas Nash on 4 April 1647. He was then a widower with eight children, owner of Abington Manor, near Northampton. A Royalist, he was knighted by Charles II in 1661, and died in 1674. *SW*

Bernardo. See Barnardo.

Bernhardt, Sarah (1844–1923), French actress who, prior to her controversial departure from the Comédie-Française in 1880, had played Cordelia and Desdemona. In 1888 she brought her *Macbeth* to Edinburgh and London, but her Delilah-like Lady Macbeth did not impress. Neither did her reprise as Ophelia (1886). The attractions of *Cléopâtre* (1890, Sardou and Moreau) and *La Mort de Cléopâtre* (1914, Maurice Bernhardt and Cain) were only derivatively Shakespearian, but as a strikingly youthful Hamlet, in Marcel Schwob's adaptation (1899), Bernhardt had many admirers. *RF*

Taranow, Gerda, *The Bernhardt Hamlet: Culture and Context* (1996)

Frank Benson as an almost holy Richard II, aptly commemorated by Vernon Spreadbury's stained-glass window at the RSC Collection in Stratford.

Berowne. See Biron.

Berri, Duke of. Present at Charles VI's council of war, *Henry V* 2.4 (mute). *AB*

Bertram marries Helen reluctantly at the King's command, *All's Well That Ends Well* 2.3, but refuses to accept her as his wife until she can obtain his ring and become pregnant by him without his help. *AB*

Bestrafte Bruder-mord, Der. This German play was published in 1781 (from a now-lost manuscript dated 1710) as *Tragoedia der bestrafte Bruder-mord oder: Prinz Hamlet aus Dännemark* (translated as *Fratricide Punished*). It appears to derive from *Hamlet* as performed by English actors in *Germany in the early 17th century, and various details—such as the use of the name Corambis for Polonius—show that they were using the first, 'bad' quarto as a *promptbook. The play, however, includes material not found there—notably an allegorical prologue and several episodes of slapstick—and has been scrutinized obsessively (but probably in vain) for echoes of the lost *ur-*Hamlet*. *MD*

Betterton, Mary (née Saunderson) (*c.*1637–1712), one of six actresses recruited by *Davenant for the public stage at the Restoration in 1660. She played Ophelia to Betterton's Hamlet in 1661, married him the following year, and while renowned for playing virtuous roles was praised by Cibber as an outstanding Lady Macbeth. *CMSA*

Betterton, Thomas (1635–1710), the greatest actor of the Restoration period, and frequently compared in skill to *Burbage and *Garrick. He began his working life apprenticed to the bookseller John Holden, a friend of Davenant and father of one of the first English actresses. Betterton's under-apprentice was Edward Kynaston. By January 1661 he had joined Davenant's Duke's Company, having performed briefly with John Rhodes's Company and with Killigrew, and had early success—recorded by *Pepys—as Hamlet. In 1662 he married the actress Mary Saunderson. In 1663 he played Sir Toby Belch, and in Davenant's versions was the definitive Henry VIII and, the following year, Macbeth. On Davenant's death in 1668 he became manager of acting (a teaching role he maintained until the end of his career in

Sarah Bernhardt in her greatest Shakespearian role, Hamlet, in 1904.

conjunction with his wife) and co-manager of the company which moved into the new theatre in Dorset Garden in 1671. In 1682 he became leader of the combined Duke's and King's Companies—the United Company—and in 1695 was one of a group of senior actors, including Elizabeth Barry and Anne Bracegirdle, who moved to Lincoln's Inn Fields following poor treatment by Rich. His company later moved to the new Queen's theatre in the Haymarket and subsequently to Drury Lane.

He was closely associated with Shakespeare in the public mind, taking the title roles in Shadwell's version of *Timon of Athens*, Dryden's *Troilus and Cressida* (1678), Tate's *King Lear* (1680), Falstaff in his own adaptation of *Henry IV*, Angelo in Gildon's version of *Measure for Measure* (1700), and *Othello*, as well as promoting and defending Shakespeare in numerous prologues. He travelled to France at least three times for theatre research and is credited with the introduction in England of a semi-operatic style of playing, frequently in association with

The frontispiece to *Hamlet* from Rowe's edition of 1709, based on Thomas Betterton's interpretation of the closet scene (3.4). Betterton's knocking over of a chair on seeing the Ghost remained a traditional piece of stage business for more than a century.

Henry Purcell, which may have influenced Shadwell's version of *The Tempest.* *CMSA*

Betty, William Henry West (1791–1874), English child star known as Master Betty and The Infant Roscius, declared at the age of 10, after seeing Sarah *Siddons perform, that he would expire if he did not become an actor. After playing leading roles including Hamlet—which he is said to have memorized in three hours—outside London, he was engaged at Covent Garden and Drury Lane late in 1803 for high fees; his sensational success led to the phenomenon known as Bettymania. William Pitt even suspended Parliament so that members could see him as Hamlet. In 1805, still only 14, he added Richard III and Macbeth to his Shakespearian repertoire. He had little success as an adult actor, but was able to retire at the age of 33 with a large fortune. *SW*

Bevington Shakespeare (1973, 1997). The updated, fourth one-volume edition of *The Complete Works of Shakespeare,* edited by David Bevington, was issued in 1997 by Longman in New York. It is more 'complete' than its predecessors by the addition of *The Two Noble Kinsmen* and 'A Funeral Elegy for Master William Peter'. This American edition originated in a revision, published in 1973, of that prepared by Hardin Craig. The 1973 revision was in turn followed by a further revision incorporating material from the Bantam edition of individual works published in 1988. The latest update retains the grouping of plays by genre, and the format of the fourth edition. A few pages are added in the general introduction to alert users to recent developments in criticism, but the straightforward introductions to individual plays, focused closely on themes and structure, are unchanged. The impression given is of an edition that avoids jargon and fashionable critical topics, and aims rather to provide for college students a clear and simple presentation of the works. Its best feature may be the excellent glosses at the foot of each double-column page of text. *RAF*

Bevis, George, and John Holland. These 'characters' have emerged as the result of editorial misreadings of stage directions in *The First Part of the Contention* (*2 Henry VI*) (they were the names of actors in Shakespeare's day). In the Oxford edition, Bevis and Holland's supposed lines are given to the first and second rebels in 4.2. A rebel called 'John' appears in 4.7, but the line 4.7.81, generally given to Bevis, is assigned to an anonymous rebel. *AB*

Beyer, Sille (1803–61), Danish translator and adapter of plays. Her versions of five Shakespeare comedies, bowdlerized and adapted in the mode of Scribe's *comédies-vaudevilles,* were popular in Danish and Norwegian theatres in the 1850s, 1860s, and 1870s. *I-SE*

Gad, B., *Sille Beyers bearbejdelse af William Shakespeares lystspil* (1974)

Bianca. (1) Younger daughter of Baptista in *The Taming of the Shrew,* she marries Lucentio. **(2)** She is Cassio's mistress in *Othello.* Without her knowledge *Iago uses her in his plot against Othello. *AB*

Bian Zhilin (b. 1910), poet and leading Chinese critic of Shakespeare in the 1950s. His most influential work includes his *translation of and critical essays on Shakespeare's four major tragedies. *HQX*

Bible. The Bible was a fundamental source in 16th-century England, a repository not only of religious 'truth', but of ancient history, moral philosophy, romance, and poetry. As such it was quoted in many different ways, through representation in literary and pictorial art to references in general conversation. Indeed, so much of the Bible had passed into common currency that it is often difficult to be sure what is and is not a biblical quotation or allusion. At the beginning of the 16th century there were only two complete English bibles but in the course of that century appeared famous translations by Tyndale, Coverdale, Cranmer, and Thomson as well as the Geneva Bible of 1560 and the Bishops' Bible of 1568. Shakespeare's poetry and drama are full of biblical references, from direct quotations and allusions to a named character or parable, to vaguer structural and linguistic echoes.

Shakespeare's familiarity with the Bible may be accounted for in various ways. Learning psalms by rote was part of the grammar-school education. Attending church, Shakespeare would have heard Scripture read directly from the Bible, probably the Bishops' text, but also from the Book of Common Prayer and from the prescribed sermons in the Book of Homilies. Nevertheless, the very specific quotations that appear in Shakespeare's work suggest that he must have read the Bible himself and can also suggest the translation he used. The Geneva Bible is his primary text, referred to throughout his career. The Bishops' Bible provides a source for the earlier plays. But there is also evidence that Shakespeare drew upon other translations and, indeed, that he was aware of contemporary disagreements over how the Bible should be translated. The contemporary debate over the translation of a word appearing in Corinthians and elsewhere as 'charity' or 'love' surfaces in *Titus Andronicus* (4.2.43) and *Love's Labour's Lost* (4.3.340–1).

Of the 42 books of the Bible that Shakespeare drew upon, *Ecclesiasticus* and *Job* seem to have been his favourites. From the former he took the text decrying excessive grief deployed in *Romeo and Juliet, Hamlet, Love's Labour's Lost,* and elsewhere. From *Job*, we have the theme of the unfortunate abandoned by friends as in *Timon of Athens,* and the idea of the guilty shunning the light which inspires the King's description of Bolingbroke in *Richard II* 3. 2. *Job* has also been suggested as a source for *King Lear.* The dramatic effect of Shakespeare's biblical quotations varies enormously. Reference to the Bible is a linguistic habit of almost every Shakespearian character and often says little about them. But it is notable that, of the two characters in Shakespeare who quote the Bible most frequently, one is the renowned devout Henry VI, and the other Richard III. Biblical quotation/allusion often appears in an ironic context, through the character of the speaker or the nature of the action. In *Titus Andronicus,* Demetrius and Chiron congratulate themselves on rape and murder with a quotation from Romans 13: 9–10 on loving one's neighbour (4.2.43). In *Othello,* the drunken Cassio discourses on the salvation of souls and his own hopes to be saved (2.3.95–100). *JKS*

Shaheen, Naseeb, *Biblical References in Shakespeare's Plays* (1999)

bibliography, the study of books as material objects and of the production and reproduction of texts. 'Enumerative' bibliography refers to a listing of books and their locations in libraries and private book collections, such as Sidney Lee's 'Census of Extant Copies of the Shakespeare First Folio' (1902). 'Analytical' bibliography, the technical study of all stages of the printing process, emerged from the New Bibliography movement in the 20th century as a consciously 'scientific' reaction to the more enumerative 'book-collectors' bibliography' that had dominated bibliographical study in the 19th century. *ER*

Bidford. See CRABTREE, SHAKESPEARE'S.

Bigot, Lord. He is one of the noblemen who discover Arthur's body and accuse Hubert, *King John* 4.3. *AB*

biographies of Shakespeare. Attempts to garner information about Shakespeare's life and career were made more or less haphazardly during the 17th century by, for instance, John *Ward, John *Dowdall, Gerard *Langbaine, Thomas Jordan, and Thomas *Fuller, but the first biographical account of consequence is Nicholas *Rowe's, published with his edition in 1709 and based in part on information gathered for him by Thomas *Betterton. Inaccurate and inadequate though it is, it was reprinted, with variations, in many subsequent editions (though not in *Johnson's and *Capell's). *Malone undertook the most thorough research to date, establishing a chronology which was long regarded as standard, and printing much new material in his edition of 1790. No less important was his exposure of the Ireland *forgeries. His incomplete attempt at a full biography appeared posthumously in the Third *Variorum (1821).

During the 19th century, contributions to biographical study came from antiquarians such as R. B. Wheler who, while providing new information, also plagiarized Rowe, and, pre-eminently, *Halliwell-Phillipps, whose voluminous, dispersed, and amazingly thorough studies have been of abiding influence and value. They reached their summation in his *Outlines of the Life of Shakespeare* which grew from 192 pages in its first edition (1881) to 848 in the two outsize volumes of the seventh (1887). *Collier's forgeries had muddied the waters in the 1830s and later, though he also made some genuine finds.

Edward *Dowden's eloquent and long-lasting *Shakspere: A Critical Study of his Mind and Art* (1875), which does not add to the documentary record, is nevertheless original in its attempt 'to connect the study of Shakspere's works with an inquiry after the personality of the author, and to observe, as far as is possible, in its several stages the growth of his intellect and character from youth to full maturity'. Also influential at this period was Sidney *Lee's *Life of William Shakespeare* (1898, greatly expanded from his article of 1897 in the *Dictionary of National Biography* and revised in later editions), long regarded as the standard life.

New information continued to come from researchers who did not write biographies, especially C. W. and H. A. *Wallace, who discovered the *Belott–Mountjoy suit in the Public Record Office in 1905. The Wallaces were American, as was Joseph Quincy *Adams, whose *Life of William Shakespeare* (1923), especially strong on Shakespeare's theatrical background, offered serious rivalry to Lee.

In 1930 appeared Sir E. K. *Chambers's monumental and still indispensable two-volume *William Shakespeare: A Study of Facts and Problems.* Making no attempt at either consecutive narrative or readability, Chambers provides an extraordinarily thorough and scholarly synthesis and appraisal of the current state of knowledge concerning every aspect of Shakespeare's life and career. In the meantime E. I. *Fripp pursued investigations into Shakespeare's Stratford affiliations culminating in the two posthumously published volumes of *Shakespeare: Man and Artist* (1938), fanciful but packed with picturesque detail about the local environment. Leslie *Hotson's enthusiastic researches in public archives concentrated rather on the London scene. Like Fripp's, his books, such as *Shakespeare versus Shallow* (1931), *I, William Shakespeare* (1937), and *Shakespeare's Sonnets Dated* (1949), are valuable rather for incidental details than for their overall theses. Far more disciplined is Mark Eccles's austere but useful *Shakespeare in Warwickshire* (1961). Also specialized in its investigations is E. A. J. Honigmann's *Shakespeare: The Lost Years* (1985), a study at once scholarly and speculative of the putative Lancashire connection.

The classic study of Shakespearian biography is S. *Schoenbaum's masterly *Shakespeare's Lives* (1970, rev. and updated 1991), intended as a preliminary study for a biography which he did not live to compose. It was followed by a continuation of Chambers's work, though in a far more accessible and humane vein, the comprehensive and superbly illustrated *William Shakespeare: A Documentary Life* (1975, revised with fewer illustrations as *A Compact Documentary*

Life, 1977), and its companion volume, *William Shakespeare: Records and Images* (1981).

As archival research becomes less fruitful—though discoveries continue to be made—biographers have tended to concentrate on interpretation of Shakespeare's life either through the society of his times or through the works. At the same time, books have sought a popular rather than, or as well as, a scholarly market, and many more or less ephemeral, sometimes fictionalized, often lavishly illustrated volumes have appeared. Though A. L. *Rowse aspired to fresh discovery, his sprightly and opinionated *William Shakespeare* (1963) is valued mainly for its setting of the historical scene. Anthony *Burgess's *Shakespeare* (1970) is written with all the flair of a successful novelist, and Garry O'Connor's intelligent if overheated *William Shakespeare: A Life* (1991) appears at times to be psychically inspired. Sounder if less flamboyant interpretations of life and career have come from M. M. Reese in *Shakespeare: His World and his Work* (1953, rev. 1980), Russell Fraser in his imaginatively written *Young Shakespeare* (1988) and *The Life and Times of William Shakespeare: The Later Years* (1992), Dennis Kay in *Shakespeare: His Life, Work and Era* (1992), and in Park Honan's full and elegant *Shakespeare: A Life* (1998).

The known facts of Shakespeare's life offer great scope for interpretation and variant contextualization. The oft-told tale will continue to be retold, fluctuating according to the knowledge, aspirations, and personality of the tellers. *SW*

Schoenbaum, S., *Shakespeare's Lives* (1970, rev. edn. 1991)

Wells, S., 'Shakespeare's Lives 1991–1994', in R. B. Parker and S. Zitner (eds.), *Elizabethan Theatre: Essays in Honour of S. Schoenbaum* (1996)

Biondello, Lucentio's servant, is beaten by Lucentio's father Vincentio, *The Taming of the Shrew* 5.1.50. *AB*

Birmingham Repertory Theatre. Founded by Sir Barry *Jackson in 1913 in a small custom-built theatre near the main railway station, it offered a wide range of plays including all of Shakespeare's, some in pioneering *modern dress. In 1971 the big new theatre opened in the civic centre. A Shakespearian or Jacobean play is staged each year. *MJ*

Birmingham Shakespeare Memorial Library (from 1968 renamed the Birmingham Shakespeare Library), founded by the local Shakespeare Club in April 1864 to mark the tercentenary and opened in 1868, housed in the Central Library. Destroyed by fire in January 1879, the collection was restored by voluntary subscription and is now part of Birmingham Central Library's collections. *SLB*

A Shakespeare Bibliography: The Catalogue of the Birmingham Shakespeare Library, Birmingham Public Libraries (7 vols., 1971)

Biron (Berowne) (his name taken from an adviser to the historical King of Navarre, the Duc de Biron) is a lord attending the King of Navarre in *Love's Labour's Lost.* In love with Rosaline, his witty conversation and mixed success in courtship of her anticipates the characterization of Benedick in *Much Ado About Nothing.* *AB*

birthday celebrations. The earliest evidence of the formal marking of Shakespeare's anniversary is a poem published in the *London Magazine*, 24 (1755), 'On the annual meeting of some Gentlemen to celebrate SHAKESPEAR'S BIRTHDAY.' Stratford-upon-Avon only got involved later: David *Garrick's *Jubilee, though intended for the playwright's 200th birthday in 1764, was held up until 1769 and took place in August rather than April so as not to clash with the London theatrical season. Nonetheless, Garrick's festival—with its public orations, and its street procession of Shakespearian characters—has exerted an immense influence on subsequent celebrations of the anniversary of Shakespeare's birth and death, notably the 1864 and 1916 tercentenaries. The current annual event follows the pattern of the 1916 festivities quite closely, and retains a distinctly Edwardian atmosphere. On the morning of the Saturday closest to 23 April the mayor and corporation of Stratford meet with invited ambassadors, academics, and others at the town hall, all wearing sprigs of rosemary (for remembrance), and in company with students and members of local amateur dramatic societies dressed as characters from the plays (in costumes borrowed from the RSC) they process (to the strains of a military band) through the town, its streets adorned with banners representing each of Shakespeare's works (unfurled, along with national and other flags, to a fanfare of trumpets, at 11 a.m.). The route traces Shakespeare's own earthly pilgrimage by passing from the Birthplace to his grave at Holy Trinity, where each member of the procession lays a floral tribute. An official lunch takes place in a marquee nearby, and includes toasts to Shakespeare's memory and (in recent years) the presentation of an award to a noted performer or writer in recognition of a lifetime's service to his works. The invited guests attend an RSC performance in the evening, and at a special Shakespeare Service the following day actors read from both Shakespeare and the Bible and an invited cleric preaches a Shakespeare Sermon. The occasion has been variously likened to Hellenic hero-cults and to the ceremonies associated in Catholic countries with local saints' days, but in keeping with its coincidence with St George's Day it remains quintessentially English, right down to the mandatory morris dancers. *MD*

Birth of Merlin, The. The *title page of the first *quarto edition (1662) of this Jacobean play ascribes it to 'William Shakespear and William Rowley'. Although *Rowley's authorship has been confirmed, the internal evidence suggesting a possible collaboration with Shakespeare is inconclusive. Thomas *Middleton was indicated as a possible collaborator towards the end of the 19th century. *The Birth of Merlin* draws from history, *romance, and the *pastoral tradition, by combining chronicle accounts of the Anglo-Saxon wars prior to the advent of King Arthur and Merlin's miraculous birth and prophecies. Particularly interesting are Donobert's stubborn daughters, who give up marriage and embrace celibacy against their father's and their suitors' wishes. *SM*

Birthplace, the name given to the half-timbered house in Henley Street, Stratford-upon-Avon, acquired, with extensive ground to the rear, by Shakespeare's father John, and where his son William is believed to have been born. The earliest evidence of John's connection with Henley Street is a fine he incurred in 1552 for creating an unauthorized muckheap there. This was likely to have been in front of a property he occupied, probably as a tenant, which may have been the house he is known to have purchased four years later in 1556. From later evidence, it is clear that this stood on the site of the south-eastern part of the present Birthplace site. In 1575, he acquired further property in the town. Its precise location is not known but, given that by 1590 his ownership of Henley Street property is known to have extended over the whole of the present Birthplace site, it is reasonable to assume that it was indeed in 1575 that this additional Henley Street property was acquired.

In plan, the present building began life as a simple rectangular structure of three bays, with close-set studding on the ground floor and square panelling above. The centre bay was the hall with a massive open hearth, between, on the north-west, the parlour, also with a fireplace, and, on the south-east, beyond a cross passage, an unheated chamber which may have served as John Shakespeare's workshop (he was a glove-maker and wool-dealer). This arrangement was matched on the first floor by three chambers reached by a staircase from the hall, probably where the present stairs are sited. Later, but before William Shakespeare's death, a separate single-bay house, now known as Joan Hart's Cottage, was built onto the north-west end of the house. The present kitchen, with chamber over, was also added at the rear at about this time.

On John Shakespeare's death in 1601, the ownership of the premises passed to his son William. By that date, Shakespeare was also the owner of New Place and had no need for the Henley Street premises as a home either for

The house now known simply as 'The Birthplace' on Henley Street, Stratford-upon-Avon: in 1552 the site of an unauthorized muckheap, now a destination of international pilgrimage.

himself or for his immediate family. The main house was therefore leased out to Lewis Hiccox, who converted it into an inn, known as the Maidenhead (later the Swan and Maidenhead). The small, one-bay house to the north-west, probably added around this time, was put to residential use. By the time of Shakespeare's death, it was occupied by his recently widowed sister Joan Hart. Under the terms of Shakespeare's will, the ownership of the whole property (the inn and Joan Hart's Cottage) passed to his elder daughter Susanna; and then, on her death in 1649, to her only child Elizabeth Nash. Elizabeth died in 1670, bequeathing it to Thomas Hart, the descendant of Shakespeare's sister Joan, whose family had continued as tenants of the smaller house after her death in 1646. The Harts remained owners of the whole property until 1806, when it was sold to a butcher, Thomas Court.

Around 1700, the Harts divided the property on different lines: the Swan and Maidenhead was reduced in size (to occupy the two south-easterly bays only). The Harts took up residence in the remaining bay of the original house and let their former cottage to tenants. These divisions survived the purchase of the whole premises by Court in 1806 and remained unchanged until 1847, when, after the death of Court's widow, the premises were again put up for sale. On this occasion, they were purchased for the nation by a body of trustees, whose successors, incorporated by private Act of Parliament, manage the property today.

The Birthplace acquired increasing importance as a literary shrine as a result of the Garrick *Jubilee of September 1769. An article on the Birthplace, complete with the earliest known drawing of the building by Richard Greene, had appeared in the July edition of the *Gentleman's Magazine*. During the Jubilee itself, the building was highlighted by a transparency hung across its windows and one of the rooms was occupied by a book and programme seller, Thomas Beckett. However, an account of a visit to the Birthplace in 1762 makes it clear that the property had been known for its Shakespearian associations for some time before then: indeed, they were mentioned by George Vertue on a visit in 1737. In these early years, it was only the part of the house occupied by the Harts which was shown to visitors and this probably accounts for the tradition that the chamber on the first floor of this section was the birthroom itself. At first it was the Harts who conducted visitors around this part of the house but in the 1790s, after they had moved away from the town, it was let to a butcher, Thomas Hornby. It was his wife Mary who achieved lasting notoriety as the custodian, immortalized by Washington *Irving as the 'garrulous old lady in a frosty red face'. Hornby died in 1817, and in 1820 Mary was eventually evicted.

Photographs taken in the mid-19th century reveal a dilapidated property, forming part of a terrace. Following the purchase of 1847, the trustees, over the next fifteen years or so, restored the property, using the earliest known drawing of the Birthplace (by Richard Greene, in 1769) as a model, but also drawing on architectural evidence as the work proceeded. From the street, the most noticeable alteration was the removal of a brick skin, built across the front of the Swan and Maidenhead early in the 19th century, and the reinstatement of three gables shown on the early drawing. There was a certain amount of replacement of decayed timbers but generally speaking the work was honestly done. Houses on either side, mostly later in date, were also demolished, leaving the Birthplace isolated from neighbouring properties.

When the refurbished premises opened to the public, the earlier division of the property was reflected in the decision to house a library and museum in the former Swan and Maidenhead part of the building, and to confine the presentation of the Birthplace proper to the traditional area. Over the years, a custom had arisen of allowing visitors to write their names on the walls of the birthroom itself. By the mid-1940s, the cumulative effect of this had become so unsightly that the decision was made, as part of a careful representation of the house, to make a full photographic record of these signatures and then to paint over them. *RB*

Deelman, Christian, *The Great Shakespeare Jubilee* (1964)
Halliwell-Phillipps, J. O., *Outlines of the Life of Shakespeare* (6th edn. 1886)
Pringle, Roger, 'The Rise of Stratford as Shakespeare's Town', in Robert Bearman (ed.), *The History of an English Borough: Stratford-upon-Avon 1196–1996* (1997)
Schoenbaum, S., *Shakespeare's Lives* (1991)

Birtwistle, Sir Harrison (b. 1934), English composer. As music director then associate director at the National Theatre in London he composed incidental music for *Hamlet* (1975), *Julius Caesar* (1977), *As You Like It* (1979), and *Coriolanus* (1984). He also wrote the concert work *For O, for O, the Hobby-Horse is Forgot* (1976), whose title derives from *Hamlet*, *Fanfare for Will* (1987), and an *Epilogue* based on 'Full fathom five' (1972). *IBC*

Bishop, Sir Henry Rowley (1786–1855), English composer. As the musical director at Covent Garden theatre (1810–24) Bishop was responsible for arranging and composing music for numerous musical adaptations of Shakespeare's plays. He borrowed heavily from other composers, while many of the lyrics in these adaptations were interpolated from other works. *IBC*

Bishop, William (1626–1700), a resident of Bridgetown in Stratford and the source of the story told by John Roberts in 1729, and subsequently dismissed as false, that two chests of Shakespeare's manuscripts were destroyed by fire (presumably at Warwick in 1694). *CMSA*

Bishops' Bible. See BIBLE.

Bjoernson, Bjoernstjerne (1832–1910), Norwegian dramatist, novelist, and poet. As director of the Christiania theatre (Oslo), 1865–7, he initiated a Norwegian Shakespeare tradition, with productions of *A Midsummer Night's Dream*, *The Winter's Tale*, *Othello*, *Macbeth*, and *Henry IV*. *I-SE*

Blanc, T., *Christiania Theaters Historie 1827–1877* (1899)

Blackamoor Child. He is the son of Aaron and Tamora, introduced in *Titus Andronicus* 4.2. *AB*

Blackfriars. In 1576, the year that James Burbage built the Theatre in Shoreditch, Richard Farrant leased from Sir William More the Upper Frater of an old Dominican monastery in the Blackfriars district of north London and used it for theatrical performances by boy players. Since the 14th century the building had served on occasion as parliament chamber of the realm and there was no official sanction for its use as a playhouse, but by pretending that the boys were merely rehearsing and by keeping the audience small and elite, Farrant and his partner William Hunnis, and later John Newman and Henry Evans, were able to run what was effectively an indoor theatre for eight years until legal wrangles between the partners brought the project to a end. In 1596 James Burbage paid £600 for this property and began converting it to become an indoor home for the Chamberlain's Men, the company whose leading actor was his son Richard and who were expecting to leave the Theatre when that playhouse's ground lease expired in 1597. A petition from important local residents objecting to the traffic and disturbance that a playhouse would bring to the Blackfriars area caused the privy council to forbid the building's use. James Burbage died in February 1597 and his sons decided to relocate the timbers of the Theatre to Bankside to create the Globe as the Chamberlain's Men's new permanent home, and to recover the lost expense by leasing the Blackfriars playhouse to a company of boy players led by the same Henry Evans who had used it 20 years earlier. Presumably discreet performances by boy players were again tolerable where performances by famous adult players were not. Evans's boys changed names and managements several times during their residency at the Blackfriars. In March of 1608 they gave a performance of George Chapman's *Conspiracy and Tragedy of Charles, Duke of Byron* which offended King James and the company was disbanded, leaving the Blackfriars playhouse vacant.

Richard Burbage's playing company was now under royal patronage as the King's Men, and he had reason to suppose that he might now be allowed to use his indoor playhouse. In August 1608 Burbage formed a seven-man syndicate—himself, John Heminges, William Shakespeare, Cuthbert Burbage, Henry Condell, William Sly, and Thomas Evans—to run the Blackfriars along the same lines as the syndicate formed to run the Globe in 1599. Plague closure prevented use of the building until late 1609, but thereafter the King's men used the open-air Globe in the summer and the indoor Blackfriars in the winter. The first of the King's Men's plays to be written specially for the Blackfriars was either Shakespeare's *The Winter's Tale* or his *Cymbeline*, although both probably also played at the Globe as did Shakespeare's later plays *The Tempest*, *All Is True* (*Henry VIII*) and *The Two Noble Kinsmen*. The Blackfriars was closed with all the other playhouses in 1642 and was pulled down in 1655.

The room which housed the playing space was a rectangle 66 feet by 46 feet (20 m × 14 m) and the stage ran across the full width of one of the short sides, although its usable width would have been reduced to something less than 30 feet (9 m) by the presence of spectators' boxes at the sides. The main body of the audience sat in the space immediately in front of the stage (roughly what would be the yard in an open-air theatre) and in galleries which ran around three walls of the room, formed into a U shape by the cutting off of two corners. The economic disposition of the audience was an inversion of the open-air arrangements: those nearest the stage at an indoor playhouse paid most. The practices and facilities of the Blackfriars can be inferred from the plays written specially for the boy players between 1600 and 1608. Spectators were allowed to sit on the stage, as they were in the public theatres from the mid-1590s. Performances were divided into five acts separated by intervals during which music was played. The audience was entirely seated, so the stage was probably not as high as stages in the public theatres, but it would need to be high enough to allow an actor to rise from underneath for the opening direction of Ben Jonson's *Poetaster* (1602): '[*Enter*] ENVY. *Arising in the midst of the stage.*' It is not certain whether actors ascended through the trap via a ladder or were raised by a mechanically operated platform, but if the latter the lack of space under the low stage would have required cutting a hole in the massive floor and fitting the machine against the ceiling of the room beneath. Descents by flight machine, with musical accompaniment, are made in Beaumont and Fletcher's *Cupid's Revenge* and in George Chapman's *The Widow's Tears*, and music plays as the actor descends. In the public theatres music was typically provided by brass instruments but for the enclosed space of the Blackfriars woodwind instruments were preferred. Operation of the flight machine in open-air playhouses was usually masked by the simulation of thunder, and the use of music alone in *Cupid's Revenge* and *The Widow's Tears* might indicate that the solid roof of the Upper Frater effectively deadened the noise of the Blackfriars flight machine.

The Blackfriars playhouse was famous for the quality of its musicians who provided entertainment before the performance as well as music during the four act intervals. When the King's Men took over the theatre they appear to have adapted their open-air practices to conform with those of the Blackfriars: thereafter they used more music in all their plays and used intervals in all performances. Absolute conformity was not possible however: as well as quieter instruments the smaller indoor theatre suited a more restrained style of vocal delivery and less movement about the stage. *GE*

Berry, Herbert *Shakespeare's Playhouses* (1987)

Gurr, Andrew, 'Playing in Amphitheatres and Playing in Hall Theatres', in A. L. Magnusson and C. E. McGee (eds.), *The Elizabethan Theatre XIII: Papers Given at the 13th International Conference on Elizabethan Theatre Held at the University of Waterloo, Ontario, in July 1989* (1994)

Smith, Irwin, *Shakespeare's Blackfriars Playhouse: Its History and its Design* (1964)

Wallace, C. W., *The Children of the Chapel at Blackfriars, 1597–1603* (1908)

Blackfriars Gatehouse, a property in the Blackfriars district of London, not far from the Blackfriars theatre, which Shakespeare bought from Henry *Walker, 'citizen and minstrel of London', for £140 on 10 March 1613. It had belonged to Mathias Bacon from 1590 until Walker bought it in 1604, and had frequently been suspected as a centre of Catholic intrigue. Part of it was built over 'a great gate'. In 1586 a Blackfriars resident, Richard Frith, had reported that 'It hath sundry back doors and byeways, and many secret vaults and corners. It hath been in time past suspected and searched for papists but no good done for want of good knowledge of the back doors and bye-ways and of the dark corners.' For some unknown reason, Shakespeare had as co-purchasers William Johnson, plausibly identified as landlord of the *Mermaid Tavern, John Jackson, possibly a shipping magnate of Hull married to the sister-in-law of Elias *James, and John *Heminges. But Shakespeare put up the money, and the others acted as his trustees. A payment of £80 in cash was made; on the day after the deed had been sealed, Shakespeare mortgaged the property back to Walker for the remaining £60, to be paid on 27 September following; this was presumably intended to allow Shakespeare time to raise the money. The trusteeship would have the effect of barring Shakespeare's widow from rights to the property, but was not necessarily entered into with this purpose. Of the extant Shakespeare *signatures, one is on the purchase deed, the other on the mortgage.

There is no evidence that Shakespeare ever lived in the house; according to his will it was let to a John Robinson, probably not the person of the same name who witnessed his will. In the spring of 1615 Shakespeare joined with several other property owners in the neighbourhood in a petition to permit Mathias Bacon, whose mother had recently died, to surrender the title deeds of the Lodging of the Prior of Blackfriars, the estate of which the gatehouse was a part. The house appears to have been demolished in the late 18th century. *SW*

Blake, William (1757–1827), English artist, poet, and philosopher, who produced during the early 1770s representations of characters from plays by Shakespeare which display the linear treatment of the human figure for which Blake is celebrated, such as *Titiana and Oberon* (pen, ink, and wash, Tate Gallery). Blake was commissioned by William Hayley to produce a series of portrait busts for a library at Felpham. These included a depiction of Shakespeare. The completed work, *William Shakespeare* (*c.*1800, Manchester City Art Gallery), employed a derivative of the *Droeshout engraving, wreathed in laurels. Blake executed numerous

William Blake's characteristic early drawing of Lear and Cordelia, produced in the 1770s.

'commercial' works, including engravings after *Fuseli, such as *Katharine, Griffiths and Patience* (F. & C. Rivington, London, 1804). *CT*

Blanche, Lady, of Spain. She is betrothed to Louis the Dauphin, *King John* 2.1. *AB*

blank verse, verse written in unrhymed lines of iambic pentameter. First employed in English by Henry Howard, Earl of Surrey, in the 1540s, it rapidly developed in the hands of Marlowe and others into the standard medium of dramatic verse. Benefiting both from the metrical flexibility of the English pentameter and from the syntactical scope permitted by enjambment, it became in Shakespeare's hands a remarkably versatile instrument capable equally of colloquial vigour and of oratorical grandeur. *CB*

blazon, a listing of the beloved's admirable physical features (coral lips, rosy cheeks, etc.) in a love poem; famously mocked in Sonnet 130. *CB*

Bloch, Ernest. See OPERA.

blocking entry. A. W. Pollard suggested that certain entries for Shakespeare's plays in the *Stationers' Register, such as those made by James Roberts for *As You Like It, Henry V*, and *Much Ado About Nothing* in 1600, were intended to block publication of these texts, and thereby keep the scripts out of the hands of rival acting companies, until their theatrical runs with the Lord *Chamberlain's Men were successfully concluded. Although there is clear evidence that early English booksellers would sometimes attempt to forestall rival booksellers by entering in the Stationers' Register projected books for which no text yet existed, it is less certain that booksellers employed such blocking entries purely in the interest of acting companies. *ER*

Bloom, Claire (b. 1931). British stage and film actress. At 17 she captivated playgoers with her dark, fragile Ophelia at Stratford. Four years later she triumphed as Juliet at the *Old Vic, by which time she had starred in Charles Chaplin's film *Limelight*. She was Ophelia to Richard *Burton's Hamlet and toured as Cordelia to John *Gielgud's King Lear. In Laurence *Olivier's film *Richard III* she played Lady Anne. Her performances as Shakespeare's maturer women (Gertrude in *Hamlet*, Constance in *King John*) were given on television, and as parts of a touring one-woman show. She has written two thoughtful volumes of autobiography. *MJ*

Blount, Edward. See COLOPHON; COPYRIGHT; FOLIOS; PRINTING AND PUBLISHING.

'Blow, blow, thou winter wind', sung by Amiens in *As You Like It* 2.7.175; the earliest surviving setting is by Thomas Arne, published *c.*1765. More recent composers include Bridge, Parry, and Quilter. *JB*

Blunt, Sir James. He is given messages from Richmond to the Earl of Pembroke and Lord Stanley, *Richard III* 5.4. *AB*

Blunt, Sir John. He is falsely reported slain, *2 Henry IV* 1.1.16 (appearing 4.3.22, mute). *AB*

Blunt, Sir Walter. He excuses *Hotspur to the King, *1 Henry IV* 1.3.69–75, and is a messenger, 3.3.163–9 and in 4.3. He is slain, 5.3, disguised as the King. *AB*

Boaden, James (1762–1839), English playwright, novelist, biographer, and scholar. Boaden confesses to being first a partisan and then an opponent of W. H. Ireland's forged Shakespeare Papers (1796). His *Inquiry into the Authenticity of Various Pictures and Prints* (1824) is an important early attempt to discriminate among the multiplying images of Shakespeare after the only fully authenticated portraits, the *Janssen bust and the *Droeshout engraving. A life of John Philip Kemble (2 vols., 1825) was followed by biographies of actresses Sarah Siddons (1827) and Dorothea Jordan (1831). In *On the Sonnets of Shakespeare* (1837) he reasonably claims to be the first to identify William Herbert, 3rd Earl of Pembroke, as the 'man right fair', and Samuel Daniel as the rival poet. *TM*

Boar's Head. See CURTAIN THEATRE; HENRY IV Part 1; HOLST, GUSTAV; INNS; KEMPE, WILLIAM; LANGLEY, FRANCIS.

Boas, Frederick Samuel (1862–1957), British academic and editor, author of *Shakspere and his Predecessors* (1896), which first applied the term 'problem plays' to *Hamlet, All's Well That Ends Well, Troilus and Cressida*, and *Measure for Measure*, on the analogy of Ibsen's modern plays dealing with social and sexual issues. *TM*

Boatswain. He rebukes the courtiers for interfering with his attempts to save his ship, *The Tempest* 1.1. *AB*

Boccaccio, Giovanni (1313–75), Italian humanist and writer, author of the *Decameron* (1353), a collection of 100 tales told by ten people over a period of ten days during quarantine in Florence. This narrative device, whereby each member of the group must tell a story to pass the time, had provided the structure of Chaucer's *The Canterbury Tales* and some of the stories told by Chaucer's pilgrims derive from the *Decameron*. The English poet was also inspired by Boccaccio's *Il Filostrato* to write his *Troilus and Criseyde*. But Boccaccio's influence upon 16th-century English literature was not dependent upon Chaucer. His *De casibus virorum et feminarum illustrium* (Concerning the Falls of Illustrious Men and Women, 1355–60) was translated into English by John Lydgate as *The Fall of Princes* (1431–8), which in turn inspired *A Mirror for Magistrates*, an important source of Elizabethan history plays. But it was the *Decameron*, translated in part into English by William Painter in 1566, for which Boccaccio was best known. In Montaigne's essay 'On Books', he complains about the tendency of comic dramatists to 'crowd into a single play five or six tales by Boccaccio'. Many English dramatists also turned to this repository of stories. It was from the *Decameron*, probably in Painter's translation, that Shakespeare took the plot of *All's Well That Ends Well* and the wager plot of *Cymbeline*. *JKS*

Bodleian Library, of the University of Oxford, formally opened in 1602. Its founder, Sir Thomas Bodley, excluded plays as 'idle bookes, & riffe raffes' but it has since become the second most important Shakespeare collection in the UK. In 1821 it acquired the library of Edmond Malone including a unique copy of *Venus and Adonis* (1593). *SLB*

Bodmer Library, established in 1951 by the private collector Martin Bodmer (1899–1971) in Cologny, near Geneva in Switzerland. It is the most important collection of early Shakespeare editions in Europe. It includes the only uncut copy of any of Shakespeare's plays printed in his lifetime and a First Folio claimed to be the finest in existence. *SLB*

http://www.ville-ge.ch/geneve/culture/musees//bodmer.htm

Bogdanov, Michael (b. 1938), British director. At Stratford-upon-Avon his productions included a radical *Taming of the Shrew* (1979) and a dashingly up-to-date *Romeo and Juliet* (1986). An internationalist and a populist, he has frequently worked abroad and has sought ways of appealing to new audiences. Since 1986 he has been director of the *English Shakespeare Company with whom he devised a popular staging of history plays; it grew between 1986 and 1989 into a seven-play cycle *The Wars of the Roses* which toured Britain and worldwide, was televised, and won awards. The company has a permanent base in Newcastle-upon-Tyne. *MJ*

Bohemia and the former Czechoslovakia. In Shakespeare's time, the kingdom of Bohemia (Bohemia, Moravia, and Silesia) was a part of the Holy Roman Empire ruled by the Austrian line of the Habsburgs. Their seat was Prague, the capital of Bohemia, from 1583 until 1612 when Emperor Rudolf II was succeeded by Matthias who moved the court back to Vienna. The Catholic and German-speaking Habsburgs were growing increasingly unpopular with the mostly Slavonic (Czech-speaking) and Protestant Czechs and Moravians who refused the Habsburg succession and invited the Protestant leader Frederick of Palatine as their king, thus starting the Thirty Years War (1618–48).

Frederick was married to *Elizabeth, daughter of James I; during their betrothal and marriage celebrations in London in 1613, a number of plays had been performed, almost half of them by Shakespeare. (These included *The Winter's Tale*, but that play's maritime Bohemia derives from its literary source, Robert *Greene's *Pandosto*, rather than from the country's real history or geography.) They also invited English strolling actors to Prague to celebrate their coronation in 1619. After the defeat of the Protestant army near Prague in 1620, the couple had to take flight, and Bohemia was exposed to long-lasting Catholicization and Germanization.

Only towards the end of the 18th century were the first translations of Shakespeare from German into Czech made and produced in Prague, among the predominant German productions. The Czech musician Jiří Benda, who was with many of his compatriots in the service of German aristocratic patrons, composed *Romeo and Juliet* (1776), one of the earliest examples of a new musical genre called *Singspiel*, a type of light opera with spoken dialogues. Benda used a German libretto which provided Shakespeare's tragedy with a happy reunion of the young lovers.

During the national revival of the 19th century, all of Shakespeare's plays were translated into Czech from English editions and most of them produced in Prague. The composer Bedřich *Smetana was a lifelong admirer of Shakespeare (though his operatic version of *Twelfth Night* remained unfinished). His colleague Antonín Dvořák composed a highly dramatic concert overture *Othello* (1892).

The tercentenary celebrations of Shakespeare's birth in 1864 and commemoration of his death in 1916 gave the Czechs the opportunity to demonstrate their striving for cultural and political independence which was reached after the end of the First World War in 1918 by the declaration of the Czechoslovak Republic. Accordingly, Shakespearian criticism (notably in the work of J. Maly) and translation (in that of Klastersky) thrived in the pre-war republic, but this tradition was tragically severed by the Second World War, during which two of the country's leading Shakespeare critics (Chudoba and Vodak) died in Nazi concentration camps, and the director E. F. Burian, similarly incarcerated, was lucky to survive.

The revival of Czech Shakespeare after the war was appropriately signalled by Burian's *Romeo and Juliet* (Prague, 1945), in which the love scenes appeared to be the dream of a dishevelled prisoner in a camp, and by a *Macbeth* (1949) in which the protagonist wore a costume deliberately suggestive of an SS uniform. The first stirrings of the 'Prague Spring' of 1968 were visible in Otomar Krejca's youth-led *Romeo and Juliet* (1963–4), designed by Josef Svoboda: both Krejca and Svoboda, symptomatically, were driven increasingly to work abroad after 1968. Important, sometimes subversive, productions of Shakespeare continued, however, notably a 1981 version of the 'bad' quarto of *Hamlet* produced at the Balustrade theatre (home territory of dramatist and future president Vaclav Havel), which provided the corpses of Act 5 with a chilling, military mass grave.

It is perhaps appropriate that the 'Velvet Revolution' of 1989 coincided with a growing interest in Shakespeare's comedies, and that the first major Czech production since should have been Jan Kacer's *The Winter's Tale* (1992), in which the Bohemian rogue Autolycus seemed an all too topical representative of the free-market chicanery that has sometimes characterized life in post-communist Prague. *ZS*

Limon, Jerzy, *Gentlemen of a Company: English Players in Central and Eastern Europe 1590–1660* (1985)

Simko, Jan, 'Shakespeare in Slovakia', *Shakespeare Survey*, 4 (1951)

Stříbrný, Zdeněk, *Shakespeare and Eastern Europe* (2000)

Vočadlo, Otakar, 'Shakespeare and Bohemia', *Shakespeare Survey*, 9 (1956)

Bohun, Edmund. Shakespeare follows *Holinshed in calling Buckingham 'Edmund Bohun', *All Is True* (*Henry VIII*) 2.1.104. Historically his name was Edward Stafford: but both Edmund and Bohun were family names, and use of the name 'Bohun', if not 'Edmund' may have been deliberate. *AB*

Bois, Jaques de. See Jaques.

Boleyn, Anne (alternative form, indicating pronunciation: Anne Bullen). In *All Is True* (*Henry VIII*) she dances with Henry VIII, 1.4; pities Katherine and is made Marchioness of Pembroke, 2.3; and appears in her coronation procession, 4.1. The historical Anne (*c.*1507–36) was beheaded for alleged adultery less than three years after the christening of her daughter Elizabeth with which Shakespeare's play closes: audiences' knowledge of this fact has often been exploited by producers of the play, who have sometimes supplied business in which Henry ominously caresses her neck. *AB*

Bolingbroke, Harry. See Richard II; Henry IV Parts 1 and 2.

Bolingbroke, Roger. A conjurer (i.e. exorcist or sorcerer) in *The First Part of the Contention* (*2 Henry VI*), he raises the spirit Asnath for the Duchess of Gloucester with the help of the witch Margery Jordan, 1.4. *AB*

Bolton, Edmund (*c.*1575–*c.*1633), historian and poet. Often in trouble for Catholic practices, Bolton around 1616, in a draft paragraph for his *Hypercritica* on historical writing, referred to Shakespeare as a model of 'the most warrantable English'. Not published until 1722, Bolton's text in print omits Shakespeare's name. *PH*

Bona, Lady. Edward IV proposes to her (by proxy) but she immediately hears he has already married Lady Gray, *Richard Duke of York* (*3 Henry VI*) 3.3. *AB*

Bond, Edward (b. 1934), dramatist. One of the most important British playwrights of the post-war period (and a key theorist of post-Brechtian political theatre), Edward Bond has made repeated and extensive use of Shakespeare in his dramaturgy, discursive writings, and practical work with actors. His major works include *Lear* (1971), an epic reworking of *King Lear*, and the speculative biographical drama *Bingo* (1973); *The Sea* (1973) contains echoes of *The Tempest*. *RS*

Bonian, Richard. See printing and publishing.

'book', the prompt copy of a play used by the book-holder in Shakespeare's theatre. The term survives on the vellum wrappers of the *manuscript plays 'The Booke of Sir Thomas Moore' and 'The Book of Iohn A kent & Iohn a Cumber', and in some entries in the *Stationers' Register: 'A booke called the booke of the m'chant of Venyce.' *ER*

Greg, W. W., *Dramatic Documents from the Elizabethan Playhouses* (1931)

Werstine, Paul, 'Plays in Manuscript', in John D. Cox and David Scott Kastan (eds.), *A New History of Early English Drama* (1997)

bookkeeper. An official play-text manuscript (or 'book') contained the essential licence from the Master of the Revels, the obtaining of which was the first task of the bookkeeper after receiving the work from the dramatist. Additionally, the bookkeeper (sometimes called a prompter or book-holder) oversaw the preparation of the individual parts (the lines of each character, written out on separate rolls), supervised the casting of roles (possibly employing a 'plat' or 'plot'), annotated the 'book' with the necessary additional directions and reminders, and remained backstage during performance to ensure that actors and properties were ready on time. Prompting, in the modern sense of jogging an actor's memory by speaking the next line, was not undertaken. *GE*

'Book of Sir Thomas More, The'. See Sir Thomas More.

Booth, Barton (?1679–1733), actor. A school-friend of Nicholas *Rowe, he began his acting career as *Betterton's protégé playing middle-sized Shakespearian roles at Queen's theatre and Drury Lane. His reputation as an intelligent tragedian, effective in conveying the passions, developed as his roles expanded at the reopening of Drury Lane in 1709–10 (he played Brutus, Othello, Horatio, for example) and when he became a partner in its management in 1713. *CMSA*

Booth, Edwin (1833–93), American actor who established an international reputation based largely on his Shakespearian performances. He undertook many Shakespearian roles (including Cassio, Laertes, Edgar, and Iago) across America before making his mark as Richard III in Boston and New York in 1857. In 1861 he made his first bid for the endorsement of London critics (cool) and audiences (somewhat warmer) as Shylock. During the 1860s and 1870s Booth added to his laurels in America, achieving his hundredth night as Hamlet—painstakingly prepared spontaneity—in 1865 under his own management, which was characterized by the high production values of its Shakespearian revivals (including *Julius Caesar* and *Othello*). Abandoning management after the loss (1873) of the New York theatre which bore his name, Booth concentrated on acting, returning to London in 1881–2 where he alternated Othello and Iago with *Irving. In 1883 he visited Berlin and Vienna where he was fêted in an entirely Shakespearian repertoire (Hamlet, Othello, Iago, Lear) playing with a German-speaking company. Back in America, he continued to perform his Shakespeare roles, making his last appearance—a mature and old-fashioned Hamlet—on 4 April 1891. In William Winter, Booth had an assiduous chronicler of his achievements. *RF*

Shattuck, Charles H., *The Hamlet of Edwin Booth* (1969)

Booth, Junius Brutus (1796–1852), English-born actor who achieved considerable success (Richard III, 1817) in London, but was routed when he played Iago to Edmund *Kean's Othello (1818), subsequently pursuing his career in America. Resembling, if not imitating, Kean, Booth's passionately demonic Richard III thrilled audiences across America, but it was as Richmond in 1855 that his son John Wilkes Booth (1839–65) began the career that was to end in his assassination of President Lincoln (14 April 1865). Of Junius Brutus Booth's ten children by his second wife, Junius Brutus Booth, jr. (1821–83), though he had his admirers as King John and Cassius, enjoyed limited success as an actor and it fell to his brother Edwin *Booth to scale the Shakespearian heights. *RF*

Borachio, sponsored by Don John, schemes to make Hero appear unfaithful to Claudio in *Much Ado About Nothing.* *AB*

Borges, Jorge Luis (1899–1986), Argentine novelist and critic. His wide-ranging admiration for English literature includes a typically compressed part-biographical, part-dreamlike, part-analytical account of Shakespeare's imagination 'Everything and Nothing' in *Dreamtigers* (1964, translated from *El hacedor,* 1960). In the magical fantasy 'Shakespeare's Memory' (1985) the narrator describes as his 'destiny' the inheritance and obligation to pass on Shakespeare's actual memory. *TM*

Boswell, James, Jr. (1778–1822), third son of James Boswell, Johnson's biographer. He collaborated with Edmond *Malone and completed his unfinished edition of Shakespeare, the so-called Third Variorum or 'Boswell's Malone' of 1821 (21 vols.), significant for its size and its exhaustive and systematic coverage of all current Shakespearian facts and problems. *TM*

Bosworth Field in Leicestershire is the scene of much of Act 5 of *Richard III.* Richard III was killed there and the Earl of Richmond crowned Henry VII in the final battle of the Wars of the Roses (22 August 1485). *AB*

Bottom, Nick, the Weaver. In *A Midsummer Night's Dream,* he takes his name from the term for an empty reel or spool used in weaving, though it obviously has additional comic implications. He is given the part of Pyramus in Quince's play, though he vaingloriously longs to play all the parts, and it is his idiocy during their rehearsal in 3.1 that inspires *Robin Goodfellow to give him an 'ass-head'. Separated from his fellow actors he encounters *Titania, who conceives a passion for him. Having been released from his enchantment and believing his adventures with the fairies are a dream (4.1), he is reunited with his companions (4.2) and in the last act they perform their play at Theseus' court.

Until the 19th century *A Midsummer Night's Dream* tended to appear as adaptations of the Bottom episodes rather than full-scale productions (the earliest known example *The Merry Conceited Humours of Bottom the Weaver* was printed 1661). Samuel *Phelps first established the role for a star actor-manager in 1853, and it remained in his repertory for 20 years. Ralph *Richardson, in 1929, was one of the first actors to rid himself of the cumbersome fully built-up head of previous ass-Bottoms, leaving him free to develop a more subtle and expressive acting style. Perhaps one of the most unusual 'translations' of Bottom into an ass was that of Timothy Spall in *Lepage's 1992 production: the French contortionist Angel Laurier, playing Puck, entwined herself around him in such a way as to make her feet ass's ears. *AB*

Shakespeare, William, *A Midsummer Night's Dream,* ed. Trevor Griffiths (1996)

Bottom the Weaver, The Merry Conceited Humours of. Robert *Cox's highly actable *droll, probably prepared in the 1640s, abbreviates *A Midsummer Night's Dream* solely to the scenes in which *Bottom appears. Its cast list provides the earliest recommendation for the doubling of the other artisans with Titania's fairies and that of Oberon with Theseus and Titania with Hippolyta. *MD*

Bouchier (Bourchier), Thomas. See CARDINAL.

Boult, a pander's servant, eventually agrees to help Marina escape prostitution, *Pericles* 19. *AB*

Bouncing Knight, The. This short 'Falstaff sketch', a compilation of the highway robbery scenes from *1 Henry IV,* was published with several other such *'drolls' in Francis Kirkman's *The Wits; or, Sport upon Sport* in 1672–3: it was probably compiled by the actor Robert Cox for clandestine performance during the Puritan Interregnum. *MD*

Bourbon, Duke of. He is a bellicose French nobleman, mentioned as having been taken prisoner, *Henry V* 4.8.77. *AB*

Bourbon, Lord. The French High Admiral appears in *Richard Duke of York* (*3 Henry VI*) 3.3 (mute). *AB*

Bowdler, Thomas and Henrietta. See FAMILY SHAKESPEARE.

Bowers, Fredson Thayer (1905–91), American academic bibliographer, significant for his radical theoretical and practical contributions to the detailed study of Elizabethan printing processes, in editions (of Dekker, Beaumont and Fletcher) favouring the preservation of original spellings and variants. Author of *On Editing Shakespeare and Other Elizabethan Dramatists* (1955) and *Textual Study and Literary Criticism* (1959). *TM*

Bowman, John (?1651–1739), actor and singer, whose long career began as a court musician performing material written for him by Purcell. In the public theatre he graduated via fops and dandies to Shakespearian character parts at Drury Lane and Queen's. William Oldys cited him as a source of information on Shakespeare. *CMSA*

boy actors. The early acting industry had no guild structure to regulate apprenticeship, but nonetheless boys were taken into theatrical companies and trained. Without guild regulation the system was ad hoc and if formal arrangements were made the boy was usually officially apprenticed to his master's secondary trade. Prepubescent boys had the stature and unbroken voices for female impersonation and Samuel Pepys called Edward Kynaston 'the loveliest lady that ever I saw in my life—only her voice not very good'. Where a boy actor's name appears in a stage direction it is often by reference to the master's name ('Enter John: Skanks Boy'). The relationships could be warm on both sides: Augustine Phillips's will left gifts to his apprentices and the wills of Alexander Cooke and Nicholas Tooley refer affectionately to their masters John Heminges and Richard Burbage respectively. Heminges left 20*s.* to his former apprentice John Rice (who had since quit the stage) and made him an overseer with Burbage for his estate, and apprentice John Pyk (or Pig) wrote a charmingly affectionate letter to the wife of his master Edward Alleyn.

An average company probably contained between two and five boy actors, aged between about 14 and 18 years. The relative scarcity of actors capable of taking female roles is the main reason that male roles dominate the drama. Frequently young female characters dress as young men in order to enter into the service of older men and the obvious homoerotic frisson which is generated indicates that the underlying maleness and youth of the female impersonator is important. Literary and historical scholarship is beginning to make sense of this phenomenon in relation to Elizabethan notions of sexuality and service. *GE*

Davies, W. Robertson, *Shakespeare's Boy Actors* (1939)
Orgel, Stephen, *Impersonations: The Performance of Gender in Shakespeare's England* (1996)

Boyce, William (1711–79), English composer. Active at Covent Garden and Drury Lane theatres (often rivalling Thomas Arne), Boyce composed dirges for *Cymbeline* (1746) and *Romeo and Juliet* (1750), set the masque in *The Tempest* (1757), wrote music for animating the statue and one song in *The Winter's Tale* (1756), and composed an *Ode to Shakespeare* (1759). *IBC*

Boydell, John (1719–1804), English print-seller and engraver. From mean beginnings as an engraver's apprentice, Boydell established a profitable practice as a seller and exporter of prints after English artists, which he commissioned himself. Commercial success bestowed public importance on Boydell, who was made alderman of Cheapward, sheriff, and lord mayor of London in 1782, 1785, and 1791 respectively. In 1786, Boydell's house and shop at Cheapside was first employed to exhibit original paintings and by 1789 the *Shakespeare Gallery was officially launched. While Boydell often stated his desire to promote artistic production, the nature of the alderman's aspirations for British painting is difficult to ascertain. The liaison between art and commerce on which his business rested often limited Boydell's patronage of promising history painters. Boydell turned down several paintings by Joseph Wright of Derby and George Romney, believing their treatment of the Shakespearian themes to lack popular appeal. During the 1790s Boydell and his gallery were lampooned in the popular press and upon Boydell's death all 22,000 lottery tickets issued to finance the gallery were sold, and it was auctioned the following year. *CT*

Boyet, a lord attending the Princess of France in *Love's Labour's Lost.* *AB*

boys. **(1)** *1 Henry VI*, see Master Gunner of Orléans **(2)** A boy is sent on an errand by Benedick, *Much Ado About Nothing* 2.3. **(3)** In *Henry V*, formerly Falstaff's page, now working for Bardolph, *Pistol, and Nim, he appears briefly in Acts 2, 3, and 4. Left to guard baggage he is slain by the French, 4.7. **(4)** A boy sings at the wedding of Theseus and Hippolyta, *The Two Noble Kinsmen* 1.1. See also Robin. *AB*

Boys, Jaques de. See Jaques.

Boys from Syracuse, The, exuberant Broadway play (1938) and Hollywood film (1940), adapted 'after a play by Shakespeare' (*The Comedy of Errors*) by George Abbott, with songs by Richard Rodgers and Lorenz Hart, the most enduring of which have been 'This can't be love' and 'Falling in love with love'. *TM*

Brabantio. See Brabanzio.

Brabanzio (Brabantio) accuses Othello of having bewitched his daughter *Desdemona before the Duke of Venice, *Othello* 1.3. *AB*

Bracciano, Orsini, Duke of (b. 1572), Elizabeth I's guest of honour at Twelfth Night celebrations in 1601, where (as he wrote to his wife) he enjoyed 'a mingled comedy, with pieces of music and dances'. Leslie Hotson conjectures the play was Shakespeare's *Twelfth Night*, although the evidence remains circumstantial. See Orsino. *CS*

Bracegirdle, Anne (*c.*1663–1748), actress whose earliest roles included Desdemona and Lady Anne. One of the highest earning and most charismatic actresses of the age, she managed Lincoln's Inn Fields with Betterton and Elizabeth Barry from 1695 and played Cordelia in Tate's *Lear*, Ophelia, and Portia (*Julius Caesar*) before her retirement in 1707. *CMSA*

Brackenbury, Sir Robert. Lieutenant of the Tower of London, he leaves Clarence to his murderers, 1.4.88–94, and refuses to let Queen Elizabeth, the Duchess of York, Lady Anne, and their companions see the Princes in the Tower, *Richard III* 4.1. *AB*

Bradbrook, Muriel Clara (1909–93), English critic, notable for wide-ranging, poetically sensitive, and theatrically informed accounts of *Shakespeare and Elizabethan Poetry* (1951), and *The Growth and Structure of Elizabethan Comedy* (1955). *Shakespeare the Craftsman* (1969), and *Shakespeare the Poet in his World* (1978) emphasize her awareness of both history and dramatic form. *TM*

Bradley, A(ndrew) C(ecil) (1851–1935), English critic, best known for *Shakespearean Tragedy* (1904) and his *Oxford Lectures on Poetry* (1909). The first is probably the most influential book of Shakespeare criticism ever published, with its detailed discussion of four plays: *Hamlet, Othello, Lear*, and *Macbeth*. More general, preliminary lectures consider 'The Substance of Shakespearean Tragedy' and 'Construction in Shakespeare's Tragedies'. The great merit of Bradley's work is his scrupulous attention to the speech and action of the plays and the reflective clarity of his commentary upon them. Bradley has subsequently been accused of paying too little attention to the plays in performance, in effect of treating them as discursive, almost novelistic, works of literature. Others have felt that he invests the characters with a life off as well as on stage. To many modern critics, this is a philosophical or theoretical weakness, an inability to consider the plays as ultimately linguistic constructs. But Bradley's directness, common sense, sometimes monosyllabic simplicity of style, and determination to take the plays seriously are precisely what continues to recommend him to subsequent generations, fully justifying his dedication of *Shakespearean Tragedy* to 'my students'. *TM*

Cooke, Katharine, *A. C. Bradley and his Influence in Twentieth-Century Shakespeare Criticism* (1972)

Bradock, Richard. See printing and publishing.

Branagh, Kenneth (b. 1960), British actor and director. Born in Belfast and trained in London, he modelled his stage and screen career on that of Laurence *Olivier. After West End success, he joined the Royal Shakespeare Company for the 1984–5 season; he played Laertes in *Hamlet*, the King of Navarre in *Love's Labour's Lost*, and an admired Henry V. Impatient with directorial dominance at the RSC, he founded his own company, Renaissance, and persuaded actors like Judi *Dench and Derek *Jacobi to direct. He played Hamlet, Benedick, Touchstone, and Coriolanus as well as directing *Twelfth Night* (later televised). He was happy to return to the RSC in 1992 under Adrian Noble's direction to play Hamlet in a very full text.

Challenged by the Olivier legend, he in 1989 adapted, directed, and starred in his own very different film of *Henry V*. His popular *Much Ado About Nothing*, filmed in Tuscany, followed in 1993. He once more challenged comparison with Olivier in his *Hamlet* (1997) set in a 19th-century court. He was Iago in Oliver Parker's film *Othello*. In his own all-singing, all-dancing *Love's Labour's Lost* (2000), conceived as a film musical, he played Berowne. *MJ*

Brandes, Georg (1842–1927), Danish writer and critic. Seen as responsible for the 'Modern

Breakthrough' in Scandinavian literature, he also influenced contemporary perception of the works of Shakespeare as fundamentally autobiographical. His massive study *William Shakespeare* (1895–6; English translation 1898) was widely read. *I-SE*

Schoenbaum, S., *Shakespeare's Lives* (1970)

Brandon. He arrests Buckingham and Abergavenny, *All Is True* (*Henry VIII*) 1.1. *AB*

Brandon, Charles. See SUFFOLK, DUKE OF.

Brandon, Sir William. One of Richmond's supporters (mute part, see RICHARD III 5.4.4). *AB*

Braunschweig, Stéphane (b. 1964), French philosopher and Germanist trained with *Vitez and influenced by *Brecht. He challenges traditional scenography: a slanted, white rectangle for *The Winter's Tale* (1994), mobile wooden panelling for *The Merchant of Venice* (1999) (both in Déprats's translation), a gigantic circular wooden structure in *Measure for Measure* (with English actors, 1997 Edinburgh Festival and Nanterre). *ISG*

brawl (branle), a dance of French origin (see LOVE'S LABOUR'S LOST 3.1.7–8), in which several couples hold hands in a line or circle (see ROUNDEL) and characteristically dance a sequence of steps sideways to left and right, but with more travel to the left. Thoinot Arbeau's *Orchesography* (1589) gives regional versions, and also branles with miming and irregular rhythms. *JB*

Brayne, John (d. before 10 August 1586), co-builder with his brother-in-law James Burbage of the Red Lion (1567) and the Theatre (1576). *GE*

Brazil. In the theatre, Shakespearian plays were first produced in Brazil early in the 19th century (just before independence, 1822), after King John VI had the São João Royal Theatre built in Rio de Janeiro in the 1810s. They were performed, however, in versions derived from French adaptations, translated by Portuguese artists such as Ludovina Soares da Costa, who worked with Brazilian actor João Caetano dos Santos, interpreter of *Macbeth* (1843), *Hamlet* (1843–4), and *Othello* (1837–60). This French influence is unsurprising: French theatrical aesthetics also shaped Brazilian comedy and the vaudeville throughout the century.

Brazilian stage Shakespeare comes of age only after the Second World War, in the work of Pascoal Carlos Magno, who offered naturalistic stagings of *Hamlet* (1948), *Romeo and Juliet*, *Macbeth*, and *A Midsummer Night's Dream* (1949), and in the career of actor and adaptor Sérgio Cardoso in the 1960s. Paulo Autran's succession of Shakespearian productions since the 1950s, including *Lear* (1996), is also remarkable. As state-sanctioned high culture, Shakespeare even served official purposes after the 1964 military coup, which in part displayed its own consolidation through officially sponsored celebrations of Shakespeare's 400th birthday, among them several hundred events, press publications, and stagings throughout the country.

Augusto Boal (exiled in 1971) criticized Shakespeare's official welcome in Brazil as a form of self-imposed cultural colonialism; his parody of *The Tempest* (1979) mocks European aesthetics and exposes various features and contradictions of popular culture. While productions have been numerous all over the country, directors have often adapted or updated plays, stressing their timelessness and universality (e.g. Amir Haddad, Cacá Rosset, Gabriel Vilella, Marcelo Marchioro). Transpositions of *Romeo and Juliet* to Brazilian culture have also been made for television (Afonso Grisolli's miniseries, 1980; a Globo TV soap opera, 1992). Antunes Filho and Ulysses Cruz have directed radical updatings, yet the counter-discursive dramaturgy and stagings that might unsettle easy universalizing have not been consistently attempted. They may, nevertheless, become one of the longer-term results of a developing postcolonial mentality in Brazilian universities.

The translations of Shakespeare available in Brazil throughout the 19th century were generally carried out in Portugal via French, as is the case with *Othelo* (Lisbon 1882) and *Hamlet* by José Antônio de Freitas (Lisbon, 1887). Victor Hugo's biography *William Shakespeare: Life and Works* (1864), which was translated into Brazilian Portuguese by Alvaro Gonçalves, added to this French bias in reception. Translators in the 20th century, however, started using modern editions in English, among them Tristão da Cunha (*Hamlet*, 1933, from a Macmillan 1904 version ed. William Aldis Wright.) Transmission increases in Rio de Janeiro and São Paulo with the work of Berenice Xavier (*The Taming of the Shrew*, 1936, and *The Merchant of Venice*, 1937), Artur de Sales (*Macbeth*, 1948), and J. Costa Neves (*King Lear*, 1948). Oliveira Ribeiro Neto's *Romeo and Juliet*, *Hamlet*, and *Macbeth* (1948), in one volume, was reprinted several times (1951; 1954; 1960). Equally important were Onestaldo de Pennafort (*Romeo and Juliet*, 1940, and *Othelo*, 1956), Péricles Eugênio da Silva Ramos (*Hamlet*, 1955, and *33 Sonnets*, 1953, both in bilingual editions), Newton Belleza (*The Taming of the Shrew*, 1960), Carlos Lacerda (*Julius Caesar*, *c.*1966), and Manuel Bandeira (*Macbeth*, 1961). As these versions went out of print, Carlos Alberto Nunes's translations of the entire canon, in print since the 1950s, became the most popular means of reception. Embellished and/or lofty styles are found in the majority of versions throughout the 1960s. Sérgio Flaksman, Bárbara Heliodora, José Roberto O'Shea, Geraldo de Carvalho Silos, and Jorge Wanderley, however, published new versions in Brazilian Portuguese in the 1990s. The metric, rhyme, and stress patterns remain a challenge to those who recreate verse translations of multiple-text plays in print, as do the uncertainties of Shakespeare's text itself, though translations to date have provided no annotations regarding the variations between *quarto and *folio texts. This important aspect of variation has been generally ignored. *'Richard II' Playtexts, Promptbooks and History: 1597–1857* is the first Latin American book about the subject of textual and theatrical transformation (Margarida G. Rauen, 1998).

The publication of several biographies of Shakespeare since the 1980s caters to the constant interest in Shakespeare. Brazilian Shakespeare criticism *per se*, though, was very scant and limited to master's and doctorate programmes in English and comparative literature until the 1990s. With the founding of the Centre of Shakespearian Studies (CESh) in 1991, President Aimara da Cunha Resende and his fellow members, mostly professors of English literature and drama, have intensified research and published articles in newspapers, journals, and proceedings, both nationally and internationally. *MR*

Gomes, Eugênio, *Shakespeare no Brasil* (1945, repr. 1961)

Brecht, Bertolt (1898–1956), German dramatist, poet, theorist, director, and founder of the Berliner Ensemble. Brecht drew on Elizabethan drama in the 1930s in creating the style he called epic theatre, and adapted ('appropriated', he said) the plays of Shakespeare and his contemporaries for political purpose, showing the need for progressive social change. His version of *Coriolanus* (first performed in 1964) resolves Shakespeare's ambiguity over the protagonist by concluding that the world can no longer afford heroes. The Berliner Ensemble's performances of Brecht's plays in London in 1956 greatly affected Peter *Hall, who drew on the company's organization and social commitment when he formed the RSC a few years later. The non-illusionist 'Brechtian' style heavily influenced Shakespeare acting and production in the 1960s around the globe. *DK*

Bretchgirdle, John (d. 1565). Appointed vicar of Stratford-upon-Avon in 1561, he probably baptized Shakespeare. He had taken his BA at Oxford in 1545 and was buried in Stratford church, leaving as bequests many learned books, Greek as well as Latin. His copy of the Latin–English dictionary *Bibliotheca Eliotae* went 'to the common use' of the scholars of Stratford school. *SW*

Bridges-Adams, William (1889–1965), British director. Having played Leontes and Prospero as an undergraduate at Oxford, he was influenced by William *Poel and *Granville-Barker. In 1919 he became director of the summer Shakespeare festivals at Stratford. In 1926 the old Memorial Theatre burned down so that in addition to staging seasons at the local cinema he was involved in planning the new theatre which opened in 1932. He directed 29 of the 36 plays in the canon, often designing them, and in his early days had to rehearse six plays in five weeks. Himself self-effacing, he occasionally invited more flamboyant people as guest directors. His resignation in 1934 reflected his frustration with the theatre's governors. He later worked for the British Council and wrote *The Irresistible Theatre* (1957). *MJ*

British Council, inaugurated in 1935 to promote British culture and language internationally. It sponsored the Marlowe Society recordings of Shakespeare plays under the direction of George *Rylands, as well as the biennial International Shakespeare Conference and **Shakespeare Survey* from 1948. *SLB*

British Empire Shakespeare Society, founded in 1901 by Greta Morritt to promote Shakespeare's works throughout the Empire by co-ordinating reading circles, dramatic readings, and costume recitals. The 'Bess' was open to both adults and children, and awarded annual prizes for elocution and essays on Shakespeare until 1939. It published an official gazette 1915–39. *SLB*

British Library, created in 1973 from the Departments of Manuscripts and Printed Books of the British Museum established in 1753. In April 1998 its catalogue listed 17,099 books by or about Shakespeare, the most important collection of Shakespeariana in the UK, including many early editions, the manuscript of *The Book of Sir Thomas More*, and the mortgage of the *Blackfriars Gatehouse, one of only six documents bearing Shakespeare's *signature. *SLB*

Britten, Benjamin (1913–76), English composer. Britten wrote incidental music for *Timon of Athens* (Westminster Theatre, London, 1935), while his chamber opera *The Rape of Lucretia* (1946) derives partly from Shakespeare's poem. His best-known Shakespearian work is his musically diverse opera *A Midsummer Night's Dream* (1960), for which he and Peter Pears reduced Shakespeare's text by about half. *IBC*

broadside ballad, a *ballad printed on a single sheet, then sung and sold by a ballad-seller, or pedlar (such as Autolycus in *The Winter's Tale*). Topics included murders, executions, and strange happenings, as well as moral admonishment and love stories (e.g. *'Greensleeves'); ballads from oral tradition were also printed. The name of the tune for each ballad is usually included, but the music is not printed; tunes may sometimes be found in instrumental arrangements from the 16th and 17th centuries. For detailed information on matching tunes to texts see Simpson (1966). *JB*

Simpson, Claude M., *The British Broadside Ballad and its Music* (1966)

brokenbacked line, a line of iambic verse that is missing an unstressed syllable before a mid-line phrasal break. This formation can sometimes seem to imply a peremptory tone or a degree of hurry from one kind of syntax to another: 'Enough to fetch him in. | See | it done (*Antony and Cleopatra* 4.1.14). *GTW*

broken music (broken consort). Two meanings were possible: disordered music, or music with *divisions. Shakespeare plays with the expression in *Henry v* 5.2.241 and *Troilus and Cressida* 3.1.49. The later term 'broken consort' (not found until well after Shakespeare's death) indicates an ensemble of mixed instruments; a standard mixed grouping in Shakespeare's time, unique to England, consisted of violin, *flute, bass *viol, *lute, *cittern, bandora (a wire-strung plucked instrument, larger than the cittern). *Morley set his *Consort Lessons* (1599, 1611) for this combination. See music. *JB*

Brook, Peter (b. 1925), British director and designer, perhaps the most influential theatrical interpreter of Shakespeare in the second half of the 20th century. Barry *Jackson brought Brook, fresh out of Oxford, to the Birmingham Rep to stage *King John* in 1945, then took him to Stratford the next year, where he directed a brilliant *Love's Labour's Lost* in a wistful mood inspired by Watteau. *Romeo and Juliet* followed in 1947, a dark version of *Measure for Measure* with John *Gielgud in 1950, and *The Winter's Tale*, also with Gielgud, in London in 1951. By the age of 25 Brook had established himself as a major director particularly attracted to lesser-known plays, whose approach involved 'making a new set of images' to recapture the surprise and danger of Shakespeare. *Titus Andronicus* at Stratford in 1955 did this forcefully; his production prompted a reversal of opinion about a play frequently called too bad to be Shakespeare's. Brook distanced spectators from its exaggerated violence through *musique concrète* and an abstract design—he was responsible for both—while Laurence *Olivier revealed an unsuspected tragic dimension to the title character. To the Warsaw critic Jan *Kott the performance clarified notions about the innate cruelty in the plays which, along with Polish performances, led to Kott's *Shakespeare our Contemporary.* Discussions between them influenced in turn one of Brook's greatest productions, a harsh and unyielding version of *King Lear* at the newly formed RSC in 1962, with Paul *Scofield in the title role, that brought the play close to the world of Samuel Beckett. (A film version directed by Brook appeared in 1970.) Still intrigued by Kott's absurdist reading of Shakespeare, Brook was back in Stratford for a remarkable *Midsummer Night's Dream* in 1970, his most widely seen and admired work, which emphasized the bestiality of Titania's love for Bottom-as-ass but was filled with athletic acting, trapezes, circus tricks, and a joyous celebration of the idea of performance. Brook's career away from Shakespeare has been equally arresting. His search for spiritual transcendence and theatrical essence led him to create the International Centre for Theatre Research in Paris in 1970, where he gathered a troupe of actors from around the globe to investigate the nature of performance, work that took them to remote villages in Africa and to paring down the means and style of production. His nine-hour version of *The Mahabharata* (1985), while criticized for its cultural insensitivity to the Indian religious epic, was an international triumph. For the Centre Brook directed three Shakespeare plays in French: *Timon of Athens* (1974), which drew on the OPEC oil crisis; an austere *Measure for Measure* (1978), which suggested a society in ruins; and what he said would be his last Shakespeare production, *The Tempest* (1990). Brook had directed the play three times before in English, but this version used a multiracial cast and borrowed the style and methods of *The Mahabharata.* He directed *Hamlet* in 2000. *DK*

Brook, Peter, *The Empty Space* (1968)
Brook, Peter, *The Shifting Point* (1988)
Brook, Peter, *Threads of Time* (1998)
Hunt, Alfred, and Reeves, Geoffrey, *Peter Brook* (1995)

'Brooke'. See Ford, Master Frank.

Brooke, Arthur (d. 1563), English poet and translator, drowned young while voyaging to New Haven to serve in the army overseas. His poem *The Tragical History of Romeus and Juliet*, over 3,000 lines long, published in 1562, adapts a French version of Bandello's narrative. Shakespeare derived elements of *The Two Gentlemen of Verona* from it, and used it extensively for the plot, local detail, and even imagery of *Romeo and Juliet.* Compressing the narrative from nine months to four or five days, he also freed it from Brooke's moralizing and expanded upon half-formed, peripheral characters to create Tybalt and Paris, Mercutio and the Nurse. *JKS*

Brooke, C. F. Tucker (1883–1946), American academic and editor, author of *The Tudor Drama* (1911), *Shakespeare of Stratford* (1926), and *Shakespeare's Sonnets* (1936). His edition of *The Shakespeare Apocrypha* (1908) consisted of plays attributed to Shakespeare but not printed in the First Folio, including seven plays added to F3 (1664). *TM*

Peter Brook's legendary 'white box' production of *A Midsummer Night's Dream* (RSC, 1970): from their circus trapezes Alan Howard and John Kane as Oberon and Puck watch Sara Kestelman and David Waller as Titania and Bottom.

'Broome'. See Ford, Master Frank.

Brough brothers. See burlesques and travesties of Shakespeare's plays.

Brutus, Decius. See Decius Brutus.

Brutus, Junius. (1) One of the Romans who vows to avenge Lucrece in *The Rape of Lucrece.* (2) The tribunes Junius Brutus and Sicinius Velutus goad Martius in the first three acts of *Coriolanus* but are dismayed when they hear he fights for the Volsces, 4.6. *AB*

Brutus, Marcus Junius. See Julius Caesar.

Bryan, George (d. 1612), actor (Strange's Men 1593, Chamberlain's Men 1596). First mentioned among the players at Elsinore in 1586 (the others were Thomas Pope and William Kempe), Bryan's name occurs in the roles of Warwick in the Induction and Damascus in 'Envy' in the plot of *2 Seven Deadly Sins* (performed before 1594, possibly by Strange's Men). Strange's Men's licence to tour, issued on 6 May 1593, names Bryan but by 21 December 1596 he was with the Chamberlain's Men and received, with John Heminges, the payment for court performances. Although identified as an actor in the 1623 Shakespeare Folio, his name is conspicuously absent from the actor lists in the Jonson folio of 1613 for plays performed in the late 1590s and early 1600s and from the company patent of 1603. Possibly he gave up acting: a George Bryan was paid as Groom of the Chamber in 1603 and in 1611–13, but the latter date extends beyond the actor's death, casting doubt on the assignment. *GE*

Buck (Buc), Sir George (d. 1623). He acted as deputy to Edmund Tilney, first regular Master of Revels, from about 1606, succeeding to Tilney's position in 1610. As Revels Master, Buck licensed plays, playhouses, and companies; censored plays; and enforced regulations against playing during Lent and plague periods. Buck was discharged in 1622 due to mental instability. *CS*

Buckingham, Duke of. (1) In *The First Part of the Contention* (*2 Henry* vi) he helps disgrace the Duchess of Gloucester, 1.4, and then the Duke of Gloucester, 3.1. He persuades the followers of Cade to disperse, 4.8 and supports Henry vi against York in the Wars of the Roses. He is based on Humphrey Stafford (1402–60), 1st Duke of Buckingham, not to be confused with Sir Humphrey Stafford in the same play. (2) He abets Richard in his ambitions in *Richard iii*, deserts him, 4.2, is led to execution, 5.1, and appears to Richard as one of the ghosts at *Bosworth, 5.5. He is based on Henry Stafford (*c.*1451–83), 2nd Duke of Buckingham. (3) He is arrested for treason, *All Is True* (*Henry viii*) 1.1, but proclaims his innocence on his way to execution 2.1. He is based on Edward Stafford (1478–1521), 3rd Duke of Buckingham. See also Bohun, Edmund. *AB*

Buckingham, George Villiers, 1st Duke of (1592–1628), James i's favourite from 1614, and a keen theatre-goer. Lois Potter suggests the role of Theseus' favourite Pirithous in *The Two Noble Kinsmen* (which originally referred to James's previous favourite Robert Carr) was cut after 1613 because of Buckingham's unpopularity. In 1628, shortly before he was assassinated, he saw *All Is True* (*Henry viii*) twice, on each occasion leaving after Buckingham's final speeches. *CS*

Bulgaria. Shakespeare's appearance on the cultural scene occurred in the middle of the 19th century in the wake of the cultural and political revival which preceded the country's liberation from Ottoman domination (1878). First mention of his name occurs in 1858 in relation to weather conditions in the British Isles. Typically, his reputation as poet and dramatist travelled before his actual work. The first undocumented amateur performance was *Romeo and Juliet* in 1868. The earliest translations, of *Julius Caesar* and *Cymbeline*, were published in 1881. In 1884 excerpts from *Macbeth* and *Hamlet* were included in the *Reader* for the schools, thus embedding them in the National Curriculum.

Performance history proper began in the 1880s with the establishment of the first professional troupes and, in 1904, of the National Theatre. Both the tragedies (especially *Othello* and *Hamlet*) and the comedies (particularly *The*

Merchant of Venice and *The Taming of the Shrew*) were performed to great acclaim between 1900 and 1944. During the communist period (1944–89), performance of almost all plays reached an apogee in technique, innovation, and political suggestion.

During the 1970s and 1980s the entire canon was translated by Valery Petrov, a version currently used as the standard stage text. The post-totalitarian 1990s have witnessed dazzling stage experiments. *BS*

Shurbanov, Alexander, and Sokolova, Boika, *Painting Shakespeare Red: An East-European Appropriation* (2000)

bull-baiting. See ANIMAL SHOWS.

Bullcalf, Peter. He is recruited to fight by Falstaff, *2 Henry IV* 3.2, but buys himself out. *AB*

Bullen, Anne. See BOLEYN, ANNE.

Bull Inn. See INNS.

Bullough, Geoffrey (1901–82), English academic, whose collection of the *Narrative and Dramatic Sources of Shakespeare* (8 vols., 1957–75) includes complete texts and excerpts from sources, as well as numerous analogues—all given in English—for every play. Bullough's meticulous scholarship, critical judgement, and expressive clarity make it an indispensable work. *TM*

Bum, Pompey. See POMPEY.

Bunbury, Henry William (1750–1811), English draughtsman. Bunbury executed several works in pencil and crayon during a Grand Tour in the late 1760s. In 1792, Bunbury was commissioned by Thomas Macklin to illustrate a Shakespeare Gallery, in competition to John *Boydell's. The gallery ran for four years, closing in 1796 in response to shifts in public taste. *CT*

Burbage, Cuthbert (1565–1636), non-playing company sharer and housekeeper (Theatre, Globe, Blackfriars), son of James Burbage, brother of Richard Burbage. As well as his familial link, Cuthbert's theatrical connections are shown by his being mentioned in the wills of William Sly, Richard Cowley, Nicholas Tooley (who died in his house), John Heminges, and Henry Condell. *GE*

Burbage, James (*c*.1531–97), actor (Leicester's Men 1572–6), builder of the Theatre and the second Blackfriars, possibly part-owner of the Curtain, father to Richard and Cuthbert Burbage. When Burbage married Ellen Brayne on 23 April 1559 he was described as a joiner, or a worker in small wooden structures such as furniture, an occupation distinct from a carpenter who made buildings. In 1567 Ellen's brother John Brayne paid for construction of a makeshift playhouse on the Red Lion farm in Stepney and in 1576 Burbage and Brayne embarked on the altogether more substantial Theatre project. A letter he wrote to the Earl of Leicester in 1572 makes it clear that Burbage was already one of his players, and Burbage is named in the company's patent of 1574, but from 1576 running the Theatre occupied all his time. Relations between Burbage and Brayne rapidly deteriorated, apparently because the former cheated his partner, and the ensuing lawsuits outlived Brayne and his widow. A deal with Henry Lanman made the Curtain playhouse 'an Esore' to the Theatre, possibly a means of selling the Curtain to Burbage and Brayne. Burbage died shortly after the frustration of his plan to move the Chamberlain's Men—led by his son Richard—into his new Blackfriars playhouse. *GE*

Burbage, Richard (1568–1619), the leading actor of Shakespeare's company, son of playhouse builder James Burbage, and younger brother to Cuthbert Burbage. Richard and Cuthbert held shares in the playhouses built by their father, but only Richard followed his father in becoming an actor. Richard's acting career began in the mid-1580s but around 1590 he was still playing minor parts, if the entrance for 'Burbage a messenger' in the 'plot' of *The Dead Man's Fortune* refers to him. The more important roles of Gorboduc and Tereus are assigned to Richard Burbage in the 'plot' of *2 Seven Deadly Sins*, but this is difficult to date. With the settlement of the Chamberlain's Men at the Theatre, his father's playhouse, in 1594 his fame rapidly increased. On 15 March 1595 Shakespeare, William Kempe, and Richard Burbage were paid for Chamberlain's Men performances given at court the previous December. Ben Jonson recorded Richard Burbage as an actor in his 1616 folio texts of *Every Man out of his Humour* (1600) and *Every Man in his Humour*

Richard Burbage, Shakespeare's leading actor: this painting, now at the Dulwich Picture Gallery, is thought to be a self-portrait.

(1601) which were first performed in 1598–9. When his fellow King's Man Augustine Phillips made a will on 4 May 1605, Richard Burbage was appointed as an executor, and in Shakespeare's will, written on 25 March 1616, Richard Burbage, John Heminges, and Henry Condell were each left 26*s.* 8*d.* to buy a ring.

Allusions to Richard Burbage's acting talent continued long after his death in 1619. A funeral elegy exists in a number of manuscript versions from shortly after his death, which despite some differences generally agree upon these lines:

No more young Hamlett, ould Heironymoe.
Kind Leer, the greued Moore, and more beside.
That liued in him, haue now for ever dy'de.
Oft haue I seene him leap into the graue,
Suiting the person which he seem'd to haue
Of a sadd louer with soe true an eye,
Thar theer I would haue sworne, he meant to dye.

The roles named here are presumably from Shakespeare's *Hamlet*, *King Lear*, and *Othello* ('the grieved Moor'), and Thomas Kyd's *The Spanish Tragedy* (*c.*1592), in which Hieronimo revenges his son's murder. The title page of the first edition of John Webster's *The Duchess of Malfi* (1623) gives Richard Burbage the part of Ferdinand, and the third printing of John Marston's *The Malcontent* (1604) has a comic induction during which Richard Burbage is identified as the actor playing Malevole. These are the only roles of which we can be certain, but the plenitude of commendations of his talent, and his seniority within the Chamberlain-King's Men makes it likely that he took leading roles in all of Shakespeare's plays from the opening of the Globe in 1599 until his retirement in the mid-1610s.

Some time before 7 October 1601 Richard Burbage married his wife Winifred, for on that day she consulted the quack doctor and astrologer Simon Forman. In his will of 3 June 1623 Nicholas Tooley referred to Richard Burbage as 'my late M[aste]r', which indicates that Tooley was Burbage's apprentice. As well as being an actor, Richard Burbage was an accomplished painter and for the Earl of Rutland's participation in the King's Accession Day tilt in 1613, Burbage painted a commemorative impresa to which Shakespeare added the motto, and for which each of them received 44*s.* *GE*

Baldwin, T. W., *The Organization and Personnel of the Shakespearean Company* (1927)

Bentley, Gerald Eades, *The Jacobean and Caroline Stage*, ii: *Dramatic Companies and Players* (7 vols., 1941)

Edmond, Mary, 'Yeomen, Citizens, Gentlemen and Players: The Burbages and their Connections', in R. B. Parker and S. P. Zitner (eds.), *Elizabethan Theater: Essays in Honor of S. Schoenbaum* (1996)

Honigmann, E. A. J., and Brock, Susan, *Playhouse Wills 1558–1642: An Edition of Wills by Shakespeare and his Contemporaries in the London Theatre* (1992)

Ingram, William, 'The Early Career of James Burbage', in C. E. McGee (ed.), *The Elizabethan Theatre x: Papers Given at the Tenth International Conference on Elizabethan Theatre Held at the University of Waterloo, Ontario, in July 1983* (1988)

Burby, Cuthbert. See PRINTING AND PUBLISHING.

Burdett-Coutts portrait, half-length, oil, named after its early 20th-century owner Burdett-Coutts. Also known as the Felton portrait after its 19th-century owner, this representation was discovered in 1792 and was (dubiously) claimed to be an original for *Droeshout's engraving by M. H. Spielmann in 1906. *CT*

Burgess, Anthony (John Burgess Wilson) (1917–93), English writer, who fancied descent from the Jack Wilson reported as singing in *Much Ado About Nothing*. *Nothing Like the Sun* (1964) fictionally recreates Shakespeare's sex life, seeming to attribute his genius to the inflammatory inspiration of syphilis. His biography of Shakespeare appeared in 1970. In *Enderby's Dark Lady* (1984), the eponymous hero prepares a libretto for a Shakespeare musical. In a climactic scene, the *Droeshout portrait comes to life, a 'talking woodcut'. *TM*

Burgh, Hubert de. See HUBERT.

Burgundy, Duke of. **(1)** He abandons his suit to marry *Cordelia after she has lost her dowry in the first scene of *King Lear.* **(2)** He arranges the Treaty of Troyes in *Henry V* 5.2. In *1 Henry VI* he allies with Talbot, 2.1, but is won round by Joan la Pucelle to the French side, 3.7. *AB*

burlesques and travesties of Shakespeare's plays. Lines from Shakespeare were parodied in his own time, but the first full-scale travesty is Thomas *Duffett's *The Mock-Tempest; or, The Enchanted Castle*, of 1674, in which Prospero's island becomes a brothel. Vigorous, amusing, and obscene, it burlesques a current production of Thomas Shadwell's operatic version of the Dryden–Davenant adaptation. Individual passages were frequently parodied during the 18th century, as in Arthur Murphy's *Life of Hamlet with Alterations* (1772), based on the ghost scenes, in which Shakespeare appears to complain of Garrick's alterations, but the heyday of burlesques employing the full framework of a play—and of theatrical burlesque in general—came in the 19th century. Travesties of *Hamlet*, *Othello*, and *Romeo and Juliet* had appeared in Vienna around the turn of the century, and in 1810 John Poole's *Hamlet Travestie*, with 'Burlesque Annotations, after the manner of Dr Johnson and Geo. Steevens Esq., and the various Commentators', was published in London. Frequently reprinted and performed, it was used for satire of *Irving as late as 1874. Poole parodies and paraphrases the play in rhymed couplets, including songs set to popular airs. Imitations include Richard Gurney's *Romeo and Juliet Travestie* (1812), the anonymous *Macbeth*, printed in *Accepted Addresses*, and *Othello Travestie* (both 1813), and an unpublished *Richard III* (1815), the first burlesque known to have been written directly for the theatre, which ends with a chorus and dance of ghosts. Other versions of the same play followed, in 1816 and 1823.

Charles Selby's *Othello, the Moor of Fleet Street* (1833) inaugurated a new phase of theatrical burlesques, many of them never published. Maurice Dowling's deplorable *Othello Travestie* (Liverpool, 1834) was so popular when given at the Strand in London that it helped to establish that theatre as a home of burlesque. The merry finale of his *Romeo and Juliet* (1837), based on Garrick's version, imitates that of Rossini's opera *La Cenerentola.* Other versions of the tragedies followed; Edward Blanchard's unpublished *Merchant of Venice* (1842) is the first to be based on a comedy. Charles Selby's *Kinge Richard ye Third* (1845), successful in America as well as England, includes a 'Gigantic Equestrian Pageant'; at the end Richard comes to life and begs the audience's favour in a finale set to 'Yankee Doodle'.

Burlesques during this period included many theatrical and other topical allusions, and around this time the pun, beloved of Victorian humorists, becomes a dominant source of comic effect. In Francis Talfourd's undergraduate jape *Macbeth Travestie* (1847) Macbeth and Banquo enter under an umbrella to be greeted by the witches with 'Hail! Hail! Hail!' Asking, 'What mean these salutations, noble thane?', Macbeth is told, 'These showers of "Hail" anticipate your "reign".' In London performances Macbeth was played by Frederick Robson, finest of burlesque actors, who scored his greatest success in Talfourd's *Shylock; or, The Merchant of Venice Preserved* (1849). Queen Victoria attended a performance in 1860, and the piece succeeded in America.

The Enchanted Isle (1848), by William and Robert Brough, treats *The Tempest* with new freedom, creating an extravaganza rather than a line-by-line travesty. William Brough's skilful and charming *Perdita; or, The Royal Milkmaid* (1856), a direct send-up of Charles *Kean's production of *The Winter's Tale*, includes a 'Grand Ballet' that achieved independent fame. Andrew Halliday's *Romeo and Juliet Travestie; or, The Cup of Cold Poison* (1859) starred Marie Wilton (Lady Bancroft), the most admired female burlesque performer of the century. The Nurse is conflated with *Dickens's Mrs Gamp, the Apothecary has a drunk scene, and in the balcony scene the lovers catch cold—'Swear not by the boon—the inconstant boon.'

The all-dancing finale to Robert and William Brough's burlesque *The Enchanted Isle; or, Raising the Wind*, 1848. Visible are Ariel ('a magic page from Shakespeare's magic volume'), Alonso, Ferdinand (played by Miss Woolgar), Miranda ('the original Miss Robinson Crusoe'), and Prospero.

Later burlesques slacken still further the relationship with the original play, and are increasingly written for amateurs, like the anonymous *Hamlet! The Ravin' Prince of Denmark!! or, The Baltic Swell!!! and the Diving Belle!!!!* (1866), heavily indebted to Poole, and full of theatrical allusions, some entirely serious. F. C. Burnand, author of *Antony and Cleopatra, or, His-tory and Her-story in a Modern Nilometre* (1866), edited *Punch* from 1880 to 1906; in his subsequent *The Rise and Fall of Richard!!!; or, A New Front to an Old Dicky* (1868) the pun is predictably rampant. The Duchess of York travesties Macbeth with 'Hang up my bonnet in the outer hall!', and Catesby and Tyrrell fall over a coal scuttle to provoke the comment 'Oh! they're more shinned against than shinning.'

This is the last major burlesque of the professional Victorian theatre. W. S. Gilbert's *Rosencrantz and Guildenstern* originally appeared in the magazine *Fun*, stimulated by Henry *Irving's sensational success in the role at the Lyceum. It contains little direct parody. Ophelia, loved by Rosencrantz, describes Hamlet in lines that glance at the oddities of actors and the disagreements of scholars:

> Some men hold
> That he's the sanest, far, of all sane men—
> Some that he's really sane, but shamming mad—
> Some that he's really mad, but shamming sane—
> Some that he will be mad—some that he *was*—
> Some that he couldn't be. But on the whole,
> (As far as I can make out what they mean)
> The favourite theory's somewhat like this:
> Hamlet is idiotically sane
> With lucid intervals of lunacy.

Hamlet is finally consigned to the Lyceum. Gilbert's play, reprinted in 1890, was acted in 1891 and again, in revised form, in 1892, when Beerbohm Tree was the special object of satire. It has been successfully revived.

Late 19th-century specimens, mostly written for amateurs and unpublished, are of decreasing interest. On the English professional stage, burlesque and extravaganza yielded to musical comedy, of which they are a forerunner. They lasted a little longer in America. Burlesques written specifically for performance by 'negro minstrels'—usually white men in black face—were popular in both continents during the middle years of the century. John Brougham's *Much Ado About a Merchant of Venice* (1868) abounds in local and topical allusions, and also contains serious social comment. *The New Version of Shakespeare's Masterpiece of 'Hamlet'* (1870) burlesqued Edwin Booth's famous performances. Later American burlesques include Charles Soule's *New Travesty on Romeo and Juliet* (1877), performed by the University Club of St Louis, and his *Hamlet Revamped* (1879), announced as 'A Travesty without a Pun'. More original is John Kendrick Bangs's *Katherine* (1888), the longest of the travesties and the only one of *The Taming of the Shrew*, notable mainly for lyrics imitative of W. S. Gilbert: 'For he's going to marry the shrew, hoo-hoo', 'Two little dudes from Pisa we', and so on. It was given a sumptuous charity performance at the Metropolitan Opera, New York, when the young soldiers for whom it was written were assisted by a church choir of 75 voices. A critic objected that 'our young men are growing up in a sufficiently light-voiced and effeminate groove without the factitious aid of corsets, crinoline and lingerie'. *SW*

Wells, S. (ed.), *Nineteenth-Century Shakespeare Burlesques* (5 vols., 1977)

Burton, Richard (1925–84), British actor. Born Richard Jenkins in a Welsh mining village he took the surname of the teacher and broadcaster who became his surrogate father. As an undergraduate in wartime Oxford he played Angelo in *Measure for Measure* and in 1951 excited Stratford audiences as Prince Hal and Henry V in the Shakespearian tetralogy. Between 1953 and 1956 at the *Old Vic he was hailed as the leading young classical actor of his generation, playing Hamlet, the Bastard in *King John*, Sir Toby Belch, Coriolanus, Caliban, and Henry V as well as alternating with John Neville as Iago and Othello. He subsequently became one of the highest-paid international film stars, marrying, divorcing, and remarrying Elizabeth Taylor and gaining a reputation for drinking and wildness. In 1964 on Broadway he played Hamlet in a production by John *Gielgud which is preserved on film. He made over 50 movies including *The Taming of the Shrew* (1967) directed by Franco *Zeffirelli and co-starring Elizabeth Taylor. *MJ*

Bragg, Melvyn, *Rich: The life of Richard Burton* (1988)

Busby, John. See PRINTING AND PUBLISHING.

Bushy. See GREEN.

Butcher, Dick the. He is a sceptical but bloodthirsty follower of Cade in *The First Part of the Contention* (*2 Henry VI*). *AB*

'But shall I go mourn for that', sung by Autolycus in *The Winter's Tale* 4.3.15. The earliest known setting is by J. F. Lampe, published *c.*1745. *JB*

Butter, Nathaniel. See IMPRINT; PRINTING AND PUBLISHING.

Butts, Dr. He draws Henry's attention to Cranmer who has been refused entry to the council chamber, *All Is True* (*Henry VIII*) 5.2. *AB*

Byam Shaw, Glen (1904–86), British director and administrator. A successful actor and teacher of acting who had never much enjoyed being on stage, he returned from war service to work at the short-lived but influential Old Vic Theatre School and with a company aiming at new audiences, the Young Vic, for which he directed his first wintry *As You Like It*. From 1952 he was co-director with Anthony *Quayle of the Shakespeare Memorial Theatre at Stratford and sole director 1956–9. He continued Quayle's policy of engaging accomplished players. His own productions were strong on narrative. They were never showy but always centred on the actors—Peggy *Ashcroft as Rosalind and Cleopatra, Michael *Redgrave as Antony. He also encouraged young directors like Peter *Hall, his chosen successor. People recall his old-fashioned courtesy. He made a rare appearance as the colonel regretting the loss of empire in the film *Look Back in Anger* (1959). *MJ*

Beauman, Sally, *The Royal Shakespeare Company: A History of Ten Decades* (1982)

Byrd, William (1543–1623), composer. The dominating musical figure in England during much of Shakespeare's life; he seems to have composed little after his last publication in 1611. *JB*

Byron, George Gordon, Lord (1788–1824), English poet. Byron's explicit rejection of Shakespeare as a dramatic model ('the worst of models—though the most extraordinary of writers') belies the saturation of Shakespearian phrasing in his dramas, and his characteristically *Romantic investment in an overreaching Macbeth and a reflective, volatile Hamlet, most visibly reworked in *Manfred* (1817) and *Don Juan* (1819–24). *NJW*

Cade, Jack. A rebel leader, Cade is slain by Iden (*The First Part of the Contention (2 Henry* VI) 4.10). Shakespeare largely follows *Holinshed's account of the rebellion. *AB*

'Cadwal' is the name given to Arviragus by Belarius in *Cymbeline.* *AB*

Caesar, Julius (102–44 BC), dictator of Rome. See JULIUS CAESAR. *AB*

Caesar, Octavius (63 BC–AD 14). In *Julius Caesar* he becomes one of the triumvirs after the murder of Caesar, and in *Antony and Cleopatra* after eliminating the other triumvirs he assumes sole leadership of the Roman Empire. *AB*

caesura, a pause within a line of verse, often coinciding with a break between clauses or sentences. In English iambic pentameter (unlike classical verse), a caesura or phrasal break may fall after any syllable from the first to the ninth. *CB*

caesura, epic (feminine). Within an iambic pentameter line, epic caesura is a phrasal break preceded by an extra unstressed syllable. Older (mainly 15th-century) poets used this pattern as a standard variation, but most 16th-century poets avoided it. Shakespeare, too, avoids it in his poems but uses it fairly frequently in his middle and later plays, evidently to vary and complicate the metrical design:

> Stealing and giv | ing odour. | Enough, no more
> (*Twelfth Night*, 1.1.7)

GTW

Cahiers élisabéthains, the chief French journal of late medieval and English Renaissance studies, was launched in 1972. It is published by the Centre d'Études et de Recherches sur la Renaissance Anglaise (Université Paul-Valéry, Montpellier, France) and is intended as a link between scholars working in its field in France and those working elsewhere in the world. An international editorial board screens submissions. Nearly all texts are written in English: abstracts in both French and English are systematically included. Two numbers are published each year, including articles, notes, and reviews of relevant critical works, theatre performances, and films. *J-MM*

Caithness, Thane of. He marches against Macbeth, *Macbeth* Act 5. *AB*

Caius is one of Titus' kinsmen in *Titus Andronicus* (mute part). *AB*

'Caius'. See KENT, EARL OF.

Caius, Dr. He is a French physician in love with Anne Page in *The Merry Wives of Windsor.* *AB*

Caius Cassius. See CASSIUS, CAIUS.

Caius Ligarius. See LIGARIUS, CAIUS.

Caius Lucius. See LUCIUS, CAIUS.

Caius Marius, The History and Fall of. First performed in 1679, Thomas Otway's play is heavily and explicitly indebted to *Romeo and Juliet*, transferring its action to the Roman civil wars of Marius and Sylla. Shakespeare's love story serves as a tragic sub-plot to Otway's depiction of the struggle between the patricians Metellus and Sylla and the plebeians' leader Marius: Marius' son is in love with Metellus' daughter Lavinia, to whom he was betrothed before Metellus defected to Sylla's rival faction, and they marry in secret despite their parents' enmity. ('O Marius, Marius, wherefore art thou Marius?', wonders Lavinia.) Although Young Marius and Lavinia are more blameless than their Shakespearian counterparts (they fall in love in compliance with their parents' original wishes, and he kills no Tybalt), they finish up in the tomb just the same, and Otway enhances the pathos of their deaths by having Lavinia awaken before Young Marius has finished dying of the poison so that they can enjoy one last brief and tormented interview. Otway's play was still being revived at intervals as late as the 1760s, and its final dialogue between the lovers was imitated in acting texts of *Romeo and Juliet* from its return to the repertory in the 1740s until well into the 19th century. *MD*

Dobson, Michael, *The Making of the National Poet* (1992)

Munns, Jessica, *Restoration Politics and Drama: The Plays of Thomas Otway* (1995)

Owen, Susan, *Restoration Theatre and Crisis* (1996)

Calchas, father of Cressida, is a Trojan priest who has defected to the Greeks in *Troilus and Cressida.* *AB*

calendar, Shakespeare's. Protestant countries, including England, still used the Julian calendar (established by Julius Caesar) in Shakespeare's day, though Catholic countries had accepted the more accurate 'New Style' Gregorian calendar in 1582 (named after Pope Gregory XIII). Consequently dates were the subject of debate, particularly the date of Easter, which was five weeks apart for Catholics and Protestants by 1599. Britain and its colonies only converted to the Gregorian calendar in 1752. At the same time New Year's Day was moved from 25 March (the feast of the Annunciation and Lady Day) to 1 January (a date which had been originally rejected by Christians because it was associated with a celebration of the god Janus). In Shakespeare's day the date of the year changed in March not January.

The following list gives the dates of festivals and other significant days, many of which are no longer celebrated, mentioned by Shakespeare in his plays.

Twelfth Night—6 January

The last day of the Christmas festival was an opportunity for carnivalesque misrule: carousing, practical jokes, and ribald impersonation of authority figures (elements which appear in *Twelfth Night*).

St Valentine's Day—14 February

Valentine's Day was traditionally associated with the pairing of birds, and is mentioned in this context in *A Midsummer Night's Dream* 4.1.138 (see also *Chaucer's *The Parliament of Fowls* (?1381)). In Elizabethan England it was celebrated with games and an atmosphere of sexual opportunity (as expressed in one of Ophelia's songs, *Hamlet* 4.5.47). It is probably no coincidence that the ancient Roman festival of Lupercalia, also a celebration of fertility, was held on the same day or thereabouts. The *Luperci* would gather in a sacred cave, sacrifice goats, and clothe themselves in the goats' skins from which they also made straps. They ran down the Palatine Hill striking anyone they met with their straps: being struck was supposed to cure infertility in women. *Julius Caesar* 1.2 is set during the celebration of Lupercalia.

Ides of March

Instead of using weeks the Romans divided their months in an irregular way originally based on the phases of the moon. Ides, from *iduare*, 'to divide', occurred in the middle of the month, on the 13th or 15th day, according to the length of the month, and originally represented the period during the full moon. Caesar is told to 'Beware the ides of March', *Julius Caesar* 1.2.20.

Dates associated with Easter

As it is today, Easter was a movable feast. In Elizabethan times the first of the dates associated with Easter, Shrove Tuesday, could fall as early as 3 February or as late as 9 March. The earliest possible date for Easter itself was 25 March. Shrove Tuesday, or Pancake Day, as it is still popularly known, is mentioned in *All's Well That Ends Well* 2.2.22–3. Shrovetide, mentioned in *2 Henry IV* 5.3.36., is the period of the few days before *Lent, when feasting and sports were customary (including football matches between villages, as at Easter). Ash Wednesday is the day after Shrove Tuesday and the beginning of fasting and abstinence of the 40-day period of Lent (ending on Easter Monday). It is mentioned in *The Merchant of Venice* 2.5.26. Friday of Easter week, Good Friday, is mentioned as a day of fasting, *King John* 1.1.235, *1 Henry IV* 1.2.114. Ascension Day is the 40th day after Easter: 'Holy Thursday'. Peter of Pomfret says John must give up his crown 'ere the next Ascension Day at noon', *King John* 4.2.151. The week succeeding the seventh Sunday after Easter, Whitsun, was a time for sports and games (especially morris dancing) and carousing (even in the churchyard itself, hence the term 'church ale'). Whitsun is mentioned: *The Winter's Tale* 4.4.134; *Henry V* 2.4.25; and is pronounced 'Wheeson' by Mistress Quickly in *2 Henry IV* 2.1.91.

May Day—1 May

Morris dancing, decorating and dancing round the maypole, the election of a summer King and Queen, and general frolicking in the woods (particularly among young people) were popular May Day activities. May Day morris dancing is mentioned in *All's Well That Ends Well* 2.2.23 and dramatized in *The Two Noble Kinsmen* 3.5; May Day morning is mentioned in *All Is True* (*Henry VIII*) 5.3.14.

Midsummer—24 June

The 24th of June was celebrated as the summer solstice (though it was actually 12 June then and 21 June now) and the feast of St John the Baptist. Midsummer is mentioned in *As You Like It* (4.1.95) and *1 Henry IV* (4.1.103), as well as in *A Midsummer Night's Dream.* Olivia says that Malvolio suffers from 'midsummer madness', *Twelfth Night* 3.4.54, referring to the revelry, magic, and atmosphere of disorientation that was associated with the moon at the summer solstice.

Lammas—1 August

Lammas Eve, the day before Lammas, is mentioned as Juliet's birthday, *Romeo and Juliet* 1.3.19. Lammastide, the season of Lammas, is mentioned in *Romeo and Juliet* 1.3.16. Lammas is from the Anglo-Saxon *hlaf-maesse*, 'loaf mass' —it was originally a harvest festival, but by Elizabethan times was merely the date on which pastures were opened for common grazing.

St Bartholomew's Day—24 August

Bartholomew-tide is mentioned in *Henry V* 5.2.306 as the hottest day of summer.

Holy-rood Day—14 September

It is mentioned in *1 Henry IV* 1.1.52 as the day of the battle between Hotspur and Douglas. Holy-rood Day was a festival commemorating the exaltation of Christ's cross after its recovery from the Persians by Heraclius in AD 628, but by Shakespeare's day was principally associated with the custom of 'going a-nutting'—like May Day, an opportunity for young people to meet in the woods.

St Lambert's Day—17 September

The day is mentioned in *Richard II* 1.1.199 as the date set by Richard for Bolingbroke and Mowbray's combat.

Michaelmas—29 September

The festival of St Michael and All Angels is mentioned in *1 Henry IV* 2.5.53 as Francis's birthday; and in *The Merry Wives of Windsor* 1.1.188 (see also Allhallowmas). It was the day on which the universities of Oxford and Cambridge and the law schools and courts of London began their terms. As with Lammas, by the Elizabethan period most of the customs associated with this day had lapsed, though it remained a time for hiring servants, initiating lawsuits, signing contracts, and harvesting and selling crops.

All Hallows Eve—31 October

The eve of All Saints is mentioned in *Measure for Measure* 2.1.121. In Shakespeare's day games were organized in order to ward off the spirits of the dead and exploit the magic associated with this night.

Allhallowmas/Hallowmas—1 November

The feast of All Saints. Simple says Allhallowmas falls a fortnight before Michaelmas (29 September), either having confused it with Holy-rood Day (14 September), or having confused Martinmas (11 November) with Michaelmas, *The Merry Wives of Windsor* 1.1.187. Prince Harry calls *Oldcastle 'All-hallown summer', *1 Henry IV* 1.2.156, a term referring to a spell of fine weather in late autumn. 'Hallowmas' and 'Hollowmas' are abbreviated forms of 'Allhallowmas', mentioned in *Two Gentlemen of Verona* 2.1.24; and *Measure for Measure* 2.1.120. Richard compares Hallowmas to the 'short'st of day' *Richard II* 5.1.80. Because of discrepancies in the Julian calendar the winter solstice was ten days earlier than it is now, consequently this made rather more sense in Shakespeare's day than it does in ours.

All Souls' Day—2 November

Catholics offer prayers for the dead on All Souls' Day, and it is the day of Buckingham's doom, *Richard III* 5.1.

St Martin's Day/Martinmas—11 November

Joan la Pucelle means a spell of unseasonably fine weather when she refers to 'Saint Martin's summer' *1 Henry VI* 1.3.110. Martlemas is another term for 'Martinmas'. Poins calls Falstaff 'Martlemas' *2 Henry IV* 2.2.95, perhaps alluding to St Martin's summer (compare Prince Harry's 'All-hallown summer'); or to Martinmas beef, fattened for slaughter by that date. *AB*

Barber, C. L., *Shakespeare's Festive Comedy* (1959)

Hutton, Ronald, *The Rise and Fall of Merry England: The Ritual Year 1400–1700* (1994)

Laroque, François, *Shakespeare's Festive World: Elizabethan Seasonal Entertainment and the Professional Stage* (1991; 1st pub. in French 1988)

Richards, E. G., *Mapping Time: The Calendar and its History* (1999; 1st edn. 1998)

Sohmer, Steve, *Shakespeare's Mystery Play: The Opening of the Globe Theatre, 1599* (1999)

Stokes, Francis Griffin, *Who's Who in Shakespeare* (1992; 1st edn. 1924)

Calhern, Louis (1895–1956), American actor-director who progressed from undistinguished stage work to a high-profile career in film (playing the title role in the 1953 MGM film of *Julius Caesar*), returning to the theatre occasionally, including *King Lear* in 1950. *RF*

Caliban. Long before the action of *The Tempest* begins, Prospero arrives on the island to find its sole inhabitant, the son of the deceased witch Sycorax. At first their relationship is harmonious: Caliban loves Prospero and shows him 'all the qualities o'th'isle' (1.2.339); and Prospero treats him 'with human care' (1.2.348) and teaches him language. However, when Caliban attempts to rape Miranda, Prospero enslaves him. During the course of the play Caliban offers his services to Trinculo and Stefano, who he mistakenly believes will be able to help him vanquish Prospero.

Critics, audiences, writers, and artists have shared a long fascination with Caliban. In the *Dryden/Davenant adaptation the low comedy of Caliban's situation was given extra impact by the addition of a female version of him, a sister. Later generations have been more interested in the tragedy of his situation: his occasionally beautiful language and miserable situation seem to invite sympathy despite his ugly appearance and violent intentions. In the last two decades of the 20th century criticism and theatre productions have often seen Caliban as a native islander. To be precise, however, he is a second-generation immigrant and the mythologies and psychology of Europeans are just as important as postcolonial perspectives in the debate over his identity. *AB*

'Calin o custure me', a *ballad tune title, probably Gaelic in origin, quoted by Pistol in *Henry v* 4.4.4. *JB*

Calpurnia is Caesar's wife in *Julius Caesar*. Frightened by a dream and ill portents she tries to persuade him not to go to the Capitol, 2.2. *AB*

Calvert, Charles (1828–79), actor, born in London. His early engagements included Southampton (1853–4, Romeo and Laertes with his future wife Adelaide Biddles as Juliet and Ophelia) and the Surrey (1855–6, Hal, Othello), but it was with *Hamlet* (1859) at the Theatre Royal, Manchester, that Calvert showed his ability to co-ordinate all the arts of the theatre in the service of the play. At the Prince's theatre, Manchester, between 1864 and 1874, he mounted eleven major Shakespeare revivals, of which *Richard III* and *Henry V* were transferred to New York.

A disciple of Charles *Kean, Calvert upheld the principles of pictorial Shakespeare and showed his intelligence and originality as an actor in his sympathetic Shylock and thoughtful Henry v. *RF*

Foulkes, Richard, *The Calverts: Actors of Some Importance* (1992)

Calvert, Louis (1859–1923), English actor-manager who upheld the Shakespearian tradition of his parents Charles and Adelaide Calvert. His career encompassed the diversity of Shakespearian staging on both sides of the Atlantic—and beyond—for half a century. Calvert acted with *Benson and *Tree, assisting the latter with his ambitious revival of *Julius Caesar* (1898), as he did Richard Flanagan with his sumptuous Shakespearian productions in Manchester where—in contrast—Calvert also staged *Richard II* (1895) in the Elizabethan style for the Manchester branch of the Independent Theatre. In 1909 Calvert was recruited for the ill-fated New Theatre, New York, where his production of *The Winter's Tale* (1910) prefigured *Granville-Barker's. Calvert remained in America, contributing an Elizabethan-style *The Tempest* to the Shakespeare tercentenary of 1916, but devoting himself increasingly to training actors in the traditions of Shakespearian acting, about which he wrote in *Problems of the Actor* (1918). *RF*

Sir Herbert Beerbohm Tree as Caliban, 1904. Tree played Caliban as a sensitive, potentially noble creature, a tragic missing link.

'Cambio'. See LUCENTIO.

Cambridge, Richard, Earl of. He is Richard Plantagenet (d. 1415), father of the Duke of York of the *Henry VI* plays. His plot with Henry le Scrope (3rd Baron of Masham, eldest son of Sir Stephen Scrope) and Sir Thomas Grey is discovered and they are sent to execution, *Henry V* 2.2. *AB*

Cambridge Shakespeare. *The Works of William Shakespeare* (1863–6), edited by William

George Clark, with at first W. Aldis Wright and later John Glover as collaborators, was published in nine volumes by Macmillan, but printed at the University Press, so that it became known as the Cambridge Shakespeare. This important edition was based on a 'thorough collation of the four Folios and of all the Quarto editions of the separate plays, and of subsequent editions and commentaries' (preface), so that in textual matters it constitutes a virtual variorum. Prefaces provide accounts of the early textual history of each of the works, and the volumes include the texts of first quartos of *Hamlet* and *Romeo and Juliet*, as well as the quartos relating to *Henry v*, *The First Part of the Contention* (*2 Henry vi*), and *Richard Duke of York* (*3 Henry vi*). Clark and Wright used the Cambridge edition as the basis for the influential one-volume *Globe Shakespeare. Both the Cambridge and the Globe editions were revised in 1891. *RAF*

Cambridge Shakespeare, New (1984, in progress). This edition is a replacement for the *New Shakespeare, completed in 1966. Whereas the New Shakespeare was edited by British scholars, the New Cambridge Shakespeare has recruited editors from other countries, especially the United States. The series aims to reflect 'current critical interests' and to be attentive 'to the realisation of the plays on the stage, and to their social and cultural settings', according to the first general editor, Philip Brockbank. The volumes are handsomely printed, with notes and collations on the same page as the text. The well-illustrated critical introductions in the first volumes added a separate stage history, but some later introductions have sought to integrate commentary on stage and film performances into critical accounts of the plays. Textual problems are treated in a 'Textual Analysis' that follows the text, as in the New Shakespeare. Beginning in 1994 with the first quarto of *King Lear*, the series is adding critical editions of the early quartos. It began to appear roughly at the same time as, and in competition with, the *Oxford Shakespeare. *RAF*

Cambridge University's major resource for the study of Shakespeare is the collection at Trinity College presented in 1799 by Edward *Capell of Shakespeare editions used in the preparation of his own edition of 1768 and his *Notes and Readings* (1774, 1779–83). *SLB*

Camden, William (1551–1623), antiquarian, historian, and teacher. Born in London, Camden was a distinguished compiler of British history and a gifted headmaster of Westminster School who won his pupil Ben Jonson's unreserved praise. Having written *Britannia* (1586), he drew partly on that work for *Remains of a Greater Work Concerning Britain* (1605), in which he glances at modern poets. In a list of nine 'pregnant wits', Camden merely cites Shakespeare's name, but on more congenial antiquarian ground, he explores the name's antecedents and variants: 'Strong-shield' or 'Breake-speare, Shake-Speare, Shotbolt, Wagstaffe'. *PH*

Camidius is given command of Antony's land army, *Antony and Cleopatra* 3.7.57–9. *AB*

Camillo, a lord at Leontes' court, helps Polixenes escape and is eventually betrothed to Paulina, *The Winter's Tale* 5.3.144–7. *AB*

Campeius, Cardinal. Sent by the Pope, he, with Wolsey, considers King Henry's proposed divorce of Katherine, *All Is True* (*Henry viii*) 2.4. *AB*

Campion, Thomas (1567–1620). He wrote three masques, and published four *Bookes of Ayres* (1610–17). Campion's *Lord's Masque*, commissioned by the Howards for Princess Elizabeth's wedding celebrations (1612–13), contains a moment reminiscent of Shakespeare's *Winter's Tale*, also performed at Elizabeth's wedding, when a row of women-statues step alive from their niches. *CS*

Canada has most often employed Shakespeare as a bulwark against other traditions or cultures. In English Canada, Shakespeare served as protection against the incursions of American commercialism; in French Canada, against imported French vaudevilles.

Despite the burden of wholesomeness imposed both by English-Scots Puritanism and French Roman Catholicism, there has been a nearly unbroken tradition of playing Shakespeare since at least the 18th century. The genealogy of Shakespeare productions may be traced back to two significant roots: British soldiers and touring companies. After the Conquest (1763), British soldiers staged plays to relieve the tedium of garrison life. However, most Shakespeare in the 18th century and up to 1914 was supplied by touring companies and such actors as Edmund *Kean, William Charles *Macready, Ellen *Terry, Tommaso *Salvini, Sarah *Bernhardt, and James O'Neill.

In the 1840s, Shakespeare societies sprang up to fill a variety of cultural needs, including self-improvement. Ladies' clubs admired Shakespeare for his creation of strong female characters; gentlemen lionized Shakespeare, the self-made man. Fuelled by British patriotism and fear of American domination, later societies (such as that founded in Toronto in the 20th century), celebrated Shakespeare's birthday, organized reading groups and competitive recitations, and occasionally produced his plays.

A wider assimilation of Shakespeare came through provincial regulation of educational institutions, where excerpts, then plays, were used as rhetorical training in schools. By the 1860s in Ontario, and shortly thereafter at all other Canadian universities, Shakespeare was firmly in place as the keystone of the honours English undergraduate programme. Canadian Shakespearian scholarship was launched with Sir Daniel Wilson's *Caliban: The Missing Link* (1873), but acquired eminence only with the extensive theoretical, interpretative, and editorial work of Northrop *Frye.

The real explosion of interest in Shakespeare, both in English and French Canada, occurred after 1945 and coincided with the growth of cities, the influx of many immigrant groups, the rapid development of technology, and debates about national identity and culture. Between 1944 and 1955, the Canadian Broadcasting Corporation presented over 60 radio adaptations of Shakespeare, including the first ever complete and chronologically arranged performance of Shakespeare's English history plays (1953–4).

Undoubtedly a major event was the creation of the Stratford Festival in Stratford, Ontario (1953), at the initiative of businessman Tom Patterson, who recruited British director Tyrone *Guthrie. Once a tent affair, the Stratford Festival is now the largest classical theatre in North America. Its inaugural production, *Richard iii* with Alec *Guinness, was greeted with wild enthusiasm and set high standards. Michael Langham's *Henry v* (1957), in which French-Canadians played the French, suggested that a unique Canadian Shakespeare might be possible. Instead, the Festival's British roots led to a dependency upon 'hired hands'—British and American directors and actors. Experimental productions gave way to an increasingly Hollywood-like emphasis on costumes, props, and gimmicks. On the whole, Stratford's influence has been architectural rather than theatrical; its thrust stage became the model for, among others, the Olivier auditorium at the National Theatre in London, and the Chichester Festival Theatre in Sussex.

While some scholars claim that the distinctiveness of Canadian Shakespeare lies in the 'conversational vitality' of its Shakespearian language, said to lack the 'operatic excesses' of the English and the 'harshness' of the American, others find distinctiveness elsewhere: for example, in Canadians' preference for Shakespeare paired with a beautiful landscape. Since the 1980s, boisterous summer Shakespeare is found not only *a mare usque ad mare* (Wolfville, Halifax, St John's, Montreal, Toronto, Saskatoon, Victoria, Vancouver, and, briefly, Ottawa), but also by the sea, in a park, or on a golf course.

In Quebec, 'Le grand Will' was historically neither part of the school curriculum nor part of the repertoire of local professional acting companies. Not translated into Québécois until 1968 by Jean-Louis Roux, Shakespeare was, in the next two decades, usually confined to being

The influential open stage of the Stratford Festival Theatre, Ontario, opened in 1953: Robin Phillips's 1977 *Richard III*, with Brian Bedford as Richard.

a vehicle, parodic or legitimizing, of cultural nationalism. Shakespeare's political face may be clearly seen in Robert Gurik's *Hamlet, prince du Québec* (1968), an allegory on Quebec politics with Hamlet as Québec, Claudius as l'Anglophonie (the English economic and political power), Gertrude as the Church in an unholy alliance with Ottawa, and the Ghost as Charles de Gaulle.

By the 1990s, Quebec became more comfortable with Shakespeare. Director/playwright /actor Robert *Lepage turned many times to Shakespeare in his explorations into multimedia, sexuality, and the act of creation itself. Alexandre Hausvater staged a cabaret-style *Lear* (1990) starring a mortally ill actor, whose visible pain and loss of physical power augmented the pathos of the play.

Despite Canada's diversity, multicultural and native Shakespeare is rare. Two notable exceptions are the Modern Times Stage Company's *Hamlet* (1999), directed by Soheil Parsa, and Louis Baumander's *The Tempest* (1987, 1989). The former, set in the Orient, costumed its actors in a mixture of kimonos, business suits, and saris, punctuated the action with gongs, and concluded with a martial arts-like duel. The latter, set on the Queen Charlotte Islands, presented Ariel as a Nanabush (native trickster).

Shakespeare's influence on Canadian culture, and drama in particular, has been mixed. The more unfortunate aspects of Shakespeare adoration may be seen in such imitative works as Charles Heavysege's *Saul* (1857), described by Coventry Patmore in its day but never since as 'scarcely short of Shakespearean'. Particularly in his status as Canada's most popular playwright, Shakespeare has also come under increasing attack for impeding the growth of a Canadian drama. Yet Canadians feel impelled to engage his works. A strong, even acerbic, tradition of rewriting Shakespeare to satirize local politics began in the 18th century. Twentieth-century rewritings, of which there are nearly 100, span a much wider spectrum of themes and issues and range from the serious to the outrageous: among them are John Herbert's *Fortune and Men's Eyes* (1967), a meditation on Shakespeare's Sonnet 29; Ann Marie MacDonald's *Good Night, Desdemona (Good Morning, Juliet)* (1990), a comic consideration of gender and genre; Norman Chaurette's *Les Reines* (1991; *The Queens*, 1992), *Richard III* reimagined from the point of view of the women of the play; Cliff Jones's *Kronberg: 1582* (1974), a pop/rock musical based on *Hamlet*; and David Belke's farcical mystery *The Maltese Bodkin* (1997). Shakespearian adaptations, inspirations, and revisions have found their way into fiction, poetry, music, radio, and television. Now firmly entrenched in schools, universities, theatres, and the public consciousness, Shakespeare has become a byword for literacy itself: Book Day Canada is celebrated on his birthday, 23 April.

IM

Benson, Eugene, and Conolly, L. W., *English Canadian Theatre* (1987)

Béraud, Jean, *350 ans de théâtre au Canada français* (1958)

Rubin, Don (ed.), *Canadian Theatre History: Selected Readings* (1996)

Tait, Michael, 'Drama and Theatre', in Carl F. Klinck (gen. ed.), *Literary History of Canada*. (1965; repr. 1973)

The Encyclopedia of Canadian Theatre on the World Wide Web: www.canadiantheatre.com

canaries, dance steps including percussive use of feet, or a lively, virtuosic couple dance involving those steps (see *Love's Labour's Lost* 3.1.11 and *All's Well That Ends Well* 2.1.73); also a tune associated with the dance. The origin of the name is unknown, despite obvious speculation about the Canary Islands. *JB*

cancel. The technical term for a page that replaces one that has been removed by the printer. The original *title page of the 1609 *quarto of *Troilus and Cressida*, for instance, which advertised the play 'As it was acted by the Kings Majesty's servants at the Globe', was cancelled during the printing process and replaced with a title page that makes no mention of a company or a theatre. *ER*

Canidius. See CAMIDIUS.

canon. The thirty-six plays in the First Folio form the authoritative canon of Shakespeare's dramatic work. But, like the universe, the Shakespearian canon is ever expanding. Heminges and Condell may have deliberately excluded collaborative plays from their collection. *Pericles*, for instance, although ascribed to Shakespeare on the title page of the 1609 quarto, was omitted from the First Folio; the play later appeared in the Third and Fourth Folios and in Rowe's editions, was excluded by Pope, but has been included in most collected editions of Shakespeare since Malone's *Supplement* (1780) to Steevens's edition. *The Two Noble Kinsmen*, ascribed to John Fletcher and Shakespeare on the title page of the 1634 quarto, appeared in the Beaumont and Fletcher Second Folio (1679) and in all subsequent editions of Beaumont and Fletcher's works, but it was not until the 20th century that the play began to be included in editions of Shakespeare.

Scholars have explored a variety of forms of internal evidence (including tests of vocabulary, imagery, verbal and structural parallels, metrical evidence, stylometry, and function word tests) in the hopes of establishing the authenticity of other plays that are attributed to Shakespeare in early printed texts, such as *The London Prodigal*, *Thomas Lord Cromwell*, *Sir John Oldcastle*, *The Puritan*, *A Yorkshire Tragedy*, and *Locrine*. But none of these plays in the 'Shakespeare Apocrypha' has been admitted to the canon. The 168 lines that Shakespeare contributed to the manuscript play *Sir Thomas More*, which was discovered in the British Museum in 1844, are widely accepted as genuine and often included in collected editions. Compelling arguments that Shakespeare was responsible for a few scenes in *Edward III* (*c.*1592) have recently propelled that play into some collected editions of Shakespeare's work, bringing the total number of plays in the canon to 40. *ER*

Wells, Stanley, and Taylor, Gary, *William Shakespeare: A Textual Companion* (1987)

Canterbury, Archbishop of. (1) Based on Henry Chicheley (Chichele) (*c.*1362–1443), his speech 'proving' King Harry's title to the French Crown (*Henry V* 1.2) is taken largely from *Holinshed. (2) See CRANMER, THOMAS. *AB*

Capell, Edward (1713–81), English Shakespearian editor. Capell's ten-volume edition of *Mr William Shakespeare his Comedies, Histories, and Tragedies* (1768) was the first to be prepared according to recognizably 'modern' principles of eclectic editing. By a process of thorough collation Capell established which of the 'old editions' would be used as the 'ground-work' for the text of each play, and incorporated into this base text readings from the other early editions at points of variance, as his editorial judgement dictated. The 1768 edition was a beautifully printed 'clean' text, accompanied by only the briefest textual notes. It was belatedly followed by Capell's remarkable explanatory apparatus, his *Notes and Various Readings* (vol. i, 1774; vols. i–iii, 1779–83), which included the *School of Shakespeare*, a collection of passages from Elizabethan and Jacobean literature chosen as illustrations of particular Shakespearian usages and cruces. The depth and originality of Capell's textual work and contextualizing scholarship was matched and exceeded only by the great variorum editors *Steevens (who was not above unacknowledged borrowing from Capell) and *Malone. *MLW*

Caphis is the servant of one of Timon's creditors in *Timon of Athens*. *AB*

Capilet, Diana. See DIANA.

Capilet, Widow. See WIDOWS.

capitalization. Capitals were used in the early modern period not only to dignify names and proper nouns, but also to provide emphasis. Capitalization, like spelling, was largely a matter of individual preference. Shakespeare's three pages in the *Sir Thomas More* manuscript reveal his characteristic habit of capitalizing initial 'C' in mid-sentence verbal forms ('Come', 'Charg', 'Cannot', 'Cry', 'hath Chidd', 'Charterd'). *ER*

captains. (1) A captain of a ship condemns Suffolk to death, *The First Part of the Contention* (*2 Henry VI*) 4.1.71–103. (2) A captain announces the arrival of Titus, *Titus Andronicus* 1.1.64–9. (3) A captain of the Welsh army announces the dispersal of his troops, *Richard II* 2.4. (4) A captain is sent by Fortinbras to Claudius, *Hamlet* 4.4. He explains Fortinbras' expedition to Hamlet in the second *quarto (see *Hamlet* Additional Passages 'J', lines 1–21). (5) A sea captain agrees to help Viola disguise herself as a eunuch, *Twelfth Night* 1.2. (6) A captain reports on the battle between Macbeth and Macdonald, *Macbeth* 1.2. (7) A Roman captain gives information to Lucius, *Cymbeline* 4.2. Two British captains arrest Posthumus, *Cymbeline* 5.5.92–5. *AB*

Capucius. See CAPUTIUS, LORD.

Capulet, Juliet's father in *Romeo and Juliet*, is the head of the family opposed to the Montagues. *AB*

Capulet, Diana. See DIANA.

Capulet, Lady. See CAPULET'S WIFE.

Capulet, Widow. See WIDOWS.

Capulet's Cousin converses with Capulet, *Romeo and Juliet* 1.5. *AB*

Capulet's Wife supports her husband in the proposed marriage of Juliet to Paris in *Romeo and Juliet*. *AB*

Caputius, Lord. He visits the dying Katherine and takes a letter from her to Henry, *All Is True* (*Henry VIII*) 4.2. He is based on the ambassador Eustace Chapuys, mentioned in *Holinshed. *AB*

Cardenio. The King's Men were paid for performing a play referred to as *Cardenno* or *Cardenna* at court on 20 May and 9 July 1613, presumably based on the story of Cardenio told in Cervantes' *Don Quixote*, which had first appeared in English translation in 1612. In September 1653 Humphrey *Moseley entered 'The History of Cardenio, by Mr Fletcher and Shakespeare' in the Stationers' Register, but there is no evidence that he ever published it. While he might have known that *Fletcher had dramatized material from *Don Quixote* elsewhere, and that he had collaborated with Shakespeare on *The Two Noble Kinsmen* (though not when), Moseley is very unlikely to have known that Shakespeare's company had given performances of a play called *Cardenno* at court—at exactly the same time, moreover, that Shakespeare and Fletcher were also collaborating on *All Is True* (*Henry VIII*) and *The Two Noble Kinsmen*. Although Heminges and Condell, for whatever reason, omitted it from the *Folio (just as they excluded *Pericles*, *The Two Noble Kinsmen*, and the mysterious **Love's Labour's Won*: see CANON), it seems almost certain that Shakespeare co-wrote *Cardenio* with Fletcher in 1612–13, and that a manuscript of the play was still extant in the 1650s.

Tantalizing glimpses of this otherwise lost play were provided in 1728 by the publication of *Double Falsehood; or, The Distressed Lovers*, 'Written Originally by W. SHAKESPEARE; and now Revised and Adapted to the Stage by Mr. THEOBALD.' Lewis *Theobald's preface to this play, which was acted with considerable sucess at Drury Lane, states that it is an adaptation of an otherwise unknown work by Shakespeare, of which he claims to possess three copies in manuscript. (One of these was said to be in the library of Covent Garden theatre as late as 1770, but the playhouse burned down in 1808.) Theobald's preface, though arguing strenuously for the play's authenticity, betrays no knowledge of either Moseley's entry in the Stationers' Register or the traces of *Cardenno*'s performances at court, so the otherwise extraordinary coincidence that *Double Falsehood* is in fact a version of the Cardenio story suggests that whatever Theobald possessed in manuscript must at least have derived from the missing Fletcher–Shakespeare *Cardenio.*

If this is the case, however, *Double Falsehood* represents *Cardenio* only at one or more removes, its language heavily rewritten for a post-Restoration stage which found Fletcher's style much more congenial than that of Shakespeare's late romances (as is demonstrated by *Davenant's version of *The Two Noble Kinsmen*, *The *Rivals*, which cuts most of the lines now attributed to Shakespeare). Nonetheless, some commentators have found lingering traces of Shakespearian imagery, and others have been impressed by the way in which *Double Falsehood* assimilates the Cardenio story to the characteristic patterns of Shakespearian romance.

MD

Frey, Charles, ' "O sacred, shadowy, cold, and constant queen": Shakespeare's Imperiled and Chastening Daughters of Romance', in C. R. S. Lenz, G. Greene, and C. T. Neely (eds.), *The Woman's Part: Feminist Criticism of Shakespeare* (1980)

Muir, Kenneth, *Shakespeare as Collaborator* (1960)

Cardinal. In *Richard III* he reluctantly agrees that the Duke of York and his mother Queen Elizabeth should be brought out of the sanctuary (3.1) that he led them to in the previous scene. He is based on Thomas Bourchier (or Bouchier) (*c.*1404–1486). In folio editions it is the Archbishop of York who leads them to sanctuary. *AB*

Carew, Richard (1555–1620), poet and antiquary. In his epistle *The Excellencie of the English Tongue*, printed in 1614, Carew cites Shakespeare as the lyric equal of the Roman poet Catullus. He adds, nevertheless, that for prose and verse the 'miracle of our age' is Sir Philip *Sidney (whom Carew had met at Oxford). *PH*

Carey, Elizabeth (d. 1635). She was the daughter of Elizabeth and Sir George Carey, and god-daughter of Lord Hunsdon, patron of the Chamberlain's Men, and Elizabeth I. Carey's marriage to Sir Thomas Berkeley on 19 February 1596 was possibly the occasion on which *A Midsummer Night's Dream* was first performed.

CS

Caribbean. Rarely mentioned in Shakespeare's plays, the Caribbean has been the site of some of the most exciting readings, adaptations, and appropriations of *The Tempest.*

The connections between *The Tempest* and the Caribbean have long been recognized, even

A CATALOGVE

of the ſeuerall Comedies, Hiſtories, and Tragedies contained in this Volume.

COMEDIES.

The Tempeſt.	Folio 1.
The two Gentlemen of Verona.	20
The Merry Wiues of Windſor.	38
Meaſure for Meaſure.	61
The Comedy of Errours.	85
Much adoo about Nothing.	101
Loues Labour loſt.	122
Midſommer Nights Dreame.	145
The Merchant of Venice.	163
As you Like it.	185
The Taming of the Shrew.	208
All is well, that Ends well.	230
Twelfe-Night, or what you will.	255
The Winters Tale.	304

HISTORIES.

The Life and Death of King John.	Fol. 1.
The Life & death of Richard the ſecond.	23
The Firſt part of King Henry the fourth.	46
The Second part of K. Henry the fourth.	74
The Life of King Henry the Fift.	69
The Firſt part of King Henry the Sixt.	96
The Second part of King Hen. the Sixt.	120
The Third part of King Henry the Sixt.	147
The Life & Death of Richard the Third.	173
The Life of King Henry the Eight.	205

TRAGEDIES.

The Tragedy of Coriolanus.	Fol. 1.
Titus Andronicus.	31
Romeo and Juliet.	53
Timon of Athens.	80
The Life and death of Julius Cæſar.	109
The Tragedy of Macbeth.	131
The Tragedy of Hamlet.	152
King Lear.	283
Othello, the Moore of Venice.	310
Anthony and Cleopater.	346
Cymbeline King of Britaine.	369

The catalogue of Shakespeare's plays from the First Folio (1623). *Troilus and Cressida*, only included in the volume at the last minute, came too late to be listed; *Pericles*, *The Two Noble Kinsmen*, and the missing *Love's Labour's Won* and *Cardenio* were left out entirely.

if their significance has been disputed. One of the play's accepted sources is William *Strachey's account of the 'wreck and redemption' of a party of English colonists heading for Virginia who were shipwrecked on the islands of the Bermudas in 1609. This is at least a New World and even North Atlantic reference point, if not quite a Caribbean one. More tellingly, Caliban is usually regarded as an anagram of the word 'can[n]bal', which has its root in the same indigenous word that also gives the term 'Caribbean'. (See TRAVEL, TRADE, AND COLONIALISM.)

When read from the Caribbean, the relationship between Prospero and Caliban has usually been seen as that between master and slave, the word by which Caliban is described in the play's 'Names of the Actors', and the play therefore read as pertaining to the history of slavery. However, the uncertainty over Caliban's parentage, provenance, and colour has allowed a considerable variation in the interpretations offered, even by those claiming to speak from Caliban's position.

The three landmarks of the reading and adaptation of *The Tempest* from the Caribbean come from three different language traditions, those of Barbados, Martinique, and Cuba: George Lamming's essay 'A Monster, A Child, A Slave', which appeared in his collection *The Pleasures of Exile* (1960); Aimé Césaire's play *Une tempête* (1969); and Roberto Fernández Retamar's essay 'Calibán', first published in the Havana journal *Casa de las Américas* in 1971.

Lamming refers to his own reading of *The Tempest* as 'blasphemous', conscious as he was both of the sacred status of Shakespeare, even in the twilight of British imperialism, and of the marginal status of a West Indian writer recently arrived in London. Ignored when it was first published, his insertion of the play into the history of the British slave trade, his probing questions about Prospero's wife, and his openly disrespectful interrogation of Prospero's psychological state subsequently became staple ingredients of the postcolonial approach to *The Tempest*. Lamming also insisted that the tide of colonial aftermath washes up on metropolitan shores, as it does with particular force in his novel *Water with Berries* (1971), in which a version of the *Tempest* story forms a violent colonial prehistory to the struggles of West Indian immigrants to make lives for themselves in London.

Césaire's *Une tempête* offers a serious and complex involvement with the Shakespearian play, an 'adaptation' which keeps close enough to its original for the variations to be striking, and which also responds to Ernest Renan's earlier continuation of the play, *Caliban: Suite de 'La Tempête'* (1878); although Césaire moves 'back' to the Caribbean (and back to Shakespeare) and therefore away from Renan's concern with European politics. The main contexts for *Une tempête* were third-world and racial issues in the late 1960s: the extended confrontation between the coloured (mixed-race) Ariel and the black Caliban becomes as central to the play as the relationship between Prospero and Caliban.

The intertexts of Roberto Fernández Retamar's 1970 essay 'Calibán' stretch back to the Uruguayan essayist José Enrique Rodó's *Ariel* (1900), to which 'Calibán' is openly responding by placing the Caribbean, in the form of Cuba, at the centre of debates about Latin American cultural identity. Fernández Retamar's defiant question was 'what is our history, what is our culture, if not the history and culture of Caliban?'; a question which has continued to form a crucial part of the cultural-political agenda in Latin America.

Creative engagements with Shakespeare have similarly emphasized *The Tempest*. The Barbadian poet Kamau Brathwaite has often responded to the play, as have the Guyanese writers David Dabydeen and Pauline Melville. Marina Warner's novel *Indigo* (1992) is largely set in the Caribbean and uses elements of the *Tempest* story and characters to tell a fictional version of the early history of English settlement in the area. In a striking variation, *A Branch of the Blue Nile* (1983), by Nobel laureate Derek Walcott, uses the Brechtian device of a group of Trinidadian actors rehearsing *Antony and Cleopatra*.

Shakespeare has been performed in the Caribbean at least since the later 17th century, with plays such as *Hamlet*, *Macbeth*, and *Romeo and Juliet* staged by travelling companies on the major islands. Jamaica, for example, where the best records survive, saw eight Shakespeare plays performed in 1781–2. *Othello* was not performed in the Caribbean until after Emancipation in 1834.

The end of the 20th century saw two Caribbean productions of Shakespeare visit the United Kingdom. In 1998 the Cuban company Teatro Buendía staged *Otra tempestad* at the reconstructed Globe (London). *Otra tempestad* goes further than other adaptations of *The Tempest* through its introduction of two new sets of characters, several from Shakespeare's other plays as well as the *orishas* (Afro-Cuban deities) who double the European parts. Then Kit Hesketh-Harvey's *The Caribbean Tempest*, equipped with new Caribbean music and spectacle but otherwise close to Shakespeare's original, and first performed in Barbados, was staged in the Royal Botanic Gardens as part of the 1999 Edinburgh Festival. *PHm*

Césaire, Aimé, *A Tempest*, trans. Philip Crispin (2000)
Fernández Retamar, Roberto, *Caliban and Other Essays*, trans. Edward Baker et al. (1989)
Hulme, Peter, and Sherman, William H. (eds.), *'The Tempest' and its Travels* (2000)
Hill, Errol, *The Jamaican Stage 1655–1900: Profile of a Colonial Theatre* (1992)
Lamming, George, *The Pleasures of Exile* (2nd edn., 1984)

Carlisle, Bishop of. One of Richard's loyal supporters (Thomas Merke, d. 1409), he is spared by King Henry, *Richard II* 5.6. *AB*

Carlyle, Thomas (1795–1881), Scottish author of *On Heroes, Hero-Worship, and the Heroic in History* (1841). In his *Hero as Poet* he presents both Dante and Shakespeare ('the greatest of Intellects') struggling heroically to transcend constricting limitations, in Shakespeare's case almost crushing his great soul to write for the Globe playhouse. *TM*

'Carman's Whistle', the title of a ribald ballad, quoted by Falstaff in *2 Henry IV*, quarto additional passage after 3.2.309; carmen or carters had a reputation for musical and sexual prowess. The ballad tune was set for *virginals by William *Byrd. *JB*

Carriers, two. They converse with each other, and briefly with Gadshill, in an inn yard, *1 Henry IV* 2.1. *AB*

cartoon Shakespeare. See STRIP-CARTOON SHAKESPEARE.

Casca is the first of the conspirators to stab Caesar (following the account in *Plutarch), *Julius Caesar* 3.1.76. *AB*

cases, large wooden trays divided into compartments used for sorting and storing type. Two cases, positioned one above the other on the *compositor's frames, were traditionally employed in early English printing-houses. Capitals were placed in the boxes of the upper case, small letters in the boxes of the lower case. Even in the current age of computer-generated type fonts, capitals are still known as 'upper case', small letters as 'lower case'. *ER*

Cassandra is a Trojan prophetess and daughter of Priam in *Troilus and Cressida* (drawn originally from *Homer). *AB*

Cassio, Michael. Othello's lieutenant, unwittingly involved in *Iago's plot against Othello, he is injured, 5.1, but given governorship of Cyprus, 5.2.341. *AB*

Cassius, Caius. Instigator of the plot against Caesar, he commands his slave Pindarus to kill him when faced with military defeat, *Julius Caesar* 5.3.45. *AB*

Castelnuovo-Tedesco, Mario See ITALY; OPERA.

Castiglione, Baldassare (1478–1529), Italian diplomat and writer whose prose work *Il libro del cortegiano* (*The Book of the Courtier*), published in an English translation by Sir Thomas Hoby in 1591, was a seminal text in the definition of Elizabethan chivalry and courtliness. Through a series of debates between various historical figures, Castiglione considered questions such as the ideal qualities of the courtier and his duty to the prince. The influence of the *Courtier* upon English Renaissance literature was one of both content and style. Not only did it inspire succeeding courtesy books, its witty exchanges may have influenced the courtship of Beatrice and Benedick in *Much Ado About Nothing*. *JKS*

cast-off copy. In order to facilitate setting by *formes, a *compositor would attempt to calculate in advance how much of his *copy would be needed to fill each printed page (so that pages 1 and 4 of a *folio, for instance, could be set and sent to the press before pages 2 and 3). Compositors who made errors in their calculations would reach the end of their stints with too little or too much copy and be forced to fill out or contract the page using such expedients as setting *prose as verse or vice versa. *ER*

catch, a simple part-song or round, e.g. *'Hold thy peace' in *Twelfth Night* 2.3.66. *JB*

Catch my Soul. See MUSICALS.

Catesby, Sir William. Drawn largely from *Holinshed, Catesby (d. 1485) is Richard's ally throughout *Richard III*. *AB*

Catharine and Petruchio. David *Garrick's three-act abbreviation of *The Taming of the Shrew*, first performed in 1754 and still in use in the 1880s, softens the play by insisting that Petruchio's mistreatment of Kate and his servants is only a temporary pretence, but nonetheless reallocates most of her speech of wifely submission to him as a concluding sermon. *MD*

Catherine. (1) A lady attending the Princess of France, she is wooed by Dumain in *Love's Labour's Lost*. **(2)** She is wooed by King Harry, *Henry V* 5.2, and claimed as his bride as part of the peace treaty with France. She is based on Catherine of Valois, 1401–37, daughter of Charles VI of France, mother of Henry VI, and grandmother of Henry VII. *AB*

Catherine the Great (1729–96), Empress of all the Russias from 1762. A fluent and avid reader of Shakespeare, albeit in French translations, Catherine corresponded extensively on Shakespeare with *Voltaire, among others: in 1786 she translated *The Merry Wives of Windsor* into Russian, and wrote a play of her own, *The Spendthrift*, based on *Timon of Athens*. Another of her own plays, *The Initial Instruction of Oleg* (1791), is a professed imitation of Shakespeare's style. *MD*

Stříbrný, Zdeněk, *Shakespeare and Eastern Europe* (2000)

Catholicism. See RELIGION.

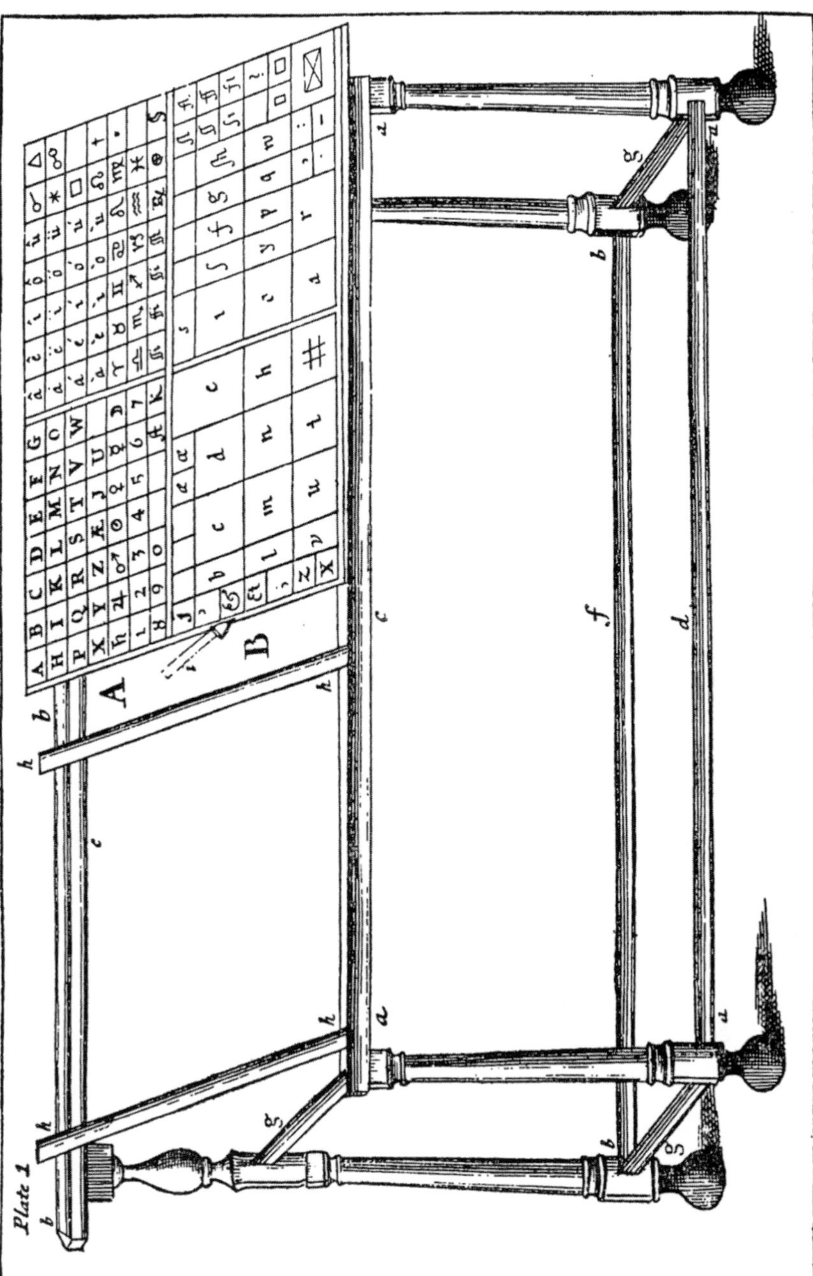

A The Upper Case (p. 29)
B The Lower Case (p. 29)
(C) The Frame (p. 31)

A 17th-century type-case. From Joseph Moxon, *Mechanical Exercises in the Whole Art of Printing* (1683–4).

Cato, Young. Son of Marcus Porcius Cato (95–46 BC), the younger Cato becomes Brutus' ally and dies at Philippi, *Julius Caesar* 5.4.8.
AB

Cattermole, Charles (1832–1900), English painter and illustrator. Amongst numerous 17th-century figure subjects, Cattermole, like his uncle George Cattermole, produced small-scale watercolours of Shakespearian scenes, with *Macbeth* a favoured theme of his stage-inspired compositions. He also executed a series of thirteen anecdotal watercolours illustrating Shakespeare's life from *Christening* to *Last Hours.*
KN

Cawdor, Thane of. This title is given to Macbeth, *Macbeth* 1.2.63–5. *AB*

Caxton, William (1421–91), translator and the first English printer. Caxton worked in the Low Countries as an agent for silk merchants and came upon printing during a business trip to Cologne. On his return to England, he set up his own press and printed the first book in English, *The Recuyell of the Histories of Troy*, in 1475. He went on to print over 70 books including Chaucer's *Canterbury Tales* and *Troilus and Criseyde*, Gower's *Confessio amantis*, and Malory's *Morte d'Arthur.* Shakespeare referred to *The Recuyell*, Caxton's own translation of a French history by Le Fevre, in the writing of *Troilus and Cressida.* *JKS*

Cayatte, André (1909–89). He produced the colour film *Les Amants de Vérone* based on *Romeo and Juliet* in 1949 (script by the poet Jacques Prévert, music by Joseph Kosma). The highly talented cast plays the beautiful love story as a timeless adventure. The carefully chosen settings of Verona create an atmosphere of mystical painting. *ISG*

Cecil, Robert (1563–1612), and his father **William** (1520–98), the most powerful ministers of their age. Comparisons between the Cecils and politic counsellors Nestor and Ulysses, who appear in *Troilus and Cressida*, were familiar from 1594. Secretary of State 1596–1608, Robert was one target of *Essex's 1601 rebellion, to which *Richard II* is linked. Robert's position as Sir William Brooke's son-in-law may have induced William Cecil (Baron Burghley from 1571) to oblige Shakespeare to change Oldcastle's name to Falstaff in *1 Henry IV.* William B. Long suggests Burghley commissioned *Sir Thomas More* to tackle anti-alien sentiment. *CS*

Celia, daughter of Duke Frederick and cousin of Rosalind in *As You Like It*, disguises herself as 'Aliena' (like Alinda in *Lodge's *Rosalynde*) and marries Oliver. *AB*

censorship. The official government censor of drama in Shakespeare's time was the Master of the Revels, to whom a playing company had to submit each playbook together with a fee. The censor's remit was never precisely defined, but successive postholders took their responsibility to be the excision of material offensive to the Church and state, broadly interpreted to include not only sedition and personal satire but also foul language and excessive sexuality. If the Master of the Revels allowed the play, he would attach his licence (a signed statement of his approval) at the end of the manuscript. Often the licence would state conditions such as 'may with the reformations [i.e. changes] be acted' or '[with] all the oaths left out'. The office of the Master of the Revels was originally established to select plays for the entertainment of Queen Elizabeth, but in 1581 Edmund Tilney was given a new patent which required 'all and every player or players . . . to present and recite before our said servant' any new work. The volume of new plays made recitation by the actors impractical and Tilney was content to read the drama by himself. Tilney was succeeded by George *Buc (who was not, as formerly thought, his nephew) in 1610, and Buc was succeeded by John Astley in 1622, who was himself succeeded by Henry Herbert in 1623. Herbert kept the job until the closure of 1642 and managed to resume some of the same functions when the playhouses opened again in the Restoration. Herbert's office book was extant until the 19th century and it provides most of what we know about the detailed operation of the censor, although it is rather later than Shakespeare's working life. If the Master of the Revels was sufficiently unhappy about a play he might refuse even a conditional licence, but we have only one record of Herbert exacting the extreme penalty: 'Received of Mr Kirke for a new play which I burnt for the ribaldry that was in it . . . £2.'

Not infrequently a play in performance at one of the London playhouses caused offence to an important person and the players were held to account. Thomas *Nashe and Ben *Jonson's *The Isle of Dogs* (now lost) was highly critical of the government and its performance at the Swan resulted in a temporary closure of all the London playhouses. Presumably the Master of the Revels could have been held responsible if such a play had been licensed, and in 1633 the players tried to blame Herbert's negligence for the offence caused by Jonson's *The Magnetic Lady*, although the Court of Commission exonerated him. An entirely separate system of censorship governed the publication of plays. Getting 'authority' or 'allowance' was a prerequisite demanded of a stationer by a Star Chamber decree of 1586, and until 1606 the authority for playbook publication was in the hands of the Bishop of London and the Archbishop of Canterbury, who governed publication generally. Unlike the performance licence which was a strict necessity, failure to secure authority for printing seems to have been casually ignored unless someone was actually offended by the work. From 1606 George Buc, later to become Master of the Revels, took over the licensing of play publication. The 'authority' needed for publication should not be confused with licence for printing given by the *Stationers' Company, the guild association for the printing trade. The Stationers' Company regulations were designed to protect the individual interests of stationers, and in particular to prevent conflicts where more than one stationer wanted to print a given text, but in deciding whether or not to give the licence the company officers would also take into consideration whether the book had authority and whether it was likely to give offence. If they were unhappy, they might license the book on condition that it not be printed until 'further', 'better', or 'lawful' authority had been obtained.

On 27 May 1606 an *'Act to Restrain Abuses of Players' was passed which made it an offence to 'jestingly or profanely speak or use the holy Name of God or of Christ Jesus, or of the Holy Ghost or of the Trinity' in a stage play, on penalty of a £10 fine. As well as effectively censoring new works, this Act also required old plays to be expurgated if they were to be revived for the stage. The Act did not cover printing, however, and the 1623 Folio of Shakespeare contains a mixture of expurgated and unexpurgated plays according to the provenance of the manuscript underlying each of them. In many cases what looks like censorship of printed plays might be something else. The first, second, and third quartos of Shakespeare's *Richard II* do not have the deposition scene which is present in the fourth and fifth quartos, and it is often assumed that the first three editions represent censorship of the potentially offensive scene. Much clearer evidence of censorship is the response of the lords *Cobham to what they perceived as satire of their ancestor Sir John *Oldcastle in Shakespeare's *1 Henry IV.* Shakespeare was forced to give Sir John a new surname, and he chose Falstaff for *2 Henry IV.*

Scholars are not in agreement about how, or indeed whether, to undo changes apparently forced onto unwilling dramatists, and modern socio-cultural studies of the entire system of relations between the theatre industry, the monarchy, and the Parliament (such as Richard Dutton's) find the Master of the Revels 'as much a friend of the actors as their overlord'. For the opposite interpretation, summarized in her book's title, see Janet Clare. *GE*

Bawcutt, N. W. (ed.), *The Control and Censorship of Caroline Drama: The Records of Sir Henry Herbert, Master of the Revels 1623–73* (1996)

Blayney, Peter W. M., 'The Publication of Playbooks', in John D. Cox and David Scott Kastan (eds.), *A New History of Early English Drama* (1997)

Clare, Janet, *'Art Made Tongue-tied by Authority': Elizabethan and Jacobean Dramatic Censorship* (1990)
Dutton, Richard, *Mastering the Revels: The Regulation and Censorship of English Renaissance Drama* (1991)
Taylor, Gary, and Jowett, John, *Shakespeare Reshaped: 1606–1623* (1993)

Central Park. See UNITED STATES OF AMERICA.

ceramics. Amongst the spate of Shakespeare representations produced around the Shakespeare *jubilee of 1769 were fanciful figurines of the dramatist and John *Milton made by the Derby factory *c.*1765–70. Similar groups including Milton and Shakespeare were later produced in Chelsea and Bow porcelain. The production of Shakespeare ceramics increased in quantity, although not necessarily in quality, throughout the nineteenth century, when likenesses of the poet based on the two principal *portrait types appeared on items such as memorial plates, toby jugs, and the tops of walking sticks. The 19th century also gave rise to the growth of curious compounds involving Shakespeare portraits, such as Staffordshire figurines of *c.*1850, founded on *Scheemakers's celebrated statue, but bearing the facial features and ermine cloak of Albert, Prince Consort. The production of Shakespeare-inspired ceramics declined during the 20th century. (See SHAKESPEARIANA.) *CT*

'Ceres', the goddess of agriculture, is a part played by a spirit in *The Tempest*'s *masque of 4.1. *AB*

Cerimon, a physician of Ephesus, restores the apparently dead Thaisa, *Pericles* 12. *AB*

Cervantes Saavedra, Miguel de (1547–1616), Spanish novelist, dramatist, and poet. His patriotic career included fighting at the battle of Lepanto (1571), and service as a government agent, before he turned to writing plays and romances. The first part of *Don Quixote* was published to immediate Spanish acclaim in 1605, though Cervantes also made many powerful enemies among those who feared Quixote was a lampoon of themselves. Part 2 was published in 1615. In the following year Cervantes died, within days of Shakespeare. Available in Thomas Shelton's translation of 1612, *Don Quixote* also proved popular in England particularly with the dramatist John Fletcher. In 1625 Fletcher adapted Cervantes' story *La Señora Cornelia* into the comedy *The Chances*. His reading of *Don Quixote*, particularly the inset story of Cardenio and Lucinda, may have inspired *Cardenio*, a lost play, thought to have been a collaboration between Fletcher and Shakespeare. *JKS*

Césaire, Aimé (b.1913), Martinican poet, playwright, and political leader; founder of the black French-language *négritude* movement. *Une tempête* (1969; *A Tempest*, 1986) is a postcolonial critique of Prospero's brave new world as a sinister dictatorship, with Caliban as a black slave stirring revolt. *TM*

'Cesario' is the name used by Viola when disguised as a eunuch in *Twelfth Night*. *MD*

Challis Shakespeare. This paperback edition of individual plays began to appear in 1980 as the first designed specifically for the 'student or non-specialist reader in Australia'. It offers a modernized text with brief notes and introductions. It was named after John Henry Challis, who died in 1880, and whose bequest made possible the foundation of a number of professorships at Sydney University. *RAF*

Chalmers, Alexander (1759–1834), a prolific editor and biographer, who produced a glossary to Shakespeare in 1797 and an attractive nine-volume edition of Shakespeare in 1805, illustrated by *Fuseli. Based on Steevens's text it reprinted prefatory material by Pope, Johnson, and Malone, and included Chalmers's own biography of Shakespeare. *CMSA*

Chalmers, George (1742–1825), a Scottish historian and antiquarian who believed in the authenticity of William Henry Ireland's forged *Shakespeare-Papers* (1795). On Ireland's confession Chalmers first wrote an *Apology for the Believers in the Shakespeare-Papers* and subsequently justified his initial belief in the *Supplementary Apology* (1799). (See FORGERY.) *CMSA*

Chamber Accounts. The accounting records of the Treasurer of the Chamber who paid out for court entertainments. This is a major source of our knowledge concerning the professional players' court performances. *GE*

Cook, David, and Wilson, F. P. (eds.), *Dramatic Records in the Declared Accounts of the Treasurer of the Chamber 1558–1642* (1961)

Chamberlain. He tells Gadshill that some wealthy travellers are about to set out, *1 Henry IV* 2.1. *AB*

Chamberlain, John (1553–1627), scholar and letter-writer. After fire destroyed Shakespeare's Globe in June 1613, the theatre was rebuilt. A letter which Chamberlain, a Londoner, sent to Alice Carleton establishes that the 'new' Globe, the 'fairest' playhouse 'that ever was in England', had opened its doors by 30 June 1614. *PH*

Chamberlain, Lord. See LORD CHAMBERLAIN.

Chamberlain's Men/King's Men. In May 1594 two privy counsellors, Henry Carey (the Lord Chamberlain) and Charles Howard (the Lord Admiral), established two acting companies, the Chamberlain's Men and the Admiral's Men, and gave them exclusive rights to perform in London at the Theatre and the Rose respectively. Shakespeare appears to have been one of the new Chamberlain's Men from the company's inception and his plays came with him, whether in his own possession or in the hands of fellow actors who performed in them for other companies we do not know.

The difficulty of distinguishing different plays on the same theme (there appears to have been more than one 'Hamlet' play in the 1590s) and of identifying single plays which might be known by more than one name (as might be the case with 'The Taming of a/the Shrew') makes the precise limits of the early Shakespeare canon uncertain. The nucleus of the company was composed of the actor-sharers George *Bryan, Richard *Burbage, John *Heminges, Will *Kemp, Augustine *Phillips, Thomas *Pope, William Shakespeare, and William *Sly. The distinctive John Sincler was not a sharer but his career can be traced through a number of Shakespeare's 'thin man' roles including Nym and Slender in *2 Henry IV*, *Henry V*, and *The Merry Wives of Windsor*, and Sir Andrew Aguecheek in *Twelfth Night*. In 1598 Francis *Meres praised Shakespeare's *The Two Gentlemen of Verona, The Comedy of Errors, Love's Labour's Lost, A Midsummer Night's Dream, The Merchant of Venice, Richard II, Richard III, Henry IV, King John, Titus Andronicus,* and *Romeo and Juliet*. Together with Shakespeare's *Henry VI* plays and *The Taming of the Shrew* this makes an impressive body of work and it is hardly surprising that the Chamberlain's Men, with such a repertory and with a state-enforced monopoly on playing on the north side of the Thames, were hugely successful. On 22 July 1596 the company's patron, Henry Carey the Lord Chamberlain, died and Lord Cobham was made Lord Chamberlain in his place. The patronage of the company passed to Henry Carey's son George, so for a while the company was officially Lord Hunsdon's Men, but in early 1597 Lord Cobham also died and George Carey received the chamberlainship, thus restoring the more impressive name to his players. Also early in 1597 died James Burbage, owner of the Theatre and the Blackfriars and father to the Chamberlain's Men's leading actor Richard Burbage. The lease on the land underneath the Theatre expired on 13 April 1597 and sometime before September 1598 the company must have started using another venue, presumably the nearby Curtain whose owner, Henry Lanham, made a profit-sharing deal with James Burbage in 1585. Unable to settle the dispute over the site of the Theatre and unable to move into the Blackfriars playhouse built by James Burbage in 1596, the Chamberlain's Men dismantled the timbers of the Theatre and reassembled them on a new site on Bankside to form the Globe, which opened some time between June and September 1599. James Burbage's sons Richard and Cuthbert inherited his Theatre and Blackfriars venues but had insufficient cash to finance the Globe project alone and so they formed a syndicate to bring in John Heminges, William Kemp, Augustine Phillips, Thomas Pope, and William Shakespeare. These actors became not only sharers in the playing company but also 'housekeepers' owning their own venue and this alignment of interests proved to be a powerful stabilizing force in the company's fortunes. William Sly stayed out of the deal initially but took up Pope's share after the latter's death in 1603. Some time after 1596 one of the original Chamberlain's Men sharers, George Bryan, dropped out and was probably replaced by Henry Condell, who became a 'housekeeper' too after Phillips died in 1605.

While the Globe was being erected in 1599 the clown William Kemp left the company and was replaced by Robert Armin, whose subtler style of humour seems to be reflected in Shakespeare's subsequent creation of reflective intellectual 'fools'. On 25 March 1603 Queen Elizabeth died and was succeeded by the King of Scotland, James VI, who became James I of England. The new monarch showed greater interest in drama than his predecessor and on 19 May 1603 he became the company's patron, changing their name to the King's Men. The following winter James demanded eight performances at court from his players, more than they had ever been asked for by Elizabeth. The company also began to tour more frequently and more widely under James's patronage, which might indicate that the new King saw his playing company as a travelling advertisement for the new reign.

In 1608 the children's company at Blackfriars disbanded temporarily after performing a play which offended James, and their manager Henry Evans surrendered his lease on the Blackfriars back to Richard Burbage. Now with royal patronage, the King's Men were able to occupy the playhouse James Burbage had built just before his death. The shareholding arrangement at the Globe had apparently proved successful for the players because they now made the same arrangement to run the Blackfriars. The new syndicate formed on 9 August 1608 was comprised of Richard and Cuthbert Burbage, John Heminges, William Shakespeare, William Sly, Henry Condell, and an outsider named Thomas Evans. Plague closure probably prevented the company using the Blackfriars until late in 1609 and, assuming that they opened it with a new play by their resident dramatist, the first performance in their new home was either Shakespeare's *The Winter's Tale* or his *Cymbeline*. With two playhouses at their disposal, the King's Men were able to use the Globe from May to September and, when the weather began to make outdoor performances uncomfortable, to move to the indoor Blackfriars for the winter. Outdoor performances had traditionally used no intervals but the tradition at the Blackfriars was to have a short break, a musical interlude, after each act. The King's Men normalized their practices by introducing act-intervals at the Globe and by moving its music room from an unseen position inside the tiring house to the balcony in the back wall of the stage. The practicalities of staging differed in the company's indoor and outdoor venues. Woodwind instruments are suitable indoors, brass outdoors, but more pressingly the small stage of the Blackfriars made sword-fighting difficult. Despite this, and presumably because they had the ingrained touring habit of accommodating to whatever space is available, the company did not immediately develop different repertories for each playhouse.

Although the Blackfriars attracted an elite audience paying high prices, the Globe's importance to the company is attested by their decision to rebuild it 'in far fairer manner than before', as Edmond Howes put it, after it burned down in 1613. Shakespeare retired around this time and was replaced by the partnership of Francis Beaumont and John Fletcher. Richard Burbage died in 1619 and was replaced by Joseph Taylor. A new patent was issued to the company on 27 March 1619, but only Heminges and Condell remained from the first patent of 1603. Heminges was by this time primarily an administrator for the company, and Condell seems to have stopped acting by the end of the 1610s. It was these two men who organized the publication of the first collected works of Shakespeare, the Folio of 1623. Playing the established masterpieces of Shakespeare and the new works of Beaumont and Fletcher, the King's Men survived intact until the general theatrical closure of 1642. *GE*

Gurr, Andrew, *The Shakespearian Playing Companies* (1996)

Knutson, Roslyn Lander, *The Repertory of Shakespeare's Company 1594–1613* (1991)

Somerset, Alan, ' "How Chances it They Travel?" Provincial Touring, Playing Places, and the King's Men', *Shakespeare Survey*, 47 (1994)

Taylor, Gary, and Jowett, John, *Shakespeare Reshaped: 1606–1623* (1993)

Wiles, David, *Shakespeare's Clown: Actor and Text in the Elizabethan Playhouse* (1987)

Chambers, Sir Edmund Kerchever (1866–1953), English civil servant and scholar. His thoroughly researched and documented *Medieval Stage* (2 vols., 1903), *Elizabethan Stage* (4 vols., 1923), and *William Shakespeare: A Study of Facts and Problems* (2 vols., 1930) are still unsurpassed as reference works, although necessarily supplemented by later investigations, including G. E. Bentley's continuation and development of *The Elizabethan Stage* into the Jacobean and Caroline era, and Samuel *Schoenbaum's documentary life of Shakespeare. After *Malone, in the 18th century, Chambers is the greatest modern researcher into original, official documents relating to dramatic history and biography, such as the records in the Patent Rolls, the Privy Council Register, the Lansdowne Manuscripts, and the Remembrancia of the City of London. Schoenbaum, his chief successor in biographical study, regarded Chambers's article on Shakespeare for the 1911 edition of the *Encyclopaedia Britannica* as the most authoritative distillation of information about Shakespeare for the next 50 years, and claimed that his British Academy lecture on *The Disintegration of Shakespeare* (1924) effectively disposed for a generation of attempts to reassign passages and sometimes whole works by Shakespeare. The fact that Chambers's logical precision and clarity of mind probably exceeded his critical sensibility cannot be regarded as a serious limitation. *TM*

Chancellor, Lord. See LORD CHANCELLOR.

Chandos portrait, oil on canvas, 552×438 mm, National Portrait Gallery. This celebrated portrait, dated *c.*1610, is the only likeness of Shakespeare thought to have been executed before his death. Traditionally attributed to John Taylor, the complex attribution history of this portrait includes George Vertue's claim that the work was painted by Richard Burbage, a celebrated actor and friend of the poet and dramatist. Vertue later made a modified notebook entry (see British Library Add. MSS, 21, 111) in which he names John Taylor as the producer of the work, information its owner (then Mr Robert Keck of the Temple, London) had gleaned from the actor Thomas Betterton, who had sold him the portrait. John Taylor (first recorded 1623, d. 1651) was identified by Mary Edmond as a Renter Warden of the Painter-Stainers' Company. Taylor is recorded in the Court Minute Books of the company several times. The Chandos portrait was bequeathed to the collection which later became the National Portrait Gallery in 1856. *CT*

Edmond, M., 'The Chandos Portrait: A Suggested Painter', *Burlington Magazine*, 124 (Mar. 1982)

Changeling Boy. He is the cause of the quarrel between *Oberon and *Titania, described in *A Midsummer Night's Dream* 2.1.18–31. *AB*

The Chandos portrait (formerly a possession of the Dukes of Chandos), the most convincing of all the paintings which have been identified as contemporary likenesses of Shakespeare. It was given to the National Portrait Gallery in 1856, where it is still catalogued as item number 1.

Chapel Lane Cottage. In 1602 Shakespeare acquired a copyhold from Walter Getley in a cottage with a garden of about a quarter of an acre (0.1 ha) in Chapel Lane, Stratford, across the road from New Place garden. On his death it passed to his daughter Susanna. *SW*

Chapel Royal, a part of the London royal household which existed to provide a children's choir, and later an acting troupe, for court entertainments. There was also a Windsor Chapel with which the Chapel Royal appears to have merged in 1576 when Richard Farrant, in association with the Chapel Royal Master William Hunnis, installed the Chapel Children in the first Blackfriars playhouse. *GE*

Chaplain. See RUTLAND'S TUTOR.

Chapman, George (*c.*1559–1634), poet and dramatist, now famous as the first translator of Homer into English, but in his time a highly successful playwright and a passionate advocate in verse of the dignity of the poet's profession. His first poems, published as *The Shadow of Night* (1594), recommend the cultivation of obscurity in poetry (making it comprehensible only to select readers), and the establishment of an intellectual meritocracy capable of competing with the Elizabethan social order. For some scholars, this book identifies him as a member of an exclusive group of intellectuals who surrounded Sir Walter *Ralegh. In 1592 the group was dubbed the 'school of atheism' by a querulous pamphleteer. One theory, now discredited, holds that *Love's Labour's Lost* (*c.*1594) is an attack on the Ralegh circle, and that Shakespeare alludes to this 'school of atheism' as the 'school of night' (4.3.251), with *The Shadow of Night* as its poetic manifesto. This theory also proposes that Chapman was the rival poet referred to in Shakespeare's Sonnets. Chapman's second book, *Ovid's Banquet of Senses* (1595), burlesques the genre of the erotic narrative poem popularized by Shakespeare's *Venus and Adonis* (1593). Its obscurity makes it less approachable than his second contribution to the genre, a pensive continuation of *Marlowe's unfinished *Hero and Leander* (1598). Chapman's translation of *Seven Books of Homer's Iliad* (1598) transformed Homer's heroes into Elizabethan soldiers and politicians, and helped Shakespeare do the same in *Troilus and Cressida* (1601–2). His best-known comedy is *All Fools* (1599), his most celebrated tragedy the extravagant *Bussy D'Ambois* (1604). Shakespeare may have modelled his late tragic heroes on the heroes of Chapman's tragedies. *RM*

Ide, Richard S., *Possessed with Greatness: The Heroic Tragedies of Chapman and Shakespeare* (1980)
Snare, Gerald, *The Mystification of George Chapman* (1989)

Chapuys, Eustace. See CAPUTIUS, LORD.

Charlecote. See LUCY, SIR THOMAS.

Charles, Duke Frederick's servant, is defeated in a wrestling match by Orlando, *As You Like It* 1.2.204. *AB*

Charles, Dauphin of France. He agrees to be viceroy of his dominions subject to King Henry VI after having been captured by the English, *1 Henry VI* 5.7. *AB*

Charles I (1600–49), King of England (reigned 1625–49). In his youth he was in the shadow of his outgoing and charismatic elder brother *Henry, whose unexpected death in 1612 placed him in a position he was poorly equipped by either nature or training to fill. His father made no secret of his disappointment in his second son, and publicly declared his preference for the favourite Buckingham. Nevertheless, and despite numerous quarrels, Buckingham became Charles's closest adviser. Together they travelled to Spain in 1623 to negotiate—unsuccessfully—a Spanish match, and his subsequent marriage in 1625, shortly after his father's death, to the French Catholic princess *Henrietta Maria, fulfilled James's great hope of an ecumenical alliance.

Charles was a quiet and intellectual man, shy to the point of prudishness, and instituted radical reforms in the court, the most visible having to do with decorum and his own privacy. He was a passionate connoisseur of all the arts, and amassed one of the greatest collections of paintings in Europe. Both he and his wife loved theatre, and Charles took an active interest in the management of the public stage, in 1634 even overruling Sir Henry Herbert on a question of censoring oaths in *Davenant's *The Wits.* During the 1630s, the decade of prerogative rule when Charles undertook to reinvent both the nation and the monarchy, the masque and drama too underwent significant developments through royal patronage. Inigo Jones's stage machinery was greatly refined and elaborated for productions at Whitehall, and perspective settings were for the first time regularly employed for drama. Few of the plays at the Caroline court were by Shakespeare; but among all the Shirley, *Beaumont and *Fletcher, *Massinger, Brome, Strode, Davenant, Townshend, and Suckling the King and Queen saw *Richard III*, *The Taming of the Shrew*, *The Winter's Tale*, *Cymbeline*, *Hamlet*, and *Julius Caesar.* Charles's copy of the Second Folio, now at Windsor Castle, includes annotations in his own handwriting, one of them retitling *Much Ado About Nothing* as 'Beatrice and Benedict'.

With the closing of the theatres in 1642, court theatre also ended, and the subsequent defeat of the Royalist cause found Charles reading Shakespeare in prison rather than watching it performed at his palace, a practice duly noted by contemporaries. One defence of his death sentence remarked that it would never have been necessary had the King 'but studied Scripture half so much as Ben Jonson or Shakespeare', while Andrew Marvell construed Charles at his execution, on a stage erected outside Inigo Jones's Whitehall Banqueting House, as a 'royal actor' on a 'tragic scaffold' (*Horatian Ode*, ll. 53–4). *Milton, in *Eikonoklastes*, deliberately used one of Charles's favourite authors against him when he likened his alleged tyranny and feigned piety to those of Shakespeare's Richard III. *SO*

Sharpe, Kevin, *The Personal Rule of Charles I* (1992)

Charles VI, King of France, accedes to the treaty in which his daughter Catherine marries King Harry (the Treaty of Troyes described by *Holinshed), *Henry V* 5.2. Historically, Charles VI (1368–1422) was insane, a state of affairs which destabilized the French governing elite and made Henry V's conquest much easier, though Shakespere suppresses this fact. *AB*

Charmian is Cleopatra's attendant, dying with her, *Antony and Cleopatra* 5.2. *AB*

Chatham, Clerk of. See CLERK OF CHATHAM.

Châtillon is the ambassador from France in *King John.* *AB*

Chaucer, Geoffrey (*c.*1340–1400), poet who played a seminal role in the development of English vernacular poetry. Chaucer's reputation in the Elizabethan age was considerable: he was heralded as the father of English poetry and as 'our English Homer' though he was also increasingly criticized for bawdiness, for the roughness of his verse, and for the obscurity of his language, with some critics confessing that they could not always understand him. The extent of Chaucer's direct influence upon Elizabethan and Jacobean literature is often difficult to gauge for he was rarely quoted and maxims that we might recognize from Chaucer were often conventional. Similarly, his plots were often available from another source.

Troilus and Criseyde was the most popular of Chaucer's works in the 16th century. Shakespeare's play follows exactly the order of events of Chaucer's poem (though in a considerably shorter time frame) from which it derives all its main characters. Perhaps the major difference is in tone. Where Chaucer felt obvious sympathy for Criseyde, Shakespeare's heroine is far more ambiguous, perhaps reflecting her degraded status in contemporary versions such as Henryson's *Testament of Cresseid.* Moreover, Shakespeare places the love story within a cynical account of the Trojan War, so that it becomes contaminated by its context and the two plots run increasingly parallel to one another. Shakespeare's earlier use of the poem in *Romeo and Juliet* was perhaps more in sympathy with

Chaucer's conception of love tragedy. Not only verbal parallels, but the emphasis upon a malign Fortune working against the comparatively innocent lovers, suggest *Romeo and Juliet*'s indebtness to Chaucer's poem.

Perhaps Chaucer's second most popular work at this time was the Knight's Tale. Again, its popularity was signalled by a number of poetic and dramatic adaptations, including two plays now lost called *Palamon and Arcite* that were apparently performed in 1566 and 1594. In *A Midsummer Night's Dream*, Shakespeare used the Knight's Tale for some details of the courtship of Theseus and Hippolyta. But at the end of his career, Shakespeare returned to Chaucer's tale and made it the foundation of *The Two Noble Kinsmen*, written in collaboration with Fletcher. The dramatists openly acknowledged their debt in the prologue which cites 'Chaucer, of all admired' as the one who has immortalized the story that is to be performed. Again the tone of Shakespeare's writing in this play differs from that of Chaucer. Here, by contrast, Shakespeare takes the story more seriously than Chaucer, leaving Fletcher to add touches of levity.

Shakespeare's reading of Chaucer was clearly wide-ranging. *The Legend of Good Women, The Book of the Duchess, The Parliament of Fowls*, the Man of Law's Tale, and the Wife of Bath's Tale are other works to which an influence can be traced. That the poet's work made a lasting impression on Shakespeare is suggested by the fact that he returned to some of these poems again and again. *JKS*

Thompson, Ann, *Shakespeare's Chaucer: A Study in Literary Origins* (1978)

Cheek by Jowl. Founded in 1981 by the director Declan Donnellan and the designer Nick Ormerod, this radical, innovative group presented classical texts in lucid productions which could readily be adapted to different playing spaces. Half their output was Shakespearian. Their celebrated all-male *As You Like It* in 1991–2 and 1994–5 went on British and worldwide tours to international acclaim. The partners have staged plays at the National and Royal Shakespeare Theatres as well as *The Winter's Tale* in Russian at the Maly theatre, St Petersburg (1997). *MJ*

Reade, Simon, *Cheek by Jowl: Ten Years of Celebration* (1991)

Chekhov, Anton (1860–1904), Russian playwright and short-story writer. Chekhov repeatedly draws on the play and character of Hamlet: for the hero of *Ivanov* (1887); for the failed intellectual of 'In Moscow' (1891) declaring 'I am a Moscow Hamlet'; and for *The Seagull* (1895), with its crucial relationships between a powerful mother, her lover, a sensitive, artistic son, and a victimized heroine—explicitly using *Hamlet* as a form of reference. *TM*

Rosalind (Adrian Lester, with headscarf) dances with Celia (Simon Coates) in Cheek by Jowl's internationally acclaimed touring production of *As You Like It* (1991–5).

Chéreau, Patrice (b.1944), French actor-director. Chéreau's career has pursued a remarkably wide-ranging trajectory, beginning with his own student theatre company in the 1960s, and subsequently extending to radical perspectives on French classical drama, notable collaborations with living artists (the scenographer Peduzzi, the playwright Koltès, the composer Boulez, the actor Desarthes), and the production of films. He played the title role of *Richard II* (1970, Marseille, then *Odéon) as a carefree clown and pleasure-seeker in an elaborate setting dominated by complex machinery. In his *Hamlet* (1988, Avignon Festival, then Nanterre), the hooves of the *Ghost's black horse resounded over an uneven wooden floor which represented an inverted fortress. *ISG*

Chester, Robert (fl. 1601). He wrote the poem *Love's Martyr* (1601), to which Shakespeare appended his most cryptic verses, 'The Phoenix and Turtle'. Chester was a long-term employee of Sir John Salusbury of Denbighshire, Wales. He contributed verses to a manuscript belonging to Salusbury, in which he shows an intimate knowledge of Sir John's affairs: they are full of obscure allusions to the women Sir John admired, and seem to mimic his master's poems, which are also full of obscure private allusions. It is thought that most of *Love's Martyr* was written to celebrate the marriage of Sir John Salusbury and Ursula Stanley in 1586. Shakespeare's 'The Phoenix and Turtle' derives its subject matter and cryptic tone from an allegory developed in Chester's poem. E. A. J. Honigmann argues—not altogether convincingly—that it, too, was written at the time of the marriage, and that this furnishes support for his theory that Shakespeare was already a member of Lord Strange's company of players by the mid-1580s. Lord Strange was Ursula Stanley's brother, and he and his company could have visited the Salusburys to take part in the wedding celebrations. But if Chester's and Shakespeare's allegories were written in 1586, why were they published in 1601? The answer may be—and here Honigmann's argument is persuasive—that the volume was issued in response to a period of crisis in Salusbury's career. In 1601 he was in financial difficulties, involved in an expensive lawsuit, and standing for election to Parliament against a powerful local rival. *Love's Martyr* may have been published in a bid to drum up support for him in London. Chester's allegory contains what seems to be a flattering character-sketch of Sir John, and a set of patriotic verses on King Arthur, doubtless intended to link Salusbury, as a Welshman, with the dominant Tudor myth. A number of prominent poets were invited to add poetic postscripts to Chester's text: they included Ben *Jonson, George *Chapman, and John *Marston, as well as Shakespeare. If it was intended to help improve Sir John's fortunes, it failed. He died in debt. *RM*

Brown, Carleton (ed.), *Poems by Sir John Salusbury and Robert Chester* (1914)

Honigmann, E. A. J., *Shakespeare: The 'Lost Years'* (1985)

Chettle, Henry (*c.*1560–*c.*1607), printer, pamphleteer, and playwright. He started life as a stationer's apprentice, then went into partnership with the printer John Danter in the 1590s. In 1592 he transcribed, from a manuscript written by the dying Robert *Greene, the last of Greene's prose works, *Greene's Groatsworth of Wit*, which Danter published. The pamphlet attacked Christopher *Marlowe as a devious atheist and Shakespeare as a plagiarist and hack. It would seem from the preface to Chettle's prose satire *Kindheart's Dream* (1592) that Marlowe and Shakespeare thought he had written *Greene's Groatsworth of Wit* himself, though he denied it vigorously. Modern critical opinion tends to share their suspicions. Chettle may also have rewritten sections of Shakespeare's *Romeo and Juliet* for the pirated edition printed by Danter in 1597. He went into more legitimate partnership with Shakespeare when they worked together, perhaps in the mid-1590s, on revisions to the play *Sir Thomas More*, which Chettle originally co-wrote (it is thought) with Anthony *Munday. He wrote a huge number of other plays—mostly in collaboration—but very few survive. *RM*

Jowett, John, 'Henry Chettle', in David A. Richardson (ed.), *Dictionary of Literary Biography*, vol. cxxxvi: *Sixteenth-Century British Nondramatic Writers* (1994)

Chetwood, William Rufus (d. 1766), bookseller, dramatist, and long-serving prompter at Drury Lane and Smock Alley, Dublin (where his pupils included Barry and Macklin), whose *General History of the Stage* (1749) is a source for the story that Davenant was Shakespeare's son. His *British Theatre* (1750), written during a period of imprisonment for debt and viewed with contempt, includes a list of Shakespeare quartos of which many are spurious. *CMSA*

chiasmus, a figure of speech in which two terms are repeated in reverse order:

> I wasted time, and now doth time waste me
> (*Richard II*, 5.5.49)

CB

Chichele (Chicheley), Henry. See Canterbury, Archbishop of.

Chichester Festival Theatre. It opened in 1962 as a summer enterprise in emulation of Tyrone *Guthrie's theatre at Stratford, Ontario. Its hexagonal auditorium and thrust stage make it ideal for Elizabethan plays, but although there have been occasional productions of Shakespeare, its middle-class audiences seem happy with starry revivals of Wilde and Coward. *MJ*

Child, Blackamoor. See Blackamoor Child.

childbirth and child-rearing. Shakespeare's plays repeatedly testify to early modern society's enormous material and psychic investments in the bearing and raising of children. Ellen *Terry lamented Shakespeare's tendency to depict parent–child relationships only as father–daughter and mother–son dyads: small children are nearly always boys (Arthur in *King John*, Young Martius in *Coriolanus*); daughters more often figure as young adults, testing the limits of paternal authority or simultaneously liberated and imperilled by a father's death (Desdemona in *Othello*, Helen in *All's Well That Ends Well*). The plays explore maternity and paternity primarily from the point of view of anxious parents. They are as interested in testing the fiction of paternity (and exploring the tensions that arise from its ultimate unknowability, in an age before genetic testing) as in representing motherhood.

In Shakespeare's time childbirth and child-rearing constituted a realm shared by adult women and small children, whose gender was not fully differentiated until the age of about 7. Yet, with a few exceptions (Titania and the Indian boy in *A Midsummer Night's Dream*, Hermione and Mamillius in *The Winter's Tale*), Shakespeare is less concerned to depict this realm than to explore the dramatic resonance of anxious male fantasies about it, and to use the danger and risk that childbirth entailed for both mother and infant as tropes that convey the male experience of vulnerability (*King Lear*, *Pericles*, *The Tempest*). *KC*

Boose, Lynda E., and Flowers, Betty S. (eds.), *Daughters and Fathers* (1989)

Pollock, Linda, *Forgotten Children: Parent–Child Relations from 1500 to 1900* (1983)

Rose, Mary Beth, 'Where are the Mothers in Shakespeare? Options for Gender Representation in the English Renaissance', *Shakespeare Quarterly*, 42 (1991)

Children of Paul's. See children's companies.

Children of the Chapel. See children's companies.

Children of the King's Revels. See children's companies.

Children of Windsor. See children's companies.

children's companies. Rosencrantz's speech about 'an eyrie of children, little eyases' (*Hamlet* 2.2.340) was probably written in 1606–8 and refers to the Blackfriars Boys company whose success—and the politically dangerous drama it was based upon—threatened the King's Men. Venues for performances by all-boy playing companies were built in St Paul's cathedral in 1575 (used by Paul's Boys) and in the Old Buttery of the Blackfriars building in 1576 (used by the Chapel Children). The boys who performed in these companies were drawn from the choirs of St Paul's and the Chapel Royal in Windsor and their managers maintained the legal fiction that they were merely continuing their education by acting. Songs and dances were a major part of the performance in the plays performed by these early companies, and the subject matter seems to have been largely classical. When John *Lyly began writing for an amalgamation of Paul's Boys and the Chapel Children the drama became more sophisticated and introduced a number of innovations (especially themes of cross-dressing and mistaken identity) which influenced Shakespeare. In 1584 the first Blackfriars playhouse was closed by its landlord, but the Paul's continued until 1590 when, in circumstances still mysterious (probably related to Lyly's involvement in the Martin Marprelate controversy), it too closed.

In 1599 the Paul's playhouse reopened in another part of the same building and in 1600 Richard Burbage leased the second Blackfriars playhouse to the same Henry Evans who had managed the first Blackfriars, and all-boy performances resumed. The drama of this revival was markedly different from the earlier phase: strong sexual innuendo predominated in plays such as Jonson, Marston, and Chapman's *Eastward Ho* and Marston's *The Dutch Courtesan* for the Blackfriars Boys and surprising violence in Marston's *Antonio and Mellida* and *Antonio's Revenge* for the Paul's Boys. The Paul's and Blackfriars playhouses ceased in 1608, the former apparently after being denounced by puritan William Crashawe and the latter because a production of Chapman's *Conspiracy of Byron* enraged the French ambassador. The Blackfriars Boys continued at the Whitefriars playhouse. Another company of children, Beeston's Boys, flourished at the Cockpit, Drury Lane, from 1637 to 1642. *GE*

Gair, Reavley, *The Children of Paul's: The Story of a Theatre Company, 1553–1608* (1982)
Shapiro, Michael, *Children of the Revels: The Boy Companies of Shakespeare's Time and their Plays* (1977)

'Child Rowland to the dark tower came', fragment of an old Scottish ballad quoted by Edgar in *The Tragedy of King Lear* 3.4.170. Child Rowland was a son of King Arthur. *JB*

Chimes at Midnight. See WELLES, ORSON.

China is a relatively new member in the world Shakespeare community. Being one of a small select number of Western literary figures whose work was introduced into China at the beginning of the 20th century, Shakespeare has won unusual popularity with over a billion Chinese people and has been regarded as one of the few world-famous literary giants who have given people insights into themselves and enriched their barren lives, and in whose work people have found wisdom, happiness, and entertainment. In the first issue of *Shakespeare Studies* published by the *Shakespeare Society of China in 1983, Shakespeare is said to have attained the same prestige as Karl *Marx, the great teacher of ideology to the Chinese in the 20th century, and this is the most enthusiastic praise the Chinese have ever given to a man of letters outside China.

It was not until 1903 that the works of Shakespeare became known for the first time in China through the *translation of ten stories from Charles and Mary *Lamb's *Tales from Shakespeare* by an unknown translator into classical Chinese. In 1922, Tian Han, the late chairman of the Chinese Dramatists' Association in the 1950s and a noted playwright himself, tried his hand at rendering *Hamlet*, the first attempt to translate a Shakespeare play into Chinese. Since then, all of Shakespeare's plays have been rendered into Chinese and some have appeared in over a dozen different versions by various hands, among whom two deserve special credit: *Zhu Shenghao and *Liang Shiqui. From the very beginning, translation has been the chief means of introducing Shakespeare to Chinese readers and also the basis of staging of Shakespeare's plays and Shakespeare criticism in China.

The first serious theatrical performance of a Shakespeare play was that of *The Merchant of Venice* in Shanghai in 1930. In the last two decades, stage performances of Shakespeare's plays have reached a wide audience in China. The performance of *The Merchant of Venice* by Beijing Youth Art Theatre, which held about 200 shows between 1980 and 1982, offers an impressive, but not isolated, example of the reception of his plays on the Chinese stage. Two Shakespeare festivals, organized by the Shakespeare Society of China, were held in Beijing and Shanghai in 1986 and 1994. In addition to *huaju*, which bears a close resemblance to a Western drama and is the normal means of staging Shakespeare's plays, there have been some experiments to adapt Shakespeare's plays to Peking opera and other Chinese local dramatic forms.

Shakespeare's plays began to be taught in China in the 1930s. Now seminars on Shakespearian drama are usually offered to English majors at the graduate level in Chinese universities and colleges while the translated version of Shakespeare's plays is often included in the reading list for students majoring in Chinese literature or foreign literature.

Serious Shakespearian criticism in China did not commence until after 1949, although the first Chinese critical essay on Shakespeare appeared in 1918. Since mainland China remained, from 1949 to the late 1970s, rather isolated, the glorious cultural heritage of the Chinese people and traditional Chinese thinking surprisingly did not seem to bear a significant influence on the interpretation of Shakespeare by early Chinese scholars and critics. On the contrary, a political and ideological approach was the dominant mode in Shakespeare criticism in mainland China up to the early 1980s. The basic principles followed in the criticism of modern Chinese literature—chiefly 'socialist realism'—were adopted by the majority of early Chinese critics of Shakespeare. For those critics, the 'purpose' of writing was profoundly important for their discussion of Shakespeare. They believed that Shakespeare was moulding and guiding public opinion for the rising bourgeois class, a conclusion drawn chiefly from their analyses of the age the dramatist lived in, of his life, and of the tone in his plays. In most of the critical essays published before the late 1980s, discussion of Shakespearian 'themes' usually took up the most space and, according to those critics, there was always a fundamental thesis in every one of Shakespeare's plays, often a political and ideological one, which reflects the playwright's bourgeois standpoint and his belief in humanism. The rigid limitations of this political and ideological approach to Shakespeare had hindered greatly Chinese critics and had often resulted in rather biased and unsatisfactory interpretations of Shakespeare's plays.

A change began to be observed in criticism published in mainland China in the late 1980s and especially in the 1990s, when China opened its door more and more to Western technology and economic structures and Chinese writers and critics obtained easier access to world Shakespeare scholarship. The founding of the Shakespeare Society of China in 1984 and the 1986 and the 1994 Shakespeare festivals further stimulated Shakespeare studies both in literary and dramatic circles in China. Chinese critics have now increased their interest in some much discussed subjects in Shakespeare's plays, such as Hamlet's indecision, the theme of forgiveness, and Shakespeare's emphasis on human interests and values. It is encouraging to see that there is now among Chinese critics more tolerance for the aesthetic concepts of the West and fewer scornful attacks on Western Shakespearian scholarship than was the case in the 1950s and early 1960s. A group of younger scholars and critics, obviously aware of the political and ideological approach to Shakespeare, has proposed to re-evaluate the early criticism published in China, to treat Shakespeare's plays as dramatic art, to absorb the essence of world Shakespearian scholarship in the last several hundred years, and to develop a Chinese interpretation of the plays on the basis of a Chinese sensibility. *HQX*

Butterfield, Fox, 'The Old Vic Takes "Hamlet" to China', *New York Times*, 25 Nov. 1979
He, Qixin, 'China's Shakespeare', *Shakespeare Quarterly*, 37 (1986)
Zhang, Xiaoyang, *Shakespeare in China: A Comparative Study of Two Traditions and Cultures* (1996)

Chiron is the younger of Tamora's two surviving villainous sons in *Titus Andronicus*. *AB*

Cholmeley, Richard, company patron, dates of birth and death unknown. A group of recusant players under Cholmeley's patronage toured in Yorkshire from 1606 to at least 1616 using only printed play-texts for their repertory. When tried for sedition these players insisted (falsely, it turned out) that they had not strayed from the printed texts, apparently thinking that this gave them a kind of surrogate licence from the Master of the Revels who had licensed the original manuscripts underlying the printing. One of the actors reported that at Candlemas 1609–10 they performed 'Perocles prince of Tire', which was undoubtedly the work of Shakespeare and Wilkins, and 'Kinge Lere', which might have been Shakespeare's (his quarto was the most recent) but equally might have been the old chronicle history of *King Leir* printed in 1605. *GE*

Sisson, C. J., 'Shakespeare Quartos as Prompt-Copies', *Review of English Studies*, 18 (1942)

chorus, the speaker and the part spoken by an extra-dramatic character who supplies background information and commentary in the drama. In Shakespeare's *Henry v* and *Pericles* a chorus provides a series of links within the drama, but usually the role is more limited: in *Romeo and Juliet* the chorus precedes Acts 1 and 2 only, and in *The Winter's Tale* 'Time, the Chorus' bridges the sixteen-year gap between Acts 3 and 4. Inductions (such as Rumour's at the start of *2 Henry iv*) and prologues (as before *Troilus and Cressida*) fulfil the choric scene-setting function, but those which exhort the audience to attend carefully (such as before *All Is True* (*Henry viii*) and *The Two Noble Kinsmen*) may have been used only on the first performance. *GE*

Christian criticism has several aspects. First, in identifying specifically Christian references, applications, and meanings in Shakespeare's works. Living within an official though turbulent Christian culture, Shakespeare was certainly thoroughly familiar with the Bible, probably in its Bishops' Bible translation (1568). One play title (*Measure for Measure*) is directly adapted from the Gospel of St Matthew (see Richmond Noble, *Shakespeare's Biblical Knowledge*, 1935). Second, in exploring the highly charged theological questions of good and evil, salvation and damnation, sin and expiation which are central to the tragedies, while the so-called Romances resonate with the words 'grace' and 'faith' (see R. Mushat Frye, *Shakespeare and Christian Doctrine*, 1963). Third, in demonstrating Shakespeare's personal sectarian allegiance, supposedly Catholic, established during a putative stay in Lancashire in the 1580s. Many critics respond to Shakespeare's sceptical humanism, but Peter Milward's various books, including *Shakespeare's Religious Background* (1973), plead the alternative case. *TM*

Christopher, Sir. He is a priest who takes a message from Lord Stanley to Richmond, *Richard iii* 4.5 (based on Christopher Urswick (d. 1521)). *AB*

chronology. The chronological ordering of the plays in the Shakespeare canon is based on various strands of interconnecting evidence: references in datable sources such as Francis Meres's list of twelve of Shakespeare's plays in *Palladis Tamia* (1598), records of court performances, Henslowe's records of performances at the Rose playhouse, entries in the Stationers' Register, dates on the title pages, and topical allusions in the plays themselves (such as the double eclipse of sun and moon in 1605 alluded to in *King Lear*). Since Shakespeare's habits of writing appear to have changed over time, scholars have brought different types of internal evidence—changes in verse, metrics, imagery, vocabulary—to bear on chronological problems with varying degrees of success. Edmond *Malone, for instance, was the first to observe that Shakespeare used more rhymed verse in his early plays than in his later works, but subsequent scholars have pointed out that while Malone's dictum is generally true, Shakespeare's earliest plays actually contain very little rhymed verse.

Although there is general scholarly consensus about which plays fall into Shakespeare's early, middle, and late periods, there is substantial disagreement about the precise dates for individual plays. In a classic study of 'The Problem of Chronology' (1930), E. K. Chambers argued that Shakespeare's first two plays, dating from 1590–1, were *The First Part of the Contention* (*2 Henry vi*) and *Richard Duke of York* (*3 Henry vi*), and that *The Two Gentlemen of Verona* and *The Taming of the Shrew* were written several years later, in 1593–5. The editors of the New Oxford Shakespeare (1986), having undertaken a major reassessment of the evidence for chronological placement, agree with Chambers that Shakespeare's earliest plays were indeed written in 1590–1 but conclude that his first two efforts were *The Two Gentlemen of Verona* and *The Taming of the Shrew*.

The list below gives the plays and poems in the order of composition proposed by the Oxford Shakespeare (with the proviso that most of the dates are necessarily provisional rather than definitive):

1590–1 *The Two Gentlemen of Verona*
1590–1 *The Taming of the Shrew*
1591 *The First Part of the Contention* (*2 Henry vi*)
1591 *Richard Duke of York* (*3 Henry vi*)
1592 *1 Henry vi*
1592–3 *Titus Andronicus*
1592–3 *Richard iii*
1592–3 *Venus and Adonis*
1593–4 *The Rape of Lucrece*
1594 *The Comedy of Errors*
1594–5 *Love's Labour's Lost*
1595 *Richard ii*
1595 *Romeo and Juliet*
1595 *A Midsummer Night's Dream*
1596 *King John*
1596–7 *The Merchant of Venice*
1596–7 *1 Henry iv*
1597–8 *The Merry Wives of Windsor*
1597–8 *2 Henry iv*
1598 *Much Ado About Nothing*
1598–9 *Henry v*
1599 *Julius Caesar*
1599–1600 *As You Like It*
1600–1 *Hamlet*
1601 *Twelfth Night*
1602 *Troilus and Cressida*
1603–4 *Sir Thomas More*
1603 *Measure for Measure*
1603–4 *Othello*
1604–5 *All's Well That Ends Well*
1605 *Timon of Athens*
1605–6 *The History of King Lear*
1606 *Macbeth*
1606 *Antony and Cleopatra*
1607 *Pericles*
1608 *Coriolanus*
1609 *The Winter's Tale*
1610 *Cymbeline*
1611 *The Tempest*
1613 *All Is True* (*Henry viii*) *ER*

Chambers, E. K., *William Shakespeare: A Study of Facts and Problems* (1930)
Wells, Stanley, and Taylor, Gary, *William Shakespeare: A Textual Companion* (1987)

Church. See RELIGION.

Cibber, Colley (1671–1757), a successful actor, manager, and dramatist who began his theatrical career playing small parts for the United Company at Drury Lane. He achieved prominence in the lead role of his own *adaptation of *Richard iii* (1699), and was appointed Poet Laureate in 1730. Endlessly involved in feuds and theatre politics, his *Apology for the Life of Mr. Colley Cibber* (1740) is a valuable source of stage history. He played Gloucester, Iago, Edmund, and Wolsey but, best suited to comedy, Shallow was considered his finest role. His final appearance was as Pandulph in his adaptation of *King John, Papal Tyranny.* *CMSA*

Cibber, Susannah Maria (1714–55), an actress, who was the sister of Thomas Arne and briefly, scandalously, the second wife of Theophilus Cibber. She began her stage career as a singer and became a fine dramatic actress, famed for conveying tenderness, whose roles included Desdemona, Isabella, Lady Anne, and a particularly affecting Constance. Her performances for *Garrick at Drury Lane, including playing opposite him as Ophelia, Cordelia, and Perdita, were considered her best Shakespearian work, although her Juliet to Spranger *Barry's Romeo at Covent Garden was well received. *CMSA*

Cibber, Theophilus (1703–58), actor, manager, and writer whose career, which began in 1720 when he joined the Drury Lane company co-managed by his father, was often driven by expediency and overshadowed by an outrageous private life and theatre politics. An early role was Prince Edward in his own adaptation of *Henry vi* (1723), and a style best suited to comic playing (Lucio, Slender, Pistol) did not preclude him attempting Romeo to his 14-year-old daughter Jenny's Juliet (in his version published in 1748) or Othello to her Desdemona. He drowned in a shipwreck travelling to perform in Dublin. *CMSA*

Cicero is a senator in *Julius Caesar* (not included in the conspiracy). Marcus Tullius Cicero (106–43 BC) was a philosopher, orator, and statesman. *AB*

Cimber, Metellus. See METELLUS CIMBER.

cinema. See SHAKESPEARE ON SOUND FILM; SILENT FILMS.

Cinna is one of the conspirators in *Julius Caesar* (L. Cornelius Cinna the younger). *AB*

Cinna the poet, a friend of Caesar's, is mistaken for Cinna the conspirator and killed by the plebeians, *Julius Caesar* 3.3. *AB*

cinquepace (sinkapace), one of a family of couple dances imported from France and Italy, including the *galliard, tourdion, and la *volta; also an alternative name for the galliard. The unit of five steps implied by the name fits to a six-beat bar: four springing kicks on the first four beats, with a jump through the fifth beat, timed so as to land on the sixth beat. *JB*

Cinthio (Giovanni Battista Giraldi) (1504–73), Italian dramatist and professor of rhetoric. Cinthio wrote a number of Senecan-style tragedies and some dramatic criticism but was best known in England as the author of the *Hecatommithi* (1565?), a collection of prose tales narrated by travellers on board a ship. Cinthio's work may have inspired Shakespeare to write two plays back to back using tales from the *Hecatommithi.* The tragi-comic 'Disdemona and the Moor' served as the main source for *Othello.* The story of Epitia provided the framework for *Measure for Measure.* Verbal similarities between the Italian 'Disdemona' and Shakespeare's tragedy, and the fact that no English translation seems to have existed, suggest that Shakespeare read the *Hecatommithi* in Italian. *Measure for Measure* is more obviously indebted to an English adaptation of Cinthio's tale, George Whetstone's play *Promos and Cassandra,* published in 1578. *JKS*

Citizen of Angers. He refuses the feuding kings in *King John* entrance to the town, but suggests the marriage of Louis the Dauphin to Blanche as a basis for peace, 2.1. *AB*

Citizen of Antium. He directs the disguised Coriolanus to Aufidius' house, *Coriolanus* 4.4.6–11. *MD*

citizens of the watch appear in *Romeo and Juliet* 3.1 at the murders of *Mercutio and Tybalt. *AB*

cittern, a wire-strung instrument played with a plectrum, associated with popular music. It might have a grotesque carved head, hence the reference in *Love's Labour's Lost* 5.2.604. *JB*

city comedy, a kind of satirical drama prominent in the early 17th century, of which Ben *Jonson was the chief exponent. It exposes the follies and vices of London life, as in Jonson's *Bartholomew Fair* and *The Devil is an Ass* (1614, 1616), or Marston's *The Dutch Courtesan* (1605). *CB*

Ciulei, Liviu (b. 1923), Romanian director-designer who has staged Shakespeare internationally. In English his *Hamlet* (Washington, 1978) was notable, as were *The Tempest, As You Like It,* and *A Midsummer Night's Dream* during his tenure as artistic director at the Guthrie Theatre in Minneapolis in the 1980s. *DK*

City. The historic core of London, the City is the administrative and financial centre of the capital, also known as the Square Mile. The modern boundaries of the City reflect those imposed by the Roman and medieval walls which protected early London. In Shakespeare's day the City's opposition to theatrical performances within its jurisdiction, from the 1570s onwards, led to the exile of the playhouses to outlying districts such as Shoreditch and *Bankside. *RSB*

Inwood, S., *A History of London* (1998)

Clarence, Duke of. **(1)** George, Duke of Clarence (1449–78), deserts his elder brother Edward (who later becomes King Edward IV) in *Richard Duke of York* (*3 Henry VI*) 2.6 but they are reunited, 5.1. In *Richard III* Edward has him imprisoned, and he is stabbed by two murderers employed by his younger brother Richard (who becomes Richard III), 1.4.263. **(2)** Thomas Duke of Clarence (*c.*1388–1421), younger brother of Henry V, appears briefly in *2 Henry IV* and *Henry V.* *AB*

Clarence's Daughter. See CLARENCE'S SON.

Clarence's Son (Edward, Earl of Warwick, 1475–99), with his sister (Margaret Plantagenet, 1473–1541), laments his father's death, *Richard III* 2.2. *AB*

Claribel, Alonso's daughter, is married to the King of Tunis in the elaborate pre-history of *The Tempest.* She is absent from the play itself. *AB*

Clark, Jaime (1844–75), translator of Shakespeare into Spanish, of British origin. He and Guillermo *Macpherson were the first to render Shakespeare's blank verse systematically into Spanish verse (normally hendecasyllabic lines, as well as the rhymed lines as such). By his untimely death at the age of 31, Clark's unfinished *Obras de Shakespeare* in five volumes (1872–76?) contained three tragedies and seven comedies. *ALP*

Clark, William George (1821–78), English academic, one of three editors (with W. Aldis Wright and John Glover) of the first *Cambridge edition of Shakespeare (9 vols., 1863–6), including variant readings from all early and some later editions. Its one-volume version, the *Globe* (1864), created a reference standard for almost a century. *TM*

Clarke, Charles Cowden (1787–1877), English writer, friend of John Keats and partner with wife Mary in a series of enthusiastic studies of Shakespeare, including his own lectures on *Shakespeare's Characters, Chiefly those Subordinate* (1863); their joint edition of Shakespeare (1868); and their *Shakespeare Key, Unlocking the Treasures of his Style* (1879). *TM*

Clarke, Mary Cowden (1809–1908), partner of husband Charles in several Shakespeare studies, including her long superseded *Complete Concordance* (1845), and *Girlhood of Shakespeare's Heroines* (3 vols., 1850–2), often mocked for its attempt to recreate a prehistory for Shakespeare's female characters, but nevertheless an early manifestation of feminine if not feminist concerns. *TM*

Claudio. **(1)** He jilts Hero at the altar (*Much Ado About Nothing* 4.1) but marries her in the end. **(2)** See VARRUS. **(3)** Isabella's brother is sentenced to death for impregnating Juliet in *Measure for Measure.* *AB*

Claudius in *Julius Caesar.* See VARRUS.

Claudius, King, the King of Denmark who has murdered his brother and married his brother's wife Gertrude (Hamlet's parents). He is called Fengo in the *Historiae Danicae* of *Saxo Grammaticus. *AB*

Clayton, John. In March 1600 a William Shakespeare successfully sued John Clayton, a 'yeoman' of Wellington, Bedfordshire, for a debt of £7 apparently incurred in 1592. *Chambers, like Sidney *Lee, sees no reason for identifying this Shakespeare with the dramatist, but gives no cogent reasons for not doing so. *SW*

Clemen, Wolfgang (1909–90), German academic, influential as founder of the Shakespeare library in Munich, and through works on imagery and soliloquy translated into English: *The Development of Shakespeare's Imagery* (1951, expanded from *Shakespeares Bilder,* 1936), *English Tragedy before Shakespeare* (1961), *A Commentary on Shakespeare's Richard III* (1968), *Shakespeare's Dramatic Art* (1974), and *Shakespeare's Soliloquies* (1987). *TM*

Cleomenes is a Sicilian lord who with another lord, Dion, is sent by Leontes to seek the oracle to ascertain the truth about Hermione in *The Winter's Tale.* *AB*

Cleon is the husband of Dioniza and Governor of Tarsus, where Pericles relieves a famine, *Pericles* 4. *AB*

Cleopatra. See ANTONY AND CLEOPATRA. *AB*

Clerk of Chatham. He is executed by Cade, *The First Part of the Contention* (*2 Henry VI*) 4.2.109. He says his name is Emmanuel, 4.2.98. *AB*

Clifford, John. See CLIFFORD, YOUNG.

Clifford, Old Lord. One of King Henry's supporters, he successfully appeals to Cade's rebels in *The First Part of the Contention* (*2 Henry VI*) 4.7, but dies in combat with York, 5.3. Thomas Clifford (1414–55) was the 12th Baron. *AB*

Clifford, Thomas. See CLIFFORD, OLD LORD.

Clifford, Young (Lord). Young Clifford vows vengeance on the House of York for the death of his father, *The First Part of the Contention* (*2 Henry VI*) 5.3. Now called Lord Clifford he stabs the Earl of Rutland in *Richard Duke of York* (*3 Henry VI*) 1.3; with Queen Margaret kills the captured York, 1.4; but dies taunted by his enemies, 2.6. John Clifford (*c.*1435–61) was the 13th Baron. *AB*

Clifford Chambers, a village about a mile and a half (2.5 km) south of Stratford, home of Lord and Lady Henry Rainsford, close friends of the poet Michael *Drayton (1563–1631), who was probably a friend of Shakespeare. *SW*

Clink. The Liberty of the Clink, within which Shakespeare lived from at least 1596–9, was the name given to the manor of the Bishop of Winchester on *Bankside, with its first usage being recorded in 1473. The name is thought to emanate from the prison in the manor, although the earliest use of Clink for the bishops' prison is in 1486. By Shakespeare's day the name usually referred to the prison—the nearest to the Bankside theatres—which was particularly associated with debtors. *RSB*

Carlin, M., *Medieval Southwark* (1996)

Clitus. See STRATO.

Clive, Catherine (1711–85), an actress universally known as Kitty, who was most admired for her work in comedy. She played Catherine (1755–6) in *Garrick's adaptation *Catherine and Petruchio*. Earlier roles included Bianca, Ariel, and an ill-received Portia to *Macklin's Shylock in his restoration of the unadapted *The Merchant of Venice*. *CMSA*

Clopton family, a prominent Stratford family. Hugh (d. *c.*1496), lord mayor of London in 1491 (but not known to have been knighted), built *New Place, which Shakespeare bought in 1597; Sir William (1538–92) owned property in Hampton Lucy where John Shakespeare was a tenant. Clopton Manor, just outside Stratford, became the family home early in the 15th century; it was used by the conspirators in the *Gunpowder Plot (1605). In the later part of the 17th century New Place came back into the family's possession. In 1702 Sir John Clopton replaced it with a new house. *SW*

Cloten, the son of Cymbeline's Queen, is beheaded by Guiderius, *Cymbeline* 4.2. *AB*

clowns. (1) *The Two Gentlemen of Verona*. See LANCE and SPEED. (2) A clown takes a message from Titus to Saturninus, *Titus Andronicus* 4.3; Saturninus orders his execution, 4.4. (3) *Love's Labour's Lost.* See COSTARD. (4) The Gravedigger and his companion are described as 'two clowns', *Hamlet* 5.1. One of them quibbles with Hamlet. (5) *The Merchant of Venice.* See LANCELOT. (6) *Twelfth Night.* See FESTE. (7) *Measure for Measure.* See POMPEY. (8) Othello's clown dismisses Cassio's musicians *Othello* 3.1 and quibbles with Desdemona 3.4. (9) *All's Well That Ends Well.* See LAVATCH. (10) The 'Rural fellow' (*Antony and Cleopatra* 5.2.229) who brings the asp to Cleopatra, 5.2, is a clown. (11) The Old Shepherd's son who witnesses Antigonus' demise, *The Winter's Tale* 3.3, and becomes Autolycus's dupe, 4.3, 4.4, and 5.2, is a clown. See also FOOLS; TRINCULO (*The Tempest*); YORICK (*Hamlet*). *AB*

Clytus. See STRATO.

Cobbler of Preston, The. The playwright Charles Johnson began work on a short, anti-Jacobite satire derived from the Induction to *The Taming of the Shrew* early in 1716: before it had even opened at Drury Lane, however, another such play with the same title and source had already been written by Christopher Bullock, rehearsed and premièred at Lincoln's Inn Fields. *MD*

Cobham, Dame Eleanor. See GLOUCESTER, DUCHESS OF.

Cobham, Lord. See OLDCASTLE, SIR JOHN.

Cobham, William Brooke, 7th Lord (d. 1597), Lord Chamberlain (August 1596–March 1597), a descendant of Sir John Oldcastle, Lollard martyr, and model for Shakespeare's Falstaff. The Brooke family's Puritanical leanings lent added gall to this defamatory use of Oldcastle's name, which was changed to Falstaff after their objections. *CS*

Cobweb is one of *Titania's fairies in *A Midsummer Night's Dream.* *AB*

Cockpit-at-Court. See COURT PERFORMANCES; GLOBE RECONSTRUCTIONS; PALLADIO, ANDREA.

Cockpit theatre. See AUDIENCES; BEESTON, CHRISTOPHER; CHILDREN'S COMPANIES; COMPANIES, PLAYING; DAVENANT, SIR WILLIAM; THEATRES, ELIZABETHAN AND JACOBEAN.

Coleridge, Samuel Taylor (1772–1834), English poet and critic. Coleridge's thoughts and writings on Shakespeare were never collected or collated in any systematic manner, being scattered over several notebooks, mentioned in letters, written in the margin of play-texts, or reported at second hand from conversations and lectures. Editors, including H. N. Coleridge (in *Literary Remains*, 1836–9), T. M. Raysor (*Coleridge's Shakespearean Criticism*, 2 vols., 1930), and Terence Hawkes (*Coleridge's Writings on Shakespeare*, 1959; repr. as *Coleridge on Shakespeare*, 1969), have variously attempted to achieve textual accuracy, the imposition of order, selection and emphasis, and accessibility. It is likely that Coleridge had composed nearly all of his own poetry before expressing the full range of his admiration for Shakespeare. A letter of 6 December 1800 refers to the 'divinity of Shakespeare', and thereafter his tone is almost uniformly ardent and celebratory, matching and possibly emulating the enthusiasm of his German contemporary August Wilhelm von *Schlegel, who had begun his classic translation of Shakespeare into German in 1796 (Coleridge himself visited Germany from September 1798 to July 1799). The original plan of his first course of lectures was to devote five to 'the genius and writings of Shakespeare', in comparison with his contemporaries. In practice, the aesthetic and ethical elements (taste, imagination, fancy, passion) predominated over the historical and comparative, Coleridge arguing that Shakespeare was not only a natural dramatist and creator of character (as the 18th century was fully aware), but also a great poet, his works growing organically from the power of language itself. *TM*

Coleville, Sir John, 'a famous rebel' (4.2.61) arrested by Falstaff, *2 Henry IV* 4.2. *AB*

Colicos, John (b. 1928), Canadian actor. Having understudied at the *Old Vic in London and acted in the States he joined the Stratford Shakespeare Festival Theatre in his native *Canada, where from 1961 his roles included Aufidius to the Coriolanus of Paul *Scofield, Caliban, and an admired King Lear. He was Biron in *Love's Labour's Lost* and Timon of Athens when the Canadian company visited *Chichester. *MJ*

collaboration. Nearly half of the plays written for the public theatres during the early modern period were products of joint authorship. External evidence indicates that Shakespeare collaborated with John *Fletcher on at least two plays: both the Stationers' Register and the title page of the first *quarto (1634) of *The Two*

Two noble kinsmen dramatized by two memorable worthies: the first quarto of Shakespeare and Fletcher's *The Two Noble Kinsmen*, 1634.

THE TWO NOBLE KINSMEN:

Presented at the Blackfriers by the Kings Maiesties servants, with great applause:

Written by the memorable Worthies of their time;

{Mr. *John Fletcher*, and} Gent.
{Mr. *William Shakspeare*.}

Printed at *London* by *Tho. Cotes*, for *Iohn Waterson*: and are to be sold at the signe of the *Crowne* in *Pauls* Church-yard. 1634.

Noble Kinsmen attribute the play to 'William Shakespeare and John Fletcher', and the entry for the lost play *Cardenio* lists the authors as 'Mr Fletcher & Shakespeare'. Stylistic evidence strongly suggests that Fletcher may also have had a hand in Shakespeare's *All Is True* (*Henry* VIII). Similar internal evidence derived from vocabulary tests, image clusters, verbal and structural parallels, metrical tests, stylometry, and function word analysis reveals that Shakespeare may have collaborated with a number of other dramatists throughout his career: with Thomas *Middleton on *Timon of Athens*, *Macbeth*, and *Measure for Measure*; with Henry *Chettle, Thomas *Dekker, and Thomas *Heywood on *Sir Thomas More*; possibly with George *Wilkins on *Pericles*; possibly with an unknown playwright or playwrights on *1 Henry* VI and *Richard Duke of York* (*3 Henry* VI). He also probably contributed at least a scene to the anonymous play **Edward* III. The absence of *Pericles*, *Cardenio*, and *The Two Noble Kinsmen* from the First *Folio has suggested to some that *Heminges and *Condell intentionally excluded these late collaborative romances.

Renaissance playwrights who worked together on a play generally worked apart. Instead of a line-by-line collaboration, they often chose a strict division of labour, with each author assuming responsibility for particular acts or scenes. There is general scholarly agreement that Fletcher wrote the prologue, 2.2–2.6, 3.3–5.1, and 5.4 of *The Two Noble Kinsmen*, while Shakespeare was responsible for 1.1–2.1, 3.1–3.2, 5.2–5.3, and 5.5–5.6. Writing in relative isolation, one collaborator would often not know exactly what the other was doing. Shakespeare, for instance, was using a different source for his share of *The Two Noble Kinsmen* from the one Fletcher was using for his: the two dramatists apparently derived the name of the character *Pirithous from different sources. In Shakespeare's share of the play, the name is trisyllabic and spelled 'Pirithous' (the spelling in North's *Plutarch); in Fletcher's share, it has four syllables and is spelled 'Perithous' (the spelling in *Chaucer's Knight's Tale). In Shakespeare's additional scene for *Sir Thomas More*, he seems unaware of the details of the original version and of the revisions made by his collaborators. Similarly, in the text of *Timon of Athens*, the interview arranged between *Flavius and *Ventidius in a passage written by Middleton never materializes in Shakespeare's share of the play. *ER*

Bentley, Gerald Eades, *The Profession of Dramatist in Shakespeare's Time, 1590–1642* (1971)

Taylor, Gary, and Jowett, John, *Shakespeare Reshaped: 1606–1623* (1993)

Wells, Stanley, and Taylor, Gary, *William Shakespeare: A Textual Companion* (1987)

Collatine. See RAPE OF LUCRECE, THE.

Collier, Jeremy (1650–1726), clergyman most famous for his diatribe against the theatre, *A Short View of the Immorality, and Profaneness of the English Stage* (1698). While Collier vents most of his wrath on his contemporaries, he attacks Shakespeare's representation of Ophelia while praising the rejection and subsequent death of Falstaff, which he sees as a just punishment. *JM*

Collier, John Payne. See FORGERY.

Collins, Francis (d. 1617), a lawyer who worked in Stratford from at least 1600 and seems to have moved to Warwick around 1612. He drew up the indentures for Shakespeare's purchase of tithes in 1605, and in 1616 acted as overseer, witness, and possibly scribe of Shakespeare's *will, by which he received a legacy of £13 6*s.* 8*d.* *SW*

Colman, George, the elder (1732–94), a successful manager of Covent Garden who promoted the career of William Powell as a Shakespearian performer (Richard III, Othello, Romeo, Macbeth) and reworked Tate's *King Lear* for him, removing the Edgar and Cordelia love plot but retaining the happy ending. He rivalled Garrick's *Jubilee* by presenting his own Covent Garden entertainment, *Man and Wife; or, The Shakespeare Jubilee*, which included an impressive procession, and was responsible for barring the ageing *Macklin from the stage after his tartan-clad *Macbeth* was hissed in 1773. *CMSA*

colonialism. See TRAVEL, TRADE, AND COLONIALISM.

colophon. In early printing, the *imprint providing the name of the printer or publisher along with the date and place of publication did not appear on the *title page but in a colophon at the end of the book. With the adoption of title pages in the 16th century colophons became less common, but they can still be found in some 17th-century books. The First *Folio concludes with the colophon: '*Printed at the Charges of W. Jaggard, Ed. Blount, I. Smithweeke, and W. Aspley, 1623*'. *ER*

Combe family, a wealthy Protestant family in Stratford with whom Shakespeare had many links. John (b. before 1561, d. 1614) was a landowner and moneylender, frequently mentioned in Stratford lawsuits instituted to recover debts. On 1 May 1602 he and his uncle William sold Shakespeare 107 acres (44 ha) of open land in the area known as *Old Stratford to the north and east of the town for £320. The two halves of the indenture, preserved in the Records Office of the Shakespeare Birthplace Trust, show that Shakespeare was represented by his brother Gilbert. The Combe family had bought the land in 1593. According to a detailed survey made around 1625, first published in 1994, Shakespeare gave it to Susanna as a marriage settlement in 1607; in fact he bequeathed it to her in 1616, but may have retained a life interest.

John, who was unmarried, made many charitable, family, and other bequests, including £5 to Shakespeare and £60 for a tomb which may be seen in Holy Trinity church. According to Dugdale the sculpture was by Geerhart *Janssen, who also carved Shakespeare's monument. Around 1618 Richard Brathwaite, in an addition to a book called *Remains after Death*, printed 'An Epitaph upon one John Combe of Stratford-upon-Avon, a notable usurer, fastened upon a tomb that he had caused to be built in his life time.' It reads:

> Ten in the hundred here lies engraved;
> A hundred to ten his soul is not saved.
> If anyone asks who lies in this tomb,
> 'O ho!' quoth the devil, ''tis my John-a-Combe.'

In 1634, a Lieutenant Hammond, after visiting Stratford, said that Shakespeare had written 'some witty and facetious verses' on 'Mr Combe'; this story is repeated in association with the epitaph in various forms by *Aubrey, *Rowe, and other writers, one of whom states that Shakespeare wrote the epitaph at Combe's request during his lifetime. Robert Dobyns, visiting Stratford in 1673, transcribed both this and Shakespeare's epitaph, later stating that since his visit Combe's had been erased by his heirs.

Epitaphs on an unnamed usurer resembling the first couplet appeared in print in 1608 and 1614. Possibly Shakespeare elaborated a traditional quip, with a characteristic pun in 'engraved'. A 17th-century Bodleian manuscript records more charitable lines, headed 'Another Epitaph on John Combe: He being dead, and making the poor his heirs, William Shakespeare after writes this for his epitaph.' They read:

> Howe'er he livèd judge not,
> John Combe shall never be forgot
> While poor hath memory, for he did gather
> To make the poor his issue; he, their father,
> As record of his tilth and seed
> Did crown him in his latter deed.

John's brother Thomas lived in a property known as the College, near the church, probably the largest house in the town. He held a share in the Stratford tithes equal to Shakespeare's. His son William (1586–1667), educated at Oxford and the Middle Temple, was partly responsible for the attempted enclosure of common land at Welcombe in 1614. Shakespeare left his sword to Thomas's other son, also Thomas (1589–1657), a lawyer and a Protestant who died a bachelor. *SW*

'Come away, come away, death', sung by Feste in *Twelfth Night* 2.4.50. The earliest known setting is one of two versions by Thomas Arne; the first was published in 1741 and the second in 1786. More recent composers include

Brahms, Chausson, Cornelius (four versions), Stanford in the 19th century, and Dankworth, Finzi, Holst, Korngold, Moeran, Quilter, Sibelius, Vaughan Williams from the 20th century. *JB*

Comédie-Française, founded in 1680 in Molière's theatre three years after his death by Louis XIV to unite the two rival companies (Guénégaud and Bourgogne), granting royal patronage and the exclusivity of the French repertoire. Once the monopoly was abolished (1791), some actors followed Talma to the newly built Salle Richelieu (the present-day theatre); the other actors joined them when Napoleon signed a unification agreement (1802–12). Unique in the world, it is still operating as a shareholding company of actors participating in its artistic policy. The first Shakespeare play staged was Ducis's verse *adaptation of *King Lear* (1783) with Talma, who later played Hamlet, Macbeth, Othello, all in Ducis's adaptations, as individualistic romantic heroes. Sarah *Bernhardt as Hamlet created a legendary stir, Piachaud's biased version of *Coriolanus* degenerated into fascist riots (1933), Vincent's *Macbeth* (1985) faithfully followed the original, and Mesguish's flamboyant and controversial *Tempest* (1998) incorporated Richard III's seduction of Lady *Anne. *ISG*

comedy. Both classical and Renaissance apologists of the theatre regarded comedy as an inferior dramatic form, its pedagogical function being its only redeeming feature. Sir Philip *Sidney, for example, praised comedy because 'nothing', he explained, 'can more open [our] eyes than to find [our] own actions contemptibly set forth' (*Apology for Poetry*, pub. 1595). A few years later, Ben Jonson rephrased a famous Horatian maxim by declaring that his 'true scope' in writing *Volpone* (1607) was to 'mix profit with . . . pleasure'. It is therefore all the more remarkable that Shakespeare's comedies are never overtly didactic. On the contrary, in them intellectual and psychological curiosity prevails over prescriptive norms as often as wonder outweighs the local and the familiar.

Shakespeare drew extensively from earlier models. From Greek Old Comedy he borrowed the saturnalian pattern of release from restraint through recognition and clarification. From Greek New Comedy he derived a variety of dramatic elements, ranging from the Tranio–Lucentio–Bianca sub-plot in *The Taming of the Shrew* to the stock character of the *senex iratus*, which he used as a model for Leonato in *Much Ado About Nothing*. *Lyly's courtship romance inspired Shakespeare's earliest comedy *The Two Gentlemen of Verona*, whereas folklore and the native popular tradition provided the raw material for the *fairy world in *A Midsummer Night's Dream*. The Italian novelistic tradition was another popular source of plot devices and story-lines: the story of Bertram and Helen in *All's Well That Ends Well* and the main plot of *The Merchant of Venice* come from two collections of Italian tales, *Boccaccio's *Decameron* and *Il pecorone*, attributed to Ser Giovanni of Florence.

Despite the undeniable influence of earlier models, Shakespearian comedy represents a distinctive dramatic category. Its main conventions include: exotic locations (with the obvious exception of *The Merry Wives of Windsor*); cases of mistaken identity in connection with bed-tricks, identical sets of twins, disguise, and cross-dressing; the Clown, an anticipation of the Fool in *King Lear*, similarly associated with caustic wit, ironic detachment, and a subversive penchant for puns and wordplay; a sustained attempt to test the limits of representation and theatrical illusion; and the 'green-world', a partly pastoral, partly utopian dimension, such as the wood outside Athens in *A Midsummer Night's Dream* or the forest of Arden/Ardenne in *As You Like It*, where the law, parental control, and social conventions are temporarily suspended.

Romantic and festive elements in Shakespeare's comedies, along with the conventional comic resolution, which is in itself suggestive of a ritual pattern of death and rebirth leading to self-discovery, harmony, and reconciliation, are often undermined by disruptive forces, ethical blind spots, and unresolved conflicts of class and gender, which are more pronounced in the late comedies, such as *Measure for Measure* or *All's Well That Ends Well*. *SM*

Barber, C. L., *Shakespeare's Festive Comedy* (1959)
Freedman, B., *Staging the Gaze: Postmodernism, Psychoanalysis and Shakespearean Comedy* (1991)
Frye, N., *A Natural Perspective* (1965)
Levin, R. A., *Love and Society in Shakespearean Comedy* (1985)

Comedy of Errors, The *(see page 84)*

'Come o'er the bourn, Bessy, to me', snatch of song, sung by Edgar in *The History of King Lear* 13.21. The complete text and two original tunes are given by Sternfeld (1964). *JB*

'Come, thou monarch of the vine', drinking song, sung by a Boy in *Antony and Cleopatra* 2.7.110; the earliest surviving setting is by Thomas Chilcot, published *c.*1750. Nineteenth-century composers include Bishop and Schubert. *JB*

'Come unto these yellow sands', sung by Ariel in *The Tempest* 1.2.377. The earliest setting to survive is by John Banister (published 1675) for the *Dryden and *Davenant adaptation of the play; a setting published in the early 18th century has been attributed to Purcell, and it was also set by Arne *c.*1740. Twentieth-century composers include Arnold, Honneger, Martin, Quilter, Tippett. *JB*

Comical Gallant, The; or, The Amours of Sir John Falstaff. John Dennis's tidily neoclassical adaptation of *The Merry Wives of Windsor* flopped at Drury Lane in 1702: its printed text is vengefully prefaced by his essay 'A Large Account of the Taste in Poetry, and the Causes of the Degeneracy of it'. *MD*

Wheeler, David, 'Eighteenth Century Adaptations of Shakespeare and the Example of John Dennis', *Shakespeare Quarterly*, 36 (1985)

Cominius is a Roman general and Coriolanus' ally. His pleas for Coriolanus to spare *Rome from attack are disregarded (described *Coriolanus* 5.1). *AB*

commedia dell'arte, a type of improvisational comedy originating in Italy in the Middle Ages. Each performance was based upon the same stock characters, for example the lovers, the comic servant, the braggart, and the pedant, within some preconceived plot which yet allowed for improvisation. This form of comedy reached the height of its popularity and influence in 16th-century Europe. It may have become known in England through the presence of Italian players in London or the travels of Englishmen in Italy. Although there is no evidence that Shakespeare saw it, a number of his plays reflect the traditions of the *commedia*, in particular *Love's Labour's Lost* and *The Tempest*. *JKS*

Lea, K. M., *Italian Popular Comedy: A Study in the Commedia dell'Arte 1560–1620* (2 vols., 1934)

companies, playing. Before the emergence of the professional theatre industry in the second half of the 16th century, companies of travelling players made their livings from performances throughout the kingdom. The forces that shaped these troupes into the enormously successful companies of Shakespeare's time were political and economic. The provincial town authorities began to demand that players have some kind of certification (in practice, a patron) and in 1550 the London aldermen issued a decree banning 'common' players (those without a patron) from performing in the city without licence. The informal collections of players were squeezed out. In a proclamation of 16 May 1559 Elizabeth restated the responsibility of lords lieutenant and sheriffs to ensure that players were licensed and did not perform anything 'wherein either matters of religion or of the governance of the estate of the common weal shall be handled or treated'. Licensing the burgeoning theatre industry was a means of censoring it. That Robert Dudley, Earl of Leicester, took trouble to write to the Earl of Shrewsbury in June 1559 requesting that his players be allowed to perform in Yorkshire indicates that

(cont. on page 87)

The Comedy of Errors

According to an eyewitness account, 'a comedy of errors (like to Plautus his *Menaechmus*) was played by the players' during the Christmas revels at Gray's Inn on 28 December 1594: this can only have been Shakespeare's play, which is indeed based on *Plautus' comedy *Menaechmi*, and it is unlikely that the lawyers and students would have hired actors to appear at a grand festive occasion with anything but a new, or at least current, play. Although this debt to classical farce has inclined some scholars to see the play as apprentice work from the very start of Shakespeare's career, stylistic tests confirm a dating around 1594, with rare vocabulary placing it between *The Taming of the Shrew* and *Romeo and Juliet* and its heavy use of rhyme placing it early in the lyrical period initiated by *Venus and Adonis*.

Sources: The play's chief plot, in which a man searching for his long-lost twin brother is repeatedly mistaken for him (with discomfiting consequences for the sought-for twin), derives, as recognized above, from Plautus' *Menaechmi*. (This play was published in an English translation by William Warner in 1595, entered in the Stationers' Register in summer 1594, but the hypothesis that Shakespeare may have had access to this version in manuscript is hardly necessary, since Plautus' plays were already familiar to most Elizabethan grammar-school boys). Shakespeare complicates this plot by adding long-separated twin servants (the Dromios) for the twin masters (the Antipholi), drawing on another Plautus play, *Amphitruo*, which also provided the scene in which a wife shuts out her husband while unwittingly entertaining another in his place. Shakespeare, however, adds the un-Plautine frame narrative of Egeon and Emilia, derived from the Greek romance of Apollonius of Tyre (which also lies behind Shakespeare's other play about *twins, *Twelfth Night*, and *Pericles*). He also changes the setting from Plautus' Epidamnus to Ephesus, and the play abounds with allusions to St Paul's Epistle to the Ephesians, especially its strictures on marriage.

Text: The play was first printed in the Folio in 1623: inconsistencies in speech prefixes and theatrically superfluous information in some stage directions suggest that it was set from Shakespeare's *foul papers. Certain stage directions, which state which of three 'houses' (the Phoenix, the Porcupine, or the Priory) characters are to enter from, indicate that the play may have been written with indoor performance (such as at Gray's Inn) in mind: academic and court performances sometimes employed a conventional 'arcade' setting with three doors at the rear of the stage, labelled by signs. The play's careful and logical division into five acts (which would have been marked by *intervals in indoor performance) would support this view.

Synopsis: **1.1** Egeon, an old merchant, is under sentence of death for entering Ephesus, currently at war with his native Syracuse, unless he can raise a 1,000-mark ransom. Questioned by the Duke of Ephesus as to why he has entered this hostile territory, he recounts how years earlier his wife bore him identical twin sons, for whom they bought identical twin slaves born at the same time, but that in a shipwreck he and the younger son and servant were separated from his wife and the other two twins. At 18 his younger son, given the same name as his missing twin, set off with his servant in quest of their brothers: Egeon subsequently set off after them, and has arrived in Ephesus on his way home after five years' fruitless search. Moved, the Duke allows Egeon the remainder of the day to raise the ransom. **1.2** Antipholus of Syracuse and his servant Dromio of Syracuse have arrived in Ephesus: Antipholus sends his servant to their lodging to lock up his money. Shortly afterwards Dromio of Ephesus arrives and, mistaking this Antipholus for his own master, calls him home to dinner. Antipholus of Syracuse, thinking this is his own

Dromio having a joke, grows angry, asking anxiously after his money, and drives Dromio away with blows before setting off to check on his belongings.

2.1 Adriana laments the continuing absence of her husband Antipholus of Ephesus to her unmarried sister Luciana, and after Dromio of Ephesus brings the story of his beating and dismissal (and is sent back to make another attempt to bring Antipholus home) she says she would be willing to forgo the gold chain her husband has promised if only he would be faithful. **2.2** Antipholus of Syracuse, having found his money safe, meets his own Dromio and berates him for the incomprehensible invitation to dinner he in fact received from Dromio of Ephesus: after a squabble their comic banter is interrupted by the arrival of Adriana and Luciana. Adriana preaches Antipholus a sermon on marital fidelity, and she and Luciana take his and Dromio's denials of their acquaintance as mere jests. Softening, she invites him home to dinner, instructing Dromio to deny all visitors: Antipholus, though he and Dromio begin to suspect that their names are known to these strangers by magic, accepts.

3.1 Antipholus of Ephesus, together with Dromio of Ephesus and his guests Balthasar the merchant and Angelo, the goldsmith who has just completed the chain for Adriana, are locked out of his house. The enraged Antipholus decides they will all dine instead with the Courtesan, and he sends Angelo to fetch the chain so that he can give it in spite to the Courtesan. **3.2** Luciana urges Antipholus of Syracuse to maintain at least a show of marital concord with Adriana: when he responds by wooing her instead she leaves to find her sister. A horrified Dromio of Syracuse reports to his master that a fat kitchen-wench claims she is engaged to him, and after a spate of comic puns likening the wench's body to the globe the two Syracusans resolve to flee from Ephesus. While Dromio seeks a ship, Antipholus is met by Angelo, who to his amazement gives him the chain.

4.1 Angelo has met another merchant, just arrested for debt, to whom he owes exactly the sum of money now owed to him by Antipholus for the chain. Antipholus of Ephesus now arrives, sending Dromio of Ephesus to buy a rope with which to chastise his household for locking them out, and berates Angelo for failing to deliver the chain. Convinced that he has already delivered it, Angelo has Antipholus arrested for debt. Dromio of Syracuse now arrives and tells Antipholus of Ephesus he has found a ship for their escape: infuriated, Antipholus sends Dromio back to Adriana to fetch money to redeem him from imprisonment. **4.2** Adriana is enraged to hear that her husband has apparently been wooing her sister: Dromio of Syracuse reports Antipholus' arrest, and they give him the purse of money he requests. **4.3** Antipholus of Syracuse is musing on how many people he meets treat him with kindness and respect when Dromio of Syracuse, amazed to find him at liberty, gives him the money. About to leave for the harbour, they are accosted by the Courtesan, who, seeing the promised chain around Antipholus' neck, asks for it, or, failing that, for the return of the diamond ring she gave him during dinner. Convinced she is a witch, Antipholus and Dromio flee: the Courtesan, convinced they are mad, decides that the only way to secure the return of her diamond is to tell Adriana her husband has lost his wits. **4.4** Antipholus of Ephesus, still under arrest, is beside himself with violent rage when Dromio of Ephesus brings not the money to redeem him but only a rope: this behaviour helps convince Adriana, arriving with the Courtesan, Luciana, and a schoolmaster-cum-exorcist called Dr Pinch, that Antipholus is insane. Pinch tries to exorcize him and is beaten for his pains: Antipholus asserts his sanity and rebukes Adriana for locking him out, to which she insists that he dined with her: as the dispute grows louder Antipholus attacks Adriana, and both he and Dromio have to be restrained with ropes. The two are carried off homewards, bound, with Pinch, while Adriana attempts to ascertain what has been happening from the arresting officer and the Courtesan: just then Antipholus of Syracuse and Dromio of Syracuse arrive, with swords, and the others flee, convinced that the two lunatics have escaped their captors.

5.1 Angelo and his creditor the merchant are just discussing Antipholus' apparent treachery when Antipholus of Syracuse, still wearing the chain, arrives with Dromio of Syracuse: insisting that he has never denied having received the chain, Antipholus is about to duel with the vexed merchant when Adriana, Luciana, the Courtesan, and their party arrive to attempt to capture him. Antipholus and Dromio flee into a nearby priory for sanctuary, from which the Abbess appears, and asks Adriana about her husband's apparent madness. The Abbess diagnoses that he has been driven mad by Adriana's continual reproaches about his infidelity, and insists that she will nurse him back to health in the abbey: a furious Adriana demands the return of her husband to her own custody and, refused, threatens to appeal to the Duke. The Duke now arrives, bringing Egeon to the nearby place of execution. Adriana kneels before him, recounting her husband's madness and escape to the Abbey, and implores the Duke to exert his authority over the Abbess so that her husband may be returned to her. When a messenger interrupts, reporting in horror that Antipholus and Dromio have got loose and are avenging themselves on Dr Pinch, he is disbelieved until Antipholus of Ephesus and Dromio of Ephesus arrive in person. Antipholus appeals to the Duke for justice against his wife, who he claims has locked him out of his house and conspired to have him falsely imprisoned as a madman, and against Angelo, who he claims has falsely demanded payment from him for an undelivered chain. The Duke, Angelo, the merchant, the Courtesan, Antipholus, and Dromio are trying in vain to make sense of all this contradictory testimony, and the Duke has just sent for the Abbess, when Egeon steps forward, saying he has seen someone he thinks will ransom him. When he speaks to Antipholus and Dromio of Ephesus, however, both deny him, Antipholus assuring him, as the Duke confirms, that he has never seen either his father or Syracuse in his life. At this point, though, the Abbess arrives, bringing with her Antipholus of Syracuse and Dromio of Syracuse, to the astonishment of all beholders. Adriana and the Duke are trying to ascertain which is the real Antipholus, and the Syracusan Antipholus and Dromio are wondering why Egeon is here and in bonds, when the Abbess recognizes Egeon and declares that she is his long-lost wife Emilia. As the Duke at last understands that the two Antipholi and Dromios are the long-separated twins Egeon had spoken of, Emilia explains that soon after the shipwreck she was separated from the baby Antipholus of Ephesus and Dromio of Ephesus by Corinthian fishermen, who took them away from her, and subsequently became a nun in Ephesus: Antipholus of Ephesus confirms the Duke's recollection that he only came to Ephesus from Corinth later on, in military service with the Duke's uncle. The Antipholi and their various debtors and creditors untangle the events of the day, Antipholus of Syracuse assuring Luciana that he will resume his suit, now she knows he is not her brother-in-law. Antipholus of Ephesus, finally obtaining the ransom money he sent for, offers to pay it to redeem Egeon, but the Duke reprieves the old man without payment. The Courtesan gets her ring back from Antipholus of Ephesus, before the Abbess invites the entire cast to what she describes as a long-delayed christening party for her twin sons. The Dromios are the last to leave the stage: not knowing which is the elder, they go hand in hand rather than in order of precedence.

Artistic features: The play's opening scene centres on the longest passage of sheer exposition in the canon, the hundred lines of narrative spoken by Egeon before he disappears from the play until the final reunions. Despite the tight, fast-moving structure of the intervening scenes, the play is notable for other solo performances too, which similarly go beyond the normal emotional range of farce: these include Adriana's complaint, in couplets, of her husband's neglect (2.1.86–114), Antipholus of Syracuse's wooing speech, in quatrains, to Luciana (3.2.29–52), and Dromio of Ephesus' lament, in prose, about the lifetime of beatings he has suffered from his master (4.4.30–40).

Critical history: The play has often been dismissed as a formulaic exercise in Plautine farce (even by *Hazlitt), although later writers, from Charles *Knight onwards, have been more willing to be moved by the romance materials with which Shakespeare frames his borrowings from *Menaechmi*, and by the extra depth they confer on the plot of mistaken identity. Harold Brooks drew attention to the play's interest in authority, relating its discussion of marriage to *The Taming of the Shrew*, while his successors have pursued the play's allusions to St Paul on the same topic, often reflecting at the same time on the play's canny thematic juxtaposition of three phenomena which confound the notion of the single, self-determining individual, namely birth, marriage, and twinship.

Stage history: Apart from the 1594 performance at Gray's Inn, only one other performance of *The Comedy of Errors* is recorded during Shakespeare's lifetime, albeit a prestigious one, when the play was revived before James I's court during the Christmas season of 1604. Since then a high proportion of the play's stage history has been one of adaptation: it first reappeared, in 1723, in an unpublished version called *Every Body Mistaken*, succeeded in 1734 by a two-act abbreviation, similarly unpublished, called *See If You Like It*. During the 1741–2 season the original enjoyed five performances at Drury Lane, with Charles *Macklin as Dromio of Syracuse, and it was in this unlikely role that J. P. *Kemble chose to appear from 1808 onwards in his own elaboration of the cut version by Thomas *Hull, *The Twins; or, Which is Which?*, which had been in the repertory since 1762. Frederick *Reynolds produced a characteristic musical version in 1819, adorned with songs from other plays, and since then the play has continued to be shortened to a farce or extended to a musical at regular intervals. In the United States, where their style perfectly suited the emergence of vaudeville, the Dromios served as vehicles for the Placide (until 1877) and then the Robson brothers, and the play later became the basis for a long-running Broadway hit by Richard Rodgers and Lorenz Hart, *The Boys from Syracuse* (1938). In Britain notable productions featuring added music have included *Komisarjevsky's eclectic romp of the same year, Julian Slade's opera (televised in 1954, staged in 1956), and Trevor *Nunn's café-cum-circus version for the RSC (1974), although others have found the play's dramatization of a broken and uneasily restored family sufficiently compelling (and sufficiently funny) without such assistance, notably Tim Supple's small-scale, modern-dress production for the RSC (1996). *MD*

On the screen: Apart from a ten-minute silent film (1908) and the heavily transposed *The Boys from Syracuse* (1940), adaptations for television include a British film (1954) with Joan Plowright as Adriana, a West German production (1964), two British TV films of RSC stage productions (1964 and 1974) and the BBC TV production (1983). The 1974 musical version directed by Trevor Nunn, and with Dame Judi Dench as Adriana, has achieved wide circulation on video. *AD*

Recent major editions

R. A. Foakes (Arden, 1962); Stanley Wells (New Penguin, 1972)

Some representative criticism

Bishop, T. G., *Shakespeare and the Theatre of Wonder* (1996), ch. 3

Brooks, Harold, 'Themes and Structure in *The Comedy of Errors*', in *Early Shakespeare*, Stratford-upon-Avon Studies 3 (1961)

Frye, Northrop, 'The Argument of Comedy', *English Institute Essays 1948* (1949), repr. in Leonard F. Dean (ed.), *Shakespeare: Modern Essays in Criticism* (1957)

Parker, Patricia, in *Shakespeare from the Margins* (1996).

Elizabeth's demand for licensing was being heeded, and that Dudley felt the free travel of his players was important. The licensed players had such an advantage over the remaining unlicensed players that we may rely on the principle of natural selection to explain the disappearance of the latter; aggressive entrepreneurial instincts were needed to survive in the new, harsher, climate.

The first nationally prominent company emerged directly from Dudley's players when the government again moved to curtail, and so control, the acting industry. In 1583 privy counsellors Walsingham and Leicester put together an all-star troupe of players picked mostly from Leicester's Men to tour the country under the patronage of Elizabeth herself in the interests of national unity. The Queen's Men specialized in a new dramatic genre, the English history play, which was particularly suited to the Puritan sensibilities of the counsellors. The leading players of this new company were John Adams and Richard Tarlton, and throughout the 1580s the Queen's Men toured extensively and enjoyed an effective monopoly of playing in London. But the settlement of 1594 gave two new companies, the Admiral's Men at the Rose and the Chamberlain's Men at the Theatre, an effective London duopoly and the Queen's Men were forced to concentrate on touring. Staying put in particular London playhouses gave the Admiral's and Chamberlain's Men advantages which outweighed the burden of having to maintain a high turnover of new material. (Touring players can of course repeat the same play in each new town.) Because audiences knew where to see the new Admiral's or Chamberlain's play—where to see Alleyn's or Burbage's newest role—a loyal base of supporters could develop amongst the London theatre-going public. Companies with a permanent base could also benefit from their accumulated capital by investing in lavish costume collections which would have been impossibly cumbersome for travelling players, even if they could afford them. The extreme effect of these two principles—expensive costuming and high turnover of new plays—can be discerned from two facts derived from Henslowe's account book: the costume collection of a company might easily be worth more than the playhouse, and a dozen different plays might be performed in one month.

The next important development to promote the theatrical company stability upon which Shakespeare's greatest work was predicated happened by chance. Denied use of the Blackfriars playhouse, Richard and Cuthbert Burbage brought their fellow playing company sharers into a syndicate to finance the Globe playhouse, and the commonality of interest within this nucleus of sharer/housekeepers made the Chamberlain-King's Men considerably more economically stable than their competitors. At the Blackfriars a succession of companies of child actors performed outrageous satires with strong, and to modern sensibilities quite disturbing, sexual content. Although these ceased after 1608, the incorporation of two of the Blackfriars conventions, act intervals and sophisticated music, into amphitheatre playing indicates the leading companies' ability to adapt themselves to changing tastes. The new King, James, took a much greater interest in the drama than his predecessor and the leading players could expect to be summoned to play at court more often.

The history of playing from 1610 to the closure of 1642 is one of gradual bifurcation into two traditions centred on two types of venue: the open-air amphitheatres and the indoor hall playhouses. The latter were more profitable but did not see off the former, perhaps because nostalgia for the populist and robust mode of outdoor entertainment persisted amongst the players. More pragmatically, the apprentices' riot which followed the transference of Queen Anne's men from the Red Bull to the Cockpit in Drury Lane signalled the tension between the two traditions which made persistence of both a practical necessity. Specialization by social class began to emerge in the drama with the indoor plays increasingly distancing themselves from the noisy spectacle available at the amphitheatres. By the end of the period the status of the playing profession was immeasurably higher—at least for the rich sharers in the most successful companies—than it had been at the beginning. Edward Alleyn's founding of the College of God's Gift at Dulwich and Shakespeare's retirement in affluent middle age were possible only because a highly successful urban theatre industry emerged in London with extraordinary rapidity; less than half a century separates the construction of the Theatre from the publication of the Shakespeare First Folio. See also PROVINCIAL COMPANIES, TOURS. *GE*

Gurr, Andrew, *The Shakespearian Playing Companies* (1996)

Ingram, William, *The Business of Playing: The Beginnings of the Adult Professional Theater in Elizabethan England* (1992)

McMillin, Scott, and MacLean, Sally-Beth, *The Queen's Men and their Plays* (1998)

compositors. The typesetters in the printing shop were the agents directly responsible for setting Shakespeare's manuscripts into type; they were also among the earliest interpreters and editors of these texts. Compositors often introduced changes in *spelling and punctuation, and sometimes made substantive emendations as well. According to Joseph Moxon's 17th-century treatise on the art of printing, the compositor could be expected to 'read his copy with consideration; so that he may get himself into the meaning of the author'. Thus enlightened, the compositor would be able to 'discern . . . where the author has been deficient' and 'amend' his copy accordingly.

Charlton Hinman's monumental analysis of *The Printing and Proof-Reading of the First Folio of Shakespeare* (1963) identified five compositors at work on that text (Compositors A, B, C, D, and E) by their individual spelling preferences; subsequent investigators have refined Hinman's findings and detected the presence of at least four more workmen (Compositors F, H, I, and J). Once particular compositors have been identified and their individual stints have been established, textual scholars are able to characterize each compositor's working habits. Compositor E, for instance, appears to have been an inexperienced workman prone to errors such as 'terrible woer' for 'treble woe' in **Hamlet* 5.1.243. Compositor B, on the other hand, seems to have made intentional changes when his copy did not make sense to him, such as the alteration of the life-rendering 'Pelican' to 'Politician' in *Hamlet* 4.5.146. *ER*

Hinman, Charlton, *The Printing and Proof-Reading of the First Folio of Shakespeare* (1963)

Moxon, Joseph, *Mechanick Exercises on the Whole Art of Printing* (1683–4), ed. Herbert Davis and Harry Carter (2nd edn., 1962)

computers. Electronic editions of Shakespeare first began to appear at the end of the 20th century. In the 1970s, old-spelling quarto and First Folio editions were made available through the Oxford Text Archive created by Oxford University Press and T. H. Howard-Hill, editor of the single-text concordances; the *WordCruncher Bookshelf Shakespeare* (1988) derived from the text of the *Riverside Shakespeare* edited by G. B. Evans; *William Shakespeare: The Complete Works, Electronic Edition* (1988) reproduced the modern-spelling Oxford edition edited by Stanley Wells and Gary Taylor.

The Arden Shakespeare CD-ROM, introduced in 1997, was the first electronic edition to employ a hypertextual interface. It combined the full text of the plays and poems included in *The Arden Shakespeare* print editions with their introductions, commentary, and textual notes along with facsimile reproductions of each page of early folio and quarto texts and electronic versions of standard reference works, including source studies, glossaries, and bibliographies.

With the advent of the Internet and the World Wide Web, an unprecedented set of electronic resources have been made available to students and scholars, including several critical editions and facsimiles of Shakespeare's works and those of his contemporaries; the best of these are provided by the Internet Shakespeare Editions (under the general editorship of Michael Best), the Renaissance Electronic Text series, the archives of the *SHAKSPER Electronic Conference*, the University of Virginia

Electronic Text Center, the *Versions of King Lear* and *First Folio Project* undertaken at the University of Pennsylvania's Furness Shakespeare Library. Further resources include Donald Foster's *SHAXICON* database, the *Perseus* database's 'Renaissance Sources Project', and MIT's *Shakespeare Electronic Archive*, which employs early editions (transcribed and in facsimile), interactive films, and digitized versions of relevant artwork and other materials from the Folger Shakespeare Library. *ER*

Best, Michael, 'From Book to Screen: A Window on Renaissance Electronic Texts', *Early Modern Literary Studies*, 1/2 (1995)

conceit, an unusually elaborate metaphor or simile that is developed ingeniously, often as the basis of a sonnet or other lyric; but also found in dramatic speeches. *CB*

concordances and dictionaries. Editions of Shakespeare from the 18th century to the present have attempted to elucidate Shakespeare by incorporating commentary and glosses, but as the need became greater, separately printed and specialized works have appeared. The synchronic aim of semantic glossaries is exemplified in the title of Robert Nares's popular *Glossary; or, Collection of Words, Phrases, Names, and Allusions to Customs, Proverbs, etc. Which Have Been Thought to Require Illustration, in the Works of English Authors, Particularly Shakespeare, and his Contemporaries* (1822); their diachronic orientation is stressed in the selection by C. T. Onions's *Shakespeare Glossary* (1911; rev. Robert Eagleson, 1986): 'words or sense of words now obsolete or surviving only in provincial or archaic use.' Specialized glossaries, employing a variety of names, could be encyclopedic, dealing with such topics as topography and history, customs and characters; or linguistic, dealing with pronunciation and wordplay, grammar and slang; or stylistic, dealing with imagery and structure, rhetoric and allusion. The one authoritative dictionary remains Alexander Schmidt's *Shakespeare-Lexicon* (1874–5), which is comprehensive in presenting the entire vocabulary and attempting semantic description and detailed grammatical description.

Concordances were a parallel development. Their principal function was to alphabetize Shakespeare's text, laying bare otherwise inaccessible qualities and quantities. Andrew Becket, compiler in 1787 of the first Shakespeare concordance, followed Dr Johnson's suggestions in selecting 'practical axioms and domestic wisdom'. Francis Twiss's *Complete Verbal Index* of 1805 was the first attempt at listing all the main word-classes and proper nouns. Samuel Ayscough's *Index* (1821) was 'calculated to point out the different meanings to which the words are applied'.

Nineteenth-century concordances, such as those by Mary Cowden *Clarke, Mrs H. H. *Furness, and J. O. *Halliwell-Phillipps, often appeared in conjunction with editions. John *Bartlett, best known for his *Familiar Quotations* (1855), expanded his *Shakespeare Phrase Book* of 1882 to form his 1894 concordance (still in print), based on the *Globe edition. In the 20th century Oxford produced computer-generated concordances to the early texts of individual plays under the supervision of T. Howard-Hill. Marvin Spevack's nine-volume *Complete and Systematic Concordance to the Works of Shakespeare* (1968–80), keyed to the *Riverside edition, was the first to present truly complete access to the vocabulary of the plays and poems individually and collectively (the latter as well in his one-volume *Harvard Concordance*, 1973), and to the vocabulary of each character, as well as to stage directions and speech-prefixes, the 'bad' quartos, and substantive variants, each entry accompanied by statistical information. *MS*

Condell, Henry (1576–1627), actor (Chamberlain-King's Men 1598–1627) and originator with John Heminges of the 1623 Folio of Shakespeare's works. Shakespeare's friend and fellow actor, Henry Condell married Elizabeth Smart on 24 October 1596 and, according to the 1616 Folio cast list, he performed in Jonson's *Every Man in his Humour* in 1598. Condell remained in the Chamberlain-King's Men his entire career and is named in their royal patent of 1603. He appears as himself, an actor, in the metadramatic Induction to Marston's *The Malcontent* (performed at the Globe in 1604) and acted Mosca to Richard Burbage's Volpone in Jonson's *Volpone* and Surly to Burbage's Subtle in Jonson's *The Alchemist*. In 1613 Condell's name appeared in verses on the burning of the Globe and in 1616 Shakespeare left money in his will for Condell to buy a commemorative ring. Condell appears to have stopped acting in 1619 but maintained his business connection with the King's Men. Condell was not an original housekeeper of the Globe but acquired a joint interest with John Heminges by 1612; in 1608 Condell was one of the syndicate formed to run the Blackfriars. Although not a star actor, Condell's high status within his profession is attested by the responsibilities laid on him in fellow actors' wills: trustee in Alexander Cooke's (1614), executor in Nicholas Tooley's (1623), and executor in John Underwood's (1625). *GE*

Conejero, Manuel Ángel (b. 1943), Spanish professor of English, founder of the Valencia Instituto Shakespeare, and supervisor of their translations. He has published on Shakespeare (e.g. *Eros adolescente*, 1980) and the theatrical translation of his plays, organized diverse Shakespearian activities, taught drama and acting, and written various plays, in which he has acted himself. *ALP*

Conrad encourages Don John and Borachio to perpetrate their crimes in *Much Ado About Nothing*. *AB*

consort. See MUSIC.

Conspiracy Discovered, The. This short, anonymous playlet based on the Scroop–Masham–Grey scene from *Henry V* was performed in 1746. Its staging was designed to coincide with the execution of those found guilty of treason during the Jacobite rebellion of 1745–6. *MD*

conspirators with Aufidius. They take part in Coriolanus' murder, *Coriolanus* 5.6. *AB*

Constable of France. Unwisely confident of victory at Agincourt (*Henry V* 4.2.15–37), he lies among the slain, 4.8.92. He is based on Charles Delabreth, or Charles d'Albret (d. 1415), the illegitimate son of Charles le Mauvais, King of Navarre. *AB*

Constance, Lady. She claims the throne for her son Arthur, and dies after his capture, *King John* 4.2.122. *AB*

Cooke, Alexander (d. 1614), actor (King's Men 1603–14). Sometimes assumed to be the man named Sander who appears in the plot of *2 Seven Deadly Sins* (which was performed before 1594, possibly by Strange's Men), Cooke enters the theatrical record with certainty in the actor lists for Jonson's *Sejanus, Volpone, The Alchemist,* and *Catiline*, as reproduced in the 1616 Folio, and for Beaumont and Fletcher's *The Captain*. For *Sejanus, Volpone,* and *The Captain* his name appears last in the list of actors, which might mean that he played women's roles in these plays. His will indicates that he was a company sharer and that he had been apprenticed to John Heminges. *GE*

Cooke, George Frederick (1756–1812), British actor, who, after 20 undistinguished years in the provinces, made an electrifying London debut in 1800 as Richard III, which he followed with portrayals of various gradations of villainy—Iago, Shylock, Macbeth, Falstaff—whilst sinking deeper into personal dissipation. In 1810 he left for America where in his largely Shakespearian repertoire he was the prototype visiting star. *RF*

Hare, Arnold, *George Frederick Cooke the Actor and the Man* (1980)
Wilmeth, Dan B., *George Frederick Cooke: Machiavel of the Stage* (1984)

Cope, Sir Walter (d. 1614), politician. Cope, then MP for Westminster, wrote to Lord Cranbrooke in 1604 of the difficulty of finding a play which the Queen Consort had not seen. However, the actors 'have revived an old one called *Love's Labour's Lost*, which for wit and mirth', as Cope has heard, 'will please her exceedingly'. *PH*

Copeau, Jacques (1879–1949), actor, director, playwright, fine translator of Shakespeare's *Tragédies* (with Suzanne Bing, 1939) and promoter of a serious but popular theatre. He deeply influenced the modern stage. Favouring text above all, he advocated stages devoid of cumbersome sets and machinery, the 'tréteau nu', referring to the bare, movable stage of travelling companies: few props, well-chosen sets of curtains, sober costumes, and a focus on the actors. He stressed the physical and mental training of his closely knit community of actors, the 'Copiaus' (1924–9) who, in turn, like *Vilar, promoted the open-to-all theatre after the Second World War. An admirer of *Granville-Barker's *Twelfth Night*, he staged his own version in 1914 with Jouvet as Aguecheek in his Théâtre du Vieux-Colombier founded the year before, and again in 1920. *As You Like It* (1924) was a shortened version and *Much Ado About Nothing* (1936) an adaptation by Sarment. *ISG*

copy, the manuscript or printed text that the compositor followed as he set type. Title pages often advertised the authenticity of their copy: the Shakespeare First Folio asserts that the text within was 'Published according to the True Originall Copies' and Q2 *Hamlet* (1604/5) claims to have been printed 'according to the true and perfect Coppie'. The term 'original' apparently meant the authoritative copy used in the theatre, the 'book' of the play. The term 'perfect' referred to copy that had been perfected, or made whole, by reference to the playwright's original foul paper manuscript. Early English printers had a marked preference for printed over manuscript copy, even when the printed copy was heavily annotated and corrected. Of the 36 plays in the Shakespeare First Folio, a third were set up from printed quartos that had been annotated by reference to a manuscript; another third were set up from manuscript playbooks and Shakespeare's original foul papers; and a final third were set up from transcripts made by Ralph Crane and other unidentified scribes. *ER*

copyright. By entering the title of a text into the *Stationers' Register, early modern publishers or printers could establish their ownership of the *'copy' (both the physical manuscript and the text more generally) and their exclusive right to reproduce it. When Jaggard and Blount published the First *Folio, they apparently purchased sixteen of the previously unprinted plays from the King's Men and negotiated with the owners of the remaining 20 who had registered titles. John Smethwick and William Aspley, who between them held the rights to *Much Ado About Nothing*, *Love's Labour's Lost*, *The Taming of the Shrew*, *2 Henry IV*, *Romeo and Juliet*, and *Hamlet*, appear to have joined the Folio syndicate. It has been suggested that the difficulties in obtaining the rights to *Troilus and Cressida* from Henry Walley almost resulted in the play being left out of the collection altogether.

Following the publication of the First Folio, the rights were assigned to subsequent syndicates with each of the three folio reprintings. By 1709, Jacob Tonson had purchased the rights to 25 of the plays. Tonson and his successors maintained a nearly perpetual copyright in Shakespeare until 1767. (In fact, the earliest recorded use of the term 'copyright' is Tonson's reference to 'the Proprietors of the Copy-Right' in an advertisement in his 1734 edition of *The Merry Wives of Windsor*.) *ER*

de Grazia, Margreta, *Shakespeare Verbatim: The Reproduction of Authenticity and the 1790 Apparatus* (1991)
Schoenbaum, Samuel, *William Shakespeare: Records and Images* (1981)
Sisson, C. J., 'The Laws of Elizabethan Copyright: The Stationers' View', *Library*, 5th ser. 15 (1960)

Corambis. See POLONIUS.

coranto, a lively and newly fashionable dance in the early part of Shakespeare's career; see Sir Toby Belch's comparison between the coranto and *galliard in *Twelfth Night* 1.3.123. *JB*

Corbet, Richard (1582–1635), bishop and poet. Written around 1619, Corbet's holiday poem 'Iter Boreale' mentions a performance of *Richard III*. Corbet's words, 'A horse! a horse!—he, Burbidge, cried', confirm other evidence that King Richard's part had been acted by Shakespeare's prime tragedian, Richard Burbage. *PH*

Cordelia. In the first scene of *King Lear* Lear disinherits his youngest daughter because she is unwilling to compete with her sisters' protestations of unbounded love for him. The King of France agrees to marry her despite Lear's displeasure. In Act 4, she appears with a French army at *Dover and is reunited with Lear. Her forces defeated by the English in Act 5, she is imprisoned and hanged, a reprieve arriving too late. At the close of the play Lear carries her dead body on stage and begs her to speak to him again before dying himself.

Many 17th- and 18th-century readers of the play shared Samuel *Johnson's view that her death ran 'contrary to the natural ideas of justice' (1765). Audiences were spared the tragedy altogether by Nahum *Tate's 1681 version, which has her survive to marry Edgar, and which held the stage until the 19th century. The critic Lily B. Campbell saw Cordelia as a Christ figure (1952) and indeed Lear's suffering has often been seen in terms of Christian redemption. In the last half of the 20th century, however, more secular and tormented stage and film versions of the play have tended to depict Cordelia's death without sentiment. *AB*

Corin is an old shepherd in *As You Like It*. *AB*

Coriolanus *(see page 90)*

Coriolanus, Caius. See CORIOLANUS.

Cornelius. **(1)** See VALTEMAND. **(2)** The Queen's doctor in *Cymbeline*, he is rightly suspicious of her request for poison, 1.5. *AB*

cornet(t), a wind instrument fingered similarly to the *recorder, but blown like a *trumpet, with a considerable expressive and dynamic range. Used by Shakespeare and other dramatists for processional entrances and exits, or to indicate rank lower than royalty. It also became a substitute for the trumpet in the indoor theatre, and was often played in ensemble with *sackbuts. *JB*

Cornwall, Barry (Bryan Waller Procter) (1787–1874), English poet and biographer, said to have introduced Hazlitt to Elizabethan drama. His works include *Dramatic Scenes* (1819), praised by Charles Lamb as 'Elizabethan'; a biography of the actor Edmund Kean (1835); and a woodcut-illustrated edition of Shakespeare (3 vols., 1839–43), with *Memoir and Essay*. *TM*

Cornwall, Duke of. Regan's husband, he is stabbed by his servant as he blinds Gloucester, *The Tragedy of King Lear* 3.7 and *The History of King Lear* 15. *AB*

Coryat, Thomas (*c*.1577–1617), travel-writer. His idiosyncratic accounts of his journeys through Europe and Asia (such as *Coryat's Crudities*, 1611) were addressed to a group of intellectuals, among them Ben Jonson and John Donne, who met regularly at the Mermaid Tavern in London. The group is traditionally thought to have included Shakespeare. *RM*

Costard, a clown who muddles Armado's letter for Jaquenetta with Biron's for Rosaline in *Love's Labour's Lost*. *AB*

costume. Actors' costumes were their most expensive possessions, a company's wardrobe often being more valuable than its theatre. *Henslowe's accounts show that a doublet might cost £3 and a gown between £2 and £7, amounts which can be scaled by comparison with the £20 annual income of the master of the Stratford grammar school. Expensive costumes were a vital part of the visual appeal of theatre, and characters of high social rank were represented by appropriately luxurious clothing. Outside the playhouse, the wearing of such costumes by commoners was criminalized by the Sumptuary Laws, not repealed until 1604. Thomas Platter, a Swiss visitor to London,

(cont. on page 93)

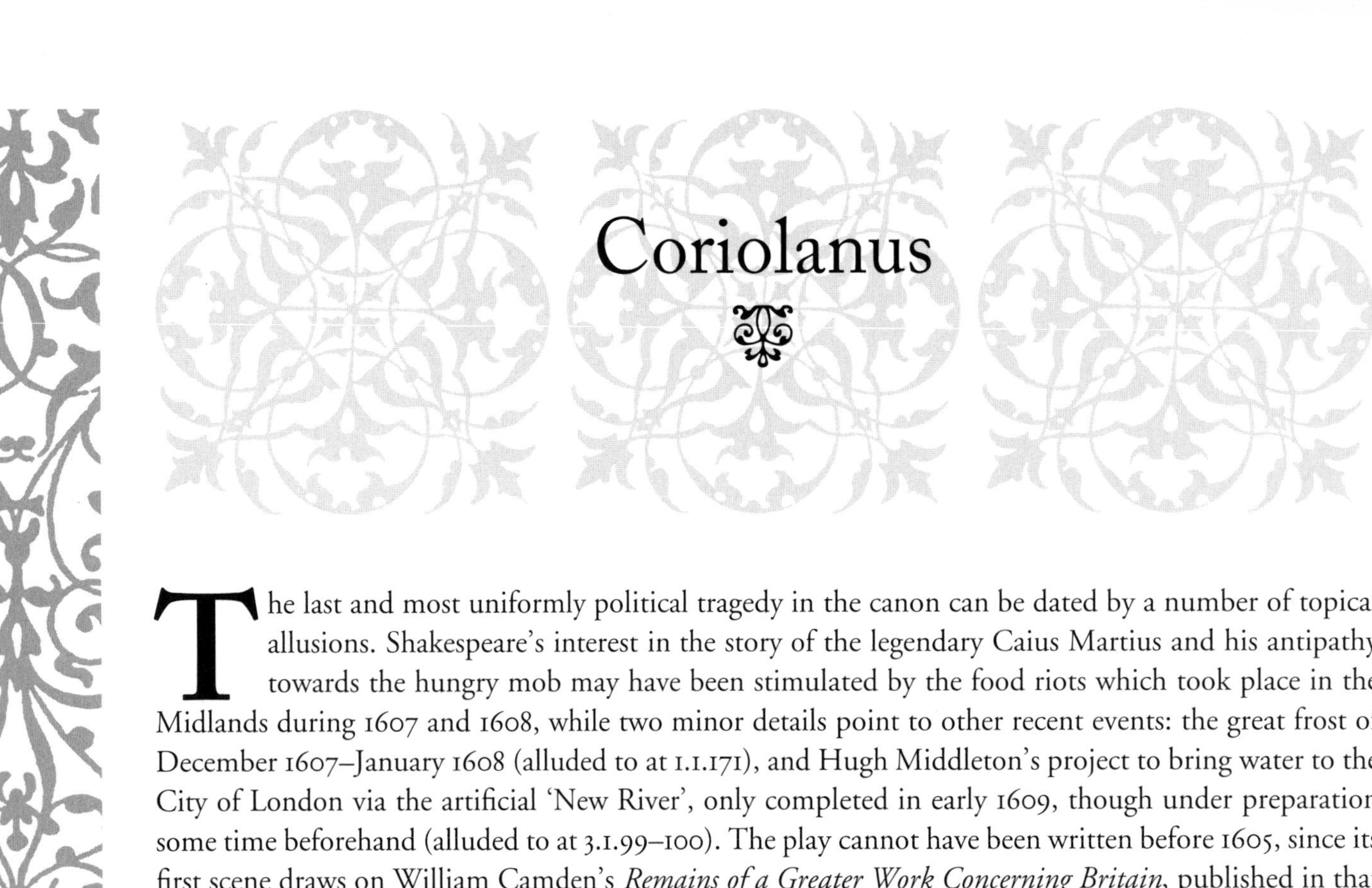

Coriolanus

The last and most uniformly political tragedy in the canon can be dated by a number of topical allusions. Shakespeare's interest in the story of the legendary Caius Martius and his antipathy towards the hungry mob may have been stimulated by the food riots which took place in the Midlands during 1607 and 1608, while two minor details point to other recent events: the great frost of December 1607–January 1608 (alluded to at 1.1.171), and Hugh Middleton's project to bring water to the City of London via the artificial 'New River', only completed in early 1609, though under preparation some time beforehand (alluded to at 3.1.99–100). The play cannot have been written before 1605, since its first scene draws on William Camden's *Remains of a Greater Work Concerning Britain*, published in that year, nor after 1609, when it was itself echoed in two separate works by authors associated with Shakespeare's company, Robert *Armin's *The Italian Tailor and his Boy* (entered in the Stationers' Register that February), and Ben *Jonson's *Epicoene* (completed later in the year). All stylistic tests place the play later than *The History of King Lear*, *Macbeth*, and *Antony and Cleopatra*, and it probably appeared shortly after *Pericles*, in spring or summer 1608.

Text: The dating of the play in 1608 is further confirmed by two details of its sole authoritative text, published in the Folio in 1623, namely the specification of cornets in some of the musical stage directions and the division of the play into acts. Both of these features are associated with indoor theatres (which could use smaller brass instruments than the public amphitheatres, and needed pauses in the action for the changing of footlights), and suggest that *Coriolanus* may have been the first of Shakespeare's plays to have been written with the *Blackfriars theatre, acquired by the King's Men in 1608, in mind. The text printed in the Folio preserves a few idiosyncrasies of Shakespeare's *foul papers (such as the occasional spelling of 'Scicinius' for 'Sicinius', which matches other examples of Shakespeare's preference for 'sc' spellings elsewhere), although other accidentals appear to be scribal. It also gives unusually full stage directions, some of them apparently the result of authorial directions being clarified and duplicated for theatrical use. It probably derives either from a promptbook transcribed from foul papers, or from a transcript of such a promptbook.

Sources: The play's depiction of the semi-legendary Caius Martius (banished from the early Roman republic in 491 BC, not so long after the events Shakespeare had narrated in *The Rape of Lucrece*) closely follows *Plutarch's 'Life of Caius Martius Coriolanus' in his *Lives of the Noble Greeks and Romans*: several major passages, notably Volumnia's appeal in 5.1 (95–183), are taken almost verbatim from Sir Thomas North's translation. Shakespeare, however, greatly expands Volumnia's role (inventing all the other episodes in which she appears), as he does that of Menenius, while Menenius' fable of the belly (1.1.85–152) shows a familiarity with other versions of this parable than Plutarch's: from Camden's *Remains*, from *Livy's version of the story in his *Annales*, and from William Averell's *Meruailous Combat of Contrarieties* (1584).

Synopsis: **1.1** Mutinous Roman citizens have banded together to avenge their hunger on the aristocrat Caius Martius, but are intercepted by Menenius, a more sympathetic patrician, who attempts to dissuade them from rebellion by telling a fable of how the parts of the body once mistakenly rose against the belly, accusing it unjustly of selfish greed. Martius himself arrives and harangues the citizens, wishing the Senate would let him kill them, and regretting that they have instead conceded the people two tribunes as representatives, Sicinius and Brutus. News arrives that a Volscian army is approaching Rome, and the senators, arriving with the tribunes, appoint an eager Martius as second-in-command under Cominius to lead a Roman force against the Volsces and their leader, Martius' arch-enemy Tullus Aufidius. Left alone, Sicinius and Brutus resolve to watch Martius, sworn enemy of their political interests, carefully. 1.2 The senators of the Volscian city Corioles, aware that the Romans have sent an army to meet their attack, send Aufidius and his troops to meet it. 1.3 Volumnia, Martius' mother, is sewing with his wife Virgilia. Delighting in Martius' military record, Volumnia has no sympathy with Virgilia's anxieties about his safety, nor, when her friend Valeria arrives to invite them out, with her refusal to leave the house while her husband is away. Valeria congratulates Virgilia on the resemblance between Martius and his young son (whom she has recently watched chasing and dismembering a butterfly), and has heard that Martius, along with his fellow commander Titus Lartius, is now besieging Corioles while Cominius leads the other half of the Roman army against the Volscian expeditionary force. 1.4–8 At the battlefront Martius reverses a Roman retreat, haranguing his soldiers and leading them into the Volscian city: the gates close behind him alone, but he survives to lead the successful taking of Corioles. Though wounded, he then joins Cominius' temporarily withdrawing force, leading a fresh and decisive assault on Aufidius' army. 1.9 Martius duels with Aufidius, driving back both him and the unwelcome fellow Volscians who take his part. 1.10 Before the victorious Roman army Cominius, despite Martius' complaints that he hates to be praised, gives Martius the title of Coriolanus for his deeds. 1.11 Aufidius, disgusted by the peace terms the Volscians have had to accept, determines to destroy his vanquisher Martius by any means, honourable or not.

2.1 Menenius is bickering with the tribunes about Martius' vices when Volumnia brings the news of his victory: to Virgilia's horror they gleefully count up how many scars he now bears. Martius, garlanded with oak and ceremonially renamed Coriolanus, is triumphantly welcomed into the city with Cominius, Lartius, and the army, and they set off for the Capitol: the tribunes, anxious that their enemy will be made consul, resolve to prevent this by provoking Coriolanus into alienating the people. 2.2 In the Capitol, Cominius gives an oration about Coriolanus' heroic deeds, which Coriolanus himself refuses to hear: the Senate name him as a consul, but this, to Coriolanus' distaste, will oblige him to appeal to the people for their acceptance by showing them the wounds he has received in their defence. 2.3 Wearing the gown of humility, Coriolanus is brought to the market place by Menenius, where he unwillingly and disdainfully requests the people's voices, which they give. After his departure, however, the tribunes persuade them to change their minds.

3.1 On their way to his investiture, Coriolanus and the senators are stopped by the tribunes, who tell him the people have withdrawn their consent: infuriated, Coriolanus rages at them, asserting that the people do not deserve political representation, and the tribunes, supported by a crowd of citizens, attempt to arrest him for treason. After a scuffle Coriolanus is persuaded to withdraw, while Menenius promises the tribunes that Coriolanus will soon answer the people's accusations in the market place. 3.2 At a patrician's house Volumnia rebukes her son for prematurely exposing his political objectives: she and the senators persuade him to speak mildly to the assembled people in order to regain the consulship he has nearly lost. 3.3 In the market place, however, the tribunes' accusations of treason goad Coriolanus into ranting against the people once more, and he is sentenced to banishment.

4.1 A stoical Coriolanus bids farewell to Volumnia, Virgilia, Menenius, Cominius, and the patricians. 4.2 Volumnia rails against the gloating tribunes. 4.3 A Roman informer tells a Volscian of Coriolanus' banishment, certain the news will encourage the regrouping Volscian army to launch a fresh attack on Rome. 4.4 Disguised, Coriolanus arrives in the Volscian city of Antium, and seeks out Tullus Aufidius. 4.5 Refusing to be denied entry by servants, Coriolanus reveals himself to Aufidius and announces that he wishes to defect to the Volscians and avenge himself on Rome. Aufidius welcomes him eagerly, to the amazement of the servants, who fear that Coriolanus will displace their master. 4.6 The mutual congratulations of Roman tribunes and people are interrupted by the news that a Volscian army, led by Coriolanus, is approaching: Menenius tells them they have deserved their impending destruction. 4.7 Aufidius, warned by his lieutenant that he appears to be Coriolanus' subordinate in their campaign, confides that he is only waiting for Coriolanus either to defeat or to refuse to attack Rome before moving against him.

5.1 Cominius returns from a wholly unsuccessful attempt to persuade Coriolanus to spare Rome, and Menenius sets off on another such embassy. 5.2 Menenius, though scorned by the Volscian watchmen, gains access to Coriolanus and Aufidius, but Coriolanus refuses to yield to his plea for mercy. 5.3 Watched by Aufidius, Coriolanus receives one last embassy from Rome before the next day's attack: Virgilia, Volumnia, Valeria, and his son Young Martius. Though he greets them with duty and love, he resolves not to accede to their request. Volumnia pleads eloquently for mercy, and at the conclusion of her speech she, Virgilia, Valeria, and Young Martius kneel before him: finally Coriolanus holds Volumnia silently by the hand before conceding, crying, that he will make peace, however dangerously to himself. 5.4 Menenius is assuring Sicinius that Coriolanus will not yield to his mother when the news arrives that he has done so. 5.5 Volumnia, Virgilia, and Valeria are welcomed back into Rome in triumph. 5.6 In Corioles, Aufidius rallies his supporters before Coriolanus arrives to report to the Volscian lords his success in obtaining a submissive peace from the Romans. Aufidius accuses him of treachery for calling off the Volscian attack at his mother's entreaty, and further provokes him by calling him 'boy': the enraged Coriolanus reminds Aufidius how often he has scarred him, and of his many victories against the Volscians. Despite the lords' attempts to keep the peace, the

Volscian people cry out for Coriolanus' death: two of Aufidius' party fatally stab him and the rest, along with Aufidius, trample his corpse. Aufidius seeks to justify the killing, but, subsiding, grants that despite the casualties he inflicted on Corioles, Coriolanus should be buried with full military honours.

Artistic features: The play is unusual for the single-mindedness with which its action builds up to a single, decisive, wordless moment, Coriolanus' yielding to Volumnia (5.3.183), while its virtuoso crowd scenes almost make the Roman people into its hero's single collective antagonist. The play has a distinctively harsh and gritty vocabulary and poetic tone throughout, thriving on rough monosyllables.

Critical history: Hazlitt's essay on the play, in *Characters of Shakespear's Plays* (1817), continues to set the agenda of much discussion of the play's political concerns. Hazlitt praises the thoroughness with which Shakespeare articulates the rival claims of aristocracy and democracy ('anyone who studies [*Coriolanus*] may save himself the trouble of reading Burke's *Reflections*, or Paine's *Rights of Man*, or the debates in both Houses of Parliament since the French Revolution or our own'), though he fears that *Coriolanus* demonstrates that poetry is innately liable to prefer dictators to the abstract claims of social justice. Before Hazlitt, commentators had tended to complain—as in their different ways did adaptors—of what *Johnson called the excessive 'bustle' of the early scenes and the inadequate business of the last, which *Dennis and other neoclassical critics had also accused of violating poetic justice. During the 19th century and the first part of the 20th much criticism of the play was similarly dedicated to showing how and why it was inferior to the earlier tragedies, with A. C. *Bradley commenting on the critical distance Shakespeare maintains between audience and characters by ironic humour and Harley *Granville-Barker praising the play's supreme, focused craftsmanship at the expense of its vitality. Frank *Harris pioneered one recurrent strain in 20th-century criticism in *The Women in Shakespeare* (1911) when he claimed that the intense mother–son bond between Coriolanus and Volumnia must have a basis in Shakespeare's own experience, and since the advent of *Freud many commentators have applied a psychoanalytic vocabulary, with greater and lesser degrees of sophistication, to the exploration of the relationship between the play's protagonist and the most fully developed older woman in the canon: the most influential example would be Janet Adelman.

Stage history: Apart from the early allusions by Armin and Jonson, there are no records of specific performances of the play before the 1680s, and its stage history thereafter is largely one of more and less propagandist adaptations until the early 19th century: Nahum *Tate's anti-Whig *The *Ingratitude of a Commonwealth* (1681), John *Dennis's anti-Jacobite *The Invader of his Country* (1719), in which Coriolanus becomes a figure for the banished Stuarts, and, later, Thomas Sheridan's version, *Coriolanus; or, The Roman Matron* (1754). This hybrid of Shakespeare's play and James Thomson's 1748 work on the same subject was still being used, in successively rewritten forms, by J. P. *Kemble for his highly successful productions (with himself in the title role and Sarah *Siddons as Volumnia) between 1789 and 1817. It became Kemble's favourite role, his own perceived arrogance and singularity in the face of his mass audience's expectations finding its perfect counterpart in Martius' imperious defiance of the Roman mob. Occasional attempts at reviving the original—in 1719, 1754, and, with Edmund *Kean as Coriolanus, in 1820—were unsuccessful, but it returned to the repertory when William Charles *Macready took the title role at Covent Garden in 1838, a part in which he was succeeded by Samuel *Phelps in 1848. Frank *Benson played Coriolanus with some success between 1893 and 1910, but the role was a disaster for Henry *Irving, who chose it as his final Shakespearian role at the Lyceum (with an equally miscast Ellen *Terry as Volumnia) in 1901. Over the 19th century as a whole the play was more successful in the republican United States, where the original had supplanted the Sheridan version (staged in Philadelphia in 1767) as early as 1796. It was the highly physical and aggressive Edwin *Forrest's greatest role, from 1831 to 1863, and he was even sculpted in the part, though some commentators preferred his successor John E. McCullough, who played Coriolanus in a more intellectually superior style in 1878.

Despite some notable revivals at the Old Vic in the 1920s, the play did not enjoy particular prominence in the 20th century until the rise of fascist movements across Europe brought it a renewed topicality. In France in 1934 the Action Française party induced the Comédie-Française to stage a version of the play which treated it as an all-out attack on democracy (stimulating violent demonstrations outside the theatre, though these failed to provoke the hoped-for military coup), and in Moscow the following year a version approved by Stalin's propagandists instead treated Coriolanus as a wholly contemptible, aristocratic, Western-style enemy of the people. The Nazis' enthusiasm for the play, which they regarded as a hymn to strong leadership, led to its banning in occupied Germany until 1953: Bertolt *Brecht's anti-Coriolanus adaptation was not acted until 1963, seven years after his death. Back in England, where attitudes to the play's protagonist have been more ambivalent, Laurence *Olivier achieved one of his greatest successes as Coriolanus, with Sybil *Thorndike as Volumnia, at the Old Vic in 1938, a role he repeated in Peter *Hall's production at Stratford in 1959, with Edith *Evans as his mother. With characteristic physical bravado Olivier made Coriolanus' death resemble the throwing from the Tarpeian rock threatened earlier by the tribunes, falling precipitately from an upper stage to dangle upside down by his ankles. His notable successors in the role have included Richard *Burton (at the Old Vic in 1954), Alan *Howard (at Stratford and on an acclaimed international tour in 1977), Ian *McKellen (in Peter Hall's uneasy modern-dress production in the National Theatre's Olivier auditorium, with a powerful Irene *Worth as Volumnia, 1984), Kenneth *Branagh (outclassed by Judi *Dench's Volumnia at Chichester in 1992) and Toby Stephens, who played Coriolanus as a sneering Regency public-school prefect in David Thacker's RSC production, with Caroline Blakiston as Volumnia, in 1994. This intelligent production was one of very few to produce the play in neither modern nor Roman dress, taking up an idea of *Hazlitt's by setting the production in the era of the French Revolution. *MD*

On the screen: The play was serialized in three parts of *The Spread of the Eagle* series (1963) for BBC TV. The BBC TV production (1983) featured Alan Howard and Irene Worth. *AD*

Recent major editions

Philip Brockbank (Arden, 1976); G. R. Hibbard (New Penguin, 1967): K. B. Parker (Oxford, 1994)

Some representative criticism

Adelman, Janet, 'Anger's my Meat: Feeding, Dependence, and Aggression in *Coriolanus*' (1978), in Murray M. Schwartz and Coppélia Kahn (eds.), *Representing Shakespeare: New Psychoanalytic Essays* (1980)

Burke, Kenneth, '*Coriolanus*—and the Delights of Faction', in James L. Calderwood and Harold E. Toliver (eds.), *Essays in Shakespearean Criticism* (1970)

Kahn, Coppélia, *Roman Shakespeare: Warriors, Wounds and Women* (1996)

Muir, Kenneth, 'The Background of *Coriolanus*', *Shakespeare Quarterly*, 10 (1959)

described one way the actors got their costumes: 'when men of rank or knights die they give and bequeath almost their finest apparel to their servants, who, since it does not befit them, do not wear such garments, but afterwards let the play-actors buy them for a few pence.' Historical accuracy in costuming was not important, and plays set in the ancient world were performed in Elizabethan dress with small additions to represent distant times and places: a curved sword to connote the Middle East, a sash to connote the Roman toga. The *Peacham drawing of what appears to be a performance of Shakespeare's *Titus Andronicus* bears out this costuming principle, but it might in fact show a performance of a German play on the same theme. *GE*

Cotes, Thomas. See folios.

Cotgrave, Randle (d. 1634?), lexicographer. He wrote *A Dictionary of the French and English Tongues* (1611), which was often reprinted throughout the 17th century. It is of great use to historians of the two languages, and hence to Shakespeare's editors. *RM*

Cottom (Cottam), John. Master of Stratford grammar school from 28 September 1579, he may have been Shakespeare's last teacher there. He had graduated from Brasenose College, Oxford, in 1566, the same year as his Stratford predecessor, Thomas *Jenkins, and had a younger brother Thomas who became a Catholic priest and was arrested in 1580, arraigned with Edmund Campion in November 1580, and executed in 1582. These events may have influenced John's resignation from his Stratford post some time after Michaelmas 1581 and before 31 January 1582, when a new teacher (probably Alexander *Aspinall) was licensed. Around 1582 Cottom, now head of the family, went to the family home at Tarnacre, in Lancashire, where he lived until his death. Tarnacre is not far from Lea, home of the Roman Catholic Alexander Hoghton whose will, in 1581, mentioned a 'William *Shakeshaft' who has been identified with the playwright. Honigmann suggests that Cottom recommended his pupil Shakespeare to Hoghton as player and teacher. *SW*

Honigmann, E. A. J., *Shakespeare: The 'Lost Years'* (1985, rev. edn. 1998)

Counter. A prison on the site of the former church of St Margaret, the Southwark Counter (or Compter), was established around 1551. Originally a lock-up, the Counter was enlarged in 1608, destroyed by fire in 1676, and rebuilt in 1685. It housed debtors (Shakespeare's references to it always consider it as a debtor's prison), as well as felons and petty offenders of both sexes. *RSB*

Carlin, M., *Medieval Southwark* (1996)

Watson, B., 'The Compter Prisons of London', *London Archaeologist*, 7 (1993)

countrymen, six. See Gerald.

couplet, a pair of rhyming verse lines, usually of the same metre and length. Shakespeare uses them to round off his sonnets and many dramatic scenes. *CB*

Court, Alexander. He is one of the soldiers who speaks to the disguised King Harry, *Henry V* 4.1. *AB*

court performances. The official reason for the existence of playing companies was to provide entertainment for the monarch in the traditional festive seasons of Christmas and Easter, and prior public performance was supposed to test and refine plays before they were taken to court. The Revels Office was initially responsible for making the costumes, properties, and sets for court performances, but from the 1580s the London theatre industry was strong enough to provide its own production materials and the Revels Office was reduced to licensing the commercial theatre and selecting from its best offerings.

Because the court moved between palaces in and around London, the players performed in a variety of rooms temporarily converted into theatres. Being called to court was lucrative and, more importantly, was a mark of royal favour which lent respectability to the leading players. *James I was more keen on theatre than his predecessor and his patronage of Shakespeare's company gave them court appearances more frequent and of longer duration than they had enjoyed under Elizabeth. The court Cockpit (a bird-fighting arena), which had been occasionally used for performance, was converted into a permanent court theatre in 1629 by James's successor Charles, under whom royal patronage of dramatic art reached its peak. *GE*

Astington, John H., *English Court Theatre 1558–1642* (1999)

Covell, William (d. 1614), divine. Covell jotted around 1595 when he was a fellow of Christ's College, Cambridge, 'Lucrecia Sweet Shakspeare' and 'Wanton Adonis. Watsons Heire'. He implies that Shakespeare is the poetic heir of Thomas Watson (d. 1592), whose love lyrics, as in the eighteen-line 'sonnets' of *The Hecatompathia* (1582), had been thought 'sweet' or mellifluous and supple. *PH*

Covent Garden theatre was designed by James Shepherd and was opened by John Rich, its first manager and holder of one of the two royal patents, in 1732. Much enlarged and restructured by Henry Holland in 1792, it was completely rebuilt after the fire of 1808, and again (the present Royal Opera House) after a second conflagration in 1856. The early playing company, led by James *Quin, competed with Drury Lane, in a rivalry that intensified from 1750 when Spranger *Barry joined Covent Garden. *Garrick's dominance at Drury Lane, however, secured the Shakespearian staging contest, with Covent Garden innovations such as *Macklin's ill-received Scottish staging of *Macbeth* (1773) doing little to redress the balance. *CMSA*

Coventry, Mayor of. See Mayor of Coventry.

Covent Garden theatre, painted by Henry Andrews (d. 1868) in 1831. In the trial scene of *All Is True* (*Henry VIII*), Charles Young's Wolsey attempts to placate Fanny Kemble's Queen Katherine, while Charles Kemble's King Henry looks on.

Cowley, Richard (*c.*1568–1619), actor (Strange's Men 1590–3, Chamberlain's/King's Men 1598–1619). The plot of *2 Seven Deadly Sins* (performed before 1594, possibly by Strange's Men) names Cowley as a lieutenant in the Induction, a soldier and a lord in 'Envy', Giraldus and a musician in 'Sloth', and a lord in 'Lechery'. Letters between Edward and Joan Alleyn in 1593 indicate that Cowley was touring with Strange's Men. It appears that in 1597 Cowley's wife Elizabeth had an affair with the astrologer Simon *Forman while consulting him professionally. By 1598 Cowley was with the Chamberlain's Men and his name is recorded in the speech prefixes of the 1600 quarto of Shakespeare's *Much Ado About Nothing* where we should expect Verges's name, indicating that he took this role. Cowley is named as a sharer in the 1603 patent to the King's Men and as an actor in the 1623 Folio of Shakespeare. In his will of 1605 Augustine *Phillips called Cowley 'my fellow' and left him 20s. in gold and Cowley's brief orally declared will of 13 January 1618 was witnessed by John *Heminges, Cuthbert *Burbage, John Shank, and Thomas Ravenscroft. *GE*

Cox, Robert (?1604–?1655), actor and writer of *drolls. No direct records exist of Cox acting before the closing of the theatres, but later commentaries assert that he achieved some fame before the Commonwealth period. In 1653 Cox was arrested apparently for a performance at the Red Bull which crossed the line between the permitted entertainments of show-dancing and the prohibited entertainment of acting. Francis Kirkman called 'the incomparable Robert Cox' the author, compiler, and performer of the drolls collected as *The Wits* (first published 1662, Kirkman's enlarged edition 1672–3) and named the Red Bull as the venue. A book called *Actaeon and Diana*, containing two plays, a jig, and a prose farce, was printed 'for the use of the Author Robert Cox' some time before 1 September 1656, the day George Thomason purchased a copy. *GE*

Kirkman, Francis, *The Wits; or Sport Upon Sport*, ed. John James Elson (1932)

Crab is Lance's incontinent *dog, *Two Gentlemen of Verona* 4.4.1–38. *AB*

'Crabbed Age and Youth', a twelve-line lyric printed as the twelfth poem in *The *Passionate Pilgrim* (1599). A fine lyric, but almost certainly not by Shakespeare, it is also the first stanza of a longer poem called 'A Maiden's Choice 'twixt Age and Youth' printed in Thomas *Deloney's *Garland of Good Will*. Not all the poems in this book are by Deloney. Though no edition survives before 1628, Thomas *Nashe refers to it in 1596. *SW*

crabtree, Shakespeare's. In 1762 the *British Magazine* published an anonymous 'Letter from the Place of Shakespeare's Nativity' written from the White Lion Inn in Stratford-upon-Avon. The correspondent claimed that his 'chearful landlord' had taken him first to the Birthplace, and then to visit 'two young women, lineal descendants of our great dramatic poet' (clearly impostors) who kept 'a little ale-house, some small distance from Stratford. On the road thither, at a place called Bidford' which is on the River Avon, some 8 miles (13 km) west of Stratford, the landlord 'showed me, in the hedge, a crab-tree, called Shakespeare's canopy, because under it our poet slept one night; for he, as well as Ben Jonson, loved a glass for the pleasure of society; and he having heard much of the men of that village as deep drinkers and merry fellows, one day went over to Bidford, to take a cup with them. He enquired of a shepherd for the Bidford drinkers; who replied, they were absent; but the Bidford sippers were at home; and "I suppose," continued the sheepkeeper, "they will be sufficient for you": and so indeed they were. He was forced to take up his lodging under that tree for some hours.'

The story grew. About 1770 John *Jordan provided a sequel, claiming that on the following morning Shakespeare's companions roused him and invited him to continue the contest, but that he refused, saying that he had drunk with

Piping Pebworth, Dancing Marston
Haunted Hillborough, Hungry Grafton,
Dadgeing Exhall, Papist Wicksford,
Beggarly Broom, and Drunken Bidford.

In 1795 Samuel *Ireland swallowed the story, writing, 'it is certain that the Crab Tree is known all round the country by the name of Shakespeare's Crab; and that the villages to which the allusion is made, all bear the epithets here given them: the people of Pebworth are still famed for their skill on the pipe and tabor: Hillborough is now called Haunted Hillborough; and Grafton is notorious for the poverty of its soil.' *SW*

Craig, Edward Gordon (1892–1966), British designer, director, and theorist. Though he directed few productions, Craig was highly influential in 20th-century Shakespeare performance. Starting with *Much Ado About Nothing* for Ellen *Terry (his mother) in 1903, he initiated a series of practical and theoretical reforms that were seized upon by later modernists. Craig's basic idea was aesthetic rather than social: he insisted that a single artist-designer-director take absolute charge of all elements of theatrical production, elevating the significance of the visual and reducing the individuality of the actors, whom he called *Übermarionetten* (super-puppets) under the director's control. His designs for Shakespeare, mostly unrealized, suggest simple symbolic solutions instead of localized or realist settings, often relying on monumental, monolithic structures to convey mood and idea. His production of *Hamlet* with *Stanislavsky at the Moscow Art Theatre (1912), though far from satisfactory to Craig, managed to suggest the fluidity and suppleness of his conception through the use of movable screens that changed configuration for each scene. His many books (e.g. *On the Art of the Theatre*, 1911; *Scene*, 1923) and his journal *The Mask* had a huge effect on subsequent practice. *DK*

Innes, Christopher, *Edward Gordon Craig* (1983)

Crane, Ralph (fl. 1555–1632). A professional scrivener who seems to have had a close association with the King's Men. In the preface to his *Works of Mercy* (1621), Crane writes that 'some employment hath my useful pen had 'mongst those civil, well-deserving men that grace the stage with honour and delight, of whose true honesties I much could write, but will comprise it (as in a cask of gold) under the kingly services they do hold'. Crane probably prepared the transcripts that served as printer's copy for the Folio texts of *The Tempest, The Two Gentlemen of Verona, The Merry Wives of Windsor, Measure for Measure, The Winter's Tale*, and *Cymbeline*.

Although Crane's transcriptions of Shakespearian texts have not survived, eight of his manuscripts of work by other dramatists are extant, including Jonson's *Pleasure Reconciled to Virtue* (1618), Fletcher and Massinger's *Sir John van Olden Barnavelt* (1619), Middleton's *A Game at Chess* (1624) and *The Witch* (1624–5), and Fletcher's *Demetrius and Enanthe* (1625). Through a detailed study of these surviving manuscripts, T. H. Howard-Hill identified Crane's characteristic habits of spelling and punctuation in order to explore the possibility that certain idiosyncratic features of the first five comedies in the Folio, such as the liberal use of colons, parentheses, hyphens, and apostrophes, may be due to Crane's influence.

The much-discussed massed entrances in three Folio texts thought to have been set up from Crane transcripts—*The Two Gentlemen of Verona, The Merry Wives of Windsor*, and *The Winter's Tale*—which list all of the characters who appear in a scene in a single opening direction regardless of whether they enter at the beginning or later, may be compared with similar directions in Crane's manuscript of *A Game at Chess* (Bodleian MS). It has been suggested that by employing this neoclassical procedure Crane intended to invest his dramatic transcripts with the trappings of antiquity, as he did in the invariably Latinate formulae he used for act and scene headings, 'Incipit Actus Quartus' and 'Finis Actus Secundij'. *ER*

Howard-Hill, T. H., 'Shakespeare's Earliest Editor, Ralph Crane', *Shakespeare Survey*, 44 (1992)

Jowett, John, 'New Created Creatures: Ralph Crane and the Stage Directions in *The Tempest*', *Shakespeare Survey*, 36 (1983)

Cranmer, Thomas (1489–1556). He secures the King's divorce from Katherine; is made Archbishop of Canterbury; crowns Anne Boleyn; and survives the charge of heresy made by Gardiner and others in *All Is True* (*Henry VIII*). *AB*

Creede, Thomas. See PRINTING AND PUBLISHING.

Creizenach, Wilhelm (1851–1919), German critic and historian of theatre, a professor at Cracow. The fourth volume of his *Geschichte des neueren Dramas* was translated as *The English Drama of the Age of Shakespeare* (1916), making many connections not only between English contemporaries of Shakespeare, but with European literature and drama. *TM*

Cressida. See TROILUS AND CRESSIDA.

crime and punishment. During the 1580s, poaching was punishable with both a fine and three months' imprisonment. It should not be surprising, then, that we have no certain knowledge whether Shakespeare actually risked that penalty by his alleged activities at Charlecote. It is always easier to write the history of punishment than that of crime, because crime prefers to keep itself hidden, whereas punishment is a matter of public record. This was all the more true in Shakespeare's time, when punishment, as an instrument of authority used to control disorder, dissent, and deviance, was a regular and highly visible fact of life: boys were publicly beaten at school, prostitutes and vagrants whipped through the city streets, and petty offenders exposed to shame and pelting in the stocks or pillory, while crowds of both sexes would gather to witness felons and traitors meeting their end on the gallows.

During Shakespeare's adult life, public opinion became increasingly aware of the causal link between poverty and crime: in *The Winter's Tale*, Autolycus has become a confidence trickster because he has lost his job as a courtier, and in *2 Henry IV* the new King grants pensions to Falstaff and his cronies expressly so that they will not be 'forced to evils' by their 'lack of means' (5.5.67). In practice, however, there was little mitigation of the penal regime. English law classified crimes on three levels according to the severity of the prescribed penalty. Lesser crimes, such as sedition, riot, libel, and perjury, were misdemeanours and attracted a range of non-capital penalties from fines to floggings. At the opposite end of the scale was treason, which could be either 'high' or 'petty', signifying respectively crimes against the state (such as the assassination of a public official, adultery committed by a queen, counterfeiting the coin of the realm, or even imagining the monarch's death) and against the order of society (such as the murder of a husband by his wife or a master by his servant). Whatever its altitude, treason was punished by an aggravated form of the death penalty. Much of what we today think of as serious crime, including murder, rape, and the various forms of theft, belonged in the middle band, felony, and was punishable by death; *witchcraft was also felonious.

There was no court of appeal in this period: a legal loophole allowed the literate to evade the death sentence in some cases, but once passed it could only be overturned by royal decree. The convict would be taken to a place of execution (usually Tyburn or Tower Hill in London) where, on the ladder of the gallows with hands tied and the noose around his neck, he would make a public speech, usually a confession, and sing a final hymn; then the hangman would push him off. At Tyburn there were about 140 such executions every year, taking place in grisly clusters during the four law terms when the courts were sitting. Felons were left to strangle under their own weight (kindly onlookers might shorten their suffering by pulling their legs), but traitors were cut down and disembowelled alive, before being cut in quarters, which were then treated with pitch and displayed around the city. (Noblemen had the privilege of being beheaded instead.) Crowds did not necessarily witness such spectacles with sadistic pleasure: some wept with humane pity for the victim, and the public hangman was the most reviled of offices, grudgingly considered the lowest possible kind of honest work. (This is why, in *Measure for Measure*, it is a step up for Pompey the bawd to be appointed temporary assistant executioner.) Accounts of the crime and execution would often appear soon afterwards as topical pamphlets and ballads.

At other times, most people's contact with criminals was probably fairly limited. Those who visited London's suburban playhouses would have travelled through districts where prostitutes operated, and the theatres themselves were often thought to be a haunt of cutpurses. However, even in cities the actual risk of becoming a victim of crime was relatively small. Accordingly, there was a strong element of fantasy in the way the period's fiction represented criminals. In part, it materialized respectable fears in the notion that the night was full of footpads and murderers who might assault a man who, like Banquo in *Macbeth*, 'walked too late' (3.6.5). But there was also a more specific conception of the underworld as a complex, highly integrated society with its own language, professional hierarchies, and codes of conduct, which Oldcastle (later Falstaff) appeals to in *1 Henry IV* when he expects thieves to be 'true to one another' (2.2.28). It is this romantic fascination which informs much of Elizabethan rogue literature, as well as Shakespeare's characterization of Falstaff, Autolycus, and the outlaws in *The Two Gentlemen of Verona*. *MW*

Emmison, F. G., *Elizabethan Life: Disorder* (1970)
Salgádo, Gámini, *The Elizabethan Underworld* (1977)
Sharpe, J. A., *Crime in Early Modern England, 1550–1750* (1984)
Sharpe, J. A., *Judicial Punishment in England* (1990)

critical history. Although criticism is strictly the attempt to explain and evaluate works of art in terms other than their own, G. Wilson *Knight, in *The Wheel of Fire* (1930), differentiates between 'criticism' (involving comparison and evaluation) and 'interpretation' (which seeks to understand a work on its own terms). In Shakespeare studies, criticism as such is often inextricable from editorial, textual, biographical, historical, linguistic, and/or purely scholarly investigation. The distinction is just as difficult now that the once informal activity of criticism has been professionalized in universities, and accompanied by a renewed codification of literary and critical theory. Because of the central place Shakespeare has come to occupy in academic education at every level, his works are now a site for contesting modes of interpretation, appropriation, and signification. In addition, there persists a broad division between literary criticism (reflecting a central canon of literature in English) and theatrical criticism (responding to the historically conditioning characteristics of live performance).

Informal criticism of Shakespeare probably begins with schoolmaster Francis *Meres's *Palladis Tamia: Wit's Treasury* (1598), in which he patriotically proposes equivalents in modern English literature for the great classical authors: Shakespeare matching Plautus for comedy and Seneca for tragedy; Ovid for love poetry; and Horace or Catullus for lyric poetry.

Classical conventions are also reflected in the presentation of the First Folio of 1623, where 36 plays are collected, in a few cases misleadingly, into genres of comedy, history, and tragedy (of which only national 'history' might properly be regarded as an Elizabethan invention); while the partial and imperfect division of individual plays into acts and scenes (with Latin designations) also reminds the reader of their classical antecedents.

The prefatory dedications and commendatory verses also raise matters which continue to occupy criticism. Shakespeare's actor-executors, John Heminges and Henry Condell, refer to the universality, popularity, and accessibility of the works; their dual status, as plays to be performed live on stage, and as texts to be read; the textual authority of the early printed editions, despite their author's inability to monitor many of them; Shakespeare's mysterious ease of composition and access to so-called 'Nature', exemplifying his spontaneous genius.

Ben Jonson, extravagantly calling the author 'my beloved', compares his achievement not only to his English predecessors and contemporaries (Chaucer, Spenser, Beaumont, Kyd, and Marlowe) but also to the great classical dramatists (Aeschylus, Euripides, Sophocles, Aristophanes, Terence, and Plautus), apparently taking for granted Shakespeare's own familiarity with their works, despite his relatively 'small Latin, and less Greek'. Jonson too draws attention to the paradox of the intrinsic theatrical impermanence of Shakespeare's plays and their literary potential to transcend any limitations of time and place. While acknowledging Shakespeare's natural gifts, Jonson is also careful to justify both the art and the effort ('sweat . . . and strike the second heat') involved in such prodigious poetic expression.

These First Folio encomia set the critical agenda for centuries to come. But note the absence of biographical or personal information. They concentrate on art and achievement. There *is* mention of the Stratford monument; the rivers Avon and Thames; the Globe, Blackfriars, and Cockpit theatres; the professional friends and aristocratic patrons. Shakespeare's appearance is commemorated in the Droeshout engraved portrait; but of family and personal life, those subjects which have so obsessed later speculators, there is nothing. Nor, on the other hand, is there the slightest doubt that William Shakespeare of Stratford-upon-Avon actually did write the plays attributed to him.

Criticism in the 17th and 18th centuries partly flourishes as an adjunct to the scholarly accumulation (often in successive editions and their accompanying biographies, from Nicholas *Rowe in 1709 onwards) of facts about Shakespeare, his theatre, and his times; and partly as an antidote to the theatrical practice of adaptation and revision. But it also represents a direct challenge and sometimes confrontation between succeeding generations of modern authors and their illustrious predecessor. In John *Dryden's *Essay on the Dramatique Poetry of the Last Age* (1672), *Preface to Troilus and Cressida* (1679), and *Essay of Dramatick Poesie* (1688), the leading author of the Restoration not only pays tribute to the 'largest and most comprehensive soul' of all modern and most ancient poets, but attributes Shakespeare's numerous defects of taste and judgement to the barbarous age in which he lived. This weighing of merits and defects seems to us unproductive, but it represents an attempt to establish permanent criteria for the assessment of value in literature against the anarchic flux of temporary fashion.

The 'enlightened' apportionment of praise and blame continues in the work of both Alexander *Pope and Samuel *Johnson. Pope's criticism, contained in the Preface to his 1725 edition, has been described as uninspired and conventional, although he does acknowledge the absurdity and irrelevance of applying Aristotelian prescriptions to Shakespeare. Johnson's own notable contribution to criticism also comes in the Preface to his edition, of 1765, in which paradoxically he appeals to both 'nature' and 'delusion' (or dramatic illusion) in defence of Shakespeare's distinctly unregulated and unclassical imagination. Johnson's praise for Shakespeare's 'just representations of general nature' and his dramatic realization of 'the genuine progeny of common humanity' reflect the importance he attached to the agreed verdict of generations of readers and spectators.

Several 18th-century essayists seem to anticipate concerns central to later criticism. Maurice *Morgann's *Essay on the Dramatic Character of Sir John Falstaff* (1777) begins an enduring fashion for isolating individual characters for analysis. Similarly, Walter *Whiter's *Specimen of a Commentary on Shakespeare* (1794), in drawing attention to the association in Shakespeare's mind of certain clusters of ideas and images, begins another process, only systematically exploited in the 20th century, of attention to the function of specific details of diction and imagery.

This period also marks the beginning of important contributions to the study and reputation of Shakespeare by distinguished European authors, including both *Voltaire's rationalist detraction and *Goethe's Romantic devotion. Although England's major *Romantic critic of Shakespeare, Samuel Taylor *Coleridge, in seeking to place Shakespeare's 'judgement' on a level with his 'genius', seems to discount any debt to German Romantic criticism, particularly that of A. W. *Schlegel, the coincidence of ideas is clear and only the precedence uncertain. The often fragmentary sources for Coleridge's own criticism (notebooks, letters, conversations, reported lectures, etc.) do define two important alternative streams of Shakespearian criticism: the 'poetic' (focusing on organic form in language) and the 'psychological' (focusing on character)—De Quincey too calls his 1823 essay 'On the Knocking at the Gate in *Macbeth*' a 'specimen of psychological criticism'.

William *Hazlitt's *Characters of Shakespear's Plays* (1817), including 'doubtful plays' as well as the accepted plays, poems, and sonnets, also emulates the romantic enthusiasm of Schlegel, in reaction to the classical reservations of Dr Johnson. Hazlitt's own insight into poetry and character is matched by his response to live performance, both in the *Characters* and in some of the companion pieces in *The Round Table* (also 1817), particularly his vivid essay 'On Mr. Kean's Iago'. John *Keats's continuous allusions to Shakespeare in his letters, particularly his identification of Shakespeare's '*Negative Capability*, that is, when a man is capable of being in uncertainties, mysteries, doubts, without any irritable reaching after fact and reason', represent another aspect of Romantic impressionism, with its elevation of Shakespeare's poetic and imaginative capacity over his intellectual judgement.

Perhaps in reaction to this, much 19th-century criticism is conducted precisely in a context of such 'irritable reaching after fact', the accumulation through documentary research of information about Shakespeare's life and times being typified by the activity and output of the *Shakespeare Society (founded 1840) and the New Shakspere Society (founded 1873). Passionate enthusiasm persists, reflected in the writings of Charles *Dickens, Herman Melville, or Fyodor *Dostoevsky; while a few sceptical detractors (notably Leo *Tolstoy) remained unimpressed by the rising cultural tide of almost universal approbation.

The New Shakspere Society attempted to use metrical and phraseological tests to establish the order in which Shakespeare wrote the plays; and, using that order, to study 'the progress and meaning of Shakspere's mind'. Much influential criticism in the 19th century reflects that speculation, both in Britain and Europe: Edward Dowden's *Shakspere: A Critical Study of his Mind and Art* (1875), responding to the German psycho-biography of *Gervinus (1849–50, translated as *Shakespeare Commentaries* in 1863). Dowden's inference of distinct periods in the growth of Shakespeare's intellect and character, while frequently scorned as unscholarly, nevertheless informed general and specialized studies of Shakespeare's 'happy' comedies, 'dark' comedies, 'great' tragedies, and 'romances' for nearly a century; and found further expression in the Danish Georg *Brandes's *William Shakespeare* (1896), which influenced writers such as Ibsen, James *Joyce, and Bernard Shaw, as well as academics such as A. C. *Bradley, in *Shakespearean Tragedy* (1904), whose detailed analysis of *Hamlet*, *Othello*, *King Lear*, and *Macbeth* is probably still the most widely consulted critical work on Shakespeare ever published, despite repeated attempts (by E. E. *Stoll, F. R. *Leavis, L. C. *Knights, and many others) to discredit its premisses.

Other early 20th-century approaches to Shakespeare were mainly characterized by comparative literary and dramatic studies; increasing attention to language and style; and a renewed recognition of the importance of stage history.

In the later 20th century the tradition of exceptional individual critics (often creative writers themselves) bringing their own literary gifts to the exposition of Shakespeare has partly been supplanted by ideologically influenced 'schools' and theories, often collaboratively and collectively reflecting the relatively new academic disciplines of politics, psychology, sociology, and cultural and women's studies. Of course, there continue to be many notable exceptions (including perhaps T. S. *Eliot, Dover *Wilson, Wilson *Knight, Muriel *Bradbrook, William *Empson, and, more recently, writers such as Harold Bloom and Ted *Hughes), in whom individual perception and even personality seem to play almost as large a part in their criticism as specialized knowledge and systematic methodology. In many respects these, and others, seem to represent what has lately been characterized and caricatured as an eclectic tradition of 'liberal humanism', bearing connotations both positive (in its elevation of individual perceptions and values) and negative (as neglecting social, historical, and political factors). A philosophical division has even revived between those who accept the *mimetic* status of art in reflecting some kind of external reality, and those for whom the only reality is subjective and perceptual.

In the contested area of ideology, the socio-economic theories of Karl *Marx and the psycho-sexual theories of Sigmund *Freud have been widely applied. Carl *Jung's formulation of a 'collective unconscious', occupied by universally recognized 'symbolic archetypes', has also found adherents.

In the past 25 years, traditional modes of exposition have continued to exist alongside sometimes mutually exclusive competing theories. Among these have flourished *structuralism; deconstruction; *cultural materialism; *new historicism; and *feminism. All have received wide professional endorsement, but probably only feminist criticism has achieved the full assent of a general non-academic audience. *TM*

The critical tradition

Bate, Jonathan, *Shakespeare and the English Romantic Imagination* (1986)

Bristol, Michael D., *Shakespeare's America, America's Shakespeare* (1990)

Dobson, Michael, *The Making of the National Poet: Shakespeare, Adaptation and Authorship* (1992)

Eastman, Arthur M., *A Short History of Shakespearean Criticism* (1968)

LeWinter, Oswald (ed.), *Shakespeare in Europe* (1963)

Ralli, Augustus, *A History of Shakespearian Criticism* (2 vols., 1959)

New approaches

Dollimore, Jonathan, and Sinfield, Alan (eds.), *Political Shakespeare* (1985)

Drakakis, John (ed.), *Alternative Shakespeares* (1985)

Greenblatt, Stephen, *Shakespearean Negotiations: The Circulation of Social Energy in the Renaissance* (1988)

Howard, Jean E., and O'Connor, Marion F. (eds.), *Shakespeare Reproduced: The Text in History and Ideology* (1987)

Lenz, Carolyn Ruth Swift, Greene, Gayle, and Neely, Carol Thomas (eds.), *The Woman's Part: Feminist Criticism of Shakespeare* (1980)

Parker, Patricia, and Hartman, Geoffrey (eds.), *Shakespeare and the Question of Theory* (1985)

Schwartz, Murray M., and Kahn, Coppélia (eds.), *Representing Shakespeare: New Psychoanalytic Essays* (1980)

Croce, Benedetto (1866–1952), Italian philosopher and literary critic. Croce, shifting discussion away from the artist's personality and mind to the work itself, with its own self-sufficient laws, represents a reaction against 19th-century criticism. *Shakespeare* (1943), extracted and translated from *Ariosto, Shakespeare, e Corneille* (1920), offers just such an analysis. *TM*

Cromwell, Oliver (1599–1658), Lord Protector. He is often wrongly accused of closing the theatres in 1650. In fact, he was fighting the Scots at the time. Theatres reopened at the Restoration in 1660. *CS*

Cromwell, Thomas (1485–1540, executed for treason), secretary to Cardinal Wolsey and later Henry VIII's chief minister. He defends Cranmer from Gardiner, *All Is True* (*Henry VIII*) 5.2. *AB*

Cross, Samuel (1568–before 1595), actor (probably Chamberlain's Men around 1594). Samuel Cross is named as a principal actor in the 1623 Folio but nowhere else in records of the company. In *An Apology for Actors* Thomas Heywood named a 'Crosse' as one of the famous actors before his time, which suggests that Cross died before Heywood came to London around 1594. *GE*

Cross Keys Inn. See INNS.

Crowne, John (*c.*1649–1703), a dramatist who amalgamated the last two acts of *The First Part of the Contention* (*2 Henry VI*) with *Richard Duke of York* (*3 Henry VI*) to create *The Misery of the Civil War* (1680), directed against the Whigs. Lady Elianor Butler, the mistress he introduced for Henry's son Edward, pursued him to the battlefield 'in man's habit'. Crowne later wrote a further political adaptation of the first three acts of *The First Part of the Contention.* *CMSA*

Cruickshank, George (1792–1878), English painter, illustrator, and cartoonist. Twenty years after illustrating Dickens, Cruickshank designed plates for Robert Brough's *The Life of Sir John Falstaff* (1857–8). This recurring interest in Falstaff is conflated with the popular genre of *fairy painting in 'The Last Scene in *The Merry Wives of Windsor*' (exhibited at the British Institution, 1857)—a genre with which Cruickshank also engaged to depict *A Midsummer Night's Dream.* His allegorical 'All the World's a Stage' (1863–5) presents Shakespeare's birth at the Globe, on a stage flanked by the figures of Comedy and Tragedy and populated by Shakespearian characters. *KN*

Cruz, Ramón de la (1731–94), Spanish playwright. He translated J. F. Ducis's adaptation of *Hamlet* for the theatre, which was the first Shakespearian play to be staged in Spain. It was entitled *Hamleto, rey [king] de Dinamarca: tragedia inglesa* and was treated merely as a tragedy of intrigue. Performances ran for five days only (Madrid, 4–8 October 1772). *ALP*

cultural materialism. A phrase originally coined by English critic Raymond Williams (*Marxism and Literature*, 1977) to describe his own unique contribution to *Marxist cultural theory. The meaning of the term was subsequently extended in the 1980s in Shakespeare (and more broadly cultural) studies to include not only Williams's work but newer currents of Althusserian Marxism, French poststructuralism, and aspects of feminist and postcolonialist theory. Cultural materialism has developed particularly as an explicitly leftist reaction to the 'old' historicism of E. M. W. *Tillyard and to Tillyard's more social-minded 'humanist' nemesis F. R. *Leavis and his numerous disciples.

The term is most often identified in Shakespeare studies with Jonathan Dollimore and Alan Sinfield, editors of the influential 1985 *Political Shakespeare: New Essays in Cultural Materialism*—the work most responsible for disseminating the term in Shakespeare studies. But it has been applied to a broad range of (mostly British) Marxist and poststructuralist-influenced critics such as Catherine Belsey, Francis Barker, Terence Hawkes, Lisa Jardine, and John Drakakis. Cultural materialism is closely allied to the 'cultural poetics' or *'new historicism' developed contemporaneously in the USA by Stephen Greenblatt and allied critics but has tended to be more explicitly Marxist and politically optimistic than its American variant. *HG*

Wilson, S., *Cultural Materialism: Theory and Practice* (1995)

Cumberland, Richard (1732–1811), prolific playwright. He adapted *Timon of Athens* for Drury Lane in 1771. He wrote an anonymous defence (1776) of his patron *Garrick whose adaptation of *Hamlet* was attacked by Arthur Murphy. *CMSA*

Cunningham, Peter (1816–69), Scottish scholar and biographer who published *Extracts from the Accounts of the Revels at Court* (1842), including for the years 1604–5 and 1611–12, the only ones extant for the Jacobean period (although sometimes questioned). He was treasurer of the London and Stratford committees that bought the *Birthplace in 1847. *TM*

'Cupid'. 'One as Cupid' (the Roman god of love) introduces the masque of Amazons, *Timon of Athens* 1.2. *AB*

Curan is one of Gloucester's retainers, *The Tragedy of King Lear* 2.1.1–13 and *The History of King Lear* 6.1–13. *AB*

Cure for a Scold, A. James Worsdale attempted to cash in on the vogue for 'ballad opera' initiated by John Gay's *The Beggar's Opera* with this 1735 'Ballad Farce of Two Acts', a hybrid of *The Taming of the Shrew* and John Lacy's adaptation *Sauny the Scot.* *MD*

Curio is one of Orsino's attendants in *Twelfth Night.* *AB*

Curtain theatre. The Curtain took its name from the parcel of land upon which it was built in Holywell in 1577, about one year later than the Theatre—with which its history is closely related—and just to the south of it. In 1585 the Curtain's owner, Henry Lanman, entered into an obscure deal with James Burbage and John Brayne, the Theatre's owners, which involved them 'taking the Curten as an Esore to their playe housse'. The modern word closest to 'Esore' is 'easer', but it is hard to see how one playhouse could 'ease' another, although William Ingram made plausible sense of the deal as a means of selling the Curtain to Burbage and Brayne for the equivalent of seven years' income, about £1,400. The Theatre appears to have stood empty for some time before being removed to form the Globe, and during this time the Chamberlain's Men were presumably using the Curtain until their new home was ready on Bankside.

Leslie Hotson identified as the Curtain the playhouse represented in the 'Utrecht' engraving owned by Abram Booth, but this has subsequently been firmly reidentified as the Theatre, although the Curtain's flag can just be made out emerging from behind an intervening roof to the right of the Theatre. Because of this misidentification a number of models of the Curtain were made from the 'Utrecht' engraving and, while quite without value concerning the Curtain, these are now reasonable guesses for the Theatre so long as the engraving's exaggeration of height is borne in mind. Chambers thought that the venue for an unnamed play seen by Thomas Platter must have been the Curtain, but recent discoveries by Herbert Berry make the Boar's Head a likelier venue. *GE*

Ingram, William, 'Henry Lanman's Curtain Playhouse as an "Easer" to the Theatre, 1585–1592', in Herbert Berry (ed.), *The First Public Playhouse: The Theatre in Shoreditch 1576–1598* (1979)

Curtis is one of Petruccio's servants in *The Taming of the Shrew.* *AB*

Cushman, Charlotte Saunders (1816–76), American actress who, after a false start in opera, inaugurated her distinguished career as Lady Macbeth in New Orleans (1836). Having honed her performance she impressed the normally critical *Macready whom she partnered during his 1843–4 tour of America, as a result of which she adopted some of his methods and took his advice to act in England. Physically mannish, Cushman shared Macready's intellectual acuity and powerful stage presence, carrying all before her as Emilia, Queen Katherine, and—crossing the gender barrier—Romeo, often to her sister Susan's Juliet. Her Hamlet and Cardinal Wolsey were less successful. The equal of *Forrest and *Booth (both of whom she partnered), Cushman was the first American actress of international stature. *RF*

Leach, Joseph, *Bright Particular Star* (1970)

Cymbeline: A Tragedy, Altered from Shakespeare. William *Hawkins's adaptation of *Cymbeline*, performed at Covent Garden in 1759, attempts the astounding feat of making Shakespeare's most wayward romance conform to the neoclassical unities of time, place, and action, as well as turning Cloten (who pays Giacomo to slander Innogen) into a traitor in the pay of the Romans. *MD*

Cymbeline, King of Britain *(see page 101)*

Czechoslovakia. See Bohemia and the former Czechoslovakia.

Charlotte Cushman (1816–76), the first American actress to achieve international distinction in Shakespearian roles, playing Romeo to her sister Susan's Juliet.

Cymbeline, King of Britain

Intricately and eclectically plotted, and producing in its last scene the most elaborate series of revelations and surprises in the canon as it snatches its multiply happy ending from the jaws of several disasters, *Cymbeline* belongs to the Jacobean vogue for tragicomedy which began with the success of Francis *Beaumont and John *Fletcher's *Philaster* in 1609. *Cymbeline* and *Philaster* are in fact closely related, and it seems most likely that Shakespeare's play was influenced by the work of his two younger colleagues—with one of whom he would later collaborate on *All Is True* (*Henry* VIII), *The Two Noble Kinsmen*, and the lost *Cardenio*. Simon *Forman records seeing *Cymbeline* performed in April 1611, when it was probably relatively new: unlike *Pericles* and *The Winter's Tale* it nowhere echoes the writings of *Plutarch which Shakespeare had consulted so heavily when composing *Timon of Athens*, *Antony and Cleopatra*, and *Coriolanus*, so it was probably composed later than both of these previous experiments with the romance genre, in 1610.

Text: The play first appeared in print in the Folio in 1623, where its text provides the first recorded instance of the name 'Imogen': one of Shakespeare's sources for the play, however, the ancient British section of *Holinshed's *Chronicles*, tells of an Innogen (wife of the legendary Brute), a name Shakespeare had earlier given to Leonato's non-speaking wife in the opening stage direction of *Much Ado About Nothing*. Since Forman's eyewitness account of seeing *Cymbeline* performed refers to its female protagonist as 'Innogen' throughout, it is almost certain that Shakespeare actually called his heroine Innogen, and that the spelling 'Imogen' only appears in the Folio through scribal or compositorial error. Otherwise the Folio text is a good one: variations in spelling, and a high incidence of parentheses (even in stage directions), suggest that it was set from a scribal copy, probably by Ralph *Crane, of an earlier transcript (whether of foul papers or a promptbook) prepared by more than one scribe.

Sources: *Cymbeline* combines three distinct plotlines, concerning, respectively, Cymbeline's dealings with the Romans, the wager on Innogen's chastity, and the exile of Belarius. Shakespeare's information about the semi-legendary king, supposed to have ascended the British throne in 33 BC, came from Holinshed's *Chronicles*, as did the account of the heroic defence of a narrow pass attributed in the play to Belarius, Guiderius, and Arviragus but deriving from an incident at the battle of Loncart (976: this is described in the Scottish section of the work which Shakespeare had consulted when writing *Macbeth*). Other minor details show that Shakespeare had also read the account of Guiderius in the second part of *A Mirror for Magistrates* (1578) and Robert Fabyan's *New Chronicle of England and of France* (1516). More centrally, the wager plot comes from *Boccaccio's *Decameron* (where it provides the ninth story on the second day), though Shakespeare draws some of its details from a version called *Frederyke of Jennen* (first printed in Dutch in 1518, translated into English in 1520, and reprinted in 1560). Much of the other material dramatized in the play—including the banishment of the hero, the jealousy of his foolish rival, and the flight of the heroine to an unjustly banished courtier's cave—derives from an anonymous Elizabethan play, *Rare Triumphs of Love and Fortune*, performed in 1582 and published in 1589.

Synopsis: 1.1 Innogen, sole remaining child of King Cymbeline (her two elder brothers having been abducted in infancy), has married the commoner Leonatus Posthumus, preferring him to her stepmother's foolish son Cloten. Her parting from the banished Posthumus—during which she gives him a diamond ring and he her a bracelet—is interrupted, thanks to the Queen's machinations, by the angry Cymbeline. At Posthumus' insistence his servant Pisanio remains with Innogen while he embarks for Rome. 1.2 Cloten, loser of a sword-skirmish with the departing Posthumus, is flattered by two lords who confide their actual contempt for him to the audience. 1.3 Pisanio describes Posthumus' departure to the yearning Innogen. 1.4 In Rome, Posthumus speaks with a Frenchman and an Italian, Giacomo, about the relative chastity of their countrywomen: despite the objections of his host Filario, Posthumus bets the mocking Italian the diamond ring and 10,000 ducats that Giacomo will be unable to seduce Innogen. 1.5 The Queen obtains what she thinks is lethal poison from the doctor Cornelius, though he, not trusting her, supplies a drug which induces only a deathlike trance: she gives it to Pisanio, saying it is a powerful medicine. 1.6 Giacomo arrives at the British court and almost convinces Innogen that Posthumus is unfaithful before his offer of himself as a replacement alerts her to his ulterior motives. Giacomo claims he was only attempting her virtue to test her, mollifies her by praising Posthumus, and persuades her to look after his trunk in her private chamber.

2.1 Cloten, angry after losing at bowls, is again mocked behind his back by two flattering lords. 2.2 After Innogen retires to bed and falls asleep, Giacomo emerges from the trunk and takes notes about the room's decor before stealing the bracelet from her arm: in doing so he further notices a distinctive mole on Innogen's left breast, before returning undetected to the trunk. 2.3 The following morning Cloten employs musicians to serenade Innogen (with the song *'Hark, hark, the lark'): antagonized by his insults to Posthumus and anxious about the loss of her bracelet, she tells him he is less valuable than Posthumus' meanest garment. 2.4 Back in Rome Giacomo, showing the bracelet and describing Innogen's mole, persuades Posthumus she has betrayed him, and is given the ring. 2.5 The enraged Posthumus rails against all women.

3.1 The Roman ambassador Caius Lucius demands payment of the annual tribute Cymbeline owes to Augustus Caesar: at the Queen's instigation he refuses, and Lucius regretfully declares war. 3.2 To his horror, Pisanio has received a letter from Posthumus instructing him to kill Innogen for her alleged infidelity, using the opportunity his letter to her will provide. This letter, which Pisanio gives Innogen, claims Posthumus is waiting for her at Milford Haven in Wales, towards which she is impatient to flee. 3.3 Outside their Welsh cave, Belarius warns his untravelled sons Polydore and Cadwal against the vices of court life: when they have gone hunting, he confides to the audience that though brought up to think he is their father they are really Guiderius and Arviragus, Cymbeline's sons, whom he stole 20 years earlier to avenge his unjust banishment. 3.4 Near Milford, Pisanio is unable to carry out Posthumus' orders, which he shows to Innogen: outraged, she renounces Posthumus and implores Pisanio to kill her as instructed. Pisanio tells her he is sure Posthumus has been deceived, but means to placate him for the time being by sending a bloodstained piece of clothing, as requested, as evidence that Innogen is dead: meanwhile he advises her to get to Rome by disguising herself as a boy and taking service as a page with Caius Lucius, who will shortly be at Milford. Leaving, he gives her the so-called medicine he had from the Queen. 3.5 Cymbeline, the Queen, and Cloten part from Caius Lucius: the King's preparations for war are distracted by the news that Innogen has vanished. Pisanio, interrogated by Cloten, shows him the letter inviting Innogen to Milford. Cloten resolves to avenge Innogen's earlier remark by dressing in some of Posthumus' clothes, going to Milford, and there killing Posthumus and raping Innogen. 3.6 Dressed as a man a hungry Innogen, now calling herself Fidele, finds Belarius' cave, where Belarius, Guiderius, and Arviragus make her welcome. 3.7 In Rome recruitment is afoot for Lucius' campaign against Britain.

4.1 Cloten, dressed as Posthumus, is near Milford. 4.2 Innogen remains at the cave while the men go hunting: she feels unwell, and takes the Queen's drug. The men see Cloten, and while Belarius and Arviragus check he is not part of a whole party seeking them, Guiderius, provoked, fights with him and decapitates him. Belarius is horrified, though Guiderius unrepentantly throws the head into a river. Arviragus finds Fidele apparently dead in the cave: sorrowfully he and Guiderius lay out the corpse and recite a dirge, 'Fear no more the heat of the sun'. Belarius lays Cloten's headless body alongside before the three depart. Innogen regains consciousness to find what she thinks is her husband's headless corpse, concluding that Pisanio and Cloten must have conspired against her. Lucius, passing by to Milford (where he expects troops from Rome led by Giacomo), is touched by what seems to be the sorrow of a page over his dead master, and takes Fidele into his service. 4.3 At court the Queen is sick with anxiety at Cloten's absence. Cymbeline learns that Roman troops have landed, but Pisanio has heard nothing from either Posthumus or Innogen. 4.4 Belarius, Guiderius, and Arviragus, despite Belarius' fear of being recognized, resolve to join the British army.

5.1 Posthumus, carrying the bloody cloth Pisanio sent, has come to Britain with the Roman army: repenting of Innogen's death, he takes off his Italian clothes and resolves to fight on the British side. 5.2 In battle, Posthumus, dressed like a peasant, defeats but spares a guilt-stricken Giacomo, who does not recognize him. 5.3–4 Cymbeline is captured but rescued by Belarius, Guiderius, Arviragus, and Posthumus: the Romans retreat. 5.5 Posthumus narrates to a British lord how Belarius, Guiderius, and Arviragus reversed a British retreat down a narrow lane into a victorious renewed assault. He decides to dress as a Roman again in the hopes of dying at British hands, and is taken prisoner. Jailed, he prays for death, imploring Innogen's forgiveness before falling asleep. In a vision the ghosts of his father, mother, and two brothers appear and call to Jupiter on his behalf. Jupiter descends in thunder, promises that he has not forsaken Posthumus, and gives the ghosts a tablet which they lay on Posthumus' breast before disappearing. Waking, Posthumus reads the riddling tablet, which he is unable to interpret, before, after bantering with his miserable jailer, he is called before Cymbeline. **5.6** Cymbeline is rewarding Belarius, Guiderius, and Arviragus for their deeds in battle, unable to find their unknown comrade Posthumus, when Cornelius brings the news both of the Queen's death and of her dying confession that she had planned to kill both Innogen and Cymbeline in her bid to make Cloten king. Lucius, Giacomo, a soothsayer, Posthumus, and Innogen, still dressed as Fidele, are brought in as captives, expecting to be killed: Lucius successfully pleads that Fidele should be spared. Instead of begging for Lucius' life in return, however, Innogen has recognized Giacomo, and with Cymbeline's support demands to know how he obtained the ring he is wearing. Giacomo confesses how he cheated in his wager with Posthumus, at which the enraged Posthumus steps forward, striking Innogen down when she tries to interrupt him: Pisanio, however, has recognized her and makes her known, though, reviving, she accuses him of giving her poison. Cornelius explains the nature of the drug he gave the Queen, which on her deathbed she had mentioned giving to Pisanio. Posthumus, Innogen, and Cymbeline embrace. Pisanio now explains where Cloten went, and Guiderius completes his narrative by boasting of having killed him. Cymbeline sentences him to death, but Belarius intervenes by revealing the true identities of himself, Guiderius, and Arviragus, to the delight of Cymbeline and Innogen, whom Belarius and the princes have already recognized as Fidele. Cymbeline spares all the remaining prisoners: Posthumus is recognized as the unknown soldier who spared Giacomo in battle, and now spares him again despite his penitent willingness to die for his crimes: and Lucius' soothsayer interprets the tablet as a prediction of the reunion of Cymbeline's family. Cymbeline embraces peace by deciding to resume paying tribute to Rome.

Artistic features: The difficulty and complexity of the play's plotting is matched by an unusual density and knottiness of syntax, from which some of *Cymbeline*'s most famously simple and affecting passages (notably the dirge, 'Fear no more the heat of the sun') can seem a relief. It is at once one of the most puzzlingly uncertain in tone, and one of the most weirdly affecting, of Shakespeare's later plays.

Critical history: Eighteenth-century comments on the play, like 18th-century adaptations (see below), predictably object to the unclassical irregularities of its plotting: Dr *Johnson famously observed that 'to remark the folly of the fiction, the absurdity of the conduct, the confusion of the names and manners of different times, and the impossibility of the events in any system of life, were to waste criticism upon unresisting imbecility, upon faults too evident for detection, and too gross for aggravation' (1765). (This did not, however, prevent contemporary engravers from choosing Giacomo's voyeurism in Innogen's chamber as one of the most frequently illustrated scenes from the late plays.) The Victorians were willing to forgive many of the play's perceived faults for the sake of Innogen ('undoubtedly one of the most exquisite of all Shakespeare's female creations', wrote Thomas Kenny in 1864), while the 20th century was more interested in explaining them by reference to the play's contexts both in the politics of the Jacobean court and in the last phase of Shakespeare's career. In terms of content, the play's interests in British unification, in imperial peace, in the masque, and even in Milford Haven—where James I's dynastic ancestor Henry VII came ashore to claim the throne—have all been explored in relation to James's cultural and political agendas: in style, its tragicomic experimentations with shocking incongruity, and its self-conscious reuse of motifs from earlier works in the Shakespeare canon (whether Juliet's potion, Othello's jealousy or Lear's loved and lost youngest daughter), have been related to similar techniques deployed less conspicuously in the other late romances.

Stage history: Forman's account of the play does not indicate where he saw it, though the masque-like special effects of 5.5 suggest it may have been written with the indoor *Blackfriars theatre in mind. It was revived at court for *Charles I and *Henrietta Maria in 1634, but was displaced later in the century by Thomas Durfey's adaptation *The Injured Princess, or, The Fatal Wager* (1682), in which Giacomo becomes a splendidly louche Restoration rake. In 1746 the original returned to the stage (despite William *Hawkins's adaptation of 1759), and in a moderately cut and transposed text *Garrick made *Posthumus one of his best-loved Shakespearian roles from 1761 until his retirement: *Kemble was equally successful in the part, with Sarah *Siddons as his slandered bride. In the 19th century Imogen (as she was then known), both innocent and married, was one of Shakespeare's favourite heroines, attracting actresses such as Helen *Faucit (who played the part for nearly 30 years, from 1837 to 1865) and Ellen *Terry (with *Irving as Iachimo, 1896). Over the next 50 years, though, the play's combination of artifice and enchantment fell from favour, and despite Peggy *Ashcroft's two triumphs as Imogen (at the *Old Vic in 1932, and at Stratford, in a fairy tale-style production by Peter Hall, in 1957) few 20th-century productions were conspicuous successes: modern dress, then novel, did not help the play in Barry *Jackson's Birmingham production of 1923 (derisively called 'Shakespeare in plus-fours'), and B. Iden-Payne's critically acclaimed attempt to direct the play on sets derived from Jacobean masques (Stratford, 1937) did not dissuade George Bernard *Shaw from producing his own critical rewriting of the last act, *Cymbeline Refinished*, in which Imogen is much less willing to forgive Posthumus for trying to kill her. John *Barton tried without success to make *Cymbeline* into a 'state of England' play in the oil crisis year of 1974, alluding in his production's designs to the vast refinery that now dominates Milford, and it is an index to directors' continuing lack of confidence in the play that the most recent RSC revival, directed by Adrian *Noble in 1997, modified the script to supply a narrator.

On the screen: A 45-minute TV version (1937) was one of the earliest British TV Shakespeare transmissions. Other

TV productions include one from the USA (1981), one from Belgium (1981), and Elijah Moshinsky's BBC TV production (1982) with Helen Mirren as Imogen, generally regarded as one of the best of the BBC series. *AD*

Recent major editions

J. M. Nosworthy (Arden, 1955) Roger Warren (Oxford, 1998)

Some representative criticism

Brockbank, J. P., 'History and histrionics in *Cymbeline*', *Shakespeare Survey* 11 (1958)

Hawkes, Terence, 'Aberdaugleddyf', *Shakespeare Jahrbuch*, 136 (2000)

Jones, Emrys, 'Stuart *Cymbeline*', *Essays in Criticism* 11 (1961)

Marcus, Leah, *Puzzling Shakespeare: Local Reading and its Discontents* (Berkeley, California, 1988)

dactyl, a metrical unit ('foot') comprising one stressed syllable followed by two unstressed syllables, as in the first half of Ariel's line 'Merrily, merrily shall I live now' (*The Tempest* 5.1.93). *CB*

Dadd, Richard (1817–86), English painter and illustrator. Dadd began exhibiting Shakespearian subjects with *The Closet Scene from* Hamlet (1840), quickly winning acclaim as an exponent of fairy painting through *Titania Sleeping*, *Puck* (both 1841), and *Come unto these Yellow Sands* (1842). These dramatically lit, theatrical compositions frame interlocking circles of dancing figures with minutely observed flora and fauna. Intensified microscopic detail crowds the surface of *Contradiction: Oberon and Titania* (1854–8), executed during Dadd's later confinement for insanity, and therefore unknown to contemporaries—as were his sketches illustrating the passions: *Love: Romeo and Juliet* (1853) and *Jealousy: Othello and Iago* (1853). *KN*

Daly, John Augustin (1838–99), American drama critic, playwright, and manager, who—in the 1890s—owned theatres bearing his name in London and New York. Realizing that by staging Shakespeare's plays he could greatly enhance his own fame and reputation, Daly produced thirteen revivals at the Fifth Avenue Theatre (1869–77) and eleven at Daly's, New York (1885–99). The plays (predominantly the romantic comedies) were heavily adapted (at least eleven of them by William Winter) to suit pictorial taste, but they featured many actors with or on the way to high reputation, in particular Ada Rehan whose Katherine was acclaimed in New York, London, and Stratford-upon-Avon. *RF*

Felheim, Marvin, *The Theater of Augustin Daly* (1956)

Dance, James (1721–74), an actor specializing in character parts, including Malvolio in Dublin and Trinculo in Edinburgh. Using the stage name James Love, he achieved prominence as Falstaff. He took larger roles for Garrick at Drury Lane from 1762 and appeared as Falstaff in *The Jubilee* (1769). *CMSA*

dance in the plays. In Shakespeare's time dancing formed a part of people's lives at all levels of society in a way that we can scarcely conceive now, and the ability to dance proficiently was an expected social accomplishment for the gentry and nobility. Not surprisingly then, the plays contain numerous allusions to dance, using terms that would have been as immediate and striking in their imagery to audiences then as they are obscure today, and providing Shakespeare with ample scope for playing on words (*brawl, *measure, *cinquepace, etc.).

Actual dancing is always linked in some way to the action of the play. Shakespeare used it to accompany, illustrate, and emphasize a change of mental or physical state, most obviously that of awakening love between a couple (Romeo and Juliet, Pericles and Thaisa, Henry VIII and Anne Boleyn). It plays a similar role in underlining the King's recovery in *All's Well That Ends Well*, and Katherine's illness in *All Is True* (*Henry VIII*). It was used to invoke or represent the supernatural (see ROUNDEL), and to celebrate a happy outcome or conclusion; three of the middle period comedies, *A Midsummer Night's Dream*, *Much Ado About Nothing*, and *As You Like It*, end with dance. Even when no dance is indicated or implied at the end of a play, it was the practice to conclude with a sung and danced theatrical afterpiece or *jig. As the five-act structure developed, dancing sometimes took place as entertainment in addition to the customary music during the intervals.

Dancing plays a part in the staged entertainments or *masques which occur within several plays. Care is still taken though to bind the dances in some way to the narrative and plot, even if only through interruption as in *The Tempest* 4.1.139. Shakespeare was probably not responsible for including the self-contained *divertissements* in *The Winter's Tale* (the satyrs' dance) and *The Two Noble Kinsmen* (the morris), which seem to have been borrowed from court masques.

Information on dance steps and style may be gained from treatises published in France and Italy during Shakespeare's lifetime (see Arbeau, *Orchesography*, 1589; Caroso, *Nobiltà di dame*, 1600); at the level of the gentry and nobility England appears to have followed continental practices in many respects. It is important to realize that in a ball, dances such as the *galliard, la *volta, and *coranto were performed by *one couple at a time*, displaying their skill to the assembled company (a point often missed in period costume productions on stage or screen). Social dances involving several couples together might include certain measures and the *pavan, when in procession; also (danced at all levels of society) the country dances and brawls. (See also BALLET.) *JB*

Arbeau, Thoinot, *Orchesography* (1589), trans. M. S. Evans (1948), ed. Julia Sutton (1967)
Brissenden, Alan, *Shakespeare and the Dance* (1981)
Caroso, Fabritio, *Nobiltà di dame* (1600), ed. and trans. Julia Sutton (1986)
Daye, Anne (ed.), *A Lively Shape of Dauncing: Dances of Shakespeare's Time* (1994)

Dancer. See EPILOGUE.

Daniel, Samuel (*c.*1563–1619), poet and playwright, whose work intersects with Shakespeare's at many points. His first publication was the Sidneian sonnet sequence *Delia* (1592), whose serious, measured verse lays the thematic foundation for variations played in Shakespeare's Sonnets (Daniel is sometimes identified as the 'rival poet' in that sequence). Alongside *Delia* he published a narrative poem, *The Complaint of Rosamond.* Written in rhyme royal, the stanza form adopted by Shakespeare in *A Lover's Complaint* and *The Rape of Lucrece*, its intimate scrutiny of sexual tyranny and female psychological torment anticipates *Venus and Adonis* as well as *The Rape of Lucrece.* The *Delia* volume may well have influenced Shakespeare's decision to publish a complaint poem along with his Sonnets in 1609. Daniel was an assiduous reviser of his writings—he prefaced his *Certain Small Works* (1607) with some verses about the process of revision—and he perhaps rewrote his academic tragedy *Cleopatra* (1594, revised 1607) after seeing Shakespeare's *Antony and Cleopatra*, which in turn contains possible echoes of Daniel's play. His epic poem *The Civil Wars between ... Lancaster and York* (1595), too, underwent many revisions. The earliest version is thought to have influenced Shakespeare's *Richard II.* In the reign of James I, Daniel became Gentleman Extraordinary of Queen Anne's Privy Chamber, and the Queen acted in two of his masques. His fine prose treatise *A Defence of Rhyme* (*c.*1603) shows a quiet confidence in his own skills which has been amply justified by his posthumous reputation. *RM*

Rees, Joan, *Samuel Daniel: A Critical and Biographical Study* (1964)

Dankworth, Johnny. See JAZZ.

Danter, John. See CHETTLE, HENRY; DERELICT PLAYS; PRINTING AND PUBLISHING.

Dardanius. See STRATO.

'Dark Lady'. All Shakespeare's sonnets unambiguously addressed to or concerned with a woman occur towards the end of the sequence, from Number 127 onwards. Most commonly characterized as 'black', in both appearance and character, she has come to be known as the 'dark lady', though the phrase itself does not occur in the Sonnets. In 1797 George Chalmers argued that all the Sonnets were addressed to Queen Elizabeth. Since then, innumerable other attempts—all doomed to failure in the absence of documentary evidence—have been made to identify the dark lady with one or more real women (including the former Anne Hathaway) of Shakespeare's time. Gerald Massey, in *The Secret Drama of Shakespeare's Sonnets* (1880), expanded his earlier claim that she was Penelope, Lady Rich. A popular candidate until she was discovered to have been fair was Mary Fitton, one of the Queen's maids of honour, disgraced in 1601 when she had a son by the Earl of *Pembroke. As her star waned, Richard *Field's French wife Jacqueline entered the lists, championed by Charlotte Stopes. Jane (or Jennet) Davenant was a natural suspect in view of her son William *Davenant's reputed willingness to believe that Shakespeare begot him. G. B. Harrison, supposing the lady to have been black all over, proposed a negro prostitute, probably the 'Lucy Negro, abbess de Clerkenwell' mentioned in the *Gesta Grayorum* (1594). In 1973, A. L. *Rowse trumpeted his conviction that she was Emilia *Lanier, revealed in the papers of Simon *Forman to have been the mistress of the Lord Chamberlain, Lord Hunsdon. Her darkness fell from the air when it was shown that Forman wrote not, as Rowse believed, that she 'was brown in youth', but that she was 'brave'. In 1997 Jonathan Bate, in *The Genius of Shakespeare*, flew a kite for the wife (first name unknown) of John Florio, sister of Samuel *Daniel.

The Dark Lady has also been linked with characters in the plays, most notably Rosaline, in *Love's Labour's Lost*, whom Biron describes as 'A whitely wanton with a velvet brow, | With two pitch-balls stuck in her face for eyes' (3.1.191–2), but also including Romeo's 'black-eyed Rosaline', Gertrude, Cressida, Mistress Quickly, and Cleopatra. *SW*

Schoenbaum, S., *Shakespeare's Lives* (1970; rev. edn. 1991)

Daughter, Antiochus'. See ANTIOCHUS.

Dauphin, Louis the. See LOUIS THE DAUPHIN

Dauphin, the. He is the boastful and bellicose eldest son of Charles VI of France in *Henry V.* *AB*

Davenant, Sir William (1606–68), putative illegitimate son of Shakespeare, the second Poet Laureate, theatre impresario, playwright, and adapter of Shakespeare. His death was reported 'just now' by Samuel Pepys on 7 April 1668. John *Aubrey recorded that Davenant would 'when he was pleasant over a glass of wine with his most intimate friends ... say that it seemed to him that he writ with the very spirit that Shakespeare [had], and was seemed contentended [*sic*] enough to be thought his son'. The tavern in Oxford owned by Davenant's parents was on the road from Stratford-upon-Avon to London but it did not offer any public accommodation and there is no evidence beyond the frequent retelling of Aubrey's anecdote to substantiate the story. However, Davenant was an avid fan of Shakespeare's work. At the age of 18 Davenant went to London and although they rejected his *The Tragedy of Albovine, King of the Lombards*, the King's Men put on his *The Cruel Brother* in 1627. Davenant's *The Colonel* was licensed on 22 July 1629 but may not have been performed, but his *The Just Italian* (1630) certainly was performed by the King's Men. In 1630 Davenant contracted syphilis and suffered disfigurement to his nose from taking mercury to cure it. When Ben Jonson broke his partnership with Inigo Jones, William Davenant took up Jonson's place and wrote his first court masque, *The Temple of Love* (1634), in 1634. Masque, play, and poetry writing occupied Davenant until the Civil War and from 25 March 1638 he received a royal pension which, although Jonson was not yet dead, was widely taken to indicate that Davenant had succeeded him as Poet Laureate.

Davenant's interest in running his own theatre is indicated by his petition of 26 March 1639 to build one in Fleet Street, and although this was refused he was appointed to succeed William Beeston as governor of the 'Beeston Boys' at the Cockpit in Drury Lane. Military service in the skirmishes which prefigured the Civil War prevented Davenant from fulfilling this commission, and in 1642 he, like many in the theatre, joined the Royalist side. In prison after defeat of the Royalists Davenant wrote his epic poem *Gondibert*, and after two years he was released unharmed, probably aided by solicitations from John *Milton amongst others. Covert theatrical performances continued throughout the Interregnum, and Davenant wrote a number of 'entertainments' which introduced innovations set to become standard theatrical practice after the Restoration: a proscenium arch, painted canvases, and female actors. The most theatrically complete of these 'entertainments' was Davenant's *The Siege of Rhodes* (1656) which was presented in revised form for the opening of Davenant's theatre, the Duke's, in 1661. In Charles II's reign Davenant at the Duke's and Thomas *Killigrew at the Theatre Royal enjoyed a theatrical duopoly in London, and both showed established classics from the pre-Commonwealth era. Davenant also adapted the earlier works: his *The Law against Lovers* (1662) was Shakespeare's *Measure for Measure* plus Beatrice and Benedick from *Much Ado About Nothing*, and his *The Tempest; or The Enchanted Island* (1667) was Shakespeare's play with the addition of sisters for Miranda and Caliban and a sweetheart for Ariel. Davenant's leading actor, Thomas *Betterton, was reputedly aided by Davenant's familiarity with the performances of John *Lowin and Joseph *Taylor who received their instructions directly from Shakespeare. This cannot be literally true since Taylor joined the King's Men in 1619, but Davenant had closer links with the Shakespearian tradition than anyone else working in the London theatre.

Davenant's adaptations of Shakespeare were only a part of his life's achievement, but having the confidence to rewrite Shakespeare's lines and to introduce technological innovations, such as '*Enter Three Witches Flying*' in his *Macbeth* (1664), brought considerable disapproval when the early 20th-century theatre industry rediscovered what it took to be 'authentic' Shakespearian practices. One of Davenant's innovations, women playing women's parts, might be judged a necessity brought about by the interruption of theatrical traditions caused by the Commonwealth suppression of drama: no boy apprentices were available when the theatres reopened. But his biographer Mary Edmond is undoubtedly right to credit Davenant with making Shakespeare available to a generation denied any access to theatrical art and his intelligent reworkings may be seen as an appropriate response to conditions utterly unlike those which obtained when the theatres were closed in 1642. *GE*

Edmond, Mary, *Rare Sir William Davenant* (1987)

Harbage, Alfred, *Sir William Davenant: Poet Venturer 1606–1668* (1935)

Davenport, James, vicar of Stratford 1787–1841 who passed on to *Malone by 1790 a story deriving from his clerk's 85-year-old father, whose family had lived close to New Place, that Shakespeare planted the mulberry tree there 'and that till this was planted there was no mulberry tree in that neighbourhood'. In 1609 James I had issued instructions to encourage the breeding of silkworms by growing more mulberry trees. *SW*

Davenport, Robert (fl. 1624), playwright. His three surviving plays, *A New Trick to Cheat the Devil* (1639), *King John and Matilda* (1655), and *The City Night-Cap* (1661), all owe some debt to Shakespeare. The Stationers' Register for 1653 claims that he co-wrote a lost play with Shakespeare, *Henry I*. *RM*

Davies, John (*c.*1565–1618), poet born at Hereford. Davies's eight-line poem, 'To our English Terence, Mr Will. Shake-speare' (1610), suggests that Shakespeare had acted royal parts on stage: 'Had'st thou not played some Kingly parts in sport, | Thou hadst been a companion for a *King*.' Davies may also imply that King James I has insufficiently honoured Shakespeare and Richard Burbage. In stanza 76 of his *The Civil Wars of Death and Fortune* (1605), he refers to those 'guerdoned not, to their deserts', and notes in the margin: 'Stage plaiers' and 'W.S. R.B.' *PH*

Davies, Thomas (?1712–85), actor, bookseller, and critic. Davies was the author of *Dramatic Miscellanies* (1785), a collection of observations on contemporary theatre and on Shakespeare's characters, especially those played by *Garrick. He introduced Boswell to Dr *Johnson in 1763, and, at Johnson's suggestion, wrote the *Life of Garrick* (1780). *CMSA*

Davy is Shallow's servant in *2 Henry IV*. *AB*

Day, John (*c.*1574–*c.*1640), one of the impecunious playwrights who wrote for the theatre-owner Philip *Henslowe. His best-known play is *The Isle of Gulls* (1606), a satirical comedy loosely based on Sir Philip Sidney's *Arcadia*, which angered James I by referring to his private life. It has also been suggested that Day wrote *Pericles* with Shakespeare. *RM*

death, as Gertrude reminds Hamlet, invoking the most persistent of consolatory topoi, is 'common'. Since 'all that lives must die, | Passing through nature to eternity' (*Hamlet* 1.2.72–3), to be human is to be mortal. Death, from this perspective, seems unproblematically universal, a simple, irreducible fact of our nature, unyieldingly the same across all societies and throughout time. If by 'death', however, we mean more than the mere cessation of animal being, it proves (like most supposedly 'natural' human experiences) to be an artefact of culture, its meanings shaped by a whole variety of local, intensely mutable beliefs and practices. Thus the death endured by Shakespeare's contemporaries, and represented in their art, was different in important respects from our own—and different also from that suffered by their medieval forebears.

In early modern England, racked by endemic social violence and decimated by recurrent epidemics of disease, death was a far more insistent presence than for us; its brutal commonness was announced by the plague pits, heaped with undifferentiated corpses, that pockmarked the ground of London, by the 'odoriferous stench' of putrefaction (*King John* 3.4.26) that leaked from the tombs crowding every church, by the systematic degradation of corpses in public anatomies (*King Lear* 3.6.34–6), and by admonitory displays of the 'rotten carcass of old Death' (*King John* 2.1.457) on gibbets and city gates. The commonness of death invested it with a levelling power that threatened to undo all the differences on which a fiercely hierarchical social order depended—a power emblematized in *Hamlet*'s graveyard, where 'imagination [can] trace the noble dust of Alexander till he find it stopping a bunghole' (5.1.199–200). In *Troilus and Cressida* the same collapse into absolute indistinction is symbolized in recurrent images of plague, and brought to startling theatrical life in the 'putrefied core' which Hector discovers beneath the sumptuous armour of the warrior whose death prefigures his own (5.9.1).

Hector's morbid antagonist, like Hamlet's gravedigging clown (who began his work 'the very day that young Hamlet was born', 5.1.144–5), resembles an uncanny summoner from the Dance of Death tradition, in which Death is endowed with a grisly personality. Widely disseminated in frescos, paintings, and prints from the 15th and 16th centuries, the *Danse Macabre*, along with the equally popular Triumph of Death, represents the nightmare of mortal undifferentiation at its most intense. In the Dance, individuals representing every rank and condition are drawn into the indiscriminate embrace of Death by cadavers who travesty the identity of each: Death comes as grinning sexton, an armoured skeleton, an 'antic' jester (*1 Henry VI* 4.7.18; *Richard II* 3.2.158); a 'fell sergeant' (*Hamlet* 5.2.288), a bony bridegroom (*Antony and Cleopatra* 4.15.100–1; *Romeo and Juliet* 4.5.65–6), an 'amorous' young lover (*Romeo and Juliet* 5.1.102–5), or a sardonic 'physician' who announces that 'death | Will seize the doctor too' (*Cymbeline* 5.5.101, 5.6.29–30). In the equally popular Triumphs, Death drives a splendid chariot over heaps of bodies in which mighty and mean lie tumbled together. '[M]ade proud with pure and princely beauty' (*King John* 4.3.35), this 'Triumphant death' (*1 Henry VI* 4.7.3) is represented as a king whose overriding authority is ironically inscribed in the very symbols of earthly power: 'within the hollow crown | That rounds the mounted temples of a king | keeps Death his court, | And there the antic sits, | Scoffing his state, and grinning at his pomp' (*Richard II* 3.2.156–9).

At the beginning of *1 Henry VI*, the funeral procession of the heroic Henry V reminds the grieving Exeter of this grim pageantry: 'Death's dishonourable victory, | We with our stately presence glorify, | Like captives bound to a triumphant car' (*1 Henry VI* 1.1.20–2); but (like their increasingly extravagant tombs) the pompous funerals of the great, organized by the College of Heralds with minute regard for the niceties of rank and honour, were designed precisely to reaffirm proper distinction in the teeth of Death's levelling assaults. Thus for Laertes his father's 'obscure burial— | No trophy, sword, not hatchment o'er his bones, | No noble rite nor formal ostentation' (*Hamlet* 4.5.211–13) seems almost more painful than his death itself.

One key to the enormous elaboration of funeral art in early modern England lay in the Reformation denial of Purgatory. This effectively silenced the whole vast industry of intercession by which medieval Catholicism had maintained a living relationship with the dead. Thus, while one part of Hamlet is convinced that the Ghost is indeed 'my father's spirit', come from Purgatory to seek his aid, the Protestant part of him repudiates the claim, knowing that the dead are beyond our reach in '[t]he undiscovered country | From whose bourn no traveller returns' (*Hamlet* 3.1.81–2). The Church asserted a continuing responsibility to prepare its members (as the Friar/Duke does in *Measure for Measure*) for the onset of death and judgement through mastery of a pious *ars moriendi*; but the dead themselves seemed abandoned. The pain of this abrupt separation informs not only *Hamlet*, but much of the proliferating writing on death, and it provided one of the animating energies of the tragic theatre, whose black hangings self-consciously mimicked the visual language of funeral (*1 Henry VI* 1.1.1), and whose 'industrious scenes and acts of death' (*King John* 2.1.376) with their defiant reaffirmations of individual identity, provided an essential secular instrument for confronting the agonizing mystery of mortal ending. *MN*

Ariès, Philippe, *The Hour of our Death*, trans. Helen Weaver (1981)
Calderwood, James L., *Shakespeare and the Denial of Death* (1987)
Neill, M., *Issues of Death: Mortality and Identity in English Renaissance Tragedy* (1997)

death mask. A plaster cast dated 1616, purporting to be Shakespeare's death mask, was brought to London from Germany in 1849: known as the Kesselstadt death mask (after a former owner), it attracted widespread interest over the next three decades, but now languishes in obscurity in a museum in Darmstadt. Claims for its authenticity are revived from time to time but have not achieved general acceptance. *MD*

Decius Brutus. One of the conspirators, he undertakes to bring Caesar to the Capitol, *Julius Caesar* 2.1.210 and 2.2.58–107. He is based on *Decimus* Junius Brutus Albinus: Shakespeare followed *Plutarch's mispelling. *AB*

Declaration of Egregious Popish Impostures, A. See Harsnett, Samuel.

Decretas tells Caesar of Antony's death, *Antony and Cleopatra* 5.1.13. *AB*

dedications. See Rape of Lucrece, The; Venus and Adonis.

deer-stealing. See Lucy, Sir Thomas.

Defoe theory, one of the wilder claims offered in the course of the *Authorship Controversy, to the effect that Shakespeare's works were written by Daniel Defoe (1660–1731): its chief exponent, appropriately, was one George M. Battey. *MD*

Deguchi, Norio (b. 1940), Japanese director. Deguchi majored in aesthetics at the University of Tokyo, and in 1974 organized the Shakespeare Theatre. The company has produced all the plays of Shakespeare in Yushi Odashima's translation. His productions are fast-moving and simple, using no scenery and no elaborate costume, and have made Shakespeare easily accessible to young audiences. *TK*

Deiphobus. One of the sons of Priam, he speaks half a line, *Troilus and Cressida* 4.1.2. *AB*

Dekker, Thomas (*c.*1572–1632), playwright and pamphleteer. Dekker was born in London and wrote about it with intense affection throughout his life. He began his career in the 1590s working for the theatrical impresario Philip Henslowe, many of whose employees were short of cash; Dekker was twice imprisoned for debt. He collaborated often, notably with Michael Drayton, Thomas Middleton, and John Ford, and rewrote other men's plays: some scholars think he revised a few of Shakespeare's. His output was prodigious: between 1598 and 1602 alone he wrote about 40 plays for the Admiral's Men. His best-known works are comedies—*The Shoemaker's Holiday* (1599), which tells the story of an eccentric shoemaker who became Lord Mayor of London, and the moralistic fairy tale *Old Fortunatus* (1599)—but he wrote well in any genre: from revenge tragedy (*Love's Dominion*, 1600) to history (*Sir Thomas Wyatt*, 1602), from civic pageant (*The Magnificent Entertainment*, 1603) to tragicomedy (*The Honest Whore*, 1604, and *The Witch of Edmonton*, 1621). During the *War of the Theatres at the turn of the century he was attacked by Ben Jonson in a series of theatrical satires, to which he responded with *Satiromastix* (1601). He also wrote many pamphlets, such as *The Wonderful Year* (1603) and *Lantern and Candlelight* (1608), which paint a vivid picture of life and death in the Jacobean metropolis. *RM*

Gasper, Julia, *The Dragon and the Dove: The Plays of Thomas Dekker* (1990)
McLuskie, Kathleen, *Dekker and Heywood: Professional Dramatists* (1994)

Delabreth, Charles. See Constable of France.

Delacroix, Eugène (1798–1863), French artist. Hailed as the leader of the 'Romantic school' of 19th-century French painting, Delacroix drew upon Shakespearian and other literary subjects throughout his career. He regarded Shakespeare as an 'imperfect genius', admiring what he saw as the psychologically powerful, 'unfinished' quality of his plays. Delacroix believed that a similar quality could be used to an even greater effect in painting and the theoretical relationship between literary and visual art became a preoccupation of his *Journal*. Favouring the pathetic elements of Shakespeare's drama, Delacroix's many Shakespeare paintings include scenes from *Hamlet*, *Othello*, and *Romeo and Juliet*. In 1843 he completed a series of sixteen lithographs with subjects taken from *Hamlet*. *RJ*

Joubin, André (ed.), *Journal d'Eugène Delacroix* (3 vols., 1932)

deletion. Evidence of Shakespeare's habit of deleting lines as he wrote is provided by the printed texts set up from his *foul papers; the compositors of these texts often either misunderstood or overlooked Shakespeare's deletion marks in the manuscript and set the cancelled version of a line or passage (known as a 'false start') as well as the line or passage that was intended to replace it. See especially *Romeo and Juliet* 3.3.40–3. *ER*

Delius, Nikolaus (1813–88), German academic, editor, and lexicographer. He published an edition of Shakespeare (1854–61) whose text was used for the so-called *Leopold Shakespeare* (1877), with Furnivall's essay on verse tests. Other publications include his *Shakspere-Lexicon* (1852); *Uber das englische Theaterwesen zu Shaksperes Zeit* (1853); and *Abhandlungen zu Shakspere* (2 vols., 1878–9). *TM*

Deloney, Thomas (d. 1600), silk-weaver, and writer of ballads and prose fiction. He originated in Norfolk and may have spent some time in Berkshire, a centre for the English silk industry. By 1586 he was in London, writing ballads, a form of poetry printed on single sheets and read by the newly literate classes involved in trade and industry. Deloney twice took the unusual step of printing his ballads in book form, as if to proclaim the value and durability of the genre he wrote in. His confidence was justified: his ballads went on being reprinted until well into the 18th century. His ballad collection *The Garland of Good Will* (1628) contains a poem, 'Crabbed Age and Youth', attributed to Shakespeare in *The* *Passionate Pilgrim. His prose narratives, too, were best-sellers till the 18th century. They include *Thomas of Reading* (1612), *Jack of Newbury* (1619), and *The Gentle Craft* (1599), part of which was adapted for the stage by Thomas *Dekker in *The Shoemaker's Holiday* (1599). Deloney's fictions celebrate the lives of successful members of the middle classes—cobblers and clothworkers—and their complex interactions with other social groups in pre-Elizabethan England. Their narratives are cleverly constructed, full of ballads, practical jokes, and lively dialogue. The death of Master Cole in *Thomas of Reading* bears a striking resemblance to the death of Duncan in *Macbeth*. *RM*

Margolies, David, *Novel and Society in Elizabethan England* (1985)
Wright, Eugene, *Thomas Deloney* (1981)

Demetrius. **(1)** He is the older of Tamora's villainous surviving sons in *Titus Andronicus*. **(2)** In *A Midsummer Night's Dream* his love for Hermia is changed by fairy magic into love for Helena. **(3)** He is a friend of Antony's who appears in *Antony and Cleopatra* 1.1. *AB*

Dench, Dame Judi (b. 1934), British actress. From drama school she went straight to the Old Vic Company in 1957 for four seasons, opening as Ophelia to John *Neville's Hamlet and later earning rave notices as Juliet in Franco *Zeffirelli's sun-baked, Italianate *Romeo and Juliet*. Thereafter she has been admired in classical and modern works, including musicals,

Judi Dench as Cleopatra to Anthony Hopkins's Antony in Peter Hall's National Theatre production, 1987.

becoming the best-loved actress of her generation. Her long association with the *Royal Shakespeare Company began in 1962 when she played Titania in *A Midsummer Night's Dream* (later filmed) and Isabella in *Measure for Measure*. In 1969 she played both Hermione and Perdita in *The Winter's Tale* and a most moving Viola in *Twelfth Night*. In 1976 she was an enchanting Beatrice as well as a brilliant Lady Macbeth in an intense, intimate version by Trevor *Nunn. She has played every Shakespearian heroine except Rosalind. At the National Theatre she scored a triumph as Cleopatra, bringing out the wit, sensuality, and earthiness. She was Volumnia to the Coriolanus of Kenneth *Branagh whom she directed earlier in *Much Ado About Nothing*. She won an Oscar for her brief appearance as Queen Elizabeth in the film *Shakespeare in Love* (1999). *MJ*

Denis (Dennis), Oliver's servant, appears in *As You Like It* 1.1. *AB*

Denmark. See Scandinavia.

Dennis. See Denis.

Dennis, John (1657–1734), critic and playwright, author of two unsuccessful adaptations which attempt to regularize Shakespeare: *The Comical Gallant; or The Amours of Sir John Falstaff* (*Merry Wives*) and *The Invader of his Country* (*Coriolanus*). His adaptation of *Coriolanus* included a critical essay assessing Shakespeare's beauties and defects. *JM*

Denny, Sir Anthony. He conducts Cranmer to Henry, *All Is True* (*Henry VIII*) 5.1. *AB*

De Quincey, Thomas (1785–1859), English essayist, author of a notable article on Shakespeare in the *Encyclopaedia Britannica* (1838) and the essay 'On the Knocking at the Gate in *Macbeth*' (1823), which he calls a 'specimen of psychological criticism', on the evocation, through sound, of sympathy and anxiety in the audience. *TM*

Derby's (Strange's) Men, the men of Ferdinando Stanley, Lord Strange (Earl of Derby from 25 September 1593), led by Edward Alleyn from 1591, containing remnants of Leicester's Men and possibly Shakespeare. In 1592 the company played 'harey the vj' (possibly Shakespeare's *1 Henry VI*) in a successful season at Henslowe's Rose. Stanley died in 1594, leaving the company without a patron (though his brother William's marriage to Elizabeth Vere in January 1595 has been proposed as the occasion for the first performance of *A Midsummer Night's Dream*). Alleyn left to form the Admiral's Men while Thomas Pope, John Heminges, Augustine Phillips, and George Bryan left to form the Chamberlain's Men. The rest of Derby's Men continued playing but were unable to break the Admiral's/Chamberlain's London duopoly. *GE*

Derby theory. The claim that Shakespeare's plays were really written by William Stanley, 6th Earl of Derby (1561–1641), was first made by James Greenstreet in 1891, but was most conspicuously (and copiously) elaborated by Abel Lefranc in France between 1919 and 1950 (see Authorship Controversy). There is in fact no reliable evidence that this Earl wrote anything, his advocates relying solely on details of his biography which they claim would have ideally fitted him to write the Shakespeare canon, such as his having visited Navarre. *MD*

Schoenbaum, S., *Shakespeare's Lives* (1970)

Dercetas. See decretas.

derelict plays. A publisher's copy rights to a text were considered to be derelict when the owner of the rights had died without heir or assignee; the copy rights would then revert to the *Stationers' Company, from which they would have to be purchased before the text could be reprinted. *A Midsummer Night's Dream* was entered in the Stationers' Register and published by Thomas Fisher in 1600, but nothing further is heard of Fisher after 1601, so Fisher's copyright was apparently deemed derelict by the publishers of the First *Folio. So too, the copyright to *Titus Andronicus* had lapsed on the death of John Danter in 1599. *ER*

Dering manuscript, one of the earliest known manuscripts of a Shakespearian play, prepared in 1622–3 for the library of the literary antiquarian Sir Edward Dering. It combines portions of *1* and *2 Henry IV* into a single play of 3,401 lines, perhaps intended for a private performance. The Dering manuscript was apparently copied from Q5 (1613) of *Part 1* and Q1 (1600) of *Part 2*; nearly three-quarters of the text was taken from *Part 1*. The adaptation divides the play into acts and scenes, cuts much of the comic material, and reveals careful attention to technical matters of stage production. Its deletions and alterations often anticipate those in later acting editions of the plays. *ER*

Yeandle, Laetitia, 'The Dating of Sir Edward Dering's Copy of *The History of King Henry the Fourth*', *Shakespeare Quarterly*, 37 (1986)

Desdemona, having eloped with Othello, follows him to his military post as governor of Cyprus. *Iago is successful in his plot to make her appear adulterous and Othello subjects her to insults and violence, finally smothering her in the last act. Her name is taken from *Cinthio's *novella* (1565) in which Disdemona is beaten to death by her husband and an Ensign (both nameless).

Desdemona may have been one of the first Shakespearian roles played by a woman on the English stage (possibly by Anne Marshall at Clare Market in 1660), but it took a long time for her character to develop into something beyond the anonymous modesty required as a foil to the star roles of Othello and Iago. Later actresses who brought interest and importance to the role included Sarah *Siddons, Fanny *Kemble, and Helen *Faucit, though during the 19th century the part became more difficult to play as racism became more pervasive and extreme: *Coleridge, for example, wrote that 'it would be something monstrous to conceive this beautiful Venetian girl falling in love with a veritable negro' (1832). Twentieth-century directors have often sought to make her tragedy one of isolation and vulnerability in the brutal world of homosocial military relations (hence Lisa Harrow's interpretation in John *Barton's 1971 production). *AB*

Hankey, Julie (ed.), *Plays in Performance: Othello* (1987)

detective fiction. See fiction.

Dethick, Sir William (1543–1612), Garter king-of-arms (a senior official of the College of Heralds) who prepared the document dated 20 October 1596 granting John Shakespeare's application for a coat of *arms and that of 1599 by which the arms could be combined with those of the *Arden family. A violent and probably corrupt man, he had many enemies. In 1602 the York herald, Ralph Brooke, accused him of granting arms to unworthy persons and of fraudulently assigning arms that already belonged to others. Shakespeare's is among the 23 names cited. *SW*

deus ex machina, a 'god from a machine', lowered mechanically to the stage in some of Euripides' plays to untangle the plot. The last scene of *As You Like It* echoes this device with the introduction of Hymen to marry off the various couples, but its most literal example in the canon is that of Jupiter's descent on an eagle in the last act of *Cymbeline*: other examples in the late romances would include Diana's appearance in *Pericles* and the divine revelations offered towards the close of *The Two Noble Kinsmen*. (See Flying.) *CB*

Deutsche Shakespeare-Gesellschaft, an open society founded in 1864 in Weimar to disseminate knowledge of Shakespeare in Germany and active ever since (currently *c.*2,500 members); from 1963 to 1993 it was politically divided into separate organizations East and West. Its public meetings feature performances, lectures, and debates; it promotes scholarship, publishes the **Shakespeare Jahrbuch*, and supports Shakespeare editions. *WH*

device, the pictorial ornament used on title pages as the trade mark of individual printers or publishers. Devices were often personalized to include the printer's initials, to represent the sign at which the bookseller carried on business, or to pun on the publisher's name, as in the framed device of a kingfisher catching a fish on the title page of Q1 *A Midsummer Night's Dream*, published by Thomas Fisher. *ER*

Devine, George (1910–66), British actor and director. While an undergraduate at Oxford he invited John *Gielgud to stage *Romeo and Juliet* with Peggy *Ashcroft and Edith *Evans as guest players. Soon he was associated with Gielgud and others in significant Shakespeare productions in London. He also devoted himself to the serious training of actors and designers and after war service taught at the short-lived but influential Old Vic Theatre School. As a freelance he staged five plays at Stratford including an innovative *King Lear* boldly designed by Isamu Noguchi. In 1956 he founded the *English Stage Company at the Royal Court, making it (at the cost of his own health) the most dynamic centre for new writing in Britain. *MJ*

Wardle, Irving, *The Theatres of George Devine* (1978)

de Witt drawing. See Swan theatre.

dialects. In Elizabethan English regional dialects were no longer employed, as they were in the Middle Ages, for literary and scientific writing, but their use survived on the stage to denote rustic speakers. Shakespeare used a conventional 'stage' dialect to disguise the courtly *Edgar, in *King Lear*, as a countryman, and national forms of speech to demonstrate the support offered to the young King Henry v, not only by his subjects in England but by those in Scotland, Wales, and Ireland too. Their dialects are suggested not primarily by vocabulary or grammar but mainly by their accents, partly realized in phonetic spelling, e.g. *pridge* for *bridge*, *gud* for *good*, and *zir* for *sir*. *VS*

Diana. **(1)** She helps Helen win Bertram in *All's Well That Ends Well.* **(2)** The Roman goddess of chastity, she appears to Pericles in a vision, *Pericles* 21. *AB*

Dibdin, Charles (1745–1814). English composer. A prolific songwriter, Dibdin played a major musical part in the Shakespeare *Jubilee celebrations at Stratford-upon-Avon in 1769. He composed a cantata, *Queen Mab*, and compiled a collection of songs sung on the occasion, including his own settings, entitled *Shakespear's Garland; or The Warwickshire Jubilee.* *IBC*

Dick. See Butcher, Dick the.

Dickens, Charles (John Huffam) (1812–70), novelist, the only English author whose prodigious gifts may justifiably be compared to Shakespeare's. Dickens's life and work are continuously informed by his familiarity with and admiration for all of Shakespeare's work, which

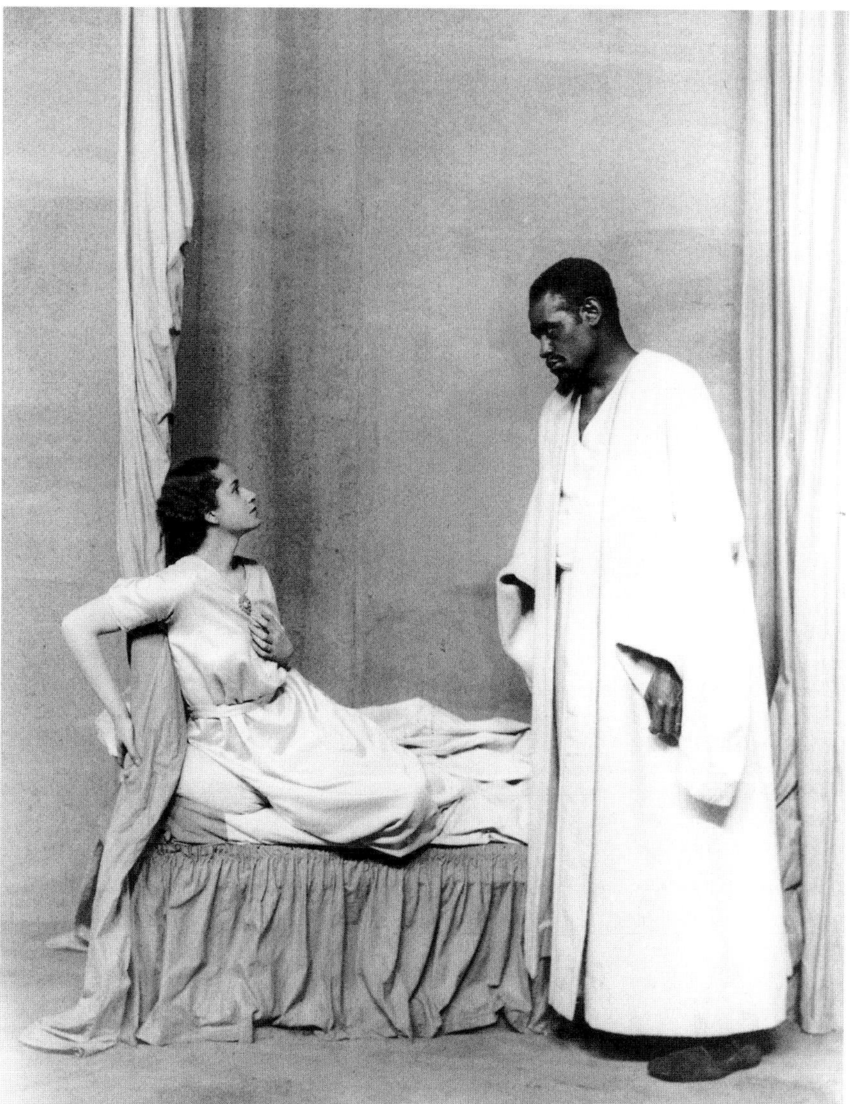

The 23-year-old Peggy Ashcroft as Desdemona, with Paul Robeson as Othello, Savoy Theatre, 1930.

undoubtedly had a transforming influence on Dickens's creative imagination. There are at least 1,000 textually supported references, echoes, and allusions in novels, essays, stories, letters, and speeches; matched only by those to the New Testament. His first speech refers to Shakespearian principles of composition and the earliest surviving fragment of manuscript is a burlesque *O'Thello* (1834); his last novel (*The Mystery of Edwin Drood*, 1870) includes echoes, allusions, and quotations from *Hamlet*, *Henry v*, and *Macbeth*; his last published article is devoted to the actor Charles Fechter as Iago and Hamlet; his last written words are a quotation from *Romeo and Juliet* ('These violent delights have violent ends', 8 June 1870). Dickens systematically studied Shakespeare (he owned several editions, chiefly the 21-volume 1821 Boswell's Malone); he performed in amateur productions; he was a member of the Shakespeare Club and the Shakespeare Society; he visited and promoted the purchase of Shakespeare's Birthplace; among his close friends were the Shakespeare scholar Charles Knight, the Shakespearian actor William Charles Macready, and the Shakespearian artist Daniel MacLise; his country home was at Gad's Hill, Falstaff's old thieving-ground; and, of course, his analogical mind draws on Shakespeare (particularly the great tragedies) in all his major novels, both in conception and in detail, from Mr Crummles's production in Portsmouth of *Romeo and Juliet* (*Nicholas Nickleby*, 1838–9, dedicated to Macready) to Mr Wopsle's impersonation of Hamlet (*Great Expectations*, 1860–1). Valerie Gager has shown (in *Shakespeare and Dickens*, 1996) how pervasively and profoundly Dickens was inspired and influenced by

Shakespeare; but also how comprehensively his own original genius transcends that and every other influence. *TM*

Digges, Leonard (1588–1635), poet. A Londoner, Digges took his BA degree at University College, Oxford, then studied abroad, but returned to live at his college. His widowed mother in 1603 married Thomas Russell, who is remembered in Shakespeare's will. The first of Digges's two tributes to Shakespeare appears in the 1623 Folio. 'To the Memory of the deceased Author Master W. Shakespeare', 22 lines long, includes the earliest known allusion to the playwright's monument at Holy Trinity church ('when . . . Time dissolves thy Stratford Monument'), and this poem establishes, once and for all, that the dramatist was the same person as William Shakespeare of Stratford. Digges's untitled 'Poets are born not made', of 68 lines, appears posthumously in John Benson's volume of Shakespeare's *Poems* (1640). *PH*

dimeter, a verse line of two feet (or beats), sometimes used in songs or (rarely) as a variation from blank verse: 'Have more than thou showest | Speak less than thou knowest,' etc. (*King Lear* 1.4.118–19). *GTW*

Diomed (Diomedes) is Cleopatra's servant. He brings Antony the news that Cleopatra is not dead, *Antony and Cleopatra* 4.15.116. *AB*

Diomedes. (1) He is one of the Greek commanders in *Troilus and Cressida.* **(2)** See DIOMED. *AB*

Dion. See CLEOMENES.

Dioniza, wife to Cleon, resolves to murder Marina out of envy, *Pericles* 15. *AB*

dirge, a poem, song, or hymn of mourning, performed at funeral ceremonies; see *Romeo and Juliet* 4.4.115. *JB*

discovery space. See STAGE DOORS; STAGE FURNITURE.

disintegration, a term coined by E. K. *Chambers to describe and castigate attempts by certain 19th-century scholars to deny Shakespeare's sole authorship of many of the plays in the recognized canon. The chief catalyst of the disintegration movement was F. G. Fleay, who argued that analysis of metrical patterns proved that parts of *The Taming of the Shrew* were written by Thomas *Lodge, that George *Peele had a hand in *Romeo and Juliet*, and that Ben Jonson wrote parts of *Julius Caesar.* Fleay's disciple J. M. Robertson saw Marlowe as the principal author of *Richard III, Richard II*, and *Henry V*, and Greene as the author of *The Two Gentlemen of Verona.* Robertson held that *Hamlet, All's Well That Ends Well, The Merry Wives of Windsor, Troilus and Cressida, Timon of Athens*, and *Pericles* all represent Shakespeare's reworking of versions of these plays originally written by George Chapman.

When Victorian disintegrators detected (rightly or wrongly) the presence of two authorial voices in the plays, they generally concluded that this was a result of Shakespeare's revising the work of other dramatists. More recent scholarship explains the presence of two or more hands in a text as evidence of collaboration. Although the 'disintegrator' label still carries pejorative connotations, there is today general agreement that Shakespeare collaborated with John Fletcher on *The Two Noble Kinsmen, All Is True* (*Henry VIII*), and the lost play *Cardenio*; with Thomas Middleton on *Timon of Athens, Macbeth*, and *Measure for Measure*; possibly with George Wilkins on *Pericles*; and possibly with an unknown playwright or playwrights on *1 Henry VI* and *Richard Duke of York*. *ER*

Chambers, E. K., *The Disintegration of Shakespeare* (1924)

divisions, embellishment of a melodic line with additional, more rapid notes, found for example in repeats of *strains in keyboard or *lute music. Extemporizing divisions was an expected musical skill in Shakespeare's time. *JB*

Doctor. He prescribes an unorthodox cure for the Jailer's Daughter's madness in *The Two Noble Kinsmen.* *AB*

Doctor, English. He announces that the King is coming to cure the sick, *Macbeth* 4.3.143–6. *AB*

Doctor of Physic. He witnesses Lady Macbeth's somnambulism and suspects her crime, *Macbeth* 5.1. *AB*

Dodd's Beauties of Shakespeare, published as two volumes in 1752, proved an immensely popular and frequently reprinted anthology and was the form in which *Goethe first read Shakespeare. William Dodd (1729–77) acknowledges an anti-editorial bias and explains rather than emends the sublime passages selected from all plays except *The Merry Wives of Windsor.* *CMSA*

Dogberry is a humorously incompetent constable who arrests and interrogates Borachio and Conrad in *Much Ado About Nothing.* *AB*

Dogberryism, a comically confused misapplication of long words, as when Dogberry claims to have 'comprehended two auspicious persons' (*Much Ado About Nothing* 3.5.44); later called malapropism. *CB*

doggerel, tediously inept verse, as in the absurd speeches of Bottom and his associates in their play of Pyramus and Thisbe in the last act of *A Midsummer Night's Dream.* *CB*

Doggett, Thomas (?1670–1721), actor, renowned for his comic playing as Sir Hugh in *Merry Wives*, Polonius, and a singing, dancing witch in *Macbeth.* A successful co-manager of Drury Lane, he used his wealth to instigate the annual watermen's race from London Bridge to Chelsea to celebrate the Hanoverian succession. *CMSA*

dogs are given names in Shakespeare more than any other kind of animal in the plays: many of them are the hunting dogs (Merriman, Clowder, Silver, Belman, and Echo in the induction to *The Taming of the Shrew*, not to mention Petruccio's spaniel Troilus (4.1.136)), and the spirits in the shapes of dogs that Prospero and Ariel set on Stefano, Trinculo, and Caliban in *The Tempest* 4.1 (Mountain, Silver, Fury, Tyrant). In the midst of his madness, Lear refers to 'The little dogs and all, | Tray, Blanch, Sweetheart—see, they bark at me' (3.6.20–1). The principal dog brought onto the stage is *Crab in *The Two Gentlemen of Verona*, though the dog in 'Pyramus and Thisbe' in *A Midsummer Night's Dream* might also have been a real animal in Shakespeare's day. Countless references are made to dogs, usually in ways that are still familiar today: as an animal worth less than a human (and therefore a frequent insult 'O damned Iago! O inhuman dog!', *Othello* 5.1.64); and though unworthy and unfortunate, sometimes faring better than particularly unlucky humans—'Why should a dog, a horse, a rat have life, | And thou no breath at all' (*King Lear* 5.3.282–3). *AB*

Garber, Marjorie, *Dog Love* (1996)

Dolabella, one of Caesar's followers, tells Cleopatra that Caesar intends to lead her in triumph, *Antony and Cleopatra* 5.1.108. *AB*

'Do me right, and dub me knight', fragment sung by Silence in *2 Henry IV* 5.3.74. 'Do me right' means 'pledge or drink my health'. The original song had music by Lassus, published in 1570. *JB*

Donalbain, younger son of Duncan, flees to Ireland after his father's murder, *Macbeth* 2.3.137. *AB*

Donne, John (1572–1631), one of the greatest English poets. Born into a Catholic family, Donne converted to the Church of England, entered the priesthood in 1615, and ended his days as Dean of St Paul's. His biographer Izaak Walton divides his literary career in two—separating the love poetry written in his youth from the religious verse of his maturity—but it is impossible to date most of his poems with certainty. He published little poetry in his lifetime, preferring to circulate his work in manuscript. His verse is both metrically and formally experimental, ranging from satire to love lyric, from sonnet to verse epistle, from elegy to hymn. In it he abandons the mythological apparatus that dominated the verse of the 1590s, as Shakespeare did in his sonnets, replacing it with questing analyses of intellectual, emotional, sexual, and spiritual problems, and wittily exploiting metaphors drawn from an abundance of contemporary discourses: philosophical, scientific, medical, cartographical, political. His protean ability to assume different roles in his poems is often described as theatrical. He is known as the founder of the 'metaphysical' school of poetry, but seems obsessed with physicality: with the difficulty of establishing relationships between lovers that outlast the moment of parting, with the problems of communicating, as a physical being, with an invisible God. His prose writings are as restlessly intelligent as his verse. *RM*

Carey, John, *John Donne: Life, Mind, Art* (1981)
Marotti, Arthur F., *John Donne, Coterie Poet* (1986)

Donnelly, Ignatius. See BACONIAN THEORY.

'Do nothing but eat and make good cheer', a carol fragment sung by Silence in *2 Henry IV* 5.3.17. The original tune is unknown. *JB*

Dorastus and Fawnia. A *droll by this title, in existence by 1703, was performed in 18th-century fairgrounds: surviving cast lists show that this was a conflation of *The Winter's Tale* and its source, *Greene's *Pandosto*. It may well have influenced later 18th-century versions of the play by *Garrick and Macnamara Morgan. *MD*

Wells, Stanley, 'A Shakespearian Droll?', *Theatre Notebook*, 15 (1961)

Dorcas and Mopsa are shepherdesses who join in the rustic raillery and sing with Autolycus in *The Winter's Tale* 4.4. *AB*

'Doricles'. See FLORIZEL.

Dorset, Marquis of. Queen Elizabeth's son and brother to Lord Gray, he flees to join Richmond, *Richard III* 4.1.91 (based on Thomas Gray, d. 1501). *AB*

Dorset, Thomas Sackville, 1st Earl of (1536–1608), poet and politician. He wrote a celebrated mythological *Induction* for the 1563 edition of *A Mirror for Magistrates*; and with Thomas Norton he wrote *Gorboduc* (1565), the first English tragedy to follow classical models and to be written in blank verse. Like *King Lear* it concerns a king who divides his kingdom between his children, with disastrous results. *RM*

Dostoevsky, Fyodor (Mikhailovich) (1821–81), Russian novelist, often compared to Shakespeare, not least by the psychoanalyst Freud, for his penetration to the depths of the human personality; and some Russian critics have argued that Shakespeare is a main inspiration for Dostoevsky's own tragic art. Encouraged to read Shakespeare by his student friend Shidlovskii, Dostoevsky knew no English, although he later memorized by heart passages of N. A. Polevoi's 1837 translation of *Hamlet*, and also used Letourneur's 1821 French version of the works. In 1849, when Dostoevsky was under sentence of death, his elder brother Mikhail sent him Ketcher's prose translations ('I thank you particularly for Shakespeare'). Dostoevsky affirmed Shakespeare's 'uncontestable aesthetic worth', admiring his truth to nature and the freedom and inconsistency of his gigantic characters; but he saw him also as a poet of despair, needing the antidote of visionary faith. There are allusions to Shakespeare in most of Dostoevsky's novels and stories, including *Poor Folk* (1846), *Crime and Punishment* (1866), *The Idiot* (1868), *The Devils* (1871), and *The Brothers Karamazov* (1879). *TM*

Levin, Iurii D., 'Dostoevskii and Shakespeare', in W. J. Leatherbarrow (ed.), *Dostoevskii and Britain* (1995)

Douai promptbooks and manuscripts. A late 17th-century manuscript owned by the Public Library in Douai, France, containing texts of *Twelfth Night*, *As You Like It*, *The Comedy of Errors*, *Romeo and Juliet*, *Julius Caesar*, and *Macbeth* transcribed from the Second Folio (1632), apparently for use in amateur productions of the plays. *ER*

Evans, G. Blakemore, 'The Douai Manuscript: Six Shakespearean Transcripts', *Philological Quarterly*, 41 (1962)

Double Falsehood. See CARDENIO.

doubling. In Shakespeare's time the number of roles in a play always exceeded the number of actors in the company, so undoubtedly actors 'doubled' (played more than one part). The evidence of printed cast lists bears out the commonsense assumption that each actor took several minor roles or else one or two major roles, thereby reducing, but not eliminating, the disproportion in the number of lines to be learnt. Detailed studies of doubling possibilities using extant play-texts as well as 'plots' are hampered by our ignorance concerning women's roles: if these were commonly played by adult men as well as boys the company would have an easier time assigning roles. Where we know the parts doubled it seems that audiences valued actorly virtuosity (displayed in pairing highly unalike characters) as well as thematic allusiveness (displayed in pairing characters who share a characteristic or a dramatic function). Doubling was intrinsic to the actor's profession so only the company fool and the most important star (Edward Alleyn is a notable case) had the opportunity to develop a speciality or 'type'. To ease moments of doubling stress an additional scene might be interpolated to give an actor time to change costumes and Henslowe's payments for 'mending' of and 'additions' to plays seem to have been for this purpose. *GE*

Douce, Francis (1757–1834), English antiquary, sometime keeper of manuscripts in the British Museum, where he worked on the catalogues of the Lansdowne and Harleian manuscript collections. He was the author of *Illustrations of Shakespeare and Ancient Manners* (2 vols., 1807), explaining, with occasional imperfections, many obscure references in Shakespeare's text. *TM*

Douglas, Earl of. 'The Douglas' (see *1 Henry IV* 5.4.25) joins *Hotspur after being defeated by him at Holmedon (described 1.1.52–61). At *Shrewsbury he fights King Henry, 5.4.38, Prince Harry, 5.4.42, and Oldcastle, 5.4.76. He is based on *Holinshed's account of Archibald, 4th Earl of Douglas (*c.*1369–1424). *AB*

Dover, the port in Kent best known for its white cliffs and its proximity to France. The surrounding area is the scene of *The Tragedy of King Lear* 4.3, 4.5, 4.6, and Act 5 (*History of King Lear* 17, 18, 20–4) (possibly also *The First Part of the Contention* (*2 Henry VI*) 4.1 and *King John* 4.1–3). *AB*

Dowdall, John (fl. 1693), a lawyer who, in a letter dated 10 April 1693, tells of a visit to Stratford where he saw the monument and grave, which he describes as 'a plain free stone', of 'our Stratford tragedian, Mr. Shakespeare'. He transcribes the epitaph which, he says, Shakespeare 'made by himself a little before his death'. Dowdall also writes that the clerk who showed him round the church and was 'above eighty years old' told him that 'this Shakespeare was formerly in this town bound apprentice to a butcher, but that he run from his master to London, and there was received into the playhouse as a servitor, and by this means had an opportunity to be what he afterwards proved. He was the best of his family but the male line is extinguished. Not one, for fear of the curse abovesaid dare touch his gravestone, though his wife and daughters did earnestly desire to be laid in the same grave with him.' *SW*

Dowden, Edward (1843–1914), Irish academic, a vice-president of the New Shakspere Society, and author of *Shakspere: A Critical Study of his Mind and Art* (1875). The German scholar *Gervinus, whose *Shakespeare Commentaries* (1863) had triggered Dowden's Dublin lectures, used verse-tests to establish four periods in Shakespeare's career. Dowden's own four periods were eventually simplified in *Shakspere* (1877) to 'In the workshop' (learning the craft of playwright); 'In the world' (dealing with history, politics, and the real world); 'Out of the depths' (coming to terms with evil and suffering); and 'On the heights' (realizing the power of repentance and forgiveness). The intellectual pitfalls of treating plays as confessional spiritual autobiography seem obvious, and were devastatingly exposed in C. J. Sisson's *The Mythical Sorrows of Shakespeare* (British Academy Lecture, 1934). That does not preclude the suggestive subtlety and elegance of Dowden's own approach, nor the persistent human impulse to find the 'mind' in the 'art'. *TM*

Dowland, John (1563–1626), composer and lutenist. Despite a European reputation he failed to achieve the position of court lutenist under Queen Elizabeth, becoming instead lutenist at the Danish court (1598–1603). James I eventually appointed him in 1612. *JB*

Downes, John (fl. 1661–1719), author, and prompter for the Duke's, United, and Betterton's companies. He wrote a history of the stage, *Roscius Anglicanus* (1708), that provides valuable connections between the Restoration and earlier periods. He suggests that Betterton was taught to play Hamlet by Davenant, who had seen it performed at Blackfriars by Taylor, who had been instructed by Shakespeare. Similarly, Betterton learned the role of Henry VIII from Davenant, who had learned it from Lowen, again as instructed by Shakespeare. *CMSA*

Drake, Nathan (1766–1836), English doctor, author of *Shakespeare and his Times, Including the Biography of the Poet, Criticisms on his Genius and Writings; a New Chronology of his Plays; a Disquisition on the Object of his Sonnets; and a History of the Manners, Customs and Amusements, Superstitions, Poetry and Elegant Literature of his Age* (2 vols., 1817), in which the theory that *'Mr W.H.', dedicatee of Shakespeare's Sonnets, is actually Henry Wriothesley, 3rd Earl of *Southampton, is first advanced. *TM*

dramatic irony, a form of irony arising from the discrepancy between what the audience knows about a character's true situation and prospects, and what that character says about them, as with Duncan's remarks upon the welcoming appearance of the castle in which he is about to be murdered (*Macbeth* 1.6.1–3). *CB*

dramatic poetry, Shakespeare's. In the 20 or 25 years of his theatrical career, Shakespeare produced 37 plays. All have survived on to modern stages; some are works of genius; and every one of them has its own stylistic and linguistic interest. Not much justice can be done to this situation in a brief note. Something might be gained by trying to analyse the significance of this or that passage extracted from *The Two Gentlemen of Verona* and *Twelfth Night* and *The Tempest.* But that significance might turn out to be intrinsic to the work as a whole. A good deal depends on what we mean by 'poetry'.

A case could be made for thinking (and the publishing history of the work would support it) that Shakespeare's best poetry, even his best *lyric poetry, is to be found in his plays. He had difficulty in handling the 'drama' of his Sonnets. In these and other poems the human story never seems to have gone quite right. Only in his plays was Shakespeare completely free to find himself as a poet. There is, of course, a latent paradox here. And it is one worth exploring, because it may explain what is exceptional about Shakespeare, who can seem somehow more three-dimensional than most other writers. He fused two forms which often exist separately and apart, even in self-contradiction. But in him they became one.

Theatre is the most public of all literary arts. (That offshoot of drama, *opera, to develop in England some decades after Shakespeare died, can rely on its visible machinery of technique, often in tension with its movingness, to a point of potential farce.) Though a play can be read, it is fulfilled only in the theatre. And the theatre makes its own, non-verbal forms: stage business of all kinds, mime, music, even silence. Any born or true dramatist, at least in Shakespeare's day, worked through the expressive meaning of things acted out in time and physically. Ezra Pound once observed that the medium of drama was not words, but bodies moving on a stage. Shakespeare showed himself a dramatist in this sense. In his first plays he is a professional and competent rhetorician, sometimes a very striking one. But in what seems to be his most theatrically inexperienced play and so possibly his earliest, *The Two Gentlemen of Verona,* he had the audacity to made one of his dramatis personae a dog—a real live animal who accompanies his master Lance onto the stage. The same dimension of sheer physical presence characterizes the peculiarly mesmeric Richard III as a 'crookback', Bottom as a braying long-eared 'ass', Falstaff a 'tun of man'—just as the most memorable character at the end of his career is Caliban, a 'savage and deformed slave'.

When Shakespeare was attacked in a pamphlet in 1592, the angry charge made against him was that a 'Shake-scene', a mere 'player', had upstaged the literate intellectuals. Perhaps the most literate and intelligent man of his time, Shakespeare was also manifestly a man of the theatre. It seems relevant that the plays whose success arouses jealousy here were his early history plays about Henry VI—relevant in the sense that history plays, a genre probably invented by Shakespeare himself, are a fully public genre, made out of the national and political history still just within the memory of his audience or of their fathers and grandfathers.

The three Henry VI plays are concluded and crowned by *Richard III,* a brilliantly worldly and claustrophobic political thriller. Linguistically, the play brings to a climax the academic rhetoric the poet perfects in these early plays, an intensely figured and formally witty verse. Powerful as *Richard III* is, and able to compete with the latest now in gangster films, not much in it would seem to foretell Shakespeare's greater poetry. And yet it possesses one long and wholly thought-provoking passage, when a quite different kind of writer seems to be taking over. In its first act Richard's elder brother, the doomed Clarence, has a dream. He has dreamed that, pushed by the lethal Richard from the deck of the ship in which they are travelling, he falls down and down to the bed of the sea:

> Methoughts I saw a thousand fearful wrecks,
> Ten thousand men that fishes gnawed upon,
> Wedges of gold, great ouches, heaps of pearl,
> Inestimable stones, unvalued jewels,
> All scattered in the bottom of the sea.
> Some lay in dead men's skulls; and in those holes
> Where eyes did once inhabit, there were crept—
> As 'twere in scorn of eyes—reflecting gems.
> (1.4.24–31)

Shakespeare was to write greater sea-poetry than this. There is a lifetime's exploration between Clarence's trudging vision and (let us say) the magical mimetic quietness with which Pericles will consign his wife's body to the seabed:

> for a monument upon thy bones,
> And aye-remaining lamps, the belching whale
> And humming water must o'erwhelm thy corpse,
> Lying with simple shells. (11.60–3)

Poetry has ceased to be rhetoric and become an enactment, a sympathetic life of words. *The Tempest* does it even more briefly: 'Those are pearls that were his eyes' (1.2.401).

The interest of Clarence's dream is that it begins this process. And it does so by making plain that poetry—Shakespeare's dramatic poetry or poetic drama—is not a mere matter of writing well. It defines the standard of a style as a capacity to meet, to rise to, the needs of a given vision or human imagination. Clarence sees, and Shakespeare is working to make us feel, a dimension of existence well beyond the hunt for power that governs the rest of the play:

> my dream was lengthened after life.
> O, then began the tempest to my soul!
> . . . Then came wand'ring by
> A shadow like an angel, with bright hair,
> Dabbled in blood. (1.4.44, 52–3)

Clarence is accused by the shadow of a young prince he has himself killed in battle. *Richard III* is made up of a sense of history as peculiarly interlocked murders, a knotted network of cunning deaths and revenges. The dream narrated here gives a wholly different perspective of meaning, of moral judgement. And that judgement is a 'dream', an inward apprehension so far from social realities as to demand the image of an ocean in which we drown alone. Shakespeare is making use of ancient symbols: the ship is the classical and Christian, medieval and Renaissance image of the ship of state; but it is also the individual soul, voyaging through this world. The public and the private interfuse here, like Clarence's remarkable image of diamonds flashing in the hollow eyes of skulls. This is the history of an individual consciousness, a poetry finding its own dramatic life.

The 'dream' is an image of dramatic poetry useful to hold on to in considering how Shakespeare's writing develops. *Romeo and Juliet* and *A Midsummer Night's Dream* are seemingly linked twin masterpieces, apparently produced immediately after *Richard III*. In his tragedy of young lovers, Shakespeare risked violating the lines of his character to allow the tough Mercutio his own 'dream' set piece, in which the fairy queen brings to sleeping human beings by night fantasies that act out the mind's secret passions. The even richer and finer comedy sends its young lovers from Athens—a symbol of high Reason in the ancient world—into the wood by night, peopled by fairies and would-be actors, to confuse and then clarify their tangled loves. When they emerge, and as the last act of the play opens, the ruler Theseus, embodying that high Reason itself, looks down with kindly patronage on the life of imagination lived out by 'the lunatic, the lover and the poet':

> as imagination bodies forth
> The forms of things unknown, the poet's pen
> Turns them to shapes, and gives to airy nothing
> A local habitation and a name. (5.1.14–17)

This is, of course, spoken by a 'shadow' in a poem, on that local habitation, the real stage of a theatre. As such, it hardly needs to be (as it is) answered by his Queen, Hippolyta, who tells him that he should give Reason a larger scope, admitting the truth to be found in dreams: a process which here entails understanding what the lovers have experienced during their night in the woods.

I glanced forward, earlier, from *Richard III* to the late romances. The debate between Theseus and Hippolyta again has its much later echo. In *The Winter's Tale*, the Queen, Hermione, innocent but on trial for her life, tells the obsessed Leontes, 'My life stands in the level of your dreams' (the image is, I think, at once that of a levelled gun and a destructive male sexuality); Leontes answers wearily, 'Your actions are my dreams' (3.2.80–1). The interchange is at once more intense than that of the earlier comedy, and briefer, more charged, more fraught; the language is now charged with implicit and inward suggestiveness, as Leontes' own nightmares darkly energize the play. Theseus in the earlier play writes down human fantasies with a high and sedate reflectiveness, and Hippolyta defends them with a more compassionate wisdom. It is Hermione, in the later, who embodies reason; while Leontes falls into an abyss of imagination where words like 'play' and 'nothing' madden him with their excess of meanings and possibilities.

Shakespeare's whole career is in this sense a meditation on the way human 'dreams' and 'actions' interconnect and inbreed. And the play between the two is a parallel to the debate between the public and the private, and, if we like, drama and poetry. In this sense, Shakespeare wrote no play that was anything but poetic. Certainly, some of his work cannot help striking a reader (in particular) as exceptionally beautiful, and therefore as more 'poetic'. Most readers would select *Twelfth Night, Antony and Cleopatra*, and *The Tempest* as spell-binding work. They have an inordinate harmony, both musical and imagistic; they have the highest possible count of gorgeous phrases and unforgettable rhythms. In the Roman play in particular, Shakespeare seems to be released by his dry dependence on his sceptical source into a kind of free flight of language, the sound of a verbal glory at once Roman-disciplined and Egypt-sensual. Yet even here, of course, the spell-binding quality—the dream dimension of imagination—can never be distinguished from dramatic meaning and function. The glamour of each of these plays has to do with what in them is aristocratic, removed, a high pastime played out within sound of the sea.

Not every play Shakespeare wrote has this musical coherence. But almost all hold together—each will possess what may be variously called 'an atmosphere', 'a world of the play', to which all dramatic elements contribute. Each is in that sense a poem. And, though obviously verse-writing will tend to indicate exalted or profound states of mind, a scene or a passage or a whole play may be in prose, may be indeed prosaic, and yet will have its place in Shakespeare's dramatic poetry. The second part of *Henry IV*, though primarily in prose, achieves something of a poetic order—does so in fact more remarkably than the brilliant *Part 1*. *Part 1* crowns the theatrical mastery the dramatist achieved in his first decade, writing through the 1590s; *Part 2* ushers in the stranger, more difficult, undoubtedly more magnificent explorations of the 1600s. The scenes of the old men in the Gloucestershire orchard (3.2, 5.3)—remembering the country dead and hearing 'the chimes at midnight'—have certainly a sombre poetry. Again, there is an effortless and unsignalled drift from verse into prose and back again in both the 'storm scenes' in *King Lear* (3.2, 4, 6 in the Folio) and the 'Dover Cliff' scene (4.6), with the prose-writing as it were justified by the conditions of natural chaos, madness, rusticity. But the imaginative range and quality of these scenes is both sustained and extreme.

It is the second half of Shakespeare's career—roughly, from *Hamlet* to *The Tempest*—which produces the greatest triumphs of dramatic poetry. And it may be material that each of these two named plays has a peculiarity of plot. Neither, strictly speaking, *has* a plot; everything in them is transmuted into experience. If 'What Happens in Hamlet' is questionable, this is because what happens in the play is less important than the feeling or meaning of what happens—and we may say something the same of all the tragedies. The most purely and alarmingly poetic must surely be *Macbeth*. Macbeth himself begins with the intuition that 'My thought, | Whose murder yet is but fantastical, | Shakes so my single state of man' (1.3.138–9): and the play shows how 'thought' and 'murder', like 'dreams' and 'actions', may make both public and private worlds fuse into one shaken 'single state of man'. Into this process each member of the audience is drawn, like the open-eyed sleepwalking Lady Macbeth (5.1).

Macbeth himself speaks, throughout his play, what is perhaps a more intense poetry than any uttered by any other chief character in the plays: a deep and strangling and ambiguous verse that lights his way downward. He is a man who dreams, and who loses himself in fantasies, without acknowledging that he is moving further and further from the real. The impassive ironies of the late romances are perhaps intended to counter this dark art. These are poetic works which from the first know just how unreal they are, and carry their conventions transparently. At the beginning of *Cymbeline*, one courtly gentleman says to another, 'Howsoe'er 'tis strange . . . | Yet it is true, sir' (1.1.66, 68): and truth in these last plays depends on the acceptance that poetry is only poetry, and that dreams are things we wake up from. But at the centre of the incomparable *Tempest* is Caliban, who given the 'noises', 'sounds', 'sweet airs', and all other dreams of the island, will cry 'to dream again' (3.2.138–46). *BE*

dramatis personae. Lists of 'the persons of the play', now a standard feature in editions of Shakespeare, are rarely found in the early printed texts. None of Shakespeare's plays printed in *quarto includes a dramatis personae. Only seven of the 36 plays in the First *Folio incorporate lists of characters; the fact that such lists appear in *The Tempest, The Two Gentlemen of Verona*, and *Measure for Measure* (three out of the first four plays in the Folio) has suggested to some that the lists were specifically drawn up by the editor when preparing copy for the collection. The dramatis personae for *2 Henry IV* and *Timon of Athens* are printed in large type on pages by themselves, suggesting that they were supplied as padding when it was found that the plays would not fill the space allotted to them.

The First Folio calls these lists 'The Names of the Actors', a misnomer since it is the names of characters rather than those of the actors that are provided. The lists are generally arranged hierarchically by social standing, with the male characters invariably preceding the females (except in the list for *Timon*, in which the women are omitted altogether: *dramatis personae non grata*). Nicholas *Rowe's 1709 edition first supplied dramatis personae for all of the plays. *ER*

Greg, W. W., *The Shakespeare First Folio* (1955)

Drayton, Michael (1563–1631), poet and playwright. Born in Shakespeare's home county of Warwickshire, Drayton started life as a servant in a noble household, and later sought to make his living as a serious professional poet. Like Samuel *Daniel he was an assiduous reviser of his work who made his name as a writer of historical poems, such as the epic *Mortimeriados* (1596), revised as *The Barons' Wars* (1603), and *England's Heroical Epistles* (1597), a collection of verse letters between famous lovers from English history. His sonnet sequence *Idea* (1619), first published as *Idea's Mirror* (1594), formed part of a series of publications in which he set out his poetic agenda: these included a collection of Spenserian pastorals, *Idea: The Shepherd's Garland* (1593), and an Ovidian cosmological poem, *Endimion and Phoebe: Idea's Latmos* (1595). By 1598 he was writing plays for the Admiral's Men. Only one survives: *Sir John Oldcastle* (1600), written with three fellow playwrights, and reprinted in 1619 as the work of Shakespeare. The play aims to rehabilitate the reputation of a proto-Protestant martyr, whose portrayal as *Oldcastle/Falstaff in Shakespeare's *1 Henry IV* had offended his descendants. Drayton's most ambitious work was the epic *Poly-Olbion* (1612), a versified historical and mythological map of Britain. According to John *Ward (*c.*1662), Drayton and Ben Jonson drank Shakespeare into the fever that killed him. *RM*

Brink, Jean R., *Michael Drayton Revisited* (1990).
Hardin, Richard F., *Michael Drayton and the Passing of Elizabethan England* (1973).

Drew family. A child-actress in London, Louisa Lane (1820–97), who at 16 was Lady Macbeth in New York, married as her third (at least) husband John Drew (1827–62), a noted Sir Andrew Aguecheek, with whom she had three children; among them were John (1853–1927), renowned as Petruchio for *Daly, and Georgiana (1856–93), who married Maurice Barrymore. *RF*

Droeshout engraving. Traditionally attributed to Martin Droeshout the younger (1601–50), the frontispiece to the First *Folio edition of 1623 has been convincingly identified as the work of Martin Droeshout the elder (*c.*1560–1642), a Flemish engraver who came to England as a Protestant refugee. An earlier proof, of 1622, was also completed. The engraving was commissioned retrospectively, as a commemorative portrait of Shakespeare, possibly by friends and partners in the Globe theatre. It has also been claimed that the image is engraved after a missing portrait by Marcus Gheeraerts. The image is cited in Ben Jonson's *Dedication to the Reader*, written for the First Folio edition. It seems likely that the artist's reputation can be largely attributed to the widespread distribution of the First Folio and to Shakespeare's fame by 1622, since Droeshout's workmanship lacks the accomplishment of artists who earned their livelihood from engraving during the period, such as Renald Elstrack and William Faithorne, displaying old-fashioned techniques far surpassed in Faithorne's engraved portraits. The image has, nonetheless, acquired iconic status and appears on cultural products as diverse as playing cards and Internet sites. *CT*

drolls, sometimes called 'droll humours', were short, usually comic playlets composed or adapted for performance in fairground booths or taverns. The form flourished during the Commonwealth, when legitimate theatrical performances were forbidden, and a number were published after the Restoration by Francis Kirkman in *The Wits; or Sport upon Sport* (2 parts, 1662, 1673). Most of the examples in this collection derive from the *Beaumont and *Fletcher canon, but three are from Shakespeare, namely *The *Bouncing Knight*, *The *Grave-Makers*, and *The Merry Conceited Humours of *Bottom the Weaver*. Known later examples of the Shakespearian droll, sadly, were rarely published: see **Dorastus and Fawnia*. *MD*

Dromio of Ephesus. The Dromios are twin slaves of the twin Antipholi in *The Comedy of Errors*. *AB*

Dromio of Syracuse. See DROMIO OF EPHESUS.

Drummond, William (1585–1649), Scottish poet. He took notes on his wide-ranging conversations with Ben Jonson in 1618–19, which record Jonson's opinion of *The Winter's Tale*, among other things. Much of his huge library survives, including annotated copies of Shakespeare's plays and poems. *RM*

drums. The military drum was associated with infantry; hence with *marches, and with the *alarums and *excursions of stage battle. See also TABOR. *JB*

Drury Lane theatre, one of the two London patent theatres granted its charter by Charles II in 1662, opened in 1663, the home of Killigrew's King's Company. Rebuilt after the fire of 1672 to a Christopher Wren design with a greater seating capacity, it was the base for *Betterton's United Company from 1682, and prospered under the joint management of Wilkes, *Doggett, and Colley *Cibber from 1711. While 1741 saw *Macklin's innovative Shylock its greatest Shakespearian period was under *Garrick's management, with John Lacy, 1747–76. In addition to staging and performing in his own Shakespearian adaptations, he was responsible for advances in playing style and the rehearsal process, for removing the audience from the stage, the introduction of de Loutherbourg's innovative stage designs, and overseeing Robert Adams's alterations of 1775.

R. B. Sheridan, with Sarah *Siddons and John Philip *Kemble as his greatest stars, followed Garrick and demolished the dilapidated theatre in 1791. Its large replacement, designed by Henry Holland, burned down in 1809, and the fourth, present building opened in 1812 with a prologue by Lord *Byron and a performance of *Hamlet*. *CMSA*

Dryden, John (1631–1700). The foremost literary figure of his age, Dryden wrote drama, poetry, and prose. He was a strong supporter of the Stuart monarchs and was named Poet Laureate by Charles II. He held this office until William and Mary came to the throne in 1688. Several of Dryden's plays are closely connected to Shakespeare's works. He collaborated with Sir William *Davenant on an adapation of *The Tempest* (1667), and returned to Shakespeare in *All for Love; or, The World Well Lost* (1678), often considered his finest play. *All for Love* is not an adaptation of Shakespeare; rather, Dryden created a Restoration play based on the story of Antony and Cleopatra. He hoped 'to imitate the Divine *Shakespeare*' in his style, choosing to abandon rhyme for the first time in his serious drama. The following year, Dryden adapted *Troilus and Cressida* as *Troilus and Cressida; or, Truth Found Too Late* (1679). The 'Truth' in the subtitle refers to Cressida's virtue; in Dryden's adaptation, Cressida remains faithful to Troilus. At the end of the play, Cressida commits suicide and Troilus is killed in battle, in contrast to the original in which both the lovers are alive at the end of the play. Dryden is also one of the first writers of English literary criticism. In his essays and prefaces to plays, poems, and translations, he comments about past and present literary practice, writing with especial care about the form and function of drama. His most famous critical work is the *Essay of Dramatick Poesy* (1668), which he structures as a debate over the proper writing of drama. He concludes that English drama provides the most 'just and lively' imitation of nature and uses Shakespeare as his example of the genius of English drama. In this work Dryden compares Shakespeare to *Homer, the first in a long line of critics to do so. Dryden's reverence for the Elizabethan playwrights also appears in his responses to Thomas *Rymer's attack on English dramatists. His first response appears in the unpublished notes 'Heads of an Answer to

Rymer' in which he attacks Rymer and avers that Shakespeare equalled the ancient Greek playwrights. He responded publicly to Rymer in a more moderate essay entitled 'The Grounds of Criticism in Tragedy', which he attached to his adaptation of *Troilus and Cressida.* In it he adheres more closely to French *neoclassical theory, sometimes censuring Shakespeare for his irregularities of form and language, but at the same time upholding the genius of Shakespeare and of English drama in general. *JM*

Du Bellay, Joachim (*c.*1520–60), French poet and member of the *Pléiade, most famous for his sonnet sequence *L'Olive,* published 1549–50, that influenced the sonnets of Daniel and Shakespeare among others. Du Bellay was renowned for his lyrical descriptions of love, sorrow, and mutability. As a young man Spenser had translated some of this poetry and his Mutabilitie Cantos may bear Du Bellay's imprint. *JKS*

Ducis, Jean-François, See FRANCE.

Duffett, Thomas (fl. 1674), playwright. He is rumoured to have been a milliner before writing his first comedy, *The Spanish Rogue,* in 1674. He is best remembered as the first exponent of Shakespearian *burlesque, since among the parodies he composed for Drury Lane theatre (of plays successful at the rival Dorset Garden) are an 'Epilogue, being a new fancy, after the old and most surprising way of *Macbeth,* performed with new and costly machines' and *The Mock Tempest; or, The Enchanted Castle* (both first performed in 1674). Unlike later exponents of the genre, however, Duffett neither shows nor expects any knowledge of Shakespeare's original texts, sending up the *adaptations then in use without any appeal to their sources. The 'Epilogue', composed for his parody of Elkanah Settle's tragedy *The Empress of Morocco,* ridicules the special-effect-ridden witches' scenes of *Davenant's *Macbeth,* while *The Mock Tempest* is a meticulous, full-length travesty of the Davenant–*Dryden adaptation *The Tempest; or, The Enchanted Island* which translates its action to contemporary low-life London. Prospero becomes a former keeper of the Lord Mayor's dog kennel who has been supplanted and reduced to superintending the Bridewell prison for prostitutes, to which his enemies are brought after being caught during the opening raid on a brothel which replaces the original's storm. Inventively obscene throughout, Duffett's burlesques, though popular in London, were considered too shocking even by contemporary Dublin audiences, and have not been performed since their own time. *MD*

Three Burlesque Plays of Thomas Duffett: The Empress of Morocco, The Mock-Tempest, Psyche Debauch'd, ed. Ronald Eugene DiLorenzo (1972)

To the Reader.

This *Figure* that thou here ſeeſt put,
It was for gentle *Shakeſpear* cut;
Wherein the *Graver* had a ſtrife
With Nature to outdo the Life.
O, could he but have drawn his Wit
As well in Braſs, as he has hit
His Face; the Print would then ſurpaſs
All that was ever writ in *Braſs.*
But ſince he cannot, Reader, look
Not on his Picture, but his *Book.*

B. J.

The Droeshout engraving of Shakespeare, with Ben Jonson's poem attesting to its accuracy, here reproduced from the Fourth Folio (1685). By this time the plate had begun to deteriorate, giving the playwright a distinctly unshaven look.

THE WITS, OR, SPORT upon SPORT.

IN

Select Pieces of DROLLERY, Digested into SCENES by way of DIALOGUE.

Together with Variety of Humors of several Nations, fitted for the pleasure and content of all Persons, either in Court, City, Countrey, or Camp. The like never before Published.

PART I.

LONDON,
Printed for *Henry Marsh*, at the Sign of the *Princes Arms* in *Chancery-Lane*. 1662.

Dugdale, Sir William (1605–86), Garter king-of-arms and antiquary of Warwickshire. A note by Dugdale, in 1653, identifies the stonemason of Shakespeare's bust at Holy Trinity church as 'Gerard Johnson' (anglicized from Gheerart Janssen), whose father was born in Amsterdam. Stratford's monument today differs from the odd sketch of it included in Dugdale's *Antiquities of Warwickshire* (1656), in which, for example, Shakespeare's face is wizened and melancholy, his elbows jut at sharp angles, and the stone pen and paper are missing. But other pictures in Dugdale's book totally misrepresent their subjects, and it is unlikely that Shakespeare's monument in the church has been altered substantially (except in colour) since 1623. *PH*

Duke Humphrey, a lost play (*c.*1613) first attributed to Shakespeare by Humphrey *Moseley, who entered it in the *Stationers' Register on 29 June 1660. The title character is generally identified with Humphrey, Duke of *Gloucester (*1 Henry VI* and *The First Part of the Contention* (*2 Henry VI*)). *SM*

Duke's Company, named after the Duke of York (the future James II) and created by Sir William Davenant in 1660. It was one of the two companies issued patents by Charles II at the Restoration. The group played initially at Salisbury Court, moved to Lincoln's Inn Fields when joined by Betterton in 1661, and to Dorset Garden theatre in 1671. It acquired the exclusive right to a number of Shakespeare's plays, and innovative use of changeable scenery and music contributed to adaptations, particularly of *The Tempest* (with Dryden) and *Macbeth*, which were influential, enduring, and popular. *CMSA*

Dull, Anthony, a constable who arrests Costard, *Love's Labour's Lost* 1.1. *AB*

Dulwich, area of south-east London in which the College of God's Gift (founded by Edward Alleyn) is situated. Alleyn and his wife Joan (Philip Henslowe's stepdaughter) moved to Dulwich from the Liberty of the Clink in 1612/13 having purchased the manor of Dulwich in 1605. Dulwich College library still holds Alleyn's papers and accounts. *RSB*

Dumain, one of the lords attending the King of Navarre in *Love's Labour's Lost*, is in love with Catherine. *AB*

Dumain, Lords. See Lord Dumain, First and Second.

The Frontispiece to *The Wits*, 1662 (an anthology of drolls which includes a 'Falstaff sketch' derived from *1 Henry IV, The Bouncing Knight*), shows Falstaff and the Hostess among other popular dramatic characters: it is not an accurate representation of any particular playhouse or performance.

Dumas, Alexandre (père) (1803–70), French playwright. Dumas's work bears the most striking and thoroughgoing orientation by Shakespeare to be found in the whole range of Romantic drama. He produced Shakespearian plays in the epic tradition of the 'Diorama' whose special effects satisfied the popular demand for elaborate stage productions with mobile scenes abounding in picturesque details. *Une fille du régent* (1846) transplants Shakespeare's *Romeo and Juliet* into an epic story of romantic love mixed with political agitation from the French Revolution. The heavily reworked tragedy of *Hamlet* (1846–7), presented as a 'modern drama', forged the immensely popular tradition of the French 'grand spectacle' under the 'July Monarchy'. Nevertheless, critics excoriated Dumas's penchant for special effects which catered to the boulevard tradition of melodrama to the detriment of poetic subtlety. *AC*

Partridge, Eric, *The French Romantics' Knowledge of English Literature (1820–1848)* (1924)

dumb shows, moments of silent action in a play where gesture is made to bear greater significance than is usual, often with emblematic meaning. Ceremonial rituals are frequently silent but the term 'dumb show' is usually reserved for the deliberate artistic suppression of dialogue where it might be expected, so creating an atmosphere of expectation. Shakespeare's dumb shows are usually contained in a play-within-the-play (such as the ones which precede 'The Murder of Gonzago' in *Hamlet* and 'Pyramus and Thisbe' in *A Midsummer Night's Dream*), but in *Pericles*, a collaboration with George Wilkins, Shakespeare made extensive use of dumb shows and choric narration in an apparent experiment in dramatic form. *GE*

Mehl, Dieter, *The Elizabethan Dumb Show: The History of a Dramatic Convention* (1965)

dump. Surviving dumps, for *lute or keyboard, are generally mournful in character, with *divisions over repeated chord sequences. The expression 'merry dumps' in *Romeo and Juliet* 4.4.132 is presumably meant ironically. *JB*

Duncan, King of Scotland. Duncan I, according to *Holinshed, was murdered by Macbeth in 1040 with Banquo's connivance. In *Macbeth* the crime is committed solely by Macbeth and his wife, 2.1–2. *AB*

Dunsinane, Macbeth's fortress, 7 miles (11 km) north-east of Perth. Macbeth is told by an apparition that he 'shall never vanquished be until | Great Birnam Wood to high Dunsinane Hill | Shall come against him' (*Macbeth* 4.1.108–10), but it is nevertheless the scene of his defeat in Act 5. *AB*

Durfey, Thomas (1653–1723), dramatist and songwriter, whose popular adaptation of *Cymbeline, The Injured Princess; or, The Fatal Wager*, added a new rape sub-plot. Pisanio's daughter Clarona is blamed for Eugenia's (Innogen's) escape from court and ordered by Cloten to be raped and hanged. Pisanio is blinded for saving her. *CMSA*

Dutch wars. In 1584, William the Silent, the Protestant leader of the Dutch opposition to Spanish rule in the *Low Countries, was assassinated at Delft. Should the Dutch resistance be annihilated altogether and Philip II regain control of the land across the North Sea, the Spanish threat to England would be significantly heightened. To prevent France from aiding the Dutch republicans, Queen Elizabeth in 1585 concluded a treaty with the Low Countries, agreeing to support them in their war of independence. Entering into war with Spain in this indirect manner, Elizabeth hoped to contain the war on the continent of Europe. Having the Dutch as her political allies and the Low Countries as a geographical buffer, she could, with the Earl of Leicester as Governor General, fight Spain at a safe distance.

Elizabeth's opportunistic stance is wryly captured in John *Marston's *The Dutch Courtesan* (1605). Here, the play's hero draws a comparison between the Virgin Queen's deft policy of securing peace at home while waging war abroad, and the London bourgeois ideal of cultivating brothels for extramarital sex to secure marital stability at home. However, the impact of the so-called Dutch wars on the history of English drama was more variegated. The Earl of Leicester's Men, performing in various Dutch locations in 1586, were the first of a continuing stream of strolling players on the continent of Europe. Numerous poets and playwrights had first-hand experience of the wars. At a very early stage, in 1586, the conflict caused the notorious death of Sir Philip *Sidney at the town of Zutphen. In addition, the wars provide a context for Christopher *Marlowe's espionage activities, and for the desire of Dr Faustus to end the conflict with his black magic. George *Chapman visited the Low Countries, probably as soldier, which would explain his stay in a Middelburg hospital in 1586. Ben *Jonson killed a man on the sconce at the city of Nijmegen, and Cyril Tourneur was present at the extended siege of Ostend (1601–4). Shakespeare absorbs the impact in a less conspicuous manner. The news of the Earl of *Essex's involvement in the projected siege of Rouen (1591–2), was reworked to provide a context in the first part of *Henry VI*. The siege of Ostend and the Somerset House Conference together fed directly into the celebration of King James's peace policy in *All's Well That Ends Well* (1604/5).

Following the peace with Spain, Elizabeth's Dutch wars were soon to be forgotten. During the early 17th century, the nation with whom Elizabeth had entered her opportunistic alliance, and which English playwrights, including Shakespeare in *The Comedy of Errors*, had long patronized ('Where stood Belgia, the Netherlands?' 'O sir, I did not look so low,' 3.2.36–7) developed into a puissant seaborne empire. The Jacobean herring debate between the two nations, the Amboyne Massacre of 1623, as well as religious and political differences of a more substantial nature, gave rise to a series of naval conflicts in which the once fortuitous allies were now one another's enemies. *TH*

Dyce, Alexander (1798–1869), Scottish scholar and clergyman. A founder member of the *Shakespeare Society in 1840, his censorious *Remarks on Mr. J. P. Collier's and Mr C. Knight's Editions of Shakespeare* (1844) breached relations with two other founding members, and his *Strictures on Mr. Collier's New Edition of Shakespeare, 1858* (1859) broke them. His own edition of Shakespeare appeared in 1857 (rev. 1866), and his *Glossary* in 1864. *TM*

East Africa. Bishop Steere's 1867 translation of *Lamb's *Tales from Shakespeare* into Swahili is an early instance of the missionary use of Shakespeare in what became in British East Africa common colonial and missionary pedagogic practice. In 1900, the University Missions to Central Africa in Zanzibar produced *Hadithi Ingereza*, a prose *translation into Swahili of versions of several plays. Kenya's premier secondary school, Alliance High School, founded by a coalition of missionary groups in 1926, not only taught but put on annual productions of Shakespeare. Ngugi wa Thiong'o writes that, as a pupil at the school, between 1955 and 1958 he saw *As You Like It*, *1 Henry IV*, *King Lear*, and *A Midsummer Night's Dream*. The presence of Shakespeare within education was strengthened during the 1950s when Makerere University College in Uganda, for a long time the only university college in East and Central Africa, developed its links with the University of London. Alan Warner in his Makerere Inaugural Lecture 'Shakespeare in the Tropics' (1954) argued that the study of English literature would make Africans 'citizens of the world' but his compatriot David Cook, also at Makerere, contributed to the study of local literatures as well as to Shakespeare. Productions of Shakespeare included one of *Macbeth*, directed by an American with the first all-black cast in the Ugandan national theatre in 1964. Milton Obote is said, as a student, to have played Caesar in *Julius Caesar*. During the colonial period expatriate colonials organized performances for regular East African Shakespeare festivals.

During and since the period leading to independence for African states, some writers have continued to promote the presence and use of Shakespeare within cultural and educative practice. Ali Mazrui, head of the Department of Political Science at Makerere, wrote in 1967 of Shakespeare's importance to African culture as 'master of the English Language' and 'great creator of human characters and eternal situations', also recommending *Hamlet* as good training for self-government. The first Swahili translations of complete Shakespeare plays are by Julius K. Nyere, as well the first president of Tanzania. In the 1960s he translated *Julius Caesar* and then *The Merchant of Venice*, the latter as *Mabepari wa Venisi* which means literally 'the capitalists of Venice'. This version, unlike his earlier translation, is said to reflect more directly his socialist position and is an instance of the attempt by some African writers to appropriate Shakespeare in the context of immediate political struggle. Nyere's translations were published by OUP in Kenya while, in 1968, S. S. Mushi's translation of *Macbeth* was published by Tanzania Publishing House. Shakespeare has been appropriated to argue more explicitly the problematics of colonialism and neo-colonialism in a series of works, notably by Ngugi in his novel *A Grain of Wheat* (1968), by Murray Carlin, whose appropriation of *Othello* in *Not now, Sweet Desdemona* was first produced at the National Theatre of Uganda, Kampala, in 1968, and, further north, by the Sudanese author Tayib Salih who narrates the experiences of a contemporary North African version of Othello in *Season of Migration to the North* (1969).

Shakespeare has also been received in other ways in various countries in Central and East Africa as a problematic and complex phenomenon. In 1948 Octav Mannoni, using Prospero and Caliban as prototypes, evolved an inferiority-dependence theory of colonialism based on his experience of the Madagascan uprising of 1947–8, ideas later to be developed by Philip Mason, a colonial official who had worked in Africa. These ideas were strongly criticized by Franz Fanon and Aimé *Césaire, famous opponents of colonialism. Ngugi wa Thiong'o, who criticized in 1981 the way in which Shakespeare, 'who had the sharpest and most penetrating observations on the European bourgeois culture', was taught to him in Kenya and Makerere as if 'the only concern was with the universal themes of love, fear, birth and death', and who, even more recently, in 1993 uses the Prospero–Caliban relationship to argue against what he sees as the neo-colonial hegemony of English, traces the beginnings of the rejection of Shakespeare and a move to the Africanization of education to the 1950s. In 1971 Wanjandey Songa was still calling for Africanization, arguing that Shakespeare was being promoted at Makerere and elsewhere at the expense of local cultures. After 1985 Shakespeare was in fact dropped from the Kenyan secondary school syllabus, but, as a result of the intervention of President Danial arap Moi, who in a public address on 25 July 1989 paid tribute to the 'universal genius' of Shakespeare, *Romeo and Juliet* was restored as a set text for the 1992 national examination.

At the end of the 20th century, while Shakespeare still features in secondary education in East African countries, there is little or no evidence of any current research at tertiary level or in the field of Shakespeare studies in general. Although, as late as 1996, F. Abiola Irene wrote in *Research in African Literatures* that 'Shakespeare's privileged position in African letters has been ensured essentially through the commanding force of his unique genius', dearth of evidence of recent new publications or performances in East African countries suggests that Shakespeare's influence, although still present, may be on the wane. *MO*

Ecclestone, William (*c.*1591–after 1623), actor (King's Men 1610–11, Lady Elizabeth's Men 1611–13, King's Men 1614–23). Ecclestone is named in a number of King's Men actor lists (including the 1623 Folio) and took the part of Kastril in Jonson's *The Alchemist.* GE

economics. See MONEY.

Eden, Alexander. See IDEN, ALEXANDER.

Edgar, son of the Earl of Gloucester in *King Lear,* is forced to flee and assumes the disguise of a 'Bedlam beggar'. AB

editing. Over the centuries, Shakespeare's texts have been edited by a remarkably diverse series of distinguished figures—including a speaker of the House of Commons (Thomas *Hanmer), the librettist of Handel's *Messiah* (Charles Jennens), and the inventor of modern chess pieces (Howard Staunton)—each of whom brought a unique set of abilities to bear on the task. In his landmark edition of 1709, the renowned dramatist Nicholas *Rowe regularized the *act and scene divisions, prefaced each play with a *dramatis personae, and supplied necessary entrance and exit directions that had been left out of the folios. In his edition of 1725, the celebrated poet Alexander *Pope regularized distinctions between verse and prose. In 1733, Lewis *Theobald, a classical philologist, introduced the practice of citing parallel passages from Shakespeare's works and from those of his contemporaries. In 1747, William *Warburton, Bishop of Gloucester, was the first to distinguish quotations from dialogue in Shakespeare's text. In 1765, the great lexicographer Samuel *Johnson applied his expertise to the elucidation of obsolete or archaic terms and made critical notes a prominent feature of his edition. The Johnson and *Steevens 'variorum' of 1773 inaugurated a tradition of the *editio cum notis variorum,* 'edition with the notes of the various commentators', that was continued by Isaac *Reed (1785), James Boswell (1821), H. H. *Furness (1871–1913), and on into the present day in the New *Variorum Shakespeare editions. W. G. Clark and W. A. Wright's *Cambridge edition of 1863 was the first to number all the lines in the works. These line numbers, reproduced in the *Globe edition (1864) and ratified by the line references in the first complete concordance to Shakespeare (1894), became standard for the next century.

For hundreds of years, the text of each new edition of Shakespeare's works was based on the one immediately preceding it: F1 was reprinted in F2, which was reprinted in F3, which was reprinted in F4. Rowe's edition was based largely on F4; Pope then based his edition on Rowe's; Theobald based his on Pope's; Johnson, in turn, used Theobald. As a matter of course, changes introduced in an earlier edition, whether as minor as a spelling correction or as major as F3's addition of seven plays, were followed by the later. Edward *Capell (1768) was the first to break with tradition by returning to the early *quarto and *Folio texts. Edmond *Malone (1790) followed Capell's example, asserting that 'every reader must wish to peruse what Shakespeare wrote, supported at once by the authority of the authentic copies . . . rather than what the editor of the second folio, or Pope or Hanmer, or Warburton have arbitrarily substituted in its place'.

Editors have long wrestled with the question of how to present plays that survive in two early versions, especially *Hamlet* and *King Lear.* The traditional lack of consensus on this issue is made manifest by the simultaneous appearance, in the early 1840s, of Charles *Knight's edition, based on the Folio texts of these plays, and John Payne *Collier's edition, based on the quartos. Historically, editors have tended to conflate the quarto and Folio texts. More recently, however, they have increasingly opted for parallel text editions or, in the case of the *Oxford Shakespeare and the *New Cambridge Shakespeare, separate editions of each textual version.

Editors undertake their task because they believe that their knowledge and insight may enable them to construct more accurate texts of Shakespeare's plays than any of the producers of previous texts (scribes, printers, other editors) were able to do. It is generally assumed that editing is an activity of historical scholarship and that an editor's own preferences ought to be subordinate to historical accuracy, but this supremely subjective enterprise invariably produces editions that are marked (or marred) by the personal idiosyncrasies of their editors. Alexander Pope, who claimed to have edited Shakespeare with 'a religious abhorrence of all innovation', is a case in point. Pope's edition drew attention to 'shining passages' with commas in the margins, relegated 'suspected passages' to the bottom of the page (about 1,500 lines in all were degraded in this manner), and highlighted distinguished scenes with an asterisk. Pope silently emended expressions he found obsolete or obscure: 'In hugger-mugger' infamously becomes 'In private' (*Hamlet* 4.5.82). His expedient for tidying up Shakespeare's metre was to replace words in metrically defective or hypermetrical lines with longer or shorter synonyms: Hamlet's dying request to Horatio 'To tell my Story' is condensed in Pope's text to read 'To tell my tale' (5.2.301).

Some scholars view Pope's edition as simply an extreme example of what they perceive to be a tradition of editorial interference with and sophistication of Shakespeare's texts. These scholars have called for the 'unediting' of Shakespeare, encouraging students to ignore edited texts and to study the plays in photographic facsimiles of the early quartos and folios with their original confusions and corruptions unobscured. ER

de Grazia, Margreta, *Shakespeare Verbatim: The Reproduction of Authenticity and the 1790 Apparatus* (1991)

Tanselle, G. Thomas, 'The Varieties of Scholarly Editing', in D. C. Greetham (ed.), *Scholarly Editing* (1995)

Werstine, Paul, 'Shakespeare', in D. C. Greetham (ed.), *Scholarly Editing* (1995)

Edmond, the Earl of Gloucester's son by his mistress, vows to supplant his older half-brother Edgar in *The Tragedy of King Lear* (spelled 'Edmund' in *The History of King Lear*). AB

Edmund. See EDMOND.

Edmund Ironside, anonymous *manuscript play, written *c.*1585–95, currently in the holdings of the *British Library (Egerton MS 1994). E. B. Everitt first advanced the hypothesis of Shakespeare's authorship in 1954. Eric Sams attempted to substantiate Everitt's theory in 1985, but failed to sway the predominant perception of the play as fundamentally un-Shakespearian.

This charming history play, redolent of the old moralities, focuses on the stark opposition between Edmund, the warlike English King, and Canute, the opportunistic Danish invader, and culminates in the slightly anticlimactic reconciliation anticipated by the play's subtitle, 'A True Chronicle History called *War hath made all friends*'. SM

education. Elementary education in Shakespeare's time was often, especially in country areas, provided informally by clergymen, itinerant teachers, and others who would attempt to instil the rudiments of grammar and arithmetic into their pupils. Shakespeare's father, brought up in a small country village, seems never to have learnt to write, though he became a successful businessman; he signed legal documents with his mark—a cross, or a pair of glover's compasses. His wife also signed with a mark, as did Shakespeare's daughter Judith, brought up in Stratford; Susanna, however, signed her name, at least in her later years. Inability to write did not necessarily imply inability to read, and intelligent people could be illiterate.

At a more formal level, children between the ages of around 5 and 7 might attend petty schools, run sometimes by women as well as by men, often untrained, though sometimes by university graduates down on their luck. Pupils were taught to read and pronounce English, to write, and to do simple arithmetic. The most basic aim was to fit them to take part in church services, and religion played a major part in education at all levels. Indeed, compulsory attendance at church, where congregations heard readings from the *Bible, the Prayer Book, and the Homilies, as well as sermons, was in itself an educational process. Shakespeare puts biblical allusions into the mouths even of his humblest characters (though Mistress Quickly, describing Falstaff's death, muddles the biblical Abraham with the mythological Arthur: *Henry V* 2.3.8–9).

The initial instrument of instruction in the petty school was a hornbook—a sheet of paper inscribed with the letters of the alphabet, a short prayer, and sometimes combinations of vowels and consonants, and then covered with a layer of translucent horn and mounted in a wooden frame with a handle. So in *Love's Labour's Lost* we learn that the pedantic Holofernes 'teaches boys the hornbook' (5.1.45) The child would progress to learn a set of prayers and the Christian catechism, and to write by imitating models in a printed copybook. Some pupils would get no further, going off to help on the farm or in the family trade or business. Others might go for a while to a secondary school to receive further instruction in reading, writing, and arithmetic, and then be sent for training in crafts or trades, often as apprentices to a master in whose household they would live. This is doubtless how John Shakespeare became a glover. The normal period of apprenticeship—available to girls as well as boys—was seven years. Shakespeare seems to portray the products of such training in the 'mechanicals', or craftsmen, in *A Midsummer Night's Dream*, who are able to read their scripts, even though Snug is 'slow of study' (1.2.63).

Boys of well-off parents, and those with talent enough to be awarded scholarships, might proceed from petty school to one of England's many *grammar schools, which ranged greatly in size, wealth, and organization. Eton and Winchester were already famous, and in London St Paul's and Westminster were richly endowed. A few schools admitted girls in the lower forms, but higher education for girls was most commonly acquired through private tuition. The Stratford grammar school dates back to the 15th century, and by a charter of 1553 became the King's New School of Stratford-upon-Avon. Its lists of pupils during the Shakespearian period no longer exist. It was modest in size, with perhaps 40 pupils taught by one master, assisted by an usher, in the room above the guildhall, both of which survive and are still used by the school. Like all grammar schools, it offered a humanist education centred on the classics, especially Latin literature and rhetoric—Greek was taught mainly in the larger schools. Boys could be admitted at the age of 7 provided they could read. They had an arduous regime, 'creeping like snail | Unwillingly to school' (*As You Like It* 2.7.145–6) with their satchels around 6.00 a.m. and continuing their studies till the late afternoon, with few holidays. Prescribed textbooks in Shakespeare's time and for centuries afterwards were the *Short Introduction of Grammar* and the *Brevissima institutio*, the latter written in Latin (but with an index using English), compiled and adapted from texts by William Lily (?1468–1523), first highmaster of St Paul's School in London. In *The Merry Wives of Windsor* 4.1 Shakespeare shows a pupil, suggestively named William, being put through his paces in Latin grammar, not very successfully, on a 'playing day' for his mother's benefit. The scene, irrelevant to the plot, is something of an indulgence, and Shakespeare is clearly drawing on his own boyhood experience. Here and elsewhere he uses phrases taken directly from Lily's grammar books; in *Titus Andronicus*, for example, he causes Demetrius to quote lines written by Horace, at which Chiron, admitting that his knowledge is second-hand, responds 'O, 'tis a verse in Horace, I know it well. | I read it in the grammar long ago' (4.2.20–24).

While learning the rudiments of Latin grammar pupils would also read elementary collections of maxims such as the *Sententiae pueriles* (1542) of Leonhard Culmann, made up of short sentences from Latin authors, and a Latin version of Aesop's *Fables*. As they progressed in learning they might go on to read—and perhaps even to act—plays by Terence and Plautus, whose *Menaechmi* and *Amphitruo* are prime sources for *The Comedy of Errors*. They would spend much time memorizing Latin writings, studying their grammatical construction, translating extracts from Latin into English and back again into Latin, and imitating classical authors. A standard work of instruction was Erasmus' *De duplici rerum ac verborum copia* (On Copiousness in Style and Subject Matter), which included among its models of composition a demonstration of some 150 ways of saying 'Thank you for your letter.' Also popular in schools were the eclogues of Battista Spagnuoli (1447–1513), known as Mantuan, whom Holofernes, in *Love's Labour's Lost*, quotes and speaks of: ' "*Facile precor gelida quando pecas omnia sub umbra ruminat*", and so forth. Ah, good old Mantuan!' (4.2.92–3) Writings such as these would have been mastered, at least by the more talented pupils, by the age of 12. The level of education acquired early in life by ordinary Stratford townspeople may be gauged from a surviving letter in Latin written to Richard *Quiney, who was in London at the time, by his son around his eleventh birthday (printed in E. I. Fripp, *Shakespeare: Man and Artist*, 1938). The boy asks for books of blank paper for himself and his brother (probably Thomas, who was to become Shakespeare's son-in-law), and expresses gratitude that his father has brought him up in the studies of sacred learning ('*educasti me in sacrae doctrinae studiis usque ad hunc diem*'). This may be in the nature of a boy's exercise, but Abraham *Sturley wrote to Quiney in Latin as a matter of course, and Thomas *Greene scribbled Latin verses on his wife's pregnancy in the midst of his notes on conversations with Shakespeare and others. If any letters written by Shakespeare ever turn up, they too could be in Latin.

In the upper forms, boys were required to speak in Latin at all times. Here they would study major Latin authors, such as Virgil, Sallust, Caesar, and Horace. *Ovid clearly made a great impression on Shakespeare, who knew the *Metamorphoses* in the original Latin as well as in Arthur Golding's English translation. He brings the book on stage in the highly Ovidian *Titus Andronicus* (4.1.42) and, by implication, in *Cymbeline* (2.2), and quotes a couplet from Ovid's *Amores* (an erotic volume to which his teachers are unlikely to have introduced him) on the title page of *Venus and Adonis*. In *The Taming of the Shrew* Lucentio, impersonating a tutor, woos Bianca under the pretext of teaching her a passage from the *Heroides*.

For Shakespeare, as an incipient dramatist, the rhetoricians were no less important than the poets. The key texts here were the pseudo-Ciceronian *Ad Herennium*, Cicero's *Topics*, and the *Institutio oratoriae* of Quintilian. Pupils were expected to compose their own elaborate orations—an exercise that must have been invaluable to the future author of, for example, *Henry V* and *Julius Caesar*.

Needless to say, education did not stop with departure from the grammar school. Some grammar-school boys would go into apprenticeship. Others would go to university, which offered training in, for instance, theology, medicine, and law. Shakespeare, like Ben *Jonson (who nevertheless prided himself on his learning), was not among them, but, for instance, his exact contemporary Christopher *Marlowe, after attending the King's School in Canterbury, proceeded on a scholarship at the age of 16 to Corpus Christi College, Cambridge. Plays were professionally performed in both Oxford and Cambridge—the first quarto of *Hamlet*, for example, declares itself to have been 'divers times acted . . . in the two Universities of Cambridge and Oxford', and an Oxford don, Henry Jackson, records seeing *Othello* in Oxford in 1610—but not, it would seem, in the colleges themselves. Grammar-school boys might also go, either directly or after university, to one of the eight Inns of Chancery or the four Inns of Court, where barristers were trained and worked. Justice Shallow's 'cousin William', still undergoing an expensive education at Oxford, is soon to proceed 'to the Inns o' Court'; Shallow himself had been trained at Clement's Inn, where he had led a life that has, according to Falstaff, grown more raffish in recollection than it was in actuality (*2 Henry IV* 3.2). *The Comedy of Errors* was acted at, and possibly commissioned for, Gray's Inn in 1594, and *Twelfth Night* had a special performance at the Middle Temple in 1602.

In Shakespeare's time as in ours, education could be acquired by personal effort as well as by formal instruction. After leaving school, Shakespeare clearly went on reading for the rest of his life. His extensive knowledge of English literature—*Gower, *Chaucer, *Arthur, *Brooke, *Sidney, *Spenser, *Greene, *Lodge, *Nashe, *Daniel, and so on—of historical writings by *Foxe and *Stow, of the chronicles of *Hall and *Holinshed and the *Mirror for Magistrates*, and of translations of *Homer, Ovid, *Plutarch, *Livy, *Boccaccio, Tasso, *Ariosto, *Montaigne, and other writers must have been acquired as it were privately, and so probably was the knowledge of French and Italian that enabled him to compose, for instance, the French episodes of *Henry V* and to read *Cinthio for *Othello*. And of course he was deeply familiar, through performance as well as reading, with the works of contemporary dramatists such as Lyly, Marlowe, Jonson, and many others (including Anon.).

The training that Shakespeare received at grammar school means that, in spite of Jonson's gibe at his 'small Latin and less Greek', he had at least as good a knowledge of Latin language and literature as a modern graduate in the classics—entirely adequate, as T. W. Baldwin has amply demonstrated, to account for the high proportion of classical, biblical, and other learned allusions in his writings. It pervasively informs his verse and prose style. And the high standard of education available to a large section of the population, in the provinces as well as in London, explains how plays as literate as those of Shakespeare and his contemporaries could achieve success in the popular theatres of his time. (See also SCHOOLS, SHAKESPEARE IN.)

SW

Baldwin, T. W., *Shakespere's Petty School* (1943)
Baldwin, T. W., *William Shakspere's Small Latine and Lesse Greeke* (2 vols., 1944)
Cressy, D., *Literacy and the Social Order: Writing and Reading in Tudor and Stuart England* (1980)

Edward III. Entered in the Stationers' Register in 1595 and published anonymously the following year, *The Reign of King Edward the Third* ('as it hath been sundry times played about the city of London') is the likeliest of the *apocrypha to have been written by Shakespeare. Although there is no external evidence linking Shakespeare's name with the play before a wholly unreliable list of plays published in 1656 (which also credits Shakespeare with writing Marlowe's *Edward II*), Edward *Capell attributed it to Shakespeare on internal evidence alone in 1760, and other commentators who have since thought that Shakespeare must have written at least parts of this attractive chronicle play have included *Tennyson, A. W. Ward, and Kenneth *Muir.

The play depicts incidents from Edward III's wars against King David of Scotland and, assisted by his son the Black Prince, against the French: in the first half of the play Edward rescues the married Countess of Salisbury from a Scots siege and subsequently courts her at length and in vain, and in the second he proves his recovery from this unvirtuous interlude by campaigning successfully in France, his victory made the more joyous by his reunion with the Black Prince, thought to have been killed. The scenes which have been most frequently credited to Shakespeare are those in which Edward woos the Countess (1.4–2.2), first commissioning Lodowick to compose a poem to her (and then preventing Lodowick from writing more than four lines of it by waxing lyrical about her himself), and is finally persuaded to renounce his adulterous suit when the Countess feigns to request Edward to kill their respective spouses and then undertakes to kill herself first. However, studies of the play since 1960—which have established, for example, that the play is mainly based on a single source, Lord Berners's translation of *The Chronicles of Froissart* (1523), rather than having taken the Countess's scenes independently from another book better known to Shakespeare, William *Painter's *Palace of Pleasure*—have generally reached the conclusion that it is the work of a single author.

The arguments that the play is all by Shakespeare rather than all by another writer (such as George Peele, the next candidate for its authorship) are complicated by uncertainties as to its date of composition, which could have been at any time between 1588 and 1595. The existence of a German play on the same subject, which may have been prompted by an Edward III play performed by English actors in *Poland in 1591, has encouraged scholars who would wish to place the play early in the Shakespeare canon, but the play's references to Lucrece and to Hero and Leander, its metre, the generally agreed superiority of the King–Countess material to the comparable but less mature scenes between Edward IV and Lady Elizabeth Gray in *Richard Duke of York* (*3 Henry VI*) and, especially, the presence of a line which also occurs in Sonnet 94 ('Lilies that fester smell far worse than weeds') suggest that if Shakespeare did write the play it must have been closer to 1594. What is certain is that Shakespeare at least knew the play—from which, if he did not write it, he derived a unique historical error about David of Scotland in *Henry V* (1.2.160–2, 293–5)—and that more and more scholars are now prepared to treat it as part of the Shakespeare canon.

MD

The Raigne of King Edward the Third (ed. Fred Lapides, 1980)
King Edward III, ed. Giorgio Melchiori in the New Cambridge Shakespeare series (1998)
Muir, Kenneth, *Shakespeare as a Collaborator* (London, 1960)
Proudfoot, G. R., '*The Reign of King Edward III* (1595) and Shakespeare', British Academy Shakespeare Lecture (1985)

Edward IV. See EDWARD, EARL OF MARCH.

Edward IV, a history play in two parts, possibly written collaboratively by *Heywood in the late 1590s. It was advertised as Shakespeare's in a bookseller's catalogue in 1654. Despite verbal parallels with *Measure for Measure*, the Shakespearian ascription is unjustified. *SM*

Edward V. See EDWARD, PRINCE.

Edward, Earl of March (1442–83). Son of Richard Duke of York, he appears briefly with his father in *The First Part of the Contention* (*2 Henry VI*) 5.1. In *Richard Duke of York* (*3 Henry VI*) he boasts of his victory over Buckingham in battle, and attempts to persuade his father to crown himself (1.1). After his father's death ('No longer Earl of March, but Duke of York' 2.1.192) he defeats the Lancastrians at Towton to become Edward IV (2.6) and marries Lady Gray (3.2). In *Richard III* his brother Richard tells him of his other brother Clarence's murder (2.1) and his own death is reported 2.3.3. *AB*

Edward, Prince. (1) The only son of Henry VI, Prince Edward (1453–71) protests against being disinherited, *Richard Duke of York* (*3 Henry VI*) 1.1; is betrothed to Warwick's daughter Anne Neville, 3.3, whom he marries; but is stabbed by Edward IV and his brothers at Tewkesbury, 5.5; and appears as a ghost to Richard III at *Bosworth (*Richard III* 5.5). **(2)** He appears as a baby in the last scene of *Richard Duke of York*. With his younger brother (also called Richard, Duke of York (1472–83)) he is taken to the Tower of London (*Richard III* 3.1) and murdered (described 4.3). Born 1470 and briefly made Edward V before his death in 1483, he was the son of Edward IV and grandson of Richard, Duke of York, of the *Henry VI* plays. *AB*

Edwards, Richard (1524–66), poet, playwright, and composer. He wrote the text and probably the music of 'When griping griefs the heart doth wound'; the opening is sung by Peter, in *Romeo and Juliet* 4.4.152. *JB*

Egeon, father of the Antipholus twins in *The Comedy of Errors*, is called Moschus in *Plautus' *Menaechmi*. *AB*

Egeus, Hermia's father, requires her to marry Demetrius in *A Midsummer Night's Dream*. *AB*

Eglamour, Sir. He helps Silvia to escape from *Milan in *The Two Gentlemen of Verona*. *AB*

Egyptian. He brings a message from Cleopatra to Caesar, *Antony and Cleopatra* 5.1. *AB*

Elbow, a 'simple constable' in *Measure for Measure*, arrests Pompey twice (2.1 and 3.1). *AB*

Eld, George. See PRINTING AND PUBLISHING.

Eleanor (Elinor), Queen (*c.*1122–1204). Mother of King John, she supports his claim to the throne against Arthur. *AB*

Elector Palatine. See Bohemia and the former Czechoslovakia; Elizabeth of Bohemia.

electronic media. Although we have come a long way from the early days of the Oxford Text Archive, when electronic texts of Shakespeare's plays were patchily available in variously edited and sporadically corrected forms, we are still in the pioneering period of the digital bard. In terms of CD-ROM text resources, there are two major items: Chadwyck-Healey's *Editions and Adaptations of Shakespeare* and *The Arden Shakespeare* CD-ROM, 'Texts and Sources for Shakespeare Studies'. Each offers access to variously mediated Q and F texts, and modernized texts: the *Arden* includes the complete *Arden 2* series, and will eventually be updated with *Arden 3* (a reminder of the instant obsolescence of all things digital). *Editions and Adaptations* includes a selection of editions (to 1836) and a range of adaptations, sequels, and burlesques; the *Arden* offers electronic versions of several standard works of reference: Bullough's *Narrative and Dramatic Sources*; Abbott's *A Shakespearian Grammar*; Onions's *A Shakespeare Glossary*; and Partridge's *Shakespeare's Bawdy*.

The world of Shakespeare editorship does not rush headlong to embrace new resources, but these CD-ROMs, along with the Chadwyck-Healey drama database, the *OED* on CD-ROM, and Ian Lancashire's *Early Modern English Dictionaries Database* (http://www.chass.utoronto.ca/english/emed/emedd.html) will surely soon be points of first resort for all editors.

Shakespeare has a massive, and growing, presence on the web. The best meta-site, providing reviews of, and links to, Shakespeare sites is *Mr William Shakespeare and the Internet* (http://daphne.palomar.edu/shakespeare/). Those with a good search engine and lots of time on their hands will be able to find many other sites which are simply bonkers: take a reality check on *The Shakespeare Authorship Web Page*, 'dedicated to the proposition that Shakespeare wrote Shakespeare' (http://www.clark.net/pub/tross/ws/will.html). 'Shaksper' is a moderated, members-only discussion list, which has some of the most eminent Shakespearians in the world as regular posters, as well as newly enthused school students (email editor@ws.bowiestate.edu to join). *JH*

Elgar, Sir Edward (1857–1934), English composer. Elgar's tone poem *Falstaff*, Op. 68, is the most vivid programme music he ever wrote, portraying the Falstaff revealed in the history plays rather than the character in *The Merry Wives*. Although there are sketches from 1902–3 *Falstaff* was only completed in 1913. *IBC*

Elinor. See Eleanor, Queen.

Eliot, Thomas Stearns (1888–1965), born American, naturalized British, poet, critic, and playwright. The contact and confrontation between the greatest 20th-century poet in English and his Elizabethan predecessor is continuous and pervasive. In his prose and poetry Eliot refers to or quotes from at least 20 of Shakespeare's works, although his essay on *Hamlet* (1919) raises more problems than it solves with its formulation of the need for an 'objective correlative' in art. The essay *Tradition and the Individual Talent* (1917) testifies to the debt all modern poets owe to their European predecessors; a debt redeemed in his poem of an old man's lost power to love and hope of spiritual rebirth, *Gerontion* (1919), which borrows both in subject matter and verbally from Tourneur, Chapman, Middleton, Jonson, and Shakespeare, creating a *pasticcio* technique and effect. This is carried to maturity in his major poem of death and rebirth, *The Waste Land* (1922), which, among many myths and legends, draws inspiration from *The Tempest*. *Marina* (1930) derives another symbol of rebirth from Pericles' reunion with his daughter. The uncompleted *Coriolan* (1931, 1932), partly inspired by *Coriolanus*, shows a counterfeit saviour, arrogantly betraying those who betray him. Eliot's work, including his plays, stands on three literary pillars—the Greeks, Dante, and Shakespeare—although his Christian inspiration eventually transcends all three. *TM*

elision, the suppression of a vowel sound, usually at the end of a word when the next word begins with a vowel: 'Th' expense of spirit ...' (Sonnet 129). *CB*

Elizabeth I (1532–1603), Queen of England (reigned 1558–1603). Her fondness for theatre was notable throughout her reign, and though she was a far less generous patron of drama than her successors *James I and *Charles I, the company playing under her name, the Queen's Men, held a monopoly on performances at court and in the city from 1583 to 1591. The major theatrical patrons during her reign, however, were court officials and privy counsellors—the Earl of Leicester, Lord Strange, Lord Howard the Lord Admiral, Lord Hunsdon the Lord Chamberlain, the Earl of Pembroke. Theatre was often, for these functionaries, a valuable means of capturing and pleasing the royal attention. From 1594, the companies that played at court were, overwhelmingly, the Lord Chamberlain's Men of Shakespeare and *Burbage, and the Lord Admiral's Men of *Henslowe and Edward *Alleyn. What plays they presented are rarely recorded. Though she must have seen most of the Shakespeare plays up to 1603, we know from the court records only that in 1598 she saw *Love's Labour's Lost*. The title page of the first quarto of *The Merry Wives of Windsor* (1602) records that this play too was performed before her, though the story that credits her with commissioning Shakespeare to write it is apocryphal, first appearing in 1702 (her purported desire to see Falstaff in love is added to the story in 1709). Unlike Peele in *The Arraignment of Paris* and *Jonson in *Every Man out of his Humour*, Shakespeare stopped short of writing roles for the Queen into any of his scripts. If her presence in the audience is implied in Oberon's apostrophe to the 'fair virgin thronèd by the west' (*A Midsummer Night's Dream* 2.1.158), the occasion of the performance that included her has not been identified—the play would have been an appropriate entertainment for an aristocratic wedding at which the Queen was a guest, but no wedding seems to fit the bill. *Richard II* clearly was felt to have a dangerous relevance to her political situation in her last years, and the three quartos published in her lifetime appeared without the deposition scene. The relevance was tragically underlined by the Earl of *Essex, who underwrote a performance of the old play as a prelude to his rebellion in 1601. After his execution Elizabeth is reported to have said, 'I am Richard the Second, know ye not that?' The only play that specifically includes her is Shakespeare's last surviving play *All Is True* (*Henry VIII*), in which her birth is initially reported to King Henry as that of 'a lovely boy', the male heir he craves, and only subsequently as 'a girl | Promises boys hereafter'—the King is not pleased, and undertips the messenger. The promised males, James and his progeny, are, in the extraordinary eulogy of Elizabeth that concludes the play, born phoenix-like from her ashes. Francis Osborne, remembering her in 1658, near the end of his life, recalls that she was 'thought something too theatrical for a virgin prince'. *SO*

Frye, Susan, *Elizabeth I* (1993)
Johnson, Paul, *Elizabeth I* (1974)
Osborne, Francis, *Historical Memoires on the Reigns of Queen Elizabeth and King James* (1658)

Elizabeth, Princess. The future *Elizabeth I appears as a baby at her christening, *All Is True* (*Henry VIII*) 5.4. *AB*

Elizabeth, Queen. See Gray, Lady.

Elizabeth of Bohemia (1596–1662), daughter of James I and Anne of Denmark. The festivities leading to her wedding in 1613 to Frederick, the Elector Palatine (later, briefly, King of Bohemia), included 20 plays in three months, eight of which were by Shakespeare. Among these were *The Tempest* and *The Winter's Tale*, the surviving texts of which were long claimed to

have been revisions reflecting the marriage; but the betrothal masque in *The Tempest* is unlikely to have been an addition, and as for the Bohemian setting of *The Winter's Tale*, Prince Frederick had no Bohemian connection whatever in 1613. Elizabeth's subsequent career reflects *King Lear* more than *The Tempest*: after her Protestant husband accepted the Bohemian throne and then lost it to Catholic invaders, James, fearing popular support for a militant reassertion of the claim, forbade her or her family ever to enter his realms. She lived thereafter in Holland, returning to England only in the last year of her life. Ironically, the present royal family descends from her. *SO*

Elizabethan Stage Society. See POEL, WILLIAM.

Elizabeth theory. One of the crowning glories of the *Authorship Controversy, the bizarre claim that Queen Elizabeth I really wrote the Shakespeare canon was made by George Elliott Sweet in *Shake-speare the Mystery* (1956). His claim rests on a peculiarly tortured reading of the Epilogue to *All Is True* (*Henry VIII*) and, obviously, requires all of the Jacobean plays to be redated, so that according to Sweet *The Tempest*, though it alludes to a shipwreck which took place in 1609, must have been written in 1582. *MD*

Schoenbaum, S., *Shakespeare's Lives* (1991)

Ellington, Duke (1899–1974), black American *jazz composer. His suite for jazz orchestra *Such Sweet Thunder* (1957) comprises twelve pieces drawing inspiration from nine different Shakespeare plays. It was dedicated to the Shakespearian Festival in Stratford, Ontario, for which he also composed incidental music for *Timon of Athens* (1963). *IBC*

Ellis-Fermor, Una (1894–1958), English academic, first general editor of the second *Arden Shakespeare, begun in 1951 as a revision of the 'old' Arden. She has written influentially on both tragedy (particularly *Timon of Athens*) and history (the idea of the statesman-king), but is perhaps best known for *Shakespeare the Dramatist* (1961). *TM*

Elliston, Robert William (1774–1831), English actor and manager, whose Hamlet, Romeo, Hotspur, and—later—Falstaff were admired, but who realized his greatest ambition when he took over Drury Lane, where he applied modern stage techniques to Shakespeare and engaged Edmund *Kean as lead, restoring *King Lear* to the stage in April 1820 (though in a version which still incorporated a good deal of Nahum *Tate's adaptation). *RF*

Murray, Christopher, *Robert William Elliston Manager* (1975)

Queen Elizabeth I bestriding her narrow kingdom like a Colossus in the Ditchley portrait, by Marcus Gheeraerts the younger, c.1592.

Elsinore, a seaport containing the fortress of Kronberg on the east coast of the Danish island of Zealand in the Sound. The castle is the scene of *Hamlet*. The 'cliff | That beetles o'er his base into the sea' described by Horatio 1.4.51–2 is imaginary (the coast is low). *AB*

Ely, Bishop of. (1) In *Richard III* he gives Richard strawberries, 3.4, but flees to join Richmond, 4.3.46. He is based on John Morton (*c*.1420–1500), who probably collaborated with Sir Thomas More in writing his *History of Richard III*, one of Shakespeare's sources. (2) He is one of those who encourage King Harry to make war on France, *Henry V* 1.2 (based on John Fordham (d. 1425)). (3) He appears at Katherine's trial, *All Is True* (*Henry VIII*) 2.4 (mute part). *AB*

Elyot, Sir Thomas (*c*.1490–1546), ambassador to Henry VIII and humanist scholar. Elyot's most famous work was *The Book of the Governor* (1531), an educational treatise which considered, among other issues, the dangers of hubris in authority, the importance of hierarchy, and the conflict between friendship and love. On these subjects Elyot may have influenced *Julius Caesar*, *Henry V* and *Troilus and Cressida*, and *The Two Gentlemen of Verona* respectively. *JKS*

Brooks, H. F., 'Shakespeare and *The Governour*', *Shakespeare Quarterly*, 14 (1963)

Ely Palace portrait, half-length, oil, dated 1603, inscribed AE. The portrait was discovered in 1845 and named after its 19th-century location when in the possession of the Bishop of Ely. The image was claimed to be an original for *Droeshout's engraving by M. H. Spielmann in 1906; it is now owned by the *Shakespeare Birthplace Trust in Stratford. *CT*

Elze, Karl (1821–89), German academic. His *Abhandlungen zu Shakespeare* was published in English as *Essays on Shakespeare* (1874); Schoenbaum describes passages on Shakespeare's doomed marriage to an older woman in his *Life of Shakespeare* (1876) as making Elze 'a Spengler of domestic life'. *Notes on Elizabethan Dramatists* dates from 1880–6. *TM*

emendation. Since the 18th century, editors have made a concerted effort to correct what they perceive to be errors in Shakespeare's texts through a process of emendation. Edward Capell defined an acceptable emendation as one that 'improves the Author, or contributes to his advancement in perfectness'. Lewis Theobald famously emended Mistress Quickly's description of the dying Falstaff in the Folio text of *Henry V*, 'for his nose was as sharp as a pen, and a Table of green fields', altering the final clause to read 'and a' babbled of green fields' (2.3.16–17). Edmond Malone distinguished between his own 'restoration' of readings from early authoritative texts and the mere conjecture practised by his predecessors who 'altered or amended as it was called, at pleasure'.

In the 20th century, the New Bibliographers championed the principle that emendation ought to be grounded in an understanding of how the corruption arose in the transmission of the text. John Dover Wilson, for instance, emended the opening line of Hamlet's first soliloquy in Q2 *Hamlet* from 'sallied flesh' to 'sullied flesh' based on an analysis of the *Sir Thomas More* manuscript which reveals that the letters 'a' and 'u' are often indistinguishable in Shakespeare's hand. If Q2 was set into type from Shakespeare's *foul papers, it would explain the 'sallied/sullied' error as well as other compositorial 'a : u' misreadings such as 'Gertrad' for 'Gertrude' and 'quietas' for 'quietus'. *ER*

Greg, W. W., 'Principles of Emendation in Shakespeare', *Proceedings of the British Academy*, 14 (1928)

Emerson, Ralph Waldo (1803–82), American poet and essayist. Shakespeare was foremost among the 'shades' to accompany Emerson for 40 years in his study at Concorde. He read contemporary criticism and the publications of the Shakespeare Society, remaining convinced that Shakespeare's truth was accessible through the text and not through secondary materials. In 'Shakspere; or, The Poet' in *Representative Men* (1850) Emerson the puritan regrets that Shakespeare's life is not more exemplary and his plays more edifying; nevertheless acknowledging the 'first poet of the world'. *TM*

Emilia. (1) *The Comedy of Errors*. See ABBESS. (2) The wife of *Iago and *Desdemona's companion in *Othello*, she unwittingly assists Iago in his plot. (3) A lady attending Hermione in *The Winter's Tale*, she announces the birth of Perdita, 2.2. (4) The sister of Hippolyta, she is beloved of both Palamon and Arcite in *The Two Noble Kinsmen*. *AB*

Emmanuel. See CLERK OF CHATHAM.

Empson, Sir William (1906–84), English academic, poet, and critic, referring extensively to Shakespeare in several studies of poetry and its language. Lines in his own poetry ('Slowly the poison the whole bloodstream fills, | The waste remains, the waste remains and kills') are widely regarded as possessing true Shakespearian power, but his continued critical importance derives from *Seven Types of Ambiguity* (1930, rev. 1947), *Some Versions of Pastoral* (1935), and *The Structure of Complex Words* (1961), in all of which (partly inspired by I. A. Richards) he relentlessly pursues the multiple meanings and larger resonance inherent in individual words of the text. His *Essays on Shakespeare* were collected in 1986. *TM*

Enchanted Isle, The*; *or, Raising the Wind upon the Most Approved Principles. See TEMPEST, THE; BURLESQUES.

enclosure, the practice of consolidating landholdings, originally scattered in strips through open fields, into compact areas, defined by hedges.

The medieval system of cultivation, by which all landholders were allocated strips in large open fields, to ensure fair distribution of good and bad land, had, by the late 15th century, come under pressure from those who saw that consolidation would be more profitable, especially when enclosed lands were given over to sheep-grazing. There was much opposition to enclosure from smaller owners and labourers whose livelihoods suffered at the expense of the larger and whose villages were sometimes depopulated. Warwickshire had witnessed enclosure riots in 1607 and the proposal in 1614 that enclosure should be applied to the common lands lying to the north-west of *Stratford was met with similar opposition from many, including the town council, whose clerk, Thomas *Greene, kept a diary of the proceedings. Shakespeare's land in *Welcombe was almost certainly part of the proposed scheme and as a leaseholder of the tithes he had an additional interest in so far as his income might be affected by change of land use. References to him in Greene's diary are unclear as to Shakespeare's stance on the proposal. Violence flared when the agents of William *Combe, the prime mover of the scheme, attempted preliminary work and the affair dragged on for several years, until the enclosure was abandoned, not occurring in Stratford, by consent and Act of Parliament, until the 1770s. In Edward *Bond's play *Bingo* (1973), based on the events of 1614–15, Shakespeare is presented as playing a prominent part. *MM*

end-stopped, punctuated at the end of a verse line or lines, the line ending at the close of a phrase, a clause or sentence: 'This blessed plot, this earth, this realm, this England, | This nurse . . .' (*Richard II* 2.1.50–1). *CB*

England's Helicon, a poetical miscellany published in 1600 under the auspices of John Bodenham (*c.*1558–1610), a wealthy literary patron. It includes verses by many of the best poets of the day, among them the lines from *Love's Labour's Lost* that had been printed in *The *Passionate Pilgrim* (1599). *SW*

England's Parnassus; or, The Choicest Flowers of our Modern Poets, an anthology published in 1600 and compiled by 'R.A.' (Robert Allott); it includes numerous extracts from Shakespeare's poems and plays, along with others mistakenly attributed to him. *SW*

English, Elizabethan. The language community into which Shakespeare was born was one in which the majority must have spoken the regional dialect of the West Midlands—a variety of English normally limited to the spoken word. The fact that it was so restricted was remarked on by John Hart, an early phonetician and spelling reformer, in 1569; he pointed out that books should not be printed 'in the manner of . . . Westerne speeches', although the *written* form was an acceptable means of communication between speakers of the same regional dialect, who might write 'according to their mother speech', and could also do so to a friend in London, who would be 'no more offended to see his writing so . . . than if he were present to hear him speak'. But if the citizens of Stratford-upon-Avon wished to converse with someone from another region, they might find it desirable to use what, by the later 16th century, had become a standard form of speech; as the critic George Puttenham remarked in 1589, the best kind of English was to be found at court, and in London and the surrounding shires up to 60 miles (100 km) around and no further. Not everyone, of course, had the opportunity of hearing London English spoken; as John Hart remarked, not everyone could have 'conference' with 'the lively voice', i.e. of Londoners.

Such unfortunates included those who had never attended a performance of a play by travelling actors, who, being London based, would have spoken Standard English. Even if Shakespeare spoke with a Warwickshire accent, he would at least have had the opportunity to hear Standard English at one of the many performances given in Stratford by itinerant companies when he was a youth; and when he came to London and began writing, he seems to have lost any trace of his regional dialect. In spite of many attempts to trace Warwickshire vocabulary, grammar, and pronunciation in his writings, no one has yet proved beyond doubt that more than a few of these regionalisms appear in his works. It is true that he depicted Edgar, disguised as a countryman in *The Tragedy of King Lear* (4.5.234–44), adopting a regional *dialect, but the only variant forms in his speech were those of the standard 'stage' dialect of the sort generally adopted by playwrights at the time, and representing a conventional form of southern English. It is somewhat strange that Shakespeare did not, in fact, exploit his Warwickshire accent, since he was happy enough to represent, in phonetic spelling, the non-standard English accents of French and Welsh speakers, and the national dialects of Scotland and Ireland.

In considering Shakespeare's employment of the language of his time the modern reader needs to know which of the many usages different from current English represent the Elizabethan norm, and in what respects they are manipulated by Shakespeare for his own dramatic purposes; and as a representative of the norm, the most appropriate material is the language of the scenes where Shakespeare is depicting everyday conversation in domestic or tavern settings, such as those which occur in the Falstaff plays. Since such scenes have won critical acclaim from Samuel *Johnson onwards for their linguistic realism (although, of course, they do not represent genuine spontaneous speech but Shakespeare's imitation of it), they provide reasonably acceptable data, which will be cited below, for the analysis of the grammar and vocabulary of Elizabethan English. They do not, however, provide accurate evidence of Elizabethan *pronunciation, since the spelling represents the sounds of 15th- and early 16th-century English, which had often changed radically by Shakespeare's time. So, for example, spellings such as *mine* and *make* in 15th-century English seem to depict simple vowels; by 1550 such vowels had changed into diphthongs through the operation of a phonetic process in Early Modern English (*c.*1400–1700) known as the Great Vowel Shift; the sound had changed but the original spelling remained. The phonetic values of such spellings are much debated but all that the non-specialist requires is the ability to recognize Elizabethan puns—much exploited by Shakespeare—where they no longer exist at the present day.

In one respect the Elizabethan writer enjoyed an unusual advantage in sometimes having a choice between different grammatical forms, one continuing the usage of the Middle Ages, and the other being a new form introduced in the 16th century and on the way to establishing itself as the sole survivor. Shakespeare could therefore choose the older or the newer form for his own dramatic purposes, the older being associated with formal usage, the newer with a more colloquial style. He also enjoyed comparable alternatives in vocabulary; the enormous influx of loan words (especially from the classics) which occurred in the 16th century offered the writer a choice between the native English term and a modern loan, with different dramatic effects.

The most important grammatical alternatives available to speakers of Elizabethan English consisted in the introduction of the unstressed auxiliary verb *do* in the basic sentence types of statements, questions, commands, and exclamations. In statements *do* was introduced in the early 16th century, for reasons which are uncertain, giving forms like *I do bring good news*, where unstressed *do* has no obvious function. No doubt the innovation proved popular with poets because it could be employed for metrical purposes, to provide unstressed syllables as in *Sweet birds do sing*; and in this function unstressed *do* survived, in verse, at least until the late 19th century. It was probably used by Shakespeare to characterize rhetorical speech like Pistol's; as a stressed auxiliary *do* has survived to denote emphasis on the associated verb. *Do* was also introduced into question sentences; the older form of question involved the inversion of subject and verb, as in *Know'st thou Gower?* while the newer form is exemplified in *Dost thou understand . . . English?* For command sentences the Elizabethan norm is without *do* as in *Sweet sir, sit*, and when *do* is introduced as in *Do thou stand for me*, it seems not to have any special function. *Do* also appears in exclamatory sentences such as *What a brawling dost thou keep!*. *Do* as an auxiliary appeared in negative sentences—the early 16th century offering alternatives such as *By my troth I care not* and the newer form *You do not know me*. A comparable choice occurs in questions like *Went you not to her yesterday?*, a variant on the newer form *Do I not bate?*, and in commands such as *Persuade me not* as opposed to *Do not betray me sir*. Several explanations have been advanced for the introduction of auxiliary *do*; one of the most compelling is the argument that since most verbs are associated with auxiliaries such as *can, may, will*, and *shall* it is reasonable to suppose that a gap came to be felt between subject and verb where no auxiliary was present, and that *do* developed by analogy to fill that gap.

The introduction of auxiliary *do* into a sentence was not the only influence on its structure; another was the effect on word order exerted by the position of adverbs and phrasal groups. If they were placed at the beginning of a sentence, it was normal in Elizabethan English to invert the following subject and verb, a change still preserved when *nor, seldom, never, rarely*, and *hardly* are in initial position, but otherwise found only in literary style, e.g. in *Down came the rain*. Differences between Elizabethan and modern English in the individual verb include the possibility in the 16th century of using a single tense form to denote both progressive and single actions; e.g. when Polonius asks Hamlet 'What do you read, my lord?' (*Hamlet* 2.2.192–3), where modern English would require the progressive tense 'What are you reading?' These 'progressive' forms began to develop in the late Middle Ages, and even by Shakespeare's time they were sill fairly unusual, being limited chiefly to verbs of frequent occurrence such as *come* and *go*. Neither of these alternatives offered the dramatist a useful choice; he could, however, exploit another pair of alternatives, i.e. the form of the third person singular of the verb (present tense). The older form was inflected in *-eth* (e.g. *singeth*) and the newer form in *-s*. The choice allowed the dramatist an extra unstressed syllable if he needed it for metrical purposes. In a few cases Elizabethan English offers alternative forms for the past participle, as in *I have wrote/written*; other grammatical differences between Elizabethan and modern English which the dramatist has at his disposal include the availability, for the purposes of emphasis, of double negation and double comparison in addition to the normal forms.

On the margins of grammar and vocabulary are certain differences between Elizabethan and current English the significance of which may not always be realized by the modern reader. Most important is the choice between *thou* and *you* when a single person is being addressed. Originally there was a simple distinction of number between these two pronouns but by the 16th century it appears that *you* (or *ye*) had come to be the norm when one person was being addressed while *thou* implied some emotional connotation, usually affection or contempt, depending on the context. There has been much discussion of the ways in which Shakespeare exploits this choice, which is, of course, no longer available except in some regional dialects. The original plural form was *ye*, now found only in religious use, and replaced by *you* which is the norm for Shakespeare. Changes have also taken place in some relative pronouns; Shakespeare could use *who* for non-human, *which* for human antecedents, while *its*, replacing *his, of it*, and *thereof*, was an innovation in his lifetime, and first recorded in 1598.

The linguistic choices described above were available to all Elizabethan dramatists, and Shakespeare merely selected those most useful for his purposes. What is more obviously Shakespearian is his lexical creativity; although other writers invented neologisms, none did so in such profusion and with such dramatic power and relevance. Some of these neologisms, such as *distrustful, reinforcement*, and *exposure*, are first recorded in his works although they are not necessarily of his invention; others are likely to be Shakespeare's own since they have some special function, e.g. to comply with the demands of metre; this must be the case with *vasty* for *vast, plumpy* for *plump*, and *enguard* for *guard*, where the affix provides an unstressed syllable. Alternatively, Shakespeare may have wished on occasion to reduce the number of unstressed syllables, e.g. by replacing *accusation* by *accuse*, and *secret and false* by *secret-false*. Another reason for the introduction of neologisms was the need to place stress in the correct position, e.g. Shakespeare's introduction of a new verb in 'The flame . . . would under-peep her lids'.

More subtle are neologisms created by Shakespeare for rhetorical reasons, such as antithesis as in 'Pay her the debt you owe her, and *unpay* the villainy you have done with her' and in 'Fathered ['possessing a father'] he is and yet he's fatherless'. Another rhetorical figure played a major part in Shakespearian drama, i.e. the pun, as in 'What a plague mean ye to colt me thus? Thou liest: thou art not colted, thou art uncolted' (colt='deceive' and 'possessing a colt'), 'uncolted' being a neologism for the sake of a pun.

The most powerful neologisms are to be found in compound words which allow Shakespeare to compress many meanings into a small space. Several such compounds are terms of contempt, e.g. *Lackbeard, Patchbreech, Tallow-face, Martext*, and *Tearsheet*—nearly all imperative compounds of a highly colloquial nature, based on a French pattern. Other neologisms are adjectives characterizing the bombastic or ornate speech of courtiers like Armado, such as *black-oppressing*, and *curious-knotted*, or occurring in genuine poetic usage such as *temple-haunting* martlet, *sky-aspiring* thoughts, *lazy-pacing* clouds, *fen-sucked* fogs, and *russet-pated* choughs.

But the dramatic energy which particularly characterizes Shakespeare's mature style owes more to his new verbs, whether based on derivation by affixes, by compounding, or by 'functional conversion', where one part of speech is used as another, e.g. noun as verb. Among the many instances of neologisms based on existing words to which affixes have been added to form new verbs are *unsphere* and *disedge*. Among the many compounds illustrative of functional conversion are *out-Herod, out-night*, and *out-Duke*, while the most powerful effects are created when single nouns are converted to verbs, e.g. 'to lip a wanton', 'still *virginalling* upon his palm' ('playing on his hand as though it were the virginals'), and are used metaphorically. *VS*

Hope, J., 'Shakespeare's "Natiue English" ', in D. S. Kastan (ed.), *A Companion to Shakespeare* (1999)

Salmon, v., and Burness, E. (eds.), *A Reader in the Language of Shakespearean Drama* (1987)

English comedians. See GERMANY; POLAND.

English Shakespeare Company. Founded in 1986 by Michael *Pennington and Michael *Bogdanov with the intent of reaching areas normally missed by English touring companies, the ESC began with a characteristically bold, imaginative, and politicized production of Shakespeare's two historical tetralogies in a 21-hour marathon. Committed to education, its schools troupe sustained the company after the Arts Council cut its funding in 1994, causing the primary troupe to disband and Pennington to leave in disgust. In 1997, the troupe re-established itself when entrepreneur Karl Watkin funded the company's move into the Tyne Theatre and Opera House in Newcastle. *BR*

English Stage Company. Founded by George *Devine in 1956 at the Royal Court theatre in

London, the company remains committed to staging vital new writing in English and significant foreign plays. Its occasional Shakespeare productions, fitting house style and artistic policy, have included a Brechtian *Macbeth* and a bleakly unredemptive *King Lear*. The Court has had a powerful influence on Shakespearian production as many of its directors, actors, and designers have gone on to the National and Royal Shakespeare companies. Two plays by the Marxist Edward *Bond, *Lear* and *Bingo*, challenged conventional assumptions about Shakespeare. *MJ*

enjambment, the unpunctuated running over of the syntax and sense of one verse line into the next. *CB*

Enobarbus, Domitius. Antony's friend, he deserts him for Caesar, *Antony and Cleopatra* 3.13, is stricken with remorse, 4.6, and dies, 4.10 (loosely based on Cn. Domitius Ahenobarbus, consul in 32 BC). *AB*

entrances and exits. The most common stage directions in Shakespeare's texts, entrances and exits are usually printed in italic, set apart from the text of the dialogue, and couched in Latin terms such as *exit*, *exeunt*, *manet*, *manent*, *solus*, and *omnes*. Entrance directions generally name the characters entering, but may also specify props, costumes, blocking, and movement as in *The First Part of the Contention* (*2 Henry* VI): '*Enter at one door Horner the armourer and his Neighbours, drinking to him so much that he is drunker; and he enters with a drummer before him and carrying his staff with a sandbag fastened to it. Enter at the other door Peter his man, also with a drummer and a staff with sandbag, and Prentices drinking to him*' (2.4.58.1–7). *ER*

epic caesura. See CAESURA, EPIC.

epilogue, a short speech delivered after the close of a play's action, by a single character (often also called the epilogue, such as the dancer who speaks the epilogue to *2 Henry* IV), usually one of the principal actors. By convention, the epilogue begs indulgence from the audience, apologizing for any tedium or inadvertent offence, and courteously invites applause. Ten of Shakespeare's plays have epilogues; these are all comedies, romances, or history plays, the use of epilogues not being found among the tragedies. *CB*

epitaph, Shakespeare's. The stone traditionally believed to mark Shakespeare's *grave in *Holy Trinity church, Stratford, bears the inscription:

GOOD FREND FOR IESVS SAKE FORBEARE,
TO DIGG THE DVST ENCLOSED HEARE.
BLESTE BE Y[E] MAN Y[T] SPARES THESE STONES,
AND CURST BE HE Y[T] MOVES MY BONES.

The stone at present in place bears no name. According to Halliwell-Phillipps, writing in 1881, by the middle of the 18th century the original stone 'had sunk below the level of the floor', and about 'fifty years ago' (but 'ninety' in the 1889 edition of his *Outlines*) 'had become so much decayed as to suggest a vandalic order for its removal, and, in its stead, to place a new slab'. 'The original memorial', he writes, 'has wandered from its allotted station no one can tell whither,—a sacrifice to the insane worship of prosaic neatness.' Nevertheless Dugdale's transcription of the epitaph in his *Antiquities of Warwickshire* of 1656 shows that the wording, if not the spelling, remained unaltered on the copy. Halliwell-Phillipps, arguing that the epitaph was probably commonplace, claimed to have found in a manuscript of about 1630 an analogous epitaph on a baker reading:

For Jesus Christ his sake forbear
To dig the bones under this bier;
Blessed is he who loves my dust,
But damned be he who moves this crust.

The curse is no doubt directed primarily at the sexton in the hope that the bones should not be dug up and dumped in the charnel house adjoining the church. The first of several 17th-century sources to ascribe the epitaph—written in the same verse form as the Epilogue to *The Tempest*—to Shakespeare himself is a manuscript compiled by Sir Francis Fane of about 1655–6. *SW*

Epitaph on Elias James. This six-line epitaph survives in two slightly different versions. One is in the same Bodleian manuscript as *'Shall I die', where it is attributed to 'W[m] Shakespeare'. The other, unascribed, is among a number of 'monumental inscriptions' in the 1633 edition of John Stow's *Survey of London*, where it is said to have been inscribed on a memorial, no longer extant, in the church of St Andrew by the Wardrobe. James, who died in 1610 leaving £10 to the poor, was a brewer in the Blackfriars area whom Shakespeare is likely to have known. *SW*

epitaphs on John Combe. See COMBE FAMILY.

epyllion, a narrative poem of medium length on some heroic or mythological subject. The term has been applied to *Venus and Adonis* and to Marlowe's *Hero and Leander*. *CB*

Eros, Antony's faithful attendant in *Antony and Cleopatra*, commits suicide when asked by Antony to kill him, 4.15. *AB*

Erpingham, Sir Thomas (1357–1428). One of Bolingbroke's supporters mentioned in *Richard* II 2.1.284, he lends King Harry his cloak, *Henry* V 4.1.24. *AB*

Escalus, an old lord, is appointed Angelo's deputy in *Measure for Measure*. *AB*

Escalus, Prince of Verona. He tries to maintain order in *Verona, *Romeo and Juliet* 1.1, and speaks the final words of the play. *AB*

Escanes. See AESCHINES.

Eschenburg, Johann Joachim (1743–1820), German scholar and translator. Author of the first German translation of the complete plays of Shakespeare (1775–82, rev. edn. 1798–1806), on whom he also published a monograph (1787), he saw his translations (in prose) rapidly overshadowed by those of *Schlegel. *I-SE*

Meyen, F., *Johann Joachim Eschenburg* (1957)

Essex, Earl of. He presents the Bastard and Falconbridge to John, *King John* 1.1. *AB*

Essex, Robert Devereux, 2nd Earl of (1566–1601), Queen Elizabeth's last favourite. Aristocratic, ambitious, impoverished, and improvident, he married *Sidney's widow, courted the Queen assiduously, participated in a number of flamboyant and inconclusive military and naval engagements, and rose to be Earl Marshal. He was sent with troops to Ireland in 1599 to quell the continuing insurgency. *Spenser praises him lavishly in the *Prothalamion* (ll. 145–56), and Shakespeare in the Chorus to Act 5 of *Henry* V imagines him 'from Ireland coming | Bringing rebellion broachèd on his sword' (ll. 31–2), but he failed ignominiously and returned without permission in disgrace. Elizabeth banished him from court. In 1601 he commissioned a revival of *Richard* II by the Chamberlain's Men, and the next day led an uprising, intending to march on Whitehall and seize the Queen; but he was stopped, arrested, tried, and promptly executed for treason. The Chamberlain's Men were interrogated about the performance, but were exonerated, and performed for the Queen the night before the execution. Elizabeth's archivist William Lambarde reports that some months later she said to him, 'I am Richard the Second, know ye not that?' Later commentators have seen Shakespearian reflections of Essex in the indecision of Hamlet, the arrogance of Achilles, the self-destructive pride of Coriolanus. *SO*

Euphronius. See AMBASSADORS.

euphuism, an elaborate prose style ornamented with numerous figures of speech. Named after Lyly's romance *Euphues* (1578), it is thought to have been parodied in *Love's Labour's Lost*. *CB*

Euripides. See CRITICAL HISTORY; DEUS EX MACHINA; GREEK DRAMA; SENECA, LUCIUS ANNAEUS.

Evans, Dame Edith (1888–1976), English actress. Although she came to possess an almost aristocratic grandeur, she began life as a milliner. She appeared in 1912 as an amateur

The Earl of Essex (1566–1601), after Marcus Gheeraerts the younger. Although they revived *Richard II* the day before his rebellion, presumably to accustom Londoners to the idea of deposing a monarch, Shakespeare's company performed before Queen Elizabeth on the eve of Essex's execution.

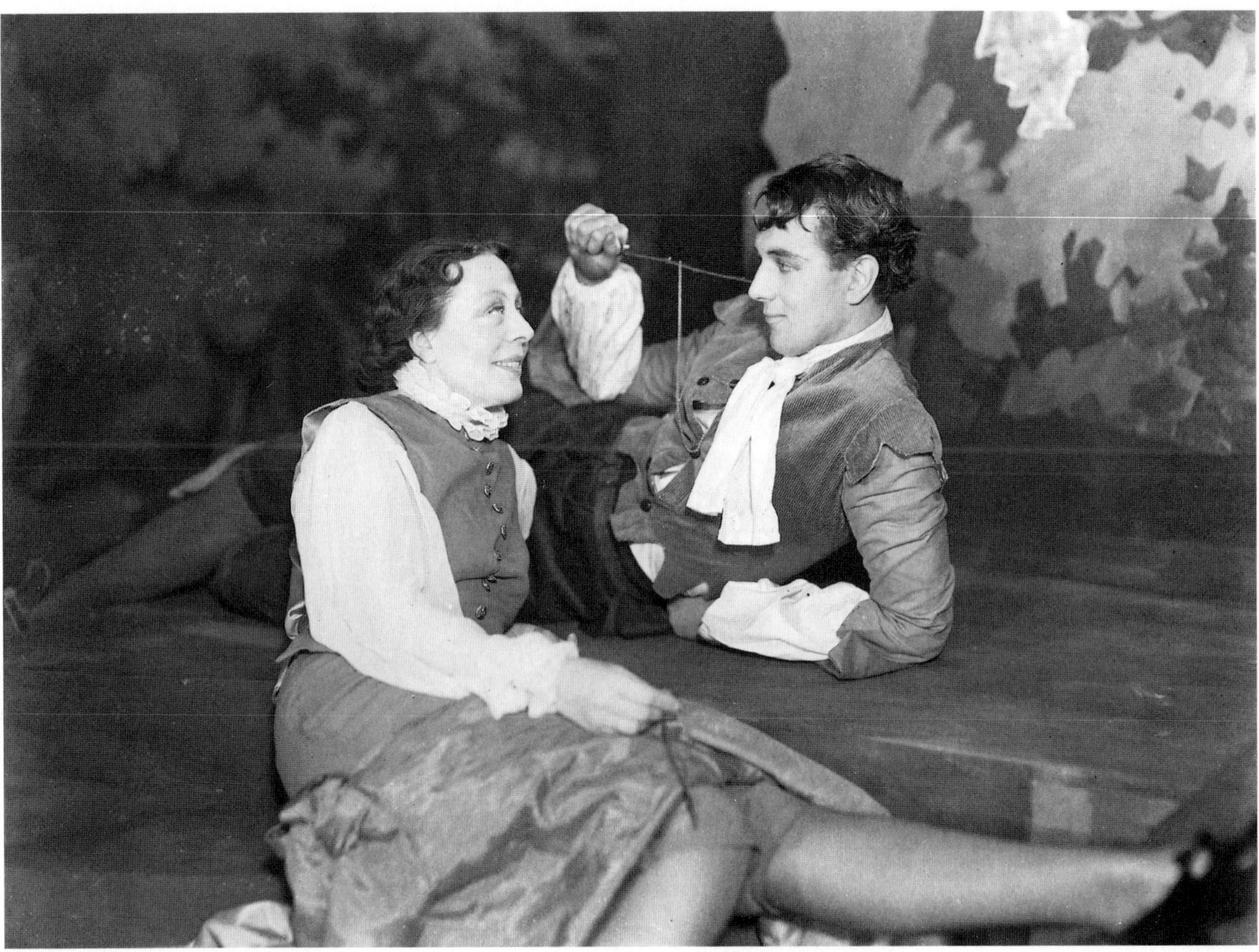

Edith Evans as a famously witty Rosalind, with Michael Redgrave as Orlando, New Theatre, 1937.

playing Cressida for William Poel; there was no going back to hats. She quickly built a reputation in London as an original and versatile actress with a special affinity for Restoration comedy. Feeling that she had failed as Helena in a starry production of *A Midsummer Night's Dream* at Drury Lane, she went to play, for very little money, ten of Shakespeare's women at the Old Vic. In New York in 1934 she played the Nurse to Katharine Cornell's Juliet, a part she repeated in London in 1936 when Peggy *Ashcroft was Juliet. Though never conventionally glamorous, she could enchant audiences with her vocal skill and timing, and at 48 triumphed as Rosalind at the Old Vic. Her Cleopatra ten years later was less happy. In maturity she played Queen Katherine in *All Is True* (*Henry VIII*) at the Old Vic as well as the Countess in *All's Well That Ends Well* and Volumnia to Laurence *Olivier's Coriolanus at Stratford. She was a devout Christian Scientist and socially a very private person. *MJ*

Evans, Sir Hugh. He is a Welsh parson who assists Slender's pursuit of Anne Page in *The Merry Wives of Windsor.* *AB*

Evans, Maurice (1901–89), British actor. Better known in the United States, of which he became a citizen in 1941, than in his native England, he gained a personal following in London when in 1934 he played Richard II and Hamlet at the Old Vic. He was immediately invited to play Romeo in America with Katharine Cornell. In New York he was soon acclaimed as Richard II and as Hamlet in an uncut Folio text. During 1945–7 he toured in his popular GI *Hamlet.* In 1960 he appeared in a dull British film of *Macbeth.* *MJ*

excursions, used in conjunction with *'alarum(s)' as a stage direction indicating movement of men in battle (e.g. *1 Henry IV* 5.4. opening). *JB*

Exeter, Duke of. **(1)** Based on Henry Holland (1430–73), he is a supporter of King Henry in *Richard Duke of York* (*3 Henry VI*). **(2)** Based on Thomas Beaufort (*c.*1375–1426), he urges his nephew the King to claim the French throne (*Henry V* 1.2.122–4) and then helps his campaign. In *1 Henry VI* his role is mainly to comment on the action, notably at the end of 3.1 and 4.1. *AB*

exploration. See TRAVEL, TRADE, AND COLONIALISM.

Exton, Sir Piers. He hears King Henry wishing to be 'rid' of Richard, *Richard II* 5.4.2, and murders him 5.5. *AB*

F. The bibliographic abbreviation for *folio: hence 'F1 [title of work]' means 'the first folio edition of [that work]', 'F2 [title of work]' means 'the second folio edition of [that work]', and so on. In Shakespeare studies 'F1' almost invariably means the Shakespeare Folio of 1623 (*Mr William Shakespeares Comedies, Histories and Tragedies*). *MD*

Fabian is Olivia's servant who joins in with the plot against *Malvolio in *Twelfth Night.* *AB*

Fabyan, Robert (d. 1513), clothier and sheriff of London. Fabyan was also an amateur historian who expanded his private diary into *The New Chronicles of England and France*, published posthumously in 1516. Holinshed, Grafton, and Halle would all turn to this history though it was Fabyan's anecdotes rather than his analysis of cause and effect that made him popular. *JKS*

facsimile editions. Pioneered in 1807, reproductions of the First Folio and the quarto editions of Shakespeare's plays proliferated after the advent of photography in the 19th century. Such facsimile editions are widely used by bibliographers and textual critics, as well as readers who wish to encounter Shakespeare's texts in their original form. Although it is generally assumed that photographic reprints present a technically exact facsimile of the original, the notoriously unreliable facsimile of the First Folio prepared by J. O. Halliwell-Phillipps in 1876 was heavily retouched in pen and ink on nearly every page. Charlton Hinman's Norton facsimile (1968) is made up of various leaves containing corrected formes from a number of actual copies, thus creating an 'ideal' copy that exists only in the facsimile. *ER*

Fair Em. The first quarto edition of this romantic comedy was published anonymously in 1590. It was catalogued as Shakespeare's in the library of King Charles II, and unconvincingly attributed to *Greene in 1675. *SM*

Fairholt, Frederick William (1818–66), English genre painter. He produced fictional *mises-en-scène* from works by English poets, a series of which, entitled *Passages from the Poets*, included scenes inspired by Shakespearian drama. The works display little artistic accomplishment, but were engraved and published in weekly magazines, serving to broaden the popular appeal of the works they illustrated. *CT*

fairies are impossible to define accurately, because the term is used for beings who range from the angry or jealous dead of a family to small and benevolent nature-spirits, with many categories in between. Fairy beliefs originate in the ancient world of the Mediterranean, where fairies take the form of childhood demons or nymphs, and by the Renaissance stories about fairies were widespread in the European countryside. Such stories were especially common in Scotland, Ireland, the Mediterranean, and Eastern Europe, and in remote parts of England like the West Country and Romney Marsh, and these stories were often cautionary tales about dangerous beings who could draw those who saw them into illness, madness, or death. Fairies could also heal, however, and many cunning folk relied on them for information about healing and also about prognostication and finding lost or buried treasure. The fairies became increasingly sought after as possible sources of wealth towards the end of the 16th century as part of both elite and popular enthusiasm for conjuration as a means of advancement, and there are numerous accounts of how these beliefs were used by the unscrupulous to rob the unwary, as celebrated in *Jonson's *The Alchemist.* Such beliefs often stemmed from Paracelsian doctrines of spirits, through which fairies came to be elected honorary servants to magicians, and that may be how demonologists began identifying them as devils. Another kind of fairy altogether came from the medieval romance, and was transformed by *Spenser's *Faerie Queene* into a rather troubled symbol of benevolence; this was a fairy who signified wealth and aristocracy, though even she could not quite escape the connotations of trickery and ambition that clustered around her diminutive relations.

Shakespeare's fairies were preceded by *Lyly and followed by others. As with his depictions of *witches, Shakespeare knew little and cared less about popular beliefs; he was no folklorist. In *A Midsummer Night's Dream*, his fairies are an amalgam of fragments of Reginald *Scot pasted on to *Ovidian gods and goddesses. *Robin Goodfellow (Puck), for example, is much more like the Ovidian and Anacreontic Cupid than like an English hob. Nevertheless, it was Puck's speeches about his mischief-making that were influential, producing some imitative poems and prose fictions which are often mistaken for folkloric sources. In fact fairies and fairy lore are supreme instances of Shakespeare's power to create popular culture; it is because of him, and specifically because of *A Midsummer Night's Dream*, that fairies become associated with lyrical bucolic idylls, and this notion in turn influences Jonson, Herrick, *Milton, and the numerous poets of the 18th century whose weakly pretty fairy verse gives fairies a bad name. Shakespeare fixed the idea of fairies, consigning some fairies forever to the dustheap and conferring immortality on his own creations. His most important portraits of fairies occur in *The Merry Wives of Windsor*, *A Midsummer Night's Dream*, and *The Tempest* (if *Ariel is really a fairy, as Trinculo claims, and not a familiar) but there are many other references, most memorably the Queen Mab speech in *Romeo and Juliet*, which exerted an enormous

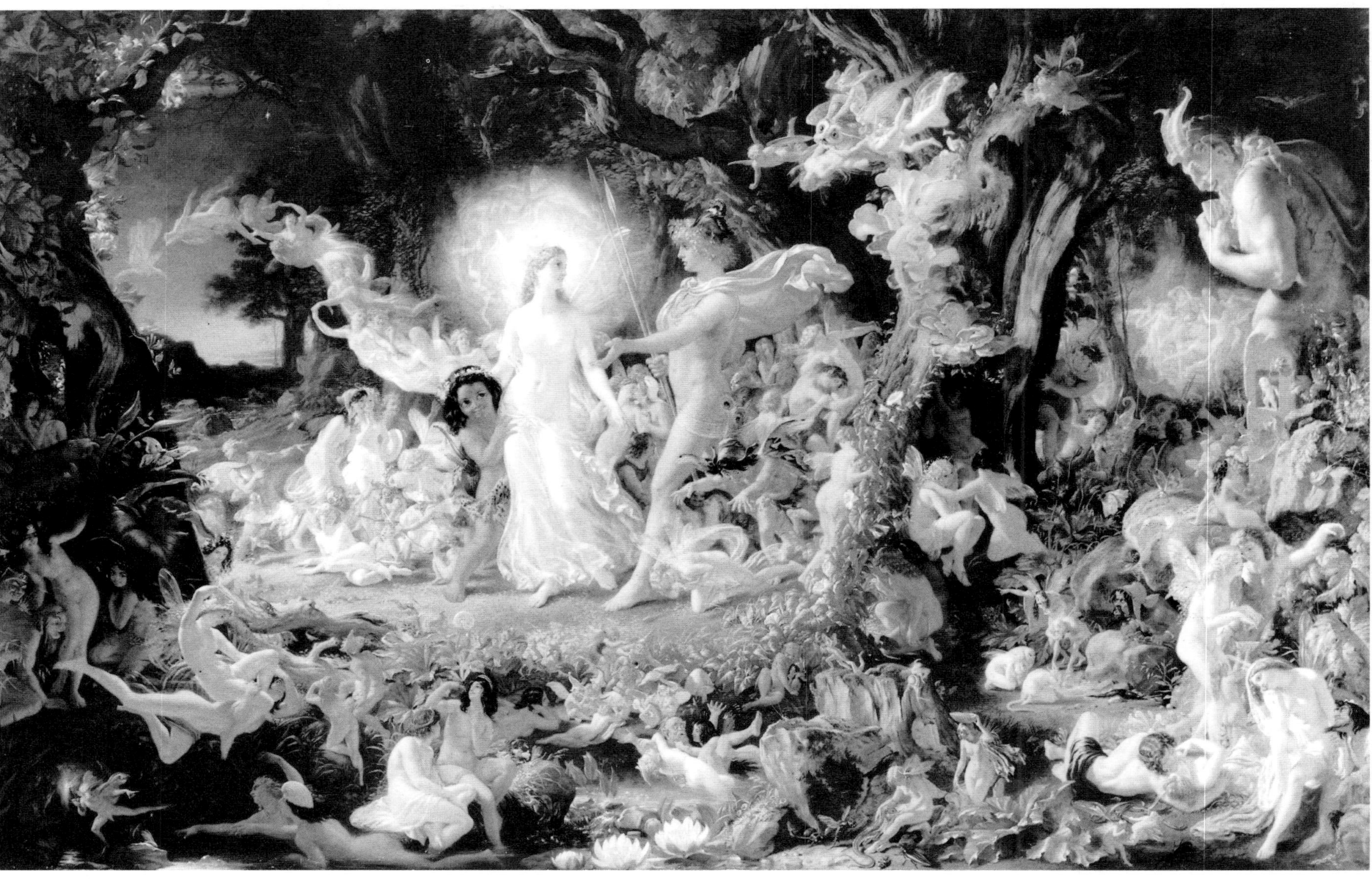

Shakespeare's portrayals of fairies licensed the imaginations of Victorian artists to pursue all sorts of erotic and surreal flights of fancy. Joseph Noel Paton's *The Quarrel of Oberon and Titania*, 1849.

influence over other, later, literary fairies. All Shakespeare's fairies are associated with jokes, tricks, and disguise; all are linked with the countryside and country life. Apart from a reference to the fairy as a fate (*Antony and Cleopatra* 4.8.12), which recalls *Holinshed's use of the term *fate* for the Weird Sisters, most brief references see fairies as one amongst many vague menaces of the night, with a few more specific allusions to fairies as child-stealers, generally as part of scenes concerning children lost to their parents in pastoral settings (esp. *Cymbeline* 3.7.14, 2.2.10, 4.2.217, 5.4.133, and *Pericles* 21.142). After Shakespeare, all fairies in English poetry became more or less funny and kindly, until the *Romantic poets revived the menacing fairy of earlier eras. In so far as his own attitude might be reconstructed, it approximates Horatio's response to a long harangue about fairies and ghosts: 'So I have heard, and do in part believe it.' *DP*

Briggs, Katherine, *The Anatomy of Puck* (1959)
Latham, Minor, *The Elizabethan Fairies* (1930)
Purkiss, Diane, *Troublesome Things* (2000)
Thomas, Keith, *Religion and the Decline of Magic* (1971)

Fairies, The. David *Garrick's musical adaptation of *A Midsummer Night's Dream* was performed anonymously in 1755, and Garrick never printed it under his own name, clearly anxious about the response which an attempt to assimilate Shakespeare to the suspect Continental genre of all-sung opera might inspire. The opera, which achieved a respectable eleven performances, omits the mechanicals entirely, and introduces songs from a wide variety of other sources, including the works of Ben *Jonson: its score was by John Smith, a pupil of Handel. *MD*

Fairy. She talks to *Robin Goodfellow, *A Midsummer Night's Dream* 2.1. *AB*

'Fair Youth'. The first 126 of Shakespeare's Sonnets are addressed mainly to a young man (usually assumed to be the same throughout), sometimes known as the 'fair youth', though the phrase does not occur. A vast amount of commentary has been devoted to attempts to determine the exact nature of the relationship, especially whether it was, or became, sexual (ostensibly denied in 20). Many attempts have been made to identify the youth (or youths) with a real person (or persons). Various words have been interpreted as clues—frequent use of 'fair', 'youth', 'beauty'; 'lovely boy' (126); incitements to marry (1–17); puns on 'will' (135–6), possible pun on 'hues' (20), and so on. He has often been supposed to be the dedicatee, *'Mr W.H.', described by the publisher as 'the only begetter of these ensuing sonnets'. A favourite candidate in both roles has been Henry Wriothesley, Earl of *Southampton, dedicatee of *Venus and Adonis* and *The Rape of Lucrece*, who was nine years younger than Shakespeare. Another is William Herbert, 3rd Earl of *Pembroke, born in 1580, dedicatee, along with his brother Philip, of the First Folio. But if 'begetter' means 'procurer' rather than 'inspirer', other possibilities open up. The name of Robert Devereux, Earl of *Essex, has often been canvassed, especially by Baconians. Hamnet Shakespeare (who died at the age of 11) has been found behind some of the poems, as has Shakespeare's brother Edmund. Father Robert Southwell, executed in 1596, the actor Will *Kempe, and Prince Harry (of the history plays) are among the more improbable candidates. *SW*

Schoenbaum, S., *Shakespeare's Lives* (1970, rev. edn. 1991)

Fairy Queen, The. This adaptation of *A Midsummer Night's Dream*, with 'singing, dancing and machines interwoven, after the manner of an opera', was first performed at Dorset Garden theatre in London in 1692 and revived, with a revised score, the following year. The script, printed anonymously, was probably prepared by Thomas *Betterton: the score was certainly composed by Henry Purcell, and, though it uses none of the original play's text, is the closest thing we have to a Purcell setting of Shakespeare. The adaptation cuts the mechanicals entirely, and adds a number of lavish special effects, including a representation of China and a masque in which Juno appears in a chariot drawn by mechanical peacocks. The huge revival of interest in baroque music since the middle of the 20th century has led to Purcell's score being recorded several times, most notably by John Eliot Gardiner in 1982, and the semi-opera has been revived in its entirety with some success, particularly by the English National Opera. *MD*

Fairy Tale, A, a two-act adaptation of *A Midsummer Night's Dream* hurriedly abbreviated by George Colman the elder at Drury Lane from a full-length version of the play which, prepared in association with David *Garrick, proved a disastrous failure in November 1763. *A Fairy Tale* opened only three days after the longer version closed, and makes something of a hasty mess of the original's structure: Theseus, Hippolyta, and the lovers disappear, leaving only the fairies and the mechanicals, who rehearse *Pyramus and Thisbe* but never get to perform it. *MD*

Faithorne engraving, attributed to William Faithorne (1616–91), English engraver. In this work, a bust of Shakespeare surmounts a representation of Lucretia and Collatius. The engraving was prefixed to an early edition of *The Rape of Lucrece* (1655). *CT*

Falconbridge, Lady. Mother of Robert Falconbridge and the Bastard, she admits the latter's father was Richard Cœur-de-lion, *King John* 1.1.253–8. *AB*

Falconbridge, Philip. See Bastard, Philip the.

Falconbridge, Robert. He claims his father's estate on the grounds of his elder brother's illegitimacy, *King John* 1.1. *AB*

Falstaff, Sir John. See Henry iv Parts 1 and 2; Merry Wives of Windsor, The; Fastolf, Sir John; Oldcastle, Sir John.

Falstaff's Wedding (1760), William *Kenrick's humorous sequel to *2 Henry iv*, was dedicated to James *Quin, a particularly popular Falstaff. In a loose political setting, the plot exploits Falstaffian stereotypes: he marries Ursula for her inheritance and fights a duel with Shallow who is vainly pursuing a loan. *CMSA*

Family Shakespeare. The Revd Thomas Bowdler (1754–1825) published the 10-volume 'Family Shakespeare' in 1818 under his own name, completing the 20-play edition published anonymously by his sister in 1807. His stated object was to remove from the works 'only those words and expressions which cannot with propriety be read aloud in a family'. In practice, he (in collaboration with his unmarried sister Henrietta, whose name was kept off the title pages lest her reputation suffer) cut any passage which in his view smacked of obscenity. So, for example, he omitted the Porter scene in *Macbeth*, and Hamlet's teasing of Ophelia before the play-within-the-play. Bowdler claimed on the title page of each volume that he added nothing to Shakespeare's text, but in fact he made changes, as at the end of *Measure for Measure*, where the last lines are replaced by an invented passage in which the Duke looks forward to reigning with Isabella as his wife, and closes with the 'royal maxim', 'To rule ourselves before we rule mankind'. The edition was attacked in the *British Critic* in April 1822, and Bowdler responded with a long defence. By 1836 the verb 'to bowdlerize' was current, with implications of crass and insensitive censoring. *RAF*

Famous History of the Life of King Henry the Eight, The. See All Is True.

Famous Victories of Henry v, The an anonymous play, first performed *c.*1586 and published in 1598, perhaps used by Shakespeare for *1* and *2 Henry iv* and *Henry v*. The text we have of the *Famous Victories* is debased and possibly piratical. The original play may have been a two-part history, concerned with the Prince's misdeeds and his development into a warrior-king. Similarities between the *Famous Victories* and Shakespeare's plays allow for the possibility that

Shakespeare knew this debased version but also provide glimpses of what the earlier play, perhaps his main source, was like. The *Famous Victories* provides the setting of the Eastcheap tavern and prototypes for the characters who gather there: Ned Poins and Gadshill, the reprobate Prince, even *Oldcastle, though as a shadow of his future self. The *Famous Victories* includes scenes that are central to *Henry IV* including the robbery at Gadshill, the derision of authority through role play, and the events surrounding the King's death. Shakespeare may also have caught the saturnalian spirit of the earlier play. *JKS*

Corbin, Peter, and Sedge, Douglas (eds.), *The Oldcastle Controversy* (1991)

fanfare. Not a term used by Shakespeare; the various signals indicated in his plays for *trumpets, *drums, etc. may be divided into the military (*alarums, charge, *parley, *retreat) and the ceremonial (*flourish, *sennet, *tucket). The music for these in Shakespeare's plays does not survive, though an idea of some military signals may be gained from *battaglia* pieces of the period, such as *Byrd's *The Battell.* *JB*

Fang and Snare are two officers who attempt to arrest Falstaff, *2 Henry IV* 2.1. *AB*

'Farewell, dear heart, for I must needs be gone', fragment of a song by Robert *Jones (from *The First Book of Songs and Airs*, 1600), sung by Sir Toby, with further extracts contributed by Feste and Malvolio, in *Twelfth Night* 2.3.98. *JB*

Farmer, Richard (1735–97), English classicist and scholar, author of *An Essay on the Learning of Shakespeare* (2nd edn. 1767). Farmer's work responds to earlier critics who claimed that Shakespeare was skilled in both Latin and Greek. He argues instead that Shakespeare relied on contemporary translations of the ancients. *JM*

Fastolf, Sir John. In *1 Henry VI* he deserts Talbot before Orléans (1.1.130–4) and again at Rouen (3.5). The outraged Talbot tears Fastolf's garter from his leg, 4.1.15. The real Sir John Fastolf (d. 1459) had been awarded the Order of the Garter in 1429 but had it taken from him 'for doubt of misdealing' (*Holinshed), though he had also deserted Talbot at Orléans. He is thought to have been part of the inspiration for Sir John Falstaff. *AB*

Father who has killed his son. See SOLDIER WHO HAS KILLED HIS FATHER.

Faucit, Helen (Saville) (1817–98), English actress from a theatrical family. She made her debut in 1836 at Covent Garden, playing Juliet, Katherine, Portia, Desdemona, and Constance in her first season. In 1837 she commenced her professional partnership with *Macready,

THE

FAMILY SHAKSPEARE,

In Ten Volumes;

IN WHICH
NOTHING IS ADDED TO THE ORIGINAL TEXT;
BUT THOSE WORDS AND EXPRESSIONS
ARE OMITTED WHICH CANNOT WITH PROPRIETY
BE READ ALOUD IN A FAMILY.

BY

THOMAS BOWDLER, ESQ. F.R.S. & S.A.

VOL. I.

CONTAINING

TEMPEST;
TWO GENTLEMEN OF VERONA;
MERRY WIVES OF WINDSOR;
TWELFTH-NIGHT: OR, WHAT YOU WILL.

LONDON:
PRINTED FOR LONGMAN, HURST, REES, ORME, AND BROWN,
PATERNOSTER-ROW.
1818.

The first complete edition of 'The Family Shakespeare'. The enormous assistance Bowdler received from his unmarried sister Henrietta is not acknowledged on the title page, since a public admission that she understood the obscene passages she marked for omission would have harmed her reputation.

during which she added Cordelia, Hermione, Rosalind, and Beatrice to her repertoire, performing them in her customary—increasingly dated—idealized style.

Helen Faucit's marriage to Theodore Martin (knighted in 1880 for his biography of Prince Albert) coincided with Macready's retirement and thereafter she acted only on special occasions such as the opening of the Shakespeare Memorial Theatre, Stratford-upon-Avon, in 1879, when she appeared as Beatrice to Barry Sullivan's Benedick. Later that year in the Calvert Memorial Performance—her age, vocal delivery, and costume notwithstanding—she evoked 'intense admiration' as Rosalind. Helen Faucit's *On Some of Shakespeare's Female Characters* (1892) was dedicated 'by permission' to Queen Victoria. *RF*

Fauré, Gabriel (1845–1924), French composer. In 1889 he composed incidental music for Edmond Haraucourt's play *Shylock* (based on *The Merchant of Venice*), which he revised as a concert suite for tenor soloist and orchestra in 1890. His incidental music for *Julius Caesar* (Théâtre Antique d'Orange, 1905) is a reworking of music originally written for *Caligula* (1888). *IBC*

'Fear no more the heat o' the sun', spoken or sung by Guiderius and Arviragus in *Cymbeline* 4.2.259. Early settings are unknown, but the lyrics became popular with English composers in the 20th century, including Geoffrey Bush, Dankworth, Walford Davies, Finzi, Gardiner, Gardner (two versions), Jacob, Lambert, Parry, Quilter, Vaughan Williams. *JB*

Fechter, Charles Albert (1822–79), actor, born in London, brought up in France where, after studying sculpture, he joined the Théâtre Français. In 1860 Fechter moved to London where he performed his innovatory Hamlet—in English—the next year. Fechter's Prince was a pale Norseman in a flaxen wig whom he embodied with subtlety and depth, eschewing the traditions of the English stage. In contrast his Othello (also 1861) was a disaster, only partially redeemed by his subsequent Iago. The attempts of the Revd J. C. M. Bellew to secure a prominent place for his protégé in the Shakespeare tercentenary were thwarted; Fechter spent his declining years in the United States. *RF*

Feeble, Francis. He is drafted into the army by Shallow and Falstaff, *2 Henry IV* 3.2. *AB*

Felix and Philiomena. According to Elizabethan Revels accounts, a performance of 'The history of felix and philiomena' by the Queen's Men took place shortly after New Year, 1585. This lost play was probably based on Jorge de Montemayor's *Diana enamorada*, and may have served as a source for *The Two Gentlemen of Verona*. *JKS*

Felton portrait. See Burdett-Coutts portrait.

feminine ending, the appearance of an additional unstressed syllable at the end of a verse line; thus in pentameter verse an eleventh syllable, as in most lines of Sonnet 87. *CB*

feminist criticism. Women's critical engagements with Shakespeare date from Margaret Cavendish's discussion of his plays in her *Sociable Letters* (1664), and have taken many forms, embracing fiction and performance as well as literary scholarship and criticism. Such engagements have often been motivated by a desire to defend or praise Shakespeare's female characters which can be described as broadly feminist. When a feminist perspective on Shakespeare began to emerge within academic literary criticism in the 1970s, it was initially informed by a similar approach. This was counterbalanced, though, by a more challenging critique of Shakespearian constructions of femininity, which argued that by underwriting certain versions of womanhood with the power of the bard, they had a pernicious cultural effect. In subsequent decades, feminist Shakespeare criticism has flourished and diversified. Committed to making connections between the critic's cultural moment and the Renaissance, feminist criticism of Shakespeare seeks both to intervene in contemporary cultural politics and to recover a fuller sense of the sexual politics of the literary heritage. If its primary effect has been to elicit fresh interpretations of the texts and their original historical location, it is also changing the way that Shakespeare is reproduced and consumed in education and in popular culture. *KC*

Barker, Deborah E., and Kamps, Ivo (eds.), *Shakespeare and Gender: A History* (1995)
Chedgzoy, Kate (ed.), *Shakespeare, Feminism and Gender: A New Casebook* (2000)

Fencing. See hunting and sports.

Fenton, Geoffrey. See Bandello, Matteo.

Fenton, Master. He is in love with Anne Page in *The Merry Wives of Windsor.* *AB*

Fenton, Richard (1746–1821), English author. He claimed in his anonymous *Tour in Quest of Genealogy through Several Parts of Wales* to own a manuscript of Shakespeare's autobiography in Anne Hathaway's handwriting, from which this work quotes. The quoted passages, however, are hardly to be taken seriously, and the whole section seems to be a satirical allusion to the Shakespearian *forgeries of William Henry Ireland. *MD*

Ferdinand, Prince of Naples, is separated from his father in the carefully managed shipwreck that opens *The Tempest*, and is subsequently introduced to Miranda, with all the hoped-for consequences, 1.2.368 ff. *AB*

Ferdinand, King of Navarre. See Navarre, Ferdinand, King of.

Feste, Olivia's jester, scorned as 'a barren rascal' (1.5.80) by *Malvolio, plots revenge in *Twelfth Night.* *AB*

fiction. In addition to his many appearances as a fictional character (see Shakespeare as a character) in novels for both adults and children, Shakespeare has been important to novelists and fiction-writers in a number of ways. From very early on in the novel's development as a genre, it was remarked that Shakespeare had affinities with the novel, not least as himself a plunderer of prose tales. Charlotte *Lennox in her *Shakespeare Illustrated* (1753–4) was the first to note his debts to the continental *novella* and to remark on how much clearer characters' motivations were in the originals. Eighteenth-century novelists, such as William Goodall in his *Adventures of Captain Greenland* (1752), frequently invoked Shakespeare as a precursor because he was felt to break literary decorums in much the same way as did the new form. Hence certain great novelists have been dubbed 'Shakespearian', a term of approval meant to connote a certain large inclusiveness of sympathy and social range—such novelists have included Sir Walter *Scott, James Fenimore Cooper, George Eliot, James *Joyce, and Victor *Hugo, to name the most outstanding.

Since *Richardson published his first novel *Pamela* (1740) it has been commonplace to use a liking for Shakespeare as a moral touchstone by which to try heroines—this has been true from Richardson's Pamela, Clarissa, and Harriet Byron, Francis Burney's Evelina, and so to Jane *Austen's Fanny Price. Equally, it has been a common technique to include a staging or reading of a Shakespeare play within the novel upon which characters comment self-revealingly or in which they participate. Perhaps the most famous examples of this would be *Dickens's *Great Expectations* (1860–1), in which, appropriately enough given the novel's concern with the absent or embarrassing father, *Hamlet* is performed, or the performance of a spurious Shakespearian medley by the King and the Duke in Mark *Twain's *Huckleberry Finn.*

More generally, certain novelistic genres have been since their inception especially prone to Shakespearian quotation and allusion, a practice that became particularly widespread in the Romantic period. (See, for example, the references to *Coriolanus* which structure the discussion of industrial relations throughout Charlotte Brontë's *Shirley*, 1849). Hence the early *Gothic novels of Horace Walpole, Ann Radcliffe, and Charles Maturin and the historical novels of Sir Walter Scott are permeated with Shakespearian epigraph, quotation, and allusion. There are several reasons for this: Shakespeare's plays, themselves regarded as committed to the messy complexities of real life in defiance of literary convention, offered an important model to chroniclers of contemporary alienation for the depiction of extreme states of consciousness, while for novelists more interested in reanimating history the varieties of his characters' personal languages, and the double-plot mechanism of the history plays themselves, modelled ways of representing the imagined past.

Finally, Shakespeare's plots have served as the armature for many novels. *Measure for Measure* is reworked in Matthew *Lewis's *The Monk* (1796); *As You Like It* serves as a reference point for the heroine of George Eliot's *Daniel Deronda* (1874–6), Gwendolen Harleth, while *Hamlet* underscores the irresolution of Eliot's eponymous hero. In the 20th century *Lear* underpins Jane Smiley's novel *A Thousand Acres* and Falstaff haunts Robert *Nye's novels. The plots of the last plays, most especially *The Tempest*, have structured romance from Scott's tales of inheritance reinstated through to the modernities and postmodernities of John Fowles's *The Magus* (1966/1977), Iris *Murdoch's *The Sea, the Sea* (1978), Margaret Laurence's *The Diviners* (1974), and Isak Dinesen's short story 'Tempests' in *Anecdotes of Destiny* (1958).

Of all of the plays, *Hamlet* and *Macbeth* have undoubtedly been the most influential in this fashion, underlying early Gothic (such as Charles Brockden Brown's *Edgar Huntly*, 1799) and its descendant, classic modern detective fictions, including Michael Innes's *Hamlet Revenge!* (1937), Marvin Kaye's *Bullets for Macbeth* (1976), and numerous others, not to mention the spoof by James Thurber, *The Macbeth Murder Mystery* (in itself a mini-essay on why these plays should have proved so tempting to the detective aesthetic). (Detective fiction has also amused itself with discovering, only in the end to destroy, sundry lost Shakespearian manuscripts: the most notable examples are Edmund Crispin's *Love Lies Bleeding*, 1948, and Michael Innes's *The Long Farewell*, 1958.) More generally, *Hamlet* underpins mainstream novels as diverse as Laurence *Sterne's *Tristram Shandy* (1759–67) and *A Sentimental Journey* (1768), Johann Wolfgang von *Goethe's *Werther* (1774) and his *Wilhelm Meister* series (1777–1829), Lillie Wyman's *Gertrude of Denmark* (1924), Virginia *Woolf's *Between the Acts* (1941), Iris Murdoch's *The Black Prince* (1973), and John Updike's *Gertrude and Claudius* (1999).

The most influential of late 20th-century critical work on Shakespeare and the novel was directed towards examining how women novelists have rethought Shakespeare's plots within their home genre (hence, in part, a resurgence of interest in Mary Cowden *Clarke's supplementary short stories *The Girlhood of Shakespeare's Heroines*, 1851–2). Here, *The Tempest* has been overwhelmingly influential, especially among women writing from a consciously postcolonial perspective—not merely American and Canadian (such as Constance Beresford-Howe's *Prospero's Daughter*, 1988, and Sarah Murphy's *The Measure of Miranda*, 1987), but also Indian and Caribbean (Suniti Nahijoshi's work, for example). African-American women writers have also found *The Tempest* peculiarly hospitable to an exploration of the intersection of race and gender: both Gloria Naylor's *Mama Day* (1988) and Toni Morrison's *Tar Baby* (1981) can be seen as critical readings of Shakespeare's last romance. *NJW*

Davies, Douglas Brooks, *Fielding, Dickens, Gosse, Iris Murdoch and Oedipal Hamlet* (1989)
Novy, Marianne (ed.), *Cross-cultural Performances: Differences in Women's Re-visions of Shakespeare* (1993)
Novy, Marianne, *Engaging with Shakespeare: Responses of George Eliot and Other Women Novelists* (1994)
Noyes, R. G., *The Thespian Mirror: Shakespeare in the Eighteenth-Century Novel* (1953)
Osborne, Laurie E., 'Romancing the Bard', in Christy Desmet and Robert Sawyer (eds.), *Shakespeare and Appropriation* (1999)
Watson, Nicola, 'Kemble, Scott and the Mantle of the Bard', in Jean Marsden (ed.), *The Appropriation of Shakespeare* (1991)

fiddler, a broader musical term in Shakespeare's time than now, applied to players of the *rebec and *lute as well as the violin (then a relatively new instrument in England), or used abusively to imply a professional musician of low status, as in *The Taming of the Shrew* 2.1.157. *JB*

'Fidele' is the name used by Innogen when disguised as a man in *Cymbeline*. *AB*

Field, Nathan (1587–1620), actor (Blackfriars Boys 1600–13, Lady Elizabeth's Men 1613–15, King's Men 1615–20) and dramatist. Nathan Field's father, the Puritan anti-theatricalist John Field, wrote *A Godly Exhortation by Occasion of the Late Judgement of God at Parris-garden* (1583) which attributed to divine displeasure the Bear Garden's fatal collapse during a Sunday performance, but he died before Nathan was old enough to be dissuaded from the theatrical life. Nathan Field's name occurs in the Blackfriars Boys' cast lists for Jonson's *Cynthia's Revels* and *Poetaster*. In the Sharers Papers of 1635 Cuthbert Burbage described Nathan as one of the 'boys growing up to be men' (the others were John Underwood and William Ostler) who joined the King's Men after the Blackfriars reverted to the Burbages in 1608, but in Field's case this happened 'in process of time', since he appears in the cast list for Jonson's *Epicoene* which was first performed in 1609 by the Blackfriars Boys, renamed the Children of the Queen's Revels, in their new venue the Whitefriars playhouse. In 1613 the Queen's Revels Children merged with the Lady Elizabeth's Men and Field stayed with this new company until he joined the King's Men, apparently in 1615. As an actor Field was at the height of his powers (second only to Burbage and subsequently Taylor in the King's Men) when he died. Field sole-authored two successful plays, *A Woman is a Weathercock* and *Amends for Ladies*, before becoming a King's Man, and he collaborated on six after: *Four Plays, or Moral Representations, in One* with Fletcher; *The Honest Man's Fortune* with Fletcher and possibly Massinger; *The Jeweller of Amsterdam* with Fletcher and Massinger; *The Queen of Corinth* with Fletcher and possibly Massinger; *The Knight of Malta* with Fletcher and Massinger; and *The Fatal Dowry* with Massinger. *GE*

Brinkley, Roberta Florence, *Nathan Field: The Actor-Playwright* (1928)

Field, Richard. See 'Dark Lady'; printing and publishing; Sonnets.

fiends. Joan la Pucelle invokes them in vain, *1 Henry VI* 5.3 (they are mute). *AB*

Fiennes, James. See Saye, Lord.

'Fie on sinful fantasy', dance song performed by the fairies in *The Merry Wives of Windsor* 5.5.92; the original music is unknown. *JB*

fife, a small transverse *flute for military use, played with *drum (separately, unlike the one-person *tabor and *pipe combination); see *Much Ado About Nothing* 2.3.14–15. *JB*

Fife, Thane of. See Macduff.

Filario (Philario) is present when Posthumus and *Giacomo set the wager on Innogen's fidelity in *Cymbeline* 1.4. *AB*

'Fill the cup and let it come', song fragment quoted by Silence in *2 Henry IV* 5.3.54; the original music is unknown. *JB*

film. See silent films; Shakespeare on sound film.

Finney, Albert (b. 1936), English actor. He proved his worth as Henry V at the Birmingham Repertory Theatre before playing lesser parts at Stratford-upon-Avon in 1959 during which he triumphantly took over from an indisposed Laurence *Olivier in *Coriolanus*. He worked in plays by John Osborne and others and in neo-realist British cinema and became an international star. He played Hamlet in the production which opened the National Theatre building on the South Bank in 1976; he also played Macbeth there in 1978. He evoked the spirit of the great Shakespearian actor-manager Donald *Wolfit in the film of *The Dresser* (1983). *MJ*

Finsbury. Fenland immediately north of the City, the manor of Finsbury was acquired by lease, by the city of London, from the Dean and Chapter of St Paul's in 1514. Golden Lane which runs through the manor was the location of the Fortune theatre, built by Philip *Henslowe in 1600. *RSB*

Levy, E., 'Moorfields, Finsbury and the City of London in the Sixteenth Century', *London Topographical Record*, 26 (1990)
Orrell, J., 'Building the Fortune', *Shakespeare Quarterly*, 44 (1993)

fires in Stratford-upon-Avon. There were three great fires in Stratford during Shakespeare's life, in 1594, 1595, and 1614. The first two, said to have broken out on a Sunday, were popularly ascribed to sabbath-breaking. The third, which started on Saturday, 9 July, destroyed 54 houses and much other property. *SW*

First Folio. See FOLIOS.

***First Part of the Contention of the two Famous Houses of York and Lancaster, The* (*2 Henry VI*)** *(see page 140)*

Fisher, Thomas. See PRINTING AND PUBLISHING.

fishermen, three. They take pity on the shipwrecked Pericles, *Pericles* 5. *AB*

Fiske, Minnie Maddern (1865–1932), American actress, who, although she made early appearances as the Duke of York in *Richard III* (1868) and Prince Arthur in *King John* (1874), showed little interest in Shakespeare, her only adult role being Mistress Page (1928). *RF*

Fitton, Mary. See 'DARK LADY'; PEMBROKE, WILLIAM HERBERT, 3RD EARL OF; TYLER, THOMAS.

Fitzwalter (Fitz-walter; Fitzwater), Lord. He challenges Aumerle and is himself challenged by the Duke of Surrey, *Richard II* 4.1. He announces the execution of two traitors, 5.6.13–16. *AB*

flags were flown over the theatres on days when performances were to be given. The de Witt drawing clearly shows one at the *Swan, the 'Utrecht' engraving shows flags over the Theatre and the Curtain, John Norden's engraved panorama *Civitas Londini* shows flags over the Globe, the Rose, the Swan, and the Beargarden, and Wenzel Hollar's Long View of London shows a particularly tall flagpole at the Hope, but none at the second Globe. It is possible that the colour of the flag indicated the genre of the play but more likely that, as with an inn sign, the flag told the illiterate the name of the venue. De Witt shows the Swan's flag bearing a swan, and an inset in Norden's *Civitas Londini* mislabels the Rose 'The Star', which is easily a misreading of a flag emblem. *GE*

Flaminius is a loyal servant of Timon in *Timon of Athens*. *AB*

Flanders. See DUTCH WARS; LOW COUNTRIES.

flats/shutters. Before the Restoration the theatres used little or no scenery, but thereafter it became usual to paint a realistic background onto canvas stretched over wooden frames (flats), often using the principle of perspective foreshortening. A shutter was two flats, each holding half the background, which could be run on grooves cut in the stage floor in order to meet on the stage. Before the Civil War masques and, less often, plays performed at court used this technology and John Webb, nephew and assistant to Inigo *Jones, brought it to the Restoration stage in his designs for William Davenant's *The Siege of Rhodes* in 1661. *GE*

Flavius. (1) The two tribunes Flavius and Murellus (spelled 'Marullus' by *Theobald and later editors), hostile to Caesar, expostulate with the commoners, *Julius Caesar* 1.1. **(2)** Also in *Julius Caesar*, Flavius is a follower of Brutus (mute, appearing 5.3 (under the name Flavio) and 5.4). **(3)** He is Timon's steward, acknowledged by Timon as the 'One honest man', *Timon of Athens* 4.3.498. *AB*

Fleance, son of Banquo, escapes when his father is murdered, *Macbeth* 3.3. (Fleance is an invention of Horace Boece, on whose *Scotorum historiae* (1527) *Holinshed based the Scottish part of his *Chronicles*, a source for *Macbeth*.) *AB*

Fleay, Frederick Gard (1831–1909), English Shakespeare scholar associated with the Victorian 'disintegrators' of the New Shakespeare Society (1873–94). Fleay championed versification analysis as an application of positivist scientific methods to literary scholarship and as the key to solving questions of chronology and authorship in the Shakespeare canon, which his analysis led him to conclude contained the work of a number of playwrights besides Shakespeare. *HG*

Fleetwood, Charles (d. 1747), controversial English manager whose period at Drury Lane 1734–44 was significant for the appointments of *Macklin as artistic manager and *Garrick as a senior player. *CMSA*

Fletcher, John (1579–1625), dramatist. Like his collaborator Francis *Beaumont, Fletcher was born into a well-connected family, but was driven to writing for the stage by financial need. Again like Beaumont, he did badly at first. His first play, an experiment in pastoral tragicomedy called *The Faithful Shepherdess* (1609), was a box-office failure, although it was admired by poets such as Ben *Jonson and George *Chapman, who contributed commendatory verses to the first edition, and later John *Milton, who echoed it in *Comus*. He preceded the printed version with a preface 'To the Reader', which defines tragicomedy for the benefit of the uncomprehending Jacobean public: 'A tragicomedy is not so called in respect of mirth and killing, but in respect it wants deaths, which is enough to make it no tragedy, yet brings some near it, which is enough to make it no comedy, which must be a representation of familiar people, with such kind of trouble as no life be questioned; so that a god is as lawful in this as in a tragedy, and mean people as in a comedy'. This definition fits many of Shakespeare's comedies as well as his late plays: in *Twelfth Night*, for instance, Viola's life is threatened by Duke Orsino, while *Measure for Measure* is heavy with the fear of death. Accordingly, the first successful tragicomedy written by Beaumont and Fletcher together, *Philaster* (1620), features a woman disguised as a page who is sent, like Viola, to woo another woman for the man she loves, and is later stabbed by him in a fit of jealousy, as if to fulfil Orsino's threats. The man, Philaster, is one of a series of tormented heroes in the Beaumont and Fletcher canon, a fusion of Hamlet and Othello, always balancing on a knife-edge between hysteria and madness. *Philaster* has much in common with Shakespeare's *Cymbeline*—both were written in about 1609—but it is not clear which came first: both Shakespeare and Fletcher had already written tragicomedies to which these plays were natural successors. It would seem that tragicomedy was simply the new genre of the moment, and that Shakespeare, Fletcher, and Beaumont sparked each other off in their efforts to develop that genre to its full potential.

Beaumont and Fletcher had good professional reasons for drawing on situations and characters from Shakespeare's work. They began by writing for children's companies, including the Children of the Queen's Revels, who were based at the Blackfriars theatre. When Shakespeare's company, the King's Men, took over the Blackfriars in 1608, Beaumont and Fletcher began to write for them, producing three of their finest plays between 1609 and 1611: *Philaster*, *A King and No King* (published 1619), and *The Maid's Tragedy* (also published 1619). After this Fletcher seems to have been groomed to succeed Shakespeare as principal dramatist for the company. He wrote three plays in collaboration with Shakespeare—the lost *Cardenio* (*c*.1612–13), *All Is True* (*Henry VIII*) (1623), and *The Two Noble Kinsmen* (1634)—before Shakespeare gave up writing for the stage. Beaumont stopped writing at about the same time as Shakespeare, and Fletcher went on to write many more plays—tragedies, comedies, and tragicomedies—both alone and with others (his chief partner after Fletcher was Philip Massinger). But when his dramatic works were published in 1647, they bore the title *Comedies and*

(cont. on page 143)

The First Part of the Contention of the Two Famous Houses of York and Lancaster (2 Henry VI)

The play was originally known and performed as *The First Part of the Contention of the Two Famous Houses of Lancaster and York, with the Death of the Good Duke Humphrey.* This title derives from the first version of the play, published in 1594. The second title is probably editorial and comes from the more familiar text of the play, longer by about a third, published in the 1623 First *Folio. Like the titles of the other plays about Henry's reign, the title *2 Henry VI* was given when the Folio presented all of the English histories in order of kings, even though Shakespeare did not compose the plays in this order.

The Contention was written in 1590–1 as the first of two parts. Its final scenes directly anticipate the opening of *Richard Duke of York* (*3 Henry VI*), written in 1591 and published in 1595. It was composed after the second edition of *Holinshed's *Chronicles* (1587, see below), and probably after publication of *Spenser's *The Faerie Queene* (1590). In September 1592 the playwright Robert *Greene parodied a line from *Richard Duke of York* (1.4.138). His allusion indicates that *The Contention* was also written prior to this date, and before theatres closed because of the plague on 23 June. On 3 March the manager-owner of the Rose theatre, Philip *Henslowe, records a 'new' performance of 'Harry the VI' in his diary. Conceivably, this entry may refer to any of the three *Henry VI* plays. But contextual evidence suggests it refers only to *Part 1*, which must have been written by August 1592, when Thomas *Nashe admired its inspiring heroism in *Piers Penniless his Supplication to the Devil.* If that is the case, *The Contention* and *Richard Duke of York* would have to have been written and performed between March and June. But this period has struck some, but not all, scholars as unrealistically brief, thus leading to the alternative theory that Shakespeare wrote *The Contention* before *1 Henry VI*. This explains several historical inconsistencies between the plays that one would not expect to find if the latter had come first, in particular the fact that *The Contention* makes no mention of *Part 1*'s ostensible hero, Talbot.

Text: The play was attributed to Shakespeare prior to the 1623 Folio by the title page of the unauthorized Pavier quarto of 1619 (Q3), which presented both *The Contention* and *Richard Duke of York* as *The Whole Contention between the Two Famous Houses, Lancaster and York.* From the late 18th century, however, Shakespeare's whole or part authorship began to be contested. Most recently the Oxford editors and Knowles (1999) continue to accept the possibility of Shakespeare's collaboration with *Greene, *Nashe, and George *Peele. Multiple authorship might explain Francis *Meres's failure to mention *Henry VI* in *Palladis Tamia* (1598), which lists other—but not all—known Shakespeare plays. Other modern editors believe Shakespeare was the sole author of *The Contention* and that the *Henry VI* plays were written in chronological order. Certain passages may sound like Greene, etc. because as a young playwright Shakespeare followed the normal early modern practice of imitating their verbal styles as he was developing his own.

Q1 of *The Contention* was entered in the Stationers' Register on 12 March 1594 and printed that year. A second edition published in 1600 (Q2) was based on Q1, as was the Pavier edition (Q3) in 1619. The provenance of Q1 has been questioned since the 18th century. One theory proposed by Edmond *Malone in 1790 was that Shakespeare revised and expanded Q1, which he believed was written by Greene and/or others. Alternatively, Dr *Johnson and Edward *Capell speculated that Q1 was some kind of report of the Folio text made from memory or shorthand. A. W. Pollard supported this view in 1909 by dividing Shakespeare quarto editions into 'Good' legitimate texts, and 'Bad' unauthorized and corrupt ones. In 1928 Madeleine Doran argued that Q1 was deliberately revised and shortened for touring performances outside London, and (independently) in 1929 Peter Alexander demonstrated that it was constructed from memory by actors who had performed the Folio version (probably Pembroke's Men after their collapse in August 1593, when they lost possession of the original playbooks). Alexander's thesis remains the accepted explanation of Q1's origins, notwithstanding valuable corrective challenges to the universal applicability of memorial reporting and to Pollard's morally inflected terminology. While Doran's arguments have also been accepted, with modifications, the derivation and purpose of Q1's often detailed stage directions continue to be disputed (namely they may be intended for readers), as do the reductions in playing personnel achieved by Q1.

Most modern scholars believe the Folio text is based on Shakespeare's manuscript, since several missing, imprecise, or discretionary stage directions suggest a draft, still open to revision, rather than a finished state or fair copy. Shakespeare also possibly revised several passages in the Folio manuscript at a later stage in his career (e.g. Clifford's speech at 5.3.31–49). Minor adjustments in the Folio, such as its elimination of Q1's Buckingham, may reflect topical political sensitivities. At several points the Folio typesetters consulted Q3 because the manuscript copy was unclear.

Sources: *The Contention* is the first of Shakespeare's English history plays to make use of Edward *Halle's *Union of the Two Noble and Illustrious Families of Lancaster and York* (1548), and the compilation edited by Raphael *Holinshed, *Chronicles of England, Scotland, and Ireland* (2nd edn. 1587). The established view is that Halle—traditionally regarded as more ideologically conservative—was Shakespeare's chief source, but recent scholarship has shifted the balance towards Holinshed. Shakespeare's presentation of Cade's rebellion in Act 4 draws on their accounts of the Peasants' Revolt of 1381. The story of Simpcox's false miracle in 2.1 is from John *Foxe's *Acts and Monuments* (the *Book of Martyrs*). Details of Eleanor Cobham's penance in 2.4 derive from a possible range of Elizabethan accounts, including *The *Mirror for Magistrates*. Robert Fabyan's *New Chronicles of England and France* (1516) is another minor source.

Synopsis: **1.1** Suffolk presents Margaret of Anjou to the English court, having wooed her by proxy for King Henry. Her lack of a dowry, and the negotiated repatriation of Anjou and Maine to the French, appals Gloucester. Winchester and Buckingham demand his removal as protector, but Salisbury is sceptical of their motives. York, alone on stage, expresses his frustrated ambitions for the crown but decides to allow factionalism to deepen before challenging the Lancastrians. **1.2** Gloucester's wife Eleanor reveals her dream of supplanting Henry and Margaret. Gloucester chides her ambitions. She hires Hume to invite witches to determine her fortunes, but he is in the pay of Winchester and Suffolk. **1.3** Seeking redress for feudal grievances, commoners mistakenly petition Suffolk and Margaret, who dismiss them disdainfully. Gloucester suppresses his rage against accusations of corruption, while Margaret tangles with Eleanor. Gloucester appoints a trial by combat between Peter, one of the petitioners, and Horner, who accuses him of saying York was true heir to the crown. York loses his bid to become regent in France to Somerset. **1.4** During Eleanor's conjuring, a spirit prophesies ominous fortunes for Henry, York, Suffolk, and Somerset. York and Buckingham interrupt the meeting and arrest the participants.

2.1 Gloucester and Winchester bicker while falconing. Gloucester exposes Simpcox's false claims of a miraculous cure of sight. **2.2** York convinces Salisbury and Warwick to support his future claim to the throne. **2.3** Eleanor is sentenced to banishment and Gloucester surrenders the protectorship. Peter defeats a drunken Horner in their trial by combat. **2.4** Eleanor does public penance and bids her sorrowful husband farewell.

3.1 Before a Parliament, Margaret leads allegations against Gloucester. Somerset reports the loss of England's remaining French territories, Gloucester is blamed and arrested, but Henry defends his innocence. Margaret, Suffolk, and York conspire with Winchester to kill Gloucester. York is dispatched to suppress an Irish rebellion. Alone on stage, York tells how he has persuaded a physically powerful Kentishman, Jack Cade, to be his stalking horse by impersonating his dead ancestor John Mortimer and inciting a civil insurrection against Lancastrian rule. **3.2** Suffolk reports Gloucester's death to Henry, who accuses him of complicity and repudiates Margaret. Gloucester's dead body is examined in his bed. Warwick concludes he was murdered and accuses Suffolk, who is exiled by Henry. Margaret and Suffolk part sadly. **3.3** Winchester, deranged and conscience-stricken, dies in his bed.

4.1 Suffolk is murdered on his way into exile by a sea captain and his crew, who express popular outrage at his and other lords' murder of Gloucester and abuse of the country's interests. **4.2–3** Cade's rebellion breaks out in Kent. The Staffords confront the rebels but are killed in battle. **4.4–7** Henry learns of Cade's advances towards London. Margaret grieves over the head of Suffolk, vowing revenge. Cade crosses London Bridge and sacks the Savoy and Inns of Court. He arrests Lord Say, charging him with corrupting the country through education, literacy, and print. Say defends himself eloquently and his words touch even Cade, but he and his son-in-law are beheaded and their heads made to kiss on poles. **4.8.** The rioters are confronted by Old Clifford and Buckingham, who offer Henry's pardon to those who will disperse, invoking the patriotic memory of Henry v's French conquests. Cade flees. **4.9** Henry pardons the rebels. York is reported to have returned from Ireland with his army, demanding the arrest of Somerset. **4.10** Cade, utterly famished, takes refuge in the Kentish garden of Alexander Iden, who fights and kills him.

5.1 Iden presents Cade's head to Henry and is knighted. York and his sons Edward and Richard, backed by Salisbury and Warwick, openly challenge Henry and his supporters. **5.2.** The first battle of St Albans. York kills Clifford, whose son vows revenge, and Richard kills Somerset. Henry and Margaret are defeated and flee to London. **5.3** The victorious Yorkists pursue them there.

Critical history: *The Contention* has frequently been better appreciated on the stage than in academic criticism, which has frequently been preoccupied with issues of text and authorship (and notwithstanding Ben Jonson's snipe: 'three rusty swords . . . Fight over York and Lancaster's long jars'). Nineteenth-century German *Romantic critics such as A. W. *Schlegel situated the play in the wider context of Shakespeare's histories as a whole, viewed as an epic national drama of political evolution. In 1944 E. M. W. *Tillyard's *Shakespeare's History Plays* adopted this interpretation but emphasized the divinely destined triumph of the Tudor dynasty: the history plays trace a pattern of national transgression, which begins with the deposition of Richard ii, a descent into civil chaos, and the restoration of order in the political marriage of Henry vii and Elizabeth of York. Since then, critics have gradually dismantled Tillyard's idealizing and totalizing premisses by studying the multiple perspectives and non-elite voices in this and other history plays that resist the notion of a monolithic ideology. The commoners' petitions and Cade's rebellion, although simultaneously comical and brutal, vividly express 16th-century traditions of popular radicalism and political protest against real social inequality and economic hardships. The play also focuses attention on the political vacuum created by Henry's personal weakness, the failures of public law and systematic justice (which collapse entirely after Duke Humphrey's death), and the destructive selfishness of the country's feudal rulers. Above all, the unceasing verbal and physical violence of the play, and its macabre spectacles of severed heads and suffering bodies, reflects the social disorder and material culture of Elizabethan society as well as late medieval England. They continue also to be read in the light of modern experiences of class conflict and political power struggles.

Stage history: *The Contention* was probably written for and performed by Lord Strange's Men, a large company able to accommodate the play's numerous roles. Q1's title page does not identify an acting company, but *Richard Duke of York*'s does: Pembroke's Men, who must also have performed *The Contention* after they came into being in May 1591. There is no further evidence of performance until John Crowne's *The Misery of Civil-War* (1680, staged 1681), a Royalist propaganda piece which adapted material from Cade's rebellion. Crowne then reworked Acts 1–3 as *Henry the Sixth* (1681), focusing popular anti-Catholic sentiment on Cardinal Winchester's murder of Duke Humphrey. From this point until the end of the 19th century, *The Contention* was performed in England only in distant adaptations, including a tercentenary revival by the Surrey theatre in April 1864. In Germany and Austria, however, strong interest in Shakespeare's histories by Romantic critics stimulated many innovative productions. F. R. *Benson mounted *The Contention* on 21 April 1899 in Stratford-upon-Avon, and again in 1906 and 1909. On the second occasion all three *Henry vi* plays were performed as a historical cycle (another idea borrowed from Germany). Benson satisfied Victorian tastes for sumptuous pageantry, but paced the action between scenes more continuously. Sir Barry *Jackson and Douglas Seale's Birmingham Repertory Theatre production in 1951 launched the play's modern stage life. Seale successfully alternated between still and lucid passages of formal verse, and explosions of factional violence. Barbara *Jefford drew serious attention to Queen Margaret's tragic role for the first time. Her powerful performance was surpassed only by Dame Peggy *Ashcroft in Peter Hall and John Barton's legendary *Wars of the Roses* for the RSC in 1963–4, later broadcast internationally in a 1965 television adaptation. Barton condensed *Part 1* and *The Contention* up to Margaret's grief for Suffolk's death into one play, *Henry vi*. He also added hundreds of lines of Shakespearian pastiche to clarify personal motives and storylines. *The Contention* was performed unadapted in Terry *Hands's well-received 1977 RSC production of the whole trilogy, a precedent followed by Michael Boyd in 2000. In 1986 Michael Bogdanov and Michael Pennington reverted to Barton's condensed format—minus his invented lines—for their spiky 'post-Falklands' production, *The Wars of the Roses*, for the *English Shakespeare Company, which toured internationally 1986–9 and is preserved on videotape. Adrian *Noble followed their format but not their production's 'radical' ideology for his two-play version *The Plantagenets* for the RSC in 1988. In America, Pat Patton based his stirring 1991 Oregon Shakespeare Festival production on Noble's *House of Lancaster*. Previous productions of *The Contention* at Ashland in 1954, 1965, and 1976 had employed strong ensemble acting and Shakespeare's full script. *RWFM*

On the screen: The play featured as one episode of the BBC's *An Age of Kings* in 1960, and in Barton's rewritten form as part of the televised *The Wars of the Roses* in 1965. Jane Howell's full-text version for BBC TV in 1983, with its Brechtian asides-to-camera and visible use of the TV studio space, had Cade (Trevor Peacock, returning as anti-hero after playing Talbot in *1 Henry vi*) leading his followers in a book-burning reminiscent of Nazi Germany. *AD*

Recent major editions

Michael Hattaway (New Cambridge, 1991); Richard Knowles (Arden 3rd series, 1999)

Some representative criticism

Berry, Edward I., *Patterns of Decay: Shakespeare's Early Histories* (1975)

Brockbank, J. P., 'The Frame of Disorder: *Henry vi*', in John Russell Brown and Bernard Harris (eds.), *Early Shakespeare* (1961)

Jones, Emrys, *The Origins of Shakespeare* (1977)

Potter, Lois, 'Recycling the Early Histories: "The Wars of the Roses" and "The Plantagenets" ', *Shakespeare Survey*, 43 (1991)

Pugliatti, Paola, *Shakespeare the Historian* (1996)

Rackin, Phyllis, *Stages of History: Shakespeare's English Chronicles* (1990)

Swander, Homer D., 'The Rediscovery of *Henry vi*', *Shakespeare Quarterly*, 29 (1978)

Tragedies Written by Francis Beaumont and John Fletcher, and it is as Beaumont's collaborator that he has entered the mythology of the theatre.

The extraordinary unity of Beaumont and Fletcher's work together provoked endless speculation about the nature of their relationship. John *Aubrey wrote: 'They lived together on the Bankside, not far from the Playhouse, both bachelors; lay together; had one wench in the house between them, which they did so admire; the same clothes and cloak, etc., between them.' After Shakespeare's retirement their plays rapidly outstripped his in popularity, and remained the most popular and influential works of the Jacobean theatre for most of the 17th century. They deserve to be better known. *RM*

Finkelpearl, Philip J., *Court and Country Politics in the Plays of Beaumont and Fletcher* (1990)
Leech, Clifford, *The John Fletcher Plays* (1962)
McMullan, Gordon, *The Politics of Unease in the Plays of John Fletcher* (1994)
McMullan, Gordon, and Hope, Jonathan (eds.), *The Politics of Tragicomedy: Shakespeare and After* (1992)
Maguire, Nancy Klein (ed.), *Renaissance Tragicomedy: Explorations in Genre and Politics* (1987)

Florence, the capital of Tuscany, figures in *All's Well That Ends Well* (Florence is the setting of 3.5 and successive scenes). Florence is also mentioned in *The Taming of the Shrew* (1.1.14 and 4.2.91) and 'Florentines' (people from Florence) in *Much Ado About Nothing* (1.1.10) and *Othello* (1.1.19 and 3.1.39). *AB*

Florence, Duke of. He appoints Bertram 'general of our horse' in *All's Well That Ends Well* 3.3.1. *AB*

Florio, Giovanni (John) (?1554–?1625), translator. The English-born son of an Italian Protestant refugee, Florio graduated from Oxford University and began to translate Italian texts into English. He produced two grammars, *Florio his First Fruits* (1578) and *Second Fruits* (1591), and an Italian–English dictionary (1598), works that Shakespeare probably knew if, as seems likely, he studied Italian himself. But Florio was most renowned for his translation of Montaigne's *Essais*, published in 1603. In a copy of *Volpone* that he gave to Florio, Ben Jonson acknowledged his debt to the translator and called him a friend to the theatre. He was certainly a friend to Shakespeare's drama and possibly to the man himself. Shakespeare and Florio may have been acquainted with one another through their shared patron Henry Wriothesley, Earl of *Southampton. Hence, Shakespeare may have had access to Florio's famous library, and the Italianate aspects of his plays may have been inspired by the literature he found there. Florio's own book, his translation of *Montaigne, is the most obvious connection between them. Passages in *The Tempest* suggest Shakespeare's use of Florio's translation, in particular Gonzalo's speech on his ideal commonwealth. *King Lear* features more than 100 words, new to Shakespeare's work, that could have been found in Florio's Montaigne. *JKS*

Florizel, the son of Polixenes, woos Perdita (who he thinks is a shepherdess) disguised as 'Doricles', a shepherd, in *The Winter's Tale* 4.4. *AB*

Florizel and Perdita. See *Winter's Tale, The*; Garrick, David.

flourish, a call on *trumpets or *cornets, perhaps extemporized, usually heralding a processional entrance; see *The Two Noble Kinsmen* 2.5 opening ('short flourish'), and also *Richard II* 1.3.122 ('long flourish'). *JB*

'Flout 'em and cout 'em', fragment sung by Stefano and Trinculo in *The Tempest* 3.2.123; the original music is unknown; Caliban tells the pair that their tune is wrong; they are corrected by Ariel on *tabor and *pipe. *JB*

Flower family. See Flower portrait; Shakespeare Memorial Theatre; Shakespeare tercentenary of 1864.

Flower portrait, half-length, oil on panel, dated 1609, inscribed 'W. Shakespeare'. Now in the *RSC collection in Stratford, the portrait is named after its former owner Mrs Charles Flower, of the Stratford brewing dynasty. Following a late 19th-century trend for identifying likely originals for Martin *Droeshout's engraved portrait, the Flower portrait was described as an original for the First Folio engraving by M. H. Speilmann in 1906. It is much more likely, however, that it is a later work based upon it. *CT*

Fluchère, Henri (1898–1987), French scholar. Fluchère gave a decisive impulse to Elizabethan studies in France after the Second World War with his *Shakespeare, dramaturge élisabéthain* (1948). He edited and prefaced Shakespeare's works for the Pléiade two-volume *Shakespeare* (1959). Many books followed including a prose translation of and introduction to *Coriolan* (1980). In 1946 he created and directed the Maison Française d'Oxford College, and in 1968 was elected Dean of the Arts Faculty at the Université d'Aix-en-Provence. In 1977, with other scholars specializing in 16th-century English literature, he launched the Société Française Shakespeare, a branch of the International Shakespeare Association, and chaired it for the first term. *ISG*

Fluellen, Captain. A Welshman in *Henry V*, he quarrels with Macmorris (3.3), Williams (4.8), and *Pistol (5.1). *AB*

flute, in Shakespeare's time a plain wooden tube with six finger holes; it came in various sizes, the most usual being the middle-sized instrument in D. The term 'flute' then might also indicate *recorder. *JB*

Flute, Francis. A bellows-mender in *A Midsummer Night's Dream*, he plays Thisbe in the play-within-the-play of 5.1. *AB*

flying. In the drama a supernatural character (for example a classical god) might best enter by being lowered from the 'heavens' over the stage, suggesting flight. The actor sat in a carriage attached by ropes to a winch in the stage cover, and the first playhouse to have a full stage cover was the Rose. In 1595 *Henslowe paid carpenters for 'making the throne in the heavens', which was the first known descent machine for flying. The Globe seems not to have been fitted with a flight machine until around 1608–9 when the King's Men brought it into conformity with their other playhouse, the Blackfriars, which had one. Shakespeare's pre-1608 supernatural characters—Hymen in *As You Like It* and Diana in *Pericles*—walk rather than fly onto the stage. Sound effects (for example thunder) or celestial music added to the impact of a supernatural descent and also helped drown the creaking of the winch. *GE*

Foersom, Peter (1777–1817), Danish actor and translator. The first to translate Shakespeare into Danish verse, he acted Hamlet in the first ever Shakespeare production at the Royal Theatre, Copenhagen, 1813. His translations of ten of the tragedies and histories (1807–18) have remained influential. *I-SE*

Rubow, P. V., *Shakespeare paa dansk* (1932)

Folger Collection. See Folger Shakespeare Library.

Folger Shakespeare. This pocket paperback edition of individual plays issued in Washington and New York between 1957 and 1964 was edited by the director of the Folger Shakespeare Library, Louis B. Wright, with Virginia A. Lamar. It was aimed at 'the general reader', and proved, with its brief and simple notes on pages facing the text, and illustrations drawn from old documents and books in the Folger Library, to be very popular for use in schools. Using the same basic format, Barbara Mowat and Paul Werstine are re-editing the series in the light of current thinking about Shakespeare's texts. *RAF*

Folger Shakespeare Library, Washington. It houses the world's largest collection of Shakespeare's printed works, including 79 copies of the First Folio and 204 quartos, among them a unique copy of *Titus Andronicus* (1594). The collection also comprises an estimated 27,000 paintings, drawings, engravings, and prints

representing or associated with Shakespeare, including the *Ashbourne (Kingston) portrait. The collection was amassed and then given to the nation in 1928 by Henry Clay Folger (1857–1930) and his wife. *SLB*

http://www.folger.edu

folios. A book in which the printed sheet is folded in half, making two leaves or four pages, is known as a folio. The prestigious folio format was used for works by the leading theologians, philosophers, and historians of the day: Holinshed's *Chronicles* (1587), Richard Hooker's *Laws* (1611), Sir Walter Ralegh's *History of the World* (1614), and William Camden's *Annals* (1615). The groundbreaking edition of Ben Jonson's *Workes* (1616) marked the first time that the *œuvre* of a playwright had ever been published in folio. But the Jonson folio had included prose and poetry as well as dramatic texts. A folio devoted entirely to plays was unprecedented before the publication in 1623 of *Mr. William Shakespeare's Comedies, Histories, & Tragedies*, the First Folio.

We know very little about the planning stages of the First Folio. It may be that Shakespeare's friends and fellow actors in the King's Men—chief among them John Heminges and Henry Condell—were planning an authorized collection of his plays when they got wind of Thomas Pavier's plans to bring out an unauthorized collection in 1619, or perhaps they got the idea from Pavier.

In their epistle 'To the great Variety of Readers', Heminges and Condell describe their task: 'It has been a thing, we confess, worthy to have been wished, that the author himself had lived to have set forth, and overseen his own writings. But since it hath been ordained otherwise, and he by death departed from that right, we pray you do not envy his friends, the office of their care, and pain, to have collected and published them.'

A syndicate of publishers was at some point formed to underwrite the venture. The colophon on the last page of the Folio is unusual in that it emphasizes the financial costs of the undertaking: '*Printed at the Charges of W. Jaggard, Ed. Blount, I. Smithweeke, and W. Aspley, 1623*'. Jaggard's association with Pavier's project no doubt involved the accumulation of rights to plays that had been printed earlier, a vital component for the production of the Folio. John Smethwick was probably invited to join the cartel because he held the copy rights to *Hamlet, Romeo and Juliet, Love's Labour's Lost,* and *The Taming of the Shrew*. Similarly, William Aspley held the rights to *2 Henry IV* and *Much Ado About Nothing*.

The imprint claims that the book was 'printed by Isaac Iaggard, and Ed. Blount'. However, Blount was only a publisher; the printing of the Folio was done entirely in the shop of William Jaggard and his son Isaac. Charlton Hinman, in his reconstruction of the events in the Jaggard printing-house, demonstrated that the printing of the 907-page Folio began early in 1622 and took nearly two years to complete, during which time as many as nine compositors worked on the project. Hinman established that the Folio was set by formes (not seriatim, as had been previously thought) and identified the pairs of type-cases used by the compositors. Apparently the copy was cast off so that two compositors could work simultaneously on the same forme, thereby speeding up composition in relation to presswork. In setting the text of *The Two Gentlemen of Verona*, for instance, Compositor C set page 30 (signature C3[v]) while Compositor A simultaneously set page 31 (signature C4[r]).

The title page advertises the plays within as 'published according to the true original copies' and Heminges and Condell distinguish their authoritative texts from some of the previously published quarto editions: 'before you were abused with diverse stolen and surreptitious copies, maimed, and deformed by the frauds and stealths of injurious impostors that exposed them; even those are now offered to your view cured and perfect of their limbs; and all the rest absolute in their numbers as he conceived them.' The publishers apparently commissioned the professional scribe Ralph *Crane to prepare transcripts of the original manuscripts to be used as printer's copy for *The Tempest, The Two Gentlemen of Verona, The Merry Wives of Windsor, Measure for Measure, The Winter's Tale,* and possibly *Cymbeline*. These were among the first plays to be printed, so it appears that Crane had an association with the Folio enterprise only in its early stages. In addition to Crane's transcripts, the Folio compositors had access to a wide variety of copy. Of the 36 plays in the Folio, twelve appear to have been set up from earlier printed quartos that had been annotated from a manuscript playbook: *Titus Andronicus, Richard III, Love's Labour's Lost, A Midsummer Night's Dream, Romeo and Juliet, Richard II, The Merchant of Venice, 1 Henry IV, Much Ado About Nothing, Hamlet, Troilus and Cressida,* and *The Tragedy of King Lear*; the playbooks themselves were apparently used as copy for only three plays in the Folio: *Julius Caesar, As You Like It,* and *Macbeth*; another nine were set from Shakespeare's foul papers: *The Taming of the Shrew, The First Part of the Contention* (*2 Henry VI*), *Richard Duke of York* (*3 Henry VI*), *1 Henry VI, The Comedy of Errors, Henry V, All's Well That Ends Well, Timon of Athens,* and *Antony and Cleopatra*; and six from transcripts made by unidentified scribes: *King John, 2 Henry IV, Twelfth Night, Othello, Coriolanus,* and *All Is True* (*Henry VIII*).

Heminges and Condell divided the plays into the generic categories of the volume's title—Comedies, Histories, and Tragedies—and apparently exercised some care in ordering the plays so that each section begins and ends with plays that had not previously appeared in quarto. The only exception to this rule is *Troilus and Cressida*, the first page of which was initially printed on the verso of the last page of *Romeo and Juliet*, in the middle of the tragedies section; the text was then reset and re-placed to come first among the tragedies—*or* last among the histories; the table of contents for the Folio omits the play and thus does not make it clear to which category it belongs. Heminges and Condell seem to have made a conscious decision not to include Shakespeare's poems in the collection, and they may have intentionally omitted some of the late collaborative plays as well (*Pericles, Cardenio,* and *The Two Noble Kinsmen*).

The first preliminary page of the First Folio consists of a verse by Ben Jonson on the *Droeshout portrait, which appears on the facing title page:

To the Reader.
This figure, that thou here seest put
It was for gentle Shakespeare cut;
Wherein the Graver had a strife
With Nature, to out-do the life:
O, could he but have drawn his wit
As well in brass, as he hath hit
His face; the Print would then surpass
All that was ever writ in brass.
But, since he cannot, reader, look
Not on his picture, but his book.
B.J.

Then follows the dedication to William Herbert, 3rd Earl of *Pembroke, and his brother Philip Herbert, Earl of Montgomery. The next item is Heminges and Condell's epistle 'To the Great Variety of Readers', two commendatory poems by Ben Jonson and Hugh Holland, the 'Catalogue of the several Comedies, Histories, and Tragedies contained in this Volume', two more commendatory verses, and finally a list of the 'Principal Actors' in the plays.

The First Folio was expected to be on the market by mid-1622; it was included in the Frankfurt book fair's catalogue as one of the books printed between April 1622 and October 1622. In the event, however, the Folio did not actually appear until very late in 1623. On 8 November 1623, Blount and Isaac Jaggard entered in the Stationers' Register their copy rights to the plays that had not been previously published:

> M[r] William Shakspeers Comedyes, Histories, and Tragedies soe manie of the said Copies as are not formerly entred to other

The 'Flower' portrait of Shakespeare, now in the RSC Collection in Stratford. The painting probably derives from Martin Droeshout's title-page engraving for the First Folio rather than being, as some have claimed, the original on which the engraving is based.

Ex dono Willi Jaggard Typographi a° 1623

MR. WILLIAM

SHAKESPEARES

COMEDIES,
HISTORIES, &
TRAGEDIES.

Published according to the True Originall Copies.

Martin Droeshout sculpsit London.

LONDON

Printed by Isaac Iaggard, and Ed. Blount. 1623.

The title page of the First Folio, 1623. This presentation copy from the publisher William Jaggard is now, along with more than 70 other copies, in the Folger Shakespeare Library in Washington.

> men. vizt. Comedyes. The Tempest. The two gentlemen of Verona. Measure for Measure. The Comedy of Errors. As you Like it. All's well that ends well. Twelft night. The winters tale. Histories. The thirde parte of Henry the sixt. Henry the eight. Coriolanus. Timon of Athens. Julius Caesar. Tragedies. Mackbeth. Anthonie and Cleopatra. Cymbeline.

The printing of the Folio was probably completed shortly thereafter—a copy at the Bodleian Library in Oxford was sent for binding on 17 February 1624—and the book was then available in bookshops for the princely sum of £1 (40 times the cost of an individual quarto).

The volume was so successful and demand apparently so great that a second edition was required within less than a decade. In 1632, Thomas Cotes, who had taken over the Jaggard shop following Isaac's death in 1627, printed the Second Folio for a syndicate of publishers that again included Smethwick and Aspley. The Second Folio was a carefully corrected page-for-page reprint of the first that made hundreds of minor changes in the text, the majority of which have been accepted by modern editors. The preliminaries of the Second Folio include John Milton's first published poem, 'An Epitaph on the Admirable Dramatic Poet W. Shakespeare'. The elegant paper stock used for the Second Folio occasioned William Prynne to lament in *Histrio-mastix* (1633) that 'playbooks are grown from quarto into folio' and that 'Shakespeare's plays are printed in the best crown paper, far better than most Bibles.'

The Third Folio appeared in 1663, with a second issue in 1664 that added *Pericles* and six apocryphal plays: *The London Prodigal*, *Thomas, Lord Cromwell*, *Sir John Oldcastle*, *The Puritan*, *A Yorkshire Tragedy*, and *Locrine*. The Fourth Folio was published in 1685; 70 pages of this edition were reprinted *c.*1700 to make up a shortage and may be considered a Fifth Folio printing. *ER*

Greg, W. W., *The Shakespeare First Folio* (1955)
Hinman, Charlton, *The Printing and Proof-Reading of the First Folio of Shakespeare* (1963)
Pollard, A. W., *Shakespeare Folios and Quartos: A Study in the Bibliography of Shakespeare's Plays 1594–1685* (1909)

Folio Society Shakespeare. The 37 volumes of this handsomely printed edition were issued between 1950 and 1976, using the text of the New Temple Shakespeare. They are chiefly notable for the introductions, of varying interest, written mainly by well-known actors and directors, among them Laurence *Olivier, Paul *Scofield, Richard *Burton, Peter *Brook, and Peter *Hall. The texts are illustrated with reproductions of costume and stage designs from the period. Thirty-five of the introductions were published as a separate book in 1978. The Folio Society have since reprinted the *Oxford edition twice. *RAF*

food and drink. The Elizabethan year (see CALENDAR) fell into feast and fast periods: both Wednesdays and Fridays were fish-eating days until 1585 and the six weeks of Lent were equally meatless except in the case of pregnant women, children, and invalids. At such times the poor ate saltfish (such as the 'poor-john' Caliban is said to smell like, *The Tempest* 2.2.25–7), while the rich might eat sprats or herrings, fresh, dried, smoked, or salted. Christmas feasting, during which open house was kept by big households, ran from 1 November right through to Twelfth Night (6 January): its special dishes included boar brawn, mince pies (still made with spiced meat), and the 'flapdragon' mentioned in *Love's Labour's Lost* (5.1.42). Other feasts would include funerals (cf. *Hamlet* on the

Here give me ſome Sack,
Says old Tun-belly'd Jack.

Shakespeare's greatest glutton, Sir John Falstaff: a popular engraving published by Bowles and Carver, *c.*1790, loosely based on earlier depictions of the actor James Quin in what became his best-loved role.

reuse of leftovers, 1.2.179–80), weddings (cf. *Taming of the Shrew* 3.3), sheep-shearing (as in *The Winter's Tale*, at which the shepherds plan to eat 'warden pie', a pear pie coloured with saffron and spiced with mace, nutmegs, ginger, prunes, and sultanas, 4.3.44–8), and harvest-home.

The richer ate three meals a day, the poorer more like two. Breakfast, served generally between 6 and 8 a.m., varied widely from the big hunting breakfasts recorded as being given for Elizabeth to private collations: the food ranged from ale, beer, or wine, boiled beef or mutton, and bread, to eggs, milk, and butter. In *Antony and Cleopatra* there is admiring talk of 'eight wild-boars roasted whole at a breakfast' (2.2.186–7). The poor would be more likely to eat some sort of cereal made into a pottage.

The main meal of the day, dinner, was served at 11 a.m. for the gentry, the middling sort eating at noon. It was laid with great ceremony on a long table, with the wine, wine cups, and basin and ewer for washing on the 'court-cupboard' (not unlike a modern sideboard; cf. *Romeo and Juliet* 1.5.6–7). The guests would for the most part be seated on joint-stools in order of social rank—hence the dramatic social solecism of Lady Macbeth's hasty command to her guests to 'stand not upon the order of your going' (*Macbeth* 3.4.118). The meal might last two, three, or four hours, and would consist of two courses, laid in prescribed patterns on the table for the diners to help themselves. The first course would consist of 'gross meats' or the equivalent on fish-days, perhaps buttered and spiced fish pies of sturgeon or salmon; the second of poultry, raised pies in 'coffins' of pastry (cf. Titus's cannibal version, *Titus Andronicus* 5.2.185–90), puddings, 'kickshaws', or 'made dishes' (e.g. fricasses, carbonadoes, hashes, collops), and salads of cooked, pickled, or raw vegetables, herbs, and flowers. The third course was the 'banquet' course. Whereas the first two courses would have been eaten in either the hall (now steadily shrinking in size) or the newly fashionable private dining parlour, the banquet 'to close our stomachs up | After our great good cheer' (*Taming of the Shrew* 5.2.9–10) would be taken in another location entirely—another room (such as the 'privy chamber' to which Wolsey's most privileged guests withdraw for their banquet, *All Is True* (*Henry VIII*) 1.3.101–2), an outside summer house, temporary or permanent, or perhaps a gazebo on the roof. There guests would be regaled on expensive sweetmeats skilfully prepared by the lady of the house—sweet biscuits and tarts, a marchpane, wet and dry 'suckets' (preserved fruits), and fresh fruit, all preceded by a 'conceited' dish of sugar sculpture made to represent a bird, animal, fish, or even, on one occasion, a castle made of sugar firing tiny guns with real gunpowder at its besiegers. The witty, whimsical, and luxurious nature of this food is reflected in Benedick's description of Claudio's affected language in *Much Ado About Nothing* as a 'fantastical banquet' (2.3.15). All told, there might be of the order of thirty different dishes for a humblish feast, though more like five or six for the country gentleman not expecting guests (compare Justice Shallow's menu in *2 Henry IV* 5.1.22–4). While the main courses were eaten on wooden, pewter, or silver trenchers depending on the wealth of the household, the banquet was served on glass plates (often hired) and eaten off wafer-thin wooden or sugar plate trenchers often decorated on the underside with a verse or epigram called a 'roundel' and read out at the end of the meal. Food was carved with a knife (often worn at the man's belt) but eaten with the fingers—forks were still a novel luxury item. Fingers were washed at the end of every course in bowls of rose-water. In between courses there might be entertainment laid on, music, a masque, or dancing—hence the appositeness of the masquing Ariel at the magic banquet in *The Tempest* (3.3.52 ff.).

Supper, by contrast, was usually very much an afterthought. Gentry supped between 5 and 6 p.m., farmers and merchants not before 7 or 8 p.m., and labourers at dusk. The meal was light—perhaps eggs and a posset (hot milk fortified with sugar, spices, eggs, and wine, brandy, or ale, and on one notable occasion with additional soporifics by Lady Macbeth, *Macbeth* 2.2.6–8).

Elizabethan England was full of the excitement of new food imports, and Shakespeare's plays reflect this. New fruits and vegetables from the Americas made their appearance: tomatoes, and potatoes both sweet and common. With Dutch refugees came asparagus, cardoons, globe artichokes, and cauliflowers, and from southern Europe the apricot, quince, fig, and melon (the real Richard II's garden would not have featured the 'dangling apricot' of 3.4.30). The more expensive or exotic the food, the more likely it was to be regarded as an aphrodisiac—hence Falstaff's excited invocation of potatoes, eringoes (the candied root of sea-holly), and kissing-comfits in *The Merry Wives of Windsor* (5.5.18–21).

In drinks, too, Falstaff proves to have expensive tastes. The generality drank ale or beer, but large quantities of claret, malmsey, madeira, and sack (a dry Spanish wine not unlike sherry), sometimes 'burnt', that is to say, heated (see *Twelfth Night* 2.3.184), were shipped in from France, Crete, Madeira, and Spain respectively. Households also produced flower and fruit wines, often for medicinal use.

Food as a source of Shakespeare's imagery was well studied by *Spurgeon, in particular bread and candy. Feasts and interrupted feasts feature importantly; see in particular *The Taming of the Shrew*, *Macbeth*, *Titus Andronicus*, *Timon of Athens*, *Antony and Cleopatra*, *As You Like It*, and *The Tempest.* But delight in food and drink in Shakespeare is synonymous with Falstaff, whose tastes provide such a sharp profile of fashionable gluttony. *NJW*

Emmison, F. G., *Tudor Food and Pastimes* (1964)
Hartley, Dorothy, *Food in England* (1954)
Lorwin, Madge, *Dining with William Shakespeare* (1976)
Paston-Williams, Sara, *The Art of Dining: A History of Cooking and Eating* (1993)
Wilson, C. Anne, *Food and Drink in Britain* (1973)

fools. In Shakespeare's time, fools or jesters were retained as providers of entertainment to both the royal court and well-to-do households like those of Olivia in *Twelfth Night* and Leonato in *Much Ado About Nothing.* They were usually male, and would often wear a distinctive costume of 'motley' (parti-coloured cloth), wear a coxcomb on their head (not the belled hood of later tradition but a removable cap), and carry a 'bauble' or carved stick, which was often a focus for phallic humour. Some were professional comedians who adopted a façade of folly, others mentally handicapped individuals, known as 'naturals', whose innocent antics were considered humorous. Their remarks could also be sharply satirical: both types of fool would be granted much greater latitude in speaking than would ordinary courtiers, although King Lear's fool is threatened with whipping when he goes too far.

Shakespeare began to use fools as stage characters with Touchstone in *As You Like It.* Scholars have postulated that he may have been responding to an innovation in a lost play by George Chapman for a rival acting company, or to the arrival in his own company of a new principal comic actor, Robert *Armin. Most of these figures, including Feste in *Twelfth Night* and Lavatch in *All's Well That Ends Well*, are professionals who are consciously wiser than the jesting roles they adopt, though the Fool in *King Lear* may be a 'natural'. All of them see and describe the plays' events in meaningful ways that are not available in normal social discourse. *MW*

Billington, Sandra, *A Social History of the Fool* (1984)
Southworth, John, *Fools and Jesters at the English Court* (1998)
Welsford, Enid, *The Fool: His Social and Literary History* (1935)

fools. **(1)** Servant of a prostitute, a fool appears briefly in *Timon of Athens* 2.2. **(2)** In *The Tragedy of King Lear* a fool accompanies Lear into the storm, but does not appear after 3.6 (*History of King Lear* 13). *AB*

foot, a patterned metrical unit (iambic, trochaic, pyrrhic, spondaic, anapaestic). See METRE. *GTW*

Foote, Samuel (1721–77), controversial English actor and writer. He was trained by *Macklin and first appeared as Othello to his mentor's Iago. Best known as a satirist (and from 1767 as owner of the Haymarket), he was particularly scornful of the Stratford *Jubilee but was himself the subject of ridicule—and some dreadful puns on his name—following the amputation of a leg. *CMSA*

Forbes-Robertson, Sir Johnston (1853–1937), English actor, who at the outset of his career (1874) came under the influence of the veteran Shakespearian actor Samuel Phelps and thereafter sought to uphold his 'histrionic pedigree'. Described by Shaw as 'essentially a classical actor', Forbes-Robertson put his natural gifts and personality to the service of his roles. In juvenile parts (Hal to Phelps's Henry IV in Manchester, 1874; Claudio with Irving and Terry at the Lyceum, 1882; and Romeo between 1880 and 1895 to a succession of Juliets, including in 1895 Mrs Patrick Campbell who also partnered him in *Macbeth* in 1898) he was judged by some to be rather insipid, but coming to Hamlet (rather late at 44 in 1897) he captured the grace, intellect and melancholy of the Dane in what for many was the definitive performance of its day. In 1913 (aged 60) he committed his legendary Hamlet to—silent—film. *RF*

Forbidden Planet, 1956, American science-fiction film, inspired by Shakespeare's *The Tempest*, directed by Fred M. Wilcox. The film is set in AD 2200. On the planet Altair Four a Prospero-like Dr Morbius (with his Miranda-like daughter Altaira) unleashes uncontrollable monstrous forces, apparently from his own id. The rock musical *Return to the Forbidden Planet* (1981) develops this. *TM*

'For Bonny sweet Robin is all my joy', snatch of a ballad sung by Ophelia in *Hamlet* 4.5.185. The tune, under a variety of titles with the word 'Robin', survives in many arrangements from the period. *JB*

Ford, Master Frank. He tests his wife by bribing Falstaff to woo her (having taken the name Brooke (Broome in the First *Folio) to conceal his identity) in *The Merry Wives of Windsor*. *AB*

Ford, Mistress Alice. With Mistress Page she devises a punishment for Falstaff, after they find he has sent them identical love letters, in *The Merry Wives of Windsor*. *AB*

Fordham, John. See ELY, BISHOP OF.

foreign words. The renaissance of learning in 16th-century England led to the enrichment of the English vocabulary with foreign words largely introduced from classical sources (often in Anglicized form) via translations from Latin and French literary and scientific texts. Because of the association of Latin with scholarship, unusual Latin loans became known as 'inkhorn' terms, whose introduction was strongly supported by some, like Sir Thomas Elyot (1490–1546), and opposed by others, like Sir John Cheke (1514–57). Shakespeare employed their misuse by lower-class speakers, like Dogberry, and their excessive use by courtly speakers, like Osric, as sources of humour and satire. *VS*

forestage, another name for an apron stage, or an extension to an apron stage. *GE*

forgery, the practice of counterfeiting an author's personal documents or works; specifically in the case of Shakespeare, counterfeiting his signature, manuscripts of his plays and poems, annotations in printed copies of his works, and historical and theatrical documents pertaining to his career.

The forgery of Shakespeare documents has a long and extensive history, beginning in his own lifetime, judging from the number of spurious plays published under his name or initials, and continuing to the present day, as manuscript experts at major auction houses and book-dealers can attest. However, the two most notorious and influential Shakespeare forgers were William Henry Ireland (1777–1835) and John Payne Collier (1789–1883).

William Ireland, the son of Samuel Ireland, a successful London book-dealer, began his forging career as a teenager by tracing over published facsimiles of Shakespeare's signatures and by acquiring old paper and mixing old formulas for ink. His forgeries included poems, personal letters (including a flattering letter sent by Queen Elizabeth I), a 'profession of faith', playhouse documents, property and mortgage deeds, promissory notes, and receipts, all purportedly signed by or involving Shakespeare. Ireland then progressed to forging partial or whole manuscripts of *Hamlet* and *King Lear* and produced partial copies of what he claimed were original manuscripts of the hitherto unknown Shakespeare plays *Vortigern and Rowena* (staged once unsuccessfully in 1796 by Richard Brinsley Sheridan at Drury Lane Theatre), *Henry II*, and *William the Conqueror*.

Samuel Ireland published some of his son's documents in 1795, convinced that they were genuine. In the next year, the editor and literary critic Edmond *Malone denounced the papers as forgeries produced under the direction of the elder Ireland in his book *Inquiry into the Authenticity of Certain Miscellaneous Papers* and in another pamphlet which was answered by Samuel Ireland, opening a contentious debate among the literary community. In the same year William Ireland finally admitted in his *Authentic Account* that he had forged the documents without his father's knowledge or assistance. Nevertheless, his attackers continued to claim his father had been complicit. In 1805 he published his *Confessions* and began trying to restore his literary reputation by claiming the unknown Shakespeare plays as his own and in writing other original plays, poems, and novels. However, after his death he and his father were again attacked, this time by C. M. Ingleby, who succeeded, incorrectly, in convincing the literary community that Samuel Ireland had indeed been the mastermind of the Ireland forgeries.

John Payne Collier was already a respected literary critic and Shakespearian editor when he claimed in 1852 to have purchased a copy of a 1632 Second Folio of Shakespeare's works owned by Thomas Perkins, alleged to have been a relative of a member of Shakespeare's acting company, the King's Men. Collier published numerous descriptions of the annotations written in Renaissance hand that he claimed to have discovered throughout the text of the 'Perkins Folio', arguing that they were taken from early Shakespearian performances. The Folio was accepted as genuine by many until subjected in 1859 to forensic examination, when it was discovered that the annotations had originally been written out in pencil and traced over in ink, and thus were modern forgeries. Many of Collier's numerous other purported Renaissance literary and theatrical finds, including Shakespeare's signature on a letter, and references to Shakespeare added to genuine theatrical documents, were then also discovered to be forgeries. In fact, the same man who had reopened the Ireland forgery case, C. M. Ingleby, exposed many of Collier's forgeries.

Yet Collier continued to work as a critic and editor, even insisting that the apocryphal play *Edward III* be assigned to Shakespeare. Collier maintained his innocence until his death. The sale of his library afterwards, however, more disastrously sealed his reputation as a forger when many of the documents in it were examined for the first time and found to be fake. Collier's most lasting legacy is that all of the numerous public and private libraries, including the important collections of the Dulwich College, Heber, and Bridgewater libraries, to which he had unsupervised access early in his career still come under suspicion of containing material that he doctored or forged.

Material exposed as Shakespearian forgeries still commands interest and attention, and today is collected in its own right. For instance, one collection of forgeries by William Ireland was auctioned at Sotheby's, London, in 1982 for £12,000 (and has since increased in value), and other items by him and Collier still find eager buyers. *GI*

Brae, E. A., *Literary Cookery* (1855)
Collier, John Payne, *Notes and Emendations to the Text of Shakespeare's Plays from Early Manuscript Corrections in a Copy of the Folio of 1632 in the Possession of John Payne Collier* (2nd edn. 1853)

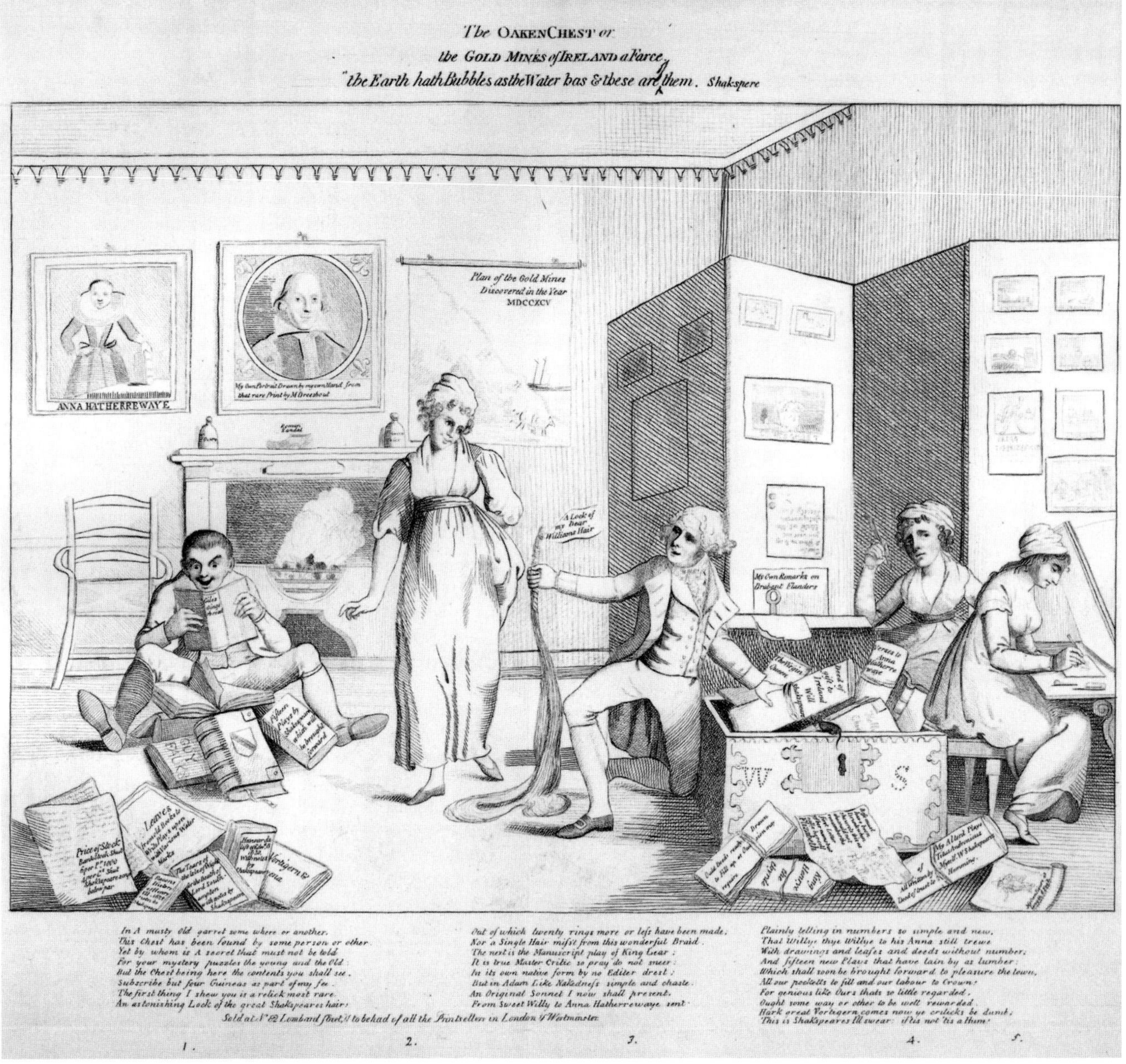

'The Oaken Chest; or, The Gold Mines of Ireland, a Farce', a satire on the Ireland forgery affair, 1796. Among the documents in the foreground are a stock-market quotation on the going rate for Shakespeare scripts.

Grebanier, Bernard D. N., *The Great Shakespeare Forgery* (1966)
Hamilton, N. E. S. A., *Inquiry into the Genuineness of the Manuscript Corrections in Mr. J. P. Collier's Annotated Shakespeare Folio 1632* (1860)
Ingleby, Clement M., *The Shakespeare Fabrications* (1859)
Ireland, Samuel, *Miscellaneous Papers and Legal Instruments under the Hand and Seal of William Shakespeare* (1796)
Ireland, William Henry, *Authentic Account of the Shakespearian Manuscripts* (1796)
Ireland, William Henry, *Confessions of W. H. Ireland* (1805)
Malone, Edmond, *Inquiry into the Authenticity of Certain Miscellaneous Papers* (1796)
Tannenbaum, Samuel A., *Shakespeare Forgeries in the Revels Accounts* (1928)
Whitehead, John, *This Solemn Mockery: The Art of Literary Forgery* (1973)

formalism is a term used to describe any critical approach which emphasizes a work's literary language and aesthetic form as opposed to its historical and cultural content. More specifically it refers to two separate trends in 20th-century literary criticism, both of which emphasized the importance of language to literary art like Shakespeare's.

The Russian Formalists (Victor Shklovsky, Roman Jakobson, Boris Tomashevsky, Boris Eikhenbaum) attempted in the 1910s and 1920s to define the specificity of literary language and forms, especially their capacity to 'defamiliarize' our perceptions of normal reality. Their work was continued in the 1970s and 1980s by structuralist and poststructuralist critics.

'American formalism' is a term sometimes applied to the American New Criticism developed by John Crowe Ransom, Alan Tate, Cleanth Brooks, and Robert Penn Warren, which championed literature from the 1940s to the 1960s as a special kind of value-laden language best studied through attention to 'the texts themselves' outside any historical context.

HG

Forman, Simon (1552–1611), astrologer and physician. Though sometimes imprisoned for illegal medical practices, Forman had a fashionable clientele of Londoners by the 1590s, and Lord Hunsdon's mistress Emilia Lanier as well as Shakespeare's acquaintances Jane Davenant and Marie Mountjoy consulted him. Friends, no doubt, helped him to get the MD degree in 1603, and yet he had keen interests in prophetic cures, the occult, and the theatre. Forman wrote the first existing accounts of Shakespeare's *Macbeth*, *The Winter's Tale*, and *Cymbeline*, along with notes on another dramatist's play, about King Richard II, which he saw at the Globe on 30 April 1611. These four reports appear in *The Book of Plays and Notes Thereof per Forman, S., for Common Policy* (that is, affording useful lessons for the common affairs of life), the authenticity of which has been questioned, but the manuscript has been reasonably established to be Forman's own. He makes errors, and may describe a drama a week or two after attending a performance. Having seen *Macbeth* at the Globe on Saturday, 20 April 1611, he mixes his report with memories of Holinshed's narrative about fairies or nymphs who stopped Macbeth and Banquo as they came 'riding through a wood'; the Globe actors were surely not on horseback. Forman recalls no cauldron scene and errs in supposing that Macbeth was made Prince of Northumberland, but he remembers vividly that at the banquet 'the ghost of Banquo came and sat down in his chair behind' the usurper. By and large, the report on *Macbeth* is an eyewitness account. Forman's entry on *The Winter's Tale* at the Globe establishes that this drama existed by the time he saw it on 15 May 1611. He was impressed by Leontes who was 'overcome with jealousy of his wife', and by the plan to have a 'cup bearer' poison Polixenes, but Forman makes no mention of Hermione's survival. Nor does he note that a bear crossed the stage in pursuit of Antigonus, though he emphasizes a wily Autolycus, in whom he typically finds a moral lesson: 'beware of trusting feigned beggars or fawning fellows.' He does not say when or where he saw *Cymbeline*; he fails to mention the Queen, calls the heroine 'Innogen' (perhaps accurately), and recounts her adventure in 'man's apparel', but neglects *Cymbeline*'s denouement. He probably watched that drama in the same year as the other plays, but not later than the summer. Having predicted the date of his death, Forman, by design or mishap, died when being conveyed across the Thames on 8 September 1611. *PH*

forme. Books were printed on large sheets of paper with a number of pages on each side, which were then folded and cut at the edges. The pages that fill either side of one sheet constitute one forme. The pages that will lie on the inside of the sheet when it is folded are the *inner forme*; those on the outside, the *outer forme*. *ER*

Forrest, Edwin (1806–72), American actor, endowed with a powerful voice and physique, which required toning down in the Shakespearian repertoire. Richard III was an early success as was Iago, and in his maturity his Othello, Macbeth, and Lear were judged to have improved following his exposure to English actors and audiences in 1836. Although Forrest won further plaudits for his Macbeth and Lear during his return to London in 1845, he also became embroiled in the disastrous rivalry with *Macready which culminated in the Astor Place riot in 1848. Though his international reputation relied heavily on Shakespeare, as a patriotic democrat Forrest had an ambivalent attitude towards British culture. *RF*

Moody, Richard, *Edwin Forrest: First Star of the American Stage* (1960)

Fortinbras. Nephew to the King of Norway, he is encouraged to march through Denmark to attack Poland, instead of claiming land in Denmark lost by his father (the previous King of Norway, also called Fortinbras). At the end of *Hamlet* he takes the Danish throne, with Hamlet's support. *AB*

'Fortune my foe', one of the most frequently used ballad tunes, especially for *broadside ballads reporting death and disaster. Many settings for lute or keyboard survive from Shakespeare's time, including variations by William *Byrd. The title first appears in a ballad licence of 1589; it is misquoted by Falstaff in *The Merry Wives of Windsor* 3.3.60. The original ballad text survives in various 17th-century *broadsides; see Claude M. Simpson, *The British Broadside Ballad and its Music* (1966). *JB*

Fortune theatre. See HENSLOWE, PHILIP; THEATRES, ELIZABETHAN AND JACOBEAN.

foul case, a type-case that had pieces of type in the wrong boxes. Since *compositors did not look at the faces of the letters as they picked them up, a foul *case inevitably led to errors. If a case was carelessly overfilled, it was easy for type to spill over from one box to another, such as from the 'a' box into the adjacent 'r' box, which would account for errors such as 'faiendship' for 'friendship'. *ER*

foul papers. A playwright's rough draft manuscript was known in the period by the descriptive term 'foul papers'. Presumably, Shakespeare's original foul papers would have been transcribed to make the official *'book' for use in the playhouse, and the foul papers thus superseded might be released by the company to a publisher. The printed texts of Shakespeare's plays that appear to derive from foul paper copy provide a unique glimpse of the playwright in the act of composition: *stage directions are frequently open-ended ('*Enter King, and two or three*', '*Enter Rosencraus and all the rest*') suggesting that when he began to write a scene, Shakespeare was undecided about (or uninterested in?) the precise number of characters who would enter; false starts reveal lines and passages deleted and revised *currente calamo*; the extraordinary variability of speech-headings (those for Lady Capulet include **Capulet's Wife*, *Wife*, *Old Lady*, *Lady*, and *Mother*) suggests that Shakespeare often conceived of characters by their relation to others onstage rather than as autonomous individuals. *ER*

Foxe, John (1516–87), English Protestant writer, exiled during Mary I's reign. His most celebrated work was the *Acts and Monuments* or *The Book of Martyrs*, published in 1563, an exhaustive history of Protestant martyrdom in England, particularly under Henry VIII and Mary I. During Elizabeth's reign this book was not only celebrated but became required reading. It was placed in churches and reprinted in shorter editions so that many households possessed a copy. Its popularity was based not only upon Foxe's dramatic style, reinforced visually in a series of woodcuts, but upon its nationalist agenda. Foxe described England as chosen by God to overthrow papacy. Among the martyrs celebrated were Sir John Oldcastle and Thomas Cranmer, figures whom Shakespeare would later represent in *1* and *2 Henry IV* and, *All Is True* (*Henry VIII*). *JKS*

France. Although the character of Falstaff left its mark when English players performed at the court of Henri IV in 1605, an interest in Shakespeare developed fairly late in France. There are decisive historical reasons for this: the lack of interest in the bard even in England, the recurrent conflicts between the two countries, and the inherent dislike of the English language by the French. The great discrepancy in theatrical aesthetics between England and France should not be overlooked as Aristotle's slightly perverted rule of the three unities (time, place, and action) prevailed on the French stage, and decency excluded verbal or corporal violence, as well as any form of vulgarity, and the principle of verisimilitude was strictly observed. So the Shakespearian corpus was altogether discarded. But as progress in the arts was currently believed to be necessary and because French tragedy had reached an impasse, some renewal was essential. So during the Age of Enlightenment the most advanced thinkers finally turned to Shakespeare, the strongest proponent being *Voltaire (François Marie Arouet, 1694–1778). As he was exiled to England on account of his free thinking between 1726 and 1729, he read the plays in the original, saw them performed (often in

The great French tragedian Jean Vilar (1912–71) as Macbeth, with Maria Casarès as Lady Macbeth, 1953.

adapted versions) at Drury Lane, and later wrote a few far-fetched imitations in regular, heroic twelve-foot alexandrines such as *Zaïre* (1732) inspired by *Othello* but set during the Crusades, which met with a great success, *La Mort de César*, and *Sémiramis*, after *Hamlet*. In his *Lettres philosophiques*, Voltaire acknowledged Shakespeare's genius in his 'monstrous farces' 'full of force and ferocity, of naturalness and the Sublime'. Pleading for a return to the text and a mixing of the genres in which the whole human condition was depicted, he wanted Shakespeare to rank among the classic playwrights alongside Corneille, Racine, and Molière. He even translated some fragments of *Hamlet* twice, first as a French piece, then keeping closer to the original. However, his early admiration then turned to an equally fierce condemnation of the bard as 'barbarous'.

As late as 130 years after Shakespeare's death, in 1746, Pierre-Antoine de La Place (1707–83) had *Le Theatre anglois* published (volumes i to v devoted to Shakespeare) along with 'Discours sur le théâtre anglais', a remarkably coherent theorization to justify his approach. Like many translators of his time, he did not translate literally, but instead worked hard to adapt this unfamiliar kind of drama to French taste. The plays were reorganized into scenes whenever characters appeared on stage, alexandrines were reserved for speeches pertaining to the 'Beautiful' or the 'Sublime', while other verse passages were in prose, and further parts only summarized (*Henry v* was dismissed in five pages) excluding any comic or vulgar transgression of the tragic genre. Pierre Le Tourneur (1737–88) took a different stand. He completed a thorough, faithful translation in 20 volumes (1776–82) which was highly praised. But it should be made clear that the first contact the French had with Shakespeare was on the page rather than on the stage. It was not until 153 years after Shakespeare's death that the plays were at last seen in France, and then exclusively under the sole name of the adaptor. The main author, Jean-François Ducis (1733–1816), wrote six tragedies after La Place, in heroic alexandrines with much altered plot and cast, allowing for long asides by confidants recalling the neoclassical style: *Hamlet* in 1769, *Romeo et Juliette* and *Le Roi Lear* in 1783, *Macbeth* in 1784, *Jean-sans-terre; ou La Mort d'Arthur* in 1791, and *Othello* in 1792, all performed at the *Comédie-Française then transferred for a time to the Odéon with great, lasting success. Very much centred on the eponymous heroes, these tragedies explore the individual destiny of exceptional characters which the famous actor François-Joseph Talma played in memorable performances until his death in 1826 (he even performed the role of Shakespeare himself in a one-act prose comedy by Alexandre Duval entitled *Shakespeare amoureux* in 1804!). With his intonation based on that of English actors, he gave life to the Shakespearian repertoire and paved the way for Romantic audiences. Shakespeare was now fashionable on stage. The interest in Shakespeare increased after the performances by English actors who were booed in *Othello* in 1822 (anti-English feeling being at its peak after the Napoleonic defeats) but highly praised in 1826–8. The players were Edmund *Kean, Charles *Kemble, and Harriet Smithson as Ophelia—whom Hector *Berlioz eventually married, mistaking theatrical illusion for reality. And so the Shakespearian myth was born. Great Romantic adaptations followed, starting with *Le More de Venise* by Alfred de *Vigny (1829) in sumptuous settings representing accurate views of Venice, Cyprus, and palace interiors and *Hamlet* by Alexandre Dumas and Paul Meurice (1847), which strayed from the original (the ghost only appears at the end as a representative of divine justice, condemning Hamlet to live and expiate his sin for having killed more characters than the evil Claudius), performed at the Comédie-Française until 1886 with Mounet-Sully (and Sarah *Bernhardt as Ophélia) in massive settings with heavy machinery, imposing long, awkward interruptions. Hamlet is the archetypal hero of the period. The stage interpretations followed the lithography by Eugène *Delacroix (from the performances he saw in London). The myth was transposed to the *opera by Ambroise Thomas (1868). Indeed music provided an outlet for the Romantic disposition as in Berlioz' *Roméo et Juliette* Symphony (1839), and the opera by Charles Gounod (1867). The cult devoted to the Shakespearian hero in black was far removed from the original, especially when performed by the great actress Sarah Bernhardt in her own Théâtre de la Renaissance in 1899. Shakespeare had then become a recurrent reference in French literature and the arts with increasing numbers of translations and adaptations. Among them was a remarkable rewriting of Le Tourneur's text in thirteen volumes by a famous historian and politician, François Guizot, who considered the dramas in a wider perspective encompassing the complete spectrum of society. But the main event was the prose translation of François-Victor *Hugo (1828–73) in fifteen volumes written during the family's exile to Guernsey between 1859 and 1865. It was introduced by his father's *William Shakespeare* commemorating the 400th anniversary of Shakespeare's birth, in which he discussed Shakespeare briefly among the geniuses of humanity, himself included. Mostly based on the Folio but including some apocryphal work such as *Edward III*, and two versions of *Hamlet* (the 1603 and 1604 quartos), this collection however does not respect the Folio classifications but groups the plays according to character types, such as 'tyrants', including *Macbeth*, *Le Roi Jean*, *Richard III*, 'jealous characters', 'tragic lovers', 'friends', and according to social categories 'family' (*Coriolan*, *Le Roi Lear*), 'society', and 'country'. This edition was to become the literary reference up to the present day but never found its way to the stage.

Towards the late 19th century Shakespearian theatre started to allow for completely antagonistic creations. The symbolist movement turned to magical drama (*Le Songe*, *Macbeth* in the ruined Gothic cathedral of Saint Wandrille in Normandy) translated by the Belgian French poet and playwright Maurice Maeterlinck. Many short-lived companies of players were set up including Camille de Sainte Croix's Compagnie Française du Théâtre Shakespeare founded in 1909. A series of lectures preceded the plays which staged junior players acting against plainly painted curtains so as not to divert the attention from the plot or the text.

As a reaction against heavy machinery, rich settings and also the cult of the hero, Aurélien Lugné-Poë (1869–1940) promoted 'Shakespeare without setting' in an article after visiting William Poel's Shakespeare Stage Society. In a memorable one-night experiment at the Cirque d'Été in Paris, he directed a debatable *Mesure pour mesure* in 1898 on a reproduction of the bare Elizabethan stage with some innovative acting in the auditorium. His success was recognized in 1913 with a version of *Hamlet* by Georges Duval 'in complete conformity with the English text' in a fixed set (a Norman arch backstage) with only a few movable painted curtains. His wife Suzanne Després was an athletic Hamlet and himself a sober Polonius.

Directors paid increasing attention to the text they chose, individual plays were translated by writers (Marcel Schwob) or poets (Pierre-Jean Jouve), and some directors even took part in the writing themselves (Jacques *Copeau for instance). In his stagings, the naturalist director André *Antoine (1858–1943) offered a meticulous reconstitution of the historical setting which was used as a great fresco in large cast productions portraying sumptuous crowd scenes: elaborate Norman arches for *Le Roi Lear* in 1905 (integral version by Pierre Loti), a complex evocation of Rome for *Jules César* in 1907, and *Coriolan* in 1910 in which the fixed set (Roman buildings covered with vines) could be partly hidden behind movable painted curtains figuring the inside of a house or a further perspective, allowing for an uninterrupted performance. During the First World War Firmin Gémier (1869–1933) staged *Le Marchand de Venise* (1917) and *Antoine et Cléopâtre* (1918) in the form of a popular theatre with massive human tableaux praising the beauty and sensuality of the body at a time when soldiers were being killed and maimed by the thousands. After the war he turned to comedies such as *La Mégère apprivoisée* and *Le Songe d'une nuit d'été* in abridged versions. Jacques Copeau (1879–1949) had a completely different approach, advocating a bare stage and minimal setting. *La Nuit des Rois* (text by Lascaris much revised by Copeau) at the Théâtre du Vieux Colombier, 1914, is a landmark in modern theatre with its stylized setting: light grey curtains on three sides of a proscenium, a single set, and a touch of melancholy in the interpretation of Sir Andrew (after Granville-Barker's interpretation). He furthered his staging renovation (abstract architecture with a backstage gallery) in *Le Conte d'hiver* (1920). Charles Dullin (1885–1949) preferred adaptations (*Richard III* by André Obey, *Jules César* and *Le Roi Lear* by Simone Jollivet) to translations, which allowed a quicker, efficient performance. In his own portrayal of Richard III (1933), which was the main role of his long career, he played a grinning, devious, deformed villain, lurching stealthily from the darkened openings of the circular setting. A few months later in February 1934 a highly political version of *Coriolan* by René-Louis Piachaud, with impressive crowds all giving the, sadly, then fashionable Roman salute, led to right-wing riots in the streets of Paris and the resignation of the Comédie-Française administrator.

Since the Second World War the interest in Shakespearian theatre has never failed. The plays are conceived for large audiences such as the open-air Avignon Festival where Jean *Vilar (1912–71) premièred *Richard II* at the 1947 opening season and staged a hieratic *Macbeth* in 1953, Roger *Planchon gave a post-Brechtian *Richard III* in 1966, Georges Lavaudant a flamboyant *Richard III*, and Jean-Louis Benoît yet another French creation, *Henry V*, as a tribute to Sir Laurence *Olivier's film. In the cultural centres based in suburbs which were created after the war, directors have developed various perspectives: Jean Dasté (1904–94) in Saint-Étienne emphasized the role of the actors (*Mesure pour mesure* was meant for transformable spaces) while Gabriel Garran in Aubervilliers (*Henry VIII*, *Coriolan*) and Bernard Sobel in Gennevilliers (*Hamlet*, *Le Roi Jean*, *Coriolan*), under Brechtian influence, aimed at political awakening. Large audience stagings range from Robert Hossein's superproduction of *Jules César* (the actors speaking through portable microphones from the audience) to Ariane *Mnouchkine's most impressive cycle of plays transposing the masculine warlike code of honour of medieval England into Kabuki for *Richard II* and *Henry IV*, and the feminine fluidity of *La Nuit des Rois* into Kathakali, on a bare stage in which the only props were multicoloured silks of great beauty.

Under the influence of Antonin Artaud's *The Theatre of Cruelty*, Peter *Brook advocated a more intimate, empty space left only to the actors and the text (Jean-Claude Carrière's prose adaptations): *Timon d'Athènes*, *Mesure pour mesure*, and *La Tempête* all with a multi-ethnic cast created an intense experience. Stuart Seide who translates the plays himself gave a shortened two-evening rendering of the three parts of *Henry VI* illustrating the blindness of sheer violence and false alliances; his *Romeo et Juliette*, in an immense sculptural setting, showed the lack of responsibility undermining society.

Some younger directors punctuate their careers with outstanding full-version texts: Stéphane *Braunschweig staged *Conte d'hiver*, *Measure for Measure* with an English cast (both invited to the Edinburgh Festival), and *Le Marchand de Venise*; Laurent Pelly directed a very witty *Peine d'amour perdue*, and a severe *Roi Jean* in modern dress. On the other hand many rewritings explore a single aspect of a tragic theme, such as the ascent of a tyrant like Richard III, *Gloucester-Materiau Shakespeare* by Matthias Langhoff or *Cacodémon-Roi* and *Richard III de Shakespeare . . .*, both by Bernard Chartreux.

Some plays, such as *Hamlet*, are great favourites and have been staged by very different directors. Antoine Vitez directed an austere six-hour performance with a white set opening onto a long perspective; Patrice Chéreau, in Yves Bonnefoy's version, explored the mental instability of the hero; in his 1977 psychoanalytical approach Daniel Mesguich had several actors playing Hamlet in surroundings entirely made of mirrors, including the floor; and in his 1986 version he took on the title role as a theatre director which he played from the side of the stage. Young companies sometimes prefer rare plays (*Troilus et Cressida* by L'Emballage Théâtre conceived as a cartoon in a bare white set) while amateur companies favour comedies such as *A Midsummer Night's Dream*. Some directors such as Jean-Pierre Vincent (*Macbeth*, *Tout est bien qui finit bien*) say they return to the Shakespearian repertoire for a lesson in perfect theatre which will regenerate their creativity.

It is true that French cinema does not include many Shakespearian films but Shakespeare proves a safe bet on stage with a profusion of extremely diversified performances aimed at audiences ranging from critical scholars to teenagers who might thus have their first theatrical experience in an otherwise virtual environment. As a further testimony to Shakespeare's lasting popularity, the third La Pléiade edition will come out in a bilingual collection under the direction of the leading current translator Jean-Michel Déprats for the plays and Henri Suhamy for the poetical works. Shakespearian studies received a dramatic impetus from eminent scholars with the creation of the *Société Française Shakespeare by Henri *Fluchère in 1977 which has been successively chaired by Jean Fuzier, Marie-Thérèse Jones-Davies, Richard Marienstras, and Jean-Marie Maguin. Many university theses cover fields of research demonstrating that Voltaire's early appeal has been answered: Shakespeare is certainly part of French culture from the university to the stage. *ISG*

France, King of. **(1)** He grants Helen's request for Bertram as her husband, *All's Well That Ends Well.* **(2)** He claims the disinherited *Cordelia as his Queen in the first scene of *King Lear.* See also Charles VI, King of France; Philip, King of France; Louis, King. *AB*

France, Princess of. She and her ladies are courted by the King of Navarre and his lords in *Love's Labour's Lost.* *AB*

Francesca (Francisca) is a nun of 'the votarists of Saint Clare', *Measure for Measure* 1.4. *AB*

Francis, a drawer (barman) in *1 Henry IV*, is teased by Prince Harry and Poins, 2.5. *AB*

Francis, Friar. See Friar Francis.

Francisco. **(1)** He is a soldier relieved at his post by Barnardo, *Hamlet* 1.1. **(2)** He is a lord shipwrecked with Alonso on Prospero's island in *The Tempest.* *AB*

Fratricide Punished. See Bestrafte Brudermord, Der.

Frederick, Duke. He is the father of Celia and usurping Duke in *As You Like It.* *AB*

Freeman, Thomas (b. *c.*1590), poet. Having taken his BA at Magdalen College, Oxford, in 1607, Freeman published chiefly epigrammatic verse. In his sonnet 'To Master W. Shakespeare' (1614), he praises the dramatist's wit, and implies that 'needy new-composers' borrow as much as they can from Shakespeare's plays. *PH*

freemen's songs. See three-man songs.

Freud, Sigmund (1856–1939), Austrian psychoanalyst. Freud's theories of the human psyche, so pervasive in the literature and criticism of the 20th century, were themselves partly derived from the evidence provided by mythology, literature, and art, particularly Shakespeare and Dostoevsky, that most human mental activity is unconscious, and that the primary source of psychic energy, even in childhood, is sexual: 'The poets and philosophers before me discovered the unconscious.' He began reading Shakespeare aged 8, and was always impressed by his powers of expression and extraordinary insight into the human mind. His knowledge of English was good, although his numerous references and quotations are mainly from the Schlegel–Tieck German translation. Commentary upon the plays is widely dispersed throughout his collected works, sometimes focused on 'exceptional' characters such as Richard III and Lady Macbeth ('Some Character-types met with in Psycho-Analytic Work', 1915); sometimes on patterns of myth and dream as revealed in plays such as *The Merchant of Venice* and *King Lear* ('The Theme of the Three Caskets', 1913); sometimes on the disabling neuroses and complexes of parent–child relationships, as in his comparison of the characters of Oedipus and Hamlet (*The Interpretation of Dreams*, 1900, 1914; see also Ernest Jones, *Hamlet and Oedipus*, 1949). Late in life, Freud, always susceptible to the idea of 'family romance' (the discovery of a secret, noble ancestry), became convinced by J. T. Looney's 1920 argument for Edward de Vere, Earl of *Oxford, as the 'true' author of Shakespeare's plays. However uncertain his current scientific status, Freud remains a major force in modern literature and criticism. *TM*

Friar Francis officiates at both the weddings of *Much Ado About Nothing*, 4.1 and 5.4. *AB*

Friar John tells Friar Laurence that he has not delivered his letter to Romeo, *Romeo and Juliet* 5.2. *AB*

Friar Laurence. In *Romeo and Juliet* his attempts to help the young couple ultimately contribute to the circumstances which cause their deaths. *AB*

'Friar Lodowick'. See Vincentio.

Friar Peter aids the schemes of the disguised Duke Vincentio in *Measure for Measure*. *AB*

Friar Thomas. In some editions the friar who appears in *Measure for Measure* 1.3 is given this name. *Johnson first suggested that he is identical with Friar Peter. *AB*

Fripp, Edgar Innes (1861–1931), English antiquarian and cleric, specializing in Stratford archives, history, and associations. Products of his local enthusiasm included *Master Richard Quyny* (1924), *Shakespeare's Stratford* (1928), *Shakespeare's Haunts Near Stratford* (1929), and *Shakespeare Studies Biographical and Literary* (1930). *Shakespeare: Man and Artist* (2 vols., 1938) was published posthumously. *TM*

Froissart, Jean (?1333–?1400), French historian and poet who travelled extensively in England. His *Chroniques*, a four-volume history of the Hundred Years War, included a sympathetic account of the deposition of Richard II, partly based on Froissart's observations at the time. Translated into English by Lord Berners and published 1523–5, the *Chroniques* was probably one of Shakespeare's sources for *Richard II*. *JKS*

Froth, a foolish gentleman, is arrested with Pompey by Elbow in *Measure for Measure*. *AB*

Frye, Northrop (1912–91), Canadian academic and critic, influential, in *The Anatomy of Criticism* (1957), for confronting the contradictions of literary criticism with the methodological discipline of science. Frye's invigorating command of 'archetypes' in literature also informs his best Shakespearian criticism: *A Natural Perspective* (1965) and *The Myth of Deliverance* (1983). See also *Northrop Frye on Shakespeare* (1986). *TM*

Fukuda, Tsuneari (1912–94), Japanese writer. Fukuda majored in English at the University of Tokyo, and in the 1950s emerged as a highly intelligent playwright. In 1956 he translated and directed *Hamlet*, which captivated audiences with its speed and energy. His translations of Shakespeare are noted for the attention to the dynamism of Shakespearian language. *TK*

Fulbrook, a former royal park between Stratford and Warwick associated in the 18th century with the legend that in his youth Shakespeare poached deer. *SW*

Fuller, Thomas (1608–61), divine. Fuller's *The History of the Worthies of England* (1662) includes the first printed biographical account of Shakespeare, who is described as a man of 'very little learning'. More colourfully, Fuller imagines wit-combats in which Shakespeare was 'the English man of War', and Ben Jonson a slower 'Spanish great Galleon'. *PH*

'Full fathom five', sung by Ariel in *The Tempest* 1.2.399; it is one of the very few Shakespeare songs to have music surviving (by Robert *Johnson) which is likely to have been used in a production during his life, even though Johnson's setting was not published until 1660 (see Wilson, John). Another 17th-century setting is that by Banister (1675); more recent composers include Arnold, Honegger, Howells, Ireland, Martin, Parry, Stravinsky, Sullivan, Tippett, Vaughan Williams. *JB*

'Funeral Elegy, A', a poem of 578 lines published independently in 1612 as 'A Funeral Elegy: in memory of the late virtuous Master William Peter of Whipton near Exeter'. The title page states that it is 'By W.S.', and the same initials appear at the end of the dedication, to William Peter's brother John. William Peter, a Devon gentleman of independent means, was born in 1582 and educated at Oxford, where he appears to have lived on and off from 1599 to 1608. He married a Devon woman, daughter of wealthy parents, in January 1609; they had two daughters. On 15 January 1612 he was stabbed to death near Exeter in a dispute over a horse after a hard day's drinking. The memorial poem was registered for publication nineteen days later by Thomas Thorpe, publisher in 1609 of Shakespeare's Sonnets. No bookseller is named on the title page. Only two copies are known, both in Oxford.

Written in alternately rhyming iambic pentameters interspersed occasionally with couplets, the poem harps insistently on the dead man's virtues in competent but laboured verse while providing little substantiation of its eulogy. It was largely ignored until the appearance in 1989 of the book *Elegy by W.S.: A Study in Attribution* by Donald Foster. Here, Foster concluded that the author was either William *Strachey or Shakespeare; in 1996, he came out firmly in favour of Shakespeare, with support from a number of fellow American scholars. The poet writes cryptically of some shame that he has endured; supporters of Shakespeare's authorship have tried to link this with that fact that Shakespeare's Sonnets show consciousness of some 'vulgar scandal stamped upon my brow' (Sonnet 112), but the allusions are unspecific. It is puzzling that although at the time he died William Peter had been married for three years, the poet refers to the woman 'who these nine of years | Lived fellow to his counsels and his bed', raising suspicion that in spite of claims of intimacy the two men were not actually well acquainted. Conceivably the poem was written at the request of the victim's relatives, perhaps in the attempt to redeem a reputation sullied by the manner of his death.

Even those who support the poem's attribution to Shakespeare admit that it has little merit. It bears few if any obvious resemblances to the way Shakespeare was writing at the end of his career. Among other obstacles to belief in his authorship are the poet's two references to himself as young: Shakespeare was 47 at the time of composition. The poem is not printed in the Oxford edition, but was added in the Norton and to the revised Riverside and Bevington editions of 1997. *SW*

Foster, Donald, '*Elegy by W. S.*': *A Study in Attribution* (1989)

'Forum: A Funeral Elegy by W. S.', in Leeds Barroll, (ed.), *Shakespeare Studies*, vol. xxv (1997)

Furness, Horace Howard (1833–1912), American scholar and editor. His New Variorum edition of Shakespeare began in 1871 with *Romeo and Juliet*. Furness had published eighteen volumes of his *New Variorum* when he died in 1912, and the work was continued by H. H. Furness, Jr., J. Q. Adams, and H. E. Rollins. After 1936 it was issued under the auspices of the Modern Language Association of America. The comprehensiveness of the volumes is indisputable, although in the nature of things each passing year produces an exponential growth in the amount of annotation to be included, inevitably slowing down the rate of completion. *TM*

furniture. See stage furniture.

Furnivall, Frederick James (1825–1910), English literary scholar and editor with a wide range of interests. Furnivall founded and headed the New Shakespeare Society (1873–94) in an attempt to organize and modernize what was then a largely amateur English Shakespeare scholarship. The Society became embroiled in a vituperative debate over the propriety of the verse analysis and theories of disintegration it propagated in this project and disbanded as a result. Furnivall founded a number of other literary societies, was active in Christian Socialism, and was an early participant in what became the *Oxford English Dictionary* project. *HG*

Fuseli, Henry (1741–1825), English artist of Swiss origin. Born Johann Heinrich Fussli, the artist received a broad and scholarly education on the Continent, aligning himself with the Anglophile scholar Johann Jacob Breitinger at an early stage. While his father and extended family were well known as accomplished artists, Fuseli, a self-styled intellectual, became preoccupied with the canonical and mythological literatures of northern Europe—from Shakespeare to the *Nibelungenlied.* Two early drawings, executed during Fuseli's sojourn in Berlin, depict scenes from *King Lear* and *Macbeth.* Fuseli's exposure to London's established artistic community and the visual wealth of the metropolis from 1764 encouraged him to divert his energies from philosophy and literature to painting. The artist's decision to leave for Rome in 1770 indicated the seriousness of his artistic intentions, which were later displayed in his submissions to Royal Academy exhibitions and the *Shakespeare Gallery. Boydell's gallery offered an opportunity to unite Fuseli's early preoccupations with atavistic elements in northern literature and his artistic talent. Works such as *The Witches in Macbeth* (1783, *RSC Collection and Gallery) and *Titania and Bottom* (1790, Tate Gallery) display the artist's aptitude for mythic narrative and his idiosyncratic approach to human physiognomy. Fuseli's treatment of the human figure was heavily criticized in the popular press, who slandered many of Fuseli's exhibits as the works of a madman. On 20 April 1785, *the Morning Post and Daily Advertiser* wrote of Fuseli's *Mandrake*, 'here is genius run mad, and however strange his witches, their daughters seem more fashionable beings'.

The artist ceased to produce paintings for the Shakespeare Gallery after 1790, considering his patron Boydell to be keenly pursuing the project for lucrative ends. *CT*

Painted by H. Fuseli R.A.
Engraved by Ja^s. Parker.
MIDSUMMER-NIGHT'S DREAM.
Act 2. Scene 1.
A Wood ——— Puck
Pub^d. Septr. 29. 1799, by J. & J. Boydell, N°. 90, Cheapside; & at the Shakspeare Gallery, Pall Mall.

Henry Fuseli's characteristically vigorous and idiosyncratic painting of Puck (Robin Goodfellow), engraved by James Parker, 1799. Fuseli shared with his Romantic contemporaries a passionate interest in Shakespeare's depictions of the supernatural.

Gadshill assists *Oldcastle, *Russell, and *Harvey in robbing some travellers, *1 Henry IV* 2.3. Gads Hill is also the name of the place (to the west of Rochester) where the robbery takes place. *AB*

Gaedertz, Karl Theodor (1855–1912), German librarian. His 1888 *Zur Kenntnis der altenglischen Bühne* (An Introduction to the Early English Stage) included Johannes de Witt's *c.*1596 drawing of the Swan theatre, together with Arend van Buchels's copy of his friend's *Observationes Londinienses*. The original drawing is now in Utrecht. *TM*

galleries, the wooden structures forming the auditorium seating around the stage and the yard (at the open-air playhouses) or around the stage and the pit (at the indoor hall playhouses), usually built to provide three levels of seating stacked vertically. At most of the open-air playhouses these structures formed the main, virtually circular, body of the venue and had the typical Tudor 'overhang' (each upper level being larger than the one upon which it rests) seen in houses of the period. At the indoor playhouses the galleries were attached to the walls of the existing hall, but cutting off the corners in order to make a U shape. *GE*

galley, a wooden tray with a false bottom, approximately the size of a printed page, into which a *compositor would transfer lines of type after he had set them up in his composing stick. When the page of text was complete, the type-block would be tied together with string and transferred from the galley to a flat table, the imposing stone, where it would be assembled with other pages for printing. *ER*

galliard, a more virtuosic type of *cinquepace with emphasis on male display. Footwork might include 'cutting capers', the equivalent of the entrechat in ballet; see *Twelfth Night* 1.3.115–28. *JB*

Gallus is sent with Proculeius to Cleopatra, *Antony and Cleopatra* 5.1.69, and is part of Caesar's train, 5.2 (mute role). *AB*

Gambon, Sir Michael (b. 1940), Irish actor. In 1962, Gambon began his acting career at the Gaiety, Dublin. Memorable roles include Othello for Birmingham Repertory Theatre (1968), Macbeth for the Forum (1968), Coriolanus for Liverpool Playhouse (1969), Benedick for the National Theatre, Antony in *Antony and Cleopatra*, and Lear for the Royal Shakespeare Company (1982). *BR*

Gamelyn, Tale of, an anonymous 14th-century narrative poem which influenced Thomas Lodge's *Rosalynde*, and thus, indirectly, *As You Like It*. The argument that Shakespeare drew upon *Gamelyn* directly is based on verbal echoes and minor plot details shared by *Gamelyn* and *As You Like It* but not found in Lodge. *JKS*

'Ganymede' is the name Rosalind takes when disguised as a boy in *As You Like It*. *AB*

Gardener. The Queen and her ladies overhear the Gardener's politically inflected conversation, *Richard II* 3.4. *AB*

Gardiner first appears as Wolsey's protégé and Henry's secretary in *All Is True* (*Henry VIII*). He becomes Bishop of Winchester and leads the attack on Cranmer, Act 5. He is based on Stephen Gardiner (*c.*1483–1555), Bishop of Winchester 1531. *AB*

Gardiner, William (1531–97), a wealthy and corrupt justice of the peace in Southwark. In 1596 Francis Langley, owner of the Swan theatre, accused him and his stepson William Wayte (d. 1603) of endangering his life; Wayte, apparently acting as Gardiner's agent, countered with similar accusations against Langley and William Shakespeare. Leslie Hotson (*Shakespeare versus Shallow*, 1931) found that Gardiner cheated Wayte of his inheritance, and proposes that in *The Merry Wives of Windsor*, Shakespeare satirizes Gardiner as Shallow and Wayte as Slender. Wayte died of the plague. *SW*

Gargrave, Sir Thomas. In *1 Henry VI* 1.6, Talbot, Sir William Glasdale, Salisbury, and Sir Thomas Gargrave are looking at the French defences at the siege of Orléans. Gargrave and Salisbury are killed by a cannon shot. *AB*

Garnet, Henry (1555–1606), a Jesuit priest executed for involvement with the Gunpowder Plot. The Porter in *Macbeth* may refer to Garnet's equivocation during the trial, when he declares 'Faith, here's an equivocator' (2.3.8), and in 'Here's a farmer that hanged himself' (2.3.4), 'Farmer' being Garnet's alias. *CS*

Garrick, David (1717–79), actor, manager, and writer, and often credited with ensuring Shakespeare's 18th-century survival and reputation. Born in Hereford, the third of seven children of Peter Garrick and Arabella Clough, he returned with his family to Lichfield where his father was stationed with the dragoons, and where he received his early education. He was taught subsequently by *Johnson at Eidal and they set off for London together in 1737.

His first play, *Lethe; or, Aesop in the Shades*, with a prologue by Johnson, was presented at Drury Lane in 1740 and the same year he performed at St John's Gate, the premises of the *Gentleman's Magazine* where Johnson worked and lodged. His early professional appearances were anonymous but he began to perform under his own name after his triumphant reception as Richard III at *Goodman's Fields in October 1741. He became most closely associated with Drury Lane, playing Hamlet in his

SHAKESPEARE
Can British gratitude delay,
To him the glory of this Isle;
GARRICK.
To give the festive day,
The song, the statue, the devoted pile?
is most respectfully inscribed.

'Garrick reciting the Ode at the Jubilee, surrounded by Shakespearean characters', by Robert Edge Pine, engraved by Caroline Watson, 1784. This posthumous tribute to the 18th century's greatest actor characteristically identifies him as Shakespeare's earthly spokesman.

opening 1742 season, and sharing its management with Lacy from 1747, and over a long career his name became synonymous with Shakespeare.

As an actor, 'a master both in tragedy and comedy' (*Johnson), he was acclaimed as Lear (1742, coached by *Macklin), as Hamlet (1742 and his own adaptation of 1772), and as Macbeth, Benedick, Romeo, Posthumus, and Leontes. While famed for a naturalistic playing style, his moments of extravagant artifice such as his start at the apparitions in *Richard III* and Hamlet's hair standing on end as he encounters the Ghost were hugely popular moments. He was frequently painted in role and many of the finest portraits are now in the possession of the Garrick Club.

Garrick's adaptations, usually reduced to the main plot and presented in three acts, re-established popular Shakespeare and his versions of *The Taming of the Shrew* (*Catherine and Petruchio*), *The Winter's Tale* (*Florizel and Perdita*), *A Midsummer Night's Dream* (*The Fairies*), and *Romeo and Juliet* survived well beyond his era. He extolled Shakespeare in many of the prologues and epilogues he wrote for new productions and new theatres, and his 'Ode to Shakespeare' proved the most enduring feature of his 1769 Stratford *Jubilee and its subsequent London staging.

As a manager Garrick reformed stage practice, banishing the public from the playing and backstage areas and abolishing the practice of admitting spectators for half price at the end of the third act. He introduced new costumes, a large corps of dancers, and, most innovatively, employed John Oram as a scene-painter and, from 1773, used the lighting and mechanical systems of scenery of Philippe de Loutherbourg. He promoted new acting talent and, always in competition with Covent Garden, established Drury Lane as the premier Shakespeare theatre.

In a letter to William Powell of 1764 Garrick advised 'Never let your *Shakespear* be out of your hands, or your Pocket—Keep him about you, as a Charm.' He collected editions (he lent his quartos to George *Steevens in 1765) and Shakespeariana, and erected a Temple to Shakespeare in the grounds of his house at Hampton. His grand funeral at Westminster Abbey, with a mourning procession not far removed from his own stage practice, attested to his achievements, his public popularity, and his success in making acting, the stage, and Shakespeare socially acceptable and of national significance. *CMSA*

Gascoigne, George (1542–77). At various times a law student, courtier, farmer, and soldier, Gascoigne was also a highly innovative poet and dramatist. Whilst fighting in the Dutch wars, he published *A Hundred Sundry Flowers* (1572), a collection of poetry and prose including one of the earliest English novels, *The Adventures of Master F.J.*, which tells the story of an adulterous affair and was condemned as libellous. Gascoigne returned to England in 1574 to a scandal and had to revise the edition, republishing it the following year as *The Posies*. He then worked hard to improve his reputation, publishing many didactic works whilst finding increasing favour for his poetry. On the brink of triumph, having just acquired a wealthy patron, poetic fame, and a position at court, Gascoigne died. He was a pioneer in various genres including satire, literary criticism, and drama. *Jocasta* (1566) is the first recorded English translation of a Greek drama. Another play of the same year, *Supposes*, a loose translation of Ariosto's *I suppositi*, is the first extant prose comedy in English. One of the 'supposes' or confusions of identity that Gascoigne used in this play formed the basis of the Bianca sub-plot in *The Taming of the Shrew*. *JKS*

Gastrell, Francis (d. 1772), a vicar (not of Stratford) who in 1756 bought from Sir John Clopton the house that had replaced Shakespeare's New Place, along with its gardens. Following altercations with the corporation he had the house demolished in 1759. Around the same time he or his wife—in order to vex his neighbours, according to Dr Johnson—cut down the *mulberry tree supposed to have been planted by Shakespeare, to the great profit of souvenir manufacturers. *SW*

Gates, Sir Thomas (fl. 1596–1621), Governor of Virginia, wrecked off Bermuda en route to the colony in the *Sea-Adventure* in 1609. Various accounts of the incident, including William Strachey's in Samuel Purchas's *Pilgrims*, Richard Rich's *News from Virginia*, and Sylvester Jourdan's *A Discovery of the Bermudas*, are possible sources for *The Tempest*. *CS*

gatherers were the collectors of money from spectators at the playhouses. This was the only playhouse occupation open to both men and women. *GE*

Gaunt, John of. He is Richard's uncle and Bolingbroke's father in *Richard II*. Richard uses his death (2.1), hastened by Bolingbroke's banishment (see 1.3.134–7), as an occasion to confiscate his land (2.1.160–3). He is based on the Duke of Lancaster (1340–99), fourth son of Edward III, Bolingbroke's father by his first wife Blanche, and an ancestor of the Beaufort-Tudor line (i.e. Henry VII) by his third wife Catherine Swynford. *AB*

Gautier, Théophile (1811–72). One of the most perspicacious literary critics of his time period, Théophile Gautier advocated the graphic realism of Shakespearian dramatic expression, all the while deploring the lack of historical veracity in French adaptations which tended to border on the ridiculous due to exaggerated exotic details. More significantly, Gautier was one of the few critics to understand fully that the success of French adaptations depended largely upon textual modifications—purifying the language, plotting, and characterization—quintessential elements for creating symmetrical works in harmony with the implacable logic of the French temperament. *AC*

Gautier, Théophile, '*Hamlet*' in *Histoire de l'art dramatique* (6 vols., 1858–9), vol. iv.

Geijer, Erik Gustaf (1783–1847), Swedish historian and poet. His *Macbeth* (1813), modelled on *Schiller's version, was the first Swedish translation of a Shakespeare play; it was written after a stay in England where Geijer saw *Kemble in *Hamlet* and *Cooke as Shylock. *I-SE*

Geijer, E. G., *Impressions of England* (1932)

Genest, John (1764–1839), English cleric. His history of the stage, *Some Account of the English Stage from the Restoration in 1660 to 1830* (10 vols., 1832), provides a basis and source of reference for all later histories. *TM*

Geneva Bible. See Bible.

Gentleman, Francis (1728–84), actor, playwright, and dramatic critic. Gentleman wrote *The Dramatic Censor; or, Critical Companion* (1770), a series of essays on specific plays, almost a third of which are devoted to Shakespeare's works. He illustrates his commentary with numerous quotations from the plays and references to contemporary productions. Gentleman was also responsible for the introduction and notes to John *Bell's acting edition of Shakespeare. His copious notes stress the plays in performance and provide a record of the staging of Shakespeare during the 18th century. Gentleman is particularly enthusiastic regarding Garrick's renditions of Shakespeare's works. *JM*

Geoffrey of Monmouth (d. 1154), Oxford canon and historian whose *Historia regum Britanniae* (*c.*1137) described British history from Brut's founding of the nation to the reign of King Arthur. The *Historia* was extremely popular in the Middle Ages and its influence extended into the 16th century when it formed the basis for a number of English histories, in particular *Holinshed's *Chronicles*. Whilst Shakespeare certainly had recourse to the latter, he may also have used Geoffrey's work directly, in the Latin text since no English translation existed. A few details in *King Lear* and *Cymbeline*, absent from Holinshed, suggest this. *JKS*

George III (1738–1820), King of England (reigned 1760–1820), who remarked in 1785 (before his madness): 'Was there ever such stuff as great part of Shakespeare? only one must not say so! But what think you?—What? Is there not sad stuff? What?—What? I know it's not to be said! but it's true. Only it's Shakespeare, and nobody dare abuse him' (in Fanny Burney's *Letters and Diaries*, 1846). *TM*

Gerald, a schoolmaster in *The Two Noble Kinsmen*, teaches country folk a morris dance which they perform to Theseus and his companions, 3.5. *AB*

Gerard, John (1545–1612), herbalist, superintendent of Burghley's gardens. His *Herbal; or, A General History of Plants* (1597)—a description of plants, their localities, medical virtues, and nomenclature—provides a useful gloss for the resonances of plant references in Shakespeare's plays, including *King Lear* and *Love's Labour's Lost*. *CS*

Germany. Within Shakespeare's lifetime English players travelling to courts and towns of Central Europe acquainted German audiences with professional acting, performed garbled versions of some Shakespeare plays from their repertoires, and left a few literary offshoots behind, such as a play by the Duke of Brunswick derived from *Titus Andronicus* and A. Gryphius' farce *Peter Squenz* adapted from *A Midsummer Night's Dream*. But their migrations practically ended with the Thirty Years War. Shakespeare's name remained unknown; an encyclopedia first mentioned it in 1682 with obvious lack of first-hand knowledge.

Reliable knowledge came in the 18th century via France, especially through *Voltaire's reports from London and French editions of *Addison's *Spectator*. A rationalist culture and a classicist aesthetic was thus confronted with Shakespeare's unruly art. The first German translation, C. W. von Borck's *Julius Caesar* in alexandrine verse (1741), immediately met with the authoritative verdict on the play's disregard for Aristotelian unities pronounced by J. C. Gottsched, who, however, also published an essay by J. E. Schlegel in which criticism of plot and structure was balanced by an appreciation of 'natural' characterization, long before *Lessing, in his *Literaturbrief* (1759) and later in the *Hamburgische Dramaturgie* (1767–8), declared that Shakespearian drama was indeed compatible with the true spirit of Aristotelian rules and recommended Shakespeare, and English drama in general, as a model better suited for German drama than what the tyranny of French classicism had imposed upon it. Though Lessing's views, indebted as they were to English classicist critics from *Dryden and *Pope to Dr *Johnson, were not so radical as to deserve later comparisons with the glorious battles in the Prussian wars with which they coincided, they did spark off an enthusiasm for Shakespeare that resulted in a cult. While C. F. Weisse's *Richard III* (1759) and *Romeo and Juliet* (1768) were still classicist 'imitations', a solid basis for the cult was provided by C. M. *Wieland's translation, mostly in prose, of 22 plays (1762–6), which, while paying attention to the critical notes in the Pope–Warburton edition, insisted on translating Shakespeare's faults along with his beauties. Wieland's interest in the literary presentation of the marvellous explains his predilection for *The Tempest*, of which he arranged an amateur performance in his home town Biberach (1761), the first one of a 'pure' Shakespeare play in Germany. His translation was later revised and completed by J. J. *Eschenburg (1775–82).

A substantial body of Shakespearian drama thus being available to German readers, its literary quality came to be debated with increasing intensity. While classicist objections never quite subsided, avant-garde writers extolled Shakespeare passionately, insisting that the work of an original genius should not be judged by normative (not even Aristotelian) rules—a point developed philosophically by J. G. Hamann and given resonance by his pupil J. G. Herder, who, in *Blätter von deutscher Art und Kunst* (1773), praised Shakespeare's art, along with Ossianic and Nordic popular poetry, as resulting from an act of independent creation, analogous to the divine one. Hence young dramatists of the 'Storm and Stress' movement, such as H. L. Wagner, F. M. Klinger, R. Lenz, and the young *Goethe, felt encouraged to create unrestrained prose plays the powerful formlessness of which outdid Shakespeare in Shakespeare's name.

Professional performances of Shakespeare's own plays were less daring. F. L. *Schröder, who in 1776 launched a series of ten productions in Hamburg, beginning with *Hamlet*, used his own adaptations of Wieland's and Eschenburg's translations and kept revising them for subsequent productions, always avoiding what might be offensive to middle-class audiences. Domesticating Shakespeare plays for the stage was, indeed, general theatre practice. Even J. W. Goethe, for all his lifelong interest in Shakespeare, came to realize that his poetry was too vast for the stage, imposed classic control on his influence, and, as theatre director in Weimar, reduced *Romeo and Juliet* to the essentials required by the plot (1811). In his novel *Wilhelm Meisters Lehrjahre* (1795) he described a process that leads the semi-autobiographical hero from a subjective reading of *Hamlet* to an objectified performance; the resulting interpretation also fuelled the permanent Teutonic preoccupation with this tragedy in political, philosophical, and fictional contexts. *Schiller's early plays, too, were indebted to Shakespeare; he often referred to him in his correspondence with Goethe and eventually convinced himself that the 'naive' nature of Shakespearian drama had to be transformed into a more idealist, 'sentimentalist' mode, and tried to do so in his translation of *Macbeth* (1801).

Dissenting pleas for unchanged performances came, around 1800, from the Romantic school. This followed logically from an appreciation of Shakespeare's autonomous organic poetry, whose total effect depends on the interrelatedness of all its elements, as A. W. *Schlegel explained in his critical writings. This enabled him to achieve a metrical translation of sixteen plays, including all the histories (1797–1810), which paid sensitive respect to the nuances of form as well as to semantic meaning. It shared its style with German serious drama of that period, which adopted blank verse as its medium, and thus constituted an intense act of appropriation. After Schlegel abandoned the project and before it was completed under the supervision of *Tieck in 1833, the book market encouraged several rival translators to come forward; among the earliest were *Voss (distinguished translator of Homer) and his sons, whose harsher alternative (1818–29) strove to be faithful to the otherness and even the obscurities of the source text, aiming at enriching German poetic language instead of merely using it. Other complete translations trying to be either more spiritual or more popular included those of J. Meyer (1824–34), J. W. O. Benda (1825), and Philip Kaufmann (1830–6), but the 'Schlegel–Tieck' one continued to be admired for its beauty and achieved a privileged status. Tieck himself assiduously studied Shakespeare's texts and their historical background and ascribed to Shakespeare numerous anonymous plays, some of which he translated; as a poet he dealt with Shakespeare's life and theatre in several novellas, and exploited the ironic mode of Shakespearian comedy in his own plays; and his stage production, in 1842, of *A Midsummer Night's Dream* was unusually close to the original principle of consecutive acting.

The Romantic approach to Shakespeare came under attack after 1830, when it was blamed—by *Heine, for instance—for its lack of a theoretical framework. Scholars came forward to provide it. In the wake of Hegel, *Ulrici diagnosed the unifying ideas of each play, and *Gervinus exhibited Shakespeare's ethical ideals for Germans to look up to. But their idealist theorizing and eulogizing itself was challenged by historical assessments of Elizabethan theatre conditions (G. Rümelin) and also by quests for realist drama (H. Hettner). More controversies followed; the Shakespeare cult was attacked (by the dramatist C. G. Grabbe as early as 1827) and defended vigorously by the dramatist's admirers. And yet Shakespeare's impact upon 19th-century German culture was omnipresent, not only on dramatists such as G. Büchner, H. Kleist, F. Grillparzer, or F. Hebbel, some of

whom aimed at a kind of symbiosis between Greek and Shakespearian dramatic form; but also on visual artists—Boydell's English precedent encouraged several 'Shakespeare Galleries', among whose participants were F. A. M. Retzsch, W. von Kaulbach, L. Richter, A. Menzel, and others; on composers of songs and operas from *Mendelssohn to *Wagner; on novelists fictionalizing Shakespeare's life (H. König, 1839) or exploring Shakespearian themes, as did J. Eichendorff or A. Stifter.

Shakespeare's productive reception, later praised as having shaped the German mind, subsided after the 1860s, when Germany was on its way towards national unity. The veneration was then institutionalized, most ostentatiously by the foundation in Weimar of the *Deutsche Shakespeare-Gesellschaft in 1864, whose intention of popularizing Shakespeare's work may have been more ambitious than what was practicable with learned publications and a revision of the 'Schlegel–Tieck' translation (1867–71). But performances became frequent everywhere; newly polished collective translations were provided by men of the theatre (F. Dingelstedt, 1867; F. Bodenstedt, 1867–81); leading actor-managers such as H. Laube or E. and O. Devrient emphasized the visual effect made possible by the technical resources of advanced theatres. The Duke of Meiningen's troupe, which travelled all over Europe, became famous for its historicist designs and choreographed crowd scenes of *Julius Caesar* and *The Merchant of Venice*. Near the end of the 19th century, however, such opulence was rejected by Jocza Savits, who, on his Munich Shakespeare Stage, like Poel in London, by restoring Elizabethan acting conditions once again appealed to his audiences' active imagination.

By 1900, Shakespeare's appropriation as the 'third German classic' (alongside Goethe and Schiller), as propagated for half a century, seemed definitive (if only for another 50 years), theoretically buttressed as it came to be by *Gundolf's cult book *Shakespeare und der deutsche Geist* (1911). This permitted ongoing performances in both the First and the Second World Wars, when most authors of enemy nations were banned from the stage. Theatre artists revealed fresh aspects—M. Reinhardt, for instance, who ever since his Berlin production of *A Midsummer Night's Dream* (1905) had used techniques of the realist theatre to explore the realms of the Shakespearian imagination, or L. Jessner, who experimented with expressionist stylization, especially in his *Richard III* (1920), and also the emerging *Brecht, whose concept of a non-Aristotelian epic theatre was to have a profound influence. Such innovation, including modern-dress performance, was, however, rejected during the Third Reich, when fitting political and heroical interpretations were imposed upon many Shakespeare plays, if only in theory. Performances remained more or less traditional until well into the 1950s, supported by the dominance of the Schlegel–Tieck translations, which to many appeared unsurpassable except by God's special grace. Attempts to replace their poetic beauty by a more modern and more theatre-conscious style were nevertheless made—by Hans *Rothe, for instance, who from 1922 used a free, colloquial idiom that elicited conservative protest and was temporarily banned by the Nazis; or by Richard Flatter's efforts to render the theatrical energies of Shakespeare's versification. In the later 20th century, alternative translations were often commissioned for theatre productions (from, for instance, Erich Fried or Frank Günther) or else shaped in the production process itself.

After the Second World War, claims to a specifically German Shakespeare collapsed along with German nationalism. Instead, Shakespeare's reception was affected by the political East–West division of the country, especially when the 1964 quatercentenary of his birth was also marked by the ideological splitting-up of the Deutsche Shakespeare-Gesellschaft, accompanied by aggressive propaganda on both sides. In East Germany (GDR), the Socialist Union Party assumed dictatorial control of theatre politics and decreed that Shakespeare was to be part of the humanist-realist cultural heritage and that performances were to suggest the resolution of historical conflicts in the socialist present—a principle whose dramaturgic realization remained a matter of debate and was increasingly subverted in practice. But Brecht's adaptation of *Coriolanus*, posthumously produced by his pupils of the Berliner Ensemble (1964), became an international event. In West Germany (FRG), a new generation levelled protest against restorative post-war tendencies, and the theatre contributed to it by subjecting classics such as Shakespeare to iconoclastic treatments and adaptations inspired by the theatre of the absurd, Artaud's theatre of cruelty, and again Brechtian concepts, if not by the deconstructivist theorizing that was in the air. The resulting pluralism of Shakespeare productions did not always go into postmodern extremes, as did those by Peter *Zadek or Günter Heyme that polarized audiences in the 1970s. Even so Shakespeare never ceased to be the author most frequently performed in both East and West Germany, and since 1990 in reunited Germany as well. Indeed the disappearance of the East German state from history was reflected in two major productions, one of *Hamlet* in Berlin directed by Heiner *Müller which also included the latter's *Hamletmachine*, and one, in Weimar, of *A Midsummer Night's Dream* by L. Haussmann. In any case trends of both performance and criticism by now tend more easily to cross national boundaries. *WH*

Blinn, Hansjürgen, *Der deutsche Shakespeare/The German Shakespeare* (1993)

Hortmann, Wilhelm, *Shakespeare on the German State: The Twentieth Century* (1998)

Stellmacher, Wolfgang (ed.), *Auseinandersetzung mit Shakespeare* (2 vols., 1976, 1985)

Williams, Simon, *Shakespeare on the German Stage 1586–1914* (1990)

By the early 19th century Shakespeare had already been adopted as an honorary father of German literature. In 'The apotheosis of Schiller', *c.*1805, the spirit of the writer who had established himself as Germany's national playwright is eagerly welcomed into Heaven by the English dramatist he had imitated.

Gertrude, Queen. Hamlet's mother, on the death of her husband King Hamlet, has married his brother King Claudius, before *Hamlet* begins. *AB*

Gervinus, Georg Gottfried (1805–71), German scholar. His *Shakespeare* (4 vols., 1849–50), translated into English as *Shakespeare Commentaries* (1863), offers a trial table of the order of Shakespeare's plays and uses verse-tests to divide the works into four periods, attempting to trace the development of Shakespeare's art as a coherent whole. *TM*

Gesta Grayorum, an account of entertainments at Gray's Inn during Christmas 1594–5, including 'Dancing and Revelling with Gentlewomen; and after such Sports, a Comedy of Errors (like to *Plautus* his *Menechmus*) was played by the Players'. Shakespeare's play might have been written for this indoor performance: it is suitably short and has a five-act structure unsuited to the open-air amphitheatres of the time. *GE*

Bland, Desmond (ed.), *Gesta Grayorum; or, The History of the High and Mighty Prince Henry Prince of Purpoole, Anno Domini 1594* (1968)

'Get you hence, for I must go', sung by Autolycus, Dorcas, and Mopsa in *The Winter's Tale* 4.4.295. A setting attributed to Robert *Johnson may have been used in the original production. *JB*

Ghost of Banquo. See Banquo.

Ghost of Caesar. See *Julius Caesar*.

Ghost of Hamlet (the late King of Denmark). He describes his murder and tells his son Hamlet to take revenge, *Hamlet* 1.5. *AB*

Ghost of King Henry VI. He appears to Richard III at *Bosworth. *AB*

Ghost of Posthumus' mother. See Ghost of Sicilius Leonatus.

Ghost of Prince Edward. He appears to Richard III at *Bosworth. *AB*

Ghost of Sicilius Leonatus. The ghosts of Posthumus' father Sicilius Leonatus, and his unnamed mother and brothers, appear to Posthumus in a dream, *Cymbeline* 5.5. *AB*

ghosts. A ghost is usually the spirit of a dead person, but even this may go too far. In Shakespeare's day, people preferred to speak of apparitions or spirits, suspending the question of what kind of entity they faced. Once the Reformation had abolished Purgatory, orthodox Protestant theology claimed that since damned spirits could not return, and blessed ones would not wish to, then any entity claiming to be a deceased person was a deceit of the devil. However, orthodox theology was often ignored by popular culture. The 16th and 17th centuries did see a number of poltergeist stories; poltergeists could be the spirits of the dead, or could be devils or intrusive witches whose spirits could walk abroad separately from their bodies. On the other hand, revenants accepted as genuinely the spirits of the dead also appeared. After the battle of Edgehill in 1642, for instance, the battle site was said to be haunted by the Royalist army, led by their deceased standard-bearer. Generally, such ghosts shared with the ghosts of the stage a purpose of amending some fault or rectifying an incomplete life. They confessed to unsolved crimes, or drew attention to buried treasure, or insisted that overdue loans be repaid, or called on the living for vengeance. Sometimes, again as on the stage, they were general warnings of disturbed times to come.

Ghosts in the theatre in any case owed less to such notions than to the conventions of Roman tragedy and comedy; both *Seneca and *Plautus use ghosts as dramatic devices, to reveal hidden aspects of the plot, or to set revenge in motion. Shakespeare's early and highly Senecan *Richard III* is accordingly thick with ghosts; Richard is ambushed by an entire legion of them at the end, and there are many references to them in the history plays. See among others *2 Henry IV* 2.3.39; *1 Henry VI* 1.1.52, 4.7.87, 5.2.16—a typical Senecan appearance by the ghost of Talbot; *The First Part of the Contention* (*2 Henry VI*), 3.2.160, 230, 372; *King John* 3.3.84; *Richard II* 3.2.158; and *Henry V* 4.0.28, where the Chorus imagines Henry's army as already a ghost army, like that at Edgehill. Any murdered person in the Shakespearian *œuvre* is likely to make a ghostly appearance, if not on stage then at least in the minds of one or more surviving characters; Tybalt, for example (*Romeo and Juliet* 4.3.55). This of course anticipates the three great stage appearances by ghosts in the Shakespearian canon: Julius Caesar, Banquo, and the elder Hamlet, all of whom appear for reasons which harmonize both with classical tradition and with popular culture; they are murder victims, and they come to punish those who have wronged them. Although *Hamlet*, in particular, canvasses questions of belief in a thoroughly intellectual fashion, these are never really resolved; the Ghost's authenticity remains open to question until the end, though (*pace* a famous essay by G. Wilson *Knight) no one ever suggests he is a demon, as Protestants might have hoped. Rather, the question seems to be whether the Ghost should have the power to drive the plot and turn the play into the kind of Senecan bloodbath in which a ghost might feel at home. Whether the dead should have authority over the living is one of the central questions of both tragedy and ghost stories, which is just one reason why it seems natural to think of them together. *DP*

Felton, D., *Haunted Greece and Rome: Ghost Stories from Classical Antiquity* (1999)
Lavater, Ludwig, *De spectris, lemuribus et magnis atque insolitis fragoribus* (1570), trans. *Of Ghostes and Spirits Walking by Night* (1572)
Thomas, Keith, *Religion and the Decline of Magic* (1971)

ghosts of Posthumus' brothers. See Ghost of Sicilius Leonatus.

Giacomo (Iachimo; Jachimo) deceives Posthumus into thinking Innogen has been unfaithful with him in *Cymbeline.* *AB*

Gide, André (1869–1951), French writer. Under the pen of André Gide translations of Shakespeare began to burgeon with the original robust force and provocative flavour particular to Elizabethan dramatic expression. His translation of *Hamlet* marked an unprecedented moment in the history of French interpretations of the English bard. In dispensing with alexandrines, Gide succeeded in restoring the original mixture of prose and blank verse to plays deprived of the unconventional literary language which had been the hallmark of Shakespearian art. In so doing, Gide put an end to the vogue for French neoclassicism whose aftermath had extended over into the 19th century. *AC*

Shakespeare, W., *Œuvres complètes: Hamlet*, trans. André Gide (1959)

Gielgud, Sir John (1904–2000), British actor and director of great fame. In a career of 75 years he appeared in countless productions internationally in theatre, film, radio, and television, and was deluged with awards and honours, including a knighthood in 1953. Along with Laurence *Olivier, Gielgud became synonymous with high standards and conscientiousness in acting. His remarkable voice, which he put to powerful effect in Shakespeare, was nonetheless a point of controversy because he often used it with rhetorical flourishes that recalled earlier models of elocution. Olivier complained that Gielgud was vocally out of touch with the modern age; Gielgud later recognized the justice of this view, yet well into the 1950s and 1960s could be heard singing Shakespeare's lines on stage, particularly in platform recitals like *The Ages of Man* (1958). The grand-nephew of Ellen *Terry, Gielgud's Shakespearian fame began at the Old Vic in 1929 with three characteristic roles: Antonio in *The Merchant of Venice*, Richard II, and Oberon. In the 1930s, while becoming a matinée idol in other work and appearing in many films, he also appeared in numerous Shakespeare plays. Hamlet and Prospero were preferred parts—he played Hamlet over 500 times—and he invested both with great intelligence and a sense of melancholy. The rivalry with Olivier reached a high point in 1935 in Gielgud's own production of *Romeo and Juliet*, designed by *Motley and with Peggy *Ashcroft and Edith *Evans. Gielgud played Mercutio to Olivier's Romeo, then after six weeks the two switched roles, highlighting their contrasting vocal styles. Gielgud first played Lear when he was only 26, and in 1940 was directed in the role for a short period by his idol Granville *Barker, who had come out of retirement for the occasion. Gielgud first appeared at Stratford in 1950, as Angelo in a memorable production of *Measure for Measure* by Peter *Brook, and the next year was Leontes in Brook's imagistic version of *The Winter's Tale* in London. As he grew older he maintained a vigorous presence on stage and film, often playing bitter old men in contemporary plays like Edward *Bond's *Bingo* (1974, where the role was that of William Shakespeare) or Harold Pinter's *No Man's Land* (1975), and directing a number of productions himself. Though he took fewer Shakespeare parts, he was seen to great effect at the National Theatre as Prospero (1974) and Caesar (1977). He seemed to have said his farewell to Shakespeare as the lead in Peter Greenaway's film *Prospero's Books* (1991), but recorded a radio Lear for the BBC three years later. On his 90th birthday in 1994 the Globe theatre in Shaftesbury Avenue was renamed for him. His six books of memoirs (e.g. *Stage Directions*, 1963; *An Actor and his Time*, 1979; *Notes from the Gods*, 1994) are most readable and useful. *DK*

Morley, Sheridan, *The Authorised Biography of John Gielgud* (2001)
Tanitch, Robert, *Gielgud* (1988)

Gilburne, Samuel (fl. *c.*1594–?1620), actor (King's Men 1605). Gilburne is named in the actor list in the 1623 Folio. He was apprenticed to Augustine Phillips, whose will left him 'the sum of 40 shillings and my mouse coloured velvet hose and a white taffeta doublet suit, my purple cloak, sword, and dagger, and my bass viol'. *GE*

Gildon, Charles (1665–1724), critic, editor, and playwright. Gildon wrote numerous essays on literature, including an effective response to Thomas Rymer's attack on *Othello* and a continuation of Gerard *Langbaine's catalogue of

English drama. He also wrote an operatic adaptation of *Measure for Measure* (1700). After the publication of Rowe's edition of Shakespeare, disreputable publisher Thomas Curll brought out a so-called volume vii of the *Works* containing Shakespeare's poems as well as two critical essays by Gildon, one a history of the stage and the second, 'Remarks on the Plays of Shakespeare', the first extensive discussion of Shakespeare's works. *JM*

Giovanni (Fiorentino), Ser (14th century), Italian writer, author of a collection of prose tales called *Il pecorone* (*The Dunce*), published in 1558. This collection seems to have been read by Shakespeare in the Italian as it was not published in English until 1632. The main plot of *The Merchant of Venice* and details of *The Merry Wives of Windsor* have been attributed to this source. *JKS*

Girlhood of Shakespeare's Heroines. See CLARKE, MARY COWDEN.

Giulio Romano. The supposed statue of Hermione in *The Winter's Tale* is said to be his work (5.2.96). Giulio (or Julio) Romano (1492–1546) was a painter, architect, and student of Raphael: see also ART. *AB*

Glamis, Thane of. This is one of Macbeth's titles. *AB*

Glasdale (Gladesdale; Glansdale), Sir William. See GARGRAVE, SIR THOMAS.

Glasgow Citizens' Theatre. Founded in 1943 by James Bridie, in a Victorian theatre, now splendidly refurbished, in the working-class area of the Gorbals, it has since 1969 staged at popular prices visually stunning, audacious productions (including Shakespeare and the Jacobeans), often featuring cross-dressing and nudity. *MJ*

Coveney, Michael, *The Citz* (1990)

Glendower, Owen. See GLYNDŴR, OWAIN.

Gl'ingannati, anonymous play, one of three Italian plays on the theme of mistaken identity (the others written by Niccolo Secchi and Curzio Gonzaga), all called Gi'inganni (*Deceits*). Of these, *Gl'ingannati* was the most popular. First published in 1537, it had run into eight editions by 1585 and had been translated into French several times. In 1595 it was performed in Latin at Cambridge University. There is no evidence that Shakespeare knew it. However, in 1602 John *Manningham noted a similarity between *Twelfth Night* and an Italian play called *Inganni*. Of these three plays, *Gl'ingannati* is the closest to Shakespeare's comedy. *JKS*

Globe Centre. See GLOBE THEATRE RECONSTRUCTIONS.

Globe Shakespeare (1864). Prepared by William George Clark and William Aldis Wright as a spin-off from their *Cambridge Shakespeare, this one-volume edition of the *Works* became for a long time a standard compact Shakespeare, offering a plain text of all the works, with a glossary at the end of the volume. Although it retained such features as the traditional scene locations added in the 19th century, e.g. 'Another part of the island' (*Tempest* 2.1), it was textually advanced for its time, and continued to be used long after it began to seem outdated, largely because the revised Globe edition of 1891 supplied act, scene, and line references to the works for *Bartlett's *Concordance*. *RAF*

The definitive romantic Hamlet for the 20th century: John Gielgud as Hamlet, New Theatre, 1934.

Globe theatre. The primary playing space of the Chamberlain-King's Men between 1599 and 1608, and thereafter their summer venue alternating with the indoors Blackfriars playhouse in winter. The Globe was located in the *Bankside district of south London, famous for its animal-baiting rings and brothels, and near to the *Rose theatre operated by Philip *Henslowe. Built from the recycled timbers of the company's previous home, the Theatre, the Globe was an open-air, virtually circular, amphitheatre with a diameter of between 80 and 100 feet (24–30 m) and a thatched roof. Although associated with several of Shakespeare's most famous plays which received their first performance in it, the Globe was built because James *Burbage's intended new home for the company, the indoors Blackfriars playhouse, was prevented from opening in 1596 by the objection of local residents. Despite its inauspicious beginning, the

Globe's long-term economic success is attested by the decision to rebuild it 'far fairer' than before after it burnt down during a performance of Shakespeare's *All Is True* (*Henry VIII*) on 29 June 1613. The appearance of this second Globe is recorded in Wenzel *Hollar's Long View of London (1641), the preliminary sketch for which, supplemented by information obtained during the archaeological excavations of 1989–90, was used as the basis of the modern replica of the first Globe which was officially opened on Bankside in 1999 (see GLOBE THEATRE RECONSTRUCTIONS).

The Globe was owned and operated by a syndicate of the leading players in the *Chamberlain's Men. Hitherto playhouses were owned by entrepreneurs working singly or in pairs to build and maintain venues hired out to acting companies for a share of the takings, usually the money collected in the galleries, with the income from standing spectators going to the actors. Expenditure on the abortive Blackfriars project left James Burbage without sufficient capital to provide a replacement for the Theatre but by forming a syndicate and by taking the Theatre's timbers with them, the Chamberlain's Men were able to finance the Globe. Thus leading members of the acting troupe, such as Shakespeare, were also shareholders ('housekeepers') in their own theatre. This arrangement proved to be particularly stable and the same procedure was followed when, in 1608, the Blackfriars project was resumed.

Because the Globe's timbers were merely those of the *Theatre reassembled on a new site, and because it is unlikely that the old joints in the wood were sawn off and remade, the new building must have been the same size and shape as its predecessor. The Theatre's name was intended to evoke the Roman amphitheatres whose circular shape it emulated, and the Globe's name extended this association to assert the microcosmic correspondence of the world of drama and the world of everyday life. This correspondence was made explicit in a number of Shakespeare's plays written for the Globe, for example in Jaques' comment that 'All the world's a stage' (*As You Like It* 2.7.139) and in Hamlet's polysemic reference to 'this distracted globe' (*Hamlet* 1.5.97), meaning his head, the theatre, and the world. There is, however, little evidence to support the frequently repeated claim that the Globe's identifying flag represented Hercules supporting the earth and nothing at all to suggest that its motto was 'Totus Mundus Agit Histrionum' (the 'whole world moves the actor', but often mistranslated as 'all the world's a stage').

The second Globe, recorded by Hollar, was built on the foundations of the first and so presumably it was the same size and shape. If so, the original groundplan of the Theatre, built in 1576, survived in this form until the closing of the playhouses in 1642. Hollar's sketch of the second Globe was made with an accurate optical instrument, but estimates of the Globe's size derived from this sketch are undermined by his multiple sketching lines and by detail hidden behind obstacles. Even if the modern replica is as much as 10% too large the increase in average human body size over the last 400 years renders the replica about as relatively roomy to us as the original was to its users. Contemporary accounts record audiences as numerous as 3,000, about 1% of the London population. With its stage extending into the middle of the yard, the Globe allowed an actor to stand almost at the centre of a densely packed cylinder of spectators, although experiments in the replica do not conclusively show that this central spot is the ideal place to deliver the most powerful lines of Shakespeare's plays.

Twenty-nine plays of the period, fifteen of them by Shakespeare, seem to have had their first performance at the first Globe. None calls for a character to 'fly' and so it is unlikely that the Globe had a flight machine when first built. Shakespeare's first use of flight was in *Cymbeline* (written 1608) and around this time staging practices at the Globe were brought into line with practices at the Blackfriars, so presumably a flight machine was then added to the Globe. Dramatic use of below-stage space is evinced by the stage direction 'ghost cries from under the stage' (1.5.157) in the second quarto of Shakespeare's *Hamlet* and by music from 'under the stage' (4.3.10) in Shakespeare's *Antony and Cleopatra*, but extensive exploitation of the 'hell' (as it was called) would have been limited by the marshiness of the land on which the Globe was built. *GE*

Gurr, Andrew, and Orrell, John, *Rebuilding Shakespeare's Globe* (1989)

Globe Theatre reconstructions. Built from the transplanted timbers of the *Theatre, and rebuilt after the fire of 1613, the Globe theatre was in some sense always a reconstruction. Modern attempts to produce a working replica of the original Globe, however, date only from 1900, when William *Poel petitioned the London County Council for a site on which to build a replica, but was denied. The desire to have Shakespeare's plays performed in a museum approximating to their first home has since then been particularly associated with the *United States. John Cranford Adams designed a replica for the 1933–4 Chicago World's Fair, and although Adams's design was discredited by scholars in 1948, it was not until 1971, at the 1st World Shakespeare Congress, that Shakespearian scholars arrived at another feasible design. Several modern reconstructions have since been attempted around the world, notably in San Diego (California), Tokyo, and Prague.

In 1924, W. W. Braines determined the Globe's original location, in what had by then become a rather Dickensian district of derelict warehouses, but it was not until 1970 that a formal campaign was initiated to build a replica of the theatre as close as possible to this site. In that year the American actor Sam Wanamaker (1919–93) formed the Globe Playhouse Trust, using much of his own capital to buy Bankside properties. In the planning and design process, Wanamaker worked closely with the stage historian Glynne Wickham, the then director of the *Shakespeare Institute, Terence Spencer, and designer Richard Southern. The four men decided to reconstruct the original 1599 Globe for which Shakespeare wrote the majority of his plays, rather than the rebuilt 1614 Globe about which more was known.

In April 1972, Wanamaker tried to spark interest in the reconstruction by organizing a Shakespeare's birthday celebration featuring lectures by academics such as Nevill Coghill and Jan *Kott and a reading by John *Gielgud. That summer he produced Keith Michell's *Hamlet*. During the summer of 1973, he produced the Tony Richardson-directed *Antony and Cleopatra* starring Julian Glover and Vanessa *Redgrave. In 1975, a temporary metal structure was erected to produce the Oxford University Dramatic Society's *Pericles* and Charles *Marowitz's *Hamlet*. Unfortunately, all three seasons were financial failures.

In the 1980s, the reconstruction project picked up steam, with theatre historians Andrew Gurr and John Orrell and designer Theo Crosby becoming major driving forces in planning the reconstruction. In 1982, the International Shakespeare Globe Centre Trust was founded to co-ordinate fund-raising for the project, and Gurr and Orrell were instrumental in determining the final 100-foot (3-m) diameter and 300-foot (90-m) circumference for the new building. Crosby found a location in Southwark where the three-storey reconstruction (33 feet (10 m) to the eaves, 45 feet (14 m) overall) would not be dwarfed by its surroundings. Much of this decade was spent controversially negotiating possession of this site against those who wanted to use it for council houses: even some Shakespearian scholars, suspicious of what they saw as a bid to displace local people in the interests of the transatlantic 'heritage industry', sided against Wanamaker's project. Crosby also resolved that the Globe should be reconstructed using only materials and technologies available to original contractor Peter *Street. During the actual reconstruction, architect John Greenfield and master carpenter Peter McCurdy followed this resolution devoutly. However, certain exceptions were made to accommodate both modern safety regulations (such as the need to fireproof the thatching, install a sprinkler system, and include well-marked exits) and contemporary theatrical demands (such as floodlights to enable evening performances).

In 1989, construction workers demolishing an office building accidentally uncovered the foundations of the *Rose theatre. Encouraged by the find, archaeologists excavated part of the site of the original Globes. They uncovered the foundations of a turret stairwell attached to a section of outer wall and a section of the interior gallery wall. Unfortunately, the location of subsequent buildings limited further investigation to sonar. The excavation proved that the Globe had 20 (not 24) sides and provided valuable information about the original bays. In 1992, trial bays were constructed. By 1993, shortly before Wanamaker's death, a rough stage was ready for the Bremer Shakespeare Company's German production of a (translated and cut) *The Merry Wives of Windsor*. By 1995, newly named artistic director Mark Rylance was ready to assay a workshop season in the nearly complete Globe, and the theatre opened for a 'preview' season in 1996 with *The Two Gentlemen of Verona*. 'Shakespeare's Globe', as it is known, built into a complex called the International Shakespeare's Globe Centre (including an exhibition space, conference facilities, restaurants, and a reconstruction of Inigo *Jones's indoor Cockpit-at-Court theatre), officially opened in 1997 with Richard Olivier's production of *Henry V*, with Rylance in the title role. To date its acting company has performed only in the summer months (to large, multinational audiences largely composed of people who rarely attend other theatrical events), although a permanent year-round repertory using the Inigo Jones theatre during the winter is envisaged. In general its productions have been warmly enjoyed by the audiences they have attracted, but have not pleased critics.

In 1999, several practical structural changes were made, including reducing the bases of the two central pillars and extending the balcony to allow more room for musicians and provide a better playing space. A side effect of this change was that the discovery area was enlarged, making it visible to the entire audience. *BR*

Day, Barry, *This Wooden 'O': Shakespeare's Globe Reborn* (1996)
Mulryne, J. R., *Shakespeare's Globe Rebuilt* (1997)
Orrell, John, *The Quest for Shakespeare's Globe* (1983)
Shakespeare Survey, 52 ('Shakespeare and the Globe') (1999)

Gloucester, Duchess of. (1) Dame Eleanor Cobham (d. 1454) practises sorcery against King Henry, *The First Part of the Contention* (*2 Henry VI*). **(2)** Eleanor de Bohun (d. 1399) appeals to Gaunt to avenge her husband's murder in *Richard II* 1.2. *AB*

Gloucester, Duke of. (1) Humphrey (1391–1447) was the youngest son of Henry IV. In *2 Henry IV* he appears in 4.3 and 5.2. He aids his brother's campaign in France in *Henry V*. In *1 Henry VI*, now Lord Protector, he quarrels with the Bishop of Winchester (later called Cardinal Beaufort). Still Protector in *The First Part of the Contention* (*2 Henry VI*) he falls after the disgrace of his wife, the Duchess of Gloucester, and is found murdered, 3.2. **(2)** Richard (1452–85) was the fourth son of the Richard, Duke of York, of the *Henry VI* plays. For his role in *The First Part of the Contention* (before he is made Duke of Gloucester) see RICHARD, CROOKBACK. Also see RICHARD DUKE OF YORK (3 HENRY VI) and RICHARD III. *AB*

Gloucester, Earl of. Drawn in part from the Prince of Paphlagonia in *Sidney's *Arcadia*, his fate echoes that of Lear in *King Lear*. *AB*

Gloucestershire, an English county mentioned twice by *Slender in *The Merry Wives of Windsor* 3.4.42–3 and 5.5.177. In *Richard II* *Northumberland finds himself in the 'high wild hills and rough uneven ways' of Gloucestershire, 2.3.2–5 (see also 5.6.3). In *2 Henry IV* Falstaff's reference to it at 4.2.79 indicates that it is the home of Shallow and Silence in 5.1 and 5.3, and therefore also the scene of Falstaff's recruiting, 3.2. See also *1 Henry IV* 1.3.241 and 3.2.176. *AB*

Glyndŵr, Owain. He defeats and captures Mortimer (described *1 Henry IV* 1.3.92–111). Mortimer marries Glyndŵr's daughter and Glyndŵr joins him in supporting *Hotspur's rebellion, though neither is present at *Shrewsbury (Act 5). Glyndŵr's death is announced *2 Henry IV* 3.1.98. He is based on Owain ap Gruffydd (*c*.1359–*c*.1416), Lord of Glyndŵr (Glendower). *AB*

Gobbo, Lancelot's father, gives Bassanio a 'dish of doves' he had originally intended for Shylock, *The Merchant of Venice* 2.2.129. *AB*

Gobbo, Lancelot. See LANCELOT.

Godfrey, Derek (1924–83), British actor. With his fine voice and often sardonic appearance, he was a loyal company actor who revealed an intuitive grasp of the dark characters in Jacobean plays by Ford, Marston, and Webster. At the Old Vic from 1956 his Shakespearian parts included Iachimo and Enobarbus and at Stratford from 1960 Orsino, Hector, Petruchio, and Malvolio. *MJ*

'god of love that sits above, The'. Fragment of a mid-16th-century ballad sung by Benedick in *Much Ado About Nothing* 5.2.25; the tune exists under various titles, including 'Turkeyloney'. *JB*

Goethe, Johann Wolfgang von (1749–1832), major German poet. Goethe's early attraction to Shakespeare, stimulated by *Dodd's *Beauties*, Wieland's translations, and Herder's enthusiasm, influenced his historical prose tragedy *Götz von Berlichingen* (1773). In his novel *Wilhelm Meisters Lehrjahre* (1795) the semi-autobiographical protagonist is involved in a production of *Hamlet*. As theatre director in Weimar (1791–1817), Goethe staged some Shakespeare plays himself, including *King John* (1791), *Hamlet* (1795), *King Lear* (1796), and a reduced *Romeo and Juliet* (1811). His own later tragedies are subjected to classic control, while he continued to value Shakespeare's place in the history of poetry rather than of theatre, as his essay *Shakespeare und kein Ende!* (Shakespeare and No End!, 1815) reveals. *WH*

Golding, Arthur. See OVID; SOURCES.

Gollancz, Sir Israel (1864–1930), English academic, British Academy secretary (1903). He edited the *Temple Shakespeare* (40 vols., 1894–6) and, for the tercentenary of Shakespeare's death, *The Book of Homage to Shakespeare* (1916). He founded the Shakespeare Association, arranging lectures and meetings and publishing books and monographs, including a series of quarto facsimiles. *TM*

Goneril is Lear's eldest daughter and wife to Albany in *The Tragedy of King Lear* (spelled 'Gonoril' in *The History of King Lear*). Her marriage fails and her sister Regan becomes her rival for the love of Edmond/Edmund. *AB*

Gonzaga, Curzio, Italian author of *Gl'inganni*, published in 1592, one of three plays of that title which may have influenced Shakespeare's *Twelfth Night*. Its relationship to the latter is slight. The strongest link is the fact that in Gonzaga's play the disguised woman calls herself Cesare. *JKS*

'Gonzago'. See PLAYERS.

Gonzalo, one of Alonso's attendants, is shipwrecked with him on Prospero's island in *The Tempest*. *AB*

Goodbody, Buzz (Mary Ann) (1947–75), British director. Goodbody joined the RSC from the feminist Women's Street Theatre in 1967, and in 1974 became artistic director of The Other Place. Her radical, populist productions included a notable *King John* (1970), a minimalist *King Lear* (1974), and a challenging *Hamlet* (1975): her suicide just before its press night cut short a brilliant career. *MD*

Callaghan, Dympna, 'Buzz Goodbody: Directing for Change', in Jean Marsden (ed.), *The Appropriation of Shakespeare* (1991)

Goodfellow, Robin. See ROBIN GOODFELLOW.

Goodman's Fields theatre, the second theatre on a site near the Tower of London, was opened by Thomas Odell *c*.1730. First managed and later owned by Henry Giffard, who rebuilt it, it was the venue for *Garrick's first public but anonymous appearance as Harlequin in 1741. *CMSA*

Goring, Marius (1912–98), British actor. Stylish and intellectual, he was as much at home acting in French and German as in English. He toured Europe with the Compagnie des Quinze. At the Old Vic in 1940 he co-directed John Gielgud in *The Tempest* and played Ariel. At Stratford-upon-Avon he played Richard III and Octavius Caesar in 1953, returning in 1962 as a self-flagellating Angelo. *MJ*

Gosson, Henry. See PRINTING AND PUBLISHING.

Gosson, Stephen (1554–1624), playwright and anti-theatrical polemicist. His three assaults on the immorality of the stage, *The School of Abuse* (1579), *An Apology of the School of Abuse* (1579), and *Plays Confuted in Five Actions* (1582), were the most intelligent and widely imitated texts of the Elizabethan anti-theatrical lobby. *RM*

Gothic literature, fiction driven by the macabre, fantastic, or supernatural, in exotic settings of castles, ruins, subterranean caverns, and wild landscapes. The first Gothic novel, Horace Walpole's *The Castle of Otranto* (1765), was programmatically Shakespearian. Walpole borrowed the plot of guilt and remorse laced with supernatural terror from *Macbeth* and *Hamlet*, supplied comic servants for ironic contrast, set his action in a 16th-century Italy full of danger and sexual intrigue derived from the problem plays, took the romance of the lost heir from the last plays, and saturated his text with Shakespearian tags and epigraphs. His successors, Ann Radcliffe, Matthew *Lewis, and Charles Maturin, would elaborate these strategies; *Byron and *Scott would send them up; and the interview between Hamlet and his father's ghost would remain an important model throughout the 19th century. It continues to haunt the Gothic novel's surviving descendant, detective *fiction. *NJW*

Gough, Matthew. See SCALES, LORD.

Gough, Robert (d. 1624), actor (King's Men by 1611 to 1624), brother-in-law of Augustine Phillips. Gough was probably the 'R. Go' named in the plot of *2 Seven Deadly Sins* (performed before 1594, possibly by Strange's Men) and his being called 'Mr' Gough in a stage direction in *The Second Maiden's Tragedy* (first performed 1611) suggests that he was by then a King's Men sharer. Gough played Peregrine in Jonson's *Volpone* and is named in the 1619 King's Men patent and in the 1623 Folio list of actors. *GE*

Gounod, Charles François. See FRANCE; OPERA.

Governor of Harfleur. He surrenders Harfleur to King Harry, *Henry V* 3.3.127–33. *AB*

Gower. (1) He is a messenger in *2 Henry IV* 2.1. (2) Based on the poet John *Gower, he acts as a Chorus, summarizing and commenting on the action and bridging the years in *Pericles*. He speaks mainly in the octosyllabic couplets of the *Confessio amantis* (a source of *Pericles*). *AB*

Gower, Captain. He is an English captain, friendly with Fluellen, in *Henry V*. *AB*

Gower, John (*c*.1325–1408), English poet and contemporary of Chaucer. Gower published a number of allegorical and didactic works on moral and social issues including *Speculum meditantis* (*c*.1378), *Vox clamantis* (*c*.1382) and most famously *Confessio amantis*, published in English in 1390 and 1393. The latter, a collection of tales illustrating the seven deadly sins, was popular in 16th- and 17th-century England. *The Comedy of Errors*, *A Midsummer Night's Dream*, and *The Merchant of Venice* may all have drawn upon it. In particular, Gower's retelling of the story of Apollonius of Tyre inspired a number of plays and prose works on this theme. Shakespeare's *Pericles* certainly draws upon it to the extent that a number of passages of the play appear to be paraphrases of the *Confessio*. Moreover, Shakespeare explicitly acknowledged his debt by writing Gower into the play as the Chorus who presents the drama, describes the gaps in time across which it moves, and offers, in the Epilogue at least, a moral perspective on the action. Gower would have been recognizable to the audience not only because he named himself and was associated with the Apollonius story, but because he spoke in the octosyllabic verse of the *Confessio*. *JKS*

Gower memorial, Stratford-upon-Avon, completed in 1888 by Lord Ronald Gower. The memorial is comprised of a seated figure of Shakespeare, surmounting a plinth shrouded with laurels. The monument's base is embellished with statues of Lady Macbeth, Hamlet, Falstaff, and Hal. *CT*

Gowrie conspiracy, an alleged plot in 1600, against King *James VI of Scotland, resulting in the deaths of John Ruthven, Earl of Gowrie, and his brother Alexander, Master of Gowrie, and the abolition of the name of Ruthven.

John and Alexander Ruthven were two of the sons of William, 1st Earl of Gowrie, executed in 1584 for plotting with other ultra-Protestant lords. William had impoverished himself in the service of the Crown whilst Treasurer of Scotland, leaving a debt of more than £80,000 which King James owed to his son John, when he was restored to his dignities in 1592. The non-payment of this debt was a source of discontent to the Earl.

In August 1600, King James, hunting at Falkland, was allegedly lured to Gowrie's house in Perth by an urgent message brought by Alexander, Master of Gowrie. After dinner, the Master and the King retired upstairs, where a quarrel broke out and the King, later claiming an attempt on his life, called for help from a window. In the mêlée both the Earl and his brother were slain. James claimed that he had foiled a plot to abduct or kill him, but supporters of the Ruthvens suggest that it was in fact a scheme by James to rid himself of an inconvenient debtor and a family he distrusted. The true story will probably never be known. Theories put forward include an assault on the virtue of the Master by the King and revenge against a fancied lover of Queen *Anne.

A play based on these events was twice performed in 1604 by the King's Players but may have been subsequently banned because, as John Chamberlain suggested in a letter of 18 December that year, it was 'unfit that Princes should be played on the Stage in their Lifetime'. *MM*

Chambers, E. K., *William Shakespeare: A Study of Facts and Problems* (1930)
Kay, Dennis, *Shakespeare: His Life, Work and Era* (1992)

Grafton, Richard (*c*.1513–1572), printer of two early bibles in English and responsible for editing and publishing Edward Halle's *Union of the Two Noble and Illustrious Families of Lancaster and York* in 1548. Grafton's own English history, the *Chronicle at Large* (1569), was based closely on Halle's work and may have supplemented Shakespeare's reading of Halle, particularly in the first tetralogy. *JKS*

grammar school, Stratford-upon-Avon. It was, in Shakespeare's day, conducted in premises, still standing, belonging to the Stratford Corporation. It had its origin in the educational provision made by the town's medieval Guild of the Holy Cross, whose members paid for the construction of a purpose-built schoolroom in 1427/8. In 1482 Thomas Jolyffe provided this school with a generous endowment. The guild was suppressed in 1547, but the arrangements made for continuing the payment of the schoolmaster's salary suggest that the school continued in existence. Under the town's charter of incorporation of 1553, it was formally re-established as a free grammar school, with the corporation responsible for the payment of the schoolmaster's salary and the provision and maintenance of appropriate accommodation.

The effigy of John Gower in Southwark cathedral, near the Globe. Shakespeare took the plot of *Pericles* from one of the books that here provide Gower's pillow, *Confessio Amantis*: the actor who first played Gower may have worn an imitation of this effigy's costume.

MERCY
PITY
ARMIGER SCUTUM NIHIL A MODO FERT SIBI TUTUM
REDDIDIT IMMOLUTUM MORTI GENERALE TRIBUTUM
SPIRITUS EXUTUM SE GAUDEAT ESSE SOLUTUM
EST UBI VIRTUTUM REGNUM SINE LABE STATUTUM
Vox Clamantis
Confessio Amantis

'What is your genitive case plural, William?' (*Merry Wives of Windsor* 4.2.52). The interior of the Stratford grammar school: a late and not very reliable tradition claims that Shakespeare's desk was the third from the front on the left-hand side.

No records of the school itself have survived, and knowledge of its operations is confined mainly to the arrangements made for the appointment and payment of the schoolmasters and to the expenditure by the corporation on the upkeep of the buildings. A persuasive case has been made, on the evidence of the plays, that Shakespeare had a grammar-school *education, and, as his father was a leading figure in the town, it is very likely that this was the school that Shakespeare attended. *RB*

Fox, Levi, *The Early History of King Edward VI School Stratford-upon-Avon*, Dugdale Society Occasional Paper no. 29 (1984)

Orme, Nicholas, *Education and Society in Medieval and Renaissance England* (1989)

Grandpré, Lord. A French commander, he speaks disparagingly of the English army before Agincourt, *Henry V* 4.2.38–55, but lies among the slain 4.8.99. *AB*

Granville-Barker, Harley (1877–1946), English actor, director, playwright, and critic, influenced by William *Poel, for whom he played Richard II at a single matinée in 1899 and, in 1903, *Marlowe's Edward II. His first Shakespeare production, in 1904, was *The Two Gentlemen of Verona* at the Court theatre, London, with Lewis Casson in the small role of Sir Eglamour and himself as Speed. The first of his revolutionary productions at the Savoy was *The Winter's Tale*, in 1912, with his first wife, Lillah McCarthy, as Hermione and Henry Ainley as Leontes. Its innovatory use of an almost complete text and of an apron stage, of non-realistic backgrounds painted on silk drops, the stylization of movement, and the speed of the speaking provoked hostility in some critics, but others hailed it as a return to true Shakespearian values. It was followed by, and for a while played along with, a *Twelfth Night* in which only 20 lines were cut, and which was far more successful with the public, partly because of the play's greater familiarity. In 1914 came *A Midsummer Night's Dream* whose breaks with tradition included the casting of Oberon as a man, the use of folk tunes arranged by Cecil Sharp in place of Mendelssohn's incidental music, and gilded fairies.

For each production Barker (who adopted the hyphenated form of his name around 1921) prepared an acting edition sold for sixpence (roughly the price of a quarto in Shakespeare's time) in which the text was preceded by a 'Producer's Preface' outlining his directorial principles. These were the forerunners of his *Prefaces to Shakespeare*, originally conceived as introductions to a projected multi-volume edition known as The Player's Shakespeare. Seven volumes only appeared, from 1923 to 1927. Some of these pieces were later revised as the *Prefaces to Shakespeare*, first series 1927 (*Love's Labour's Lost*, *Julius Caesar*, and *King Lear*), second series 1930 (*The Merchant of Venice*, *Cymbeline*, and new prefaces to *Romeo and Juliet* and *Antony and Cleopatra*). Prefaces to *Othello* appeared in 1945 and to *Coriolanus*, posthumously, in 1947. More revisions were made for the two-volume edition of 1946–7, and *More Prefaces to Shakespeare*, collecting the early work, appeared in 1974. These writings, unique in their time in their combination of scholarship with detailed practical attention to the texts' theatrical values, exercised an immense influence for the good on mainstream 20th-century Shakespeare production. Granville-Barker, more of a textual purist than Poel but less austere in the visual aspects of his staging, believed that the director should above all trust and serve the author.

He virtually retired from the theatre during the 1920s, but in 1940 assisted Lewis Casson in directing John *Gielgud as Lear at the *Old Vic in a production which showed that the play could succeed in a full text played in Elizabethan costume. *SW*

Kennedy, Dennis, *Granville Barker and the Dream of Theatre* (1985)

Gratiano. See Graziano.

grave, Shakespeare's. Shakespeare's supposed gravestone in *Holy Trinity church, Stratford-upon-Avon, bears an *epitaph but no name; the tradition that it is his dates back well into the 17th century. According to Halliwell-Phillipps, the present stone is a replacement, dating from the late 18th or early 19th century, for the original. It is prominently situated before the steps leading to the altar rails; most of the other stones in the row are dedicated to members of his family. Shakespeare's monument is placed on the wall to the left of the row. Its laudatory inscriptions mention only his surname. This, along with certain features of its design, has led to the conjecture that it was intended to surmount a tomb on which more facts would have been inscribed but that this part of the plan was abandoned. In the floor, close to the monument, is the stone commemorating Shakespeare's widow. Although Anne died seven years after her husband, her stone, not his, lies directly under the monument. To the right of Shakespeare's stone are those commemorating Thomas *Nash, then Shakespeare's son-in-law Dr John *Hall, then Hall's wife Susanna. The other two stones in the row are not dedicated to members of Shakespeare's family. The one at the extreme right, which is badly defaced but dates from the early 18th century or later, is partly covered by the altar steps, which project forward at this point.

It is often said that Shakespeare had the right to be buried in the church rather than the churchyard because he was a tithe-holder. This does not adequately explain why his gravestone lies not merely in the chancel but as close to the altar as it is possible to get. There are no gravestones in the chancel other than the row made up mainly of members of Shakespeare's family. The floor is paved with black and white lozenge-shaped slabs. In some old churches the entire chancel floor is covered with gravestones. Shakespeare died in 1616. The members of his family whose stones lie on either side of his died respectively in 1623, 1647, 1635, and 1649. It seems possible that at some point the Stratford chancel floor was relaid, that decaying gravestones were removed and replaced by the merely decorative stones that lie there now, and that at the same time some or all of the gravestones most worthy of note were preserved and replaced in the star spots.

Donald Calthorp as Puck (Robin Goodfellow) with the First Fairy in Harley Granville-Barker's fluid, vivid, and colourful production of *A Midsummer Night's Dream*, Savoy Theatre, 1914.

Shakespeare's gravestone itself is short. Anne's stone measures 5 feet (1.5 m); the others are 5 feet 7 inches (1.7 m) long. Shakespeare's is only 3 feet 7 inches (1.1 m) in length. This might be because it has been broken or cut off and the remnant discarded, or it could be hidden under the altar steps, like part of the stone at the other end of the row.

And may there be any connection between the shortness of the stone and the fact that it bears no name? His widow's stone bears a memorial brass inscribed with Latin verses but is otherwise unmarked. The three neighbouring stones dedicated to members of Shakespeare's family are carved with both a coat of arms and a memorial inscription.

It seems odd that there is nothing on the stone carved with what is generally believed to be Shakespeare's epitaph to link it with Shakespeare. Yet several 17th-century visitors to Stratford transcribed the epitaph as his, and the belief has persisted. Nicholas Rowe, writing in 1709, said that the stone lay 'underneath' the monument, which might mean that at that time it lay directly below it, with the result that no identification was necessary. But the shortness of the stone and the absence of any identification may arouse suspicion that at some time it was carved with an inscription in addition to the epitaph, or even that it, too, bore a memorial brass.

Though the altar steps seem not to have been in place when the stone at the end of the row was laid, they are depicted very much as they are now in a painting attributed to Sir William Allan belonging to the Shakespeare Birthplace Trust which shows Sir Walter *Scott, who visited Stratford in 1828, paying tribute at the grave. Conceivably, then, a part of the original stone lies hidden under the steps, and might be carved with Shakespeare's name or bear marks indicating that it once bore a memorial brass. This could be investigated: but only by someone bold enough to run the risk of invoking Shakespeare's curse. *SW*

Gravedigger and companion. See CLOWNS.

Grave-Makers, The. An anonymous *droll composed for clandestine performance during the Commonwealth, consisting entirely of Hamlet's dialogue with the gravediggers in 5.1. It is significant that this scene had come iconically to stand in for the entire play as early as the 1650s. *MD*

Gray (Grey), Lady (1437–92). In *Richard Duke of York* (*3 Henry VI*) Edward IV makes her his consort. In *Richard III*, now Queen Elizabeth, she fails to protect her sons from Richard, but nevertheless promises her daughter in marriage to him, 4.4. *AB*

Gray, Lord. He is executed by Ratcliffe, *Richard III* 3.3, and his ghost appears at *Bosworth. Sir Richard Gray (or Grey, d. 1483) was Dorset's brother and youngest son of Queen Elizabeth (Lady Gray) by her first husband Sir John Gray. *AB*

Gray, Terence (1895–1986), British director. Originally an archaeologist, he ran from 1926 to 1933 the innovative Festival Theatre at Cambridge which had more in common with continental than with insular English stage practice. He remodelled a dilapidated old playhouse by stripping away the proscenium and footlights, and staged aggressively anti-realist productions. Though some found his approach to Shakespeare iconoclastic (Rosalind disguised as a Boy Scout, Celia as a Girl Guide; Aguecheek on roller-skates), others thought his banishing of illusion and stress on stylization achieved an almost Elizabethan dimension. *MJ*

Marshall, Norman, 'Terence Gray and the Festival Theatre Cambridge', in *The Other Theatre* (1947)

Gray, Thomas (1716–71), English pre-Romantic poet, author of the famous *Elegy*. Gray praises Shakespeare's poetry, anticipating later image criticism, in a 1742 letter to his Eton school-friend and fellow poet Richard West (1716–42): 'In truth, Shakespeare's language is one of his principal beauties . . . every word in him is a picture.' (See POEMS ON SHAKESPEARE) *TM*

Gray's Inn. See COMEDY OF ERRORS, THE; GESTA GRAYORUM; INNS OF COURT.

Graziano (Gratiano). **(1)** A friend of Antonio and Bassanio, he marries Nerissa in *The Merchant of Venice*. **(2)** Brabanzio's brother, he is in Cyprus, *Othello*, Act 5, to witness events at the climax of the tragedy. *AB*

Greece. Extracts from Shakespeare began to appear in Greek translation from 1818, but the earliest published translation of a complete play was Iakovos Polylas's *The Tempest*, in prose (Corfu, 1855). Since then notable translations of individual plays have been made by Dimitrios Vikelas (five tragedies, 1876–82), Angelos Vlachos (five tragedies, 1904–5), Constantinos Theotokis (four plays, 1914–30), Michael Damiralis (21 plays, in prose, 1928–9), Klearchos Kartheos (seven plays, 1932, 1938, 1939, 1947, 1950, 1955, 1964), Vassilis Rotas, the complete works (1970s).

The earliest known performances by Greek actors took place outside Greece: *Julius Caesar* in Constantinople, *Othello* in Odessa (1863), and *Hamlet* and *Othello* in Smyrna (1866–7). Nikolaos Lekatsas (1847–1913) triumphed as Othello, Hamlet, Lear, and Romeo in Athens in 1882, using Vikelas's translation, and in 1883 played these roles on tour in Turkey, Romania, Russia, Egypt, and Cyprus.

At least six plays were given at the Royal Theatre in Athens from 1900 to 1908 and in 1922 Emilios Veakis played Macbeth and Othello 'subtly and without bombast'. In 1926 Marika Kotopouli was a fine Lady Macbeth, and Alexis Minotis succeeded as Antony in *Julius Caesar*. Shakespeare productions increased in popularity during the 1930s, when Katerina Andreadi (b. 1909) toured the country with successful productions of *Othello* and *The Merchant of Venice*. Katina Paxinou (1900–73) delighted as Olivia in 1935, and 1937 saw an acclaimed production of *Hamlet* by Dimitris Rontiris with Veakis, Paxinou, Minotis, and Manos Katrakis in the leading roles. Later, the State Theatre of Northern Greece presented a number of plays, giving, for instance, *The Taming of the Shrew* in thirteen towns in 1965. During the later part of the 20th century Shakespeare's plays have rivalled the classic native drama in popularity.

During the 19th century, criticism was confined to introductions to translations. Costis Palamas (1859–1943) published 'Miranda', a poem (1892), and C. P. Cavafy (1863–1933) two essays on Shakespeare as well as 'King Claudius', a poem. Nikos Kazantzakis (1883–1957) wrote *Othello Returns*, a play, in 1937, and published an ode to Shakespeare (1938). His travel book *England* (1941) discusses Shakespeare at length. Other important contributions are *Othello* (1932), a critical study by Pelos Katselis, *Eros and Time* (1938) by Dimitris Kapetanakis, and *Shakespeareana* (1959) by Stathis Dromazos. Alexis Solomos's *Theatrical Notebook* (1962) examines Shakespeare's art, as does Minotis's *Experimental Theatre Education* (1972). Panos Karagiorgos's *Shakespeare Studies* (1995) contains a dozen essays on Shakespeare's life and works and includes a Greek Shakespeare bibliography. *PK*

Greek drama. In *Hamlet* 2.2, Polonius praises the actors' abilities: 'Seneca cannot be too heavy, nor Plautus too light.' The representatives of tragedy and comedy chosen are not Greek but Roman. In this respect, Polonius describes the preferences of the English Renaissance theatre which knew Greek drama second hand, through Roman adaptations. Plautus and Terence adapted the Greek New Comedy to their Roman style, largely through their adaptations of Menander's comedies. Seneca produced his own versions of tragedies by Sophocles, Euripides, and Aeschylus. The drama of ancient Rome seems to have been favoured by 16th-century readers and audiences. Even some Renaissance scholars who had studied Greek tragedies in their original language adjudged Seneca to be the equal of his classical predecessors.

Since Jonson described Shakespeare as having 'small Latin and less Greek', the absence of any direct Greek influence upon Shakespeare's work has often been attributed to this problem of accessibility. Greek was not taught at grammar schools and it is highly unlikely that Shakespeare knew more than a few words, certainly not enough to read a play. Nevertheless, there were Latin translations of all extant Greek tragedies and there is evidence of performances in English of Terence, Euripides, Sophocles, and Plautus before 1560, though not on the public stage. On this basis, similarities have been proposed between for example *King Lear* and Sophocles' *Oedipus Coloneus*, and *Hamlet* and Sophocles' *Electra*. Emrys Jones has argued for the widespread influence upon Shakespeare of Euripides' *Hecuba*. Nevertheless, whilst Shakespeare was profoundly interested in classical mythology and history, and whilst his plays share some structural and thematic features with their Greek predecessors, Shakespeare's 'classical' drama was Roman and not Greek. *JKS*

Baldwin, T. W., *Shakespeare's Small Latine and Less Greeke* (2 vols., 1944)
Jones, Emrys, *The Origins of Shakespeare* (1977)
Whitaker, Virgil K., *Shakespeare's Use of Learning: An Inquiry into the Growth of his Mind and Art* (1953)

Green, a supporter of Richard, is condemned with Bushy by Bolingbroke, *Richard II* 3.1.

AB

Greenblatt, Stephen. See NEW HISTORICISM.

Greene, John (*c.*1575–1640), and **Thomas** (d. 1640). John Greene was a lawyer of Clement's Inn who also became much involved in Stratford's legal affairs. He became a trustee of Shakespeare's *Blackfriars Gatehouse in 1618, acting for Susanna Hall (see SHAKESPEARE, SUSANNA). His brother Thomas, also a lawyer, was Stratford's town clerk from 1603 to 1617. He had studied at the Middle Temple from 1595, was called to the Bar in 1600, and continued to keep chambers in London. In diary entries of 1614 and 1615 he regularly writes of 'my Cosen Shakespear'. The exact relationship is unclear, but an earlier 'Thomas Greene, alias Shakspere' had been buried in Stratford in 1590. Greene's first children to be baptized in Stratford were named Anne (1603/4) and William (1607/8); the Shakespeares may have been their godparents. Thomas's diary includes a Latin poem written in December 1614 when his wife was about to have another child; he may be the Thomas Greene who published as a booklet a competent poem, *A Poet's Vision and a Prince's Glory*, in honour of King James in 1603, and a sonnet printed in the 1605 edition of Drayton's *The Barons' Wars*. In 1609, while waiting to move into their own house, he and his family lived at *New Place. His diary entries on the *Welcombe enclosure crisis, which include notes on conversations with Shakespeare and John *Hall, hint vividly at the turmoil it induced, and at his personal anxieties about it. He left Stratford in 1617 for London, where he had a successful career as a barrister. *SW*

Greene, Joseph (1712–90), master of Stratford grammar school from 1735 until 1772. Greene made a number of contributions to the study of Shakespeare's life and in particular to his local background. In 1746, he played a leading part in the restoration of Shakespeare's bust in Holy Trinity church, and was involved in the Garrick *Jubilee celebrations of 1769. *RB*

Fox, Levi (ed.), *Correspondence of the Reverend Joseph Greene*, Dugdale Society Publication 23 (1964)

Greene, Robert (1558–92), prose-writer, poet, and playwright. Greene was extremely interested in his own image and carefully constructed himself as a libertine and then as a devout penitent in a number of semi-autobiographical works including *Greene's Groatsworth of Wit* and *The Repentance of Robert Greene*, published after his death. He described with some relish his dissolute behaviour in Italy where he travelled after completing a BA at Cambridge. He became notorious in England for drunkenness, blasphemy, and lechery, and for having abandoned his wife and child. His early death was attributed by Gabriel Harvey, an enemy, to a surfeit of wine and pickled herrings. But for all this celebrated self-indulgence, Greene was a prolific writer who achieved success in various genres, from his euphuistic novels to imitations of Greek romances, *Menaphon* and *Pandosto*, from his dramatic adaptation of Ariosto's *Orlando furioso* to the famous coney-catching pamphlets which chronicled London's criminal underworld.

Greene's career began in 1583 when he completed an MA at Oxford and published *Mamilia*, a courtesy book for Elizabethan women, written in the euphuistic style. Greene's considerable debt to *Lyly in the early part of his career is further apparent in *Euphues, his Censure to Philautus* published in 1587. But it was also in this year that Greene seems to have written his first play, *Alphonsus, King of Aragon*, suggesting his indebtedness to another contemporary, Christopher *Marlowe. *Alphonsus* features a tyrannical and bombastic hero whose rise to power against fearful odds is the play's main action. But the play did not achieve the success of Marlowe's *Tamburlaine*, and comparison between the plays was to Greene's disadvantage. Greene defended *Alphonsus* but abandoned this style, casting aspersions against Marlowe in his later works. He turned to romantic comedy with *Friar Bacon and Friar Bungay* (*c.*1589) and *James IV* (1591). It was in this dramatic form that Greene became the innovator. His interweaving of main and sub-plots, fusion of history and comedy, and creation of courageous and sympathetic heroines provided a model for Shakespearian comedy.

That Greene perceived himself in relation to, if not in competition with, Shakespeare is suggested by *Greene's Groatsworth of Wit*. Here, Greene famously warned his fellow playwrights against the 'upstart crow, beautified with our feathers, that with his tiger's heart wrapped in a player's hide, supposes he is as well able to bombast out a blank verse as the best of you'. Here Greene quotes a line from *Richard Duke of York* (*3 Henry VI*) suggesting that the identity of this upstart crow is Shakespeare, a connection made explicit by Henry *Chettle. This criticism can be interpreted in various ways: as an attack on Shakespeare's presumption in challenging the university-educated dramatist; as an accusation of plagiarism in general; as an attack on Shakespeare's plagiarism of Greene. It has been suggested that the *Henry VI* plays were based on early plays by Greene or written in collaboration with him. If Shakespeare's debt to the dramatist in *Henry VI* remains obscure, it is blatant in *The Winter's Tale*, based on Greene's novel *Pandosto: The Triumph of Time* (1588). When *The Winter's Tale* was performed in 1611, Greene had been dead for nineteen years, his play was old, and its genre and subject matter recognizably old-fashioned. But Shakespeare's recurrence to *Pandosto* in this play, and to *Friar Bacon and Friar Bungay* in *The Tempest*, suggests the long shadow Greene cast over the 'upstart's' work. *JKS*

Davis, Walter K., *Idea and Act in Elizabethan Fiction* (1969)

Gesner, Carol, *Shakespeare and the Greek Romance: A Study of Origins* (1970)

'Greensleeves' was originally a *broadside ballad, licensed in 1580; it is mentioned twice in *The Merry Wives of Windsor* (2.1.60 and 5.5.19). The earliest surviving version of the tune (based on the **passamezzo antico*) is in William Ballett's MS Lute Book (*c.*1600). *JB*

Greenwich Palace. Birthplace of Henry VIII, Mary, and Elizabeth, the Greenwich estate came into Crown ownership in 1447 with the palace being developed by Henry VII and Henry VIII. It was used as a venue for performances for royalty and their guests but was more popular with the Tudor than the Stuart monarchs.

RSB

Cherry, B., and Pevsner, N., *The Buildings of England. London 2: South* (1990)

Greet, Sir Philip Barling Ben (1857–1936), English actor-manager, who, after an apprenticeship with Sarah Thorne, made his London debut as Caius Lucius (in *Cymbeline*) in 1883, followed by the Apothecary in Mary *Anderson's *Romeo and Juliet* (1884). In 1886 Greet set up in management, specializing in open-air performances of Shakespeare and contributing to the Stratford-upon-Avon festivals. By 1914 Greet had long-established networks for his companies in America as well as Britain, but he answered Miss *Baylis's patriotic call to the Old Vic, where by 1918 he had produced 24 Shakespeare plays to which schools matinées were central. Greet continued to promote Shakespeare in education and encouraged the founding of the *Open Air Theatre in Regent's Park (1933), appearing as Touchstone and Friar Laurence. *RF*

Isaac, Winifred F. E. C., *Ben Greet and the Old Vic: A Biography of Sir Philip Ben Greet* (1964)

Greg, Sir Walter Wilson (1875–1959), English librarian and bibliographer. Together with A. W. Pollard and R. B. McKerrow he revolutionized the textual study of Shakespeare and his contemporaries in the 20th century, directing attention to what survived of Elizabethan dramatic documents and manuscripts (in *Dramatic Documents of the Elizabethan Playhouses*, 1931); to the early printed editions of Elizabethan and later plays (in *A Bibliography of the English Printed Drama to the Restoration*, 4 vols., 1939–59); and above all to the printing and publication of Shakespeare's own plays (in *Principles of Emendation in Shakespeare*, 1928, *The Editorial Problem in Shakespeare*, 1942, 2nd.

edn. 1951, and *The Shakespeare First Folio*, 1955). His vast knowledge of the early English book trade, including copyright and censorship, is reflected in *Some Aspects of London Publishing between 1550 and 1650* (1956). Greg's textual principles included: the complete and accurate collation of all early printed copies; the crucial selection of a single authoritative copy text; no emendation of that text without clearly demonstrable error (subjective eclecticism in the choice of readings was anathema); and the exact reproduction of original spelling. At the time, this represented a methodological revolution, and even now, only the exact reproduction of original spellings has been largely abandoned. *TM*

Gregory. (1) He is one of Petruccio's servants (see *The Taming of the Shrew* 4.1.108 and 122). **(2)** One of Capulet's servants, he and his fellow servant Samson instigate a brawl, *Romeo and Juliet* 1.1. *AB*

Gremio is an old rich suitor of Bianca in *The Taming of the Shrew* (called Cleandro in *Ariosto's *I suppositi*, one of Shakespeare's sources). *AB*

Greville, Fulke (1554–1628), poet, patron, politician, and friend of Sir Philip Sidney. He wrote (probably before 1600) an intelligent collection of sonnets and lyrics, *Caelica*, and the political closet dramas *Mustapha* and *Alaham* (1633). David Lloyd claimed in 1655 that Shakespeare was Greville's servant in his youth. *RM*

Grey, Lady. See GRAY, LADY.

Grey, Sir Richard. See GRAY, LORD.

Grey, Thomas. See DORSET, MARQUIS OF.

Grey, Sir Thomas. See CAMBRIDGE, RICHARD, EARL OF.

Griffith, the gentleman usher of Katherine in *All Is True* (*Henry VIII*), appears 2.4 and 4.2. He is based on Griffin Richardes, her receiver-general. *AB*

Griffith, Elizabeth (1727–93), Anglo-Irish, briefly an actress in Dublin and Covent Garden. She wrote *The Morality of Shakespeare's Drama Illustrated*, dedicated to Garrick, in 1775. She provides summaries of 36 plays, uses quotation to illustrate general and specific moral points, and comments on character. *CMSA*

Grimestone, Edward (?1528–99), translator of S. Goulart's *Histoires admirables et memorables de nostre temps* (1606). The work, which Grimestone published in 1607, contains an analogue for the Isabella plot in *Measure for Measure*, in which the victims are husband and wife (not siblings) and there is no final forgiveness. *CS*

groundlings, Hamlet's amusing name for the spectators in the yard open-air amphitheatre (3.2.11), derives from the fact that they stood on the ground, but may also allude to the name of a fish with a large open mouth and small body. *GE*

Grumio is Petruccio's jocular servant in *The Taming of the Shrew.* *AB*

Guiderius kills Cloten, *Cymbeline* 4.2, but is tacitly forgiven by Cymbeline (his father) at the end of the play. *AB*

Guild chapel, Stratford-upon-Avon. It stands on the corner of Church Street and Chapel Lane. Its lofty nave and prominent tower date from a late 15th-century rebuilding while it was still in use by the Guild of the Holy Cross. Following the suppression of the guild in 1547, ownership of the chapel passed to the Stratford Corporation. In John Shakespeare's year as chamberlain (1563/4) payments were made for the defacement of its images. Whether this included the whitewashing over of the wall-paintings, rediscovered in 1804, remains in doubt. *RB*

Davidson, Clifford, *The Guild Chapel Wall Paintings at Stratford-upon-Avon* (1988)
Styles, Philip, 'Stratford-upon-Avon', in *Victoria History of the County of Warwick*, vol. iii (1945)

Guildenstern. See ROSENCRANTZ.

Guildford, Sir Henry (1489–1532). He welcomes the ladies to Wolsey's feast, *All Is True* (*Henry VIII*) 1.4. *AB*

guilds, also known as livery companies, were formal structures that regulated crafts and trades in the city of London. Livery companies became the principal socio-economic organizations as the legal practice of crafts and trades could only be undertaken by freemen. Freedom of the city could only be obtained through guild membership. *RSB*

Archer, I., *The Pursuit of Stability: Social Relations in Elizabethan London* (1991)
Rappaport, S., *Worlds within Worlds: Structures of Life in Sixteenth-Century London* (1989)

Guinness, Sir Alec (1914–2000), British stage and film actor. He early impressed critics in parts like Osric and Aguecheek at the Old Vic, where in 1938 he played Hamlet in modern dress and in its entirety under Tyrone Guthrie's direction. After war service he returned to the Old Vic Company and gave brilliant, subtle performances as the Fool to Laurence Olivier's Lear, and as a wily Menenius in *Coriolanus.* Never a romantic actor, he divided critics as Richard II and again in 1951 when he both directed and played in *Hamlet.* Later Guthrie invited him to head the first Shakespeare festival at Stratford, Ontario, as Richard III and as the old King in *All's Well That Ends Well.* He became a major star in films. He was hurt by the reviewers' hostile reception of his Macbeth in a Brechtian production at the Royal Court in 1966. He was Shylock at Chichester in 1984. His autobiography recalls many talented, eccentric players, some of them Shakespearians. *MJ*

Guinness, Alec, *Blessings in Disguise* (1985)
O'Connor, Garry, *Alec Guinness, Master of Disguise* (1994)

Gundolf, Friedrich (1880–1931), German academic. His 1911 *Shakespeare und der deutsche Geist* (Shakespeare and the German Spirit) and 1928–9 *Shakespeare: Sein Wesen und Werk* (Shakespeare: His Life and Work) were notable agents in the 20th-century cultural exchange between Britain and Germany. His translations of the plays appeared between 1908 and 1923. *TM*

Gunpowder Plot (1605), a conspiracy of certain younger Catholic gentry to remove King *James from the throne of England, and restore Catholicism.

Before his accession to the throne of England in 1603, James VI of Scotland had been approached, as the heir of Mary, Queen of Scots, by the leading Catholics in England, to whom he made non-committal promises of toleration. The hopes thus raised were dashed when, in his first Parliament, he supported the enactment of increasingly harsh penal laws. Led by Robert Catesby, of Ashby St Legers, Northamptonshire, a group of young men determined to blow up Parliament when it met. Their plan was to kill the King and the Prince of Wales, and proclaim as queen the young Princess Elizabeth, who would be educated as a Catholic monarch. Most of the conspirators had Midland connections, the exception being Guy Fawkes, a Catholic mining expert recruited to supervise the digging of a tunnel under the Parliament House. Postponements in summoning Parliament delayed execution of the plot for ten months and it is certain that the government knew at least the broad outline, although it is impossible to determine whether Burghley orchestrated events to suit his purposes. In early November 1605 most of the conspirators were in Warwickshire, ready to seize Elizabeth from Combe Abbey, near Coventry, and, on the discovery of Fawkes in the cellars of Westminster on 5 November, fled north through the Midlands, being finally surrounded at Holbech House, Staffordshire, where Catesby and three others died. The rest were captured and either died in prison or were executed for treason.

Most English Catholics were appalled by news of the plot, realizing the slim chance of success, and that failure would lead to further repression. The peripheral involvement of the Jesuits gave the government the opportunity to invoke the severest penalties against Catholic clergy who, the evidence suggests, had been strongly against the plot.

References to the events of 1605 have been proposed in *King Lear* and *Macbeth*, both first performed around 1606. In September and October 1605 a double eclipse of the sun and moon was assumed to presage ill times. The events of the following months seemed to justify the foreboding and Shakespeare probably drew on this in *King Lear* 1.2.100–6, *Gloucester remarking, 'These late eclipses in the sun and moon portend no good to us . . . Love cools, friendship falls off, brothers divide; in cities, mutinies; in countries, discord; in palaces treason.' In *Macbeth* the references are more oblique but more numerous. Allusions to the plot occur most notably in the speech of the *Porter whose remarks about equivocation appear to refer to the allegations that the Jesuits encouraged lying in the cause of religion (2.3.7–11). The analogy is possibly continued in the equivocal prophecies of the Weird Sisters, telling Macbeth that he would 'never vanquished be until | Great Birnam Wood to high Dunsinane Hill | Shall come against him' (4.1.107–9) and further bolstering his confidence with the assurance that 'none of woman born | Shall harm Macbeth' (4.1.96–7) *MM*

Fraser, Antonia, *The Gunpowder Plot: Terror and Faith in 1605* (1996)

Gurney, James. He attends Lady Falconbridge, *King John* 1.1. *AB*

Guthrie, Sir Tyrone (1900–71), English director, knighted in 1961. The great-grandson of the Irish actor Tyrone Power, Guthrie made his mark as an inventive Shakespearian director starting with *Measure for Measure* (1933) at the Old Vic. In 1937 he directed Laurence *Olivier in a famous *Hamlet* that toured to Elsinore and a *Henry V* that influenced Olivier's film version. A modern-dress *Hamlet* in 1938 starred Alec *Guinness. After the war Guthrie experimented with the open stage with the designer Tanya Moiseiwitsch, a collaboration which culminated in the creation of the Stratford Shakespearian Festival in Ontario, which Guthrie led from 1953 to 1957. A stage of vaguely Elizabethan architecture was placed in the middle of a huge canvas tent, with the audience seated in a semicircle around it; drawing on the traditions of William *Poel and *Granville-Barker, Guthrie established a lively choreographic method that was widely imitated (see page 65). His first productions (*Richard III* and *All's Well That Ends Well* in 1953, both with Guinness, and a Wild West *Taming of the Shrew* in 1954) foregrounded the actors and the verse in simple settings that often relied on ceremonial movement. Guthrie and Moiseiwitsch collaborated on a second version of their open plan in Minneapolis in 1963, in a house subsequently called the Guthrie theatre, and their work affected construction of new spaces in Chichester, Sheffield, and elsewhere, just as Guthrie's dynamic style of direction greatly affected Shakespeare production in the second half of the 20th century. *DK*

Guthrie, Tyrone, *A Life in the Theatre* (1959)

H

Haberdasher. He presents Katherine with a hat, which Petruccio rejects, *The Taming of the Shrew* 4.3.62–85. *AB*

Hacket, Marian. See Hostess.

Hackett family. James Henry Hackett (1800–71) was an American actor-manager, whose Falstaff was acclaimed for its symmetry of intellect and sensuality in America (1828) and England (1833). A keen student of Shakespeare, Hackett wrote detailed descriptive notes of Edmund *Kean's Richard III (pub. 1959). By his second wife, the English-born actress Catharine Lee Sugg (1797–1848), Hackett had a son, James Keteltas (1869–1926), who played leading Shakespearian roles under *Daly and collaborated with Joseph Urban in a scenically significant revival of *Othello* (1914). *RF*

Hagberg, Karl August (1810–64), Swedish scholar and Shakespeare translator. Initially a classicist and translator of Aristophanes, he produced the first Swedish translation of the complete plays of Shakespeare (1847–51). Remarkable for its imaginative transmission of Shakespeare's language, it remains a national classic. *I-SE*

Hakluyt, Richard (?1552–1616), English clergyman and geographer who attempted to fan the flames of colonial ambition with his travel-writing, in particular *The Principal Navigations, Voyages and Discoveries of the English Nation ...* published in 1589 and expanded into three volumes (1598–1600). Shakespeare's familiarity with this work is suggested by some of the exotic details of Othello's travel narratives, while *Twelfth Night* refers to 'the new Map, with the augmentation of the Indies', included in the second edition (3.2.74–5). *JKS*

Hal. *Oldcastle/Falstaff's name for Prince Harry in the *Henry IV* plays. *AB*

Hales, John (1584–1656), English scholar. Gildon (1694) and Rowe (1709) report an old debate at Eton, on Shakespeare's superiority to the Ancients. Contestants included Sir John Suckling, William Davenant, Endymion Porter, Hales himself, and Ben Jonson. Gildon makes Hales the initiator; Rowe, Ben Jonson. Whatever the cause, Shakespeare's reputation triumphed. *TM*

Hall, Arthur. See Homer.

Hall, Elizabeth (1608–70), Shakespeare's last descendant, daughter of his eldest child Susanna *Shakespeare and her physician husband John *Hall. Eight at the time of Shakespeare's death, she was left most of his silver in his *will. After her mother's death she inherited a lot more of her grandfather's estate, and lived in *New Place for a while with her first husband, Thomas *Nash. After Nash's death she remarried John Bernard (d. 1674) and moved to Northamptonshire. In her will she bequeathed Shakespeare's *birthplace to her cousin George Hart, and New Place to her husband, whose heirs sold it. *MD*

Hall, John (*c.*1575–1635), Shakespeare's son-in-law, born in Bedfordshire and (like his father Dr William Hall) a physician. He graduated from Queens' College, Cambridge, in 1593–4 and took his MA in 1597. Though he is not known to have taken a medical degree, he may have studied medicine in France, perhaps at Montpellier. He settled in Stratford at some unknown date, and his father's assistant Mathew Morris appears to have followed him; his master bequeathed him £4 and all his astrology and astronomy books in 1607 so that he could teach these skills to John.

John Hall married Susanna *Shakespeare on 5 June 1607. Her father gave her 107 acres (43 ha) of land in *Old Stratford when the marriage was arranged. They may have lived in the house in Old Town now known as *Hall's Croft. Their only child *Elizabeth was baptized on 21 February 1608. In 1613 their marriage was afflicted by scandal; Susanna sued John *Lane for defamation after he had stated that she suffered from a venereal infection adulterously contracted. Hall was an executor of Shakespeare's will, for which he was granted probate in London on 22 June 1616. New Place was the family home at least from the time of Shakespeare's death in 1616 until Hall died on 25 November 1635. His gravestone in the chancel of Stratford church carries a flattering Latin epitaph.

Hall enjoyed considerable fame as a physician in and beyond Warwickshire, and treated a wide range of patients, some humble, some distinguished, including the Earl of Warwick, the Earl and Countess of Northampton, and the poet Michael *Drayton. Although he was a Protestant with Puritan leanings, he did not refuse to treat members of the many recusant families living in the area. In 1626 Charles I, on his coronation, offered him, and many others, a knighthood as a money-raising ruse. Hall refused, paying a fine of £10 instead. After twice refusing to serve as a burgess because of the demands of his practice, he accepted election to the town council in 1632; in that year one of his patients complained bitterly that the magistrates ought not 'to lay this burden upon you whose profession is to be most abroad and cannot be effected by an apprentice as theirs may'. His period of office was turbulent, and he was fined for missing sessions. In January 1633 he was rebuked for making 'abusive speeches' against the bailiff, and in October was expelled for 'the breach of orders wilfully and sundry other misdemeanours contrary to the duty of a burgess ... and for his continual disturbances at our halls'. In 1635 he and his friend the Puritan vicar Thomas Wilson sued the corporation on the grounds that, though Hall had sold his lease of the tithes to the corporation for at least £100 less than they were worth in the hope of boosting the vicar's salary, it had been reduced, and also that they had failed to maintain the schoolmaster's salary. He took an active part in the affairs of the church, to which he presented a carved pulpit in 1629, and was churchwarden in 1628–9.

Hall died, a wealthy man, in 1635. By an oral will dictated to his son-in-law Thomas *Nash, he left property and money to his wife and daughter and his 'study of books' to Nash, with permission to burn his manuscripts 'or else do with them what you please'. His widow sold two of his manuscripts, 'both intended for the press', to James Cooke, a Warwick surgeon, who translated parts of them from Latin and in 1657 published Hall's *Select Observations on English Bodies*. It records many picturesque case histories, including those of Hall's wife and daughter, but not his father-in-law. One of the manuscripts, owned successively by David Garrick and Edmond *Malone, is now in the British Library; the whereabouts of the other—if it survives—is unknown. It has often been stated that the notebooks record no cases before 1617, but although this is the earliest date explicitly mentioned, some of the case studies predate it. Nevertheless, if the other manuscript were to turn up it might tell us more about the illnesses of Shakespeare's family, and perhaps even of Shakespeare himself. *SW*

Lane, J., *John Hall and his Patients: The Medical Practice of Shakespeare's Son-in-Law* (1996)

Hall, Joseph (1574–1656), satirist and later Bishop of Exeter and Norwich. Hall's *Virgidemarium* (1597, 1598) alludes to Edward *Alleyn playing Tamburlaine (book I, third satire), arguably an influence on Ulysses' description of Patroclus as 'a strutting player, whose conceit | Lies in his hamstring' in *Troilus and Cressida* (1.3.153–4). *CS*

Hall, Sir Peter (b. 1930), English director and manager, founder of the *Royal Shakespeare Company. After literary study at Cambridge, Hall worked in Oxford and London before directing *Cymbeline* (1957) and *Coriolanus* (1959) at Stratford, the latter starring *Olivier. In 1960 he assumed the management of the Shakespeare Memorial Theatre, which he renamed the Royal Shakespeare Theatre, and his changes were revolutionary. By the next year he had formed the Royal Shakespeare Company along European ensemble lines, with actors, directors, and designers on multi-year contracts, and had opened the Aldwych theatre as a London home. He also bid for dramatically increased government subsidy, expanded the mandate to include new plays, and encouraged radical revisions like Peter Brook's *King Lear* of 1962. He was surprisingly effective with all of his projects and soon the RSC was producing some of the most exciting theatre in the world. Hall's own directing was central to the new enterprise, particularly *The Wars of the Roses* (1963–4), the history plays from *Richard II* to *Richard III* performed in seven parts in celebration of Shakespeare's quatercentenary. Adapted with John Barton and influenced by Brecht as well as by Jan Kott's view of the histories as a cycle of unending bloodshed, the productions abandoned ideas of royal elegance for rough-hewn leather, clanging metal, and a sense of the horror and futility of war. Hall's *Hamlet* of 1965, with the young David Warner as a contemporary, conversational student, struck a chord for a generation. Hall resigned as director of the RSC in 1968 to pursue opportunities in opera and contemporary plays but was soon invited to replace Olivier as director of the National Theatre, a post he held for fifteen years from 1973, despite difficulties with the new building and declining subsidies. Knighted in 1977, he directed some ten Shakespeare plays at the National, the most notable being *Coriolanus* (1984) and a trilogy of the last plays (*Cymbeline*, *The Winter's Tale*, *The Tempest*) as his farewell in 1988. He founded the Peter Hall Company that year, directing a series of high-profile productions at the Old Vic and elsewhere including *The Merchant of Venice* (1989), *Hamlet* (1994), and *King Lear* (1997). He returned to Stratford for *All's Well That Ends Well* (1992). *DK*

Hall, Peter, *Peter Hall's Diaries*, ed. John Godwin (1983)

Hall, Peter, *Making an Exhibition of Myself* (1993)

Halle, Edward (*c.*1498–1547), lawyer and historian to Henry VIII. Halle's admiration for the Tudor monarchy inspired him to compose *The Union of the Two Noble and Illustrious Families of Lancaster and York*, in which Henry Richmond ends the cycle of bloodshed caused by the murders of Richard II and Henry VI. Published posthumously by Richard Grafton in 1548, the *Union* was to form the basis for various works of English chronicle history, in particular *Holinshed's *Chronicles*. It was particularly renowned for its emphasis on the horrors of civil war and the inevitability of divine retribution, and for its portrayal of characters such as Richard II and Joan of Arc. The *Union*'s influence upon Shakespeare is most apparent in the *Henry VI* plays. *JKS*

Halliday, F(rank) E(rnest) (1903–82), English schoolmaster. Author and compiler of *A Shakespeare Companion* (1952, rev. edn. 1964), an alphabetical guide to every aspect of Shakespeare; *Shakespeare: A Pictorial Record* (1956); and *Shakespeare in his Age* (1960). Sometimes disparaged as popularizations, such compendia, if accurate and adequately documented, serve an educational function. *TM*

Halliwell-Phillipps, James Orchard (1820–89), English scholar. A founding member of the Shakespeare Society (1840), he published a *Life of Shakespeare* in 1848; an edition in fifteen volumes (1853–61); and from 1850 onwards a series of Stratford archives and legal documents, many of them collected into his *Outlines for the Life of Shakespeare* (1881). A scholar of great determination, not seeking controversy, his career was nevertheless marked by public scandal: as a young man, he was accused of stealing rare books and manuscripts from Trinity College, Cambridge; in his maturity he was hounded by his father-in-law Sir Thomas Phillipps for the theft and mutilation of one of two extant copies of the first quarto of *Hamlet*; his old age was marred by disputes with the New Shakespeare Society, the Birthplace Trustees, and the corporation of Stratford—the town which furnished him with most of his genuine and important biographical discoveries. *TM*

Hall's Croft is a timber-framed house in Old Town, Stratford-upon-Avon, named after John *Hall, believed, on the evidence of an early 19th-century statement, to have lived there from the time of his marriage to Shakespeare's elder daughter Susanna in 1607 until 1616, when, on Shakespeare's death, he and his family moved into *New Place. The oldest part of the present structure, the Hall and Parlour, with range of small rooms behind, dates from the early 17th century. This was an addition to an existing building, which was later reconstructed, probably towards the end of the 17th century. Around 1630, some fifteen years after Hall and his wife had moved to New Place, a free-standing kitchen was built at the rear, probably replacing an earlier building. Then, some 20 years later, the two separate structures were linked together by a new staircase hall. For many years the building continued in use as the residence of town gentry and then, from the late 18th century until around 1850, of professional men, mainly solicitors and doctors. It was then converted into a private school. In 1913 it was sold to an American, Josephine Macleod, who took up residence there with her sister Betty Leggett, the widow of a millionaire founder of a New York grocery business. Together they carried out considerable restoration work. Betty died in 1931 and in 1943 Josephine made the house over to her niece, the Countess of Sandwich. Her daughter sold the house to the Shakespeare Birthplace Trust in 1949. Following restoration, it was opened to the public in 1951. *RB*

Hallström, Per (1866–1960), Swedish novelist, dramatist, and poet. His translation of the complete plays of Shakespeare, 1922–31, was the

Hall's Croft, the house inhabited by Shakespeare's daughter Susanna and his prosperous son-in-law Dr John Hall from their marriage in 1607 until they moved into New Place on Shakespeare's death in 1616.

first to challenge the classic Swedish translation by *Hagberg. It contains remarkable poetry but has proved less speakable and actable. *I-SE*

Donner, H. W., 'Some Problems of Shakespearian Translation', *Shakespeare Translation*, 1 (1974)

Hamlet, Prince of Denmark *(see opposite page)*

Hamlet Studies was founded by R. W. Desai, its editor, in 1979. It is the only journal devoted exclusively to a single work by Shakespeare and publishes articles, notes, book and theatre reviews, and occasional digests of articles on *Hamlet* in other publications. *SLB*

Hamlett, Katherine (d. 1579), spinster of Tiddington, close to Stratford, drowned in the Avon on 17 December 1579. The coroner's jury concluded that she died accidentally while 'going with a milk pail to draw water at the River Avon', but *Fripp, stimulated by her surname, speculated that she committed suicide and that the story of Ophelia 'was fashioned out of the Poet's youthful recollections' of her death. *SW*

Hamlet Travestie. See BURLESQUES AND TRAVESTIES OF SHAKESPEARE'S PLAYS.

Hampton Court was developed by Cardinal Wolsey, who presented it to Henry VIII in 1525. Henry further developed the site, particularly the Great Hall which can be regarded as the oldest surviving English playhouse. The King's Men played at Hampton Court, over Christmas 1603/4, for *James I and Queen Anne with over 30 plays being performed that Christmas. *RSB*

Osborne, J., *Hampton Court Palace* (2nd edn. 1990)

Hands, Terry (b. 1941), English director. In 1964, Hands co-founded the Everyman Theatre, Liverpool, serving as artistic director until 1966 when he became artistic director of the *Royal Shakespeare Company's touring troupe, Theatre-Go-Round. He served as associate director for the RSC (1967–77) and consultant director at the *Comédie-Française (1975–80). In 1978, he was made co-artistic director of the RSC with Trevor *Nunn. When Nunn left in 1986, Hands became sole artistic director and chief executive director. Although his directing has been criticized as overly concept driven, he received considerable praise for directing Shakespeare's history plays, most of which featured Alan *Howard. He has also had great success directing comedies, such as *Much Ado About Nothing* (1982) and *Love's Labour's Lost* (1990). In 1997, Hands became artistic director of the fledgling Theatr Clywd, hoping to turn it into a National Theatre for Wales. In 2000, he directed Kelsey Grammer's Broadway debut as Macbeth. *BR*

handwriting. The only extant examples of Shakespeare's handwriting are six *signatures on legal documents, the two brief monosyllables 'By me' on his *will, and the three pages he contributed to the *Sir Thomas More* manuscript. The idiosyncrasies of Shakespeare's handwriting have been analysed in minute detail by palaeographers. In three of the signatures, Shakespeare places an ornamental dot within the final loop of the 'W'. Another characteristically Shakespearian letter formation is the 'p' in the Blackfriars Gatehouse mortgage deed of 1613, in which a descender is followed by a cross-stroke and then a third stroke to finish off the top of the loop; the same formation appears in the three instances of 'peace' in line 50 of the *More* fragment.

(cont. on page 183)

Hamlet, Prince of Denmark

The one Shakespearian tragedy from which almost every speaker of English can quote at least one or two phrases, *Hamlet* is also one of the most difficult to date. *The Revenge of Hamlet Prince [of] Denmark*, 'lately acted by the Lord Chamberlain his servants', was entered in the Stationers' Register in July 1602, and printed in quarto in 1603 as *The Tragical History of Hamlet, Prince of Denmark*: this edition attributes the play to Shakespeare but is drastically shorter than either a subsequent quarto (1604/5, 1611, 1622, 1637) or the play as printed in the Folio (1623). Contemporary allusions to *Hamlet* are complicated by the existence of an earlier play on the same story, cited by Thomas Nashe in 1589, documented in the repertory of the Admiral's Men in 1594 and mentioned by several other writers, but this lost *'ur-*Hamlet*', already in existence before Shakespeare is known to have written anything, is very unlikely to have been a first draft of Shakespeare's own. It is not listed among his works by *Meres in 1598, for example, and a possible pun in Nashe would attribute it plausibly to Thomas *Kyd. External and internal evidence between them suggest that Shakespeare wrote his own *Hamlet* around the turn of the 17th century: Gabriel Harvey refers approvingly to Shakespeare's play in a manuscript note written between 1598 and early 1601, while stylistic evidence, although in some respects contradictory, places it just before *Troilus and Cressida*, around 1600.

Text: The discrepancies between the three substantially different texts of the play have vexed its editors ever since the publishers of the 'good' quarto of 1604–5, indignantly distinguishing their version from the apparently illicit 'bad' quarto printed the previous year, declared it to be 'newly imprinted and enlarged to almost as much again as it was, according to the true and perfect copy'. It seems likeliest that Shakespeare wrote *Hamlet* in about 1600 (producing the version printed as the 'good' quarto), but had revised it by 1602 to produce the acted version which was printed in the Folio and which also lies behind the first, 'bad' quarto of 1603 (a *reported text, very probably assembled by the hired actor who played Marcellus, Valtemand, and Lucianus, whose scenes are more fully and accurately rendered than the rest of the play). There is no complete assent on the relations between the three texts, however: some editors have favoured the 'good' quarto, insisting that the Folio text, though in places puzzlingly superior, mainly reflects unauthorized cuts by actors, while others, including those of the Oxford edition, see the Folio as Shakespeare's own mature revision of his earlier draft. The 'bad' quarto, further disputed over by editors, is also valuable despite its obvious errors and inconsistencies (and eminently actable, as sporadic modern revivals have demonstrated): its vivid stage directions may supply genuine details of the play's early performances omitted by the other printed versions, and its variations in character names—Polonius, for example, is here called Corambis, and Reynaldo is Montano—may result from an accidental conflation with the lost ur-*Hamlet*, in which the reporter had perhaps also acted.

Sources: Shakespeare's chief source was the Norse folk tale of Amleth, written down in Latin by the Danish historian *Saxo Grammaticus (fl. *c.*1200) and expanded by the French writer François de *Belleforest in his *Histoires tragiques* (7 vols., 1559–80), though it is possible that Shakespeare knew the story only at second hand via the lost earlier play. Belleforest's version was translated into English in 1608 in a version, *The Historie of Hamblet*, which itself incorporates phrases from Shakespeare's play, but the savage old Scandinavian legend is worlds away from the Renaissance tragedy

Shakespeare made of it. Although Saxo provides the originals for most of Shakespeare's main characters and much of his plot (while Belleforest further supplies the adultery of Amleth's mother and uncle before the murder of his father), in the old story no ghost has to return to demand vengeance. The identity of the King's killer is not a secret, and Amleth, feigning near-idiocy as a ruse, needs no prompting to undertake his revenge against the usurper. Deported to England, he kills his companions, as in the play, by tampering with their commission, but he reaches England himself (where he marries the King's daughter) before returning in disguise to get the entire court drunk while they celebrate his supposed death, upon which he burns down their hall, kills his uncle, and proclaims himself king. It is impossible to imagine Belleforest's Amleth commissioning the performance of 'The Murder of Gonzago', musing in the graveyard, or making fun of Osric, and Shakespeare's additions to this material (if they do not derive from the ur-*Hamlet*, as we know from Nashe the Ghost does) also include Ophelia's madness, Laertes' revenge and the character of Fortinbras.

SYNOPSIS: **1.1** Sentries at the Danish royal castle of Elsinore are insisting to the student Horatio that they have seen a ghost resembling the late King Hamlet when the Ghost appears again: they resolve to tell the old King's son, Hamlet. **1.2** The new King Claudius, old Hamlet's brother, recounts to his court that he has married his brother's widow Gertrude, and sends ambassadors to Norway to protest against young Fortinbras' plans to repossess by force the lands won from his royal father by old Hamlet. With the consent of Laertes' father, the counsellor Polonius, Claudius permits Laertes to return to his studies in France, before turning to his silent, black-clad nephew Prince Hamlet, urging him, with Gertrude's backing, to abandon his excessive grief over his father's death, and denying him permission to return to university at Wittenberg. Left alone, Hamlet reflects in horror over his mother's hasty remarriage before his fellow student Horatio and the sentry Marcellus arrive to narrate the apparition of the silent ghost: Hamlet agrees to meet them on the battlements that night. **1.3** Laertes, taking leave of his sister Ophelia, warns her against trusting Hamlet as a suitor: after Polonius has seen Laertes off, with many proverbs, he too urges her to break off her relationship with the Prince. **1.4–5** On the battlements, the ghost of Hamlet's father beckons the Prince away from his companions, and relates how, so far from having died of a snake bite as was announced, he was murdered in his sleep by Claudius, who had already seduced Gertrude: he urges Hamlet to spare Gertrude but to avenge him on Claudius, before departing, asking to be remembered. Hamlet vows to remember nothing else, and when his companions return, though he does not recount what the Ghost has told him, he swears them to secrecy, hinting that he may feign madness later on.

2.1 Polonius sends a servant, Reynaldo, to spy on Laertes' conduct in Paris, before a shocked Ophelia recounts how she has been visited by Hamlet, apparently mad: Polonius decides Ophelia's rejection of Hamlet has driven him insane, and resolves to inform Claudius. **2.2** Claudius and Gertrude welcome Rosencrantz and Guildenstern, student companions of Hamlet summoned from Wittenberg, whom they send to the Prince to attempt to discover the cause of his mental disorder. Claudius receives the ambassadors he earlier sent to Norway, who recount how a rebuked Fortinbras has now redirected his efforts against Poland, before Polonius expounds his theory that Hamlet's madness has been caused by frustrated love. They plan to spy on Hamlet at a future, engineered meeting with Ophelia, but meanwhile Polonius alone meets Hamlet, who insults him repeatedly under a guise of insanity and speaks darkly of Ophelia. Polonius is replaced as his interlocutor by Rosencrantz and Guildenstern, from whom Hamlet exacts an admission that they have been sent by Claudius and Gertrude, and to whom he expresses his profound disenchantment with life before reviving when they tell him an acting company is on its way. They discuss theatrical affairs before the players arrive, when Hamlet has their chief tragedian recite a speech about the destruction of Troy. He confidentially requests them to act 'The Murder of Gonzago' before Claudius and the court, with a new additional speech by himself. Left alone, Hamlet berates himself for seeming so much less impassioned about his father's murder than the player does about the legendary Queen Hecuba, but concludes that by watching Claudius' response to the play, which resembles his father's death, he can satisfy himself as to his uncle's guilt.

3.1 Disappointed by Rosencrantz and Guildenstern's report, Claudius hides with Polonius to watch Hamlet encounter Ophelia. Hamlet arrives, and reflects on suicide, action, and the fear of death before seeing Ophelia, whom he hysterically instructs to retreat to a nunnery: after he leaves, Ophelia laments that he has lost his reason. Claudius, distrusting his nephew, resolves to send him to England, while Polonius undertakes to overhear, unseen, a conversation between Hamlet and Gertrude. **3.2** Hamlet instructs the players on the art of acting before briefing Horatio about the secret purpose of the performance he has commissioned, urging him to watch Claudius. The court arrives and settles to watch the play. A player queen makes promises of eternal fidelity to a player king, vowing never to remarry should he die: while the player king sleeps, his nephew Lucianus pours poison into his ear, just as the Ghost had described the means of his own murder. At this point Claudius rises and demands lights, and the court disperses in disarray, Hamlet and Horatio agreeing that Claudius is guilty. Rosencrantz and Guildenstern, and then Polonius, summon Hamlet to speak privately with his mother. **3.3** Claudius, alarmed, tells Rosencrantz and Guildenstern they must take Hamlet to England at once. Alone, he prays that he may be forgiven for murdering his brother despite his inability to renounce Gertrude and the crown. Hamlet, unseen, finds him at prayer, and is about to kill him, but postpones his vengeance until another occasion for fear of sending his uncle's soul to Heaven rather than to

Hell. 3.4 Polonius hides behind the arras in Gertrude's closet: Hamlet arrives and retorts so violently to her rebukes that she fears he may kill her. Polonius cries out and Hamlet, thinking it is Claudius, stabs him fatally through the arras. Hamlet, hinting at his father's murder, and comparing pictures of his father and his uncle, reproaches his mother for her remarriage: as he rants, the Ghost, unseen by Gertrude, reappears and urges him not to be distracted from his revenge. Hamlet assures Gertrude he is not insane and makes her promise secrecy before dragging off Polonius' body. 4.1–3 Claudius, learning of Polonius' death from Gertrude, sends Rosencrantz and Guildenstern to seek Hamlet: with great difficulty they bring the morbidly joking prince before Claudius, who tells Hamlet he is to be sent at once to England for his own protection but who discloses in soliloquy that he is sending letters along with the Prince instructing the English authorities to kill him. 4.4 Fortinbras leads his army, by permission, across Danish territory. (In the 'good' quarto of the play, Hamlet, on his way to England, sees this and reflects self-critically on the contrast between Fortinbras' vigorous ambition and his own slow revenge.) 4.5 Ophelia, mad since her father's death, comes to Gertrude and to Claudius, singing distractedly: Laertes, at the head of a mob, arrives to demand vengeance for Polonius' death, for which he blames Claudius, but his anger dissipates when he sees his sister, who distributes herbs. Claudius promises to explain the circumstances of Polonius' death and to assist Laertes' revenge against the real criminal. 4.6 Horatio receives a letter from Hamlet explaining that he alone has returned to Denmark on board a pirate ship which intercepted his. 4.7 Claudius, conspiring with Laertes, also receives word from Hamlet: the two resolve that Laertes shall kill Hamlet as if by accident in a fencing match, Laertes' unblunted point made the more lethal by venom, with a poisoned drink ready for the Prince should this fail. Gertrude arrives and narrates how the mad Ophelia has drowned.

5.1 Two gravediggers are jesting at their work. Hamlet, arriving with Horatio, banters with one of them, before learning that one of the skulls they have just uncovered is that of the jester Yorick he knew as a child. His reflections on mortality are interrupted by Ophelia's funeral procession, and when Laertes leaps into her grave in extravagant grief Hamlet steps forward, declares himself to the assembled court, and leaps in too. The struggling Laertes and Hamlet are parted, and Claudius promises Laertes that their planned revenge will be immediately put into motion. 5.2 Hamlet tells Horatio how, on board ship, he secretly unsealed Rosencrantz and Guildenstern's letter to the English King and, discovering its contents, substituted a forgery telling the King to have Rosencrantz and Guildenstern killed instead. The affected courtier Osric brings Laertes' challenge to a fencing bout, which a fatalistic Hamlet, despite his forebodings, accepts. Claudius, Gertrude, and their court arrive and, after ceremonial apologies, Hamlet and Laertes duel. Hamlet is winning at first, and declines the poisoned cup, from which Gertrude unwittingly drinks. Laertes wounds Hamlet, but in a scuffle they exchange rapiers and he too is wounded with the envenomed point. Gertrude collapses, knowing she has been poisoned, and dies, and the dying Laertes tells Hamlet of the plot to kill him, blaming Claudius. Hamlet stabs Claudius and forces him to drink some of the remaining poison: he dies, and Hamlet and Laertes exchange forgiveness before Laertes' own death. Hamlet prevents Horatio from drinking poison, begging him to live on in order to tell his story, and, after hearing the approach of Fortinbras' army and prophesying that Fortinbras will be the next king, the Prince dies. Fortinbras, accompanied by the English ambassadors who have come to report the deaths of Rosencrantz and Guildenstern, takes control and makes arrangements for Hamlet's military funeral.

Artistic features: *Hamlet* is characterized by an unprecedented range of dramatic techniques and styles, but the most central is that of the soliloquy: Hamlet's 'O that this too too solid flesh would melt . . .' (1.2.129–58), 'O, what a rogue and peasant slave am I . . .' (2.2.553–607), and 'To be, or not to be . . .' (3.1.58–90) are among the most famous opportunities in the world's theatrical repertoire for an actor to exhibit consciousness in action. The play combines a powerful impression of design (with, for example, its careful parallels between the families of Hamlet, Laertes, and Fortinbras) with an equally strong effect of casual improvisation, its inset stories (and, indeed, its play-within-a-play) perpetually cut short by new circumstances. The Prince himself seems to step outside the conventions of the *revenge tragedy to reflect on his own predicament and comment on his own volatile impromptu performances in the successive episodes which overtake him, to such an extent that, despite being the most familiar play in the world, *Hamlet* still seems one of the most excitingly unpredictable, its ending as abrupt and tragic an interruption as ever.

Critical history: It would be impossible, even in a book-length study, to do full justice to any more than the bare outlines of this play's impact, not just in literary criticism and on the stage, but on Western culture at large: its characters have entered the realm of myth, and its motifs have been endlessly reworked, in *fiction (*Gothic and otherwise), *painting, *opera, and *film no less than in subsequent drama (from *Middleton's *Revenger's Tragedy* through 19th-century *burlesque to *Chekhov and *Stoppard and beyond). It has, indeed, had a profound effect on conceptions of Shakespeare himself, the rumour that Shakespeare originally played the Ghost (recorded by *Rowe in 1709) shaping many subsequent views of Shakespeare's relations to his texts and their latter-day interpreters.

The play has held such an important place in the literary canon that the history of writing about *Hamlet* is practically the history of literary criticism itself, successive interpreters and schools of thought inevitably having to try out their ideas, sooner or later, on this most celebrated and enigmatic of texts. In the 18th century strict *neoclassical critics such as *Voltaire objected to the indecorous gravediggers and to the concluding proliferation of onstage deaths, but its English popularity never wavered, Dr *Johnson defending its range and variety. The *Romantics found Hamlet's interview with the Ghost particularly sublime, and were above all preoccupied with the Prince's apparent paralysis of will, *Coleridge and *Hazlitt reflecting on the relations between thought and action in ways heavily influenced by *Goethe and *Schlegel. From then until the late 20th century much writing about the play was dominated by the question of Hamlet's character, his sanity or otherwise, and why he delays. A. C. *Bradley influentially found the core of the play's power in its juxtaposition of the scope of human thought with the limitations of mortality: other scholars continued to worry at a number of more local questions which the play deliberately leaves unresolved, such as the extent of Gertrude's guilt, the nature of the Danish succession, and the precise status of the Ghost (who, apparently on temporary release from Purgatory, seems to belong to a Catholic theology rather than a Protestant one). The emergence of *Marxist criticism saw the Prince variously lauded as a revolutionary ahead of his feudal time and reviled as a vacillatingly uncommitted bourgeois intellectual, but the play has been more central to the development of *psychoanalytic criticism, and indeed of psychoanalysis itself. Since the time of *Malone *Hamlet* had been regarded as especially revealing of Shakespeare's own emotional nature (its plot occasionally related both to the death of Shakespeare's father John in 1601 and to the death of his son Hamnet in 1596), and in 1919 T. S. *Eliot famously declared the play an artistic failure on the grounds that Shakespeare's depiction of Gertrude did not supply an adequate 'objective correlative' for the private sense of disgust with which he felt the play was nonetheless overburdened. Eliot's concerns substantially overlap with those of Sigmund *Freud, who refers to the play in outlining his theory of infantile repression in *The Interpretation of Dreams* (1900), and whose idea that Hamlet is immobilized in part because he too desires Gertrude and has entertained murderous wishes against his father was influentially developed by Ernest Jones in *Hamlet and Oedipus* (1949). Since then Hamlet's dealings with Gertrude and Ophelia have continued to preoccupy psychoanalytic criticism and the *feminist and deconstructive strains which have derived from it, while historically inclined commentators of different shades have related the play to the fall of the Earl of *Essex, the Elizabethan succession crisis, Renaissance attitudes to *death, the Reformation, and the philosophy of *Montaigne, among much else.

STAGE HISTORY: The play seems to have been an immediate success, performed in London, the universities, the provinces, on the Continent, and even at sea, as allusions by *Keeling, *Ratsey, and others, and the existence of *Der *Bestrafte Bruder-mord*, testify. The role of the Prince was almost certainly created by Richard *Burbage, and was assumed after his death by Joseph *Taylor. Popular enough to survive in performance during the Puritan Interregnum, albeit only as the *droll *The *Grave-Makers*, the play was assigned to *Davenant's company at the Restoration, since which time an unbroken line of leading actors have measured themselves against its title role, starting with *Betterton (from 1661 until his retirement more than 40 years later) and extending through *Garrick, *Kemble, *Kean, *Macready, *Sullivan, *Forrest, *Booth, and *Irving to *Barrymore, *Gielgud, *Olivier, *Burton, *Pennington, and *Branagh, among many others. It would in fact be hard to list any major anglophone actors who have not played Hamlet. The play has been equally important, since the early 19th century, in the theatres of (in particular) *France, *Germany, *Russia, and *Scandinavia: furthermore the title role's sensitive qualities have attracted not only actors but actresses, including Sarah *Siddons, Asta Nielsen, and, most famously, Sarah *Bernhardt. Long even without editorial conflation of the quarto and Folio versions, the play has usually been shortened in performance, the Fortinbras plot often disappearing entirely: over the course of his career Garrick gradually restored many formerly cut lines, but at the expense of the gravediggers, whom he excised, along with Ophelia's funeral and Laertes' death, in 1772. Broadly speaking, the 18th-century Hamlet was less indecisive than the Romantic one exemplified by Kemble, Kean, and their Victorian successors, who was an idealized figure too complex and imaginative for the corrupt world in which he found himself. In the 20th century, this tradition was notably sustained by Gielgud, who played the role at different times between 1930 and 1944, while his contemporary Olivier experimented with a Freudian approach to the Prince's psychology in 1937. Since then the Prince has often been played less sympathetically (David *Warner's sullen student in Peter *Hall's production of 1965, and Ben *Kingsley's determinedly ungraceful Prince in Buzz *Goodbody's of 1970, stand out), while the play's interest in an isolated, anxious, and possibly disordered consciousness has lent it ideally to the methods and concerns of modernism and postmodernism, notable avant-garde readings of the play including those of Charles *Marowitz, Peter *Brook, Heiner *Müller, and Robert *Lepage. *MD*

ON THE SCREEN: A five-minute French version (1900) is the earliest on record, but the significant achievements on silent film are the 1913 *Hamlet* with Sir Johnstone Forbes-Robertson in the title role, and Svend Gade's film with Asta Nielsen as the Prince (1920). Ernst Lubitsch's 99-minute *To be or not to be* (1942) might be seen as opening the way for the sound films that were to follow, but the best-known *Hamlet* remains Laurence *Olivier's 1948 film, in which the 40-year-old Olivier played the title role and was director. There is about the camera's elegiac journey into and through the loneliness of the Prince a nostalgia which arguably reflects the mood of post-war Europe. Sixteen years later the Russian director Grigori *Kozintsev made his *Hamlet* (1964). Like Olivier's, it was filmed in monochrome, but Kozintsev dramatized his images in a more arresting way. There is a starkly elemental basis to his cinematography and his is a more vigorously political view of the play than Olivier's. Less cinematic was Tony *Richardson's adaptation (1969) of his Round House theatre production, with Nicol *Williamson as a Hamlet who was more student than Prince. Franco *Zeffirelli's *Hamlet* (1990) with Mel Gibson in the title role is a move away from psychological complexity, and is more consciously an attempt to present the drama in a fragmented cinematic style. Using little more than 30% of the full text, Zeffirelli's priority was clearly to target a young audience with a racy film made up of short-duration shots. Kenneth *Branagh's *Hamlet* (1996) incorporates the First Folio text uncut with some additions from the second quarto. The complete version lasting over four hours is filmed on a lavish scale and the cast lists an array of famous names even in the small parts. The inclusion of a number of American film actors moves the film away from the British tradition of casting established stage actors for Shakespeare film roles. A shortened two-hour version has been edited from the original. Branagh's choice of late 19th-century costuming contrasts with Michael Almereyda's modern-dress version, released in 2000, with Ethan Hawke as a New York businessman Prince and Sam Shephard as the Ghost. *AD*

RECENT MAJOR EDITIONS

Harold Jenkins (Arden 2nd series, 1982); Philip Edwards (New Cambridge, 1985); George Hibbard (Oxford, 1987)

SOME REPRESENTATIVE CRITICISM

Alexander, Peter, *Hamlet, Father and Son* (1955)

Bradley, A. C., *Shakespearean Tragedy* (1904)

Dietrich, Julia, *'Hamlet' in the 1960s: An Annotated Bibliography* (1992)

Eliot, T. S., 'Hamlet and his Problems' (1919), in *Selected Essays* (1932)

Ferguson, Margaret, '*Hamlet*: Letters and Spirits', in Patricia Parker and Geoffrey Hartmann (eds.), *Shakespeare and the Question of Theory* (1985)

Foakes, R. A., *Hamlet versus Lear* (1995)

Mander, Raymond, and Mitchenson, John, *Hamlet through the Ages* (1952)

Neill, Michael, *Issues of Death: Mortality and Identity in English Renaissance Tragedy* (1998)

Raven, Anton A., *A 'Hamlet' Bibliography and Reference Guide, 1877–1935* (1936)

Robinson, Randal F., *'Hamlet' in the 1950s: An Annotated Bibliography* (1984)

Rose, Jacqueline, 'Sexuality in the Reading of Shakespeare: *Hamlet* and *Measure for Measure*', in John Drakakis (ed.), *Alternative Shakespeares* (1985)

Showalter, Elaine, 'Representing Ophelia', in Patricia Parker and Geoffrey Hartmann (eds.), *Shakespeare and the Question of Theory* (1985)

Weitz, Morris, *'Hamlet' and the Philosophy of Literary Criticism* (1964)

Wilson, John Dover, *What Happens in 'Hamlet'* (1934)

Shakespeare's unusual open 'a' with a horizontal spur at the back appears in a signature from 1612 as well as in the *More* manuscript. This practice of leaving the 'a' open at the top like a 'u' may help explain the frequency of *a : u* misreadings in texts set into type from Shakespeare's foul papers: 'Gertrad' for *'Gertrude', 'sallies' for 'sullies', 'rain' for 'ruin', and 'quietas' for 'quietus' in the second *quarto of *Hamlet*. Similarly, Shakespeare's habit of writing lower-case 'e' with the loop reversed may lie behind the many *e : d* misreadings in the printed texts of his plays, such as 'didst' for 'diest' in Q2 *Hamlet*. *ER*

Dawson, Giles E., 'Shakespeare's Handwriting', *Shakespeare Survey*, 42 (1990)

Schoenbaum, Samuel, *William Shakespeare: Records and Images* (1981)

hangings. See DEATH; HELL; STAGE DECORATION, ELIZABETHAN.

Hanmer, Sir Thomas (1677–1746), Speaker of the House of Commons. After retiring from Parliament, Hanmer produced an opulent edition of Shakespeare published by the Clarendon Press at Oxford (1744). Hanmer's editorial method was lax (he took his text from Alexander *Pope's earlier edition and made no attempt to collate it with other texts), but the edition itself was lavishly produced, with illustrations and a costly binding. Although William Warburton attacked Hanmer's lack of historical and textual accuracy, the sales of Hanmer's edition soared while Warburton's rival edition was remaindered. Pope ridicules Hanmer in *The Dunciad* 4 (II. 105–18). *JM*

Harbage, Alfred (1901–76), American academic, author of influential studies of *Shakespeare's Audience* (1941) and *Shakespeare and the Rival Traditions* (1952); editor of *Annals of English Drama 975–1700* (1940, rev. S. Schoenbaum, 1964), and of the single-play series the Pelican Shakespeare (1956–67), and its collection as *The Complete Works* (1969). *TM*

Hardy, Robert (b. 1925), English actor. In 1949, Hardy joined the Shakespeare Memorial Theatre where he played Banquo (1949), Oberon (1959), and Edmund (1959). Since then he has made a speciality of 'quality' television costume drama, his roles including Coriolanus in *The Spread of the Eagle* (1963), Hal/Henry V in *An Age of Kings* (1960), and Leicester in *Elizabeth R* (1971). *BR*

Harfleur, Governor of. See GOVERNOR OF HARFLEUR.

Harington, Sir John (1561–1612), Queen Elizabeth's godson. Harington was a court favourite commended for his witty epigrams. He became one of Essex's entourage and followed the Earl to Ireland, though he took no part in the rebellion which finally led to the Earl's execution. After Elizabeth's death, Harington remained at court as tutor to Prince Henry. His literary works include a collection of miscellaneous verse called *Nugae antiquae*, not published until 1769, and, most importantly, a celebrated translation of Ariosto's *Orlando furioso*, published in 1591, which he claimed had been commissioned by Elizabeth herself. Shakespeare probably knew Ariosto's romance through Harington's translation. *JKS*

'Hark, hark, the lark', an aubade (dawn song), sung by a musician in *Cymbeline* 2.3.19. An anonymous MS setting from Shakespeare's time or not long after has been attributed to Robert *Johnson, in which case it may have been used in an early production. The best-known setting since is *Schubert's 'Standchen' (1826), with translation by *Schlegel. *JB*

Harlequin's Invasion: A Christmas Gambol (1759), a Shakespearian entertainment devised by *Garrick and the first pantomime to feature a speaking Harlequin, celebrated military victories against the French, promoted English culture, featured a replica of *Scheemakers's monument, and concluded with the singing of 'Heart of Oak', Garrick's popular, patriotic song. *CMSA*

Harlequin Student; or, The Fall of Pantomime, with the Restoration of the Drama, by Henry Giffard, possibly *Garrick's London debut, was performed at Goodman's

Fields in 1741. It concluded with a speech by Jupiter promoting Shakespeare above 'Foreign Mimes' and the display of a replica of *Scheemakers's *Westminster abbey monument. *CMSA*

harp, an important instrument in Shakespeare's time, but with little surviving repertoire since playing depended on extemporization and memory. It was smaller than the modern concert harp; tone might be altered to produce a buzzing sound with 'brays', metal pins brought just into contact with the strings near the tuning pegs. *JB*

Harris, Frank (James Thomas) (1856–1931), Irish journalist. Harris believed he had discovered the man behind the dramatic mask: first in 'The True Shakespeare' (*Saturday Review*, Mar. 1898); later *The Man Shakespeare and his Tragic Life Story* (1909) became a popular sensation by interpreting the plays as the intimate autobiography of a turbulent soul. In *The Women of Shakespeare* (1911), Harris recreates four influential women: his mother, his wife, his mistress, and his daughter Judith. Harris's play *Shakespeare and his Love* (1910) disputes unsuccessfully the imaginative right to Mistress Mary Fitton with Bernard Shaw's *The Dark Lady of the Sonnets* (1910). *TM*

Harris, Henry (*c.*1634–1704), a prominent actor (and perhaps scene-painter) with Davenant's Duke's Company, he played Horatio to Betterton's Hamlet in 1661, Romeo in 1662, then a range of comic and serious roles including Andrew Aguecheek and a praised Wolsey. In 1671 he became joint manager of Dorset Garden theatre with Betterton. *CMSA*

Harrison, George Bagshawe (1894–1991), English academic. Author of *Shakespeare: The Man and his Stage* (1923), and *Shakespeare under Elizabeth* (1933), which speculates on the black prostitute Lucy Negro as a possible Dark Lady. His widely diffused Penguin editions of each play (1937–59) were based on the Folio text, but with only limited annotation. *TM*

Harrison, William (1534–93), English clergyman and historian, author of *An Historical Description of the Island of Britain.* This work was published as part of *Holinshed's *Chronicles* in 1577 and again, in expanded form, in the *Chronicles* of 1587. Shakespeare may have turned to Harrison's account of pre-Christian Britain for *King Lear.* *JKS*

Harry, Prince. See Henry IV Parts 1 and 2; Henry V.

Harsnett, Samuel (1561–1631), Protestant chaplain and polemicist who served in 1599 as licenser for books, responsible for censoring seditious material. By authorizing a history which celebrated *Essex at the height of the Irish debacle, Harsnett was threatened with imprisonment but managed to avoid that fate. In the same year he published his *Discovery of the Fraudulent Practices of John Darnel*, followed by a longer study, *A Declaration of Egregious Popish Impostures*, in 1603. Both exposed the Catholic practice of exorcism as a pernicious trick closely related to those deceptions practised on the contemporary stage. That Shakespeare knew the *Declaration* is made clear by *King Lear.* Deep structural and symbolic parallels have been perceived between the two. More obviously, Edgar's physical 'mortification' as Poor Tom and much of what he says to create the impression of madness derive from the description of those who are equally fraudulent in Harsnett's tract. The *Declaration*'s influence may also have extended to *Pericles* and *The Tempest.* *JKS*

Brownlow, F. W., *Shakespeare, Harsnett and the Devils of Denham* (1993)

Greenblatt, Stephen, 'Shakespeare and the Exorcists', in Patricia Parker and Geoffrey Hartmann (eds.), *Shakespeare and the Question of Theory* (1985)

Salingar, Leo, in *Dramatic Form in Shakespeare and the Jacobeans* (1986)

Hart, William (d. 1616), Shakespeare's brother-in-law, husband of Joan *Shakespeare. Their marriage is not found in the Stratford register, and he is first recorded in the entry for the baptism of his son, also William, on 28 August 1600. At the christening of his second son and at his burial on 17 April 1616—a week before Shakespeare died—he is identified as a hatter. *SW*

Harvard, John (1607–38), founder of Harvard University; son of Robert Harvard, a Londoner who in 1605 married Katherine Rogers in Stratford. They lived in Southwark near the Globe. In 1596 her father Thomas, a prosperous butcher, had rebuilt his house in the High Street, Stratford, with splendid carved-wood decorations. Now known as Harvard House, it is administered by the Shakespeare Birthplace Trust. *SW*

Harvey, in *1 Henry IV*, is one of *Oldcastle's (Falstaff's) companions. Harvey was Shakespeare's first name for Bardolph, changed at the same time as Oldcastle's name was changed to Falstaff and Rossill (*Russell) to Peto. *AB*

Harvey, Gabriel (*c.*1550–1631), poet, pamphleteer, and controversial Cambridge academic. In 1580 he published his correspondence with Edmund *Spenser, *Three Proper, and Witty, Familiar Letters*, which discusses their experimental efforts to compose English verse in classical metres. Later he became embroiled in a literary quarrel with Thomas *Nashe, who goaded him into writing *Pierce's Supererogation* (1593), stuffed with intriguing critical assessments of contemporary writers. The quarrel ended when both men (with several others) had their works publicly burned by the Church in 1599. Harvey scribbled valuable notes all over the books in his vast library. Some of these pertain to Shakespeare. *RM*

Harvey, Sir John Martin (1863–1944), English actor-manager who, after fourteen years with *Irving (1882–96), established himself independently. He gradually introduced Shakespeare into his repertoire: *Hamlet* (1904), less dominated by the Prince than was usual; a surprisingly debonair and picturesque Richard III; *The Taming of the Shrew* as Petruchio to his wife Nina de Silva's (1869–1949) Katherine, with Sly present throughout and the scenery changed in the audience's view; and a patriotic *Henry V* in the Elizabethan manner in 1916. *RF*

Harvey, Sir William (d. 1642), courtier. Harvey in 1598 married the third Earl of *Southampton's widowed mother. He has been linked hypothetically with 'Mʳ W. H.' in the dedication to *Shakespeares Sonnets* (1609), and with 'W Har', who in *Epicedium* (1594) alludes to Shakespeare's *Lucrece.* *PH*

Hastings, Lord. (1) In *Richard Duke of York* (*3 Henry VI*) he is one of Edward IV's supporters, helping him escape Warwick (4.7.82). In *Richard III* he refuses to help Richard seize the throne (3.2), is accused by him of protecting the 'witch' Jane Shore, and executed (3.4). His ghost appears at *Bosworth. He is based on William, Lord Hastings (*c.*1430–83). **(2)** One of the rebel leaders in *2 Henry IV*, he is sent to execution with the Archbishop of York and Mowbray by Prince John, 4.1. He is based on Sir Ralph Hastings (d. 1405). *AB*

Hastings, Sir Ralph. See Hastings, Lord.

Hathaway, Anne (?1555–1623), Shakespeare's wife, daughter of Richard Hathaway (d. 1581), whose father John held land and a house called Hewlands (see Anne Hathaway's Cottage) in Shottery, near Stratford, in 1556. One of seven children, she was born in 1555 or 1556, judging by the inscription on the brass marking her grave, which says that she was 'of the age of 67 years' at her death on 6 August 1623. Her father left her 10 marks to be paid on her marriage. Her brother Bartholomew succeeded to his father's copyhold when their mother died, in 1599. In 1610 he paid £200 to buy the house and other property outright. He left them to his son John in 1621, naming John *Hall as overseer of his will; the house belonged to his descendants till 1838.

A record of Shakespeare's courtship may survive in the wordplay of his Sonnet 145, which ends:

> 'I hate' from hate away she threw,
> And saved my life, saying 'not you.'

On 27 November 1582 the Bishop of Worcester licensed marriage 'inter Wm Shaxpere et Annam whateley de Temple grafton'. That 'whateley' is a simple error is suggested by a bond of 28 November, in the large sum of £40, by which Fulk Sandells and John Rychardson of Stratford exempted the Bishop from liability if there was any irregularity in a marriage between 'william Shagspere' and 'Anne hathwey of Stratford in the Dioces of worcester maiden.' Sandells had been overseer of Richard Hathaway's will, and Rychardson a witness. As a minor, Shakespeare could not marry without his father's consent; presumably Sandells and Rychardson had to testify, among other things, that he had it.

The licence gave permission to marry after one asking of the banns, which were forbidden from Advent Sunday (2 December in 1582) to 13 January. This is presumably because Anne was pregnant: their first child, *Susanna, was baptized on 26 May 1583. The marriage licence suggests that Anne may have been living at Temple Grafton, though the bond describes her as of Stratford. The marriage is not recorded in the Stratford register, but could have been solemnized at one of the neighbouring villages, Temple Grafton, Bishopton, or *Luddington, for none of which the records survive. Twins, *Hamnet and *Judith, were baptized in Stratford on 2 February 1585. In 1601 Anne was mentioned in the will of Thomas *Whittington as holding money on his behalf.

The Shakespeares' first house of their own appears to have been *New Place, which William bought in 1597. Shakespeare must have spent much time in London, though his many recorded business transactions in Stratford-upon-Avon and the neighbourhood suggest that he frequently returned to the area, and he seems to have lived there permanently in his last years. He does not mention Anne by name in his *will, though he left her 'my second best bed with the furniture'. She would have been legally entitled to a share in her husband's estate, along with the right, which she seems to have exercised, to continue to live in New Place. A late 17th-century legend says that she and her daughters wished to be buried in her husband's grave (see Dowdall, John). Her gravestone lies next to his, and immediately below his monument, in the chancel of Stratford-upon-Avon church. A brass plate carries an inscription written perhaps by her son-in-law John *Hall:

> Heere lyeth interred the body of Anne wife of William Shakespeare who departed this life the 6th day of August 1623 being of the age of 67 yeares:

> Vbera, tu mater, tu lac, vitamque dedisti:
> Vae mihi: pro tanto munere saxa dabo?
> Quam mallem amoueat lapidem bonus Angelus orem!
> Exeat, ut Christi corpus, imago tua.
> Sed nil vota valent; venias cito, Christe! resurget
> Clausa licet tumulo mater et astra petet.

Translated, these Latin elegiacs mean:

> Breasts, O mother, milk and life thou didst give. Woe is me—for so great a boon shall I give stones? How much rather would I pray that the good angel should move the stone so that, like Christ's body, thine image might come forth! But my prayers are unavailing. Come quickly, Christ, that my mother, though shut within this tomb, may rise again and seek the stars.

We have no direct information other than that given here about the relationship between Shakespeare and his wife. Schoenbaum, in his *Compact Documentary Life* (not in the original), reproduces a drawing, dated 1708, by Sir Nathaniel Curzon purporting to be of 'Shakespear's Consort' which is preserved in a copy of the Third *Folio, and the *forgeries of William Henry Ireland include a love letter from her husband. *SW*

Schoenbaum, S., *William Shakespeare: A Documentary Life* (1975, compact edn. 1977)

Hauptmann, Gerhart (1862–1946), German dramatist. Despite the naturalism of his early plays, Hauptmann was constantly involved with Shakespeare. He adapted *The Tempest* in his play *Indiphodi* (1920), arranged *Hamlet* for the Dresden stage (1927), wrote a play on the hero's student life (*Hamlet in Wittenberg*, 1936) and a novel about a *Hamlet* performance that also alluded to Goethe's *Wilhelm Meister*. *WH*

hautboy, or shawm, a loud double reed wind instrument and ancestor of the oboe; 'hautboys' occurs as a stage direction for scenes of banqueting and entertainment, e.g. *Timon of Athens* 1.2.opening. *JB*

Hawkins, William (1722–1801), English clergyman and poet. As professor of poetry at Oxford, he delivered the first-ever series of lectures devoted to Shakespeare (1751–6). He also wrote a strongly nationalistic adaptation of *Cymbeline* (1759) in which he attempted to make the play more modern and thus more 'rational'. *JM*

hay (hey), dancers interweaving by passing each other alternately to left and to right. References in *Love's Labour's Lost* 5.1.147 and in Heywood's *A Woman Killed with Kindness* suggest that the hay was considered a dance in its own right, as well as a choreographic device. *JB*

Haydn, Franz Josef (1732–1809), Austrian composer. His only known Shakespeare setting is the canzonetta 'She never told her love' (1795) from *Twelfth Night*. The incidental music for *King Lear* (1806) attributed to Haydn is almost certainly the work of others (possibly K. D. Stegmann or Josef von Blumenthal). *IBC*

Hayman, Francis (1708–76), English painter and illustrator. After early success as a scene painter, Hayman established a remunerative practice as a portrait painter. His living sitters included David *Garrick and Mrs *Pritchard, and he also executed a full-length retrospective portrait of Shakespeare, sometimes known as the 'Willett portrait', now in the *RSC Collection and Gallery. In 1741, Hayman was commissioned by entrepreneur Jonathan Tyers to decorate the supper-boxes at Vauxhall Gardens with pastoral and dramatic subjects: the results included scenes from *King Lear*, *Hamlet*, *Henry v*, and *The Tempest*. Hayman also produced designs for Thomas Hanmer's edition of Shakespeare plays, published in 1744, and for Charles Jennen's unfinished edition, abandoned in 1770. *CT*

Hayward, Sir John (?1564–1627), author of the *First Part of the Life and Reign of Henry the Fourth*, published, with a dedication to the Earl of Essex, in 1599. In 1600, Hayward was imprisoned for his work, which Shakespeare may have seen in manuscript and used as a source for *Henry iv*. *CS*

Hazlitt, William (1778–1830), English critic. Together with A. W. *Schlegel and Samuel Taylor *Coleridge, one of the key figures in *Romantic Shakespearian criticism. His *Characters of Shakespear's Plays* (1817), strongly influenced by the 1815 English translation of Schlegel's lectures, was the first inexpensive play-by-play survey aimed at a wide readership. As in much criticism of the period, there is an emphasis on the interpretation of the leading roles in the plays, but by 'characters' the title means 'distinctive traits'—Hazlitt's aim was to sketch pen-portraits of the unique 'characteristics' of each play. His own prose style plays a part in some of the richest characterizations: the essay on *Coriolanus* is abrasive, that on *Macbeth* antithetical, on *Hamlet* inward-looking.

Hazlitt is most notable as a reader of the tragedies, though he also included an influential contrast between Shakespeare and Ben *Jonson in his *Lectures on the English Comic Writers* (1819). Like the other Romantics, he identified especially with the Prince of Denmark ('It is *we* who are Hamlet'). His disquisition on the politics of *Coriolanus* ('The language of poetry naturally falls in with the language of power') led to a fierce dispute with the Tory critic William Gifford. Hazlitt wrote venomously of the hypocrisy of the powerful, and liked minor characters who showed up their betters: Barnardine in *Measure for Measure* 'is a fine antithesis to the morality and the hypocrisy of the other characters in the play'.

Hazlitt's abiding principle was 'sympathy', the idea of the artist's capacity to transcend egotism: 'The striking peculiarity of Shakspeare's mind was its generic quality, its power of communication with all other minds—so that it contained a universe of thought and feeling within itself, and had no one peculiar bias . . . His genius shone equally on the evil and on the good, on the wise and the foolish, the monarch and the beggar.' John *Keats heard Hazlitt speak to this effect in *Lectures on the English Poets* (1818) and went on to develop his theory of the poet as a chameleon who delights as much in an Iago as an Imogen.

Hazlitt was a passionate theatre-goer, although he was infuriated by the practice of adapting Shakespeare's text and by the weakness of the minor players in the star-based theatrical economy of early 19th-century London. He was generous in his praise of those actors who embodied the art of sympathetic impersonation, notably Sarah *Siddons for her Lady Macbeth, John Philip *Kemble for his Coriolanus, Eliza *O'Neill for her Juliet, and Edmund *Kean for a succession of roles, beginning with Shylock and Richard III. He described Kean's performance as Othello in the third act as 'the finest piece of acting that was ever seen', but admired his Iago almost as much. Hazlitt, who collected his theatrical notices in *A View of the English Stage* (1818), was Kean's greatest apologist; his reviews played a major part in the actor's rise to celebrity following his 1814 Drury Lane debut. *JBt*

Hazlitt, William, *Complete Works*, ed. P. P. Howe (21 vols., 1930–4)
Bate, Jonathan (ed.), *The Romantics on Shakespeare* (1992)
Bate, Jonathan (ed.), *Shakespearean Constitutions: Politics, Theatre, Criticism 1730–1830* (1989)
Bromwich, David, *Hazlitt: The Mind of a Critic* (1983)
Kinnaird, John, *William Hazlitt: Critic of Power* (1978)
White, R. S. (ed.), *Hazlitt's Criticism of Shakespeare: A Selection* (1996)

headless line, a line of iambic verse that is missing an initial unstressed syllable, sometimes implying a degree of abruptness: 'Stay, the King hath thrown his warder down' (*Richard II* 1.3.118). Not to be confused with otherwise normal iambic lines that begin with a trochaic foot: 'Near to the King in blood, and near in love' (*Richard II* 3.1.17) *GTW*

'Heart's Ease', a popular song or tune referred to by Peter in *Romeo and Juliet* 4.4.128. Two *broadside ballad tunes survive. *JB*

heavens. Early playhouses such as the Theatre and the Curtain had no substantial cover over the stage, only a turret-like tiring house with perhaps a short pentice extension. By 1595 the Rose was fitted with a full cover which provided protection for the actors' (and soon after, the onstage spectators') costumes, and all subsequent playhouses copied this innovation. The underside of the cover, the heavens, was brightly painted with astral bodies and figures from classical mythology and from the zodiac on a background of marbling. Shakespeare's characters commonly allude to the heavens: in *Titus Andronicus* 4.3 Titus and Marcus fire arrows towards it, Othello swears by 'yon marble heaven' (3.3.463), Timon of Athens speaks of 'the marbled mansion all above' (4.3.192), Hamlet finds no pleasure in 'this brave o'erhanging, this majestical | roof fretted with golden fire' (2.2.302–3), and in *Cymbeline* Giacomo commits to memory the detail that 'The roof o' th' chamber | With golden cherubins is fretted' (2.4.87–8). *GE*

Hecate, originally a Greek divinity, had evolved into the ruler of demons and *witches by Shakespeare's day. She appears in *Macbeth* 3.5 and 4.1. Many scholars have seen her lines as interpolations, probably by Thomas *Middleton. *AB*

Hector, the Trojan champion in *Troilus and Cressida*, is killed treacherously by Achilles' Myrmidons, 5.9. He is based on medieval interpretations of the character from *Homer's *Iliad.* *AB*

'Hector'. See ARMADO, DON ADRIANO DE.

Heine, Heinrich (1797–1856), German poet. He criticized previous *Romantic views of Shakespeare in *Die romantische Schule* (1836). In *Shakespeares Mädchen und Frauen* (Shakespeare's Maidens and Women, 1839), one of the first 19th-century books on the subject, his digressive and often ironical texts accompany a series of engraved portraits; they also contain a vindication of Shylock. Shakespeare appears as a character in Heine's epic poem *Atta Troll* (1847). *WH*

Helen. (1) According to Homeric legend, her abduction by Paris caused the Trojan War. She appears in *Troilus and Cressida*, 3.1. **(2)** The heroine of *All's Well That Ends Well*, an orphan under the protection of the Countess of Roussillon, who falls unrequitedly in love with Bertram, but wins him through her relentless resourcefulness. Editors often prefer 'Helena', though she is called Helen except in stage directions (and once, in 1.1). **(3)** She is Innogen's lady-in-waiting, *Cymbeline* 2.2. *AB*

Helena. (1) Her love for Demetrius in *A Midsummer Night's Dream* is eventually requited, thanks to fairy magic. **(2)** *All's Well That Ends Well.* See HELEN. *AB*

Helenus, one of Priam's sons, is a Trojan warrior and priest in *Troilus and Cressida.* *AB*

Helicanus, a lord of Tyre, is offered the crown, *Pericles* 8, but defers accepting it out of loyalty to the missing Pericles. *AB*

hell. The area underneath the stage, often used to represent the underworld. Hellish characters could emerge through a trapdoor set in the stage or, if the underside of the stage was not boarded in, through the hangings which concealed the understage area. Occasionally an actor or musician might perform from within the hell, as when the Ghost of Hamlet's father cries 'Swear' from under the stage (1.5.151) and when 'Music of the hautboys is under the stage' in *Antony and Cleopatra* (4.3.10). *GE*

Helpmann, Sir Robert (1909–96), Australian actor and all-round man of the theatre. With some experience as a dancer in his native land he joined Sadler's Wells Ballet in London, excelling in character parts. At the Old Vic in 1937 he played Oberon in a lavish *Midsummer Night's Dream* and in 1942 choreographed a surrealist ballet *Hamlet* to a scenario by his lover Michael *Benthall under whose direction he often acted. He played Hamlet for the Old Vic in 1944 and in Stratford in 1945, where he also played a foxy King John and a malevolent Shylock but was frustrated in his desire to add the shrew Katherine. During Benthall's long, successful directorship of the Old Vic he both appeared in and directed plays by Shakespeare and also played Shylock, Petruchio, and Angelo in an Australian tour with Katharine Hepburn as co-star. After Benthall's death in 1974 he ran the Australian National Ballet. A cruelly accurate mimic, he seems to have been more feared than loved by his fellows. *MJ*

Heminges, John (1566–1630), actor (Strange's Men by 1593, *Chamberlain's/King's Men 1596–1630) and business manager for the King's Men. Heminges was about to become free of his apprenticeship as a grocer when he married Rebecca Knell, the 16-year-old widow of William Knell (a Queen's Men actor), on 10 March 1588. By May 1593 Heminges was an actor with Strange's Men and by the end of 1596 Heminges was a Chamberlain's Man, receiving with George Bryan the payment for their court performances; throughout his career, especially after 1611, Heminges's business skill was as important as his acting. In 1599 Heminges became one of the original *Globe housekeepers and in 1608 one of the *Blackfriars housekeepers, and he managed to increase his shares to a one-quarter holding in each by the time of his death. Heminges probably owned the taphouse which adjoined, and which in 1613 caught fire from, the first Globe and he certainly had a house (possibly also a taphouse) adjoining the second Globe. In 1611 Heminges's daughter Thomasine married the King's Man William Ostler who died intestate on 16 December 1614 leaving his widow shares in the company playhouses over which father and daughter fought in the courts. The legal records of this battle are an important source of our knowledge about the ownership of the playhouses. Heminges appears as himself in the Induction to *Marston's *The Malcontent* and is named as an actor in company cast lists for *Jonson's *Every Man in his Humour*, *Every Man out of his Humour*, *Sejanus*, *Volpone*, *The Alchemist*, and *Catiline*. A surviving copy of Jonson's 1616 folio has a handwritten Jacobean annotation assigning Heminges the part of Corbaccio in *Volpone* alongside Nathan Field as Voltore, and since the latter did not the join the King's Men until 1616 Heminges's acting career seems to have lasted until his early fifties. In 1619 Heminges's wife Rebecca died and in 1623 he and Henry Condell produced the Shakespeare *Folio. Towards the end of his life Heminges was almost solely responsible for the business affairs of the King's Men. After his death in 1630, Heminges's son William sold Globe and Blackfriars shares to the King's Man John Shank, triggering the dispute recorded in the Sharers Papers. *GE*

Henderson, John (1747–85), actor. He was an immediate sensation as Hamlet at Bath in 1772 (followed by Richard III, Benedick, and Hotspur). *Garrick's jealousy allegedly delayed his London debut but he achieved success as Shylock for *Colman at the Haymarket and, while continuing to play Hamlet and a range of roles, he excelled as Iago. *CMSA*

hendiadys, a rhetorical figure in which two terms, usually nouns, are coupled by 'and' to form a single complex idea, where one would expect a noun qualified by an adjective: 'a tale | Told by an idiot, full of *sound and fury*' (instead of *furious sound*), *Macbeth* 5.5.26–7. *CB/GTW*

Henley Street, the street in Stratford in which Shakespeare's father was living by 1552, when he was fined for making a dungheap there, and where he owned property at the time of William's birth in 1564. His house, now known as the *Birthplace, passed to William on his father's death. *SW*

Henri IV (1553–1610), King of Navarre and France. Henri de Bourbon, King of Navarre, succeeded his cousin Henri III as King of France in 1594: his accession may have motivated Shakespeare's depiction of the King of Navarre in *Love's Labour's Lost*. He was a Huguenot Protestant, greatly admired in England until his conversion to Roman Catholicism, to secure the succession, reportedly with the words 'Paris vaut bien une messe' (Paris is well worth a mass). Thereafter he was often cited as a model of French faithlessness and hypocrisy. His claim to the French throne depended on the Salic Law, firmly rejected by the King's advisers in *Henry V*. It is probably also relevant that the Duke of Bourbon is represented in the play as a pompous braggart. *SO*

Wormersley, David, 'France in Shakespeare's *Henry V*', *Renaissance Studies*, 9/4 (Dec. 1995)

Henriad. A modern nickname for the Second *Tetralogy, particularly the two *Henry IV* plays and *Henry V*, coined by anology with *Virgil's *Aeneid*. It implies that these plays are Shakespeare's epic, with Prince Harry, later Henry V, as their epic hero. *MD*

Henrietta Maria (1610–66), Queen of England, consort of *Charles I, posthumous daughter of *Henri IV of France and Marie de Médicis. Her marriage to Charles as Prince of Wales was a triumph of *James I's ecumenism, and she maintained her Roman Catholic faith throughout her life. From her arrival in England, she was an enthusiastic patron of theatre, not only dancing in *masques, but commissioning plays in which she and her ladies took speaking roles. These were widely condemned and frequently cited as touchstones for the immorality of the court, but the debate they engendered opened the way to the domestication of actresses on the English stage at the Restoration—the word 'actress' was first used in reference to her. After the murder of the Duke of Buckingham (1628), she became the King's chief confidante and adviser, and was often blamed for his unpopular policies. During the Civil War she actively supported the Royalist cause, raising money and troops. She fled to France in 1644, returning to England with Charles II in 1660. *SO*

Henry IV (1366–1413), King of England (reigned 1399–1413 after supplanting *Richard II), surnamed Bolingbroke. See Richard II; Henry IV Part 1; Henry IV Part 2. *AB*

Henry IV Part 1 *(see page 188)*

Henry IV Part 2 *(see page 193)*

Henry V (1387–1422), King of England (reigned 1413–22). See Henry IV Part 1; Henry IV Part 2 (in which he is depicted as Prince Harry); Henry V. *AB*

Henry V *(see page 196)*

Henry VI (1421–71), King of England (reigned 1422–71, though his rule was contested from 1455 onwards). See Henry VI Part 1; First Part of the Contention, The; Richard, Duke of York. *AB*

Henry VI Part 1 *(see page 200)*

Henry VI Part 2. See First Part of the Contention, The.

Henry VI Part 3. See Richard Duke of York.

Henry VII. See Richmond, Henry, Earl of.

Henry VIII. See All Is True.

Henry VIII (1491–1547), King of England (reigned 1509–47). See All Is True; religion. *AB*

Henry, Prince. Son of King John, he is present at his father's death, *King John* 5.7, becoming Henry III. *AB*

Henry, Prince of Wales. See Henry IV Parts 1 and 2; Henry V.

Henry Frederick, Prince of Wales (1595–1612), elder son of *James I and Anne of Denmark. Outgoing and charismatic, his character was antithetical to that of his withdrawn, intemperate, and awkward father. He had military ambitions; his investiture as Prince of Wales in 1610 was celebrated with *Prince Henry's Barriers*, an extended display of jousting for which Ben *Jonson wrote introductory speeches and Inigo *Jones designed stage sets and costumes; and subsequently on New Year's Day 1611 with Jonson's and Jones's *Oberon*, in which he danced the role of the fairy prince—the masque was originally planned to conclude with martial games, but the King demanded a more courtly and pacific culmination. His politics were aggressively Protestant, in contrast to his father's commitment to accommodation with the Catholic powers on the Continent. From the age of 14 he maintained a large and increasingly influential court, and was an enthusiastic patron of the arts. Under the guidance of Arundel, Salisbury, and Inigo Jones (whom he employed as his surveyor), he amassed in a short period one of the greatest art collections in England at the time, which after his death formed the nucleus of his brother Charles's superlative collection. He strongly supported his sister *Elizabeth's marriage to Frederick the Elector Palatine, and deplored his father's plans to marry him to a Catholic princess, though he was forced to acknowledge publicly that this was a matter of state, not of his choosing. He reportedly proposed following his sister and brother-in-law to Germany at the head of a Protestant army of liberation—something the heir to the throne would certainly not have been permitted to do. His death from typhoid fever at the age of 18, a few months before his sister's marriage, was devastating to the nation's morale, and it was widely rumoured that he had been poisoned by Catholic sympathizers. According to Anthony Weldon in 1650, the King himself was the prime suspect. *The Winter's Tale* was written in 1610, two years before Henry's death, but the play—with the sudden death of Prince Mamillius, and the marriage of his sister Perdita to a future king of Bohemia—must have had an eerie topicality when it was performed during the festivities leading to the royal wedding in February 1613. *SO*

Strong, Roy, *Henry Prince of Wales* (1986)
Weldon, Anthony, *The Court and Character of King James* (1650)

(cont. on page 192)

Henry IV Part I

Immediately and enduringly popular, this rich and assured sequel to the events dramatized in *Richard II* (1595) was probably composed and first acted in 1596: the changes to certain characters' names, discussed below, was probably connected with court performances at the end of that year.

Text: The play was entered in the Stationers' Register in February 1598 (as 'The history of Henry the IIIIth with his battle of Shrewsbury against Henry Hotspur of the North with the conceited mirth of Sir John Falstaff'), and was published in at least two quarto editions in the same year (the earliest known of which survives only in an eight-page fragment). Five more appeared before the publication of the Folio (in 1599, 1604, 1608, 1613, and 1622), and its early texts also include the *Dering manuscript, though this derives from the 1613 quarto rather than from an independent source. The Folio, which retitles the play *The First Part of Henry the Fourth*, also draws its text from the 1613 quarto, but removes all oaths in scrupulous compliance with the *Act to Restrain the Abuses of Players. This was not the first time the play had undergone censorship: when first composed its greatest comic character was called Sir John Oldcastle, but a descendant of this real-life historical figure (who was regarded as a Protestant hero, and features in *Foxe's *Book of Martyrs*), insisted on its being changed. (This was either William Brooke, 7th Lord *Cobham—Elizabeth's Lord Chamberlain from August 1596 until his death the following March—or his son Henry, 8th Lord Cobham.) Even the play's altered text, though, retains traces of the original name (Sir John is called 'my old lad of the castle' by the Prince, 1.2.41–2), as well as the original names of two of his tavern companions (Harvey and Russell, changed to Bardolph and Peto, probably for fear of offending the earls of Bedford, whose surname was Russell, and Sir William *Harvey, who was about to marry the dowager Countess of Southampton). There is some evidence that the substitution of 'Falstaff' (a name based on that of the cowardly Fastolf who appears in *1 Henry VI*) was not always made in performance even after 1596. The Oxford edition, consequently, restores not only the fat knight's blasphemies but his original surname, but maintains the continuity of the sequence by calling him only Sir John in speech prefixes throughout this play and the subsequent *Merry Wives of Windsor* and *2 Henry IV*.

Sources: Shakespeare drew both the name and the reprobate character of Oldcastle from an anonymous play about Prince Harry's wild youth, sudden reformation, and glorious kingship, *The *Famous Victories of Henry V*, entered in the Stationers' Register in 1594 and printed in 1598: this work undoubtedly influenced not only *1 Henry IV* but the rest of the Second *Tetralogy, but the surviving text offered by the 1598 edition is so evidently garbled and truncated that it is hard to tell how much. For his historical material Shakespeare also consulted *Holinshed and Samuel *Daniel's *The First Four Books of the Civil Wars* (1595), while his comic scenes draw broadly on the traditions of medieval mystery and morality plays.

Synopsis: **1.1** King Henry IV speaks of his long-standing desire to mount a crusade, but this scheme has to be postponed once more when news arrives that after a fierce battle Edmund Mortimer has been taken prisoner by the Welsh rebel Glyndŵr. In the north, however, Harry Percy, known as Hotspur, has won a great victory against the Scots—causing the King to envy Northumberland for having such a valiant son, unlike the dissipated Prince Harry—but at the instigation of his uncle Worcester Hotspur has refused to deliver more than one of his prisoners to the King, who has summoned them to Windsor to explain themselves. **1.2** In London the King's eldest son Prince Harry is bantering with the fat old knight Sir John when Poins invites them to take part, along with three other confederates, in a highway robbery planned for the following morning at Gads Hill: Poins privately suggests that he and Harry should allow Sir John and the others to commit the robbery alone and should subsequently rob them of the spoils, in disguise, meeting them in the evening in Eastcheap to hear how they explain their loss. Alone, Harry confides that he is only pursuing this career of

Orson Welles as Falstaff with Jeanne Moreau as Doll Tearsheet in Welles's film adaptation of both parts of *Henry iv, Chimes at Midnight*, 1967.

idleness for the time being, the better to amaze the world when he finally stages his reformation. **1.3** The King confronts Worcester, Northumberland, and Hotspur with their refusal to deliver their prisoners. After Worcester is dismissed for insolence, Hotspur claims he only failed to do so because tactlessly asked for them by an effeminate courtier in the immediate aftermath of the battle, and he has now made it clear that he will hand them over as soon as the King pays Mortimer's ransom. The King, however, insists that Mortimer, who has married Glyndŵr's daughter, is a traitor, and, refusing to believe Hotspur's account of Mortimer's combat with the Welshman, reiterates his demand for the prisoners. Left alone, Northumberland and the angrily voluble Hotspur, soon rejoined by Worcester, reflect on the ingratitude of the man they helped to make king in Richard II's place and on Richard's alleged choice of Mortimer as his heir, and Worcester, when Hotspur has finally calmed down sufficiently to listen, outlines an eagerly seconded plot to combine their forces with those of the Scots, the Welsh, and the Archbishop of York against the King.

2.1 Before dawn at an inn, two carriers and a chamberlain meet Gadshill, on his way to take part in the planned highway robbery. **2.2** The robbers, including Prince Harry, Poins, Gadshill, and an already exhausted Sir John, meet, and after the Prince and Poins slip away to disguise themselves the travellers arrive and are robbed. **2.3** In disguise the Prince and Poins easily rob their confederates, who run away. **2.4** Hotspur, having angrily read a letter from someone declining to join the rebellion, is asked by his wife Lady Percy why he has been so sleepless and agitated: declining to tell her of the conspiracy, he only promises that though he must set off shortly she will follow the next day. **2.5** At the Boar's Head Tavern in Eastcheap, Prince Harry has been fraternizing with the bar staff, and he and Poins perplex the drawer Francis. Sir John and the other robbers arrive, Sir John railing against the Prince's absence from the robbery and its sequel, and in reply to Harry's promptings he gives an increasingly exaggerated account of how they were robbed of their booty, claiming to have fought eleven of over 50 attackers in single combat, killing at least seven. When Harry finally confronts him with the truth he claims to have known his identity all along and to have instinctively declined to fight against a true Prince. News arrives of the rebellion, and in a mock-play an undaunted Harry rehearses for the upbraiding he expects to receive from his father for his absence from court, Sir John playing the King and urging the Prince to banish all his idle companions except Sir John. When they swap roles the Prince as King urges Sir John as Harry to banish Sir John, and hints that in time he himself will indeed do so. Nonetheless when officers come seeking to arrest Sir John and his associates for the robbery Harry protects them, concealing the fat knight behind an arras, where he falls asleep. Having sent the officers away on a false trail Harry picks the sleeping Sir John's pocket and finds a bill for little food and much drink. He promises to repay the robbed travellers, and undertakes to obtain Sir John a place in the King's army during the impending civil war.

3.1 In Wales Mortimer, Hotspur, and Glyndŵr divide a map of England and Wales into the three parts each hopes to receive after the defeat of King Henry, supervised by Worcester, who does what he can to moderate Hotspur's impatience with Glyndŵr's grandiloquent claims to possess magic powers. Along with Lady Percy comes Mortimer's wife, who can speak only Welsh to her monoglot anglophone husband: interpreted by her father Glyndŵr, she laments his impending departure, and sings a Welsh song. 3.2 King Henry reproaches Harry at length for his cheapening of himself among the taverns, comparing him unfavourably to Hotspur and to his own younger self, but is appeased by Harry's promise to win back his honour in combat against Hotspur: the royal forces set off to confront the rebels at Shrewsbury. 3.3 Sir John accuses the Hostess of allowing his pocket to be picked of valuables: Harry arrives, busy with military preparations, and having confronted the bluffing Sir John with the truth about what was taken from his pocket assigns him an infantry command.

4.1 Worcester, Hotspur, and the Scots commander Douglas receive news that Northumberland is sick and will not be present with his forces at the impending battle: Sir Richard Vernon brings further news, that the royal army is gathering, including both the King himself and the unexpected Prince Harry, and that Glyndŵr's army will not be ready in time for the battle. 4.2 In Warwickshire Sir John has accepted bribes to exempt able-bodied men from conscription and has instead mustered a regiment with which he is ashamed to be seen: Prince Harry, passing with Westmorland, comments on their poverty, and urges an unenthusiastic Sir John to hurry their march lest he miss the battle. 4.3 The rebels, disputing whether their outnumbered forces should give battle at once, are visited by Sir Walter Blunt, sent by the King to learn of their grievances: Hotspur outlines their cause and questions the King's right to the crown, promising to send Worcester to parley with him the next morning. 4.4 The Archbishop of York, anxious about the outcome of the battle, musters forces to defend himself should the rebels lose at Shrewsbury.

5.1 Worcester outlines the rebels' grievances to the royal party, including Harry, who offers to fight Hotspur in single combat: the King promises to pardon them if they will abandon their rebellion, but Harry has little hope the offer will be accepted, and the royal army makes ready for battle. Sir John, left alone, reflects on the frail vanity of honour, preferring survival. 5.2 Worcester does not tell his fellow rebels of the King's offer of clemency, convinced that even if the young impetuous Hotspur is forgiven he and the older rebels never will be, and they prepare for immediate battle. 5.3 In the fighting Douglas kills Blunt, who is one of many royal troops disguised as the King, and is disappointed to learn from Hotspur of his real identity. Sir John, whose own soldiers have been decimated, is met by Harry, who is furious to find that Sir John's pistol case contains only a bottle of sack. 5.4 Harry, though wounded, declines to leave the field. He rescues his father from the assault of Douglas, then duels with Hotspur, while Sir John, spectating, is apparently killed by the Scot. The Prince kills Hotspur and speaks regretfully of his courage, then, seeing Sir John lying beside him, laments his disreputable friend. When Harry has left, though, Sir John gets up, and, resolving to claim to have killed Hotspur himself, wounds his corpse and lifts it onto his back. Harry arrives with his younger brother John of Lancaster and is astonished to find Sir John alive and willing to make such boasts, but undertakes not to hinder Sir John from receiving an unearned reward. 5.5 The battle won, the King sentences Worcester and Vernon to death. Harry reports that Douglas has been captured, and is allowed to have him set free as a tribute to his valour. The King divides his forces so that they may follow up this victory against the remaining rebels throughout the kingdom.

Artistic features: The play is the first of Shakespeare's histories to weave together tragedy and comedy (into the 'double plot' influentially analysed by William *Empson): its mainly prose scenes in which Prince Harry seems disloyally to prefer the company of his surrogate parent Sir John to that of his real father provide a comic counterpoint to the political rebellion with which King Henry is confronted in the main plot. The play is remarkable for the range of distinctive voices and vocabularies with which it supplies its characters, from the realistic common speech of the carriers to the chivalric idealism of Hotspur, with Prince Harry's centrality to its design underlined by his protean ability to operate across all of them.

Critical history: The play's initial popularity is attested by the proliferation not only of early editions but of allusions, principally to Sir John, who has dominated much writing about the entire Second Tetralogy. Largest in conception as well as in bulk of all Shakespeare's comic characters—the funnier and the apparently freer for his running combat with the realities of chronicle history—Sir John captivated the imagination of the (equally corpulent) Dr *Johnson ('*Falstaff*, unimitated, unimitable *Falstaff*, how shall I extol thee? Thou compound of sense and vice; of sense which may be admired but not esteemed, of vice which may be despised, but hardly detested'), inspired a pioneering essay on Shakespearian characterization by Maurice *Morgann (1777), and has been preferred to the calculating Prince who will eventually reject him by commentators from *Hazlitt through *Bradley to *Auden and beyond. Outside the long-running discussion of Sir John's career—which has variously depicted him as a representative of Vice, a ritual sacrificial substitute for the King, and an image of national fertility, an ancient but undying personification of the English people—the play has usually been discussed in relation to Shakespeare's view of history, and to 16th-century views of national destiny more generally. The Second Tetralogy has often been seen, from the early 20th century onwards, as showing England's fall from Richard II's lost Eden and its providential reunification and redemption under Henry V, a view associated particularly with E. M. W. *Tillyard. He and subsequent commentators have pointed out that the England of *1 Henry IV* seems far less remote from Shakespeare's own times than the more recent events dramatized in the First *Tetralogy (with Hotspur embodying a nostalgic idea of feudal valour doomed to defeat at the hands of modern politicians like King Henry and his son), and have related the play plausibly to the interests of the Tudor nation-state, an institution for which critics have in general expressed progressively less enthusiasm since Tillyard's own time. In an influential essay the American *new historicist Stephen Greenblatt compared Harry's strategies among the common people of Eastcheap with those of 16th-century English colonists in the New World, while King Henry's attempts to subdue the Welsh have been repeatedly compared to Queen Elizabeth's efforts to put down rebellions in *Ireland.

STAGE HISTORY: Early records of performances, especially at court, are complicated by the different titles under which both *1 Henry IV* and its immediate sequel seem to have gone: it was certainly acted before the Flemish ambassador in 1600, and the plays referred to as *The Hotspur* and *Sir John Falstaff* at the wedding of Princess *Elizabeth in 1612–13 were probably the two *Henry IV* plays. The two were combined in the *Dering manuscript for a private, amateur performance in around 1623, and *Part 1* was performed at court in 1625 (as *The First Part of Sir John Falstaff*) and in 1638 (as *Oldcastle*, unless this was the collaborative *Sir John Oldcastle* written in 1600 to counter Shakespeare's depiction of the knight, though this seems less likely). In the public theatres, it is generally assumed that Richard *Burbage created the role of the Prince, but the identity of the original Sir John is uncertain: *Malone claimed to have seen a document which assigned the part to *Heminges. The role, however, was certainly one of the best loved of the entire pre-war repertory: in 1699 James Wright could still remember the applause *Lowin received in it before the Civil War. Sir John was popular enough to be acted even under Cromwell in the *droll *The *Bouncing Knight* (and to become one of the first Shakespearian characters depicted pictorially, on the title page to the anthology in which the droll was later printed, *The *Wits*). At the Restoration in 1660 this play about the successful defeat of a rebellion was one of the first Shakespeare plays to be revived: in the hands of *Killigrew's King's Company it became a firm favourite with Samuel *Pepys. The subsequent stage history of the play has often been shaped by which of its major roles leading actor-managers have preferred. *Betterton played Hotspur in 1682 but graduated to Sir John in 1700 (reviving both *2 Henry IV* and *The Merry Wives of Windsor* to give himself even more scope), and this trajectory was repeated by James *Quin, who excelled as the fat knight from the early 1720s until his retirement in 1753. *Kemble, however, was too thin and too dignified to move beyond Hotspur (whom he first played in 1791), leaving the role of Sir John to his brothers, first Stephen and then Charles, who in 1824 became one of the first 19th-century producers to well-nigh bury the play under historically researched costumes and sets (which necessitated extensive cuts and transpositions of scenes). The Victorians found the tavern scenes coarse, and the play fell from favour, though Samuel *Phelps was a notable Sir John in 1847 and, at Drury Lane, in 1864, in a production otherwise best remembered for its spectacular pictorial recreation of the battle of Shrewsbury.

In the 20th century the play gradually regained some measure of its earlier popularity, though unlike *Richard III* it has never attracted very much interest outside the nation whose history it dramatizes, Sir John seeming as inexplicably English a joke as Mr Punch. Barry *Jackson staged a full text of *1 Henry IV* in 1913, and revived both it and *2 Henry IV* for Shakespeare's birthday in 1921, anticipating subsequent directors who have sought to stage the Second Tetralogy as a grand, Wagnerian sequence. At the Old Vic in 1930 John *Gielgud played Hotspur to Ralph *Richardson's Prince Harry, and another conspicuous production of that decade found the music-hall comedian George Robey playing a widely praised Sir John, in 1935. The legendary production of the century, though, of both *1 Henry IV* and *2 Henry IV*, took place at the Old Vic in 1945, when Ralph Richardson returned to the play as an alert, mercurial Sir John, Laurence *Olivier played a fiery, stammering Hotspur, and Sybil *Thorndike played the Hostess. Another impressive cast was assembled six years later in Stratford, where Anthony *Quayle played Sir John, Michael *Redgrave Hotspur, Harry Andrews the King, and Richard *Burton Prince Harry. Peter *Hall mounted an impressive production for the RSC in 1964, with Ian Holm as Harry, part of an ambitious presentation of the Second Tetralogy which staged it as a prelude to the First, famously condensed into the three-part *The *Wars of the Roses*. This immense undertaking was repeated, in a very different manner, by Michael *Bogdanov's *English Shakespeare Company in 1985–6, with Michael *Pennington as a cold Harry and John Woodvine as a memorably cynical Sir John. *MD*

ON THE SCREEN: The earliest version for BBC TV (1959), an abbreviation in the tradition of *The *Bouncing Knight* entitled *The Gadshill Job*, aimed to attract younger viewers.

More memorable was the BBC TV series *An Age of Kings* (1960), allotting four out of its fifteen parts to the *Henry IV* plays. A two-hour adaptation of *1 Henry IV* on American television was transmitted in the same year. BBC TV screened full versions of both parts of *Henry IV* in 1979, and in 1995 John Caird adapted them for BBC television.

On film, Orson *Welles's *Chimes at Midnight* (1965), which draws on both *Henry IV* plays, stands as a classic. Welles makes Falstaff the dramatic centre of his adaptation, and it is clearly Welles's affinity with Falstaff's condition which gives the film its poignancy. *AD*

RECENT MAJOR EDITIONS

A. R. Humphreys (Arden, 1960); David Bevington (Oxford, 1987); Herbert and Judith Weil (New Cambridge, 1997)

SOME REPRESENTATIVE CRITICISM

Auden, W. H., 'The Prince's Dog', in *The Dyer's Hand* (1962)
Bradley, A. C., 'The Rejection of Falstaff', in *Oxford Lectures on Poetry* (1909)
Empson, William, *Seven Types of Ambiguity* (1930)
Greenblatt, Stephen, *Shakespearian Negotiations* (1988)
Helgerson, Richard, *Forms of Nationhood* (1994)
Tillyard, E. M. W. *Shakespeare's History Plays* (1944)
Wilson, Dover John, *The Fortunes of Falstaff* (1943)

Henry Irving Shakespeare. This edition of the *Works*, with introductions by various scholars to the individual plays, and numerous illustrations, was published in eight volumes in 1890, and reissued in ten in 1906. It aimed to assist those who wished to read the plays aloud or prepare an acting version for private or public use. Here the influence of Irving is to be seen, in the use of wavy lines at the side of passages in the double-column texts of the plays to mark them as capable of being omitted without 'any detriment to the story or action of the play' (preface). *RAF*

Henryson, Robert (?1425–?1500), Scottish poet who wrote a sequel to *Chaucer's *Troilus and Criseyde* entitled *The Testament of Cresseid* (1493). This work was partly responsible for the hostile representation of Cressida in 16th-century English literature: Henryson's character is a prostitute punished with leprosy. The *Testament* may have come to Shakespeare's attention through Thynne's edition of Chaucer which, from 1532, included this poem. *JKS*

Henslowe, Philip (1555/6–1616), theatre entrepreneur (the *Rose, the Fortune, the Hope). Philip Henslowe was apprenticed to one Henry Woodward who died in 1578 and whose widow, Agnes, Henslowe married in 1579. Agnes was much older than Philip but not, as is often assumed, much wealthier and she already had two daughters. In 1587 Henslowe and John Cholmley built the Rose playhouse and in 1592 Henslowe recorded expenditure on a substantial enlargement of it. Also in 1592 Agnes's daughter Joan married the actor Edward *Alleyn who led an amalgamation of Strange's Men and Admiral's Men performing at the Rose. In 1595 Henslowe paid for further work at the Rose and towards the end of the century (possibly as a result of competition from the Swan and the *Globe) Henslowe and his stepson-in-law Alleyn planned a new square open-air playhouse, the Fortune, located north of the river in the parish of St Giles without Cripplegate, which opened in 1600. In 1613 Henslowe built the multi-purpose Hope playhouse near to the site of the old Beargarden on *Bankside.

Much of what we know about the Elizabethan theatre business comes from Henslowe's book of accounts and memoranda commonly (but misleadingly) known as his 'Diary' which was deposited among other papers at the College of God's Gift at Dulwich founded by Alleyn and opened in 1617. Recorded in the account book are Henslowe's pawn transactions, personal and business debts and loans, receipts from his theatres, expenditure on costumes, and an inventory of the Admiral's Men's stage properties. Critical work on these records in the early 20th century characterized Henslowe as a ruthless exploiter of actors, but recent work has tended to ameliorate this view. *GE*

Henslowe's 'Diary', ed. W. W. Greg (2 vols., 1908)
Cerasano, S. P., 'Philip Henslowe, Simon Forman, and the Theatrical Community of the 1590s', *Shakespeare Quarterly*, 44 (1993)

heraldry, the practice of allotting specific coats of arms and badges to families for easier identification on the field of battle.

Originally devised for swift and accurate identification of armed men, heraldry is a discipline of simple devices and limited use of colour which, in a defined system of presentation, can be used to show marriage and family relationships. Badges developed as personal cognizances and in the 15th century, under the system loosely defined as 'bastard feudalism', were used to identify the adherents of particular families or factions.

By the later Middle Ages, the right to a coat of arms had become a matter for social pride and strict control. The College of Arms was first incorporated by Richard III in 1483 and from that date heralds, originally neutral messengers between rulers, became arbiters of status.

Shakespeare was influenced by heraldry both professionally and personally, applying for a coat of arms on behalf of his father, granted in 1596. These arms exemplify the system, depicting a spear, displayed diagonally, in an allusion to the family name. In his works Shakespeare uses heraldry most particularly in the history plays, where frequent references are made to the arms or badges of the chief protagonists. Richard, Duke of Gloucester, is referred to as 'abortive, rooting, hog' (*Richard III* 1.3.225), alluding to his personal badge of the white boar, whilst his brother Edward IV, one of whose badges was a sun in splendour, is in the same play punningly referred to as 'this son of York' (1.1.2).

Elsewhere, Shakespeare attributes coats of arms to non-historic characters and uses the specific heraldic terms for colours: gules, sable, azure, to intensify an effect; 'Head to foot, now is he total gules' (*Hamlet* 2.2.259–60), 'My sable ground of sin I will not paint | To hide the truth' (*The Rape of Lucrece* 1074). Other formal heraldic words used liberally are 'blazon', 'crest', 'badge'. *MM*

heralds. (1) In *The First Part of the Contention* (*2 Henry VI*) a herald summons Gloucester to Parliament, 2.4.71. **(2)** In *Henry V* a herald delivers the list of the dead at Agincourt to King Harry, 4.8. **(3)** In *Othello* 2.2, a herald announces a 'triumph' to celebrate the defeat of the Turks and Othello's nuptials. **(4)** In *The Tragedy of King Lear* 5.3.102–6, a herald summons anyone who calls Edmond a traitor to combat (*History of King Lear* 24.109–13). **(5)** In *Coriolanus* 2.1.159–63, a herald announces Martius' new name of 'Coriolanus'. *AB*

Herbert. See PEMBROKE.

Herbert, Sir Henry (1595–1673), Master of the Revels (1623–73). Herbert bought his mastership from Sir John Astley, and his collection of papers (extant until 1818) is an important source of information concerning the Caroline stage. (See CENSORSHIP.) *GE*

Bawcutt, N. W., (ed.), *The Control and Censorship of Caroline Drama: The Records of Sir Henry Herbert, Master of the Revels 1623–73* (1996)
Dutton, Richard, *Mastering the Revels: The Regulation and Censorship of English Renaissance Drama* (1991)

Herbert, Sir Walter. One of Richmond's supporters, he speaks one line, *Richard III* 5.2.19. *AB*

(cont. on page 199)

Henry IV Part 2

A darker more worldly play than its exuberant predecessor, *2 Henry IV* was probably begun soon after *1 Henry IV*, in 1597, but it may have been laid aside while Shakespeare composed *The Merry Wives of Windsor*: the fact that the February 1598 entry in the Stationers' Register for *1 Henry IV* does not refer to it as 'Part 1' probably indicates that *Part 2* had not then been performed. It must pre-date *Henry V*, however, which could have been completed by late 1598, and so was probably finished and first performed during the spring or summer of 1598.

Text: The play was entered in the Stationers' Register in August 1600, and appeared in quarto in the same year, as *The Second Part of Henry the Fourth* ('Continuing to his death, and coronation of Henry the Fifth. With the humours of Sir John Falstaff, and swaggering Pistol. As it hath been sundry times publically acted by the right honourable the Lord Chamberlain his servants. Written by William Shakespeare.'). This text—set from Shakespeare's own *foul papers—was reissued, probably in the same year, with the addition of Act 3 Scene 1, omitted from the original printing. The play reappeared in the Folio in 1623 in a text derived from a promptbook but 'corrected' by a compositor who, wishing to make the text more literary, also consulted a transcript of the play derived from the quarto version. The Folio text restores material apparently cut from the earlier editions at the insistence of the censors, as well as showing some evidence of independent authorial revision. Much of the censored material (such as Lord Bardolph's advice on planning a rebellion in 1.3 and the Archbishop's recapitulation of the rebels' grievances in 4.1) refers to the fate of the deposed Richard II, and it has usually been assumed that the stirrings of what would become the Earl of *Essex's rebellion had by 1600 made these speeches look uncomfortably topical. The Folio text has been purged of oaths in compliance with the *Act to Restrain the Abuses of Players, but seems otherwise complete, though in one respect the play does respond to earlier censorship. Although Shakespeare had by now adopted the surname Falstaff for Sir John (though in the quarto one speech prefix still calls him Oldcastle), the play's Epilogue carefully points out that he is not Oldcastle—thereby, however, drawing attention to the fact that in *1 Henry IV* he was.

Sources: As with *1 Henry IV*, Shakespeare drew on the anonymous *The Famous Victories of Henry V*, *Holinshed's *Chronicles* and Samuel *Daniel's *Civil Wars*, here supplemented by Sir Thomas Elyot's *The Governor* (1531), which supplied the story of Prince Harry's dealings with the Lord Chief Justice. In this play, though, more space is given to the invented adventures of Sir John compared to the historical events of Henry IV's reign.

Synopsis: In an Induction, Rumour, wearing a robe decorated with images of tongues, explains that the play is about to show false reports about King Henry's victory at Shrewsbury reaching the malingering Northumberland. **1.1** Lord Bardolph brings Northumberland the supposed news that their fellow rebels have defeated the royal army at Shrewsbury, where the King has been mortally wounded and Northumberland's son Hotspur has killed Prince Harry: the servant Travers, however, has heard that the rebels have been defeated and Hotspur killed. The truth of Travers's version of events is confirmed in full by an eyewitness, Morton, who adds that an army led by Prince John and the Earl of Westmorland is on its way northwards. Northumberland, throwing away his pretended sickness, rages, but is calmed by Morton and Lord Bardolph, who reassure him that their rebellion is not fully defeated yet, especially since the Archbishop of York is mustering large numbers to their cause. **1.2** Sir John, accompanied by a small page given him by Prince Harry for the sake of the comic contrast between their sizes, is accosted by the Lord Chief Justice, who we learn has earlier been struck by Prince Harry: though Sir John at first attempts continually to change the subject, he makes it clear that Sir John's part in the highway robbery (depicted in *1 Henry IV*) is well known, rebukes him for misleading Prince Harry, and tells him he has only escaped punishment because of his reputedly good service at the battle of Shrewsbury. He also points out that Sir John has now been sent northwards with

Prince John's forces specifically to separate him from Prince Harry, upon which Sir John, posing as an indispensable war hero, requests the loan of £1,000 towards his expenses. After the Justice leaves, refusing, Sir John sends begging letters to several other figures, reflecting that the limp he has acquired through either venereal disease or gout will at least make him look more eligible for a military pension. **1.3** The Archbishop of York, Mowbray, Hastings, and Lord Bardolph discuss the prospects of their rebellion, comforted to reflect that only a third of the King's forces can march against them, the rest divided between opposing Glyndŵr in Wales and fighting the French: the Archbishop comments on the fickleness of public opinion, as Henry Bolingbroke's former supporters are now rallying to them, nostalgic for the dead Richard II.

2.1 Mistress Quickly has Sir John arrested for breach of promise, explaining, before the Lord Chief Justice, who happens to pass, that he has lived at her expense for many years, owes her money, and has promised her marriage. Sir John attempts to convince the Justice that she is mad, but finally takes her aside, renews his promises to her, and convinces her to pawn her silver in order to lend him yet more money: Mistress Quickly even invites him to supper, asking whether he would like the prostitute Doll Tearsheet to be there too. The Justice receives discouraging news of the King's illness. **2.2** Prince Harry, in self-disgusted conversation with Poins, confides that he is sad about his father's sickness though he knows Poins will think him a hypocrite to say so. Sir John's companions Bardolph and the Page bring the Prince a letter in which Sir John warns him that Poins has been boasting that the Prince will marry his sister, though Poins denies this. Harry and Poins learn that Sir John is to dine at the tavern in Eastcheap with Doll Tearsheet and resolve to spy on him there disguised as bar staff. **2.3** Northumberland, about to set off to join the Archbishop's forces, is dissuaded by his daughter-in-law Lady Percy, Hotspur's widow, who argues that since Northumberland betrayed her lamented husband he should not keep his word to others. She is seconded by Northumberland's wife, and Northumberland decides to fly to Scotland until the success or otherwise of the rebellion is more evident. **2.4** In a private room at the tavern Sir John, dining with Mistress Quickly and Doll Tearsheet, is interrupted by the swaggering Pistol, who, after ranting in garbled fragments of Marlovian verse, is finally expelled, after a scuffle, by Bardolph. To the strains of music Sir John takes Doll on his knee, watched and overheard by the disguised Prince and Poins, and speaks disparagingly of the Prince before kissing her, lamenting his age. The Prince and Poins confront him, and he claims to have been deliberately dissuading sinners like Doll from loving the Prince, for his own good. Prince Harry is called away to his father, reproaching himself for wasting his time at the tavern during a crisis, and Sir John too is summoned to join the army, sending back, however, to summon Doll to him before he does so.

3.1 King Henry, in his nightgown, envies his subjects the freedom from anxiety that comes with sleep, before reflecting with Warwick and Surrey on his betrayal, prophesied by Richard II, by the nobles who helped him to power. Warwick, comforting him with the news that Glyndŵr is dead, persuades him to go to bed for fear of worsening his sickness. **3.2** In Warwickshire Sir John is welcomed by his old acquaintances Justice Shallow and Justice Silence, where he chooses recruits from among a number of villagers: the fittest of them, Mouldy and Bullcalf, offer bribes, through Bardolph, to be exempted from military service, and Sir John does not select them despite Shallow's protests, picking the unimpressive Feeble, Wart, and Shadow instead. Alone, Sir John reflects with amusement at the discrepancy between the insignificant Shallow he remembers and the tales he now tells of his wild youth, planning to fleece him on his return from the impending campaign.

4.1 In the forest of Gaultres, the Archbishop of York, Thomas Mowbray, and Lord Hastings have just heard that Northumberland will not be joining them when Westmorland arrives from the approaching royal army: they outline their grievances to him, and give him a written text of their demands, which he undertakes to give to the royal army's commander, Prince John. The Archbishop and Hastings try to reassure Mowbray that the King will be willing to make peace with them and will keep to any terms agreed. This is confirmed at a parley between the two armies by Prince John, who promises that all their demands will be met, and drinks with them to peace: as soon as the rebels have dismissed their army, however, he arrests them for capital treason, promising that though they will be executed the grievances to which they have drawn his attention will be redressed. **4.2** Sir John meets a rebel commander, Coleville, who, hearing of his adversary's identity, surrenders in terror: Sir John hands him over to Prince John, who arrives with Westmorland and soldiers pursuing fleeing rebels, and Coleville is sent to York to be executed. The nobles set off for London, where the King's sickness has worsened. Sir John reflects that Prince John's cold nature is the result of insufficient drinking, a fault from which Harry is free, and speaks eloquently of the beneficial effects of consuming sherry-sack. **4.3** On his sickbed, the King speaks of Prince Harry and his anxiety about the chaos that may befall his kingdom when he inherits the throne: Warwick tries in vain to reassure him that the Prince is only studying his present companions, and will renounce them in due course. Westmorland brings news of the defeat of the Archbishop's forces, and Harcourt news that Northumberland and his Scottish and English confederates have been defeated by the Sheriff of Yorkshire, but this good news brings on a seizure, and the King sleeps, the crown beside him on the pillow, while his nobles speak of omens prophesying his death. Prince Harry arrives, and watches over his father while the others depart: alone with the sleeping King he reflects on the cares that come with the crown and then, sorrowfully convinced that his father has died, takes it and puts it on. After he has left, however, the King awakens, and becomes convinced that his son has taken the crown, wishing him dead: alone with Harry he upbraids him at length, lamenting the riotous reign he is convinced the Prince longs for. A weeping Harry convinces him of the truth, however, and they are reconciled, the King advising Harry that although his inheritance of the crown will be less controversial than his own snatching of it from Richard he should be sure to distract his people with military campaigns abroad to prevent further domestic rebellions. Convinced he is dying, he learns that the room in which he collapsed is called the Jerusalem Chamber, and reflects that it was once prophesied that he would die in Jerusalem but he had always hoped this would be on the crusade he has never been able to lead.

5.1 On his way back from the campaign, Sir John has arrived at Shallow's house, where he sees the overbearing servant Davy effectively running the entire household: Sir John plans to keep Prince Harry amused with stories and jests involving Shallow. 5.2 The Lord Chief Justice learns to his sorrow from Warwick that the old King has died, and much of the court assembles, including Prince John and his brothers Clarence and Gloucester, all deeply apprehensive about how they will be treated now that the wild Prince Harry has inherited the throne. When Harry arrives, however, he speaks with dignity, promising a well-governed reign, and in response to the Lord Chief Justice's defence of his earlier decision to send him to prison the new King warmly ratifies his position at the head of the judicial system. 5.3 Sir John, his page, and Bardolph are dining, along with Silence, at Justice Shallow's house, the meal punctuated by Silence's unexpected bursts of song, when Pistol arrives in a state of incomprehensible excitement. He brings the news that Prince Harry has inherited the crown, upon which Sir John, convinced that thanks to the new King's friendship he will have unlimited power and scope, sets eagerly off for London. 5.4 Mistress Quickly and Doll Tearsheet are arrested by beadles, accused of taking part, with Pistol, in a fatal beating. 5.5 Sir John, Shallow, Pistol, Bardolph, and the Page eagerly await King Henry V's coronation procession, the more so since Sir John has borrowed £1,000 from Shallow on his expectations from the new King: Sir John confidently expects, too, to be able shortly to procure Doll Tearsheet's release from prison. When the King and his attendants arrive, however, he refuses to recognize Sir John, publicly renouncing his former ways, and declares that if Sir John comes within 10 miles (16 km) of him again he will be put to death. After his departure, Sir John insists that the King will send for him privately later on, but the Lord Chief Justice returns to commit him and his followers to the Fleet prison. Prince John approves, and has heard a rumour that the King means shortly to launch a military campaign in France. An epilogue promises a sequel which will include comic scenes involving Princess Catherine of France, and in which Sir John—who is not Oldcastle, we are reminded—may go to France and die of a sweat.

Artistic features: The play in many respects recapitulates that of *1 Henry iv* in a minor key, the Machiavellian defeat of the rebellion a far cry from Hotspur's heroic death at Shrewsbury, while the sub-plot, though exquisitely funny, is tinged throughout with a melancholy which is only underlined by the potential pathos of Sir John's final rejection at the hands of Henry v. The scene of the evening at Shallow's house in Gloucestershire, punctuated by the memories of old men and culminating in the news of a king's death, has no equal as a simultaneously comic, lyrical, and rueful dramatization of the passage of time.

Critical history: The critical history of this play is in practice impossible to disentangle from that of *Part 1*, and to a lesser extent the remainder of the Second *Tetralogy: see the reading list appended to the entry on *1 Henry iv*.

Stage history: *2 Henry iv* has only rarely been acted wholly independently of *Part 1*: since at least the time of the *Dering manuscript the plays have been largely inseparable in the theatre no less than in criticism. The earliest post-Restoration revival came when *Betterton produced a cut version in which he extended his depiction of Falstaff, but the play was better known in the 18th century for the role of Pistol, memorably played by Theophilus *Cibber (who was nicknamed Pistol for the rest of his career). In the 19th century it was revived by *Macready in 1821 to mark the coronation of George iv (a production which later visited New York), and from then onwards more attention seems to have been paid to the role of Justice Shallow, which Samuel *Phelps doubled with the King in 1853 and at intervals thereafter. In the 20th century Laurence *Olivier's performance as Shallow alongside Ralph *Richardson's poignant but impish Falstaff, at the New Theatre in 1945, entered the realms of legend.

On the screen: See Henry iv Part 1. *MD*

Recent major editions

Giorgio Melchiori (New Cambridge, 1989); A. R. Humphreys (Arden 2nd series, 1966); René Weis (Oxford, 1998)

Some representative criticism

See the reading list appended to the entry on *Henry iv Part 1*.

Henry v

The culmination of Shakespeare's mature sequence of English histories, *Henry v*, the last play of the Second *Tetralogy, is comparatively easy to date thanks to an uncharacteristic topical reference. At the start of Act 5 the Chorus explicitly compares Henry v's welcome back to London after his campaign in France to the anticipated welcome the Earl of *Essex would receive should he return victoriously from his current expedition against Tyrone's rebellion in Ireland (5.0.30–5). Essex's planned campaign was common knowledge as early as November 1598, but this passage, and probably the rest of the play too, is more likely to have been written between the Earl's departure in March 1599 and his return in disgrace that September.

Text: The play was first printed in *quarto in 1600, said to have been 'sundry times played by the Right Honourable the Lord Chamberlain his servants', and reappeared in the Folio of 1623 in a version derived from Shakespeare's own *foul papers. The quarto is in many respects corrupt, apparently a memorial reconstruction (see REPORTED TEXT) assembled by actors who had appeared in a version of the play shortened for performance by a small cast (perhaps on a provincial tour), but it seems to derive from a later authorial text of the play than does the Folio. In particular, the quarto chooses to follow Shakespeare's historical sources in not representing the Dauphin as a combatant at Agincourt, giving the lines he speaks there in the Folio to the Duke of Bourbon.

Sources: Shakespeare again worked from the materials he had used in the *Henry iv* plays, namely the chronicles of *Holinshed and *Halle and the anonymous play *The Famous Victories of Henry v*. It is possible that he was also influenced by other contemporary plays on this subject, now lost.

Synopsis: The Chorus speaks a prologue, lamenting the inadequacy of the theatre to so great a subject and imploring the audience to use their imaginations. **1.1** The Archbishop of Canterbury and the Bishop of Ely are anxious that the new King, whose transformation from reveller to statesman they applaud, may support a measure heavily taxing the Church: the Archbishop has attempted to dissuade him from this by offering a large grant towards a military expedition urging his title to the French crown. **1.2** Before receiving a French embassy, King Harry calls upon the Archbishop to explain his right to the French throne, which he does at some length, urging Harry to attack France. The Archbishop is seconded by Ely and a number of English nobles including the King's uncle the Duke of Exeter, who convince Harry that he can mount a campaign in France while satisfactorily garrisoning England against potential Scottish invasion. The French ambassador is admitted with a message from the Dauphin, who has heard of Harry's plans to claim French territory and, as a comment on his youth and alleged frivolity, has sent a barrel of tennis balls as a present. The King dismisses the ambassadors after promising that he will soon avenge this mockery in full, and sets the preparations for his campaign in motion.

2.0 The Chorus describes the country's eager preparations for the war, but also outlines a French-funded conspiracy to assassinate the King at Southampton. **2.1** Corporal Nim and Ensign Pistol quarrel about Nim's former fiancée the Hostess, Mistress Quickly, whom Pistol has married: they are prevented from duelling by Bardolph, and by a summons home to the bedside of their sick master Sir John Falstaff, broken-hearted over his rejection by Harry (dramatized at the end of *2 Henry iv*). **2.2** At Southampton the King, about to embark with his forces for France, is advised by the traitors Scrope, Cambridge, and Grey against showing mercy to a drunk who has shouted abusively at him, but has the man released. He then presents the three traitors with what he says are their commissions but are in fact their indictments for capital treason, decrying their treachery and refusing them mercy by their own earlier advice. They confess and apologize before being led away to execution, and the King embarks. **2.3** Pistol,

Nim, Bardolph, and the Boy are also leaving for France, sorrowful over the death of Sir John, which is poignantly narrated by the Hostess, from whom they part. 2.4 King Charles of France is making arrangements to defend his realm against King Harry, whom the Dauphin scorns to take seriously despite the misgivings of King Charles and the Constable: Exeter arrives as Harry's ambassador, delivering his claim to France, demanding an immediate response, and passing on Harry's personal defiance to the Dauphin. King Charles insists on a night in which to consider his reply.

3.0 The Chorus asks the audience to imagine Harry's army crossing the Channel and laying siege to Harfleur. 3.1 Harry urges his troops to make one more assault on the breach in Harfleur's walls. 3.2 Bardolph is eager enough to join the attack but Nim, Pistol, and the Boy would rather stay alive: they have to be driven towards the breach with blows by the Welsh captain Fluellen. The Boy remains behind and comments on the cowardice and petty thieving of his associates, whom he plans to leave. 3.3 Fluellen laments to his English comrade Captain Gower that the operation to lay mines under Harfleur's walls is not being carried out according to proper military precedent, for which he blames the Irishman, Captain MacMorris, who arrives in the company of the Scots captain Jamy. MacMorris, furious himself at the mismanagement of the mines, is in no mood to enter into a discussion about military discipline with Fluellen, and is especially touchy about Fluellen's reference to his nationality, but they postpone their quarrel to another occasion when they hear a parley sounded. King Harry urges the Governor of Harfleur to surrender, threatening that his soldiers will otherwise commit rape, infanticide, and other atrocities when they finally gain entrance, and the Governor capitulates, having received word that the Dauphin will not be able to send reinforcements. Harry plans to retire to Calais with his increasingly sickly army. 3.4 At the French court the Princess Catherine is learning English from her gentlewoman Alice, naming parts of the body and finding the English words 'foot' and 'gown' shockingly immodest. 3.5 King Charles's nobles are astonished that the English have hitherto been so successful, lamenting that their women are taunting them for being less virile. Detaining the Dauphin with him, King Charles sends an immense force against Harry led by the Constable of France, first sending the herald Montjoy to ask what ransom Harry will pay to be spared. 3.6 Fluellen has been impressed by Pistol's valiant language, but is disillusioned when Pistol asks him to intercede with Exeter to have Bardolph spared from hanging after being caught looting: Gower confirms that Pistol is a fraud. The King arrives and receives a progress report from Fluellen, including the news of Bardolph's execution, which the King endorses. Montjoy arrives with King Charles's request that Harry name his ransom: Harry, however, though admitting that his army is enfeebled by sickness and few in number, says he will not decline a battle, ordering his soldiers to encamp for the night and be ready to fight the next morning. 3.7 The French nobles, eager for battle, scoff at the supposedly doomed English: Bourbon [in the Folio, the Dauphin] brags absurdly about his horse.

4.0 The Chorus describes the two armies the night before the battle—the over-confident French dicing for English prisoners, the demoralized English being cheered by the King in person—and apologizes that the stage is so inadequate to the task of representing the battle of Agincourt. 4.1 During the night King Harry borrows a cloak from Sir Thomas Erpingham and wanders incognito among his soldiers: he is defied by Pistol for calling himself a friend of Fluellen, and approvingly overhears Fluellen reproaching Gower for speaking too loudly so close to the enemy army. He then joins a discussion among three common soldiers, Bates, Court, and Williams, about the justice of the King's war and his responsibility for its casualties: Williams insists that the King's declaration that he will not be ransomed is so much cynical propaganda, and he and Harry exchange gloves, by which they will recognize one another again, so that they may take up this quarrel after the battle. Alone, Harry laments the responsibilities laid on him by his subjects, ill compensated by the idle ceremonies of royalty, and prays that God will make his soldiers brave, imploring pardon for his father's crime in usurping the crown from the murdered Richard II. 4.2 In the morning the French nobles eagerly prepare for battle. 4.3 The English nobles, their army outnumbered by five to one, bid farewell to one another, Warwick wishing their numbers were swelled by 10,000 of those at home who will do no work on this day: arriving from reviewing his troops the King overhears and rebukes him, saying the fewer they are the more honour they will share. In a stirring oration Harry claims that on this day, the feast of St Crispin, the heroic deeds of this small band of brothers will forever be remembered. Montjoy comes with one final appeal that Harry should negotiate a ransom instead of fighting, but Harry defies him, allowing the Duke of York to lead the English vanguard into battle. 4.4 In the fighting Pistol takes a French prisoner, with whom, using the Boy as interpreter, he negotiates a ransom. The Boy is anxious that the English camp is currently guarded only by boys. 4.5 Some of the French nobles are appalled that their army is losing, all order confounded: Bourbon leads them back into the battle, preferring death to the shame of defeat. 4.6 Exeter tells the King how York and Suffolk have died together in chivalric brotherhood: seeing the French regrouping, Harry orders the English to kill their prisoners. 4.7 Fluellen and Gower are horrified that the French have killed the English boys who were guarding the camp. Fluellen praises Harry, proud that the King was born in Monmouth, and makes a far-fetched comparison between Harry and Alexander the Great, likening Alexander's killing of his friend Cleitus to Harry's rejection of Falstaff. The King, angry to have heard of the slaughter of the boys, receives Montjoy, who concedes defeat. Fluellen congratulates the King for living up to the example of his ancestors and for being proud to be Welsh: heralds go to count the dead. Harry speaks with

Williams, who does not recognize him; he then gives Fluellen the glove he had from Williams the previous night, telling him whoever challenges it is a traitor and should be arrested, but he sends Warwick and Gloucester to follow and prevent any mischief. **4.8** Williams challenges Fluellen's glove and Fluellen tries to have him arrested: the King arrives with Warwick, Gloucester, and Exeter, however, explains his trick, reveals the identity of the man Williams challenged the previous night, and rewards Williams by returning his glove filled with gold coins. A herald brings the lists of the dead from both sides: the French have lost 10,000, including the Constable and many nobles, while the English have lost only 25 men all told. The King attributes the victory to God and decrees a mass.

5.0 The Chorus describes the King's triumphant return to London, but says the play will not show this, cutting ahead to his return to France for the peace negotiations. **5.1** Fluellen has been affronted by Pistol on St David's Day and mocked for wearing a Welsh leek in his cap: he now seeks out Pistol, cudgels him and makes him eat the leek, with Gower's approval. Pistol, alone, laments that the Hostess has died of venereal disease, but looks forward to returning to England, resuming his career as a bawd and pickpocket, and passing off the marks of his beating as heroic war wounds. **5.2** At a grand summit between Harry and his delegation and the French court, Burgundy laments the damage the war has done to French agriculture, urging the swift conclusion of a peace: while his nobles discuss their proposed settlement with King Charles and his Queen, Harry remains with Alice and the Princess Catherine, whose marriage to Harry is one of the English demands under discussion. In a mixture of English and French Harry woos Catherine, assuring her that he loves France so well that he means to keep it, and on her concession that she will marry him if her father agrees he kisses her, much to her shock. Burgundy, finding them kissing on his return with the negotiators, jests elaborately. King Charles has agreed to all the English terms, including his daughter's marriage to Harry, except the requirement that he should officially call Harry the heir to France. At Harry's insistence, however, he cedes this point, and peace is concluded, the nobles looking forward to Harry and Catherine's wedding. The Chorus speaks an epilogue, in the form of a sonnet, reminding the audience that despite Harry's triumphs his son Henry VI lost France and allowed England to fall into renewed civil wars.

ARTISTIC FEATURES: The Chorus's speeches contain some of Shakespeare's most exciting and ambitious poetry, reaching towards the territory of epic, and the King's two great orations, 'Once more unto the breach' (3.1) and 'This day is called the Feast of Crispian' (4.3.18–67), are classics of English patriotic rhetoric. The play is more double-edged, however, than these frequently quoted passages may suggest: its depiction of warfare never precisely matches the glamorous and heroic pictures conjured by the Chorus, while its protagonist, aptly parodied by his comic counterpart Pistol, is both more insecure and more Machiavellian than the 'warlike Harry' promised in the Prologue.

CRITICAL HISTORY: The success with which the play has monopolized the representation of the historical Henry V has often led commentators to conflate Shakespeare's Henry with the real one, and this in turn has exacerbated a tendency to identify the play solely with its titular hero. *Romantic critics, from *Hazlitt to W. B. *Yeats and beyond, tended to disparage Henry as somehow mechanical, convinced that as a true poet Shakespeare must have preferred his more contemplative protagonists, such as Hamlet and Richard II, to anyone so decisive and successful. Much 20th-century commentary, particularly before 1950, was interested in relating this play to the design of the Second *Tetralogy as a whole, often presenting Henry as Shakespeare's culminating ideal of English kingship (a view particularly associated with E. M. W. *Tillyard): since then critics have more often been divided between those who accuse the play of jingoism, or at best of complicity with Tudor policy in *Ireland and elsewhere, and those more interested in highlighting Shakespeare's awareness of the contradictions and moral problems implicit in Harry's attack on France.

STAGE HISTORY: The play was revived at court in 1605, but the extant evidence suggests that it did not achieve the same popularity in its own time as the *Henry IV* plays or *Richard III*, something for which it would wait until the 18th century. When it was first revived, however, it appeared only in pieces, the Fluellen–Pistol scene appearing in Charles Molloy's farce *The Half-Pay Officers* in 1720 and some of the rest of the play the following year in Aaron Hill's adaptation **King Henry the Fifth; or, The Conquest of France by the English*. The original was first revived in 1735, during the wave of patriotism that preceded the War of Jenkins's Ear, and from then on a succession of wars with France kept it in the repertory for most of the rest of the century: it was revived at Covent Garden, for example, in every single season during the Seven Years War (1756–63). *Garrick cast himself as the Chorus in 1747, but the role was more usually cut, and the increasingly spectacular style in which the play was mounted mandated further cuts over the ensuing years. Major actors taking the role of Henry included *Kemble, *Macready, *Phelps, and, in New York, George Rignold, whose 1875 production lost even more of Shakespeare's text to make way for a grand recreation of Harry and Catherine's betrothal ceremony. In England the role became a favourite of Frank *Benson from 1899 onwards: his athletic ascent of the proscenium arch in full armour during 'Once more unto the breach' and his subsequent vaulting over the walls of Harfleur remain legendary, although he had strong competition during the Boer War years from Lewis Waller. The play was much revived during the First World War (Sybil *Thorndike played the Chorus at the Old Vic) and remained a favourite during the inter-war years, with Laurence *Olivier playing his first Henry in 1937. Since the Second World War interpretations of the title role have been largely shaped by their response to his portrayal, filmed in 1944, with some actors closely following his approach (such as Alan *Howard in Terry *Hands's important Stratford production of 1975), some reacting strongly against it (such as Michael *Pennington, playing Henry as a cold cynic in Michael *Bogdanov's production of 1985–6), and some attempting to do both, notably Kenneth *Branagh, who first played the role in Adrian *Noble's ambivalently post-Falklands War production for the RSC in 1984. *MD*

On the screen: The two outstanding *Henry v* films were made by Laurence Olivier (1944) and Kenneth Branagh (1989) who, like Olivier before, was director and played the title role. Olivier's film, despite its vigorous wartime patriotism, remains a classic, exploiting with imaginative brilliance cinema's ability to embrace a range of visual styles and to effect transitions in time and place, and between theatre and cinema. With *Walton's rousing orchestral score punctuating the soundtrack with sparkle and wistfulness, it is the first sound film to establish both artistic stature and public appeal for filmed Shakespeare. Branagh's *Henry v*, made for an audience far more suspicious of the glamorization of war, has been seen as a reaction to Olivier's film. Yet Branagh incorporates and modifies some of Olivier's devices. His is a profoundly searching Henry, with none of the easy RAF-style nonchalance so evident in Olivier's portrayal: he finds the body of the slain Boy at Agincourt, for example, and carries it, grieving, across the battlefield. *AD*

Recent major editions

Gary Taylor (Oxford, 1982); A. J. Gurr (New Cambridge, 1992); T. W. Craik (Arden 3rd series, 1998)

Some representative criticism

Battenhouse, R. W., '*Henry v* as Heroic Comedy', in R. Hosley (ed.), *Essays on Shakespeare and Elizabethan Drama in Honour of Hardin Craig* (1963)

Meron, Theodor, *Henry's Wars and Shakespeare's Laws* (1993)

'Hercules'. See Mote.

Herder, Johann Gottfried von (1744–1803), German philosopher, historian, and critic. His admiration for English ballads, Ossianic poetry, and Shakespeare influenced *Goethe, and contributed to the developing intuitive, irrational Sturm und Drang (Storm and Stress) movement in late 18th-century German literature. *TM*

Her Majesty's theatre, Haymarket. In 1897 H. Beerbohm *Tree opened this opulent playhouse on a site of theatrical prominence since 1704. Its stage was designed to frame his visually lavish productions of Shakespeare and other authors. George Robey appeared there as Falstaff in 1936. It now houses big-scale musicals. *MJ*

Hermia, daughter of Egeus, refuses his demand for her to marry Demetrius. She escapes into the woods outside Athens with Lysander in *A Midsummer Night's Dream.* *AB*

Hermione, Leontes' Queen, is falsely condemned as an adulteress in *The Winter's Tale.* *AB*

Hero, Leonato's daughter, is jilted at the altar by Claudio who believes her to be unfaithful in *Much Ado About Nothing.* *AB*

heroic couplets, pairs of rhymed iambic pentameter lines, typically but not always end-stopped and thus allowing an effect of completeness. Shakespeare uses them to round off all his sonnets and some dramatic scenes. *CB*

Herrera Bustamante, Manuel (1779–1834), Spanish army officer and author of *Estudio crítico sobre las tragedias de Shakespeare*, the first piece of Spanish Shakespearian criticism independent of translations, which he wrote in London in 1829 (he was of liberal sympathies and was exiled in England between 1823 and 1833). His study, unpublished and now lost, was reported to be lengthy and entirely consonant with A. W. *Schlegel's critical principles. *ALP*

'He that has and a little tiny wit', sung by the Fool in *The Tragedy of King Lear* 3.2.74; apparently adapted from *'When that I was and a little tiny boy' in *Twelfth Night.* *JB*

hexameter. See alexandrine.

Heyes, Thomas. See printing and publishing.

'Hey Robin, jolly Robin, tell me how thy Lady does', a three-part *catch by William Cornysh (d. 1523); sung as a solo by Feste in *Twelfth Night* 4.2.73. *JB*

Heywood, Thomas (1573/4–1641), poet, playwright, and miscellanist. In the preface to *The English Traveller* (1633) Heywood claims to have had a hand in some 220 plays, but only 20 or so survive. His best plays fall, broadly speaking, into two categories: lively studies of domestic and marital politics, often in a middle-class setting, such as *The Wise-Woman of Hogsdon* (1638), *The English Traveller*, and his tragicomic masterpiece, *A Woman Killed with Kindness* (1607); and spectacular dramatizations of classical myth and legend, such as *The Rape of Lucrece* (1608)—a strange musical tragedy which may be echoed in Shakespeare's *Cymbeline*—and his Ovidian theatrical epic in five instalments, *The Golden Age* (1611), *The Silver Age* (1613), *The Brazen Age* (1613), and the two parts of *The Iron Age* (printed in 1652). *The Iron Age*, which deals with the Trojan War, owes much to Shakespeare's *Troilus and Cressida*, but Heywood conceives his audience very differently. Where Shakespeare's difficult play evokes the exclusive atmosphere of a private performance, Heywood's *Ages* are designed 'the ruder censures to refine, | And to unlock the casket, long time shut, | Of which none but the learned keep the key, | Where the rich jewel (poesy) was put' (*The Silver Age* 1.1.12–15). They are full of humour, of action rapidly switching between comedy and pathos, of special effects and musical interludes, and are based on another first-class piece of entertainment, Heywood's mythological narrative poem *Troia Britanica* (1609). Some have argued that Heywood wrote *Pericles* and that Shakespeare revised it. He also published the most elaborate defence of the English stage of its times, *An Apology for Actors* (1612). In it he complains that some of his poems had been published under Shakespeare's name in the 1612 edition of *The Passionate Pilgrim*, and adds, with characteristic modesty, that they are not good enough to be Shakespeare's. *RM*

Baines, Barbara J., *Thomas Heywood* (1984)

McLuskie, Kathleen, *Dekker and Heywood: Professional Dramatists* (1994)

Higgins, John. See Mirror for Magistrates, The.

highways subscription. On 11 September 1611 Shakespeare was listed among 71 contributors 'towards the charge of prosecuting the bill in parliament for the better repair of the highways and amending divers defects in the statutes already made'. *SW*

Hilliard miniature. A miniature by Nicolas Hilliard (1547–1619), now in the Victoria and Albert Museum, has sometimes been

(cont. on page 202)

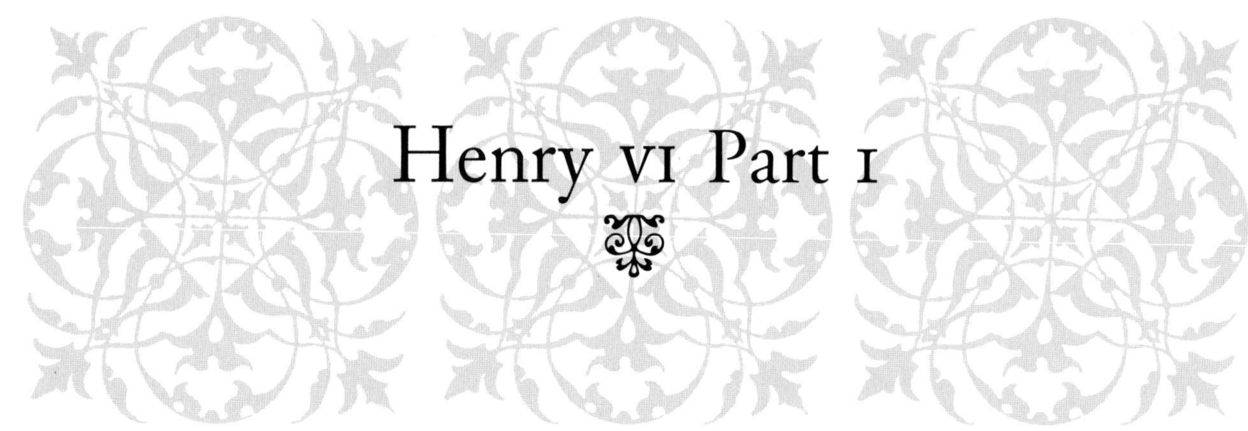

Henry VI Part 1

On 3 March 1592 the manager-owner of the *Rose theatre, Philip *Henslowe, recorded a 'new' performance of 'Harry the VI' in his diary. While this may conceivably allude to any of the three *Henry VI* plays, contextual evidence suggests it refers only to *Part 1*. (There is no early edition to help with the question of dating, since *1 Henry VI* did not appear in print until the appearance of the First Folio in 1623.) The box-office receipts of £3 16*s.* 8*d.* set a record that season, and the play was performed another fifteen times by Lord Strange's Men over the next ten months. Thomas *Nashe attested to its popularity in August that year in *Piers Penniless his Supplication to the Devil.* He invokes the inspiring deeds of *Part 1*'s warrior hero, Lord Talbot, to defend the theatre against moralistic attacks and as a 'reproof to these degenerate effeminate days of ours': 'How would it have joyed brave Talbot, the terror of the French, to think that after he had lien two hundred years in his tomb he should triumph again on the stage, and have his bones new-embalmed with the tears of ten thousand spectators at least, at several times, who in the tragedian that represents his person imagine they behold him fresh bleeding!'

Some scholars believe *Part 1* was written before these dates but after *The First Part of the Contention* (*2 Henry VI*) in 1590–1, and also *Richard Duke of York* (*3 Henry VI*) in 1591. Although *Part 1* presents events early in Henry's reign that are continued by those plays, there are historical anomalies between *The Contention* and *Part 1* that one would not expect to find if the latter had come first, in particular the fact that *The Contention* makes no mention of Talbot. The *Stationers' Register entry for 8 November 1623 covering the play's Folio publication also misleadingly records 'The Third Part of Henry the Sixth', even though *Richard Duke of York* had long been in print. The numbering thus refers to *Part 1*'s first publication after the other *Henry VI* plays had been issued, and perhaps to its sequence of composition. It must have been written after the second edition of *Holinshed's *Chronicles* (1587, see below), as well as the publication of *Spenser's *The Faerie Queene* (1590). The play's action may allude to English military expeditions to France between 1590 and 1591, particularly the Earl of *Essex's (ultimately unsuccessful) siege of Rouen, October 1591–January 1592.

Authorship: Although it first appeared in the authoritative 1623 Folio, *Part 1* is perhaps the least likely of the *Henry VI* plays to be wholly by Shakespeare, whose authorship has been questioned since the 18th century. Collaborative writing might explain Francis *Meres's failure to mention *Henry VI* in *Palladis Tamia* (1598), which lists other—but not all—known Shakespeare plays. Modern scholars and editors have argued that Thomas Nashe wrote Act 1 and perhaps other scenes, which may partly explain his enthusiastic notice of the play. Other possible collaborators are Robert *Greene and George *Peele. Other recent editors, however, such as Cairncross (Arden edition, 1962) and Hattaway (Cambridge, 1990), argue that Shakespeare was the sole author, and that the play's episodic design, monochromatic characterization, and stylistic unevenness indicate Shakespeare writing at an earlier stage in his career, before the superior achievements of *The First Part of the Contention* and *Richard Duke of York.*

Sources: *1 Henry VI* skilfully telescopes wide-ranging and often diffuse accounts in Edward *Halle's *Union of the Two Noble and Illustrious Families of Lancaster and York* (1548), and the compilation edited by Raphael Holinshed, *Chronicles of England, Scotland, and Ireland* (2nd edn. 1587). The established view is that Halle—traditionally regarded as more ideologically conservative—was Shakespeare's chief source, but some scholars have questioned this priority. Robert Fabyan's *New Chronicles of England and France* (1516) probably supplied information for 1.3 and 3.1, while Geoffrey of Monmouth's medieval *Historia regum Britanniae*, *Froissart's

Chronicles (trans. 1523–5), and John *Stow's *Chronicles of England* (1580) are sources for individual minor details.

Synopsis: **1.1** Henry v's state funeral is disrupted by news of the loss of conquests in France and the nobles' quarrelling, especially between Humphrey, Duke of Gloucester, and Henry Beaufort, Bishop of Winchester. **1.2** The French are beaten back after trying to disperse the English siege of Orléans. Joan la Pucelle presents herself as a holy peasant maid divinely destined to liberate France; she recognizes Charles the Dauphin without ever having seen him, and defeats him in a test of combat. **1.3** A violent brawl between Gloucester, Winchester, and their men is dispersed by the Mayor of London. **1.4** The Master Gunner of Orléans fires upon a tower from where Talbot and the English have surveyed the French defences. Salisbury is mortally wounded. **1.5–6** Joan disarms Talbot and captures Orléans. The victorious French celebrate her victory on the city walls.

2.1 Using scaling-ladders, Talbot, Bedford, and Burgundy assault Orléans and drive out the French. **2.2–3** Salisbury's funeral. The Countess of Auvergne invites Talbot to visit her castle, where she tries to take him prisoner, but he secretly forearms himself with a troop of soldiers. **2.4** In the Temple Garden, Richard Plantagenet, Somerset, and their supporters display their rival loyalties by plucking white and red roses, symbolizing the beginning of the Wars of the Roses. **2.5** York visits the dying Edmund Mortimer, heir to Richard ii but long imprisoned by the Lancastrians. He describes Plantagenet's dynastic claim to the throne deriving from Edward iii.

3.1 Gloucester and Winchester quarrel before the young Henry, who creates Plantagenet Duke of York. Henry leaves to be crowned in France. **3.2** Joan la Pucelle leads the French in disguise to take Rouen. The English are first defeated in battle but then recover the city. **3.3** Joan persuades Burgundy to switch sides to support the French. **3.4** Henry creates Talbot Earl of Shrewsbury. Vernon and Basset, respective supporters of York and Somerset, challenge each other.

4.1 Henry's coronation is interrupted by the banishment of John Fastolf, disgraced for cowardice. Henry tries to mediate Vernon and Basset's quarrel, unwittingly favouring the latter and infuriating York. **4.2** Talbot challenges the French before the walls of Bordeaux. **4.3** York blames Somerset's lack of co-operation for his inability to rescue Talbot, as the French recapture more towns. **4.4.** Somerset blames York for his delay in sending aid and Talbot's imminent defeat. **4.5** Talbot's son John vows to accompany his father in battle. **4.6.** Talbot rescues him when he is endangered. **4.7** Talbot dies after his dead son is brought before him. Lucy solemnly claims their bodies from the victorious and scoffing French.

5.1 The French offer Henry the Earl of Armagnac's daughter in peace negotiations. Winchester is made a cardinal. **5.2** The Parisians revolt against Charles and Joan. **5.3** Joan is captured by York while raising demonic spirits. Suffolk captures Margaret of Anjou and woos her for Henry's queen so that she may secretly become his paramour. Margaret's father René consents to give her to Henry, but without any dowry and on condition that Anjou and Maine are returned to French rule. **5.4** Joan denies knowing her old father and is condemned to the stake by York. He and Winchester negotiate a peace with the French, who agree in the hope of gaining future advantage. **5.5.** Suffolk persuades Henry to accept Margaret as his queen over the English nobles' objections.

critical history: Until recently, *1 Henry vi* attracted little critical attention. The play's arguably collaborative origins have suppressed interest on the grounds that it is not fully or genuinely Shakespearian. Its stylistic hybridity and loose structure have also been taken as a sign of apprentice work, especially if *Part 1* is positioned as the first play of the *Henry vi* trilogy, near the beginning of Shakespeare's professional career, while literary critics have missed the dramatic unity and aesthetic refinement they value in Shakespeare's later histories. An exception to these negative assessments was made by 19th-century German critics such as A. W. *Schlegel, who situated the play in the wider context of Shakespeare's histories as an epic national drama of political evolution from feudalism. In 1944 E. M. W. *Tillyard's *Shakespeare's History Plays* adopted this interpretation but emphasized a pattern of national transgression and redemption. The retributive consequences of originally deposing Richard ii continue in *Part 1* with the premature death of the heroic Henry v. The subsequent plunge into domestic factionalism and humiliation in France is ultimately corrected by the triumph of Henry vii and the Tudor dynasty, which united the Lancastrian and Yorkist lines. Since the 1970s critics have dismantled the monolithic ideology and rigid historical pattern of Tillyard's so-called 'Tudor myth' by observing the multiplicity of causal agencies and historical perspectives in this and other history plays. *Part 1* certainly endorses the idea that civil dissension and weak central authority—continually admonished in Elizabethan government writings—led to English losses in France during the Hundred Years War and the beginnings of the Wars of the Roses at home. But there is little in the play to connect these events with any metaphysical pattern of divine retribution. The focus is on secular history and personal agents making military and political decisions with predictable human consequences. Taking their cue partly from the conspicuous stage success the play has enjoyed in the past 50 years, theatre-minded critics have also observed how *Part 1* experiments with the full physical resources and configuration of the Elizabethan stage in boldly innovative ways, especially the use of the theatre gallery for vertically oriented assaults and multiply focused action on several levels. Stage productions have also pointed the way for feminist studies of Joan's subversion of traditional gender and social hierarchies. These critics have also noted the resemblance between Joan's various symbolic personae and public roles and those played by Elizabeth i.

Stage history: Henslowe's diary entry indicates *1 Henry vi* was written for and performed by Lord Strange's Men at

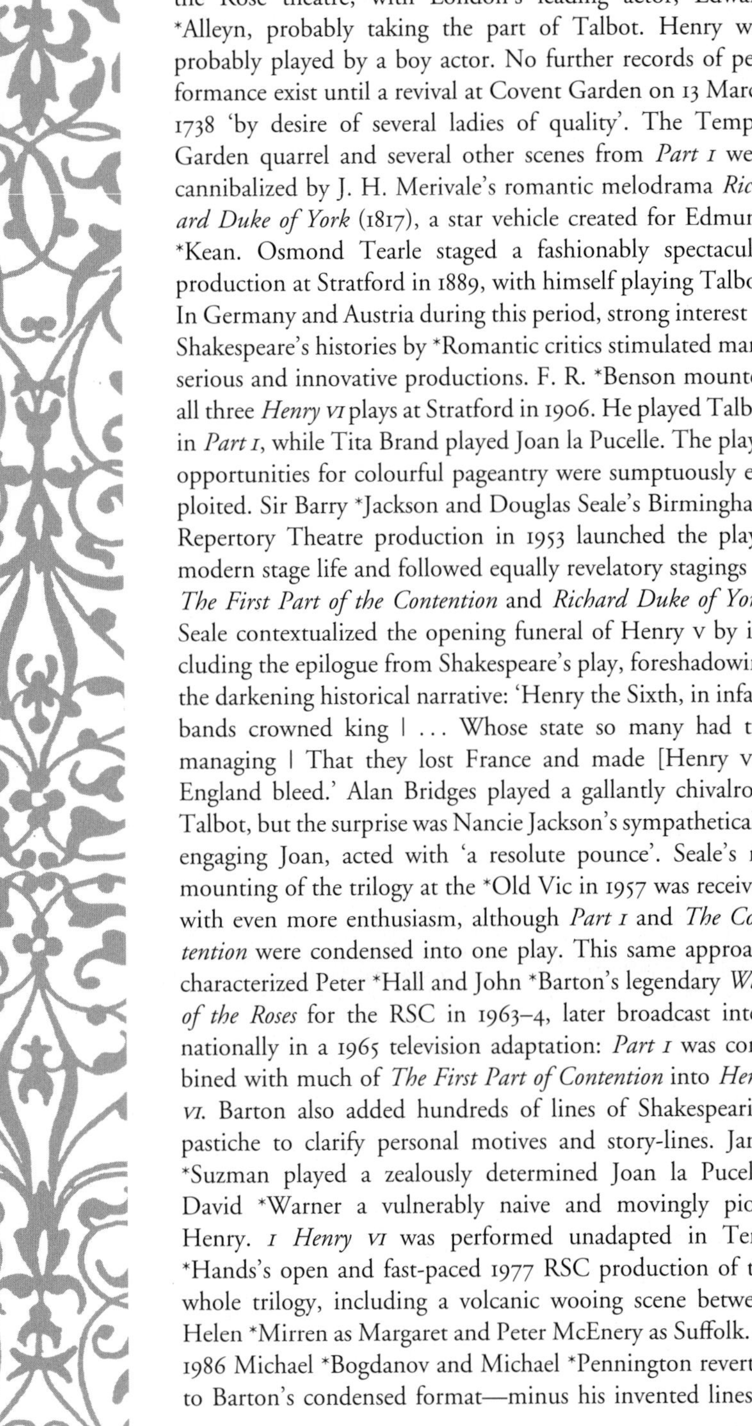

the Rose theatre, with London's leading actor, Edward *Alleyn, probably taking the part of Talbot. Henry was probably played by a boy actor. No further records of performance exist until a revival at Covent Garden on 13 March 1738 'by desire of several ladies of quality'. The Temple Garden quarrel and several other scenes from *Part I* were cannibalized by J. H. Merivale's romantic melodrama *Richard Duke of York* (1817), a star vehicle created for Edmund *Kean. Osmond Tearle staged a fashionably spectacular production at Stratford in 1889, with himself playing Talbot. In Germany and Austria during this period, strong interest in Shakespeare's histories by *Romantic critics stimulated many serious and innovative productions. F. R. *Benson mounted all three *Henry VI* plays at Stratford in 1906. He played Talbot in *Part I*, while Tita Brand played Joan la Pucelle. The play's opportunities for colourful pageantry were sumptuously exploited. Sir Barry *Jackson and Douglas Seale's Birmingham Repertory Theatre production in 1953 launched the play's modern stage life and followed equally revelatory stagings of *The First Part of the Contention* and *Richard Duke of York*. Seale contextualized the opening funeral of Henry V by including the epilogue from Shakespeare's play, foreshadowing the darkening historical narrative: 'Henry the Sixth, in infant bands crowned king | ... Whose state so many had the managing | That they lost France and made [Henry V's] England bleed.' Alan Bridges played a gallantly chivalrous Talbot, but the surprise was Nancie Jackson's sympathetically engaging Joan, acted with 'a resolute pounce'. Seale's remounting of the trilogy at the *Old Vic in 1957 was received with even more enthusiasm, although *Part I* and *The Contention* were condensed into one play. This same approach characterized Peter *Hall and John *Barton's legendary *Wars of the Roses* for the RSC in 1963–4, later broadcast internationally in a 1965 television adaptation: *Part I* was combined with much of *The First Part of Contention* into *Henry VI*. Barton also added hundreds of lines of Shakespearian pastiche to clarify personal motives and story-lines. Janet *Suzman played a zealously determined Joan la Pucelle, David *Warner a vulnerably naive and movingly pious Henry. *1 Henry VI* was performed unadapted in Terry *Hands's open and fast-paced 1977 RSC production of the whole trilogy, including a volcanic wooing scene between Helen *Mirren as Margaret and Peter McEnery as Suffolk. In 1986 Michael *Bogdanov and Michael *Pennington reverted to Barton's condensed format—minus his invented lines—for their spiky 'post-Falklands' production, *The Wars of the Roses*, for the *English Shakespeare Company, which toured internationally between 1986 and 1989. Adrian *Noble followed their format but not their 'radical' ideology for his two-play version, *The Plantagenets*, for the RSC in 1988. In America, Pat Patton based his stirring 1991 Oregon Shakespeare Festival production on Noble's 'House of Lancaster'. Previous productions of *Part I* at Ashland in 1953, 1964, and 1975 had employed strong ensemble acting and Shakespeare's full script. *RWFM*

On the screen: Inspired by Brecht's self-conscious approach to theatricality, Jane Howell directed a playful but often intense production for BBC television, first broadcast in 1983. Trevor Peacock's Talbot and Brenda Blethyn's Joan were curiously matched as unheroic, down-to-earth, but knowing outsiders on their respective sides. Henry was played, as usual in modern productions, by an adult actor—the ascetic and benign Peter Benson, who succeeded in making Henry 'both pathetically ineffectual and truly saintly'. *AD*

Recent major editions

Andrew S. Cairncross (Arden 2nd series, 1962); Michael Hattaway (New Cambridge, 1991); Edward Burns (Arden 3rd series, 2000)

Some representative criticism

Berry, Edward I., *Patterns of Decay: Shakespeare's Early Histories* (1975)

Brockbank, J. P., 'The Frame of Disorder: *Henry VI*', in John Russell Brown and Bernard Harris (eds.), *Early Shakespeare* (1961)

Jackson, Gabriele Bernard, 'Topical Ideology: Witches, Amazons, and Shakespeare's Joan of Arc', *Renaissance Quarterly*, 29 (1988)

Jones, Emrys, *The Origins of Shakespeare* (1977)

Leggatt, Alexander, 'The Death of John Talbot', in John W. Velz (ed.), *Shakespeare's Histories A Quest for Form and Genre* (1996)

Marcus, Leah, *Puzzling Shakespeare: Local Reading and its Discontents* (1988)

Potter, Lois, 'Recycling the Early Histories: "The Wars of the Roses" and "The Plantagenets" ', *Shakespeare Survey*, 43 (1991)

Rackin, Phyllis, *Stages of History: Shakespeare's English Chronicles* (1990)

Taylor, Gary, 'Shakespeare and Others: The Authorship of *Henry the Sixth, Part I*', *Medieval and Renaissance Drama in England*, 7 (1995)

Warren, Roger, ' "Contrarieties Agree": An Aspect of Dramatic Technique in *Henry VI*', *Shakespeare Survey*, 37 (1978)

identified as a likeness of Shakespeare: see portraits. *CT*

Hinman, Charlton (1911–77), American academic. Hinman's technical study *The Printing and Proof-Reading of the First Folio of Shakespeare* (2 vols., 1963) is based on an investigation of 80 copies of the First Folio in the Folger Shakespeare Library in Washington. By tracing individual pieces of type Hinman was able to reconstruct the sequence of printing; to identify individual compositors; to establish the order of type-formes through the press; and to determine the limited degree of proof-correction. His *Norton Facsimile: The First Folio of Shakespeare* (1968) uses 30 original copies to produce a composite photographic facsimile, with introduction and specimen proofs. *TM*

Hippolyta. **(1)** The Queen of the Amazons, having suffered military defeat by Theseus, is to marry him in *A Midsummer Night's Dream.* **(2)** Her wedding to Theseus is again dramatized in *The Two Noble Kinsmen.* *AB*

hired men. The majority of actors were not sharers in a playing company but were merely hired men expected to double several minor roles and paid a contract rate (5*s.* to 10*s.* a week) rather than a share of the profits. The term also covered musicians and non-performing playhouse personnel such as tiremen and stagekeepers. *GE*

historical novel. See FICTION.

history. Plays based on English history flourished in the second half of the 16th century and declined soon after the death of Elizabeth I in 1603. A popular genre, the history play was the product of a high demand for new plays for the public stage and the rise of strong nationalist feelings following the Protestant Reformation and the commercial wars with European countries, such as the Anglo-Spanish conflict which culminated with the defeat of the Armada in 1588.

The history play has no classical precedents. It derived its structure from English medieval morality plays and its primary material from official Tudor historiography, such as Raphael *Holinshed's *Chronicles of England, Scotland, and Ireland* (1587), Edward *Halle's *The Union of the Two Noble and Illustrious Families of Lancaster and York* (1548) and Polydore Vergil's *Anglica historia* (1534).

Shakespeare wrote ten history plays: *King John, Henry VIII,* and the two tetralogies, which cover the Wars of the Roses from the deposition of King Richard II in 1398 to the accession of Henry VII in 1485. Shakespeare wrote the tetralogies in reverse order: the three parts of *Henry VI* and *Richard III* were written in the early 1590s, *Richard II,* the two parts of *Henry IV,* and *Henry V* in the late 1590s.

The popularity enjoyed by the history play on the Elizabethan stage can also be explained in terms of the broader cultural history of the period. Elizabethan dramatists were attracted by the rhetorical and dramatic potential of the current conflict between a residual, Christian view of history as a divine, providential pattern, and the emergent, humanist notion of history as *magistra vitae* and source of political and pragmatic lessons for the Machiavellian ruler.

There is no critical consensus on the vexed issue of which view of history Shakespeare's historical plays subscribe to. In his *The Elizabethan World Picture* (1943) and *Shakespeare's History Plays* (1944), E. M. W. *Tillyard argued that Shakespeare's history plays represent a nationalist enterprise celebrating the providential restoration of order following the accession of the first Tudor king to the English throne in 1485. In 1957, Irving Ribner concentrated instead on the influence of Italian humanism on the English history play. Recent criticism tends to reject both approaches, by pointing out that conflicting views of history encouraged Shakespeare and his contemporaries to question the very idea of the universality of the human condition, on the one hand, and of the viability of secular institutions, such as monarchical absolutism, on the other. Greater attention is therefore paid to episodes such as the deposition scene in *Richard II,* revived on the eve of the *Essex conspiracy against Queen *Elizabeth in 1601. Equally popular with contemporary critics of Shakespeare's histories is Henry V's failure to persuade Private Williams of the King's genuine concerns for the welfare of his soldiers, while visiting his troops in disguise the night before the battle of Agincourt. *SM*

Holderness, Graham, et al., *Shakespeare and the Play of History* (1987)

Morse, David, *England's Time of Crisis: From Shakespeare to Milton. A Cultural History* (1989)

Ribner, Irving, *The English History Play in the Time of Shakespeare* (1965)

Tillyard, E. M. W., *The Elizabethan World Picture* (1943) *SM*

History and Fall of Caius Marius, The. See CAIUS MARIUS, THE HISTORY AND FALL OF.

History of King Lear, The (Shakespeare). See KING LEAR.

History of King Lear, The. Nahum *Tate's adaptation of *King Lear* was first performed in 1681, during the Exclusion Crisis (when the Whig party were attempting to disinherit the future James II in favour of Charles II's illegitimate son the Duke of Monmouth), and some of its alterations to Shakespeare's plot—particularly its focus on Edmund, and its happy ending in which the King is restored—may have been dictated by political considerations. The happy ending, though (a deliberate or instinctive return to Shakespeare's sources), endured long after the Exclusion Crisis had been forgotten, as did Tate's neat provisions of straightforward motive. His Cordelia, for example, only refuses to humour Lear in the love-test because she does not wish to be married off to either France or Burgundy: she is already in love with Edgar, to whom she will finally be betrothed (with the approval of both Lear and Gloucester, who is also spared) at the end of the play.

Tate clearly admired Shakespeare's tragedy (anticipating subsequent editors by drawing on both the Folio and quarto texts in preparing his adaptation), but felt it needed adjustment to fit

Cordelia, with her confidante Arante, is rescued by the disguised Edgar from Edmund's two hired ruffians in Nahum Tate's enduringly popular adaptation *The History of King Lear*. This mezzotint, after a painting by Leta van Bleeck, depicts Susannah Cibber as Cordelia.

the Restoration theatre's notions of characterization and decorum: in a preface he called it 'a heap of jewels, unstrung and unpolished'. In particular Tate excised the Fool entirely, finding his jokes and his diction incompatible with the dignity of tragedy, and in this he was supported by most commentators on *King Lear* for more than a century, who regarded the Fool as an unforgivable concession to Shakespeare's vulgar audience. *The History of King Lear* was progressively altered by successive 18th-century actors and managers—*Garrick restored many of Shakespeare's lines at the expense of Tate's, and in 1768 George Colman the elder eliminated the romance between Cordelia and Edgar altogether—but Tate's happy ending (preferred even by Dr *Johnson, though lamented by Samuel *Richardson) was not laid aside until Edmund *Kean's production of 1823, and the Fool was not restored until William Charles *Macready's in 1838. *MD*

Clark, Sandra (ed.), *Shakespeare Made Fit: Restoration Adaptations of Shakespeare* (1997)
Maguire, Nancy Klein, 'Nahum Tate's *King Lear*: "The King's Blest Restoration" ', in Jean Marsden (ed.), *The Appropriation of Shakespeare* (1991)
Spencer, Christopher (ed.), *Five Restoration Adaptations of Shakespeare* (1965)
Tate, Nahum, *The History of King Lear*, ed. James Black (1975)

Hoby, Sir Edward. See Castiglione, Baldassare; Richard II.

Hoffman. A 1656 bookseller's catalogue lists this tragedy as Shakespeare's. However *Henslowe's 'Diary' more reliably reports that *Chettle received payment for writing a 'tragedie called Hawghman', which was first performed at the Fortune. *SM*

Hogarth, William (1697–1764), English painter and engraver. His most celebrated theatrical portrait, painted around 1745 and much engraved, is *David Garrick as Richard III* (now at the Walker Art Gallery, Liverpool), a work which is influenced by French baroque portraits. In 1757, Hogarth completed a double portrait of *Garrick and his wife, which shows Garrick seated on a chair made from wood supposedly taken from Shakespeare's *mulberry tree. Known chiefly for his graphic satires, in 1728 Hogarth produced an engraving of Henry VIII and Anne Boleyn ousting Catherine of Aragon and Cardinal Wolsey from influential positions at court, from Shakespeare's *All Is True* (*Henry VIII*), at the time of the coronation of George II. Upon its publication, the print was read as an analogy for Tory hopes that the new King would remove the Prime Minister, Walpole, from office. *CT*

'Hold thy peace', a *catch or round sung by Sir Andrew, Sir Toby, and Feste in *Twelfth Night* 2.3.68. Two tunes survive for the words. *JB*

Holinshed, Raphael (d. *c.*1580), editor, translator, and historian. He began his career as a translator with the publisher Reginald Wolfe, who proposed that he compile a history of the world from the time of the Flood to *Elizabeth I. Wolfe died before he could see the early fruits of this labour, the publication in 1577 of *The First Volume of the Chronicles of England, Scotland, and Ireland . . . from the First Inhabiting unto the Conquest.* As well as historical accounts, it included a sociological and geographical description of each country. The work was a collaborative effort by Holinshed, William Harrison, Richard Stanyhurst, Edmund Campion, and Richard *Hooker. These men must have worked on the second expanded edition published in 1587 after Holinshed's death.

In the 1590s, the revived interest in English *history resulted in a fashion for plays on historical subjects. The *Chronicles* may have contributed to this fashion. Certainly, Holinshed's work was an invaluable source for poets and dramatists at this time. Not only was it the most complete account of British history published so far but its descriptions provided ideal background material for drama. It was also relatively easy to read. Holinshed had condensed his chief source *Halle considerably, excising some of the moral comment and narrating events in his own plainer style. Although Shakespeare probably used Halle in the original, his main source for the history plays was Holinshed's *Chronicles* (1587). Indeed, it stands alongside North's *Plutarch as his primary dramatic source, providing material for *Macbeth*, *King Lear*, and *Cymbeline*, as well as for all the English history plays. Shakespeare's borrowings vary from details of plot and character to the paraphrasing of whole speeches. Perhaps more interesting, though less tangible, is Holinshed's historiographic influence. The *Chronicles* is the work of a number of writers drawing upon different historical sources. The juxtaposition of various opinions, often with little attempt to arbitrate between them, makes for a more complex and non-committal view of history than was usual. Shakespeare's history plays are full of such ambiguities. The most obvious example is the tension in *Henry V* between different representations of the King. In his account of the reign, Holinshed includes a eulogy to Henry but also describes the King's troubled conscience on his deathbed and laments the human cost of the French wars. The tensions in Shakespeare's play may reflect Holinshed's divided mind. *JKS*

Holland. See Dutch wars; Low Countries.

Holland, Henry. See Exeter, Duke of.

Holland, Hugh (d. 1633), poet. A fellow of Trinity College, Cambridge, Holland contributed a sonnet to the First Folio (1623). Shakespeare is eulogized for 'dainty Plays' and especially for 'Tragedies'. After the Globe's applause, he has gone to 'Death's public tiring-house'. *PH*

Holland, John. See Bevis, George.

Holland, Philemon. See Livy; Pliny; Plutarch.

Hollar, Wenceslaus (1607–77), Czech engraver, active in England 1636–77. From drawings made at the top of *St Mary Overies church (now Southwark Cathedral), he executed the celebrated topographical Long View of London (engraving, 1647). The work depicted both sides of the Thames and includes the most reliable picture we have of the exterior of the second Globe, as well as other *Bankside theatres. This ambitious engraving was etched onto six plates and is annotated with names of the chief buildings depicted. *CT*

Holm, Sir Ian (b. 1931), British actor. His long association with the *Royal Shakespeare Company dates from 1964. Small of stature, he was cast in parts like Ariel, Puck, and Lear's Fool, but in the history cycle *The Wars of the Roses* he played Richard Crookback and went on to trace Prince Hal's development from youthful roisterer to politically adroit king. In 1967 he experienced a trauma and could not face live audiences until 1993. He appeared memorably in films and in television. In 1997 in the intimate Cottesloe at the National Theatre he was a great King Lear in a production later televised. *MJ*

Hordern, Michael, *A World Elsewhere* (1993)

Holofernes, a schoolmaster in *Love's Labour's Lost*, takes the part of Judas Maccabeus in the performance of 'The Nine Worthies', 5.2. He was probably based on the stock pedant of the **commedia dell'arte*, though various scholars have suggested a real-life original: John *Florio, Richard Mulcaster, or Thomas Hunt. *AB*

Holst, Gustav (1874–1934), English composer. Holst's one-act opera *At the Boar's Head*, Op. 42 (1924), is based on the tavern scenes from *Henry IV*, and uses traditional 17th-century English dance music. It also includes settings of Sonnets 12 and 19. Holst earlier set 'It was a lover and his lass' as a partsong (1890s) and 'Come away death' as a six-voice madrigal (*c.*1900). *IBC*

Holy Trinity church, Stratford-upon-Avon, stands in all probability on the site of an Anglo-Saxon minster, established by the 8th century. A settlement grew up around it, which was left undisturbed when, at the end of the 12th century, a new town was laid out on land to the north. This explains why today the church stands some distance from what is now the town centre. The success of this new town led to a rapid growth in population and, in the middle of the 13th century, to an almost complete rebuilding of the church. This is represented today by the transepts which have survived further periods of reconstruction. In the early 14th century the two nave aisles were rebuilt and the tower arch reconstructed. At the same time, a chantry was established, served by five priests, who soon afterwards assumed full control of the church. The rector became warden (later dean) and a college for the priests was built on adjoining land to the west. At the end of the 15th century, the old chancel was completely rebuilt by Dean Thomas Balsall, but leaving undisturbed an earlier building built against the north wall, the basement part of which became a charnel house. The last major alteration was made soon afterwards, probably under the direction of Balsall's successor Ralph Collingwood, when a clerestory was built above the nave arcades, the roof raised, and the great west window inserted. Subsequent alterations and restorations have not altered fundamentally the appearance of the church, with the exception of the present spire, added in 1763 to replace a smaller timbered one, and the demolition of the charnel house building around 1800.

The college was suppressed at the Reformation in 1553 and its property, including the tithes, confiscated by the Crown. In 1553, the income from these tithes was granted to the newly formed Stratford Corporation, out of which it was to pay the vicar's salary.

Several 17th-century accounts survive of visits to Holy Trinity church, specifically and often exclusively containing mention of Shakespeare's grave and effigy, but the first account to imply that the visitor had been drawn there as an act of homage is William Hall's of 1694. However, it is clear that, even when the Birthplace and Anne Hathaway's Cottage had been identified, the church remained for many years the principal item on the visitor's itinerary. *RB*

Bearman, Robert, 'Holy Trinity Church, Stratford-upon-Avon', *Archaeological Journal*, 128 (1971)

Pringle, Roger, 'The Rise of Stratford as Shakespeare's Town', in Robert Bearman (ed.), *The History of an English Borough: Stratford-upon-Avon 1196–1996* (1997)

Styles, Philip, 'Stratford-upon-Avon', in *Victoria History of the County of Warwick*, vol. iii (1945)

Holywell. The Liberty of Holywell, in the parish of St Leonard's, Shoreditch, was where the *Theatre (1576) and *Curtain (1577/8) playhouses were built. The Liberty's name and status was derived from a well within the Augustinian priory of St John the Baptist, Holywell, located between Shoreditch High Street and *Finsbury fields. *RSB*

Homer is generally identified as the author of the two seminal epic poems of the classical world, the *Iliad* and the *Odyssey*. The earliest written versions of what were originally oral poems date from the middle of the 8th century BC.

The *Iliad* dramatizes the siege of the city of Troy or Ilion (as it was also known) in Asia Minor by a Greek expedition led by Agamemnon of Mycenae. The purpose of the Trojan War was to recover Helen of Sparta, the beautiful wife of Menelaus, Agamemnon's brother. She had been abducted by Paris of Troy. The *Odyssey* tells of the turbulent return home from Troy to Ithaca of the resourceful Odysseus. It was his ruse of the wooden horse which caused the fall of Troy.

Shakespeare did not know Homeric epic in the Greek original, but he probably would have seen a version of George Chapman's *Seven Books of the Iliads* (1598) or Arthur Hall's *Ten Books of Homer's Iliads* (1581) before writing the satirical and anti-heroic Trojan War play *Troilus and Cressida*. The Troy story was, however, available in a number of other classical sources that Shakespeare knew well, such as *Aeneid* 2 (the source of most of the Troy material in *Hamlet*), and Ovid's *Metamorphoses* 13. *RW*

Troilus and Cressida ed. David Bevington, Arden 3rd series (1998)

Griffin, Jasper, *Homer* (1980)

Silk, Michael, *Homer: The Iliad* (1987)

homoeroticism. See SEXUALITY.

homosexuality. See SEXUALITY.

'Honour, riches, marriage, blessing', sung by Ceres and Juno in *The Tempest* 4.1.106; the original music is unknown. *JB*

Hooker, Richard (?1554–1600), theologian. He wrote *Of the Laws of Ecclesiastical Polity*, first published in 1593. This robust defence of the Church of England contains an eloquent passage on the necessity of Order, on which Shakespeare drew for Ulysses' speech on degree in *Troilus and Cressida* (1.3). *CS*

Hope theatre. See ANIMAL SHOWS; FLAGS; HENSLOWE, PHILIP; SWAN THEATRE.

Horatio is Hamlet's confidant in *Hamlet*. *AB*

Hordern, Sir Michael (1911–95), British actor. Coming to Stratford in 1952 as a mature actor, he played Jaques, Menenius, and Caliban, occasionally giving by his inflections new point to familiar lines. At the *Old Vic from 1953 his successes included Polonius, King John, Malvolio, Cassius, and Ulysses in *Troilus and Cressida*. Under Jonathan *Miller's meticulous, probing direction he played a very human King Lear, first on stage and later on BBC television. At Stratford in 1978 he was Prospero; and in *Love's Labour's Lost* his Don Armado recalled Don Quixote. *MJ*

horn. Made from animal horn or metal, it is a signalling instrument for huntsmen (*The Taming of the Shrew* Induction 1.13), messengers (*Richard Duke of York* 3.3.160), and sowgelders. *JB*

Horner, Thomas, an armourer accused of treason by his servant Peter Thump *The First Part of the Contention* (*2 Henry VI*) 1.3. Gloucester sentences them to single combat, which the terrified Thump wins 2.3.98, Horner confessing as he dies. A historical account (eventually published in John Noorthouck's *New History of London*, 1773) says that the armourer (William Catur) entered the lists drunk (at Smithfield, 1446) and was killed by his servant (John David) who later confessed slander. *AB*

hornpipe. Little is known about the dance in Shakespeare's time. The music was in triple metre; the common-time 'sailor's' hornpipe is much more recent. Also a reed instrument incorporating an animal horn. *JB*

horses are the second most frequently named animals in Shakespeare (after *dogs). They include Sir Andrew *Aguecheek's Capulet (*Twelfth Night* 3.4.278) and *Hector's Galathe (*Troilus and Cressida* 5.5.20). They are very frequently mentioned throughout the plays, as means of transport ('Therefore to horse, | And let us not be dainty of leave-taking, | But shift away', *Macbeth* 2.3.142–4) and as possessions of value ('The King, sir, hath wagered with him six Barbary horses', *Hamlet* 5.2.112). In Shakespeare's day horses were also essential in battle as Richard III finds out to his cost. The importance of the horse for the combatant is parodied by Shakespeare in Bourbon's panegyric to his 'mistress' Pegasus, *Henry V* 3.7. *AB*

Hortensio, Lucentio's rival for Bianca in *The Taming of the Shrew*, forswears her for a widow. *AB*

Hortensius' Servant, Titus' Servant, and Philotus' Servant (servants of Timon's creditors) appear in *Timon of Athens* 3.4, to demand repayment of debts. *AB*

Hostess. **(1)** She berates Sly in *The Taming of the Shrew* (Induction 1), and could be the 'fat alewife' named as Marian Hacket (Induction 2.20). **(2)** See also QUICKLY, MISTRESS. *AB*

hosts. **(1)** The Host of Julia's lodgings takes her (disguised as 'Sebastian') to see Proteus serenade Silvia. **(2)** The Host of the Garter Inn loses his horses in *The Merry Wives of Windsor* 4.5 (probably Evans and Caius' plot, see 3.1.109–12), and helps Fenton win Anne Page. *AB*

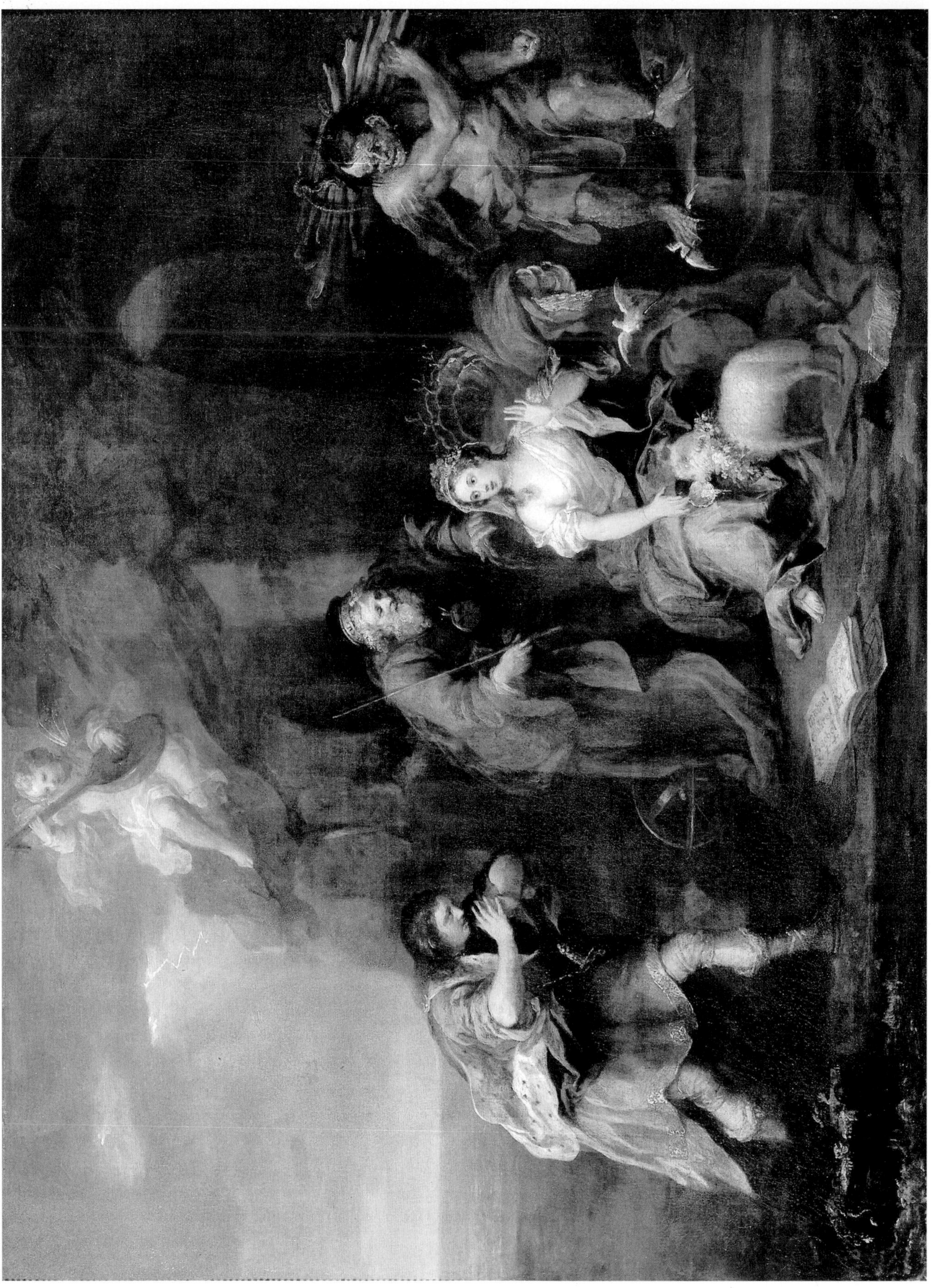

Hôtel de Bourgogne, the first public theatre in France, built in 1548 in the market district of Paris and used for over 200 years. The theatre was built in a rectangular room about 109 by 44 feet (33 × 13 m), the approximate size and shape of English indoor hall playhouses of Shakespeare's time. The Hôtel de Bourgogne had an upper playing space and flying machinery, and its main stage could employ perspective scenery as well as the more traditional use of multiple stage 'houses' representing diverse locations. *GE*

Wiley, W. L., 'The Hôtel de Bourgogne: Another Look at France's First Public Theatre', *Studies in Philology*, 70 (1973)

Hotson, Leslie (1897–1992), born in Canada, variously resident in America and England, a scholar specializing in literary detection from original documents, most famously in his *Death of Christopher Marlowe* (1925). Of his Shakespeare researches, *Shakespeare versus Shallow* (1931); *I, William Shakespeare* (1937); *Shakespeare's Sonnets Dated* (1949); *The First Night of 'Twelfth Night'* (1954), and *Mr W.H.* (1964) all infer from contemporary documents and records a complex network of associations, allusions, and identifications (not always accepted by other scholars) among Shakespeare's friends and acquaintances in London and Stratford—including Francis Langley, Thomas Russell, Leonard Digges, and William Hatcliffe. *Shakespeare's Wooden O* (1959) offers an in-the-round reconstruction of the Elizabethan theatre. *TM*

Hotspur (Henry Percy) appears with his father Northumberland as a supporter of Bolingbroke in *Richard* II. In *1 Henry IV* he leads the rebellion against Henry, but is killed by Prince Harry at *Shrewsbury, 5.4.85.

Historically, Harry Percy (1364–1403) was older than Henry IV, though Shakespeare casts him as a strong-willed and ambitious young counterpart to the dissipated Prince Harry. Stage productions of *1 Henry IV* have traditionally played off the youthful, heroic tragedy of Hotspur against the mature, abundant comedy of the tavern scenes. There were many memorable 20th-century Hotspurs: Matheson Lang in Beerbohm *Tree's production (1914) started a stage tradition which lasted for decades of giving Hotspur a stammer; and Laurence *Olivier's dedication to the part extended to spending three hours each night putting on a ginger beard and wig (1945). The convention of playing this aristocrat with a working-class northern accent—followed, for example, by Timothy Dalton (1981)—dates from the 1950s. *AB*

McMillin, Scott, *Henry IV Part One*, in J. R. Mulryne and J. C. Bulman (eds.), Shakespeare in Performance series (1991)

housekeepers, the owners of a playhouse, to be distinguished from the sharers in a playing company, although from 1599 several Chamberlain's Men (including Shakespeare) were both. *GE*

Houseman, John (1902–88), American producer and director. Hungarian by birth, English by schooling, he collaborated with Orson *Welles in New York on the voodoo *Macbeth* and the anti-fascist *Julius Caesar.* He produced films in Hollywood, including *Julius Caesar* (1953). From 1956 to 1959 he directed the American Shakespeare Festival at Stratford, Connecticut. He published three volumes of memoirs. *MJ*

Howard, Alan (b. 1937), English actor. Gifted with a striking physique and what one reviewer called 'the great voice of the classical stage', Howard dominated the *Royal Shakespeare Company stage during the late 1960s and 1970s, playing nearly all the kings in the Terry *Hands-directed history cycle. He also doubled Theseus and Oberon in Peter *Brook's *A Midsummer Night's Dream* (1970–3) and played Coriolanus (1977) and Mark Antony in *Antony and Cleopatra* (1978). After leaving the stage in the 1980s to spend time with his family, he returned in the early 1990s, playing Macbeth (Royal National Theatre, 1993) and Lear (Old Vic, for Peter *Hall, 1997). *BR*

Howard, James (*c*.1630–*c*.1680), author of a lost, late 17th-century adaptation of *Romeo and Juliet.* In his tragicomedy the lovers survived to heal the civil rifts. *CMSA*

Howard, Thomas. See Surrey, Earl of.

Howes, Edmund (fl. 1607–31), chronicler. In a continuation he added to the fifth edition of John Stowe's *Annals of England* (1614), Howes in 1615 listed 'excellent Poets' of Queen Elizabeth's reign. With attention to various 'priorities' including social rank, he places '*Shakespeare* gentleman' thirteenth, among 27 poets. *PH*

'How should I your true love know', sung by Ophelia, to her own lute accompaniment, in *Hamlet* 4.5.23. The opening words, and also a tune apparently sung at Drury Lane in the late 18th century, both relate to the 16th-century ballad 'Walsingham'; in this, an old man, driven mad by lost love in his youth, asks a traveller from Walsingham if he or she has seen his true love. The ballad tune was used for fine sets of keyboard variations by William *Byrd and John Bull. *JB*

Hubert takes Arthur into custody, and under John's orders he prepares to put out his eyes, but he is unable to complete the task, *King John* 4.1. Hubert de Burgh (d. 1243), Duke of Kent, was a powerful statesman during the reigns of John and Henry III. *AB*

Hudson, Henry Norman (1814–86), American scholar and cleric. He published *Lectures on Shakespeare* (1848); an edition (1852–7); and *Shakespeare: His Life, Art, and Characters* (2 vols., 1872). According to Hudson the Sonnets are exercises, only thrown into the form of personal address—those addressed to the young man being in fact to Anne *Hathaway. *TM*

Hughes, Margaret (d. 1719), one of the first English professional actresses. She appeared with the King's Company in the 1660s, possibly as Desdemona, and played Charmian in Sedley's version of *Antony and Cleopatra.* The mistress of Prince Rupert, she is the subject of a provocative portrait by Lely. *CMSA*

Hughes, Ted (Edward James) (1930–98), English Poet Laureate, 1984–98. Hughes once chided his first wife, the poet Sylvia Plath, with knowing only thirteen of Shakespeare's plays, and in both his reading and writing he returned always to Shakespeare. His poetic preoccupation with birds, animals, and the English countryside (even in their more savage and destructive aspects) does seem to suggest Shakespearian affinities. *Shakespeare and the Goddess of Complete Being* (1992) attempted, without convincing all readers, to identify his own mythic and mystic obsessions in the works of Shakespeare, focusing particularly on *Venus and Adonis* and *King Lear. Tales from Ovid* (1998) vividly translates the mythic murders, rapes, and mutilations of Shakespeare's favourite author for a modern audience, and was itself dramatized for the Royal Shakespeare Company in 1999. The final moving moment of Hughes's thanksgiving service in Westminster Abbey on 13 May 1999 was the unidentified, disembodied, recorded voice of the dead poet reciting the dirge from *Cymbeline.* *TM*

Hughes, William, an identity hypothesized by Thomas Tyrwhitt (1730–86) from line 7 of Sonnet 20: 'A man in hue, all hues in his controlling.' Oscar *Wilde adopts the name for the beautiful boy actor in *Portrait of Mr W.H.* Samuel Butler discovered a sea-cook of this name. *SW*

Hugo, François-Victor (1828–73), French translator. Former journalist and second son of the distinguished man of letters, artist, and politician Victor Hugo, he translated the whole Shakespearian corpus into French in fifteen volumes after the Folio (but he adopted a different genre classification, and included two translations of *Hamlet* based on the early

William Hogarth's slightly biblical vision of *The Tempest* 1.3, 1735–40. Hogarth helped to establish scenes from Shakespeare as an important part of any British painter's subject matter.

quarto) during his family's political exile to Guernsey. Although still a literary milestone, this prose version never found its way to the stage. *ISG*

Hugo, Victor Marie (1802–85), French poet, playwright, and novelist. One of the beacons of the Romantic reform movement, Hugo was among the most fervent partisans of English drama during the Restoration period in France. With the inception of his literary salon, the 'Cénacle' (1829), bourgeois and anticlerical liberals joined the aristocratic and monarchist Romantics with the intention of overthrowing the old school of their classical forefathers. Hugo's rallying forces promulgated a new dramatic style capable of expressing not only the supple laws of nature through the run-on line, but above all the unruly spirit of Shakespeare through the alliance of tragic and comic genres. In his *'Preface' to Cromwell* (1830) Hugo cited Shakespeare as his precedent for defending the total autonomy of the aesthetic voice. In proclaiming 'The poet must only take counsel from nature, from truth and from inspiration which is also a form of truth and nature,' Hugo planted the seeds of dramatic discontent which would trigger off 'the battle of *Hernani*' in 1830. He later published an equally enthusiastic critical study, *William Shakespeare* (1864). *AC*

Hull, Thomas (1728–1808), Anglo-Irish actor and playwright. He played a wide range of secondary roles—Friar Laurence, Buckingham, Edgar, Pisanio—in Dublin, Bath, and, from 1759, Covent Garden. He adapted Shadwell's *Timon of Athens*, abridged *The Winter's Tale*, and wrote two versions of *The Comedy of Errors*. *CMSA*

humanism is a philosophical and critical system of values with several applications relevant to Shakespeare: **(1)** the Renaissance revival of interest in the secular Greek and Latin classics, literae humaniores; **(2)** human experience as the criterion for man's knowledge of himself, God, and Nature; **(3)** the attribution of positive value to individual human life. Shakespeare and the French essayist Montaigne (1533–92) may be regarded as foremost among contemporaries in their consistent expression of humanist values. The related term 'liberal humanist', implying rational tolerance for a plurality of critical opinion, has in recent times become as derogatory in the mouths of the more doctrinaire literary theorists as 'humanist' itself once was in those of religious absolutists. *TM*

Hume, Sir John. In *The First Part of the Contention (2 Henry VI)* he is bribed by Cardinal Beaufort and Suffolk to undermine the Duchess of Gloucester. With fellow priest John Southwell, two unnamed priests, Roger Bolingbroke, and Margery Jordan, he is arrested for performing witchcraft. Hume, Southwell, Bolingbroke, and Jordan are condemned to death, 2.3.5–8. *AB*

Humphrey, Duke of Gloucester. See GLOUCESTER, DUKE OF.

Hungary. The genesis of Hungarian Shakespeare is strongly linked with the cultural movements of national awakening of the late 18th century. After a few sporadic references to the playwright (György Szerdahelyi, 1776; György Bessenyei, 1777), the first translations were based on German adaptations: *Romeo and Juliet* (Sándor Kun Szabó, 1786), *Hamlet* (Ferenc Kazinczy, 1790). Kazinczy's *Hamlet* was the text of the first Shakespeare performance in Hungarian (1793, Kolozsvár (Cluj)).

The reformation and standardization of the vernacular played a central role in Hungarian nation formation and Shakespeare's plays were ideal touchstones for these efforts. Parallel with the initiatives to found the Hungarian National Theatre in Pest (1837) there had been repeated demands to translate all Shakespeare plays directly from English. The greatest translations of the first half of the 19th century today still belong to the national canon of the Hungarian Shakespeare: *Julius Caesar* (1847) and *King Lear* (1856) by Mihály Vörösmarty and *Coriolanus* (1848) by Sándor Petőfi.

A decade after the abortive war of independence against Habsburg Austria (1848–49), Anasztáz Tomori initiated and financed the translations of Shakespeare's complete works. János Arany became a central figure in the enterprise: in addition to co-ordinating the work in general, he translated *Hamlet* (1867), *King John* (1867), and *A Midsummer Night's Dream* (1864). He was a dominant member of the first Hungarian Shakespeare Committee (1860), under whose aegis the first complete series of Shakespeare plays was published between 1864 and 1878.

The second committee was established (1907) to promote further Shakespeare studies in Hungary. Its publication series (*Magyar Shakespeare-tár*, 1908–22) offered valuable contributions to historical scholarship. Its plans to revise and republish the existing translations were frustrated by the two World Wars and were only completed in 1948 (ed. László Országh and Kálmán Ruttkay). This edition included a few classical translations but was mainly dominated by new works by outstanding poets and translators such as Mihály Babits, Dezsö Kosztolányi, Dezsö Mészöly, Miklós Radnóti, György Somlyó, Lörinc Szabó, and István Vas.

In the first half of the 20th century, Shakespeare became an 'in-house' author of the Hungarian National Theatre. The most celebrated directors of their time produced memorable 'Shakespeare cycles': Sándor Hevesi (director of the National: 1922–32) and Antal Németh (1935–44). After the war, Shakespeare's popularity continued: there were eight Shakespeare productions in the National Theatre between 1945 and 1949. During the 1950s, Shakespeare was claimed to be a 'proto-communist' author: his plays were heavily appropriated by socialist realism. In the 1960s Miklós Gábor's outstanding performances as Hamlet, Romeo, Iago, and Richard III were internationally acclaimed.

In 1955 an edition of Shakespeare plays was published (with more than a dozen new translations) and the poems were added in 1961. (Both were edited by László Kéry.) The contemporary 'Shakespeare scene' is co-ordinated by the third Hungarian Shakespeare Committee (1987). Its current president, István Géher, edited (with Mária Borbás) a collection of Shakespeare translations (1988). Hungarian scholars' recent monographs published in Great Britain and the United States—such as those by Péter Dávidházi and Tibor Fabiny—have increasingly helped to expand the dialogue on Shakespeare between Hungary and other countries. *ZM*

Hunnis, William (d. 1597), Master of the Chapel Royal (1566–97), poet, composer. Hunnis, together with Richard Farrant and Henry Evans, ran the first Blackfriars playhouse from 1576 to 1584. *GE*

Smith, Irwin, *Shakespeare's Blackfriars Playhouse: Its History and its Design* (1964)
Stopes, C. C., *William Hunnis and the Revels of the Chapel Royal* (1910)

Hunsdon, George Carey, 2nd Lord (1547–1603), Lord Chamberlain from 1597. Despite being patron of Lord Hunsdon's—later the *Chamberlain's—Men, Hunsdon petitioned against *Burbage's plans for a playhouse at *Blackfriars in 1596, resistance which forced Burbage to move to the south bank when the Theatre's lease ran out in 1599. *CS*

Hunsdon, Henry Carey, 1st Lord (1526–96), Lord Chamberlain from 1583 to his death in 1596. He was patron of Shakespeare's acting company (later the Chamberlain's Men), formed in 1594. His mistress Emilia *Lanier was proposed by A. L. Rowse as a candidate for the *Dark Lady of Shakespeare's *Sonnets*. *CS*

Hunsdon's Men. See CHAMBERLAIN'S MEN/KING'S MEN.

Hunt, Hugh (1911–93), British director. Younger brother of the mountaineer Lord Hunt, he became after war service the first director of the Bristol Old Vic, 1945–9. His success led to his taking over the *Old Vic Company in London after the departure of Laurence Olivier and Ralph Richardson. Under his regime the Vic moved from the West End to its restored theatre in Lambeth. Hunt's book *Old Vic Prefaces*

(1954) outlined his own directorial approach. He later ran the Elizabethan Theatre Trust in *Australia and in 1961 became the first professor of drama at Manchester University. *MJ*

Hunt, Leigh (1784–1859), English writer and dramatic critic, who from 1805 in the *Examiner* and other journals chronicled one of the great periods of English acting, a task to which he was ideally suited. No admirer of the stately John Philip Kemble, Hunt was prevented, being in prison, from seeing Edmund Kean's debut as Shylock in 1814 and proclaimed his disappointment at his Richard III, but was won over by his Othello, which he hailed as 'the masterpiece of the living stage'. *RF*

Leigh Hunt's Dramatic Criticism 1808–31, ed. L. H. and C. W. Houtchens (1949)

Hunt, Simon, master of Stratford grammar school from 1571 to 1575 after graduating from Oxford in 1568. He may have been the Simon Hunt who matriculated from the University of Douai in 1575, became a Jesuit in 1578, and died at Rome in 1585, but another man of the same name died in Stratford in or before 1598, leaving £100. *SW*

hunting and sports. Belarius in *Cymbeline* hunts for his daily food, but his circumstances are special. Hunting in Shakespeare is normally for exercise or sport. The animals said to be hunted include lion, panther, bear, wolf, hare, boar, fox, and deer. Only deer, however, are treated in a way that seems to reflect personal knowledge and experience. The other animals are stereotypes for ferocity or, in the case of the hare and the fox, resourcefulness and cunning. But deer are referred to and deer-hunting scenes presented with a wealth of technical terms correctly used and from a large number of different aspects. We hear of 'a jolly troop of huntsmen' with their horns and hounds, see keepers carrying crossbows, are told of poachers breaking into parks and rascal deer breaking out of them, of stags locking horns, and of the ceremonies at the end of a hunt. We are invited to sympathize with the deer at bay that does not know which way to turn and with the fatally wounded deer 'straying in the park, seeking to hide herself'. There are also constant puns and double entendres (heart/hart, deer/dear, suitor/shooter, stand) which would have fallen flat if stag-hunting had not been recognized as a part of real life even though most people could not afford to take part in it themselves.

The same is true of falconry. Though birds could be shot (*Taming of the Shrew* 5.2.47–51), they are far more often said to be flown at. Direct descriptions of falconry or allusions to it by way of simile or metaphor occur throughout the plays and cover every aspect of the sport. We are assumed to know how hawks are caught and trained and flown, how strong their sex-drive is, how their young behave, and are even expected to recognize the technical term ('imp') for repairing a broken wing (*Richard II* 2.1.294). Nevertheless, Shakespeare does not use what Ben Jonson's young bucks call 'the Hawking language' (*Underwood* 44.72) if that means the

'A braggart, a rogue, a villain, that fights by the book of arithmetic!' (*Romeo and Juliet* 3.1.101–2). The Continental, 'geometrical' method of fencing scorned by Mercutio, from the aptly named Gerard Thibault's *L'Academie de l'espée* (1618).

pretentious and archaizing jargon of the falconry manuals. Instead his language seems to have been that of practising falconers. The likelihood is that he spoke of falconry from his own personal experience, as is also suggested by his having chosen a falcon to figure in his family coat of arms.

Fishing, conducted by line, hook (or 'angle'), and bait, is recognized by Shakespeare as a gentleman's occupation. Antony spent his days fishing (*Antony and Cleopatra* 1.4.4) and the Wooer in *Two Noble Kinsmen* (4.1.53 ff.) went 'angling in the great lake that lies behind the palace'. But such moments are rare. Nearly all allusions to it are metaphorical and confined to its more obvious aspects, like fishing for approval ('great opinion') in *Troilus and Cressida* 4.4.103. One may therefore suppose that the sport held little attraction for Shakespeare. Indeed if Cleopatra's remark about fish with a hook in their 'slimy jaws' (*Antony and Cleopatra* 2.5.13) reflects personal sentiment he may have found it positively unpleasant.

The most important pastime in Shakespeare's plays, however—if any activity with such drastic consequences can be called such—is fencing, and here again the playwright both displays and presumes an extensive and up-to-date technical vocabulary. The rapier—a narrow, two-edged, lightweight, and pointed sword—had only been introduced into England around the middle of the 16th century, and the language used by fashionable fencing manuals (and, less reputably, by professional fencing instructors, who enjoyed the same vagabond status as common players) was still largely Italian. Mercutio, for example, ridiculing what he regards as Tybalt's pedantic duelling style, mimics him with the words 'Ah, the immortal *passado*, the *punto reverso*, the *hai*' (*Romeo and Juliet* 2.3.23–4), while the more Anglicizing Host in *The Merry Wives of Windsor* tells Caius he hopes 'To see thee fight, to see thee foin, to see thee traverse . . . to see thee pass thy punto, thy stock, thy reverse, thy distance, thy montant' (2.3.22–5). Although all gentlemen were expected to be adepts at self-defence (the word 'fence' is merely an abbreviation of 'defence', and Shakespeare uses the two forms interchangeably), duelling with the rapier was associated with an over-scrupulous obsession with personal honour (as dramatized in Thomas *Middleton and William *Rowley's *A Fair Quarrel*, 1617): characteristically, Shakespeare explores both the tragic possibilities of this vogue (in *Romeo and Juliet* and *Hamlet*) and the comic (in the abortive duel between Viola and Aguecheek in *Twelfth Night*, and in Touchstone's disquisition on 'the lie direct' in *As You Like It*). These depictions of the modern rapier are a far cry from Shakespeare's treatment of the medieval broadsword, still associated with the now-obsolete trial by single combat (as in *Richard II* 1.3), but increasingly felt to be a vulgar weapon for common brawlers (cf. Hotspur's dismissive reference to the slumming Prince Harry as 'that same sword-and-buckler Prince of Wales', *1 Henry IV* 1.3.228). *MP*

Madden, D. H., *The Diary of Master William Silence: A Study of Shakespeare and of Elizabethan Sport* (1897)

Pope, M., 'Shakespeare's Falconry', *Shakespeare Survey*, 44 (1992)

Sieveking, A. Forbes, 'Fencing', in *Shakespeare's England* (1916)

Huntington Library, San Marino, California. It specializes in English and American literature, history, and art. It holds 50% of the titles printed in England before 1641 and 95% of all English plays and masques of the period, including a collection of early Shakespeare editions second only to the *Folger's in the USA. *SLB*

http://www.huntington.org

Huntsman. He reluctantly accompanies the freed Edward IV, whom he was supposed to be guarding, *Richard Duke of York* (*3 Henry VI*) 4.6. *AB*

huntsmen, two. They accompany the Lord, *The Taming of the Shrew* Induction 1. *AB*

'hunt's up, The', a popular 16th-century ballad tune mentioned by Juliet in *Romeo and Juliet* 3.5.34. *JB*

Huon de Bourdeaux, a French romance, translated into English in 1534, and possibly adapted for the stage in the early 1590s, features a fairy king called Oberon. In anticipation of *A Midsummer Night's Dream*, the romance associates Oberon with a forest in which travellers expect enchantment. It also asserts that the humans' future happiness will depend upon the fairy's generosity. *JKS*

Hutt, William (b. 1920), Canadian actor, director. Noted for his crisp voice, extremely technical acting style, and captivating stage presence, due partly to his 6-foot 2-inch (1.87 m), height Hutt has been a mainstay of the Stratford Shakespeare Festival (Ontario) since 1953. His roles include: Lear—which he has played four times, first as a member of the Canadian Players (1962) then three times at Stratford (Ontario), most recently in 1996—Prospero (1975, 1999), and Leonato (1998). Directing credits include *As You Like It* (1972) and *All Is True* (*Henry VIII*) (1986). In 1969, he was made Companion of the Order of Canada, Canada's highest honour. *BR*

Hymen is the god of marriage. **(1)** He presents Rosalind to her father and Orlando in the last scene of *As You Like It*. **(2)** He leads the wedding procession at the beginning of *The Two Noble Kinsmen*. *AB*

hyperbole, rhetorical exaggeration:

> His legs bestrid the ocean; his reared arm
> Crested the world.
> (*Antony and Cleopatra* 5.2.81–2)

CB

Iachimo. See Giacomo.

Iago, Othello's 'ancient' or ensign, declares his intention of taking revenge on Othello for promoting Cassio ahead of him in the first scene of *Othello.* He skilfully convinces Othello that his wife *Desdemona has been adulterous with Cassio. He wounds Cassio, murders Roderigo, whom he has involved in his plots, and also kills his own wife Emilia who exposes his crimes in the final scene.

Some of the great 18th- and 19th-century tragedians were better at playing Iago than Othello (there was a stage tradition of playing the roles alternately)—among them *Garrick, J. B. *Booth, and *Macready. During the 19th century there was a temptation to make Iago a stage villain complete with black wig and heavy black eyebrows, and it was not until *Irving and *Fechter that star actors chose to rest their reputations on Iago rather than Othello. In the 1920s many actors followed Irving in playing him as a mortally frivolous intellectual: *Olivier famously broke this pattern by suggesting a thwarted homosexual passion for Othello. In the wake of the Second World War new kinds of Iago have emerged as motiveless evil has come to seem more mundane. Notable Iagos have included Emrys James's disgruntled NCO (John *Barton, 1971, a reading subsequently developed by both Ian *McKellen and Simon Russell Beale); Bob Hoskins's criminal psychopath (Jonathan *Miller, BBC, 1983); Christopher Plummer, who matched the stature and power of James Earl *Jones's Othello (Winter Gardens, New York, 1982); and David Suchet's homosexual Iago (Terry *Hands, 1985). *AB*

Hankey, Julie (ed.), *Plays in Performance: Othello* (1987)

iambic, composed of metrical units ('feet') in which one unstressed syllable is followed by one stressed syllable. The dominant metre of English verse, it permits variations, especially in its five-stress or pentameter form, in which syllables may diminish or augment their degree of stress, often with notable expressive effect. *CB/GTW*

Ibsen, Henrik (1828–1906), Norwegian playwright and poet. Ibsen, familiar with Shakespeare from his professional career as a *dramaturg*, later, for his 'problem' plays of contemporary life, sought to reject the artificial devices of blank verse, soliloquy, mistaken identity, overheard conversations, intercepted letters. But the structure of *Ghosts* (1881), with its dead father, powerful mother, and sensitive son, bears many resemblances to *Hamlet*; and some of the symbolism of his last play *When We Dead Awaken* (1899) seems to echo Shakespearian 'romance'. *TM*

Iden (Eden), Alexander. He discovers the starving Cade in his garden and kills him, *The First Part of the Contention* (*2 Henry VI*) 4.9, receiving a knighthood and money as a reward, 5.1. He was Sheriff of Kent at the time of the Cade rebellion (1450). *AB*

'If wishes would prevail with me', sung by Pistol, and continued by the Boy, in *Henry V* 3.2.15. The original tune is unknown. *JB*

illustrations. Early 18th-century editions of Shakespeare's plays (such as Nicholas *Rowe's, 1709) often included handsome frontispieces. Alexander *Pope's edition of 1723, for example, offered George Vertue's celebrated engraved portrait depicting Shakespeare, in a cartouche, wearing Van Dyck dress. A milestone in illustrated versions of Shakespeare, however, came in 1740, with the publication of Lewis *Theobald's *Works of Shakespeare*, expensively illustrated by the French engraver Hubert François Gravelot. In 1744 a comparable text was published with illustrations after designs by Francis *Hayman. Illustrations to Shakespeare plays became increasingly sentimental as the century progressed, such as those in the 1785 popular edition commissioned by John *Bell. Bell's celebrated editions included stage portraits of contemporary actors 'in character' drawn by aspiring artists early in their careers such as John Keys Sherwin and Johann Heinrich Ramberg. The portraits were engraved by Charles Grignon and often represented fictional compilations of the action, costume, or roles played by the actors depicted. Numerous illustrated versions were produced during the 19th century, such as Cassell's *New Royal Quarto*, 1864, illustrated by H. C. Selous, which included fictional Shakespearian *mises-en-scène*, also published in the *Illustrated London News* to promote the edition. Reasons for the decrease in, and eventual disappearance of, illustrated versions of the plays during the 20th century are difficult to ascertain, though the genre survives after a fashion further downmarket in the *strip-cartoon edition. *CT*

Illyria, an indefinite region of coast to the east of the Adriatic Sea, is the scene of *Twelfth Night.* Although nothing is said explicitly about the nature of the place in this play, a reference in *The First Part of the Contention* (*2 Henry VI*) to 'Bargulus, the strong Illyrian pirate' (4.1.108) suggests that Shakespeare chose this setting with Antonio, the 'salt-water thief' (5.1.65), in mind. *AB*

imagery, a modern critical term for the totality of references to perceptible things and actions to be found—usually but not exclusively in such figures of speech as metaphor and simile—within a poem or play. In the 1930s it became a central concept in the redirection of Shakespearian interpretation away from dramatic action and character, towards poetic 'theme': the work of G. Wilson *Knight in *The Wheel of*

One of the earliest illustrations to Shakespeare, the frontispiece to *The Tempest* in Rowe's edition (1709). The artist has been so heavily influenced by contemporary stage performances that his depiction of the storm owes more to Davenant and Dryden's adaptation *The Tempest; or, The Enchanted Island* than to Shakespeare's play.

Fire (1930) and its sequels proposed that patterns of recurrent imagery not only produced the special atmosphere of each play but also indicated its deeper themes, of love, death, harmony, or chaos. In a more statistical investigation, Caroline *Spurgeon's book *Shakespeare's Imagery and What it Tells us* (1935) claimed that each play was dominated by a distinctive 'cluster' of images, e.g. of light and darkness in *Romeo and Juliet* and of disease in *Hamlet*; and that these were clues to Shakespeare's personal mentality and habits, revealing his good knowledge of housework and gardening, his sympathy for horses and small boys, and his passion for health and cleanliness. Although it has tempted some to forget that the plays are after all plays, the analysis of imagery remains a significant part of Shakespearian study. *CB*

Imogen. See CYMBELINE.

impresa. On 31 March 1614 Thomas Screvin, steward to Francis Manners, 6th Earl of Rutland, recorded payment of 44*s.* 'to Mr Shakespeare in gold about my lord's impresa' and another payment of the same amount 'to Richard Burbage for painting and making it'. The actor Burbage was a talented painter, and the association with him makes it likely that 'Mr Shakespeare' is William. The impresa—an allegorical device, with a motto, painted on a paper shield (cf. *Pericles* 6.16–48)—was made to be borne by the Earl at a tournament on the King's Accession Day, 24 March 1613. *SW*

imprint. The imprint on the *title page of early Shakespearian texts provides the names of the printer and/or publisher along with the place and date of publication. The imprint also informed retailers where copies of a book could be purchased wholesale: 'Printed for Nathaniel Butter, and are to be sold at his shop in Paul's Churchyard at the sign of the Pide Bull near St. Austin's Gate' (Q1 *King Lear*). *ER*

India. Shakespeare sailed towards India in 1607: two performances of *Hamlet* apparently took place aboard the *Hector* commanded by William Hawkins, who was on his way to the court of the 'Great Mogol' (see TRAVEL, TRADE, AND COLONIALISM). Over the next four centuries, Shakespeare's plays, on the stage as well as in the classroom, were to become a central feature of the English presence and its legacy in India. As the privileged core of colonial English education, they were used to bolster ideas of English superiority over the culture and literature of the 'natives'. On the stage, Shakespeare was staple fare for amateur theatricals of the English resident in India as well as for Indian students of European-style colleges all over the country. Western-style public theatres were established in Calcutta, Bombay, and Madras partly on the strength of their adaptations and translations of Shakespeare's plays.

In Calcutta, among the first performances at the Hindu theatre, established 1831, were scenes from *Julius Caesar*. In 1848 the San Souci theatre saw a young Bengali actor, Baisnab Charan Addy, act Othello opposite an Englishwoman, Mrs Anderson, playing Desdemona. Such casting was revolutionary for its time as black Othellos were opposed on English stages until the early 20th century. In 1872, Girishchandra Ghosh started the famous National Theatre, and himself played star roles such as Macbeth. *Bhanumati Chittavilasa*, the 1852 adaptation of *The Merchant of Venice* into Bengali, is reckoned to be one of the earliest Indian adaptations of any foreign play.

In Bombay, the first public performances of Shakespeare took place in the Bombay theatre, established in 1849. Soon after, the 'Hindu Dramatic Corps' was born, with the aim of enacting the same kind of plays but in Indian languages. Over the next seven decades, the Marathi, Gujarati, and especially the Parsi stages constantly performed their versions of Shakespeare. Ganapatrao Joshi became famous as the 'Garrick of Maharashtra', playing Hamlet, Othello, and Macbeth from 1882 until his death in 1922. Balvantrao Jog was known for playing Ophelia, Desdemona, and Lady Macbeth. Jayshankar, who played Desdemona (Sundari) in an extremely successful Gujarati adaptation of *Othello*, continued to call himself by that name throughout his career. Aga Hashr Kashmiri was the most prolific adapter of Shakespeare in Urdu for the Bombay stages in the late 19th and early 20th centuries and was nicknamed 'Shakespeare-e-Hind' (Shakespeare of India). Shakespeare was also performed on private stages, especially those patronized by royalty—a performance of *Cymbeline* at the festivities during the wedding of the Maharaja of Baroda in 1879 reportedly lasted nearly six hours! The Maharaja of Mysore also encouraged Shakespearian adaptations although in southern India public theatres did not stage English plays with the same fervour as in Calcutta or Bombay.

In the 1920s Shakespeare entered Indian cinema as theatre companies switched to the new medium—Sohrab and Rustem Modi, for example, changed their theatre group into the Stage Film Company in order to film their popular version of *Hamlet* (*Khoon ka Khoon*, literally 'Blood for Blood'). The advent of cinema marked a decline of travelling companies with their Shakespearian repertoires. This is documented by Merchant–Ivory's film *Shakespeare Wallah* (1965), which tells the story of the English actor-director Geoffrey Kendal's travelling troupe Shakespeariana, which toured India extensively from the 1940s to the early 1960s, playing in palaces, public theatres, clubs, schools, and colleges. Shakespeariana included Indian actors such as Utpal Dutt, later a star on the Bengali stage and screen, as well as the Bombay film idol Shashi Kapoor.

Hundreds, if not thousands, of adaptations and translations of Shakespeare exist in various Indian languages. In 1934, R. K. Yajnik listed over 200; a more recent bibliography estimates over 2,000, although it is still hard to estimate exact numbers since many playscripts have been lost. These adaptations play freely with Shakespeare's plots and themes, adapting them to Indian theatrical and social conditions and thus implicitly challenging the reverential attitude that colonial educationists sought to instil in Indians, and which still dominates classroom approaches to Shakespeare. Today, Shakespeare continues to be widely taught, although some critics have challenged his centrality, and to be performed in educational institutions. On the English-language stage, his plays are generally performed in a bland and adulatory fashion, but, adapted into Indian languages, they can result in vital experimentation, as is the case with productions of the National School of Drama during the 1970s or more recent adaptations of *Lear* and *Othello* into the dance-drama form of Kathakali. Habib Tanvir, a well-known director, has adapted *A Midsummer Night's Dream* into the Chattisgarhi style of folk theatre. In the 1980s, Mizo-language performances of Hamlet in the north-eastern state of Mizoram acquired the status of a popular cult. *Kaliyattam*, a 1997 film in Malayalam directed by Jayaraj, sets *Othello* among a troupe of Thaiyyam dance-drama performers in Kerala. If Shakespeare lives in India today, it is as a dramatist transformed by his encounter with indigenous traditions, languages, and political concerns. *AL*

Kendal, Geoffrey, *The Shakespeare Wallah* (1986)

Loomba, Ania, '*Hamlet* in Mizoram', in Marianne Novy (ed.), *Cross-cultural Performances* (1993)

Loomba, Ania, ' "Local-Manufacture Made-in-India Othello Fellows": Issues of Race, Hybridity and Location in Postcolonial Shakespeares', in Ania Loomba and Martin Orkin (eds.), *Postcolonial Shakespeares* (1998)

Yajnik, R. K., *The Indian Theatre, its Origins and its Later Developments under European Influence* (1934)

Zarilli, Philip B., 'For Whom is a King a King? Issues of Intercultural Production, Perception and Reception in a Kathakali *King Lear*', in Janelle G. Reinelt and Joseph R. Roach (eds.), *Critical Theory and Performance* (1992)

Indian Boy. See Changeling Boy.

induction, in the Shakespearian canon, a term used for Rumour's introductory monologue in *2 Henry IV* and the Christopher Sly scenes that open *The Taming of the Shrew*. See prologue. *CB*

Ingon, a village in the parish of Hampton Lucy about 2 miles (3 km) north of Stratford, home of Shakespeare's uncle Henry *Shakespeare, who also farmed land at the nearby *Snitterfield. John *Shakespeare leased Ingon Meadow between 1568 and 1570, and in 1575 paid £10 for a lease of 14 acres (5.5 ha) there. *SW*

Ingratitude of a Commonwealth, The; or, The Fall of Caius Martius Coriolanus. Nahum *Tate's adaptation of *Coriolanus* was first performed in November 1681, and, as its preface makes clear, was intended to draw topical parallels between Shakespeare's Roman plebeians and the contemporary Whig party. Apart from its political fellow-feeling with Coriolanus, this unsuccessful adaptation is most notable for its ending which, reversing the strategy he had employed on *King Lear*, Tate makes as gory and tragic as possible: not only does Coriolanus die on stage but so do Aufidius, his lieutenant, Young Martius, and Virgilia, while Volumnia, understandably, goes mad. *MD*

McGugan, Ruth, *Nahum Tate and the Coriolanus Tradition in English Drama, with a Critical Edition of Tate's The Ingratitude of a Common-Wealth* (1987)

Innogen. See Cymbeline.

inns. Before the construction of the first permanent theatre spaces in London in the 1560s and 1570s, the large yards of the inns of the city of London were being used for dramatic performance. The yards, designed for the unloading of wagons, were enclosed on three or four sides and had galleries around their edges which provided access to the rooms available for nightly rental. With the addition of a portable stage an inn-yard made an effective theatre with space for spectators standing around the stage and under or within the galleries. The first recorded performances were at the Saracen's Head, Islington, and the Boar's Head, Aldgate, in 1557. The Red Lion used to be thought an inn-playhouse, but new evidence shows that, despite the unlikely sounding name, this was a farm converted to a playhouse in 1567.

Until 1594 playing companies moved between different city inns in winter, and the suburban playhouses in the summer. In 1594 the Privy Council banned all playing at city inns and allowed only two companies, the Admiral's Men and the Chamberlain's Men, at two specified suburban venues: the *Rose and the *Theatre, respectively. Glynne Wickham thought that players using an inn probably preferred one of its interior halls to its exposed yard for their performance since this would give them protection from the winter elements and would also please the innkeeper, who would not want to lose the use of his yard for unloading wagons. But wagons were probably unloaded early in the morning and late at night so for most of the day no conflict existed, and moreover Oscar Brownstein showed that the annual migration between city inns and suburban amphitheatres was prompted more by plague restrictions than by concerns of comfort. (Receipts for the Boar's Head galleries on 24 and 26 December 1599 suggest that outdoor playing was practical in winter.) However, it is quite possible that the Cross Keys and the Bell inns allowed only indoor performance since they never put on the exclusively outdoor entertainment of sword-fighting 'prizes' which were popular at the rival Bull and the Bell Savage inns. We know of only one inn being permanently converted into a playhouse: the Boar's Head in 1598. A Privy Council order of June 1600 banned all playing at inns and no subsequent performances are recorded. *GE*

Brownstein, Oscar, 'A Record of London Inn-playhouses from *c.*1565–1590', *Shakespeare Quarterly*, 22 (1971)

'The Saracen's Head, Islington: A Pre-Elizabethan Inn Playhouse', *Theatre Notebook*, 25 (1971)

Berry, Herbert, *The Boar's Head Playhouse* (1986)

Wickham, Glynne, *Early English Stages 1300 to 1660* (3 vols., 1963), ii: *1576 to 1660*, part I.

Inns of Court. The four Inns of Court—Gray's Inn, Lincoln's Inn, Middle Temple, and Inner Temple—were established in the 13th century to teach the practice of law as well as to teach history, music, and dancing. The Halls of the Inns were used for indoor performances with revels being performed for members of the Inn and the public. *RSB*

Bland, D. S., *Three Revels from the Inns of Court* (1984)

Megarry, Sir Robert, *Inns Ancient and Modern: A Topographical and Historical Introduction to the Inns of Court, Inns of Chancery, and Serjeant's Inn* (1972)

Weinreb, B., and Hibbert, C. (eds.), *The London Encyclopedia* (1983)

Instituto Shakespeare, a translating team at the English Department of Valencia University, Spain. It was formed in 1978 with the purpose of producing new translations of Shakespeare's plays into Spanish free verse, supervised by Manuel Ángel *Conejero, in the service of theatrical effectiveness. Translators included Juan Vicente Martínez Luciano, Vicente Forés, and Jenaro Talens, though the group changed in the 1990s. By 1999 they had published eleven translations, most of them in bilingual editions, with introductions and notes by various scholars (Cátedra, Madrid). *ALP*

interludes. The word 'interlude' was used from the 14th century for a short dramatic performance, given on its own or during an interval within a longer entertainment. Henry Medwall's *Fulgens and Lucrece* (probably 1497) and Nicholas Udall's *Jack Jugeler* (1535–60) show the genre's usual moralism, and the latter also its use of characteristic names in Dame Coye and Jenkin Careaway. *Elizabeth I allowed her father's *Lusores Regis* (Players of the King's Interludes) to disintegrate, and the entertainment 'Pyramus and Thisbe' in *A Midsummer Night's Dream* parodies the genre's lack of sophistication. Interludes by Thomas Heywood, John Rastell, and others, however, encouraged a movement away from the abstract morality towards a more localized and particular dramatic form. They may also have exercised a specific influence upon later plays, including the two parts of *Henry IV*. *JKS/GE*

Craik, T. W., *The Tudor Interlude* (1958)

International Shakespeare Association (ISA). It came into being formally in 1974 as a result of recommendations made at the first World Shakespeare Congress, held at the University of British Columbia in 1971, to establish an international association which would provide an advisory committee for planning further world congresses and undertake a number of specified co-operative tasks. Since its creation, the headquarters of the association have been at the Shakespeare Centre in Stratford-upon-Avon. It is administered by an executive committee which represents the international nature of its work and membership. Sir John *Gielgud was its president from its foundation until his death in 2000. Membership is open to any person who wishes to support its objects and accepts its articles, and is not restricted to professional academics. The ISA's central commitments, outlined in its constitution, are to link the work of the various Shakespeare associations and societies and to advise on the foundation and development of new associations worldwide; to support an information centre, covering research, publication, translation, and performance; to circulate a diary of future performances, conference, and graduate courses; to aid travel in the interests of Shakespeare scholarship and performance; and to co-ordinate and support requests for finance for internationally co-operative projects. The ISA has organized six World Shakespeare Congresses in co-operation with the relevant national Shakespeare association, each on a special theme: 'Shakespeare, Pattern of Excelling Nature' in Washington (1976), 'Shakespeare, Man of the Theatre' in Stratford-upon-Avon (1981), 'Images of Shakespeare' in Berlin (1986), 'Shakespeare and Cultural Traditions' in Tokyo (1991), 'Shakespeare and the Twentieth Century' in Los Angeles (1996), and 'Shakespeare and the Mediterranean' in Valencia (2001). The proceedings are published. The ISA also organizes regular International Conferences for Teachers of Shakespeare in conjunction with the Shakespeare Birthplace Trust. Since 1979 it has published a series of Occasional Papers reprinting lectures sponsored by the ISA in different parts of the world. Authors have included playwrights, academics, and actors. It produces an annual newsletter. *SLB*

International Shakespeare Conference. See Shakespeare Institute.

International Shakespeare's Globe Centre. See globe reconstructions.

interpolations, lines or passages suspected of having been introduced into a text without authorization. The process of identifying interpolations can be highly subjective. The Fool's prophecy in *King Lear* (3.2.79–96), for instance, is viewed by some as an interpolation, whereas others see it as a perfectly germane authorial element of the text. It has also been suggested that the *masque in 4.1 of *The Tempest* and the two songs in *Macbeth* were late interpolations into Shakespeare's text. *ER*

Intervals. See act and scene divisions.

'In youth when I did love', a misquoted poem, 'The aged lover renounceth love', by Thomas, Lord Vaux (1509–56), sung by the First Clown (Gravedigger) in *Hamlet* 5.1.61. Music survives; see Sternfeld, *Music in Shakespearean Tragedy* (1964). *JB*

Iras, one of Cleopatra's attendants, dies just before Cleopatra's suicide, *Antony and Cleopatra* 5.2.287. *AB*

Ireland. With an ideal of 'civilizing' Ireland (or at least of converting it to Protestantism), Munster and Ulster were colonized by the English during the 16th century in a policy that aroused considerable resentment among the native population. By 1595, a crisis point had been reached and the so-called Nine Years War was under way. Hugh O'Neill, Earl of Tyrone, broke out in open rebellion, banding together 'Gaels' and 'Old English' hostile to Elizabeth and defeating English forces at Yellow Ford in 1598. Licking his wounds, Robert Devereux, the Earl of *Essex, withdrew to England in 1599, his Irish campaign a disaster. It was left to Charles Blount, Lord Mountjoy, to subdue this recalcitrant outpost. While Tyrone was quashed at Kinsale in 1601, he was still recognized, in 1603, as chief lord of Ulster under the Crown. As a result, King *James, despite his subsequent 'plantation' scheme in Ireland, was obliged to continue to allow over-mighty subjects to rule the country in his name.

In Shakespearian drama can be glimpsed an acute responsiveness to the 'Irish problem'. There are numerous (mainly negative) references to Ireland in the early works, including the comedies. Even in the history plays, the theme of a garden turning into a wilderness refracts contemporary accounts of Ireland as a fertile environment with a savage underside. Coinciding with the beginning of the Nine Years War is the reference in *Richard II* to 'rough rug-headed kerns', a typically barbed construction of the Irish as ethnically marginal and morally unregenerate.

But Shakespeare also contemplated in greater detail the situation of a territory in a vexed relation to the policies of central government. From the scene involving the four captains in *Henry V* emerges a trenchant investigation into the processes of shoring up an unstable national identity. In particular, the question posed by MacMorris, the Irish captain—'What ish my nation?' (3.3.66)—has been read as a subtle undermining of Henry's imperializing project. The Chorus's complimentary reference to the Earl of Essex's Irish campaign notwithstanding, the play as a whole, it has been argued, stands as a critique of an English nation that requires the conquest of France (and Ireland) to heal its internal divisions.

After 1599, Ireland is a much less obvious presence in Shakespeare's *œuvre*, probably because the Nine Years War was an increasingly delicate topic for representation. Yet the later plays are still haunted by 'Irish' ghosts. *King Lear* and *Othello* present themselves respectively as dramas preoccupied with the unity of 'Britain' and the nature of hybridized identity, areas of concern with multiple Irish associations. *The Tempest* might also be seen as having an Irish dimension, since the island, like Ireland, is in the process of developing from a kingdom to a colony: it is a domain caught between two territorial vocabularies.

If Ireland was of interest to Shakespeare, Shakespeare has certainly been of interest to Ireland. Over the course of the 18th century, Shakespeare was a regular feature of the dramatic repertoire of the Dublin theatres at Aungier Street and Smock Alley. The dramatist continued to be staged in Dublin during the 19th century in both public and private performances. Since the close of the 19th century, and the cultural and national resurgence of Ireland in the literary imagination, Shakespearian performance has been somewhat eclipsed; nevertheless, there have been notable 20th-century productions at the Abbey, the Gaiety, and the Gate in Dublin, at the Lyric in Belfast, and at community festivals dotted around the country, and Shakespeare continues to exercise an influence on Irish dramatic traditions.

Indeed, no doubt because of his complex 'national' status, Shakespeare, in Ireland, has been a favourite port of call for indigenous playwrights and artists. In the plays of both O'Casey and *Shaw, Shakespearian structures and situations can be easily detected. *Joyce was fascinated by Shakespearian 'artist' figures; *Yeats dropped in on the Bard to negotiate his own relationship to Ascendancy culture; and Seamus Heaney has found in the dramatist opportunities to further poetic representations of national crises. In Irish history, politics, and culture, Shakespeare has proved an abiding presence. *MTB*

Baker, David J., *Between Nations: Shakespeare, Spenser, Marvell, and the Question of Britain* (1997)
Burnett, Mark Thornton, and Wray, Ramona (ed.), *Shakespeare and Ireland: History, Politics, Culture* (1997)
Highley, Christopher, *Shakespeare, Spenser and the Crisis in Ireland* (1997)
Murphy, Andrew, *But the Irish Sea betwixt Us: Ireland, Colonialism, and Renaissance Literature* (1999)
OhAodha, Micheál, *Theatre in Ireland* (1974)

Ireland, Samuel. See FORGERY.

Ireland, William Henry. See FORGERY.

'Iris', messenger of the gods, is played by a spirit in *The Tempest*'s *masque of 4.1. *AB*

irony, a subtly humorous perception of incongruity in which an apparently straightforward statement or event is given another significance by its context. This may take the form of verbal irony, in which what is said is not what is meant (as in some rhetorical figures such as litotes and meiosis), or of situational irony (e.g. 'dramatic irony'), which plays on the discrepancy between an audience's superior awareness of events and a character's blindness to them. *CB*

Irving, Sir Henry (1838–1905), English actor-manager, knighted (the first actor) 1895; funeral in Westminster Abbey. Her precocious nephew's recitals of Shakespeare disturbed Sarah Penberthy, who was intent upon giving him the benefit of strict Methodist upbringing in the Cornish mining village of Halsetown, but the future actor was not to be deterred from his vocation by religious prejudice any more than by his ungainly physique or unmelodious voice. Irving persevered through an exceptionally long and industrious apprenticeship during which, hardly being the conventional juvenile lead, his lot was more likely to be Sylvius, Hortensio, or Osric than Orlando or Hamlet. Nevertheless, during his gruelling years (1856–66) in the provinces, Irving was an eager pupil of such masters as Charles *Calvert in Manchester, who cast him as Mercutio in 1864 for the Shakespeare tercentenary, but it was at his own behest that Irving played Hamlet for his benefit there later that summer. The local press found Irving deficient in voice and physique, but commended his intelligence and determination.

Following his sensational success as Mathias in *The Bells* at the Lyceum theatre for the Batemans in 1871, Irving claimed Hamlet (1874), Macbeth (1875), Othello (1876), and Richard III (1877), but opinion generally fell far short of enthusiasm. As Hamlet his voice was considered jerky, his movements angular, and his bearing lacking in dignity; he did not strive to make points but to give a consistent reading of the melancholy, benign Prince in the grip of moral poison.

Irving inaugurated his own regime at the Lyceum with Hamlet (30 December 1878), followed by his dignified Shylock (1 November 1879). In 1881 he alternated Othello and Iago with Edwin *Booth; in 1882 came his rather mature Romeo and his witty and gallant (except to Beatrice) Benedick; in 1884 his sombre Malvolio prompted a divided reaction; his Macbeth (1888) was riven with guilt; his Cardinal Wolsey, one of many clerical characters, was a compelling portrait of pride and mental torture; and his carefully conceived Lear was largely inaudible on the first night (1892). He convinced even *Shaw as Iachimo, but not as Richard III (both 1896); and no one was convinced by his Coriolanus (1901).

Consistency of interpretation was the hallmark equally of Irving's individual Shakespearian performances and of his productions at the Lyceum, where he sought to harmonize all the arts of theatre in the service of the play. No slavish antiquarian, he encouraged his designers to capture the mood of the play as he also did with lighting and music. Many members of the acting company set up in management on the Irving model to which Shakespeare's plays were indispensable. Shakespeare was Irving's motive and cue: at the Lyceum, where he created a national theatre in all but name (and subsidy); on his eight tours as cultural ambassador to North America and his continuing visitations to the provinces of Britain. Irving produced attractive editions of his (substantially cut and rearranged) acting versions and the *Henry Irving Shakespeare, edited by himself and Frank A. Marshall, published in eight handsome volumes (1892), stands as a lasting memorial. *RF*

Hughes, Alan, *Henry Irving, Shakespearian* (1981)
Irving, Lawrence, *Henry Irving: The Actor and his World* (1951)

Irving, Washington (1783–1859), American author. His *Sketch Book* (1819–20) describes the Stratford *Birthplace in 1815 as 'a small and mean-looking edifice' and his guide (Mary Hornby) as 'a garrulous old lady' exhibiting a collection of bogus relics: limitations long past, and now forever transcended in the Birthplace's millennium refurbishment. *TM*

Isabel, Queen. Charles VI's consort in *Henry V*, she blesses the marriage of King Harry and Catherine 5.2.354–63. The historical Isabel (1370–1455) was considerably more lascivious and factious than Shakespeare's presentation of a peace-loving matron would suggest. *AB*

Isabella, a novice in *Measure for Measure*, is told by Angelo that if she has sex with

Henry Irving as Shylock, 1879.

him, she can save her condemned brother Claudio. *AB*

'I shall no more to sea', a fragment sung by Stefano in *The Tempest* 2.2.41; the original tune is unknown. *JB*

Isidore's Servant. See VARRO'S SERVANT.

Israel. Short passages of Shakespeare were translated into Hebrew during the early 19th century from Russian and German versions, but the first full translations were from the English. Hebrew versions of *Othello* (1874) and *Romeo and Juliet* (1878) were made by Isaac Edward Salkinson, an Eastern European Jew who emigrated to England, converted to Christianity, and became a minister and a missionary. Written in a language which was not yet spoken, they were essentially closet dramas. Translations by other hands followed: *Macbeth*, from Schiller's version, and, from the English, *The Taming of the Shrew*, *King Lear*, and *Hamlet*, all published in Eastern Europe late in the 19th century. Whereas the early Hebrew translations strove for dignity, beauty of expression, and preciseness of rendering, Yiddish translations, starting with *Julius Caesar* (Warsaw, 1886), were written in a racy vernacular, devoid of literary pretensions, often quite crude. They too were meant for reading.

With the early 20th-century growth of Yiddish theatre in America, some of the tragedies—mainly *Hamlet*, *Othello*, and *Romeo and Juliet*—became popular, initially in melodramatic interpretations. Yiddish theatre reached its artistic peak at the Moscow Jewish State Theatre, in 1935, with an internationally acclaimed *King Lear*, acted by the legendary Solomon Mikhoels. Shortly after, Yiddish culture was to become a mere relic of Jewish life before the Holocaust.

From the 1940s, translations were mainly the work of poets residing in the then Palestine, often commissioned by one of the theatres. Foremost among them was the Russian-born Avraham Shlonsky, who translated *King Lear* and *Hamlet* from the Russian in the early 1940s. To the same generation of translators belong the poets Nathan Alterman and Leah Goldberg. Later translators include Raphael Eliaz, Ephraim Broido, T. Carmi, Dan Miron, David Avidan, Dan Almagor, Shimon Sandbank, Avraham Oz, Ehud Manor, Meir Wieseltier, and Dori Parnes.

The first professional Hebrew production of Shakespeare was *Twelfth Night*, translated by the poet Shaul Tchernichovsky, at the Habimah theatre, in 1930. In 1936, Leopold Jessner directed *The Merchant of Venice* at the Habimah, with the Russian-born actor Aharon Meskin. The appropriateness of the play's performance in Israel was debated heatedly. Habimah staged the play again in 1959, with Tyrone *Guthrie as director and Tanya Moiseiwitsch as designer. The production was criticized as the work of a Gentile director, unable to understand the distress caused to Jews by the play. The production most harshly basted for alleged anti-Semitism was the first one directed by an Israeli-born director, Yossi Yizraeli, at the Cameri theatre, in 1972. In 1995, the Israeli director Hanan Snir directed a production at the Nationaltheater of Weimar. The clash between Jews and Germans, working together on Shakespeare's anti-Semitic play, was brought to a head through the decision to set the play in the officers' mess at Buchenwald concentration camp, close to Weimar. The production was brought to Israel where it created a furore.

Shakespeare is the most frequently performed playwright on Israeli stages, and his plays are translated regularly for new productions. In the early years of the Hebrew theatre, celebrated foreign directors were invited over, bringing with them the latest theatrical innovations. More recently, visiting foreign companies, performing in English as well as in a variety of other languages, have exposed the local audience to the latest trends and interpretations (Royal Shakespeare Company, Shared Experience, Cheek by Jowl, Stary Teatr from Cracow, Rustaveli Teatr from Tbilisi, the Nationaltheater of Weimar). The British director Steven Berkoff has had a considerable influence on the Israeli scene in a number of ways. He brought over his company to perform *Hamlet*, then *Coriolanus*, with himself in the leading role, worked as director in various Israeli theatres, and directed in 1999 a highly successful Hebrew *Hamlet* at the Haifa Municipal Theatre, with Doron Tavori.

Shakespeare research in Israel is fairly recent. Most of it is written in English and published abroad, and very little has been written in Hebrew. Among contemporary scholars are Ruth Nevo, Zvi Jagendorf, Avraham Oz, Hanna Scolnicov, and Elizabeth Freund. *HS*

Almagor, D., 'Shakespeare in Israel: A Bibliography, 1950–1965', *Shakespeare Quarterly*, 17 (1966)

Almagor, D., 'Shakespeare in Hebrew Literature, 1794–1930: Bibliographical Survey and Bibliography', in *Festschrift for Shimon Halkin* (1975) (in Hebrew)

Golomb, H., 'Shakespearean Re-generations in Hebrew: A Study in Historical Poetics', in A. Oz (ed.), *Strands Afar Remote: Israeli Perspectives on Shakespeare* (1998)

Prager, L., 'Shakespeare in Yiddish', *Shakespeare Quarterly*, 19 (1968)

italics, a cursive version of roman type. Italic was first used as a text type in the early 16th century, but it was found to be less legible than roman and thereafter generally employed as the secondary and subordinate type in conjunction with roman. In the printing of Shakespeare's early texts, italic type was used primarily for speech-headings, *stage directions, and proper names. *ER*

Italy. Despite Shakespeare's overwhelming interest in Italy as an at least nominal setting for comedies, Italy was at first slow to take any interest in Shakespeare. The first printed reference to Shakespeare in Italian appeared in 1668, in Lorenzo Magalotti's account of a journey to England where the author provides a list of about 25 'Poets': 'Spens, Drayton, Shakespier . . .'; in the list, 'Bemont', 'Flescher', and 'Dreiden' are described as 'comico' (author of comedies), and 'Conte di Orerey' (Roger Boyle, Earl of Orrery) as 'tragico' (author of tragedies). No qualification is attached to Shakespeare.

The next appeared only in 1726, when Antonio Conti published a play entitled *Il Cesare*. In a letter which precedes the text, 'Sasper' as author of *Julius Caesar* is described as the English Corneille but criticized for his disregard of the classical unities. In 1729, in the 'Life of Milton' which introduces his translation of *Paradise Lost*, Paolo Rolli cited Shakespeare as the inventor of blank verse ('verso sciolto') and also as the initiator, like Dante, of the national language: he also praised the histories and affirmed that anything which is neither sublime nor elegant in Shakespeare's plays is the addition of contemporary playwrights. But until the 1770s, the evaluation of the plays was coloured by *Voltaire's *neoclassical idea of their author as a great tragic poet who lacked regularity and good taste. Such an evaluation was expressed, among others, by the playwright Carlo Goldoni who, like most 18th-century Italian writers, read the plays in a French translation. The 'Discours sur Shakespeare et sur Monsieur de Voltaire' by Giuseppe Baretti (1777) is the first substantial essay by an Italian critic and the first seriously to counteract Voltaire's classicist bias. Baretti was a friend of Dr *Johnson, and the 'Discours' is permeated by the influence of Johnson's prefaces; however, the importance of the essay goes beyond a vigorous defence of Shakespeare's 'irregularities' for—by affirming the idea of the artist's freedom—Baretti prepared the ground for the *Romantic debate and pointed to Shakespeare as the figure in whose name the new ideas on art were to be championed. The Romantic battle was fought in Italy in essentially the same terms as in the rest of Europe. It was inspired by the translation, which appeared in 1817, of the influential *Course of Dramatic Literature* by A. W. *Schlegel and by the works of Mme de Staël (*De la littérature*, 1800, *De l'Allemagne*, 1813, and the essay 'On the Manner and Utility of Translations', 1816). Although a few well-known critics attacked Staël's ideas, in the end the opinion of her defenders (Berchet, Pellico, Visconti, Tommaseo) prevailed. But it was mainly the critical work of Alessandro Manzoni, especially his 'Lettre à M. Chauvet sur l'unité de temps et de lieu dans la tragédie' (1819, pub. 1823), that most contributed to overcoming the idea of Shakespeare as undisciplined genius in whose work beauty is an unpremeditated effect. So much so that when the critic Pagani-Cesa revived the objections of the classicists (*Sovra il teatro tragico italiano*, 1825), he met with universal opposition. Even one of the artificers of the Italian 'Risorgimento' and of Italian national unity, Giuseppe Mazzini, in two articles published in the 1830s in *Antologia*, a critical journal of the Romantics, engaged in a vigorous defence of the Romantic perspective, producing critical observations of remarkable insight. The next critic who deserves to be mentioned is Francesco de Sanctis; in his twelve lectures on Shakespeare, held in Naples in 1846–7 and published only in 1919 and in 1926 by Benedetto Croce, and in his imposing *Storia della letteratura italiana* (1870–1), Shakespeare is discussed in a critically conscious perspective which is far from both the neoclassicist bias and the Romantic excess. In 1919, Croce published his seminal essay 'Ariosto, Shakespeare, Corneille', in which he pleads against biographism, dismantles the moralistic criticism *à la* Tolstoy as being simplistic, and argues for a reading of Shakespeare's world as a world of insoluble contrasts. Starting in the 1930s, the critical activity of Mario Praz gave an unprecedented impulse to English studies. His brilliant writings on the 17th century significantly contributed to preparing the ground for the study of Shakespeare. Since the 1960s, the academic study of Shakespeare has flourished in Italy, with most major schools of contemporary criticism ably represented. In the 1990s, Italy's first chair of 'Shakespeare criticism' was held by Agostino Lombardo, who is also editor of a series on Shakespeare.

The first translation of a Shakespeare passage was that of Hamlet's soliloquy 'To be or not to be' by Paolo Rolli (1739), and the first translation of a play was that of *Julius Caesar* by Domenico Valentini (1756); late 18th-century translations include *Othello* and *Hamlet* by Alessandro Verri, and *Othello*, *Macbeth*, and *Coriolanus* by Giustina Renier Michiel. During the first two decades of the 19th century, Michele Leoni translated the tragedies and published them in separate volumes. The first complete prose translation was attempted by Carlo Rusconi (1838), and the first complete verse translation by Giulio Carcano (1875–82), who called Shakespeare 'the inspirer of all modern literature'. The first attempt at translating the Sonnets was made by Oliveri (1890), who was followed by de Marchi (1891), Sanfelice (1898), and Darchini (1908). Between 1911 and 1934, Diego Angeli produced another verse translation of the complete plays. Praz edited a translation of the *Complete Plays* by various authors (1943–7); in 1961 there appeared a translation of the complete plays by Cesare Vico Lodovici, followed in 1964 by that of Gabriele Baldini. Melchiori edited and introduced a translation of the *Complete Plays* by various authors (1976–91). Translations by various authors are in progress for the publisher Garzanti; Lombardo is translating the complete plays in separate volumes. There have been several translations of the Sonnets (the most important are those, with introductions and annotations, by Melchiori, 1965, and Serpieri, 1991); selections have been translated by a few poets (Quasimodo, Montale, Ungaretti); Q1 of *Hamlet* has been edited, introduced, and translated by Serpieri (1997). Actor and playwright Eduardo de Filippo has translated *The Tempest* into Neapolitan dialect (1984).

The first musical and choreographic adaptation of a Shakespeare play was a *ballet inspired by *Othello* by choreographer and dancer Salvatore Viganò (1820). But adaptations and rewritings of Shakespeare plays have mainly concerned the musical theatre. The operas by Giuseppe *Verdi (*Macbeth*, 1847: libretto by F. M. Piave, in collaboration with A. Maffei;

Otello, 1887, and *Falstaff*, 1893: librettos by Arrigo Boito, who also wrote a libretto for F. A. Faccio's *Amleto*, 1865) greatly contributed to a wider knowledge of Shakespeare's work. Other Italian opera composers and musicians were also inspired by Shakespeare's plays: Rossini (*Otello*, 1816), Zandonai (*Giulietta e Romeo*, 1922), and Malipiero (*Giulio Cesare*, 1935 and *Antonio e Cleopatra*, 1938). In the years immediately following the Second World War, Castelnuovo-Tedesco composed *33 Shakespeare Songs* from Shakespeare's plays. Adaptations and rewritings have been attempted, among others, by Giovanni Testori (*Ambleto*, 1972 and *Macbetto*, 1974) and Carmelo Bene (*Otello*, *Riccardo III*, and different versions of *Hamlet* from Laforgue's French translation).

The staging of Shakespeare's plays in Italy started later than in other European countries. At the end of the 18th century, there were two isolated attempts at interpretations of abridged texts of *Hamlet* by Antonio Morrocchesi (1791) and Francesco Menichelli (1795). During the first half of the 19th century, other isolated attempts, including *Othello*, first interpreted by Francesco Lombardi and later by Gustavo Modena, who is considered the master of all later Shakespearian interpreters, did not meet with the favour of the public. Modena's production, based on a rather mangled text, was taken by the audience as a farce, and loudly hissed and interrupted. The first Italian actor who may be considered a Shakespeare interpreter is Alamanno Morelli, a pupil of Modena who, using texts that he himself reduced, was a neuropathic Hamlet (1850) and, later, a remarkable Macbeth. But the first who attracted the attention of the public and who seriously tackled the question of the interpretation of Shakespeare's characters was Ernesto *Rossi. His acting style (between 1856 and 1896 he played Othello, Hamlet, Romeo, Macbeth, Richard III, Lear, Prospero, Mark Antony, Brutus, and Shylock) appeared romantically exuberant and instinctive, but was sustained by strenuous study. If Rossi is mainly remembered as Hamlet, Tommaso *Salvini became legendary as Othello (his interpretation inspired Verdi's opera). From the 1850s until 1903, he interpreted various roles (Lear, Hamlet, Macbeth, Coriolanus, Romeo, and, towards the end of his career, Iago) in a classic vein that was especially praised for the perfect control of the expressive means. Adelaide Ristori was the most notable 19th-century female interpreter of Shakespeare. She is mainly remembered as Lady Macbeth, a role that she constructed as a monstrous figure, in a tragic style of great impact. In the last two decades of the century, Giovanni Emanuel, generally appreciated for his versatility, interpreted Hamlet, Othello, and Lear. Ermete Novelli is remembered as Shylock, a role in which he gave proof of his talent as a mime, in a comic vein deriving from the *commedia dell'arte* characters; in her twenties, the great Eleonora Duse played Juliet, Ophelia, Cordelia, and Desdemona and was later to be a memorable Cleopatra (1888). A new style, tending towards naturalistic interpretation, was that of Ermete Zacconi who, in the first years of the 20th century, played the roles of Hamlet, Macbeth, Othello, and Petruccio. Mario Fumagalli was especially successful as protagonist and director of *King Lear* (1910). Between the 1890s and the 1940s, Ruggero Ruggeri was a spiritual Hamlet, a subtle Iago, a tormented Macbeth, and a brilliant Jaques, with tones which exalted the phonic values of the Italian language. In the 1930s, Alessandro Morissi was the first of a long line of 'Freudian' Hamlets. Starting in the 1950s, Renzo Ricci interpreted Hamlet, Mercutio, Achilles, Petruccio, Richard III, and Lear, relying on a voice of exceptional musicality. In the post-war years, the emphasis shifted from actor to production: directors like Luchino Visconti, Luigi Squarzina, Franco Enriquez, Luca Ronconi, Orazio Costa, and Gabriele Lavia have elaborated different directorial styles for the interpretation of Shakespeare. Giorgio *Strehler, with his twelve productions of Shakespeare plays, was certainly the most intellectually alert and innovative of the Italian directors. Of special interest are the experiments of Carmelo Bene, the *enfant terrible* of Italian theatre, who produced a series of textual manipulations (using the formula: 'from Shakespeare according to C.B.') which he staged and interpreted in a highly sophisticated style of great visual, acoustic, and conceptual impact. Bene staged five different versions of *Hamlet* from Shakespeare-Laforgue (*Amleto*, 1961, 1967, and 1974; *Hommelette for Hamlet*, 1987 and *Hamlet Suite*, 1994); *Romeo e Giulietta* (1976); *Richard III* (1977); *Othello* (1979); and *Macbeth* (1983). Starting in the 1970s, a close collaboration of directors with academic critics (Strehler and Squarzina with Lombardo, Lavia with Serpieri) has been one of the most interesting features of the staging of Shakespeare's plays. *PP*

Bragaglia, L., *Shakespeare in Italia* (1973)
d'Amico, S. (ed.), *Enciclopedia dello spettacolo* (9 vols., 1954–62)
Lombardo, A., 'Shakespeare in Italy', *Proceedings of the American Philosophical Society*, 141/4 (1997)
Rasi, L., *I comici italiani* (3 vols., 1897–1905)

'It was a lover and his lass', sung by two pages in *As You Like It* 5.3.15; composed by Thomas *Morley and published in 1600, the same year as the first performance of the play. If the song came out before the play, then the words may not be by Shakespeare; much discussion has centred on this issue. The song's lack of dramatic function, unusual in the plays, does make it seem like an *interpolation. *JB*

'It was the Friar of orders grey', fragment of a bawdy ballad sung by Petruccio in *The Taming of the Shrew* 4.1.131. The original tune is unknown; see Pete Seng, *The Vocal Songs in the Plays of Shakespeare* (1967) for the complete text. *JB*

Jackson, Sir Barry (1879–1961), English manager, director, designer, and playwright, the founder of the Birmingham Repertory Theatre in 1913. Using his own substantial inheritance, Jackson funded the first purpose-built regional theatre in Britain and Ireland, which he made into a laboratory for theatrical experiment and change. He produced a wide range of work in Birmingham, London, and at the Malvern Festival, which he founded in 1929, that invigorated British theatre between the wars. He had two important managerial connections to Shakespeare. First, he mounted three modern-dress productions in the 1920s which insisted that a Shakespeare for the post-war generation required the light of contemporary fashions, manners, and politics. *Cymbeline* (1923) remained in Birmingham but *Hamlet* 'in plus-fours' (1925, the year he was knighted) and *Macbeth* set in the Great War (1928) moved to London and international fame. (Though they are rightly associated with Jackson's name, only *Cymbeline* was directed by him, the other two by his regular colleague A. J. Ayliff.) Second, from 1945 to 1948 Jackson was director of the Shakespeare Memorial Theatre; his first move was to bring along the young Peter *Brook and Paul *Scofield as part of a revitalization of moribund Stratford traditions. *DK*

Jackson, John, Shakespeare's fellow trustee in the purchase of the *Blackfriars Gatehouse, possibly the Yorkshire-born merchant (*c.*1575–1625) of this name, a frequenter of the *Mermaid Tavern, who married Elias *James's sister-in-law. *SW*

Jacobean tragedy, a term used for a cluster of sombre dramatic works dating from the reign of *James I (1603–25). Although most of Shakespeare's own mature tragedies belong to this period, the term usually refers to non-Shakespearian works, of which the principal examples are *The Revenger's Tragedy* (1607, by Tourneur or *Middleton), John *Webster's *The White Devil* (1612) and *The Duchess of Malfi* (1613), Middleton's *The Changeling* (with Rowley, 1622) and *Women Beware Women* (1627); Ford's *'Tis Pity She's a Whore* (1633), which may be post-Jacobean, is usually included. Once overshadowed by Shakespeare, these works were redeemed by the critical essays of T. S. *Eliot in the 1920s. *CB*

Jacobi, Sir Derek (b. 1936), English actor. After playing Hamlet as a schoolboy with the National Youth Theatre, he went up to Cambridge where his many roles included Prince Hal and Edward II. His student performance in Marlowe's tragedy, repeated out of doors at Stratford-upon-Avon, led to his engagement at the Birmingham Repertory Theatre. As a founder member of Laurence *Olivier's National Theatre 1963–71, he played Laertes, Cassio, Touchstone, and the King in *Love's Labour's Lost.* From 1971 he played with the Prospect Company in London and on tour; his roles included Hamlet. In 1982 he was Benedick and Prospero at the *Royal Shakespeare Company to which he returned in 1993 as Macbeth. He appears in Kenneth *Branagh's films of *Henry V* (Chorus) and *Hamlet* (Claudius). Though sometimes regarded as a golden-voiced Shakespearian, he has given subtle performances on television and in films. *MJ*

Jaggard, William (fl. 1591–1623) and **Isaac** (fl. 1613–27), printers and publishers of the Shakespeare First Folio. William Jaggard was admitted to the Stationers' Company in 1591, after which he rose quickly in the book trade and acquired a number of key monopolies: he leased the rights to publish playbills from James Roberts; he obtained the sole rights to print the Ten Commandments (a royal warrant of 1604 ordered all parish churches to display copies of the Ten Commandments printed exclusively by William Jaggard); and in 1610 he secured the position of printer to the City of London.

Jaggard produced sermons, Puritan devotionals, illustrated books of heraldry and science, popular ballads, and literature, including *The Passionate Pilgrim* (1599) with its title-page attribution to 'W. Shakespeare'. Some authors complained about the frequency of typographic errors in books from Jaggard's press. Thomas Heywood claimed that Jaggard's refusal to include an errata slip in *Troia Britanica* (1609) was calculated to place 'fault upon the neck of the author'. The printing shop's errors may be attributable to William Jaggard's failing eyesight, probably a result of a sexually transmitted disease and its treatment. His son Isaac was admitted to the Stationers' Company in 1613 and no doubt assumed increasing responsibilities for the family business as his father's blindness progressed.

In 1619, the Jaggards printed nine quartos of Shakespeare's plays for the publisher Thomas Pavier. These individual quartos were intended to be bound together to form a collection. The King's Men apparently heard about Pavier's planned collection and invoked the protection of authority. In May of that year, the Lord Chamberlain ordered that 'no plays that his majesty's players do play' should be printed without their consent. It seems that presswork was already completed on a number of these quartos, which are correctly dated '1619', but others were falsely dated, probably with the intention to pass them off as remainders of earlier editions.

Despite the Jaggards' association with Pavier's illicit project, the King's Men turned to them when they were planning the authorized collection of Shakespeare's plays. Work on the First Folio began early in 1622 and was not

completed until late in 1623. By early November, William Jaggard had died. He is named in the colophon as one of the publishers and Isaac is named on the title page as the printer. *ER*

Hinman, Charlton, *The Printing and Proof-Reading of the Shakespeare First Folio* (1963)
Bracken, James K., and Silver, Joel (eds.), *British Literary Booktrade, 1475–1700* (1996)

jailers. (1) A jailer takes Egeon into custody, *Comedy of Errors* 1.1.156. (2) A jailer has custody of Antonio, *Merchant of Venice* 3.3 (mute part). (3) A jailer refuses to let Paulina see Hermione but brings Emilia to her and allows her to take baby Perdita, *The Winter's Tale* 2.2. (4) Two jailers imprison Posthumus, *Cymbeline* 5.5.94. One discusses hanging with him, 5.5.245 ff. (5) A jailer consents to an unorthodox cure for his mad daughter, *The Two Noble Kinsmen* 5.4. *AB*

Jailer's Brother. He captures the Jailer's Daughter and brings her back to her father, *The Two Noble Kinsmen* 4.1. *AB*

Jailer's Daughter. She sets Palamon free, *The Two Noble Kinsmen* 2.6, and is driven mad by unrequited love for him. *AB*

James I (1566–1625), King of England (reigned 1603–25). Elizabeth I's distant cousin James VI, King of Scotland, succeeded her on the English throne in 1603. He had been a notable patron of drama in Scotland, and himself composed a masque for the Marquess of Huntley's marriage in Edinburgh in 1588. One of his first official acts as King of England was to take the major theatrical companies under the patronage of members of the royal family. Shakespeare's company, the Lord *Chamberlain's Men, became the King's Men. This testifies to their pre-eminence in the London theatre world, and constituted an important social advancement for the players, who, as members of the royal household, wore the royal livery and were thereby raised to the gentry. They thereafter formally referred to themselves as Gentlemen, the King's Servants. They entertained the King regularly, often with plays by Shakespeare (see REVELS OFFICE AND ACCOUNTS): there were Jacobean court performances during Shakespeare's lifetime of *Othello, The Merry Wives of Windsor, Measure for Measure, The Comedy of Errors, Henry V, Love's Labour's Lost, The Merchant of Venice, King Lear, The Tempest, The Winter's Tale, Julius Caesar, Much Ado About Nothing, The Two Noble Kinsmen* and *Cardenio* (Shakespeare's two collaborations with Fletcher, the latter now lost), and possibly also of *As You Like It, A Midsummer Night's Dream*, and both parts of *Henry IV*. Of the 20 plays presented at court by the King's Men during the Christmas season preceding the wedding of James's daughter Princess *Elizabeth to the Elector Palatine in 1613, eight were by Shakespeare. Though there is no record of a court performance of *Macbeth*, the play is deeply cognizant of the company's royal patron, both in its treatment of Banquo, James's ancestor (who in the chronicles is fully Macbeth's accomplice in the murder of Duncan, but is entirely exculpated by Shakespeare), and in its extensive focus on *witchcraft, a subject on which James considered himself an expert. The apparition that the witches summon up for Macbeth—a vision of eight generations of Scottish kings descending from Banquo—brings the play down to the present: the eighth generation is James's mother Mary Stuart, the eighth king is King James. It has been suggested, plausibly, though not all editors agree, that the moment following this, when the witches conclude their ominous predictions and perform songs and dances to 'show the best of our delights | That this great king may kindly say | Our duties did his welcome pay' (4.1.147–8), indicates that the text of the play included in the *Folio (the only surviving text) was prepared specifically for a performance before King James. Elements of the Jacobean royal style have also been detected in the Duke's withdrawal from the court and from active governance in *Measure for Measure*, in the occulted language of *Cymbeline* and *The Winter's Tale*, and in the quasi-mystical idealization of monarchy in *Macbeth, The Winter's Tale*, and *All Is True* (*Henry VIII*). *SO*

Goldberg, Jonathan, *James I and the Politics of Literature* (1983)
Willson, David H., *King James VI and I* (1967)

James, Elias. See 'EPITAPH ON ELIAS JAMES'.

James, Henry (1843–1916), American novelist and essayist. James directly refers to Shakespeare in memoirs, letters, prefaces, notebooks, and criticism; and indirectly, as a 'precedent', through novels such as *The Portrait of a Lady* (1881), *The Princess Casamassima* (1886), and *The Tragic Muse* (1890). Between 1873 and 1896 he reviewed eleven productions of Shakespeare, and *The Birthplace* (1903) reflects on the life of the artist, through the caretakers of a Shakespeare shrine in Stratford. James admired the works for 'realist' rather than 'symbolist' qualities, but in 1903 expressed scepticism of either Shakespeare's (or indeed *Bacon's) actual authorship of the plays. *TM*

James, Richard (1592–1638), librarian. Writing to Sir Richard Bourchier around 1625, James observed that because in the play '*Harrie the fift*' (for *Henry IV*?), Sir John *Oldcastle's name seriously had offended 'personages descended from his title', Shakespeare was forced to change the name 'Oldcastle' to 'Falstaff'. *PH*

James I theory. One of the less widely publicized lunacies of the *Authorship Controversy, the claim that James I found time from his duties as King of Scotland and England to write the Shakespeare canon was first made, for no obvious reason, by Malcolm Little, later known as Malcolm X, during a debate in the Norfolk Prison Colony in Massachusetts. *MD*

Churchill, R. C., *Shakespeare and his Betters* (1958)
[Haley, Alex], *The Autobiography of Malcolm X* (1965)

Jameson, Anna Brownell (1794–1860), Anglo-Irish writer. Her *Memoirs of the Loves of the Poets* (1829) may be the first to suggest that some of the Sonnets are addressed in the Earl of Southampton's name to Elizabeth Vernon. *Characteristics of Women* (1832) uses Shakespeare's heroines as role-models to provide an antidote to 'the condition of women in society, as at present constituted, [which] is false in itself, and injurious to them'. *TM*

Jamy, Captain. He is a Scot in *Henry V* who has a conversation with *Fluellen and *MacMorris, 3.3. *AB*

Janssen bust, Shakespeare's funerary monument, erected in *Holy Trinity church, Stratford-upon-Avon, after his death in 1616. Traditionally attributed to Geerhart Janssen (sometimes Anglicized to Garret Johnson), the bust is thought to post-date the poet's death by four years. The work comprises a limestone bust lodged under a classicized pediment surmounted by the poet's coat of arms and two putti. Beneath the effigy is an inscription written in rhyming couplets. Little is known of the obscure sculptor who executed the bust. An English sculptor of Dutch origin, Janssen (the younger) pursued his father's profession: Geerhart Janssen the elder, an immigrant from the duchy of Gelderland, is likely to have been his teacher. Several derivative versions and copies exist, including a free-standing bust and plaster copy of the head (both at the *National Portrait Gallery) and a plaster copy of the effigy, pediment, and embellishments (*Folger Collection). Despite the bust's evident acceptance by the playwright's family and friends as at least an adequate likeness, Shakespeare's admirers have usually preferred to imagine him as the more dashing, less corpulent figure depicted in the *Chandos and *Soest portraits. *CT*

Japan. When the works of Shakespeare first became fully accessible to theatre audiences and readers in Japan, their author had been dead for almost two centuries and a half. When he was alive and active, Japan still retained its ties with other countries and so Shakespeare may have

King James I and VI, patron of Shakespeare's acting company from 1603, painted by Mytens, 1621. The portrait characteristically incorporates James's chosen motto, 'Beati pacifici' ('blessed are the peacemakers').

Shakespeare's monument in Holy Trinity church, Stratford-upon-Avon, *c.*1620, by Geerhart Janssen.

been known to some Japanese, but no record remains to prove this. From the early 16th century onwards, the Japanese government consistently tightened control over visitors from abroad and for more than two centuries Japan had virtually no contact with the rest of the world. When the country reopened its gate in 1854, it started to 'modernize' itself by importing every kind of product of Western civilization. Literature was no exception, and Shakespeare was eagerly received as the epitome of high culture.

This does not mean, however, that his plays were easily accessible to the general public. In order to make them accessible, the earliest translators of Shakespeare chose one of two ways. They either retold them as stories in prose, just as Charles and Mary *Lamb had done—the Lambs' *Tales from Shakespeare* was also translated—or they adapted them as the kind of drama most familiar to the general public, namely Kabuki. Thus the first full-scale Japanese production of Shakespeare, *Sakura-doki Zeni no Yononaka* (*Cherry Blossom Time and Money Makes the World Go Around*) (1885) was a Kabuki adaptation of *The Merchant of Venice* performed by Kabuki actors.

Such flirtation with the indigenous tradition can be found even in the works of the major translator of Shakespeare, Shoyo Tsubouchi. The first translation of Shakespeare he published was that of *Julius Caesar*, and while it retained virtually all the speeches in the original, it also contained a lot of descriptive passages which are not in the original at all and the whole work reads like a script for Bunraku puppet theatre. Eventually Tsubouchi translated the complete canon of Shakespeare and later translations show his effort to move away from the world of Kabuki and Bunraku. This had its irony because the more faithful to Shakespeare he tried to be the more he realized the difficulty of inventing an adequate style in Japanese. In grammar, syntax, and metrical system Japanese shares nothing with English, and if one tries to obey the prosodic principles of Japanese, as some earlier translators did, the result is likely to be both verbose and ludicrous. The sense of difficulty was shared by two of Tsubouchi's successors, Tsuneari Fukuda and Junji Kinoshita. They both tried to find a style neither too archaic (as Tsubouchi's style sometimes tends to be) nor too colloquial and prosaic, and to a considerable extent they succeeded in creating a new kind of theatre language. Their translations are totally unlike a Kabuki script, and naturally enough they were used by actors of the Shingeki school rather than Kabuki.

Shingeki, which literally means 'new theatre' or 'new drama', began as an attempt to produce a Japanese equivalent of modern realistic theatre in Europe. It suffered from a lack of accurate historical perspective because literary works belonging to different historical periods were introduced to Japan simultaneously. The fact that the two playwrights who were most popular among the first Shingeki artists were Shakespeare and *Ibsen would show the intrinsic paradox of the genre. It also suffered from a lack of tradition because it tried to establish itself by revolting against the old and popular genre, Kabuki. Thus it used to be unthinkable for Shingeki actors to work with Kabuki actors in the same production, and for many decades Western plays, including plays by Shakespeare, were performed only by Shingeki actors.

After the end of the Second World War the situation gradually changed and there were attempts to fill the gap between the old and the new. Probably the epoch-making production was *Richard III* (1964) directed by Tsuneari Fukuda in which the central character was played by a noted Kabuki actor with Shingeki actors playing supporting roles. Today such productions are quite common and one of the most memorable would be *Macbeth* (1976) with a Kabuki actor who specializes in female roles playing Lady Macbeth. The director was Toshikiyo Masumi, who as a leading member of Haiyu-za (Actor's Theatre), one of the most influential Shingeki companies, has also presented a number of more modernist-oriented Shakespearean productions. Younger directors such as Yukio *Ninagawa and Tadashi Suzuki use techniques of Noh and Kabuki more extensively and consciously, and their productions, when successful, can be understood as a happy fusion of the indigenous and the alien. Thus Shakespearian productions in Japan began by following the rules of the tradition and then tried to reject them and finally accepted them again in a more sophisticated way.

Perhaps a similar favourable change is to be found in Shakespearian scholarship in Japan as well. English is the most widely studied foreign language in the country and most major universities have an English department where Shakespeare often occupies a central place in the curriculum. Unfortunately, however, works of Japanese scholars used to be little known outside Japan mainly because most of them were written in Japanese and more often than not they were imitative of the works of scholars from English-speaking countries. But the situation has changed. In 1991 the Shakespeare Society of Japan, which was established in 1962 and has more than 800 members, hosted the 5th World Congress of the *International Shakespeare Association in Tokyo, and scholars from abroad realized that Japanese Shakespearians today have a more comfortable relation with their own culture and tradition than their predecessors.

The best-known Shakespeare-related works from Japan, however, are the films of Akira *Kurosawa. *Throne of Blood* (1957), *The Bad Sleep Well* (1960), and *Ran* (1985) transposed *Macbeth*, *Hamlet*, and *King Lear* to a Japanese setting, and the result was an intriguing interpretation of Shakespeare. Less well known but no less significant is a group of literary works inspired by Shakespeare. One should mention novels and short stories based on *Hamlet* such as *The Diary of Claudius* (1912) by Naoya Shiga (1883–1971), *The Testament of Ophelia* (1931) by Hideo Kobayashi (1902–83), *The New Hamlet* (1941) by Osamu Dazai (1909–48), and *Hamlet's Diary* (1955) by Shohei Ooka (1909–88). Japanese intellectuals have been fascinated by this particular play, and again their interpretation shows what can happen when an encounter takes place between two apparently different but similarly old traditions. Transplanting Shakespeare to Japanese soil has not been easy, but it seems he has firmly taken root. *TK*

Sasayama, Takashi, Mulryne, J. R., and Shewring, Margaret (eds.), *Shakespeare and the Japanese Stage* (1998)
Uéno, Yoshiko (ed.), *Hamlet and Japan* (1995)

Jaquenetta, 'a country wench', is courted by Costard and Armado in *Love's Labour's Lost*. *AB*

Jaques (traditionally pronounced Jay-quees). A lord attending Duke Senior, who is living in banishment in *As You Like It*. Though melancholy and moralistic, he says he is 'ambitious for a motley coat' (2.7.43) (that is, he wants to be a jester) and is said by the Duke to have been a 'libertine' (2.7.65). He banters with Orlando (3.2) and 'Ganymede' (4.1) and dissuades Touchstone from marrying Audrey in the woods (3.3).

*Hazlitt considered him to be 'the only purely contemplative character in Shakespeare' (1817), and because of the breadth and depth of his musings his lines have often been conflated with Shakespeare's own voice, perhaps more than any other character in the works, particularly in the famous speech which begins 'All the world's a stage' (2.7.139–66). In the second half of the 20th century directors tended to react against this by casting actors capable of playing him as unattractively cynical and jaded, such as the slouching Richard *Pasco in a grubby white suit who had the air of a man who 'knew that his breath smelt vile, but also that no-one would dare tell him' (Stratford, 1973: review by Peter Thomson, *Shakespeare Survey*, 27 (1974)). *AB*

Jaques de Bois (Boys). Brother to Oliver and Orlando, he announces the restoration of Duke Senior, *As You Like It* 5.4.149–64. *AB*

jazz. The fusion of Shakespeare and jazz has been somewhat limited. The most famous jazz-inspired Shakespeare setting is Leonard Bernstein's **West Side Story* (1957), a modernized musical version of *Romeo and Juliet* (see MUSICALS). Also composed that year was Duke *Ellington's *Such Sweet Thunder*, a suite of twelve pieces for jazz orchestra inspired by Shakespeare's works and written in collaboration with Billy Strayhorn. John Dankworth's *Shakespeare & All That Jazz* (recorded by Cleo Laine) contains settings of various Shakespearian lyrics, including three for *Twelfth Night* composed originally for the City of London Festival in 1964. The work also includes the songs 'The Compleat Works' and 'Dunsinane Blues'. *IBC*

Jefford, Barbara (b. 1930), English actress. One of the most versatile and accomplished performers of her day, Jefford was able to record in 2000 that she had appeared in 32 of Shakespeare's plays. An award-winner at RADA, she came to prominence at Stratford in 1950–4, notably as the fierce Isabella of Peter *Brook's *Measure for Measure* who held an electrifying pause before kneeling to ask pardon for Angelo, sometimes for minutes at a time. She added to her repertoire of heroines at the Old Vic, 1956–62 (among them Imogen, Portia, and Lady Macbeth), and embarked on Shakespeare's maturer women as Gertrude in Peter Hall's *Hamlet*, which opened the Lyttleton auditorium at the National in 1976. A subsequent return to the RSC included appearances as Volumnia (1989, a role she repeated for the Almeida in 2000) and the Countess in *All's Well That Ends Well* (1992). *MD*

Jenkins, Thomas (fl. *c.*1568–80), master of Stratford-upon-Avon grammar school from 1575 to 1579, so probably Shakespeare's most influential teacher. He came from London, son of an 'old servant' of Sir Thomas White, founder of St John's College, Oxford, where in 1566 he took his BA and was elected to a fellowship. In the same year he was granted leave for two years 'that he may give himself to teach children'. He took his MA in 1570 and in 1572 the college granted him a lease of 'Chaucer's House' in Woodstock. He appears to have taught at Warwick before moving to Stratford in 1575. He resigned in 1579, having received £6 from his successor, Thomas *Cottom or Cottam, 'in consideration of my departure from the school of Stratford-upon-Avon'. *Fripp's suggestion that Shakespeare 'burlesqued him in the character of Sir Hugh Evans' in *The Merry Wives of Windsor* relies on the mistaken assumption that he was Welsh. *SW*

Jessica, Shylock's daughter in *The Merchant of Venice*, disguises herself as a boy to elope with Lorenzo, 2.6. *AB*

Jeweller. He appears in *Timon of Athens* 1.1 with a jewel for Timon. *AB*

Jew of Venice, The. The adaptation of *The Merchant of Venice* prepared by George Granville, Lord Lansdowne (1666–1735) in 1701 held the stage until Shakespeare's original was revived in 1740–1. Although the play loses much of its comedy, including the Gobbos, Granville's Shylock is a less tragic and dignified figure than Shakespeare's: he accepts Antonio's invitation to dinner, for example, and when asked to toast his mistress, he drinks to 'Interest upon Interest'. The play is best remembered for its prologue, in which the ghosts of Shakespeare and Dryden lament the spread of homosexuality since Shakespeare's time and Shakespeare expresses gratitude for Granville's 'polishing' of his play. *MD*

Handasyde, Elizabeth, *Granville the Polite* (1933)
Wilson, J. H., 'Granville's "Stock-Jobbing Jew" ', *Philological Quarterly*, 13 (1934)

Jews. Despite the popular belief that 'there were no Jews in Shakespeare's England', Jews in small numbers had begun returning to England not long after their expulsion in 1290. By the reign of *Elizabeth I, small groups of

Marranos—Iberian Jews who practised their faith in secret—could be found in both London and Bristol (the total number of Jews in England during the Tudor and Stuart reigns at any one time probably did not exceed 150 or so). Londoners interested in meeting those raised in the Jewish faith could visit the Domus Conversorum, a converts' house on Chancery Lane, where a handful of poor Jewish converts could be found throughout most of the 16th century.

Much of what we know about Jews who lived in Shakespeare's England comes from Iberian Inquisition records. For example, according to the prisoner of war Pedro de Santa Cruz, repatriated to Madrid in 1588, it 'is public and notorious in London' that 'by race they are all Jews, and it is notorious that in their own homes they live as such observing their Jewish rites'. We know from other testimony that these Jews observed such holidays as Passover and Yom Kippur. The community was well enough established that Salomon Cormano, the envoy of the Jewish Duke of Metilli, had no difficulty finding fellow Jews to pray with during his official visit to London in 1592.

Among the Jews residing in England during the Tudor period were Roderigo *Lopez, Elizabeth's physician, who was put to death in 1594 for conspiring against the Queen. There were also court musicians of Italian descent—the Lupos, Bassanos, and Comys—brought over by Henry VIII. Occasionally, a Jew was officially invited into the country: Marco Raphael, who resided in England for three years, was brought from Italy by Henry VIII in an unsuccessful attempt to justify Henry's divorce from Queen Catherine. Another Jew, Yehudah Menda, from Barbary, had been living in England for five years when he was publicly converted by John *Foxe in 1577 at All Hallows' church in London. One of the few Jews who was not of Iberian descent, Joachim Gaunse of Prague, served as Sir Walter *Ralegh's 'mineral man' on the Roanoke expedition, and later fell foul of local authorities in Bristol when in an argument with a local clergyman he spoke disparagingly of Jesus ('there was but one God, who had no wife nor child').

The physical presence of this small number of Jews among the many thousands of aliens living in Elizabethan London matters far less than the extraordinary preoccupation at the time with Jewish questions: Were the Jews racially and nationally different? What role should England play in the conversion and restitution of the Jews? Post-Reformation England also experienced a growing interest in the study of Hebrew and in Jewish religious practices. Jewish questions—and characters—would find their way into works of many writers of the period, including Christopher *Marlowe, John *Donne, Francis *Bacon, Thomas *Nashe, Andrew Willet, and of course, Shakespeare. *JS*

Katz, David S., *Jews in the History of England: 1485–1850* (1994)
Katz, David S., *Philo-Semitism and the Readmission of the Jews to England 1603–1655* (1982)
Roth, Cecil, *A History of the Jews in England* (1940, 3rd edn. 1960)
Shapiro, James, *Shakespeare and the Jews* (1996)

jig. (1) A lively dance; the music from Shakespeare's time is often in simple rather than compound metre.

(2) A short verse *ballad on a comic, often sexual, theme accompanied by vigorous dancing and performed in the theatre as an afterpiece to the main play (cf. Hamlet's comment on Polonius, *Hamlet* 2.2.503). Richard *Tarlton appears to have excelled in this entertainment and made it ubiquitous. Thomas *Platter describes how, after a play about Julius Caesar, 'they danced together admirably and exceedingly gracefully, according to their custom, two in each group dressed in men's and two in women's apparel', suggesting that the jig was toned down if it followed a tragedy. At the other extreme of dignity was probably the bergomask dance by Bottom and Flute after their performance as Pyramus and Thisbe in *A Midsummer Night's Dream.* *JB/GE*

Baskervill, C. R., *The Elizabethan Jig and Related Song Drama* (1929)

Joan la Pucelle. Champion of the French forces in *1 Henry VI*, her offer of body and soul to *fiends, 5.3, fails to save her from the English. Based on the national heroine of France, Joan of Arc (1412–31). Shakespeare has followed the anti-French history of *Holinshed. *AB*

Joan of Arc. See JOAN LA PUCELLE.

Jodelle, Étienne (1532–73), French dramatist and poet, member of the Pléiade, whose sonnets lamenting the poet's separation from his patron may have influenced Shakespeare's Sonnets. Jodelle's most famous work was *Cléopatre Captive*, a play published in 1553. Minor similarities between this work and *Antony and Cleopatra* are probably attributable to their common source in *Plutarch rather than to Shakespeare's familiarity with Jodelle. *JKS*

'Jog on, jog on', sung by Autolycus in *The Winter's Tale* 4.3.123; it occurs with music and two further stanzas in John Playford's *Catch That Catch Can* (1667). *JB*

John, a rebel, is among Cade's followers in *The First Part of the Contention* (*2 Henry VI*) 4.7. *AB*

John (*c.*1167–1216), King of England (reigned semi-officially during his brother Richard I's absence on the Crusades until his return in 1194, then officially after Richard's death in 1199). See KING JOHN. *AB*

John and Robert are servants of Ford in *The Merry Wives of Windsor.* They carry Falstaff in a basket, 3.3, and throw him in the Thames (3.5.4–5). *AB*

John, Don. He is Don Pedro's illegitimate brother, who conspires against Claudio and Hero in *Much Ado About Nothing* (see 1.3.60–4). *AB*

John, Friar. See FRIAR JOHN.

John Falstaff, Sir. See HENRY IV PARTS 1 and 2, MERRY WIVES OF WINDSOR, THE; OLDCASTLE, SIR JOHN.

John, Prince. See JOHN OF LANCASTER, LORD.

John, Sir. See PRIESTS.

John of Gaunt. See GAUNT, JOHN OF.

John of Lancaster, Lord. In *1 Henry IV* he is commended by Prince Harry after *Shrewsbury, and sent with Westmorland to quell the northern rebels. In *2 Henry IV*, now called Prince John of Lancaster, he sends a number of rebels to their deaths (4.1.339–49 and 4.2.70–1). Editors usually give him a small part in *Henry V* under the name of the Duke of Bedford (historically he was not at Agincourt, and in the Oxford edition his lines are given to his brother Clarence). In *1 Henry VI*, again under the name of Duke of Bedford, he is Regent of France. In 1.1 he hears of losses in France. He recaptures Orléans, 2.1, but dies of an illness before Rouen, 3.5. The third son (1389–1435) of Henry IV, he was created Duke of Bedford 1414 and Regent of France 1422. *AB*

John Oldcastle, Sir. See OLDCASTLE, SIR JOHN.

John Talbot. Talbot's son, he is killed at Bordeaux, *1 Henry VI* 4.7. He is based on Lord Lisle, who was killed by Talbot's side at Castillon in 1453. *AB*

Johnson, Arthur. See PRINTING AND PUBLISHING.

Johnson, Charles (1679–1748), playwright. He adapted *As You Like It* into **Love in a Forest* (1723), adding the 'rude mechanicals' from *A Midsummer Night's Dream* to its final act. His topical rewrite of the Induction to *The Taming of the Shrew*, *The *Cobbler of Preston* (1716), for Drury Lane competed with a play of the same title by Christopher Bullock at Lincoln's Inn Fields. *CMSA*

Johnson, Robert, a Stratford innkeeper. An inventory of his goods written on 5 October 1611 by the schoolmaster Alexander *Aspinall mentioned 'A lease of a barne that he holdeth of M[r] Shaxper, xx[li].' He had lived in Henley Street since at least 1591. The barn still belonged to

Shakespeare's granddaughter when she made her will in 1670. *SW*

Johnson, Robert (*c.*1583–1633), composer. From 1604 he was a lutenist at the court of James I; settings of songs from *Cymbeline*, *The Winter's Tale*, and *The Tempest* have been attributed to him. *JB*

Spink, Ian (ed.), *Robert Johnson: Ayres, Songs and Dialogues* (1961)

Johnson, Samuel (1709–84), essayist, lexicographer, literary historian and critic, Shakespearian editor. Johnson's edition of *The Plays of William Shakespeare* (1765) was anticipated by his initial statement and example of editorial method in the *Miscellaneous Observations on the Tragedy of Macbeth* (1745), and the formal subscription *Proposals* (1756).

Johnson's preface to his edition is one of the monuments of 18th-century criticism, and marked an important turning point from classicism towards what would become *Romanticism. His assessment of Shakespeare begins with a fundamental statement of mimetic theory: 'Nothing can please many, and please long, but just representations of general nature.' Shakespeare is distinguished as 'above all modern writers, the poet of nature'. His characters are 'the genuine progeny of common humanity', recognizable to us because they embody general truths of human experience. Hence Johnson questions the 'rules' of *neoclassical dramatic criticism. It is nonsense in his view to complain, as *Voltaire and Thomas *Rymer had done, of Shakespeare's breaches of the unities of time and place. Dramas, like other imitations, are not 'mistaken for realities, but . . . bring realities to mind'; the audience knows itself to be in a theatre, and can therefore readily accept the movement of the scene from Alexandria to Rome, and from one year to another. Equally, Johnson defends on mimetic grounds the Shakespearian mixture of *tragedy and *comedy, which exhibits 'the real state of sublunary nature, . . . in which, at the same time, the reveller is hasting to his wine, and the mourner burying his friend'.

Johnson argued for a contextualized evaluation and understanding of Shakespeare as of other writers. Shakespeare should be estimated in the light of 'the age in which he lived, and . . . his own particular opportunities'. In his *Proposals* Johnson insisted that an editor must 'endeavour to read the books which the author read, . . . and compare . . . the works of Shakespeare with those of writers who lived at the same time'. Though Johnson was less of a literary antiquary than some of his contemporaries, he possessed, through his work on the *Dictionary*, an unsurpassed knowledge of the language of Shakespeare and his contemporaries.

Johnson was a principled textual editor. In his discussion in the preface of text-editorial procedure, still an important document of its kind, Johnson asserts his understanding of the superior authority of the First *Folio (1623). He argues for a movement away from conjectural emendation and towards a determined attempt to find and explain meaning in the surviving wordings of 'the old text', a determination exemplified in the close and rigorous readings of his commentary to the plays. Though Johnson's edition is not in the fullest sense a *variorum, his notes engaged with the work of previous editors (especially those of his most immediate forerunner, *Warburton), and provided the basis of the variorum annotations of *Steevens, *Reed, and *Malone. *MLW*

Johnson on Shakespeare, ed. Arthur Sherbo (1968) (vols. vii and viii of the Yale edition of the *Works* of Samuel Johnson)
Hagstrum, Jean, *Samuel Johnson's Literary Criticism* (1967)
Jarvis, Simon, *Scholars and Gentlemen: Shakespearian Textual Criticism and Representations of Scholarly Labour, 1725–1765* (1995)
Parker, G. F., *Johnson's Shakespeare* (1989)

Johnson, William. See Blackfriars Gatehouse.

Jones, Ernest (1879–1958), Welsh psychoanalyst and biographer. His *Oedipus-Complex as an Explanation of Hamlet's Mystery* (1910) and *Hamlet and Oedipus* (1949) argue that a guilty Hamlet is reluctant to kill Claudius because of his fulfilment of Hamlet's own unconscious incestuous desires—a *Freudian theory which remains pervasive and persistent. *TM*

Jones, Inigo (1573–1652), architect and court masque designer. With his nephew-assistant John Webb, Jones brought Sebastian Serlio's perspective scenery to the English stage. Jones's finest building design, as Surveyor of Works, was the 1622 Banqueting House in Whitehall which still stands. *GE*

Orgel, Stephen, and Strong, Roy (eds.), *Inigo Jones: The Theatre of the Stuart Court* (2 vols., 1973)

Jones, James Earl (b. 1931), American actor. Jones, noted for his resonant, bass voice, is the son of actor Robert Earl Jones. His roles include Oberon (1961), Othello (1963), Claudius (1972), and Lear (1973) at the New York Shakespeare Festival, and a famous Othello, with Christopher Plummer's Iago, at Stratford, Connecticut (1981). *BR*

Jones, Robert (fl. 1597–1615), composer. He published five books of songs for voice and *lute, and one book of *madrigals. His song *'Farewell, dear heart' is quoted in *Twelfth Night* 2.3.98. *JB*

Jonson, Ben (1572–1637), poet and playwright. His father, a minister, died before Ben's birth; his mother then married a bricklayer. With financial support from an unknown patron Jonson attended Westminster School, but left early to become first his stepfather's apprentice, then a soldier in the Netherlands. By 1597 he was writing plays—mostly in collaboration with other authors—for the theatre owner Philip *Henslowe. He rapidly rose to become one of the most eminent dramatists of the Jacobean period. He published his *Works* in 1616 (an unprecedented act of self-confidence for a popular playwright), was awarded a royal pension of 100 marks a year, and spent the rest of James's reign writing court *masques, a form of entertainment which he raised to a highly sophisticated level. With the accession of *Charles I his fortunes changed. He was dropped by the court as a writer of masques, and his popularity as a playwright waned. But he remained perhaps the most respected and imitated poet of his time, and a volume of over 30 elegies on him, *Jonsonus Virbius* (1638), was published after his death.

Jonson himself was partly responsible for defining his relationship to Shakespeare. He refers, in his affectionate verses on Shakespeare in the First *Folio (1623), to his late rival's 'small Latin, and less Greek', told William Drummond in their *Conversations* of 1618–19 that Shakespeare 'wanted art', and wrote in his *Discoveries* (*c.*1630) that Shakespeare's 'wit was in his own power; would the rule of it had been so too'. All this seems to identify Shakespeare as a 'natural' phenomenon, whose easy inventiveness contrasts with Jonson's hard-won classical erudition and the scrupulous care he took over his writing. But Jonson's First Folio verses offer an extraordinarily generous tribute to the skill as well as the talent of his friend, and in his later plays—particularly *The New Inn* (1629)—he paid him the compliment of adapting the conventions of Shakespearian comedy to his own ends. Jonson was hugely inventive himself in his adaptation of classical dramatic models to the needs of the English stage, and his engagement with the radical social and economic transformations of urban life in his own time is as conspicuous in his plays as his learning. So is his engagement with politics. He was twice imprisoned for his part in writing scandalous theatrical satires (*The Isle of Dogs* (1597), with Thomas *Nashe, and *Eastward Ho* (1605), with George *Chapman and John *Marston), and his most painstakingly classical play, *Sejanus* (performed 1603), presents a devastating portrait of a corrupt political system for which he was summoned to appear before the Privy Council to answer charges of treason. He was also passionately concerned with experimental modifications to current theatrical practice. These concerns were at the root of his involvement in

Ben Jonson, Shakespeare's greatest (and fattest) colleague and rival, by Abraham van Blyenberch, c.1618.

the so-called 'War of the Theatres' between 1600 and 1602, in which he engaged, through a series of plays, in a ferocious verbal battle with some of the playwrights—including Marston and Thomas *Dekker—against whose work he sought to define his own. The main thing that distinguishes Jonson from Shakespeare is that Jonson mostly wrote about modern times and urban places—a procedure that sometimes got him into trouble—while Shakespeare, on the whole, did not.

His great comedies, *Every Man in his Humour* (1601), *Volpone* (1607), *Epicoene* (1616), *The Alchemist* (1612), and *Bartholomew Fair* (1631), offer dynamic analyses of the relationships between a wide range of social groups in the early modern city, and of the habits, economic aspirations, and linguistic peculiarities that govern each group. In the late 1590s he was the foremost exponent of the 'comedy of humours', which imagined the city in terms of the elements or 'humours' whose balance or imbalance determined the physical condition of the human body, according to contemporary medical theory. If the city is a body, the operations of its component parts are less important than the way they combine to enable the urban body to function. Jonson's tightly plotted and immaculately timed dramas, which nevertheless burst at the seams with various kinds of barely controlled linguistic and material excess, are filled with fashion victims, confidence tricksters, professionals, tradesmen, social climbers, religious bigots, whores, criminals, and members of the gentry, who, together with the institutions they represent, comprise the grotesque yet vigorous internal organs of the metropolis. Their language—ranging from rapid-fire dialogue to monomaniacal soliloquy, from luxuriant verse to jargon-ridden babble—often resembles, or mimics, the sales-pitches of stall-holders in the busy London markets, or the private negotiations between merchants and tradesmen. In their mouths everyday objects and ordinary people undergo astonishing transformations as they are enlisted in the citizens' projects to improve their social or economic fortunes. Jonson's plays are rich with theatrical performances—financial scams, entertainments, disguises, seductions, and the self-advertising gimmicks of successful or unsuccessful posers—attesting to his awareness that plays themselves are only the most conspicuous of the many theatrical devices that drive the early modern economy. They offer an unrivalled insight into the desires and anxieties of Londoners in the 1590s and 1600s.

Shakespeare's plays often have outlandish magic in them. Jonson found magic enough in the metamorphoses being worked in his own rapidly changing culture. His comedies offered a model for comic theatre which continued to hold the stage for centuries, and which arguably comes closer to modern comic conventions, on stage and on the screen, than the comedies of Shakespeare. Many people now agree that he was Shakespeare's greatest literary contemporary. *RM*

Barton, Anne, *Ben Jonson, Dramatist* (1984)
Burt, Richard, *Licensed by Authority: Ben Jonson and the Discourses of Censorship* (1993)
Donaldson, Ian, *Jonson's Magic Houses: Essays in Interpretation* (1997)
Partridge, Edward B., *The Broken Compass: A Study of the Major Comedies of Ben Jonson* (1958)

Jordan, Dorothea (1761–1816), best known as an English comic actress with a naturalistic and affecting playing style. She was an immediate success as Viola at Drury Lane in 1785. Later roles included Rosalind, Julia, Ophelia, and Imogen. She was the subject of many portraits (Hoppner, Romney, Stothard) and, during her affair with Prince William (William IV), of caricatures. *CMSA*

Tomalin, Claire, *Mrs Jordan's Profession* (1994)

Jordan, John (1746–1809), English poet and local historian. Jordan, born at Tiddington, near Stratford-upon-Avon, was educated at the village school until 1756, and was then put to learn his father's trade of wheelwright. His evident academic abilities, however, led him to seek advancement by way of antiquarian and Shakespeare studies. By 1776 he had composed *Welcombe Hills, near Stratford-upon-Avon, a Poem*, published by subscription the following year. By 1786 he had compiled a history of Stratford, eventually published by J. O. Halliwell, in a much abbreviated form, as *Original Collections on Stratford-upon-Avon* (1864). During 1790, Jordan was in correspondence with Edmond *Malone when the latter was collecting material for his biography of Shakespeare, sending him a manuscript account of Shakespeare and his relatives. This was also later edited by Halliwell as *Original Memoirs and Historical Accounts of the Families of Shakespeare and Hart* (1865). These two works are the earliest written source for much of the Shakespearian folklore circulating in the town at the end of the 18th century but the former also represents the first attempt to write a history of Stratford. In 1792 Samuel Ireland visited Stratford, and Jordan guided him round the principal sights. Ireland proved a more gullible recipient of Jordan's collection of Shakespeare folklore, some of which appeared in print for the first time in his *Picturesque Views of Shakespeare's Avon* (1795). Jordan died on 25 June 1809, and was buried alongside his wife in the churchyard of Holy Trinity, Stratford-upon-Avon. *RB*

Schoenbaum, Samuel, *Shakespeare's Lives* (1991)

Jordan (Jourdain), Margery. See BOLINGBROKE, ROGER.

Joseph, Nathaniel, Nicholas, Peter, and **Philip** are all Petruccio's servants, in attendance in *The Taming of the Shrew* 4.1. *AB*

Jourdan, Sylvester (d. 1650), traveller on board the *Sea-Adventure* in 1609 when it was wrecked off the coast of the Bermudas on its way to the English colony at Virginia. On his return to England, Jourdan published an account of his experiences called *A Discovery of the Bermudas, Otherwise Called the Isle of Devils* (1610), a likely minor source for *The Tempest.* *JKS*

journals. Shakespeare journals, in the history of their development, mirror the gradual professionalization of Shakespeare studies. In the mid-19th century they served to record the researches of amateur critics and scholars. Later they encouraged and catered for the popular enthusiasm for Shakespeare's works and, under the guidance of professional teachers, supported the first formal study of Shakespeare in the universities. In more recent years they have provided a forum for increasing academic specialization. The Shakespeare Society's *Papers* (1844–9) were the first publication which could be described as a Shakespeare journal. During the society's existence (1840–53) it issued 48 volumes of primary materials for the illustration of Shakespeare and his contemporaries, successors, and predecessors. Four of these, published at irregular intervals, were devoted to collected papers by its members, including J. P. Collier and J. O. *Halliwell-Phillipps, of insufficient length or importance to form a separate volume. Its successor, the *New Shakespeare Society, in its *Transactions* (1874–92), attempted to adopt the rigorous scientific method required of Darwin's contemporaries. Series 1 of its publications records the proceedings of its meetings, the papers read, and the discussions which followed. Contributors included F. J. *Furnivall, Sidney *Lee, William *Poel, and F. G. Fleay. Meanwhile, the *Shakespeare *Jahrbuch* of the German Shakespeare Gesellschaft, founded in 1865, had from the beginning many of the characteristics now associated with university periodicals, regular publication, with reports and reviews of performance and an exhaustive annual bibliography. Unlike its British counterparts it was not primarily a vehicle for the research of its members but a source of information for its readers. In the first decades of the society's history it had a national focus, and all material published in the *Jahrbuch* was in German until the 1890s when the first English articles appeared. Twenty years later its members included many individuals and institutions from English-speaking countries and the *Jahrbuch* became international in its scope. From 1911 until 1924 it transcended politics as the only specialist Shakespeare journal in existence. *Shakespeariana* (1883–93), the first American journal devoted to Shakespeare, put into practice its country's democratic and capitalist principles and started life as a commercial venture carrying general advertising, although it soon came under the scholarly patronage of the *New York Shakespeare Society. The journal was designed 'to furnish a recognized medium for the interchange of ideas among Shakespearian scholars' but also to encourage the popular appreciation of Shakespeare, showing a special interest in education and the work of America's Shakespeare reading societies. Its successor *New Shakespeareana* (1902–11) claimed to be 'the only magazine devoted to its exclusive field published in English'. However, the first Shakespeare journal in the USA of real significance was the *Bulletin* of the *Shakespeare Association of America, one of the aims of the society being 'to serve as a means of communication in the Shakespearean world'. It adopted the scope and ambitions of its predecessors, but under the editorship of Samuel Tannenbaum (1934–47) directed itself toward a more professional audience. The last years of the 1940s saw the birth of the two journals which now dominate Shakespeare studies: **Shakespeare Quarterly* in the USA and **Shakespeare Survey* in the UK, the former gathering wide-ranging reports of the latest scholarship and criticism, the latter produced annually and having a thematic focus. *Shakespeare Newsletter*, founded by Louis Marder in 1951, serves more informally as a bulletin of news, events, and publications. Shakespeare journals such as **Shakespeare Studies* and *Shakespeare Yearbook*, published in annual hardback volumes, have since come into existence to provide more generous receptacles for the ever-increasing flow of writing by academics. As Shakespeare studies in English-speaking countries reach saturation point these journals have become increasingly specialized: *Shakespeare Translation*, later *Shakespeare Worldwide* (1974–95); *Shakespeare on Film Newsletter* (1976–92); *Shakespeare and Schools* (1987–94); and an entire journal dedicated to a single play, **Hamlet Studies* (1979–). Elsewhere in the world, where there is an active Shakespeare society there is usually a Shakespeare journal, for example *Magyar Shakespeare-tár* (Hungary, 1908–22), *Shakespeare Renaissance* (China, 1933–5), **Shakespeare Studies* (Japan), *Shakespeare in Southern Africa* (South Africa, 1987–), *Folio* (the Netherlands, 1993–). Shakespeare's dominance in English studies has ensured that articles on his life and works appear frequently in general periodicals such as **Notes and Queries*, *Studies in Bibliography*, *Review of English Studies*. To assist the reader through this flood of material, which in 1997 was running at 4,789 items per year, bibliographies and bibliographical guides have proliferated, the most useful of which are the annual *World Shakespeare Bibliography*, published with *Shakespeare Quarterly*, and the Garland Shakespeare Bibliographies series. *SLB*

Joyce, James (1882–1941), Irish writer. In the novel *Ulysses* (published by Shakespeare and Company, 1922), chapter IX (Scylla and Charybdis) is set in the director's office of the National Library in Dublin. The hero, Stephen Dedalus, discusses Shakespeare with the poet George Russell (AE), John Eglinton, and the librarian Lyster. Following the Danish critic Georg *Brandes, Joyce (through Stephen) ironically 'proves by algebra that Hamlet's grandson is Shakespeare's grandfather and that he himself is the ghost of his own father'. In fact, fatherhood and creativity remain a central mystery of both *Hamlet* and *Ulysses*. *TM*

Jubilee. David *Garrick's pioneering festival of *bardolatry, held at Stratford-upon-Avon, was originally intended to celebrate the bicentenary of Shakespeare's birth in April 1764, but in the event took place in early September five years later (to mark the opening of the new town hall, without clashing with the London theatrical season). Garrick, who had been invited to organize the festivities by the town's corporation, presented Stratford with a painting by Gainsborough of himself with a bust of Shakespeare (later destroyed by fire), and a copy of *Scheemakers's statue of Shakespeare, which is still displayed in a niche on the town hall's west front.

The Jubilee lasted three days, during which Stratford was crowded with fashionable visitors from London: its ceremonies included a Grand Parade of Shakespeare's Characters, a masquerade ball (at which James Boswell appeared as a Corsican chief), a performance of *Arne's oratorio *Judith*, horse-racing, and firework displays. Only the indoor events survived the torrential rain which dogged the Jubilee from first to last, but fortunately Garrick had commissioned a special temporary 1,000-seat auditorium (the Jubilee Rotunda, close to what is now the site of the Royal Shakespeare Theatre) for its climax, his own performance of his poem *An Ode upon Dedicating a Building, and Erecting a Statue, to Shakespeare, at Stratford-upon-Avon*, set to music by Thomas Arne. The Ode was prefaced by a rehearsed interruption by an actor, Thomas King, whom Garrick had planted in the audience to complain, in the character of a Frenchified aristocratic fop, that Shakespeare was a low and overrated English provincial: his objections were patriotically met by a pseudo-impromptu speech in reply from Garrick, and comprehensively quashed by the Ode itself, which anticipates much *Romantic writing about Shakespeare in its emphasis on his power to create his own world, peopled by his own characters.

The Jubilee attracted enormous publicity across Europe, and helped establish both the worldwide status of Shakespeare as Britain's foremost cultural product and the fame of Stratford as a site of secular pilgrimage. (Many aspects of its design still structure the *birthday celebrations held in Stratford every April.) The rain-drenched gaudiness of Garrick's festival, however, and especially the prices charged by Stratford's landlords, came in for a good deal of satire (including George Colman's play *Man and Wife; or, The Shakespeare Jubilee*), though no one at the time seems to have been bothered by the fact that the Jubilee's proceedings did not include the performance of a single line from Shakespeare's works. On his return to London, Garrick simultaneously recouped the money he had lost on the event and reappropriated the criticism it had received by rapidly composing his own part-satirical afterpiece depicting the event, *The Jubilee*. Punctuated by the songs Garrick had written for the festival (including 'The Will of all Wills was a Warwickshire Will', which went on to become the official anthem of the Royal Warwickshire Regiment), and culminating in a rain-free staging of the Grand Procession, this became one of Garrick's most popular and lucrative plays. *MD*

Deelman, Christian, *The Great Shakespeare Jubilee* (1964)
Dobson, Michael, *The Making of the National Poet* (1992)
England, Martha W., *Garrick's Jubilee* (1964)
Garrick, David, *The Jubilee*, in *The Plays of David Garrick*, ed. H. W. Pedicord and F. L. Bergmann (6 vols., 1981), vol. ii
Stochholm, Johanne M., *Garrick's Folly* (1964)

'Judas Maccabeus' is the part Holofernes unsuccessfully attempts in the performance of 'The *Nine Worthies' in *Love's Labour's Lost* 5.2. Maccabeus (d. 161 BC) led the Judaeans against the Syrians, but the aristocrats insist on muddling him with Judas Iscariot, the disciple who betrayed Christ and then, according to legend, hanged himself. *AB*

Judith Shakespeare: A Romance, a sentimental novel by William Black (1841–98), published in 1884, is a fanciful account, with much geographical, historical, and local Stratfordian colour, of Thomas *Quiney's courtship of Shakespeare's daughter. Quiney's fidelity during Judith's delirious fever, medically supervised by Dr John *Hall, provides the touching conclusion. *CMSA*

Julia, in love with Proteus in *The Two Gentlemen of Verona*, disguises herself as 'Sebastian' to follow him. She is called Felismena in *Montemayor's *Diana*. *AB*

Juliet. **(1)** See *Romeo and Juliet*. **(2)** In *Measure for Measure* she is made pregnant by Claudio, who is condemned to death for doing so. *AB*

Julietta, Madame. This is Mistress Overdone's name for Juliet, *Measure for Measure* 1.2.71. *AB*

Julius Caesar *(see opposite page)*

Jungian criticism derives from the analytical psychology of Carl Gustav Jung (1875–1961), who postulated the existence of a collective unconscious or common racial memory manifested in recurrent images, stories, or figures, known as archetypes. These archetypes, when expressed in art, become instruments for the achievement of psychological maturity (or 'individuation') in both artist and audience. Maud Bodkin's *Archetypal Patterns in Poetry* (1934) includes an application of this to Shakespeare, as does the later criticism of Northrop *Frye. *TM*

'Juno', Jupiter's consort and goddess of marriage, is played by a spirit in *The Tempest*'s *masque of 4.1. *AB*

Jupiter, the king of the gods, helps Posthumus at the request of the ghosts of his family, and gives him a cryptic prophecy on a tablet, *Cymbeline* 5.5. *AB*

Justice. He is invited to the home of Escalus for dinner, *Measure for Measure* 2.1.266. *AB*

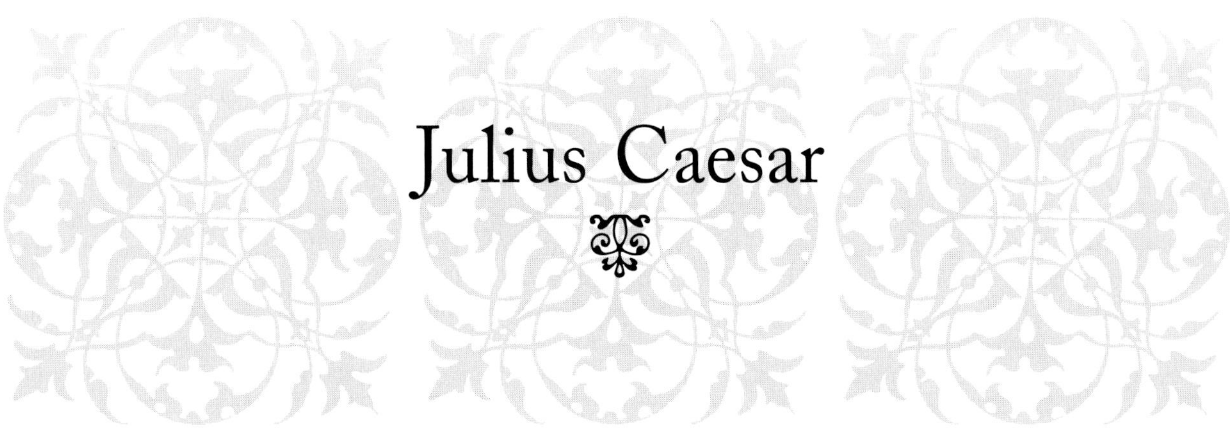

Julius Caesar

Shakespeare's most classical tragedy, as well as one of his most polished, was seen by a Swiss visitor, Thomas *Platter, on 21 September 1599: since *Julius Caesar* is not mentioned among Shakespeare's works by *Meres the previous year, draws incidentally on two works published in 1599 (Samuel Daniel's *Musophilus* and Sir John Davies's *Nosce teipsum*), and is itself alluded to in a third (Ben Jonson's *Every Man in his Humour*), this is likely to have been an early performance. In vocabulary the play has links with Shakespeare's next tragedy, *Hamlet*, while in metre it is closest to *Henry V* and *As You Like It*: it was probably composed between the two latter plays, during 1599.

Text: The play's only authoritative text is that provided by the First Folio (1623), for the most part an unusually good one, apparently prepared from a promptbook. It may record some alterations to the play made long after its première: 2.2 and 3.1, for example, seem to have been modified to allow an actor to double the roles of Cassius and Ligarius, while a line of Caesar's ridiculed as self-contradictory by Ben *Jonson in his prologue to *The Staple of News* (1625) and again in *Discoveries* (*c.*1630), 'Know Caesar doth not wrong but with just cause' (3.1.47), appears in the Folio with the offending last four words removed.

Sources: This was Shakespeare's first play to use *Plutarch's *Lives of the Noble Grecians and Romans*: it closely follows the relevant sections of Plutarch's biographies of Caesar, Brutus, and Antony, although Shakespeare compresses and transposes events at will. The Lupercal and the Ides of March, for example, which in the play seem to be successive days, are actually a month apart (see CALENDAR, SHAKESPEARE'S), while the battle of Philippi was actually two battles, the deaths of Cassius and Brutus separated by 20 days rather than the few hours which seem to intervene in the play. Plutarch, however, supplies only the barest summaries of the speeches made at Caesar's funeral by Brutus and Antony, the latter of which becomes the turning point of Shakespeare's play, as well as one of the most frequently quoted passages in the entire canon. Although here he adds material to Plutarch, in one crucial respect Shakespeare removes some: the play suppresses the detail that Brutus was suspected by many of being Caesar's illegitimate son (and that his 'unkindest cut' was delivered to Caesar's groin), exonerating him from parricide.

Synopsis: **1.1** The tribunes Flavius and Murellus rebuke a group of commoners for celebrating Caesar's victory over Pompey in the civil wars. **1.2** At the festival of the Lupercal, Caesar reminds Antony to touch his wife Calpurnia while running the ceremonial race in the hopes of curing her infertility. A soothsayer urges him to beware the Ides of March, but is dismissed as a dreamer. Left together when Caesar's party leave for the race, Brutus and Cassius discuss Caesar's increasing power, anxious, when they hear an offstage shout, that he may be proclaimed king: Cassius, working on Brutus, reminds him of his republican ancestor Lucius Junius Brutus. When Caesar returns with his followers he is angry, and asks Antony in private about the malcontented-looking Cassius: after their departure the sardonic Casca tells Cassius and Brutus how Antony offered Caesar a crown three times but he refused it, to the applause of the watching crowd, and that Murellus and Flavius have been condemned to death for removing festive decorations from images of Caesar. Brutus agrees to discuss the political situation further with Cassius, who resolves, in soliloquy, to have anonymous letters delivered to Brutus encouraging him to take an active part in a conspiracy against Caesar. **1.3** At night Casca speaks in terror of the prodigies he has seen, first to Cicero and then to Cassius, who welcomes them as omens commenting on Caesar's ambition and admits Casca to the conspiracy. Cassius sends Cinna to deliver further anonymous messages to Brutus before he and Casca go to Brutus' house to continue persuading him to join them.

2.1 In his orchard Brutus decides Caesar must be prevented from becoming a tyrant by assassination, a decision in which he is confirmed by reading the anonymous letters. His servant Lucius confirms that tomorrow is the Ides of March. Cassius, Casca, and other conspirators arrive, their faces hidden, and after a private discussion with Cassius, Brutus shakes their hands (declining to take a formal oath), ratifying their plan to kill Caesar the following day. Brutus overrules Cassius' suggestion that Caesar's close friend Antony should be killed too. Decius promises to flatter Caesar to ensure that he comes to the Capitol, where they will stab him. After the conspirators depart, Brutus' wife Portia implores him to tell her what has been on his mind, finally showing that she has wounded her own thigh to prove her stoicism: Brutus promises he will, but first admits the sickly Caius Ligarius, who is eager to join the conspiracy. **2.2** Caesar, alarmed by the omens, orders that augurers sacrifice an animal, which proves to have no heart. Calpurnia, who has dreamed of his murder, begs Caesar not to go to the Capitol, and he eventually agrees. Decius arrives, however, and persuades Caesar to change his mind, assuring him that the Senate means to crown him. Brutus and the conspirators, and Antony, arrive to accompany him to the Capitol. **2.3** Artemidorus has a letter for Caesar warning him against the conspirators. **2.4** Portia is desperately anxious for news from the Capitol.

3.1 Caesar and his party are met by the Soothsayer, who points out that the Ides of March are not yet over, and by Artemidorus, whose letter Caesar sets aside unread on the grounds that it concerns him personally. Cassius is worried that the conspiracy is about to be discovered, but Trebonius leads Antony out of the way as planned, and Metellus Cimber petitions Caesar for the repeal of his banished brother. The other conspirators kneel in his support, but Caesar insists that he is above being swayed from his purposes. Casca stabs him, followed by all the conspirators, lastly Brutus, and Caesar dies. The other senators and citizens flee: the conspirators wash their hands in Caesar's blood, planning to proclaim their act and its libertarian motives in the Forum. Antony arrives, and after asking whether they wish to kill him too, willing to die alongside Caesar, he shakes their hands, looking forward to hearing their reasons for the murder. Brutus, against Cassius' advice, permits Antony to speak at Caesar's funeral. Left alone with Caesar's body, Antony vows revenge. He tells the servant of Caesar's nephew Octavius that he means to see what his oratory can do to win over the people, after which he will discuss the future with Octavius. **3.2** Brutus ascends the pulpit before the plebeians and assures them, in prose, that though he loved Caesar he had to kill him to preserve their country's liberty: they hail him as a hero, but at his insistence they remain after his departure to hear Antony. Antony, praising the conspirators with an irony that becomes increasingly obvious, reminds the people of Caesar's virtues, shows a document he claims is his will, and, coming down from the pulpit, shows them Caesar's corpse and its wounds, inflaming them against the conspirators. Feigning unwillingness, he finally reads Caesar's will, in which according to Antony each Roman is left money and Caesar's private gardens will become public parks, upon which the crowd disperses to attack the conspirators. Hearing that Brutus and Cassius have fled the city, while Octavius and Lepidus are both at Caesar's house, he goes to join the latter. **3.3** Rioting citizens kill a poet called Cinna even though he insists that he is not the Cinna who was among the conspirators, before departing to burn the conspirators' houses.

4.1 Antony, Octavius, and Lepidus negotiate a proscription list, which includes Lepidus' brother and Antony's nephew. After Lepidus' departure Antony argues that he is not fit to share the government of Rome with them, but Octavius disagrees. They set about mustering allies and troops to meet those being raised by Brutus and Cassius. **4.2** At a private conference, Brutus accuses Cassius of betraying the conspiracy's ideals by accepting bribes: eventually they make up their quarrel, Brutus explaining his temper by revealing that he has just learned that Portia, distracted with anxiety, has killed herself. Their lieutenants Titinius and Messala are admitted to discuss strategy: Messala reports Portia's death, of which Brutus feigns a stoical acceptance. Brutus overrules Cassius, insisting that they should march immediately to Philippi to fight Antony and Octavius. After his colleagues' departure, when his staff have gone to sleep, Brutus is visited by Caesar's ghost, which promises to meet him at Philippi.

5.1 Antony and Octavius quarrel as to which shall lead the right flank of their attack before defying Cassius and Brutus to immediate battle at a parley. Cassius and Brutus part, resolved to kill themselves if defeated. **5.2–3** Brutus' forces assault those of Octavius, but leave Cassius' army at the mercy of Antony: Cassius sends Titinius to report from his camp. Seeing Titinius surrounded by cavalry, Cassius' servant Pindarus reports that all is lost, and Cassius has himself killed by him. The cavalry, however, were those of Brutus' army: finding Cassius' body, Titinius kills himself. Brutus, young Cato, and others find their bodies, but rally for another assault. **5.4** Young Cato is killed: Lucillius, claiming to be Brutus, is captured, but Antony is not deceived. **5.5** Brutus, among a few defeated followers, pauses to rest: one by one he asks three of them to kill him, saying he has seen Caesar's ghost again and knows his time has come, but each refuses. After the others fly, however, Strato agrees to hold Brutus' sword while he runs upon it, and Brutus dies saying he killed Caesar less willingly. Octavius and Antony find his body and speak of his virtues, distinguishing his high motives from those of the other conspirators.

ARTISTIC FEATURES: *Julius Caesar* is both a triumphant display of rhetoric and a stringent examination of its uses and abuses, its characters lucid and eloquent even when persuading others to adopt the most violent and primitive behaviour. It employs a much higher proportion of verse than any other play composed at this period of Shakespeare's career, determined to match its canonical classical subject with a consistently dignified style: the comic plebeians of 1.1 are swiftly dismissed, as is the comic poet who intrudes on Brutus and Cassius in 4.2.

CRITICAL HISTORY: For precisely these reasons, the play has often been more admired than loved, seen as representing Shakespeare rather self-consciously on his best artistic behaviour. It has often been chosen as a school set text, due to its edifying subject and absence of bawdy (see SCHOOLS, SHAKESPEARE IN), and has consequently retained an unfortunate aura of the classroom for many readers and commentators. Nonetheless, the admiration *Julius Caesar* has enjoyed has been genuine, consistent, and well deserved. Praised by Margaret Cavendish, Duchess of *Newcastle, during the Restoration, it became for the 18th century one of the most important plays in the canon, with Shakespeare seen as a sympathizer with Brutus' libertarian ideals: Francis *Gentleman, commenting in *Bell's edition in 1773, felt it should be a compulsory part of the syllabus at all major private schools and that all members of Parliament should be made to memorize it. (This wish was perhaps in part fulfilled by the election of a Prime Minister, Tony Blair, who as a private schoolboy was aptly cast as Antony.) It has always been especially valued in the United States, where phrases from its text littered the rhetoric of colonists during the War of Independence. Discussions of this perennially topical play have traditionally centred on the question of where its political sympathies finally lie. Brutus has generally been taken as its tragic hero (Charles *Gildon was the first critic to suggest the play should be renamed after him, in 1710), and he has been variously considered as an unambiguously endorsed personification of republican values, a Hamlet-like contemplative idealist too naive for public life, or a zealot committed to bloodless theories at the expense of flesh and blood. In the earlier 20th century the play's structural kinship with two plays about regicide, *Richard III* and, especially, *Macbeth*, was frequently noted. Since the Second World War *Julius Caesar* has enjoyed the attention of *feminist critics interested in Portia's wound and the play's general relegation of women to the margins of a political world dominated by intense relationships between men, while *poststructuralists have been fascinated by its interest in the interpretation and misinterpretation of signs and its dramatization of the relations between texts, bodies, and wills.

STAGE HISTORY: The play remained in the theatrical repertory down to the closing of the theatres in 1642 (court performances are recorded in 1612–13, 1637, and 1638), and its power in the theatre is highly praised by Leonard *Digges in his commendatory verse to Shakespeare's poems (1640). After the Restoration its potentially sympathetic depiction of an assassination easily read as regicide kept it from being revived at once, but it was back on the boards by 1671, and after 1684 Thomas *Betterton took over the role of Brutus, with lasting success. Around 1688 the version of the play in use in London theatres was slightly rewritten to make Brutus more unambiguously sympathetic (adding, for example, a last defiant dialogue with Caesar's ghost at Philippi, which remained part of its text until the retirement of J. P. *Kemble), but while it has frequently undergone minor cuts and transpositions the play was never supplanted by a full-scale adaptation (although the Jacobite statesman John Sheffield, Earl of Mulgrave, composed a heavily pro-Caesar version in two parts, *The Tragedy of Julius Caesar, Altered* and *The Tragedy of Marcus Brutus*, completed around 1716 but never performed). James *Quin played Antony in 1718 but in later years was an important Brutus, first at Drury Lane and then, throughout the 1740s and 1750s, at Covent Garden: David *Garrick, unsuccessful as Antony in *Antony and Cleopatra*, did not find any of the leading roles sufficiently commanding, and the play was not revived at Drury Lane during his entire management. Kemble's 1812 production was notable both for his upright Brutus and for its attention to the historical accuracy of the actors' togas: his most important immediate successor in the part was *Macready, who had earlier played Cassius. The play had first been performed in America in 1774, in Charleston, but enjoyed its greatest vogue during the following century (when it was played in 51 different theatres in New York alone): most famously (and infamously), it was a favourite of the *Booths, Edwin playing Brutus on tours throughout the States. A benefit performance of the play in 1738 had helped pay for *Scheemakers's statue of Shakespeare in Westminster Abbey, and another took place in New York in 1864 to pay for the statue of Shakespeare in Central Park. Edwin Booth played Brutus, Junius Booth was Cassius, and John Wilkes Booth played Antony; a year later he shot Abraham Lincoln. The play was less popular in England during the later 19th century, but enjoyed considerable success in Beerbohm *Tree's lavish production of 1898, with himself as Antony. Thereafter it became a standard feature of the repertory at Stratford under Frank *Benson, who played Caesar: it was chosen as the command performance to commemorate the tercentenary of Shakespeare's death in 1916, at the close of which Benson, still in costume, was knighted by George V. *Julius Caesar* also became a fixture at the Old Vic, where it was revived in every season from 1914 to 1923, and again in 1932, with Ralph *Richardson as a much-praised Brutus. The most famous inter-war production, however, took place at the Mercury theatre in New York, when Orson *Welles directed the play in modern dress, giving the conspiracy strong anti-fascist overtones: the idea was imitated at the Embassy theatre in London soon after the outbreak of war. Notable post-war productions have included Anthony *Quayle's in Stratford in 1950 (with Quayle as Antony and John *Gielgud as Cassius), Minos Volanakis's production of 1962 (with Robert Eddison as Cassius), and Peter *Hall's interval-free production for the RSC in 1996, with Hugh Quarshie as Antony. *MD*

ON THE SCREEN: Nine silent versions (the first made by Georges Méliès) emerged between 1907 and 1914. Material from the play was among the earliest Shakespeare scenes broadcast on BBC television (1937) and in 1938 the BBC televised the Embassy's modern-dress production, reflecting the play's relevance to the political turmoil in 1930s Europe. The film with the strongest resonance remains the 1953 cinema film directed by Joseph L. Mankiewicz with Louis

Calhern (Caesar), James Mason (Brutus), John Gielgud (Cassius), and Marlon Brando as Mark Antony. The most recent screen version is the 1979 BBC TV production, with Charles Gray as Caesar and Richard *Pasco as Brutus. *AD*

RECENT MAJOR EDITIONS

Arthur Humphreys (Oxford, 1984); David Daniell (Arden 3rd series, 1998); Marvin Spevack (New Cambridge, 1988); Norman Sanders (New Penguin, 1967)

SOME REPRESENTATIVE CRITICISM

Burckhardt, Sigurd, 'How Not to Murder Caesar', *Centennial Review*, 11/2 (1967)

Charney, Maurice, *Shakespeare's Roman Plays* (1961)

Dobson, Michael, 'Accents yet Unknown: Canonisation and the Claiming of *Julius Caesar*', in Jean Marsden (ed.), *The Appropriation of Shakespeare* (1990)

Girard, René, 'Collective Violence and Sacrifice in Shakespeare's *Julius Caesar*', *Salmagundi*, 88–9 (1990–1)

Kahn, Coppélia, *Roman Shakespeare: Warriors, Wounds and Women* (1995)

Paster, Gail Kern, ' "In the Spirit of Men there is no Blood": Blood as a Trope of Gender in *Julius Caesar*', *Shakespeare Quarterly*, 40/3 (1989)

Ripley, John, *'Julius Caesar' on Stage in England and America, 1599–1973* (1980)

Kames, Henry Home, Lord (1696–1782), Scottish judge and philosopher. Kames uses Shakespeare as an example of genius in his popular study of moral aesthetics *Elements of Criticism* (1762). Focusing on universal human nature rather than critical rules, Kames's work examines how drama arouses emotions and passions in its audiences. *JM*

Katherine (Catherine; Katharina; Katharine; Kate). (1) For Katherine/Kate, see THE TAMING OF THE SHREW. (2) *Love's Labour's Lost.* See CATHERINE. (3) *1* and *2 Henry IV*. See PERCY, LADY. (4) *Henry V*. See CATHERINE. (5) Queen Katherine/Princess Dowager in *All Is True* (*Henry VIII*) (Henry VIII's first Queen) pleads her case in court, 2.4, but dies shortly after her divorce, 4.2. She is based on Catherine of Aragon (1485–1536), daughter of Ferdinand and Isabella of Spain, married in 1509 to Henry VIII. Her first four children died in infancy, but her fifth, Mary, lived to become queen. *AB*

Kean, Charles (1811–68), English actor-manager, son of the great Edmund *Kean, who sent him to Eton. Plump of figure, facially expressionless, and vocally nasal, Charles Kean was not well endowed to enter the profession in which he was bound to be compared—unfavourably—with his father. Nevertheless, despite or because of the family name, Charles Kean had early opportunities to play Shakespearian leads in London: Romeo (1829), Richard III (1830), Iago (1833) to his father's Othello, Othello and Hamlet (both 1838); in addition to which he undertook engagements in the provinces and America. Charles Kean's Shakespeare performances were criticized for 'clap-trap effects', misplaced emphases and unceasing—but pointless—locomotion. Nevertheless, in 1848 Queen Victoria appointed Kean director of the Royal Theatricals at Windsor Castle, whither he marshalled fellow thespians to perform before their sovereign in a range of plays old and new in which the works of Shakespeare, who was rapidly assuming the status of national bard, were respectfully represented.

When, in 1851, Kean set up in management at the Princess's theatre, the Queen's patronage was undoubtedly highly conducive to attendance by those (upper) classes who had not hitherto considered theatre-going to be a proper activity. The prominence of Shakespeare's plays in the repertoire was a further inducement especially as they were produced with such painstaking antiquarian accuracy of sets, costumes, and other accoutrements as to constitute lessons in (principally British) history. In the decade of the Great Exhibition, the *Pre-Raphaelite brotherhood, and early photography, Kean captured and catered for the public taste for reconstructing and *animating* the past with all the accuracy that art, antiquarianism, and technology could deploy.

Although Kean did venture to distant places (*The Merchant of Venice, Hamlet, The Tempest*) and times (*A Midsummer Night's Dream, The Winter's Tale*), his most ambitious and successful productions were rooted in the homestead of history: *King John* (1852), *Macbeth* (1853), *All Is True* (*Henry VIII*) (1855 and 1858), *Richard II* (1858), *King Lear* (1858), and *Henry V* (1859). In addition to the historical accuracy of their every facet, these revivals were characterized by large-scale, carefully orchestrated crowd effects (foreshadowing the Saxe-Meiningen company) often in interpolated episodes, such as the entry of Bolingbroke and Richard II into London which Shakespeare was content just to describe, which were accommodated by huge (a third or more) cuts in and rearrangement of the text.

Acting tended to be subservient to scenery, but Kean's company included his formidable and talented wife Ellen (Tree) and the forthright John Ryder. Of Kean himself G. H. Lewes remarked that he is 'changing his style to a natural one'. Undoubtedly in the context of his own productions Kean's performances exceeded his youthful (lack of) promise, notably his sympathetic Richard II. To their intense disappointment the Keans' unstinting efforts on behalf of their monarch and national dramatist did not result in the hoped-for knighthood, and the couple set off on an exhausting (though remunerative) tour of America and Australia. Thus it was that the Shakespeare tercentenary found the Keans in Melbourne, where they performed four acts, each from a different play: 'so there's a hard night's work', as Mrs Kean observed. *RF*

Schoch, Richard, *Shakespeare's Victorian Stage: Performing History in the Theatre of Charles Kean* (1998)

Kean, Edmund (1787/9–1833), English actor, who pre-eminently gave expression to *Romanticism on the stage. Kean's parentage and early life are cloaked in mystery. Born and brought up in London, he was evidently something of an infant prodigy, becoming a proficient singer, dancer, fencer, acrobat, and mime. He performed on the legitimate stage as Prince Arthur at Drury Lane (1801), but, save for appearances—Rosencrantz, Polonius, and First Gravedigger—at the Haymarket (1806), spent the next thirteen years in the provinces, including York where he was a youthful Hamlet (1802).

Kean resisted the temptation of making his London debut prematurely, but when he played Shylock at Drury Lane on 26 January 1814, he caused a sensation. The Thames was frozen and the vast (3,060) auditorium less than a third full, but from his first appearance the small, swarthy actor electrified the audience. Instead of the red-haired, unkempt, conventional Jew, Kean, in a black wig, cut a presentable figure, who

Charles Kean as Richard II, from *The Illustrated London News*, 28 March 1857. In characteristic mid-Victorian fashion Kean staged episodes which Shakespeare only describes, here Richard's ignominious progress through London in the wake of Bolingbroke's triumph (described at 5.2.23–36).

provoked pity and fear as well as loathing and contempt. With each of Shylock's appearances Kean's performance grew in power and passion and by curtain-fall that privileged audience knew that—in *Coleridge's memorial words—'To see him [Kean] act is like reading Shakespeare by flashes of lightning.' The impact of Kean's performance was heightened by the contrast which it provided with the self-conscious classicism of the *Kembles (especially John Philip), prompting *Hazlitt to write (1816) that Kean had 'destroyed the Kemble religion ... in which we were brought up'.

Kean was fortunate in his chroniclers—Hazlitt, Leigh *Hunt, Coleridge, and *Keats—who, as well as being aficionados of the finer points of performance, were in sympathy with his radical—Romantic—style. When Hazlitt returned to Drury Lane on 15 February to see Kean as Richard III, he was again struck by the actor's originality ('it is entirely his own, without any traces of imitation'), the animation and vigour which he brought to the role in which 'He filled every part of the stage.' With Hamlet, a month later, Kean was departing from the vein of energetic malignity which had characterized his Drury Lane performances to date, but though Hazlitt considered him 'too strong and pointed' for the pensive Prince, he nevertheless commended the ingenuity of his interpretation and the 'tone of fine, clear and natural recitation' in which he executed the major speeches, judging overall that 'To point out the defects of Mr. Kean's performance of the part, is a less grateful but a much shorter task than to enumerate the many striking beauties which he gave to it, both by the power of his action and by the true feeling of nature.'

Although Kean had added the melancholy Dane to his credits, it was with roles rather more in tune with his own restless, mercurial, arrogant—and increasingly alcoholic—disposition that he consolidated his success. In Othello and Iago—both at Drury Lane in 1814—his 'deficiency of dignity' in the former was offset by his instinctive delicacy and in the latter he added to his portraits of restless malignity. Though his early experience had equipped him to do so, Kean did not include comedy in his mature repertoire; nevetheless, he invested some of his serious (villainous) roles with humour. Kean continued to create more Shakespeare roles. He was a rather disappointing Romeo and Macbeth, and an improbable Richard II. He reclaimed Timon of Athens, whose paroxysms he took beyond the bounds of nature; Richard, Duke of York, in an adaptation of *1–3 Henry VI*; and Posthumus (surprisingly in preference to Iachimo), along with King John, Hotspur, Coriolanus, Cardinal Wolsey, and (belatedly—in 1830—and uncomfortably) Henry V.

In June 1820, following the death of King George III, during whose prolonged period of mental instability the play had not been performed, Kean assumed the title role in *King Lear*. Hazlitt found that 'the gigantic, outspread sorrows' of Lear seemed to 'elude his [Kean's] grasp, and baffle his comprehension', whereas he rose to the intensity of passion in the curse of Goneril, achieving 'the only moment worthy of himself, and the character'.

Kean's increasingly dissolute private life inevitably had a deleterious effect on his stage work. He toured America in 1820 and in 1825, following the scandal—and trial—arising from his affair with Charlotte Cox, whose husband was an alderman and member of the Drury Lane committee. On his return from America Kean played at Covent Garden, but it was back at Drury Lane that he recovered some of his former brio as Othello to the Iago of his, now formidable, rival *Macready in 1832. The following year he gave what was to be his last performance as Othello to his son Charles's Iago. As he collapsed he moaned, 'I am dying—speak to them for me.' *RF*

Playfair, Giles, *Kean: The Life and Paradox of a Great Actor* (1939)

Keats, John (1795–1821), English poet. Keats is best known in this context for his celebration (after *Hazlitt) in his letters and marginalia of a Shakespeare of protean sympathies, generous redundancy of imagination, and natural feeling, declared the epitome of 'negative capability'—a 'chameleon' poetic stance which he contrasted to the egotistical *Milton and *Wordsworth and to which he himself aspired. *NJW*

White, R. S., *Keats as a Reader of Shakespeare* (1987)

Keeling, Captain William (d. 1620), naval commander. Off Sierra Leone, aboard the *Dragon* of the East India Company, Keeling's men performed *Hamlet* on 5 September and *Richard II* on 30 September 1607. Again *Hamlet* was acted at sea on 31 March 1608, as Keeling explained, 'to keep my people from idleness and unlawful games, or sleep'. *PH*

keepers, Mortimer's. They accompany the imprisoned *Mortimer, *1 Henry VI* 2.5. *AB*

Kemble, Charles (1775–1854), English actor, manager, and playwright, and the younger brother of Sarah *Siddons and John Philip *Kemble. His first named role was Orlando in Sheffield and he played the provinces until his 1794 London debut at Drury Lane as Malcolm to his brother's Macbeth. After a succession of minor roles he joined Covent Garden in 1803 and played Romeo but toured at home and abroad (including opening the new theatre at Brighton playing Hamlet to his wife's Ophelia) to escape the 'younger Kemble' tag. His greatest success came on his return to Covent Garden, particularly from 1820 when he became a shareholder, and he staged intelligent productions of *Macbeth*, *Julius Caesar*, *1 Henry IV*, and a memorable *King John* with historically accurate costumes by Planché. Popular performances with his daughter Fanny helped relieve the financial difficulties of management. He took the company to Paris, and in 1832 made a successful tour of North America playing Hamlet, Romeo, Benedick, and Falconbridge. He retired from the stage in 1836 with a further performance of Benedick opposite Helen Faucit's Beatrice, was persuaded to return briefly to perform for Queen Victoria, and continued to give Shakespeare readings. *CMSA*

Edmund Kean as Richard III, 1814: characteristically, the moment Cruikshank has chosen to illustrate is a convincingly abrupt start. 'To see him act is like reading Shakespeare by flashes of lightning,' claimed Coleridge.

Kemble, Fanny (Frances Anne) (1809–93), English actress, who made her debut as Juliet under her father Charles's—ailing—management at Covent Garden on 5 October 1829. With no previous professional experience and just three weeks' rehearsal the young actress relied on her emotional identification with the character rather than technique. Within two years of her triumph as Juliet, Fanny played Lady Macbeth, Portia, Beatrice, and Constance. During her 1832–3 American tour her father played opposite her as Romeo. Following her ill-fated marriage, Fanny returned to the

Charles Kemble as Romeo with Harriet Smithson as Juliet in the tomb scene, Paris, 1827. The composer Berlioz became obsessed with Smithson after seeing this production and later married her.

stage in 1847, appearing as Desdemona with Macready in 1848, but thereafter she devoted herself to performing her Shakespearian readings on both sides of the Atlantic. The author of a play—*Francis I*, 1832—on the Shakespearian model, Fanny produced multiple volumes of memoirs and has attracted several biographers. *RF*

Marshall, Dorothy, *Fanny Kemble* (1977)

Kemble, John Philip (1757–1823), English actor, manager, and playwright, the son of provincial theatre manager Roger Kemble, and brother of Charles *Kemble and Sarah *Siddons. He began to train for the priesthood at Douai but left in 1775 to become an actor, first joining a travelling company and then playing provincial theatres: he appeared as Othello to Siddons's Desdemona at Liverpool in 1778. That year he wrote to Tate Wilkinson, appending a list of the 68 roles in tragedies and 58 in comedies that he was able to play, and was employed to perform in the north-east. During his time with Wilkinson he wrote his first Shakespearian adaptation (28 more would follow): *Oh! It's Impossible*, a version of *The Comedy of Errors*. After appearing with Daly's company in Dublin he made his London debut at Drury Lane in 1783 playing Hamlet, shortly followed by Richard III and Shylock. From 1785 he appeared regularly opposite his sister: Othello to her Desdemona, Macbeth to Lady Macbeth, Posthumus to Imogen, Mark Antony to Cleopatra, and Lear to Cordelia.

His work was characterized by research and thorough preparation, leading to suggestions that some of his roles were too studious—and he was certainly less successful in romance and comedy—but such study effectively informed his *Macbeth Reconsidered; an Essay: Intended as an Answer to Part of the Remarks on Some of the Characters of Shakespeare* (1786), dedicated to Edmond *Malone and written as a response to Thomas Whately's *Remarks on Some of the Characters of Shakespeare* which claimed that Macbeth was a coward.

In 1788 he took over the management at Drury Lane and his great success as Coriolanus (with Sarah as Volumnia) led to his enduring identification with Roman roles. He opened the new theatre at Drury Lane in 1794 with *Macbeth*, extending his reputation for authenticity, stage effects, and a visual playing style (largely earned from the processions and tableaux of his 1788 *All Is True* (*Henry VIII*)) with crowds of flying witches and a full, loud orchestra. In 1803 he became the manager of Covent Garden and extended its Shakespearian repertoire, playing Wolsey, Prospero, Iago, Valentine, and Macbeth. Many of his great roles were recorded in paint, most famously in the portraits by Lawrence. He retired from the stage in 1817 with a final performance as Coriolanus, widely respected as a great tragedian and as *Garrick's successor in the promotion and playing of Shakespeare. *CMSA*

Kempe (Kemp), William (d. 1603), comic actor (Leicester's Men 1585–6, Strange's Men 1592, Chamberlain's Men 1594–9). Kempe's fame grew in the late 1580s and early 1590s from his work with Leicester's and then Strange's Men. Richard Tarlton established the improvisational clowning tradition which Kempe inherited and refined although his particular skill was in dancing and playing musical instruments rather than mockery and he wrote a number of highly popular *jigs. Kempe's name appears in a stage direction in the 1599 quarto of Shakespeare's *Romeo and Juliet* where we should expect Peter and in the speech prefixes of the 1600 quarto of Shakespeare's *Much Ado About Nothing* where we should expect Dogberry, so we may be confident that he took these roles. Other roles are speculative but David Wiles saw Kempe's style in the Clown in *Titus Andronicus*, Lance in *The Two Gentlemen of Verona*, Costard in *Love's Labour's Lost*, Bottom in *A Midsummer Night's Dream*, Lancelot in *The Merchant of Venice*, and, his acme, Falstaff in the *Henry IV* plays and in *The Merry Wives of Windsor*.

Kempe sold his *Globe share soon after the building was complete in 1599 and early in 1600 he demonstrated his extraordinary endurance by *morris dancing from London to Norwich, a feat he described in his pamphlet *Kempe's Nine Days Wonder*. It is not clear why Kempe left the King's Men, but the mocking of his style of clowning in *The Return to Parnassus* and Hamlet's demand that clowns should 'speak no more than is set down for them' (3.2.39) suggest that improvisation became unfashionable. Robert *Armin replaced Kempe as the Chamberlain's Men's clown and after a continental sojourn in 1601 Kempe was acting with Worcester's Men at the Boar's Head and the *Rose in 1602. Thereafter Kempe disappears from records until the burial of 'Kempe a man' at St Saviour's. *GE*

Wiles, David, *Shakespeare's Clown: Actor and Text in the Elizabethan Playhouse* (1987)

Kenilworth, a town 12 miles (19 km) north-east of Stratford with a splendid castle, now in ruins, where Robert Dudley, Earl of Leicester, entertained Queen Elizabeth for nineteen days in 1585. It has been speculated that Shakespeare's father took him to see the elaborate entertainments, and that the presentation of Arion in a water pageant suggested allusions in *Twelfth Night* (1.2.14) and *A Midsummer Night's Dream* (2.1.149–540). *RB*

Kenrick, William (?1725–1779), notoriously acerbic hack writer and reviewer for the *Monthly Review*. Kenrick viciously attacked Samuel *Johnson's edition of Shakespeare and subsequently lost his job. He also wrote *Falstaff's Wedding*, a comic sequel to *Henry IV* performed once at Drury Lane in 1766. *JM*

Kent, the English county, is mentioned in some of the history plays: in *The First Part of the Contention* (*2 Henry VI*) it is where the rebel *Cade comes from and where he meets his end. Its prominence in *King Lear* may be related to the fact that Kent retained different inheritance laws from the rest of England, dividing estates between all the testator's children instead of passing the whole to the eldest son. *AB*

Kent, Earl of. Banished by Lear, he is taken back into his service disguised under the name of 'Caius' (see *The History of King Lear* 24.278 and *The Tragedy of King Lear* 5.3.259). *AB*

Keysar, Robert (fl. 1605–19), a goldsmith and financier who bought an interest in the Children of the Queen's Revels in 1605 and later managed the company. They originally acted at the *Blackfriars, and in 1610 Keysar initiated an action against *Burbage and other members of the King's Men alleging that the theatre had been transferred without his agreement and claiming a share of their profits. *SW*

Killigrew, Thomas (1612–81), actor, dramatist, and manager. A strong supporter of the Royalist cause, at the Restoration he was awarded one of the two royal patents giving exclusive rights to form an acting company and build a theatre. In choosing a group of actors who had been active before the Civil War, acquiring the rights to plays performed by the old King's Company pre-1642, and in the bare staging style he adopted at his first venue, the Tennis Court in Vere Street, he was less successful than his forward-looking rival William *Davenant. In 1663 his King's Company moved to the new Theatre Royal (rebuilt by Sir Christopher Wren after a fire in 1672). Despite having exclusive rights to perform 20 Shakespeare plays, in the period to 1682, when it was joined by the Duke's Company, it produced only four: *Othello*, *1 Henry IV*, *The Merry Wives of Windsor*, and *Julius Caesar*. *CMSA*

King, Thomas (1730–1805), English actor. Drury Lane's principal comedian, he played *Garrick's foppish foil at the Stratford *Jubilee and in the London version processed as Touchstone, the role in which he was later painted by Zoffany. *CMSA*

'King Cophetua and the Beggar Maid', a ballad title mentioned in several plays, including

Kemps nine daies vvonder.

Performed in a daunce from London to Norwich.

Containing the pleasure, paines and kinde entertainment of *William Kemp* betweene *London* and that Citty in his late Morrice.

Wherein is somewhat set downe worth note; to reprooue the slaunders spred of him: many things merry, nothing hurtfull.

Written by himselfe to satisfie his friends.

LONDON
Printed by E. A. for *Nicholas Ling*, and are to be solde at his shop at the west doore of Saint Paules Church. 1600.

The title page of *Kempe's Nine Days Wonder* (1600) shows the former clown of Shakespeare's company, certainly the original Dogberry and probably the creator of such roles as Bottom and Falstaff, engaged in his publicity-stunt morris dance from London to Norwich, with his taborer Thomas Sly.

Love's Labour's Lost 4.1.65; *Romeo and Juliet* 2.1.14; *Richard II* 5.3.78; *2 Henry IV* 5.3.103. *JB*

King Henry IV Part 1. See HENRY IV PART 1.

King Henry IV Part 2. See HENRY IV PART 2.

King Henry V. See HENRY V.

King Henry the Fifth; or, The Conquest of France by the English. Aaron Hill's adaptation of *Henry V*, first acted in 1723, keeps the battle of Agincourt offstage (it is narrated in song by the Genius of England) and replaces Pistol and his associates with a new, romantic sub-plot. King Harry's spurned ex-mistress Harriet, niece of the conspirator Scroop, acts as his go-between to Princess Catherine while disguised as a page before finally stabbing herself in despair. *MD*

King Henry VI Part 1. See HENRY VI PART 1.

King Henry VI Part 2. See FIRST PART OF THE CONTENTION, THE.

King Henry VI Part 3. See RICHARD DUKE OF YORK.

King Henry VIII. See ALL IS TRUE.

King James Bible. The occasionally expressed popular belief that Shakespeare must have helped prepare the translation of the *Bible completed for King James in 1610 is based solely on the circumstance that a few famous passages from that translation and from Shakespeare's tragedies are the only specimens of Jacobean English most people ever hear. Rudyard Kipling, however, composed a whimsical short story, *Proofs of Holy Writ*, in which one of the translators consults Shakespeare and *Jonson, and in 1970 Anthony *Burgess pointed out that in the King James Bible the 46th word of the 46th psalm, translated in Shakespeare's 46th year, is 'shake', while the 46th word from the end (if one cheats by leaving out the last, cadential word, 'selah'), is 'spear'. Burgess was not rash enough to make anything of this coincidence, however. *MD*

Burgess, Anthony, *Shakespeare* (1970)

King John *(see page 240)*

King Lear *(see page 244)*

King Leir, an anonymous verse drama of the early 1590s, and the most important source for Shakespeare's *King Lear*. The play is a romance chronicle with a happy ending, and it was in existence by April 1594. It was printed in 1605 as *The True Chronicle History of King Leir and his Three Daughters*, a year before Shakespeare's *King Lear* was first performed at Whitehall on 26 December 1606.

Shakespeare's use of *King Leir* is instructive in a number of ways. Among the more noteworthy changes are his conflating two of the source's characters into the plain-speaking Kent, giving the name Oswald to its villainous Messenger, and, above all, introducing the Fool and having Cordelia die in the play. Leir's 'I am as kind as is the Pellican' (512) anticipates the 'pelican daughters' in *King Lear*, and at times Shakespeare appears to conduct a seamless cross-textual dialogue with the source, as in his casual reference to 'thy mother's tomb', an echo of the funeral of Leir's wife which opens the source play. *RW*

Bullough, G., *Narrative and Dramatic Sources of Shakespeare*, vol. vii (1973)

King Richard II. See RICHARD II.

King Richard III. See RICHARD III.

King's Company, formed by Thomas Killigrew, one of the two companies granted a patent by Charles II at the Restoration in 1660. Performing initially at the Red Bull and moving into the new Theatre Royal in Drury Lane in 1663, it acquired the rights to the Shakespearian plays performed by the old King's Men pre-1642 and included actors from the old company. *CMSA*

Kingsley, Ben (b. 1943), British stage and screen actor. The son of an English-educated Gujarati father, he won international fame in the film *Ghandi* (1980). His association with the *Royal Shakespeare Company began in 1970 with Peter *Brook's seminal *A Midsummer Night's Dream* and he was the Prince in Buzz *Goodbody's revelatory studio production of *Hamlet*. He returned to the RSC in 1988 to play Othello as a North African Arab and was Feste in Trevor *Nunn's film *Twelfth Night* (1996). *MJ*

King's Men. See CHAMBERLAIN'S MEN/KING'S MEN.

'King Stephen was and a worthy peer', sung by Iago in *Othello* 2.3.82. His last line, 'Then take thy auld cloak about thee', is the title of a Scots ballad with related words; Sternfeld's *Music in Shakespeare Tragedy* (1964) gives the tune. *JB*

Kinoshita, Junji (b. 1914), Japanese writer. Kinoshita majored in English at the University of Tokyo, and became a successful playwright in the 1940s. Many of his plays deal with subjects with socio-political relevance, and his translations of Shakespeare can be best understood as conscientious attempts to reproduce the energy of the original in a language with entirely different linguistic principles. *TK*

Kirkman, Francis See DROLLS.

Kittredge, G. L. (1860–1941), American scholar. The one-volume edition of the *Complete Works* by G. L. Kittredge published in 1936 by Ginn and Co., Boston, was eagerly welcomed. It was based on a fresh collation of the early printed texts, and retained stage directions found in quartos and the First *Folio, printing added directions and scene locations in square brackets. Brief introductions preface each text, which is printed in double columns on the page, and there is a full glossary at the end of the book. Kittredge also published over a period of some years separate annotated editions of some of the plays, and these were gathered by A. C. Sprague in *Sixteen Plays of Shakespeare* issued by Ginn in 1946. Kittredge's learned notes on the plays still repay attention, and they are notable for his concern about the sequence and timing of scenes and other problems of staging them. *RAF*

Kneller, Sir Godfrey (?1649–1723), German painter active in England 1674–1723. He produced a full-length portrait of Shakespeare, a copy of which was presented to the poet and dramatist John *Dryden. *CT*

Knight, Charles (1791–1873), English publisher, editor, and author. Knight, himself largely self-taught, was an indefatigable promoter of useful general knowledge in the 1830s and 1840s, through a series of weekly magazines. A founding member of the Shakespeare Society (1840), he published his *Pictorial Shakespeare* in weekly illustrated parts (1838–41) and his Library Edition (12 vols., 1842–4). Knight was the first to point out the extent of Anne *Hathaway's dower rights as a widow in Shakespeare's estate, even without specific acknowledgement in the *will. His own library, bequeathed to the City of Birmingham, forms the basis of a major Shakespeare collection. *TM*

Knight, G(eorge) Wilson (1897–1985), leading mid-20th-century English Shakespeare critic who helped pioneer 'spatial' or *imagery-based study in the 1930s in a development closely connected with the contemporaneous literary *modernism of T. S. *Eliot. Knight is best remembered for his books of 'interpretation' of Shakespeare plays (he thought the term 'criticism' implied an ill-suited judgemental approach to art and avoided the term) in which he developed his interpretative method in exuberant, impressionistic essays on the poetic images and symbols seen as forming unified patterns central to the meaning of the individual plays. He was widely read and imitated in mid-century North America and the UK. Most influential of his books were: *The Wheel of Fire:*

(cont. on page 242)

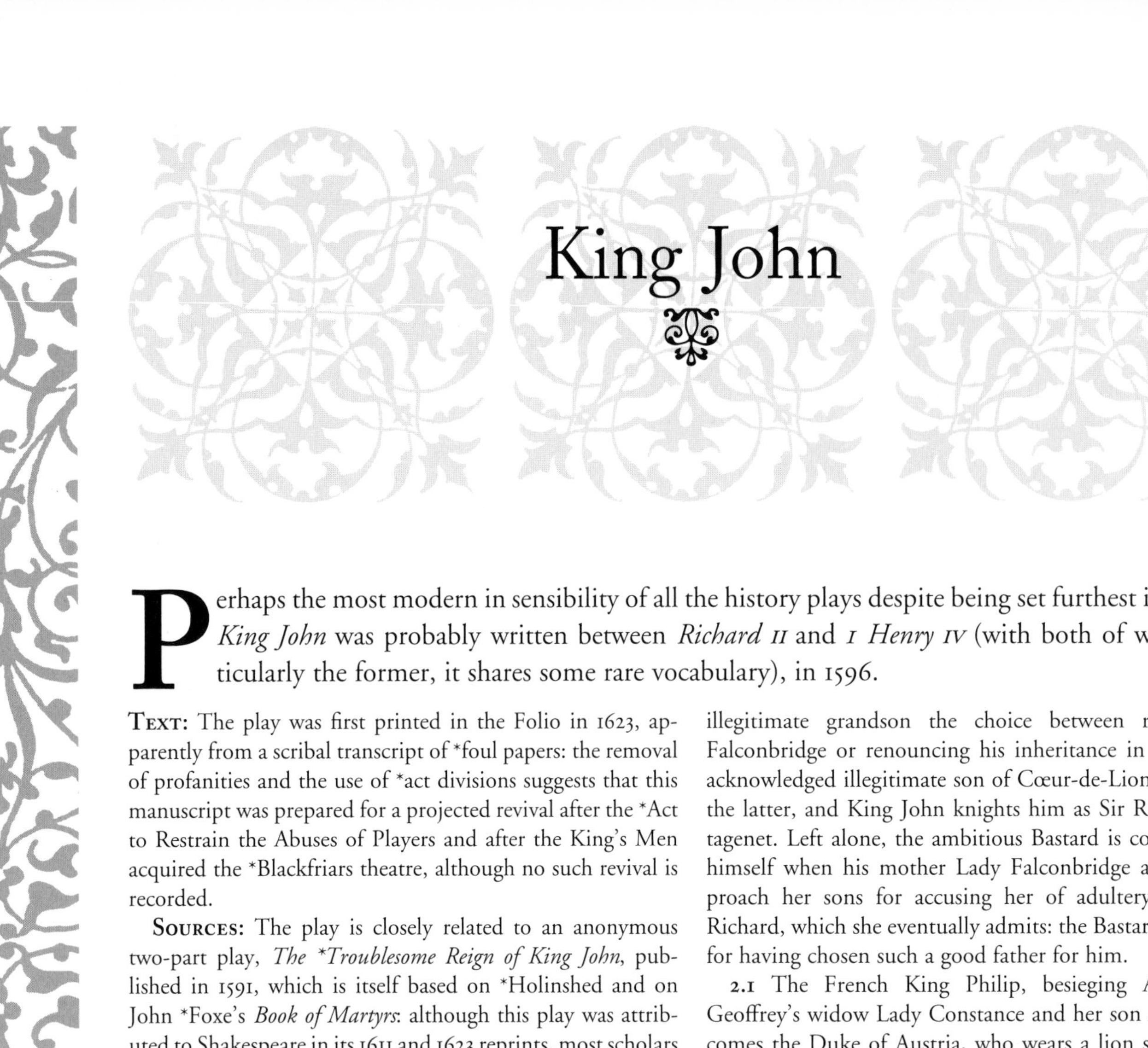

King John

Perhaps the most modern in sensibility of all the history plays despite being set furthest in the past, *King John* was probably written between *Richard II* and *1 Henry IV* (with both of which, particularly the former, it shares some rare vocabulary), in 1596.

Text: The play was first printed in the Folio in 1623, apparently from a scribal transcript of *foul papers: the removal of profanities and the use of *act divisions suggests that this manuscript was prepared for a projected revival after the *Act to Restrain the Abuses of Players and after the King's Men acquired the *Blackfriars theatre, although no such revival is recorded.

Sources: The play is closely related to an anonymous two-part play, *The *Troublesome Reign of King John*, published in 1591, which is itself based on *Holinshed and on John *Foxe's *Book of Martyrs*: although this play was attributed to Shakespeare in its 1611 and 1623 reprints, most scholars now believe that this was a source for Shakespeare's play rather than a derivative version of it. Shakespeare's condensation of *The Troublesome Reign* is marked chiefly by a toning down of its strident anti-Catholicism: the main point of the earlier play is to depict John as a fearless resister of the papacy, a comparatively incidental aspect of his presentation in Shakespeare's version.

Synopsis: **1.1** The ambassador Châtillon declares war on King John in the name of the French King Philip, who supports John's young nephew Arthur's claim to the throne: John promises to defend his title in a military campaign in France, though his mother Queen Eleanor privately admits to John that his deceased elder brother's son has the better right to the crown. The King is then asked to judge a dispute between one Philip (the Bastard) and his brother Robert Falconbridge: despite being the junior, Robert claims the lands of their father Sir Robert Falconbridge on the grounds that Philip is in fact the illegitimate son of John's late brother King Richard Cœur-de-Lion, who had sent Sir Robert away to Germany at the time the Bastard was conceived. The King, though recognizing by family likeness that the Bastard is indeed King Richard's son, points out that in law he is still rightful inheritor of Sir Robert's land, but Queen Eleanor gives her illegitimate grandson the choice between remaining a Falconbridge or renouncing his inheritance in order to be acknowledged illegitimate son of Cœur-de-Lion: he chooses the latter, and King John knights him as Sir Richard Plantagenet. Left alone, the ambitious Bastard is congratulating himself when his mother Lady Falconbridge arrives to reproach her sons for accusing her of adultery with King Richard, which she eventually admits: the Bastard thanks her for having chosen such a good father for him.

2.1 The French King Philip, besieging Angers with Geoffrey's widow Lady Constance and her son Arthur, welcomes the Duke of Austria, who wears a lion skin to commemorate his killing of King Richard Cœur-de-Lion, to their party. Châtillon brings the news that the English army is approaching, and King Philip and his allies are confronted by King John, the Bastard, John's niece Lady Blanche, and their army: the two sides taunt and defy one another, the Bastard singling out Austria for his attention. The citizens of Angers, summoned to the walls to see which of the two armies they will allow into the city, respond to the rival eloquence of King John and King Philip by saying they will recognize whoever wins a battle between the two as rightful king. The two armies battle offstage, but each returns and claims victory: the citizens of Angers are thus still unable to decide whom to favour. The Bastard, irritated with them, suggests that John and Philip should first combine to demolish Angers before settling their differences, and as the two sides prepare to take this advice a citizen of Angers, terrified, suggests that instead of further bloodshed the French and English should make peace by means of a marriage between the Dauphin and Lady Blanche. This proposal is accepted, King John offering a large dowry with his niece to assure himself against further trouble from Philip, and to pacify the absent Lady Constance and her son he declares Arthur Duke of Brittaine, Earl of Richmond, and lord of Angers. Left alone, the Bastard reflects on the calculating self-interest that governs all worldly affairs. **2.2** Lady Constance, with Arthur, is horrified to learn from the Earl of Salisbury that the French King has abandoned their cause: declining to appear before the two kings she sits on the ground in sorrow.

3.1 The new allies enter in state from the wedding between the Dauphin and Lady Blanche, and are cursed at length by Constance. She takes some comfort from the arrival of the papal legate Cardinal Pandolf, who has been sent to demand that King John allow the Pope's choice Stephen Langton to be Archbishop of Canterbury: when John defies him and the Pope, Pandolf excommunicates him and instructs King Philip to let go of his hand and declare war on him again. After much debate, the Bastard taunting Austria throughout, King Philip obeys Pandolf: Lady Blanche laments her divided loyalties. **3.2** In the ensuing battle the Bastard kills Austria and King John captures Arthur. **3.3** King John leaves Queen Eleanor in France, sends the Bastard to England to raise money from the Church, and appoints Hubert to kill Arthur. **3.4** The discomfited King Philip, the Dauphin, and Pandolf are further dismayed by the grief-stricken ranting of Constance, who unbinds her hair as a mark of her distraction. When Pandolf and the Dauphin are left alone, the Cardinal points out that King John is certain to have Arthur killed and that this, coupled with his assaults on the Church, will make him unpopular and vulnerable: he urges the Dauphin to claim the English crown through his marriage to Blanche, promising to gain Philip's support for an invasion.

4.1 Hubert has instructions to blind Arthur with hot irons, but the boy speaks so poignantly that he is unable to carry them out: instead he undertakes to protect Arthur but tell the King he has killed him. **4.2** King John has had himself crowned for a second time, an action which, as his nobles Pembroke and Salisbury point out, has made his claim to the throne look weaker rather than stronger. When the King, after hearing from Hubert, announces that Arthur has died, the nobles accuse him of murder, and leave, promising vengeance. A messenger brings the news that the Dauphin has landed with an army and that Queen Eleanor and Lady Constance are both dead. The Bastard arrives, reporting that the country is full of rumours of the King's impending fall: he has brought a prophet with him, Peter of Pomfret, who says John will give up his crown before noon on the next Ascension Day. John gives Hubert instructions to hang Peter of Pomfret at that time, and sends the Bastard to try to win the nobles back to his side. When Hubert brings news of further omens and prophecies John reproaches him for killing Arthur, eventually stinging him into confessing that Arthur is still alive, news which John instructs him to give to the nobles as soon as he can. **4.3** Disguised as a ship's boy Arthur leaps down from the walls and dies. Salisbury, Pembroke, and Bigot find the body just as the Bastard is trying to persuade them to rejoin the King instead of going over to the French, and just before Hubert arrives to tell them Arthur is still alive: they promise vengeance. Alone with Hubert, the Bastard accuses him of killing Arthur, but is eventually persuaded of his innocence: he fears John's reign cannot last.

5.1 On Ascension Day King John, making peace with the papacy, gives his crown to Pandolf, who restores it to him: he recognizes that Peter of Pomfret's prophecy has been fulfilled. The Bastard brings news that the nobles have joined with the Dauphin, who has entered London, and he chides King John for making peace with Pandolf, urging defiance. **5.2** The defecting English lords swear allegiance to the Dauphin, who refuses to make peace with King John even when Pandolf brings the news of his reconciliation to the Church. The Bastard defies the Dauphin on John's behalf and the two sides prepare for battle. **5.3** In the battle John, growing faint with fever, learns that French reinforcements have been wrecked on the Goodwin Sands: he retreats to the abbey at Swineshead. **5.4** Salisbury, Pembroke, and Bigot are dismayed to learn from the dying Count Melun that the Dauphin means to kill them if he wins the battle: at Melun's urging they set out to rejoin King John. **5.5** The Dauphin, close to victory, learns of the English lords' re-defection and of his shipwrecked reinforcements. **5.6** Hubert meets the Bastard and tells him the King has been poisoned by a monk: the Bastard, though pleased to hear of the nobles' return, reports that half his army has been drowned by the tide in the Wash. **5.7** The King's son Prince Henry has the dying King John, who has been singing in delirium, brought out into the open air, where he speaks of his longing to be cooled: he dies while the Bastard is telling him of the Dauphin's approach. The Bastard learns that Pandolf has negotiated a peace: he and the nobles kneel before Prince Henry, now King Henry III, who promises to honour his father's desire to be buried at Worcester. The Bastard observes that England is never conquered without the assistance of internal treachery but that, now the nobles have returned, it will remain invulnerable if the nation only keeps faith with itself.

Artistic features: The play is perhaps most remarkable for the sardonic way in which it depicts the shifting allegiances of international power politics, most obviously by the set-piece mock-grandeur of 2.1, 3.1, and 5.2, in which monarchs ceremonially commit perjury in the ordinary pursuit of *realpolitik*. It is appropriate in this regard that the play's largest and most conspicuous role belongs not to King John but to the Bastard, a variously cynical and patriotic commentator on the play's action.

Critical history: Although immensely popular in the theatre throughout the 18th and 19th centuries, *King John* has attracted little unmixed enthusiasm from literary critics: an anomaly among the English histories, it has often been ignored, like *All Is True* (*Henry VIII*), in favour of the two tetralogies. Commentators have usually found the play a mass of contradictions, whether between the defiant, potentially sympathetic King John of the early acts and the wavering would-be murderer of Arthur of the later (as did Charles *Knight), or between the psychological naturalism of some scenes (notably that of Constance's grief, 3.4) and the

conventionality of others (as did Barrett Wendell). It is only since the advent of Bertolt *Brecht and his view that historical dramas may exploit deliberate incongruities in the interests of concentrating an audience's mind on political ideas that the play's artistry has found defenders, although most discussions of the play remain centred on the question of Shakespeare's lack of Protestant zeal compared to that of his source.

Stage history: The first recorded performances of the play took place at Covent Garden, under the auspices of the patriotic *Shakespeare Ladies' Club, in 1737, and it held its own despite competition from a more anti-Catholic adaptation by Colley *Cibber in the year of the second Jacobite uprising, 1745. *Garrick, successfully competing with this version, cast himself as John at Drury Lane to considerable applause. The role of Constance suited itself perfectly to the style of Sarah *Siddons, who first took it in 1804, while her brother J. P. *Kemble was much admired as John. Charles Kemble's lavish 1823 revival, designed by J. R. Planché, was a milestone in the staging of Shakespeare's histories, the first of many spectacular productions intended to animate the Middle Ages with as much antiquarian accuracy as possible. Kemble cast himself as the Bastard, and though his successor *Macready played the King most Victorian actor-managers followed this choice of role, sometimes casting a girl as Arthur. More and more of the text disappeared, however, to make way for historical pageantry, Beerbohm *Tree interpolating an entire dumb show of the signing of the Magna Carta in his 1899 revival.

In the 20th century the play's set pieces of pathos fell from favour, although periodic revivals rediscovered their power: among notable Constances have been Sybil *Thorndike (1917–18, and again in 1941), while the Bastard has been played to great effect by Ralph *Richardson (1931–2), Paul *Scofield (1945), and Richard *Burton (1953). The most critically admired production of the later 20th century was undoubtedly that of Deborah *Warner for the *RSC (1988). *MD*

On the screen: Brief episodes from Beerbohm Tree's production, filmed in 1899, are the first recorded footage of Shakespearian material. Two subsequent British productions were made for television, one in 1952 and one in 1984 for BBC TV, with Leonard Rossiter as John. *AD*

Recent major editions

R. L. Smallwood (New Penguin, 1967); A. R. Braunmuller (Oxford, 1989); L. A. Beaurline (New Cambridge, 1990)

Some representative criticism

Bonjour, Adrien, 'The Road to Swinstead Abbey: A Study of the Sense and Structure of *King John*', *English Literary History*, 18 (1961)

Calderwood, J. L., 'Commodity and Honour in *King John*', *University of Toronto Quarterly*, 29 (1960)

Matchett, William H., 'Richard's Divided Heritage in *King John*', *Essays in Criticism*, 12 (1962)

Smallwood, R. L., 'Shakespeare Unbalanced: The Royal Shakespseare Company's *King John*, 1974–5', *Shakespeare Jahrbuch 1976*

Sprague, A. C., *Shakespeare's Histories: Plays for the Stage* (1964)

Interpretations of Shakespeare's Tragedy (1930); *The Imperial Theme: Further Interpretations of Shakespeare's Tragedies* (1931); and *The Crown of Life: Essays in Interpretation of Shakespeare's Final Plays* (1947). He wrote several other books on Shakespeare and other literary figures, increasingly influenced in his later works by a belief in Spiritualism and communication with his dead brother. *HG*

knights, five. They are *Thaisa's suitors, *Pericles* 6, 7, and 9. *AB*

knights, six. Three accompany Arcite and three Palamon, *The Two Noble Kinsmen*, Act 5. *AB*

Knights, L(ionel) C(harles) (1906–97), English academic. His polemical *How Many Children Had Lady Macbeth?* (1933) seeks to discredit A. C. *Bradley's extra-textual speculations. *Shakespeare's Politics* (British Academy Lecture, 1957), *Some Shakespearean Themes* (1959), and *An Approach to Hamlet* (1960) demonstrate the evaluative approach to literature and society associated with the *Scrutiny* critic F. R. Leavis. *TM*

Knolles, Richard (?1550–1610), author of *The General History of the Turks* (1603). This 1,000-page work provides details of the Venetian–Turkish wars which are the backdrop to *Othello*, whilst Knolles's story of Basso Ionuses, who murdered his wife Manto through irrational jealousy, is a possible precursor for *Othello*'s plot. *CS*

Knyvet (Knevet), Charles. See Surveyor, Buckingham's.

Komisarjevsky, Theodore (1882–1954), Russian director, designer, and author. Born Fyodor Komissarzhevsy in Venice, the half-brother of the actress Vera Komissarzhevskaya, he worked in the Russian avant-garde or synthetic style at important theatres in St Petersburg and Moscow until he emigrated in 1919. Thereafter he directed widely in England and Europe, becoming known especially as an interpreter of Russian plays (and becoming the second husband of Peggy *Ashcroft). Invited to Stratford by W. Bridges-Adams, he directed and designed a series of fanciful productions of Shakespeare that despite their outrageousness were much admired. *The Merchant of Venice* in 1932 showed a tilting view of the city, *Macbeth* in 1933 used metallic scenery, while *The Merry Wives of Windsor* in 1935 was treated as a Viennese operetta. *King Lear* (1936), with Randle Ayrton in the title role, was handled respectfully, though its setting of steep steps was unusual for Stratford. *The Comedy of Errors* (1938) and *The Taming of the Shrew* (1939), both exotic and farcical, were his most popular productions. He moved to New York soon afterwards, where he spent the last part of his career. *DK*

Korea. Shakespeare made his first appearance in Korea in an anonymous translation (1906), from the Japanese (1871), of Samuel Smiles's *Self-Help* (1859). Smiles's book was partially translated under the title of 'Jajoh Ron' (The Principles of Selp-Help) in *Joyang Boh*, a monthly journal, with a view to selecting passages suitable to the spirit of the age, as descriptions of the virtues of perseverance and hard work required for the formation of a new world of enlightenment. In a prologue, Shakespeare was portrayed as the greatest mind of his day who influenced the promotion of English cultural nationalism. He was admired as an exemplary man of discipline who rose to prominence from a humble background. This image of Shakespeare was associated with the moral code of frugality and propriety which the declining Johson Dynasty was eagerly seeking

The advent of designer Shakespeare at Stratford: Theodore Komisarjevsky's surreally out-of-drawing Venice, his own set design for *The Merchant of Venice*, Shakespeare Memorial Theatre, 1932.

in order to westernize or modernize the nation in the face of Japanese imperialism.

The treatment of Shakespeare in the 1910s characterized him as a radiant figure of wisdom. A Shakespeare quotation became a resource in cultural discourse and provided a point of reference that reinforced educational and fundamental principles of moral rectitude. *Sohnyon* (The Youth), a monthly journal edited by Nam-Son Cheh, a leading figure of the age, was characteristic in employing Shakespeare quotations for didactic and utilitarian purposes. Cheh's use of quotations was bound up with his political awareness of the need to urge young people to stand up to the Japanese occupation. He published his complete translation, via the Japanese, of *Self-Help* under the title of 'Jajoh Ron' in 1918.

The first Shakespeare film shown in Korea was Beerbohm Tree's *Macbeth* in 1917. It was with this film that Shakespeare entered the public consciousness. When Shakespeare began to have a public life, however, it was only with educated and politically conscious circles in Seoul. In the 1920s this small group of elite intellectuals were not introduced to Shakespeare's own words but to translations, via the Japanese, of Mary and Charles *Lamb's *Tales from Shakespeare*, which had been already influential in making the plays known in *Japan. The moral value of, and the lessons to be learned from, the *Tales* communicated ethical significance in relation to the values of Confucian patriarchal culture. They demonstrated that the narrative and plot elements of Shakespeare were susceptible to transference into Korean sensibility.

The first theatrical adaptation of Shakespeare was *King Lear and his Daughters* (1924), a two-act play, designed for girl students. Its provision of a happy ending, *après* *Tate, was regarded as morally and socially justifiable, and gave the play tones of emotion and sentimentality. It was printed in *Sinyohsung* (The New Woman), a monthly journal for female intellectuals.

The first Shakespeare performance in English was the Forum scene (3.2) of *Julius Caesar*, played by the drama group of Kyungsung School of Commerce in December 1925. This scene attracted most attention in the 1920s, along with the trial scene in *The Merchant of Venice*. Their popularity had much to do with the strong current of nationalism and resistance to Japanese colonial rule. The formulation of 'Geukyesool Yongoohwe' (The Theatre Arts Research Association) in 1932 proved to be a turning point in the history of Shakespearian stage production in Korea. In 1933 it held a Shakespeare Exhibition and staged *The Merchant of Venice—The Trial Scene* in Johson theatre. This event saw the shift in Shakespearian performance from the school or

(cont. on page 248)

King Lear

The third of the so-called 'great' tragedies, *King Lear* differs greatly in structure and tone from its predecessors, *Hamlet* and *Othello.* According to its entry in the Stationers' Register on 26 November 1607, it had been performed at court on 26 December 1606. This suggests composition no later than autumn 1606. The play is indebted to Samuel *Harsnett's *Declaration of Egregious Popish Impostures* and to *Florio's translation of *Montaigne's *Essais*, both published in 1603. Gloucester's reference to 'late eclipses in the sun and moon' may or may not allude to actual eclipses of September and October 1605; possible debts to *Jonson, *Chapman, and *Marston's play *Eastward Ho* and to George *Wilkins's *Miseries of Enforced Marriage* imply composition later than June 1605. The play was probably written late in 1605. Revision represented by the Folio text was made on a copy of the 1608 quarto, probably, judging by stylistic evidence, around 1610.

Text: The play was first printed, badly, in 1608. The origin of this text has been much disputed but the current view is that it derives from Shakespeare's original manuscript. It was reprinted with minor but unauthoritative improvements in 1619. Editors from the early 18th century onwards, assuming that both texts derive from a single archetype, normally conflated them, but recent research indicates that the 1608 quarto represents the play as Shakespeare first wrote it, and the Folio a substantial revision, cutting some 300 lines and adding about 100, and with many other variations. The Oxford editors first disentangled the two texts under their original printed titles of *The History* and *The Tragedy of King Lear.* The synopsis given below is based on the *History* but indicates major variations in the *Tragedy.*

Sources: Lear's story had often been told and Shakespeare appears to have known several versions. He treats it with great freedom, especially by adding Lear's madness and giving it a tragic conclusion. He knew well *The True Chronicle History of *King Leir and his Three Daughters*, a play published in 1605 but written at least fifteen years earlier. Echoes from it in many of Shakespeare's plays suggest that he may have acted in it, probably before 1594. The parallel story of Gloucester and his sons is based on episodes from Sir Philip *Sidney's *Arcadia.* Details of, especially, Edgar's speeches as Mad Tom derive from Harsnett's *Declaration*, and Florio's *Montaigne* also influences the play's vocabulary.

Synopsis: Sc. 1 (1.1) The Earl of Gloucester tells the Duke of Kent that King Lear is equally well disposed to each of his sons-in-law, the dukes of Albany and Cornwall, in sharing out his kingdom. Gloucester introduces his bastard son Edmund to Kent, saying that the bastard is no less dear to him than the legitimate Edgar. Lear enters with his daughters, Gonoril, Regan, and Cordelia, and the elder sister's husbands. Calling for a map, he declares his intention to divide his kingdom into three parts which he will share among his daughters. The King of France and the Duke of Burgundy are in waiting to learn which of them will win the hand of his youngest daughter, Cordelia. Lear asks each daughter for an expression of her love. Gonoril and Regan flatter him, but Cordelia refuses to take part in the competition. Infuriated, Lear banishes both her and Kent, who defends Cordelia. Lear announces that he will retain the name of king, and that, along with a retinue of 100 knights, he will live alternately month by month with each of his elder daughters. Burgundy refuses to marry the disinherited Cordelia, but France, perceiving her true value, accepts her. Left alone, Regan and Gonoril reveal jealousy of Cordelia and impatience with their father's weaknesses.

Sc. 2 (1.2) Edmund, declaring allegiance to the law of nature, reveals his determination to usurp his legitimate brother's inheritance. Producing a letter purportedly written by Edgar, he tricks Gloucester into believing that Edgar seeks to join with Edmund in seizing their father's estates. Edmund offers to demonstrate the truth of his allegation if Gloucester will conceal himself to overhear a conversation between the brothers. Gloucester blames recent eclipses of the sun and moon for overturning the natural order, but Edmund, in soliloquy, reveals a rationalist disposition. He tells the innocent Edgar that Gloucester is displeased with him.

Sc. 3 (1.3) Lear is staying with Gonoril. Complaining that he and his followers are riotous, she instructs her servant Oswald to treat them insolently. She will write to Regan advising her to follow a similar course.

Sc. 4 (1.4) Kent, disguised, declares unwavering loyalty to Lear, who admits him into his service. Oswald behaves insolently and Kent endears himself to Lear by mocking him. Lear's Fool warns his master in riddles and snatches of song against the consequences of his poor judgement. Gonoril complains to Lear of his retinue's behaviour; enraged, he calls for his horses, invokes a curse upon her, and leaves for Regan's home. Within moments he returns in even greater fury, having learned that 50 of his followers have been dismissed. Gonoril summons Oswald to carry a letter to Regan.

Sc. 5 (1.5) Lear also sends letters to Regan, by Kent. Lear meditates on his wrongs, punctuated by cryptic comments from his Fool.

Sc. 6 (2.1) In Gloucester's house, Curan, a servant, tells Edmund that Cornwall and Regan are approaching, and reports rumours of forthcoming wars between Cornwall and Albany. Edmund tricks Edgar, who is in hiding, into running away, convincing Gloucester by means of a mock fight that Edgar had been trying to persuade Edmund to murder their father. The duped Gloucester instigates a hunt to the death for Edgar. Cornwall and Regan join in enmity to Edgar, report receipt of Gonoril's letter, and commend Edmund, taking him into their service.

Sc. 7 (2.2) Kent threatens and insults Oswald; Cornwall orders Kent to be put into the stocks even though Gloucester points out that this will offend Lear. In soliloquy Kent tells of a letter he has received from Cordelia, in France, who knows of his course of action. He goes to sleep. The fugitive Edgar reveals to the audience his plan to assume the appearance and behaviour of a Bedlam beggar. Lear, entering with no more than his Fool and one follower, is appalled to find Kent in the stocks and goes off to question Regan. Speaking to Kent, the Fool reveals his continuing loyalty to Lear. Lear tells Gloucester of his anger that Regan and Cornwall have refused to see him. They enter, and Kent is released. Gonoril enters, and Lear is shocked that Regan welcomes her. Regan tells her father that he should return to Gonoril, dismiss half of his retinue, and then come to stay with her. Lear refuses to have anything more to do with Gonoril and says that he and his 100 knights will live with Regan. She prevaricates, saying she will accommodate no more than 25 followers, at which Lear decides he will go to Gonoril after all. When the sisters question his need for even a single follower, Lear, breaking down, threatens revenges on them both and expresses fear of madness. He departs into the night. Cornwall and Regan batten their gates against the coming storm.

Sc. 8 (3.1) A gentleman tells Kent that Lear, accompanied only by the Fool, is battling against the elements. Kent tells the gentleman of division between Albany and Cornwall and that an invasion force is on the way from France (not in *Tragedy*), and asks him to hasten to Dover to tell Cordelia of the King's plight (to give Cordelia, if he sees her, a ring which she will know comes from him (Kent), *Tragedy*).

Sc. 9 (3.2) Accompanied by the Fool, Lear rages against the storm. Kent tries to persuade him to shelter in a hovel, and they go off to look for it. (Before leaving the Fool speaks a mock prophecy, *Tragedy*.)

Sc. 10 (3.3) Gloucester, turned out of his own house, tells Edmund of division between Albany and Cornwall (and passes on news of the French invasion, *History*) (and that support for Lear's party is already on the way, *Tragedy*). Edmund, left alone, says he will instantly tell Cornwall of this and expresses determination to supplant his father.

Sc. 11 (3.4) Kent seeks to persuade Lear to enter the hovel. Before doing so, Lear prays for all who suffer in the storm, acknowledging that he has 'ta'en | Too little care of this'. The Fool, who has entered the hovel, emerges terrified by the presence of the disguised Edgar. Edgar vigorously acts the madman, and Lear assumes that Edgar has daughters who have 'brought him to this pass'. Edgar's near-nakedness provokes Lear to reflect on the basic state of 'unaccommodated man', and Lear tears off his own clothes in sympathy. Gloucester enters, shocked that Lear has 'no better company', and offers, in spite of the sisters' prohibition, to find shelter for Lear. Lear's wits are turning, and Gloucester fears for his own. They all go into the hovel.

Sc. 12 (3.5) Cornwall declares his determination to revenge himself on Gloucester. Edmund accuses his father of complicity with the powers of France, and Cornwall tells him that he will soon succeed his father.

Sc. 13 (3.6) Gloucester leaves the hovel to seek help. Lear, now fully mad, conducts a mock trial of Gonoril and Regan (not in *Tragedy*) then sleeps. Gloucester, reporting 'a plot of death' against the King, arranges for him to be carried in a litter to Dover. Edgar, left alone, reflects on the situation (not in *Tragedy*).

Sc. 14 (3.7) Preparing to take revenge on Gloucester, Cornwall sends Edmund away. Oswald reports that Lear, with a party of his knights, is on his way to Dover. Edmund leaves with Gonoril, and Cornwall gives orders for Gloucester to be bound and brought before him. Gloucester is tied to a chair and Regan plucks him by the beard as they interrogate him about the King's whereabouts. Provoked beyond endurance, Gloucester admits that he has sent Lear to Dover to protect him from his evil daughters. Sadistically, Cornwall puts out one of Gloucester's eyes. A servant who protests is stabbed to death by Regan, and Cornwall, injured in the fight, puts out Gloucester's other eye. When Gloucester calls on the absent Edmund for help, Regan reveals that it was he who told them of the help that Gloucester had given Lear. Gloucester now realizes that Edgar had been tricked. A horrified servant says he will get Tom o'Bedlam to lead Gloucester on his way to Dover, and another that he will fetch 'flax and whites of eggs | To apply to his bleeding face' (not in *Tragedy*).

Sc. 15 (4.1) The disguised Edgar encounters his father being led by an old man. Gloucester calls upon the supposedly absent Edgar for help. Edgar comes forward and his father asks him to lead him to the edge of Dover Cliff.

Sc. 16 (4.2) Gonoril welcomes Edmund. Oswald reports that her husband Albany, much changed, is refusing to oppose 'the army that was landed'. She sends Edmund to expedite Cornwall's opposition, giving Edmund a token of her love and kissing him. Albany enters and expresses horror at what the sisters have done to their father, prophesying that the heavens will take revenge. A gentleman brings news of Gloucester's blinding and reports that Cornwall has died of his wounds. Gonoril reveals fear that Regan may seduce Edmund.

Sc. 17 (not in *Tragedy*) Kent asks a gentleman why France has returned home and whether the letters describing Lear's plight moved Cordelia. The Gentleman describes Cordelia's sorrowful reaction. Kent remarks that Lear, in his more lucid moments, is too ashamed to see Cordelia.

Sc. 18 (4.3) Cordelia (entering with an army, *Tragedy*) sends soldiers to seek the mad King. A messenger brings news that the British armies are approaching. Cordelia declares that she is acting out of love for her father, not personal ambition.

Sc. 19 (4.4) The jealous Regan tries to persuade Oswald to reveal the contents of letters he is carrying from Gonoril to Edmund. She sends a token to Edmund by Oswald and offers promotion to anyone who will kill Gloucester.

Sc. 20 (4.5) Edgar persuades a suspicious Gloucester that they are close to the edge of Dover Cliff and invents a description of the view. Believing himself on the verge, Gloucester prays and leaps forward. Speaking in a different accent, Edgar approaches him as if he really had fallen. Gloucester repents his suicide attempt. Lear enters, madly reliving episodes from his past, inveighing against female sexuality and reflecting on justice and authority in a poignant mixture of reason and madness. Gloucester recognizes his voice and pays homage, and Edgar looks on, moved. Gentlemen arrive to take Lear to Cordelia, but he evades capture. Edgar asks about the impending battle and starts to lead Gloucester to safety. Oswald enters, recognizes Gloucester, and hopes to kill him so as to gain the promised reward, but Edgar fights and kills him. Dying, Oswald asks him to take the letters he is carrying to Edmund. Edgar searches his pockets and finds a letter in which Gonoril incites Edmund to kill her husband.

Sc. 21 (4.6) Kent, still in disguise, encounters Cordelia. A doctor (not in *Tragedy*) and gentleman ask if they may awaken Lear, and he is revealed (carried in, *Tragedy*) asleep, freshly arrayed. They wake him (to the accompaniment of music, *History*). At first Lear believes he is dead and that Cordelia is an angel, but slowly he comes to himself and recognizes her. He kneels to her in penitence, and she asks his blessing.

Sc. 22 (5.1) Amid preparations for war, Regan asks Edmund if he has seduced Gonoril. He replies evasively. Edgar, now disguised as a peasant, gives Albany a letter to open before the battle, claiming that, if Albany wins, Edgar will produce a champion who will bring to pass what the letter claims. Edmund admits to the audience that he has sworn love to both sisters and declares that he will have no mercy on Lear and Cordelia if they fall within his power.

Sc. 23 (5.3) The French (an, *Tragedy*) army, led by Cordelia with Lear, passes across the stage. Edgar, still disguised as a peasant, leaves his blind father in a safe place. Noises of battle are heard. Edgar, returning with news that Lear has lost and is captured with Cordelia, leads his father away.

Sc. 24 (5.3) Edmund enters with Lear and Cordelia captives, and they are led to prison. Edmund instructs a captain to follow them and to obey the orders in a note which he gives him. Albany instructs Edmund to hand over his captives. Edmund explains that he has sent them to prison. Albany says he had no right to make a decision. Regan and Gonoril vie in defending his action. Regan, saying that she is unwell, claims Edmund as her husband. Albany arrests Edmund and Gonoril on charges of high treason. Albany challenges Edmund. Regan becomes more sick, and Gonoril in an aside reveals that she has poisoned her. A herald reads a challenge on behalf of Edmund. The disguised Edgar answers it. They fight and Edgar wins. Gonoril opposes the decision but flounces off when Albany produces her letter to Edmund. Edgar reveals his identity and tells of his father's death (and of how Kent, finding them together, was so overcome with grief that he collapsed: not in *Tragedy*). A gentleman enters with news of Gonoril's suicide and Regan's death. Kent's entry in his own person to say farewell to Lear reminds Albany of Lear and Cordelia. The bodies of the evil sisters are brought on to the stage. Edmund, dying, repents and reveals that he has given orders for Lear and Cordelia to be killed. A servant is sent to try to countermand the order, but Lear enters with Cordelia in his arms. He seeks for signs that she is alive and reveals that he killed her murderer. Kent identifies himself. News arrives that Edmund is dead. Albany offers to give up the kingdom to Lear, who dies, grieving over Cordelia's body. Albany asks Kent and Edgar to rule, but Kent says he must follow his master. Albany (Edgar in *Tragedy*) rounds off the play, commending stoicism and integrity.

Artistic features: Though occasionally relieved by touches of humour, this is Shakespeare's most profoundly and philosophically intense drama, often dense in expression though with shafts of sublime simplicity, especially in Lear's reunion and reconciliation with Cordelia. It is his only tragedy with a fully developed sub-plot, or parallel story, the physical suffering of Gloucester, culminating in his blinding, running alongside the mental torment of Lear, culminating in madness. Shakespeare seems consciously to withdraw all sense of period, avoiding the Christian frame of reference which is notable in *Hamlet*, and of locality: even Dover is an idea rather than a place. The influence of the morality tradition is apparent in the exceptionally black and white characterization. Lear's Fool represents Shakespeare's most subtle and poignant development of this type of character. The play calls for acting of the highest quality but otherwise makes no exceptional demands; with doubling, it could be acted by thirteen men and three boys, and the staging calls for no special effects except an upper level at only one point.

Critical history: Nahum *Tate's adaptation *The *History of King Lear*, a skilful piece of theatrical writing which evades the play's tragic issues, held the stage from 1681 to 1845, influencing the perceptions even of critics such as *Johnson, *Hazlitt, *Coleridge, and *Lamb who acknowledged the original play's sublimity but doubted its theatrical validity. A. C. *Bradley too, though he wrote eloquently on the play in *Shakespearean Tragedy* as 'the fullest revelation of Shakespeare's power', considered it '*not* his best play'. At the same time, *Tolstoy vitriolically attacked *Lear*, eccentrically stating a preference for *King Leir*. *Granville-Barker's 'Preface', of 1927, successfully refutes Lamb's criticism of the play's actability. From G. Wilson *Knight in 1930 onwards the play's literary qualities have provoked much fine criticism from critics including R. B. Heilman, W. H. Clemen, and Winifred Nowottny. Twentieth-century critics including J. F. Danby, Barbara Everett, W. R. Elton, Jan Kott, and many others concentrated on the question of whether the play embodies fundamentally Christian values or is fundamentally pessimistic. Other topics of discussion and, sometimes, controversy have included the play's structure, its relationship to the morality tradition, the credibility of, especially, the opening scene, whether the blinding of Gloucester and the death of Cordelia are dramatically justifiable, and whether Lear dies happily or in despair. Critics such as Maynard Mack and Marvin Rosenberg have drawn on the play's performance history, and more recent criticism includes studies relating it to feminist, historicist, and materialist issues. It has also stimulated important scholarly studies feeding into criticism by for example W. W. Greg, Enid Welsford, Peter W. M. Blayney, Gary Taylor, and R. A. Foakes, along with numerous pictorial, dramatic, and fictional offshoots.

Performance history: The only recorded early performance is the one given at court on 26 December 1606. The play was acted after the Restoration, but from 1681 to 1838 in England, and to 1875 in America, all performances adopted or modified Nahum Tate's adaptation, which cuts around 800 lines, modernizes the language, omits the Fool and France, adds a love story between Edgar and Cordelia, and preserves the lives of Kent, Gloucester, and Lear. David *Garrick triumphed as Lear, and the play was adapted into French and German during the 18th century. In the Romantic period *Kemble and *Kean were outstanding in the title role. *Macready restored the Fool, played by a woman, in 1838, and the Italian *Salvini played in a shortened translation from 1882. Henry *Irving, in 1892, cut nearly half of the text. The first French production of the unadapted text was acted in 1904. *Komisarjevsky directed the play successfully at Stratford in 1936. Barker translated the principles of his 'Preface' into theatrical terms in an almost uncut text given in Elizabethan costume with John *Gielgud as Lear at the Old Vic in 1940. Donald *Wolfit was an admired Lear during the 1940s and 1950s. Peter *Brook directed Paul *Scofield in an influential Stratford production of 1962; more recent outstanding British Lears have included Brian Cox (National Theatre, 1990), Robert *Stephens (Stratford, 1993), and Ian *Holm (National, 1997). *SWW*

On the screen: The most memorable film versions of *Lear* are the two made for cinema by Peter *Brook (1971) and Grigori *Kozintsev (1969), and Michael Elliott's production for Granada Television (1983). Both Brook and Kozintsev selected remarkably articulate locations to project the world of the play, Brook's landscape being one of ice and snow, Kozintsev's one of stony barrenness. While Brook infuses his film with moments of Brechtian alienation, reminding the viewer of the medium with written captions, Kozintsev's film explores, with no over-indulgence, the emotional dimensions of the play and (unlike Brook, who eschews it) gives music (composed by Shostakovich) a major function. There is, too, a great disparity in the portrayals of Lear. Brook's Lear (Paul *Scofield) gives the impression of immense stature, and curtails the range of emotional expression in the lines. Kozintsev chose the Estonian Yuri Yarvet for his Lear. Physically small and unable to speak Russian, Yarvet impressed Kozintsev as ideal for Lear because of his eyes.

Michael Elliott's Granada production captures a rare side of Lear, played with compassion and a captivating autumnal radiance by the 75-year-old Laurence *Olivier. Jonathan *Miller's BBC TV production (1982) stressed the domestic dimensions of the tragedy, with Michael *Hordern moving about the rather confined space like a father but not like a king.

Akira *Kurosawa's *Ran* (1985) is a powerful and visually splendid adaptation of the play, with Lear's daughters transposed into the sons of the old warrior lord Hidetora. *AD*

Recent major editions

Jay L. Halio (New Cambridge, 1992; Folio based); R. A. Foakes (Arden, 1997; conflated); Stanley Wells (Oxford, 2000; quarto-based)

Some representative criticism

Bradley, A. C., *Shakespearean Tragedy* (1904)

Colie, Rosalie (ed.), *Some Facets of King Lear* (1974)

Everett, Barbara, 'The New King Lear', *Critical Quarterly* (1960)

Granville-Barker, H., *Preface* (1927 etc.)

Greenblatt, Stephen, *Shakespearean Negotiations* (1988)
Kozintsev, Grigori, *King Lear: The Space of Tragedy* (1973)
Leggatt, Alexander, *King Lear: Shakespeare in Performance* (1991)
Mack, Maynard, *King Lear in our Time* (1965)
Marcus, Leah, *Puzzling Shakespeare* (1988)
Nowottny, Winifred, 'Lear's Questions' and 'Some Aspects of the Style of *King Lear*', *Shakespeare Survey*, 10 (1958), 13 (1961)
Reibetanz, John, *The Lear World* (1977)

college stage to the public theatre. Shakespeare also provided sources for contemporary playwrights. The Romeo and Juliet story was the most fruitful source for the plays of Chee-Jin Yoo: *Daechoo Namoo* (The Date Tree, 1942), *Jamyung Goh* (The Self-Tolling Drum, 1946), and *Byul* (The Stars, 1948). Yoo appropriated the Shakespearian theme to social and political issues during the last years of the Japanese colonial occupation and after the Independence of 1945, when the country was in turmoil due to ideological conflicts between the right and the left.

During the Korean War (1950–3) Shakespeare's tragedies came to the forefront of the theatrical scene. Their astonishing popularity can be interpreted as an intellectual retreat from ideological pigeon-holing to a world of imaginative communings with the tragic characters' mental processes. After the war Shakespeare became a subject of serious academic and critical study in universities. The increasing numbers of annotated academic editions, accessible textbooks, and critical essays showed the growing use of Shakespeare as an educational instrument. Jae-Suh Cheh was the first academic to gain a Ph.D. in Shakespeare studies. His thesis entitled 'Shakespeare' (1960) was focused on Shakespeare's aesthetic perception of 'Order of Life' in his writings. Its enlarged edition with a new title 'Life and Arts of Shakespeare' was published by Bantam in the United States in 1965. The establishment of the Shakespeare Society (Association from 1982) of Korea in 1963, and its *Shakespeare Review* in 1970, was an important step forward in the recognition of Shakespeare's pre-eminence amongst English-speaking writers.

A special landmark was the celebrations marking the quatercentenary of Shakespeare's birth, in 1964. The year witnessed the publication of two different issues of a Korean translation of the complete works—one was done by Jae-Nam Kim, the other by a group of nineteen Shakespearian scholars—and the unprecedented popularity of Shakespearian performances. The canonization of Shakespeare was diffused and adopted within a public sphere wider than the universities. This was a milestone marking the beginning of a new era of his reception, and opening up a variety of Korean Shakespeares on the page, on the stage, or in the media—though not so far on film. The National Dance Company's production of *Othello* in 1997 was an innovative attempt to translate the psychological space of Shakespearian characters to Korean traditional dance. It can be regarded as the pinnacle of the ongoing process of Korean affiliations with Shakespeare. *YH*

Byung-Chul Kim, *Hankook Geundae Bonyok Moonhaksa Yongoo* (A Study of the History of Literary Translation in Early Modern Korea) (2 vols., 1975)
Joyang Boh, 1 and 2 (June and July 1906)
Min-Young Ryu, *Gaehwagee Yongeuk Sahwesa* (The Social History of Drama in the Age of Enlightenment in Korea) (1987)

Kortner, Fritz (1892–1970), Austrian actor and director. In the 1920s he was Richard III in L. Jessner's expressionist production (1920) and, adopting a more realist style, Hamlet (1926) and Shylock (1927). Returning from emigration during the Third Reich in 1950, he directed numerous impressive Shakespeare productions, mainly in Munich and Berlin. He last played Shylock on television (1969). *WH*

Kott, Jan (b. 1914), Polish critic. *Shakespeare our Contemporary* (1964) invigorated popular attitudes with a Shakespeare to be performed and spoken of in the same terms as Bertolt *Brecht or Samuel *Beckett. In some respects journalistic, the book presented a 'cruel and true' playwright who might have experienced the political oppressions and military conflicts of the 20th century. *TM*

Kozintsev, Grigori (1905–73), Russian film director. He made *Hamlet* (1964) and *King Lear* (1971), monochrome films which articulate the dramatic substance of the plays through a uniquely imaginative cinematic language. He is also known for his books *Shakespeare, Time and Conscience* (1967) and *King Lear, The Space of Tragedy* (1977). *AD*

Krauss, Werner (1884–1959), German actor, famous for his intense characterization. In Berlin he played Shylock (in Max *Reinhardt's production, 1921) and Richard III (1936). He starred in the Nazi propaganda film *Jud Süss*, and his Shylock in Vienna (1943) was notoriously and predictably anti-Semitic. *WH*

Kurosawa, Akira (1910–98), Japanese film director, whose films include *Kumonosu Djo* (*The Castle of the Spider's Web*, also known as *Throne of Blood*, 1957), based on *Macbeth*, and *Ran*, based on *King Lear* (1985). In both, the dramatic structure of the source plays is closely followed. His *The Bad Sleep Well* (1960) has looser affinities with *Hamlet*. *AD*

Kyd, Thomas (1558–94), dramatist. Little is known about Kyd's life except that it ended badly. He was arrested in 1593 on suspicion of fostering xenophobia in London. Heretical papers were found among his possessions, which he said belonged to his former room-mate Christopher *Marlowe. He was imprisoned and tortured, and died not long after his release. In the preface to Robert *Greene's *Menaphon* (1589), Thomas *Nashe hints that Kyd had written a play called *Hamlet*, now lost (and now known as the *'ur-*Hamlet*'), but presumed to have been a source of Shakespeare's play. Kyd also wrote *Soliman and Perseda* (*c.*1592), and translated a French neoclassical tragedy, *Cornelia* (1594). But his fame rests on just one dramatic achievement, *The Spanish Tragedy* (1592). This was perhaps the most influential tragedy of its time. It was printed at least ten times between 1592 and 1633, was mentioned more often in English plays than any of its competitors, and was popular on the Continent throughout the 17th century. It initiated a vogue for revenge theatre that lasted for decades, and it shares many elements with the greatest of all revenge tragedies, *Hamlet*.

Like *Hamlet*, *The Spanish Tragedy* opens with a ghost calling for retribution. The chief revenger is a father, Hieronimo, who has lost his son. Like Hamlet he is driven mad by his inability to get justice for his relative's murder, and at one stage contemplates suicide as an escape from his impasse. Hieronimo's wife too goes mad, like Ophelia, and kills herself amid a riot of devastated plants. The instrument Hieronimo finally chooses for his revenge is a play-within-a-play, anticipating Hamlet's 'Mousetrap'. He persuades the murderers to take part in his production, each of them speaking his part in a different language, and the cacophony that results graphically illustrates the terminal breakdown of communication in the Spanish court. In the course of the performance the murderers are murdered. Afterwards Hieronimo explains what has happened, then bites out his tongue to prevent the Spanish authorities from forcing him to change his story. The play ends when Hieronimo commits suicide with a penknife. In the process he asserts his right to narrate his own history more effectively than Hamlet, who left his best friend to tell the tale instead of telling it himself.

The most popular part of the tragedy seems to have been the section in which Hieronimo runs mad. Ben *Jonson was paid by Philip *Henslowe to write 'additions to Hieronimo', and these are perhaps the new mad scenes printed in the 1602 edition of the play. Something about Hieronimo's frustrated quest for justice left an indelible mark on Kyd's first audiences, and to watch or read *The Spanish Tragedy* is to encounter one of the seminal texts of the early modern theatre. *RM*

Braden, Gordon, *Renaissance Tragedy and the Senecan Tradition: Anger's Privilege* (1985)
Murray, Peter B., *Thomas Kyd* (1969)
Siemon, James R., 'Sporting Kyd', *English Literary Renaissance*, 24/3 (1994)

Kynaston, Edward (?1643–1712), actor. He was recruited at the Restoration to play women's roles and was an outstanding female impersonator, praised for his prettiness by Samuel *Pepys. He became a leading actor–shareholder of the King's Company until its amalgamation with Duke's in 1682, and for the new United Company was successful in male roles including Antony (in *Julius Caesar*) and Clarence. *CMSA*

Lacy, John (*c.*1615–1681), actor and playwright. As a member of the King's Company, under Killigrew, Lacy played clowns and character roles including Falstaff (probably in *The Merry Wives of Windsor*). He reworked *The Taming of the Shrew* as *Sauny the Scot*, *c.*1667, focusing on Grumio (Sauny) and introducing an additional taming scene in which the husband, pretending that toothache causes his wife's refusal to speak, sends for a surgeon to extract her teeth. *CMSA*

ladies, two. **(1)** They try to distract the Queen from her cares, *Richard II* 3.4. **(2)** They banter with Mamillius, *The Winter's Tale* 2.1. *AB*

Lady, Old. In *All Is True* (*Henry VIII*) she banters with Anne Boleyn, 2.3, and announces the birth of Princess Elizabeth, 5.1. *AB*

Laena, Popilius. See Popilius Laena.

Laertes. In *Hamlet*, he is killed by Hamlet in his attempt to avenge the deaths of his father Polonius and his sister *Ophelia. *AB*

Lafeu (Lafew), an old lord in *All's Well That Ends Well*, presents Helen to the King of France, 2.1, and quarrels with Paroles, 2.3 and 2.5, but takes pity on him, 5.2. *AB*

Laforgue, Jules (1860–87), French writer. His *Moralités légendaires* (Moral Tales, 1887) consist of poetic prose parodies of legendary characters and stories, including 'Hamlet or the Consequences of Filial Piety (I cannot help it.)'. Set on 14 July 1601, the tale concentrates on just two episodes from Shakespeare's play: the encounter with the actors and the graveyard scene. Laforgue's mock-serious stylistic experimentation influenced both T. S. Eliot and James Joyce. *TM*

Lamb, Charles (1775–1834) and **Mary** (1764–1847), *Romantic prose stylists. Charles Lamb's important essay 'On the Tragedies of Shakespeare Considered with Reference to their Fitness for Stage-Representation' (1811) argues for the impossibility of adequately staging Shakespeare's tragedies so as to do justice to their sublimity of character and of poetry. Deploring the painful, 'disgusting', and even unintentionally comic effect of staging, and contrasting this with the greater delight and terror to be had in reading, Lamb champions the power of the solitary reader's imagination over the shabbily populist tricks of the theatre. With his sister Mary, Lamb had already produced the *Tales from Shakespeare* (1807, never out of print since), the form in which generations of children (and, in translation, many foreign cultures) have first encountered Shakespeare. They are at once an expression of the Lambs' opinion that writing for children should counterbalance the moral with the imaginative, and the first substantial effort to provide a Shakespeare suitable for girls. *NJW*

Lamb, Charles, and Lamb, Mary, *Tales from Shakespeare* (1807), ed. Julia Briggs (1993)
Wells, Stanley, 'Tales from Shakespeare', in *British Academy Shakespeare Lectures, 1980–9* (1993)

Lambarde, William (1536–1601), keeper of the Tower of London records. When Lambarde met Queen Elizabeth at Greenwich Palace on 4 August 1601, she called herself 'Richard II', and complained that a 'tragedy' about him 'was played forty times in open streets and houses'. Lambarde neither mentions Shakespeare's *Richard II*, nor identifies the very popular 'tragedy'. *PH*

Lambert, Edmund (d. 1587). In 1578, John *Shakespeare mortgaged part of his wife's *Wilmcote inheritance to her brother-in-law Edmund Lambert. When, two years later, John failed to redeem the mortgage, Lambert retained possession of the property. After Lambert's death in 1587, John Shakespeare tried to regain possession from Lambert's son and heir John. In the litigation which followed, John Shakespeare argued that John Lambert had promised an extra £20 provided that the Shakespeares and 'their eldest son William' handed over the estate outright. This is the only mention of William during the so-called 'lost years'. *SW*

Lampe, John Frederick (*c.*1703–51), German composer, mostly resident in Britain. He contributed two songs to *The Winter's Tale* (Covent Garden, 1741) and all the music for the mock-opera *Pyramus and Thisbe* (Covent Garden, 1745). He also composed (or arranged) the music for choruses sung between the acts 'in the Manner of the Ancients' in a production of *King John* (Dublin, 1750). *IBC*

Lancaster, Duke of. See Gaunt, John of.

Lancaster, John of. See John of Lancaster, Lord.

Lance (Launce) is Proteus's 'clownish' servant and long-suffering owner of the dog Crab in *The Two Gentlemen of Verona.* *AB*

Lancelot, a clown, servant to Shylock, leaves his service for that of Bassanio in *The Merchant of Venice.* *AB*

Lane, John (1590–1640). He was sued by Susanna Hall on 15 July 1613 in the consistory court at Worcester because 'about five weeks past the defendant reported that the plaintiff had the running of the reins'—i.e. suffered from gonorrhoea—'and had been naught with Ralph Smith' at the house of John Palmer, a gentleman of Clopton. He was excommunicated. Technically a gentleman, in 1619 he was prosecuted for rioting and libelling the vicar and aldermen and charged by the churchwardens for drunkenness. *SW*

Langbaine, Gerard, the younger (1656–92), dramatic biographer and critic. Langbaine catalogued English drama in works such as *An Account of the English Dramatick Poets* (1691), providing short biographical accounts of playwrights along with lists of their plays. Langbaine also cited the sources and popularity of plays. *JM*

Langham, Michael (b. 1919), British director. He first directed plays during six years as a prisoner of war, and later at Stratford and the *Old Vic. In 1955 he succeeded Tyrone *Guthrie as head of the Festival Theatre, Stratford, Ontario, staging many plays including *Henry V* (with Québécois actors as the French), subsequently seen at the Edinburgh Festival (1956), and *Love's Labour's Lost* and *Timon of Athens*, repeated at Chichester (1964). He ran the Guthrie theatre in Minneapolis from 1971 until 1980. *MJ*

Langley, Edmund de. See York, Duke of.

Langley, Francis (1547/8–1602), builder of the *Swan playhouse and investor in the Boar's Head. *GE*

Ingram, William, *A London Life in the Brazen Age: Francis Langley 1548–1602* (1978)

Langtry, Lillie (1852–1929), British actress, whose stage career was founded on her social connections and personal attractions. She found scope to exploit the latter as Rosalind (1882) discarding, as Ganymede, the traditional boots and trunks for tights alone. She also attempted Lady Macbeth (New York, 1889) and—a decidedly modern—Cleopatra (1890). *RF*

language. See English, Elizabethan.

Lanier, Emilia (1569–1645), poet. A. L. Rowse argued, on the basis of what is written about her in Simon *Forman's diary, that Lanier was the *'Dark Lady' of Shakespeare's sonnets. While his argument is unconvincing, Rowse did Lanier a service by drawing scholarly attention to her work for the first time. The daughter of a court musician, Lanier spent her early years in the household of the Countess of Kent. Before she was 20 she became the mistress of Elizabeth's Lord Chamberlain Lord *Hunsdon, whose son she bore in 1593, soon after her marriage to another court musician. In 1597 she consulted the astrologer Simon Forman to find out whether her husband would be knighted. Forman's notes on the consultation provide information about her early life, as well as about his hopes of getting her into bed. In 1611 she published her only surviving collection of poems, *Salve Deus Rex Judaeorum* (Hail, God, King of the Jews). This makes her the first Englishwoman to print a substantial book of original poetry in a bid to attract patronage. It opens with a series of dedicatory poems addressed to aristocratic women, representing them as a mutually supportive female community. This is followed by a narrative poem which combatively asserts the central role played by women (Eve, the Virgin Mary, Pilate's wife, the daughters of Jerusalem) in the Christian tradition. It ends with 'A Description of Cookham', which celebrates an English country house as a lost feminist paradise. The skill she displays in this volume suggests that she wrote a good deal more which has been lost. *RM*

Grossman, Michael (ed.), *Aemilia Lanyer: Gender, Genre, and the Canon* (1978)
Woods, Susanne (ed.), *The Poems of Aemilia Lanyer* (1992)

la Pucelle, Joan. See Joan la Pucelle.

Lartius, Titus. A Roman general in *Coriolanus*, he witnesses Martius' prowess at Corioles and is left in charge of the town. *AB*

last plays, a modern term for the plays Shakespeare wrote after about 1607, particularly the *romances *Pericles*, *The Winter's Tale*, *Cymbeline*, *The Tempest*, and *The Two Noble Kinsmen* and the most romance-oriented of the histories, *All Is True* (*Henry VIII*). *MD*

Latin America. Spanish-speaking Latin America has enjoyed a quite different relationship with Shakespeare from that of Portuguese-speaking *Brazil. In the theatre, a handful of Shakespeare's plays were already well known at the beginning of the independent era, whether in their original language, in French or Italian *translations, or in the few but steadily multiplying Spanish versions then available. In Argentina and Uruguay productions began as early as the mid-1810s (translated and produced by Luis Morante, who later worked in Chile), while in Mexico *Hamlet* was first staged in 1821. Throughout the 19th century productions by European companies, mainly Spanish, were relatively frequent: even an Italian, cross-gendered *Hamlet* played by Giacinta Pezzana successfully toured the subcontinent in 1878. Among the Spaniards who staged Shakespeare in Mexico was Leopoldo Burón, who in 1880 and 1886 produced two different versions of *Hamlet*; the latter, by the local writers Manuel Pérez and Francisco López, was one of the earliest native translations to enjoy a favourable response from audiences and critics.

In the first half of the 20th century, interest in other plays grew. In 1903 Emilio Thuillier staged *The Taming of the Shrew*, perhaps for the first time in Mexico, and in 1924 the Argentine company of Vittore-Pomar produced a *Tempest* that would tour every major city south to north. In the following decades, *Hamlet*, *Othello*, *Macbeth*, and *King Lear* continued to be frequently staged, but other plays—e.g. *A Midsummer Night's Dream*, *The Merchant of Venice*, *The Tempest*—began to attract Latin American theatre-makers and theatre-goers with an appeal that has yet to cease. Unsurprisingly, in the second half of the century Shakespeare has been the only playwright whose works are standards with the professional, community, and middle and higher education theatres.

As elsewhere, Shakespeare's works have been the subject of adaptation and experimentation by both well-established and young directors and companies as often as they are conventionally approached. The National Theatre of Montevideo, for instance, has seen as many performances of straightforward *Lears* (like the one directed by Eduardo Schinca in 1996) as there have been alternative renderings of other plays in the same city, such as the adaptation of *Hamlet* by Mary Vázquez for the company El Galpón in the early 1990s. Individual directors through the years—such as the Mexicans Seki Sano in the 1950s, José Solé in the 1960s, Héctor Mendoza in the 1970s, Jesusa Rodrigues in the 1980s, and Martin Acosta in the 1990s—or groups undergoing similar processes of experimentation at the same time—e.g. the productions of *Macbeth* by the company La Máscara of Cali (1977), *Richard III* by the Popular Theatre of Bogotá (1987), and *King Lear* by the Free Theatre of Bogotá (1979), all from Colombia—testify to the firm hold of Shakespeare in Spanish-speaking Latin America. A recent development must not pass unrecorded: the translation and performance of Shakespeare in an indigenous language. In 1990, in the Mexican state of Michoacán, Juan Carlos Arvide promoted and directed a production of *Hamlet* translated into the Purepecha language by Lucas Gómez and Gilberto Gerónimo, adapted to a pre-Columbian setting, and performed entirely by members of the native community of Zacán.

Translations of Shakespeare in Spanish-speaking Latin America go back to the 19th century, and throughout the 20th remain mostly the unpublished result of performative need rather than the outcome of editorial projects. In fact, many productions still rely on translations made in Spain (the work of Luis *Astrana Marín in particular). Several major Latin American writers have translated Shakespeare, but none has approached the task systematically. Among the best known are the Chilean Nobel laureate Pablo Neruda's *Romeo and Juliet*, and the Mexican novelist Luisa J. Hernández's *King Lear*. A unique printing was 'Three versions of *Hamlet*', one volume containing translations of the *Folio and first *quarto texts by Guillermo Macpherson and Pablo Canto, introduced by the Dominican Pedro Henríquez Ureña for Losada, Buenos Aires, 1940. Recently Joaquín Gutiérrez, from Costa Rica, has translated and published

Macbeth and *Hamlet* exclusively for the page. Still, in countries like Uruquay and Argentina there are translators and dramaturgs whose steady work has been published only in a limited fashion (Idea Vilariño), or not at all (Mercedes Rein). Doubtless the finest translations of individual sonnets are by the Colombian Mario Reyes, issued in 1964. The only systematic endeavour in translation to date has been the 'Proyecto Shakespeare' by the Universidad Nacional Autónoma de México (UNAM), which aims at publishing the entire canon in individual volumes, introduced and annotated. So far sixteen translations have been issued in the course of nineteen years, fourteen of which are the work of Ma. Enriqueta González Padilla, head of the project; another four are in process. Among her collaborators are Federico Patán, Luz Aurora Pimentel, Marcel Sisniega, and Alfredo Michel Modenessi.

The academic study of Shakespeare in Spanish-speaking Latin America is far from systematic, although several important writers and scholars have approached Shakespeare either as a subject among many, or as an excuse to make or support a comment of a different nature. The list includes the Mexicans Alfonso Reyes and Nobel laureate Octavio Paz; the Argentine Jorge Luis *Borges, whose 'Everything and Nothing' is perhaps the greatest if also shortest text on Shakespeare in Spanish; the Uruguayan José Enrique Rodó; and the Peruvian Mario Vargas Llosa. Short, and mostly topical, pieces are published by writers and scholars who now and then try their hands at the subject without actually pursuing it as a discipline. Among the few attempts at focusing on Shakespeare as a specific subject of academic, long-term study are Margarita Quijano's *Hamlet and its Critics* (Mexico City, 1964); Emilio Armaza's *Shakespeare, the One and Only*, on the identity of Shakespeare (Lima, 1966); and Ulises Schmill's *The Boar's Way*, a study of *Macbeth* (Mexico City, 1983).

The School of Philosophy and Literature of UNAM is probably the only one offering specific courses on Shakespeare as an essential part of its curriculum in English literature. Prologues to the plays in translation have become the usual vehicles to publish some ideas and findings of an academic kind, as is the case with the collaborators in UNAM's 'Proyecto Shakespeare'. Otherwise, scholarly attempts are preserved only as dissertations, seldom reaching any further than the school's classrooms or library. On the other hand, some of the few scholarly books that are not edited in *Spain have been translated into Spanish in Latin America, often belatedly. Instances of this are Dover *Wilson's *The Essential Shakespeare* (1964); Arnold Kettle's compilation *Shakespeare in a Changing World* (1966); and Frances Yates's *Shakespeare's Last Plays* (1986). In contrast to their closeness in the theatrical field, in this field Shakespeare and Spanish-speaking Latin America are still worlds apart. *AMM*

Laughton, Charles (1899–1962), British stage and screen actor. An inspired, self-tortured performer, who loathed his moon-faced appearance, he made his name in London as a stage actor of great originality. In 1933 he was already a major film actor when Tyrone *Guthrie invited him to the Old Vic to play Shakespeare for the first time. As Henry VIII, Angelo, Prospero, and Macbeth, he fascinated and divided critics. Hollywood reclaimed him. In 1959, already in poor health, he played Bottom and King Lear at Stratford-upon-Avon, where again there was a sense of greatness missed. *MJ*

Callow, Simon, *Charles Laughton: A Difficult Actor* (1987)

Launce. See LANCE.

Laurence, Friar. See FRIAR LAURENCE.

Lavatch, the clown, is the Countess of Roussillon's servant in *All's Well That Ends Well.* *AB*

Lavinia, the victim of rape and mutilation, is eventually killed by her father, *Titus Andronicus* 5.3. *AB*

law. Shakespeare's frequent use of legal language (notably in the Sonnets) and his fascination with the possibilities of law as a source of dramatic material have led some commentators (notably John, Lord Campbell, in 1859) to imagine that Shakespeare had worked as a legal clerk during his *'lost' years. More recently it has been shown that other Elizabethan drama was even more legalistic in its vocabulary, in what was a very litigious society, while some commentators have found a kinship between the plays of the period and the practice of arguing 'moots' (hypothetical cases, often with elaborate narrative ramifications) in legal apprenticeships (though it is unlikely that Shakespeare ever had any such training himself). Lawyers and the legal apprentices of the Inns of Court would have been an important component of Shakespeare's audience, and having picked up some legal jargon and experience of court procedure (perhaps from his father's litigation and, later, the *Belott–Mountjoy suit) he was fairly well equipped to explore some aspects of contemporary legal debate in his plays.

Shakespeare's interest in the law is most obvious in *The Merchant of Venice* and *Measure for Measure.* Though legal procedure in these plays is set in *Venice and *Vienna respectively and is unrealistic to say the least, many critics have seen the triumph of mercy and leniency over the severity of the letter of the law in both plays as exploring the 16th-century adjustment of English common law to the practice of equity in the Court of Chancery. However, the tone of many of the references to law and lawyers is cynical in Shakespeare's plays: notably the First Clown's (Gravedigger's) mock-legal quibbling at Ophelia's graveside, followed by Hamlet's more direct, but still broadly comic, critique of the lawyer and 'his 'quiddits . . ., his quillets, his cases, his tenures, and his tricks' (*Hamlet* 5.1). 'The first thing we do, let's kill all the lawyers' is the rebellious cry of Cade's follower the Butcher in *The First Part of the Contention* (*2 Henry VI*) 4.2.78, and the play clearly expects its audience to understand his sentiment, if not to endorse his proposed course of action.

The many trials and trial-like scenes are among the most emotionally charged moments of Shakespeare's plays, often hinging on the testimony of women, such as Desdemona's defence of Othello in front of the Venetian senate (1.3), and Queen Hermione's and Queen Katherine's respective defences of themselves before their husband-kings in *The Winter's Tale* (3.2) and *All Is True* (*Henry VIII*) (2.4). The accused 'join-stool' which stands in for Gonoril, however, remains silent in Lear's fantasized trial after the storm in *King Lear* (Scene 13, not included in the *Folio version of the play). The newly crowned Henry V signals his respect for the law by retrospectively endorsing the authority of the Lord Chief Justice to punish his younger self at the end of *2 Henry IV*, and in *Henry V* much is made of his insistence on his legal claim to France by the detailed refutation of Salic Law expounded by the Archbishop of Canterbury. More often, though, tension in the drama derives from the incompetent or immoral administration of the law, whether practised by the lowly Dogberry in *Much Ado About Nothing* or by the dukes, princes, and kings elsewhere in the canon. Richard II's inability to arbitrate effectively between Bolingbroke and Mowbray, for example, and his later flouting of the laws of inheritance, precipitate his tragedy. *AB*

Campbell, John, Lord, *Shakespeare's Legal Acquirements Considered* (1859)
Cohen, Walter, '*The Merchant of Venice* and the Possibilities of Historical Criticism', *English Literary History*, 49 (1983)
Ives, E. W., 'The Law and the Lawyers', *Shakespeare Survey*, 17 (1964)
Keeton, George Williams, *Shakespeare's Legal and Political Background* (1967)
Phillips, O. Hood, *Shakespeare and the Lawyers* (1972)
Sokol, B. J., and Sokol, Mary, *Shakespeare's Legal Language* (2000)
Tucker, E. F. J., 'The Letter of the Law in *The Merchant of Venice*', *Shakespeare Survey*, 29 (1976)
Zeeveld, W. Gordon, *The Temper of Shakespeare's Thought* (1974)

Law against Lovers, The. Sir William *Davenant's first adaptation of Shakespeare was first acted early in 1662. It is a hybrid of *Measure for Measure* and *Much Ado About Nothing*, largely cast in rhyming couplets, in which Benedick is Angelo's brother: in between sparring verbally with Beatrice he fights in earnest in a cavalier uprising against his brother's puritanical regime. The Duke, self-restored to power at the close, parallels the newly restored Charles II, while Angelo turns out to have been virtuous at heart all along: in the last act he reveals that he propositioned Isabella only to test her morals, and (as in Shakespeare's main sources for *Measure for Measure*) they marry. The play was well received, and encouraged Davenant to re-write further Shakespeare plays to fit them to the modes and concerns of his own time. *MD*

'Lawn as white as driven snow', sung by Autolycus in *The Winter's Tale* 4.4.219. The earliest surviving musical setting is in John *Wilson's *Cheerful Airs or Ballads* (1660). *JB*

Lear, King. See *King Lear*.

Leavis, F(rank) R(aymond) (1895–1978), English academic, editor of the journal *Scrutiny* (1932–53), credited, by Leavis himself, with the dethronement of the critical ideas represented by A. C. *Bradley. His article 'Diabolic Intellect and the Noble Hero' (*Scrutiny* (1937), repr. in *The Common Pursuit*, 1952) stresses Othello's self-dramatizing, obtuse, and brutal egotism, vitiating the more traditional heroic version. *TM*

Le Beau, one of Duke Frederick's courtiers, warns Orlando to flee, *As You Like It* 1.2. *AB*

Lee, Sir Sidney (1859–1926), English academic, editor of the *Dictionary of National Biography* (1891), in which his first biography of Shakespeare appears (vol. 51, 1897), later expanded into a quasi-official *Life of Shakespeare* (1898, and fourteen later editions). Lee's original *Life*, the longest in the *DNB*, is regarded, despite some errors of factual detail, as striking a balance between presentation of the facts and discussion of the achievement, on the whole rejecting the current personalist approach, though not always consistently. His full-scale *Life*, expanded to 500 pages, undertakes to give verifiable references to all the original sources of information, rejecting the pseudo-fictional excesses of his predecessors; in fact, Lee does not always fully acknowledge some of his own notable changes of mind over time. Other publications include *Stratford-on-Avon from the Earliest Times to the Death of Shakespeare* (1885); *Shakespeare and the Modern Stage* (1906); and *Shakespeare and the Italian Renaissance* (1915). *TM*

Lefranc, Abel. See DERBY THEORY.

Legh, Gerard (d. 1563), writer on heraldry, whose *Accidence of Armoury* (1563), a dialogue concerning armorial bearings, included the story of King Lear, and an account of Alexander's armour which may have inspired a joke in *Love's Labour's Lost* (5.2.571–2). It also features an anecdote about a tailor which anticipates a scene in *The Taming of the Shrew* (4.3). *JKS*

Legouis, Émile (1861–1937), French academic and literary historian. Author, with Louis Cazamian, of the once-standard *Histoire de la littérature anglaise* (1924), and of *Shakespeare* (1899). *TM*

Leicester, Robert Dudley, Earl of (?1532–1588), known for his lavish entertainments at Kenilworth, near Stratford, and patron of a company of players, Leicester's Men, who performed in London and the provinces, including Stratford, in the 1570s and 1580s. In the myth about Shakespeare's youthful deer-poaching, Leicester induces Sir Thomas *Lucy to drop charges. *CS*

Leicester abbey is the place of Cardinal Wolsey's death in *All Is True* (*Henry VIII*), described by Griffith to Katherine, 4.2.17–30. *AB*

Leicester's Men. See COMPANIES, PLAYING.

Leigh, Vivien (1913–67), British actress. One of the great beauties of her time, she achieved international film stardom as Scarlett O'Hara in *Gone with the Wind* (1939). Earlier in the London theatre she had played Titania in Tyrone *Guthrie's Victorian-romantic *A Midsummer Night's Dream* as well as Ophelia at Elsinore to the Hamlet of Laurence *Olivier, whom she later married. They starred together in an unsuccessful Broadway *Romeo and Juliet*. During 1951 they played Antony and Cleopatra in London and New York. They led a memorable season at the Shakespeare Memorial in Stratford in 1955 when she was Viola and Lady Macbeth, as well as Lavinia in Peter *Brook's *Titus Andronicus*. Some critics, notably Kenneth *Tynan, would never grant that she was a stage player of the first rank. After a much publicized divorce, though often in poor physical and mental health, she acted on stage and screen and she played Viola during an Australian tour. *MJ*

Lembcke, Edvard (1815–97), Danish teacher, poet, and translator. He was the author, competent rather than exciting, of the first complete (except for *Titus Andronicus* and *Pericles*) Danish translation of Shakespeare's plays (1861–73), having revised existing translations and added his own. *I-SE*

Rubow, P. V., *Originaler og Oversættelser* (1929)

Lennox (Lenox) is a Scottish thane who first appears in attendance on Duncan, *Macbeth* 1.2. *AB*

Lennox, Charlotte (*c.*1729–1804), novelist and critic. She became a writer, praised and supported by Fielding, *Richardson, and *Johnson, after an unsuccessful stage career. She produced the first published collection of source material, with criticism, comparison, and commentary, for 22 Shakespeare plays: *Shakespeare Illustrated; or, The Novels and Histories on which the Plays of Shakespear are Founded, Collected and Translated from the Original Authors with Critical Remarks* (3 vols., 1753–4). While concerned that this publication might injure Shakespeare's reputation for originality and invention (though she often points out that Shakespeare's sources are usually clearer about motivation than the plays he makes of them), Lennox felt that her work underlined Shakespeare's more important talents for characterization and representation of life. *CMSA*

Doody, Margaret Anne, 'Shakespeare's Novels: Charlotte Lennox Illustrated', *Studies in the Novel* 19 (1987)

Lent. From 1579, playhouses were supposed to close during Lent but the order was frequently repeated (suggesting non-compliance) and in 1618 Master of the Revels George *Buck sold to John *Heminges a dispensation limiting the restriction to just Sundays, Wednesdays, and Fridays and the whole of Easter week. *GE*

Leonardo, Bassanio's servant in *The Merchant of Venice*, appears in 2.2. *AB*

Leonato is the Governor of Messina and father of Hero in *Much Ado About Nothing*. *AB*

Leonine. Ordered by Dioniza to kill Marina, he fails in his attempt, *Pericles* 15.140–1. *AB*

Leontes. See WINTER'S TALE, THE.

Leopold Shakespeare. This one-volume edition, undated (1877), and so called because it was dedicated to Prince Leopold, the youngest son of Queen Victoria, uses the text of Nicolaus Delius' edition published in Leipzig in 1854. It is notable for including *The Two Noble Kinsmen* and *Edward III*, as well as for a long introduction by F. J. *Furnivall proposing a revised chronological ordering of the texts, one close to that now generally accepted. Furnivall had published in 1874 his book *The Succession of Shakespeare's Works*. *RAF*

Lepage, Robert (b. 1957), Québécois actor and director. For Théâtre Repère in Quebec he directed a series of Shakespeare plays in 'tradaptions' in the 1990s that looked at issues relating to the subservient role of French-speakers in *Canada. In *Romeo and Juliette* (*sic*, 1989) the Montagues spoke English and the Capulets French. *A Midsummer Night's Dream* at the Royal National Theatre in London (1992) used mostly British actors—many of them people of colour, legatees of the empire—and a

Vivien Leigh as Lavinia in Peter Brook's production of *Titus Andronicus*, Stratford, 1955. The red streamers trailing from her bandaged wrists provided an abstract representation of her mutilation.

large pool of mud and water in the centre of the stage to represent the wood. Lepage also wrote, directed, and acted in *Elsinore* (1996), a one-man adaptation of *Hamlet*. *DK*

Lepidus. In *Julius Caesar* he is present at Caesar's assassination (3.1, an addition to Shakespeare's historical sources), and becomes one of the triumvirs. In *Antony and Cleopatra* he tries to keep the peace between Antony and Octavius Caesar (1.4 and 2.2) but is overthrown and imprisoned by Caesar (reported 3.5.6–11). He is based on Lepidus M. Aemilius (d. 13 BC). *AB*

Lessing, Gotthold Ephraim (1729–81), German dramatist and critic. In his *17th Literaturbrief* (1759) and in *Hamburgische Dramaturgie* (1767–69) he justified Shakespeare from a rationalist point of view and recommended English drama in general as a model preferable to that of French classicism. His plea paved the way towards classic German drama. *WH*

Letourneur, Pierre (1736–88), French translator. Letourneur's liberal translation of the Shakespearian repertoire (in 20 volumes, 1776–83) testifies to an unprecedented, proto-Romantic attempt to modernize Shakespeare's style by alternating prose and verse, thus putting an end to the traditional classical interpretations of *Voltaire (who was horrified) and La Place. Nevertheless, the desire to 'improve' Shakespeare, really no more than the desire to obviate ridicule, is still evident in passages that might offend a Parisian audience's sense of propriety or produce an unacceptably comic effect in the middle of a serious scene. Consequently, some of Hamlet's quibbles and the obscenities in his language to *Ophelia were omitted or placed among the notes. Equally, a hero could not be allowed to speak disrespectfully to his father's spirit, and in Hamlet's remarks to his father's subterranean ghost 'boy' became 'étranger', 'truepenny', 'ombre royale', and 'old mole', 'invisible fantôme'. Likewise Ophelia was not merely 'sewing' in her closet when Hamlet burst in, but 'occupée à broder'. Such substitutions were intended to please a public for whom the prosaic handkerchief in *Othello* had to be transformed into a 'bandeau de diamants'. *AC*

Bailey, H. P., *Hamlet in France from Voltaire to Laforgue* (1964)

Leveridge, Richard (1670–1758), English bass singer and composer. He is principally remembered for his incidental music (often wrongly attributed to *Locke) for the *Davenant adaptation of *Macbeth* (1702), though, anticipating *Britten, he also composed a mock Italian opera based on the mechanicals' play from *A Midsummer Night's Dream*, *Pyramus and Thisbe: A Comic Masque* (1716). So popular was Leveridge's *Macbeth* score that even when Shakespeare's 'original' was restored (1744) the singing and dancing witches were retained. Leveridge's music remained in use in London theatres until well into the 19th century. *IBC*

Lewis, Matthew 'Monk' (1775–1818), English novelist. The extravagant *Gothic novel that made Lewis's (nick-)name, *The Monk* (1796), rewrites *Measure for Measure*: Lewis borrows its Catholic setting, derives its hypocritical principal character Ambrosio from Angelo, and elaborates his proposed transgression into a series of satanic crimes. *NJW*

Liang Shiqui (1903–87), the first Chinese writer to translate all of Shakespeare's plays. He began his *translation in 1922 and his work was completed and published in Taiwan in 1967. *HQX*

liberties, land, either in monastic or royal ownership, which was free from the jurisdiction of the civic authorities. After the Henrician dissolution, liberties became the focus of certain commercial activities (particularly animal-baiting and acting) which were subject to control within civic areas. The Liberty of the *Clink, on *Bankside, was the focus of much of this, and hence became the most important theatre district, but north of the river the *Blackfriars theatre, too, occupied a similar geographical loophole. *RSB*

licensing. See CENSORSHIP; PRINTING AND PUBLISHING.

Lieutenant of the Tower. He apologizes to King Henry, *Richard Duke of York* (*3 Henry VI*) 4.7, for confining him, but brings Richard of Gloucester to him, 5.6. *AB*

Lieutenant to Aufidius. He discusses Coriolanus with Aufidius, *Coriolanus* 4.7. *AB*

Ligarius, Caius. He is one of the conspirators in *Julius Caesar*, based on Quintus Ligarius. Caius is *Plutarch's name for him, followed by Shakespeare. *AB*

lighting. Open-air playhouses used available daylight supplemented by cresset-lights (oil-soaked rope burning in a metal basket) in the early evening. Putting the stage in the north-east corner of the yard would have maximized the sunlight on the stage, but although the Rose's stage was so located, the stage of the *Globe seems to have been in the shaded south-east corner. The indoor hall playhouses relied heavily on candles throughout the performance, enabling visual illusions such as the gradual increase in lighting intensity (by lighting additional candles) immediately prior to a scene of night (achieved by quickly extinguishing most of the candles) in order to increase the subjective feeling of being plunged into darkness. *GE*

'Light o' love', a ballad tune title quoted in *The Two Gentlemen of Verona* 1.2.83, in *Much Ado About Nothing* 3.4.40, in *The Two Noble Kinsmen* 5.4.54, and in several other contemporary plays too. *JB*

Lillo, George (?1691–1739), playwright. The author of *The London Merchant; or, The History of George Barnwell* (1731), which influenced much subsequent European drama by its willingness to take a middle-class apprentice as its tragic hero, was himself profoundly influenced by Shakespeare and the Elizabethans. He adapted the apocryphal **Arden of Faversham*, used *Macbeth* as a model for his *Fatal Curiosity* (1736), in which a wife urges her husband to murder and rob the guest who turns out to be their son, and in 1738 rewrote the last section (Scenes 15–22) of *Pericles* as *Marina*, which he dedicated to the *Shakespeare Ladies' Club. *MD*

Limoges. See AUSTRIA, DUKE OF.

Lincoln, Bishop of. Henry VIII's confessor, he admits he counselled him to divorce Katherine, *All Is True* (*Henry VIII*) 2.4.208 ff. *AB*

Lincoln's Inn. See INNS OF COURT.

Lincoln's Inn Fields, west of the city of London, was the site of three theatres, occupied by *Davenant's Duke's Company from 1661 to 1671, briefly by the King's Company, and by *Betterton from 1695 to 1705. The theatre that opened in 1714 was one of London's two patent houses until 1732. *CMSA*

Ling, Nicholas. See PRINTING AND PUBLISHING.

Linley, Thomas, Jr. (1756–78), English composer. Before his tragically early death in a boating accident, Linley composed two major Shakespearian works. *A Lyric Ode on the Fairies, Aerial Beings and Witches of Shakespeare* (which sets an imitation of *Garrick's Jubilee Ode written by French Lawrence when still a schoolboy at Winchester) was performed at Drury Lane in 1776, and his splendid incidental music for *The Tempest* the following January. His Storm Chorus for *The Tempest* proved particularly popular for many years. *IBC*

'Lion'. See SNUG.

Lisle, Lord. See JOHN TALBOT.

litotes, a figure of speech, related to meiosis, which affirms something indirectly and ironically by understatement ('we have seen better days'—*As You Like It* 2.7.120), most commonly using negation ('Nor do we find him forward to be sounded'—*Hamlet* 3.1.7). *CB*

Li tre saltiri (The Three Satyrs), an Italian play in the *commedia dell'arte* tradition which bears resemblances to the plot of *The Tempest.* The action takes place on an island ruled by a magician and features the attempt by a native and some shipwrecked men to steal the magician's book and usurp his power. *JKS*

livery. As the household servants of their patron, sharers in a playing company were given distinctive clothing (livery) identifying their master. In 1604 each of the King's Men (including Shakespeare) received 4½ yards (4 metres) of red cloth for James I's delayed coronation procession. *GE*

Livy (Titus Livius) (50 BC–AD 17) was the author of a famous history of Rome called *Ab urbe condita libri.* Its second book treats of Rome after the expulsion of the Tarquins, and Shakespeare may have used this in *The Rape of Lucrece.* In 1601 Philemon Holland's English translation of Livy, *The History of the World,* appeared; Shakespeare drew on it for *Othello* and *Coriolanus.* *RW*

Dorey, T. A., *Latin Historians* (1966)
Baldwin, T. W., *William Shakspere's Small Latine & Lesse Greeke* (2 vols., 1944)

Llorca, Denis (b. 1931), French director. Representative of the 1970s, his Shakespeare productions favoured a sense of pleasure and magic: these included *Henry IV* (1972), *Falstaff* (1974), *Hamlet,* using white masks (1975), *Twelfth Night* with an all-male cast (1971), *Romeo and Juliet* (1978) with five actresses. He has since retired from the live theatre. *ISG*

Lloyd, William Watkiss (1813–93), English classical scholar, historian, biographer, and critic. His essays on the life and plays of Shakespeare appeared in 1856, to accompany the edition of Samuel Weller Singer. His 35 *Critical Essays on the Plays of Shakespeare,* which follow the Folio order and selection, with the addition of *Pericles,* were collected in 1858, and are still occasionally consulted by lecturers lost for inspiration. *TM*

locality boards. In *An Apology for Poetry* Philip *Sidney refers to a theatrical convention which indicates that written labels identified fictional locations: 'What child is there, that coming to a play, and seeing "Thebes" written in great letters upon an old door, does believe that it is Thebes?' Presumably entrance through such a door indicated that the ensuing scene occurred in the place named in the label. It is not clear whether this practice was confined to certain venues in certain periods but Shakespeare's use of scene-setting dialogue seems to obviate it. *GE*

Locke, Matthew (*c.*1621/3–1677), English composer. Although he composed incidental music for *Davenant's adaptation of *Macbeth* (1673), little survives; most of the 'famous' music, often erroneously attributed to him, is actually by *Leveridge. Locke also contributed substantial instrumental pieces to the Davenant–Dryden adaptation of *The Tempest* (1667). *IBC*

Locrine. The original *title page (1595) suggests that this pseudo-historical *tragedy was 'overseene and corrected' by W.S. The editors of the third *Folio included it in their collection, although Shakespeare's role, if any, was probably limited to copy-editing for publication. *SM*

Lodge, Thomas (1557/8?–1625), poet, dramatist, and prose-writer, son of the lord mayor of London, and University Wit. Lodge's literary career spanned many genres including contemporary satire, literary criticism (*A Defence of Poetry,* 1580), two plays (*The Wounds of Civil War,* 1588, and *A Looking Glass for London and England,* 1590), and various pastoral romances. It was the romance *Rosalynde, Euphues Golden Legacy,* published in 1590, that garnered Lodge the most praise in his lifetime and caught Shakespeare's attention. Its popularity was probably a considerable part of its attraction for the dramatist who took it as the main source for *As You Like It.* Indeed, the title of Shakespeare's play may allude to the dramatist's sense that he was giving the public what it wanted. *Rosalynde* provided all the main action of *As You Like It* and was also a source of those pastoral conventions which defined the meeting of aristocrats and shepherds in the bucolic landscape, and their poetic expressions of love. Shakespeare fulfilled audience expectations but also made the romance more naturalistic by excising some of *Rosalynde*'s violence and melodrama, and by introducing a broader social perspective. The satirical humour of Shakespeare's Rosalind, Touchstone, and Jaques exposes the pretentiousness of pastoral romance but only Jaques resists the conventional happy ending. *JKS*

Lodovico, Brabanzio's kinsman on Venetian state business in Cyprus, helps uncover the truth of events at the end of *Othello.* *AB*

'Lodowick, Friar'. See VINCENTIO.

London. Capital of the United Kingdom, the dominant natural feature that has shaped the development of London is the River Thames, which runs through the Thames Valley to the sea. Originally slow moving and much wider than now, the Thames was and is a major influence in settlement patterns and activity, dictating both areas suitable for occupation and locations suitable for crossing. Glacial erosion and deposition during the last Ice Age (*c.*10,000 years ago) caused the formation of gravel islands capped with sand (eyots) along the south bank of the Thames whilst cutting terraces through the steeper, higher topography of the north bank. It is in the marshy land in between the eyots on the south bank that the archaeological evidence of London's Tudor and Stuart playhouses has been recorded: the damp soils being perfect for the preservation of archaeological remains.

Before establishing control in Britain, the Romans probably forded the Thames in the area of modern-day Westminster, as this was the lowest fordable point in the river. Once control had been established (*c.* AD 50) the Romans began to establish a permanent settlement on the north bank of the Thames on two flat-topped gravel hills (now Ludgate Hill and Cornhill) which rose above the Thames. Topography also dictated the location of the first bridge across the river, in the vicinity of modern-day London Bridge, as it was here that the Thames was narrow enough to bridge (about half a mile (1 km) wide at high tide) but deep enough to bring in ocean-going vessels. The bridge meant that Londinium became the focus and hub of a road network linking the south-coast ports with the remainder of the country. *Southwark, at the southern end of the bridge, became the entry point to London from the south.

The 5th century saw the decline and end of the Roman administration in London and a shift in the focus of settlement to the west of the walled Roman town, with the main Saxon settlement (Lundenwic) located around modern-day Covent Garden. However, from the 9th century onwards people moved back into the walled, Roman town and from the late Saxon/early medieval period the City again became the focus of settlement. It was this expanding medieval city that Shakespeare entered in the late 1580s.

The London that Shakespeare knew was a changing city with economic and social pressures challenging the established order. The wealth of London's ruling elite, derived from commerce, land, and patronage, had brought increasing contact and liaison with European traders and merchants and led to London's development as a centre of European commerce and trade. In particular the trade in English wool with the Florentine cloth industry (with Italian merchants bringing spices and luxury cloth) kick-started London's economy and led to huge migration from the provinces. Despite high mortality, this led to a dramatic increase in London's population in the 16th and 17th centuries: the best guesses permitted by uncertain evidence suggest the city grew from a population of *c.*200,000 in 1600 to *c.*400,000 in 1650.

The growth of London's population through internal migration and immigration and the

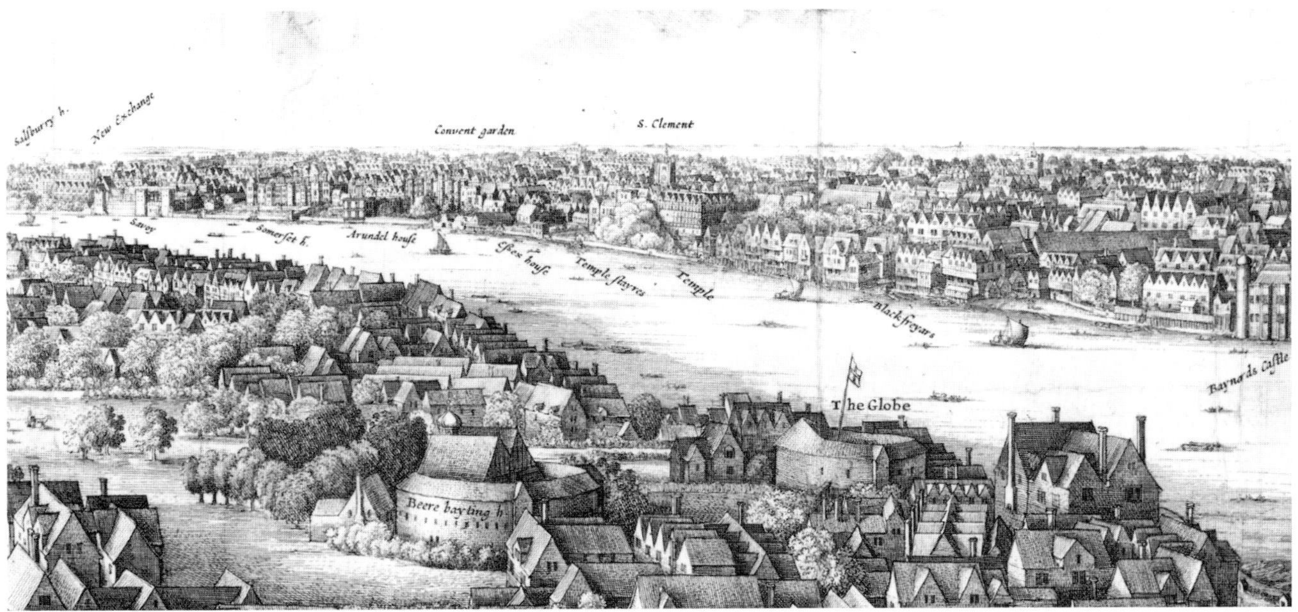

The second Globe (1614), rebuilt after the fire of 1613, from Wenceslaus Hollar's remarkably accurate Long View of London (1641). Hollar mistakenly labelled the Globe 'Beere-bayting house' and gave the label 'The Globe' to the nearby Paris Garden bear-baiting arena.

love/hate relationship that London held with foreign traders, merchants, and residents are recurring themes through London's history and development. For historians the records, diaries, and letters of overseas visitors, traders, diplomats, and residents provide valuable evidence of London life and, in particular, of London life in the 16th and 17th centuries. The pleasures offered by London also attracted large numbers of country gentlemen, to the extent that one observer suggests this led to a neglect of public duties and a shortage of justices, deputy lieutenants, and commissioners for the muster elsewhere in the country.

The pleasures included the opportunity to take part in trade and industry, to get access to education, and to get access to London's variety of entertainment. Cloth had replaced wool as England's major export with one estimate suggesting that, in the 16th century, over 20% of London's workforce was involved in some aspect of the making of clothes. The increase in industrial activity, to meet the needs of the growing population, saw the dirtier industries (leather manufacturing, glass and pottery manufacturing, etc.) moved to the south and east, away from the noses of the city. At the same time, these new industrial areas, with their immigrant workforce, led to the decline in the power and influence of the city-based guilds.

It was this city of contradictions (a cosmopolitan trading centre in which inhabitants lived in fear of at least one of the many threats (the mob, increasing migrant population, infectious diseases, and God) that provided the cultural, social, and economic conditions in which playhouses developed—illustrating, in their turn, an increasing freedom enjoyed by London's citizens. After the Henrician dissolution of the monasteries, large tracts of land both within and adjacent to the city were available for new forms of development. The advantage of the old monastic *liberties was that they remained of dubious judicial authority, with neither the city, the Crown, nor the local justices being able (or willing) to maintain control over these areas. This provided players (and bearwardens) with the opportunity to erect permanent, purpose-built structures in which they could provide entertainment for London's growing population.

The development of permanent, purpose-built playhouses encapsulates some of the contradictions of early modern London and this appears to be borne out by the effect of Tudor Poor Law legislation, particularly the 1572 Act for the Punishment of Vagabonds. This is the most repressive of the Tudor Poor Laws, with fencers, bearwardens, and common players included in the definition of rogues, vagabonds, or sturdy beggars. The penalty, under the 1572 Act, for an initial offence of being convicted as a rogue, vagabond, or sturdy beggar was to be whipped and have a hot compass iron (of about an inch) bored through the gristle of the right ear. The penalty for a second offence under the same Act was to be condemned as a felon, whilst the penalty for a third offence was death and forfeiture of land and goods. To avoid being convicted as a rogue, vagabond, or sturdy beggar, one needed either to have land or to have a master—an incentive, if one were needed, for groups of travelling actors to obtain a noble patron.

At the same time, the nobility had an incentive to find a group of players to master. In an age of *patronage, favour, and sinecure, representation at court could be the beginning or end of an illustrious career. One way to curry favour was to provide entertainment for the monarch and the monarch's visitors. Contemporary documents contain evidence of groups of actors (and bearwardens with their bears) entertaining the monarch at significant holiday times (Christmas, Easter, Whitsuntide, etc.) and providing entertainment for visiting dignitaries. Permanent, purpose-built places of entertainment provided such professionals with a venue in which to perfect their art.

The architectural heritage and development of theatres—particularly the open-air/amphitheatre type structures—appears as multifaceted as the social and economic history of their development. Cartographic evidence appears to show the development of the open-air theatres following the form taken by the animal-baiting pits. The earliest cartographic evidence of animal-baiting is from a 1542 manuscript map of Southwark (sometimes known as Long Southwark) which locates a bullring along the west side of Borough High Street but the map does not provide any architectural information. The 'Agas' map (*c.*1562) and the Braun and Hogenberg map of 1572 both show animal-baiting pits and provide an image of the type of structure we now associate with animal-baiting and the outdoor playhouse—the circular or polygonal, timber-framed structure with timber galleries surrounding an open, central yard. Elsewhere, both in and adjacent to the city, inns and existing buildings within the old

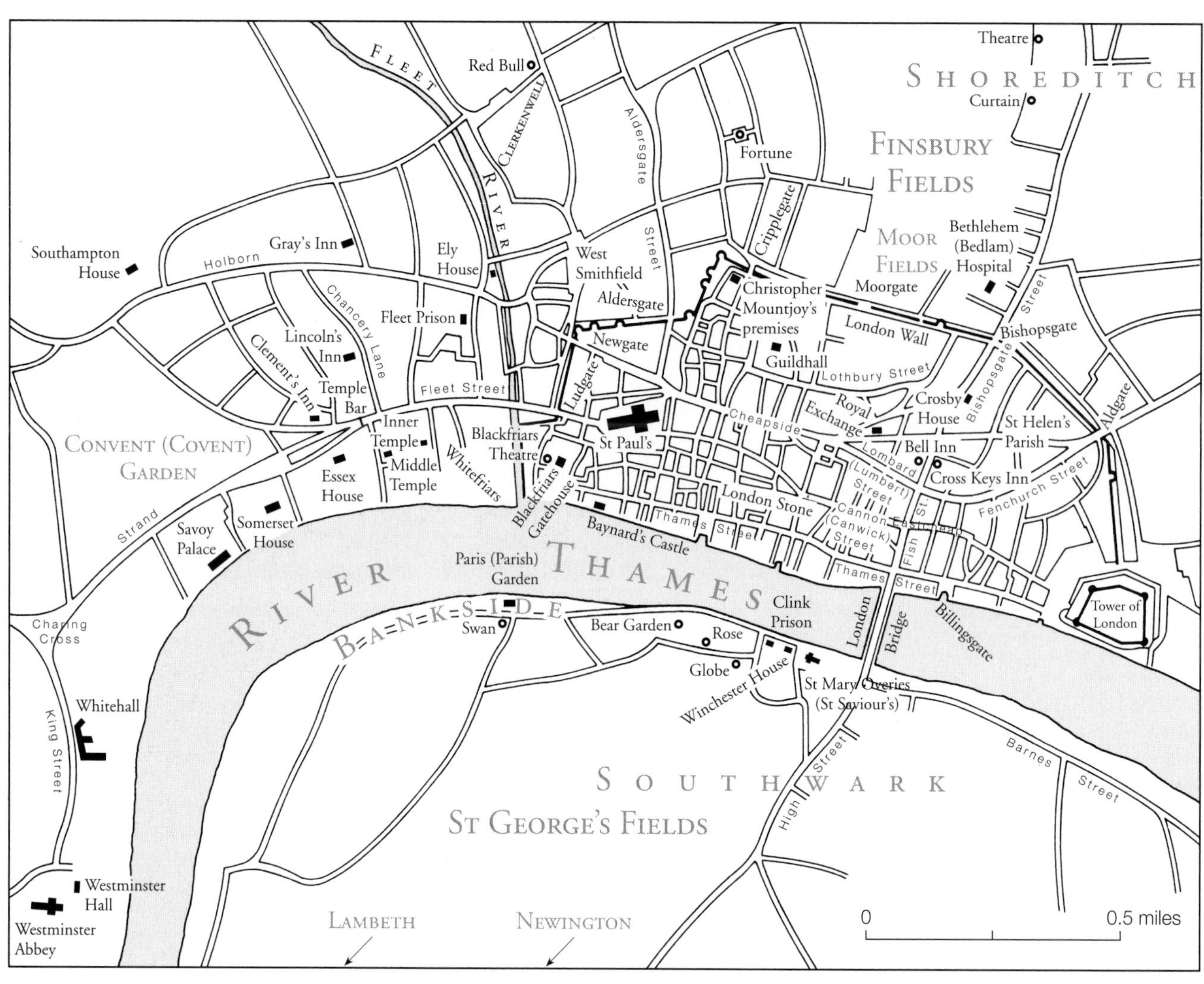

London in Shakespeare's time

monastic liberties were adapted and used for playing.

The chronology of the demise of London's playhouses is less certain than previously thought, with evidence emerging that Puritan leaders and supporters visited theatres as a means of leisure. It seems possible that the playhouse Closure Orders of 1642, 1647, and 1648 were instigated by concerns about public order, rather than by a religious crusade: the soldiers' raids of January 1649, for example, on the Red Bull, Salisbury Court, the Fortune, and the Phoenix were undertaken with a view to removing potential points of public meeting and disorder before the trial of the King. That some playhouses continued to exist and continued to provide spectacle throughout the period of the Civil Wars, to 1660, does not now seem to be in doubt. Political, military, and economic circumstance led to a reduction in the number of venues and performances although the Restoration of the monarchy witnessed a new impetus for drama and dramatic venues. *RSB*

Gurr, A., *The Shakespearean Stage 1574–1642* (3rd edn. 1992)
Inwood, S., *A History of London* (1998)
Johnson, D., *Southwark and the City* (1969)
Survey of London, XXII, *Bankside (The Parishes of St. Saviour and Christchurch Southwark)* (1950)
Weinreb, B., and Hibbert, C. (eds.), *The London Encyclopedia* (1983)
Weinstein, R., *Tudor London* (1994)

London, Mayor of. See MAYOR OF LONDON.

London Prodigal, The (pub. 1605). This humorous *comedy of manners, or city comedy, was written around 1603–5 and reprinted as Shakespeare's in the Third *Folio. Despite the ascription to Shakespeare on the original title page, its authorship remains controversial. *SM*

Longespée, William de. See SALISBURY, EARL OF.

Longleat manuscript. A pen and ink drawing made by Henry Peacham of a scene from *Titus Andronicus*, dated 1595, provides the only extant contemporary illustration of a Shakespearian production. The manuscript leaf, now in the library of the Marquess of Bath at Longleat, includes a *stage direction that does not appear in any printed text, 'Enter Tamora pleadinge for her sonnes going to execution,' followed by a transcript of lines 1.1.104–21 and 5.1.125–44 from the play. The drawing has occasioned much comment (some denying that it depicts Shakespeare's play at all, some treating it as infallible evidence as to how *Titus* looked in early performances), while its details have been the basis for various conflicting accounts of Elizabethan theatrical costuming. Some of the characters' outfits make gestures towards classical Roman attire whereas others, most obviously the soldiers to the left, appear to be in Elizabethan costume. *ER*

Cerasano, S. P., ' "Borrowed Robes", Costume Prices, and the Drawing of *Titus Andronicus*', *Shakespeare Studies*, 22 (1994)
Metz, Harold G., 'Titus *Andronicus:* A Watermark in the Longleat Manuscript', *Shakespeare Quarterly*, 36 (1985)

long lines, lines of hexameter (infrequent) or heptameter (rare). Because the six-foot line, unlike the pentameter, tends to divide in half, Shakespeare sometimes uses it to emphasize a contrast: 'To have what we would have, we speak not what we mean' (*Measure for Measure* 2.4.118). *GTW*

Longueville is one of the three lords who attend the King of Navarre in *Love's Labour's Lost*: he falls in love with Maria. Many editors since *Pope have called him 'Longaville'. *AB*

Looney, Thomas. See OXFORDIAN THEORY.

Lopez, Roderigo (d. 1594). The Queen's physician, he was a Portuguese crypto-*Jew executed in 1594, accused of trying to poison *Elizabeth at the instigation of King Philip of Spain. Graziano's tirade against Shylock as a wolf (*lupus*) 'hanged for human slaughter' in *The Merchant of Venice* (4.1.133) may refer to Lopez. *CS*

Lord Chamberlain. In *All Is True* (*Henry VIII*) he is a 'comptroller' (controller, organizer) at Wolsey's feast (1.4), and one of the Council which arraigns Cranmer (5.2). *AB*

Lord Chamberlain. One of the most powerful of court officials, the Lord Chamberlain was responsible for assigning lodgings in the palace, for the court's travel arrangements, for the reception of overseas dignitaries, and for the court's entertainments including plays. The Revels Office, and its Master, were but part of the Lord Chamberlain's vast responsibility. Henry Carey, Lord *Hunsdon, was appointed Lord Chamberlain on 4 July 1585 and in May 1594 he formed a playing company, the *Chamberlain's Men, which included Shakespeare. Henry Carey died on 22 July 1596 and the office passed to William Brooke, 7th Lord *Cobham. At this time Shakespeare's company reverted to the name of Henry's son George Carey (the 2nd Lord Hunsdon) and so were Hunsdon's Men. Fortunately for Shakespeare's company Cobham—who objected to his ancestor Sir John *Oldcastle being mocked when Shakespeare's *1 Henry IV* played at court over Christmas 1596—died on 5 March 1597 and George Carey was appointed to the chamberlainship; the company again had an influential patron. The Lord Chamberlain's office remained responsible for overseeing the theatre industry until 1968 and its records (which include, for example, the Sharers Papers) are a major source of our dramatic knowledge. *GE*

Lord Chancellor. In *All Is True* (*Henry VIII*) he presides at the meeting of the Council (5.2) and formally accuses Cranmer of heresy. *AB*

Lord Chief Justice. He derides Falstaff, *2 Henry IV*, 1.2. His fears for his position after the death of Henry IV prove unfounded, 5.2. *AB*

Lord Dumain, First and **Second.** The brothers hatch a plot for Paroles's downfall, *All's Well That Ends Well* 3.6, which they later carry out. *AB*

Lord Marshal. He officiates at the Coventry lists, *Richard II* 1.3. *AB*

lords. **(1)** Finding Sly lying drunk a lord decides to play a practical joke on him in the Induction to *The Taming of the Shrew.* **(2)** A Roman lord breaks down, leaving Lucius to tell the story of the wrongs done to his family, *Titus Andronicus* 5.3. **(3)** Two lords attend the Princess of France, *Love's Labour's Lost* 2.1. **(4)** Lords recount Jaques's speech on the fallen stag, *As You Like It* 2.1. Other lords attend Duke Frederick, 2.2. **(5)** Four lords are presented as potential husbands to Helen, *All's Well That Ends Well* 2.3. **(6)** A lord discusses Scottish affairs with Lennox, *Macbeth* 3.6. **(7)** A lord is a voice of moderation amidst the hysteria of Acts 2 and 3 of *The Winter's Tale.* **(8)** Two lords accompany Cloten, *Cymbeline* 1.2 and 2.1, one of them making sarcastic asides. A Briton lord listens to Posthumus' account of the battle against the Romans, *Cymbeline* 5.5. *AB*

Lords Room. A number of contemporary references indicate that a part of the playhouse auditorium had this name, although whether one or more lords is meant is unclear—any possessive apostrophe we apply must be speculative—and we should remember that 'room' commonly meant 'space' rather than 'chamber'. The standard work by W. J. Lawrence identified the Lords Room as the balcony behind and above the stage as seen in de Witt's drawing of the *Swan, but this generates a number of problems. In 1592 *Henslowe paid for a ceiling to be installed in the Lords Room at the *Rose and for another in 'the room over the tirehouse', so it would seem that the Lords Room was not the room over the tiring house. Sir John Davies's epigram 'In Sillam', written in 1595 or 1596, describes a gallant sitting on the stage at a playhouse instead of choosing either 'the best and most conspicuous place' or else the stage balcony. This suggests that the Lords Room was either not 'the best and most conspicuous place'—as we would expect of an aristocrat's seat—or it was not in the stage balcony. In addition to these problems it is difficult to imagine the aristocrats putting up with

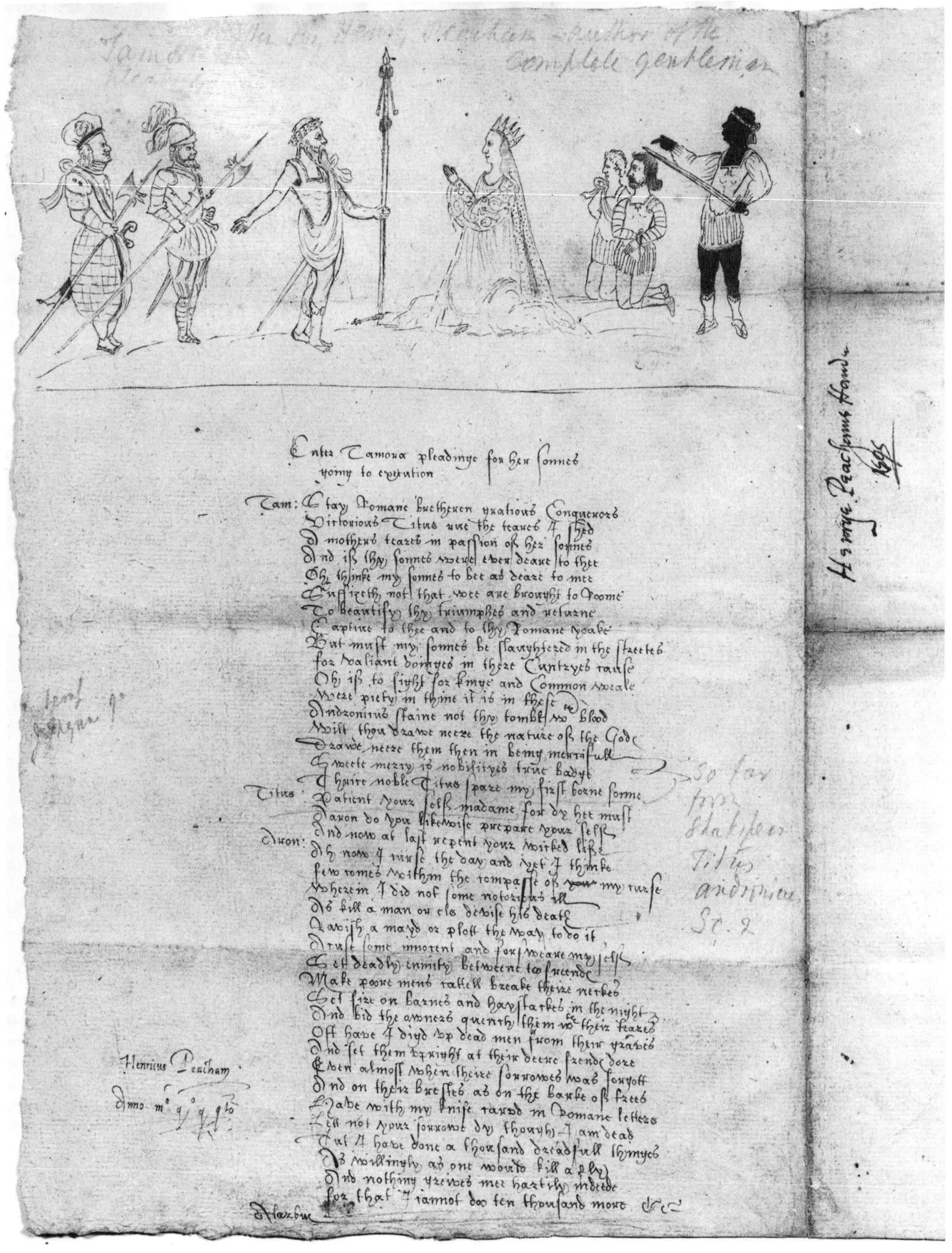

The Longleat MS, attributed to Henry Peacham and dated 1595, though it appears to conflate Tamora's plea in the opening scene of *Titus Andronicus* with a subsequent moment from Aaron's role (since he should not be armed at this moment) provides our only contemporary image of a Shakespeare play in performance.

extremely poor sightlines to the 'discoveries' which were a recurrent feature of the drama. It is probable that, like the 'gentlemens roomes' described in the contract to build the Fortune, the Lords Room was in the lowest auditorium gallery directly adjacent to the stage. *GE*

Egan, Gabriel, 'The Situation of the "Lords Room": A Revaluation', *Review of English Studies*, 48 (1997)

Lawrence, W. J., *The Elizabethan Playhouse and Other Studies* (1912)

Lorenzo elopes with Jessica in *The Merchant of Venice*. *AB*

'lost years' of William Shakespeare. The period between 1585, when Shakespeare's twins were baptized in Stratford, and 1592, when Robert *Greene obliquely alluded to him in his *Groatsworth of Wit*, are often known as the 'lost years', since there is no documentary evidence about him except in a reference in a court case involving Edmund *Lambert. A starting date of 1585 for this period presupposes that he remained in Stratford until his family was established, but some conjectures about his employment, whether in or out of Stratford, before he became an actor concern the period between leaving school—whenever that was—and marrying. *Dowdall reported that he had been apprenticed to a butcher. *Malone, who had been a barrister, deduced that he must have been employed 'in the office of some country attorney', and many others, including E. I. Fripp (who thought that legal imagery often obtruded inartistically into the works), agreed. Duff Cooper (a soldier), who wrote a book called *Sergeant Shakespeare* (1949), was not the first to show that he must have been a soldier. William Bliss, on the other hand (*The Real Shakespeare*, 1947), proposed that he had circumnavigated the globe with Drake on the *Golden Hind*. E. B. Everitt (*The Young Shakespeare*, 1954) saw him as a scrivener. John *Aubrey's report that 'he had been in his younger years a schoolmaster in the country' had behind it the testimony of William *Beeston, whose father had acted with Shakespeare. It has been used to support the hypothesis that the William *Shakeshaft named in the will of Alexander Houghton in 1581 is Shakespeare, though Shakeshaft is not explicitly called a teacher (and of course 1581 pre-dates the 'lost years'). *SW*

Honigmann, E. A. J., *Shakespeare: The 'Lost Years'* (1985, rev. edn. 1998)

Louis, King. Warwick and Margaret unite with Louis against Edward IV in *Richard Duke of York* (*3 Henry VI*) 3.3. He is based on Louis XI (1423–83), King of France, the first cousin of both Henry VI and Margaret. *AB*

Louis the Dauphin. **(1)** *Henry V*. See DAUPHIN. **(2)** In *King John* his marriage to Blanche does not prevent him from taking up arms against her uncle, John. He is based on Louis (1187–1226), who succeeded to the French throne as Louis VIII in 1223. *AB*

Loutherbourg, Philip James de (1740–1812), French designer. He was born in Strasbourg and studied art in Paris before moving to London in 1771 and presenting *Garrick with revolutionary staging plans for Drury Lane. Innovative in his use of perspective, as well as lighting and costume, he may have designed for *Richard III*, and his moving scenic display *Eidophusikon* (1781) was a device adopted by Edmund *Kean for the staging of *King Lear* in 1820. *CMSA*

Love in a Forest. Charles Johnson's short-lived 1723 adaptation of *As You Like It* tidies up Shakespeare's comedy on *neoclassical lines, cutting Touchstone and all the rustic characters, and pairing off Celia with Jaques instead of an unforgiven Oliver. Apologizing in a prologue, Johnson makes it clear that he would rather see Shakespeare's plays as potential aristocratic gardens than as forests of Arden:

> Forgive our modern author's honest zeal,
> He hath attempted boldly, if not well:
> Believe, he only does with pain and care,
> Presume to weed the beautiful parterre.

MD

Lovel, Lord. He is one of Richard's henchmen in *Richard III*. He appears in Act 3 of *Folio editions. *AB*

Lovell, Sir Thomas. Present at Wolsey's banquet in *All Is True* (*Henry VIII*) 1.4, he also conducts Buckingham away from his trial, 2.1. *AB*

'Love, love, nothing but love', sung by Pandarus in *Troilus and Cressida* 3.1.111. The original music is unknown. *JB*

Lover's Complaint, A *(see page 262)*

Love's Labour's Lost *(see page 264)*

Love's Labour's Won Francis *Meres lists a play by this title among Shakespeare's works in 1598, and we know that it even got into print in quarto: *Love's Labour's Won* is listed in an extant bookseller's catalogue compiled in August 1603. Scholars have suggested that this may have been the original title of another Shakespeare play known by a different title after 1598, but no comedy written before 1598 and not mentioned by Meres fits this title. It seems almost certain that before 1598 Shakespeare had written a comedy called *Love's Labour's Won*, possibly a sequel to *Love's Labour's Lost*, which for some reason failed to get into the Folio, but no copies of the quarto have yet come to light. Anyone finding one should contact the editors of this volume immediately. *MD*

Baldwin, T. W., *Shakspere's Loves Labours Won* (1957)

Low Countries. The earliest contacts between the Elizabethan stage and the Low Countries date from the late 16th century. At this time, the strolling players, on their way to Germany and beyond, first performed in venues like Amsterdam, Utrecht, Leiden, Brussels, and Ghent. This explains how *Titus Andronicus* became a model for Jan Vos's *Aran and Titus* (1641), why *The Taming of the Shrew* was first translated and performed in the early 1650s, and how in 1651 *Richard III* became a source for Lambert van den Bosch's *Red and White Rose of Lancaster and York*, a chronicle play glancing at the regicide of *Charles I and the Cromwellian protectorate.

With the rise of French classicism in the 1660s, interest in Shakespearian drama declined, despite words of admiration from critics like Justus van Effen and J. C. Weyerman. As *Voltaire's voice prevailed, spectatorial writings of English origin became the main Shakespearian conduits for many years. Around the mid-18th century R. M. van Goens and Hieronymus van Alphen were the first to renounce normative poetics, cultivating an image of Shakespeare founded on the early German *Romantics' views of individual genius and the imagination. In 1778, the publisher Albrecht Borchers initiated the first *translation project, using both the Edward *Capell text and J. J. *Eschenburg's German prose translation. Until well into the 19th century, however, the Dutch translations of Jean François Ducis's classicist French pseudo-Shakespeare held their position, in the study and on the stage. Only around the middle of the century (with Jurriaan Moulin, the Dutch novelist Jacob van Lennep, and the Ghent poet Napoleon Destanberg) did the professional translation of Shakespeare from the original English come into its own, culminating in Dutch renderings of the complete works by A. S. Kok (1880) and L. A. J. Burgersdijk (1877–85). Burgersdijk's translation of *The Merchant of Venice* premièred in 1880 with Louis Bouwmeester as Shylock. This was to become the most popular Dutch Shakespeare interpretation of all time, with over 2,000 performances worldwide, including one at Stratford-upon-Avon on 3 August 1921. Abroad, Bouwmeester would perform in Dutch, his supporting cast in English. The late 19th century also saw the rise of Shakespeare criticism in the Low Countries. This included literary interpretation, but also produced valuable work on the cultural relations between the English and Dutch stages in the 17th century (H. E. Moltzer and J. A. Worp).

During the 20th century, Shakespeare's popularity in the Low Countries only increased. His plays continue to be translated, and the list of distinguished translators has come to include Jacques van Looy, Bert Voeten, Dolf Verspoor, and Gerrit Komrij, as well as the Fleming Willy Courteaux, who is responsible for the only translation into Dutch of the complete plays

(cont. on page 263)

A Lover's Complaint

Shakespeare's poetic depiction of a seduced and abandoned woman, the last and at 329 lines the shortest of his narrative poems, was published at the end of the Sonnets when they first appeared in quarto in 1609. Although it uses the same rhyme-royal stanza as *The Rape of Lucrece* (1593–4), the poem shares some imagery, phrasing, and rare vocabulary with *All's Well That Ends Well*, *Hamlet*, and *King Lear*, and was probably composed when Shakespeare was revising and completing his sonnet sequence, possibly while the theatres were closed by plague in 1603–4.

Text: The whole of the 1609 volume (*see* SONNETS) appears to have been set from a transcript rather than from an authorial holograph. *A Lover's Complaint* is at times misleadingly punctuated, but otherwise the 1609 text poses few problems. The poem reappeared in 1640 in the printer John Benson's pirated *Poems: Written by W. Shakespeare, Gent.*, but this text merely reprints that of the 1609 quarto and has no authority.

Sources: *A Lover's Complaint* has no specific single source, but, like *The Rape of Lucrece*, draws on a well-established poetic tradition which goes back to *Ovid's heroic epistles. The dramatization in verse of the sorrows of unfortunate women had more recently featured in *The *Mirror for Magistrates* (1559, reprinted and augmented thereafter), a collection of poems in which historical figures lament their fates, and the form had been adopted by Samuel *Daniel, whose *Complaint of Rosamond* (1592), the lament of Henry II's ill-fated mistress, employs the same rhyme-royal stanza.

Synopsis: The narrator describes hearing the echoing voice of a woman lamenting in a valley, and then seeing her, wearing a straw hat, her beauty faded with time and grief. She sits beside a river, weeping, reading and tearing up love letters, throwing gifts of jewels into the water, and breaking rings (ll. 1–56). An old man grazing his cattle nearby comes and sits with her and asks what is the matter and whether he can help (ll. 57–70). The remainder of the poem, from line 71 onwards (the start of the eleventh of 47 stanzas), is given over to her reply. She first explains (ll. 71–84) that she is not as old as she looks: her beauty has in fact been damaged by sorrow as a consequence of her wooing by a young man she goes on to describe at length (85–133). Young and almost androgynously beautiful, with brown curling hair, eloquent, and a brilliant horseman, his gifts, especially of rhetoric, made him universally popular. She explains that though many women desired him and sought to own pictures of him, she did not pursue him herself, and at first was immune to his charms, recognizing that he was capable of perjury and had seduced others (ll. 134–75). She only fell when he made the speech she goes on to quote (ll. 176–280), in which he claimed that his previous amours had all been mere lusts of the flesh, while his vows to her were the first he had ever made sincerely. He showed her locks of hair different women had given him, together with gifts of jewels, which he then gave to her, tokens of conquest passed on to his conqueror: he even showed her a gift he had received from a love-struck nun. All these women were in love with him, but he only with her, he claimed, and they all share in his sorrow at her refusal and join in wishing her to accept him. At the close of this speech he wept (ll. 281–7), and the lady laments to her auditor that these dissembling tears overcame her, so that she wept too, seduced (ll. 288–301). She feels that he was such a skilled hypocrite, able even to preach chastity as part of a plot to seduce, that no one could resist him, and she is convinced that were he to repeat his attentions she would even now be persuaded to give up her repentance and be seduced again (ll. 302–29).

Artistic features: The poem shares some of the formality, as well as some of the concerns, of *The Rape of Lucrece*, but this poem, its central woman seduced rather than raped, deliberately eschews the dramatic and conclusive ending of its predecessor. Part of its strength lies in its vivid depiction of a psychological state from which neither the woman nor the poem seems able to imagine an escape, condemned endlessly to re-enact to herself the drama of her own undoing. The 'complaint' of the title may be either the inset complaint of the woman, or the complaint of her seducer which it quotes: in either case, neither the rural old man to whom she speaks nor the narrator who overhears them is able to place the woman back into a wider world outside her own self-tormenting consciousness.

Critical history: While the long-ignored Sonnets were rehabilitated at the end of the 18th century, *A Lover's Complaint* had to wait until the 1960s before many scholars were willing to concede that Shakespeare had even written it. Most editors of the Sonnets, considering their publication to have been unauthorized, omitted this poem, believing it to have been an inferior work foisted on Shakespeare by Thomas Thorpe. It was only after Kenneth Muir and MacDonald P. Jackson independently vindicated the poem's authenticity in 1964 and 1965 that more commentators began to find the poem of interest, particularly in relation to the Sonnets it follows. It was pointed out that in placing this poem after the last of the Sonnets Shakespeare might have been following the examples of Thomas *Lodge and Samuel Daniel, who had both appended poems in which seduced women lament their falls to their own sonnet sequences, and most modern criticism of *A Lover's Complaint* has taken up this suggestion. The poem is now usually regarded as a deliberate coda to the Sonnets, and critics have looked for ways in which it takes up their thematic concerns, particularly with the ethics of dissimulation (the seducer of *A Lover's Complaint* is, among other things, a consummate actor) and the use and abuse of praise. *MD*

Recent major editions

John Kerrigan (New Penguin, 1986); Katharine Duncan-Jones (Arden 3rd series, 1998); Stanley Wells (Oxford, 1985); each of these prints the poem as the coda to the *Sonnets*

Some representative criticism

Jackson, MacDonald P., *Shakespeare's 'A Lover's Complaint': Its Date and Authenticity* (1965)

Muir, Kenneth, *Shakespeare the Professional* (1973)

since Burgersdijk. The complete Shakespeare in Frisian was produced by Douwe Kalma (1956–63). Nine complete translations of the Sonnets are available.

Shakespeare has come to be performed ever more frequently, and a gallery of notable theatricals has formed. Actor-director Eduard Verkade (1878–1961), in the tradition of Gordon *Craig, determined the face of *Hamlet* for five decades. Willem Royaards (1867–1929), a *Reinhardt adept, produced epoch-making productions of *A Midsummer Night's Dream* and *Twelfth Night*. More recently, the innovative directorial skills of Hans Croiset, Erik Vos, Franz Marijnen, and Gerardjan Rijnders have met with great acclaim. Remarkable actors include Albert van Dalsum as Macbeth (1937), Richard III (1947), and Lear (1964); and Ko van Dijk as Othello (1951, 1964) and Macbeth (with Ank van der Moer as Lady *Macbeth, 1957).

The plays are also often performed by amateur companies, like the Shakespeare company at Diever, which celebrated its 50th anniversary in 1997. In 1993, the Shakespeare Society of the Low Countries was founded. Its biannual journal *Folio* first appeared in 1994. (See also Dutch Wars.) *TH*

Lowin, John (1576–1653), actor. Lowin was apprenticed to goldsmith Nicholas Rudyard at age 17 and was an actor in Worcester's Men in 1602–3 at the Rose but in 1603 he began his association with the King's Men, which was to last the rest of his long career. Lowin appears to have joined Shakespeare's company as a hired man since he is in the 1603 cast list for Ben *Jonson's *Sejanus* but not in the company patent. In the Induction to *Marston's *The Malcontent* (performed in 1604) Lowin plays himself, the actor, helping his fellows eject gallants who attempt to take up seats on the *Globe stage. Lowin published a mildly Puritan pamphlet called *Conclusions upon Dances* in 1606 and in 1607 he married a widow, Joan Hall. In his *Historia histrionica* (published in 1699) James Wright claimed that 'Lowin used to act, with mighty applause, *Falstaff, Morose, Volpone*, and *Mammon* in *The Alchemist*; [and] *Melantius* in *The Maid's Tragedy*'. John Downes, in his *Roscius Anglicanus* (published 1708), attributed the quality of *Betterton's performance in the role of Shakespeare's Henry VIII to instruction transmitted via William *Davenant 'who had it from old Mr *Lowin*, that had his instructions from Mr. Shakespeare himself'.

Lowin was apparently a large man, judging from consistent comments on his characters' appearance and from his picture (when aged 64) in the Ashmolean Museum, Oxford. A number of his roles are men whose outspokenness borders on gruffness, although more significant is the range of his roles which in his 50s included Domitianus Caesar in Philip Massinger's *The Roman Actor*, Eubulus in Massinger's *The Picture*, and Undermyne in John Clavell's *The Soddered Citizen*. After John *Heminges's death in 1630 Lowin became joint manager of the company with Joseph *Taylor but he continued to act and thus may be considered the origin of the theatrical tradition of 'actor-manager'. *GE*

Bowers, Rick, 'John Lowin: Actor-Manager of the King's Company, 1630–1642', *Theatre Survey*, 28 (1987)

Lucan (AD 39–65), Roman poet, the grandson of *Seneca, forced to commit suicide by the Emperor Nero. His epic poem *Bellum civile* or *Pharsalia*, an account of the civil wars between Caesar and Pompey, is a probable source for *Julius Caesar*. Shakespeare may have used the Latin edition published in 1589, or *Marlowe's English translation of book I which circulated in manuscript before its publication in 1600. *JKS*

Jones, Emrys, *The Origins of Shakespeare* (1977)

Luce. See Nell.

Lucentio falls in love with Bianca in *The Taming of the Shrew* and disguises himself as a teacher under the name 'Cambio' to woo her. *AB*

Lucetta, Julia's servant in *The Two Gentlemen of Verona*, tries to get her to read Proteus' letter, 1.2. *AB*

Lucian (*c.*120–200), Greek satirist who wrote mainly in the form of dialogues. One such dialogue, *Timon Misanthropus*, is a possible source for *Timon of Athens*. Available to Shakespeare in a Latin translation by Erasmus, and in French and Italian, Lucian's dialogue may also have influenced the dramatist indirectly, through the anonymous *Timon* comedy which survives only in manuscript. *JKS*

Luciana is Adriana's sister in *The Comedy of Errors*. *AB*

'Lucianus'. See players.

Lucilius, Timon's servant, is given money by him to marry the woman of his choice, *Timon of Athens* 1.1. *AB*

(cont. on page 266)

Love's Labour's Lost

At once Shakespeare's most airy comedy and his most sustained discussion of language, *Love's Labour's Lost* was probably composed in 1594 and 1595. It is listed among Shakespeare's works by *Meres in 1598, and appeared in the same year in a quarto edition which boasts that the play was acted before Queen Elizabeth 'this last Christmas' (which may mean either 1597–8 or 1596–7). The play's heavy use of rhyme suggests it belongs to the 'lyrical' period initiated by *Venus and Adonis* (1592–3): in rare vocabulary it is closely linked to *Romeo and Juliet* (1595) and *A Midsummer Night's Dream* (1595), but stylistically it seems to be earlier. Probable allusions in Act 5 to the Christmas revels at Gray's Inn in 1594 suggest that the play was composed, or at least completed, early in 1595.

Text: The surviving 1598 quarto of the play claims to be 'Newly corrected and augmented', but in all probability this is an exaggeration and the edition is merely a reprint of a now lost earlier edition of the same year. The text seems to have been set, fairly carelessly to judge by certain passages which seem to preserve two successive drafts of the same speech (in 4.3), from Shakespeare's own *foul papers. The play was reprinted in the *Folio in 1623, directly from the quarto text, but with some corrections made apparently from a promptbook.

Sources: No specific source is known for the play's plot, although it clearly alludes to the historical French court: King Henri of Navarre did have two lords called the Maréchal de Biron and the Duc de Longueville, who served as commanders in the French civil war from 1589 to 1592. Biron was widely known in England, since he became an associate and adviser of the Earl of *Essex when he led an English force to Henry's aid. It has been conjectured that the main story of *Love's Labour's Lost* may derive from a now-lost account of a diplomatic visit to Henry in 1578 made by Catherine de Médicis and her daughter Marguerite de Valois, Henry's estranged wife, to discuss the future of Aquitaine, but this is by no means certain. What is much clearer is that the play's subplot is peopled by Shakespeare's variants on familiar comic types from Italian **commedia dell'arte*, which abounds in pedants (like Holofernes), braggarts (like Don Armado), rustic priests (like Sir Nathaniel), rural clowns (like Costard), and pert pages (like Mote).

Synopsis: **1.1** Ferdinand, the King of Navarre, has three of his lords, Biron, Longueville, and Dumaine, sign a declaration vowing that they will study with him for three years, not seeing a woman throughout that time: Biron is sceptical about the scheme, but eventually signs anyway. The rustic constable Dull, on the instructions of the Spaniard Don Armado (from whom he brings an affected letter), brings the country swain Costard to the King; Costard is condemned to a week's fasting for having been caught in the royal purlieus with the wench Jaquenetta. **1.2** Armado confesses to his punning page Mote that he is in love with Jaquenetta. Dull brings Costard with the King's instruction that Armado guard him and make him fast for a week. Armado undertakes to write poetry about his love.

2.1 The Princess of France arrives on an embassy to Navarre from her father, accompanied by three ladies, Maria, Catherine, and Rosaline, and three lords, one named Boyet: having heard of the King's vow she sends Boyet ahead to him, and while he is away the three respective ladies discuss the King's three respective fellow students. When the King and his three colleagues arrive the Princess presents him with a letter from her father, demanding back a share of Aquitaine in recompense for the full repayment of a loan: while the King reads it Biron is wittily rebuffed by Rosaline, with whom he attempts to flirt. The King agrees to accommodate the Princess while they await the arrival of documents which will establish whether or not the whole loan has already been repaid. Each of his lords privately asks Boyet the name of one of her ladies: Dumaine is attracted to Catherine, Longueville to Maria, and Biron to Rosaline, while Boyet tells the Princess he thinks the King himself is falling in love with her.

3.1 Armado sends Mote to fetch Costard, with whom he means to entrust a love letter to Jaquenetta. Costard, after a bantering quarrel with Mote about hurting his shin, is left with three farthings for delivering the letter. Biron arrives and gives Costard a shilling to deliver a letter to Rosaline; left alone, he reflects on the demeaning absurdity of his having fallen in love with her.

4.1 The Princess, out hunting with her ladies, meets Costard, who does not know which of them is Rosaline: he gives the Princess Armado's letter by mistake, which Boyet reads aloud to general amusement. Costard jests with Boyet and the ladies. 4.2 The schoolmaster Holofernes and the priest Nathaniel are being learnedly witty at the expense of Dull, and Holofernes is showing off his pedantry to Nathaniel, when the illiterate Jaquenetta and Costard arrive to ask Nathaniel to read them the letter Jaquenetta has received from Armado: unfortunately Costard has given her Biron's letter to Rosaline, which Holofernes tells her to take to the King. 4.3 Biron has been writing more poetry for Rosaline: hiding, he overhears the King reading aloud his own poem to the Princess. The King in turn hides when he sees Longueville approach, and both he and Biron overhear Longueville reading out a poem he has composed for Maria. Longueville then hides, and all overhear Dumaine sighing in rhyme for Catherine. Longueville steps forward and reproaches Dumaine: the King steps forward and reproaches Longueville for hypocrisy: then Biron steps forward and reproaches all of them. His triumph is short-lived, however, as Jaquenetta and Costard arrive with his own letter to Rosaline, which he at first tears up but then confesses to. Biron urges his colleagues to lay aside their unnatural vow and set about their wooing.

5.1 Nathaniel and Holofernes, discussing Armado's pretensions to linguistic style before a silent and uncomprehending Dull, are interrupted by Armado's arrival, with Costard and Mote: he has been sent confidentially by the King to commission an entertainment to be performed for the Princess. Holofernes decides they shall stage a pageant of the Nine Worthies. 5.2 The Princess and her ladies scoff at the respective love letters they have received. Boyet brings news that the King and his three lords are approaching, disguised as Muscovites: the women exchange masks, so as to trick their suitors into wooing the wrong people. The men arrive, posing as Muscovites, prefaced by a speech from Mote which, despite prompting, he forgets: all four are taken in by the trick and each is dashed by the witty rebuffs of his partner before they leave, discomfited. The women scoff behind their backs, and when they return undisguised they pretend not to have recognized them, lamenting that they have had their time wasted by foolish Russians. Biron forswears all affectation and pretence to wit in his future wooing, and finally understands how he and his companions have been ridiculed. Costard arrives to ask whether the Nine Worthies should perform, and despite the King's misgivings the Princess insists the pageant should proceed. Mocked by their spectators, speaking in archaic verse, Costard impersonates Pompey the Great, Nathaniel (who forgets his words) plays Alexander the Great, Mote plays the infant Hercules strangling snakes in his cradle, but Holofernes' performance as Judas Maccabeus is dashed by heckling. Armado appears as Hector, and is even more dashed by Costard's public claim that Jaquenetta is two months' pregnant by him: the two nearly come to blows, but at this point the entertainment is interrupted by the coming of a messenger, Mercadé. He brings the news that the Princess's father has died. The women at last listen seriously to the mens' love-suits, but will give no answer until they meet again in a year and a day: Rosaline makes Biron promise to spend the intervening period telling his jokes in a hospital. Armado returns, and before the King and his lords and the princess and her ladies part he and the rustics perform a song of spring and winter, 'When daisies pied'.

Artistic features: The play is marked by long passages of sustained punning, and by a heavy use of rhyme: even when not reading aloud from love letters, the aristocratic characters frequently speak in sonnets.

Critical history: Until the 19th century very few critics found a good word to say about *Love's Labour's Lost*, which seemed to most commentators to represent Shakespeare simultaneously at his most self-indulgent and his most datedly Elizabethan. Francis *Gentleman, relegating the play to the eighth volume of *Bell's edition in 1774, called it 'one of Shakespeare's weakest compositions..., he certainly wrote more to please himself, than to divert or inform his readers or auditors'. Enthusiasm grew over the following century, albeit often of a qualified sort. *Hazlitt, though admitting it had charm, found it pedantic, while *Coleridge enjoyed the play primarily as an intelligent game at the expense of the ideals of Renaissance humanism. Victor *Hugo initiated one enduring strand in the play's critical history in the preface to his translation of the play, when he attempted to show that it was a specific satire on Elizabeth's court, directly inspired by the relationship between the Earl of *Southampton (according to Hugo, the original for Biron, as well as for the *'Fair Youth' of the Sonnets) with Elizabeth *Vernon. (The quest for topical or allegorical significance in the play has been pursued more recently by Frances Yates and her followers). The play only came into its own critically with the dawning of the aesthetic movement at the end of the century, when commentators such as Walter Pater and Algernon Charles *Swinburne began to celebrate the play's studied artifice and pose of insubstantiality instead of lamenting it. Since then critics have, however, looked for sterner things in the play, whether its questioning of the limitations of comedy (notably by the bereavement which cuts off its marital ending), its alleged attempt to beat the *University Wits at their own game, its views of language, identity and social hierarchy, or its understanding of the pastoral and the festive.

Stage history: The courtly tone of the play, together with its comparative brevity, has led some to speculate that it may have been written for performance at an annual revel of one of the *Inns of Court, but there is no direct evidence for this beyond the possibility that the missing **Love's Labour's Won* was a sequel, played the following year and depicting the renewal of the courtships postponed for a year at the end of this play. The play was certainly acted before Elizabeth (see above), and a private performance took place at *Southampton's house over Christmas 1604–5, according to a letter from Sir Walter *Cope. After this, though, the play disappeared from the stage, regarded as the least rescuable of all Shakespeare's comedies (though the transplanted concluding song for many years adorned revivals of *As You Like It*): an anonymous adaptation published in 1762, *The Students*, was never performed, and when *Love's Labour's Lost* was finally staged by Elizabeth *Vestris at Covent Garden in 1839 it enjoyed the distinction of being the last play in the canon to have been revived. Vestris was highly praised as Rosaline, but the play was not revived again until it flopped in 1857, with Samuel *Phelps as Armado. (During the 19th century, however, an adaptation of the play in French sometimes served as a replacement libretto for *Mozart's *Così fan tutte*, regarded at the time as immoral.) *Love's Labour's Lost* was chosen (partly for its obscurity) to be acted on Shakespeare's birthday at the Shakespeare Memorial Theatre in Stratford in 1885, but sporadic revivals there and elsewhere (including a musical version in 1919) failed to establish it in the repertory. The young Tyrone *Guthrie produced it twice, first at the Westminster theatre in 1932 and then four years later at the *Old Vic (with Michael *Redgrave as the King), but neither production was a hit, though the play did become something of a favourite at the *Open Air Theatre in Regents Park in the mid-1930s. The first production really to establish the play was Peter *Brook's delicate, bitter-sweet revival at Stratford in 1946, with Paul *Scofield as a melancholy Armado and designs suggestive of the paintings of Watteau. Since then it has been revived much more frequently: notable RSC productions, for example, have included John *Barton's, set in a wooded Elizabethan park, in 1977–8 (with Michael *Pennington as Biron and Jane Lapotaire as Rosaline), Barry Kyle's in 1984 (with Josette Simon as Rosaline) and Ian Judge's in 1994–5, set in a *Zuleika Dobson*-esque Edwardian Oxford on the eve of the First World War. *MD*

On the screen: The earliest of five silent films was made in 1912, unsuited as the medium seems to such a word-oriented play. The Bristol Old Vic production (1964) was recorded on television to mark the 400th anniversary of Shakespeare's birth. Elijah Moshinsky directed the BBC TV production in an 18th-century setting (1984). Kenneth *Branagh's version, heavily cut and featuring song-and-dance routines to music by Cole *Porter and others, which appeared in 2000, has so far been the least critically acclaimed of his films. *AD*

Recent major editions

John Kerrigan (New Penguin, 1982); G. R. Hibbard (Oxford, 1990); Henry Woodhuysen (Arden 3rd series, 1998)

Some representative criticism

Barber, C. L., *Shakespeare's Festive Comedy* (1959)
Hoy, Cyrus, '*Love's Labour's Lost* and the Nature of Comedy', *Shakespeare Quarterly*, 13 (1962)
Yates, Frances, *A Study of 'Love's Labour's Lost'* (1936)

Lucillius (Lucilius) is a friend of Brutus and Cassius in *Julius Caesar*. He is taken prisoner at Philippi, 5.4. *AB*

Lucio asks Isabella to intercede for Claudio, and slanders Duke Vincentio, in *Measure for Measure*. *AB*

Lucius. **(1)** Titus' eldest son in *Titus Andronicus*, he takes revenge on Saturninus and is made emperor at the end of the play. **(2)** See Lucius, Young. **(3)** He is Brutus' boy servant who sleeps as Caesar's ghost appears to Brutus, *Julius Caesar* 4.2. **(4)** He is a lord who gives Timon four horses (mentioned 1.2.181–3), but refuses to give him a loan, *Timon of Athens* 3.2. His servant is also called by the name 'Lucius', *Timon of Athens* 3.4.3. **(5)** See Lucius, Caius.

Lucius, Caius. He is a Roman ambassador and then general in *Cymbeline*. *AB*

Lucius, Young. He is Lucius' son in *Titus Andronicus*. Lavinia uses his copy of *Ovid to indicate that she has been raped, 4.1. *AB*

Lucius' Servant. See Lucius.

Lucrece. See Rape of Lucrece, The.

Lucullus sends Timon a gift of greyhounds but refuses to give him a loan, *Timon of Athens* 3.1. *AB*

Lucullus' Servant appears briefly, *Timon of Athens* 3.1. *AB*

Lucy, Sir Thomas (1532–1600). According to a popular legend, the young Shakespeare poached deer from the estate of Sir Thomas Lucy of Charlecote, near Stratford-upon-Avon. The Sir Thomas of Shakespeare's boyhood lived from 1532 to 1600 and built the great house of Charlecote, which still stands. He also owned, through his wife Joyce Acton, rich estates at Sutton in Worcestershire. He was knighted by the Earl of Leicester at Charlecote in 1565, and Queen Elizabeth visited him there in 1572. He was a prominent figure in Stratford-upon-Avon, with a household of about 40 servants and retainers. William *Camden and other heralds attended his funeral, and his effigy in armour is still to be seen in Charlecote church.

The legend that Shakespeare poached Sir Thomas's deer is first mentioned by Richard Davies in a manuscript dated between 1688 and 1708 in which Lucy is identified with 'Justice Clodpate'—i.e. Shallow in *The Merry Wives of Windsor*. *Aubrey does not mention the tale, but in 1709 *Rowe reported *Betterton's saying that Shakespeare had been prosecuted by Lucy, wrote a ballad about him, and was consequently obliged to escape to London. William Oldys and Edward *Capell quoted what was said to be the 'first stanza of that bitter ballad' transmitted by 'several old people at Stratford' who vouched that it had been stuck on Lucy's park gate. The legend has formed a picturesque incident in many accounts of Shakespeare's life, but according to Eccles, 'The Sir Thomas Lucy who died in 1600 had no park in Warwickshire, though he had a coney warren, and the whole story seems to be a late invention.' His heir was his son, also Sir Thomas (1551–1605), who in 1618 was licensed to impale a park at Charlecote. *SW*

Lucy, Sir William. He is a messenger who appears in *1 Henry VI* 4.3, 4.4, and 4.7. *AB*

Luddington is a small village close to Stratford, reputedly the scene of Shakespeare's marriage to Anne *Hathaway. Its registers for the period do not survive. According to a Victorian biographer, S. W. Fullom, a very old resident claimed to have seen 'the ancient tome in which it was registered'. Other residents confirmed this, but said that the curate's housekeeper 'one cold day burnt the register to boil her kettle'. *SW*

Ludwig, Otto (1813–65), German author of realist novellas and plays, whose eventual self-abandonment to the admiration and copious annotation of Shakespeare's plays (published posthumously in 1874) was said to have caused the premature extinction of his remarkable creative talent. *WH*

Luhrmann, Baz. See ROMEO AND JULIET; SHAKESPEARE ON SOUND FILM.

lute, a plucked string instrument central to music-making in Shakespeare's time, among both amateurs (including Queen Elizabeth) and professionals. It has a fine surviving repertoire; John *Dowland was the leading exponent and composer. *JB*

Lyance, the name of land at Hatton, later known as Moat Farm, about 7 miles (11 km) from Stratford, which was in the hands of the Shakespeares of *Rowington and *Wroxall from 1547 to 1578. *SW*

Lyceum theatre. A big theatre built in 1834 just off the Strand, it was from 1878 the fiefdom of Henry *Irving, whose major productions of Shakespeare, often co-starring Ellen *Terry, drew fashionable audiences. In 1902 it was reconstructed as a music hall. Due for demolition in 1939, it was restored in 1996 and now houses large-scale musicals. *MJ*

Lychorida, Thaisa's nurse, brings the newborn Marina to Pericles (*Pericles* 11) and becomes her nurse. *AB*

Lydgate, John (*c.*1370–1451), priest and prolific poet. Lydgate is best known for his *Troy Book* (1412–21), an English poem based on a Latin prose account of the Trojan Wars. The *Troy Book* was highly esteemed in 16th-century England and was one of Shakespeare's sources for *Troilus and Cressida.* *JKS*

Lyly, John (*c.*1554–1606), novelist and dramatist, one of the *University Wits, who aspired to be Master of the Revels but eventually became a member of Parliament. His prose romance *Euphues; or, The Anatomy of Wit* (1578), followed two years later by *Euphues, and his England* (1580), established a vogue for a literary style based on rhetorically balanced sentences featuring antimetabole and antithesis and employing abundant metaphors and similes. This style, dubbed 'euphuism', was frequently imitated by Lyly's contemporaries, most obviously *Lodge and *Greene, and sometimes satirized. It was also a central feature of his courtly comedies of the 1580s, *Sapho and Phao* (1584), *Campaspe* (1584), *Gallathea* (1585), and *Endimion* (1588), whose popularity was such as virtually to dictate the form of comedy for years to come.

Shakespeare was undoubtedly influenced by the style, themes, and structure of Lyly's drama. The absurdity of love and the wittiness of courtship characteristic of Lyly are central to Shakespeare's comedies. Concerned with setting up a debate through language rather than through action, Lyly's static forms are reflected in *Love's Labour's Lost* and *As You Like It*, both renowned for their thinness of plot. Another aspect of form that Shakespeare may have borrowed and developed is the juxtaposition of different groups of characters, noble and artisan, god and mortal. Moreover, Lyly's preoccupation with mistaken identity may have influenced Shakespeare. *Gallathea*'s examination of inconstancy, through the literal transformation of its characters and linguistic images of vacillation, has marked similarities with *A Midsummer Night's Dream.* In *As You Like It*, Ganymede's image of woman as constantly changing, 'moonish', may relate directly to the eponymous character in Lyly's *The Woman in the Moon* (?1593). Other works which have been thus linked include *Euphues* and *The Two Gentlemen of Verona*, *Endimion* and *The Merry Wives of Windsor*, *Campaspe* and *Timon of Athens.* *JKS*

Mincoff, Marco, 'Shakespeare and Lyly', *Shakespeare Survey*, 14 (1961)
Scragg, Leah, *The Metamorphosis of 'Gallathea': A Study in Creative Adaptation* (1982)

Lymoges. See AUSTRIA, DUKE OF.

lyric, a short poem expressing the mood or thought of a single speaker, whether real or fictional. This need not be intended for singing, and the term embraces literary sonnets etc., as well as songs. *CB*

lyric poetry, Shakespeare's No full account of Shakespeare's lyric poetry could ignore the lyrics in the plays—'Full fathom five thy father lies' or 'Was it the heavenly rhetoric of thine eye'—but here I mention only the revealing stanza sung in *The Merchant of Venice* during Bassanio's choosing of the casket. That brief question-and-answer poem argues that it is not in the heart, nor in the head, but solely in the eye that 'fancy' (or sexual attraction) is bred, fed, and ultimately extinguished:

> Tell me, where is fancy bred,
> Or in the heart, or in the head?
> How begot, how nourishèd?
> Reply, reply.
> It is engendered in the eyes,
> With gazing fed; and fancy dies
> In the cradle where it lies.
> (*The Merchant of Venice* 3.2.63–9)

This unequivocal belief in the erotic compulsion of sight governed, as perplexing theme, most of Shakespeare's lyric poetry. In the seriocomic *Venus and Adonis* (1593), Venus is taken by the looks of 'rosecheeked' Adonis, with his 'round enchanting' dimples; in the tragic history of *The Rape of Lucrece* (1594), Tarquin inflames his lustful gaze by watching 'the silent war of lilies and of roses' in Lucrece's blushing face; in the vein of pathos, the betrayed maid of *A Lover's Complaint* (published as a tailpiece to the Sonnets in 1609) sighs still after her faithless but fatally handsome lover; and the speaker of the Sonnets (1609) is infatuated with the beautiful young man.

Since the Sonnets are by common consent Shakespeare's greatest lyric achievement, I will turn first to them. Because of Shakespeare's intense subjection to beauty of visage, the chief epistemological concern of the Sonnets is the haunting fear of discrepancy between the physical exterior and the moral interior of the beloved. Sonnet 54—dwelling on this theme—will serve as a typical example of Shakespeare's manner of developing the three alternately rhymed quatrains and concluding couplet of the sonnet form that has come to bear his name.

The speaker begins by contrasting the beautiful but odourless canker roses to those 'true' roses from which perfume can be distilled:

> O how much more doth beauty beauteous seem
> By that sweet ornament which truth doth give!
> The rose looks fair, but fairer we it deem
> For that sweet odour which doth in it live.
> The canker blooms have full as deep a dye
> As the perfumèd tincture of the roses,
> Hang on such thorns, and play as wantonly
> When summer's breath their maskèd buds discloses;
> But for their virtue only is their show
> They live unwooed and unrespected fade,
> Die to themselves. Sweet roses do not so;
> Of their sweet deaths are sweetest odours made:
> And so of you, beauteous and lovely youth,
> When that shall fade, by verse distils your truth.

The sonnet's first notable linguistic means is a cascade, in lines 1–6, of self-duplicating language—'beauty beauteous'; 'sweet ornament . . . | . . . sweet odour'; 'fair . . . fairer'; 'rose . . . | roses'. This reduplicative lexicon vanishes entirely in lines 7–10, only to reappear (further emphasized by grammatical parallelism) in lines 11–13—'Sweet roses. . . | sweet deaths . . . | sweetest odours . . . | . . . beauteous.' Although the word 'truth', too, is duplicated in the sonnet, the duplication (l. 14) comes so long after the initial instance (l. 2) that it serves only to give conclusiveness to conclusion, differing thereby from the earlier duplication of close-packed heaps of luscious words; and 'truth' of course differs radically in semantic category from the 'natural' words about roses.

We must explain, then, why Shakespeare writes lines 7–11 in a different mode of expression, and ask whether the second heap of sweetness and odours and roses (ll. 11–13) replicates the first or changes it. The second of these questions is more easily answered: the earlier heap speaks of the life ('live', 1. 4) of roses, the later one of the death ('deaths', 1. 12) of roses. Two different 'odours' are in question: the first is the natural odour of the living rose, the second the distilled odour of perfume. There is another difference: in the first set of rose-expressions, the rose is externally 'fair', and only its inner odour is 'sweet': in the second set—in which the rose is sweet, its death is sweet, and its distilled odours are sweet—external 'fairness' has vanished from the equation. In lieu of 'fairness' and 'odour' as categories of outside and inside, the poet substitutes (in 1. 9) 'show' and 'virtue'—moral words connected in category to the word 'truth'.

Such distinctions are the very stuff of Shakespeare the poet: he liked nothing better than to subdivide scholastically any available object or concept. Divide roses in general into unscented canker roses and perfumed 'true' roses. Divide a *living* 'true' rose into its fair exterior and its *sweet* fragrant essence; divide a *dead* 'true' rose into its *sweet* death and its subsequent *sweet* distillation. Find a pun: the canker blooms have a 'dye' and they indeed 'die', but their death is not 'sweet'. Draw a chart of similarities between true roses and canker roses: both are deep dyed, both hang on thorns, both play wantonly as the zephyr discloses their covered buds. But to this list of similarities introduce the fatal point of non-similarity: because one cannot distil the odourless canker roses into perfume, they suffer sexual and social ostracism, and die alone. Then point your moral.

The eye falls in love (as the casket-song says) with fairness, not with sweetness (an invisible moral virtue); one can be as sexually undone by a canker rose as by any true rose. Therefore the second quatrain of the sonnet, introducing the canker rose, is the most sensual, the most seductive, the most teasing, the most wanton in language. The kiss of summer's breath, intent on encouraging the erotic 'masked buds' to unclose themselves, is substituted for the kiss of the lover, who began by mistakenly judging truth to be merely an 'ornament'.

In addition to the rich exploitation of contrary lexicons, Shakespeare—because of his experience with drama—tends to vary speech-acts throughout a poem. Here, the speaker begins with a moral proposition—'O how much more'; continues with direct description of sensuous experience—'and play as wantonly'; passes into emblem—'Of their sweet deaths are sweetest odours made'; and ends with an adjuration and prophecy—'And so of you, beauteous and lovely youth'. The varying speech-acts of the Sonnets, together with their fecundity of lexicon and metaphor, are made to mimic the evolving gestures of the mind behind them.

In the sonnet sequence, discrepancy between exterior and interior makes itself felt slowly, as Shakespeare's speaker gradually loses faith in the fidelity of both the young man and the dark lady. The intellectual ingenuity of the effort to explain away betrayal leads Shakespeare's speaker into elaborate 'logical' antitheses (the poet's favourite figure) and to many emblems of truth and falsehood (the rose, the wolf in sheep's clothing, the bad angel, and so on). A grim comedy pervades some of the sonnets, not least 144, which, taking as its convention the struggle (found in medieval drama) between a good and a bad angel for the soul of Everyman, blasphemes against its religious origin by revising the expected plot: in Shakespeare's version, the good and bad angels go off together as a sexual couple, leaving the bewildered Everyman behind.

Even in the so-called 'impersonal' sonnets, there can exist a dark personal irony. In 129, the famous sonnet on lust, we first see the speaker in hellish *retrospective* recollection of his own past actions ('Th'expense of spirit in a waste of shame'); this gradually changes to *chronological* recollection (how sexual attraction felt at the time, i.e. heavenly, if brief and ultimately unreal—'A bliss in proof and proved, a very woe; | Before, a joy proposed; behind, a dream'). In the knowing chiasmus of the couplet, the phrase 'well knows' stands for retrospective recollection, and the phrase 'none knows well' for chronological recollection; and by this adroit reversal the couplet represents the helpless circuit between our chronological perception of our life as we live it (hoping for joy), and our devastating sense of our life as we look back on it (aware of our mistakes):

All this the world well knows, yet none knows well
To shun the heaven that leads men to this hell.

The language of the Sonnets is racy, dramatic, lurid, and even pugnacious (''Tis better to be vile than vile esteemed', 121) when it is not being courtly, abject, pleading, and strategic ('Let me not to the marriage of true minds', 118). In both sorts of poems, as the plight of Shakespeare-the-speaker is analysed and formally enacted by Shakespeare-the-author, an ironic distance separates the sufferer from his expert portrayer. By animating his sequence with four main protagonists—the speaker, the young man, the dark lady (mistress to both), and a rival poet—Shakespeare added immensely to the dramatic play of the (normally dyadic) genre. And by ingenious, if covert, verbal schemes (such as frequently compelling the same root-word to appear in each of the four units of a sonnet (cf. 7, where the root-word is 'look'), Shakespeare joyfully complicated for himself the writing wager.

Shakespeare's longer poems, with their elaborate erotic conceits, conscious rhetoric, and stately pentameter rhyme-schemes (*ababcc* for the mythological *Venus and Adonis*; rhyme royal—*ababbcc*—for both the aristocratic *The Rape of Lucrece* and the pastoral *A Lover's Complaint*) prefigure and confirm the deceptions of fair appearance that vex the Sonnets. Throughout Venus's teasing and petulant sexual debate with the reluctant Adonis, we are instructed by Shakespeare's urbane and experienced Ovidian narrator, who points the moral:

Were beauty under twenty locks kept fast,
Yet love breaks through, and picks them all at last.
(ll. 575–6)

Frustrated of her desire (as Adonis resists her and is killed by the boar) Venus, in the most didactic passage of the poem, lays a curse on human love (a curse that comes true in the Sonnets). The diction and rhythmical movement are conspicuously less original in this youthful epyllion than in the best poems of the sonnet sequence:

Sorrow on love hereafter shall attend.
It shall be waited on with jealousy,
Find sweet beginning, but unsavoury end;
  Ne'er settled equally, but high or low,
  That all love's pleasure shall not match his woe. (ll. 1136–40)

The deceptions of fair appearance are marked once more in *The Rape of Lucrece*: Tarquin, says Lucrece, 'beguiled' her with 'outward honesty, but yet defiled | With inward vice'. The poem is one long tracking of the mortal effect of Tarquin's rape—itself provoked by the careless boasts, by Lucrece's husband, of her beauty. Shakespeare's narrator (commenting on Lucrece's long inner debate on the proper course to take) is given to ceremonious sententiae about love, shame, evil, and the relations between the sexes, moralizings which are nonetheless—in spite of their rather stiff presentation—often ahead of their time:

No man inveigh against the withered flower,
But chide rough winter that the flower hath killed.
Not that devoured, but that which doth devour,
Is worthy blame. O, let it not be held
Poor women's faults, that they are so full-filled
  With men's abuses. Those proud lords, to blame,
  Make weak-made women tenants to their shame.
(ll. 1254–60)

The dramatist in Shakespeare relished the insoluble nature of Lucrece's dilemma: were she to have resisted, Tarquin would have left her dead in bed with one of her male servants, shaming her and her husband in perpetuity; were she to submit to Tarquin and afterward accuse him, she could be thought to be concealing a voluntary submission on her part; and so her only resort—in order to preserve her husband's honour and her own, and to ensure the punishment of Tarquin—is to make good her tale by suicide. At the end of the poem, the Romans, seeing her violated body borne through the streets, expel the tyrannical house of Tarquin and establish Rome as a republic, thereby giving political, as well as moral, force to Lucrece's self-sacrifice.

The secure moral viewpoint of the narrator of *Lucrece* (and of its heroine) disappears in *A Lover's Complaint.* Its narrator is almost invisible, and the overheard voice of the seduced and betrayed maiden dominates the poem. The moral is not even equivocal: if, says the lovesick girl, her seducer (who greatly resembles—in his beauty, his carelessness, and his amorality—the young man of the Sonnets) were to return, she would—such was his beauty, so entrancing was his tongue—willingly succumb to him again. The Spenserian elaborations of pathetic complaint make this poem (whose attribution to Shakespeare has been contested) less appealing to the modern reader than the vigorous Sonnets, but we can see its plot as another version of that perennially deceiving discrepancy between appearance and character, 'show' and 'virtue', on which—from the 'lascivious grace' of the young man to the vicious 'honesty' of Iago—Shakespeare expended so much of his lyric and dramatic energy.

There remains Shakespeare's enigmatic and beautiful elegy of married constancy 'The Phoenix and Turtle' (written in trochaic tetrameter). The two birds, 'co-supremes and stars of love' who have perished 'in a mutual flame', are celebrated in a liturgy (in thirteen *abba* quatrains) followed by a threnody (in five *aaa* tercets). The style is one of metaphysical concision: 'Two distincts, division none: | Number there in love was slain' (ll. 27–8). In its confidence that a kind of love exists in which a 'concordant twain' live in exemplary fidelity, Shakespeare's terse formal elegy stands as the Platonic opposite to his corrosive lyric and narrative investigations of human sexual fallibility. *HV*

Lysander is in love with, and eventually permitted to marry, Hermia in *A Midsummer Night's Dream.* *AB*

Lysimachus is overcome with shame when he meets the virtuous Marina in a brothel, *Pericles* 19. *AB*

M., I. James Mabbe (1572–1642), a fellow of Magdalen College, Oxford, is probably the 'I.M.' who wrote a brief elegy for the First Folio (1623). In the poem, Shakespeare leaves the 'world's-stage' for 'the grave's-tiring-room', but lives on in print to renewed applause. *PH*

Macbeth (*c.*1005–1057), King of Scotland (reigned after defeating King Duncan in battle in 1040, and was himself killed by rebels under Malcolm in 1057). See MACBETH. *AB*

Macbeth *(see opposite page)*

Macbeth, Lady. See MACBETH.

Macbeth nach Shakespeare. See MACBETH.

Macbett, 1972 French play by Romanian-French author Eugène Ionesco (1909–94). Ionesco's ironic version of *Macbeth* constitutes an 'absurdist' critique of Shakespeare's heroic tragedy, exposing a brutal and banal cycle of ambition, conspiracy, and assassination, in which some scenes and speeches are replayed verbatim by different characters. The First Witch transforms herself into 'Lady Duncan', who then seduces a compliant Macbett. The triumph of Macol (Shakespeare's Malcolm) brings only crueller tyranny. *TM*

Macbird. See MACBETH.

'Maccabeus, Judas'. See 'JUDAS MACCABEUS'.

McCarthy, Lillah (1875–1960), English actress, wife of Harley *Granville-Barker from 1906 to 1917 and his managerial partner. Noted for her statuesque beauty and eloquent voice, she gave enticing performances in his productions at the Savoy as Hermione and Viola (1912) and Helena (*A Midsummer Night's Dream*, 1914). *DK*

McCullough, John (1832–85), Irish-born American actor in the heroic mould, whose successes included Richard III, Hamlet, King Lear, and Othello. When he played the latter role at Drury Lane in 1881 his performance was considered old-fashioned, but effective in a rather coarse way. *RF*

Macduff finds the murdered Duncan (*Macbeth* 2.3) and begins to suspect Macbeth, whom he kills at the end of the play in revenge for the murder of his family. Shakespeare broadly follows *Holinshed's account of Macduff, the Thane (later Earl) of Fife. *AB*

Macduff, Lady. She and her children are killed by Macbeth's henchmen, *Macbeth* 4.2. *AB*

Machiavelli, Niccolò (1469–1527), Italian political philosopher who became notorious for his ruthlessly pragmatic ideas. Machiavelli served as assistant secretary of state to the Florentine republic until the return of the Medici caused him to be exiled in 1512. Nevertheless, it was to the Medici that Machiavelli dedicated *Il principe* (*The Prince*), which he wrote in 1513 urging them to unite the country against the French invaders. As the chance of this happening became remote, Machiavelli decided not to publish this treatise or his *Discorsi* (*Discourses*) written from 1513 to 1517. It was not until after his death in 1532 that *The Prince* was published and the ideas within it became the focus for lengthy and heated debate across Europe. Machiavelli recognized moral exigencies and condemned rulers for excessive brutality. Nevertheless, he allowed that violent or immoral acts could be justified in the pursuit of a unified and self-sufficient state. He distinguished the successful prince from the ideal Christian ruler, implying that spiritual and ethical values had no place in the political sphere. He also emphasized the need to take risks and to accept one's dependence upon chance. These ideas were condemned by moralists in England and France as demonic and an incitement to tyranny. In 1576 Innocent Gentillet published a denunciation of *The Prince*, the *Contre-Machiavel*, which was translated into English in 1602. But long before then, the words 'Machiavellian' and 'Machiavelism' had passed into the English language and the Machiavel had become a stock dramatic type, brought onto the stage at the beginning of Marlowe's *The Jew of Malta* and claimed as an influence by Richard of Gloucester in *Richard Duke of York* (*3 Henry VI*) (3.2.193). Shakespeare may not have read *The Prince* but he advertised his awareness of 'Machiavelism' through direct reference and characterization, and through the creation of a savage political world in which a pious Christian king like Henry VI is entirely at a loss. *JKS*

machines in the Elizabethan theatre. Little was needed to adapt the mechanical winches used in the Elizabethan construction industry for theatrical *flying from the 'heavens' and for unassisted ascent from or descent into 'hell', but once settled at permanent playhouses the companies were slow to give up the minimalist habits required for touring. No play written for the Globe requires a mechanical elevator platform beneath the trapdoor set into the stage—simple steps will do for the descending actor—and not until Shakespeare's *Cymbeline* (1610), when Jupiter descends on an eagle, was flight called for. Philip *Henslowe was ahead of his rivals, paying for the flight machine at the Rose in 1595. *GE*

Mack, Maynard (b. 1909), American academic, editor, and critic. His 'The World of Hamlet' (*Yale Review*, 41, 1952) discusses the imagery of the play; and *King Lear in our Time* (1965) considers both the play's literary mode and several modern productions, including Peter *Brook's versions on stage and film. *TM*

(cont. on page 275)

Macbeth

Possibly Shakespeare's most intense tragedy, and certainly his most Jacobean—in that its interests in *Scotland, in *witches, and in the Stuarts' ancestor Banquo suggest that Shakespeare was here deliberately catering to the tastes of his company's patron King *James—*Macbeth* was probably first performed in 1606. The Porter's remarks about equivocation and treason appear to allude to the trial of the *Gunpowder Plot conspirators, which took place from January to March of 1606, and the First Witch's undertaking to condemn a ship called 'the Tiger' to 81 weeks of storms (1.3.6–24) may allude to a real ship of that name which reached Milford Haven in June 1606 after a traumatic voyage of just that duration. Banquo's ghost may be glanced at in two plays written in 1607, the anonymous *The *Puritan* and perhaps *Beaumont and *Fletcher's *The Knight of the Burning Pestle*. Internal evidence, moreover, particularly the play's metre, also suggests that *Macbeth* was composed in 1606, after *King Lear* but just before *Antony and Cleopatra*: Macbeth even mentions Antony (3.1.58) in a manner which suggests that Shakespeare was already revisiting *Plutarch in preparation for the latter tragedy while composing his Scottish play.

Text: *Macbeth* was first printed in the *Folio in 1623, which provides its only authoritative text, unfortunately in many ways a defective one. The play is unusually short: many editors have suspected cutting, wondering, for example, whether the murderers' description of the killing of Banquo was originally a separate scene between 3.3 and 3.4, or whether King Edward the Confessor originally made an appearance in 4.3. More conspicuously, three episodes in which the goddess Hecate appears in person to the Witches (3.5, 4.1.38–60, 141–8), which have little or no effect on the plot and are different in style to the surrounding dialogue, seem to be non-Shakespearian *interpolations. Since these episodes call for the performance of two songs found in Thomas *Middleton's play *The Witch*, it is now generally believed that the text of *Macbeth* in the Folio derives from a promptbook of the play as adapted by Middleton for a later Jacobean revival.

Sources: Shakespeare's principal source was *Holinshed's account of the reigns of Duncan and Macbeth, supplemented by material borrowed from elsewhere in Holinshed's history of Scotland: Lady Macbeth, for example, is largely based on the wife of Donwald, who prompted her husband to kill King Duff. Shakespeare restructures Holinshed's material, however, making the historical Macbeth's long and peaceful reign look like a short-lived usurpation, and framing his play by the appearance of the three witches who tempt Macbeth and Banquo with their prophecies. Shakespeare may have consulted other accounts of Macbeth's reign too, including George Buchanan's *Rerum Scoticarum historia* (1582) and Andrew of Wyntoun's poem *The Original Chronicle of Scotland* (*c.*1424), in which Macbeth is incited to kill Duncan by three women who appear to him in a dream. It is likely that Shakespeare also knew of a playlet by Matthew Gwinne, *Tres sibyllae*, performed before King James at St John's College, Oxford, in 1605. The three sibyls of the title reminded James that they had once prophesied endless dominion to Banquo's descendants, and saluted him in turn with the words 'Hail, thou who rulest Scotland!' 'Hail, thou who rulest England!' 'Hail, thou who rulest Ireland!' (cf. 1.3.46–8).

Synopsis: 1.1 Three witches agree to meet again on a heath in order to accost Macbeth after the day's battle. **1.2** King Duncan, fighting against the rebel Macdonald, receives a report from a bleeding captain about Macbeth's valiant deeds in the battle: Macbeth has killed Macdonald, and he and his comrade Banquo have met the fresh assaults of Macdonald's Norwegian allies. Ross brings the news that Macbeth has defeated the King of Norway and his associate, the traitorous

Thane of Cawdor: Duncan condemns Cawdor to death and confers his title on Macbeth. 1.3 The three witches hail Macbeth by his current title, Thane of Glamis, and then as Thane of Cawdor and as future king: before vanishing they tell Banquo that though he will not be king his descendants will. Ross and Angus bring the news that Macbeth is now Thane of Cawdor: reflecting on the witches' prophecy, now partly fulfilled, Macbeth is already imagining the murder of Duncan. 1.4 Duncan, after hearing a report from his son Malcolm of the death of the former Cawdor, welcomes Macbeth and Banquo, before declaring Malcolm the Prince of Cumberland and his heir. Duncan means to be Macbeth's guest at Inverness, towards which Macbeth sets off to inform his wife, conscious that he must now remove both Malcolm and Duncan if the witches' prophecy is to be fulfilled. 1.5 Lady Macbeth reads a letter from Macbeth describing his meeting with the witches, and, aware of the conscience which may hold back his ambition, she is ready to urge him on to the murder of Duncan. A servant brings the news of Duncan's impending arrival: Lady Macbeth calls on the forces of darkness to make her cruel and unwomanly enough to be an instigator of Duncan's murder. When Macbeth arrives she urges him to dissemble with Duncan and promises to do her part. 1.6 Duncan and his nobles, including his sons Malcolm and Donalbain along with Macduff, the Thane of Fife, are welcomed to Inverness by Lady Macbeth. 1.7 Briefly alone while Duncan dines, Macbeth reflects in horror on the crime he is on the verge of committing, for no motive but ambition, and when Lady Macbeth comes to find him he renounces their plot to kill the King. By taunting him for unmanliness and inconstancy, however, she persuades him to resume his original purpose, saying she will get Duncan's chamberlains drunk so that the Macbeths can make it appear that they are the culprits.

2.1 After midnight, Banquo and his son Fleance are met by Macbeth: Banquo opens the subject of the witches, but Macbeth says they will discuss them on another occasion. After the departure of Banquo and Fleance, Macbeth, awaiting the bell which will be Lady Macbeth's signal that it is time to kill Duncan, sees a vision of a dagger, at first clean but then bloodstained, beckoning him towards Duncan's chamber. The bell rings and he goes to commit the murder. 2.2 Lady Macbeth, having drugged Duncan's grooms and left their daggers ready for her husband to use, awaits Macbeth. When he arrives he is terrified by what he has done and fearful of discovery, convinced he has heard a voice cursing him with eternal insomnia: he is still clutching the bloodstained daggers, which Lady Macbeth has to take back to Duncan's chamber. Macbeth feels he will never be able to get his hands clean of the blood. He is frightened by the sound of knocking at a door: Lady Macbeth leads him away to wash his hands and change into a nightgown. 2.3 A drunken porter, also disturbed by knocking, indulges a fancy that he is the porter at the gates of Hell before finally admitting Macduff and Lennox, to whom he discourses about the effects of drink. Macbeth arrives and conducts Macduff, calling by appointment to awaken the King, to Duncan's door: Lennox describes the ominous storms of the past night. A horrified Macduff brings the news of Duncan's murder and awakens the household while Macbeth and Lennox go to the chamber: Lady Macbeth, Banquo, Macbeth, Lennox, Malcolm, and Donalbain assemble and learn both of Duncan's death and of Macbeth's sudden killing of the two apparently guilty chamberlains on reaching the fatal chamber with Lennox. While Macbeth is explaining that righteous anger overcame his judgement, Lady Macbeth faints. Banquo urges the others to dress and arm themselves: left alone, Malcolm and Donalbain, convinced that they too are intended victims, resolve to flee. 2.4 Ross is discussing further omens with an old man when Macduff arrives: he reports that it is thought the two chamberlains had been paid to kill Duncan by the fugitive Malcolm and Donalbain, and that Macbeth, chosen as Duncan's successor, has gone to Scone to be crowned. Although Ross means to attend the coronation, Macduff is on his way home to Fife.

3.1 Banquo recognizes that the witches' prophecies to Macbeth have been fulfilled, and suspects him of Duncan's murder; he wonders if their remarks about his own descendants will also come true. Macbeth, arriving with Lady Macbeth, Lennox, Ross, and other nobles, invites Banquo to a feast that evening and asks in detail about where he and Fleance mean to ride that afternoon. Dismissing his court, the insecure Macbeth summons two murderers, reflecting bitterly on the pointlessness of his crime if Banquo's descendants are destined to inherit the throne. He instructs the murderers to kill Banquo and Fleance. 3.2 Lady Macbeth also feels that their achievement of an anxious throne is worthless. When Macbeth arrives, envying the dead Duncan's freedom from fear, she urges him to feign cheerfulness at the feast. He hints darkly at the impending murder of Banquo and Fleance but does not confide that he has already commissioned it. 3.3 The two murderers, joined by a third, kill Banquo, but Fleance escapes. 3.4 Macbeth is called away from the feast by the two murderers, who report their partial success. Rejoining the party, he alone sees Banquo's ghost sitting in his place, and speaks in guilty horror. Taking him aside, Lady Macbeth rebukes him for his visible distraction, and after the ghost leaves he is able to compose himself and apologize to his guests for what he claims is merely an indisposition. The ghost returns, however, and Macbeth speaks to it in such terror that Lady Macbeth has to dismiss the company. Left alone with his wife, Macbeth comments on Macduff's absence from the feast, and resolves to consult the witches again. 3.5 The three witches are rebuked by Hecate for their dealings with Macbeth: Hecate is summoned away by spirits, with whom she sings. 3.6 Lennox, recognizing that Macbeth is responsible for the murders of Duncan and Banquo, talks with a Lord, who reports that Macduff has gone to the English court to join Malcolm and to urge the English king to provide military aid against Macbeth.

4.1 The witches, subsequently joined by Hecate, prepare a dreadful potion. Macbeth arrives and insists that they call forth their spirits to provide him with further insights into the future. An armed head warns him to beware of Macduff; a bloody child tells him he cannot be harmed by any man born of woman; and a crowned child holding a tree tells him he will never be defeated until Birnam Wood comes to Dunsinane. Encouraged, Macbeth insists that the witches tell him whether Banquo's descendants will indeed rule Scotland: to his horror he is shown a procession of eight kings, the last holding a mirror, with Banquo's ghost smiling and indicating that they are his descendants. After the witches vanish, Lennox brings the news that Macduff has fled to England. Alone, Macbeth resolves to have Macduff's family killed at once. 4.2 Lady Macduff laments her husband's absence to Ross, and speaks of it with her young son after Ross leaves. A messenger warns that they are in immediate danger, and flees: shortly afterwards murderers arrive, stab the boy to death, and pursue the screaming Lady Macduff. 4.3 In England Malcolm speaks warily with Macduff, professing a suspicion that he may have been sent by Macbeth, especially since he has left his family in Macbeth's power. Malcolm goes on to tell Macduff that he is unfit to be king in Macbeth's place, claiming to be lascivious, greedy, and generally vicious: when Macduff, despairing for Scotland, finally repudiates him, Malcolm says he is now convinced of Macduff's sincerity and is in fact innocent of all crimes, having maligned himself only as a test. He has indeed already secured English aid. A doctor tells of the English King's miraculous ability to cure scrofula. Ross brings the news that Macduff's wife, children, and servants have all been killed: overcome by grief and self-reproach, Macduff vows revenge on Macbeth.

5.1 A gentlewoman has brought a doctor to witness Lady Macbeth's habitual sleepwalking: Lady Macbeth duly arrives, obsessively washing her hands, and speaking guiltily of Duncan's murder and the deaths of Lady Macduff and Banquo. 5.2 Scottish nobles, including Lennox, go to Birnam to rendezvous with Malcolm's English army. 5.3 At Dunsinane Macbeth, convinced of his invulnerability, learns of the English army's approach: he reflects that he may as well die, however, having forfeited the respect and friendship that make life worth living. He asks the doctor about Lady Macbeth's health, but despairs of a cure for her sorrows. Angry and coarse with his staff, he dons his armour. 5.4 Malcolm instructs his army to carry boughs cut in Birnam Wood as camouflage. 5.5 Macbeth, with his servant Seyton and soldiers, learns that Lady Macbeth is dead: he feels life is futile. A messenger brings the news that Birnam Wood is apparently coming to Dunsinane: Macbeth feels that he is doomed, but resolves to fight defiantly. 5.6 Malcolm places the English nobleman Siward and his son in the vanguard of their army. 5.7 In the battle Macbeth, convinced he can only be killed by a man not born of woman, kills Young Siward. 5.8 Macduff seeks Macbeth. 5.9 Siward tells Malcolm Macbeth's castle has surrendered. 5.10 Macduff confronts Macbeth: they fight, but Macbeth tells Macduff of his presumed invulnerability. Macduff, however, tells Macbeth he was born by Caesarean section. Despairing, and cursing the witches' equivocation, Macbeth still refuses to surrender, and the two resume their combat. Macbeth is killed. 5.11 Malcolm and his nobles, knowing they have won the battle, await news of the missing. Siward stoically accepts the reported death of his son. Macduff brings Macbeth's head, and Malcolm is hailed as King of Scotland: he makes his nobles earls.

Artistic features: The structure of *Macbeth* resembles that of *Julius Caesar*—following the tense, suspense-filled preparations for an assassination, after which the perpetrators fall into discord and anticlimax—but Shakespeare's focus on the consciousness of Macbeth and his wife, achieved by a succession of extraordinarily dense and rich soliloquies, goes far beyond his comparatively dispassionate investigation of Brutus' more intellectual motivations. The vividness with which the play thus renders the psychological experiences not only of committing murder but of anticipating and remembering doing so, coupled with its depiction of the witches, make even reading the play seem a genuine engagement with the forces of evil, an effect no doubt partly responsible for the superstition according to which it is unlucky to mention *Macbeth* by name in the precincts of a theatre.

Critical history: *Macbeth* has been of crucial importance not only to Shakespeare's reputation as a master of tragic pity and terror, possessed of uncanny psychological insight, but also to the work of subsequent artists, whether writers (from *Byron to the authors of countless *Gothic novels and detective thrillers), musicians such as *Verdi, painters such as *Fuseli, or film-makers from Hitchcock (on whom the play exerted a palpable influence) to *Welles, Polanski, and *Kurosawa. In the modern theatre alone, the play's offshoots range from the American political skit *Macbird* (an attack on President Johnson, 1965, one of a long line of *Macbeth* *burlesques and travesties) to Heiner *Müller's radical adaptation *Macbeth nach Shakespeare* (1972) and Ionesco's **Macbett* (1972). Quite apart from anything else, the play has influenced all subsequent notions of *ghosts and *witches.

The force with which *Macbeth* depicts terror and the supernatural gave it a special place in the canon for 18th-century and *Romantic commentators, with their interest in the sublime, while the density of its *imagery has made it a perennially important test case for studies of Shakespeare's style. Although the success with which Sir William *Davenant's verbally simplified adaptation displaced Shakespeare's text from the stage between the 1660s and the 1740s suggests that Restoration playgoers found this very density objectionable, *Macbeth* was by the mid-18th century one of the most highly regarded of the tragedies. Dr *Johnson, who cites it more often than any other play in his *Dictionary*, found it more satisfactorily moral than most of Shakespeare's work. Romantic critics were less interested in the play's morality than in its intense theatrical and psychological effects; *Macbeth*, for example, inspired one of Thomas *De Quincey's best literary essays, 'The Knocking at the Gate' (*London Magazine*, 1823). Following *Coleridge, many 19th-century critics examined how Shakespeare created the play's distinctive atmosphere: A. C. *Bradley, for example, in *Shakespearean Tragedy* (1904), pursued the play's recurrent references to darkness, anticipating 20th-century discussions (by *Spurgeon and others) of its imagery of blood. This increased sense of the play's literary technique led to an impatience with earlier, realist accounts of its plot and characters, famously voiced in L. C. *Knights's 1933 essay 'How Many Children Had Lady Macbeth?' The play has fascinated *psychoanalytic criticism since the time of *Freud himself (who felt that the play resembled a dreamlike account of Elizabeth I's presumed guilt over the execution of Mary, Queen of Scots), with *feminist critics in particular pursuing the connections between the uncertain gender of the witches, Lady Macbeth's imagined unsexing, and the mother-ripping birth of Macduff. Historically oriented critics, meanwhile, continue to muse on the play's relations to Jacobean politics.

STAGE HISTORY: Although *Macbeth* probably enjoyed its first performances in 1606, the first to be recorded took place in April 1611, when the astrologer and diarist Simon *Forman saw it at the Globe. Forman was especially struck by the prophecies, Banquo's ghost, and the sleepwalking scene, but despite his interest in supernatural affairs he says nothing of the cauldron scene, or Hecate, and refers to the witches as 'fairies or nymphs'. It was probably a little after this, around 1613, that Middleton adapted the script, adding Hecate, and a tendency to elaborate on the witches' scenes would be even more spectacularly visible when the play enjoyed its next recorded revivals 50 years later. Sir William Davenant rewrote the play to suit the tastes and concerns of Restoration audiences and the scenic possibilities of Restoration playhouses in 1664. As well as developing its opportunities for music and special effects (with singing, flying witches, a cloud for Hecate to ride, and a disappearing cavern for the apparition scene), Davenant updated the play's interest in the Stuart monarchy, so that his usurping, regicidal Macbeth becomes a figure analogous to Oliver Cromwell and his Malcolm to the recently restored Charles II. More pervasively, Davenant simplified Shakespeare's diction, cut the indecorous Porter, and gave the play an unambiguous, symmetrical moral scheme by expanding the roles of Macduff and Lady Macduff to make them into virtuous counterparts to the Macbeths.

With Thomas *Betterton and his wife Mary in the leading roles, this adaptation was immensely successful (Samuel *Pepys saw it eight times in less than four years, describing it as 'a most excellent play in all respects, but especially in divertisement'), and Macbeth remained one of Betterton's greatest roles down to his retirement in 1709. His most important successor in the part as reshaped by Davenant was James *Quin, who played it at different times from 1717 (at *Drury Lane) until 1751 (by which time he had moved to *Covent Garden), but by then his dignified, oratorical performance as Macbeth, and indeed the lucidly neoclassical script he was using, had been overshadowed by the arrival of David *Garrick. In 1744 Garrick advertised *Macbeth* at Drury Lane 'as written by Shakespeare' ('What does he mean?', Quin is said to have remarked, 'don't I play Macbeth as written by Shakespeare?'), and though his own version retained Davenant's operatic witches and still excludes the Porter and the murder of the Macduffs' children (as well as supplying Macbeth with a longer and more penitent onstage dying speech), from Garrick onwards the great soliloquies of Shakespeare's script, and the unaltered dialogues between Macbeth and his Lady (played with particular success by Hannah *Pritchard), were again the heart of the play.

Since Garrick's time, however, *Macbeth*, though one of Shakespeare's most regularly revived tragedies, has occasioned more conspicuous disasters in the theatre than successes (another factor, perhaps, contributing to actors' superstitions about the play), and the much shorter role of Lady Macbeth has been far luckier for performers than that of her husband. Charles *Macklin was ahead of his time in his 1773–6 production at Covent Garden, which gave the play a consistent, 'authentic' old Scottish design, much ridiculed. Between 1777 and 1817 Lady Macbeth was by common consent Sarah *Siddons's greatest role, but her brother J. P. *Kemble's Macbeth was less successful. Edmund *Kean cut some of Davenant's added witch material in 1814 (the rest disappeared finally from Samuel *Phelps's revival of 1847), and he was followed by William Charles *Macready, who played Macbeth (in tartans) between 1820 and 1848. Macready's performance, however, is remembered less vividly than that of his Lady Macbeth, Charlotte *Cushman, just as Henry *Irving's nervy and unwarlike Thane (*Lyceum, 1875, 1888) was a critical flop compared to Ellen *Terry's Lady Macbeth. Cushman upstaged the American actor Edwin *Forrest just as successfully during his visit to London in 1845, and Forrest's own Macbeth is remembered principally for its riot-provoking rivalry with that of Macready in New York in 1849, which further contributed to the play's evil reputation.

Unequivocally successful 20th-century revivals of the play were equally rare. Sybil *Thorndike and Flora *Robson were both praised as Lady Macbeth, but opinions were divided about the Macbeths offered by the most prominent Shakespearian actors of the time. John *Gielgud, in 1930 at the *Old Vic, was sensitive and introverted but unsoldierly; Donald *Wolfit forceful but mannered (1937, 1945–6, 1953); Laurence *Olivier was felt to be simplistic opposite Judith *Anderson's operatic Lady at the Old Vic in 1937, but was more impressive in Glen *Byam Shaw's Stratford production in 1955. Notable disasters include Barry *Jackson's 'tweedy' modern-dress production (1928), Orson *Welles's 'voodoo' design (1936), and Peter O'Toole's notoriously gory, melodramatic performance (1976). Perhaps the period's only legendary success was Trevor *Nunn's studio production for the *RSC in 1976, with Ian *McKellen and Judi *Dench. Further afield, meanwhile, the play inspired Welcome Msomi's popular Zulu adaptation *uMabatha*, premièred in Natal in 1972, which toured throughout the world between 1973 and 1998. *MD*

On the screen: The earliest recorded film of *Macbeth* is a one-minute scene shot in America (1905). The cinema adaptations of the play have had a more enduring impact than any television version. Still vigorously discussed are Orson Welles's *Macbeth* (1948), *Kurosawa's *Throne of Blood* (1957), and Roman Polanski's *Macbeth* (1971). The places, the atmospheric dimensions, and the spatial detail referred to in the dialogue afford the cinematographer more elaborate opportunities than can effectively be accommodated on the television screen. Welles, Kurosawa, and Polanski each adopt different priorities in visualizing the drama; Welles dramatizes an amorphous universe, Kurosawa incorporates both Noh theatricalization and samurai realism, and Polanski counterpoises scenic realism with powerful acting and strong projection of dialogue. The play also provided the basis for an American gangster film, *Men of Respect* (1991), but its most interesting film version probably remains the one that got away, the film of *Macbeth* which Olivier planned after his stage performance in 1955 but was unable to finance.

George Schaefer's American TV adaptation (1954, remade 1960) featuring Maurice *Evans and Judith Anderson drew scant praise from the critics, though Michael *Hordern's Banquo shone memorably in the later version. The television film (1979) of Trevor Nunn's famous RSC in-the-round production is historically interesting but suffers from the inevitable distancing which the camera brings to such a production, though it remains more effective than the foggy BBC TV production (1982) with Nicol *Williamson and Jane Lapotaire. *AD*

Recent major editions

Kenneth Muir (Arden 2nd series, 1951); Nicholas Brooke (Oxford, 1990); A. R. Braunmuller (New Cambridge, 1997)

Some representative criticism

Adelman, Janet, in *Suffocating Mothers: Fantasies of Maternal Origin in Shakespeare, Hamlet to The Tempest* (1978)

Bartholomeusz, Dennis, *Macbeth and the Players* (1969)

Bradley, A. C., in *Shakespearean Tragedy* (1904)

Brooks, Cleanth, 'The Naked Babe and the Cloak of Manliness', in *The Well-Wrought Urn* (1947)

Garber, Marjorie, in *Shakespeare's Ghost Writers: Literature as Uncanny Causality* (1987)

Knights, L. C., in *Explorations* (1946)

Knights, L. C., *Some Shakespearean Themes* (1959)

Orgel, Stephen, 'The Authentic Shakespeare', *Representations*, 21 (1988)

Orgel, Stephen, '*Macbeth* and the Antic Round', *Shakespeare Survey*, 52 (1999)

Spencer, Christopher (ed.), *Davenant's Macbeth from the Yale Manuscript* (1961)

Spurgeon, Caroline, in *Shakespeare's Imagery* (1935).

McKellen, Sir Ian (b. 1939), English actor. As an undergraduate at Cambridge, he played many parts including Justice Shallow and in 1962 was Henry V in repertory at Ipswich. His star quality was established in 1969 when he played both *Marlowe's Edward II and Shakespeare's Richard II at the Edinburgh Festival, in London, and on television, though his Hamlet in 1971 disappointed most critics. In 1972–4 he was a co-founder of a co-operative, the Actors' Company; his parts included Edgar in *King Lear* and Giovanni in Ford's *'Tis Pity She's a Whore.* At Stratford in 1976 he played Romeo and Leontes and excelled in Trevor Nunn's intense studio production of *Macbeth*, later portraying a suppressed, paranoid Iago in a similarly intimate production by Nunn of *Othello.* Over several years at the National Theatre he has acted Coriolanus, Kent in *King Lear*, and a ruthless, fascistic Richard III in a production set in a version of 1930s London. This latter concept he re-explored in a prize-winning film version, directed by Richard Loncraine (1996). A gay activist, McKellen has also spoken out against elitism and racialism in London theatres. In 1999 he played Prospero at the Yorkshire Playhouse, Leeds. *MJ*

Mackenzie, Henry (1745–1831), English novelist, playwright, and editor of and major contributor to the *Mirror.* His observations on *Hamlet* in this weekly, Edinburgh-based periodical (23 Jan. 1779–27 May 1780) were praised by *Bradley for their response to Hamlet's charm and their discernment of Shakespeare's intentions. *CMSA*

McKerrow, Ronald Brunlees (1872–1940), British bibliographical scholar. With A. W. Pollard and W. W. Greg, he transformed the understanding of Shakespeare *quartos and *folios by systematically investigating the nature and transmission of extant early printed copies, rather than relying on later derivative editions. *An Introduction to Bibliography for Literary Students* (1927) pioneers the study of early printed books in the process of transmission from manuscript to print. Unfortunately, despite an influential *Prolegomena for the Oxford Shakespeare* (1939), setting out the principle of printing Shakespeare's works as nearly as possible in the form in which he left them, his own edition never reached publication. *TM*

Macklin, Charles (1699–1797), actor and playwright. He was born in Ireland, and his early career, possibly as a strolling player, is obscure. From 1725 he alternated minor, often comic roles in London theatres (Touchstone, Osric/Gravedigger, Sir Hugh) with periods in the provinces. In 1735 he killed a fellow actor, and his reputation for violence endured. He achieved overnight fame in 1741 playing a dignified, tragic Shylock, which contrasted with the low comic norm, in a *Merchant of Venice* largely reclaimed from Granville's 1701 adaptation *The *Jew of Venice.* In the same season he played Malvolio. From 1742 he helped train actors, including preparing *Garrick for King Lear, and ran a school of oratory in 1753. In 1744 he hired the Haymarket and attempted to evade the Licensing Act with performances of *Othello* offered as the 'free' second half of a fee-paying concert of music. Despite a rift with Garrick he opened for him as Shylock when he took over Drury Lane in 1747 and subsequently played Iago to his Othello. In 1773 he staged a memorable *Macbeth*, partly in Scottish costume, and retired from the stage in 1789 when his memory failed while playing Shylock. *CMSA*

McManaway, James Gilmer (1899–1980), American scholar, acting director of the *Folger Shakespeare Library in Washington (1946–8), editor of the important journal **Shakespeare* Quarterly, and, with Jeanne Addison Roberts, of *A Selective Bibliography of Shakespeare: Editions, Textual Studies* (1975). *TM*

MacMorris, Captain. He is an Irish officer who quarrels with *Fluellen, *Henry V* 3.3. *AB*

Macpherson, Guillermo (1824–98), translator of Shakespeare into Spanish. Born in Gibraltar, he held consular posts in Cadiz, Seville,

Ian McKellen as a chain-smoking, fascist Richard III in Richard Loncraine's film version, 1996.

Madrid, and Barcelona. He and Jaime *Clark were the first to render Shakespeare's blank verse systematically into Spanish verse (usually hendecasyllabic lines, as well as the rhymed lines as such). He translated 23 of Shakespeare's plays (*Dramas de Shakespeare*, 1873). The 1885 reprint of his versions contained an introduction by Eduardo Benot which was remarkable for its perceptiveness. *ALP*

Macready, William Charles (1793–1873), English actor. Born in London, he made his acclaimed debut as Romeo on 7 June 1810 under his father's—financially challenged—management in Birmingham. During the next four years with his father's company in the provinces the youthful Macready essayed 70 roles including Hamlet, Hotspur, Richard II, and Othello. His initial London Shakespearian performances at Covent Garden (Othello and Iago in October 1816) did not impress, but he triumphed as Richard III (25 October 1819). Already Macready was directing his attention to the restoration of Shakespeare's original texts and to thorough rehearsals, concerns which would distinguish his own management of that theatre (1837–9) and Drury Lane (1841–3).

In the interim Macready encompassed—comedy apart—the range of the Shakespearian repertoire—Coriolanus and Cassius, Hubert, Cardinal Wolsey, Henry V, Leontes, Prospero, and Shylock—but he excelled in the major tragedies, particularly as Macbeth and King Lear. To them he brought a strong physical presence, powerful—if mannered—vocal delivery, and above all a searching intelligence which revealed character psychology. John Forster hailed his Lear as 'the only perfect picture that we have had of Lear since the age of Betterton'. This was in his landmark revival at Covent Garden (25 January 1838) in which he restored the Fool. In *Coriolanus* and *Henry V* at that theatre and *As You Like It* and *King John* at Drury Lane, Macready implemented the principles of Shakespearian production (authentic text, well-rehearsed cast, historically accurate scenery and costumes) which were to set the standards for decades. By the time he retired in 1851 Macready could take personal credit for the greatly enhanced status of the theatre, central to which had been his achievements in Shakespeare, who had formed the core of Macready's three American tours and the model for several new plays written for him. His diaries are a major resource. *RF*

Downer, Alan S., *The Eminent Tragedian William Charles Macready* (1966)

Trewin, J. C., *Mr Macready: A Nineteenth-Century Tragedian and his Theatre* (1955)

madrigal, secular vocal music in parts, imported to England from Italy in the late 1580s and then imitated by many composers, including *Morley and *Weelkes. The partsongs in Shakespeare's plays are simple *catches and *three-man songs in the English tradition. *JB*

Maecenas, after trying to reconcile the triumvirs in *Antony and Cleopatra* 2.2, encourages Caesar's attack on Antony, 4.1. He is based on C. Cilnius Maecenas (d. 8 BC), friend of Octavius Caesar, best known as the patron of *Virgil and Horace. *AB*

Maidenhead Inn and **Woolshop** are names by which parts of Shakespeare's *Birthplace were previously known. Soon after John *Shakespeare's death in 1601, his three-bay house in

Henley Street was let to Lewis Hiccox, who converted it into an inn known as the Maidenhead (later Swan and Maidenhead). It continued in the same use until the sale of the premises in 1847, although, around 1700, it was reduced in size, to occupy the two south-easterly bays only. The Woolshop was the part of the Birthplace property which, because it was originally unheated, is thought to have been John Shakespeare's business premises (he was a glove-maker and wool dealer). It occupied the south-east bay of the house, beyond the cross-passage. *RB*

Malcolm, Duncan's oldest son, leads the English forces against Macbeth, *Macbeth* 5.6. *AB*

Mallarmé, Stéphane (1842–98), French poet. An unhappy English teacher but a highly praised Symbolist poet, he discussed Shakespeare in an influential article (*La Revue indépendante,* 1 November 1886) focusing on Mounet-Sully's performance of Hamlet in the five-act verse drama by Dumas and Meurice, *Comédie-Française, 1886. He described the inner dilemma of the melancholy prince as a lonely shadow of himself playing a solitary tragedy, thus defining 'Hamletism', the late 19th-century trend, characterized by the metaphysical uneasiness of a dual personality. *ISG*

Malone, Edmond (1741–1812), Anglo-Irish scholar. Born in Dublin, graduated from Trinity College, and called to the Irish Bar in 1767, he settled permanently in London in his mid-thirties. Having inherited an ample income after his father's death, he devoted himself to the study of English letters. His literary projects include editions of William Goldsmith (1780) and John Dryden (1800), and substantial assistance to James Boswell on his *Life of Johnson.* He busied himself, too, with such occasional efforts as the exposure of the two great literary *forgers of the day, Thomas Chatterton and William Henry Ireland. His main efforts, however, centred on Shakespeare, beginning with the first sustained attempt to establish the *chronology of Shakespeare's work (1778) and culminating in two editions of Shakespeare's *The Plays and Poems,* the first in ten volumes (1790) and the second, completed posthumously by James Boswell the younger, in 21 (1821).

Believing no limits should be set on Shakespeare studies until 'every temporary allusion shall have been pointed out, and every obscurity elucidated', he was in his own time mocked as well as admired. He is now considered among the greatest of Shakespearian scholars. He is credited for both his use of primary materials and his respect for accuracy. His exhaustive 'investigations' extended to old plays and tracts, records of Chancery, parish registers, wills and letters, and documents in the Exchequer and Lord Chamberlain's Office; he was the first to use both *Henslowe's 'Diary' as well as *Strachey's 1610 account of the discovery of the Bermudas. His concern with accuracy is apparent in both his biographical and historical accounts as well as his textual efforts. In his unfinished factual *Life of Shakspeare* and his documentary *Account of the English Stage,* he strives to distinguish verifiable facts from received accounts. His textual labours are similarly driven by the desire to separate the authentic Shakespeare from the spurious. He scrutinizes *Pericles* and the *Henry VI* plays in order to single out Shakespeare's hand, cordons off the *apocryphal works of the Third Folio from the canonical, and supplants *Benson's hybridized 1640 *Poems* with the Sonnets of the 1609 quarto. The same impulse determines his selection of copy texts for the plays; hoping to bypass the mediations of intervening printers and scholars, he returns to the early *quartos and *Folio and aims at the ideal of reproducing them verbatim. In one notorious instance, his obsession with authenticity led to the whitewashing of Shakespeare's bust in Stratford, subsequently discovered to have in its original state been painted.

However determined to return to an unmediated Shakespeare, Malone unquestionably built on the work of the long succession of 18th-century editors which preceded him. At the same time, the basis of the modern textual apparatus is recognizable in his efforts: the establishing of authentic texts, the commitment to factual accuracy, the need for a chronology to co-ordinate his life and his works, and a historical background to differentiate Shakespeare's times from the present. In addition to the two monumental editions which incorporated his Shakespearian projects, Malone's legacy to Shakespeare scholarship includes the better part of his extensive library, now at the Bodleian Library, Oxford. *MG*

Grazia, Margreta de, *Shakespeare Verbatim: The Reproduction of Authenticity and the 1790 Apparatus* (1991)

Martin, Peter, *Edmond Malone Shakespearean Scholar: A Literary Biography* (1995)

Schoenbaum, S., *Shakespeare's Lives* (1991)

Malone Society, a scholarly organization, founded by R. B. *McKerrow in 1896 and named in honour of Edmond *Malone, devoted to the republication (usually in facsimile) of Elizabethan plays and dramatic documents, including many Shakespearian *quartos. *SLB*

Malvolio, Olivia's steward in *Twelfth Night,* is disproportionately humiliated after disparaging the jester Feste (1.5) and scolding Sir Toby Belch and his companions for their noisy revelry (2.3): he finally leaves the stage with one of the most ominous exit-lines in all comedy, 'I'll be revenged on the whole pack of you' (5.1.374).

Malvolio has tended to attract 'star' actors more than any other role in *Twelfth Night,* perhaps unsurprisingly given that he is of central importance to some of Shakespeare's funniest scenes. A wide range of interpretations have included the old and cold—John Lowe (1939), Ernest Thesiger (1944), Roger Mitchell (1960), Nigel Hawthorne in Trevor *Nunn's film version (1996)—and the young, oily, and upwardly mobile—John Abbott (1937), Laurence *Olivier (1955). Whether he deserves his punishment, and what we are to make of his intended revenge, has usually worried literary critics more than audiences. *AB*

Mamillius is the young son of Leontes and Hermione. His death is announced, *The Winter's Tale* 3.2.142–4. *AB*

Manningham, John (d. 1622), diarist. A law student at the Inner Temple, Manningham jotted memoranda in a notebook later known as his *Diary* (1868). In his Hall in February 1602, he watched a performance of *Twelfth Night,* probably not its first. Then on 13 March he recorded a ribald anecdote. Richard *Burbage, who played Richard III, had a tryst with a lady whom Shakespeare got to first. Already 'at his game' when Burbage arrived, Shakespeare sent word that 'William the Conqueror was before Richard III'. Embellished with new details, the anecdote was first printed in Thomas Wilkes's *A General View of the Stage* (1759). *PH*

Mansfield, Richard (1854–1907), American actor-manager who was compared to Henry *Irving. His productions were lavish spectacles and his performances were forceful; his Shakespearian successes included Henry V—'with his *panache* always in evidence'—Shylock, and Richard III—with 'a hump like a camel'. *RF*

Mantell, R(obert) B(ruce) (1854–1928), Scottish-born actor whose efforts to establish himself in the United States only succeeded when he introduced the robuster tragic and historical Shakespearian roles (Richard III, King John, Shylock, Macbeth, Othello, and Lear) into his repertoire, achieving surprising popularity with audiences more attuned to melodrama. *RF*

Mantua, the Italian city, is the scene of parts of *The Two Gentlemen of Verona*; Romeo's place of exile in *Romeo and Juliet*; and in *The Taming of the Shrew* the Pedant is told ''Tis death for anyone in Mantua | To come to Padua', 4.2.82. *AB*

Mantuanus, Baptista Spagnolo (1448–1516), an Italian Carmelite monk, also known as Mantuan, renowned for his pastoral poetry. His Latin eclogues, translated into English in 1514 by George Turberville and published in 1567, were extremely popular in 16th-century England and formed part of many *grammar schools' curricula. In *Love's Labour's Lost,* the

'This does make some obstruction in the blood, this cross-gartering, but what of that?' (*Twelfth Night* 3.4.19–21). Henry Ainley as Malvolio in Harley Granville-Barker's production, Savoy theatre, 1912.

pedant Holofernes quotes Mantuan and invokes him by name (4.2.93–9). *JKS*

manuscript plays. Although the original manuscripts of Shakespeare's plays have not survived (with the exception of the three pages in the collaborative manuscript play *Sir Thomas More*), there are a dozen extant dramatic manuscripts from the period that provide information about the ways in which play scripts were prepared for the stage. Of particular interest are the layers of addition, revision, playhouse annotation, and *censorship in the playbook of Thomas *Middleton's *The Second Maiden's Tragedy* (1611), which was performed by the King's Men when Shakespeare was still an active member of the company, and Philip *Massinger's autograph copy of *Believe as You List* (1631), heavily annotated for use as prompt copy by the *bookkeeper for the King's Men. *ER*

Greg, W. W., *Dramatic Documents from the Elizabethan Playhouses* (1931)
Werstine, Paul, 'Plays in Manuscript', in John D. Cox and David Scott Kastan (eds.), *A New History of Early English Drama* (1997)

Marcellus is a soldier of the night watch on the battlements at *Elsinore. He sees the *ghost of Hamlet's father, *Hamlet* 1.1 and 1.4. *AB*

marches in Shakespeare's plays were accompanied by the *drum (muffled for dead marches), occasionally with the *fife too; a passage in *1 Henry VI* 3.7.29–35 suggests that English and French marches each had a distinctive drum rhythm. *JB*

Marcius. For Caius *Martius* Coriolanus, see CORIOLANUS. For his son, see MARTIUS, YOUNG.

Mardian, Cleopatra's eunuch, is sent by her to tell Antony that she has killed herself, 4.14 (and does so, 4.15). *AB*

Margaret. (1) Daughter of René Duke of Anjou, she is captured by Suffolk, *1 Henry VI* 5.5, and her marriage with King Henry is arranged. In *The First Part of the Contention* (*2 Henry VI*), now Suffolk's mistress, she quarrels with the Duchess of Gloucester, 1.3, and helps plot the Duke of Gloucester's death, 3.1. She openly mourns the death of Suffolk, 4.4. In *Richard Duke of York* (*3 Henry VI*) she is one of those who taunt and stab York, 1.4, but by the end of the play is herself defeated and her husband and son murdered (5.5 and 5.6) by Richard of Gloucester. In *Richard III* she curses all the members of the House of York, especially Richard, 1.3. Shakespeare's character has little to do with the historical figure of Margaret of Anjou (1430–82). She is his only character to appear in four plays: her most celebrated impersonator was undoubtedly Peggy *Ashcroft in the *RSC's *The Wars of the Roses*, 1964. **(2)** Hero's gentlewoman is mistaken for Hero by Claudio during her night-time tryst with Borachio, *Much Ado About Nothing* (described 3.3.138–56). *AB*

Margareton (Margarelon; 'Bastard' in *speech-prefixes). He is the illegitimate son of Priam. He challenges Thersites, *Troilus and Cressida* 5.8. *AB*

Maria. (1) A lady attending the Princess of France, she is wooed by Longueville in *Love's Labour's Lost*. **(2)** She is Olivia's gentlewoman and chief architect of the plot against Malvolio (in gratitude for which Sir Toby Belch marries her). *AB*

Mariana. (1) Betrothed to Angelo but rejected by him, she agrees to help Isabella in *Measure for Measure*. **(2)** Widow Capilet's friend in *All's Well That Ends Well* 3.5. *AB*

Marín, Luis Astrana. See ASTRANA MARÍN, LUIS.

Marina, daughter of Pericles and Thaisa, is carried away by pirates (*Pericles* 15) and sold to the proprietors of a brothel (16). *AB*

Mariner. He sets Antigonus and baby Perdita on the coast of Bohemia, *The Winter's Tale* 3.3. *AB*

Markham, Gervase (?1568–1637), writer. Markham is sometimes imagined to be the *'rival poet' of Shakespeare's Sonnets. Raised in Nottinghamshire, he soldiered briefly in the Low Countries, and in 1595 addressed an elegant sonnet to the Earl of Southampton. Later he rose to a captaincy in Ireland under the Earl of *Essex. *PH*

Marlovian theory. The notion that some or all of Shakespeare's plays were in fact written by Christopher *Marlowe, despite his meticulously attested death in May 1593 (mentioned when Phebe quotes from Marlowe's *Hero and Leander* in *As You Like It* 3.5.82–3), was first developed during the heyday of the *Authorship Controversy by a San Francisco lawyer, William Gleason Zeigler, who in 1895 published a bizarre historical novel, *It Was Marlowe: A Story of the Secret of Three Centuries*. According to Zeigler, Marlowe's death was only faked, and he lived on in secret until 1598, producing all of Shakespeare's best plays during these five extra years. Zeigler's hypothesis (despite the problems involved in redating plays which allude to the Jacobean era to dates of composition between 1593 and 1598) was supported by an obscure Ohio professor, T. C. Mendenhall, who published elaborate numerical graphs of Shakespearian and Marlovian vocabulary in the *Popular Science Monthly* of December 1901 which made the two playwrights' work look statistically similar, despite their obvious differences of style. The idea was further taken up in 1931 by Gilbert Slater, whose *Seven Shakespeares* alleges that the Shakespeare canon was really written by a committee which included Marlowe (supposed to have returned from a simulated death under Shakespeare's name in 1594), as well as Sir Francis *Bacon, the Earls of *Derby, *Oxford, and *Rutland, Sir Walter *Ralegh, and Mary Herbert, Countess of Pembroke.

These fantasies were understandably ignored, however, until the Marlovian theory was reinvented by a determined Broadway press agent, Calvin Hoffman. In 1955 Hoffman published *The Murder of the Man Who Was 'Shakespeare'*, a sufficiently lurid piece of work to have attracted wide press coverage at the time. Based, it claims, on nineteen years of research (which sadly failed to produce any documentary evidence), the book outlines a scenario according to which Sir Francis Walsingham, head of Elizabeth I's secret service, employed a team of agents to murder a nameless foreign sailor and pass the corpse off as Marlowe's in 1593, while Marlowe fled to the Continent, avoiding the enemies who had threatened him. Marlowe then allegedly returned undercover to spend the rest of his life in hiding, writing new plays and poems for Walsingham, who, determined that these works should not languish in obscurity, passed them on to an actor called Shakespeare, insisting that he should pass them off as his own. Hoffman explains all this, in so far as he does, by alleging that Walsingham wished to protect Marlowe because he was his homosexual lover, and deduces that Marlowe must have died before 1623, when Walsingham must have covertly sponsored the publication of the First Folio, title page, testimonials, astonishingly plausible attributions to Shakespeare, and all.

Although Hoffman's theory attracted one or two followers (including a lawyer, Sherwood E. Silliman, who dramatized the theory in *The Laurel Bough*, 1956, and David Rhys Williams, author of *Shakespeare thy Name is Marlowe*, 1966), it is now largely forgotten: picturesquely dotty as it is, it has been unable to distract very much intellectual attention from the genuinely fascinating topic of Marlowe's actual literary influence on Shakespeare. *MD*

Hoffman, Calvin, *The Murder of the Man Who Was 'Shakespeare'* (1956)
McMichael, George, and Glenn, E. M. (eds.), *Shakespeare and his Rivals* (1962)
Schoenbaum, S., *Shakespeare's Lives* (1970, rev. edn. 1991)
Wraight, A. D., *The Story that the Sonnets Tell* (1994)

Marlowe, Christopher (1564–93), poet and playwright, one of the most brilliant of early modern English dramatists. The son of a shoemaker, he went to Cambridge on a scholarship, and may have been recruited there as a spy. He is thought to have worked on and off as a government spy for the rest of his life. After graduating he joined the army and went to the Netherlands, where he got involved in counterfeiting money and was sent home in disgrace. In 1589 he was imprisoned after a fight in which a man was killed. Later he joined the group of freethinkers surrounding Sir Walter *Ralegh. In 1593 he was summoned to appear before the Privy Council, accused of heresy, and released on bail while evidence was gathered against him. Some of this evidence survives in the form of the 'Baines Note', which vividly lists Marlowe's 'damnable opinions' on religious and sexual matters. While on bail he was stabbed to death in a guesthouse in Deptford, supposedly in a quarrel over a bill, but perhaps for some other reason connected with his espionage activities (one of the men present at his death, Robert Poley, was a government agent). The few details we have of Marlowe's life make it sound as busy and as full of intrigue as any of his plays.

His first play, *Tamburlaine* (published 1590), was performed in 1587, and it took the London stage by storm. Its prologue announces Marlowe's intention to revolutionize English verse, to set it free from the 'jigging veins of rhyming mother-wits' and fill it instead with 'high astounding terms', and the play triumphantly fulfils this ambitious promise. Its flamboyant use of contemporary rhetorical techniques, its arrogant exploitation of classical myth and Asian geography, and its flagrant disregard for crude moral imperatives set radical new standards for the new generation of Elizabethan playwrights. Marlowe followed *Tamburlaine* with a series of equally popular and influential exercises in theatrical virtuosity: *2 Tamburlaine* (1590), *Doctor Faustus* (printed 1604), *The Jew of Malta* (printed 1633), *Edward II* (printed 1594), and *The Massacre at Paris* (printed *c.*1594). Some of these were still being performed and imitated until well into the 17th century.

The Massacre at Paris was probably written with Thomas *Nashe, and Marlowe also collaborated with Nashe in writing the tragicomedy *Dido Queen of Carthage* (1594). This is closer in tone to *Ovid than to *Virgil, populated with irresponsible gods and self-centred heroes, and opening with a saucy homoerotic love scene. In this play, as in all Marlowe's works, the classical literary tradition so revered by Elizabethan schoolmasters becomes an inexhaustible repository of scandalous erotic narratives. He drew repeatedly on Ovid's *Metamorphoses*, a familiar text in schools, but crossed these with Ovid's controversial *Elegies*. Marlowe's fine translations of the latter circulated in manuscript and print throughout the 1590s, and were publicly burned by order of the Church in 1599. His narrative poem *Hero and Leander* (written *c.*1592) is his most ebulliently Ovidian text. It takes place in a pagan world where the gods are always interfering with the sexual affairs of mortals, and where mortals struggle to satisfy their own desires against overwhelming odds. Its fusion of myth, eroticism, and satire was hugely influential, both before and after its publication in 1598.

Hero and Leander resembles Shakespeare's *Venus and Adonis*, but nobody knows which came first. The doubt is symptomatic of the relationship between the two writers: this might best be described as a dialogue, in which ideas, plots, and stylistic techniques circulate from Marlowe to Shakespeare and back again up to the moment of Marlowe's death. Marlowe's effect on the young Shakespeare was so pervasive that some scholars have attributed parts of Shakespeare's early plays to Marlowe (and on scholarship's lunatic fringe, contributors to the *Authorship Controversy have attributed the late ones to him too: see *Marlovian theory). The protagonist of *Richard III* mimics the devious political machinations of Marlowe's villains, and *Richard II* looks like an admiring response to Marlowe's *Edward II*. *Titus Andronicus*, with its plot partly based on the *Metamorphoses*, its shocking transformation of ancient Rome into a 'wilderness of tigers', and the control exerted over events by a murderous outsider, Aaron, is one of Shakespeare's most Marlovian productions. Another is *The Merchant of Venice*, which like *The Jew of Malta* uses a Jewish protagonist to probe the moral and economic values of contemporary Christianity. But the transference of material between the playwrights was not all one way. Marlowe probably wrote *Edward II* in response to the popularity of Shakespeare's three plays about Henry VI. The Machiavellian villain of Marlowe's play, Mortimer Junior, may recall Richard III. So too may the Guise in *The Massacre at Paris*, who orchestrates the genocide of French Protestants for the benefit of an English Protestant audience, just as Shakespeare's Richard implicates his Elizabethan audience in his jovial demolition of the English social hierarchy. The rivalry between these young contemporaries seems to have been richly fruitful for both.

In Shakespeare's plays of the later 1590s, imitation of Marlowe gradually gives way to affectionate parody: the description of the sack of Troy in *Dido Queen of Carthage* parodically recalled by the First Player in Act 2 of *Hamlet*, Pistol remembering *Tamburlaine* in *2 Henry IV* (2.4.154–8), Phoebe, quoting *Hero and Leander* in *As You Like It* (3.5.83–4). This last is Shakespeare's only clear allusion to a contemporary poet. After about 1600 his references to Marlowe become more oblique. But one thing is certain: without Marlowe's poems and plays the works of Shakespeare would have been very different. *RM*

Bradbrook, M. C., 'Shakespeare's Recollections of Marlowe', in Philip Edwards, Inga-Stina Ewbank, and G. K. Hunter (eds.), *Shakespeare's Styles: Essays in Honour of Kenneth Muir* (1980)

Brooke, Nicholas, 'Marlowe as Provocative Agent in Shakespeare's Early Plays', *Shakespeare Survey*, 14 (1961)

Cartelli, Thomas, *Marlowe, Shakespeare and the Economy of Theatrical Experience* (1991)

Shapiro, James, *Rival Playwrights: Marlowe, Jonson, Shakespeare* (1991)

Marlowe, Julia (1866–1950), American actress. Marlowe was famous for playing young heroines, such as Viola (1887, 1907), Rosalind (1889), and Imogen (1893). Her scholarly and intelligent acting bridged Romantic and realistic styles. By 1924, Marlowe had reportedly played more Shakespearian roles than any other actress, many opposite her husband E. H. Sothern. *BR*

Marlowe Society. Founded at Cambridge University in 1907 for student productions of neglected Elizabethan drama, the Marlowe, commissioned by the British Council and directed by George *Rylands, broke new ground with its audio *recordings, released on the Argo label between 1958 and 1964, of the Complete Works, unabridged (in Dover Wilson's *Cambridge edition). A mixture of student and professional actors perform. *JKC*

Marowitz, Charles (b. 1934), American director, dramatist, and critic; founder of the innovative Open Space theatre company in London. Having worked as assistant to Peter *Brook, from 1965 on he staged a series of radical adaptations and collages of classic, canonical texts, including *Hamlet*, *Macbeth*, *Othello*, *The Shrew*, *Measure for Measure*, and *The Merchant of Venice* (collected as *The Marowitz Shakespeare*, 1978). *TM*

Marprelate controversy. See Nashe, Thomas; religion.

marriage in Shakespeare's world was not just a matter for the wedded couple, but was a crucial social institution that situated the married pair in a complex network of relationships to the extended family, the household, and the wider community. In post-Reformation England, there were very few institutions that sustained a life of elective celibacy, and in effect the only alternative to marriage for women was domestic service, essentially a transitional life-stage experience rather than a permanent option. Transitions between the childhood home, domestic service, and marriage shape the plots of several of Shakespeare's early comedies (e.g. *The Comedy of Errors*, *The Merchant of Venice*). The cultural prescription and economic necessity of marriage were especially determining of women's life chances: T.E.'s statement in *The Law's Resolutions of Women's Rights* (1632) that 'all women are married or to be married' is exemplified by the expectation that women must be either 'maid, wife or widow' that resonates in *Measure for Measure* and *All's Well That Ends Well*.

Work on marriage and the family in Shakespeare in recent decades has been informed by developments in the social history of these institutions. The immense influence of Lawrence Stone's magisterial but not uncontroversial book *The Family, Sex and Marriage in England 1500–1800* (1977) has given way to more varied explorations of the status of husband and wife, and the nature and quality of the relations between them, as these matters are represented both in prescriptive writing and in Shakespeare's plays. Such work has constituted one of the key sites in Shakespearian criticism where fundamental questions about what we might expect the relation between drama and social history to be have been posed, though no easily agreed answers have been generated. To take just one example, marriages such as that between Macbeth and his 'dearest partner of greatness' (1.5.10) have been adduced as evidence both for the rise of the affective companionate marriage in which both husband and wife understand themselves as embarked on a joint emotional and social enterprise, and equally as an instance of the irreconcilability of the competing demands of heterosexual marriage and the homosocial culture of aristocratic masculinity.

The relation between marriage as a social practice and the aesthetic work it accomplishes in shaping dramatic action and generic form has been much discussed in recent criticism, especially by *feminist scholars who have played a key role in reinvigorating discussions of Shakespearian marriages. Working in and against the structures of New Comedy, the teleology of marriage is what gives the romantic comedies their generic identity, though when the religious and sexual consummation of marriage is deferred beyond the ending of the play, questions can be posed about how far theatrical pleasure and social imperatives are reconcilable (*Twelfth Night*, *Measure for Measure*). In the dramas of British history which Shakespeare composed in the 1590s, the purpose of marriage is primarily dynastic, and the theatrical strategies of comedy are borrowed to underpin marriage as political resolution with the pleasures of narrative closure (*Richard III*, *Henry V*). Dramas of cuckoldry (or supposed cuckoldry) such as *Othello*, *Cymbeline*, and *The Winter's Tale* play out an anxiety about female sexuality within marriage which in the comedies of Shakespeare's contemporaries is linked to the question of property, but in these tragically inflected representations of aristocratic marriage takes on a more psychological cast. Throughout the canon, then, Shakespeare uses a variety of theatrical and generic strategies to explore the dramatic consequences of the often conflicted relations between love, marriage, and other social imperatives. *KC*

Belsey, Catherine, *Shakespeare and the Loss of Eden* (1999)

Hopkins, Lisa, *The Shakespearean Marriage: Merry Wives and Heavy Husbands* (1998)

Rose, Mary Beth, *The Expense of Spirit: Love and Sexuality in English Renaissance Drama* (1988)

Marshal. He officiates at Simonides' banquet, *Pericles* 7. *AB*

Marshal, Lord. See Lord Marshal.

Marston, John (?1575–1634), English dramatist who forsook the stage in 1609 to become a priest (at Christchurch Priory in Hampshire). After graduating from Oxford in 1594 Marston joined his father's law practice at the Middle Temple, where he began to publish satires, at first pseudonymously. His writing for the *children's companies (beginning with *Antonio and Mellida* and *Antonio's Revenge*, 1599–1600) may have helped to inspire the discussion of satirical juvenile drama in *Hamlet* (2.2.337–62): in any event he became involved in the *'War of the Theatres' against *Jonson, though they were later reconciled. His later plays include the bitter, tragicomic *The Malcontent* (printed in 1604), which with its disguised Duke and atmosphere of sexual corruption shares key elements with *Measure for Measure*; the comedy *The Dutch Courtesan* (*c.*1604); and a comedy which takes its title from a Shakespearian subtitle, *What You Will* (1607). *MD*

Martext, Sir Oliver. He is a clergyman who is prevented by *Jaques from marrying Touchstone and Audrey in the forest, *As You Like It* 3.3. *AB*

Martius. (1) *Titus Andronicus.* See Quintus. (2) Caius *Martius* Coriolanus. See Coriolanus.

Martius, Young. He is the young son of Coriolanus. He speaks two lines, *Coriolanus* 5.3.128–9. *AB*

Marullus. See Flavius.

Marx, Karl. See Marxist criticism.

Marxist criticism. By the end of the 20th century Marxism had long ceased to be a unitary political philosophy, having developed over its 150-year history into an extraordinary array of competing theories ranging from the most vulgar or tyranny-abetting economic determinisms to some of the most sophisticated intellectual projects of the 20th century. Marxist criticism of Shakespeare has varied accordingly. All Marxist criticism is characterized by the belief that art and literature are interrelated with the societies which produce them, but further generalization is impossible.

The German radical philosopher and social theorist Karl Marx (1818–83) himself was an avid admirer of Shakespeare and quoted him frequently throughout his works, often decoratively, at times more substantively, as in the discussion in his *The Economic and Philosophic Manuscripts of 1844* of Timon's tirade on gold in *Timon of Athens* (4.3.26–45), in which Marx saw expressed his own ideas on money as an alienated human power destructively ruling over humanity.

Perhaps because of these Marxian precedents, perhaps because Shakespeare was already associated with nationalist resistance against Napoleon in much of Central and Eastern Europe, Shakespeare was a major subject for both theatrical production and literary criticism in the socialist and communist movements of 19th- and 20th-century Europe—and in the last days of Soviet-imposed rule in Eastern Europe, Shakespearian productions were often vehicles of political protest and resistance. Characteristically Shakespeare was a hero for both sides in the major debate of mid-20th-century Marxist literary criticism, championed both by anti-modernist Georg Lukács for his consummate artistic representation of social 'typicality' and by pro-modernist Bertolt *Brecht as a predecessor of Brecht's anti-realist epic theatre.

As Marxism metamorphosed into a variegated component of avant-garde thought in Western Europe after the Second World War and as the radicalizing 1960s spawned theoretically sophisticated literary-critical methodologies not only in Western Europe but in the UK and the USA, new Marxist-inspired work on Shakespeare began to proliferate. There were several individual attempts at explicitly Marxist interpretations of Shakespeare. The German critic Robert Weimann and the American Walter Cohen, to take outstanding examples, each developed unique Marxist contributions to Shakespeare studies. But Marxism was perhaps most influential as a component of broader developments. From the 1980s on Marxism in Shakespeare studies became a part of a larger synthesis including *feminism, postcolonial theory, *psychoanalysis, and poststructuralism more generally, variously referred to as cultural studies, *new historicism, or *cultural materialism. Even while resisting the label 'Marxist', both the new historicism chiefly associated with Stephen Greenblatt in the USA and the cultural materialism of Catherine Belsey, Alan Sinfield, Jonathan Dollimore, and many others in the UK incorporate Marxist themes in their emphasis on literature as a product of broad cultural and ideological processes mediating social and political power.

Ironically other elements of Marxist literary theory have provided other themes for some of the most forceful critiques of the new historicism and cultural materialism. Michael Bristol in *Carnival and Theater* (1985) developed the ideas on carnival of the *sui generis* Marxist cultural critic Mikhail Bakhtin into a provocative criticism of what he sees as an overemphasis on power in the new historicism, while Jean Howard has incorporated feminism and theories of nationalism into a developing Marxist-influenced synthesis. Graham Holderness, Terence Hawkes, Hugh Grady, and Richard Halpern (among others) have developed Marxist-influenced analyses of Shakespeare as a cultural phenomenon, and Terry Eagleton showed the possibilities of combining Marxism and deconstruction in the analysis of Shakespeare. *HG*

Cohen, Walter, 'Political Criticism of Shakespeare', in J. E. Howard and M. F. O'Connor (eds.), *Shakespeare Reproduced: The Text in History and Ideology* (1987)

Mary Arden's House was the name given, until 2000, to a timber-framed farmhouse in Wilmcote, a hamlet in the parish of Aston Cantlow. It was so called on the strength of a tradition (which cannot, however, be traced back beyond the 1790s) that it was owned by Robert Arden, and may therefore have been the home of his daughter Mary until her marriage to John *Shakespeare. In 1891, when the *Shakespeare Birthplace Trust was placed on a legal footing by private Act of Parliament, it was charged with the duty of purchasing 'as and when the opportunity shall arise . . . the house at Wilmcote known as the house of Mary Arden his [Shakespeare's] mother'. This was achieved in 1930, when the property next came up for sale, and, after extensive restoration (including the removal of the early 19th-century stucco) was opened to the public. In 2000, however, the true location of the Arden homestead was identified as the neighbouring Glebe Farm, and the name Mary Arden's House transferred to it. The former Mary Arden's House has been renamed Palmer's, after Adam Palmer, the owner in the 1580s.

Robert Arden, who died in 1556, was a well-to-do husbandman with eight daughters. In 1550, when he made arrangements for the future division of his estates, four were still unmarried. Mary was one of these and she was still single on Robert's death six years later. By that time, her father had married again, taking as his second wife a widow, Agnes Hill, who had four young children of her own.

Palmer's, with the exception of the lean-to structure at the rear, dates from the 16th century. The south face, with extensive use of decorative timber, must originally, as now, have been the 'front'. The biggest difference between the building today and the 16th-century farmhouse is at the eastern end. This bay, with elaborate herring-bone decoration in its gable, was originally a cross wing at least two bays deep. By the 18th century, however, the bay (or bays) at the rear had been demolished, and the lean-to added. The central section of the house, a two-bay hall, was originally open to the roof. To the east was the cross wing. The bay to the west, with cross passage and kitchen, may have been built at the same time, though there is some structural evidence to suggest that it may have been added slightly later.

At the rear of the property is a complex of farm buildings, including, in one range, a dovecote, an open-fronted cowshed and small barn with cider press, together with a stable and large barn now housing a display of farming equipment. These form part of the Shakespeare Countryside Museum which is continued in another complex of farm buildings to the west. This, formerly known as Glebe Farm, has now been identified as the *Ardens' family residence, a copyhold property, held of the lord of the manor, which Robert Arden bequeathed to his wife Agnes (Mary's step-mother) and which was recorded as late in her tenure in a 1587 survey. The main part of the farmhouse itself, originally built with an open hall in its central bay, has been dendochronologically dated to 1514. A wing was added to the west end soon afterwards, and this was extended northwards early in the 18th century.

The Ardens' copyhold title passed from Agnes Arden to her son-in-law, John Fullwood, and then descended in his family until 1662. It was then sold off by the lord of the manor and in 1738 later owners disposed of it to augment the living of the neighbouring parish of Billesley,

Mary Arden's House, Wilmcote, the 16th-century farmhouse (formerly known as Glebe Farm) identified as the girlhood home of Shakespeare's mother in 2000.

hence its traditional name, Glebe Farm. A few years later, more lands and buildings were added to this glebe which recent research has further established represent the freehold premises in Wilmcote which had come to John Shakespeare on his marriage to Mary Arden. These John had then mortgaged to his brother-in-law, Edmund Lambert, whose son John kept them in his possession despite legal cases brought against him by the Shakespeares.

The buildings of Glebe Farm were bought by the Shakespeare Birthplace Trust in 1968, but it was not until 1978, on the death of the sitting tenant, that occupancy was obtained.

Palmer's was bequeathed, in 1584, by Adam Palmer to his son Edmund, and has a well-documented history thereafter. Its mistaken attribution as the home of the Arden family can be traced back no earlier than 1794, when it featured in correspondence between Samuel *Ireland and John *Jordan. Jordan also executed the earliest known drawings of the house, though none were published during his lifetime. It was another 80 years or so before uncritical attributions of the property as Mary Arden's House became a regular feature of tourist guides. *RB*

Alcock, N. W., 'Topography and land ownership in Wilmcote, Warwickshire', unpublished report, May 2000.

Halliwell-Phillips, J. O., *Outlines of the Life of Shakespeare* (London: Longmans, 2 vols, 6th edn. 1886).

Meeson, Bob, 'Glebe Farm, Wilmcote, Warwickshire: an architectural analysis', unpublished report, 2000.

Schoenbaum, Samuel, *Shakespeare's Lives* (Oxford: Oxford University Press, 1991).

Styles, Philip, 'Aston Cantlow' in *Victoria History of the County of Warwick*, vol. 3 (London: Oxford University Press, 1945).

Masque of the Inner Temple and Gray's Inn, a masque written by Francis *Beaumont (perhaps with Francis *Bacon's assistance) to celebrate the marriage of Princess *Elizabeth and the Elector Palatine in 1613. It was performed in the banqueting hall at Whitehall along with various plays including *The Tempest.* One of the antimasques was borrowed by Shakespeare and Fletcher for *The Two Noble Kinsmen.* *JKS*

masques were quasi-dramatic entertainments performed at court which combined music and dancing and, especially in their blossoming under *James I, elaborate scenery and spectacle. Masques were often written to celebrate a particular event—a royal birthday or a marriage—and performed by a company made up of professionals and members of the court before a banquet; the culmination being a mass dance joining performers with the audience. Typically the characters of a masque would be classical deities or abstract qualities such as a Virtue and Beauty, contrasted with rustic figures, and the story would represent an archetypal conflict proceeding to resolution. Originally a carnivalesque folk celebration with the traditional themes of inversion and transgression, the courtly form became highly formalized in the Jacobean collaborations of Inigo *Jones and Ben *Jonson. As set-designer Jones emulated the elaborate perspective designs of the Italian Sebastian Serlio which were best seen from a focal point—where the monarch sat—and which used complex machinery to transform the scene as if by magic. To match Jones's visual effects Jonson wrote poetic dialogue of the highest order.

In 1608 Jonson introduced the innovation of an 'antimasque' in which grotesque figures (antics) danced before the main masque, for which reason the word 'antemasque' is also sometimes used. Although new to the court masque, the Jonsonian contrast was really a reintroduction of the folk element of inversion. The fullest extant eyewitness account of a masque is by the Venetian chaplain Orazio Busino describing a performance of Jonson's *Pleasure Reconciled to Virtue* in 1618, ending with an exhausting communal dance and an unseemly rush for food which sent the glassware crashing to the floor of the Banqueting House. *GE*

Bevington, David, and Holbrook, Peter (eds.), *The Politics of the Stuart Court Masque* (1998)

Orgel, Stephen, *The Jonsonian Masque* (1965)

Orgel, Stephen, *The Illusion of Power* (1975)

Welsford, Enid, *The Court Masque: A Study in the Relationship between Poetry and the Revels* (1927)

Massinger, Philip (1583–1640), dramatist. Massinger was born into the gentry—a fact he never forgot—but by about 1613 he was in prison for debt and appealing to the theatre-owner Philip *Henslowe to bail him out. For the next few years he collaborated with John *Fletcher, writing for Shakespeare's company, the King's Men; twelve of these collaborations were published in the first folio of Beaumont and Fletcher's plays (1647). Some scholars have argued that he, rather than Fletcher, was Shakespeare's collaborator in *The Two Noble Kinsmen* and *All Is True*. After Fletcher's death Massinger succeeded him as the company's principal dramatist. His highly critical portrayals of autocratic rulers in plays like *The Duke of Milan* (1623) and *The Maid of Honour* (1632), together with his bold choice of topics connected with contemporary politics in, for instance, the lost first version of *Believe as You List* (1631), have led to a recent resurgence of critical interest in him as a daring exploiter of the theatre's resources for political ends. Some of his work, such as his fascinating account of conflict and conversion in the Ottoman Empire, *The Renegado* (1630), suggests that he was sympathetic to Catholicism. His best-known play is a funny and disturbing analysis of 17th-century class warfare, *A New Way to Pay Old Debts* (1633). It features the courageous, flamboyant, and utterly unscrupulous financier Sir Giles Overreach, a part played with huge success by the great actor-managers of the late 18th and early 19th centuries. *RM*

Howard, Douglas (ed.), *Philip Massinger: A Critical Reassessment* (1985)

Master Gunner of Orléans. The Master Gunner tells his son to watch for the English while he is away from his cannon, *1 Henry VI* 1.6. The boy fires it himself and kills Salisbury and Gargrave. *AB*

Master Gunner of Orléans's Son. See MASTER GUNNER OF ORLÉANS.

Master of a ship. **(1)** He and his Mate demand 1,000 crowns ransom each for their prisoners, *The First Part of the Contention* (*2 Henry VI*) 4.1.16. **(2)** He tells the Boatswain to 'Bestir' at the beginning of *The Tempest*. *AB*

Master of the Revels. The Office of the Revels, overseen by its Master, existed to provide entertainment for the court and the official reason for the existence of Elizabethan playing companies was to meet this need; by public performance the players could maintain a state of perpetual readiness for court performance. In 1581 Edmund *Tilney (Master from 1579 to 1610) was given the patent to license all playbooks for public performance and when George *Buck succeeded to the office in 1610 he brought to it his responsibility (held since 1606) for the licensing of printed plays. Buck was succeeded by John Astley in 1622, who was himself succeeded by Henry Herbert in 1623. Herbert kept the job until the closure of 1642 and his office book is an important source of our knowledge of play licensing and *censorship in the period. *GE*

Clare, Janet, *Art Made Tongue-tied by Authority': Elizabethan and Jacobean Dramatic Censorship* (1990)
Dutton, Richard, *Mastering the Revels: The Regulation and Censorship of English Renaissance Drama* (1991)

'master, the swabber, the bosun and I, The', sung by Stefano in *The Tempest* 2.2.45. The original melody is unknown, but it very closely fits a 16th-century tune, 'The Leather Bottel'. *JB*

Mate, Master's. See MASTER OF A SHIP.

Mathews, Charles James (1803–78), English comic actor, whose *métier* fell outside the Shakespeare repertoire. He was involved in several managerial enterprises with his wife Madame Vestris, including Covent Garden (1839–42), where *Love's Labour's Lost* (1839) and *A Midsummer Night's Dream* (1840) were notable successes. *RF*

Matthews, James Brander (1852–1929), American academic, playwright, and critic, who founded the Theatre Museum at Columbia University. His *Shakespeare as a Playwright* (1913) brings to bear his own practical and theoretical experience of drama. *TM*

Mayor of Coventry. He appears with Warwick, *Richard Duke of York* (*3 Henry VI*) 5.1 (mute). *AB*

Mayor of London. **(1)** He complains about the riotous behaviour of the feuding followers of Gloucester and the Bishop of Winchester, *1 Henry VI* 1.3 and 3.1. **(2)** He is one of Richard's supporters in *Richard III*. **(3)** He is thanked by Henry, *All Is True* (*Henry VIII*) 5.4.69–70 (mute part). *AB*

Mayor of St Albans. He sends for a beadle to whip Simpcox, *The First Part of the Contention* (*2 Henry VI*) 2.1.144. *AB*

Mayor of York. He reluctantly admits King Edward to the city of York, *Richard Duke of York* (*3 Henry VI*) 4.8. *AB*

measure, a dance term with various meanings: it could signify, according to context, a dance, a specific choreography, a step sequence, or a unit of steps. This ambiguity, combined with the word's more usual meaning, is exploited by Shakespeare on several occasions, e.g. in *Romeo and Juliet* 1.4.9–10. *JB*

Measure for Measure *(see page 284)*

medicine. Renaissance medical theory was based on that of ancient Greece. The main authority was still Galen, a writer of the 2nd century AD who had been physician to the Roman Emperor Marcus Aurelius. Its most important doctrine was that of the four humours. Our bodies were thought to be composed of blood, phlegm, black bile, and yellow bile just as the world at large consisted of earth, air, fire, and water. The underlying principle was the opposition between hot and cold, wet and dry. Blood was hot and moist, yellow bile hot and dry, black bile cold and dry, phlegm cold and moist. Each predominated in turn as one went through the stages of life. Health depended on always keeping the right balance or temperature.

Distemperature was not itself a disease but a prelude to it. When Henry IV complained that 'rank diseases grew near the heart' of his kingdom, Warwick reassured him: 'It is but as a body yet distempered | Which to his former strength may be restored | With good advice and little medicine (*2 Henry IV* 3.1.40–2). A similar progression is described in *The Comedy of Errors* 5.1.79–87: the husband of a jealous wife is said to get no recreation; this leads to 'melancholy' (i.e. black bile); and 'melancholy' brings 'a huge infectious troop Of pale distemperatures and foes to life'.

Another cause of disease was bad air due to natural conditions. Caliban's wish 'All the infections that the sun sucks up | From bogs, fens, flats, on Prosper fall, and make him | By inchmeal a disease' (*The Tempest* 2.2.1–3) assumes this miasma theory. But infection or contagion of the air could be caused by people too. 'Men take diseases, one of another,' said Falstaff, and hoped that a sense of discipline could be caught in the same way (*2 Henry IV* 5.1.69); Olivia said one might fall in love as quickly as one might catch the *plague (*Twelfth Night* 1.5.285): the fear of contagion led to plague-sufferers being left alone (*The Two Gentlemen of Verona* 2.1.19) with an isolation order put on their houses (*Romeo and Juliet* 5.2.9–11).

In both prevention and cure the physician's prime concern was to control the balance of the humours. He had various means at his disposal. He could recommend a change of air or of diet, administer a concoction of herbs (perhaps made to his own special recipe and charged at a high price), purge the patient, or, in the case of fever or threatened fever, bleed him.

The justification for bloodletting before the discovery of the circulation of the blood in 1628 by William Harvey was eminently logical. Blood was thought to be the final and most purified form of our food and drink, and to be distributed through the body by the veins. It started in the liver, and had to be used up by the

(cont. on page 287)

Measure for Measure

Shakespeare's ambivalently comic treatment of power, sexuality, and repression belongs very much to the early years of the Jacobean period. According to the *Revels accounts for 1604–5, the first recorded performance of *Measure for Measure* took place at court on 26 December 1604. Several topical allusions in the text suggest a slightly earlier date of composition. A passing reference in the opening lines of 1.2 to the final stages of a war between the Duke of Vienna and the King of Hungary might be an allusion to the peace settlements with Spain which King James I signed at Hampton Court on 18 August 1604. It has been suggested that these lines might refer to the Duke of Holst, Queen Anne's brother, who levied an army in London in December 1604 to support the new Protestant ruler of Hungary. However, Mistress Overdone's complaint in the same scene provides another set of allusions to memorable events which occurred in London in the winter of 1603–4. The Overdone–Pompey exchange in 1.2 might also be another allusion to the King's proclamation of 16 September 1603 calling for the demolition of houses in the suburbs of London. The hypothesis that *Measure for Measure* was not a new play when it was staged at court in December 1604 is further reinforced by the fact that Shakespeare might have decided to write the play while performances at the Globe were suspended between 19 March 1603 and 9 April 1604 because of the plague.

Text: *Measure for Measure* was entered in the *Stationers' Register by Edward Blount and Isaac *Jaggard on 8 November 1623: it was never printed in a *quarto edition prior to its inclusion in the 1623 Folio. The Folio text was transcribed by Ralph *Crane, probably from a promptbook. Crane is likely to have supplied the list of characters, where the Duke, who is otherwise never referred to by his proper name in the play, is called Vincentio.

The text shows some signs of adaptation: the Boy's song, 'Take, O take those lips away', at the beginning of Act 4 may be a late interpolation from *Fletcher's *Rollo, Duke of Normandy* (1616–19), and the Duke's subsequent monologue 'O place and greatness' (too short to allow Isabella to inform Mariana about the Duke's plans) was probably transposed by the later adapter responsible for introducing the act division with the original monologue, 'He who the sword of heaven will bear', which is longer and more suitable as an act-break. More tampering must have occurred in 1.2, where the news of Claudio's arrest is divulged twice: the first part of 1.2 was probably added to the promptbook by a later adapter, probably Thomas *Middleton. This later addition was probably meant to replace the original exchange, but Crane transcribed both by mistake.

Sources: Of the three main plot-components upon which *Measure for Measure* is based—'the corrupt magistrate', 'the ruler in disguise', and 'the bed-trick'—only the first one derives from the play's main sources, the fifth *novella* of the eighth decade in *Cinthio's *Hecatommithi* (1565), its dramatic rendition *Epitia* (1573), and *Whetstone's *Promos and Cassandra* (1578). The stock character of the ruler in disguise, which enjoyed sweeping popularity on the early Jacobean stage (see, for example, Middleton's *The Phoenix*, *Marston's *The Malcontent* and *The Fawn*, and Sharpham's *The Fleer*), might derive from Elizabethan history plays, such as *Heywood's *King Edward IV* (1600), the anonymous **Fair Em* (1590), or *Peele's *King Edward I* (1593), where the encounter between the disguised ruler and his subjects is the focus of the dramatic tension. The bed-trick, which Shakespeare used again in *All's Well That Ends Well*, has famous precedents in the Italian novelistic tradition but also in the

Old Testament (Genesis 38), Plautus' *Amphitruo*, and Malory's *Le Morte d'Arthur*.

Synopsis: 1.1 The Duke leaves *Vienna straight after appointing Angelo as his substitute. Angelo is younger and more inexperienced than the old councillor Escalus and asks the Duke to test him before handing the rule of the city over to him. The Duke refuses to delay his departure any further. 1.2 Lucio's banter with two gentlemen is interrupted by Mistress Overdone's announcement that Claudio is being carried off to prison for getting Juliet with child. Mistress Overdone informs Pompey, the pimp, that because of a new proclamation her brothel and other houses of ill-repute in the suburbs will be pulled down. Lucio meets Claudio on his way to prison. The latter explains that although Juliet is 'fast' his wife, following a private exchange of vows between them, they have not been married in the church because Juliet's relatives oppose the match. Claudio will be sentenced to death as a result of Angelo's decision to revive an ancient law, which the Duke had failed to enforce for years. Claudio hopes that his sister Isabella will plead with the strict deputy for his life. 1.3 The Duke explains to Friar Thomas that he had to leave Vienna because of his failure to enforce the law and that Angelo was appointed to restore order on his behalf. The Duke will go back to Vienna disguised as a friar in order to keep an eye on his deputy. 1.4 Lucio goes to the convent where Isabella is about to take her vows and persuades her to plead with Angelo for Claudio's life.

2.1 Elbow, a constable, takes Pompey and Froth to court for attempting to corrupt his wife. Elbow's malapropisms bring the trial to an end and both Pompey and Froth are let off with a warning. 2.2 Isabella is brought before Angelo and she pleads for her brother's life. Her arguments grow stronger and Angelo is attracted both by the strength of her rhetorical powers and by her chastity. Angelo tries to repress his feelings for Isabella and wonders why he should be tempted by such a chaste creature as Isabella, since he has never been tempted by a woman before. 2.3 The Duke, disguised as a friar, goes to the prison and lectures Juliet about her share of responsibility for what has happened to her and Claudio, but fails to comfort her. 2.4 Isabella goes back for a second meeting with Angelo, who tells her that he will spare her brother only if she agrees to give up her virginity to him. Isabella threatens to report him, but Angelo is confident that his 'false' will overweigh her 'true', because of his spotless reputation and his privileged position as the Duke's deputy.

3.1 The Duke visits Claudio in prison pretending to be his 'ghostly father', a religious figure in charge of a penitent or one near death. His lesson in *ars moriendi* seems to persuade Claudio that life is not worth living after all, but as soon as Isabella hints at Angelo's indecent proposal, Claudio begs her to comply with Angelo's request. Isabella scolds Claudio for asking her to sacrifice her virtue. The Duke approaches Isabella and persuades her to trick Angelo into sleeping with his former fiancée Mariana, who had been spurned by Angelo a few years earlier following the loss of her dowry. They agree that Isabella will persuade Angelo to meet her in the dark, so that he will mistake Mariana for Isabella and spare her brother's life. 3.2 On his way out of the prison, the Duke meets Lucio, who slanders him. Because he is still in disguise, the Duke cannot refute Lucio's allegations.

4.1. Mariana, who is still in love with Angelo, welcomes the Duke's plans and agrees to go to Angelo pretending to be Isabella. 4.2 Pompey, who is now in prison himself, is appointed personal assistant to Abhorson, the executioner. The Duke realizes that Angelo has failed to keep his word and has ordered Claudio's execution. The Duke is therefore forced to inform the Provost that he is acting on the Duke's behalf and that he wishes him to delay Claudio's execution. He also suggests that the Provost should pretend that Angelo's orders have been carried out and that Claudio is dead, by sending Angelo the severed head of Barnardine, another prisoner who is shortly to be executed. 4.3 Barnardine spoils the Duke's plans by refusing to be executed. He claims to be too drunk and therefore unfit to die. The Duke instead sends Angelo the head of Ragozine, another prisoner who has fortunately just died in prison. The Duke lies to Isabella about Claudio's execution. She believes him dead and Lucio tries to comfort her, taking once more the opportunity to slander the Duke, by blaming him for leaving his subjects at the mercy of the strict deputy. 4.4 Angelo and Escalus learn of the Duke's imminent homecoming. 4.5 The Duke finalizes the arrangements for his homecoming, instructing Friar Peter to help Mariana and Isabella report Angelo to the Duke after his reinstatement as the supreme ruler in Vienna. 4.6 Still unaware of the friar's true identity, Isabella and Mariana are also instructed by the Duke.

5.1 The Duke meets Angelo and Escalus at the city gates. Isabella is brought before him and accuses Angelo of deflowering her. The Duke pretends to ignore the truth and, despite Lucio's interference, proceeds to have Isabella arrested for slandering his deputy. Friar Peter announces that a witness can corroborate Isabella's accusations. Mariana enters wearing a veil and promises to reveal her identity only when her husband bids her to do so. Mariana claims that Angelo is her husband and that they have already consummated their marriage. Angelo accuses Mariana of lying and the Duke pretends to side with him. Friar Peter asks that another witness be brought before the Duke. The Duke exits and re-enters wearing his disguise as a friar. When Lucio accidentally unmasks him, Angelo finally realizes that the Duke has known the truth all along. He begs to be executed but the Duke orders him to marry Mariana in order to restore her reputation, ordering his execution immediately after the ceremony. Mariana pleads for his life and asks Isabella to do the same. Isabella argues that Angelo should be spared because Claudio was at least punished for a crime he actually committed, while Angelo was in the event prevented from taking her virginity. Angelo is finally forgiven when the Duke orders the Provost to unmask a prisoner whose execution had been delayed and the prisoner turns out to be Claudio. The Duke asks Isabella to marry him.

Artistic features: *Measure for Measure* has been perceived as an exceptionally complex and 'dark' comedy, or tragicomedy, mostly because of its peculiar structure and characterization. Whereas the first half of the play explores the moral issues raised by Claudio and Isabella's potentially tragic ordeal, the second half is largely devoted to the Duke's efforts to orchestrate the happy ending. The comic resolution, however, is remarkably fraught with tension, embarrassing silences (such as Isabella's failure to respond to the Duke's proposal) and disappointing reunions, and fails to provide an answer to the moral issues raised in the first half. The characters themselves are never single-mindedly evil or entirely sympathetic. Isabella is one of Shakespeare's most articulate heroines, but may seem harsh and self-righteous in her adamant conviction that 'more than our brother is our chastity'. Angelo is a hypocritical coward and yet he is also a self-conscious villain, who wonders at the mystery of his own fall from grace. The Duke aims to appear as a merciful ruler but resorts to spying, scheming, and acting as a meddling busybody throughout the play. Shakespeare seems therefore intent on systematically undercutting his characters' ideals so as to show them as painfully human and fallible.

Critical History: *Measure for Measure* has always had a mixed critical reception: its moral complexity irritated *Johnson but pleased *Hazlitt; the personal shortcomings of its characters alienated *Coleridge but moved *Ulrici. Twentieth-century critics have replicated this split by reading this comedy as either a *problem play (as did *Tillyard and Schanzer) or as a Christian allegory of mercy and forgiveness (as did Wilson *Knight 1930, Roy Battenhouse, and Neville Coghill). Recent criticism is similarly divided in its assessment of this play in relation to the political and social institutions of its time. Some critics regard the low characters as ultimately subversive, while others argue that *Measure for Measure* exemplifies the systematic suppression of diversity. A feminist and a materialist critic have, for example, remarked that if 'feminist criticism . . . is restricted to exposing its own exclusion from the text' (Kathleen McLuskie, 1985), a materialist critic 'looking for evidence of resistance . . . [will] find rather further evidence of exploitation' (Jonathan Dollimore, 1985).

Stage history: The *Revels accounts for 1604–5 report the only recorded performance prior to the closure of the London theatres in 1642. During the Restoration, *Measure for Measure* was revived in two heavily adapted versions, *Davenant's *The *Law against Lovers* (1662) and Charles *Gildon's *Measure for Measure; or, Beauty the Best Advocate* (1700), which cuts the low characters and instead fills out the play by having Angelo listen to Purcell's opera *Dido and Aeneas* in instalments in a fruitless bid to take his mind off Isabella. The Shakespearian original was restored to the stage in 1720, often understood as a warning against prime ministerial government, but most 18th-century productions were heavily cut. *Measure for Measure* disgusted the Victorians, but appealed to 20th-century audiences. Tyrone *Guthrie's 1933 production at the Old Vic was only moderately successful, despite its star-studded cast, which included Charles *Laughton as Angelo. The next remarkable production this century was Peter *Brook's at Stratford-upon-Avon, remembered for Paul *Scofield's foppish Lucio and for Barbara *Jefford's dramatic pause before she knelt down to plead for Angelo's life in Act 5, which was never less than 30 seconds long and sometimes far longer. The cultural changes ushered in by the late 1960s led directors John *Barton and Trevor *Nunn to depart from Brook's optimistic interpretation of the Duke: their 1970 and 1990 productions emphasized the oppressive nature of the Duke's regime and Isabella's plight in Act 5. More sympathetic Dukes, however, have included Michael *Pennington's in Barry Kyle's production (1978) and Daniel Massey's in Adrian *Noble's (1984), opposite Juliet Stevenson's powerful Isabella. *SM*

On the screen: The earliest film recorded was a 1913 Italian version. A 90-minute adaptation, again from Italy (1942), was followed by a more substantial German television film (1963). The BBC TV version (1978), though recognizing its Gothic elements, presented the play as a comedy. David Thacker's later BBC TV production (1994) is memorable for updating the play socially (into a world of televised courtrooms) and for taking a much more serious view of the action. Like Barton's stage production, it left the question of Isabella's marriage unresolved. *AD*

Recent major editions

N. W. Bawcutt (Oxford, 1991); Brian Gibbons (New Cambridge, 1991); J. W. Lever (Arden 2nd series, 1965)

Some representative criticism

Bloom, Harold, *William Shakespeare's 'Measure for Measure'* (1987)

Dollimore, Jonathan, 'Transgression and Surveillance in *Measure for Measure*', in Jonathan Dollimore and Alan Sinfield (eds.), *Political Shakespeare* (1985)

Foakes, R. A., *Shakespeare, The Dark Comedies to the Last Plays* (1971)

McLuskie, Kathleen, 'The Patriarchal Bard: *Measure for Measure* and *King Lear*', in Jonathan Dollimore and Alan Sinfield (eds.), *Political Shakespeare* (1985)

Watts, C., *Shakespeare: 'Measure for Measure'* (1986)

Wood, Nigel, *Theory in Practice: 'Measure for Measure'* (1996) time it got to the furthest parts, like the water in an irrigation channel (hence the remark in *Coriolanus* 1.1.153 about the 'great toe' being 'the worst in blood'). If there was still any blood over, there could be trouble. The excess might simply erupt in pimples, boils, and the like, but a more serious consequence, blood being hot, could be a fever. The most obvious remedy for this was to stop eating (whence our saying 'starve a fever') and so stop blood being produced, but the quicker way, as Biron puts it in *Love's Labour's Lost* (4.3.95–6), was to cut into a vein and let the excess blood out 'in saucers'.

Less relevant for therapy was the function assigned to the arteries and the nerves. The arteries were thought to contain a refined form of air—'life-breath' or 'vital spirit'—which was pumped through the body by the heart for the purpose of ventilation. Thus the body could be called 'a confine of blood and breath' (*King John* 4.2.247), and at a less serious level it could be argued that too much academic study, 'universal plodding', creates dullness because it 'prisons up | The nimble spirits in the arteries' (*Love's Labour's Lost*, 4.3.301–2).

The nerves were tiny tubes by which sensation passed from the body to the brain and the power of voluntary motion from the brain to the body. The medium of communication was an extremely refined form of air—'soul-breath' or 'animal spirit'—created within the brain, and the brain itself was, according to some, 'the soul's frail dwelling-house' (*King John* 5.7.3). These words were spoken as the King lay dying, and so at a solemn moment. In another play at a romantic moment Lorenzo explains to Jessica that her appreciation of music is due to her spirits (*Merchant of Venice* 5.1.70), and goes on to add that the same holds true for animals. Earlier in the play (3.2.63–4) and in a different, lighter, context, the song 'Tell me where is fancy bred, | Or in the heart or in the head' alludes to the same question, for though the brain as the seat of thought was orthodox doctrine according to Galen, it was nevertheless possible to follow Aristotle and assign this role to the heart.

Shakespeare's wide knowledge of medical theory is not displayed pedantically for its own sake. It comes out in the natural conversation of his characters and is for the most part unobtrusive. It can also be surprisingly up to date. The idea that the spirits are the substance of the soul seems to be due to Telesius who published it (in Latin) in 1590. Telesius also, following Argenterius (1565), drew no distinction between the vital and the animal spirits—and Shakespeare, unlike most of his contemporaries, does not distinguish them either. One imagines that he must have learnt of these ideas by talking about them, and that he may therefore have numbered doctors among his friends. At any rate his eventual son-in-law John *Hall was one, and it is noteworthy that, except for Doctor Caius in *Merry Wives*, who is made fun of for being a Frenchman, doctors are always treated with respect. They are never, as they often have been by poets and satirists, attacked as either mercenary or murderous. *MP*

Hoeniger, F. D., *Medicine and Shakespeare in the English Renaissance* (1992)
Pope, M., 'Shakespeare's Medical Imagination', *Shakespeare Survey*, 38 (1985)
Simpson, R. R., *Shakespeare and Medicine* (1959)

meiosis, a figure of speech that belittles what it describes; or an understatement.

> Landlord of England art thou now, not king
> (*Richard II* 2.1.113)

CB

Melun, Count. Mortally wounded, he warns the English lords that Louis the Dauphin will betray them, *King John* 5.4. *AB*

Melville, Herman (1819–91), American novelist. Melville himself hoped that Nathaniel Hawthorne would emulate Shakespeare's achievement for America, but most critics feel that Melville's own epic-tragedy *Moby-Dick* (1851) comes nearest to fulfilling that function, Captain Ahab evoking King Lear, and Pip the Fool (see Charles Olson, *Call Me Ishmael*, 1947). Melville was always drawn to Shakespeare's tragic vision, his power of darkness, his capacity for invoking savage nature, and several versions of Iago (Jackson in *Redburn*, 1849; Babo in *Benito Cereno*, 1855; and Claggart in *Billy Budd*, 1924) surface throughout his work. *TM*

memorial reconstruction. See REPORTED TEXT.

Menander. See GREEK DRAMA; PLAUTUS; TERENCE.

Menas. He tries to persuade Pompey to kidnap Antony and Caesar at the banquet on his galley, *Antony and Cleopatra* 2.7. *AB*

Mendelssohn, Felix (1809–47), German composer. Mendelssohn's tremendously popular, and substantial, music for *A Midsummer Night's Dream*, Op. 61, received its first public performance in Berlin in 1843 (although the overture, Op. 21, had already been written in 1826) and was soon adopted on the British stage. The music contains the famous Wedding March. *IBC*

Menecrates comments on the will of the gods, *Antony and Cleopatra* 2.1. *AB*

Menelaus is the husband of Helen and brother of Agamemnon in *Troilus and Cressida*, based on the character of the same name who plays a more prominent part in *Homer's *Iliad*. *AB*

Menenius Agrippa, Coriolanus' friend, vainly attempts to dissuade him from attacking Rome, *Coriolanus* 5.2. *AB*

Menteith is a Scottish thane who first appears with the other thanes who are to join Malcolm and the English forces against Macbeth, *Macbeth* 5.2. *AB*

Mercadé brings the Princess of France the news of her father's death, *Love's Labour's Lost*, 5.2.711–13. *AB*

Merchant of Venice, The *(see page 288)*

merchants. (1) A merchant of Ephesus gives Antipholus of Syracuse helpful advice, *The Comedy of Errors* 1.2. **(2)** A second merchant is owed money by Angelo, *The Comedy of Errors* 4.1. **(3)** A merchant appears in the first scene of *Timon of Athens* and is cursed by Apemantus. *AB*

Merchant Taylors' School, originally located in Suffolk Lane in the *City of London, was founded in 1561 by Richard *Mulcaster, under whom it became a hotbed of educational drama. Plays acted at court by Merchant Taylors' boys include *Ariodante and Genevra* (1583), a possible source for *Much Ado About Nothing*. The school's alumni include Edmund *Spenser. *RSB*

Mercutio, in *Romeo and Juliet*, accompanies Romeo to the Capulet masque, and talks among other things of 'Queen Mab' in one of Shakespeare's most famous speeches (1.4.55–95). He vainly attempts to summon Romeo by teasing him about Rosaline before he and Benvolio leave the masque without him (2.1). The next morning he indulges in elaborate word games with Romeo and is with him when he encounters the Nurse (2.3). In 3.1 he fights with Tybalt and is mortally wounded when Romeo tries to stop them, in revenge for which Romeo kills Tybalt.

In many ways Mercutio is a parallel figure to Romeo, the complexity, lyricism, and imagination of his language balancing Romeo's. Actors have sometimes exchanged the two roles, as did John *Gielgud and Laurence *Olivier in 1935. When Mercutio is killed the tone of the play changes, losing some of its romantic energy as the tragedy gathers pace. In the 19th century he was seen as a 'mercurial and spirited' young gentleman (*Hazlitt, 1817) but more recent productions have seen a darker side to his character, as does *Zeffirelli's film version (1968) in which John McEnery as Mercutio is intellectual, macabre, and perhaps a little mad. *AB*

Levenson, Jill, *Shakespeare in Performance: Romeo and Juliet* (1987)

Meres, Francis (1565–1647), critic and clergyman. Born in Lincolnshire, Meres entered Pembroke College, Cambridge, where he took his BA. He later claimed to be 'Master of Arts of both Universities'. Before moving to a Rutland parish, he lived in London where in 1597 and

(cont. on page 291)

The Merchant of Venice

Shakespeare's perennially popular, and perennially controversial, comedy of religious conflict was entered in the *Stationers' Register on 22 July 1598, and is mentioned in Francis *Meres's *Palladis Tamia* soon afterwards. *The Merchant of Venice* cannot have been more than two years old then: the passage in which Shylock cites the story of Jacob and Laban (1.3.70–89) shows the influence of Miles Mosse's tract *The Arraignment and Conviction of Usury* (1595), and the play is unlikely to have been written before 1596, since a reference at 1.1.27–9 to 'wealthy Andrew' probably alludes to a Spanish ship, the *St Andrew*, captured in the Cadiz expedition that summer. Internal, stylistic evidence links the play's metre and vocabulary to those of the *Henry IV* plays, and it was probably composed during the same period, around 1596–7.

Text: The Stationers' Register calls the play *The Merchant of Venice, or Otherwise Called The Jew of Venice*, possibly reflecting Shakespeare's original subtitle, but when it appeared in quarto in 1600 it did so as *The Most Excellent History of the Merchant of Venice. With the Extreme Cruelty of Shylock the Jew towards the Said Merchant, in Cutting a Just Pound of his Flesh: and the Obtaining of Portia by the Choice of Three Chests.* This remains the only authoritative text for the play, serving as the basis for a further quarto printed by the *Jaggards for Pavier in 1619 (fraudulently dated '1600') and for the text published in the 1623 Folio, which adds, however, a number of stage directions (mainly musical cues) which may derive from the additional consultation of a theatrical manuscript. Fortunately it is a generally reliable text, deriving either from a fair copy in Shakespeare's own hand or from an accurate transcript of such a manuscript.

Sources: Shakespeare's play, as the quarto's subtitle suggests, brings together two widely known folk-tale motifs, the story of the pound of flesh and the story of the three caskets. Many of the play's most important elements are already present in the Florentine writer Ser *Giovanni's version of the pound of flesh plot, a story known as 'Giannetto of Venice and the Lady of Belmont'. In this story a merchant borrows from a Jew in order to fund his protégé Giannetto's repeated attempts to woo the Lady of Belmont, who will only marry the man who can first pay a contestant's fee and then stay awake long enough to seduce her. Giannetto falls asleep on his two first attempts, before the Lady's maid warns him not to drink the wine which the Lady always offers her suitors before bed, which she drugs: he is thus enabled to win her. As in the play, the Jew is foiled in his attempt to exact a pound of flesh from the defaulting merchant. Shakespeare knew the pound of flesh story from other sources too, one of which, Alexander Silvayn's *The Orator* (translated in 1596), influenced his own trial scene. In rewriting the story of Giannetto as that of Bassanio, Shakespeare replaced the seduction test with the choice of the three caskets, a motif also available to him in many forms, in John *Gower's *Confessio amantis*, in *Boccaccio's *Decameron*, and in the anonymous *Gesta Romanorum*. It is possible that Shakespeare was not the first playwright to combine the pound of flesh and the casket plots: Stephen Gosson's *The Anatomy of Abuses* (1579) refers to a now lost play called *The Jew*, which represents, he reports, 'the greediness of worldly choosers and the bloody minds of usurers'. Whether or not this vaguely described play served as a source for *The Merchant of Venice*, Shakespeare must have been conscious as he wrote his own play about a Jew of another, Christopher *Marlowe's black farce *The Jew of Malta* (*c*.1589). In Marlowe's play the titular Machiavellian villain-hero, Barabas, is betrayed by his daughter Abigail, who falls in love with a Christian, and becomes a nun after Barabas has her suitor killed. The elopement and conversion of Shylock's daugher Jessica, significantly, is an addition by Shakespeare to his chief, prose, sources. Marlowe's play had enjoyed a new lease of life in 1594, when it was revived by the *Admiral's Men, apparently to capitalize on the anti-Semitism exacerbated by the execution that June of Elizabeth I's Jewish-Portuguese physician Roderigo *Lopez on dubious charges of attempting to poison the Queen: some commentators regard Graziano's reference to 'a wolf ... hanged for human slaughter' (4.1.132–7) as a punning allusion to Lopez's fate (*lupus* is Latin for 'wolf').

Synopsis: 1.1 Antonio, a Venetian merchant, will not be cheered up by his associates, even the frivolous Graziano. Left alone with his friend Bassanio, who already owes him much money, he learns of Bassanio's desire to woo an heiress of Belmont called Portia, for which Bassanio will need further money. Antonio urges Bassanio to borrow money on his credit for this purpose. 1.2 In Belmont, Portia reflects on her late father's will, which obliges her to marry whichever suitor correctly chooses between three chests of gold, silver, and lead: she speaks disparagingly of the suitors listed by her waiting-woman Nerissa. Nerissa speaks of Bassanio, but they are interrupted by news that a fresh suitor has arrived, the Prince of Morocco. 1.3 Bassanio is negotiating a loan of 3,000 ducats, for three months, with the Jewish usurer Shylock. When Shylock sees Antonio approaching he speaks in an aside of his hatred of him, but when Antonio arrives, Shylock, though reminding him of many public insults, speaks affably in defence of usury, and despite Antonio's renewed profession of enmity offers to lend the 3,000 ducats at no interest, insisting only—professedly in fun—that Antonio should sign a bond specifying that if he defaults Shylock will be entitled to a pound of his flesh.

2.1 The Prince of Morocco agrees to vow, before making his choice of casket, that if he chooses wrongly he will remain unmarried forever. 2.2 Lancelot Gobbo debates the morality of running away from his master Shylock, finally deciding to do so. When his blind father arrives he pretends to be a stranger and announces his own death, before revealing his identity and announcing his intention of leaving Shylock's service. When Bassanio enters, the Gobbos beg that Lancelot may join his staff, to which Bassanio agrees. Bassanio is subsequently met by Graziano, whom he permits to accompany him to Belmont on condition that he behave soberly. 2.3 Shylock's daughter Jessica bids farewell to Lancelot, giving him a letter to Bassanio's friend Lorenzo, with whom she plans to elope. 2.4 Lorenzo, among his revelling friends, receives Jessica's letter, which directs him to take her from her father's house, disguised as a page, that night. 2.5 Shylock, invited out to dine with Antonio and associates, bids farewell first to Lancelot and then, despite misgivings, to Jessica. 2.6 Lorenzo, disguised among his friends, receives Jessica as she climbs from her window disguised as a boy, bringing much of Shylock's gold and jewellery. Antonio urges Graziano to join Bassanio on board their ship for Belmont. 2.7 Morocco chooses between the three caskets, which all bear mottoes: the lead 'Who chooseth me must give and hazard all he hath', the silver 'Who chooseth me shall get as much as he deserves', and the gold 'Who chooseth me shall get what many men desire'. To Portia's relief he chooses the gold casket, which contains a death's head bearing a poem, 'All that glisters is not gold ...' 2.8 Salerio and Solanio, associates of Bassanio, discuss Shylock's anguish at the loss of his daughter, Antonio's tender parting from Bassanio, and rumours that a Venetian ship, possibly one of Antonio's, has been wrecked. 2.9 Portia's next suitor, the Prince of Aragon, chooses the silver casket, which contains a fool's head and another mocking poem. As he departs, news arrives that another, Bassanio, is approaching.

3.1 Solanio and Salerio are discussing the wreck of one of Antonio's ships when Shylock arrives and accuses them of complicity in Jessica's elopement: distraught, he is consoled only by the news of Antonio's losses, and promises to pursue his revenge against him as ruthlessly as would a Christian. Left alone with Tubal, Shylock learns of Jessica's extravagance with the money and jewels she took with her, alternating between grief at this and vengeful glee as he hears further of Antonio's impending bankruptcy. 3.2 Though Portia begs him to postpone his choice, Bassanio, to the accompaniment of a song ('Tell me, where is fancy bred ...?'), reflects prudently on the caskets' mottoes and correctly chooses the lead one: within is a picture of Portia and a poem which instructs him to claim her with a kiss. Portia formally gives herself and her estate to him, with a ring which she urges him to wear forever. Graziano now announces that Nerissa has promised to marry him should Bassanio succeed; Portia and Bassanio give their blessing. Lorenzo and Jessica arrive, together with Salerio, who brings Bassanio a letter from Antonio: it tells him that, all his seaborne ventures having failed, he is at Shylock's mercy. Bassanio explains to Portia that Antonio incurred this lethal debt on his behalf, and she immediately postpones their marriage, sending him to Venice with money in the hopes of persuading Shylock to let Antonio live. 3.3 On the eve of the pound of flesh falling due, Shylock refuses to hear Antonio's pleas for mercy. 3.4 Portia hands over her house to Lorenzo's keeping, saying she and Nerissa will stay in a nearby convent while Bassanio and Graziano are in Venice, but after Lorenzo's departure she sends her servant Balthasar on an errand to her relative, the lawyer Bellario, and explains to Nerissa that the two of them will in fact go to Venice in male disguise. 3.5 Lancelot banters with Jessica about her conversion to Christianity. Jessica and Lorenzo speak admiringly of Portia and Bassanio.

4.1 Before the Duke, Shylock, though offered his 3,000 ducats, insists on his pound of flesh. Bassanio offers twice the sum, which Shylock also refuses. Antonio professes a stoical acceptance of death while Shylock sharpens his knife. The Duke threatens to adjourn the court until he has received legal advice from Bellario: instead he receives a letter sending a young expert in his place, Balthasar, who is really Portia in disguise, accompanied by Nerissa as clerk. Portia speaks eloquently to Shylock, urging him to show mercy, but he refuses, and she concedes his legal right to the pound of flesh. Bassanio and Graziano, in Portia and Nerissa's hearing, each tell Antonio they would sacrifice their wives to save him.

Antonio has exposed his breast for Shylock's incision when Portia announces that since the bond mentions no blood, Shylock's estate will be forfeit to the state if he sheds any while cutting his pound of flesh. Baffled, Shylock accepts 9,000 ducats in place of the flesh, but Portia insists he is entitled only to the flesh, not even to the 3,000 ducats he originally loaned. Shylock is about to leave when Portia announces that as an alien who has sought to kill a Venetian he is liable to the death penalty, and his possessions must be divided between Antonio and the state. The Duke spares Shylock's life and offers to waive the state's claim to half Shylock's wealth, requiring only a fine. Antonio in his turn says he will only borrow half Shylock's estate and give it after Shylock's death to Lorenzo, to whom he insists Shylock bequeaths all his other possessions, and he further insists that Shylock should convert to Christianity. Shylock leaves, unwell. The disguised Portia and Nerissa, gratefully offered gifts by Bassanio and Graziano, demand their respective wedding rings: at Antonio's insistence the men hand them over.

5.1 Lorenzo and Jessica, outside Portia's house, listen to music by moonlight. Portia and Nerissa, no longer disguised, return home, followed separately by Bassanio, Antonio, and Graziano. Nerissa upbraids Graziano for giving her ring to the clerk, and Bassanio soon has to admit he gave his to the lawyer. Portia and Nerissa claim they will not sleep with their husbands, but only with the lawyer and his clerk: only when a penitent Antonio intercedes on Bassanio's behalf does Portia produce the ring again, at first claiming to have obtained it in bed from the lawyer before revealing her deception. Portia further gives Antonio news that three of his argosies have arrived safely, and gives Lorenzo the deed by which Shylock has made him his heir.

ARTISTIC FEATURES: Combining the logics of both the fairy tale and the financial market place—or perhaps revealing their secret kinship—*The Merchant of Venice* is one of Shakespeare's most tightly structured comedies, both narratively and thematically. The questions raised by the lead casket's motto, 'Who chooseth me must give and hazard all he hath', resonate throughout its two interwoven plots as they scrupulously weigh the competing claims of religion and civil society, justice and mercy, marriage and friendship. Shylock, the first of the mature comedies' great antagonists, owes some of his enduring impact not only to his formal status as the comedy's tragic scapegoat and his religious status as an embodiment of Judaic *law in a Christian community nominally committed to love and mercy, but to the skill with which Shakespeare invests his comparatively short role with its own distinctive voice.

CRITICAL HISTORY: Responses to this play have for most of its history been dominated by responses to Shylock. The question of Shakespeare's attitude to the *Jews has been debated since the time of Nicholas *Rowe, and from the early 19th century onwards many commentators have seen the play as essentially sympathetic to Shylock: *Hazlitt insisted that he was presented as, finally, an object of pity, while *Heine, remembering an English theatre-goer weeping 'The poor man is wronged!' at the end of Act 4 (in *Shakespeares Mädchen und Frauen*, 1839), opined that even if Shakespeare had consciously intended Shylock to be a monster his humanity had led him to write a vindication of the Jews. The argument between those who insist that Shakespeare was exposing his Christians' hypocrisy rather than attacking Judaism, and those who claim that all Elizabethans were automatically anti-Semitic and would have found Shylock's torments hilarious, continues to this day, though since the early 20th century accounts of Shylock's significance (such as that offered by *Auden in 1948) have been more inclined to see him in thematic relation to the play's other outsider, Antonio. Antonio's erotically charged patron–client relationship with Bassanio has come under considerable scrutiny over the last century, while *psychoanalytic criticism has been interested in the symbolism of the play's plots since *Freud's own remarks on the play (in *Psychopathology of Everyday Life*, 1914). Portia, meanwhile, offered as a role-model to the countless Victorian schoolgirls required to memorize her oration on mercy, has been studied in relation to the other cross-dressed heroines, and her successful replacement of Antonio as Bassanio's chief benefactor has been of much interest to recent *feminist criticism.

STAGE HISTORY: In the theatre, the history of *The Merchant of Venice* has largely been a history of great Shylocks. According to the quarto, the play was popular in its own time, and the *Revels accounts record two court performances in 1605, but the play's next recorded performances were only in the form of George Granville's adaptation *The *Jew of Venice* in 1701. It was only in 1741 that the original play returned to the stage, with Charles *Macklin as a fierce, methodically prepared Shylock (a role he retained to his retirement in 1789). Macklin's most notable successors included J. P. *Kemble (with Sarah *Siddons as Portia), Edmund *Kean, who played Shylock wholly sympathetically in 1814 (replacing his traditional red beard with a small black one), William Charles *Macready, Charles *Kean, and, most famously, Henry *Irving, whose aristocratic, proud Shylock, first seen at the *Lyceum in 1879 (with Ellen *Terry as Portia), was a summit of his career. With actor-managers so frequently casting themselves as Shylock, the play sometimes finished at the close of his part, with Act 5 cut entirely. The 20th century, however, with its shift towards the director (well exemplified by *Komisarjevsky's fantastically designed debut production at Stratford in 1932), saw a movement towards more balanced productions, using fuller texts. The period's troubled history, however, emphatically kept the spotlight on Shylock, whether played as an unsympathetic caricature (as in Max *Reinhardt's Cubist production of 1921, and in several notorious revivals in *Germany during the Nazi period) or as a wronged victim (as he was by George C. Scott in New York in 1962, and by Laurence *Olivier in Jonathan *Miller's production of 1970). Although the play continues to divide Jewish audiences and actors (it has been much performed and discussed in

*Israel, and has inspired combative adaptations such as Arnold Wesker's *The Merchant*, 1976), the role of Shylock has increasingly attracted Jewish players, among them Dustin Hoffman, Warren Mitchell, Antony *Sher, and Henry Goodman, whose meticulous performance dominated Trevor *Nunn's *National Theatre production, set in a just-pre-Nazi Central Europe, in 1999. *MD*

On the screen: Nine silent versions were made between 1902 and 1926. Of the memorable television versions, five were made for the BBC after 1947, culminating in the Jonathan Miller production (1980) with Warren Mitchell (Shylock) and Gemma Jones (Portia). Most impressive was Jonathan Miller's television adaptation of his National Theatre stage production (1970), with Laurence Olivier as an Edwardian Shylock whose off-screen wailing after his final exit gave his agony an indelible poignancy. Frank Finlay's Shylock for BBC TV (1972) was seen as significant in touching the role with comedy, so sharpening the question about the place of the play in the post-Holocaust world. *AD*

Recent major editions

Jay L. Halio (Oxford, 1993); John Russell Brown (Arden, 1955); M. M. Mahood (New Cambridge, 1987)

Some representative criticism

Auden, W. H., 'Brothers and Others', in *The Dyer's Hand* (1948)

Brockbank, Philip, 'Shakespeare and the Fashion of These Times', *Shakespeare Survey*, 16 (1963)

Edelman, Charles, 'Is This the Jew that Shakespeare Drew? Shylock on the Elizabethan Stage', *Shakespeare Survey*, 52 (1999)

Gross, John, *Shylock: A Legend and its Legacy* (1992)

Jardine, Lisa, 'Cultural Confusion and Shakespeare's Learned Heroines', in *Reading Shakespeare Historically* (1996)

Lelyveld, Toby, *Shylock on the Stage* (1960)

Lever, J. W., 'Shylock, Portia and the Values of Shakespearean Comedy', *Shakespeare Quarterly*, 3 (1952)

Shapiro, James, *Shakespeare and the Jews* (1995)

1598 he met literary men and prepared his uniquely informative *Palladis Tamia. Wit's Treasury. Being the Second Part of Wit's Commonwealth*, registered on 7 September 1598 and published late that year. Though full of similitudes and routine panegyrics, the book is valuable for its lack of originality and reflection of current views. Importantly, Meres refers to Shakespeare's 'sugared Sonnets among his private friends'; possibly these are not surviving poems, but it is clear that some Shakespeare sonnets circulated by September 1598. Even more usefully, we learn about dramas which existed by that date, although Meres's list is not exhaustive and is meant to point up Shakespeare's double superiority in the theatre's two main genres. For 'Comedy', Meres cites *The Two Gentlemen of Verona, The Comedy of Errors, Love's Labour's Lost, Love's Labour's Won, A Midsummer Night's Dream*, and *The Merchant of Venice*. For 'Tragedy', he mentions *Richard II, Richard III, Henry IV, King John, Titus Andronicus*, and *Romeo and Juliet*. Unless it is an alternative name for an existing comedy **Love's Labour's Won* refers to a missing play, and Meres, evidently, was not mistaken to list that title. *PH*

Merke, Thomas. See Carlisle, Bishop of.

Mermaid Tavern, a tavern in Bread Street, London, in which, according to Thomas *Coryat, writing in 1615, aristocrats and intellectuals assembled on the first Friday of each month during the early years of the 17th century for convivial conversation. A verse letter of uncertain date and authorship, often ascribed to *Beaumont, addressed from the country to *Jonson, speaks nostalgically of the 'full mermaid wine' and the 'things' done and spoken there:

> Words that have been
> So nimble, and so full of subtle flame,
> As if that everyone from whom they came
> Had meant to put his whole wit in a jest
> And had resolved to live a fool the rest
> Of his dull life.

There is no evidence that Shakespeare was a member of the circle. The legend that the Mermaid was the scene of the 'wit combats' which according to Thomas *Fuller took place between Shakespeare and Jonson derives from William Gifford in his 1816 edition of Jonson. *SW*

Merry Devil of Edmonton, The. A popular comedy, dated *c.*1602–3, possibly written by *Dekker or *Drayton. It was attributed to Shakespeare by Humphrey *Moseley in 1653 and then included in 'Shakespeare Volume I' in Charles II's library: see apocrypha. *SM*

Merry Wives of Windsor, The *(see page 292)*

Messala brings Brutus and Cassius the news that the triumvirate have executed many senators, including Cicero, *Julius Caesar* 4.2, but is himself reconciled with Octavius Caesar and Antony, 5.5. He is based on M. Valerius Messalla, who fought on the republican side at Philippi but later became one of Augustus Caesar's generals. *AB*

messengers. There are many unnamed messengers in Shakespeare's plays, some of whom occasion very dramatic or significant moments: **(1)** A messenger appears 'with two heads and a hand', *Titus Andronicus* 3.1.232, to tell Titus his voluntary mutilation has been pointless. **(2)** A messenger announces the approach of Don Pedro, Claudio, and Benedick, giving Beatrice the opportunity to make sarcastic remarks about Benedick, *Much Ado About Nothing* 1.1. **(3)** A messenger tells an incredulous Macbeth that Birnam wood is moving, *Macbeth* 5.5. *AB*

Mahood, M. M., *Playing Bit Parts in Shakespeare* (1998)

metaphor, the most imaginatively powerful of rhetorical figures, in which one thing, idea, or action, is referred to by the name of another, and thus some quality shared by the two terms is assumed without being specified: 'the bubble reputation' (*As You Like It* 2.7.152). *CB*

Metellus Cimber is one of the conspirators in *Julius Caesar*, based on L. Tillius Cimber. *AB*

metonymy, a figure of speech that substitutes for the thing meant some quality or property associated with it. Most commonly a quality, in the form of an adjective, stands in place of the noun: 'a flagon of Rhenish', i.e. of wine (*Hamlet* 5.1.175), 'the quick and dead', i.e. people (ibid. 247). *CB*

metre, the pattern of measured syllables recurring in lines of verse. In English, this refers to the expected number of stressed syllables in a line (usually four or five), and often also to the total number of syllables in the line (usually eight or ten). The predominant metre of Shakespeare's work is iambic pentameter, i.e. normally a line of ten syllables, alternately unstressed and stressed, but with many variants. See blank verse: also alexandrine; anapaest; anaptyxis; brokenbacked line; caesura; caesura, epic; couplet; dactyl; dimeter; elision; end-stopped; enjambment; feminine endings; foot; headless line; heroic couplets; iambic; long lines; pentameter; Pyrrhic foot; short lines; spondee; squinting line; synaeresis; syncope; tetrameter; trimeter; trochee; weak ending. *CB/GTW*

Wright, George T., *Shakespeare's Metrical Art* (1988)

(cont. on page 295)

The Merry Wives of Windsor

Shakespeare's only comedy set in his homeland (with the exception of the Induction to *The Taming of the Shrew*), and his closest to the mainstream tradition of English farce, may also be his only play composed for a specific state occasion. According to a tradition first recorded by John *Dennis in 1702, the play was personally commissioned by Queen *Elizabeth, who, added *Rowe in 1709, particularly wished to see Falstaff in love. This unlikely piece of hearsay may have a kernel of truth, in that the play's last act alludes to the ceremonies of the Order of the Garter, to which Shakespeare's patron George Carey, Lord *Hunsdon, the Lord Chamberlain, was admitted at Windsor early in 1597. These ceremonies were followed by a Garter Feast at the Palace of Westminster on St George's Day, 23 April, attended by the Queen, and the play's topical references to the Order of the Garter suggest that *The Merry Wives of Windsor* may have been composed expressly for performances associated with this event. The play may thus have enjoyed a royal première on Shakespeare's 33rd birthday: in any event its rare vocabulary, quite apart from its leading role, links it closely with the *Henry IV* plays (1596–8), and since it calls Sir John Falstaff throughout rather than Oldcastle it must post-date the censorship of *1 Henry IV*. Royal command performance or not, the play was almost certainly composed in 1597 or 1598.

Text: The play was entered in the *Stationers' Register in January 1602, and was printed in the same year in a quarto that was subsequently reprinted in 1619: a much fuller and more reliable text appeared in the *Folio in 1623, and was itself reprinted in quarto in 1630. The two early quartos preserve an abbreviated and sometimes clumsily rewritten text of the play, apparently adapted from a memorial reconstruction (see REPORTED TEXT) prepared by an actor who had played the Host, but it is nonetheless a useful one, since the Folio text—visibly prepared from a transcript by the idiosyncratic scribe Ralph *Crane—is apparently based on a promptbook which had undergone both expurgation (in compliance with the *Act to Restrain the Abuses of Players, 1606) and censorship. Lord *Cobham, who had already complained about Shakespeare's treatment of his ancestor Oldcastle, seems to have objected to Ford's alias as 'Brooke' (the Cobhams' family name), which the Folio text alters to 'Broome' (though preserving, meaninglessly, some of the puns occasioned by the original pseudonym). The confusing incident involving the theft of the Host's horses, apparently incorporating allusions to the German Count Momplegard (finally elevated to the Garter *in absentia* in 1597 after much embarrassing importunity), also seems to have been censored, but is irrecoverably truncated in both extant texts.

Sources: No single source for this play is known, though its plot draws on widespread literary traditions, most obviously that of the Italian novella (exemplified, for example, by the work of Ser *Giovanni). With its good-natured plot of a comic elopement in a realistic English provincial setting, the play resembles Henry *Porter's *Two Angry Women of Abingdon*, published in 1599, but Porter's comedy may have been influenced by Shakespeare's rather than vice versa. A long-standing tradition regards Justice Shallow as a hostile portrait of Sir Thomas *Lucy, alleged to have prosecuted the young Shakespeare for deer-poaching, though Leslie Hotson (in *Shakespeare versus Shallow*, 1931) claimed him more plausibly as a hit at the Surrey justice William *Gardiner.

Synopsis: **1.1** Justice Shallow calls at Master Page's house in Windsor, hoping to recommend his foolish nephew Slender as a suitor to Page's daughter Anne: he is incensed against Sir John Falstaff, also a dinner guest at the Pages', who has been poaching his deer. The Welsh parson Evans attempts to make peace between Shallow, Sir John, and Sir John's followers Bardolph, Nim, and Pistol, who have earlier got Slender drunk and robbed him. Finally left alone with Anne, Slender is socially inept. **1.2** Evans sends a letter, via Slender's servant Peter Simple, to Mistress Quickly, housekeeper to the French physician Dr Caius and a friend of Anne, urging her to promote Slender's suit. **1.3** Sir John, staying at the Garter Inn, successfully recommends Bardolph to his Host as a tapster. Sir John then explains to Nim and Pistol that he means to gain money by seducing Mistress Ford and Mistress Page, and gives them love letters to deliver: when they refuse this dishonourable errand he dismisses them, entrusting the letters instead to his page Robin. Nim and Pistol decide to avenge themselves by warning Ford and Page. **1.4** Mistress Quickly is telling Simple she will recommend Slender to Anne when Dr Caius returns unexpectedly: she hides Simple in a closet, where Caius finds him. Furious to learn of Simple's errand—since he himself wishes to marry Anne—Caius sends a challenge to Evans. After Caius's departure, the well-born Fenton arrives, also hoping to be recommended to Anne.

2.1 Mistress Page is affronted by the letter she has received from Sir John: Mistress Ford arrives, similarly agitated by her own letter, and when the two women compare notes they discover Sir John has written identically to each. They decide to avenge themselves on him by feigning compliance only to delay him at the Garter until he is bankrupt, deliberately arousing Ford's causeless jealousy at the same time. Ford and Page arrive, receiving their warnings from Pistol and Nim: Page laughs his off, but the jealous Ford is troubled. The two wives leave with Mistress Quickly, whom they intend to use as go-between to Sir John. Ford arranges with the Host to visit Sir John under the alias of Brooke: he, the Host, Page, and Shallow leave in the hopes of seeing the intended duel between Evans and Caius. **2.2** At the Garter Mistress Quickly tells Sir John that both wives, ignorant of each other's affairs, are in love with him, and that Mistress Ford sends word her husband will be absent from his house tomorrow between ten and eleven: she begs Robin, a potential go-between, for Mistress Page. Ford, sending Sir John a bottle of sack, subsequently arrives as Brooke, and privately explains that he has long desired Mistress Ford himself but despairs of overcoming her virtue unless she is first seduced by a more accomplished lover. Sir John delightedly accepts the money Brooke offers him to seduce Mistress Ford, and tells him gleefully of his appointment with her the following morning. Alone, Ford, horrified that his worst fears are apparently justified, rejoices that at least he now stands a chance of averting his cuckolding. **2.3** Caius and his servant John Rugby are waiting for Evans to arrive and fight: the Host, Shallow, Page, and Slender arrive, and the Host promises not only to lead Caius to where Evans is but to bring him to a farmhouse where he may woo Anne.

3.1 Evans is also waiting, with Simple, for Caius, trying to maintain his courage by singing: when Shallow, Slender, and Page and at last the Host and Caius arrive, the jovial Host reveals that he has deliberately been averting the duel by sending the would-be combatants to separate places. Caius and Evans, reconciled, plan to avenge themselves on the Host for this indignity. **3.2** Ford, learning that Mistress Page now employs Sir John's page, is astonished at Page's unsuspicious nature. Page arrives, assuring Slender that he supports his suit with Anne although Mistress Page favours Caius, and though the Host thinks that Anne herself will prefer Fenton. Ford takes Caius and Evans with him towards his house, expecting to surprise Sir John with his wife. **3.3** Mistresses Ford and Page are preparing for Sir John's arrival, having their servants bring a large laundry basket and hiding Mistress Page in another room. Sir John arrives and woos Mistress Ford, swearing that her suspicion that he is also courting Mistress Page is groundless: on a pre-arranged cue from Robin, Mistress Page enters, announcing that the jealous Ford is on his way with armed men to search the house, and the two women hide Sir John in the laundry basket, in which he is carried out by two servants just as Ford, Page, Caius, and Evans arrive. When their combined search of the house fails to find Sir John, the baffled Ford has to apologize to the company. **3.4** Fenton is reassuring Anne that although at first, as her father suggests, he only wooed her for her money, he now loves her truly, when Shallow, Slender, and Mistress Quickly arrive: Slender is as incompetent a wooer as ever. Page and Mistress Page arrive: Page rebukes Fenton for his persistence, favouring Slender, whom Anne tells her mother she does not wish to marry. Left alone, Mistress Quickly admits she has been accepting gifts from all three of Anne's rival suitors. **3.5** A chilled Sir John, who has been tipped from the basket into the Thames with the laundry, orders some mulled sack. Mistress Quickly apologizes on Mistress Ford's behalf and tells him to come again between eight and nine, when Ford will be out birding. Ford then arrives as Brooke for a progress report, and learns both how Sir John escaped him among the laundry and of his next impending appointment with his wife.

4.1 Mistress Page's young son William is given a Latin lesson by Evans, much misconstrued by Mistress Quickly. **4.2** Sir John is again wooing Mistress Ford when Mistress Page again brings news that the jealous Ford is approaching: Sir John refuses to enter the laundry basket again, and the women instead arrange to dress him as Mother Prat, a suspected witch. Before Page, Caius, Evans, and Shallow, Ford triumphantly ransacks the laundry basket, baffled not to find Sir John, and himself unwittingly drives Sir John, disguised as Mother Prat, out of the house, beating him with a cudgel. After the men depart, the wives agree to inform their husbands of the whole story, hoping this will have cured Ford's jealousy forever, and resolve to punish Sir John further only with their husbands' co-operation. **4.3** Bardolph requests three horses from the Host for a mysterious German duke, who has apparently booked the Garter for a week already, obliging the Host to turn away his other guests. **4.4** The Pages and the Fords, laughing over Sir John's misadventures to date, plot that the two wives should invite Sir John to meet them, disguised as the legendary horned spirit Herne the Hunter, at Herne's Oak in Windsor Park at midnight, where Sir John can be ambushed by Anne, William, and other children disguised as fairies and then exposed to public ridicule. It is agreed that Anne Page will be dressed as the queen of the fairies: Page plans secretly to arrange Slender's elopement with her, though his wife still prefers Caius. 4.5 Simple has come to the Garter, hoping to consult Mother Prat, supposedly seen entering Sir John's rooms, about Anne Page's fortune. The Host learns from Bardolph, Evans, and Caius that the German duke was a hoax and his horses have been stolen. Mistress Quickly brings Sir John the letter appointing his midnight rendezvous. 4.6 Fenton arranges with the discomfited Host for a vicar to be ready to marry him to Anne between midnight and one: she has feigned compliance with both her father's plot that she should elope with Slender and her mother's that she should elope with Caius, but really plans to run away with Fenton.

5.1 Sir John agrees to the rendezvous, and tells Ford as Brooke of his escape and sufferings in the guise of Mother Prat. 5.2 Page and Shallow check that Slender knows how he is to identify the figure with whom he is to elope: he and Anne will both be dressed in white. 5.3 Mistress Page similarly briefs Caius, who expects Anne to be in green. Anne, Evans, and the other pretended fairies are already lying in wait in a pit near Herne's Oak. 5.4 Disguised as a satyr, Evans marshals his fairies. 5.5 The amorous Sir John, wearing horns, awaits Mistress Ford: she arrives, with Mistress Page, and he is delightedly preparing to enjoy both when, hearing a noise, they flee in pretended panic. Evans and the fairies appear, with Anne dressed as a fairy and Mistress Quickly as the fairy queen: Sir John hides, convinced he is witnessing fairy revels and in grave danger, as they recite verses blessing Windsor and the Garter emblems. The fairies find Sir John, testing his purity with lighted tapers, then pinching him as a punishment for his sins (to the song 'Fie on sinful luxury . . .'): meanwhile Caius steals away with a fairy in green, Slender with one in white, and Anne leaves with Fenton. The pretended fairies disperse at a sound of hunters, and are replaced by the Pages and the Fords, who confront Sir John and reveal their various stratagems. Evans joins in their sermonizing. Slender arrives, indignant at discovering that the fairy in white was a boy, followed by Caius, whose fairy in green was also a boy: the newly-weds Fenton and Anne then arrive, and on Ford's advice the Pages accept their new son-in-law. All, including Sir John, set off for Windsor to laugh about the night's events.

ARTISTIC FEATURES: The play uses less verse than any other Shakespeare play, and features more devices familiar from later situation comedies, such as comic stage accents (Welsh and French) and malapropisms (or, less anachronistically, Quicklyisms). Nonetheless its harmonious, magic-haunted conclusion is recognizably akin to the worlds of *A Midsummer Night's Dream* and *As You Like It*.

CRITICAL HISTORY: Apart from a long-running argument about whether the Sir John of this play lives up to his appearances in the *Henry IV* plays, *The Merry Wives of Windsor* has occasioned very little critical discussion, although some modern criticism has related it usefully to the *city comedies favoured by some of Shakespeare's colleagues, such as *Jonson and *Middleton.

STAGE HISTORY: As its multiple early editions suggest, the play was popular before the Civil War (played at court in 1604 and in the 1630s), and it was revived in unadapted form soon after the Restoration in 1660. Despite *Dennis's short-lived adaptation *The *Comical Gallant* (1702), the original play has remained popular ever since, often starring actors already established as Sir John in *Henry IV* (from *Betterton through *Quin to Beerbohm *Tree and beyond), though many important performers have also been attracted to the role of Ford (including *Kemble and Charles *Kean), and to those of the wives themselves (including Anne *Bracegirdle and Elizabeth *Barry, Madge Kendal and Ellen *Terry, the *Vanbrugh sisters, Peggy *Ashcroft and Edith *Evans). Modern directors have found possibilities in the play too: *Komisarjevsky gave it a Viennese setting at Stratford in 1935, Terry *Hands has directed it twice, and in 1985 Bill Alexander successfully staged the play for the *RSC in a kitsch, mock-Tudor 1950s setting, the wives comparing letters under adjoining hairdryers. It remains true, however, that this unabashedly middlebrow play has enjoyed its greatest acclaim as an *opera, its musical transformations including Otto Nicolai's *Die lustigen Weiber von Windsor* (1848) and *Verdi's last masterpiece *Falstaff* (1893). *MD*

ON THE SCREEN: Historically interesting screen versions include the BBC TV transmission of Glen *Byam Shaw's Christmassy Stratford production (1955), with Anthony *Quayle, and the 1982 BBC TV production with Ben *Kingsley (Ford) and Richard Griffiths (Sir John). *AD*

RECENT MAJOR EDITIONS

Giorgio Melchiori (Arden 3rd series, 2000); T. W. Craik (Oxford, 1989); David Crane (New Cambridge, 1989)

SOME REPRESENTATIVE CRITICISM

Barton, Anne, 'Falstaff and the Comic Community', in Peter Erickson and Coppélia Kahn (eds.), *Shakespeare's Rough Magic: Renaissance Essays in Honor of C. L. Barber* (1985)

Bradley, A. C., 'The Rejection of Falstaff', in *Oxford Lectures on Poetry* (1909)

Bruster, Douglas, in *Drama and the Market in the Age of Shakespeare* (1992)

Evans, Bertrand, in *Shakespeare's Comedies* (1960)

Green, William, *Shakespeare's Merry Wives of Windsor* (1962)

Vickers, Brian, in *The Artistry of Shakespeare's Prose* (1968)

metrical tests. Scholars have long assumed that Shakespeare had characteristic metrical habits, which can be used to distinguish his work from that of his contemporaries, and that those habits changed over time, such that statistical analyses of metrical irregularities may be of use in determining the order in which the plays were composed. Attempts to establish the authenticity and chronology of Shakespeare's works by means of metrical tests began in 1857 with the publication of Charles Bathurst's *Remarks on the Differences in Shakespeare's Versification.* In founding the New Shakespeare Society in 1873, F. J. *Furnivall stated that ascertaining the order of the plays by metrical tests would be one of the society's principal objectives. A year later, F. G. Fleay tabulated the total number of lines of blank verse, rhymed verse, and prose in each play, along with short and long lines, and lines with redundant syllables. Fleay's tables became the standard guide used by the 'distintegrators' to reject suspect plays and passages as non-Shakespearian. In 1930 E. K. Chambers pointed out many inaccuracies in Fleay's tables, cited the deficiencies of verse-tests conducted by other investigators, and concluded that 'in view of all the uncertainties attaching to the metrical tests, I do not believe that any one of them or any combination of them can be taken as authoritative in determining the succession of plays'.

In the wake of Chambers's critique, scholars have approached metrical tests with some caution. A 'metrical index' developed by Karl Wentersdorf and further refined by MacD. P. Jackson and others attempts to be comprehensive in charting a multitude of changes in the features that together make up Shakespeare's blank verse style (including *feminine endings, *alexandrines, variations in stress in iambic pentameter lines, extra mid-line syllables, extra syllables, and overflows) that may have application to questions of chronology and authorship of Shakespeare's plays. *ER*

Chambers, E. K., *William Shakespeare: A Study of Facts and Problems* (1930)

Jackson, MacDonald P., 'Another Metrical Index for Shakespeare's Plays: Evidence for Chronology and Authorship', *Neuphilologische Mitteilungen*, 95 (1994)

Wells, Stanley, and Taylor, Gary, *William Shakespeare: A Textual Companion* (1987)

Wentersdorf, Karl, 'Shakespearean Chronology and the Metrical Tests', in *Shakespeare-Studien* (1951)

Mexico. See LATIN AMERICA.

Michael is a follower of Cade, *The First Part of the Contention* (*2 Henry VI*) 4.2. His lines announcing the approach of the Staffords are given to a messenger in the Oxford edition. *AB*

Michael, Sir. He takes letters from the Archbishop of York, and reassures him about their military action, *1 Henry IV* 4.4. *AB*

Middle Temple. See INNS OF COURT; MANNINGHAM, JOHN; TWELFTH NIGHT.

Middleton, Thomas (1580–1627), playwright, poet, and pamphleteer. His father was a prosperous bricklayer, wealthy enough to send him to Oxford. Before 1600 he wrote poetry, including a set of satires, *Micro-Cynicon* (1599), and an imitation of Shakespeare, *The Ghost of Lucrece* (1600). By 1601 he was 'accompanying the players' in London. He collaborated with *Webster and others on a lost play for the Admiral's Men in 1602, but a year later the plague closed the theatres and he started writing pamphlets, among them the flashy urban satire *The Black Book* (1604). Throughout his career he collaborated often, on pamphlets, on plays, and on the many pageants he devised for the City of London. His most frequent collaborator was Thomas *Dekker, but he also worked with Shakespeare on *Timon of Athens* (published 1623). The title pages of two more of his plays—*The Puritan* (1607) and *A Yorkshire Tragedy* (1608)—claim (improbably enough) that Shakespeare wrote them, but there is a much better case for believing that Middleton revised Shakespeare's *Macbeth,* since it incorporates two songs from his tragicomedy *The Witch* (not published until 1778). In the mid-1600s Shakespeare was the principal dramatist for the King's Men and Middleton his anonymous assistant; but it would not be long before Middleton was presenting the company with some of its most remarkable successes.

From 1604 to 1606 Middleton wrote, on his own, a series of plays for a children's company, the Paul's Boys. These include three scintillating city comedies: *Michaelmas Term* (1607), *A Mad World my Masters* (1608), and *A Trick to Catch the Old One* (1608), all modelled on the cunningly plotted comedies of Terence. Then in about 1606 he wrote his first great tragedy for the King's Men, *The Revenger's Tragedy* (1607), often attributed to Cyril Tourneur. The revenger of the title first appears clutching a skull, in a pastiche of the graveyard scene from *Hamlet,* but he soon becomes absorbed—linguistically, morally, and through the disguises he adopts—into the degenerate world of the aristocracy on whom he has sworn vengeance. This is one of the hallmarks of Middleton's drama: characters who strive to set themselves apart from the social classes or values they despise find themselves inextricably enmeshed in them. His best comedy, *A Chaste Maid in Cheapside* (printed in 1630), revolves around the interdependence between a decayed aristocracy and the emergent middle classes, to whom the aristocrats turn for the sexual and economic regeneration of their family fortunes. A similar blurring of social and moral borderlines occurs in his two great tragedies, *The Changeling* (printed 1653), written with William Rowley, and *Women Beware Women* (printed 1657). In the former, a governor's daughter falls in love with a merchant, for whose sake she has her fiancé killed, then becomes sexually entangled with the gentleman she hired to do the killing. The play derives much of its intensity from her desperate efforts to convince herself that her values remain unchanged as she changes partners. In *Women Beware Women* the wife of a mercantile husband—a nobleman's factor or business agent—grows weary of her confinement in his house and has an affair with a duke, to which her husband retaliates by having an affair with a noble widow. In all three of these last-mentioned plays, young women are the ultimate victims of what Middleton depicts as a general tendency to substitute commercial values for other methods of measuring human worth. Women are exchanged between men as expensive luxury commodities, and struggle to gain a measure of control over the various sexual transactions in which they are caught up. They invariably die in the attempt; even Moll, the heroine of *A Chaste Maid in Cheapside,* goes through a mock death and funeral before her sufferings can achieve a comic resolution.

Middleton's biggest contemporary success was the satirical comedy *A Game at Chess* (1625), an attack on *James I's negotiations for a Spanish marriage alliance, which had the first long run in theatrical history (9 days) before being suppressed by the authorities. Otherwise he was apparently not much admired in his own lifetime. But his reputation rose to unprecedented heights in the 20th century. One reason for this is the skill with which he represents the responses of Jacobean city-dwellers—especially women—to the pressures exerted on them by their urban environment. Another is the astonishing metaphorical and thematic unity of his plays, and the ingenuity of their plotting. The new edition of his complete works by Oxford University Press should confirm his status as one of the greatest dramatists in the English language. *RM*

Chakravorty, Swapan, *Society and Politics in the Plays of Thomas Middleton* (1996)

Friedenreich, K. (ed.), *'Accompaninge the Players': Essays Celebrating Thomas Middleton, 1580–1980* (1983)

Heinemann, Margot, *Puritanism and Theatre: Thomas Middleton and Opposition Drama under the Early Stuarts* (1980)

Taylor, Gary, (ed.), *The Complete Oxford Middleton* (2001)

Midsummer Night's Dream, A *(see page 296)*

Milan, the main city of Lombardy, is mentioned in *The Tempest* (Prospero is the 'rightful'

(cont. on page 299)

A Midsummer Night's Dream

One of Shakespeare's most perfect achievements in comedy, or perhaps in any other genre, *A Midsummer Night's Dream*—with its exuberant range of poetic styles, metres, and rhyme-schemes—clearly belongs to the lyrical period of his career that also produced *Love's Labour's Lost*, *Richard II*, and *Romeo and Juliet.* It has close links with the latter play (which in Mercutio's 'Queen Mab' speech displays a similar conception of *fairies), of which the play-within-the-play staged by the 'mechanicals', 'Pyramus and Thisbe', is almost a burlesque. Indeed, Shakespeare's departures here from *Ovid's version of the Pyramus and Thisbe story seem to be shaped by the plot of *Romeo and Juliet*, suggesting that *A Midsummer Night's Dream* was written soon after it, in 1595. Other evidence, too, ties the play to the 1594–6 period: it was certainly extant by 1598, when it is listed by *Meres, and its references to disrupted weather (2.1.88–114) suggest composition between mid-1594 and late 1596, a disastrous period for English agriculture. A familiar hypothesis that the play was specifically written for performance at an aristocratic wedding seems implausible (elaborate courtly entertainments were more prevalent in the Jacobean period, and the earliest known example of a play commissioned for a wedding is Samuel *Daniel's *Hymen's Triumph*, 1614), but if the play were acted privately in association with such a function the likeliest candidates are the nuptials of the Earl of Derby with Elizabeth Vere (1595) and those of Thomas Berkeley with Elizabeth Carey (1596).

Text: The play, entered in the *Stationers' Register in October 1600, appeared in quarto in the same year, and this quarto was reprinted in 1619 (though this second quarto is fraudulently dated '1600'). The quarto text seems to have been set from Shakespeare's *foul papers: some of its mislineation probably results from confusion over revisions jotted in their margins. The text printed in the *Folio in 1623 was set from a copy of the second quarto (reproducing some of its errors), but one which had been supplemented by reference to a promptbook. This promptbook had clearly been used in relatively late revivals of the play: one stage direction mentions the musician William *Tawyer; a cut of 'God warrant us' and 'God bless us' at 5.1.314–15 suggests compliance with the 1606 *Act to Restrain the Abuses of Players; and the newly imposed act divisions suggest the introduction of intervals, not used by the King's Men before around 1609. But the bulk of the Folio's amendments to stage directions and the attributions of speeches may date from early in the play's performance history, and are probably authorial.

Sources: Most of the plot is Shakespeare's own invention, though the play draws on a number of literary sources. The most important is *Chaucer's Knight's Tale, to which Shakespeare would return, with *Fletcher, nearly 20 years later, dramatizing it as *The Two Noble Kinsmen.* Chaucer's story provides the basis for Shakespeare's depiction of Theseus and Hippolyta's marriage, which it juxtaposes, furthermore, with a rivalry between two men for the same woman, source for the competition between Lysander and Demetrius over Hermia. Shakespeare, however, adds a second woman, Helena, who has earlier been jilted by Demetrius, and thereby repeats the pattern of love intrigues he had deployed in *The Two Gentlemen of Verona. A Midsummer Night's Dream* is pervasively indebted to Ovid, most obviously for Pyramus and Thisbe, but also for the name Titania, an alternative name for Diana (hence the fairy queen's reference to the Indian boy's mother as 'a vot'ress of my order', 2.1.123) and also for Circe (who transformed her lovers into beasts, a habit echoed in Titania's infatuation with the 'translated' Bottom).

The name Oberon for the fairy king derives from the French romance **Huon de Bordeaux*, and also appears in Robert *Greene's *James IV* (*c.*1591). *Robin Goodfellow was well known in folklore, and Shakespeare may also have read about him in Reginald *Scot's *Discovery of Witchcraft* (1584). The transformation of Bottom owes much to *Apuleius' *The Golden Ass*, written in Latin in the 2nd century and translated into English in 1566, while Bottom's anxiety about bringing a lion among ladies (3.1.25–30) may derive from a real incident at the Scottish court (reported in a pamphlet, *A True Reportary*, 1594) when a lion was excluded from the entertainments at Prince *Henry's baptismal feast because its presence 'might have brought some fear to the nearest'.

Synopsis: 1.1 Four days before their wedding, Theseus, Duke of Athens, and the Amazonian Queen Hippolyta whom he has conquered are visited by Egeus, accompanied by his daughter Hermia and her two suitors: Egeus complains that Hermia refuses to marry his choice, Demetrius, because she has been wooed by Lysander, and demands that she be put to death, as Athenian law allows, unless she marries Demetrius. Lysander points out that Demetrius formerly wooed Helena, who still loves him, but despite this Theseus supports Egeus, declaring that unless Hermia agrees to marry Demetrius she must accept either death or a vow of eternal celibacy. Left alone, Lysander and Hermia arrange to meet in nearby woods the following night and flee to his aunt's house beyond Athens's borders, where they may marry. They confide this in Helena, who arrives bewailing Demetrius' preference for Hermia, and who decides to betray their elopement to Demetrius and accompany him when he goes in pursuit. **1.2** Led by Quince the carpenter, a team of artisans meet to cast the play of 'Pyramus and Thisbe' which they hope to perform at Theseus' wedding: *Bottom the weaver has ambitions to play most of the roles, but finally agrees to confine himself to Pyramus. They arrange to rehearse privately in the woods.

2.1 In the woods Robin Goodfellow, a puck who serves the fairy king Oberon, meets a fairy servant of their queen, Titania, with whom Oberon has fallen out because she will not part with an Indian changeling boy she keeps as an attendant. Oberon and Titania meet, accusing one another of over-familiarity with Hippolyta and Theseus respectively, and Titania recounts how their quarrel has affected the climate, confusing the seasons. Oberon urges her to make peace by yielding up the boy, but she refuses, explaining that she loved his mortal mother, and departs with her train. Oberon resolves to defeat her by applying the magic juice of a flower, love-in-idleness, to her eyes as she sleeps, which will make her fall in love with the next creature she sees: he sends Robin to fetch it. Meanwhile he watches Demetrius, unable to find Hermia and Lysander, rebuking Helena, who follows him off despite his disdain, and when Robin returns with the love-juice, Oberon, determined to punish Demetrius, instructs Robin to find a man wearing Athenian clothes and apply some of the love-juice to his eyes when the woman he scorns is nearby. **2.2** Titania's fairies sing her a lullaby, 'You spotted snakes . . .': while she sleeps Oberon drops the love-juice on her eyelids. Lysander and Hermia arrive, benighted, and settle themselves to sleep (apart, at her insistence): Robin, assuming Lysander to be the Athenian Oberon intended, applies the love-juice to his eyes. Lysander is awakened by the arrival of Helena, whom Demetrius flees, and falls in love with her: although she is outraged at what she thinks is his mockery, Lysander pursues her off. Hermia awakens from a nightmare and finds herself alone.

3.1 The artisans meet, and Bottom insists that they alter their script to point out that Pyramus and Thisbe do not really die and the lion is only Snug the joiner dressed up: after further discussion they agree that the play's characters must include the moonshine by which the lovers meet and the wall through whose cranny they speak. As they rehearse, Robin arrives, and mischievously transforms Bottom's head into that of an ass. Bottom cannot understand why his colleagues flee, assuming they are playing a joke, and sings to keep up his courage. Titania awakens, sees Bottom, and falls in love with him: she appoints four fairies to be his attendants and leads him away to her bower. **3.2** Robin tells a delighted Oberon of Titania's love for the transformed Bottom, but when Hermia arrives, accusing Demetrius of killing the missing Lysander, it becomes clear that Robin has enchanted the wrong Athenian. While Demetrius, eluded by Hermia, sleeps, Oberon sends Robin to fetch Helena and applies the love-juice to Demetrius' eyelids. Helena arrives, pursued by the besotted Lysander, and when Demetrius awakes and also falls in love with her she concludes that both are mocking her. When Hermia arrives, lamenting Lysander's defection, Helena decides she too must be a participant in this cruel game, and accuses her of betraying their childhood friendship. The incensed Hermia decides Helena must have lured Lysander away by pointing out her superior height, and after the two rival men leave to fight, Helena has to run away from her. Oberon accuses Robin of negligence and instructs him to lead Demetrius and Lysander astray and use the love-juice to restore Lysander's love for Hermia before day breaks. Robin, feigning the respective would-be duellists' voices, keeps them apart. **3.3** Misled by Robin, Lysander and Demetrius, still hoping to fight, independently settle to sleep: Helena arrives too, and also sleeps, as does Hermia. Robin applies the love-juice to Lysander's eyes, with a spell to restore his affection to Hermia.

4.1 Titania arrives with Bottom and his fairy attendants: after these have been dismissed, the two sleep. Oberon reports to Robin that the enchanted Titania has given him the changeling, and proceeds to undo the spell: waking, Titania at first thinks her passion for Bottom was a dream before seeing him asleep. Robin removes Bottom's ass-head: Oberon and Titania, reconciled, dance, and leave, as does Robin. Theseus, Hippolyta, and Egeus arrive, hunting, and find the four lovers, who awaken, restored to themselves and to each other, and attempt to explain what has been happening. Theseus overrules Egeus, declaring that Hermia may marry Lysander, and Helena Demetrius, when he marries Hippolyta. The lovers, uncertain as to whether they are dreaming, follow Theseus and his party towards Athens. Bottom awakes, awestruck at the recollection of experiences which he too thinks must have been a dream, which he hopes to have Quince make into a ballad. **4.2** The artisans are distraught at Bottom's absence and their missed opportunity to perform, but to their delight he rejoins them and they leave for the palace.

5.1 Hippolyta and Theseus discuss the lovers' reported experiences, which Theseus puts down to overactive imagination. As the two other newly-married couples join them, Theseus considers what entertainment should while away the time before bed, and despite being warned how amateurishly bad 'Pyramus and Thisbe' is he chooses the artisans' play. Quince duly mis-recites a prologue, and his cast enact the story of Pyramus and Thisbe in dumb show. Punctuated by derisive comments from its audience, the play, written in archaic and comically inept rhyme, proceeds. Snout the tinker explains that he is playing the Wall through which Pyramus and Thisbe converse. Bottom as Pyramus and Flute the bellows-mender as Thisbe arrange to meet at Ninus' tomb. After Starveling, bearing a lantern, has finally explained that he represents the man in the moon, Thisbe arrives and flees from Snug as the lion, who worries her dropped mantle. Pyramus finds the mantle, concludes that Thisbe has been eaten by the lion, and kills himself: Thisbe returns, finds his body, and kills herself too. Theseus declines their offered epilogue, and Bottom and Flute dance a bergomask instead before leaving. After the three couples have retired to bed, Robin arrives, sweeping with a broom, followed by Oberon, Titania, and their train, who bless the house and the three married couples, warding off birth defects from their children. Left alone, Robin speaks an epilogue, advising the audience to dismiss the play as a dream if they have not enjoyed it, but promising to improve if the audience applauds.

Artistic features: As well as showing off some of Shakespeare's most dazzling *dramatic poetry—which, with its evocation of the minutely-detailed woodland world of Robin Goodfellow and his colleagues, has shaped all subsequent notions of *fairies—*A Midsummer Night's Dream* offers some of his most piercing reflections on the nature of theatre and the imagination themselves. The Mozartian interweaving of its different layers of plot and artifice has never been equalled: it is understandable why the play should have attracted not only painters and illustrators (from *Fuseli through *Dadd and beyond) but operatic composers, from Purcell to Benjamin *Britten.

Critical history: Popular in its own time and beyond ('Pyramus and Thisbe', for example, profoundly influenced the pioneer of English nonsense poetry John *Taylor), *A Midsummer Night's Dream* fell from favour after the Restoration, dismissed as a self-indulgent novelty for most of the 18th century: Dr *Johnson called it 'wild and fantastical', while Francis *Gentleman, annotating *Bell's edition in 1774, spoke of 'a puerile plot, an odd mixture of incidents, and a forced connexion of various styles'. The *Romantics, however, completely revalued the play's elements of fancy, and over the course of the 19th century *A Midsummer Night's Dream* was taken ever more seriously by literary critics: Georg *Brandes, recognizing its seminal importance to his Romantic precursors, identified the play as a bridge between *Spenser and Shelley. Twentieth-century critics variously mined the play for elements of folk May-games (treating its comedy as a sort of fertility ritual), pursued its lines of thought about the nature of theatrical make-believe, and considered its potentially troubling representations of the relations between the sexes. Louis Montrose, in one of the most influential of *new historicist essays, related the play's animus against virginity and its depictions of the tamed Amazon Hippolyta and the defeated Titania to imputed male anxieties about the dominance of England's real-life fairy queen, Elizabeth I.

Stage history: A range of allusions suggest the play was frequently revived in Shakespeare's own time and afterwards: it was acted at court in 1604, and was popular enough to survive even during the Interregnum in the form of Robert *Cox's *droll *The Merry Conceited Humours of *Bottom the Weaver*. After the Restoration the play was revived in London and also at the Smock Alley theatre in Dublin, but seemed suddenly dated and artificial in a theatrical repertoire now dominated by contemporary satirical comedy: *Pepys, seeing it in 1662, called it 'the most insipid ridiculous play that ever I saw in my life'. Thereafter its stage history for most of the next century and a half is one of successive *adaptations: *Betterton's *The *Fairy Queen* (1692), *Garrick's *The *Fairies* (1755), George Colman's *A *Fairy Tale* (1763), and the independent fortunes of 'Pyramus and Thisbe,' transplanted into Charles Johnson's **Love in a Forest* (1723) and made into separate mock-operas by Richard *Leveridge (1716) and Frederick *Lampe (1745). An attempt by Garrick, in collaboration with Colman, to revive the whole play in 1763 was, instructively, a flop: the play was too various, and too much of an ensemble piece, to fit the 18th-century theatre. Regarded as too poetical for the stage by *Hazlitt—disappointed by Frederick *Reynolds's pantomime-like musical version of 1816—the play had to await the displacement of the actor-manager by the designer and the director before coming into its own. The most important revival of the Romantic period took place in *Germany in 1843, supervised by the translator, *Tieck, who used *Mendelssohn's famous incidental music (1826). At last seized upon by designers, the play was ever more lavishly staged by Elizabeth *Vestris, Samuel *Phelps (self-cast as Bottom, the favourite role of actor-managers), and Charles *Kean, whose production included an 8-year-old Ellen *Terry entering as Robin Goodfellow on a pop-up mushroom. This tradition of spectacle peaked in Beerbohm *Tree's production (1900): his wood featured real live rabbits. More indicative of 20th-century *Dreams* to come was Harley *Granville-Barker's controversial 1914 production at the Savoy, with its gilded, other-worldly, puppet-like fairies. Since then the play has been both immensely popular (one of the most frequently revived in the canon, especially in outdoor venues: it appeared every year at the *Open Air Theatre in Regent's Park between 1932 and 1940 and has nearly done so ever since) and a directors' playground, successive productions veering between spectacle and minimalism, nostalgia and eroticism. Notable revivals have included Max *Reinhardt's eclectic spectacular of the 1920s (the basis for his later film), Tyrone *Guthrie's gauzily Victorian production of 1937 (with Vivien *Leigh as Titania and Ralph *Richardson as Bottom), the successive incarnations of Peter *Hall's Elizabethan production of 1959 (also filmed), and, most famously, Peter *Brook's 'white box' production for the *RSC in 1970, the play's magic translated into the terms of the circus. Brook's influence has haunted subsequent directors of the play, notably Adrian *Noble. The play's depiction of amateur drama, coupled with its equal balance of roles and indestructibly comic plotting, has made it a perennial favourite of amateur companies. *MD*

On the screen: The play clearly offers attractive possibilities for visual realization. The earliest version was an eight-minute sequence shot in America (1909). The year 1935 brought to the screen the Max Reinhardt film featuring Olivia de Havilland as Hermia, Mickey Rooney as Puck, and James Cagney as Bottom, so asserting a claim by Hollywood film actors for Shakespearian roles. Between 1937 and 1981 there were eight British television productions based on the play, the last being the visually elaborate BBC TV version produced by Jonathan *Miller (with Elijah Moshinsky as director), some of its framed compositions alluding to 17th-century Dutch paintings.

Peter Hall's film (1969), based on his earlier stage production, had a mixed reception. It juxtaposes in an arresting way expressionism and realism, and boasts an impressive cast (including Diana *Rigg, Helen *Mirren, Judi *Dench, Ian *Richardson, and Ian *Holm), but its documentary camera techniques can seem at odds with the illusory worlds of the play. In 1984 Celestino Coronado made a memorably imaged film of the Lindsay Kemp London stage production. Adrian Noble's film (1996), based on his own RSC production, uses a boy's dream as a central narrative device, linking the cinematic world of Theseus' court with the more theatrically minimalist woods. Michael Hoffman's less intellectually cogent Hollywood film (1999) sets the play in 19th-century Italy, crassly punctuating its soundtrack with famous operatic arias. *AD*

Recent major editions

Peter Holland (Oxford, 1994); Stanley Wells (New Penguin, 1967); Harold F. Brooks (Arden 2nd series, 1979); R. A. Foakes (New Cambridge, 1984)

Some representative criticism

Barber, C. L., in *Shakespeare's Festive Comedy* (1957)

Barton, Anne in *Shakespeare and the Idea of the Play* (1962)

Dent, R. W., 'Imagination in *A Midsummer Night's Dream*', *Shakespeare Quarterly*, 15 (1964)

Leggatt, Alexander, in *Shakespeare's Comedy of Love* (1974)

Montrose, Louis, ' "Shaping Fantasies": Configurations of Gender and Power in Elizabethan Culture', *Representations*, 1 (1983)

Young, David P., *'Something of Great Constancy': The Art of 'A Midsummer Night's Dream'* (1966)

Duke of Milan) and is the scene of parts of *The Two Gentlemen of Verona.* *AB*

Milan, Duke of. **(1)** Father of Silvia in *The Two Gentlemen of Verona*, he finally agrees to her marriage with Valentine, 5.4. **(2)** For Prospero, see Tempest, The. **(3)** *The Tempest.* See Antonio. *AB*

Milford Haven, on the coast of Pembrokeshire, was the landing place of *Richmond in August 1485 before he defeated Richard III at *Bosworth. Pisanio is instructed to kill Innogen there, *Cymbeline* 3.4.28. *AB*

Milhaud, Darius (1892–1974), French composer. In 1936–7 he composed incidental music for *Julius Caesar* and *Romeo and Juliet* (both performed in Paris) and for *Macbeth* (Old Vic theatre, London). He also wrote incidental music for a parody of *Hamlet* (Paris, 1939) and C.-A. Puget's adaptation of *The Winter's Tale* (Paris, 1950). *IBC*

Miller, Jonathan (b. 1934), British stage and television director and cultural critic. Formerly a doctor, he remains fascinated by neurology and the workings of the mind. He entered professional theatre in the satirical revue *Beyond the Fringe* (1961). He has an international reputation as a director, especially of opera. His Shakespearian productions always express a view of the play, whether in early work with Oxbridge amateurs (*Julius Caesar* set in a de Chirico forum, a Renaissance *Hamlet*) or his work at the National Theatre (*Measure for Measure* set in Freud's Vienna, *The Merchant of Venice* with Laurence *Olivier as Shylock in a social setting redolent of Henry James). In 1980–1 he reinvigorated the hitherto stuffy BBC Shakespeare Television Series, producing thirteen and directing six of the plays. He twice directed *The Tempest* as a myth of colonialism, and he brought out the Oedipal conflicts in *Hamlet* by staging it alongside *Ibsen's *Ghosts* and *Chekhov's *The Seagull.* His adventurous seasons at the *Old Vic (which included Eric Porter in *King Lear*) were abruptly terminated in 1990 by the theatre's owners. *MJ*

Miller, Jonathan, *Subsequent Performances* (1986)

Millington, Thomas. See printing and publishing.

Milton, John (1608–74), political pamphleteer, Latin secretary to the Council of State under Cromwell, and the greatest poet of the 17th century. His first published work was the sonnet 'On Shakespeare', included without attribution among the commendatory verses in the Second *Folio (1632). It appeared definitively as Milton's only in the 1673 *Poems*, where it is dated 1630. In it, the 22-year-old Milton credits Shakespeare with 'easy numbers' and 'delphic lines'. A year later, in 'L'Allegro', the delphic element had disappeared, and Milton's cheerful man heard 'Sweetest Shakespeare, fancy's child | Warble his native woodnotes wild'. The many echoes of Shakespeare in the *Masque ... at Ludlow* (*Comus*, 1634), however, reveal a much broader appreciation of the complexity and depth of Shakespearian verse—Comus greets the Lady with the words of Ferdinand greeting Miranda, and his seductive arguments speak a language learned as much from Angelo, Othello, and Cleopatra as from Oberon. Shakespeare is implicitly invoked in the prefatory note on the verse of *Paradise Lost* to justify the absence of rhyme; and the earliest sketch for the epic (according to Milton's nephew Edward

Philips), Satan's monologue at the opening of book 4, is deeply indebted to *Macbeth*, as is the figure of Satan generally. In *Eikonoklastes* (1649) Milton cites as the prototype of the hypocritical *Charles I Shakespeare's Richard III. The tragic models recalled in the preface to *Samson Agonistes* are exclusively classical, but *King Lear* and *Coriolanus* resonate throughout the work. If, as Milton told *Dryden, 'Spenser was his original', so, even more profoundly, was Shakespeare. *SO*

Minola, Baptista. See BAPTISTA MINOLA.

miracle plays, a form of drama based on biblical texts, popular in England from the 14th century until the late 16th century when the government took active measures to prohibit it. The miracle plays derive from the introit plays of *c.*950–1250, part of the liturgy of the Catholic Church, performed at the festivals of Easter and Christmas. Gradually, the plays moved outside the church, laymen joined the cast, and Latin was replaced by the vernacular. What had initially been single scenes became a series or cycle of plays under the control of local guilds rather than the Church, of which the most famous examples are the York, Towneley (Wakefield), Chester, and Coventry cycles. In the 14th century, the most popular occasion for these performances was the feast of Corpus Christi so that 'Corpus Christi cycles' became a generic term. References to such popular figures of miracle plays as Herod can be found in many 16th- and 17th-century plays including those of Shakespeare. *JKS*

Miranda, Prospero's daughter, witnesses the wreck of Alonso's ship; listens eagerly to Prospero's account of his life; and meets Ferdinand with whom she falls in love, *The Tempest* 1.2. Her match with Ferdinand is accepted by the end of the play by their reconciled fathers.

Miranda's upbringing was sufficiently fascinating to *Dryden and *Davenant for them to create other versions of her, a sister Dorinda and a man who has never seen a woman before, Hippolito, in their 1667 *adaptation of the play *The Tempest; or, The Enchanted Island.* Miranda's ignorance of social and sexual mores remained appealing to many of Shakespeare's admirers through to the 19th century and beyond. Coleridge, for example, thought Miranda Shakespeare's 'favourite character' and greatly admired 'the exquisite feelings of a female brought up in a desert, yet with all the advantages of education, all that could be given by a wise, learned, and affectionate father' (1811–12). However, as Stephen Orgel has argued in his Oxford edition of *The Tempest* (1987), precise attention to Miranda's lines reveals a much more troubling version of her as an individual and in relation to her father than many stagings of the play have dared to suggest. *AB*

Mirren, Helen (b. 1945), English actress. After training with Michael Croft's National Youth Theatre, Mirren played Cleopatra at the Old Vic in Croft's *Antony and Cleopatra* (1965). Cleopatra, a role she reprised with the *Royal Shakespeare Company in Adrian *Noble's acclaimed production (1982) and again at the *National Theatre (opposite Alan Rickman in a critically disastrous revival in 1998), is typical of the powerful, seductive characters Mirren excels at playing. In 1967, she joined the RSC, where her roles included Hero (1968), Cressida (1969), Lady Macbeth (1974), and Queen Margaret in the *Henry VI* plays (1977). Drawn increasingly to film and *television, she can be seen in the BBC Shakespeare series as Rosalind (1978), Titania (1981), and Imogen (1982). *BR*

Mirror for Magistrates, The, a collection of verse biographies of famous historical figures published by William Baldwin in 1559 and 1563. The first *Mirror* contained nineteen lives, all written from the perspective of the dead subject who lamented his downfall, usually attributing it to some crime or fault that brought retribution upon him. After Baldwin's death, John Higgins continued the work, publishing in 1574 and 1587 *The First Part of the Mirror for Magistrates*, which contained new lives plundered from ancient British history. Thomas Blenerhasset's *Second Part* (1578) covered the period from Caesar's invasion of Britain to the Norman Conquest. Clearly, Baldwin had come up with a winning formula, a kind of history that emphasized the divine nature of royal authority and the nemesis incurred if this authority were violated. In his dedication to the 1559 edition, he presented the work as 'a mirror for all men as well noble as others' to see the 'slippery deceits' of Fortune and the 'due reward for all kinds of vices'. Shakespeare's debt to the *Mirror* is apparent in the plots and characters of many of his English history plays as well as in *King Lear* and *Cymbeline.* The suicide of Cordila in Higgins's poem may have influenced the ending of *King Lear.* For the scene of Clarence's murder in *Richard III*, Shakespeare borrowed details and a gruesome joke from Clarence's tragedy in the *Mirror.* *JKS*

Prior, Moody E., *The Drama of Power: Studies in Shakespeare's History Plays* (1973)

mislineation. Blank verse is sometimes mislined, wrongly divided, or set as prose in the early printed texts of Shakespeare's plays. Mislineation may indicate that scribal transcripts were being used as printers' copy, but in many instances the compositors may have departed from their copy and intentionally set verse as prose in order to conserve space and cover up errors in casting off. *ER*

misprints. Mistakes in the printing of Shakespeare's early texts can be attributed to a wide variety of factors, including compositors misreading their manuscript copy (especially when setting from Shakespeare's original *foul papers), working from a *foul case, or accidentally setting a piece of type upside down (such that 'you' reads 'yon'). *ER*

Mnouchkine, Ariane (b. 1939), French visionary founder and director of the Théâtre du Soleil since 1964 (now based in La Cartoucherie de Vincennes, a former cartridge warehouse near Paris). Mnouchkine promotes a radical, political theatre which favours collective training, improvisation, and grand visual effects: pet projects have included plays on the French Revolution, sequences of Oriental history and classical drama, and a long-term collaboration with the feminist playwright and theorist Hélène Cixous. Mnouchkine first came to Shakespeare in the early 1960s as associate director on an English student production of *Coriolanus.* Her *A Midsummer Night's Dream*, translated by her fellow actor Léotard, was played on a circus-ring covered with furs (1968, Cirque de Montmartre, and London), conveying a dreamlike, sensuous animality. Her widely acclaimed but controversial Shakespeare cycle (1981–4) consisted of three plays (out of the twelve originally planned) given in her own versions: *Richard II* (1981), *Twelfth Night* (1982), and *1 Henry IV* (1984). These productions transposed Elizabethan codes of honour into the aesthetics of Japanese Kabuki theatre and Indian Kathakali (though their red-nosed clowns came from the **commedia dell'arte* tradition). Although sometimes accused of cynically plundering other cultures for spuriously exotic effects (a criticism similarly levelled at the later work of Peter *Brook, with whom Mnouchkine is often compared), Mnouchkine's productions have exerted a visible influence on directors of Shakespeare throughout the West. *ISG*

Mock-Tempest, The. See BURLESQUES AND TRAVESTIES OF SHAKESPEARE'S PLAYS; DUFFETT, THOMAS.

modern dress, the use of contemporary costumes for classic plays. The Elizabethans had loose ideas about earlier periods and were not conscious of anachronisms, as evidenced by the Peacham drawing of *Titus Andronicus* (in the *Longleat manuscript) which shows Roman togas and 16th-century garb together. It was common in the 17th and 18th centuries to dress actresses in gowns with a contemporary cut, but

Ariane Mnouchkine rehearsing her production of *Twelfth Night*, Festival d'Avignon, 1982.

the self-conscious use of modern clothing became possible only after the historically minded productions of the 19th century, like those of Charles *Kean, where efforts were made to set the plays in precisely rendered periods. Like the Elizabethan-dress Shakespeare of William *Poel, these productions tried to erase all evidence of the present moment. The first major use of modern dress for Shakespeare in the 20th century was in a production of *Hamlet* by Max *Reinhardt in Berlin in 1920. In England the movement is associated with Barry *Jackson, who began with *Cymbeline* at the Birmingham Rep in 1923 and caused a sensation with *Hamlet* in London in 1925. Directed by H. K. Ayliff, the production used short skirts and fashionable 'bobbed' hairdos for the women, cigarettes, cocktails, syncopated dance music, and plus fours for Hamlet. *Macbeth* in 1928 set the action in the First World War. It has since become common to dress the plays in modern attire, sometimes to pull the action away from any specific period, more often to indicate a direct parallel with a present circumstance. A parallel movement has preferred to set the plays in identifiable periods between Shakespeare's and the present (*Hamlet* in Napoleonic dress, for example), while productions with a postmodern bias have often used eclectic or historically mixed costumes. The advantages of modern dress are many, but contemporary dress in English-speaking performances comes at the price of a conflict between the archaism of the language and the modernity of the clothes. *DK*

modernist criticism. Modernism was an international movement in the arts and literature characterized by radical experiments with aesthetic time and space and a revolt against 19th-century realism. With roots in 19th-century French Symbolism, modernism established itself in English-speaking cultures around 1910 and was the dominant aesthetic until the rise of postmodernism (seen by some as a continuation of modernism, however) late in the 20th century. Both international Shakespeare theatrical productions and English literary studies were markedly influenced by new modernist currents as the century developed, and in Shakespeare studies the shift from 19th-century preoccupations with character and plot to 20th-century emphases on myth, poetic images, and symbols was clearly related to the new modernist literary techniques and themes of James *Joyce, T. S. *Eliot, Virginia *Woolf, and William Faulkner. T. S. Eliot was a pivotal figure in this movement, and works of G. Wilson *Knight, the American New Critics Cleanth Brooks and Robert Heilman, the British *Scrutiny* critics F. R. *Leavis, L. C. *Knights, and Derek Traversi, and historicists E. M. W. *Tillyard and followers can all be characterized as instances of modernist criticism displaying the influence of modernist aesthetics. *HG*

Grady, Hugh, *The Modernist Shakespeare: Critical Texts in a Material World* (1991)
Halpern, Richard, *Shakespeare among the Moderns* (1997)

Modern Receipt, The. John Carrington's polite *adaptation of *As You Like It*, subtitled *A Cure for Love* and printed at its author's expense in 1739, is heavily influenced by Charles Johnson's **Love in a Forest* (1723) but shows considerably less enthusiasm for Shakespeare's original play. It was never intended to be performed, and probably never will be. *MD*

Modjeska, Helena (1840–1909), Polish actress who based her international career on a substantially Shakespearian repertoire (sixteen roles), initially performing in Polish or English. Perceptive and sensitive, her interpretations were overwhelmingly sympathetic, from her mercurial and intelligent Rosalind to her exonerative Lady Macbeth. *RF*

Mohun, Michael (?1616–84), trained as a boy actor by Christopher *Beeston. He may have performed for Prince Charles (Charles II) at Antwerp. At the Restoration he worked for the King's Company in secondary roles including Edgar, Cassius, and Iago. *CMSA*

Moiseiwitsch, Tanya (b. 1914), British designer associated with the open stage movement. With Tyrone *Guthrie she designed the stage of the Stratford Festival Theatre in Ontario in 1953. Her work was characterized by simple settings and costumes that accented character rather than period, often relying on portable banners and hangings to establish place and mood. For *Richard III*, the inaugural production in Ontario, she used large, ritualistic costumes; a modern dress *All's Well That Ends Well* in the same season, however, was restrained, cool, and elegant. *DK*

Molyneux, Emerie (fl. *c.*1590–1600), cartographer whose map of the world, the 'Hydrographical Description', published in 1598–9, is mentioned in *Twelfth Night* (3.2.74–5). Shakespeare may have come across it in his reading of *Hakluyt's *Navigations*. *JKS*

Monarcho (fl. *c.*1570–90), a delusional Italian who entertained the Elizabethan court with his fantasies. His name became a byword for foolery or lunacy and is mentioned in *Love's Labour's Lost* (4.1.98) and *All's Well That Ends Well* (1.1.106). *JKS*

Monck, Nugent (1878–1958), British director. A professional who had assisted William *Poel, he preferred working with amateurs and in 1911 founded the Norwich Players. For 40 years, first in an old inn and later at the Maddermarket theatre, which approximated to an Elizabethan playhouse, he staged some 300 plays including all of Shakespeare's. His productions were admired for their pace and, on occasion, for their pageantry and crowd scenes. At Stratford-upon-Avon in 1946 he directed *Cymbeline* and in 1947 *Pericles* (minus its first act). Monck is a character in David Holbrook's novel *A Play of Passion* (1978). *MJ*

Monck, Nugent, 'The Maddermarket Theatre and the Playing of Shakespeare', *Shakespeare Survey*, 12 (1959)

money. The 'universal equivalent' of all other commodities, money in Shakespeare is important from many perspectives. These include the dramaturgical, in which money is passed from hand to hand—perhaps most typically in the form of purses, as stage properties—signifying much about the personal and social relations of the playworld in question; the moralistic, in which acquisitiveness, possessiveness, and liberality may be alternately decried or praised; the thematic, in which such topics as husbandry and usury figure importantly in works like the Sonnets and *The Merchant of Venice*, among many others; and the linguistic, in which, for example, puns and other wordplay are made on such irresistible denominations as the 'crown', 'angel', 'cross', and 'dollar'.

Shakespeare uses a variety of monetary designations, including, where appropriate, terms for classical and foreign currency. Among the coins circulating in England mentioned by Shakespeare (real money at this time consisted wholly of coins, and not paper notes), those listed below are among the more important. They are listed in escalating order of value with the common abbreviation supplied.

The penny (1*d.*) was a silver coin for which the word 'pence' is the collective plural. The silver farthing was worth a quarter of a penny. A halfpenny was of course half a penny; a groat was worth fourpence (4*d.*); and a sixpence (popularly called a 'tester') was worth six pennies, or 6*d.* The shilling (*s.*) was a silver coin worth twelvepence (12*d.*). The crown was originally a gold coin worth five shillings (5*s.*), but later was minted in silver (as was the half-crown); it is the coin that Shakespeare most often uses to indicate large sums of money. The angel was a gold coin worth ten shillings (10*s.*). The ryal or rose noble was a gold coin worth fifteen shillings (15*s.*). A gold farthing (farthing noble) was worth a quarter of a noble. The sovereign was a gold coin valued at one pound sterling (20*s.* or £1). In addition to these English coins, a wide variety of foreign coins regularly circulated in England, among which were the French crown (valued around 6*s.*), the Dutch florin (a gold coin of two denominations, worth

2*s.* and 3*s.* 3*d.*, respectively), the Spanish ducat (worth approximately 6*s.* 4*d.*), and the crusado (cruzado), a Portuguese coin stamped with a cross (its value is estimated variously, between 2*s.* and 10*s.*). Also notable is Shakespeare's use of insignificant denominations like the 'doit' and 'denier' in expressions of contempt.

It should be noted that the coinage was often debased (lowered in value through the admixture of alloy) and strategically revalued. The preceding values are implied only for Shakespeare's lifetime; even during this time, some of these coins would draw alternative evaluation, owing to the introduction of foreign money and the competition between coinage of various metals (as was the case, for instance, with the silver farthing and the copper farthing minted by Lord Harington in 1613), and even between various weights of the same metal. For this reason, coins in the works of Shakespeare and his contemporaries are often identified with the monarch under whom they were minted.

Although Shakespeare's characters often refer to precise sums of money, the fact that they frequently do so in numbers rounded to the hundreds, thousands, and even hundreds of thousands suggests that we are to take these sums as only general markers of value. And while it is tempting to seek the modern-day equivalence of various sums mentioned both in the plays and in documents surrounding Shakespeare's life and career, this can be a frustrating task. One of the most difficult, and dangerous, of scholarly endeavours is the attempted conversion of currency valuations from one time to another. The problem with such an endeavour is that standards of living, desires, practices, available goods—in a word, life itself—differ so greatly from one period to another that we are left acknowledging the essentially untranslatable nature of value. *DB*

Fischer, Sandra, *Econolingua: A Glossary of Coins and Economic Language in Renaissance Drama* (1985)

Jones-Davies, M. T. (ed.), *Shakespeare et l'argent* (1993)

monsters. The display of 'monsters' was an important element of Elizabethan and Jacobean culture. In fairground sideshows, theatrical exhibitions, cabinets of curiosities, and royal entertainments, 'monsters' took pride of place, stimulating, in the process, an extensive literature devoted to their celebration and explication. Under the title of 'monster', moreover, could be brought together a gamut of non-normative types, ranging from the physically anomalous animal to the differently bodied *Homo sapiens*. It is through *Caliban in *The Tempest* that Shakespeare's fascination with 'monsters' is best illustrated. The 'savage and deformed slave' is repeatedly represented in terms of contemporary 'monstrous' discourses, as the variously ethnically charged, origin-related, and theatrically oriented commentaries upon him suggest. But Shakespeare is no less drawn to the ways in which metaphorical 'monsters' can be put to thematic use. Thus discussion of 'monstrous births' in *Othello* illuminates the processes whereby the hero is corrupted, while the 'monstrous' accusations levelled at the body of Richard III highlight the twisted and dislocated condition of the English state. Isolated references throughout the rest of the Shakespearian corpus demonstrate the pervasiveness and utility of 'monsters' to the writer's imaginative enterprise. *MTB*

Montacute (Montague), John de. See Salisbury, Earl of.

Montacute (Montague), Thomas de. See Salisbury, Earl of.

Montagu, Elizabeth (1720–1800), English philanthropist, patron, and leader of the Blue-Stocking circle, she published her popular and influential *Essay on the Writings and Genius of Shakespear* in 1769. Chiming with the national mood of enthusiasm for Shakespeare and animosity against the French, it offered a witty defence of Shakespeare against the criticisms of *Voltaire through an exploration of the function, effect, and rules of drama, a character study of Macbeth, and a comparison between *Julius Caesar* and Corneille's *Cinna*. *CMSA*

Montague, Romeo's father, is the head of the house of Montague which feuds with the house of Capulet in *Romeo and Juliet*. *AB*

Montague, Lady. See Montague's Wife.

Montague, Marquis of. Warwick's brother in *Richard Duke of York* (*3 Henry VI*), he affirms his loyalty to King Edward, 4.2, but is next seen as part of Henry's court, 4.7, and is killed at Barnet on the Lancastrian side (mentioned 5.2.40). *AB*

Montague's Wife appears in *Romeo and Juliet* 1.1 and 3.1. Her death, caused by grief at her son Romeo's banishment, is announced at 5.3.209–10. *AB*

Montaigne, Michel de (1533–92), French nobleman and essayist. As a young man Montaigne practised law in Bordeaux and also resided frequently at court. In 1571, aged 38, he retired to his country estate, to the tranquillity of his extensive library, where he began his writing career. He published two volumes of *Essais* in 1580 before emerging from his seclusion to travel through Germany and Italy and to hold the position of mayor of Bordeaux. At the end of his second term, Montaigne returned to the *Essais*, publishing an expanded version of the first two volumes and a new third volume in 1588. He continued revising these works until his death.

The *Essais* cover a remarkable range of subjects. Montaigne juxtaposes pieces on the nature of cannibals and of smells with considerations of death, the education of children, and the power of the imagination. He argues with wit and erudition, deploying many classical texts, as well as historical and contemporary examples, to make his points. Montaigne described these pieces as *Essais* (Trials) and thus coined a new literary term, but he professed to have no interest in expanding literary horizons or in educating his readers. In the preface to the first volume, he described himself as the substance of his book and subsequently confessed that 'there is no reason why you should waste your leisure on so frivolous and unrewarding a subject'. However, far from being frivolous, this quest for self-knowledge was central to Montaigne's sceptical philosophy. He explains that men's certainties are shaped by received wisdom which has in many cases subsequently been disproved, or by customs which are only applicable to the Western world. Montaigne's God exists at a great distance from man and cannot be reached by human wisdom. These arguments led Montaigne to conclude that the only wisdom man could realistically strive for was knowledge of himself.

And yet, certainty on this subject also evaded the author, who found the self to be characterized by vacillation and contrariness. It continually evaded his grasp. It is this conception of identity that led to comparisons between the Montaigne of the *Essais* (available through John Florio's translation published in 1603 and perhaps earlier in manuscript form) and Shakespeare's Hamlet. A number of Hamlet's reflections, that there are things outside his own philosophy, that he is both virtuous and vicious depending upon his own perspective, that his motives are unfathomable, and so on, suggest verbal and thematic parallels between *Hamlet* and the *Essais*. A similar prevailing theme of questioning and doubt in *Troilus and Cressida* and *Measure for Measure* has been attributed to the *Essais*, whilst *King Lear* may recall Montaigne's *Apology for Raimond Sebonde* in its sense of man's distance from God. Nevertheless, Shakespeare's only obvious debts to Montaigne occur in *The Tempest*: Gonzalo's vision of his commonwealth (2.1.149–70) derives from the essay 'On Cannibals', whilst Prospero's decision to be merciful (5.1.21) echoes the essay 'On Cruelty'. The nature of Shakespeare's relationship with Montaigne continues to be a matter of debate. *JKS*

Ellrodt, Robert, 'Self-Consciousness in Montaigne and Shakespeare', *Shakespeare Survey*, 28 (1975)

Robertson, John M., *Montaigne and Shakespeare* (1909)
Salingar, Leo, in *Dramatic Form in Shakespeare and the Jacobeans* (1986)

Montano, the Governor of Cyprus, is wounded by Cassio, *Othello* 2.3. He disarms Othello and pursues Iago, 5.2. *AB*

Montemayor, Jorge de (*c.*1521–61), Portuguese-born poet and novelist who spent most of his life in Spain. Montemayor was renowned in Renaissance Europe for his Spanish prose romance *Diana enamorada* (1542), which exerted a considerable influence upon the Renaissance pastoral tradition. Its narrative of pastoral lovers pursuing one another in disguise, its use of love potions, and its breaking up of its action with songs inspired many French, Italian, and English imitations. Shakespeare may have read the *Diana* in Bartholomew Yonge's English translation, not published until 1598 but apparently available in manuscript for some sixteen years before this date, or in the French translation of Nicholas Colin (1578). Echoes of the *Diana* have been found in *A Midsummer Night's Dream* and *As You Like It*, but its presence is most pronounced in *The Two Gentlemen of Verona*. The love-triangle of Proteus, Julia, and Sylvia strongly recalls that in Montemayor's romance where Felismena, disguised as a man, woos another woman for her lover Felix. *JKS*

Montgomery, Sir John. He threatens to withdraw his support for Edward unless he claims the title of king, *Richard Duke of York* (*3 Henry VI*) 4.8. *AB*

Montjoy (Mountjoy) is the French herald in *Henry V*, who asks King Harry to consider his ransom (3.6) but ultimately begs for permission to count the French dead (4.6). *AB*

monuments. The erection of commemorative monuments to Shakespeare gathered pace after 1740, when William Kent produced a design for a statue of Shakespeare to be placed in Poets' Corner, *Westminster Abbey (see SCHEEMAKERS). John Cheere later produced a bust copied from Scheemakers's statue, which was donated (along with a full-sized copy of the statue) to Stratford town hall by David *Garrick in 1769. In 1789, Thomas Banks completed a bas-relief sculpture entitled *Shakespeare Seated between the Dramatic Muse and the Genius of Painting*, which was displayed on the façade of the *Shakespeare Gallery and is now in the Great Garden of *New Place. Subsequent monuments include C. C. Walker's *Monument to Shakespeare, Heminges, and Condell*, in St Mary's churchyard, Aldermanbury, London, and the *Gower memorial in Stratford: see also PORTRAITS; JANSSEN BUST; STATUARY. *CT*

'Moonshine'. See STARVELING, ROBIN.

Moorfields, an area of moorland to the north of the Roman and medieval city wall of London, used by Londoners for gardens, pasture, quarrying, skating, the dog houses of the city's common hunt, and other recreational activities. The earliest Elizabethan *playhouse was located close by, in Shoreditch. *RSB*

Levy, E., 'Moorfields, Finsbury and the City of London in the Sixteenth Century', *London Topographical Record*, 26 (1990)

Moors. Shakespeare's use of the term Moor remains notoriously imprecise, despite extensive scholarship on the subject. The term is most immediately associated with Othello, 'the Moor of Venice', the villainous Aaron in *Titus Andronicus*, and the Prince of Morocco in *The Merchant of Venice*. The confused etymology and use of 'Moor' in the 16th century suggests that Shakespeare, like his contemporaries, lacked a specific geographical or ethnographic comprehension of the term. Derived from the Greek, a Moor was understood to be an inhabitant of ancient Mauretania, which corresponded to contemporary Morocco and Algeria. However, the Greek root was also associated with 'dark' or 'dim'. The Greek term became 'Maurus' in Latin, which throughout the Middle Ages took on the more ethnographic sense of black. The presence of Muslims believed to originate from Mauretania throughout the Iberian peninsula also led to the term being used as a synonym for Muslim. The confusion over what Shakespeare meant when he referred to Moors emerges from this tripartite conflation of the term, between inhabitants of North Africa, black, and Muslim. John Pory, in his translation of Leo Africanus' *History and Description of Africa* (1600), often believed to be one of the sources for *Othello*, claims that Moors 'are of two kinds, namely white or tawny Moors, and Negroes or black Moors'. Significantly, whilst both Othello and Aaron refer to their dark skin colour, the Prince of Morocco is explicitly labelled as 'a tawny Moor'. Whenever the term is used in Shakespeare it is invariably derogatory and defined in opposition to white ethnicity and 'civilized' Christianity, although critical debate still rages as to whether or not this indicates that Shakespeare's characterization of Moors influenced and prefigured subsequent racist thinking. *JBn*

Bartels, Emily, 'Making More of the Moor: Aaron, Othello, and Renaissance Refashionings of Race', *Shakespeare Quarterly*, 41 (1990)
Barthelemy, Anthony Gerard, *Black Face, Maligned Race: The Representation of Blacks in English Renaissance Drama from Shakespeare to Southerne* (1987)

Mopsa. See DORCAS.

moralist criticism may be defined as the attempt to find moral, social, and cultural values in Shakespeare—as his continued presence in the national curricula of many countries, often as a broader secular alternative to narrowly dogmatic religious education, confirms. John *Dryden and Samuel *Johnson's complaints that Shakespeare's works lack moral purpose represent a tendency (whose most notorious exemplar is Thomas *Rymer's *Short View of Tragedy*, 1693) in Enlightenment criticism which perhaps finds a modern counterpart in the extreme reaction of the Russian novelist Tolstoy to Shakespeare (*Shakespeare and the Drama*, 1904) and the morally serious revaluations of F. R. *Leavis, L. C. *Knights, and the journal *Scrutiny*. A contrary view would be that all art is ultimately anarchic, subversive play. *TM*

morality plays, an English dramatic form, popular from the late 15th to the mid-16th century, primarily characterized by its use of allegory to convey a moral lesson. The characters were abstractions, for example, Good Counsel, Hypocrisy, False Dissimulation. Easily the most popular plot was the psychomachia, in which the characters battled for the possession of a representative man. The latter's main enemy was a character called the Vice, an instrument of the devil, if not a devil himself, who would try to insinuate himself into the confidences of the subject, thus to corrupt him. Notable examples of the morality play include *The Castle of Perseverance*, *Nature*, and *Lusty Juventus*. Towards the mid-16th century, the form became increasingly secular and realistic and exerted a considerable influence over the work of dramatists such as *Kyd and *Marlowe. In particular, the memory of the Vice lingered on in Elizabethan drama. References to this character occur in *Richard III*, *1 Henry IV*, and *Twelfth Night*. Critics have argued that Shakespeare's Aaron, Richard III, Iago, and Falstaff owe a considerable debt to the exuberance and cunning of the Vice. This ancestry may also account for the difficulty of explaining the motives of Shakespeare's villains. The Vice simply hated goodness because he was a villain. *JKS*

Bevington, David, *From 'Mankind' to Marlowe: Growth and Structure in the Popular Drama of Tudor England* (1962)
Spivack, Bernard, *Shakespeare and the Allegory of Evil: The History of a Metaphor in Relation to his Major Villains* (1958)

Moratín, Leandro Fernández de (1760–1828), Spanish poet and playwright. He was the first to translate a Shakespearian play from the English (*Hamlet*, 1798, under the pseudonym 'Inarco Celenio'; the previous version, by Ramón de la *Cruz, being from the French). His introduction, biography of Shakespeare, and extensive critical notes which accompany the translation are a valuable document of a characteristically

18th-century mind divided between 'the beauties and the imperfections' of Shakespeare. *ALP*

More, Sir Thomas (1478–1535), Lord Chancellor of England from 1529 until his disgrace in 1534 for refusing to recognize his master *Henry VIII's marriage to Anne Boleyn, a refusal which would lead to his execution. As well as the celebrated *Utopia* (1516), he composed a *History of King Richard III* (written before 1513, published in 1543) which lies behind the chronicles from which Shakespeare created *Richard III*. He is the protagonist of the collaborative play **Sir Thomas More*, to which Shakespeare contributed two scenes. *AB*

'Morgan'. See BELARIUS.

Morgann, Maurice (1726–1802), English politician, philosopher, and author of *An Essay on the Dramatic Character of Sir John Falstaff* (1777). Convinced that other critics have misunderstood the character of Falstaff, Morgann dedicates his essay to proving that Falstaff is not a coward but rather a man of courage and honour. Morgann vindicates Falstaff by rejecting logical deduction in favour of subjective, emotional response. His impressionistic essay imagines a virtuous past and hypothetical biography (including military service) for Falstaff and uses this as the basis for his interpretation of *1 Henry IV*, proving that Falstaff is indeed an honourable figure. *JM*

morisco. See MORRIS DANCE.

Morley, Thomas (*c.*1557–1602), composer. He studied with William *Byrd and became a proponent, publisher, and imitator of the new Italian *madrigal style (which Byrd did not care for). His treatise *A Plain and Easy Introduction to Practical Music* (1597) is an important historical source on many aspects of music-making in Shakespeare's time.

Much speculation, based on little evidence, has taken place over the extent of Morley's collaboration and possible friendship with Shakespeare. The two have been linked through the composer's setting of *'It was a lover and his lass', and also, incorrectly, through the song *'O mistress mine', which Morley did not compose, but arranged instrumentally in his *First Book of Consort Lessons* (1599) for mixed consort (see BROKEN MUSIC). *JB*

Morocco, Prince of. He is one of Portia's unsuccessful suitors in *The Merchant of Venice*. *AB*

Morozov, Mikhail (1897–1952), influential *Russian academic, translator, and critic. His important works include *Shakespeare on the Soviet Stage* (1947). *TM*

morris dance. Referred to in *All's Well That Ends Well* 2.2.23 and *Henry V* 2.4.35 (where the dance is associated with May Day and Whitsun respectively), and performed on May morning in *The Two Noble Kinsmen* 3.5. The 'wild Morisco' in *The First Part of the Contention* (*2 Henry VI*) 3.1.365, despite the bells on the legs and similarity of the name, appears to be a different kind of dance: a solo display, similar in character to the *morisques* described by Arbeau (1589), and more closely linked to the early Renaissance *moresca*. *JB*

Mortimer, Lady. She is Mortimer's inconveniently monoglot wife and Glyndŵr's daughter, *1 Henry IV*; she appears in 3.1, where she speaks and sings in Welsh. *AB*

Mortimer, Edmund. (1) In *1 Henry VI* 2.5 he is brought in a chair, decrepit with age, to advise Richard Plantagenet (later the Duke of York), whom he names his heir, before his death. The 5th Earl of March (1391–1424) was on good terms with Henry V (contrary to what the scene suggests) and died aged 33 of the plague. **(2)** Sir Edmund Mortimer (1376–1409) forms an alliance with *Glyndŵr (marrying his daughter) and *Hotspur (who is married to his sister) against King Henry in *1 Henry IV*. He is confused by Shakespeare and *Holinshed with the preceding Edmund Mortimer (his nephew). *AB*

Mortimer, Sir John (b. 1923), English playwright, novelist, and barrister. His 1977 fictional 'entertainment' *Will Shakespeare* was based upon and a prelude to six television plays, shown on ATV in 1978, directed by Peter Wood, with Tim Curry as Shakespeare. Mortimer, 'not with the assurance of history, but with the liberty of fiction', attempts to explore 'why such an apparently calm course [as Shakespeare's] was forever inwardly troubled with storms of bitterness, self-hatred, and rejection of the world'. *TM*

Mortimer, Sir John, and **Sir Hugh.** They are uncles of York who fail to save him from defeat at the battle of Wakefield, *Richard Duke of York* (*3 Henry VI*) (see 1.2.62–75 and 1.4.2). *AB*

Morton describes the battle of *Shrewsbury to Northumberland, *2 Henry IV* 1.1. *AB*

Morton, John. See ELY, BISHOP OF.

Moseley (Mosely), Humphrey (d. 1661), prestigious Royalist bookseller, publisher, and freeman of the *Stationers' Company. On 9 September 1653 he entered *The *Merry Devil of Edmonton* as by Shakespeare, and the lost *Henry the First and Henry the Second* as by Shakespeare and Davenport; on 29 June 1660 he similarly entered three lost plays, **Duke Humphrey*, *The History of King Stephen*, and *Iphis and Iantha*, as Shakespeare's. These attributions have always been treated with scepticism. *SM*

Mote, originally 'Moth', pronounced 'mote' (meaning speck), of which 'moth' was a variant spelling. **(1)** Armado's page in *Love's Labour's Lost*, he is given the part of the infant Hercules in the performance of 'The Nine Worthies'. Legend has it that Hercules strangled two snakes as a baby in his cradle. **(2)** He is one of Titania's fairies in *A Midsummer Night's Dream*. *AB*

Moth. See MOTE.

'Motley', collective pseudonym—from Jaques's line in *As You Like It*, 'Motley's the only wear' (2.7.34)—for costume- and set-designers Sophie Harris (1900–66), her sister Margaret Harris (1904–2000), and Elizabeth Montgomery (1902–93). The three attended Queen Anne Art School and afterwards made money by selling sketches of actors at the *Old Vic theatre. There they met Sir John *Gielgud, who asked them to design costumes for *Romeo and Juliet* (1932). Their economical yet functional designs, revolutionary for their suggestive, representational nature, became a widely accepted alternative to historically accurate designs. Around 280 productions from 1927 to 1978 boasted 'design by Motley'. *BR*

Mouffet, Thomas (d. 1604), physician, entomologist, and poet. Mouffet's poem 'Of the Silkworms, and their Flies' (published in 1599) includes a retelling of the Pyramus and Thisbe legend which was thought to have influenced *A Midsummer Night's Dream*. This view has been strongly challenged, not least on the grounds that the poem was probably written after Shakespeare's play. *JKS*

Duncan-Jones, Katherine, 'Pyramus and Thisbe: Shakespeare's Debt to Moffett Cancelled', *Review of English Studies*, 32 (1981)

Mouldy, Ralph. He is recruited to fight by Falstaff, *2 Henry IV* 3.2, but buys himself out. *AB*

Moulton, Richard Green (1849–1924), English academic, based in Chicago. His *Shakespeare as a Dramatic Artist: A Popular Illustration of Scientific Criticism* (1885) moves away from the dominant biographical interpretation offered by the likes of *Dowden, towards a more text-based approach. *TM*

Mountjoy. See MONTJOY; BELOTT–MOUNTJOY SUIT.

'Mousetrap, The', Hamlet's name (3.2.226, perhaps a flippant coinage?) for the tragedy performed by the *players, otherwise called 'the murder of Gonzago' (*Hamlet* 2.2.539). *AB*

Mowbray, Thomas. He is accused by Bolingbroke of embezzlement and of murdering the Duke of Gloucester (Thomas of Woodstock, youngest son of Edward III), *Richard II* 1.1. He is based on the 1st Duke of Norfolk (1366–99) in whose custody Gloucester died, though, according to *Holinshed, Mowbray had incurred Richard's displeasure for having tried to save him, contrary to his orders. *AB*

Mowbray, Lord Thomas. He is one of the rebels treacherously caught and executed by Prince John, *2 Henry IV* 4.1, and the eldest son of the Thomas Mowbray of *Richard II*. *AB*

Mozart, Wolfgang Amadeus (1756–91), Austrian composer. Mozart did not set any Shakespeare himself. However, the music from his opera *Così fan tutte* was reworked by Delibes and Prosper Pascal into a version of *Love's Labour's Lost* entitled *Peines d'amour perdues!*, which was first performed in Paris in 1863. He was contemplating an opera based on *The Tempest* at the end of his life. *IBC*

Mr W.H., the mysterious dedicatee of the first edition of Shakespeare's Sonnets. The identity of 'Mr W.H.' has been endlessly discussed, and so has his function. The initials at the end of the dedication are those of the publisher Thomas Thorpe, not of Shakespeare; and 'begetter' might have a range of meanings, including 'inspirer', 'originator', and 'procurer' (i.e. of the manuscript for the printer). A prime candidate as inspirer has been Henry Wriothesley, Earl of *Southampton, dedicatee of *Venus and Adonis* and *The Rape of Lucrece*, and often regarded as the *'Fair Youth' of the Sonnets. This, however, requires the assumption that the initials are deliberately reversed, presumably so that the dedicatee's identity would be apparent only to those in the know, and that 'M^r^' (for Master) is also part of the disguise. Some scholars favour William Herbert, Earl of *Pembroke, one of the dedicatees in 1623 (seven years after Shakespeare died) of the First *Folio. A case has been made for Sir William *Harvey, Southampton's stepfather, on the grounds that he could have got hold of the manuscript and passed it on to Thorpe. Receding from plausibility, it has been proposed that the initials mean 'William Himself', or are a misprint for 'W.S.', and that Thorpe is dedicating the volume to its author. Oscar *Wilde, elaborating on a remark made by Thomas *Tyrwhitt to *Malone, and building on supposed puns in Sonnet 20 on the word 'hue', posited an otherwise unknown but beautiful boy actor called William Hughes, making this fancy the basis of his entertaining story 'The Portrait of Mr W.H.' Various historical bearers of the name—none of them actors—have been discovered, including a sea-cook mentioned by Samuel Butler in his edition of the Sonnets (1899). Leslie Hotson, in *Mr W.H.* (1964), set forth the claims of a William Hatcliffe. If Thorpe's use of initials was intended to conceal the truth from all but a select band of readers in his own time, he must be considered wholly successful. *SW*

Schoenbaum, S., *Shakespeare's Lives* (1970, rev. edn. 1991)

Mucedorus, a popular romantic comedy set in Spain, published in 1598 and revised in 1610. Attempts to identify Shakespeare as the reviser have failed, although the play was catalogued as Shakespeare's (see APOCRYPHA) in the late 17th century. *SM*

Much Ado About Nothing *(see opposite page)*

Muir, Kenneth (1907–96), English academic, distinguished for more than 60 years across the spectrum of Shakespeare studies in research, scholarship, and criticism. His Arden editions of *Macbeth* (1951) and *King Lear* (1952) remain standard; his *Shakespeare's Sources* (1957, rev. 1977) revealed the breadth of Shakespeare's literary antecedents; and *Shakespeare as Collaborator* (1960) reclaimed several plays once regarded as *apocryphal. He edited **Shakespeare Survey* (1965–80), and was a pillar of the International Shakespeare Conference and the *International Shakespeare Association. A lifelong commitment to Labour politics and a cosmopolitan cultural perspective informed but never distorted his habitual scholarly accuracy, lucidity, and economy. *TM*

mulberry tree. A year before he demolished Shakespeare's former Stratford home *New Place in 1759, the Revd Francis Gastrell cut down a mulberry tree which had grown in its garden. One of his reasons for so doing was that he was tired of being asked for cuttings from it by early *bardolatrous pilgrims convinced that it had been planted by Shakespeare himself, and he was able to sell the tree for a considerable sum to one Moody, a Birmingham-based manufacturer of, among other things, souvenir tobacco-stoppers. Although Shakespeare's patron *James I had encouraged the planting of mulberry trees in the Midlands during 1609 in a short-lived bid to foster a native silk industry, there is no evidence to confirm that the tree had indeed been planted by Shakespeare: the earliest written reference to it dates only from the 1740s. However, the tree's posthumous fame was firmly established at Garrick's *Jubilee in 1769 (where it was made the subject of one of the song lyrics Garrick composed for the occasion), and it has been calculated that by the end of the 18th century enough relics purporting to be made of the wood of the true mulberry had been sold to have consumed a whole copse of mulberry trees. The most famous of these was a chair designed for Garrick by William *Hogarth. *MD*

Mulcaster, Richard (*c*.1530–1611), educational theorist and headmaster of the *Merchant Taylors' School, where he taught Edmund *Spenser and perhaps Thomas *Jenkins, Shakespeare's schoolmaster at Stratford. His *Elementary* (1582) argues that many boys would benefit from being taught in English as well as in Latin, and defends English as a medium for serious writing. *RM*

Müller, Heiner (1929–96), German dramatist. In the tradition of *Brecht, he propagated communist ideals, but became increasingly critical of actual conditions in (former) East Germany. He translated and co-translated several Shakespeare plays; more independent adaptations are his gruesome *Macbeth* (1971), his intertextual *Anatomie Titus Fall of Rome* (1984), and his subversive text *Hamletmachine* (1977). *WH*

multiple setting. To present a story taking place in multiple locations the actors usually cleared the stage between scenes to signify the shift to a new place, but an occasionally employed alternative was 'multiple setting' or 'simultaneous staging' in which widely separated locations were presented onstage together. In Shakespeare's *Richard III* 5.3 the camps of Richard and Richmond are represented by two tents onstage—which conveniently allows ghosts to address both combatants—and in Jonson, Chapman, and Marston's *Eastward Ho* 4.1 Slitgut remains up a pole to view rescues, depicted on the stage below him, which occur across several miles of the Thames. In *An Apology for Poetry* Philip *Sidney mocked the over-use of this technique in plays which 'have Asia on the one side, and Africa on the other'. *GE*

Munday, Anthony (1560–1633), playwright, poet, and writer of many varieties of prose. After a spell as a bookseller's apprentice, he enrolled at the English College at Rome in 1579, probably as a government spy. He published a journalistic account of these experiences, *The English Roman Life*, in 1582. During the 1580s he wrote anti-Catholic propaganda and informed against Catholics as well as writing and translating prose romances. Between 1594 and 1602 he produced plays for the Admiral's Men, after which he concentrated on writing *pageants for the city of London and on revising the *Survey of London* by John Stow. In the early 1590s he wrote, perhaps with Henry Chettle, the first version of the history play **Sir Thomas More*, which fell foul of the censors and was rewritten by other playwrights, including Shakespeare. It was never acted. His play based on the Robin Hood legends, *The Downfall of Robert, Earl of Huntingdon* (pub. 1601), seems to have been popular—he followed it with two sequels—and may have influenced *As You Like It*. Finally, *Sir John Oldcastle* (1599) was co-written by Munday, Michael Drayton, and others to capitalize on the success of Shakespeare's *Henry IV* plays, and the scandal they had provoked by

(cont. on page 310)

Much Ado About Nothing

Shakespeare's popular comedy of reputation and repartee is not listed among his works by *Meres in mid-1598, but must have been written by early 1599, when the comedian Will *Kempe, accidentally mentioned in the quarto edition of 1600 as the original Dogberry, left Shakespeare's company. It was probably composed in 1598 and first performed that autumn, a dating confirmed by internal evidence: in rare vocabulary it is closely related to *2 Henry IV* and *Henry V* (1597–8, 1598–9) and the incidence of colloquialisms in its verse places it before *As You Like It* (1599).

Text: The 1600 quarto was clearly set from Shakespeare's own *foul papers. This authorial draft was apparently fairly untidy: as well as sometimes preserving the names of actors Shakespeare had in mind as he wrote (Kempe for Dogberry and Richard *Cowley for Verges), the speech prefixes are often inconsistent, while entrances and exits are often omitted, and one *mute character, Leonato's wife Innogen, is mentioned in the opening stage directions to the first two acts but never says or does anything and is never mentioned. The Folio text (1623) reprints the play from a copy of the quarto supplemented, here and there, by the consultation of a promptbook, from which certain stage directions have been added or elaborated.

Sources: The main plot of *Much Ado About Nothing*—the story of Hero's defamation—derives from one of the most widely disseminated narratives in European Renaissance culture, which Shakespeare probably knew in many different forms. It appears as the story of Ginevora in *Ariosto's *Orlando furioso* (1516, translated into English by Sir John *Harington in 1591), and as the story of Fenicia in *Bandello's *Novelle* (1554, translated into French in *Belleforest's *Histoires tragiques*, 1559), while English versions include those of George *Whetstone (in *The Rock of Regard*, 1576) and Edmund *Spenser (in book 2 of *The Faerie Queene*, 1590). The story had already been dramatized in English at least twice, once as *A History of Ariodante and Genevra*, acted at court in 1583, and once as *Fedele and Fortunio* (1585), an adaptation, probably by Anthony *Munday, of Luigi Pasqualigo's *Il Fedele* (1579). The more comical story of Beatrice and Benedick, however, seems to be Shakespeare's own invention (though some commentators feel that their repartee shows the influence of the exemplary witty dialogues between courtly ladies and gentlemen supplied in *Castiglione's *Il libro del cortegiano*, 1528, translated by Sir Thomas Hoby as *The Book of the Courtier*, 1561), as do the doings of Dogberry and Verges.

Synopsis: **1.1** Leonato, Governor of Messina, together with his daughter Hero and niece Beatrice, learn of the approach of Don Pedro, Prince of Aragon, who has just defeated his illegitimate half-brother Don John (to whom he is now reconciled) in a military campaign: among his party are the young Count Claudio and his friend Benedick, about whom Beatrice, Benedick's long-time conversational adversary, makes disparaging jokes. Leonato welcomes Don Pedro, and Beatrice and Benedick, both scorners of romantic love, exchange witty insults. The bashful Claudio, left with Benedick, confides despite his friend's disdain for marriage that he means to woo Hero. Don Pedro promises to assist by courting Hero while disguised as Claudio at the evening's masked ball and winning Leonato's consent to the match. **1.2** Leonato is told by his brother Antonio that he has heard that Don Pedro seeks to marry Hero. **1.3** The malcontented Don John, with his companion Conrad, learns from Borachio of his brother's plan to woo Hero for Claudio, and hopes to thwart it.

2.1 At the masked ball, Don Pedro (whom Hero has been advised to accept if he proposes) speaks in disguise to Hero. Beatrice speaks to a disguised Benedick, whom she feigns not to recognize, of his faults. Don John, pretending to take the masked Claudio for Benedick, tells him Don Pedro is wooing Hero for himself. Claudio, cast down, laments this apparent betrayal. Benedick is more affronted at the account of himself he has heard from Beatrice, whom he describes scornfully to Don Pedro: when Beatrice reappears, with Claudio, Hero, and Leonato, he rudely leaves. Don Pedro reassures Claudio that he has wooed Hero only on Claudio's behalf, and the match is agreed, to mutual satisfaction. Don Pedro banters with Beatrice. After her departure, he undertakes that, with the help of Leonato, Claudio, and Hero, he will trick Benedick and Beatrice into falling in love during the week that intervenes before Claudio and Hero marry. **2.2** Borachio promises Don John he will prevent the marriage between Claudio and Hero by arranging that on its eve Claudio shall see him courting Margaret, Hero's gentlewoman, in Hero's clothes at Hero's window and thus think Hero unfaithful. Don John promises him 1,000 ducats as a fee. **2.3** In the orchard Benedick, reflecting on Claudio's transformation from soldier to lover, hides to overhear a conversation between Don Pedro, Leonato, and Claudio. After hearing a song by Balthasar, 'Sigh no more, ladies', Don Pedro, pretending not to have noticed the concealed Benedick, asks Leonato whether it is true that Beatrice is in love with Benedick. He and Claudio confirm and elaborate this story and, praising Beatrice, the three say they will not tell Benedick because he would only scorn her. Satisfied that Benedick has heard, they leave to initiate a corresponding stratagem against Beatrice, whom they send to call Benedick to dinner. Left alone Benedick, completely taken in, repents of his earlier attitude and promises to reciprocate Beatrice's imputed love. After she bids him in to dine, Benedick, alone, twists her straightforward and unenthusiastic remarks into subtle messages of love.

3.1 Hero arranges for Beatrice, apparently unperceived, to overhear a conversation with her gentlewoman Ursula in which Hero reports that Benedick is deeply in love with Beatrice and deserves better than the insults he would receive if he told her of it. Alone, the deceived Beatrice undertakes to reciprocate Benedick's love. **3.2** The day before the wedding Don Pedro and Claudio banter with Benedick, who will not admit that he has fallen in love, but nonetheless leaves for a private conference, presumably about the possibility of marrying Beatrice, with Leonato. Don John tells Claudio and Don Pedro that Hero is disloyal, promising to show them a man entering her chamber window that night: Claudio says that if this proves true he will shame Hero at the intended wedding. **3.3** The constable Dogberry, with his partner Verges, gives the Watch comically ill-worded advice as to how to discharge their duties during the night. After Dogberry and Verges leave, the Watch overhear Borachio boasting to Conrad about how he has been wooing Margaret at Hero's window, successfully persuading the watching Claudio and Don Pedro (placed at a distance by Don John) that Hero is false. The Watch arrest both men. **3.4** Hero, Beatrice, Ursula, and Margaret are dressing on the morning of the wedding, Margaret joking at the expense of the apparently converted Beatrice and Benedick. **3.5** Dogberry and Verges come to tell a preoccupied Leonato about the arrested Borachio and Conrad, whom they hope to interrogate in his presence, but are so long-winded and inept that he dismisses them to proceed on their own.

4.1 At the wedding service, conducted by Friar Francis, Claudio gives Hero back to her father, accusing her, with the support of Don Pedro and Don John, of falsehood, and recounting that he saw her entertain a lover at her chamber window the previous night. Hero faints before her three accusers leave. Leonato, convinced of her guilt, wishes she were dead, but Friar Francis, questioning her as she revives, is persuaded of her innocence. Leonato and Benedick agree, on the Friar's advice, to conceal Hero, giving out that she has died. Left together, Beatrice and Benedick admit they love one another. Beatrice asks Benedick to prove his love by avenging the slander of Hero: he agrees to challenge Claudio to a duel. **4.2** The inept and self-important Dogberry and Verges, with the Sexton and the Watch, question Borachio and Conrad. The Sexton realizes that the supposedly dead Hero was slandered by Don John, who has stolen away, and goes to tell Leonato. Dogberry, insisting when Conrad calls him an ass that this too should be written down, brings his prisoners after him.

5.1 Leonato refuses Antonio's attempts to comfort him: when they meet Don Pedro and Claudio, they accuse Claudio of killing Hero by his defamation, but he declines to fight with either, and they leave, Don Pedro still maintaining the truth of Claudio's accusation. Benedick arrives and, despite flippant remarks from Don Pedro and Claudio, challenges Claudio to a duel, and leaves. When Dogberry, Verges, the Watch, and their prisoners Borachio and Conrad arrive, Don Pedro and Claudio are appalled to learn how they have been deceived. Brought by the Sexton, Antonio and Leonato join them, and a penitent Borachio confesses to Leonato his share in Hero's supposed death. Don Pedro and Claudio beg Leonato to impose what penance he will for theirs: Leonato instructs Claudio to vindicate Hero's reputation to the people of Messina, to bring an epitaph to her tomb that night, and to be ready the following morning to marry a daughter of Antonio's, said to resemble Hero, in her place. Borachio assures Leonato that Margaret was unaware of the malicious plan in which she was a participant. **5.2** Benedick has been trying to write love poems for Beatrice: the two are talking when Ursula brings the news that Hero has been cleared and the slanderous Don John has fled. **5.3** At Leonato's family tomb Claudio reads out and places an epitaph for the wronged Hero, and a hymn is sung, 'Pardon, goddess of the night'. Claudio and Don Pedro leave to change out of mourning in time for the planned wedding. **5.4** At Leonato's bidding Antonio is ready to present a veiled Hero to Claudio as if she were his daughter. Friar Francis, his faith in Hero vindicated, agrees to marry Beatrice and Benedick at the same time. Don Pedro and Claudio arrive: Antonio brings Hero, Beatrice, Margaret, and Ursula, all veiled, and shows Claudio which he is to marry. Claudio vows to marry the veiled Hero, thinking she is Leonato's niece: she then reveals her face, asserting her innocence. The Friar promises to explain everything to the overjoyed Claudio after the wedding ceremony. Meanwhile Beatrice and Benedick, beginning to realize how they were tricked, come close to disowning their mutual affection before their friends produce a love sonnet written by Benedick and a love letter by Beatrice as evidence of it, and they agree to wed, Benedick disavowing his former opposition to marriage. Benedick calls for music that all the reconciled friends and lovers may dance before the wedding, and when news arrives that Don John has been captured and brought back to Messina Benedick urges Don Pedro to postpone all thoughts of him and his due punishment until the following day.

Artistic features: Less lyrical than the other mature comedies, with the exception of *The Merry Wives of Windsor*, *Much Ado About Nothing* nonetheless looks forward, in the depiction of Hero's 'resurrection', to the late romances (particularly *The Winter's Tale*). Its closest kinship, however, is with the early *The Taming of the Shrew*, with which it shares a structure contrasting naive, romantic attitudes to love (such as those of Lucentio or Claudio) with more pragmatic and sceptical ones. Benedick and Beatrice, quarrelling in prose all the way to the altar, often resemble Petruccio and Katherine: Beatrice, for example, admitting to herself that she loves Benedick, promises to reform her character in terms of which Petruccio would certainly approve: 'I will requite thee, | Taming my wild heart to thy loving hand' (3.1.111–12).

Critical history: Although their relationship occupies what is nominally only the sub-plot, it is the more protesting and reluctant couple who have dominated responses to the play, which seems to have been nicknamed 'Beatrice and Benedick' (the title *Berlioz would use for his operatic version) from early in its stage history (by, for example, *Charles I). Combining the play with elements of *Measure for Measure* in 1662 (as *The *Law against Lovers*), William *Davenant borrowed only Beatrice and Benedick from this play, their repartee decisively influencing the subsequent development of Restoration comedy. The play has been one of the most popular of the mature comedies since the mid-18th century, though it has never inspired as rich a critical literature as *The Merchant of Venice*, *As You Like It*, or *Twelfth Night*. *Hazlitt praised Dogberry, regularly hailed since as an all too convincing depiction of petty officialdom, but from his day to this the main plot of the play has elicited little but apologies, with criticism on the subject mainly dedicated to exploring or explaining Claudio's inadequacies as a comic protagonist. His behaviour towards Hero, variously excused and vilified as wholly conventional, and the play's suggestions of a woman-centred world which finally prevails against the barrack-room assumptions of the soldiers, have, however, recommended the play to the attention of *feminist critics, while others have found in Friar Francis's stratagem not only an anticipation of the last plays but glimpses of Shakespeare's views on *religion.

Stage history: *Much Ado About Nothing* was one of the plays acted at court in May 1613 to celebrate the marriage of Princess *Elizabeth, and according to Leonard *Digges's commendatory poem (1640) was one of Shakespeare's most popular comedies. Beatrice and Benedick reappeared at the Restoration only as the laughing cavaliers of *Davenant's adaptation, but the original made brief returns to the stage in the 1720s and 1730s (displaced between 1737 and 1741 by another adaptation, the Reverend James Miller's *The Universal Passion*, which crosses the play with Molière's *La Princesse d'Élide*). It was finally established in the repertory forever when David *Garrick wittily chose the role of Benedick for his first performances on returning to the stage after his honeymoon in 1748, opposite Hannah *Pritchard's Beatrice. Since then the bantering couple's most notable representatives have included J. P. *Kemble and Dorothea *Jordan (1798), Mr and Mrs Charles *Kean (1858), Mr and Mrs Charles *Calvert (1865), Henry *Irving and Ellen *Terry (1882), Lewis Casson and Sybil *Thorndike (1927), John *Gielgud and Peggy *Ashcroft (1931, 1950, 1955), and, in John *Barton's production of 1976 (set in the British Raj), Donald *Sinden and Judi *Dench. Dench herself directed the play for Kenneth *Branagh's Renaissance company in 1988–9 (with Branagh as Benedick and Samantha Bond as Beatrice), a production which anticipated many elements of his subsequent film. Modern productions of the play, like Barton's, have often stressed the military world inhabited by its male characters: this was especially true of *Cheek by Jowl's award-winning 1998 production, their last Shakespearian revival, which followed Barton in dressing Don Pedro's officers in uniforms of the British colonial period.

MD

On the screen: The earliest recorded screen version was an American *silent film of 1909. Scenes from the play were among the earliest Shakespeare television extracts to be transmitted (1937). Russian films were made in 1956 and 1973. *Zeffirelli directed an impressive British cast (including Maggie *Smith, Derek Jacobi, and Frank Finlay) in a stage production later adapted for television (1967), followed by a BBC TV version (1978) with Michael York as Benedick, originally scheduled to open the complete BBC series but replaced in 1984 by Stuart Burge's TV production. On a grander scale Kenneth Branagh filmed the play (1993) in a lavish Italian setting, with himself and his then wife Emma Thompson as Benedick and Beatrice among a part-Hollywood cast.

AD

Recent major editions

Arthur Humphreys (Arden 2nd series, 1981); F. H. Mares (New Cambridge, 1988); Sheldon P. Zitner (Oxford, 1994)

Some representative criticism
Cook, Carol, 'The Sign and Semblance of her Honour: Reading Gender Difference in *Much Ado About Nothing*', *Publications of the Modern Language Association* (1986)
Evans, Bertrand, in *Shakespeare's Comedies* (1960)
Everett, Barbara, '*Much Ado About Nothing*', *Critical Quarterly*, 3 (1961)
Levin, Richard, in *Multiple Plot in English Renaissance Drama* (1971)
Leggatt, Alexander, in *Shakespeare's Comedy of Love* (1974)
Rossiter, A. P., in *Angel with Horns* (1961)

characterizing the Protestant martyr Oldcastle as a felonious glutton. *RM*

Eccles, Mark, 'Anthony Munday', in J. W. Bennett (ed.), *Studies in English Renaissance Drama* (1959)
Turner, Celeste, *Anthony Munday: An Elizabethan Man of Letters* (1928)

'Murder' is impersonated by Demetrius in *Titus Andronicus* 5.2. *AB*

murderers. Unnamed assassins in Shakespeare's plays include the following: **(1)** The stage direction at the beginning of *The First Part of the Contention* (*2 Henry VI*) 3.2 requires 'two men' to lie on the Duke of Gloucester's 'breast, smothering him in his bed'. The Second Murderer has regrets. **(2)** In *Richard III* assassins are hired by Richard to kill Clarence, 1.3. The First Murderer kills him, 1.4, the Second has misgivings and says he will refuse the fee, 271–3. **(3)** Two assassins are hired by Macbeth, *Macbeth* 3.1, to kill Banquo and his son (though Fleance escapes, 3.3). In 4.2 murderers kill *Macduff's son and chase his wife (Ross reports that 'Wife, children, servants, all | That could be found' were slaughtered, 4.3.212). *AB*

Wiggins, Martin, *Journeymen in Murder: The Assassin in English Renaissance Drama* (1991)

'Murder of Gonzago, The'. See 'Mousetrap, The'.

Murdoch, Dame Iris (1919–99), Anglo-Irish novelist and philosopher. Bradley Pearson, the hero of *The Black Prince* (1973), conquers his impotence only when, after a series of discussions about *Hamlet*, his young mistress Julian Belling comes to him disguised as the 'Black Prince'. In *The Sea, the Sea* (1978), a 60-year-old Shakespearian theatre director faces, Prospero-like, his 'wifeless, childless, brotherless, sisterless' existence. *TM*

Todd, Richard, *Iris Murdoch: The Shakespearian Interest* (1979)

Murellus. See Flavius.

Murphy, Arthur (1727–1805), English playwright. In youth Murphy wrote vigorously in defence of Shakespeare against *Voltaire in the *Gray's Inn Journal* ('with us islanders Shakespeare is a kind of national religion in poetry'), and he later wrote a splendid attack on *Garrick's rewritten version of *Hamlet* (1776, published in Jesse Foot's biography of Murphy, 1811). His biography of Garrick (1801) remains an important source for the study of 18th-century Shakespeare. *MD*

Murry, John Middleton (1889–1957), English writer and critic, husband and promoter of Katherine Mansfield. Author of *Keats and Shakespeare* (1925); *Shakespeare* (1936), which places *King Lear* behind *Coriolanus* in achievement; and *Countries of the Mind* (2 vols., 1922, 1931), which includes a notable essay on 'A Forgotten Heroine of Shakespeare'. *TM*

Muscovy. In *Love's Labour's Lost* the King of Navarre and his lords disguise themselves as Muscovites (Russians). See *Russia and the former Soviet Union. *AB*

music has a vital, and integral, role in Shakespeare's work, whether in explicit cues for music (present in all the plays except *The Comedy of Errors*), the wealth of musical imagery (employed in the poems, such as Sonnet 8 or *The Rape of Lucrece* 1121–41, as well as in the drama), or the sheer musical resonance of Shakespeare's writing. The extent and function of music in the plays varies considerably, depending on the nature of the work. Almost all the tragedies and all the history plays require 'signal' music—alarums, *sennets, marches, and other military *flourishes, interrupting and charging the atmosphere as they signal the entrance (or exit) of important figures or the start of important events. Particular instruments could suggest a location or occasion, evoke an atmosphere, and even indicate the status of the characters on stage. Some of the associations remain obvious today: *drums accompanying marching, *horns for the hunt, *trumpets heralding royalty. Other timbres no longer carry their original significance: *cornets for dignitaries not high enough in rank to merit trumpets, *hautboys for banquets, consorts of *flutes or *recorders for rituals of death and transfiguration. In *A Midsummer Night's Dream* the conventions of signal music are used to comic effect: as we reach daylight and the resolution of the action, horns, appropriately, are employed to announce the arrival of the hunting Duke, whereas the opening of the mechanicals' play a little later is marked by the inappropriately self-important and over-ceremonious use of trumpets.

Instrumental music is important for creating or enhancing the atmosphere where words are silent, or as a backcloth for speech that is often melancholy and reflective. There are numerous cues for 'soft music', one of the most poignant being in *King Lear* (Scene 21), where music's curative powers help temporarily to restore Lear's sanity. In the fourth act of *All Is True* (*Henry VIII*) Katherine goes to sleep to 'sad and solemn music' that continues as she dreams. The peaceful music (and vision), painfully at odds with her waking condition, intensifies the audience's pity for her. In a different way, soft music is particularly effective as an accompaniment to Richard II's soliloquy in Pomfret Castle (5.5.41–63) and, more positively, the dialogue between Jessica and Lorenzo at Belmont in *The Merchant of Venice* (5.1.69–88). These speeches are especially notable for their rich musical imagery.

Instrumental music is employed in other functional ways. It is used for magical, or apparently magical, events, such as the coming to life of Hermione's statue in *The Winter's Tale* and the apparitions of the banquet in *The Tempest.* It is used ceremonially, to accompany the coronation procession in *All Is True*, the laying of the coffins in *Titus Andronicus*, and the bearing away of the hero's body at the end of *Coriolanus.* And it is used joyfully, especially to accompany dances. While some of these, such as that which closes *Much Ado About Nothing*, are mostly there for pure entertainment, others serve a more dramatic purpose. The dances in *Romeo and Juliet* and *All Is True* are the critical occasions when the two main characters in each play first meet, while the dance of shepherds and shepherdesses in *The Winter's Tale* allows the disguised Polixenes to question the old shepherd about his son while the son is present but otherwise occupied. In *A Midsummer Night's Dream* the dance of fairies at the very end of the play is particularly important for affirming the sense of resolution and harmony that has finally been reached in the play. Sometimes, however, music is used to emphasize the distance in understanding between characters. One very dramatic instance of this occurs in the fourth act of *Romeo and Juliet.* The (presumably) jolly and brash music which is required to accompany the happy Paris as he approaches the Capulet house to marry Juliet is in stark contrast to the state of shock that is about to grip the household as they discover Juliet's apparently dead body. The sudden triviality and inappropriateness of the music heightens the pathos of the scene, and serves as a symbol of the obliviousness of the elders of both houses to the needs and turmoil of their children. The dialogue which ensues between the suddenly redundant musicians, who resolve to stay and cadge a free meal despite the family's bereavement (4.4.170–1), gives a wonderful glimpse of the stoical opportunism of the profession.

The addition of words and the use of the human voice allow for even more diverse functions of music in the plays. The healing and soothing power of music is evoked in several instances when songs are called for but no lyrics provided, such as Marina's song in *Pericles*, the Welsh song in *1 Henry IV*, and Lucius' song for Brutus in *Julius Caesar*. In contrast, broken snatches of songs are used to portray the disturbed state of many characters. Comic instances of this include: the nervous Parson Hugh Evans, in *The Merry Wives*, mixing up the words of a psalm with a secular love song; Mistress Quickly feigning innocent normality when suddenly disturbed by her master Caius, also in *The Merry Wives of Windsor*; and the singing of various drunken characters in *Twelfth Night* and *The Tempest*. A poignant, more extended example is Desdemona's fragmented singing of the Willow song in *Othello*. Snatches of song are also used to depict madness, whether the very painful broken mind of Ophelia in *Hamlet*, or the assumed madness of Petruccio in *The Taming of the Shrew*, and are a normal mode of communication for clowns and fools.

The remaining songs cover a wide variety of moods and functions. There are celebratory songs, such as in the wedding masques in *As You Like It* and *The Tempest*, and there are the more solemn dirges and laments of *Cymbeline* and *Much Ado About Nothing*. *Love's Labour's Lost* and *Twelfth Night* both end, a little surprisingly, with reflective songs, a sad tinge belying the apparently happy resolution of the plays. The association of love with music is made explicit in the opening words of *Twelfth Night*: 'If music be the food of love, play on'; yet there are few actual love songs. Indeed, music's power seems to fail in the serenades *'Who is Silvia?' (*Two Gentlemen of Verona* 4.2.38–52) and 'Hark, hark, the lark' (*Cymbeline* 2.3.19–25). However, in both cases it is the serenader who, not being the right lover (and therefore in some way 'false'), is unable to harness that power. The only 'true' serenade is Benedick's attempt in *Much Ado About Nothing* (5.2.24–8), but this is given comic treatment, its awkward poetry reflecting Benedick's awkwardness at being a conventional lover. Earlier in the play there is an interesting use of song as Balthasar sings *'Sigh no more, ladies'. Led to expect a sentimental love song celebrating Claudio and Hero's engagement, it is puzzling to hear lines like 'Men were deceivers ever' and 'To one thing constant never'. However, the intention is to help set up the appropriate mood for introducing a discussion of Beatrice (from whom such sentiments might well be heard), knowing that Benedick is hidden nearby.

Music is heavily associated with magic, hence its importance in *A Midsummer Night's Dream* and *The Tempest* and the use of a song as the 'fairies', as Falstaff believes them to be, taunt him in *The Merry Wives of Windsor*. Songs are also used to emphasize the 'other-worldness' of the banished Duke's court in the Forest of Arden in *As You Like It*. There are songs commenting on corrupt courts (in *Troilus and Cressida* and *As You Like It*) and songs that mark the passing of time as other activities are occurring, such as *'Tell me, where is Fancy bred?' in *The Merchant of Venice* (3.2.63–72) and *'Blow, blow, thou winter wind' in *As You Like It* (3.1.175–94). And there are songs, such as those by the Gravedigger in *Hamlet* and Autolycus in *The Winter's Tale*, whose prime purpose is to provide relief from the tragedy of the plays. Indeed, the relentless tragedy of the opening three acts of *The Winter's Tale* is made all the more stark by the total absence of music, contrasted with almost an excess of singing and dancing in the fourth act.

No instrumental music survives that can be associated for certain with a production during Shakespeare's lifetime, and musical information from the stage directions and play texts in the quartos and First Folio is often unclear or vague, with inconsistent use of musical terms: printed editions were intended for the reader rather than the performer. If one examines musical directions in the plays of Shakespeare's contemporaries too, as Manifold (*The Music in English Drama*, 1956) has done in some detail, then it becomes possible to reach firm conclusions about the meaning of some expressions, but not others. Of the various types of ceremonial trumpet signal, for example, sennet and *tucket emerge with precise meanings, but flourish seems at times a more generalized term.

Musicians at the Globe and in other theatres did not form an integrated ensemble, but consisted of separate groups from different backgrounds: the actors themselves, who were expected to be musically versatile; the trumpeters, probably with military training; and the players of hautboys or shawms, who may have been drawn from the local waits, and, if so, could doubtless play a variety of instruments. Actors when singing might accompany themselves on the *lute, as indicated for Ophelia with her song fragments in *Hamlet* 4.5; clowns and others too played *tabor and *pipe, for example Ariel, in *The Tempest* 3.2, when correcting the tune sung by Stefano and Trinculo.

The placing of musicians in the playhouse is not always clear from surviving descriptions. In private theatres the musicians' performing area was called the *'music room', suggesting a standardized location, and various references to music 'above' imply this was in the gallery over the stage. There was a tradition that musicians should be heard from behind a curtain, and not be seen unless involved in the action; two out of three illustrations of indoor theatre stages (all from after Shakespeare's death) show the centre of the gallery appropriately curtained. Yet in the remaining picture the audience occupies the centre space, and in the only representation of an open or public theatre stage, a problematic copy of de Witt's sketch of the *Swan (*c.*1596), the entire gallery is occupied by what appears to be audience. Positioning evidently varied on occasions to produce a particular effect; in *Antony and Cleopatra* for example, the sound of hautboys playing under the stage is regarded as a puzzling omen by a group of soldiers before battle (4.3).

Shakespeare's use of music reflects changes in compositional style and performance practice which took place throughout Europe during his career, summarized in musical history as the transition between the Renaissance and baroque eras. A major development was the burgeoning of secular music, both vocal and instrumental, including at court level the emergence of opera in Italy and increasingly elaborate *masques under *James I in England. Many of the later plays incorporate some kind of staged entertainment or masque, with only three of the eleven plays from *Timon of Athens* onwards lacking such a scene. Settings of songs from the last plays sometimes display the dramatic and declamatory characteristics of early opera (e.g. *'Get you hence' and *'Hark, hark, the lark') and during this final period traditional *ballads are quoted less frequently.

Taste in instrumental timbre was changing too; Renaissance instruments such as the *bagpipes, *rebec, and *regal descended the social scale as their raucous sound went out of fashion. This move towards tonal refinement coincided with the need for gentler sounds in private theatres such as the Blackfriars, not only to please the audience, but also to avoid annoying the neighbours. Cornets replaced trumpets, and soft instruments, including the *organ, were played in the intervals. Music came to take on a more extensive role in the theatrical event as a whole, with performances before the play too. But the popular custom in the public theatres of ending a play with a sung and danced afterpiece or *jig was not approved of in private theatre productions.

It has been argued that the standard six-piece English mixed or 'broken' consort of the period (see BROKEN MUSIC) formed an ensemble in some Shakespeare plays; it was certainly a line-up used for professional entertainment in other contexts. Circumstantial evidence includes that of a German visitor to the Blackfriars theatre in 1602 who was delighted with the playing of a mixed consort for an hour before the play (unnamed) began. It may be that the combination was associated more with the private theatre; productions at the reconstructed Globe theatre in London have demonstrated the need for loud instruments to make an impact in the outdoor acoustic, over a sometimes noisy audience. With so many gaps in our knowledge of music on the Shakespearian stage, theories of common practice must be treated with caution.

Music has remained intertwined with Shakespeare down the centuries since his own time. Some of the most important *adaptations of the Restoration were musical: *A Midsummer Night's Dream* and *The Tempest*, for example, were both turned into semi-operas. *A Midsummer Night's Dream* became *The *Fairy Queen*, with splendid music by Henry Purcell, while *Dryden and *Davenant's rewritten *The Tempest* was given music by a group of composers including Matthew *Locke and Pelham Humfrey. (A subsequent score was misattributed to Purcell for many years). Both these plays continued to attract much musical attention during the 18th century, including being set as all-sung operas by J. C. Smith in 1755 and 1756. Music went with magic, tragic as well as comic: hence William Davenant's alteration of *Macbeth* into a semi-opera, with singing and dancing witches. The music for this was originally composed by Matthew Locke. It was reset by John Eccles around 1695, but it was Richard *Leveridge's setting of 1702 that took the theatres by storm, accompanying all major London productions of *Macbeth* until well into the 19th century, long after Shakespeare's 'original' play had been restored.

Other important musical practices in the Restoration included the use of specially composed act music—instrumental music to be played between the acts of a play—and the addition of masques to several works. Of particular note is the insertion of Purcell's *Dido and Aeneas*, divided into four entertainments, into Charles *Gildon's adaptation of *Measure for Measure* (1700), which then served as the vehicle for the first public performance of Purcell's opera.

During the 18th century the interpolation of additional songs was often dictated by the presence of good singers, and their relative acting abilities. Another important factor governing the introduction of music was the desire to emulate on stage major events in real life. Hence the coronation scene in *All Is True* (*Henry VIII*) became an impressive spectacle, with music, around the time of the coronations of George II in 1727 and George III in 1761. Music seems to have become even more important in Shakespeare performances in the 19th century. The comedies were often crammed full of songs, notably in the productions mounted by Frederick *Reynolds and Henry *Bishop, with lyrics normally taken from several Shakespeare plays and from other poets, and the music adapted and arranged from various composers. When *Mendelssohn's music for *A Midsummer Night's Dream* was first performed in London in 1844 so popular did it prove that it became almost obligatory in productions of the play for almost a century (and, indeed, was used in a Guildford theatre as late as 1965).

Productions of Shakespeare's plays since the 1900s have, on the whole, tended to follow one of three trends when choosing music. The first is the historical approach, trying to use 'authentic' music and instruments (along with costumes and so on) from Elizabethan times, pioneered by *Poel and now associated with the *Globe reconstruction on Bankside. The second is the use of serious contemporary music, which has sometimes been very experimental: Roberto Gerhard's music for *King Lear* (1955), for example, was one of the earliest works in this country to use *musique concrète*. The third is the adoption of music of a more popular style, especially for productions set in a particular decade, such as the 1920s, or set in present times.

Starting with the semi-operas of the Restoration there have been several hundred reworkings of Shakespeare's plays into *operas, operettas, and *musicals. From the 20th century there have also been a number of important film scores, notably those by William *Walton for Laurence *Olivier's films. Shakespeare's plays, too, have inspired a large number of orchestral works, such as *Tchaikovsky's fantasy overture *Romeo and Juliet*, and smaller instrumental pieces. Even as early as the 17th century lyrics from the plays started to be set as art songs independent of the stage, and there have been many musical settings of passages from the plays not originally intended to be sung, a striking example being Ralph *Vaughan Williams's *Serenade to Music* (1938), which is based on Lorenzo and Jessica's dialogue in *The Merchant of Venice* (5.1.54–110). *A Shakespeare Music Catalogue* (1991) lists over 20,000 arrangements and settings written for stage productions or otherwise inspired by Shakespeare's works; there seem to be no signs of this industry abating. *JB/IBC*

Gooch, Bryan, and Thatcher, David, *A Shakespeare Music Catalogue* (1991)

Hartnoll, Phyllis, (ed.), *Shakespeare and Music* (1964)

Long, John H., *Shakespeare's Use of Music*, i: *A Study of the Music and its Performance in the Original Production of Seven Comedies*; ii: *The Final Comedies*; iii: *The Histories and Tragedies* (1955, 1961, 1971)

Manifold, J. S., *The Music in English Drama* (1956)

Naylor, Edward, *Shakespeare and Music* (1896, rev. edn. 1931)

Seng, Peter J., *The Vocal Songs in the Plays of Shakespeare: A Critical History* (1967)

Sternfeld, F. W., *Music in Shakespearean Tragedy* (1963)

(For further bibliography, see SONGS IN THE PLAYS and BROADSIDE BALLAD).

musicals. Among the earlier Shakespearian successes on the modern light musical stage were the Rodgers and Hart musical *The Boys from Syracuse* (1938) (based on *The Comedy of Errors*), Cole Porter's *Kiss me Kate* (1948) (derived from *The Taming of the Shrew*), and *The Belle of Mayfair* (1906) and the Sondheim/Bernstein *West Side Story* (1957) (both versions of *Romeo and Juliet*). In America in the 1960s and 1970s there was a spate of 'mod-musicalized' Shakespeare plays, which included: Galt MacDermott, John Guare, and Mal Shapiro's *Two Gentlemen of Verona* (1971); a Canadian *Rockabye Hamlet* (1974); *Pop* (1974), based on *King Lear*; and an *Othello* derivative in the 'blaxploitation' mode entitled *Catch my Soul* (1968). More recent musicals have included the 'western' musical *The Merry Wives of Windsor, Texas* (1988) and *Return to the Forbidden Planet* (1989), a work based on *The Tempest* (via the film **Forbidden Planet*) using rock and roll numbers from the 1950s and 1960s. Gaston Serpette's operetta *Shakespeare!* (1899) is about an English dog, and not the dramatist. *IBC*

music of the spheres, a Renaissance concept derived from Pythagoras, in which the proportional movement of the planets was linked to musical *proportion. There are several allusions in Shakespeare (e.g. *Twelfth Night* 3.1.109). *JB*

music room. Musicians in the Elizabethan theatre were located behind the scenic wall, either hidden within the tiring house or else in a balcony overlooking the stage. Prior to 1609 music used in plays at the Globe comes from 'within', suggesting somewhere out of sight inside the tiring house, but thereafter the music tends to come from 'above', indicating that the stage balcony was used. At the Blackfriars the stage balcony was always occupied by the musicians, whose lengthy pre-performance recitals were famously excellent and who, unlike the musicians in open-air theatres, which used continuous performance until 1609, also played between the acts. It seems likely that when the King's Men took over the Blackfriars in 1608–9 they regularized the musical arrangements by adopting Blackfriars practice (visible musicians in the balcony playing music between the acts) at both playhouses, much as they adopted the Blackfriars observance of intervals and use of a flight machine. *GE*

Hosley, Richard, 'Was There a Music-Room in Shakespeare's Globe?', *Shakespeare Survey*, 13 (1960)

Mustardseed is one of Titania's fairies in *A Midsummer Night's Dream.* *AB*

mutes. These are characters who are referred to in Shakespeare's plays but do not appear (such as the 'brave son' of the Duke of Milan, *The Tempest* 1.2.440–1) or those mentioned in stage directions who do not speak and are not referred to by others (such as 'Innogen', wife of Leonato in the first stage direction of *Much Ado About Nothing*, edited out in modern editions). *AB*

Mutius is one of Titus' sons, killed by him, *Titus Andronicus* 1.1.287, as he attempts to stop Titus from pursuing Lavinia. *AB*

'My heart is full of woe', a popular song mentioned by Peter in *Romeo and Juliet* 4.4.131. *JB*

Myrmidons, Achilles' personal guard, are instructed to kill Hector in *Troilus and Cressida* (5.7) and carry out their instructions, 5.9. *AB*

mystery plays. See MIRACLE PLAYS.

myth criticism. See JUNGIAN CRITICISM.

N

Naples, the capital of the former kingdom of Naples and Sicily in Italy, is ruled by Alonso in *The Tempest.* René, Duke of Anjou, has the title of King of Naples in the *Henry VI* plays. *AB*

Naples, King of. See Alonso.

Nash, Anthony (d. 1622) and **John** (d. 1623), brothers, friends of Shakespeare, who left each of them 26*s.* 8*d.* to buy mourning rings. They had witnessed the deed by which Shakespeare bought land from John and William *Combe in 1602. Anthony also witnessed agreements by Shakespeare in 1605 and 1614. John, like Shakespeare, was a lessee of Stratford tithes. Both brothers seem to have been prosperous, especially Anthony. In 1619 John, sued in Star Chamber, was described by the Attorney General as the leader of rioters who threatened to flay the new Puritan vicar, Thomas Wilson, in church, crying out 'hang him, kill him, pull out his throat' and circulating scurrilous verses. Anthony's elder son *Thomas, who inherited property from his father, married Shakespeare's granddaughter Elizabeth *Hall in 1626. *SW*

Nash, Thomas (1593–1647), eldest son of Shakespeare's friend Anthony *Nash. Christened at Stratford on 20 June 1593, he married Shakespeare's granddaughter Elizabeth *Hall in 1626. He had studied law at Lincoln's Inn, but seems not to have practised, perhaps because his father had left him well provided for. For a time Elizabeth and he owned the house next door to *New Place now known as Nash's House. John *Hall left him his 'Study of Bookes' and his manuscripts in 1635; these must have included some books, at least, that had belonged to Shakespeare. He died childless on 4 April 1647, and his gravestone, carved with the combined arms of Nash, Hall, and Shakespeare, lies next to Shakespeare's in the chancel of *Holy Trinity church. *SW*

Nashe, Thomas (1567–*c.*1601), pamphleteer and playwright. Born in East Anglia, he went to Cambridge, and took up writing as a profession after gaining his BA in 1586. His tragedy *Dido Queen of Carthage* (1594), written with his fellow student Christopher *Marlowe, is sometimes dated to their Cambridge years; the speech on the death of Priam performed by the First Player in Shakespeare's *Hamlet* (2.2.452–520) has sometimes been identified as a parody of it. His preface to Robert *Greene's *Menaphon* (1589) alludes to the *ur-*Hamlet.* In the late 1580s he was employed by the Church to write pamphlets against the Puritan satirist Martin Marprelate, and much of his time in the 1590s was devoted to composing a series of excoriating attacks on the scholar Gabriel Harvey, such as *Have with You to Saffron Walden* (1596). His best-known work, *The Unfortunate Traveller* (1595), is a fictional travelogue recording the adventures of an impudent page as he travels through a Europe ravaged by plague and war in the time of Henry VIII. In 1598 Nashe fled back to East Anglia after writing a controversial satirical comedy, *The Isle of Dogs,* with Ben *Jonson and others; there he wrote *Lenten Stuff* (1599). His most popular poem was *The Choice of Valentines,* a pornographic pastiche of the Ovidian narrative poetry popularized by Shakespeare's *Venus and Adonis.* All his writings were publicly burned by order of the Church in 1599. He is remembered now as the most energetically inventive prose stylist of the 16th century. *RM*

Hutson, Lorna, *Thomas Nashe in Context* (1989)

Nathaniel. See Joseph.

Nathaniel, Sir. He is a curate in *Love's Labour's Lost* who plays Alexander the Great (conqueror of Asia in the 4th century BC) in the performance of 'The *Nine Worthies', 5.2. *AB*

nationalism. The centrality of Shakespeare's history plays to the development of English national consciousness, and their commitment to a grand religious vision of national destiny, used to be taken for granted by anglophone literary critics in the era of the British Empire. Certainly Shakespeare's interest in the national past, far greater than that of his rivals *Fletcher and *Jonson, played a significant part in his retrospective promotion as Britain's national poet during the two centuries following his death. As the favourite literary figurehead of an emergent middle-class culture, Shakespeare played a posthumous role, too, in subsequent national movements across Europe, most conspicuously in *Germany.

The question of Shakespeare's relations to nationalism, both in his own time and since, came to new prominence in Shakespeare studies at the end of the 20th century, a development prompted in part by the new pressures on 'Britishness' exerted by the European Union, by multiculturalism, and by the resurgent national movements of *Wales, *Scotland, and *Ireland. It has reflected, too, the increasing prominence of scholars from North America within Shakespeare studies, many of them less enthusiastic about the Tudor nation-state and its imperial successor than were their Anglophile predecessors. Some recent studies of Shakespeare's history plays have stressed (with some disapproval) the unusual extent to which they identify the country with the monarchy, while others have explored Shakespeare's complicity or otherwise with *James I's desire to unite England and Scotland—pointing out, for example, that Shakespeare's two plays set in ancient Britain, *King Lear* and *Cymbeline,* were both written under James (as was *Macbeth,* which concludes by celebrating the Anglicization of Scotland's thanes as earls), while the earlier *Henry V* already seems to adumbrate the invention of a modern

Britain by including Irish, Scots, and Welsh officers in Henry's army. *MD*

Dobson, Michael, *The Making of the National Poet: Shakespeare, Adaptation and Authorship, 1660–1769* (1992)
Helgerson, Richard, *Forms of Nationhood: The Elizabethan Writing of England* (1992)
Kelly, Henry Ansgar, *Divine Providence in the England of Shakespeare's Histories* (1970)
McEachern, Claire, *The Poetics of English Nationhood, 1590–1612* (1996)

National Portrait Gallery, London. Established in 1856 as a repository for portraits of patriotic, historical, and literary importance, the gallery's collection was founded with the acquisition of the *Chandos portrait of Shakespeare in 1856: four more Shakespearian likenesses had been added by 1914. *CT*

National Theatre, Royal. The long political campaign to have in England a state-supported National Theatre comparable to continental institutions was launched with a pamphlet *A Home for Shakespeare* in 1848. By 1907 William Archer and Harley *Granville-Barker had published *A National Theatre: A Scheme with Estimates*, but, although committees met and a site in South Kensington was acquired, nothing had been achieved by the outbreak of the Second World War. The *Old Vic Company in London and the Shakespeare Memorial Theatre in Stratford each contended to become the nucleus of a national theatre. Successive post-war governments dithered, and it was the London County Council's offer of a site on the South Bank of the Thames which finally prompted parliamentary approval. In 1963 the first director Laurence *Olivier assembled an acting company and production team at the borrowed Old Vic theatre, opening with *Hamlet*. By the time the National took possession of the architect Denys Lasdun's complex of three theatres on the South Bank in 1976, Olivier had been succeeded by Peter *Hall, whose opening play was also *Hamlet*. Richard Eyre became director in 1988 and Trevor *Nunn in 1997. All four men and their associates directed notable productions of Shakespeare—under 10% of the repertoire. Whatever the aims of the early campaigners, the NT (Royal since 1988) is not a home for Shakespeare alone. A second national theatre, the *Royal Shakespeare Company, is committed to staging a predominantly Shakespearian repertory at Stratford, in London, and on tour. *MJ*

Callow, Simon, *The National Theatre and its Work. 1963–97* (1997)

Navarre, Ferdinand, King of. With three of his attendants he swears to study and to avoid women for three years, but they are forced to break their vows when the Princess of France and her attendants arrive on an embassy in *Love's Labour's Lost.* *AB*

Neilson, Adelaide (1846–80), English actress who, following a deprived childhood, worked as a Shakespeare-reciting barmaid before putting her natural beauty and intelligence to good effect on the stage, making her London debut as Juliet (1865), a role in which she was acclaimed—as she was as Rosalind, Viola, and Isabella—on both sides of the Atlantic. *RF*

Neilson, Julia (1868–1957), English actress and member by marriage (to Fred) of the *Terry dynasty. As Rosalind and Beatrice (to her husband's Benedick) she relied on her radiant beauty and was not above plagiarizing more accomplished performers, but her Constance (for *Tree, 1899) was unexpectedly impressive. *RF*

Nell. (1) She is the 'kitchen wench' described by Dromio of Syracuse, *Comedy of Errors* 3.2. Her part in 3.1 is usually given to another servant of Adriana's named Luce. **(2)** She is one of the dancers tutored by Gerald the schoolmaster in *The Two Noble Kinsmen.* *AB*

neoclassicism was the guiding intellectual force behind most of the Shakespeare criticism and stage *adaptations in England from the Restoration through the 18th century. Influenced by the celebrated French neoclassical culture of the court of Louis XIV, English neoclassical critics like Thomas *Rymer emphasized the 'rules' of tragedy as defined in Aristotle's *Poetics* and criticized Shakespeare for violations of unity, diction, verisimilitude, and morality. Rymer's contemporary John *Dryden modified this approach, agreeing that Shakespeare was 'irregular' in many ways but defending his plays as works of natural genius. By the end of the neoclassical era, Samuel *Johnson expressed what had become an English consensus, that the strictly defined neoclassical rules did not apply to a Shakespeare who had become the English national poet. *HG*

Nerissa, Portia's waiting-gentlewoman, marries Graziano in *The Merchant of Venice.* *AB*

Nerval, Gérard de (1808–55), French essayist and critic. The long-running series of dramatic articles which Nerval published in major literary reviews constitute one of the 19th century's most authoritative accounts of canonical English plays adapted for the French stage: they include an incisive critical assessment of the reception of Shakespeare's major works presented in the original text by an English troupe of actors in 1822, 1827, and 1845. Nerval's account of responses to the three English visits reveals the extent to which the French public's appreciation of Shakespeare was dictated by oscillating cultural and political trends under the July Monarchy. Shakespearian drama had been recuperated by the French Romantics as an immensely popular form of entertainment, but this vogue was affected by vacillating periods of Anglophobia (1822) and of Anglomania (1827), and finally tailed off into a period of relative apathy in the 1840s. *AC*

Juden, B., and Richer, J., (eds.), *Le Journal de Macready, La Revue des lettres modernes*: 'Macready et *Hamlet* à Paris', 9 (1962–3)
Nerval, Gérard de, 'Les Acteurs anglais' (1844), in *Œuvres complètes*, ed. J. Guillaume and C. Pichois (1989)

Nestor is one of the Greek commanders in *Troilus and Cressida*. In *Homer's *Iliad* he is a wise old counsellor. *AB*

Netherlands, the. See Low Countries.

Neville, Anne. See Anne, Lady.

Neville, Cicely. See York, Duchess of.

Neville, George. See Abergavenny, Lord.

Neville, John (b. 1925). A Londoner of striking good looks, he played several seasons at the *Old Vic, progressing from Shakespeare's young lovers to encompass Aguecheek, Henry V, Richard II, Hamlet, and (in alternation with Richard *Burton) both Iago and Othello. He was a highly successful director of the Nottingham playhouse, 1963–8, where his own parts included Coriolanus, Angelo, and Iago to the Othello of the film star Robert Ryan. Having played at the Festival Theatre, Stratford, Ontario, he settled in *Canada, running theatres in Edmonton, Alberta, and Halifax, Nova Scotia, only occasionally acting in Britain. *MJ*

Neville, Ralph. See Westmorland, Earl of.

Neville, Richard. See Salisbury, Earl of.

New Cambridge Shakespeare. See Cambridge Shakespeare, New.

Newcastle, Margaret Cavendish, Duchess of (*c.*1625–1673), author of poetry, plays, a biography of her husband, autobiography, and, in Letter CXXIII of her *Sociable Letters* (1664), the first published criticism of Shakespeare. Written to a possibly fictional female correspondent, the piece defends Shakespeare from *neoclassical attacks, ascribing them to envy and malice. She argues for his superior imaginative power in creating convincing representations of a range of characters: 'It expresses and declares a greater wit, to express, and deliver to posterity, the extravagancies of madness, the subtlety of knaves, the ignorance of clowns ... than to express regularities ... for 'tis harder to express nonsense than sense.' Cavendish writes about Shakespeare as a literary artist but has a strong awareness of performance and, while drawing attention specifically to some female characters, is alluding to a range of roles when she asserts, 'he presents passions so naturally, and misfortunes so probably, as he pierces the souls of his readers with such a true sense and feeling thereof, that it forces tears through their eyes, and almost persuades them, they are really actors, or at least present at those tragedies'. Cavendish's final defence is to suggest that it is further evidence of Shakespeare's wide-ranging 'wit' and 'eloquence' that he 'wanted subjects . . . to work on, for which he was forced to take some of his plots out of history'. *CMSA*

New Criticism, the dominant form of academic literary criticism in the USA and UK between about 1940 and 1970, characterized by close readings of decontextualized literary texts and an aesthetics of complex meaning, irony, and unity under tension. The term is most properly applied to the American variant developed at Vanderbilt University by John Crowe Ransome, Cleanth Brooks, Alan Tate, Robert Penn Warren, and others, but these critics had in turn been influenced by ideas of T. S. *Eliot and the 'practical criticism' developed at Cambridge by I. A. Richards and William *Empson. Their ideas and methods closely parallel the independently developed criticism of F. R. *Leavis and his followers in the UK, now often also called New Critical in consequence. New Criticism in this broad sense spread throughout academia after about 1955 and waned markedly after 1970. Shakespeare was a major figure for New Criticism from the beginning, for example, in the famous essay on an image in *Macbeth* by Cleanth Brooks in his *The Well-Wrought Urn* (1947). New Criticism was most at home with lyric poetry, and tended to treat the plays too as lyrics, in which its exponents characteristically found a tension-filled unity of complex signification. *HG*

new historicism, a term coined by the American critic Stephen Greenblatt to describe his own and related approaches to the study of literature (superseding Greenblatt's earlier coinage, 'cultural poetics'). It emphasizes contextualizing a work of literature within its larger milieu, and studying both the meaning and the function of the work as an element in a larger matrix of social power. Most characteristically, new historicists like to take an apparently unrelated minor text or historical anecdote from the Elizabethan period and prove that it exemplifies the same dominant ideologies they find informing Shakespeare's texts.

In its most characteristic forms in Shakespeare studies, the new historicism has drawn on elements of *Marxism, the social theory of Michel Foucault, the anthropological theory and methods of Clifford Geertz, and a wide array of contemporary social theorists. It has taken as a particular polemical opponent previous 'aestheticist' approaches to literature epitomized for new historicists by *New Critics and Northrop *Frye.

Perhaps the earliest identifiable new historical work was Stephen Orgel's *The Illusion of Power: Political Theater in the English Renaissance* (1975), but its coming to the forefront of Renaissance studies was marked by the publication of Stephen Greenblatt's *Renaissance Self-Fashioning: From More to Shakespeare* (1980). Other prominent new historicists in Shakespeare and early modern studies include Jonathan Goldberg, Catherine Gallagher, Louis Montrose, Leah Marcus, and Leonard Tennenhouse. The new historicism has clear intellectual affiliations with British *cultural materialism, but a number of different emphases and practices: rather than emphasizing the possibility of dissent, it has characteristically argued that any instances of apparently 'subversive' ideas in Shakespeare are always already contained, serving only to prove the dominance and necessity of the status quo. *HG*

Veeser, H. A. (ed.), *The New Historicism* (1989)

Newington Butts theatre. See THEATRES, ELIZABETHAN AND JACOBEAN.

New Place was the name of the house once standing on the corner of Chapel Street and Chapel Lane, Stratford-upon-Avon, which Shakespeare purchased in 1597. It was built towards the end of the 15th century by Hugh Clopton, the younger son of a local squire, who had made a business fortune in London, serving as lord mayor in 1492. John Leland, on his visit to Stratford-upon-Avon around 1540, described it as a 'praty howse of brike and tymbar'. Referred to in Clopton's will as his 'Great House', and later as 'New Place', it was reputedly the second largest house in the town (the largest being the College in Old Town, which, until the Reformation, had housed the priests who served the parish church). In 1576 it was bought from the Cloptons by William Underhill, who sold it, in May 1597, to William Shakespeare. We do not know exactly how much he paid, but a figure of around £120 has been suggested. At a time when a house could change hands for as little as £25, Shakespeare's outlay is strong evidence of his financial success as an actor and playwright in London. This became the family home, where Shakespeare lived when not in London, where he made his will in January 1616, and where he died in April of the same year.

The house descended in Shakespeare's family until the death of John Barnard, the second husband of Shakespeare's granddaughter Elizabeth, in 1674. It was then sold to Sir Edward Walker, who left it to his daughter, the wife of John Clopton. In this way it passed back into the ownership of the family that had built it. Around 1700, John Clopton radically altered, if not rebuilt, the house, as a wedding present for his second son Hugh. To Hugh can be attributed the story, recorded in 1733, that Queen *Henrietta Maria lodged at New Place in 1643, and there is other evidence from this period that the house had never lost its Shakespearian associations. Following Hugh Clopton's death, his trustees, in 1756, sold New Place to the Revd Francis Gastrell, who, three years later, demolished it: this reputedly arose out of irritation caused by increasing numbers of literary pilgrims wishing to view the property, although there is also evidence of a more mundane dispute between Gastrell and the Stratford Corporation over other matters.

The property as reconstructed in 1700 is recorded in a number of drawings but there also survives a drawing and plan by George Vertue, from memory, and recollections of Richard Grimmitt, recorded in 1767, on which to base a reconstruction of the house as it was in Shakespeare's day. A five-bay timbered building fronted the street through which the visitor entered a courtyard, with the house proper on the far side. In the centre of the courtyard was a well, a feature which survives today. Some foundations and cellars have also been exposed to view although there is uncertainty on the question of whether they belong to the original house or the reconstructed residence of 1700.

With this property went a substantial amount of land comprising not only ground immediately to the rear of the house but, by Shakespeare's time, a large garden area reaching further down Chapel Lane in one direction and across the backs of neighbouring Chapel Street properties in the other. In subsequent years, some of this land was built over whilst other parts became detached from New Place proper. However, in the early 1860s J. O. Halliwell led a fund-raising campaign to bring the premises back under a single ownership in order to preserve them as a memorial to Shakespeare. This was achieved by 1876 and the property vested in the *Shakespeare Birthplace Trust in 1891. Soon after the First World War, and under the direction of Sir Ernest Law, the gardens were redesigned in a style which would have been familiar to Shakespeare: a geometric Knot-Garden, immediately to the rear of the site of New Place, and the Great Garden beyond with its long border.

Today the site of New Place and the Knot-Garden is reached through the neighbouring property to the north. This is known as Nash's House, after Thomas *Nash, the first husband of Shakespeare's granddaughter Elizabeth, who owned it. *RB*

Bearman, Robert, *Shakespeare in the Stratford Records* (1994)

George Vertue's 1737 sketch of New Place, Shakespeare's family home in Stratford for the last 20 years of his life, provides the best surviving evidence of how the second-largest house in Stratford looked before it was first redeveloped (1700) and then demolished (1759).

This Something by memory and ye description of **Shakespears House** which was in Stratford on Avon. where he livd and dyed. and his wife after him 1623.

This the outward appearance towards the Street. the gate and entrance, (at the Corner of chappel lane / the chappel. X. founded by Sr. Hu. Clopton. who built it and the Bridge over Avon.

besides this front or outward gate there was before the House it self (that Shakespeer livd in.) within a little court yard. grass growing there — before the real dwelling house. this outside being only a long gallery &c and for servants.

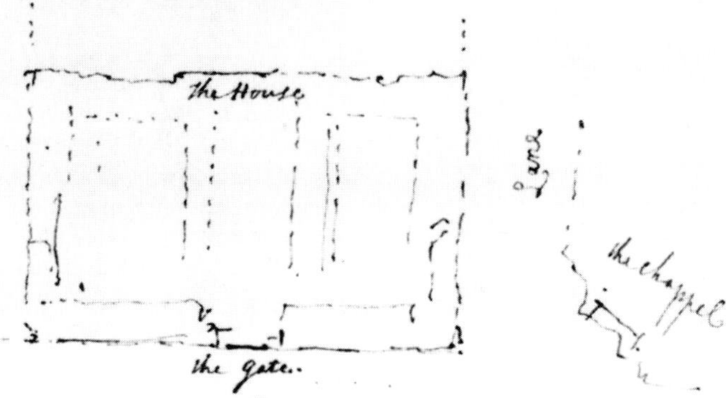

This House of **Shakespears** was pulld down about 40 years ago and then was built a handsome brick house. by. and now in posession of the Cloptons.

Halliwell, J. O., *An Historical Account of New Place, Stratford-upon-Avon* (1864)
Pringle, Roger, 'The Rise of Stratford as Shakespeare's Town', in Robert Bearman (ed.), *The History of an English Borough: Stratford-upon-Avon 1196–1996* (1977)
Tennant, Philip, *The Civil War in Stratford-upon-Avon* (1996)

New Shakespeare (Cambridge, 1921–66). The critical introductions to the earlier volumes in this important edition of the works, written by 'Q' (Sir Arthur *Quiller-Couch), are in belletristic style and largely forgotten, but the textual work of John Dover *Wilson proved enormously influential. By 1947, when his notable edition of *Macbeth* appeared, he had taken complete charge of the series, and wrote his own challenging critical accounts of the plays. Later on he collaborated with G. I. Duthie, J. C. Maxwell, Alice Walker, and Peter Ure. But Dover Wilson's is the name associated with the overall plan of a series that was the first to bring A. W. Pollard's recognition of the authority of the quartos (1916–17) and Sir Edmund Maunde Thompson's discovery of Shakespeare's hand in **Sir Thomas More* (1916) to bear on the editing of Shakespeare. Dover Wilson's full discussions of the copy for the texts became required reading after *The Tempest* appeared in 1921, a volume that included a facsimile of a passage from the manuscript of *Sir Thomas More.* Dover Wilson's fondness for inventing elaborate stage settings and directions (e.g. 'on one side the land slopes gently down to the shore', *The Tempest* 3.2; 'he leads them down to the sea', *Antony and Cleopatra* 2.6) had become something of a joke by the time the series was completed, but much of his lively writing, critical and textual, bears rereading.
RAF

New Shakespeare Society, founded in 1873 by F. J. *Furnivall who defined its purpose as getting the plays 'as nearly as possible in the order' in which they were written so as to study 'the progress and meaning of Shakespeare's mind'. The society, which was disbanded in 1894, held lectures and published primary materials. *RF*

New Temple Shakespeare (Dent, 1934–6). This handsomely printed pocket edition of the individual works, with wood cuts by Eric Gill, was edited by M. R. Ridley. Each volume has a brief introduction, plain text on the page, and sketchy notes and glosses at the end. It was innovatory in three respects: first, in relegating act and scene divisions to the top margin in order to maintain the flow of the action; second, in returning to a lighter punctuation, in accordance with early printed texts; and third, where *quarto and *Folio texts exist for the same play, in using brackets to enclose passages found only in one or the other, and not in both. Ridley's edition bears no relation, except in name, to the first Temple Shakespeare edited by Israel Gollancz over a period of years from 1894. *RAF*

New Variorum Shakespeare (1871, in progress). Horace Howard *Furness, a Philadelphia lawyer, joined the Shakespeare Society of the city in 1860, and became involved in their serious study of the plays. In 1866 they began to study the texts of *Romeo and Juliet*, and this led to Furness's idea of replacing the so-called Variorum edition of 1821 with a new Variorum edition, beginning with this play. At first he thought of basing his work on the text and notes of the *Cambridge Shakespeare (1863–6), which led to a quarrel with W. Aldis Wright, one of the editors of this edition; but the quarrel was soon resolved when Furness dropped his initial idea, and instead adopted the reading preferred by a majority of the best editors. Also, the New Variorum *Romeo and Juliet*, published by J. B. Lippincott in Philadelphia in 1871, not only gives readings of old editions, but notes 'the adoption or rejection of them by the various editors' (preface, p. vii). This volume soon established an international reputation for Furness, as well as numerous offers of help and emendations for his future work. *Macbeth* appeared in 1873, a huge two-volume *Hamlet* in 1877, and *King Lear* in 1880. By 1912, when Furness died, editions of thirteen plays had appeared, and another, *Cymbeline*, was in the press. Furness's son, Horace Howard, Jr., worked on a further five plays. After his death in 1930, Matthias Shaaber and Matthew W. Black continued to work on *Richard II* and *2 Henry IV*, but it was not until after the Modern Language Association of America took charge of the project that these plays and four other volumes were brought out between 1936 and 1955. Lack of funding then halted the project until 1973, and further volumes began to appear in 1977, now published by the Association. The New Variorum has established itself as a basic resource for research on Shakespeare's works.
RAF

New York Shakespeare Festival, theatre company founded by Joseph Papp in 1954. Though housed in the Public Theatre in the East Village, the centre of Shakespeare operations remains the Delacourt theatre in Central Park, an open-air stage built in 1957 where the Festival offers free performances in the summer. A large number of multicultural American actors and directors have worked there, and non-Shakespearian activities have made the company one of the chief producing organizations in New York. Since 1993 the artistic director has been George C. Wolfe. *DK*

New York Shakespeare Society, founded in 1885 by Appleton Morgan and others. It published *Shakespeariana* (1889–93), the first American journal devoted exclusively to Shakespeare, *New Shakespeareana* (1902–11), the Bankside Shakespeare edition (1888–1906), and the Bankside Restoration Shakespeare (1907–). The society, refounded in 1982, now meets as a Columbia University Seminar.
SLB

New Zealand. Shakespeare has been a presence in New Zealand culture since 1769, when a copy of his works sailed on the famous voyage of the bark *Endeavour* during which Captain James Cook claimed New Zealand as British territory. Waves of later migrants then brought with them Victorian double-column small-type Shakespeares. Throughout the 19th century, travelling players performed Shakespeare in the Theatres Royal of the scattered settlements of the colony; and in more informal surroundings, such as the 1846 *Macbeth* H. F. McKillop saw when, to the 'uproarious . . . laughter of the crowd', Macbeth enlivened 'some long soliloquy' by singing and dancing the sailor's hornpipe. Itinerant Shakespeare continued until the 1920s, when Alan Wilkie's company toured Shakespeare throughout New Zealand. The cinema curtailed such tours, which were followed by the sophisticated amateur productions staged by the writer Ngaio Marsh. Her finely honed Shakespeares entertained New Zealanders from 1942 to 1972. From the 1960s local repertory companies, from Dunedin's Globe to Auckland's Theatre Corporate, regularly performed Shakespeare. Their efforts were supplemented by tours of the *RSC (1997) and the *National Theatre (1998) (both recalling the celebrated visit of the *Old Vic Company, with Laurence *Olivier, in the 1940s). By the 1990s also, outdoor summer Shakespeares were enthusiastically received throughout the country.

The Shakespeare market was fuelled by the compulsory reading of his works in secondary schools and universities. This began in the 1870s with the introduction of state education and the founding of university colleges. By the year 2000 school leavers were still required to study Shakespeare; and his texts were a prevalent if no longer an absolute requirement of university training in literature. Students were well served by their instructors. John MacMillan Brown, professor at Canterbury College, was a renowned lecturer and prolific writer on Shakespearian topics. His writings and those of his contemporaries are listed in Percy Marks's pioneering *Australasian Shakespeareana: A Bibliography of Books, Pamphlets, Magazine Articles . . . Printed in Australia and New Zealand, Dealing with Shakespeare and his Works* (1915). After the Second World War, increased professionalization and access to microfilm, facsimiles, and rare book collections made possible more serious contributions to scholarship. New Zealand scholars were acclaimed for work in bibliography (D. F. McKenzie), attribution (MacD. P. Jackson), and literary/cultural studies (Michael Neill).

New Zealand writers return frequently to Shakespeare. Katherine Mansfield (the nation's most famous expatriate writer) read Shakespeare obsessively; a pattern repeated in the autobiography and fictions of Janet Frame, New Zealand's greatest living writer. M. K. Joseph's satirical campus fiction *A Pound of Saffron* (1962) invents a Machiavellian drama lecturer who stages a scandalously multiracial *Antony and Cleopatra.* Ngaio Marsh's detective novels often use Shakespearian motifs and clues. Her last novel *Light Thickens* (1982) features a lavish, neo-medieval production of *Macbeth.* Later writers have been more playfully postcolonial. Mike Johnson's surrealist *Lear: The Shakespeare Company Performs Lear at Babylon* (1986) imagines the play as performed in a plague-ridden future. *Pouliuli* (1977) by the Samoan New Zealand writer Albert Wendt rewrites *King Lear* as the crisis of a Samoan elder. Jean Betts's plays *Revenge of the Amazons* (1983) and *Ophelia Thinks Harder* (1994) burlesque *A Midsummer Night's Dream* and *Hamlet.* Pacific Underground's *Romeo & Tusi* delighted crowds in the late 1990s, weaving a production of Shakespeare's play into a fable of Samoan/Maori conflict: Shakespeare's lines emerge as healing and energizing. Many New Zealanders still engage in orthodox *bardolatry, crafting tapestries as New Zealand's gift to the reconstructed *Globe in London, and flocking to annual Shakespeare in Schools contests, where a 'speech straight' is the 'taste of . . . quality' (*Hamlet* 2.2.433–4). Marked by such contradictions, Shakespeare in New Zealand remains in a state of productive flux. *MH*

Frame, Janet, *To the Is-land: An Autobiography* (1983)
Houlahan, Mark, 'Shakespeare in New Zealand', in Roger Robinson and Nelson Wattie (eds.), *The Oxford Companion to New Zealand Literature in English* (1998)
Marsh, Ngaio, *Black Beech and Honeydew: An Autobiography* (1966)
Neill, Michael, 'Post-colonial Shakespeare? Writing away from the Centre', in Ania Loomba and Martin Orkin (eds.), *Post-colonial Shakespeares* (1998)

Nicanor. See ADRIAN.

Nicholas. See JOSEPH.

Nicolai, Otto (1810–49), German composer. His popular opera *Die lustigen Weiber von Windsor*, based on *The Merry Wives of Windsor* and first staged in Berlin in 1849, has remained in the repertory due to its charming melodies and carefully crafted comic situations. With a libretto by Hermann Mosenthal it also includes material from *Twelfth Night*, *2 Henry IV*, and *A Midsummer Night's Dream.* *IBC*

Nicoll, Allardyce (1894–1976), Scottish theatre historian, author of *British Drama* (1925); *The Development of the Theatre* (1927); *History of English Drama 1660–1900* (6 vols., 1952–9); *World Drama from Aeschylus to Anouilh* (1949); *Shakespeare* (1952); and *The Theatre and Dramatic Theory* (1962). He was the first editor (1948–66) of **Shakespeare Survey* and the founder and first director of the *Shakespeare Institute, for research and postgraduate study, in Stratford (1951–61). His work as a theatre historian has sometimes been underestimated as the product of an encyclopedic card index, but this completely misses the intellectual acuity and stylistic precision of his critical writing. *TM*

Nim. In *The Merry Wives of Windsor* Falstaff becomes angry with Nim and Pistol because they will not deliver his letters to Mistress Ford and Mistress Page, 1.3. Their revenge is to tell the women's husbands, 2.1. In *Henry V*, Nim quarrels with Pistol over Mistress Quickly, 2.1. He is hanged with Bardolph for looting, 4.4. Spelled 'Nym' in Folio editions, 'Nim' in the first quarto, his name was slang for 'to steal': his favourite word is 'humour', and the cast list of *2 Henry IV* aptly classifies him as an 'irregular humorist'. *AB*

Ninagawa, Yukio (b. 1935), Japanese director. Originally an actor, Ninagawa made his directorial debut in 1967 and quickly established himself as one of the leading figures of artistically and politically radical 'underground theatre'. In 1974 he directed *Romeo and Juliet* for a commercial company in Tokyo with a Kabuki actor playing Romeo, and since then has directed many other Shakespeare plays. His productions are usually dominated by visually impressive scenery with strong Oriental flavour such as a huge Buddhist altar (*Macbeth*, 1980), a Noh stage (*The Tempest*, 1987), and a rock garden (*A Midsummer Night's Dream*, 1994). Actors often wear traditional Japanese costume, and frequently acting techniques of Noh and Kabuki are assimilated. Most of these productions were successfully presented outside Japan and earned the director an international reputation. Ninagawa directed *Peer Gynt* (1994) with an English-speaking cast and *King Lear* (1999) for the *Royal Shakespeare Company. Later he was based at the Saitama Arts Theatre in Japan, where he hoped to mount all of Shakespeare's plays. *TK*

nineteenth-century Shakespearian production. During the first decade of the 19th century, *Drury Lane and *Covent Garden, which, as holders of the patents granted by King Charles II in 1660, enjoyed a monopoly on legitimate drama in London, were burnt down. When rebuilt both theatres held in excess of 3,000. The consequences were an increasing emphasis on the visual and the spectacular and a reliance on powerful vocal delivery and emphatic gesture from the actors.

Covent Garden was presided over by the dignified John Philip *Kemble, who with his sister Sarah *Siddons and younger brother Charles formed the theatre's 'first family'. As an actor Kemble was deliberate in delivery and statuesque in stance, lacking his sister's emotional force; as a manager he made far-reaching initiatives. He extended the Shakespearian repertoire, reintroducing long-neglected pieces to the extent that his collected edition of 1815 comprised 26 plays; he began to discard the accretions of adaptors such as *Dryden, returning to original Shakespeare, albeit cut and rearranged; with the architect and antiquarian William Capon he produced historically accurate sets (a Gothic *Macbeth*, 1794, an Anglo-Norman *Hamlet*, 1812) and costumes; he marshalled hitherto undreamt of numbers of extras (240 for *Coriolanus*, 1806); and in the year (1817) he retired, gas-lighting was installed at Covent Garden. The family tradition was upheld by Charles Kemble whose revival of *King John* in 1823 was supervised by J. R. *Planché, an expert in costume and heraldry. Thus the playbill cited sources (in Worcester cathedral and elsewhere) for the costumes.

In 1832 Charles Kemble was a leading witness before the Select Committee appointed to inquire into the laws affecting dramatic literature. Throughout his lengthy testimony Kemble staunchly defended the monopoly, claiming that only large theatres with experienced companies could adequately represent 'such plays as *Coriolanus* or *Julius Caesar*', though he conceded that '*Hamlet* may be done in a small theatre'. The monopoly was abolished in 1843, but in the interim William Charles *Macready, as manager of Covent Garden (1837–9) and Drury Lane (1841–3), showed what the resources of the patent houses properly managed could achieve in the production of Shakespeare's plays. He set the standard with *King Lear* at Covent Garden (25 January 1839): discarding *Tate, restoring the Fool, rehearsing the whole cast—processions, marches, groups—thoroughly, setting every scene from castle to druid circle appropriately, and summoning the 'dreadful pother' with unprecedented verisimilitude. Refusing to exploit *Lear*'s success with a long run, Macready applied his high standards to further Shakespeare revivals at Covent Garden (*Henry V* 'with pictorial illustrations from the pencil of Mr [Clarkson] Stanfield') and at Drury Lane (*King John*, 'an animated picture of those Gothic times').

Madame *Vestris, who had succeeded Macready at Covent Garden, also applied the principles of careful preparation and antiquarianism to her revivals of *Love's Labour's Lost* (1839) and *A Midsummer Night's Dream* (1840), both with J. R. Planché, who went on to contribute his historical expertise to *The Taming of the Shrew*, which Ben Webster staged in the Elizabethan style at the Haymarket in 1844. By then the monopoly was abolished and any theatre could stage Shakespeare. That 'minor' theatres (such as the Surrey) had long included Shakespeare in their bills, evading the law by interspersing songs, was indicative of the popular appeal of the plays to the expanding artisan population of London. In these theatres the plays were presented and appreciated as rattling good stories with thrilling theatrical moments which brought the occupants of the pit and the gallery to the edge of their benches. Their enjoyment was now legitimized and the Britannia, for example, indulged in such novelties as having each act performed by a different Hamlet. It was a rather more refined populist urge which Samuel *Phelps brought to Islington in 1843, where at Sadler's Wells theatre he offered 'an entertainment selected from the first stock drama . . . at a price fairly within the habitual means of all'. During his eighteen years' tenure of Sadler's Wells Phelps staged 32 of Shakespeare's plays, including such rarities as *Timon of Athens* and *Pericles*, in productions characterized by relatively authentic texts, specially prepared, though not pedantically 'accurate', scenery and costumes, and thoroughly rehearsed ensemble acting.

The suggestion that the abolition of the patent theatres' monopoly should be accompanied by the establishment of a *National Theatre with Shakespeare's plays as its centrepiece fell on deaf ears, but in 1848 Queen Victoria instituted the 'Windsor Theatricals', in emulation of European court theatres, appointing Charles *Kean as director. Thither Kean marshalled his profession for performances of which Shakespeare's plays formed a significant part. With his personal status enhanced, Kean set up in management at the Princess's theatre, where through the 1850s he staged his spectacular Shakespearian revivals, 'realising', as he wrote in the playbill for *King Richard II* in 1857, 'the scenes and actions which he [Shakespeare] describes . . . exhibiting men as they once lived'. To this end the plays were ruthlessly cut and rearranged, but Kean's productions with their historically accurate costumes, armour, furniture, and sets—in which the 'join' between the two and three dimensional was scarcely perceptible—succeeded in attracting a new educated audience to his theatre. When the *Shakespeare tercentenary of 1864 was celebrated Phelps had left Sadler's Wells and Charles Kean was in *Australia, whither English actors, for whom America had long been a visiting or permanent destination, were venturing primarily in search of personal fortune, but in so doing laying the foundations for a substantially British—Shakespearian—repertoire in these new English-speaking lands.

In England during the 1860s and 1870s it was in Manchester that the traditions of Shakespearian staging were most effectively upheld. There at the Prince's theatre, between 1864 and 1874, Charles *Calvert mounted eleven Shakespeare revivals. Although Calvert proclaimed his admiration for Phelps, who appeared in two of the revivals, his greater debt was to Charles Kean, whose influence was apparent in the choice of plays, the acting editions, the practice of interpolating 'episodes' such as Henry V's return to London, the attention to historical accuracy and the deployment of the muses of music, painting, movement, and history to create as complete an illusion of reality as possible. The contribution of the scenic artists was particularly important (and noticeable) and Calvert's team, which included the Grieves, the Telbins, George Gordon, Walter Hann, and Hawes Craven, formed a link between Kean and *Irving. With *Henry V*, first seen in Manchester in 1872, Calvert's influence spread all over America (starting in New York in 1875, with George Rignold in the lead) and Australia. Indeed when Richard Mansfield staged *Henry V* at the Garden theatre, New York, in 1900, with the purpose of showing that the American theatre could hold its own with Europe's, he followed the detail of Calvert's scene order and business.

Amongst Calvert's Manchester company was a young actor serving a lengthy provincial apprenticeship, who in 1878 opened his own management at the *Lyceum theatre, London, with *Hamlet*, appearing in the title role as he had done fourteen years earlier with Calvert. Henry Irving's idiosyncrasies of speech and physique made him an unconventional Shakespearian actor; nevertheless, according to Edward Gordon Craig, 'Irving thought only as an actor'. Thus, although he engaged distinguished academicians (Burne-Jones, Ford Madox Ford) to design scenery and employed a talented team of scene-painters (Craven, Telbin, Harker), the ultimate criterion was not historical authenticity but theatrical effectiveness. Accordingly for Cardinal Wolsey he discarded the robe of authentic red (from Rome) in favour of one of a rosy dye produced in England. Although his 1879 production of *The Merchant of Venice* was prompted by a visit to the Levant, the most striking feature of the design for the trial scene is the sheer distance contrived (through the use of diagonals) for Irving's exit as Shylock. The escalating costs of these Shakespearian productions could not be recouped at the Lyceum, but though finance was a factor in his eight North American tours, Irving also saw himself as an ambassador (if not missionary) introducing American audiences to Shakespeare and setting standards for the profession there to follow.

It was early (1881) in Irving's reign at the Lyceum that the Duke of Saxe-Meiningen's company made its influential visit to London. Their meticulously rehearsed and historically accurate productions were much admired—the forum scene in *Julius Caesar* being particularly celebrated—but theirs was essentially the method of Charles Kean, carried forward with the advantage of generous state subsidy, a luxury which no British theatre enjoyed. Herbert Beerbohm *Tree, the actor-manager widely regarded as Irving's heir, was proud of the fact that his Shakespearian revivals (from 1897 at Her/His Majesty's) were sustained by 'public opinion as revealed by the coin of the realm'. He was equally unrepentant about his use of all 'the arts and sciences' to achieve such successes as *Julius Caesar* (1898), seen by 240,000 people in London alone, the forum scene of which with designs by Alma-Tadema could stand comparison with the Saxe-Meiningen company's down to the individualized actions of each member of the crowd.

Another actor-manager who acknowledged the influence of the Saxe-Meiningen company, but whose resources were far more modest than Tree's, was Frank *Benson, who, after a short engagement with Irving, took over a touring Shakespearian company in 1883 and made it his life's work to take Shakespeare to audiences all over Britain and beyond. In the *Cornhill Magazine* for May 1900 the eminent Shakespeare scholar Sidney *Lee summarized Benson's creed: that Shakespeare's plays should be acted constantly and in their variety; regular changes in the programme with no play enjoying a disproportionately long run; every part should be played by an actor trained to speak blank verse; no play should be adapted for the sake of one part; scenery should be simple and subordinate to the dramatic interest.

For the first half of 1884 Benson's stage-manager was William *Poel, latterly manager of the Royal Victoria Hall (the *Old Vic) for Emma Cons, whose niece, Lilian *Baylis, was to turn to Shakespeare in despair. In 1877 Poel had founded the Elizabethans, a company of 'professional ladies and gentlemen' dedicated to creating 'a more general taste' for Shakespeare; in 1881 he staged the 'bad' quarto of *Hamlet* on a bare platform in St George's Hall, London, with himself in the title role. In 1893 Poel produced *Measure for Measure* on what was intended as a reconstruction of the Fortune theatre which was placed (inauthentically) within the proscenium arch at the Royalty theatre. The following year Poel established the Elizabethan Stage Society which, until 1905, staged plays by Shakespeare and his contemporaries in the Elizabethan manner. Eccentric and erroneous as much of Poel's work now appears, it provided a vital corrective to the prevailing pictorialism of 19th-century Shakespearian production and influenced *Granville-Barker's seminal productions of *The Winter's Tale* and *Twelfth Night* (both 1912) and *A Midsummer Night's Dream* (1914). Nevertheless the dominant style of Shakespearian production at the end of the 19th century was that prefigured at the beginning by J. P. Kemble: visually spectacular, usually historically accurate sets and costumes; the authentic Shakespearian text, albeit cut and rearranged; and an essentially pictorial style of acting.

Styles and trends in Shakespearian production were increasingly international as improved travel facilitated the movement of actors, often complete with their own company and sets. From America Edwin *Booth, Mary *Anderson, Augustin *Daly, and Richard Mansfield took on the challenge of staging Shakespeare on a scale equalling or excelling their British rivals.

In his article on 'Shakespeare and Stage Costume' (*Nineteenth Century*, May 1885) Oscar *Wilde wrote: 'In fact, everywhere that Shakespeare turned in London he saw the apparel and appurtenances of past ages, and it is impossible to doubt that he made use of his opportunities.' The passage of time meant that only a portion of the apparel and appurtenances which Wilde found it impossible to doubt that Shakespeare had used in his plays had survived, but that did not deter producers from using every means—antiquarian and artistic—to realize them for the adornment of Shakespeare's plays and the entertainment and erudition of their audiences.

RF

Foulkes, Richard (ed.), *Shakespeare and the Victorian Stage* (1986)
Odell, George C. D., *Shakespeare from Betterton to Irving* (2 vols., 1920)

'Nine Worthies'. The figures appearing in the pageant performed for the King of Navarre and his guests in *Love's Labour's Lost* 5.2. *AB*

No Bed for Bacon (1941, repr. 1999), a comic historical novel, by Caryl Brahms (Doris Caroline Abrahams) and S. J. Simon (Seca Jascha Skidelsky), in which Shakespeare pursues his dramatic art and Francis Bacon a 'second-best bed'. Its vivid but tongue-in-cheek depiction of Elizabethan life, and its plot in which a stage-struck Lady Viola moonlights in drag as a boy actor with Shakespeare's company, thereby inspiring *Twelfth Night*, clearly lie behind the film *Shakespeare in Love* (1998, co-scripted by Tom *Stoppard), which uses this novel as shamelessly as Shakespeare used *Cinthio or *Holinshed. *TM*

Noble, Adrian (b. 1950), English director. Serving as associate director for the Bristol Old Vic theatre from 1976 to 1979, Noble gained recognition for daring, innovative interpretations of *Titus Andronicus* (1978) and *Timon of Athens* (1979). He joined the *Royal Shakespeare Company as a resident director in 1980, becoming an associate director in 1982 and artistic director in 1991. Noble is noted for his faith in well-spoken poetic language as the cornerstone of a good Shakespearian production as well as for his love of spectacular staging. Both his *King Lear* productions (1982, 1993) were highly acclaimed. His productions can be poignant without being heavy-handed; for example, he directed *Henry V* in 1984—just two years after the Falklands conflict—with the young Kenneth *Branagh in the title role, 'to try to understand the attraction of war as well as its horror'. His playful *A Midsummer Night's Dream* (1994, subsequently made into a film under Noble's direction), which echoed elements of *Brook's production, included the muscular Barry Lynch as an unconventionally large and sexualized Puck. *BR*

noise, collective noun for a group of instruments, e.g. 'a noise of fiddles', or of instrumentalists, like the band summoned to play at Mistress Quickly's tavern: 'see if thou canst find out Sneak's noise. Mistress Tearsheet would fain hear some music', *2 Henry IV* 2.4.11–12.

JB

Nokes, James (d. 1696), actor, whose comic playing was admired and copied by Colley *Cibber. He took women's roles at the Restoration and was dubbed 'Nurse Nokes' for his performance as the Nurse in Otway's version of *Romeo and Juliet*, *The History and Fall of *Caius Marius*. Other roles included Polonius and he may have played the Fool to *Betterton's Lear.

CMSA

'No more dams I'll make for fish', sung by Caliban, drunk, in *The Tempest* 2.2.179. The original tune is unknown. *JB*

Norfolk, Duke of. **(1)** In *Richard Duke of York* (*3 Henry VI*) he appears, 1.1 and 2.2, as a supporter of York. **(2)** Father of Surrey, he is put in command at *Bosworth in *Richard III*. **(3)** *All Is True* (*Henry VIII*). See Surrey, Earl of.

AB

Normandy, in the north of France, was temporarily occupied by Edward III and conquered by Henry V in 1419. In *The First Part of the Contention* (*2 Henry VI*), Cade executes Lord Saye for 'giving up' Normandy (4.7.25), which was indeed reclaimed by the French in 1450.

AB

North, Sir Thomas. See Plutarch.

Northcote, James (1746–1831), English painter, who turned to history painting after finding himself unable to create a lucrative portrait practice. His collaboration with John *Boydell, proprietor of the *Shakespeare Gallery, proved long and fruitful, since he shared Boydell's ambitions for its commercial success. Northcote's subjects were largely drawn from the English history plays and often employed old master precedents, such as his supplement to *Richard III*, *Burial of the Royal Children*, which draws from 17th-century religious paintings of the deposition and entombment of Christ. The artist's paintings from Shakespeare were praised for their treatment of stories familiar to the popular viewer. A journalist writing in the *Public Advertiser* of 28 May 1789 claimed of Northcote: 'of English history he has given us English pictures ... invoked with that energetic air ... that Baronial hardihood.'

CT

Northumberland, Earl of. **(1)** A Lancastrian, he nevertheless pities the captured York, *Richard Duke of York* (*3 Henry VI*) 1.4. Henry Percy (1421–61) was the 3rd Earl of Northumberland, grandson of *Hotspur. **(2)** In *Richard II*, he is one of Bolingbroke's supporters. In *1 Henry IV* he joins his brother *Worcester and his son Hotspur in the rebellion against Henry IV (1.3), but, 'crafty-sick' (*2 Henry IV* Induction 37), avoids the battle of *Shrewsbury where his son dies. His plans for revenge come to nothing, and his own defeat is announced, *2 Henry IV* 4.3.97–101. Henry Percy (1342–1408) was the 1st Earl of Northumberland. **(3)** See Siward. *AB*

Northumberland, Lady. She advises her husband the Earl of *Northumberland to escape to Scotland, *2 Henry IV* 2.3.50–2. *AB*

Northumberland manuscript, a manuscript dating from *c.*1598 containing several essays and speeches by Francis *Bacon, the *title page of which is covered with annotations, possibly in the hand of Adam Dyrmonth, including the name 'Mr ffrauncis Bacon', many repetitions of the name 'William Shakespeare', the titles 'Rychard the second' and 'Rychard the third', a quotation from *The Rape of Lucrece* (ll. 1086–7), and a variant spelling of the word '*honorificabilitudinitatibus*' from *Love's Labour's Lost* (5.1.41). *ER*

Norton, Thomas (1532–84), poet, translator, and anti-Catholic agitator. He wrote the important tragedy *Gorboduc* (1565) with Thomas Sackville, later Earl of Dorset. It shares both its source (Geoffrey of Monmouth's *History of the Kings of Britain*) and elements of its plot with Shakespeare's *King Lear*. *RM*

Norton Shakespeare. The well-illustrated Norton one-volume Shakespeare, general editor Stephen Greenblatt, appeared in 1997 to challenge other student editions designed mainly for the American academic market (such as the *Riverside and the *Signet). Its text is basically that of the *Oxford Shakespeare (1986), as is its ordering of the works. Unlike other one-volume editions, it is printed with a single column per page, with glosses in the right margin, and some longer notes at the foot of the page. The works are printed in chronological order, though the dating of many plays remains speculative, and titles are sometimes taken from early quartos as embodying acting versions, rather than from the 1623 Folio. *2 Henry VI* thus becomes *The First Part of the Contention of the Two Famous Houses of York and Lancaster*, a title derived from the 1594 quarto, although the control text for this play is that in the Folio. The edition seems to be designed in part to destabilize the usual patterns of one-volume editions. So it includes three texts of *King Lear*, quarto and Folio texts on facing pages and a composite text. The 'economics of publishing and the realities of bookbinding' (p. xii), however, prevented the editor from including multiple texts of other variant plays in a volume that runs to 3,400 pages. The powerful general introduction and the introductions to the individual plays contributed by Greenblatt, Walter Cohen, Jean Howard, and Katharine Eisaman Maus show the influence of *new historicism, and are very much of their time in their concern with darker resonances in the plays, and with such issues as gender and cross-dressing. The Norton edition provides very full documentation in relation to Shakespeare, and includes an essay by Andrew Gurr on 'The Shakespearean Stage'. *RAF*

Norway. See SCANDINAVIA.

Notes and Queries was founded in 1849 by William J. Thoms with the epigraph 'when found, make a note of (Captain Cuttle)' as 'a medium for intercommunication for literary men, artists, antiquaries and genealogists, etc.' Now addressed to 'readers and writers, collectors and librarians', it publishes brief factual articles, requests for information, and reviews, of which a substantial percentage have always concerned Shakespeare. *SLB*

novel. See FICTION.

Nunn, Trevor (b. 1940), British director. After undergraduate acting and directing at Cambridge he scored a success at the *Royal Shakespeare Company with a stylized production of *The Revenger's Tragedy* in 1966 and soon became artistic director. In eighteen years at Stratford he directed a wide range of plays on the main stage. Soon after The Other Place (seating 140) opened he staged an enthralling, simple *Macbeth* and subsequently *Othello*. Both survive on videotape. His *Comedy of Errors* (1976) won a prize for Best Musical. From 1981 Nunn amassed a personal fortune, staging hit musicals like *Cats* and *Les Misérables* in London and worldwide. He directed a feature film of *Twelfth Night* in 1996. A year later he became the fourth director of the *National Theatre, where his eclectic productions have included an epic *Troilus and Cressida* and a more intimate, naturalistic *Merchant of Venice*. His involvement with the Shakespearian stage has extended to marriages to two Shakespearian actresses, Janet *Suzman and Imogen Stubbs. *MJ*

nurses. (1) A nurse brings Aaron's child to him, *Titus Andronicus* 4.2, and he murders her (4.2.144). **(2)** Juliet's Nurse in *Romeo and Juliet* tells anecdotes of Juliet's early childhood at her first appearance (1.3). She is present at the first meeting of Romeo and Juliet and acts as a go-between in 2.3, 2.4, and 3.3. She breaks the news of Tybalt's death to Juliet (3.2) and advises Juliet to marry Paris when Romeo is banished (3.5), after which Juliet ceases to confide in her. She discovers Juliet's apparently dead body (4.4).

There is, no doubt, some irony intended in her name Angelica (4.4.5), as her decrepit physical state (made much of by her in 2.4) and her questionable moral values (her role in creating Juliet's predicament) are anything but angelic. In some productions she has been made into an ancient crone to contrast with Juliet's beauty, youth, and innocence (notably Peter *Brook's 1947 production in which, according to the *News Chronicle*, she was 'racked by every ailment known to pathology'). Pre-20th-century productions preferred a more benign version of her, and her lines, many of which are bawdy in tone, were severely cut. Lines intact, she is one of the most colourful and developed of the comic characters in the tragedies. The role was a speciality of Dame Edith *Evans: more recent Nurses have tended to be less rustically Chaucerian, closer in social tone to governesses than to wet-nurses. *AB*

Levenson, Jill, *Shakespeare in Performance: Romeo and Juliet* (1987)

Nye, Robert (b. 1939), English novelist. Nye has specialized in robust and linguistically exuberant recreations of mythical or fictional characters, sharing some of Anthony Burgess's—and Shakespeare's own—enthusiasm for bawdry, puns, lists, and neologisms in *Falstaff* (1976), *Mrs Shakespeare* (1993), and *The Late Mr Shakespeare* (1998). *TM*

Nyerere, Julius (1922–99), President of the United Republic of Tanzania 1964–85. He was regarded as the most cultured of modern African statesmen; austere and incorruptible in his personal life; severe and even autocratic in dealing with opponents to his administration, and ready to use force to put down rebellion or to overthrow regimes in Uganda, the Comoros, and the Seychelles. To the end of his life he was known in Swahili as 'mwalimu', or teacher. Not surprisingly, for an experienced statesman named Julius, he was drawn to Shakespeare's political plays, and his publications include translations of *Julius Caesar* and *The Merchant of Venice* into Swahili. See EAST AFRICA. *TM*

Nym. See NIM.

Oberon is the king of the *fairies in *A Midsummer Night's Dream.* Angry with his consort Titania because she refuses to part with the changeling boy, he tells *Robin Goodfellow to fetch a magic herb with which to drug her (a herb subsequently used on Lysander and Demetrius too).

In the 19th century, Oberon was usually a singing part for a woman. In the 20th century, most often played by male actors, the attempt to make him other-worldly has moved towards giving him either fantastic costumes or very little costume at all. With the advent of electricity he was given lights in his headdress by Frank *Benson and Beerbohm *Tree (both 1900), although Benson's use of the new technology was abandoned when the battery concealed in the actor's wings leaked over him. Various reviewers have described the Oberons they have seen as resembling insects or birds (beetles, Michael *Benthall 1957 and Patrick Kirwan 1914; a bluebottle, Robert *Helpmann 1938; a dragonfly, Benthall 1954; a cockatoo, Paul *Scofield 1982; and an Aztec bird, George *Devine 1954). In the second half of the 20th century Oberon has become an increasingly sinister figure as critics and directors have become more alive to the play's dark sexual undercurrents: at the same time the role has often been doubled with that of Theseus (and that of Titania with Hippolyta, doublings first recommended by Robert *Cox in the 1640s), suggesting that the fairy king is in some sense the rational Duke's unconscious. *AB*

octave. See SONNET.

Octavia is Caesar's sister in *Antony and Cleopatra.* Her marriage with Antony is arranged, 2.2. *AB*

octavo, the format of a book in which the printed sheet was folded in half three times, making eight leaves or sixteen pages. Although the *quarto format was standardly used for single-text printings of Shakespeare's plays, the octavo format was employed for most early editions of the narrative poems. *ER*

Odashima, Yushi (b. 1930), Japanese translator. Odashima majored in English at the University of Tokyo, where he later worked as a professor of English. Together with Shoyo Tsubouchi, he is one of the two Japanese who have translated the complete canon of Shakespeare. His translations have successfully recreated the original in contemporary Japanese, and he is regarded as a great popularizer of Shakespeare. *TK*

Odéon, Théâtre de l', founded in 1780, at times dependent on the Comédie-Française. It was run between 1906 and 1914 by André *Antoine, who directed *Julius Caesar, Coriolanus,* and *Romeo and Juliet.* It was conceded to the Renaud-*Barrault company (and staged Bonnefoy's adaptation of *Julius Caesar* in 1960), and is now Théâtre de l'Europe, originally under the direction of Giorgio *Strehler. When the *National Theatre's productions of *King Lear* (directed by Deborah Warner) and *Richard III* (directed by Richard Eyre) visited in 1991, they were the first Shakespeare plays to be performed with French subtitles. *ISG*

Oehlenschläger, Adam (1779–1850), Danish Romantic poet and playwright. Instrumental in introducing Shakespeare into Scandinavia, he translated *A Midsummer Night's Dream* (1816) and wrote plays influenced by Shakespeare. His *Amleth* (1847) goes back to *Saxo and creates a happy ending for a heroic Prince. *I-SE*

Hanson, K. S., 'Adam Oehlenschläger's Romanticism', *Scandinavian-Canadian Studies*, 2 (1986)

office book. See MASTER OF THE REVELS.

Okes, Nicholas. See PRINTING AND PUBLISHING.

Okhlopkov, Nikolai (1900–67), Soviet director. His *Hamlet* (Moscow, 1954) was set in a massive pair of gates that looked like an iron curtain and presented Denmark as a literal prison. The play had been banned during and after the Second World War: this was the first major *Hamlet* in the USSR after Stalin's death. *DK*

Old Athenian. See ATHENIAN, OLD.

Oldcastle, Sir John. Known as Lord Cobham (*c.*1378–1417), he was a Lollard leader (the Lollards followed John Wyclif's heresies of scepticism originating in anticlericalism). Though acquainted with Prince Henry (later Henry V), he was condemned for treason and heresy and executed in 1417. He was venerated as a martyr by John *Foxe (1516–87) and others during Shakespeare's lifetime. Sir John Falstaff's name was originally Oldcastle in *1 Henry IV* (as in one of Shakespeare's sources, *The Famous Victories of King Henry V*), but Shakespeare changed it because of pressure from Oldcastle's descendants the *Cobhams after the play had been performed but before the first *quarto was registered in February 1598 (see also HARVEY; RUSSELL). *AB*

Old Lady. See LADY, OLD.

Old-Spelling Shakespeare (1907–9). An ambitious project to issue all Shakespeare's works in 40 volumes 'in such a form as would have harmonized with the poet's own orthography' (Prospectus) was part of the plan for the Shakespeare Library, general editor Israel Gollancz. These old-spelling texts, edited initially by F. J. *Furnivall and W. G. Boswell-Stone, and from 1908 by Boswell-Stone and F. W. Clarke, included modern stage directions in brackets, collations, and brief textual notes. They were handsomely printed in a limited edition, beginning with the comedies in 1907. Only thirteen plays were issued, as the project was then halted. It was not until 1986 that another modern old-spelling edition was published, as part of the *Oxford Shakespeare. *RAF*

Old Stratford, that part of the parish of Stratford-upon-Avon which lay outside the medieval borough boundary, where Shakespeare bought 107 acres (43 ha) of land in 1602 from William and John *Combe. It was leased for farming to Thomas (d. 1611) and Lewis (d. 1627) Hiccox. The latter was to set up an inn, the Maidenhead, later the Swan and Maidenhead, in the eastern wing of the property now known as Shakespeare's *Birthplace. *SW*

Old Vic theatre. Located in the Cut, off Waterloo Road, it is the fifth oldest standing theatre in London. Originally the Royal Coburg (built 1818), it provided broad melodrama but also hosted six appearances by Edmund *Kean (1831). It was redecorated in 1833, renamed the Royal Victoria Theatre after the future Queen, and soon became known affectionately as the 'Old Vic'. Struggling financially, it was bought by social worker Emma Cons in 1880 and opened as a temperance music hall managed by William *Poel. In the 1900s, Cons began staging Shakespearian scenes during concert interludes. In 1914, Cons's niece Lilian *Baylis, now controlling the theatre, mounted the first entirely Shakespearian season. The following season, Baylis put Ben *Greet in charge of production. A series of great actors such as Sybil *Thorndike, John *Gielgud, Edith *Evans, Peggy *Ashcroft, and Richard *Burton contributed to the theatre's success. It housed the *National Theatre Company under Laurence *Olivier and later Peter *Hall from 1963 to 1976. It housed the Prospect Theatre Company (1979–81) until the company disbanded, causing the theatre to close until 1983: it later provided a London base for Peter Hall's own company. In 1997, the building was almost sold, but in 1998 supporters established a trust to ensure that the theatre would survive. *BR*

Oldys, William (1696–1761), biographer and antiquarian who, with *Johnson, compiled the *Harleian Miscellany*. His notes form the 'Additional Anecdotes' in *Steevens's 1778 edition of Shakespeare and are a source for such myths as the existence of a Stratfordian model for Falstaff, Shakespeare's performance as Adam in *As You Like It*, and Shakespeare's paternity of *Davenant. *CMSA*

Oliva, Salvador (b. 1942). Catalan poet and translator of Shakespeare. His translations were first conceived to subtitle and dub the BBC Television Shakespeare series. He casts blank verse into Catalan free verse, and aims at a close poetic and dramatic rendering. Having started in the 1980s, Oliva is the most prolific of modern translators of Shakespeare into any Spanish language: he has translated all the plays, as well as the Sonnets. *ALP*

Oliver is the villainous older brother of Jaques (de Bois) and Orlando in *As You Like It*. The parallel character in *Lodge's *Rosalynde* is Saladyne, who is killed rather than undergoing a conversion. *AB*

Olivia, a countess in *Twelfth Night*, is loved by Orsino but falls in love with his servant 'Cesario'. The parallel character in *Rich's *Apolonius and Silla* is Julina. *AB*

Olivier, Lord (Sir Laurence) (1907–89), British stage and film actor and director. At 15 as Kate in a school version of *The Taming of the Shrew* this son of a high Anglican vicar attracted the praise of Dame Ellen *Terry. By 1930 he was a name in the West End and by 1939 a lauded Hollywood star. Meanwhile in 1935 in London he had performed the parts of Romeo and Mercutio in succession with the more classical John *Gielgud. Olivier's animal magnetism and impetuous verse-speaking provoked debate. The next year he appeared as Orlando in a coy film of *As You Like It*. He confirmed his position as a major stage actor at the *Old Vic in 1937–8 when under Tyrone *Guthrie he played Sir Toby Belch, Henry V, Hamlet, Macbeth, Iago, and Coriolanus. He divorced his first wife and married the beautiful film star Vivien *Leigh, and in 1940 they collaborated on a disastrous *Romeo and Juliet* on Broadway. Released from war service he adapted, directed, and starred in the imaginative, patriotic Technicolor film of *Henry V* (1944), which moved from a stylized opening at Shakespeare's Globe to realistic battle scenes. In the peak years 1944–8 along with Ralph *Richardson he led the fabled Old Vic seasons in the West End. His Shakespearian roles alone displayed his versatility: Hotspur and Justice Shallow in the two parts of *Henry IV*, Crookback in *Richard III*, and King Lear. His second Shakespearian film as director and star was *Hamlet* (1948), shot in black and white. The Old Vic did not re-engage him and he went into management. In 1951 he appeared with Vivien Leigh in London in a Festival of Britain production of *Antony and Cleopatra*, repeated in New York. The third and last of his remarkable Shakespeare films was *Richard III* (1955): he played the hunchback King with a relish which has been much imitated. Leading the season at Stratford-upon-Avon in 1955 with Vivien Leigh, he played a brooding Macbeth and (under Peter *Brook's direction) a great and moving Titus Andronicus as well as a rather fussy *Malvolio. He returned to Stratford to give a strikingly physical performance as Coriolanus in 1959. His appearance as the comedian Archie Rice in John Osborne's *The Entertainer* brought him in close touch with younger actors and directors at the *Royal Court, including the actress Joan Plowright who (following his second divorce) became his wife. When the long-delayed *National Theatre became a reality Olivier, as the leader of his profession, was the obvious candidate as first director. From 1962 to 1973 in temporary quarters at the Old Vic he built up an acting ensemble and production team drawing not on old associates like Richardson but on young directors, actors, and designers from the Royal Court, including Plowright. His Shakespearian contributions included directing the opening *Hamlet* with Peter O'Toole as well as a visually charming *Love's Labour's Lost*. He played an arresting, arrogant Othello in blackface (less convincing when filmed), and a 19th-century Shylock (under Jonathan *Miller's direction) reminiscent of a Rothschild financier. By the time he reluctantly yielded his post to Peter *Hall, he had survived a series of major illnesses, and he never acted in the new National Theatre complex where the largest, open-stage auditorium is named the Olivier. No longer able to sustain a part on stage, he appeared on film and television; his King Lear was screened by Granada Television. Uniquely honoured, he garnered Oscars, honorary doctorates, and a peerage. The memorial service for Lord Olivier of Brighton OM in Westminster Abbey was televised like a royal event: his chosen epitaph, recalling his Hamlet, was 'Goodnight, sweet Prince.' *MJ*

'O mistress mine', sung by Feste in *Twelfth Night* 2.3.38. Much debate has taken place over whether the popular tune of the same title arranged by Thomas *Morley in *The First Book of Consort Lessons* (1599) is the right one for the lyrics; if it is, then the song probably pre-dates the play and the words therefore may not be Shakespeare's. The title is found as an opening to other early English songs.

The song was set by many late 19th- and early 20th-century composers, including Coleridge-Taylor, Dankworth, Finzi, Korngold, MacCunn, Parry, Quilter, Stanford, Sullivan, Warlock, and *Vaughan Williams. *JB*

'On Ben Jonson'. According to an anecdote in the papers of Nicholas Burgh (*c.*1650) in the Bodleian Library, Shakespeare and *Jonson, 'being merry at a tavern, Master Jonson having begun this for his epitaph: "Here lies Ben Jonson, | That was once one", he gives it to Master Shakespeare to make up, who presently writes: "Who while he lived was a slow thing, | And now, being dead, is nothing." ' In another version, found among the papers of Thomas Plume in Maldon, Essex, Jonson wrote, 'Here lies Ben Jonson, | Who was once one', where-

'Upon the King . . .' Laurence Olivier as Henry v the night before Agincourt, from his film version (1944).

upon 'Shakespeare took the pen from him, and made this:

> Here lies Benjamin—
> With short hair upon his chin—
> Who while he lived was a slow thing,
> And now he's dead is no thing.'

SW

O'Neill, Eliza (1791–1872), an actress who had already made her name (as Volumnia, Constance, and Juliet) in her native *Ireland before her sensational Covent Garden debut as Juliet in 1814. Greatly admired (not least by Talma) and regarded as a successor to Mrs *Siddons, Eliza O'Neill's career ended with her marriage in 1819. *RF*

onomatopoeia, the use of words that seem to imitate the sounds they refer to:

> Sometimes a thousand twangling instruments
> Will hum about mine ears.
>
> (*The Tempest* 3.2.135–6)

CB

Open Air Theatre, Regent's Park. Often regarded as a tourist attraction, this playing area on the greensward of a royal park has afforded pleasure to many (some seeing their first play by Shakespeare) as well as giving young players like Ralph Fiennes their first work. The champion of such pastoral playing was Ben *Greet, a founding father in 1932–3; its longest serving exemplar was the stentorian Robert *Atkins who frequently directed and acted in the park, 1933–61. Stars like Gladys Cooper and Anna Neagle were happy to don Rosalind's doublet and hose for a short summer season; admired regulars included Leslie French as Ariel and Puck. The repertoire has never been restricted to Shakespeare's pastoral comedies. In 1975 a more permanent theatre with up-to-date technology was constructed, further modernized in 1999–2000. Under David Conville and Ian Talbot production values became more sophisticated than was possible within Atkins's limited budget. *MJ*

opera. No literary figure has inspired so many operas as Shakespeare, with nearly 300 operas to date (and many failed attempts) based wholly or in part on his works, including two on *The Rape of Lucrece* and one on *Venus and Adonis.* Admittedly, of these 300 only *Verdi's masterpieces *Otello* and *Falstaff* currently rank in the top 50 most frequently performed operas, though there are good recordings of several of the other Shakespearian operas, which are periodically revived. The most often set plays are (in order): *The Tempest* (the play requiring the most music), *A Midsummer Night's Dream* (arguably the most musical play in terms of its poetry), *Hamlet* (always the most popular of the plays), *Twelfth Night,* and *Romeo and Juliet.* The plays which have not yet received operatic treatment are: *Titus Andronicus,* the *Henry VI* plays, *King John,* and *Richard II.* Although Shakespearian operas have been composed all over Europe, the Americas, and in the Far East, this brief survey will concentrate on the

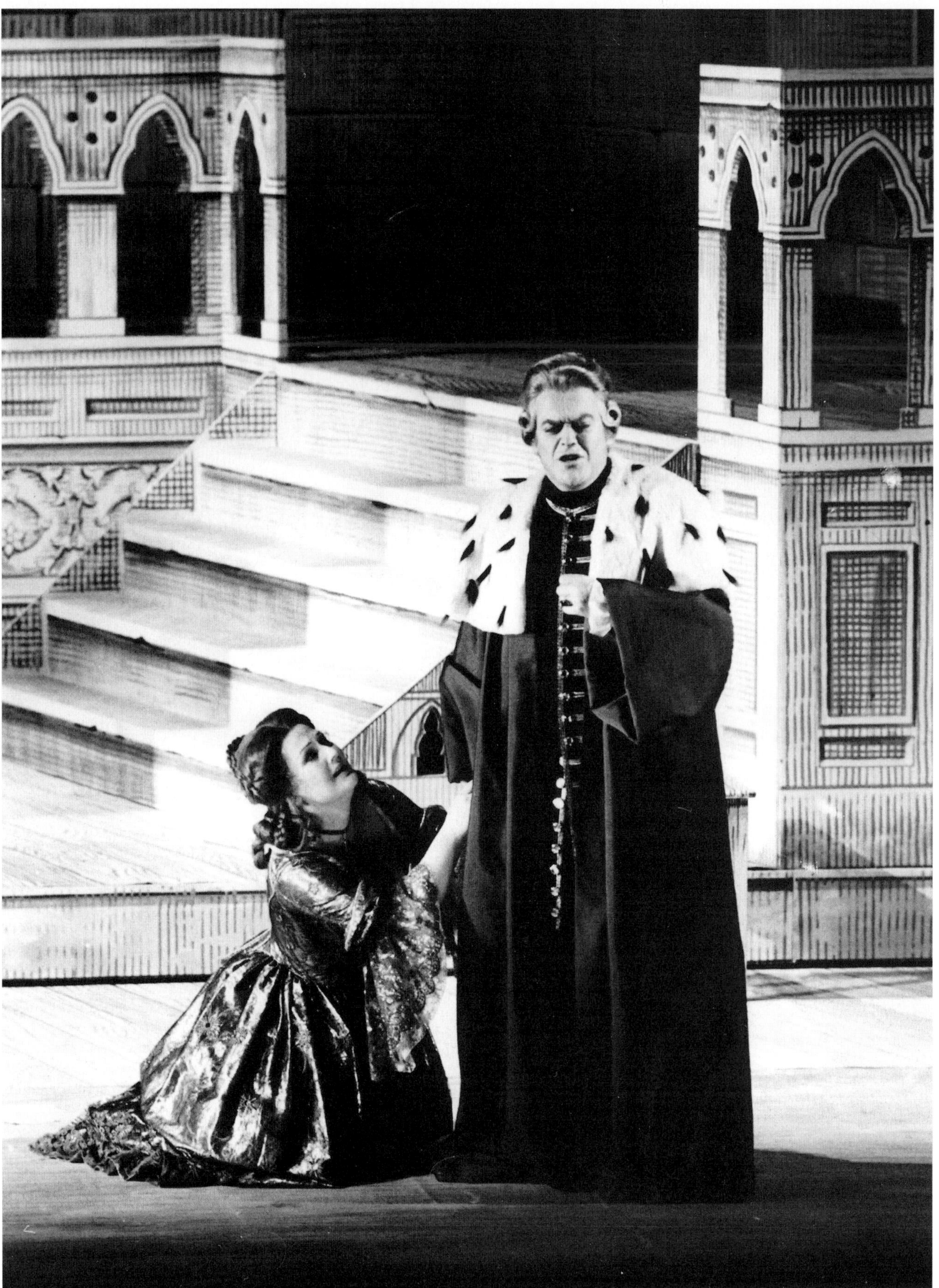

Heroine and antagonist as soprano and bass: Isabella (Sabine Hass) pleads with Friedrich [Angelo] (Hermann Prey) in the Bavarian State Opera's 1983 production of Richard Wagner's opera *Das Liebesverbot* (1836), based on *Measure for Measure*.

better-known, mainstream Western compositions.

Because of the very different nature, and demands, of opera compared with legitimate drama, Shakespeare's plays cannot be turned into opera simply by setting all the words to music. (The one attempt to do so, John Barkworth's *Romeo and Juliet*, performed in Middlesbrough in 1916 and London in 1920 and 1926, was not a success.) Instead, much pruning and tightening up of both text and plot is required: in effect an opera libretto is a type of translation. Abroad, librettos often underwent a kind of double transformation, being prepared from foreign-language translations (not always of the highest standard) and even adaptations of the plays. More often than not, Shakespearian operas have also reflected the prevailing dramatic and operatic tastes of the time. Thus, these operas, while clearly relating to Shakespeare's works on one level, are often at many different removes from their sources. This is particularly vividly demonstrated in the English operas.

The earliest Shakespearian operas are the so-called semi-operas, or dramatic operas, composed in England during the Restoration, namely: *Macbeth* (*Davenant's adaptation, 1664, with music first by Matthew Locke and later by John Eccles and then Richard Leveridge), *The Tempest; or, The Enchanted Island* (Davenant and *Dryden, 1667, set by various composers including Locke, Pelham Humfrey, John Banister, and Giovanni Battista Draghi, and later by John Weldon), and *The *Fairy Queen* (1692, with music by Henry Purcell, adapted from *A Midsummer Night's Dream*). For centuries the English were uncomfortable with all-sung operas in English. These Shakespearian Restoration dramatic operas, with plots and language heavily altered from their originals, contained vocal and instrumental music and spoken dialogue, but had a particular emphasis on the use of splendid scenery, costumes, and stage machines. Essentially, English opera at the time was a multisense experience, appealing as much to the eye as to the ear. Also, in contrast to continental opera, none of the principal characters had singing roles. Naturally, such spectacles were very expensive to produce, and they became less frequent in the 18th century.

As Italian opera became more popular in England at the end of the 17th century and beginning of the 18th, so there developed a strong anti-Italian opera sentiment. This feeling expressed itself in the one-act mock-opera *Pyramus and Thisbe* (1716), a work derived from *A Midsummer Night's Dream* and set to music by Richard Leveridge. This text was revised and set to music by John Frederick Lampe in 1745. Like its predecessor, Lampe's work ridiculed Italian operatic convention and called for an alternative English form of musical entertainment. Although both these pieces enjoyed moderate popularity on the stage, the most effective attack on Italian opera during this period was John Gay's parody *The Beggar's Opera* (1728), which used ballad tunes rather than more sophisticated newly composed music. *The Beggar's Opera* spawned a large number of other ballad operas, of which the only Shakespearian one was James Worsdale's two-act ballad farce *A *Cure for a Scold* (1735), based on *The Taming of the Shrew*.

Despite this discomfort with all-sung English opera, several attempts were made in the 18th century to create all-sung English Shakespearian operas. In 1755 John Christopher Smith composed *The *Fairies*, a three-act all-sung opera in Handelian style with a libretto (by *Garrick) based on the first four acts of *A Midsummer Night's Dream*; the following year he set *The Tempest* in similar fashion. Both operas were supplemented with lyrics from other authors, such as Milton and Dryden, and *The Tempest* included material from the Restoration adaptation of the play. Although successful enough at the time, neither opera was performed for more than one season, probably because of the difficulty in engaging singers of sufficient merit. Seventeen years later, in 1773, at Garrick's prompting Captain Edward Thompson adapted *Love's Labour's Lost* (the one Shakespeare play that was never performed in the Restoration and 18th century) as an opera. Thompson's text is very close to Shakespeare's, but was not quite completed, perhaps because of a major falling out with Garrick, and none of it was ever set to music. Finally, there appears to have been an operatic version of *The Tempest* at Covent Garden theatre in December 1776. Reduced to three acts on account of all the extra music, this was still principally a spoken drama with lots of music rather than a true opera.

At Covent Garden theatre in the early 19th century Frederick *Reynolds prepared texts for a number of Shakespearian 'operas' of this type, continuing the tradition of freely adding lyrics from other authors or from other plays, with the music often arranged from or composed by a number of composers. Similar treatment was given to *The Merry Wives of Windsor* (1824) at Drury Lane theatre, with music principally by Charles Edward Horn. This period, however, also witnessed an 'authentic', Rossini-influenced opera in Michael Balfe's two-act *opera buffa Falstaff* (Her Majesty's theatre, London, 19 July 1838).

Other genuine operas followed in the 20th century. A sense of nationalism, combined with a rediscovery of folk music, inspired Gustav *Holst to use traditional 17th-century English dance music in his one-act opera *At the Boar's Head* (1924), based on scenes from the *Henry IV* plays. Also caught up in this movement was Ralph *Vaughan Williams, whose four-act opera *Sir John in Love* (1924–8), derived from *The Merry Wives of Windsor*, also employs English folk songs as part of its musical language. Of more recent operas, those by Benjamin *Britten have proved of international significance. Britten's *A Midsummer Night's Dream* is particularly notable for having a libretto that is very close to Shakespeare's original (though reduced in length to about half).

As Shakespeare's works became known abroad, so their potential for operatic transformation quickly became apparent. However, since Shakespeare's plays are not entirely original in their source material, it is not always easy to determine to what extent an opera in a foreign language can truly be said to be derived from Shakespeare rather than from sources in common. For example, Apostolo Zeno and Pietro Giovanni Pariati wrote a *Hamlet* libretto, *Ambleto*, that was set to music by Francesco Gasparini (Venice, 1706), Domenico Scarlatti (Rome, 1715), and Giuseppe Carcani (Venice, 1742). Their source was *Saxo Grammaticus' *Historia Danica*, which also lies behind Shakespeare's play. Many other *Hamlet*, *Caesar*, and *Coriolanus* operas are likewise not directly derived from Shakespeare's works.

The earliest Italian operas generally accepted as Shakespearian were, in fact, first produced outside Italy. Francesco Maria Veracini's *Rosalinda* (1744), based on *As You Like It*, Ferdinando Bertoni's *Il duca d'Atene* (1780), derived from *The Taming of the Shrew*, and Pietro Carlo Guglielmi's *Romeo e Giulietta* (1810) were all first performed in London. Stephen Storace's *Gli equivoci* (1786), the only operatic version of *The Comedy of Errors* before the 20th century and one of the finest early Shakespearian operas, has the unusual distinction of being an Italian opera composed by an Englishman and premièred in Vienna, with an Italian libretto (by *Mozart's librettist Lorenzo da Ponte) based on a French translation of the play. (Storace reused much of the material from *Gli equivoci* in his London operas *No Song, no Supper*, 1790, and especially *The Pirates*, 1792.) Other Italian operas from this time include Gaetano Andreozzi's *Amleto* (Padua, 1792), Luigi Caruso's *La tempesta* (Naples, 1799) and *Falstaff; ossia, Le tre burle* (Vienna, 1799) by Antonio Salieri (1750–1825), a prolific Italian opera composer who lived and worked mostly in Vienna.

Although not the most popular subject matter (when turning to British literature in search of plots, Italian librettists often went first to Sir Walter *Scott), Shakespeare's plays continued to attract operas by Italian composers in the 19th century, including one by Gioachino Rossini (1792–1868), the most important Italian composer of the first half of the 19th century. *Otello; ossia, Il moro di Venezia*, which includes some music from Rossini's earlier works, was first performed in Naples in 1816. For its revival in Rome, 1819, it was given a happy ending. Giovanni Pacini's *La gioventù di Enrico V* (Rome, 1820) and Salvario Mercadante's opera of the same title (Milan, 1834) are unusual for being based on episodes in the two *Henry IV* plays. But Vincenzo Bellini's *I Capuleti e i Montecchi* (Venice, 1830), for long considered one of the finest Shakespearian operas of this period, proves on closer analysis of the text not in fact to be derived from Shakespeare at all but from his Italian sources.

The second half of the 19th century in Italy is dominated by Giuseppe Verdi's masterpieces *Otello* (Milan, 1887) and *Falstaff* (Milan, 1893), preceded by the stirring *Macbeth* (Florence, 1847). Arrigo Boito, Verdi's librettist for his last two operas, prepared his first Shakespearian libretto for Franco Faccio's *Amleto* (Genoa, 1865), a work, however, of finer literary than musical merit. In the 20th century more notable Italian Shakespearian operas include Gian Francesco Malipiero's *Antonio e Cleopatra* (Florence, 1938), *Giulio Cesare* (Genoa, 1936), and *Romeo e Giulietta* (the second act of *Mondi celesti e infernali*, 1950) and Ottorino Respighi's *Lucrezia* (Milan, 1937). More recent operas include the unperformed *All's Well That Ends Well/Giglietta di Narbona* (1955–8), and the prize-winning *The Merchant of Venice/Il mercante di Venezia* (Milan, 1961), both by Mario Castelnuovo-Tedesco (1895–1968).

Although Italy produced arguably the finest Shakespearian operas, Shakespeare has been more frequently set by German composers. *The Tempest* in particular was a great favourite of late 18th- and early 19th-century Romantics, while *Twelfth Night* and *The Winter's Tale* also attracted a number of settings. Even Richard Wagner (1813–83) was tempted by Shakespeare. His opera *Das Liebesverbot; oder, Die Novize von Palermo*, based, rather unusually, on *Measure for Measure*, was, however, a failure and was performed just once in his lifetime, at Magdeburg on 29 March 1836. The only German Shakespearian opera to obtain any enduring popularity is Otto *Nicolai's *Die Lustigen Weiber von Windsor* (Berlin, 1849). More recent German operas include Aribert Reimann's *Lear* (Munich, 1978) and Hans Gerfor's *Der Park* (Wiesbaden, 1992), a 'psychological interpretation' of *A Midsummer Night's Dream*. In France Shakespeare's works have also had an important influence on the operatic world, though, in complete contrast to Germany, for example, there are no French operas on *The Tempest*. Instead, on the whole, the French have been more attracted to the tragedies. Nevertheless, the earliest French Shakespearian opera appears to be Papavoine's *Le Vieux Coquet; ou, Les Deux Amies* (Paris, 1761), based on *The Merry Wives of Windsor*. *Romeo and Juliet*, however, was the subject of operas by Nicolas-Marie Dalayrac (Paris, 1792), Daniel Steibelt (Paris, 1793, one of the most successful early Shakespearian operas) and, in 1867, a fine work by Charles François Gounod (1818–93) with much sumptuous music. *Macbeth* caught the attention of two composers early in the 19th century: Hippolyte-André-Baptiste Chelard (Paris, 1827) and Louis Alexandre Piccinni (Paris, 1829). Of greater artistry and success, however, were Hector *Berlioz's *Béatrice et Bénédict* (1860–2) and a musically rich setting of *Hamlet* (1868) by Ambroise Thomas (1811–96), containing some of his most splendid music (and a happy ending). Thomas's other Shakespeare opera is *Le Songe d'une nuit d'été* (Paris, 1850) which rather than being the setting of *A Midsummer Night's Dream* its title suggests is a biographical fantasy about Shakespeare himself. The writer (a yearning tenor) is redeemed from his corrupting association with Falstaff (here a real-life gamekeeper) by the inspiring intervention of Queen Elizabeth, who poses in diguise as Shakespeare's muse and stirs his soul with some magnificent coloratura arias. An operatic *Henry VIII* (Paris, 1883) by Camille Saint-Saëns (1835–1921), however, is based not on Shakespeare but on Calderón's play *La cisma in Inglaterra*. Ernest Bloch's opera *Macbeth* (Paris, 1910) was originally written in French but was translated into Italian and into English and, after revivals in a number of European towns, received its first major American performance at the University of California at Berkeley in 1960. Bloch (1880–1959) was Swiss, not French, and assumed American nationality in 1924.

With the exception of M. Cooney's *Hamlet* (New York, 1870), all the many North American Shakespearian operas were composed as recently as the 20th century (although Harry Rowe Shelley's *Romeo and Juliet* dates from as early as 1901). The USA has been particularly important for the development of lighter Shakespearian operatic forms, such as *musicals and rock operas. However, there have also been more serious works, such as Samuel Barber's *Antony and Cleopatra* (New York, 1966). Barber (1910–81) was commissioned to compose this opera to celebrate the reopening of the New York Metropolitan Opera at the Lincoln Center. Unfortunately the production (by *Zeffirelli) was a disaster, and the most expensive flop in the Metropolitan Opera's history. *IBC*

Gooch, Bryan N. S., and Thatcher, David, *A Shakespeare Music Catalogue* (1991)

Hartnoll, Phyllis (ed.), *Shakespeare and Music* (1964)

Sadie, Stanley (ed.), *The New Grove Dictionary of Opera* (1992)

Schmidgall, Gary, *Shakespeare and Opera* (1990)

Ophelia, Polonius' daughter and Laertes' sister, is warned away by them from Hamlet, who has been wooing her. Polonius orders her to speak to Hamlet while he and the King spy on them in the 'nunnery scene' (*Hamlet* 3.1) and she also appears in 3.2. In 4.5, now insane, she is brought before the King and Queen. Gertrude describes her death by drowning, 4.7, and there is a confrontation between Laertes and Hamlet at her burial, 5.1.

On one level Ophelia's madness is easily explicable: her father forces her to betray Hamlet and he has apparently gone mad, rejected her, and killed her father. However, none of the characters links her madness with these events explicitly, and her part is lightly sketched, leaving it tempting to fill in the gaps. Laurence *Olivier is by no means alone, for example, in declaring that Hamlet 'is not just imagining what is beneath Ophelia's skirts, he has found out for himself' (1937, though he seems to have changed his mind for the film version in 1948: *Branagh's film version, by contrast, supplies flashbacks to a nude bedroom scene). In some stage productions the violent language of the nunnery scene has been accompanied by violent groping: Jonathan Pryce's Hamlet, for example, was particularly physical with Harriet Walter's Ophelia in 1980. The 19th century preferred their Ophelias more innocent: on stage the bawdier verses of her mad songs were cut, and in fiction Mary Cowden *Clarke, in 'Ophelia: The Rose of Elsinore' (from *Girlhood of Shakespeare's Heroines*), explained how Ophelia had learned them from a seduced and abandoned peasant girl. An enduring fascination with Ophelia's psychology (visible, for example, in the *Pre-Raphaelite Millais's hugely popular painting of her death) was accompanied by a sentimentality which, Elaine Showalter has argued, affected the way that madness in real women was perceived. *AB*

Showalter, Elaine, 'Representing Ophelia: Women, Madness, and the Responsibilities of Feminist Criticism', in Patricia Parker and Geoffrey Hartmann (eds.), *Shakespeare and the Question of Theory* (1985)

oral traditions. Perhaps all Shakespeare's plays derive material not just from printed texts but from a variety of unwritten forms, from *fairy tales, gossip, superstitions, *ballads, *jigs, and mummings. To trace such borrowings we are paradoxically reliant upon written records which will only exist if this information was finally thought worthy of preservation.

Sixteenth- and 17th-century drama is itself an important resource in studying oral traditions.

The oral culture of Britain may be traced from the Anglo-Saxon society wherein the retainers or *comitatus* of a great lord would gather to hear the narrative performed by the poet and accompanied by harp, to the 11th–14th-century minstrel tradition. With the invention of print, minstrels in their medieval form largely disappeared, becoming balladeers selling broadsheets of their songs and singing to advertise their wares, or stage-players. Nevertheless, for the considerable percentage of the population of Elizabethan England still illiterate, this oral culture continued. Whilst more than 4,000 *ballads were printed before 1600, they continued to be produced and transmitted orally. The popular festive rites of a particular town or village continued to be passed on from year to year without being fixed through literacy. Memory was a much more important and reliable tool than it is now.

Some of the plots that Shakespeare turned into drama clearly have their roots in the fairy tale. The choice between three caskets in *The Merchant of Venice* or between three daughters of whom only the youngest is good in *King Lear* derives ultimately from folk tales, as does the wicked stepmother of *Cymbeline. The Taming of the Shrew* recalls a tradition of stories about scolds. Even *Hamlet* was a popular Danish legend before *Belleforest's French translation made it more accessible in written form. Shakespeare probably drew upon his own knowledge of superstition, fairy lore, and *ghost stories for *A Midsummer Night's Dream* and *Macbeth.* The ballad tradition was also an important influence upon his work, supplying 'old' and 'fantastical' tales such as are proffered by Autolycus in *The Winter's Tale,* tales to which the play's improbable drama is likened. There are snatches of ballads in many of Shakespeare's plays, performed by *Ophelia, *Desdemona, and, of course, Autolycus.

The influence of various festive kinds of oral performance is also apparent. The *jig was a popular kind of dancing performed to the music of a pipe or tabor that often had a vocal accompaniment. In the 16th century, jigs became a common conclusion to stage plays. Although they varied in content, there was often a narrative précis improvised beforehand and some kind of structure to the dancing, usually a competition in which the *fool triumphed. One specific kind of jig in which the Robin Hood tradition, a popular subject of ballads, prevailed was the *morris dance. The dancers competed for the favour of a lady, usually called Maid Marian, in a kind of ritual combat, often featuring the hobby-horse. Another kind of festive combat was the mumming. These plays were based on the conflict between St George and his adversary, the Turkish knight, and sometimes a dragon. St George is killed in the course of the action but miraculously brought back to life through the attentions of the Doctor. Yet another popular festive rite passed on through oral tradition rather than through any written text was the charivari or skimmington ride, an opportunity for neighbours to protest at the perceived wrongdoing of one of their number by means of a noisy procession with the subject represented in effigy.

Some of these popular forms, particularly the Robin Hood plays, were deliberately appropriated for the stage and Shakespeare's plays include a number of references to them: Jack Cade as morris dancer in *1 Henry VI* (3.1.365–6), the mention of 'the old Robin Hood of England' in *As You Like It* (1.1.111), the reference to jigs and the hobby-horse in *Hamlet* (3.2.126–9), the morris dance in *The Two Noble Kinsmen* (3.5). Parallels have also been identified between the St George mummings and *Coriolanus* and between the combat between Carnival and Lent and *Henry IV.* *JKS*

Barber, C. L., *Shakespeare's Festive Comedy: A Study of Dramatic Form and its Relation to Social Custom* (1959)

Liebler, Naomi Conn, *Shakespeare's Festive Tragedy: The Ritual Foundations of Genre* (1995)

Smith, Bruce R., *The Acoustic World of Early Modern England* (1999)

orchestra, in the Roman theatre the space directly in front of the stage reserved for the senators. In his drawing of the *Swan, Johannes de Witt labelled as 'orchestra' the auditorium gallery adjacent to the tiring house, presumably to indicate that this was the place (known as the *lords room) where the most socially elevated members of the audience sat. The reorganization of spectating positions in the *Restoration theatre gave the position in front of the stage to the musicians who, by transference from the old name for this location, became known as the orchestra in the early 18th century. *GE*

organ. Although Shakespeare's play texts do not refer to the organ, the instrument was used in the indoor theatre; Marston's tragedy *Sophonisba* (1606) indicates an organ in ensembles playing between the acts. *JB*

Orlando, mistreated by his eldest brother Oliver, escapes to the forest of *Ardenne in *As You Like It.* The parallel character in *Lodge's *Rosalynde* is Rosader. *AB*

Orléans, Bastard of. See BASTARD OF ORLÉANS.

Orléans, Duke of. One of the noblemen at Agincourt, he is taken prisoner (*Henry V* 4.8.76). He is based on Charles, Duke of Orléans (1391–1465). *AB*

'Orpheus with his lute', sung by a Gentlewoman in *All Is True* (*Henry VIII*) 3.1.3, to her own lute accompaniment; the earliest setting to survive is by Matthew *Locke, published 1667. Nineteenth- and 20th-century settings include those by Bishop, Coates, Gurney, Kodaly, Quilter, Rubbra, Stenhammer, *Sullivan, and *Vaughan Williams. *JB*

Orsino, the Duke of Illyria, is rejected by Olivia and is ultimately betrothed to Viola in *Twelfth Night.* His name may have been adapted from Orsini, Duke of *Bracciano, who was in London during the winter of 1600–1. *AB*

Osric, an effete courtier, acts as an umpire during the fencing match of *Hamlet* 5.2. *AB*

Ostler, William (*c.*1585–1614), actor (Blackfriars Boys 1601–8, King's Men 1608–14). Ostler first enters the dramatic record via the actor list for *Jonson's *Poetaster* (performed 1601), printed in the 1616 Jonson folio. In the Sharers Papers of 1635 Cuthbert *Burbage described Ostler as one of the 'boys growing up to be men' (the others were John *Underwood and Nathan *Field) who joined the King's Men when the *Blackfriars reverted to the Burbages in 1608. Ostler subsequently appeared in actor lists for the King's Men's performances: Jonson's *The Alchemist* and *Catiline*; Webster's *The Duchess of Malfi* in the role of Antonio; and Beaumont and Fletcher's *The Captain, Bonduca,* and *Valentian.* In 1611 Ostler married Thomasine Heminges, daughter of John *Heminges, and soon after he acquired shares in the Globe and the Blackfriars which were the subject of a legal dispute between Thomasine and her daughter after Ostler died intestate on 16 December 1614. An epigram by John Davies, printed around 1611, described Ostler as 'sole King of Actors'. *GE*

Oswald, Goneril's steward in *King Lear,* is challenged by Kent (*Tragedy of King Lear* 2.2; *History of King Lear* 7) and killed by Edgar (4.5.249; *History* 20.242). *AB*

Othello *(see page 330)*

Other Place. See ROYAL SHAKESPEARE COMPANY.

'O' the twelfth day of December', snatch sung by Sir Toby in *Twelfth Night* 2.3.81. The ballad of 'Musselburgh Field' opens similarly; the music is unknown. *JB*

'ousel cock so black of hue, The', sung by Bottom in *A Midsummer Night's Dream* 3.1.118. The original tune is unknown, but the early 17th-century tune 'Woodicock' fits well, as suggested by Professor John Ward. *JB*

outlaws capture Valentine and Speed in *The Two Gentlemen of Verona* 4.1, then Silvia, 5.3, the Duke of Milan and Thurio, 5.4. *AB*

(cont. on page 334)

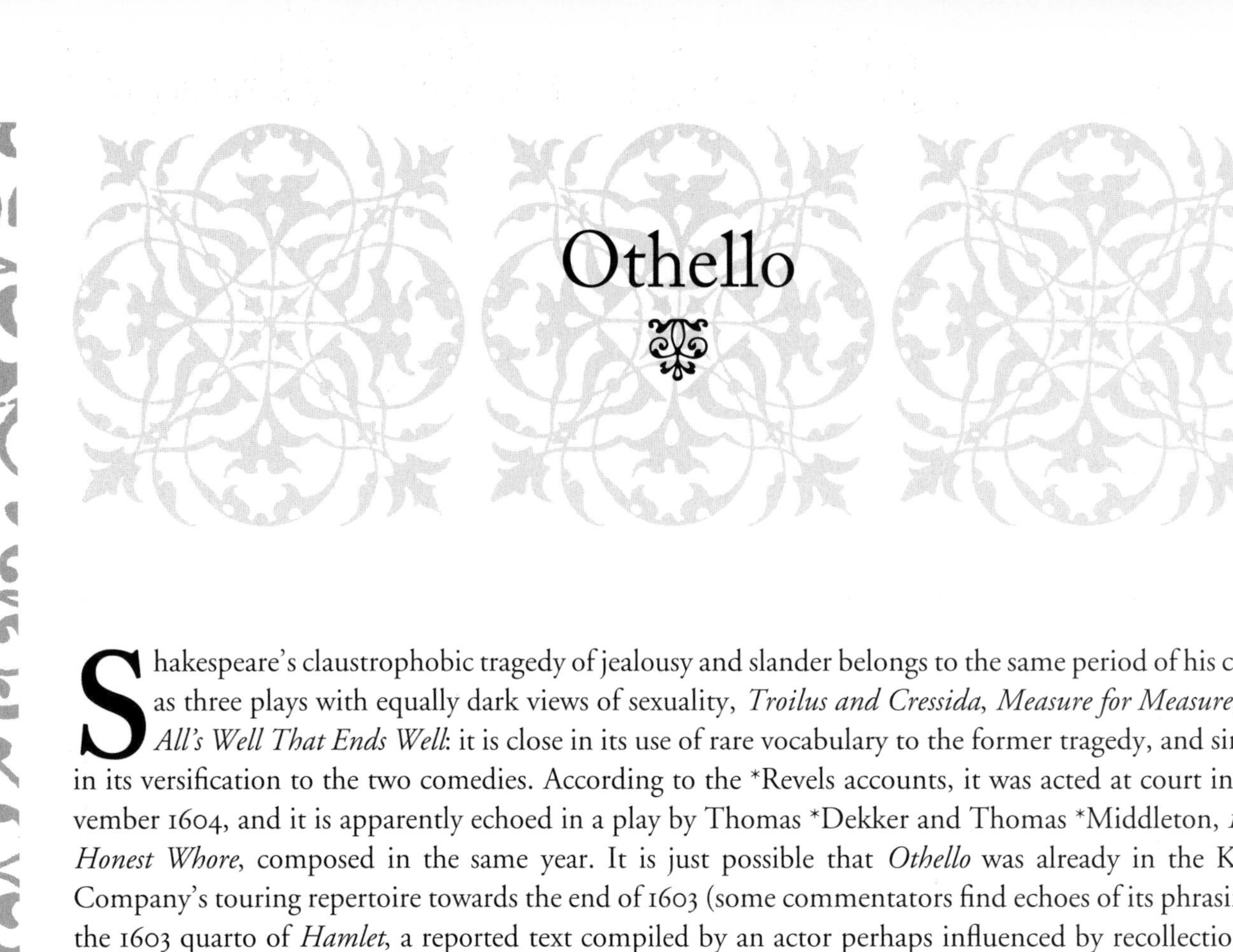

Othello

Shakespeare's claustrophobic tragedy of jealousy and slander belongs to the same period of his career as three plays with equally dark views of sexuality, *Troilus and Cressida*, *Measure for Measure*, and *All's Well That Ends Well*: it is close in its use of rare vocabulary to the former tragedy, and similar in its versification to the two comedies. According to the *Revels accounts, it was acted at court in November 1604, and it is apparently echoed in a play by Thomas *Dekker and Thomas *Middleton, *1 The Honest Whore*, composed in the same year. It is just possible that *Othello* was already in the King's Company's touring repertoire towards the end of 1603 (some commentators find echoes of its phrasing in the 1603 quarto of *Hamlet*, a reported text compiled by an actor perhaps influenced by recollections of *Othello*), but it seems likeliest that the play was composed in late 1603–4 and first acted in 1604, especially since its account of the Turkish navy is informed by Richard Knolles's *History of the Turks*, published only in autumn 1603.

Text: The play first appeared in quarto in 1622, and reappeared in the Folio the following year. The differences between these two texts make *Othello* one of the most complicated plays to edit in the canon, and they are compounded by the fact that both seem to have been set from manuscripts that had already been transcribed by fairly independent-minded scribes. The quarto, the only Shakespearian quarto divided into acts, seems to derive from a presentation copy of the play prepared from Shakespeare's *foul papers by a scribe who sometimes had trouble making sense of their details, and who sometimes intervened to expand and clarify stage directions for the benefit of readers. The Folio text, 160 lines longer and different in wording at over 1,000 points, seems to have been set from a later manuscript incorporating Shakespeare's subsequent revisions, prepared by an even more intrusive scribe with different tastes. As well as having been expurgated in compliance with the *Act to Restrain the Abuses of Players (1606), the Folio has fewer and less detailed stage directions, and more punctuation, and insists on spelling out in full some words and expressions contracted in the quarto. The Oxford edition, favouring Shakespeare's revisions, incorporates the new passages found only in the Folio (which include Desdemona's Willow song, and an increased emphasis on Emilia's role in the last act), but in other respects follows the unexpurgated and less scribally sophisticated quarto.

Sources: Shakespeare derived most of the plot for *Othello* from a story in *Cinthio's *Hecatommithi* (1565), which he must have read either in the original Italian or in a French translation published in 1584. In this rather squalid prose tale, an ensign lusts after his Moorish captain's Venetian wife Disdemona, and avenges her rejection of his advances by persuading the Moor that she has committed adultery with his friend, a captain. The ensign substantiates his allegation by stealing a handkerchief from Disdemona while she is fondling her baby, planting it in the captain's room, and showing the Moor the captain's wife copying its embroidery. Convinced of his wife's guilt, the Moor collaborates with the ensign to beat her to death in her chamber with a sand-filled stocking, and they then pull down the ceiling in order to make the murder look like an accident. Disdemona's relatives, though, learn the truth and eventually kill the Moor in revenge, and the ensign dies horribly under torture. Shakespeare both promoted and ennobled the Moor to create the first black tragic hero in Western literature, though the name he gave him may consciously echo a comedy: in Ben *Jonson's *Every Man in his Humour* (1598), the obsessively (and groundlessly) jealous husband is called Thorello (later renamed Kitely when Jonson rewrote the play to set it in London instead of Italy). Shakespeare moved the action to the earliest days of Othello and Desdemona's marriage, adding the characters of Brabanzio and the gullible disappointed suitor Roderigo, and set this relationship between a Moor and a Venetian against the backdrop of Venice's wars against the Ottoman Empire. Cyprus was attacked by the Turks in 1570 and fell the following year, but in the play military conflict gives place to marital once the characters reach Cyprus. Exotic details in Othello's speeches suggest a familiarity with *Pliny's *Natural History* (translated by Philemon Holland in 1601): *see also* TRAVEL, TRADE, AND COLONIALISM, MOORS.

SYNOPSIS: 1.1 The ensign Iago, enraged that the Moorish general Othello has made Cassio his lieutenant instead of him, has Roderigo awaken the Venetian senator Brabanzio and inform him that his daughter Desdemona has eloped with Othello. Horrified, Brabanzio raises a hue and cry. 1.2 Iago, concealing his enmity, warns Othello against Brabanzio's wrath. Cassio brings Othello a summons to the Duke. Brabanzio arrives with officers, accusing a calm Othello of having seduced his daughter by sorcery: all depart for the palace, Brabanzio confident that the Duke will support him. 1.3 The Duke learns that a hostile Turkish fleet is bound for Cyprus. When Othello arrives the Duke says he must be sent immediately against the Turks, before Brabanzio makes his accusation against the Moor. Sending for Desdemona as a witness, Othello eloquently describes how she fell in love with him when, invited by her father, he related his past military escapades and exotic adventures. Challenged by Brabanzio on her arrival, Desdemona says her first duty is now not to him but to her husband Othello: heartbroken, Brabanzio refuses the Duke's consolation. The Duke sends Othello to defend Cyprus: neither Brabanzio nor Othello wishes Desdemona to stay at her father's house during his absence, and she herself insists on accompanying her husband. Othello gives order that she shall travel to Cyprus in the conduct of Iago. Left with Iago, Roderigo despairs of ever enjoying Desdemona, but Iago, promising that her marriage to Othello will prove fragile, urges Roderigo to provide himself with money and come to Cyprus, undertaking to help him cuckold the Moor as part of his own revenge. Alone, Iago speaks of his hatred of Othello and a rumour that the Moor has cuckolded him, and hatches a plan to persuade Othello that his wife is unfaithful with Cassio.

2.1 Montano, governor of Cyprus, awaits news of the Turkish fleet, soon reported to have been wrecked in continuing storms. Cassio arrives from Venice, anxious for the safety of Othello's ship. Iago, his wife Emilia, Desdemona, and Roderigo arrive on another vessel, and receive a courtly welcome from Cassio. Iago banters misogynistically with Desdemona as she awaits Othello's arrival, and watches as she speaks with Cassio, certain he can use their friendship to their undoing. Othello arrives and is blissfully reunited with Desdemona before confirming the destruction of the Turkish fleet. Left with Roderigo, Iago tells him Desdemona is in love with Cassio, and outlines a scheme by which this new rival may be discredited: placed in charge of the watch that night, Roderigo will provoke Cassio into a brawl. Alone, Iago claims he too desires Desdemona, to avenge his own alleged cuckolding by Othello, and hopes that by convincing the Moor she is false with Cassio he may enjoy Othello's favour. 2.2 A herald announces feasting in honour of Othello's marriage. 2.3 Leaving Cassio in charge, Othello retires to bed with Desdemona. Iago gets Cassio drunk among members of the Cypriot garrison, singing 'And let me the cannikin clink' and 'King Stephen was a worthy peer'. Iago alleges that Cassio is a drunkard, a story apparently confirmed when Cassio drives in Roderigo, who has succeeded in provoking him to fight. Montano tells Cassio he is drunk, and they also fight. An alarm bell summons Othello to quell this brawl: he interrogates the participants, and Iago, feigning to defend Cassio, blames the incident on the lieutenant. Othello cashiers Cassio before leading Desdemona, roused by the fray, back to bed. Alone with Iago, Cassio laments the loss of his reputation: Iago advises him to woo Desdemona to plead for his reinstatement. Alone, Iago reflects with satisfaction on his hypocrisy. A bruised Roderigo arrives, dissatisfied with Iago's progress on his behalf, and is reassured. Alone again, Iago plans to have his wife advise Desdemona to support Cassio's suit, and to arrange for Othello to find Cassio soliciting Desdemona.

3.1 The next morning Cassio has musicians play outside Othello's apartments: they are dismissed by a clown, whom Cassio sends to fetch Emilia. Iago arrives and undertakes to lead Othello away while Cassio speaks with Desdemona. A sympathetic Emilia promises to bring Cassio to her. 3.2 Othello arranges to meet Iago at the citadel. 3.3 Desdemona and Emilia promise Cassio to do all they can to persuade Othello to reinstate him: he takes his leave when he sees Othello and Iago approaching, a departure to which Iago insinuatingly draws Othello's attention. Desdemona speaks on Cassio's behalf, but Othello postpones the subject and asks to be left alone for a while. Iago, alone with the Moor, questions him about Cassio's role in his courtship, and at Othello's increasingly anxious and impatient promptings suggests that Othello should watch Desdemona carefully lest she be engaged in an affair with Cassio, warning against jealousy, and promising to help Othello investigate the situation. Alone, Othello, trusting Iago's supposed honesty, is convinced of Desdemona's infidelity, though when she returns his faith revives: nonetheless he complains of a headache, for which she offers a handkerchief to bind his brow, which he drops. When the troubled couple leave Emilia picks the handkerchief up, recognizing it as Othello's first gift to Desdemona, for which Iago has been asking, and which she gives him on his return. Iago, alone, plans to leave it in Cassio's lodging. Othello returns, already visibly distracted with jealousy, and demands that Iago prove the truth of his allegations. Iago claims he has overheard Cassio dreaming of illicit encounters with Desdemona and has seen him with the handkerchief. Othello vows revenge: Iago vows to serve it. Othello commands Iago to kill Cassio and means to kill Desdemona himself. 3.4 Desdemona sends the clown to fetch Cassio. She is troubled about the loss of the handkerchief, which Emilia denies having seen. Othello arrives, and Desdemona tells him she has summoned Cassio: he feigns a cold and asks for the handkerchief. When she says she has lost it he tells her it was magically charmed to ensure the continuance of mutual love, given to his mother by a sorceress, and that its loss is ominous: as his questioning about it grows more urgent, she attempts to change the subject back to Cassio, which enrages him further until he leaves. Desdemona and Emilia are alarmed by this unwonted behaviour. Cassio arrives with Iago, but Desdemona explains that Othello is uncharacteristically vexed and will not hear his suit. Desdemona decides Othello must be anxious about state affairs, and the two women go to seek him. Cassio is accosted by his mistress Bianca, who is suspicious when he asks her to copy the embroidery on Desdemona's handkerchief, which he has found in his chamber.

4.1 Othello, told by Iago that Cassio has admitted sleeping with Desdemona, falls into a fit. While Iago gloats, Cassio arrives: Iago has him wait nearby. When Othello recovers, Iago hides him where he may watch Cassio talking, as Iago claims, about his liaison with Desdemona: he then converses flippantly with Cassio about the doting Bianca. Othello, watching, is convinced Cassio is laughing about Desdemona, and is even more enraged when he sees Bianca give Cassio back the handkerchief. Alone again with Iago, Othello asks Iago to fetch him poison for Desdemona: Iago persuades him instead to strangle her in bed, and promises to kill Cassio before midnight. Desdemona arrives with Lodovico, a Venetian senator who has brought letters: Othello, with increasing fury, reads that he is to return to Venice, leaving Cassio in his place, and strikes Desdemona. She is leaving in tears, but he calls her back before dismissing her again, eventually storming off himself. Lodovico is astonished. 4.2 Emilia tells Othello Desdemona is innocent, but he dismisses her as a bawd, telling her to keep the door while he speaks with Desdemona. He accuses his wife of whoredom, discounts her denials, and insultingly gives Emilia money as he leaves. Desdemona, weeping, speaks with Iago and Emilia, vowing eternal fidelity despite Othello's mistreatment. After the women leave, Roderigo comes to accuse Iago of merely leading him on: Iago promises he will soon enjoy Desdemona so long as he is prepared to kill Cassio. 4.3 After supper, Othello, leaving to walk with Lodovico, bids Desdemona prepare for bed and dismiss Emilia. Undressing with Emilia's help, Desdemona sings the Willow song ('The poor soul sat sighing by a sycamore tree'). The two women discuss infidelity, which Desdemona can hardly believe any woman would commit: Emilia, however, argues that wives should revenge themselves in kind against unfaithful husbands.

5.1 Iago sets Roderigo on to kill Cassio in the dark, but Cassio wounds Roderigo, and Iago, attacking unseen from behind, is able to wound Cassio only in the leg. Hearing his cries, Othello is satisfied that Cassio is dying and, inspired by Iago's example, goes to kill Desdemona. Lodovico, with Brabanzio's brother Graziano, hears the wounded men: Iago, feigning to help, stabs Roderigo, then pretends horror on finding him dead. When Bianca arrives Iago accuses her of being behind the incident, and when Emilia comes he sends her to tell Othello of what has happened. 5.2 Othello comes, with a light, to the sleeping Desdemona and kisses her tenderly, though convinced of her guilt. When she awakens he tells her to pray, as he is about to kill her. Desdemona protests her innocence and that of Cassio, weeping when Othello tells her he is dead: he smothers her and conceals her body behind the bed curtains as Emilia calls for admittance, bringing the dismaying news that Roderigo is dead and Cassio wounded. Desdemona, regaining consciousness, tells Emilia she has been falsely murdered but insists Othello was not her killer before dying. Othello, however, admits killing her, explaining to a horrified Emilia that he did so because he learned from Iago that she had committed adultery with Cassio. Emilia calls for help and confronts Iago, who arrives with Montano and Graziano. Graziano says the sight of Desdemona's body would drive Brabanzio to despair had he not already died of grief over her marriage. Othello says he saw Cassio with Desdemona's handkerchief: aghast, Emilia declares how she gave the handkerchief to her husband. Realizing the truth, Othello runs at Iago, but Montano disarms him: Iago stabs Emilia before fleeing, pursued by Montano. Emilia, still reproaching Othello with Desdemona's innocence, dies. Othello produces another sword and laments over Desdemona's body, intending suicide. Lodovico, Montano, and a crippled Cassio enter with Iago under guard, whom Othello wounds before being again disarmed: Othello asks forgiveness of Cassio, and asks why Iago has so conspired against him. Iago says he will never speak again. Cassio and Lodovico, with the help of letters found on Roderigo, unravel Iago's machinations: Lodovico says Othello must be taken to Venice. Othello, however, asking to be remembered fairly, along with his services to the state, stabs himself, just as he once stabbed a Turk who had beaten a Venetian. He dies kissing Desdemona. Lodovico, leaving to report these tragic events in Venice, urges Cassio, now governor of Cyprus, to have Iago tortured to death.

Artistic features: The diction of *Othello* is unusually polarized between the glamorous, exotic music of the Moor's poetry and the harsh cynicism of his ensign's soliloquies: this has contributed to the play's attractiveness to operatic composers such as *Verdi, who have translated Othello into a tenor and Iago into a baritone. Partly through these soliloquies, *Othello* exploits *dramatic irony more relentlessly than any other play in the canon, letting us know of 'honest' Iago's treachery from its opening scene onwards but denying that knowledge to the rest of the cast until the final act. The play's intensity is assisted by the absence of any sub-plot, and by the skill with which Shakespeare compresses the narrative he found in Cinthio: it is this compression which gives rise to the famous 'double time' effect, whereby the play's events seem at once to take place with terrible swiftness over only two or three days (so that there is no time for Othello to realize the truth) and yet to encompass enough time for Iago's allegations to be plausible.

CRITICAL HISTORY: The subject of more 17th-century allusions than any other Shakespeare play except *The Tempest*, *Othello* was already established as one of Shakespeare's greatest achievements long before Thomas *Rymer made his ineffectual attack on it in 1693 (describing it as 'a bloody farce', a view which would be developed more sympathetically in W. H. *Auden's account of Iago's scheme as a terrible practical joke). Samuel *Johnson and William *Hazlitt alike praised the rich contrasts between its characters and the skill of its design. *Iago influenced *Milton's dramatization of Satan, and would fascinate the *Romantics, *Coleridge finding in his soliloquies (with their excess of potential rationalizations for his crimes) 'the motive-hunting of motiveless malignity'. Although some 19th-century Americans (including Joseph Quincy *Adams) found the play's depiction of interracial marriage objectionable (and even Coleridge refused to see Othello as black, preferring to envisage him as an aristocratic Arab), most 19th-century critics found Othello convincingly noble. It was only in the 20th century, when T. S. *Eliot took issue with A. C. *Bradley's account of the play, that some began to adopt Iago's view of Othello as a bombastic self-deceiver. This argument between pro- and anti-Othello factions has now been largely displaced by the discussion of Shakespeare's attitude to *Moors, and whether Othello's unquestioning assumption that adulterous wives should die is intended to be seen as confirming the racist views expressed by Brabanzio and Iago. Iago's interconnected obsessions with class, race, and gender have indeed helped to keep the play central to much current critical discourse, whether *feminist, *Marxist, or *psychoanalytic.

STAGE HISTORY: The quarto reports that the play was acted at both the *Blackfriars and the *Globe, and an eyewitness account of a performance in Oxford in 1610 confirms the power the play exerted on the Jacobean stage. Still in the repertory through the 1630s, it was revived in unadapted form at the Restoration (so that *Desdemona was one of the first roles to be played by a woman on the English professional stage) and few seasons have gone by without a revival since. Outside the English-speaking world, the play has been especially popular in *Russia. The roles of Desdemona and Iago are discussed elsewhere. Great Othellos have included *Betterton, *Quin, Spranger *Barry, J. P. *Kemble, and Edmund *Kean, whose frightening, animalistic performance in the role was one of his greatest from 1814 until his death (after collapsing onstage in Act 4) in 1833. The American Ira *Aldridge was the first black actor to play Othello, a role he played almost everywhere except in his own country between 1826 and 1865, but the role remained predominantly a blackface one (from *Forrest and *Booth to *Salvini and *Forbes-Robertson) until the advent of Paul *Robeson, who first played it at the *Old Vic in 1930 and last in Stratford in 1958 and whose record-breaking Broadway run in the role in 1943 greatly distressed white supremacists. Laurence *Olivier's Othello for the *National Theatre in 1963, a magnificent egotist who reverts to barbarism, was in retrospect the last possible flowering of the blackface tradition: non-black actors who have played the role since (such as Anthony Hopkins and Ben *Kingsley) have preferred to make the role less African. Patrick *Stewart even played a white Othello among an otherwise all-black cast in Washington in 1998. Nowadays some black actors refuse the part on the grounds that in making an exotic spectacle of Othello's blackness the play is innately racist, but it has elicited towering performances from the likes of James Earl *Jones and Willard White, and Janet *Suzman's production at the Market Theatre in Johannesburg in the late 1980s, with John Kani in the title role, made an eloquent protest against apartheid. *MD*

ON THE SCREEN: The most interesting *silent film is the 93-minute German *Othello* (1922) directed by Dmitri Buchowetzki, with Emil Jannings as the Moor. The four best-known sound cinema films are those made by Orson *Welles (1952) and Sergei Yutkevich (1955), Stuart Burge's film with Olivier as Othello (1965), and the *Othello* directed by Oliver Parker (1995). Pre-eminent among those filmed for television are Janet Suzman's Johannesburg production (1988) and Trevor *Nunn's RSC production with Willard White as the Moor (1990).

Despite its unimpressive Venice sequences, Welles's film, with its Moroccan location brilliantly exploited for dramatic contrasts, stands in a class of its own. Yutkevich's *Othello*, shot in colour and originally with Russian dialogue, is profoundly memorable for its visual impact, with stone, sea, and sky as elements in the film's language. Burge's film of John Dexter's National Theatre production is historically important for its capturing of Olivier's immense performance, though his stage projection is somewhat overpowering for the camera. While Jonathan *Miller's BBC TV *Othello* (1981) featuring Anthony Hopkins was criticized for its failure to give Othello the necessary dramatic weight, the two stage productions filmed for television focus well on characters other than the Moor. Parker's Othello is Laurence Fishburne, an American black actor whose portrayal has been seen as capitalizing on the recent media dramatization of the O. J. Simpson trial. Kenneth *Branagh plays Iago. *AD*

RECENT MAJOR EDITIONS

E. A. J. Honigmann (Arden 3rd series, 1997); Kenneth Muir (New Penguin, 1968); Norman Sanders (New Cambridge 1984)

SOME REPRESENTATIVE CRITICISM

Auden, W. H., 'The Joker in the Pack', in *The Dyer's Hand* (1948)

Bradley, A. C., in *Shakespearean Tragedy* (1904)

Callaghan, Dympna, 'Othello was a White Man', in *Shakespeare without Women: Representing Gender and Race on the Renaissance Stage* (2000)
Eliot, T. S., 'Shakespeare and the Stoicism of Seneca', in *Selected Essays* (1932)
Empson, William, in *The Structure of Complex Words* (1951)
Gardner, Helen, *Othello*: A Retrospect, 1900–67', *Shakespeare Survey*, 21 (1968)
Leavis, F. R., in *The Common Pursuit* (1952)
Stallybrass, Peter, 'Patriarchal Territories: The Body Enclosed', in Margaret Ferguson, Maureen Quilligan, and Nancy Vickers (eds.), *Rewriting the Renaissance* (1986)

Overdone, Mistress. A bawd in *Measure for Measure*, she is sent to prison, 3.1.464. *AB*

Ovid (Publius Ovidius Naso) (43 BC–AD 17) was Shakespeare's favourite classical poet: 'for the elegancy, facility, and golden cadence of poesy . . . Ovidius Naso was the man. And why indeed "Naso" [nose] but for smelling out the odoriferous flowers of fancy, the jerks of invention' (*Love's Labour's Lost* 4.2.122–5). The epitome of style, the preceptor of love, Ovid was exiled from Rome to Tomis on the Black Sea for an offence against the Emperor Augustus. Hence Touchstone among the exiles in Arden: 'I am here with thee and thy goats as the most capricious poet honest Ovid was among the Goths' (*As You Like It* 3.3.5–6). At school Shakespeare would have been drilled in extracts from Ovid's works in their original Latin—first brief passages in textbooks for the teaching of grammar and rhetoric, then more substantial sections of the poems themselves.

Ovid's love poems, the *Amores*, are among the key precedents for the Sonnets; each sequence is a set of variations on the moods of love, shifting rapidly between different poses and tones. The *Fasti*, which linked major events in Roman history and mythology to the calendrical year, provided the principal source for *The Rape of Lucrece*. The *Amores* could have been read in *Marlowe's translation, but the *Fasti* were only available in Latin. When Ben *Jonson wrote of Shakespeare's 'small Latin' he was measuring with the yardstick of his own prodigious learning—by modern standards, Shakespeare had perfectly adequate Latin.

Ovid's *Heroides*, imaginary verse-epistles from women in mythology who are deserted by their lovers (e.g. Ariadne on Naxos, Dido after the departure of Aeneas from Carthage), were widely studied in school, where a frequent exercise was to imitate them. They are cited in the tutoring scene in *The Taming of the Shrew* (3.1.28–9), which also alludes playfully to Ovid's notorious *Ars amatoria* or 'art of love'. Like *Lyly and Marlowe, Shakespeare found in the *Heroides* models for a character's solitary self-examination at moments of emotional crisis.

The influence of these shorter works pales beside that of Ovid's magnum opus, the *Metamorphoses* (written before his exile in AD 8). About 90% of Shakespeare's allusions to classical mythology refer to stories included in this epic compendium of tales. Shakespeare knew the book in both the original Latin and Arthur Golding's 1567 English translation. Golding's language influenced, for example, the bristles on the boar in *Venus and Adonis* and the 'babbling' of the nymph Echo to whom Viola compares herself in *Twelfth Night* (1.5.262). Shakespeare frequently referred to the stories in the *Metamorphoses* as parallels or paradigms for the emotional turmoil of his characters. Where Ovid told of bodily metamorphoses wrought by extremes of passion, Shakespeare translated these into psychological transformations and vivid metaphors. Ovid was especially important for his representation of female feeling.

Shakespeare was most Ovidian at the beginning and the end of his career. Both his early narrative poems are based on Ovidian sources. *Venus and Adonis* takes a 100-line story from the third book of the *Metamorphoses* and expands it into more than 1,000 lines of elegant artifice. Shakespeare wove into the narrative structure elaborate arguments for and against the 'use' of beauty. For this, he pulled together different parts of Ovid: the witty persuasions to love are in the manner of the *Amores* and the *Ars amatoria*, while the figure of the vain youth has something of Narcissus and that of the forward woman more than a little of Salmacis, who seduces another gorgeous but self-absorbed boy, Hermaphroditus (*Metamorphoses* 4). *Lucrece* combines the Ovidian narrative of Tarquin's act of rape with a long lament in the tradition of female 'complaint' which descends from the *Heroides*. Tarquin's ravishing stride returns as a sinister image in several of the plays.

If *Venus and Adonis* and *The Rape of Lucrece* are poetic explorations of, respectively, the light and the dark sides of desire, then *A Midsummer Night's Dream* (written soon after) and *Titus Andronicus* (written or revised in 1594) are their dramatic equivalents. *Titus* is explicitly patterned on the story of the rape of Philomel in book 7 of the *Metamorphoses* (some fifteen years after *Titus* Shakespeare returned to this tale in *Cymbeline*, where Giacomo notices in Innogen's bedchamber that 'She hath been reading late, | The tale of Tereus. Here the leaf's turned down | Where Philomel gave up'—2.2.44–6). A copy of Ovid's book is actually brought on stage in *Titus* (4.1) and used as a plot-device: by pointing to the story of Philomel, raped in the secluded woods by her brother-in-law Tereus, Lavinia indicates that she too has been violated. Titus then acts out his revenge in deliberate homage to that of Procne, Philomel's sister: 'For worse than Philomel you used my daughter, | So worse than Progne I will be revenged' (5.2.193–4)—Procne tricked Tereus into eating his own son, whereas Titus goes one better and bakes both Tamora's sons in his pie.

In *A Midsummer Night's Dream* the metamorphic power of the flower 'love-in-idleness' is Ovidian. Bottom's assumption of the ass's head plays on animal transformation, while 'Pyramus and Thisbe'—which includes clanking verse that may parody the 'fourteener' of Golding's translation of the *Metamorphoses*—is a comical staging of one of Ovid's most tragic stories of doomed love (*Metamorphoses* 4). Ovid's great theme is the inevitability of change. Book 15 of the *Metamorphoses* offers a philosophical discourse on the subject, mediated via the philosophy of Pythagoras. It was from here that Shakespeare got many of those images of transience that roll through the Sonnets, but *A Midsummer Night's Dream* is his chief dramatic celebration of how something positive and potentially enduring can grow from change: 'And all their minds transfigured so together | More witnesseth than fancy's images, | And grows to something of great constancy' (5.1.24–6).

Though no subsequent comedy has transformation woven so fully into its texture as this, Ovid was of continued importance in Shakespeare's later work in the genre. At the climax of *The Merchant of Venice*, Lorenzo and Jessica duet upon a sequence of Ovidian lovers—Pyramus and Thisbe, Dido, Medea. The myth of Actaeon, transformed into a hart and torn to pieces by his own hounds as punishment for his gaze upon the naked goddess Diana bathing, is alluded to in both *The Merry Wives of Windsor* and *Twelfth Night*. The Golden Age before the earth was scarred by property-ownership, legal codes, and empire-building (*Metamorphoses* 1) is an important point of reference in both *As You Like It* and *The Tempest*.

In *The Winter's Tale*, Perdita, flowers in hand, invokes Proserpina (4.4.116), whose abduction to the underworld by Dis (*Metamorphoses* 5) symbolizes the coming of winter, her recovery the return of spring. Florizel, meanwhile, compares his mock-transformation of dress and rank to the disguises of the Ovidian gods (4.4.25–31). The reanimation of Hermione is modelled on the bringing to life of Pygmalion's ivory statue (*Metamorphoses* 10).

Shakespeare's most sustained passage of Ovidian imitation is Prospero's renunciation of his rough magic (*The Tempest* 5.1.33 ff.). That Shakespeare went to the *Metamorphoses* so late in his career shows that his Ovidianism was no mere young man's affectation; that Prospero's speech is modelled on the words of Ovid's witch Medea (*Metamorphoses* 7) raises questions about the 'whiteness' of his magic. *JBt*

Barkan, Leonard, *The Gods Made Flesh: Metamorphosis and the Pursuit of Paganism* (1986)
Bate, Jonathan, *Shakespeare and Ovid* (1993)
Carroll, William, *The Metamorphoses of Shakespearean Comedy* (1985)
Nims, J. F. (ed.), *Ovid's Metamorphoses: The Arthur Golding Translation* (1965, repr. 2000)
Taylor, Tony (ed.), *Shakespeare's Ovid* (2000)

Oxford, Earl of. A Lancastrian in *Richard Duke of York* (*3 Henry VI*), he is captured at the battle of Tewkesbury, 5.5.2. In *Richard III* he speaks two lines, 5.2.17–18. He is based on John de Vere (1443–1513), 13th Earl of Oxford. On the 17th Earl, see OXFORDIAN THEORY. *AB*

Oxford English Dictionary, commonly known as *OED* and now in its second edition (1986). It is constructed on historical principles, using quotations, listed chronologically, to illustrate the various senses of a word, as well as providing etymology, pronunciation, and derivatives. It includes nearly all the vocabulary of important authors from 1590 to 1660, including Shakespeare. *SLB*

Oxfordian theory, a term for what has since the mid-20th century been the most visible strand in the *Authorship Controversy, the claim that Shakespeare's works were in fact written by Edward de Vere, 17th Earl of Oxford (1550–1604). De Vere published verse and also wrote comedies, though these do not survive (they are mentioned by *Meres in *Palladis Tamia*, quite independently of Shakespeare's). His involvement with the theatre extended to employing *Lyly as a secretary, and patronizing an acting company from 1580 onwards, Oxford's Men, who seem to have mainly toured the provinces and were absorbed by Worcester's Men after 1602. De Vere was a notorious figure at Elizabeth's court, violent and irresponsible: he killed a servant when only 17, and his many subsequent quarrels included a brawl with the family of a lady-in-waiting he had impregnated and a conspiracy against *Sidney. In between squandering his estate, fighting in Flanders, and feuding, however, he established a reputation as a good dancer and musician.

The view that de Vere supplemented his more public involvement with poetry and the theatre by secretly writing the Shakespeare canon in his spare time was first put forward by the unfortunately named Thomas J. Looney in *'Shakespeare' Identified* (1920). Already convinced that Shakespeare could not have written his own works, Looney hit upon Oxford as the true author after noticing that his poem 'Women', anthologized in *Palgrave's Golden Treasury*, was written in the same (common) stanzaic form as *Venus and Adonis.* Looney offered no explanation as to why or how de Vere should have published mediocre work under his own name and masterpieces under Shakespeare's, nor why the deception should have been kept up by the compilers of the Folio, and he had to argue that the Shakespeare plays visibly written after de Vere's death in 1604 must have been subsequently revised by others. An exception was *The Tempest*, which Looney simply dismissed as inauthentic.

Despite the theory's shortcomings it attracted followers in the 1920s and 1930s (most notoriously Sigmund *Freud), and was further developed in the 1950s by Charles and Dorothy Ogburn, who in the 1,300-page *This Star of England* claimed that Oxford had been secretly married to Queen *Elizabeth and that the *Fair Youth of the Sonnets was their hitherto unacknowledged son, the Earl of *Southampton. Since the 1980s the Oxfordian theory has been enthusiastically propagated by one of de Vere's descendants, the Earl of Burford (sometimes to the embarrassment of his father, the current Earl of Oxford), who has successfully appealed, in particular, to the displaced snobbery of wealthy Texans. *MD*

Bate, Jonathan, in *The Genius of Shakespeare* (1998)
Matus, Irvin Leigh, *Shakespeare, in Fact* (1999)
Schoenbaum, S., *Shakespeare's Lives* (1970, rev. edn. 1991)

Oxford Shakespeare (1) 1982, in progress; (2) 1986. **(1)** A new 'Oxford Shakespeare', one work to a volume, began to appear, under the general editorship of Stanley Wells, in 1982. Like the New *Cambridge edition that began life at almost the same time, this series is based on a fresh appraisal of the texts by scholarly editors, as well as a concern with performance, and uses illustrations to enliven the substantial critical introductions. It also provides a collation and notes on the same pages as the text. Its format and printing style suggest a more sober approach than that of the New Cambridge, but in their general aims the two editions appear to be much alike.

(2) *The Complete Works*, general editors Stanley Wells and Gary Taylor, published by Oxford University Press, together with a second volume containing an edited 'original spelling' text, and often referred to as the Oxford Shakespeare, appeared in 1986. It is based on a comprehensive rethinking both of the textual basis for each of the plays, and also of the best way to present them for present-day readers. The works are printed in a newly determined chronological order, which often challenges previous assumptions, though the dating of many plays and poems remains speculative. This means, for instance, that *1 Henry VI* follows *2 Henry VI*, here titled *The First Part of the Contention of the Two Famous Houses of York and Lancaster.* (The title is taken from the quarto, although the control text for this play is the Folio). The effect is destabilizing, as is this edition's choice of texts, preferring, where possible, those associated with the stage rather than those thought to be derived from Shakespeare's drafts or *'foul papers'. The edition thus subverts a tradition of textual criticism that argued for recovering as nearly as possible what was in Shakespeare's manuscript. The edition also acknowledges that Shakespeare may have *revised his plays, most notably by printing two texts of *King Lear*, based on the quarto and the Folio, and also by relegating to a list of 'Additional Passages' the lines found in the second quarto of *Hamlet* but not in the Folio text. Another innovatory feature of the edition is the provision of numerous stage directions that help the reader to visualize the staging, so that 'Enter Ghost' (*Hamlet* 1.1.37) becomes 'Enter the Ghost in complete armour, holding a truncheon, with his beaver up.' Some critics of the edition have been troubled that these editorial interventions are often not marked as such, and others protested that such innovations as renaming Falstaff, a character of mythic repute, as *Oldcastle (in *1 Henry IV*), are ill advised. The edition was published with double-column plain text on the page, very brief prefaces to each of the works, a glossary at the end of the book, and a general introduction that includes a brief explanation of the thinking that went into the edition. A full account of this thinking was later published separately in *William Shakespeare: A Textual Companion* (1987). The text of the Oxford Shakespeare has been taken over, with some modifications, into the *Norton Shakespeare (1997), which adds the full apparatus that American students expect. *RAF*

Oxford University Dramatic Society (OUDS, pronounced 'owds') was formed in 1885 by undergraduates and limited by the university to the performance of the classics, especially Shakespeare. The involvement of professionals (including John *Gielgud) as guest directors and designers has sometimes attracted national reviews. It has launched many theatrical careers, among them those of Peter *Brook and Kenneth *Tynan. *SLB*

oxymoron, a compressed paradox, in which complete opposites qualify one another:

> Feather of lead, bright smoke, cold fire, sick health
> (*Romeo and Juliet* 1.1.177)

This figure of speech is particularly associated with *Petrarch, and became a cliché among his English imitators. *CB*

Pacino, Al. See RICHARD III; UNITED STATES OF AMERICA.

Pacorus, son of Orodes I, King of Parthia, invaded Syria unsuccessfully, dying in battle 38 BC. His body is paraded in triumph by Ventidius, *Antony and Cleopatra* 3.1. *AB*

Padua, in the north of Italy, was a famous university town and a centre of art and literature in the Middle Ages. It is the scene of much of *The Taming of the Shrew*. *AB*

Page, Anne. In *The Merry Wives of Windsor* she elopes with Fenton, but is forgiven by her mother and father, who had intended her for Caius and Slender respectively. *AB*

Page, Mistress Margaret. See FORD, MISTRESS ALICE.

Page, Master (George). Father of Anne and William, he rejects Nim's information that Falstaff is pursuing his wife, *The Merry Wives of Windsor* 2.1, and advises Ford to do the same. *AB*

Page, William. Younger brother of Anne Page, his Latin grammar is tested by Sir Hugh Evans, *The Merry Wives of Windsor* 4.1.

pageants. Professional players were hired to perform in public events celebrating the installation of officials such as the lord mayor of London. On 31 May 1610 the investiture of Prince *Henry as Prince of Wales was celebrated with a sea-pageant on the Thames in which Richard *Burbage and John *Rice performed as tritons. In recompense, Burbage and Rice were allowed to keep their costumes which probably were reused for *Caliban and *Ariel-as-sea-nymph in *The Tempest*. *GE*

pages. **(1)** *Taming of the Shrew*. See BARTHOLOMEW. **(2)** In *Richard III* a page is sent to fetch Tyrrell, 4.2. **(3)** *Love's Labour's Lost*. See MOTE. **(4)** Mercutio's Page is sent to fetch a surgeon, *Romeo and Juliet* 3.1.94. Paris's Page alerts the watch, *Romeo and Juliet* 5.3. **(5)** *The Merry Wives of Windsor*. See ROBIN. **(6)** Falstaff has a page in *2 Henry IV*, possibly the same person as Robin and the Boy in *The Merry Wives of Windsor* and *Henry V* respectively. **(7)** Two pages sing *'It was a lover and his lass' to Touchstone and Audrey, *As You Like It* 5.3. **(8)** A page summons Paroles, *All's Well That Ends Well* 1.1.183. **(9)** A page banters with Apemantus, *Timon of Athens* 2.2. **(10)** A page attends Gardiner, *All Is True* (*Henry VIII*) 5.1. *AB*

Painter. He and a Poet present their work to Timon, *Timon of Athens* 1.1; they are reviled by him in the woods, 5.1 *AB*

Painter, William (*c.*1540–94), schoolmaster, fraudulent clerk at the Tower of London, translator. Painter's *Palace of Pleasure* (1566–7) is a collection of prose tales, mainly from *Boccaccio, *Bandello, and *Cinthio, in Painter's own English translations. As a repository of plot material, it may have been a particular favourite of Shakespeare's: the outlines of *The Rape of Lucrece, Romeo and Juliet, The Merry Wives of Windsor, Timon of Athens*, and *All's Well That Ends Well* are all found in these volumes. Painter translated with such conscientiousness that he made few alterations to his sources, though he may have been responsible for the protagonist's name in *Romeo and Juliet* being Romeo, not Romeus as in *Brooke. *JKS*

painting. Although illustrators had been providing frontispieces to the plays since *Rowe's edition of 1709, the first depictions on canvas of scenes from Shakespeare belong to the 1730s, when British artists such as *Hogarth identified these as a properly native subject matter at a time of increasing cultural nationalism. As the century progressed the search for sublime and national-historical subjects brought painters repeatedly to the great tragedies, especially *King Lear*, depicted, for example, in Francis *Hayman's decorations for Vauxhall Gardens (1741), James *Barry's *Lear Weeping over the Body of the Dead Cordelia* (1786–8, now in the Tate Gallery), and the early drawings of William *Blake. *Fuseli, meanwhile, found inspiration in the live theatre (returning repeatedly, for example, to compositions derived from actors' movements in *Macbeth*), and in the supernatural characters of the tragedies and comedies alike. Art and politics were again compounded in the opening of *Boydell's *Shakespeare Gallery in 1789, which appealed to national sentiment as Britain prepared for war with revolutionary France. Paradoxically, it was the collapse of the print trade with France that also contributed to the gallery's sale in 1803.

Later in the 19th century, scenes from plays by Shakespeare set in Italy and in historically distant eras provided material that met the artistic agenda of the *Pre-Raphaelite Brotherhood, who aspired to pre-industrial standards of artistic production, while less idealistic history painters mined the Roman plays for subjects of classical violence and voluptuousness. The 20th century's preference for abstraction, however, led to the virtual disappearance of Shakespearian scenes as a subject for major painters, and despite some noteworthy commissioned portraits of actors in Shakespearian roles (such as those held in the *RSC Collection in Stratford) it is hard to imagine the plays being rediscovered as such in the age of Damien Hirst. *CT*

Pakistan. See INDIA.

Palamon, Arcite's rival for Emilia, is to marry her at the end of *The Two Noble Kinsmen*. *AB*

Palladio, Andrea (1508–80), Italian architect, builder of the Teatro Olimpico in Vicenza in 1583. Palladio's neoclassical designs were based on principles of harmonious proportion derived from mathematical ratios, especially 1:2, 3:4, 2:3, and 3:5. Inigo *Jones's absorption of Palladian principles is evidenced in his Whitehall Banqueting House of 1622 and the Cockpit-at-Court playhouse conversion of 1629. *GE*

Ackerman, James S., *Palladio* (1966)
Wittkower, Rudolf, *Palladio and English Palladianism* (1974)

Palmer, John, actors: 'Gentleman' Palmer (1728–68) made his Drury Lane debut in the 1748–9 season playing Graziano, Lennox, and Cassio. At his illness and death his roles were inherited by 'Plausible Jack' Palmer (1744–98, no relation) who, after an indifferent career to that point, became one of the most versatile actors and best comedians of his day with successes as Falstaff, Sir Toby Belch, and Henry VIII. *CMSA*

Pandar. See PANDER.

Pandarus. Owing much more to *Chaucer's version of the character than *Homer's Greek hero, he is the uncle of Cressida and intermediary between her and Troilus in *Troilus and Cressida.* *AB*

Pander. Sometimes given the proper name 'Pandar', he owns the brothel in *Pericles.* *AB*

Pandolf, Cardinal. He is a papal legate who excommunicates John, *King John* 3.1, forcing King Philip of France to end his new alliance. (He is 'Pandolph' or 'Pandulpho' in the First *Folio and 'Pandulph' in *Holinshed.) *AB*

Panthino. The servant of Antonio, he advises him to send Proteus to the Emperor's court, *The Two Gentlemen of Verona* 1.3. *AB*

paradox, an expression that is or appears puzzlingly self-contradictory: 'the truest poetry is the most feigning' (*As You Like It* 3.3.16–17). *CB*

parallel texts. Several of Shakespeare's plays, including *Hamlet* and *King Lear,* survive in two or more early versions. Editors since the 19th century have often printed the textual versions in parallel columns in order to facilitate study and analysis of their differences. *ER*

The Parallel King Lear 1608–1623, ed. Michael Warren (1989)
The Three-Text Hamlet, ed. Paul Bertram and Bernice W. Kliman (1991)

'Pardon, goddess of the night', sung, probably by a musician or musicians (the text is unclear), in *Much Ado About Nothing* 5.3.12. The original music is unknown. *JB*

Paris. One of Priam's sons in *Troilus and Cressida,* he is wounded by Menelaus (mentioned 1.1.110), whose wife Helen he has abducted. They fight again, 5.8. *AB*

Paris, County. Intended by Capulet for Juliet, he bitterly laments her supposed death, *Romeo and Juliet* 4.4.68–73. He is slain by Romeo, 5.3.73. *AB*

Paris Garden. See ANIMAL SHOWS; THEATRES, ELIZABETHAN AND JACOBEAN.

parison, parallelism of construction in successive clauses or lines:

> My manors, rents, revenues, I forgo;
> My acts, decrees, and statutes I deny
> (*Richard II* 4.1.212–13)

CB

parley, a *trumpet signal indicating a meeting between opposing parties, or a ceasing of hostilities (e.g. *1 Henry IV* 4.3.31). *JB*

Parnassus plays, the collective name for three anonymous plays, *The Pilgrimage to Parnassus, The First Part of the Return from Parnassus,* and *The Second Part of the Return from Parnassus,* written between 1598 and 1602 and performed at St John's College, Cambridge. The theme is several young scholars' attempts to find occupations, and in the final part two of them try to join the *Chamberlain's Men. During their audition, William *Kempe disparages university plays and university men, in particular *Jonson, to whom Shakespeare has given 'a purge that made him beray his credit', which suggests that Shakespeare too indulged in personal satire. In *First Part of the Return from Parnassus* are disparaging allusions to Shakespeare's *Venus and Adonis* and *The Rape of Lucrece.* *GE*

Anon., *The Three Parnassus Plays (1598–1601),* ed. J. B. Leishman (1949)
Glatzer, Paula, *The Complaint of the Poet. The Parnassus Plays: A Critical Study of the Trilogy Performed at St John's College, Cambridge, 1598/99–1601/2, Authors Anonymous* (1977)

Paroles, a cowardly braggart who falls victim to the conspiracy of his comrades in *All's Well That Ends Well.* *AB*

Parry, Sir Hubert (1848–1918), English composer. He set a large number of Shakespeare's songs and sonnets, either as solo songs or as partsongs. Many were published in his twelve-volume collection *English Lyrics* (1885–1920) or in *A Garland of Shakespearian and Other Old Fashioned Songs,* Op. 21 (1874). *IBC*

parts. Players of Shakespeare's time were not given the entire script of a play to rehearse, but only their 'part' or 'side' written out with cues indicating when to commence a speech (cf. *A Midsummer Night's Dream* 3.1.92–5). The only extant 'part' is for Edward *Alleyn's title role in Robert *Greene's *Orlando furioso,* in the form of a scroll over 17 feet (5 m) long. *GE*

Pasco, Richard (b. 1926), British actor. Having won attention as Berowne, Henry V, Angelo, and Hamlet at the Bristol Old Vic, he went on to play leading parts for the *Royal Shakespeare Company, notably both Richard II and Bolingbroke (alternating with Ian *Richardson) in 1973 and Timon of Athens in 1980. *MJ*

passamezzo (passy-measures), a livelier version of the *pavan; also chord sequences, associated originally with the dance, which formed the basis for many popular song and dance tunes throughout Europe from the late 16th century onwards: *'Greensleeves' is based on the minor or Dorian mode *passamezzo antico.* The eight-bar phrase structure may explain Sir Toby (*Twelfth Night,* 5.1.198) calling the drunk surgeon (whose eyes are set at 'eight i'th' morning') a 'passy-measures pavan'. *JB*

Passionate Pilgrim, The, a collection, ascribed to Shakespeare, of 20 short poems, mostly amorous, some of them mildly erotic, published in 1599 by William *Jaggard. The first edition survives only in part of one copy; the second followed in the same year. It opens with versions of two of Shakespeare's Sonnets (138 and 144), perhaps in order to capitalize on Francis *Meres's reference, in the previous year, to Shakespeare's 'sugared sonnets among his private friends'. The remaining poems include three extracts from *Love's Labour's Lost* along with several other short poems known to be by writers other than Shakespeare: two by Richard *Barnfield, one by Bartholomew Griffin, a version of *Marlowe's 'Come live with me and be my love', and the last stanza of the reply to that poem attributed to Sir Walter *Ralegh. For no clear reason, the first fourteen poems are followed by a second title page promising 'Sonnets to Several Notes of Music'. The eleven poems not definitely known to be by writers other than Shakespeare are included in the Oxford edition, with a statement that the ascription is very doubtful.

A third edition, of 1612, adds poems from Thomas *Heywood's *Troia Britannica* (1609). In his *Apology for Actors,* published in the same year, Heywood protested against the 'manifest injury' of printing writings by him 'in a less volume, under the name of another, which may put the world in opinion I might steal them from him'. Acknowledging his lines unworthy of Shakespeare, Heywood declared 'the author'—i.e. Shakespeare—'much offended with Master Jaggard that, altogether unknown to him, presumed to make bold with his name'. Probably as a result, the original title page was cancelled and replaced with one that did not mention Shakespeare. *SW*

passy-measures. See PASSAMEZZO.

Pasternak, Boris (1890–1960), Russian novelist, poet, and translator. Unable to publish his own poetry under the tyrant Stalin, he became the official translator of Shakespeare into Russian. His *Gamlet* (*Hamlet*) and *Korol Lir* (*King Lear*) were used in films by *Kozintsev. A poem linking Hamlet and Christ is the first of the hero's poems printed at the end of his banned novel *Doctor Zhivago* (1958). *TM*

pastoral, a kind of imaginative literature taking its characters and settings from an idealized conception of the unhurried life of shepherds and shepherdesses. In prose or verse, in drama or lyric, it provides an escapist picture of rural tranquillity and idleness in which actual sheep-tending is displaced by amorous conversation and song, and real shepherds by noble exiles from the corruptions of city and court. Paradoxically a sophisticated literary treatment of imagined simplicity, this tradition originated in ancient Greek and Latin poetry—the *Idylls* of Theocritus, the *Eclogues* of *Virgil—and was revived in 16th-century Italy, notably by Sannazzaro, Tasso, and Guarini. English pastoral was inaugurated by *Spenser's verse eclogues in *The Shepheardes Calendar* (1579) and further developed in *The Arcadia* (1590), a prose romance by *Sidney. Shakespeare's use of pastoral conventions, which can include an element of apparently 'anti-pastoral' realism about country matters, is most evident in *As You Like It* and *The Winter's Tale*, and fainter echoes of them can be felt in *A Midsummer Night's Dream* and *Love's Labour's Lost*. For these works he drew upon contemporary English pastoral romances, notably *Greene's *Pandosto* (1588) and *Lodge's *Rosalynde* (1590). *CB*

Pater, Walter Horatio (1839–94), English academic, influential in the *fin de siècle* aesthetic movement with *Studies in the History of the Renaissance* (1873) and *Marius the Epicurean* (1885). Essays on *Measure for Measure* (1874), *Love's Labour's Lost* (1878), and *Shakespeare's English Kings* were collected in *Appreciations* (1889). *TM*

pathetic fallacy, a mild form of poetic personification in which human motives are attributed to inanimate nature or non-human creatures (e.g. 'the scolding winds', *Julius Caesar* 1.3.5). John Ruskin, who coined the term, commended Shakespeare for his sparing use of such metaphors, by comparison with later 'morbid' poets. *CB*

Patience, Katherine's waiting woman, attends her *All Is True* (*Henry* VIII) 4.2. *AB*

Paton, Sir (Joseph) Noel (1821–1901), Scottish painter and illustrator. Paton earned recognition for himself and the proliferating genre of *fairy painting with *The Reconciliation of Oberon and Titania*, winning a prize in the high-profile 1847 Westminster Hall competition. Characterized by a profusion of minutely observed detail, *The Reconciliation* and its pendant *The Quarrel of Oberon and Titania* (1849, see page 134) teem with encounters between naked fairies—generating sexual undertones absent from his later *Oberon and the Mermaid* (1883). Paton illustrated Shakespeare's plays throughout his career: from *The Tempest* (Chapman & Hall, 1845) through to William Mackenzie's *The National Shakespeare* (1888–9). *KN*

Patroclus, based on *Homer's character of the same name, is killed by the Trojans (his body is produced, *Troilus and Cressida* 5.5.16), spurring his friend Achilles back into action. *AB*

patronage, in a Renaissance literary context, the social convention by which authors (and acting companies (see COMPANIES, PLAYING)) would receive protection, support, or subsidy from wealthy individuals, families, or institutions, in return for furthering their reputations, either simply by associating them with their work or by actively praising them in it (in flattering dedications, if nowhere else). More broadly, 'patronage' is a term for the entire pyramid-shaped social structure by which a network of mutual favours and obligations extended from the monarch downwards through the aristocracy and beyond.

Until well into the 18th century, most writers seeking to publish works with any literary pretensions at all both needed and sought patronage: Shakespeare was no exception, dedicating his narrative poems to the Earl of *Southampton and later, according to the dedication of the First Folio, attracting the benign attention of the earls of *Pembroke. The development of the commercial theatre, however, could offer writers an alternative source of income—albeit a meagre and precarious one if, as most did, they remained freelance. Although the Lord *Chamberlain's Men of course depended collectively on the patronage of the Lord Chamberlain, Shakespeare was from the mid-1590s onwards—as a shareholder in the theatre company for which he wrote—more independent of individual patronage than were many of his literary contemporaries.

The Shakespeare canon abounds in depictions of patron–client relations, both artistic—as in Timon's dealings with the Poet and the Painter in *Timon of Athens*—and more general—as in the relationship between Antonio and Bassanio in *The Merchant of Venice*. As this latter example may suggest, the terms in which a client solicits the favours of a patron, and those by which a patron promises favours, can be close to the language of love, and some have detected an erotic dimension to Shakespeare's own dealings with Southampton on the strength of the dedications to *Venus and Adonis* and *The Rape of Lucrece*. *MD*

Bergeron, David M., *Practicing Renaissance Scholarship: Plays and Pageants, Patrons and Politics* (2000)
Brennan, Michael, *Literary Patronage in the English Renaissance: The Pembroke Family* (1988)
Schmidgall, Gary, *Shakespeare and the Poet's Life* (1990)

Paulina, Antigonus' wife in *The Winter's Tale*, defends Hermione in spite of Leontes' anger in Acts 2 and 3. She reunites them, and, long since bereaved of Antigonus, agrees to marry Camillo, 5.3. *AB*

pauses. See CAESURA.

pavan, a sedate dance in common time performed by one couple or in procession; it went out of fashion during Shakespeare's lifetime. Musically it was often succeeded by the livelier *galliard. *JB*

Pavier, Thomas. See QUARTOS.

pay. See HIRED MEN.

Payton, John (fl. 1760–1800), a Stratford alderman who lived in Shottery. A street in modern Stratford is named after him. The master bricklayer Joseph Mosely, who found the document known as the Spiritual Last Will and Testament of John *Shakespeare in the *Birthplace in 1757, later gave it to Payton, who around 1789 sent it to *Malone, who printed it in 1790. In the interim John *Jordan had tried unsuccessfully to publish a copy in the *Gentleman's Magazine*. *SW*

Peacham, Henry (?1576–?1643), author and artist. His *Truth of our Times* (1638) contains an account of *Tarlton playing when Peacham was a London schoolboy; his *Complete Gentleman* (1622) provides insight into London playgoing. A sketch of *Titus Andronicus* with an extended quotation (*c*.1595) is attributed to Peacham: see LONGLEAT MANUSCRIPT. *CS*

Peaseblossom is one of Titania's fairies in *A Midsummer Night's Dream*. *AB*

Pedant. He is a travelling schoolmaster whom Tranio persuades to impersonate Vincentio in *The Taming of the Shrew* 4.2. *AB*

Pedro, Don. He arranges the betrothal of Claudio to Hero, but becomes convinced of her infidelity, in *Much Ado About Nothing*. *AB*

Peele, George (1556–96), playwright and poet. After attending Christ Church, Oxford, he wrote a series of plays and entertainments which helped revolutionize the theatrical use of verse. His best-known plays are *The Arraignment of Paris* (1584) and *The Old Wives Tale* (1595). The first is a pastoral play—one of the earliest in English—which ends with *Elizabeth I being offered a golden apple by the goddess Diana; the second is a cheerful adaptation of various motifs from folk tale and romance. He also wrote two energetic history plays and a melodious biblical drama, *David and Bethsabe* (1599). *RM*

'Peg a Ramsay', the title of a popular dance and ballad tune, quoted by Sir Toby in *Twelfth Night* 2.3.73. *JB*

Pelican Shakespeare. This paperback edition, designed for an American market, was produced between 1956 and 1967. Shakespeare's works were separately edited by noted scholars under the general guidance of Alfred Harbage. He emphasized the flow of action in the plays by omitting scene locations and relegating act and scene divisions to the margins. With very brief introductions and light glossing at the foot of the page, the volumes offered attractively presented texts at an initial price, in the USA, of 65c: in many respects they resembled the *Penguin and New Penguin editions. The Pelican series was revived in 1999 under the general editorship of A. L. Braunmuller and Stephen Orgel. *RAF*

Pembroke, Earl of. (1) Edward IV orders Pembroke and Lord Stafford (both mute) to 'prepare for war' against Henry, *Richard Duke of York* (*3 Henry VI*) 4.1.127–8. **(2)** He vows revenge for Arthur's death, *King John* 4.3, and joins the French, but returns to John in time to see him die. *AB*

Pembroke, Henry Herbert, 2nd Earl of. See PEMBROKE'S MEN.

Pembroke, Mary Herbert, Countess of (1561–1621), third wife to Henry Herbert, 2nd Earl of Pembroke, and sister of Philip *Sidney. A patroness of poets, including Ben *Jonson, Herbert initiated courtly interest in *Seneca, translating Garnier's *Marc Antonie* (1592), echoes of which occur in *Antony and Cleopatra.* Dover *Wilson speculates that Herbert commissioned Shakespeare's first seventeen sonnets. *CS*

Pembroke, Philip Herbert, 4th Earl of (1584–1650), younger son of Henry and Mary Herbert. Possibly called Philip after his uncle Philip *Sidney, he was a munificent patron and lifelong benefactor of the artist Van Dyck and playwright Philip *Massinger. John *Heminges and Henry *Condell, joint editors of Shakespeare's posthumous First *Folio in 1623, dedicated the work to Philip and his brother William. The dedicatory epistle to this 'incomparable pair of brethren' is testimony to an established connection between Shakespeare and the Herberts, and their long-standing generosity towards the playwright, noted in the dedication as their 'servant Shakespeare'. As Heminges and Condell wrote, 'your [lordships] have been pleased to think these trifles something heretofore, and have prosecuted both them and their author living, with so much favour [that . . .] the Volume asked to be yours'.

Philip was known for his hasty temper, and was frequently embroiled in brawls at court, including a quarrel with Shakespeare's patron, the Earl of *Southampton, over a game of tennis in 1610. Despite this, Philip remained a firm favourite of *James I, becoming gentleman of the bedchamber in 1605, and retaining the position until James's death in 1625—continued favour that owed much to the comeliness of his person, and his passion for *hunting and field sports.

Philip married Susan Vere, daughter of the 17th Earl of Oxford, in 1604, and was created Earl of Montgomery in 1605, succeeding his brother William as Earl of Pembroke in 1630. *CS*

Pembroke, William Herbert, 3rd Earl of (1580–1630), eldest son of Henry and Mary Herbert, educated by the poet Samuel *Daniel. Like his brother Philip, co-dedicatee of Shakespeare's First *Folio (1623), William was an enthusiastic patron of the arts. His beneficiaries included Ben *Jonson, Philip *Massinger, and Inigo *Jones. John *Aubrey remembers William as 'the greatest Maecenas to learned men of any peer of his time or since', and according to Edward Hyde, Earl of Clarendon, his liberality exceeded both his own considerable fortune, and that of his wife Mary Talbolt.

William was disgraced, and imprisoned briefly in 1601, for an affair with Mary Fitton, believed by some to be Shakespeare's *Dark Lady. Despite getting Fitton pregnant, William refused to marry her, making her at least the fourth well-born woman he had declined to wed—the previous three being Elizabeth *Carey (1595); Bridget Vere, Lord Burghley's granddaughter and daughter of the 17th Earl of Oxford (1597); and a niece of Charles Howard, Earl of Nottingham (1599).

Dover *Wilson conjectures that William's reluctance to marry induced his mother Mary to commission Shakespeare to write seventeen sonnets advocating marriage to mark William's 17th birthday in 1597 (Sonnets 1–17). This identification of William Herbert as *'Mr W.H.', to whom the publisher Thomas Thorpe dedicated the Sonnets in 1609, was first floated by James Boaden in 1837.

Suppőrters of William Herbert as 'W.H.' find further evidence in Francis Davison's *Poeticall Rhapsody* (1602), in which Davison celebrates William's 'lovely . . . shape'. Another suggestive allusion is Thorpe's reference to himself as 'the Well-wishing Adventurer', which may celebrate William's incorporation as a member of the King's Virginia Company in 1609. This connection with the Virginia Company may have allowed Shakespeare access to unpublished accounts of the wreck of the *Sea-Adventure* in 1609, an incident on which he based *The Tempest,* especially William *Strachey's *Reportary,* later published in Samuel Purchas's *Pilgrims* (1625). *CS*

Pembroke's Men, an obscure playing company, under the patronage of Henry Herbert, 2nd Earl of Pembroke (?1534–1601), known mostly from the title pages of their plays. Their *The Taming of a Shrew* has some relation to Shakespeare's *The Taming of the Shrew,* their *Richard Duke of York* is a memorial reconstruction of the play printed as *3 Henry VI* in the Shakespeare Folio of 1623, and their *Titus Andronicus* is Shakespeare's. It seems likely that Shakespeare was one of Pembroke's Men before he, and several of the others, joined the *Chamberlain's Men in 1594. Other Pembroke's Men were John *Sincler, Gabriel *Spencer, Robert Shaw, and possibly Richard *Burbage. The company probably played at the *Theatre in 1592–3 and broke in 1594, to be re-formed in 1597 for a brief season at the Langley's *Swan playhouse before their production of *The Isle of Dogs* caused that playhouse's closure. The company survived Ben *Jonson's murder of Gabriel Spencer in 1598, occupying the *Rose after the Admiral's Men left it for the Fortune in 1600, only to break forever with the death of their patron on 9 January 1601. *GE*

Penguin Shakespeare. Penguin Books began a revolution in publishing with their sixpenny pocket paperbacks, and included in their early lists an edition of Shakespeare. The first six titles appeared in 1937, attractively printed, with a plain text uncluttered by scene locations, a very brief introduction, and some notes and a short glossary at the end. The editor, G. B. Harrison, preferred Folio texts as closer to what he supposed was acted, but included in brackets passages found only in quartos. The series was superseded by the New Penguin Shakespeare (1967–), which retained the plain text format, but gave individual editors of the various works freedom to determine the text in the light of current scholarship. This new edition also provided much more substantial critical introductions, extensive commentaries, and accounts of textual problems. The general editor, T. J. B. Spencer, soon brought in Stanley Wells as his associate editor. In the plays the scenes are numbered in the margins, so that the stage directions and text seem to run on from one scene to the next. Both series have been very popular, and the New Penguin Shakespeare has been much used by schools, and also by acting companies, including the *Royal Shakespeare Company. *RAF*

Pennington, Michael (b. 1943), British actor, renowned for his grace of movement and mellifluous speaking of verse. Having acted at Cambridge, he played Angelo, Berowne, and

William Herbert, 3rd Earl of Pembroke, by Isaac Oliver, certainly an important patron of Shakespeare (and as such a co-dedicatee of the First Folio), and possibly the 'Mr W.H.' of the Sonnets.

Hamlet with the *Royal Shakespeare Company, 1974–81. He co-founded with Michael *Bogdanov the *English Shakespeare Company and toured worldwide in their popular seven-play *Wars of the Roses* (1986–9), later videotaped. He rejoined the RSC in 1999 to play Timon of Athens. *MJ*

pentameter, a verse line of five feet. Although there are other kinds (such as anapaestic pentameter, occasionally used by Browning), the most important form of pentameter is iambic. In English, iambic pentameter (five predominantly iambic feet) is the standard metre of blank verse, heroic couplets, sonnets, and rhyme royal. *CB/GTW*

Pepys, Samuel (1633–1703), diarist. He began writing his *Diary* in 1660 when a civil servant in the Naval Office and continued the record, in cipher and shorthand, until 1669 when his eyesight began to fail. Among much else, it provides a remarkable account of the social experience of theatre-going and of the *Restoration theatre's innovations (particularly the introduction of actresses, Shakespearian *adaptations, and the development of stage effects), in addition to commenting on performers and performances. For example, he records visits to *Macbeth* (in *Davenant's adaptation): 'From hence to the Duke's house, and there saw "Macbeth" most excellently acted, and a most excellent play for variety' (28 December 1666); 'and thence to the Duke's house, and saw "Macbeth", which, though I saw it lately, yet appears a most excellent play in all respects, but especially in divertisement, though it be a deep tragedy; which is a strange perfection in a tragedy, it being most proper here, and suitable' (7 January 1667); 'So to the playhouse, not much company come, which I impute to the heat of the weather, it being very hot. Here we saw "Macbeth", which, though I have seen it often, yet is it one of the best plays for a stage, and variety of dancing and music, that I ever saw' (19 April 1667); 'I was vexed to see Young (who is but a bad actor at best) act Macbeth in the room of Betterton, who, poor man! is sick: but, Lord! What a prejudice it wrought in me against the whole play' (16 October 1667); 'Thence to the Duke's playhouse, and saw "Macbeth." The King and Court there; and we sat just under them and my Lady Castlemayne, and close to the woman that comes into the pit, a kind of loose gossip, that pretends to be like her' (21 December 1668). Pepys was nearly as fond of the Davenant–Dryden adaptation of *The Tempest*, but other Shakespearian comedies pleased him less: he dismissed *A Midsummer Night's Dream*, for example, as 'the most insipid ridiculous play that ever I saw in my life' (29 September 1662). *CMSA*

Percy, Henry. (1) See NORTHUMBERLAND, EARL OF. (2) See HOTSPUR. *AB*

Percy, Lady. *Hotspur's wife (b. 1371), called 'Kate' by him, appears in *1 Henry IV* 2.4 and 3.1, and as a widow in *2 Henry IV* 2.3. *AB*

Percy, Thomas. See WORCESTER, EARL OF.

Perdita is the daughter of Hermione and Leontes in *The Winter's Tale*. The parallel character is Fawnia in *Greene's *Pandosto*, Shakespeare's chief source. *AB*

Perdita; or, The Royal Milkmaid. See BURLESQUES AND TRAVESTIES OF SHAKESPEARE'S PLAYS.

performance criticism, in Shakespeare studies, a term for the kind of analysis of Shakespeare's plays which considers them as scripts only fully realized in performance, rather than solely as literary works to be read on the page.

Despite the anti-theatrical perspective of many 18th-century editors, and the dominant *Romantic and 19th-century view of Shakespeare as a poet whose works only happened to take the form of plays, this has always been a strong element in Shakespeare criticism (exemplified, for example, by *Hazlitt, and by professional theatre reviewers from Leigh *Hunt onwards), but it has been newly prominent since the mid-20th century, as the academic study of Shakespearian drama has extended from the library and the classroom and into the theatre. The amount of space which major editions of the plays such as the *Arden devote to considerations of performance (both in Shakespeare's time and since) has increased immensely since the 1970s, for example, while series such as *Shakespeare in Performance* (Manchester University Press, 1984–) and *Shakespeare in Production* (Cambridge University Press, 1996– , the successor to *Plays in Performance*, 1981–) have proliferated.

Much contemporary performance criticism draws on semiotics, and, in reading performance as a social as well as an aesthetic event, incorporates some form of cultural theory. An influential work was Raymond Williams's chapter on *Antony and Cleopatra* in his *Drama in Performance* (1954): since then important exponents of performance criticism have included J. L. Styan, Dennis Kennedy, and Peter Holland. *MD*

Dobson, Michael, 'Shakespeare on the page and stage', in Stanley Wells and Margreta de Grazia (eds.), *The Cambridge Companion to Shakespeare* (2001)
Holland, Peter, *English Shakespeares* (1997)
Kennedy, Dennis, *Looking at Shakespeare* (1993)
Wells, Stanley, (ed.), *Shakespeare in the Theatre: An Anthology of Criticism* (1997)

performance times, lengths. Ordinarily at open-air and indoor hall playhouses the performances began at 2 p.m. and 3 p.m. and lasted two to three hours; the elite indoor venues probably had more latitude to run late than did the amphitheatres. At court the performances were always at night, and quite possibly the authorities in towns visited by touring companies were flexible, since an unanticipated performance would draw a larger crowd if it began after the working day was finished. No contemporary reference to performance lengths is shorter than the *Romeo and Juliet* Prologue's 'two-hours' traffic' and a few go as high as three hours, which is a variation of +/− 20% around a norm of 2.5 hours. Surviving play-texts, on the other hand, vary by as much as +/− 50% around a norm of about 2,600 lines, with a tendency to longer plays in the later years. Whether plays were routinely cut for performance remains a matter of argument. *GE*

Gurr, Andrew, 'Maximal and Minimal Texts: Shakespeare v. the Globe', *Shakespeare Survey*, 52 (1999)

Pericles *(see page 342)*

periphrasis, a figure of speech in which something is referred to by circumlocution where a more direct expression is available:

> As he is but my father's brother's son
> (*Richard II* 1.1.117)

CB

Perithous. See PIRITHOUS.

perspective. Stage scenery can be made to appear three dimensional by illusionistic techniques of painting based upon perspective foreshortening, but this technique was not used in the theatres until the Restoration. Artificial perspective effects require spectators to view from within a predefined focal area and so demand a seated audience all of whose members are looking in approximately the same direction, as in a hall playhouse; open-air playhouse conditions, with spectators all around the stage, are quite unsuited to perspective effects. Sebastiano Serlio's mid-16th-century work on theatre perspective illusions was absorbed by Inigo *Jones and his assistant-nephew John Webb and emerged in the elaborate court *masques and in the perspective techniques of the Restoration theatres. *GE*

Campbell, Lily B., *Scenes and Machines on the English Stage during the Renaissance: A Classical Revival* (1923)
Orrell, John, *The Human Stage: English Theatre Design, 1567–1640* (1988)

Peter (1) Peter is the Nurse's servant in *Romeo and Juliet*. (2). See JOSEPH. *AB*

Peter, Friar. See FRIAR PETER.

Peter of Pomfret is a prophet hanged by John, *King John* 4.2. *AB*

Peter Thump. See HORNER, THOMAS.

(cont. on page 344)

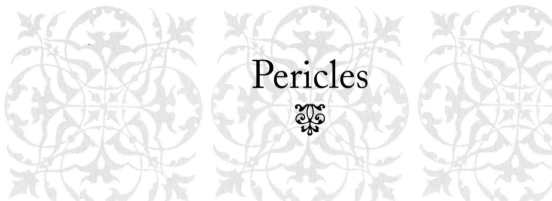

Pericles

Conclusive external evidence shows that the first and most deceptively simple of Shakespeare's late romances was written no later than 1608. A manuscript copy of the play, most probably the *promptbook used by the King's Men at the *Globe, was entered in the *Stationers' Register by Edward Blount on 20 May 1608. In the same year, George *Wilkins published a novel called *The Painful Adventures of Pericles Prince of Tyre*, which is clearly based on the play. The Italian ambassador Giorgio Giustinian saw a production of *Pericles* during his visit to London between January 1606 and November 1608, and it is referred to as 'new' in a pamphlet, **Pimlico*, of 1609.

Text: The only extant text of *Pericles* is a pirate *quarto edition published by Henry Gosson in 1609. The text of the play was reconstructed either by one of the actors playing a minor role or by two reporters, who transcribed the text of the play surreptitiously, as it was being performed at the Globe. The 1609 quarto is a very poor text, where verse is printed as *prose and prose as verse, the *stage directions are few and sketchy, and blatant mistakes abound. Perhaps because of the textual shortcomings of this edition, *Pericles* was not included in the 1623 *Folio, although it was added to the Third Folio, along with several *apocryphal plays. Although the original quarto does not divide the play into acts (and is followed in this respect by the Oxford edition), later editions conventionally break it up into five, starting Act 2 at Scene 5 (after the Antioch incidents and the relief of Tarsus), Act 3 at Scene 10 (after the wedding of Pericles and Thaisa), Act 4 at Scene 15 (after the storm and its immediate consequences), and Act 5 at Scene 20 (after Marina's release from the brothel).

A considerable amount of effort has gone into establishing the origins of Wilkins's 1608 *The Painful Adventures*. The theory that Wilkins's novel served as a source for the play has been repeatedly confuted, although the assumption that the novel contains passages from an earlier play on the subject has found some supporters. Many modern editions, including the Oxford, take the view that the novel in part derives from the play, and use it to emend the defective quarto text.

Sources: The story of Pericles derives from the Greek romance of Apollonius of Tyre, which had already been retold several times, most importantly in John *Gower's *Confessio Amantis* (1393): Gower himself features as the Chorus in Shakespeare's play. The other main source, which Shakespeare followed as closely as Gower, is Laurence *Twine's *The Pattern of Painful Adventures* (1576). Twine's influence is especially noticeable in the brothel scenes in Act 4. Given that the main hero is called Apollonius in both sources, editors since *Steevens have argued that Shakespeare may have borrowed the name 'Pericles' from a character in *Sidney's *Arcadia*.

Synopsis: 1 The presenter Gower introduces himself and the main characters involved in the Antioch episode, namely King Antiochus the Great, who is having a secret incestuous affair with his daughter, and Pericles, the King of Tyre, who has travelled to Antiochus' court to woo the fair Princess. The King has devised a riddle, which his daughter's suitors must solve in order to gain her hand. If they fail they lose their lives. Pericles is brought before Antiochus: professing his love for the Princess, he is granted the opportunity to solve the riddle. Pericles deciphers the riddle, which reveals the King's incest. Knowing that either revealing this secret or pretending not to have solved the riddle will bring about his death, Pericles gives a riddling answer, whereby he warns the King without exposing him. The King grants Pericles more time to solve the riddle only in order to arrange to have him murdered by Thaliard. Pericles, conscious of the danger, flees. 2 Pericles confides his troubles to Helicanus, who urges him to leave Tyre. 3 Thaliard arrives at Tyre straight after Pericles' departure. 4 Pericles arrives at Tharsus, formerly a rich town, whose resources have been wasted by its proud citizens, and delivers them from famine by giving them corn. The rulers

Cleon and Dioniza swear allegiance to Pericles in return for his generosity. 5 As Gower, with the help of a dumb show, explains, Pericles receives word of Thaliard's mission and decides to resume his travels, which are brought to an end by a sea-storm. Pericles suffers shipwreck and is cast ashore near Pentapolis among fishermen. After offering Pericles food and shelter, they recover his father's armour from the sea. Pericles decides to wear it and take part in a joust which Simonides, King of Pentapolis, has organized to test the valour of his daughter's suitors. 6 The joust is preceded by a parade and the interpretation of the emblematic shields and mottoes carried by the six suitors. Pericles is mocked for his modest apparel. The joust takes place offstage. 7 Pericles wins but looks melancholic and refuses to eat at the banquet. Simonides and his daughter Thaisa also lose their appetite: Thaisa is charmed by the mysterious knight and her father is too keen to discover his origins to care about food. Simonides sends his daughter over to Pericles to enquire about his identity. Pericles refrains from disclosing his real identity and introduces himself as a lord from Tyre. 8 In Tyre, Pericles' lords complain about the protracted absence of their King and offer Helicanus the crown. Helicanus asks them to wait and search for their King for another year. 8a Pericles, brought to a bedchamber, requests a stringed instrument on which to play. 9 Simonides dismisses the other suitors, then tests Pericles by confronting him with a forged love letter to Thaisa. He pretends to be angry while Pericles begs Thaisa to tell her father that he has never importuned her with love. Simonides, now certain of his daughter's feelings and Pericles' virtue, suddenly grants them his consent to marry. 10 Gower describes the joyful celebration of their wedding, and with the help of a dumb show narrates its sequel: Thaisa is pregnant when a second letter reaches Pericles, announcing that Helicanus will be crowned king should Pericles fail to return within the following six months. Pericles discloses his real identity and although Simonides is happy to find out that his son-in-law is a king, he is sad to see him and his daughter depart for Tyre. 11 The sea journey to Tyre is interrupted by another storm. Thaisa apparently dies in childbirth: at the superstitious sailors' insistence, Pericles casts her body overboard, sealed in a box. He decides to take Marina, his newly born baby, to Tharsus. 12 Cerimon, a lord of Ephesus, manages to revive Thaisa, washed up on his coast, from her deathlike slumber. 13 Pericles arrives at Tharsus and hands Marina over to Cleon and Dioniza. 14 Cerimon takes Thaisa, unable to remember Marina's birth, to the temple of Diana in Ephesus. 15 Gower tells how after Marina grows into a charming and talented young woman, Dioniza, forgetful of her debt to Pericles, plans to have her murdered in order to enhance her own daughter's chances of an advantageous marriage. Leonine, hired to kill Marina while she is walking along the seashore, is interrupted by the arrival of pirates, who kidnap Marina. 16 In Mytilene, a pander and a bawd complain that they are short of healthy young women to initiate to their trade. Their man Boult is sent to the market to search for female slaves. Boult comes back with the pirates who agree to sell Marina to the Bawd. Marina regrets that Leonine was too slow to dispatch her. The Bawd attempts to let Marina into the secrets of the sex trade, but Marina refuses to collaborate. 17 Cleon arraigns his wife for betraying Pericles' trust. 18 Gower describes Pericles' arrival at Tharsus and his suffering following the discovery of Marina's death, on which he swears to spend the rest of his life mourning the loss of his wife and daughter, his hair unshorn. 19 Virtuous Marina converts the Bawd's customers. Lysimachus, the Governor of Mytilene, apparently a regular client despite a subsequent claim that he is there solely to gather evidence against the Bawd, visits the brothel and is left with Marina, who persuades him she is genuinely a virgin and no prostitute: he leaves promising to help. The Bawd, outraged by Marina's behaviour, orders Boult to deflower her, but she persuades him she will be more profitably employed in respectable activities such as sewing, weaving, and dancing. 20 Gower narrates Marina's establishment as a singer and embroiderer, and the arrival of Pericles' ship at Mytilene. 21 Lysimachus enquires after Pericles' distemper and suggests that Marina might be able to cure him. Marina is sent for and sings to the silent Pericles. He initially pushes her away, but his interest is aroused by her defiant reaction: Marina claims to have suffered as much as he and to have royal ancestors. Pericles finally looks at her and notices her resemblance to Thaisa. Marina reveals her name and father and daughter are finally reunited. Diana appears to Pericles in a dream and directs him to Ephesus. 22 Gower narrates the arrival of Pericles and his party at Diana's temple, where Thaisa is among the vestals. 23 When Pericles narrates his story, Thaisa faints, and, reviving, is reunited with Pericles and Marina. Gower's epilogue recommends endurance in the face of adversity.

Artistic features: The most prominent, and most vilified, feature of *Pericles* is the uneven quality of its dramatic and poetic diction, often mock-medieval in style. The differences in style, characterization, and structure between Acts 1 and 2 and the second half of the play are remarkable, even allowing for the shortcomings of the reporters of the first pirate edition of 1609 and the idiosyncrasies of its compositors. Critics and editors have therefore argued that *Pericles* was either hastily revised by Shakespeare or written collaboratively with William *Rowley, Thomas *Heywood, John *Day, or, more plausibly, George *Wilkins. Both hypotheses help to account for the rambling plot and the scanty characterization in Acts 1 and 2 and the sudden improvement at the beginning of Act 3. Particularly admired for its psychological and dramatic complexity is the reunion between Pericles and Marina in Act 5. Although neither the revision nor the collaboration theory have been convincingly confuted, critics now tend to emphasize the structural unity of the play, which is reinforced by the constant presence of the sea and the re-emergence of the incest motif, and Shakespeare's reliance on music, magic, and supernatural intervention, which is typical of the late romances.

CRITICAL HISTORY: In his *Ode to Himself* (1629), Ben *Jonson famously referred to *Pericles* as a 'mouldy tale'. Many critics after him criticized the 'absurdity' of its plot and the lack of consistency of its characterization. In *An Essay on the Dramatic Poetry of the Last Age* (1672), Dryden remarked on the 'lameness' of the plot and the 'ridiculous' and 'incoherent' qualities of the story: fooled by the play's conscientiously naive style and manner, he thought *Pericles* must have been Shakespeare's first play. This view was even endorsed by *Malone, who dated the play *c.*1592. Because *Pericles* abounds in what *neoclassical critics regarded as serious formal flaws, its authorship was regularly contested. *Rowe included it in his 1709 edition of Shakespeare's *Complete Works*, but *Pope, *Theobald, *Warburton, Dr *Johnson, *Capell, and others omitted it from the *canon. Malone, who believed that Shakespeare wrote at least some parts of the play, reintroduced it in his 1780 edition. Many critics have remarked on Shakespeare's unusual reliance on his sources. Malone noticed that Shakespeare 'pursued the story exactly as he found it'. In 1898, Albert Henry Smyth defined *Pericles* as the 'most singular example in Elizabethan literature of a consistent copying of a venerable and far-travelled story'. In 1956, Maxwell observed that the 'complicated episodic narrative of the sources is followed in a fashion unparalleled in Shakespeare'. In 1976, Northrop *Frye reached a similar conclusion: '*Pericles* seems to be a deliberate experiment in presenting a traditional archetypal sequence as nakedly and baldly as possible.' After almost two centuries of critical neglect, the play is now praised for its power to move. The reunion between father and daughter in Act 5, which is often compared to the climactic reunion between Lear and Cordelia at the end of *King Lear*, Act 4, was T. S. *Eliot's main source of inspiration for his poem 'Marina'. More generally, critics now tend to regard *Pericles* as the first of the last plays, in that, despite the obvious flaws of its text, it anticipates several elements of the romances. Shakespeare, for example, uses Gower to bridge the temporal gaps between adjacent episodes in *Pericles* in ways which parallel the use of Time as chorus in *The Winter's Tale.*

STAGE HISTORY: *Pericles* was an immense theatrical hit in 1608, possibly Shakespeare's largest: Q1 was printed twice in 1609 and four new reprints were published before the outbreak of the Civil War in 1642. *Pericles* was the first of Shakespeare's plays to be revived when the London theatres reopened in 1659–60: the young Thomas *Betterton was highly praised for his performance in the leading role. The play was not performed again until George *Lillo adapted it as *Marina* in 1738, omitting the first two acts. The play had hardly any stage revivals until Robert *Atkins's 1921 production at the *Old Vic. In 1939 Robert Eddison played Pericles at the *Open Air Theatre in Regent's Park: after the war, Paul *Scofield played the title role twice (in 1947 and 1950), and Douglas *Seale directed a successful production at the *Birmingham Repertory Theatre in 1954. This revival established an enduring directorial tradition of emphasizing the fairy-tale qualities of the plot and Shakespeare's unusual use of pageantry, followed, for example, by Glen *Byam Shaw's Stratford production the following year, with Geraldine McEwan as Marina. It remains, however, one of Shakespeare's least-revived plays, a situation unimproved by Phyllida Lloyd's short-lived production at the *National Theatre's Olivier auditorium in 1991. *SM*

ON THE SCREEN: The only extant screen version is a slightly literal-minded BBC TV production of 1983, with Mike Gwilym as Pericles and Juliet Stevenson as Thaisa. *AD*

RECENT MAJOR EDITIONS

F. D. Hoeniger (Arden 2nd series, 1963); J. C. Maxwell (New Cambridge, 1956); Philip Edwards (New Penguin, 1976)

SOME REPRESENTATIVE CRITICISM

Arthos, J., '*Pericles, Prince of Tyre*: A Study in the Dramatic Use of Romantic Narrative', *Shakespeare Quarterly*, 4 (1953)

Barber, C. L., ' "Thou That Beget'st Him That Did Thee Beget": Transformation in *Pericles* and *The Winter's Tale*', *Shakespeare Survey*, 22 (1969)

Massai, Sonia, 'From *Pericles* to *Marina*: "While Women are to be had for Money, Love, or Importunity" ', *Shakespeare Survey*, 51 (1998)

Peto brings news to Prince Harry, *2 Henry IV* 2.4.358–63. See also RUSSELL. *AB*

Petrarch (Francesco Petrarca) (1304–74), Italian humanist and poet who combined diplomatic missions abroad with the humanist quest for long-neglected classical works. He translated and published many such works whilst writing some of his own prose and verse compositions in Latin. Petrarch's sonnets, dedicated to his beloved Laura, were published in collections called the *Canzoniere* and *Trionfi*. Their structure, themes, and conceits established a convention in sonneteering which lasted for more than 200 years, first imitated in England at the court of Henry VIII by Sir Thomas Wyatt and Henry Howard, Earl of Surrey. Shakespeare often wrote in the Petrarchan style, most notably in his own Sonnets and in *Romeo and Juliet* which includes a direct reference to Petrarch (2.3.36–7), but he was also part of a contemporary anti-Petrarchan movement and sometimes ridiculed the pretensions and frustrations of the Petrarchan lover. *JKS*

Petruccio (Petruchio). See TAMING OF THE SHREW, THE.

Phaonius, Marcus. See POETS.

Phebe. See PHOEBE.

Phelps, Samuel (1804–78), English actor-manager, born in Devon. After an eleven-year provincial apprenticeship, which included Richard III, Hamlet, Macbeth, Othello, and Lear, Phelps made his London debut (for Ben Webster at the Haymarket in 1837) as Shylock, reviewed as judicious and correct rather than striking or remarkable. In the engagements with *Macready which followed Phelps generally found himself cast in subservient roles, or kept idle, though he seized such opportunities as Macduff (1837), Hubert (1842), and, alternating with Macready, Othello and Iago (1839).

Following the abolition of the patent theatres' monopoly in 1843, Phelps set up in management (initially with Mrs Warner) at *Sadler's Wells theatre in Islington with the professed objective of presenting 'the first stock drama in the world ... [performed by] a Company of acknowledged talent ... in a theatre where all can see and hear, and at a price fairly within the habitual means of all'. In the opening production of *Macbeth*, Phelps as the Thane was acclaimed by experienced critics (who credited him with greater energy and reality than Macready) as well as local audiences. Thenceforward Shakespeare was established as the 'house dramatist', with revivals of 32 of his plays during the next eighteen years. These productions were characterized by a (relatively) full text, ensemble acting, and costumes and sets, of which gauzes and dioramas were regular features, which illuminated rather than swamped the play. Although he was indisputably the leading actor Phelps ensured that his performances harmonized with the production as a whole. Thus Henry Morley wrote that Phelps's Bottom 'was completely incorporated with the *Midsummer Night's Dream*, made an essential part of it, as unsubstantial, as airy and refined as all the rest'.

Following the termination of his management in 1862, Phelps continued to work as an actor in London and the provinces (especially in Manchester with *Calvert), where his Shakespearian performances established a tradition for young actors to follow, notably Johnston *Forbes-Robertson, who played Hal to Phelps's Henry IV, which the veteran actor doubled with Justice Shallow. The high point came in the Jerusalem chamber encounter between father and son, with Phelps's broken emphasis on 'Harry' ('Come hither, Harry') maximizing the pathos of their affectionate reconciliation. *RF*

Allen, Shirley, *Samuel Phelps and the Sadler's Wells Theatre* (1971)

Philario. See FILARIO.

Philemon is Cerimon's servant, *Pericles* 12. *AB*

Philharmonus. See SOOTHSAYERS.

Philip. See JOSEPH.

Philip, King of France. He supports Arthur's claim to the English throne in *King John*. *AB*

Phillips, Augustine (d. 1605), actor (Strange's Men 1593, Chamberlain's-King's Men 1598–1605). Phillips is named as taking the role of Sardanapalus in 'Sloth' in the plot of *2 Seven Deadly Sins* which was performed before 1594, possibly by Strange's Men. A touring licence issued to Strange's Men by the Privy Council names Phillips, but by 1598 he had joined the Chamberlain's Men, appearing in the actor lists for *Jonson's *Every Man in his Humour* and *Every Man out of his Humour*, and *Sejanus*, as printed in the 1616 folio. When the syndicate to run the Globe was formed in 1599 Phillips was a member, and on 18 February 1601 he was called upon to explain to Chief Justice Popham and Justice Fenner why the company had performed Shakespeare's *Richard II*, which dramatizes usurpation, at the Globe on the eve of *Essex's rebellion and at the request of his supporters. Phillips's name appears in the King's Men's patent of 1603 and the actor list of the 1623 Folio of Shakespeare's plays. The circumstances of Phillips's marriage are unclear, but Simon *Forman's notes suggest that he was twice rejected in marriage suits before being accepted by Anne, who survived him. In his will Phillips left money to his fellow actors (including Shakespeare) and costumes, properties, and musical instruments to his apprentice Samuel *Gilburne. *GE*

Philo, Antony's friend in *Antony and Cleopatra*, only appears in the first scene. *AB*

Philostrate, Theseus' Master of the Revels, appears (mute) in the first scene of *A Midsummer Night's Dream*. (In *quarto editions he also introduces the interlude of the 'hard-handed men' in Act 5, but the Folio reassigns these speeches to Egeus). *AB*

Philoten, the daughter of Dioniza, is described by Gower, *Pericles* 15, but does not appear. *AB*

Philotus' Servant. See HORTENSIUS' SERVANT.

Phoebe (Phebe in the *Folio), loved by Silvius in *As You Like It*, herself falls in love with *'Ganymede'. *AB*

'Phoenix and Turtle, The', a *lyric poem—also known as 'The Phoenix and the Turtle'—ascribed to Shakespeare when it appeared, untitled, as one of the 'Poetical Essays' by various authors, including the playwrights Ben *Jonson, George *Chapman, and John *Marston, in Robert *Chester's *Love's Martyr; or, Rosalind's Complaint* (1601, repr. 1611). It was later included in John Benson's 1640 edition of Shakespeare's poems.

Chester's *Love's Martyr* is a long poem described as 'allegorically showing the truth of love in the constant fate of the phoenix and turtle' (i.e. turtle dove). The 'poetical essays' appended to it are called 'Divers poetical essays on the former subject, viz. the turtle and phoenix, done by the best and chiefest of our modern writers, with their names subscribed to their particular works; never before extant.' How Shakespeare came to be involved in the enterprise is not known; he appears to have read Chester's poem before writing his own, a 67-line allegorical elegy which mounts in intensity through its three parts. First it summons a convocation of benevolent birds, with a swan as priest, to celebrate the funeral rites of the phoenix and the turtle dove, who have 'fled | In a mutual flame from hence'. Then the birds sing an anthem in which the death of the lovers is seen as marking the end of all 'love and constancy'.

> So they loved as love in twain
> Had the essence but in one,
> Two distincts, division none.
> Number there in love was slain.

Their mutuality was such that 'Either was the other's mine'. Finally Love makes a funeral song

> To the phoenix and the dove,
> Co-supremes and stars of love,
> As chorus to their tragic scene.

This threnos—funeral song—is set off by being written in an even more incantatory style than what precedes it; each of its five stanzas has three rhyming lines, and the tone is one of grave simplicity.

The poem, often regarded as one of the most intensely if mysteriously beautiful of Shakespeare's works, is usually assumed to have been composed not long before publication, though Honigmann (see CHESTER, ROBERT) dates it as early as 1586. Its affinities and poetical style seem to lie rather with Shakespeare's later than his earlier work. In subject matter it appears to have irrecoverable allegorical significance. Various scholars have identified one or other of the phoenix and the turtle with the dedicatee Sir John Salisbury and his wife, Queen Elizabeth, her collective subjects, the Earl of *Essex, Shakespeare himself, and even the Italian philosopher Giordano Bruno (who died at the stake in 1600). G. Wilson *Knight, one of the poem's most passionate advocates, supposed that 'the Turtle signifies the female aspect of the male poet's soul'. *SW*

Underwood, R. A., *Shakespeare's 'The Phoenix and the Turtle': A Survey of Scholarship* (1974)

Phoenix theatre. See BEESTON, CHRISTOPHER.

Phrynia and Timandra (Tymandra), both mistresses of Alcibiades, are given gold and verbal abuse by Timon, *Timon of Athens* 4.3. *AB*

Picasso, Pablo (1881–1973), Spanish artist. In 1964 Picasso made a series of twelve drawings on the theme of Shakespeare and *Hamlet* to commemorate the quatercentenary of Shakespeare's birth, as well as a number of related 'portrait' heads of the poet. The *Hamlet* series was published the following year in Louis Aragon's *Shakespeare* (published by Éditions Cercle d'Art, 1965). *RJ*

Pimlico, an anonymous pamphlet printed in 1609, refers to a crowd swarming as if at a 'new-play' such as '*Pericles*'. Hence *Pericles* must have existed, and still been relatively new, when *Pimlico* was registered on 15 April 1609. *PH*

Pinch, Dr. He attempts to exorcize the supposedly possessed Antipholus of Ephesus and

Dromio of Ephesus in *The Comedy of Errors* 4.4: he derives from 'Medicus' in *Plautus' *Menaechmi.* *AB*

Pindarus. See CASSIUS, CAIUS.

pipe, in Shakespearian usage, specifically the three-holed pipe played with the *tabor (see *Much Ado About Nothing* 2.3.15); also used as a term for wind instruments generally. *JB*

piracy. See REPORTED TEXT.

Pirithous (Perithous), Theseus' friend and attendant, describes Arcite's fatal accident, *The Two Noble Kinsmen* 5.6.48–85. *AB*

Pisanio, Posthumus' servant, is commanded by him to kill Innogen in *Cymbeline.* *AB*

Pistol is at the centre of the tavern brawl in *2 Henry IV* 2.4. In 5.3 he announces the death of Henry IV and in 5.4 witnesses Sir John's rejection by the new King and is taken with Sir John and others to prison. In *The Merry Wives of Windsor* he refuses to act as Sir John's go-between and betrays him to Ford (2.1). In *Henry V*, now married to Mistress Quickly, he joins Harry's French campaign after Sir John's death. In France his quarrels with Fluellen culminate when the latter forces him to eat a leek: by now the revelations of his dishonesty and cowardice render him a pathetic as much as a comical figure, completing the picture of the disintegration and decay of Harry's old set of acquaintances.

Actors have made the most of the flamboyantly bombastic side of the role: most famously, Theophilus *Cibber was nicknamed 'Pistol', both for his superlative performance as such and for his alleged offstage resemblance to the character. In modern times, though, the role, with its swaggering mock-Marlovian jargon, has become less easily comprehensible, and directors have often resorted to elaborate comic stage business: in Trevor *Nunn's 1982 *2 Henry IV*, for example, Pistol's eviction from the tavern was accompanied by much chasing up and down the immense set and firing of his gun. Michael *Bogdanov (1986) had him in motorbike leathers bearing the label 'Hal's Angels' and a T-shirt which, alluding to the punk group the Sex Pistols and the title of their collected works, read 'Never mind the bollocks; Here comes Pistol'. *AB*

Hodgdon, Barbara, *Shakespeare in Performance: Henry IV Part Two* (1993)

pit. The area of ground-level seating nearest the stage of an indoor hall playhouse such as the Blackfriars, corresponding in location and relative low cost to the yard in the open-air amphitheatres. A thrust stage projecting into the pit would be surrounded by seats. *GE*

Pitt Press Shakespeare. This early *schools edition of the individual plays began to appear in 1893, and was intended by the editor, A. W. Verity, for 'schoolboys' aged 14 and up. It offered them a short introduction describing aspects of each play, its characters, and giving an outline of the story. The plain text was followed by extensive notes and a glossary, so no schoolboy could complain of shortage of information. *RAF*

Place Calling Itself Rome, A (1973), a modernized English version of *Coriolanus* by John Osborne (1929–94). Given Germany's turbulent modern history, Bertolt *Brecht (*Coriolanus*, 1951–3) and Günter Grass (*The Plebeians Rehearse the Uprising*, 1966) have produced the major 20th-century dramatic reactions to Shakespeare's republican Rome. However, Caius Martius' reactionary political opinions, capacity for demotic invective, and mother-fixated sexual nausea make Osborne a powerful apologist in this angry play. *TM*

plague was unhappily frequent in Shakespeare's London, but its causation was not known. The disease is transmitted by the bite of an infected rat flea. The flea, though, will only bite humans when it has infected and killed all the local rats. This means that there are no rats around when an epidemic breaks out and their part in the process is not evident. Moreover the rat flea, unlike the human one, cannot hop far, so that people who are just visiting the sick are unlikely to get infected. However the flea can live for weeks without food if the humidity and temperature are right for it. The clothing and bedding of plague victims are particularly dangerous, as are wooden buildings, earthen floors, rubbish heaps, and dunghills. Hence the poor suffered far more in an epidemic than the rich.

Medical opinion never suspected the flea or the rat, and the disease was normally thought to be spread by contagion from the air and from infected sufferers (see MEDICINE). Therefore, when plague struck, one of the first measures taken by the authorities to prevent it spreading was to close the playhouses. This was no light matter for the actors' companies—for instance between 1603 and 1613 the theatres were closed for a total of 78 months. Even if they managed to get engagements to play outside London it still meant a curtailment of their activities. Indeed it has been suggested, on the plausible assumption that Shakespeare only wrote a play when there was an immediate demand for one, that the gaps in his dramatic creativity and his seemingly early retirement can be largely accounted for by these closings of the theatre.

If so, epidemics of the plague were more important for Shakespeare than for his characters, who neither catch it nor die from it. Plague and pestilence are words more often used in cursing than to describe a real medical event. Once or twice they are used jokingly to refer to falling in love, as when Biron says, 'They have the plague, and caught it of your eyes' (*Love's Labour's Lost* 5.2.422). And there is an even more unexpected, though perfectly logical, use. If bad air helped spread the disease, good air should prevent it. Pomanders were used for this purpose. But one could extend the principle to young and healthy people. 'The plague is banished by thy breath', says Venus, dreamingly, of Adonis (*Venus and Adonis* 510). 'Methought she purged the air of pestilence', says Orsino of Olivia (*Twelfth Night* 1.1.19). It is an attractive thought: one only wishes it could have been true. *MP*

Barrol, E. F. L., *Politics, Plague, and Shakespeare's Theatre* (1991)
Slack, P., *The Impact of Plague in Tudor and Stuart England* (1985)

plague regulations. A large crowd gathering in a confined space, such as a playhouse, was thought to give ideal conditions for transmission of the plague, and the Privy Council closed the playhouses when the weekly death toll exceeded 50 (reduced under James I to 30). *GE*

Barroll, Leeds, *Politics, Plague, and Shakespeare's theatre* (1991)
Wilson, F. P., *The Plague in Shakespeare's London* (1927)

Planché, James Robertson (1796–1880), English playwright and antiquarian, who became Somerset Herald (1866). His prolific and diverse output extended to some 150 theatrical pieces (extravaganzas, pantomimes, and librettos, including Weber's *Oberon*, 1826), scholarly works such as his *History of British Costume* (1834), his *Recollections and Reflections* (1872), and designs for several Shakespeare plays. His costumes for Charles *Kemble's *King John* (1823) broke new ground by setting the play in its historical period, even citing 'Authorities for the Costumes' on the playbill. Planché worked on Madame *Vestris's notable productions of *Love's Labour's Lost* and *A Midsummer Night's Dream* and Ben Webster's Elizabethan-style *The Taming of the Shrew* (1844). *RF*

Planchon, Roger (b. 1931), French actor, director (Théâtre de la Cité, Villeurbanne, near Lyon) and playwright, who has explored the full range of the French repertoire. His *Richard III* (1966 Avignon Festival, then Villeurbanne) was influenced by post-*Brechtian theories. He played the title roles in *Antony and Cleopatra* and *Pericles* (1978) in sets recalling well-known epic films. *ISG*

Plantagenet, Edward. See AUMERLE, DUKE OF; YORK, DUKE OF.

Plantagenet, Lady Margaret. See CLARENCE'S SON.

Plantagenet, Richard. (1) Duke of York, see I Henry VI; THE FIRST PART OF THE CONTENTION; RICHARD DUKE OF YORK. (2) See CAMBRIDGE, RICHARD, EARL OF.

Platter, Thomas (1574–1682), Swiss traveller. Born in Basle, Platter took his medical baccalaureate at the Université de Montpellier, and later visited England from 18 September to 20 October 1599. Writing in a difficult German dialect, he noted that on 21 September he crossed the Thames and observed a tragedy about Julius Caesar, performed 'with approximately fifteen characters', in 'the straw-thatched house' ('steüwine Dachhaus'). He may report on an unknown 'Caesar' drama; but it is probable that he saw Shakespeare's *Julius Caesar*, and that he offers the earliest report of any dramatic performance at the newly built *Globe. The most approved modern translation of Platter's remarks on the play is Ernest Schanzer's, in 'Thomas Platter on the Elizabethan Stage', *Notes and Queries*, 201 (1956). *PH*

Plautus (*c*.254–184 BC), Roman comic dramatist who wrote in the tradition of the New Comedy, popular in 4th-century Greece and exemplified by the work of Menander. Of the 130 plays attributed to Plautus in the 1st century BC, 21 survive, more than any other classical playwright and a testament to his contemporary success. Plautus was one of the causes célèbres of Renaissance humanism, admired for his witty and vivacious style and for the intricacy of his comic plots. Henry VIII commanded the performance of two of his plays at court and throughout the 16th century there were numerous continental translations and adaptations of his plays. Stephen Gosson complained that early English drama 'smelt of Plautus'. The Plautine mode of comedy was based upon stock characters, including the crafty servant or the braggart soldier (*miles gloriosus*), which often figured in early English comedy. Perhaps most Plautine, however, was the plot of confusion or error based on mistaken identity in which these characters appeared. This could be the deliberate deception practised by the stock character of the trickster or that practised by nature through the phenomenon of twins. In *The Comedy of Errors*, Shakespeare combined the 'errors' of two Plautine comedies, *Menaechmi* and *Amphitruo*, to compound the possible confusion. *The Comedy of Errors* also employs the Plautine convention of a child lost and found, and of a family reunited. *The Taming of the Shrew*, *Twelfth Night*, and *All's Well That Ends Well* all contain elements of Plautine comedy. Shakespeare probably read the *Menaechmi*, and other Plautine plays (*Amphitruo*, *Rudens*, and *Mostellaria*), in Latin. *JKS*

Miola, Robert S., *Shakespeare and Classical Comedy: The Influence of Plautus and Terence* (1992)

Riehle, Wolfgang, *Shakespeare, Plautus and the Humanist Tradition* (1990)

playbills, public notices advertising that plays were to be performed, attached to posts in the surrounding district. No playbills have survived from Shakespeare's time, so we cannot be sure how much detail was given. Richard Vennar's advertisement for his entertainment *England's Joy* at the Swan in 1603 was fraudulent—he planned to steal the receipts without giving a performance—so it cannot be regarded as a typical playbill. *GE*

playbook, the official play-text manuscript (or 'book'), containing the essential licence from the Master of the Revels. From this valuable document—which ordinarily never left the theatre—the bookkeeper would have actors' parts copied, and he might also annotate the playbook with reminders and additional directions to help him run the performance from offstage. The word promptbook is equivalent, although prompting (in the sense of reminding actors of their lines) does not seem to have happened in Shakespeare's time. *GE*

'Player King'. See PLAYERS.

'Player Queen'. See PLAYERS.

players. (1) As part of a lord's deception of Sly in the Induction, they perform the bulk of *The Taming of the Shrew*. (2) After much advice from the Prince, they perform the play presented by Hamlet to King Claudius, *Hamlet* 3.2. The Player King plays Duke Gonzago, and the Player Queen his wife Baptista. Other parts are the Prologue and the poisoner Lucianus. *AB*

players' quartos. See QUARTOS.

Players' Shakespeare. This rather grand large-paper limited edition, published by Ernest Benn, set out to print Shakespeare's plays 'litteratim from the First Folio of 1623', with line-blocks by various artists, among them Paul Nash, and long introductions by Harley *Granville-Barker. The edition ran out of steam after seven plays had been published between 1923 and 1927. It provided the occasion for Granville-Barker to develop *performance criticism' in what later became well known as his 'Prefaces' to Shakespeare; the first three of these (to *Julius Caesar*, *King Lear*, and *Love's Labour's Lost*) were published in a separate volume in 1927. *RAF*

playhouses. See THEATRES, ELIZABETHAN AND JACOBEAN.

playing companies. See COMPANIES, PLAYING.

Pléiade, French literary movement founded in 1549 by five university students including Joachim du Bellay and Pierre de Ronsard. Named after the Alexandrian society of the 3rd century BC, the group was inspired by the great writers of Greece and Rome, in particular Pindar and Anacreon, and by contemporary Italian literature. In dismay at the state of French literature, the Pléiade set out to reform it by importing the style, vocabulary, and themes of these classical and contemporary models into French poetry. The Pléiade's translations and imitations of classical lyric, and its innovations in the sonnet form, influenced English Renaissance poetry. *JKS*

Pliny (AD 23/24–79), equestrian, rhetorician, and author of many works of history and rhetoric of which only the *Naturalis historia* survives. This is a study of the physical universe with sections on botany, geography, metallurgy, and human and animal biology. It was translated as *Natural History* or *History of the World* by Philemon Holland in 1601. That Shakespeare knew Pliny's work is suggested by descriptions of exotic lands and peoples in *Othello*. Features drawn from Pliny include the Anthropophagi, Arabian trees which drop medicinal gum, and a description of the Pontic Sea (1.3.127–44, 5.2.359–60, 3.3.456–63). *JKS*

'plots'. Scene-by-scene outlines of plays written on large sheets of paper and posted in early playhouses. Plots reminded actors when and in what character they were to appear, while alerting backstage personnel when specific properties were required and when music or noises were called for. Seven 'plots' or 'platts' from the period are extant, including two from the *Admiral's or Strange's Men *c*.1590 and five dating from 1597–1602. *ER*

Plummer, Christopher (b. 1929), Canadian actor. With Broadway experience behind him, he was the first Canadian-born actor to play leading parts in the Stratford Festival, Ontario, 1956–67, beginning with Henry V and going on to Hamlet, Leontes, Mercutio, Macbeth, Aguecheek, and Antony—absenting himself in 1961–2 to play Richard III and Benedick for the *Royal Shakespeare Company in Stratford and London. In New York he has played Iago in *Othello* (1982) and the title role in a disastrous production of *Macbeth* with Glenda Jackson (1988). He also starred in a one-man show *Barrymore*, based on the life of the self-destructive Shakespearian player. *MJ*

Plutarch (L.[?] Mestrius Plutarchus) was born in Chaeronea to the west of Delphi in *c*. AD 46, and he died after AD 120. This makes him a direct contemporary of the great Roman historian Tacitus and, during his younger years, of the Emperors Claudius and Nero.

Plutarch wrote in his native Greek and was a prolific essayist, philosopher, biographer, and historian. He was best known in the Renaissance for his *Parallel Lives*, of which 23 have survived. In nineteen of them the biographiesof famous Greeks and Romans such as

Alexander the Great and Julius Caesar are compared.

Plutarch is an accomplished narrator who uses vivid anecdotes and colourful cameos to bring his characters to life. In the 'Life of Alexander' he famously noted that, as Sir Thomas North's translation puts it, 'The noblest deeds do not always show men's virtues and vices, but oftentimes a light occasion, a word, or some sport, makes men's natural dispositions and manners appear more plain than the famous battles won.' For Plutarch history was a stage on which great men shaped the world according to their moral inclinations. It is fitting that the other collection of extant works by this much-travelled writer, who quietly ended his life at Delphi as a priest, should be called the *Moralia*.

Plutarch's influence on Shakespeare is hard to overestimate. Shakespeare knew Plutarch's *Lives* in the 1579 English version by Sir Thomas North (North in turn translates the French text of Jacques Amyot) and the *Moralia* in the 1603 translation by Philemon Holland. Plutarch's writings provided material for *Titus Andronicus*, *A Midsummer Night's Dream*, *Timon of Athens*, and, probably, for the nomenclature of *The Winter's Tale*. It is, however, in *Julius Caesar*, *Antony and Cleopatra*, and *Coriolanus* that Shakespeare's use of Plutarch is most thorough.

While the chronological spread of Plutarchan material across the canon suggests that Shakespeare was steeped in Plutarch from the start and drew on him for each one of his dramatic genres, these three Roman plays dramatize material from Plutarch's *Lives* and, in the case of *Antony and Cleopatra*, the *Moralia* as well. Shakespeare repeatedly telescopes his source materials from the *Lives*, and his uses range from direct verbal echoes between text and source to artful rewritings of Plutarch. At times, as in the case of Enobarbus' tribute to Cleopatra's magic at Cydnus, the intertextual play between the source and the drama is so intimate that Shakespeare must have worked with a copy of North's Plutarch at his elbow, as he did with *Holinshed in *Henry v* and a handful of other *sources such as, for example, *Greene's *Pandosto* (for *The Winter's Tale*) and *Brooke's *Romeus and Juliet*. Shakespeare generally transcends Plutarch's moral homilies by attributing them to particular characters in his plays. *RW*

Bullough, Geoffrey, *Narrative and Dramatic Sources of Shakespeare*, vol. v (1964)
Spencer, T. J. B., *Shakespeare's Plutarch* (1964)
Stadter, Philip A. (ed.), *Plutarch and the Historical Tradition* (1992)

Poe, Edgar Allan (1809–49), American poet and story-writer. Comments on Shakespeare occur in 'Letter to B—', from the preface to *Poems* (1831) and in the *Southern Literary Messenger* (1836), where he contrasts the 'hideous and unwieldy' spirit of Samuel *Johnson with the 'airy and fairy-like' creations of the 'immortal Shakespeare!' *TM*

Poel, William (1852–1934), English actor and director who dedicated his life to reforming Shakespearian performance. An antiquarian at heart and always a bit of a crank, Poel was caught between a zealous study of the Elizabethan stage and a fanatical hatred of the Victorian theatre. He began by directing (and taking the main role in) the 'bad' quarto of *Hamlet* at St George's Hall in London in 1881 in Elizabethan dress. After the publication of the de Witt sketch of the *Swan theatre in 1888, Poel set about to discover how stage practice in Shakespeare's time resided in Shakespeare's texts. Believing that the plays had been buried under the silt of subsequent production styles, he insisted that only by taking them out of the proscenium theatre and discovering Elizabethan performance methods could they be adequately understood. For *Measure for Measure* in 1893 (in which he played Angelo) he built what he considered to be a replica of the Fortune theatre as a portable structure and placed it on the stage of the Royalty theatre, jutting out partly into the auditorium, adding ladies and gentlemen as 'spectators' in Elizabethan costume matching that of the actors. He founded the Elizabethan Stage Society in 1895 and until 1905 directed a number of its productions, starting with *Twelfth Night* and continuing with *Richard II* (1899, with Harley *Granville-Barker in the title role), *Everyman* (1901), *Romeo and Juliet* (1905), and lesser-known plays by Shakespeare's contemporaries. In the 1920s he directed **Fratricide Punished*, **Arden of Faversham*, *Sejanus*, and plays by *Rowley and *Chapman. He refused a knighthood in 1929 because he would not be allied with other theatrical knights whose work he abhorred. Though his productions were usually marred by idiosyncratic notions of vocal tone and delivery, and though his understanding of Elizabethan acting was seriously flawed, he had great influence on the general 20th-century project of invigorating Shakespeare by simple and open staging. His inheritors include Granville-Barker and Tyrone *Guthrie, who succeeded in part because they followed Poel's ideal rather than his practice. *DK*

Poel, William, *Shakespeare in the Theatre* (1913)
Speaight, Robert, *William Poel and the Elizabethan Revival* (1954)

poems on Shakespeare. The First *Folio of Shakespeare's works (1623) included five commemorative verses in its introductory material, two by Ben *Jonson, one by Hugh *Holland, one by Leonard *Digges, and one, by I. *M., for whom a number of authors have been proposed. The Second Folio (1632) added three more; the anonymous 'Upon the Effigies of my Worthy Friend', *Milton's epitaph 'What need my Shakespeare for his honoured bones . . .', and 'On Worthy Master Shakespeare and his Poems' by I.M.S. The most influential of these pieces has been Jonson's 'To the Memory of my Beloved, the Author Mr William Shakespeare: And What He Hath Left Us', which was reprinted in all the major 18th-century collected works and has adorned many more complete editions since. It has been read biographically, '—thou hadst small Latin, and less Greek'; has articulated Shakespeare's 'immortality', 'He was not of an age, but for all time!'; it described, presciently, his status as an international figure and a source of national pride, 'Triumph, my Britain, thou hast one to show, | To whom all scenes of Europe homage owe'; and contributed the enduring descriptor 'Sweet swan of Avon'.

These points were developed by many subsequent poets, building on Jonson and developing Milton's metaphors for Shakespeare's instinctive imaginative power—'fancy's child' who 'warble[d] his native woodnotes wild' ('L'Allegro', *c.*1631)—and shifting from epitaphic commemoration to a celebration of skill and pride in national achievement. Thomas *Gray's 'The Progress of Poesy' (1751–4) supplied Shakespeare with an appropriate literary pedigree and made an implicit comparison with the classics as the Nine Muses forsook Parnassus and sought out Albion where, 'Far from the sun and summer-gale, | In thy green lap was Nature's Darling laid, | What time, where lucid Avon stray'd.'

Such sentiments, often exploited for commercial or political reasons and frequently using snatches of quotation, were made explicitly chauvinistic in theatrical prologues and epilogues, and rapidly became part of a standard language of *bardolatry. A good example is provided by Philip Frowde's 1727 prologue to Lewis *Theobald's *Double Falsehood*:

> Such Shakespeare's genius was . . . let Britons boast
> The glorious birth, and, eager, strive who most
> Shall celebrate his verse; for while we raise
> Trophies of fame to him, ourselves we praise:
> Display the talents of a British mind,
> Where all is great, free, open, unconfined.

The culmination of such material was the songs and verses written for the 1769 Stratford *Jubilee and its London dramatization, which celebrated 'Warwickshire Will', 'The *Mulberry Tree', 'Sweet Willy O' ('The pride of all nature'), and, in 'Roundelay', 'Avon's Banks, where Shakespear's bust | Points out, and guards his sleeping dust'. The hyperbolic chorus of David *Garrick's Ode, the Jubilee's centrepiece, left other poets little else to say—'The lov'd, rever'd, immortal name! | Shakespeare! Shakespeare! Shakespeare!'—although many went on trying, notably Matthew *Arnold. *CMSA*

'Poetomachia'. See 'WAR OF THE THEATRES'.

poetry, dramatic. See DRAMATIC POETRY.

poetry, lyric. See LYRIC POETRY, SHAKESPEARE'S.

poets. **(1)** A poet interrupts the discourse of Cassius and Brutus, *Julius Caesar* 4.2. The incident is based on *Plutarch's account of the poet Marcus Phaonius who supposedly ended the quarrel by making Cassius laugh. **(2)** See PAINTER. *AB*

Poins, Edward (Ned). He is a companion of Prince Harry and practical joker in *1* and *2 Henry IV*. *AB*

Poland is mentioned in several of Shakespeare's plays, but nowhere, with one exception, is the country's presence more than incidental. The exception is *Hamlet*, where Poland plays an important role, providing, along with Norway, the background of international politics. Shakespeare's Poland, however, is both confused and confusing. Old Hamlet 'smote the sledded Polacks on the ice' (1.1.66), though it took *Malone to restore the sense of 'Poles' from Q2's and F's 'Pollax'—an Elizabethan spelling of pole-axe. The context, however, confirms his emendation, since Poland has always been in the eyes of the English a northern country ('Poland winter' is mentioned in *The Comedy of Errors*), and the image of people, or troops, travelling on sleds stirs the imagination and gives local colour to the Baltic wars. It is further confirmed by another allusion to Poland, the name of the garrulous courtier known in the first quarto as 'Corambis': 'Polonius' is simply the Latin for 'Polish'. The name seems slightly ironic: as the Lord Chamberlain (?) of the Danish court, dealing with international politics, Polonius is responsible for the permission given to the Norwegian army to march against Poland. Polonius further reveals the play's confusion about Poland when he uses the word 'Danskers' in his conversation with Reynaldo ('Inquire me first what Danskers are in Paris', 2.1.7). The context implies that this means Danes, but in usual Elizabethan and Jacobean usage the word meant a citizen of Dansk, or Danzig (in German) or Gdańsk (in Polish). Shakespeare appears to have confused *dansk* (Danish), *Danske* (Danes) with *Dansk* (Danzig or rather *Gdańsk*) and *Dansker* (a citizen of Dansk or Gdańsk), the only writer of the period to do so. The linguistic affinity probably led the poet to think that Denmark bordered with Poland, where Dansk was the major city and harbour: hence his apparent ignorance of the fact that in order to reach Poland from Denmark by land, Fortinbras' army would have to pass through three other countries, namely, Holstein, Mecklenburg, and Pomerania. All Danish or Swedish invasions of Poland in the 16th and 17th centuries were sea invasions; military clashes with Norway are not recorded.

Shakespeare may have heard about Gdańsk (and Elsinore) from his fellow actors, many of whom in the late 1590s ventured tours on the Continent, where shortly Gdańsk was to become one of the centres of their activity. During Shakespeare's own lifetime his plays were performed there. And in around 1610 a public theatre was built in that city, which accommodated *c.*3,000 spectators and which was reminiscent of the Fortune playhouse in Shakespeare's London (a reconstruction project of the Gdańsk theatre is in progress). Also, from around 1617, the kings of Poland kept English players at their courts, and in fact Poland was the only country in Europe where the activity of English actors continued uninterrupted during the Thirty Years War. One of the best-known English comedians, Robert Reynolds, who gained fame under the stage name 'Pickleherring', died in Warsaw in or shortly before 1642 and his wife was given a pension by King Vladislaus IV, perhaps the first known example of an actors' pension scheme in Poland.

In the 17th century Shakespeare was performed in German prose translations. The first Polish translations (free adaptations rather, based on German renditions) and productions of Shakespeare appeared towards the end of the 18th century, and were the creations of Wojciech Bogusławski. His 1797 production of *Romeo and Juliet* in Lwów is considered the first Polish performance of Shakespeare; this was soon followed by *Hamlet* (1798), *Othello* (1801), *King Lear* (1805), and *Macbeth* (1809), which became permanent pieces in theatre repertories. After the failure of the November Uprising in 1831, in the Russian sector of partitioned Poland, Shakespeare disappeared from the stage for over thirty years: the Tsarist censors did not approve the frequent conspiracies against rulers and government in general presented in the plays. Shakespearian productions continued in the other parts of divided Poland, especially under Austrian rule (with two important cultural centres, Lwów and Kraków). These early productions were always abridged, adapted, and altered to suit the taste of the period, and it was not until around the middle of the 19th century that Shakespeare appeared unamended on the Polish stage. It was Stanisław Koźmian, the theatre manager and director in Kraków, who introduced nearly 20 new productions of Shakespeare in the last quarter of the 19th century, including *Twelfth Night*, *A Midsummer Night's Dream*, and *As You Like It*—all in new translations from the original. Around this time, following a relative relaxation of censorship, Shakespeare enjoyed a comeback in Warsaw, and some of Poland's leading actors and actresses, such as Helena Modrzejewska (who gained international fame as *Modjeska) and, later, Ludwik Solski and Karol Adwentowicz became Shakespeare's great promoters.

In the period between the wars, in the reborn Poland, perhaps the greatest productions of Shakespeare were those directed by Leon Schiller, and the memorable Shakespearian roles were played, among others, by Aleksander Zelwerowicz, Kazimierz Junosza-Stępowski, and Stefan Jaracz along with Stanisława Wysocka (the first Polish actress to play Hamlet, with Teresa Budzisz-Krzyżanowska being the most recent example). In the post-war period the greatest Shakespearian productions were directed by Willam Horzyca, Konrad Swinarski, Jerzy Jarocki, Adam Hanuszkiewicz, and Andrzej Wajda; best remembered are the roles of Jacek Woszczerowicz, Gustaw Holoubek, Zofia Kucówna and Jadwiga Jankowska-Cieślak, to mention just a few. Despite its fuzziness about Poland's geography, *Hamlet* has featured prominently in recent Polish theatrical history, and in one respect has generally done so in an unusually full text. The scene in which Hamlet converses with a captain of the Norwegian army that is marching against Poland (4.4.9–29), often cut from productions elsewhere, has generally been retained in Poland, where this depiction of a foreign military threat has often been crucial for political interpretations of the play (as in Andrzej Wajda's production of 1981). On average there are about a dozen new Shakespearian productions in Polish theatres every season, and some Polish television productions of Shakespeare are equally notable for their artistic and intellectual quality. In 1993 an annual international Shakespeare Festival was started in Gdańsk.

Several translations of the complete plays have appeared (the last one was completed in the 1970s by Maciej Słomczyński), whereas the most recent attempt, undertaken by Stanisław Barańczak, is still in progress. Individual plays have enjoyed varying popularity both on the stage and in translation (*Hamlet* is the leader with 23 translations). As far as Shakespeare criticism goes, Jan *Kott's *Shakespeare our Contemporary* has won international acclaim and has influenced theatre directors around the world, including such prominent figures as Peter *Brook. There is a Shakespeare Association of Poland, and recent Shakespeare scholarship is represented by the work of Przemysław Mroczkowski, Henryk Zbierski, and Marta Gibińska. *JL*

Stříbrný, Zdeněk, *Shakespeare and Eastern Europe* (2000)

Pole, William de la. See SUFFOLK, EARL OF.

Polixenes is the King of Bohemia and father of Florizel in *The Winter's Tale*. The corresponding character in Shakespeare's source, *Greene's *Pandosto*, is Egistus. *AB*

Pollard, Alfred William (1859–1944), English bibliographer. With W. W. Greg and R. B. McKerrow, initially through the Bibliographical Society's journal *The Library*, Pollard revolutionized not only the bibliographical and textual study of all early English printed books, but specifically that of Shakespeare, mainly by the careful investigation and analysis of all the earliest printed copies, in both quarto and folio. His main publications are: *Shakespeare Folios and Quartos* (1909); *Shakespeare's Fight with the Pirates* (1917); and *The Foundations of Shakespeare's Text* (1923). Some of the information at his disposal has been supplemented or superseded, but not the intellectual rigour of his approach. *TM*

Polonius, father of *Ophelia and Laertes in *Hamlet*, is killed by Hamlet, 3.4.23. He is called Corambis in the first *quarto. *AB*

'Polydore' is the name given to Guiderius by Belarius in *Cymbeline*. *AB*

Pompey. Mistress Overdone's servant, he is interrogated by Elbow and Escalus, *Measure for Measure*, giving his full name as Pompey Bum (2.1.205–7). He later becomes Abhorson's assistant (4.2.14–17). *AB*

'Pompey'. Costard takes the part of Pompey the Great (Cn. Pompeius Magnus, 106–48 BC) in the performance of 'The Nine Worthies', *Love's Labour's Lost* 5.2. *AB*

Pompey (Pompeius), Sextus (75–35 BC). Son of Pompey the Great, he makes a short-lived treaty with the triumvirs, *Antony and Cleopatra* 2.6. His defeat by Caesar is announced, 3.5. *AB*

'poor soul sat sighing by a sycamore tree, The'. See Willow song.

pop music. Although those conspicuous 'New Elizabethans' the Beatles were prevailed upon to act out 'Pyramus and Thisbe' from *A Midsummer Night's Dream* in a TV special in the year of Shakespeare's 400th birthday, 1964 (with Ringo as Lion), and used an extract from a *radio production of *King Lear* in the fade-out to 'I am the Walrus' (1968), the influence of Shakespeare on anglophone pop music has predominantly been in the quotation of single lines of text, often simply as titles, such as B. A. Robertson's 'To be or not to be', David Essex's 'A Winter's Tale', and Dire Straits' love ballad 'Romeo and Juliet'. A more abstract Shakespearian influence can be seen in Elvis Costello's 'The Juliet Letters' (written in collaboration with the Brodsky Quartet), and the Smiths' song 'Shakespeare's Sister'. Bands adopting Shakespeare-inspired names include 'Shakespear's [*sic*] Sister' and 'Romeo's Daughter'. Two notable rock-based musical versions of Shakespeare's plays are *Drei Herren aus Verona* (Nuremberg, 1972) and **Return to the Forbidden Planet* (London, 1989), a sci-fi version of *The Tempest* loosely based on the 1956 film **Forbidden Planet*. Perhaps surprisingly, translated Shakespeare has been used frequently as a source for pop lyrics in Eastern Europe. *IBC*

Grzegorzewska, Malgorzata, 'Wooing in Festival Terms: Sonneteering Lovers, Rock and Blues', in Jonathan Bate et al. (eds.), *Shakespeare and the Twentieth Century* (1998)

Pope, Alexander (1688–1744), poet and Shakespearian editor. Pope's six-volume edition of Shakespeare's *Works* (1725) was the product of a poet rather than a specialized philologist or dedicated Shakespearian scholar. Though Pope carried out some textual collation, and made innovative use of the Shakespearian *quartos, he was less concerned to explain difficulties and resolve variance on rational or critical grounds than to mediate his author for what were perceived to be more cultivated contemporary tastes. Pope's text is in part constructed and presented according to aesthetic criteria. The 'most shining passages' are pointed out by marginal quotation marks, or preceded by an asterisk. Some lines which Pope thought 'excessively bad', on the basis of their verbal quibbles or *conceits, he 'degraded' from the text itself to the foot of the page. Pope's preface is an important document of early 18th-century English criticism, characterizing Shakespeare, despite his 'great defects', as an original genius, the great poet of nature, and famously comparing the Shakespearian drama, in its strength and irregularity, to 'an ancient majestick piece of *Gothick* Architecture'. *MLW*

Dixon, Peter, 'Pope's Shakespeare', *Journal of English and Germanic Philology*, 63 (1964)
Hart, John A., 'Pope as Scholar-Editor', *Studies in Bibliography*, 23 (1970)
Jarvis, Simon, *Scholars and Gentlemen: Shakespearian Textual Criticism and Representations of Scholarly Labour, 1725–1765* (1995)

Pope, Elizabeth, née Young, (*c*.1740–97), a leading actress with a broad range. She made her debut as Imogen for *Garrick at *Drury Lane in 1768. She specialized in young innocents—Perdita, Juliet, Miranda—and played Cordelia to Garrick's Lear at the end of his career. She joined *Covent Garden in 1779 where her more mature roles, some performed with her husband, Alexander, included Queen Katherine, Lady Macbeth, and Mrs Ford. *CMSA*

Pope, Thomas (d. 1603), actor (Strange's Men 1593, Chamberlain's Men 1597–1603). First mentioned among the players at Elsinore in 1586 (the others were George *Bryan and William *Kempe), Pope's name occurs in the role of Arbactus in 'Sloth' in the *plot of *2 Seven Deadly Sins* (performed before 1594, possibly by Strange's Men). Strange's Men's licence to tour, issued on 6 May 1593, names Pope but by 27 November 1597 he was with the Chamberlain's Men and received, with John *Heminges, the payment for court performances. His name appears in the actor lists for *Jonson's *Every Man out of his Humour* and *Every Man in his Humour* in Jonson's 1616 folio, and in the actor list in the Shakespeare Folio of 1623. In 1599 he was one of the original *Globe housekeepers, but he is not mentioned in the King's Men's patent of 19 May 1603. His will indicates that he also had a share in the Curtain playhouse. *GE*

Popilius (Popillius) Laena (Lena) (historically 'Laenas'), a senator who alarms Cassius by wishing him well and then speaking to Caesar just before the assassination, *Julius Caesar* 3.1. *AB*

popular culture. It is an accident of history that Shakespeare and popular culture seem to modern audiences an odd couple. For many previous generations, Shakespeare and popular culture would have seemed an obvious match. The public theatre for which he wrote occupied the bottom rung of early modern literary institutions, its questionable reputation shaped by its commercialism, its consciously broad appeal, and its predilection for sensationalism and low humour, qualities we have come to associate with popular culture rather than the high art with which Shakespeare is now routinely identified. Shakespeare's transformation from popular playwright to highbrow icon, largely a 20th-century phenomenon, is the result of several developments. Most important of these were the displacement of stage performance by *film, *radio, and *television, and the institutionalization of English as an academic discipline. Professionalized study of Shakespeare established canons of authenticity that tended to treat popular appropriations of Shakespeare as degraded versions of the 'legitimate' Shakespeare found in the historical researches of scholars and in performances by professional theatrical companies. However, many have begun to reassess the function of Shakespeare in popular culture. Taking their cue from *cultural materialist criticism, *performance criticism, and cultural studies, scholars have analysed how Shakespeare's works and cultural authority have been used and reinvented, particularly in popular culture. If, scholars argue, Shakespeare exists not in a single authoritative form but in multiple performances, pop Shakespeare ought to be included within the newly broadened continuum of Shakespearian 'performance'. Many have recognized that audiences encounter Shakespeare through the mediation of cultural institutions of which the mass media is a powerful and, for many, a primary source of ideas about Shakespeare. Most important to this sea-change, however, has been the revived ideal of a popular Shakespeare fostered throughout the 1990s, prompted largely by the box-office success of Shakespeare film. Since popular culture's interest in Shakespeare tends to be cyclical, a response to a perceived 'trend', Shakespeare has become a newly insistent point of reference in the mass media, particularly in film, television, and genre fiction. Current interest in pop Shakespeare belatedly acknowledges that for modern audiences it is Shakespeare's appearance in the mass media, and not in the work of the academy, that lends his work cultural legitimacy.

The ubiquity of Shakespeare in popular culture hardly needs demonstration. Shakespeare's likeness is perhaps one of the most recognizable images in the world, functioning something like a trademark in the popular imagination. Shakespeare himself regularly appears as a character in popular *fiction, ranging from cameos—as in 'The Bard', an episode of the TV show *The Twilight Zone* (1963)—to full-blown fictional biography—as in Neil Gaiman's series on Shakespeare for the *Sandman* comics (1991) or Erica Jong's bestseller *Shylock's Daughter* (1995). Allusions to his works abound in *advertisements, sermons, political speeches, self-help books, radio and television shows, movies, popular drama, rock and *pop music, comic books, erotica, and genre fiction, in addition to being the subject matter of mass-produced collectibles such as *ceramics, dolls, toys, games, *statuary, prints, stamps, and cards (see SHAKESPEARIANA).

Shakespearian plots and characters have provided the basic armature for popular works in many genres, including westerns, science fiction, detective fiction, *Gothic romances, X-rated films, cartoons, and, most recently, teen movies. Some of these adaptations remain relatively faithful to their Shakespearian originals—*Men of Respect* (1991), a modernized *film noir* rendition of *Macbeth*, provides a good example. More typical, however, are popular works which might best be characterized as 'free variations' on Shakespearian motifs, works that negotiate between Shakespeare's works and the conventions, thematics, and iconography of popular culture. Where popular works depend upon recognition of the Shakespearian subtext or allusion, they tend to refer to those plays most widely taught or to lines, plots, or characters that have passed into common parlance—the balcony scene from *Romeo and Juliet*, 'To be or not to be', Hamlet's discoursing to the skull of Yorick, Lady Macbeth's sleepwalking scene. Conversely, 'proper' Shakespearian productions are increasingly shaped by conventions and allusions taken from popular culture—*Olivier's *Hamlet* (1948) and *Welles's *Othello* (1952) both borrow themes and motifs from 1940s *film noir*. In many cases, the variation is so 'free' that the relationship to Shakespeare is not immediately recognizable and thus a matter of some debate. To what extent do stories of young lovers blocked by their families—a favourite of adolescent fiction and romance novels—owe specifically to *Romeo and Juliet*? Need the typical reader perceive the parallels between Gloria Naylor's novel *Mama Day* (1988) or the science-fiction film **Forbidden Planet* (1956) and *The Tempest* to appreciate the works? Such problems open larger theoretical questions: to what end is Shakespeare being used if the use is not perceived by a popular audience? Do such parallels testify to Shakespeare's status as a persistent master narrative, to certain archetypes of which Shakespeare and contemporary popular works are both exemplars, or to the interpretative ingenuity of *bardolaters anxious to project Shakespeare into every nook and cranny of cultural production?

Just as popular culture appropriates Shakespeare in a dizzying variety of forms and modes, so too works of popular culture display a complex—and contradictory—range of attitudes towards Shakespeare. Central to those attitudes is an awareness of Shakespeare's prestige, what Pierre Bourdieu has dubbed 'cultural capital', and of the tension in the cultural market place between highbrow and lowbrow. Frequently Shakespeare serves as a metonym for ideologically charged concepts—literature, classical theatre, highbrow culture, intellectualism—against which popular culture defines itself. Even so, popular conceptions of Shakespeare are hardly monolithic. Shakespeare is often treated as a repository of 'universal' truths, invoked to underwrite a particular claim—as in political speeches or advertisements—or to elevate the cultural register of the work—as in the case of book or movie titles. In the science-fiction film *The Postman* (1997), for example, the protagonist's concern with preserving a cultural legacy in a post-apocalyptic America takes the form of reciting Shakespeare. Shakespeare has also served to confer an aura of artistic authenticity on culture industries, particularly at moments of crisis. Early in the century *silent film adopted Shakespeare to counter claims that the movies were a corrupting influence, a process repeated in different ways in the mid-1930s with the talkies and in the 1950s and 1960s with early television. Even the sex industry has fought off threats of censorship by grafting Shakespeare onto erotica. This gloss of artistic legitimacy extends to the individual Shakespearian actor, as Paul Rudnick chronicles in his play *I Hate Hamlet* (1994). Just as often, however, legitimization operates in the opposite direction: Shakespearian performances by film or TV stars and productions of Shakespeare on film, TV, and radio confer the imprimatur of stardom on Shakespeare and remove the taint of elitism and antiquarianism. Indeed, many cases of popular Shakespearian appropriation partake of what might be called reciprocal legitimization, through which Shakespeare and popular media exchange different types of cultural prestige.

Other popular adaptations remain ambivalent or sceptical about Shakespeare's cultural authority, making it and its agents subjects of critique. Since mass culture typically establishes itself as 'popular' by demonizing the highbrow, Shakespeare has served as a symbolic target or, occasionally, as an unlikely ally. The vicissitudes of reading Shakespeare for class or performing Shakespeare in a school production are staples of TV and film partly because they are part of the audience's shared experience, but also because they provide opportunities for taking issue with 'proper' Shakespeare. Comedy groups such as the Reduced Shakespeare Company or Shakespeare Skum target the class-coded canons of stylistic decorum that underlie 'authentic' Shakespeare. Such canons of taste are closely linked for modern audiences to the quaint, quasi-scriptural ring of Shakespearian language, another favourite target for satirists. But critique can extend far beyond stylistic decorum to those institutions that use Shakespeare to purvey a notion of 'proper' culture and thereby protect their own class privilege. Indeed, popular culture often situates Shakespeare in those cultural institutions that reproduce and regulate his high-cultural status. Such is the case with the campy horror film *Theatre of Blood* (1973), in which disgruntled actor Edward Lionheart makes Shakespearian murder scenes the gruesome instruments of his revenge against those critics who have rejected his performances. *Theatre of Blood* makes explicit what is implicit in pop renderings of Shakespeare: a contest between cultural constituencies for authority, a struggle that makes Shakespeare the cultural icon both weapon and prize. In the 1990s, a number of works have made the contestatory ideal of a popular Shakespeare a central concern, among them the films *Looking for Richard* (1995), *A Midwinter's Tale* (1995), and *Shakespeare in Love* (1998). The sheer variety of popular Shakespeariana testifies that Shakespeare remains a powerful resource in popular culture, even as the media with which he has long been associated, the page and the stage, have been dethroned by the screen and the 'zine. (See also UNITED STATES OF AMERICA.) *DL*

Burt, Richard, *Unspeakable ShaXXXspeares* (1998)
Garber, Marjorie, 'Shakespeare as Fetish', in *Symptoms of Culture* (1998)
Hawkins, Harriett, 'From "King Lear" to "King Kong" and Back: Shakespeare and Popular Modern Dramas', in *Classics and Trash* (1990)
Levine, Lawrence W., *Highbrow/Lowbrow.* (1990)

Porter, Cole (1891–1964), American composer. His masterpiece is the *musical *Kiss Me Kate*, based on *The Taming of the Shrew*, first performed in Philadelphia and New York in 1948. Many of its individual songs gained independent popularity, notably 'Brush up your Shakespeare'. A film adaptation was made in 1953.

IBC

Porter, Eric (1928–95), British actor. He played a range of parts in repertory at Birmingham and Bristol and at the *Old Vic in London, notably Jaques and Bolingbroke. Between 1960 and 1965 he was a pillar of the *Royal Shakespeare Company, excelling as Malvolio, Leontes, Ulysses, Macbeth, Shylock, and Bolingbroke. He returned in 1968 to play an impressive King Lear. He became a household name for playing Soames in the BBC television *Forsyte Saga* (1967) and won major awards for stage performances, but never quite achieved the recognition he deserved. *MJ*

Porter, Henry (d. 1599), a playwright who wrote for the Admiral's Men between 1596 and 1599. His one surviving play, *The Two Angry Women of Abingdon* (printed in 1599), was successful enough to spawn two sequels. This bawdy farce ties itself in complicated knots around the feud between the two angry women of the title and the efforts of their husbands and children to reconcile them. Much of it is set at night, and it has affinities with *A Midsummer Night's Dream* and *The Merry Wives of Windsor*. Porter may have been killed by his fellow playwright John Day in 1599. *RM*

porters. **(1)** A porter attends the Countess of Auvergne, *1 Henry VI* 2.3. **(2)** A porter tells Lord Bardolph where to find Northumberland, *2 Henry IV* 1.1. **(3)** A porter admits Macduff and Lennox to Macbeth's castle, *Macbeth* 2.3. **(4)** A porter and his man try to contain the crowds eager to see *Elizabeth I's christening, *All Is True* (*Henry VIII*) 5.3. *AB*

Porter's Hall. When Philip Rosseter's lease on the Whitefriars playhouse expired he obtained a royal patent (dated 3 June 1615) to build a playhouse in Porter's Hall in Blackfriars. The Porter's Hall playhouse was not long open when the Privy Council, under pressure from the London Corporation and presumably also the local residents, closed the playhouse by exploiting a flaw in the patent: since 1608 Blackfriars had not been 'in the suburbs' as the patent had stated, but within the City. *GE*

Portia. **(1)** She is a rich heiress of Belmont who according to her father's will must accept the suitor who chooses the right casket of three in *The Merchant of Venice*. The Princes of Morocco and Aragon choose incorrectly, but Bassanio, whom Portia favours, is successful (3.2). Hearing of Antonio's plight she disguises herself as 'Balthasar', 'a young doctor of Rome'; saves Antonio with a legal quibble at the Venetian court; and humbles Shylock (4.1). Ellen *Terry's overt (by Victorian standards) advances to Bassanio and crucial use of feminine intuition in the trial scene were the result of the actress's developing proto-feminism. Since the Second World War, directorial attempts to integrate the Belmont romantic comedy with the Venetian tragedy have resulted in some interesting if less attractive Portias: notably Joan Plowright, whose calculating, mature Portia was very much a reflection of the Machiavellian world of Venetian business politics in Jonathan *Miller's 1970 production; and Deborah Findlay's smugly racist Portia in Bill Alexander's daring 1987 production. **(2)** She is Brutus' wife, who entreats him to confide in her, *Julius Caesar* 2.1. Her death is announced, 4.2.201.

AB

Bulman, James C., *Shakespeare in Performance: The Merchant of Venice* (1991)

portraits Speculation regarding the date of the *Chandos portrait aside, no depiction of Shakespeare made during his lifetime exists today. This absence has provided an opportune space for the scholarly, fantastic, and political projections of art historians, private collectors, *advertisers, comedians, journalists, and even publicans. Shakespeare's likeness has been avidly sought out, copied, forged, appropriated, invented, and capitalized upon. The two iconic representations at the heart of this cultural phenomenon are the *Droeshout engraving of 1623 and John Taylor's oil portrait of *c.*1610, known as the Chandos portrait. These images were used as sources by artists commissioned to produce early portraits of Shakespeare, such as Michael Van der Gucht, who produced a design for a derivative of the Chandos portrait with allegorical figures in 1709. Throughout the 18th century, the principal appropriations of Shakespeare portraiture were, however, commercial in function. The London publisher Jacob Tonson incorporated the Chandos portrait into his shop sign and trademark, and the same portrait was engraved for Paul Rapin-Thoyras's highly successful *History of England* (1725), which went into eight editions between 1725 and 1789.

The 19th century witnessed a spate of 're-discovered' originals allegedly used by Martin Droeshout in engraving the First Folio portrait. These images included the *Ely Palace, *Flower, and *Ashbourne portraits. This trend—intimately linked to the growth of *bardolatry—was exemplified by the appearance, in 1814, of an image in the style of a late 16th- or early 17th-century Dutch portrait, identified as Shakespeare's likeness, which came into the possession of Dunford, a prosperous publisher. The painting was later identified as a forgery.

Original portraits of Shakespeare continued to be produced during the 19th century, and most frequently appeared as engraved frontispieces to new editions of the plays. Depicting the sitter alongside attributes serving both to identify and elevate him has been one of the principal conventions of portraiture since the 16th century. It is, therefore, common to find Shakespeare not only shown with pen and scroll in hand, as in the statue by Louis François *Roubiliac commissioned by *Garrick (1758, now at the British Library), but portrayed alongside characters from the plays. The frontispiece to *Knight's Pictorial Shakespeare* (1838), for example, was executed by the Dalziel Brothers and depicts the dramatist alongside his characters, forging a link between creator and creations worthy of Old Testament narratives.

In the wake of the successful construction of Shakespeare as a national hero (ratified, in 1847, by the purchase of the dramatist's *birthplace and its transformation into a national shrine) the spurious 'identification' of portraits with obviously non-authentic provenances became especially frequent during periods of national crisis. In the period preceding the explosion of hostilities in 1914, one such 'discovery' was announced in Llandudno, Wales, and a portrait of 'Shakespeare' signed by 'Jo Taylor' was later exhibited at Earl's Court, London. Another mis-identification of a 17th-century Dutch portrait, likely to have represented an Old Testament prophet, and incorrectly attributed to Frans Hals, was made in the *Reynolds News* on 5 November 1944.

Renewed momentum was given to the identification of Shakespeare portraits by the institutionalization of Art History as an academic discipline. A celebrated instance of this phase of portrait identification is that relating to a portrait miniature of a young man by Nicholas *Hilliard. In 1977, Leslie *Hotson argued that the sitter was indeed Shakespeare, and wrote a detailed iconological account of the piece. Hotson claimed that Shakespeare was represented as Mercury (the amethyst-coloured hat supposedly referring to the god) and that the youthful hand grasped by the sitter was that of Apollo. Hotson's view of the portrait, however, was not shared by other scholars, and Sir Roy Strong later identified the sitter as Lord Thomas Howard, later 1st Earl of Suffolk.

The use of Shakespeare portraiture for purposes other than commemoration of the dramatist himself shows no sign of abating. The Droeshout engraving appeared on the initial screen of the British Library's computer catalogue until 1999, above the institution's claim to world-class status as 'the leading resource for research, innovation and scholarship'. Seemingly endowed with boundless authority and powers of historical and scholarly validation, yet executed in a style that was anachronistic in its own day, the Droeshout portrait testifies to the value still placed upon Shakespeare's authorial presence. *CT*

Engler, Balz, 'Shakespeare in the Trenches', *Shakespeare Survey*, 45 (1991)
Hotson, Leslie, *Shakespeare by Hilliard* (1977)
Pointon, Marcia, 'Shakespeare, Portraiture, and National Identity', *Shakespeare Jahrbuch*, 133 (1997)
Scharf, George, *A Few Observations Connected with the Chandos Portrait of Shakespeare* (National Portrait Gallery, Mar. 1865)
Spielmann, Marion H., *The Portraits of Shakespeare*, vol. x of The Stratford Town Edition (1906–7)
Strong, Roy, 'No Man's Hand', *The Times*, 6 Oct. 1977

Portugal was, apparently, of limited interest to Shakespeare: England's oldest ally is mentioned in his writings only twice, once as one of several foreign countries in which banished xenophobic rioters would themselves be foreign (*Sir Thomas More*, Add.II.D., 141–5), and once solely for its proximity to the depths of the Bay of Biscay ('My affection hath an unknown bottom, like the Bay of Portugal', *As You Like It* 4.1.197–8). Reciprocally, Portugal's interest in Shakespeare was slow to develop. An 18th-century *Hamlet* opera (Francisco Luis Ameno's *Ambleto em Dania*, *c.*1755) was based on an Italian or Spanish version of the story rather than directly on Shakespeare's play, and when a few Shakespeare plays began to appear in Portuguese (and subsequently *Brazilian) theatres in the later 18th and 19th centuries they too had been heavily adapted from translations into other languages (Rebello da Silva's *Othello*, 1856, for example, is a sentimental prose adaptation of de *Vigny's French translation). It took a monarch to initiate a tradition of translating Shakespeare directly from English into Portuguese, Louis I, who published his *Hamlet* anonymously in 1877. His notable successors included Bulhão Pato and Antonio Petronillo Lamarão. In the 20th century a translation of the Complete Works was carried out by the Faculty of Letters at the University of Coimbra, and the coming of age of a Portuguese Shakespeare industry was marked by a major conference in Lisbon in 1987. *MD*

Coloquio sobre Shakespeare, 7, 8 e 9 de maio de 1987 (1987)
de Mello Moser, Fernando, *Discurso inacabado: ensaios de cultura portuguesa* (1994)
Michaelis de Vasconcellos, Carolina, 'Shakespeare in Portugal', *Shakespeare Jahrbuch*, 15 (1880)

Posthumus Leonatus, banished when his marriage to Innogen is discovered, makes a wager with Giacomo that he will not be able to seduce her in *Cymbeline*. *AB*

postmodernism. (1) The aesthetic and literary period following 20th-century modernism, variously said to have begun in 1945, 1965, or 1980 and marked by an aesthetics of disunity, anti-hierarchy, flatness, ironyless irony, and decentred subjectivity. Many critics see its impact on Shakespeare after about 1980 in avant-garde (or merely eclectic) theatrical productions and in poststructuralist literary criticism.

(2) According to French social theorist François Lyotard, postmodernism (or postmodernity) is the intellectual problematic arising from the collapse of central assumptions of long-term modernity (seen as having begun in the Enlightenment). In this view modernity or (long-term) modernism had been marked by teleological narratives of progress and increasing rationality which are now revealed as ideological. 'Postmodernist' in this connection denotes those theories and theorists which share Lyotard's diagnosis, usually including Nietzsche, Foucault, and other poststructuralists, and hence this term is sometimes used in Shakespeare studies to designate poststructuralist critiques of rationality and teleology. At other times the term is used in a conflated sense, combining meanings (1) and (2). *HG*

poststructuralism. See STRUCTURALISM AND POSTSTRUCTURALISM.

Powell, William (?1735–69), English actor. He was trained by *Garrick, and covered many roles during his absences abroad. Success in London was followed by summer seasons at Bristol, where he became a popular actor-manager. In 1767 he acquired a part-share in *Covent Garden theatre, where he played major Shakespearian roles including Hamlet. *CMSA*

Pre-Raphaelite Brotherhood, a society formed in 1848 by the English artists William Holman Hunt, John Everett Millais, and Dante Gabriel Rossetti, with four friends. The Pre-Raphaelites identified in Shakespeare an ideal they could harness to their attempt to revitalize British art with noble ideas and fidelity to nature: in 1848 Rossetti and Hunt prepared 'a list of Immortals, forming our creed', wherein the 'first class' comprised Jesus and Shakespeare. Hunt chose episodes dramatizing moral conflict in *Valentine Rescuing Sylvia from Proteus* (1851) and *Claudio and Isabella* (1850–3). Millais's luminous *Ferdinand Lured by Ariel* (1849) enlivened popular *fairy painting with an innovative realism which also characterizes his *Ophelia* (1852) (see page 354). Like the latter, Rossetti's sketches *Hamlet and Ophelia* (*c.*1854–9) and *The Death of Lady Macbeth* (*c.*1876), and his painting of the pining *Mariana* (1868–70), all explore tragic Shakespearian women—a theme popular with followers of the movement after 1853, when the formal Brotherhood ceased. *KN*

Priam is King of Troy and father of Hector, Deiphobus, Helenus, Paris, Troilus, and Margareton in *Troilus and Cressida*. (According to Homeric legend, and the joke Pandarus recounts at 1.2.156–8, he had 50 sons.) *AB*

priests. (1) A priest greets Hastings, *Richard III* 3.2, who whispers something to him. He is named 'Sir John' at line 105. **(2)** A priest tells Laertes that *Ophelia's 'death was doubtful', *Hamlet* 5.1.221. **(3)** A priest testifies that Olivia and Sebastian have married, *Twelfth Night* 5.1.154–61. *AB*

Prince of Verona. See ESCALUS, PRINCE OF VERONA.

princes, five. See KNIGHTS, FIVE.

Princes in the Tower. See EDWARD, PRINCE.

Princess's theatre. See KEAN, CHARLES.

printing and publishing. In Shakespeare's time the printer of a book owned the type and the press. The publisher acquired the manuscript, paid for copies of it to be printed, and sold them wholesale. The imprint on a Shakespearian *quarto usually identifies the printer (often only by his initials, perhaps to emphasize the greater importance of the publisher), the publisher, and the bookshop (usually the publisher's own) in which copies of the book could be purchased wholesale: 'Printed at London by P.S. for Thomas Millington, and are to be sold at his shop under Saint Peter's Church.'

The publisher would acquire a manuscript that he deemed publishable, register it in the *Stationers' Register, and obtain approval of the text by the ecclesiastical authorities (or by others to whom this task had been delegated, such as the *Master of the Revels). The publisher would select a master printer and the two would then decide on the format, type size and design, paper quality, and the number of copies likely to be sold. The publisher would supply the printer with the manuscript to be printed and a sufficient amount of paper for the print run.

The master printer would decide whether the text would be set into type by a single *compositor or by a number working simultaneously, in which case the copy would have to be cast off. The compositor would set individual lines of type in a composing stick, transfer these to a *galley which made up a page, and then transfer his galleys to the imposing stone where they would be positioned to make up a *forme. When the forme was completed, it would be tightly wedged into an iron frame and delivered to the pressman, who would place it on the bed of the press. While one pressman inked the type in the forme, another placed a sheet of slightly dampened paper on a hinged frame covered with parchment, the 'tympan'. The tympan was then folded over the type and rolled under the upper plate of the press, the 'platen'. The pressman pulled on the bar, causing the platen

A London printing-house of Shakespeare's day, from Stephen Batman's *The Doom Warning All Men to Judgement* (1581). One pressman (right) is removing the sheet which has just been printed from the tympan, while another inks the type-bed in readiness for the next pull. At the rear a compositor (right) is sitting at a case of type, setting from the copy held before his eyes in a copy-holder, while his colleague may be making press corrections.

to press the tympan on the inked type and taking the impression. A proof sheet would be pulled, and read against the manuscript. Any necessary corrections would then be made in the metal type.

John Everett Millais's *Ophelia* (1852), the most enduringly popular of all Pre-Raphaelite paintings. In common with Victorian producers such as Charles Kean, Millais chose to show a scene which Shakespeare only describes.

A single press could print about 250 sheets per hour. If an edition consisted of 800 copies, it would be possible to print all copies of one forme in approximately three hours. This rate of speed would enable the pressmen to print one side of a sheet in the morning, and then print the other in the afternoon while the pages were still wet. At the rate of one sheet per day, an average-sized play quarto of twelve sheets would take two weeks to machine in a shop with a single press. If time was of the essence, the job might be shared by two or more printing-houses.

When all sheets of the book had been printed and dried, they were ready to be folded and collated for binding. Generally, however, only a few books were bound, usually to be used as display copies. The remainder were warehoused as sheets to be distributed to retail booksellers. Any bookseller who belonged to the Stationers' Company could purchase books published in London at controlled wholesale prices from other company members.

Peter Blayney has estimated that a publisher's total costs for producing a run of 800 copies of a play quarto (including the price of acquiring the manuscript, the costs of licence and registration, and the amount paid to the printer) would average 2.7*d.* per copy. The publisher would therefore set the wholesale price at 4*d.* and the unbound play quarto would then retail at approximately 6*d.* a copy. The only recorded prices paid for Shakespeare's plays before 1623 are 5*d.* for the 1600 quarto of *2 Henry IV* and 8*d.* for the 1595 octavo of *Richard Duke of York* (*3 Henry VI*). Publishers might hope to realize substantial profits if demand merited a second edition, in which case the publisher's only outlay would be the costs of printing.

Shakespeare's first printed works, *Venus and Adonis* (1593) and *The Rape of Lucrece* (1594), came from the printing-house of Richard Field (1561–1624), a native of Stratford who later printed *Love's Martyr* (1601), a collection of verse that included Shakespeare's 'The Phoenix and Turtle'. The popularity of the narrative poems in Shakespeare's lifetime is well attested: *Venus and Adonis* appeared in nine editions and *The Rape of Lucrece* in five. The history plays also sold well. The three plays published by Andrew Wise in the years 1597–8—*Richard II*, *Richard III*, and *1 Henry IV*—turned out to be Shakespeare's best-selling plays, each appearing in five quarto editions before the publication of the First Folio in 1623.

Certain printers seem to have specialized in play quartos. Thomas Creede (fl. 1578–1617) printed the first quartos of *The First Part of the Contention* (*2 Henry VI*), *Henry V*, *The Merry Wives of Windsor*, *Pericles*, and the second quarto of *Romeo and Juliet*, as well as the second, third, fourth, and fifth quarto reprints of *Richard III*. The premier printer of play texts, George Eld (fl. 1603–24), was responsible for 34 play quartos, including *Troilus and Cressida* (1609), as well as *Shakespeare's Sonnets* (1609). Even as small a printing job as a play quarto might occasionally be shared by two shops: for the first quarto of *Romeo and Juliet* (1597), sheets A–D were printed by John Danter while sheets E–K were printed by Edward Allde. Peter Short and Valentine Simmes shared the printing of *Richard III* (1597). The printing of the quarto of *Pericles* was shared by William White and Thomas Creede.

The list below provides the printers, publishers, and distributors (in those cases in which the publisher did not serve as his own distributor) of the first editions of Shakespeare's plays and poems:

Venus and Adonis (1593)
- Printer: Richard Field
- Publisher: Richard Field

The Rape of Lucrece (1594)
- Printer: Richard Field
- Publisher: John Harrison

Titus Andronicus (1594)
- Printer: John Danter
- Publisher: John Danter
- Distributors: Thomas Millington and Edward White

The First Part of the Contention (1594)
- Printer: Thomas Creede
- Publisher: Thomas Millington

Richard Duke of York (1595)
- Printer: Peter Short
- Publisher: Thomas Millington

Romeo and Juliet (1597) Q1
- Printer: Edward Allde and John Danter
- Publisher: [Cuthbert Burby?]

Richard II (1597)
- Printer: Valentine Simmes
- Publisher: Andrew Wise

Richard III (1597)
- Printer: Peter Short and Valentine Simmes
- Publisher: Andrew Wise

1 Henry IV (1598)
- Printer: Peter Short
- Publisher: Andrew Wise

Love's Labour's Lost (1598)
- Printer: William White
- Publisher: Cuthbert Burby

Romeo and Juliet (1599) Q2
- Printer: Thomas Creede
- Publisher: Cuthbert Burby

2 Henry IV (1600)
- Printer: Valentine Simmes
- Publisher: William Aspley and Andrew Wise

A Midsummer Night's Dream (1600)
- Printer: [Richard Bradock?]
- Publisher: Thomas Fisher

The Merchant of Venice (1600)
- Printer: James Roberts
- Publisher: Thomas Heyes

Much Ado About Nothing (1600)
- Printer: Valentine Simmes
- Publisher: Andrew Wise

Henry V (1600)
- Printer: Thomas Creede
- Publisher: John Busby and Thomas Millington

The Merry Wives of Windsor (1602)
- Printer: Thomas Creede
- Publisher: Arthur Johnson

Hamlet (1603) Q1
- Printer: Valentine Simmes
- Publisher: Nicholas Ling and John Trundle

Hamlet (1604/5) Q2
- Printer: James Roberts
- Publisher: Nicholas Ling

King Lear (1608)
- Printer: Nicholas Okes
- Publisher: Nathaniel Butter

Shakespeare's Sonnets (1609)
- Printer: George Eld
- Publisher: Thomas Thorpe
- Distributors: William Aspley and John Wright

Troilus and Cressida (1609)
- Printer: George Eld
- Publisher: Richard Bonian and Henry Walley

Pericles (1609)
- Printer: Thomas Creede and William White
- Publisher: Henry Gosson

Othello (1622)
- Printer: Nicholas Okes
- Publisher: Thomas Walkley

Mr William Shakespeares Comedies, Histories, & Tragedies (The First Folio, 1623)
- Printer: William and Isaac Jaggard
- Publishers: William Jaggard, Edward Blount, John Smethwick, and William Aspley

ER

Blayney, Peter W. M., 'The Publication of Playbooks', in John D. Cox and David Scott Kastan (eds.), *A New History of Early English Drama* (1997)

Williams, George Walton, *The Craft of Printing and the Publication of Shakespeare's Works* (1985)

Pritchard, Hannah (1709–68), English actress and singer. She began her career playing light comic roles in ballad opera and pantomime and became one of the most versatile performers of her day. At *Drury Lane from 1735 she played the Duchess of York, Lady Anne, Lady Macduff, Anna Bullen, and Desdemona, and scored her first major success as Rosalind in the 1740 revival of *As You Like It* with song settings by *Arne. She first appeared with *Garrick in 1742, playing Gertrude to his Hamlet and Queen Elizabeth to his Richard III, a professional relationship which strengthened when she joined his company in 1747 and played Gertrude, Viola, and Emilia. She triumphed as Lady Macbeth the following year, her passionate intensity becoming the definitive model for the role and proving a perfect foil for Garrick's Macbeth. In 1749 she played Beatrice to his Benedick, in 1754 was Catherine in the première of his adaptation *Catherine and Petruchio*, and in 1755 played Hermione in his *Florizel and Perdita*. Renowned for her natural playing style, good voice, and charm, her achievements are recorded on a memorial tablet next to Shakespeare's monument in *Westminster Abbey.

CMSA

private theatres. See THEATRES, ELIZABETHAN AND JACOBEAN.

Privy Council, a group of about ten advisers to the monarch which met daily to decide matters of policy and of law. Many regulations concerning the theatre industry emerged directly from the Privy Council and countered antitheatrical orders from the London corporation.

Lord *Hunsdon, the *Chamberlain's Men's patron, was a privy counsellor. *GE*

'problem plays' (sometimes 'problem comedies' or 'dark comedies'), a term coined by F. S. *Boas for *Troilus and Cressida*, *Measure for Measure*, and *All's Well That Ends Well*, which, according to W. W. Lawrence, 'clearly do not fall into the category of tragedy, and yet are too serious and analytic to fit the commonly accepted conception of comedy'. This grouping of early Jacobean plays has sometimes been extended by the inclusion of *Timon of Athens*, *Twelfth Night*, and even *Hamlet* and *Othello*. Although mainly concerned with genre, the term 'problem play' also recalls the Ibsenite drama of the 1890s, implying a play with an intellectual interest in a particular social issue. It has fallen into comparative disfavour in more recent criticism, which has pointed out that few of Shakespeare's other plays fit the simple generic categories of comedy and tragedy any more comfortably. *MD*

Lawrence, W. W., *Shakespeare's Problem Comedies* (1931)
Tillyard, E. M. W., *Shakespeare's Problem Plays* (1949)
Wheeler, Richard, *Shakespeare's Development and the Problem Comedies* (1981)

Proculeius. He is sent with a message from Caesar to Cleopatra *Antony and Cleopatra* 5.1. He captures her, 5.2. *AB*

profanity. See Act to Restrain Abuses of Players.

Prokofiev, Sergei (1891–1953), Russian composer. In 1933 he composed incidental music for a play based partly on *Antony and Cleopatra* (from which he derived an orchestral suite, *Egypatin Nights*, Op. 61), and in 1938 he wrote music for a production of *Hamlet* (Op. 77) in Leningrad. His most famous Shakespearian music, however, is his splendidly evocative *ballet music for *Romeo and Juliet* (Op. 64) which, initially rejected in Moscow, was first staged in Brno in 1938. *IBC*

prolepsis, a figure of speech in which something is described prematurely in terms that are not yet applicable: 'I am dead, Horatio' (*Hamlet* 5.2.285). *CB*

prologue, a preliminary speech announcing the subject or setting of a play, usually spoken in verse by a single chorus figure. Seven of Shakespeare's plays use this device. More substantially dramatic introductions—such as the introductory monologue by Rumour in *2 Henry IV*, and the frame-story of Christopher Sly in *The Taming of the Shrew*—are called inductions. *CB*

Promos and Cassandra. See Whetstone, George.

Promptbook. See playbook.

pronunciation. It is often said, usually by Americans, that the spoken English of Shakespeare's day was closer in sound to present-day American English than it was to current British 'received pronunciation'. There is some truth in this with regard to certain vowel sounds: most 16th-century English dialects, for example, even at court, were still rhotic, i.e. they pronounced the 'r' in 'hard', as do many present-day English dialects in rural areas and almost all American ones outside Harvard. On the other hand, for Shakespeare as for his present-day compatriots 'clerk' rhymed with 'bark', and when it came to consonants he and his contemporaries seem to have pronounced theirs with a force and distinctness long vanished from most American usage: for many the 'k' and 'g' in 'knight' and 'gnaw' were still enunciated, while the pronunciation of words like 'mission' and 'vision' as disyllables with a soft medial 'sh' or 'zh' sound had only begun to supplant an older and more strenuous sounding of 'mis-yon' or 'viz-yon'. But as this last example may suggest, the most important fact about Elizabethan pronunciation was that it was in a process of change, with all sorts of different phonetic usages still contending for dominance, so that generalizations comparing an imaginary Shakespearian 'norm' with any notional present-day one are innately suspect.

Self-conscious about their pronunciation for the first time—as about their *spelling, and the extent to which it should be phonetic—the English produced a number of books on the subject in Shakespeare's period (among them John Hart's *An Orthography*, 1569, and Richard *Mulcaster's *The First Part of the Elementary*, 1582), which together with the evidence of rhyme, puns, and metre supply a good deal of information about how their speech must have sounded. Some sounds were always different from their standard modern equivalents, on either side of the Atlantic. The 'ea' vowel in 'feat', for instance, was never the same as the 'ee' in 'feet', but instead was closer to the long 'a' of 'fate': 'beat', 'bait', and 'bate' thus sounded more or less alike (as they still do in many northern English dialects), and so did 'mead', 'maid', and 'made'. It is clear, however, that in other instances different pronunciations existed side by side, and that Shakespeare, when not supplying characters with particular *dialects, felt perfectly free to use different variants interchangeably according to the demands of rhyme or scansion rather than as markers of class or region. 'Toil', for example, might sound either as in present-day standard English or like a rhyme for 'pile' (as in 19th-century Cockney, and hence modern Australian). Shakespeare and his contemporaries were at their freest when stressing polysyllables: long words recently coined from Latin could be made to fit the stress-patterns of verse pretty much as the occasion required. This sometimes leaves modern actors—when faced with a line which asks them to say 'c*o*rrosive' or 'dem*on*strate' or 'sep*u*lchre'—with a choice between sounding metrical but affected or comprehensible but unrhythmic.

The quest for 'authenticity' in the staging of Elizabethan drama exemplified by the work of William *Poel and the builders of the reconstructed *Globe has rarely extended from performing on Elizabethan-style stages in Elizabethan costumes to performing in Elizabethan dialects. Some contemporary directors, however, notably John *Barton, still wax lyrical about the superior physicality of 16th-century pronunciation (which Barton discusses, and memorably attempts to simulate, in his *Playing Shakespeare* television series), and Barry Rutter's Northern Broadsides company conscientiously shun received pronunciation, instead speaking Shakespeare's lines as though all his characters came from working-class Yorkshire in a bid to provide a comprehensible modern equivalent for the imagined lost vernacular hardness of Elizabethan usage. *MD*

Barton, John, *Playing Shakespeare* (1984)
Dobson, E. J., *English Pronunciation 1500–1700* (2 vols., 1957)
Smith, Bruce, *The Acoustic World of Early Modern England* (1999)

proofreading. A trial print of a sheet was generally made before printing began; this 'proof' was then read against copy by a 'corrector' who marked errors on the proof and returned it to the *compositor for correction in the metal type. The first sheets of a print run might be provided to reassure the corrector that the changes had indeed been implemented; these would often be checked as the rest were being printed, resulting in books that were made up of sheets in different states of correction. *ER*

properties. Among the items in Philip *Henslowe's inventory of 'all the properties for my Lord Admiral's men' (taken on 10 March 1598) are a 'rock', a 'tomb', and a 'hell mouth', which presumably were lifelike, and others such as 'the city of Rome' and a 'rainbow' which must have been representative. The 'dragon for fostes' (*Marlowe's *Doctor Faustus*) and the 'cauldron for the Jewe' (Marlowe's *The Jew of Malta*) were obviously kept for particular plays and the small number of other general-purpose items accords with the sparsity of directions requiring properties in the drama. Curtained beds are commonly needed and the Admiral's Men had a 'bedstead' and a 'wooden canopy', the latter presumably being a multi-use booth structure. The most numerous handheld items are eight 'vizards', eight lances, and six crowns (sorted into imperial and plain). Anything not worn or carried by an actor would have to be transported by stagehands in full view of the audience and this potential disruption—together with the exigencies of touring—would encourage dramatists to minimize use of larger properties. *GE*

proportion, in music, the note value ratios within a particular time signature and the tempo relationships between different time signatures (see *Richard II* 5.5.43). The term is also applied to the frequency ratios of pitches. *JB*

proscenium, a Renaissance word for the stage and so used as a label in de Witt's drawing of the *Swan, but subsequently used to refer to the arrangement in post-Restoration theatres (and some Stuart *masques) where the acting space is recessed behind an arch. Another term for this arrangement is the 'picture frame' stage. *GE*

prose. With a few notable exceptions (*The Merry Wives of Windsor, Much Ado About Nothing, As You Like It, Twelfth Night*), Shakespeare's plays rely more on verse than on prose. Shakespeare's use of prose is therefore marked, and often triggered by, an identifiable context: comedy (including the comic scenes of histories and tragedies); speech between lower-class characters; sub-plots; madness; letters and proclamations. Because comedy favours prose, the proportion of prose to verse found in Shakespeare's plays rises steadily from the early to the mid-period, as Shakespeare switches from histories to comedies, and then falls away again with the late tragedies.

The contexts favouring prose are mostly informal ones, but prose can be formal (Brutus' funeral speech in *Julius Caesar* can be contrasted with Antony's emotional verse reply) and even pompous (Armado in *Love's Labour's Lost*). There are also instances of characters slipping in and out of verse and prose in the same scene, apparently marking transient emotional states (*Troilus and Cressida* 3.2). Prose provided Shakespeare with a useful stylistic resource, and it is notable that after four prose-free early histories (*1 Henry VI, Richard Duke of York* (*3 Henry VI*), *King John, Richard II*), he never wrote another play entirely in verse.

Linguistic approaches to Shakespeare's prose, such as those pursued by Vivian Salmon, have looked to it as evidence for Elizabethan spoken English, and these studies can now be compared with findings from non-literary texts such as court depositions (as in the work of Wright). Many prose passages in Shakespeare do indeed show the grammatical features we associate with speech. In the following exchange, note the use of simple clauses and sentence fragments joined by syndetic or asyndetic co-ordination; repetition; ellipsis; and the apposition of noun phrases or use of relative clauses to provide elaborated information:

> PRINCE HARRY. ... tell me, Jack, whose fellows are these that come after?
> SIR JOHN. Mine, Hal, mine.
> PRINCE HARRY. I did never see such pitiful rascals.
> SIR JOHN. Tut, tut, good enough to toss, food for powder, food for powder. They'll fill a pit as well as better. Tush, man, mortal men, mortal men.
> WESTMORLAND. Ay, but Sir John, methinks they are exceeding poor and bare, too beggarly.
> (*1 Henry IV* 4.2.61–9)

Literary-stylistic approaches to Shakespeare's prose (such as those of Jonas Barish and Brian Vickers) have stressed the rhetorical tradition, which provided Elizabethan writers with various models for prose style. The two most influential models are usually termed 'Ciceronian' and 'Senecan'—though the use of these terms should not necessarily be taken as implying direct influence of Latin models (and there is considerable variation within, and even sharing of features between, the styles).

'Ciceronian' is applied to prose styles which favour long sentences containing many subordinate clauses, often embedded within each other, and using many rhetorical figures, especially those involving balanced elements and parallelism. The 'periodic sentences' thus produced often have a highly Latinate vocabulary. This style is formal, favouring noun clauses as subjects and objects, and often postponing the main verb, or distancing it from the subject. Word order is frequently disrupted, producing a formal effect, and the impression of control and prior planning. This style was brought to a notorious extreme in the 16th century by John *Lyly in his novel *Euphues* (1578), and in *1 Henry IV*, when Sir John pretends to be King Henry rebuking Hal for his dissolute life, he adopts a mock-euphuistic style, laden with balanced clauses, antithetical structures, and elaborate comparisons:

> SIR JOHN. Harry, I do not only marvel where thou spendest thy time, but also how thou art accompanied. For though the camomile, the more it is trodden on, the faster it grows, yet youth, the more it is wasted, the sooner it wears. That thou art my son I have partly thy mother's word, partly my own opinion, but chiefly a villainous trick of thine eye, and a foolish hanging of thy nether lip, that doth warrant me. If then thou be son to me, here lies the point. Why, being son to me, art thou so pointed at? Shall the blessed sun of heaven prove a micher, and eat blackberries?—A question not to be asked. Shall the son of England prove a thief, and take purses?—A question to be asked. There is a thing, Harry, which thou hast often heard of, and it is known to many in our land by the name of pitch. This pitch, as ancient writers do report, doth defile. So doth the company thou keepest. For Harry, now I do not speak to thee in drink, but in tears; not in pleasure, but in passion; not in words only, but in woes also.
> (*1 Henry IV* 2.5.402–20)

In contrast to the highly subordinated (or hypotactic) Ciceronian style, the 'Senecan' model uses co-ordination and juxtaposition (or parataxis) to give the impression of thought as it happens. Simple clauses are laid next to each other. Subjects are plain noun phrases. Effects are achieved over short, rather than long, distances. While seeking the appearance of being unplanned, this style is nonetheless often highly rhetorical. Sir John has a tendency towards the Ciceronian even when speaking in his own person, but his catechism on 'honour' displays many of the features of this type of prose: the sense of thoughts being sparked from one clause to the next; short clauses, and sentence fragments; rhetorical figures based on the repetition of individual words rather than phrases:

> PRINCE HARRY. Why, thou owest God a death. *Exit*
> SIR JOHN. 'Tis not due yet. I would be loath to pay him before his day. What need I be so forward with him that calls not on me? Well, 'tis no matter; honour pricks me on. Yea, but how if honour prick me off when I come on? How then? Can honour set-to a leg? No. Or an arm? No. Or take away the grief of a wound? No. Honour hath no skill in surgery, then? No. What is honour? A word. What is in that word 'honour'? What is that 'honour'? Air. A trim reckoning! Who hath it? He that died o' Wednesday. Doth he feel it? No. Doth he hear it? No. 'Tis insensible, then? Yea, to the dead. But will it not live with the living? No. Why? Detraction will not suffer it. Therefore I'll none of it. Honour is a mere scutcheon. And so ends my catechism.
> (*1 Henry IV* 5.1.126–40)

JRH

Barish, Jonas, *Ben Jonson and the Language of Prose Comedy* (1960)
Salmon, Vivian, and Burness, E., *A Reader in the Language of Shakespearean Drama* (1987)
Vickers, Brian, *The Artistry of Shakespeare's Prose* (1968)
Wright, L., 'Syntactic Structure of Witnesses' Narratives from the Sixteenth-Century Court Minute Books of the Royal Hospitals of Bridewell and Bedlam', *Neuphilologische Mitteilungen*, 96 (1995)

prosopopoeia, an important poetical figure of speech in which something or someone incapable of speech or hearing (because inanimate, dead, absent, or imaginary) is spoken to or heard from; more broadly translated as 'personification':

Dear earth, I do salute thee with my hand (*Richard II* 3.2.6) *CB*

Prospero. See TEMPEST, THE.

Prospero's Books. See TEMPEST, THE.

prostitution in the London of Shakespeare's time was transacted largely, though not exclusively, in the variant-quality brothels of *Bankside, the location, too, of many theatres. Ambulant prostitutes often sought business in the playhouses, bear gardens, and taverns. Some worked part-time as seamstresses, as Nell Quickly's comments in *Henry v* (2.1.31–4) imply. Though most of Shakespeare's plays mention it, only five depict prostitution: *The Comedy of Errors* (if one regards the Courtesan as a professional), *Measure for Measure, 2 Henry iv, Timon of Athens*, and *Pericles. Othello*'s Bianca has traditionally been regarded as a whore, because called such in the play, but so, unjustly, are both of the other female characters. No partner for Bianca other than Cassio is mentioned, nor are financial transactions. Doll Tearsheet of *2 Henry iv* is Shakespeare's only character to call herself a 'whore' without disowning the term. Her whipping by beadles, who scapegoat her and Quickly for Pistol's violence, is realistic, as is her death, mentioned in *Henry v*, from venereal disease, a fate of many from unhygienic conditions and incompetent treatments. Mistress Overdone's care for Kate Keepdown's illegitimate child in *Measure for Measure* seems unusually kind, as pregnant women were generally ejected from brothels. The Church long profited from prostitution through licensing and the leasing of land and buildings. In *1 Henry vi*, Gloucester chastises Cardinal Winchester's granting of indulgences for prostitution (1.3); 'Winchester geese' was one of many early modern slang terms for prostitutes (cf. Pandarus' epilogue to *Troilus and Cressida*). Most brothel prostitutes endured conditions like those discussed in *Pericles*. *KS*

Burford, E. J., *The Bishop's Brothels* (1993)

Stanton, Kay, ' "Made to write 'whore' upon?": Male and Female Use of the Word "Whore" in Shakespeare's Canon', in Dympna Callaghan (ed.), *A Feminist Companion to Shakespeare* (2000)

protection of players. On 27 December 1624 the *Master of the Revels, Sir Henry *Herbert, signed a document protecting 22 men from arrest without the prior authorization of himself or the Lord Chamberlain. These men were described as 'employed by the King's majesty's servants in their quality of playing as musicians and other necessary attendants' and as many as half were musicians, perhaps the beginnings of a theatre orchestra. *GE*

Cutts, John P., 'New Findings with Regard to the 1624 Protection List', *Shakespeare Survey*, 19 (1966)

Proteus, in love with Julia, forswears her for Silvia in *The Two Gentlemen of Verona*. His name is that of the old man of the sea from Greek mythology who constantly changes shape. The parallel character in *Montemayor's *Diana* is called Felix. *AB*

provincial companies, tours. In Shakespeare's time the majority of playing companies seldom or never performed in London but rather followed established touring routes across the countryside, stopping for a few days in each town to play in the town hall or a large inn. Because they were not settled, information about the companies resides in provincial records, and the overall picture of non-London drama is only now beginning to emerge from the *Records of Early English Drama* project. All companies were essentially provincial touring companies until, in 1594, the *Chamberlain's Men and the *Admiral's Men were granted a duopoly in London. *GE*

Provost. He superintends the prison in *Measure for Measure*, helping 'Friar Lodowick' (Duke Vincentio) to undermine the severity of Angelo's sentences. *AB*

psychoanalytic criticism is the application of Sigmund *Freud's theories of the unconscious to the interpretation of literature. It was initiated by Freud himself in an analysis of Shakespeare's *Hamlet* as a manifestation of Oedipal conflict. Freud's ideas were subsequently developed by his disciple Ernest *Jones in the classic *Hamlet and Oedipus* (1949), and by numerous other amateur and professional critics. Psychoanalytic criticism has a long 20th-century history marked by competing developments of Freud's theory. In Shakespeare studies Norman Holland combined American ego psychoanalysis and *formalism when psychoanalysis was in disfavour in an academic world dominated by *New Criticism and historicism. After the demise of New Criticism around 1970, psychoanalytic approaches became more prominent in Shakespeare criticism, through the work of critics like C. L. Barber, Richard Wheeler, and Coppélia Kahn. The theories of object-relations psychoanalysts D. W. Winnicott and Melanie Klein have influenced American *feminist critics like Janet Adelman while French psychoanalyst Jacques Lacan's complex synthesis of Freud, *structuralism, and poststructuralism has become prominent in recent years, often in combination with feminism and/or *Marxism. *HG*

Holland, Norman N., *Psychoanalysis and Shakespeare* (1964)

Schwartz, Murray, and Kahn, Coppélia, (eds.), *Representing Shakespeare: New Psychoanalytic Essays* (1980)

Publius. (1) Marcus Andronicus' son, he helps bind and gag Chiron and Demetrius, *Titus Andronicus* 5.2.162. **(2)** A senator in *Julius Caesar*, he is 'quite confounded with this mutiny' (the assassination of Caesar), 3.1.86. *AB*

Pucelle, Joan la. See JOAN LA PUCELLE.

Puck. See ROBIN GOODFELLOW.

Pudsey, Edward (fl. 1596–1602), compiler of a commonplace book containing quotations from various plays performed around 1600, including Ben *Jonson's plays, John *Marston's *Antonio* plays, and *The Merchant of Venice*. The inaccuracy of most citations suggests they were noted down during or soon after performance, not taken from a printed text. *CS*

Pujante, Ángel-Luis (b. 1944), Spanish professor of English and translator of Shakespeare. He has written on various aspects of Shakespeare and *Middleton. His translations attempt to be faithful to Shakespeare's poetic expressiveness and to the dramatic nature of his works. He renders Shakespeare's blank verse into Spanish free verse, except for the rhymed passages, which he translates as such. Starting in 1986, by 1999 he had published fourteen translations with introductions and notes (Espasa, Madrid). In 1998 he was awarded the National Prize of Literary Translation for his version of *The Tempest*. *ALP*

punctuation. A coherent system of punctuation, which did not exist in the classical or medieval periods, was probably first mandated by Renaissance printers. Given the almost complete absence of punctuation in Shakespeare's contribution to the **Sir Thomas More* manuscript, some scholars have concluded that punctuation marks in the printed texts of his plays are probably the compositors' rather than Shakespeare's. And yet, the humour of Peter Quince's prologue in *A Midsummer Night's Dream* (5.1.108–17) depends upon its deliberate mispunctuation: as Theseus observes, 'This fellow doth not stand upon points' (5.1.118). *ER*

puns, jokes, subtle or coarse, that exploit either the possibilities of homophones (i.e. words that sound the same but have different meanings: son/sun, sole/soul) or different senses of the same verbal form, e.g. in polite and in slang uses ('Will': testament/wish/William/penis). Shakespeare's notorious devotion to punning gives rise both to unprompted double meanings such as the 'son of York' who shines away wintry discontent (*Richard iii* 1.1.2) and to his characteristically dramatic punning in which one character wrests a different sense from a word just used by another, e.g. the Cobbler's jokes in *Julius Caesar* 1.1. *CB*

Purcell, Henry (1658–95), English composer. Purcell is often wrongly credited with some splendid, early 18th-century music for the Restoration operatic version of *The Tempest* (published by the Purcell Society but now thought to be mostly by John Weldon), although he did write one song for Dorinda, 'Dear pretty youth'

(1695). He composed incidental music for Thomas Shadwell's adaptation of *Timon of Athens* (1694) and his opera *Dido and Aeneas* was cleverly incorporated into Charles *Gildon's adaptation of *Measure for Measure* (1700). His most substantial Shakespeare contribution was for the Restoration adaptation of *A Midsummer Night's Dream* entitled *The *Fairy Queen* (1692, rev. 1693). Purcell's contribution is a set of self-contained *masques within each of the acts of the play. The masques, which include not a word of Shakespeare, are additional entertainments bringing in new and somewhat exotic characters, such as a Drunken Poet, Night, Mystery, Secrecy, and a Chinese man and woman. *IBC*

Puritan, The, a satirical play published in 1607, more similar in style to Jonsonian than Shakespearian comedy. Attributed to Shakespeare in a bookseller's catalogue of 1656, this member of the *apocrypha was most probably written by *Middleton. *SM*

Puritanism. See ANTI-THEATRICAL POLEMIC; RELIGION.

Pushkin, Alexander Sergeyevich (1799–1837), national poet of *Russia. In 1605 an anonymous writer compared *Hamlet* to events at the court of the Russian Tsar Boris Godunov. In 1825 Pushkin based his tragedy *Boris Godunov* on the popular Shakespearian model, preferring it to French classical exemplars. Pushkin deliberately turned to Shakespeare from *Byron, reading the works in *Letourneur's 1821 French translation, and studying, at the same time, A. W. *Schlegel on dramatic art. In an 1830 draft preface to *Godunov* he confessed, 'I imitated Shakespeare's free and broad portrayal of characters, and his casual and simple delineation of types.' Elsewhere, Pushkin repeatedly praises Shakespeare's blank verse, boldness of invention, lifelike speeches, and many-sided characters—of whom Hamlet and Falstaff are representative. *TM*

Puttenham, George (1529–90) and **Richard** (?1520–?1601), nephews of Sir Thomas *Elyot, both contenders for the authorship of *The Art of English Poesy*, a highly influential work of Elizabethan literary criticism, published anonymously in 1589 but later attributed to one 'Master Puttenham'. George had published a collection of poetry a few years earlier, making him the more likely author. *The Art of English Poesy* probably contributed to Shakespeare's knowledge of rhetorical figures and to the debate on art and nature in *The Winter's Tale*. *JKS*

Rushton, W. L., *Shakespeare and 'The Arte of English Poesie'* (1909)

'Pyramus'. See BOTTOM, NICK.

'Pyramus and Thisbe', the play-within-the-play rehearsed and performed by the artisans in *A Midsummer Night's Dream*, with Bottom and Flute in the title roles. *AB*

Pyrrhic foot, a metrical unit consisting of two unstressed syllables; in English, a device of metrical variation only. 'And in | his mantle muffling up his face' (*Julius Caesar* 3.2.187). *CB/GTW*

Q, the bibliographic abbreviation for *quarto: hence 'Q1 *Hamlet*' (or *Hamlet* Q1') means 'the first quarto edition of *Hamlet*', 'Q2 *Hamlet*' means 'the second quarto edition of *Hamlet*', and so on. *MD*

'Q'. See Quiller-Couch, Sir Arthur.

quartos. A book in which the printed sheet is folded in half twice, making four leaves or eight pages, is known as a quarto. Renaissance play quartos were about the size and shape of modern comic books and sold for sixpence. About half of Shakespeare's plays were printed during his lifetime, usually in quarto format (see printing and publishing).

The acting companies for which Shakespeare wrote held the legal copy rights to his manuscripts. Theatre historians have traditionally maintained that the players were reluctant to allow their plays to be printed, either because they feared losing exclusive acting rights to another company or because they believed that the sale of printed texts might reduce the demand for performance. Thomas *Heywood referred to certain play-texts as being 'still retained in the hands of some actors, who think it against their peculiar profit to have them come in print'. And yet, when unauthorized versions of Shakespeare's plays occasionally reached print, the acting companies—whether motivated by commercial interests or pride—moved quickly to supersede these texts with authorized versions: Q1 *Romeo and Juliet* (1597) was soon followed by Q2 (1599), advertised as 'newly corrected, augmented, and amended'; similarly, Q1 *Hamlet* (1603) was followed hard upon by Q2 (1604/5), which claimed to be 'newly imprinted and enlarged to almost as much again as it was, according to the true and perfect copy'. The earliest extant quarto of *Love's Labour's Lost* (1598), advertised as 'newly corrected and augmented', may also have been intended to replace an earlier and incomplete edition.

The first of Shakespeare's plays to appear in print—*Titus Andronicus* (1594), *The First Part of the Contention* (*2 Henry VI*) (1594), and *The True Tragedy of Richard Duke of York* (*3 Henry VI*) (1595)—were part of a wave of 27 play quartos printed between December of 1593 and May of 1595. Given that the theatres had been closed in the *plague years 1592–3, A. W. Pollard argued that the unemployed players were motivated by financial hardship to sell their manuscripts during this period. But since most of these quartos were, in fact, published *after* the theatres reopened, Peter W. M. Blayney has suggested that acting companies may have been prompted to flood the market with printed plays as a means of advertising the reopening and generating renewed interest in the stage after a two-year lull. Observing that a large number of plays owned by the Chamberlain's Men were printed in the years 1599–1600, Gary Taylor has proposed that the company may have been trying to raise capital around the time of their move into the *Globe theatre.

Nine early quartos were printed from Shakespeare's own *foul paper manuscripts: *Titus Andronicus* (1594), *Richard II* (1597), *Love's Labour's Lost* (1598), Q2 *Romeo and Juliet* (1599), *Much Ado About Nothing* (1600), *2 Henry IV* (1600), *A Midsummer Night's Dream* (1600), Q2 *Hamlet* (1604), and *The History of King Lear* (1608). Another four quartos seem to have been printed from fair copy transcripts of the foul papers: *1 Henry IV* (1598), *The Merchant of Venice* (1600), *Troilus and Cressida* (1609), and *Othello* (1622). Eight quartos may represent reported texts: *The First Part of the Contention* (*2 Henry VI*) (1594), *Richard Duke of York* (*3 Henry VI*) (1595; technically an octavo rather than a quarto), Q1 *Romeo and Juliet* (1597), *Richard III* (1597), *Henry V* (1600), *The Merry Wives of Windsor* (1602), Q1 *Hamlet* (1603), and *Pericles* (1609). (For a list of the printers and publishers of each of these quarto editions, see printing and publishing.)

During Shakespeare's lifetime, there was a thriving industry devoted to reprinting his plays, especially the histories: *Richard II*, *Richard III*, and *1 Henry IV* were each reprinted five times in quarto between the years 1597 and 1615. Remarkably, there was not a single Shakespearian play published in the three years following the dramatist's death in 1616. In 1619, Thomas Pavier, who owned the rights to several history plays, reprinted ten of Shakespeare's works, including *The First Part of the Contention* (*2 Henry VI*) and *The True Tragedy of Richard Duke of York* (*3 Henry VI*), which were joined together with a common title, *The Whole Contention*, along with Q3 *Pericles*, Q2 *The Merry Wives of Windsor*, Q2 *The Merchant of Venice*, Q2 *A Midsummer Night's Dream*, Q2 *King Lear*, and Q3 *Henry V*. The supposition that these individual quartos were intended to be bound together to form a collection of Shakespeare's plays is encouraged by the signatures, which are continuous from *The Whole Contention* through to *Pericles*. The King's Men apparently heard about Pavier's planned collection and invoked the protection of authority. On 3 May 1619, the court of the Stationers' Company had before it a letter from the Lord Chamberlain, whereupon it was ordered that in the future 'no plays that his majesty's players do play' should be printed without the consent of the King's Men. It seems that presswork was already completed on a number of Pavier's texts, which are correctly dated 1619; but the question was what to do with the plays yet to be printed. W. W. Greg suggested that since 'it was no longer safe to put the current date on the titles . . . it was decided that the dates on the titles should

be those of the editions that were being reprinted, so that if necessary the reprints could be passed off as copies of the same, or at any rate as twin editions of the same date'. Thus, Pavier's quartos of *King Lear* and *Henry V* were dated '1608', and *The Merchant of Venice* and *A Midsummer Night's Dream* were dated '1600'.

The substantial number of quartos that appeared in 1622—Q1 *Othello*, Q6 *Richard III*, Q6 *1 Henry IV*, Q4 *Romeo and Juliet*, and Q4 *Hamlet*—may indicate that publishers were attempting to capitalize on the renewed interest in Shakespeare generated by the advance publicity for the First *Folio. Another spate of quarto reprints appeared in and around 1632, the year in which the Second Folio was published, suggesting again that quartos were being offered as less expensive alternatives for readers who could not afford to purchase folio volumes.

The Shakespearian quartos published in the latter half of the 17th century often present the version of the play that was then current on the Restoration stage. In the 'players' quartos' of *Hamlet* (1676, 1683, 1695), for instance, the diction is modernized and the scenes and passages that were omitted from the production (which starred Thomas *Betterton) are marked with marginal inverted commas. The 1674 and 1695 quartos of *Macbeth* reproduce *Davenant's adaptation of Shakespeare's play, 'with all the alterations, amendments, and additions'. *ER*

Blayney, Peter W. M., 'The Publication of Playbooks', in John D. Cox and David Scott Kastan (eds.), *A New History of Early English Drama* (1997)

Wells, Stanley, and Taylor, Gary, *William Shakespeare: A Textual Companion* (1987)

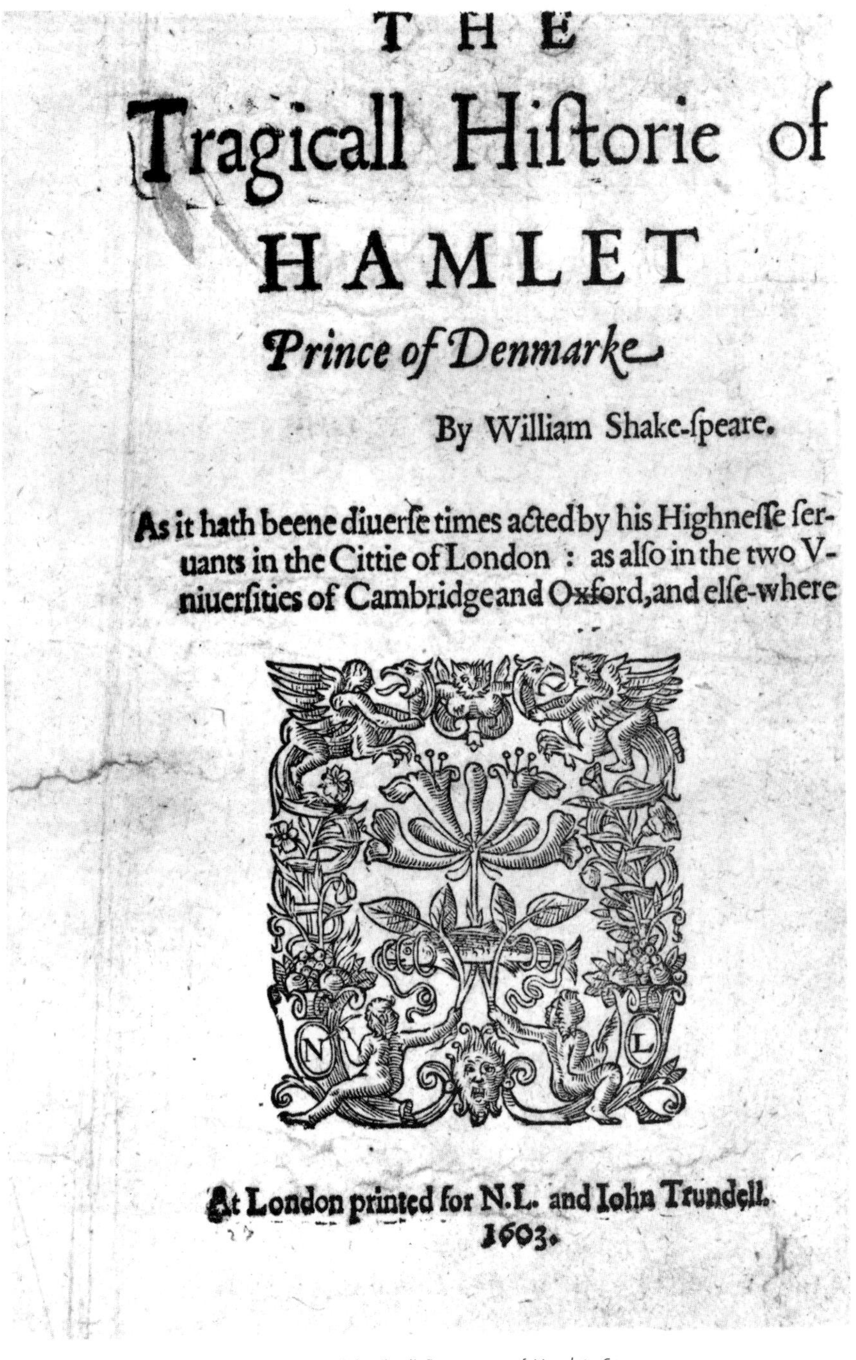
THE
Tragicall Hiſtorie of
HAMLET
Prince of Denmarke
By William Shake-ſpeare.
As it hath beene diuerſe times acted by his Highneſſe ſeruants in the Cittie of London : as alſo in the two Vniuerſities of Cambridge and Oxford, and elſe-where
At London printed for N.L. and Iohn Trundell.
1603.

The title page of the 'bad', first quarto of *Hamlet*, 1603.

Quayle, Sir Antony (1913–89), British actor and director. Having played at the *Old Vic before distinguished war service, he impressed as Enobarbus in a London *Antony and Cleopatra*. At Stratford-upon-Avon in 1948 he played Claudius, Iago, and Petruchio and directed two plays, impressing the governors, who appointed him director, 1949–56. An astute administrator, he enlisted actors of the calibre of Peggy *Ashcroft and John *Gielgud. His major achievement was the 1951 cycle of history plays; he co-directed and played Falstaff. His other comic parts included Bottom and Pandarus. He was impressive as Coriolanus and as Aaron in *Titus Andronicus*. Playing Othello on an Australian tour he was outshone by Leo McKern as Iago (who was soon replaced). He later acted *Marlowe's *Tamburlaine the Great* in North America, toured Britain as King Lear for the Prospect Theatre Company (1978), and in 1981 set up his own, unsubsidized touring company, Orbit, for which his roles included Prospero. *MJ*

Queen Anne's Men. See companies, playing; Stratford-upon-Avon, Elizabethan, and the theatre.

Queen Margaret; or, Shakespeare Goes to the Falklands, an anonymous satirical parody published in *The Economist* (Christmas 1982), exemplifies the survival of Shakespearian *burlesque. In this skit 213 extracts from Shakespeare's plays are adapted, with embarrassing appropriateness, into a three-act drama for Margaret Thatcher and the other political protagonists (British, American, and Argentine) of the Falklands military campaign. *TM*

queens. (1) Wife of Cymbeline and mother of Cloten (by her first husband), she hatches various evil plots which are uncovered in her deathbed confession, reported by Cornelius, *Cymbeline* 5.6.25–61. (2) Wife of Richard II, she last sees him on his way to the Tower, *Richard II* 5.1. Historically, Richard's wife at this

THE

Tragicall Hiſtorie of

HAMLET,

Prince of Denmarke.

By William Shakeſpeare.

Newly imprinted and enlarged to almoſt as much againe as it was, according to the true and perfect Coppie.

AT LONDON,
Printed by I. R. for N. L. and are to be ſold at his ſhoppe vnder Saint Dunſtons Church in Fleetſtreet. 1604.

The title page of the 'good', second quarto of *Hamlet*, 1604.

time (Isabella, daughter of Charles VI of France) was only 11 or 12 years old. (3) Three queens successfully plead with Theseus to avenge their husbands by raising a force against Creon, *The Two Noble Kinsmen* 1.1. *AB*

Queen's Men. See COMPANIES, PLAYING; STRATFORD-UPON-AVON, ELIZABETHAN, AND THE THEATRE.

Quickly, Mistress. In *1 Henry IV* she appears as the hostess of a tavern in Eastcheap and has an argument with Sir John (3.3). In *2 Henry IV*, now a widow, she tries to have him arrested for debt, 2.1, and claims that he has promised to marry her. She is one of the protagonists in the 'tavern brawl' scene (2.4) and is taken to prison with Doll Tearsheet in 5.4. In *Henry V*, now married to Pistol, she describes the death of Falstaff in a celebrated prose speech which is at once comic and moving, 2.3.9–25, and her own death is announced, 5.1.77. In *The Merry Wives of Windsor* she is *Caius' housekeeper. Falstaff does not know her when he meets her (is she the same character as in the other plays?—compare *2 Henry IV* 2.4.386–8). She appears disguised as the fairy queen at the end of the play. She is frequently mistaken or unwittingly tactless in her choice of words, sometimes producing double entendres (conceding of Falstaff's conversation, for example, 'A did in some sort, indeed, handle women', *Henry V* 2.3.34). Shakespearian critics, consequently, often prefer the term 'Quicklyism' for this comic device to the commoner but here anachronistic 'malapropism' (a term derived from Sheridan's Mrs Malaprop in *The Rivals*, 1775).

Mistress Quickly's lines were severely bowdlerized in the 19th century. The tavern brawl scene was often omitted because, according to Constance Benson, who played the role in the 1890s, 'no principal actress will condescend to speak but two speeches'. Twentieth-century directors have also cut her lines: the arrest of Quickly and Tearsheet has often been dispensed with, for example, because it has appeared digressive, though it has also been played as a brutal prefiguration of a police-state to come under Henry V (as in Michael Attenborough's RSC production, 2000). Memorable Mistress Quicklys have included June Watson in Michael *Bogdanov's 1986 production (who repeatedly hit the men on stage in the groin with her shopping bag), Judi *Dench in Kenneth Branagh's film of *Henry V* (1989), and Margaret Rutherford in Orson *Welles's *Chimes at Midnight* (1966), an ageing female counterpart to Falstaff. *AB*

Quiller-Couch, Sir Arthur (1863–1944), English writer, editor, and critic, in some respects the archetypal 'liberal man of letters'. Known as 'Q', he edited several influential *Oxford Books*: of *English Verse*; *Ballads*; *Victorian Verse*; and *English Prose*. *Shakespeare's Workmanship*, based on his Cambridge lectures, dates from 1918, but his widest readership was gathered by the earlier volumes of the Cambridge *New Shakespeare, jointly edited with John Dover *Wilson, for which 'Q' wrote the general introduction as part of the first volume, *The Tempest* (1921). *TM*

Quin, James (1693–1766), actor and manager. He was born in London and gave his earliest performances in Dublin. He came to prominence in the 1716–17 season at Drury Lane where his roles included Gloucester and Guildenstern. His subsequent popularity and reputation rests largely on his personation of Falstaff, whose lifestyle his was thought to resemble, and the role is recorded in pictures by *Hayman and McArdell, and in Bow, Derby, and Staffordshire figurines. He is also the subject of portraits by *Hogarth, Gainsborough, and Hudson.

In fact Quin had a large Shakespearian repertoire: from 1718 he was at Lincoln's Inn Fields where he played Othello, Cymbeline, Hector and Thersites, Lear, Buckingham, and the Duke in *Measure for Measure*, as well as Falstaff in *The Merry Wives of Windsor* and *1 Henry IV*. He played Apemantus in the opening season (1732) of the new *Covent Garden theatre, and Othello, Falstaff, Brutus, and the Ghost in *Hamlet* at Drury Lane the following year, roles to which he added Jaques in 1740. For most of the 1740s and early 1750s he appeared regularly at Covent Garden and with his contrasting, somewhat old-fashioned declamatory style was seen as the rival of the more naturalistic *Garrick at Drury Lane. The two were friends and occasionally performed together (Quin as Falstaff and Garrick as Hotspur in 1746), and Garrick wrote the epitaph for Quin's tomb in Bath abbey. *CMSA*

Quince, Peter. He is a carpenter in *A Midsummer Night's Dream* who allots the parts to the actors of 'Pyramus and Thisbe' and himself speaks the prologue, 5.1.126–50. *AB*

Quiney, Richard (before 1577–1602). Father of Judith *Shakespeare's husband, and writer of the only surviving letter addressed to Shakespeare. Alderman of Stratford-upon-Avon in 1588 and bailiff in 1592, he regularly visited London on town affairs. In 1598 he was there to petition for a more favourable charter and for tax relief because of declining trade and hardship caused by fires in 1594 and 1595. On 25 October 1598 while staying at an inn near St Paul's he wrote a letter endorsed 'To my loving good friend and countryman Mr William Shakespeare deliver these.' Whoever was to bear the letter appears to have been expected to know where to find him—presumably in London. It reads:

> Loving countryman,
> I am bold of you as of a friend, craving your help with £30 upon Mr Bushell's and my security or Mr Mytton's with me. Mr Roswell [probably Thomas *Russell] is not come to London as yet and I have especial cause. You shall friend me much in helping me out of all the debts I owe in London, I thank God, and much quiet my mind which would not be indebted. I am now towards the court in hope of answer for the dispatch of my business. You shall neither lose credit nor money by me, the Lord willing, and now but persuade yourself so as I hope and you shall not need to fear but with all hearty thankfulness I will hold my time and content your friend and if we bargain farther you shall be the paymaster yourself. My time bids me hasten to an end and so I commit this [to] your care and hope of your help. I fear I shall not be back this night from the court. Haste. The Lord be with you and with us all, Amen. From the Bell in Carter Lane, the 25 October 1598.
>
> Yours in all kindness,
> Ric[hard]. Quiney

As the letter was found among Quiney's papers it seems not to have been delivered, and we do not know whether Shakespeare lent the money. It was a large sum, and Quiney may have been asking for it on Abraham *Sturley's behalf rather than personally, quite possibly as a business transaction on which Shakespeare would receive interest. A letter to Quiney from Sturley written a few days later indicates that Quiney was optimistic of success; but Sturley was sceptical. *SW*

Quiney, Thomas (1589–?1662–3), Shakespeare's son-in-law, husband of Judith *Shakespeare. He was baptized at Stratford on 26 February 1589, the third son of Richard *Quiney. By 1608 he was managing his widowed mother's business as a tavern-keeper and wine merchant, and in 1611 rented the tavern next to his mother's house in High Street. He married Judith Shakespeare on 10 February 1616 and less than six weeks later, on 26 March, was prosecuted for 'incontinence' with Margaret Wheeler, who, with her child, had been buried on 15 March. In July, Thomas and Judith moved to the Cage, a building which still stands on the corner of High Street and Bridge Street. They had three sons (see SHAKESPEARE, JUDITH). His name appears from time to time in Stratford records until at least 1650, and in 1655 his brother Richard left him an annuity. His death is not recorded, but there is a gap in the register in 1662–3. *SW*

Quintus is one of Titus' sons in *Titus Andronicus*. With his brother Martius he is executed for the murder of Bassianus, 3.1, who has really been killed by Demetrius and Chiron. *AB*

radio, British. From the earliest days of British broadcasting Shakespeare's plays have figured as part of the radio drama repertory, as individual full-scale productions, in special seasons, and as selected extracts in more general programmes. Plays about Shakespeare and features concerned with such matters as his contemporary world, the authorship question, and the Shakespeare industry have also been much in evidence. Despite Orson *Welles's activities with the Mercury Theatre of the Air in America in the late 1930s and the enterprising broadcast of *Brecht's adaptations of *Hamlet* and *Macbeth* by German radio in 1927, the richest tradition of radio Shakespeare has been that of the BBC.

Probably because written for an essentially bare stage and learned as cue parts, Shakespeare's plays have proved adaptable to radio, with its reliance on expressive language and suggestive sound effects. Scenes are set and characters repeatedly named in Shakespeare's dialogue while exits, entrances, and significant gestures and expressions are often registered verbally—'Here comes the Duke ...'; 'But look! amazement on thy mother sits ...' Radio production lacks the visual effects, costume, and audience reaction of theatre, but Shakespeare's text offers a rich stimulus to the auditory imagination. Radio's emphasis on words, moreover, chimed with the 20th-century shift away from elaborately realistic staging, act drops, and *intervals promoted by William *Poel and Harley *Granville-Barker.

The first British radio broadcasts of Shakespeare quickly followed the October 1922 formation of the British Broadcasting Company. Speeches from *Much Ado About Nothing* and *All Is True* (*Henry VIII*) and the quarrel scene from *Julius Caesar* were broadcast on 16 February 1923; on 15 May, extracts from *Macbeth*; on the 21st, the Hubert and Arthur scene from *King John* (with Ellen *Terry); on the 23rd, the trial scene from *A Merchant of Venice*, then, on 28 May, came the first full-scale (although much-cut) BBC *adaptation, with Howard Rose's production of *Twelfth Night*. *King Lear* (1925) and *The Tempest* (1926) followed. The year 1928 saw Shakespeare thoroughly established in the radio drama repertory with adaptations of *Henry V*, *Macbeth*, *A Midsummer Night's Dream* (cut to an hour and broadcast 'for schools'), *Hamlet*, and *King Lear*. The *BBC Annual* (1935) registers eighteen broadcasts of Shakespeare plays between 1930 and 1934. Val Gielgud, head of drama at the BBC from 1929, discussing in his memoirs the demand for high-quality radio plays, identified Shakespeare as 'the indispensable ballast of respectable output'.

The Dramatic Control Panel, introduced in 1927–8, and extended in 1932, enabled the intercutting of dialogue, sound effects, and music, produced in various studios. A rush of new productions from the late 1960s responded to the introduction of stereophonic effects. Although the earliest productions were broadcast live, the development of recording discs, magnetic tape, and, eventually, digital tape enabled increasingly sophisticated editing of productions. It also allowed storage for the archive and repeat broadcasting.

Radio made Shakespeare in performance available for the first time to many in its massive audience (already a million listeners in 1924). This was particularly the case up to 1939 when there was a single national station. With the 1946 addition to the Light and Home Services of the Third Programme, for more specialist and avant-garde material, this channel increasingly became the home of Shakespeare production, gaining for it greater freedom to experiment, but losing the wider audience. Between 1950 and 1978 there were 81 Shakespeare productions on the Third to 34 on the Home Service and just one on the Light Programme.

Already by 1930, Shakespeare broadcasts, most frequently scheduled for Sunday evenings, were identified with holidays. Regular 'birthday productions' followed that of *Henry V* on 23 April 1928, and broadcast Shakespeare has been in evidence in times of national celebration and emergency, with large-scale series presented as national events. A 1944 'Theatre in Wartime' adaptation of *Twelfth Night*, with Wendy Hiller as Viola, broadcast first on the Home Service (1 November 1944) and then to the Forces in Africa (8 November 1944) and the Pacific (10 November 1944), was preceded by an announcement that it had previously played 'to munitions workers all around the country'. Incidents from the history plays featured in the 26-episode *Vivat Rex* that ran in Elizabeth II's jubilee year, 1977, and the BBC paid tribute to its own history by celebrating its sixtieth anniversary (2 October 1982) with a new production of its first broadcast Shakespeare, *Twelfth Night*. To celebrate the Millennium a series of seventeen new productions, to be immediately available on cassette and compact disc, was begun in 1999.

There is overlap between the plays which appear most frequently in the theatrical repertoire and on the radio. The first set of plays in the 1999 'Shakespeare for the Millennium' series were *Hamlet*, *A Midsummer Night's Dream*, *Julius Caesar*, and *Romeo and Juliet*. Nevertheless, radio has also proved an imaginative host to productions of plays that, until recently, were scarcely seen in the theatre, including, in the 1980s, productions of *Pericles*, *King John*, and *Cymbeline*. There have also been notable productions of *Henry VI* (1946), *Titus Andronicus* (1952), and *Timon of Athens* (1952; 1974). As well as Nahum *Tate's version of *King Lear* (7 November 1960), various *apocryphal works, such as *The Book of Sir Thomas More* (28 August 1951; 25 December 1983), have figured, including, in a

'Shakespeare Apocrypha' series in 1956, *Edward III, A *Yorkshire Tragedy, and, again, *Sir Thomas More.

Broadcast Shakespeare has sometimes involved direct transfer of successful stage productions but, more often, new adaptations have been commissions. Actors have often been drawn from the BBC Drama Repertory Company, sometimes with the addition of stars from the theatre. Lewis Casson and Sybil *Thorndike were among the earliest. John *Gielgud, Peggy *Ashcroft, Ralph *Richardson, and Alec *Guinness figured frequently as, more recently, have Harriet Walter, Alec McCowen, Michael Maloney, and Juliet Stevenson. The shorter rehearsal periods for radio work (usually between four and six days) and the need to commit to a single recording, instead of a season, have enabled radio producers to attract particular acting combinations that might have proved difficult to achieve in the theatre or to make more widely available celebrated interpretations of a role: radio Lears, for example, have included Donald *Wolfit (26 April 1949), John Gielgud (14 November 1951), Michael *Redgrave (29 December 1953) and Alec Guinness (15 December 1974). Cathleen Nesbitt, who doubled Viola and Sebastian in the 1923 *Twelfth Night*, was responsible for many of the early adaptations, and producers particularly associated with radio Shakespeare have included Val Gielgud, John Tydeman, and Raymond Raikes.

There have been numerous full-text radio productions (including a notable *Cymbeline* in 1986) since an *Othello* seriously overran its allotted spot in a live broadcast of 1932. But most radio versions have involved cutting, those for the Third Programme (later, Radio Three) tending to be longer than those for the Home Service (Radio Four). The norm is two to two and a half hours, with a ten-minute break midway. Adaptations have involved more or less extensive sound and music cues, usually with some increase in naming—'Signior Fabian', 'Sir Toby'—as a new character arrives. In the period up to the Second World War, most productions included an announcement of time and place and many made more extensive use of a narrator to describe the scene, the opening situation, and aspects of the action.

As radio audiences became accustomed to the medium and drama producers came to trust their audiences and the Shakespeare text, debate on the need for narration subsided. Increasingly, producers have let the dialogue and sound signals common to radio drama do this work. Change of location is indicated by swelling or receding volume, by footsteps, the opening or closing of a door, or by brief musical interludes, perhaps a few chords strummed on a lute or guitar. A sudden multiplicity of voices would suggest a court or crowd scene; birdsong, a garden; wind and rain, a heath; waves and seagulls, a seashore. Gesture is signalled by the sound of crackling parchment, the clink of money changing hands, the swish of a sword being drawn. A personal microphone, as used for Cordelia's asides in the 1951 *King Lear*, could create a startling intimacy with the audience. Occasional productions have introduced a modern soundtrack—espresso machines, vespas, and modern dance music enliven the Verona of the Millennium *Romeo and Juliet* (3 October 1999).

Readings of the narrative poems and selections from the Sonnets have been frequent, in complete programmes (22 April 1956; 21 May 1981) or as part of themed or more general poetry features. The full sonnet sequence was delivered in twelve short programmes (beginning 18 January 1959) and Italian, French, and German versions were read in 'Shakespeare Translated' (22 November 1968). Short scenes, speeches, and *songs have figured recurrently in 'Favourite Characters' programmes and such features as 'Shakespeare and his Musicians' (16 December 1948) or 'Shakespeare and the Death Penalty' (25 April 1956) which drew on material from *Measure for Measure*. In 1977, '*King Lear* through the Ages' dramatized the performance history of the play from *Tate and *Betterton to *Brook and *Scofield. Fictional accounts of Shakespeare's life and his relationship with his wife and his fellow actors and dramatists have fuelled plays and features throughout broadcasting history, contributing to the identification of Shakespeare as the National Poet on the National Network. *JC*

The BBC Annual Report, subsequently, *The BBC Yearbook*
The BBC Sound and Written Archives
Briggs, Asa, *The History of Broadcasting in the United Kingdom* (5 vols., 1995)
Chothia, Jean, *English Drama 1890–1940* (1996)
Drakakis, John, (ed.), *Radio Drama* (1981)
Gielgud, Val, *British Radio Drama, 1922–56* (1957)

Ragusine (Ragozine) is a pirate whose head is substituted for Claudio's to present to Angelo (*Measure for Measure* 4.3.66–78). *AB*

Ralegh, Sir Walter (*c*.1554–1618), courtier, poet, and writer of prose. Born into a prominent family in Devon, Ralegh fought in France before attending Oxford and the Inns of Court. In 1580 he went to Ireland to serve under Lord Grey. Here he met Edmund *Spenser, who represented him as the squire Timias in *The Faerie Queene* (1590), and who addressed a famous letter to him describing his plan for the poem. On returning from Ireland he became a favourite of Elizabeth's at court, and it is to this period that most of his poems are assigned. These include a sardonic reply to Christopher *Marlowe's poem 'The Passionate Shepherd to his Love', published as Shakespeare's in *The *Passionate Pilgrim* (1599). He is sometimes identified as the *'rival poet' in Shakespeare's Sonnets. In 1592 he was imprisoned for marrying one of Elizabeth's maids of honour without permission. After his release he led an expedition to Guiana, a land which he described in seductive terms in one of his finest prose works, *The Discovery of . . . Guiana* (1596). With other accounts of New World voyages this had a pervasive influence on Shakespeare's *The Tempest*. Raleigh returned to royal favour in 1597, but was tried for treason by James I in 1603, and spent the rest of his life in prison, apart from one more disastrous expedition to Guiana. While in prison he wrote his most celebrated work, a monumental—and unfinished—*History of the World* (1614). *RM*

May, Steven W., *Sir Walter Raleigh* (1989)

Raleigh, Sir Walter (1861–1922), English academic, author of *Shakespeare* (1907) in the series 'English Men of Letters'. Once regarded as one of the most civilized short books on the subject, it is now felt to be too susceptible to biographical myth and too negligent of documentary fact. *TM*

Hawkes, Terence, 'Switter-Swatter: Making a Man of English Letters', in *That Shakespeherian Rag* (1986)

Rambures, Lord. He banters with the other French commanders before Agincourt, *Henry V* 3.7 and 4.2, but lies among the slain, 4.8.94. *AB*

Ran See Kurosawa, Akira.

'Rape' is impersonated by Chiron, *Titus Andronicus* 5.2. *AB*

Rape of Lucrece, The *(see opposite page)*

Rare Triumphs of Love and Fortune, an anonymous play, first performed *c*.1582 and published in 1589. Similarities between this work and Shakespeare's late plays, in particular *Cymbeline* and *The Tempest*, have suggested that the *Rare Triumphs* may have been revived on the Jacobean stage. Its enduring appeal is suggested by its fifteen reprints between 1610 and 1670. Like the *Rare Triumphs*, *Cymbeline* features the separation of lovers through banishment and their reconciliation by Jupiter. Bomelio, an exiled courtier turned magician who lives in a cave and whose magic books are stolen, may be a prototype of Prospero. *JKS*

Ratcliffe, Sir Richard. He is one of Richard's henchmen in *Richard III*. *AB*

Ratsey, Gamaliel (d. 1605), highwayman, hanged in 1605. In the pamphlet *Ratseis Ghoaste* (one of several pamphlets and ballads in which he appears), Ratsey advises the leader of an itinerant company of players to perform in

(cont. on page 369)

The Rape of Lucrece

Presumably the 'graver labour' promised in the dedication to *Venus and Adonis* (1593), Shakespeare's narrative of rape and suicide was entered in the *Stationers' Register in May 1594 (as *The Ravishment of Lucrece*) and published in quarto in the same year. In rare vocabulary it is linked with *Titus Andronicus*, *1 Henry VI*, and *Richard III*: it was probably the next work Shakespeare composed after *Venus and Adonis*, in 1593–4.

Text: The quarto is well printed, presumably from Shakespeare's own manuscript, by Richard Field, the Stratford-born printer also responsible for the first edition of *Venus and Adonis*: six further editions followed during Shakespeare's lifetime, and another three had appeared by 1655. The title page of the first edition calls the poem *Lucrece*, but the head title and running titles call it *The Rape of Lucrece.*

Sources: Like *Venus and Adonis*, this poem derives from the work of Shakespeare's favourite classical author *Ovid, but for this tragic narrative Shakespeare turned from the mythological *Metamorphoses* to Ovid's historical *Fasti* ('chronicles'), which he probably consulted in the original Latin. He also shows a familiarity with the earliest account of the Lucrece story, written by *Livy around 25 BC (five centuries after Lucrece's death), which had been translated in William *Painter's *Palace of Pleasure* (1566). Two earlier English versions of this semi-legendary material lie behind his own, that of *Chaucer (in *The Legend of Good Women*) and perhaps that of John *Gower (in *Confessio amantis*). Shakespeare's literary treatment of the story shows the influence of the 'complaint' tradition exemplified by the **Mirror for Magistrates* (1559), in which the ghosts of historical figures bemoan their fates in verse. This tradition had recently been developed by Samuel *Daniel in *The Complaint of Rosamond* (1592), which uses the same *rhyme-royal stanza, and Shakespeare would return to this genre with his own *A Lover's Complaint* (*c*.1603–4).

Synopsis: A dedication, signed 'William Shakespeare', commends the poem to the attention of 'the Right Honourable Henry Wriothesley, Earl of *Southampton and Baron of Titchfield' in unusually affectionate terms: 'The love I dedicate to your lordship is without end . . . [w]hat I have done is yours; what I have to do is yours, being part in all I have, devoted yours.' The Argument which follows, summarizing the content of the poem in Latinate prose, supplies many details of the story which the poem itself either omits or mentions only fleetingly, particularly the events leading up to the rape and its political consequences. (Assuming it to be authorial, it is the longest specimen extant of Shakespeare's non-dramatic *prose.) It recounts how during the reign of King Tarquinius Superbus, who had obtained the throne unelected through the murder of his father-in-law, a group of Roman noblemen were engaged in the siege of Ardea, among them the King's son Sextus Tarquinius (the poem's Tarquin) and Collatinus (the poem's Collatine). They fell to discussing the virtues of their wives, which they resolved to test by riding quickly back to Rome together to see how they were occupied in their husbands' absence: all were amusing themselves except Collatinus' wife Lucretia (Lucrece), who was virtuously spinning among her maids. Sextus Tarquinius, desiring her, subsequently returned privately to her house at Collatium ('Collatia' in the sources, which Shakespeare seems erroneously to have thought a suburb of Rome), where he was welcomed and lodged: during the night he crept to Lucretia's chamber, raped her, and fled. The following morning Lucretia summoned her father and husband, told them what had happened, and stabbed herself to death after vowing them to revenge: with the assistance of Junius Brutus, they used Lucretia's death to incense the Roman people against the Tarquins, who were banished, and the monarchy was replaced by a consular republic.

The first section of the poem focuses primarily on Tarquin's consciousness. At its opening he is already speeding alone towards Collatium (ll. 1–7), the origins of his lust recounted briefly in flashback (ll. 8–49): Lucrece welcomes him, unsuspecting, and later he retires to bed (ll. 50–126). Alone, he reflects on his intended crime before rising and lighting a torch (ll. 127–89): the next thirteen stanzas (ll. 190–280) are his soliloquy, dilating on the danger and dishonour of his intentions but finally resolving to pursue them nonetheless. Stealing through the house, he forces each lock which intervenes on the way to Lucrece's chamber, ignoring the reproaches constituted by these, by a draught that nearly extinguishes his torch, and by the evidence of Lucrece's virtuous sewing (ll. 281–336): at last he forces his way into her room (ll. 337–71). There follows a set-piece description of Lucrece asleep as Tarquin sees her (ll. 372–420), before she is awakened by his hand at her breast (ll. 421–69). Challenged, he tells her, drawing his sword, that if she refuses him he will kill her and a slave, making it appear he caught them in bed together, whereas if not she can keep his violation a secret (ll. 470–539). She pleads in vain (ll. 540–666), and Tarquin, extinguishing the light and silencing her with her nightdress, forces her (ll. 667–86). He immediately experiences a revulsion of feeling, and creeps away in shame, longing for the morning which Lucrece wishes would never come (ll. 689–749).

From here the poem concentrates on Lucrece's perspective. Embarking on her lengthy, rhetorical complaint, she apostrophizes night, time, and opportunity (ll. 750–966), and curses Tarquin (ll. 967–1022), before resolving on suicide, as much for Collatine's sake as for her own: she will tell him everything (ll. 1023–78). As morning approaches, she rebukes the sun for rising and the birds for singing, comparing herself to the ravished Philomel who was transformed into the nightingale (ll. 1079–148), and finally concludes that suicide (which, with an anchronistically Christian perspective, she regards as a sin against her soul) is preferable to a shamed life (ll. 1149–76). She decides that suicide will save her reputation, and that her husband can vindicate her through revenge on Tarquin (ll. 1177–211). She calls her maid, who weeps to see her mistress's grief: after Lucrece asks about Tarquin's departure, the maid asks the cause of her sorrow, but Lucrece will not tell, sending for ink and paper (ll. 1212–95). Lucrece writes briefly to Collatine, summoning him home (ll. 1296–365). Awaiting his return, she meditates on a painting of besieged Troy, described at length, which she apostrophizes, finally tearing its likeness of the traitorous Sinon because reminded of Tarquin (ll. 1366–568). When her husband arrives, with other lords, she describes what has happened, withholding the name of her rapist until all the men have vowed to avenge her, then stabs herself to death (ll. 1568–729).

Lucrece's bleeding corpse is described, and the lamentation of her father Lucretius, with whose grief that of Collatine competes (ll. 1730–806). Junius Brutus, however, abandoning the folly he has assumed as a disguise, rallies the men to renew their vow of vengeance (ll. 1807–48). The poem's final stanza briefly recounts that they subsequently displayed Lucrece's corpse in Rome, thereby winning the Roman people to agree to the banishment of the Tarquins (ll. 1849–56).

Artistic features: The discrepancies between the Argument and the poem itself—which shows very little interest in the public consequences of Tarquin's crime, preferring to dramatize the private experiences of rapist and victim—have led some commentators to conclude that the Argument was not written by Shakespeare, but the differences probably reflect its function, to provide the standard account of the story on which the poem offers an artistic variation. The poem proper is intensely dramatic, and would frequently be recalled by Shakespeare in his subsequent writings for the stage, primarily his Roman tragedies but in other plays too: Hamlet, like Lucrece, reflects in grief on the represented sufferings of Hecuba, and both Macbeth and *Giacomo liken themselves to Tarquin. Modern readers, however, who have generally preferred *Venus and Adonis*, often find that its drama is dissipated rather than enhanced by its forceful display of rhetoric.

Critical history: The popularity reflected by the proliferation of early editions of *The Rape of Lucrece* is confirmed by allusions and imitations: it was praised by Thomas *Freeman in 1614 ('Who loves chaste life, there's *Lucrece* for a teacher'), and imitated by Thomas *Middleton (in *The Ghost of Lucrece*, 1600), Thomas *Heywood (in his play *The Rape of Lucrece*, published in 1608), and John Quarles, whose 'Tarquin Banished; or, The Reward of Lust' was appended to the 1655 edition of Shakespeare's poem. After this, though, the poem fell from favour, ignored throughout the 18th century, and despite *Coleridge's grudging admission of its eloquence most 19th-century readers were more interested in the Dedication's hints at the nature of Shakespeare's relationship with Southampton than in the poem's literary qualities. In the 20th century, however, it was at least partly rehabilitated, although much criticism has concentrated on its anticipation of later works. Its subject matter has attracted both feminists and their opponents. Perhaps predictably, it was a favourite poem of Ted *Hughes, who found in it a key to Shakespeare's entire output as a tragedian. *MD*

Recent major editions

The Poems, ed. Hyder Rollins (New Variorum, 1938); *The Poems*, ed. F. T. Prince (Arden 2nd series, 1960); *The Narrative Poems*, ed. Maurice Evans (Penguin, 1989); *The Poems*, ed. John Roe (New Cambridge, 1992)

Some representative criticism

Allen, D. C., 'Some Observations on *The Rape of Lucrece*', *Shakespeare Survey*, 15 (1962)

Kahn, Coppélia, 'The Rape in Shakespeare's *Lucrece*', *Shakespeare Studies*, 9 (1976)

Stimpson, Catharine, 'Shakespeare and the Soil of Rape', in C. R. S. Lenz, G. Greene, and C. T. Neely (eds.), *The Woman's Part: Feminist Criticism of Shakespeare* (1983)

London, where his Hamlet will rival Burbage's, but to return to the provinces with enough money to buy 'some place of worship'. This may be a topical reference to Shakespeare's upward social mobility. The pamphlet provides one of the most detailed pictures extant of *provincial actors in Shakespeare's time. *CS*

Ravenscroft, Edward, see TITUS ANDRONICUS.

reading and the book trade. The book trade in Shakespeare's England, sometimes mistakenly assumed to be a primitive cottage craft undertaken in open-air market stalls, was a thriving industry supported by a national infrastructure for distribution and marketing. Early London bookshops were substantial buildings, often four storeys tall, identified by the pictorial signs mentioned on title-page advertisements: 'to be sold in Paul's Churchyard at the sign of the Green Dragon'. The centre of the London book trade was Paul's Cross Churchyard, in which more than 30 bookshops flourished, but bookshops could also be found throughout the city, especially along major thoroughfares and around focal points such as bridges, city gates, and public buildings.

Although the trade in printed plays was a relatively small part of the bookselling business, a contemporary observed that play *quartos were printed in substantial numbers to satisfy the reading audience of the early 17th century: 'our quarto-playbooks have come forth in such abundance, and found so many customers, that they almost exceed all number, one study being scarce able to hold them, and two years time too little to peruse them all.' Play quartos would usually be sold without bindings, although readers who had collected a number of dramatic quartos might have them bound as a single volume.

Several of Shakespeare's fellow dramatists apparently felt some discomfort in publishing plays intended for performance as if they were literary texts designed to be read. In an address 'To the Reader' that prefaces the first printed edition of *The Malcontent* (1604), John *Marston apologizes that 'scenes invented merely to be spoken should be enforcively published to be read'. Marston goes on to characterize the reading text as subordinate to the experience of seeing the play performed: 'the unhandsome shape which this trifle in reading presents may be pardoned, for the pleasure it once afforded you when it was presented with the soul of lively action'. A letter-writer in 1638 tells her correspondent that reading plays is a lacklustre expedient to be adopted only when one has no access to the London theatre: 'I could wish myself with you ... to see the *Alchemist*, which I hear this term is revived, and the new play ... but for want of these gentle recreations, I must content myself here, with the study of Shakespeare, and the history of women, all my country library'.

Printed plays were clearly regarded by some as 'light' reading. In Abraham Cowley's poem 'A Poetical Revenge' (1636), one schoolboy curses another who has offended him: 'may he | Be by his Father in his study took | At Shakespeare's plays, instead of my L. Cooke'. In an epistle 'to the comic play-readers' of *The Roaring Girl* (1611), Thomas *Middleton suggests, however, that reading plays might actually prevent one from engaging in more seditious pursuits: 'you shall find this published comedy good to keep you in an afternoon from dice, at home in your chambers'.

Humphrey *Moseley clearly had the needs of his readers in mind when he decided not to include reprints of plays that had already been published, such as *The Two Noble Kinsmen*, in his 1647 folio of *Beaumont and *Fletcher's works: 'And indeed it would have rendered the book so voluminous that ladies and gentlewomen would have found it scarce manageable, who in works of this nature must first be remembered'. It has been suggested that with his emphasis on 'ladies and gentlewomen', Moseley is envisioning a play-reading audience made up largely of women. *ER*

Blayney, Peter W. M., *The Bookshops in Paul's Cross Churchyard* (1990)

Hackel, Heidi Brayman, 'Printed Drama in Early Libraries', in John D. Cox and David Scott Kastan (eds.), *A New History of Early English Drama* (1997)

rebec, a bowed instrument of Arabic origin, with a small pear-shaped body and three strings. During Shakespeare's life it was being superseded by the violin and decreasing in importance and status. *JB*

recitations and one-person shows. In his *London Labour and the London Poor*, first published in 1851, Henry Mayhew described how one youthful reciter delivered Othello's 'Most potent, grave and reverend signiors' with such force that he felt compelled to explain, 'When I act Shakespeare I cannot restrain myself, it seems to master my very soul.' The reciter's pitch was the Commercial Road and Walworth Road and his best-ever receipts were at a public house near Brick Lane. At the other extreme the actor-manager Charles *Kemble gave his first reading before Queen Victoria at Buckingham Palace on 24 April 1844, when *Cymbeline* was selected by the Prince Consort. Thereafter Kemble gave readings of Shakespeare across the country, attracting the likes of the dissenting minister who told him that 'though I abominate the stage ... yet I am a patron of Shakespeare in my social hours'. Kemble's daughter Fanny continued the tradition, increasingly preferring readings to stage performances, especially when they were by invitation at Eton College. Other notable exponents of the Shakespearian reading were Mr and Mrs German Reed and the Revd J. C. M. Bellew, a friend of Charles *Dickens—himself hugely popular as a reader from his own novels—whose most ambitious reading was the whole of *Hamlet* with actors whose duty was to suit the action to the word as Bellew recited the play.

It was in education that the differing approaches to readings of Shakespeare were entwined: in the Working Men's Institutes; the improving 'entertainments' which clergymen such as the Revd Julian Young (son of actor Charles Mayne Young, and rector of Ilmington) provided for their parishioners; and the compulsory learning of 'three hundred lines of good poetry' (usually Shakespeare) which was required of pupils in elementary schools.

The Shakespearian one-person show—requiring no scenery, and no director—has remained a staple of classical actors between productions: exponents have included John *Gielgud, Ian *McKellen (whose own, which he toured extensively during the late 1980s, featured him as both Romeo and Juliet in the balcony scene), and Claire *Bloom. *RF*

recorder. The Renaissance instrument of Shakespeare's time came in many sizes and had a stronger sound than the later baroque type, familiar as today's school descant. See *Hamlet* 3.2.332 and *A Midsummer Night's Dream* 5.1.123. *JB*

recordings. Following demonstrations of the 'perfected phonograph' in 1888, Emile Berliner's gramophone of 1895, and the foundation in 1898 of the London Gramophone Company (subsequently HMV, then EMI), the technology to enable the recording of sound has become increasingly sophisticated. Shakespeare recordings have been in evidence from the earliest days of the wax cylinder, through the short-playing 78 revolutions per minute (rpm) shellac discs of the 1930s and the long-playing 33 1/3 rpm vinylite discs (LPs) and reel-to-reel tapes of the 1950s, to the widely available audio-cassettes, compact discs (CDs), videotapes, and digital recordings of the present. The industry of making sound recordings of Shakespeare's works has flourished most visibly in Britain.

The first recordings were concerned rather with registering the voices of actors than with the Shakespeare text as such. Although sequences of just two, then four, minutes, were possible until well into the 20th century, short monologues by such renowned Shakespearians as Edwin *Booth, Henry *Irving, Beerbohm *Tree, and Ellen *Terry were recorded between 1890 and the First World War. Between the wars, Hamlet's 'O! what a rogue and peasant slave ...' and 'How all occasions do inform ...', and Macbeth's 'Is this a dagger ...?' were recorded on 78s by such stars as Henry Ainley and John *Barrymore (HMV) and included with other famous soliloquies and educational intent on Johnston *Forbes-Robertson's two-disc 'How to Speak Shakespeare' (Columbia, 1928). More evidently collectors' items were *Gielgud's acclaimed *Hamlet* on a mammoth set of ten 78s and Orson *Welles and the Mercury Company's *Macbeth* on nine (Columbia Masterworks). It was only in the 1950s that abridged versions of whole plays could be preserved on single LPs and full-text versions on sets of two or three discs, while stereo sound, developed in the 1960s, enabled a more convincingly dramatic interaction of voices.

The first substantial LP recording venture was the *British Council's 1958 commissioning from the Cambridge *Marlowe Society of the entire canon of plays and poems unabridged (Argo). Completed for the 1964 Shakespeare quatercentenary, it was an important cultural event. Although somewhat uneven, the whole became an invaluable resource for language teachers worldwide and stimulated numerous other recording projects. Where the Marlowe used a mixture of student and professional actors, the Shakespeare Recording Company of New York, between 1960 and 1968, cast famous actors in leading roles and exploited new stereo effects in recording some 32 plays (Caedmon).

Numerous other projects in the post-Second World War period presented Shakespeare in a variety of forms. The 'Living Shakespeare' series from Odhams (FCM production) offered leading classical actors (Donald *Wolfit in *King Lear*, Michael *Redgrave in *Hamlet*, Peggy *Ashcroft in *The Merchant of Venice*), in 26 plays, each abridged to a single LP, with a narrator providing continuity. Extracts from the soundtrack of *Olivier's *Henry v* were reproduced on disc and, on cassette, such BBC work as the 1984 *King Lear*, with Alec *Guinness, which presented the Folio text with modifications for radio. Significant productions by such companies as the *Old Vic, the *National Theatre, the *RSC, and the Renaissance Theatre Company are also on record: *Zeffirelli's 1965 National Theatre *Much Ado About Nothing* (HMV), and the Folio Theatre Players' *Henry viii* with Lewis Casson and Sybil *Thorndike are only two among many. In 2000 there were eight different recordings of *Hamlet* available in British record shops.

As well as single-play recordings, extracts are widely used in showcase anthologies such as Irene Worth's *Her Infinite Variety*. Gielgud included various excerpts on his *Seven Ages of Man* collection (Columbia). Richard ii's 'For God's sake let us sit upon the ground' is spoken as prologue to the RSC's *The Hollow Crown* (Argo, 1962). As well as five distinct recordings of the complete Sonnets, individual songs and sonnets recur in various general recitals and several, orchestrated by Johnny Dankworth, are sung by Cleo Laine on *Shakespeare and All that Jazz* (Fontana).

With the advent of the personal stereo in the 1980s, recordings, increasingly available on audio-cassette, have been used rather for individual than communal listening and this has led to a marked resurgence of recordings of Shakespeare. All seventeen productions in BBC radio's 'Shakespeare for the Millennium', begun in 1999, and involving such actors as Amanda Root, Timothy West, Juliet Stevenson, and Michael Maloney, are available simultaneously with the broadcasts on CD and cassette, while 'Audiobooks'—unabridged performances for cassette and CD (Penguin and Naxos)—are already a feature of early 21st-century recording.

Recording has enabled the dissemination of contemporary performance but digital recording, with its capacity to reproduce early recordings, with whistles, scratches, and other interference minimized, also allows better acccess to the performance styles of earlier generations. Thus, 'Great Shakespeareans' (Pavilion Records) includes the voices of Edwin *Booth in 1890 and John Gielgud in 1930, speaking Othello's 'Most potent, grave and reverend signiors' speech, as well as pre-1914 contributions from Beerbohm Tree, Lewis Waller, and Ben *Greet. A great range of Shakespeare performances, including those directly recorded from stage or broadcast, are now preserved in the sound archives of major theatre companies, the British Library, and the Library of Congress, but are also available as never before, for educational, domestic, and individual listening. *JC*

Bauer, R., *Historical Records, 1898–1909* (1937, 1946)

Junge, E., 'World Drama on Record', *Theatre Research* (1964)

Ross, A., *British Documentary Sound* (1977)

Weiss, A. J., 'A Selective Discography of Shakespeare's Plays', in H. Roach (ed.), *Spoken Records* (1970)

Whittington, J. (comp.), *A Checklist of the Archives of Recorded Poetry and Literature in the Library of Congress* (1981)

recusancy. See RELIGION.

Red Bull Inn. See INNS.

Red Lion, a farm in Stepney in the garden of which John Brayne, James *Burbage's brother-in-law, constructed the first playhouse in 1567. The galleries were a single storey and the stage was 40 feet by 30 feet by 5 feet high (12 m × 9 m × 2.7 m) with an attached turret—the purpose of which is unclear—reaching some 30 feet (9 m) above the ground. The entire structure was cheap (under £20 compared to the Theatre's £700), rested on the ground without foundations, and there is no evidence that it lasted beyond the summer of 1567. Spurious speculation about 'lewis' braces—suggesting a winch at the top of the turret—has arisen from a simple error in transcribing the construction contract. *GE*

Berry, Herbert, 'The First Public Playhouses, Especially the Red Lion', *Shakespeare Quarterly*, 40 (1989)

Loengard, Janet S., 'An Elizabethan Lawsuit: John Brayne, his Carpenter, and the Building of the Red Lion Theatre', *Shakespeare Quarterly*, 34 (1983)

Redgrave, Sir Michael (1908–85), British stage and film actor. Both his parents were actors. At Cambridge he acted and wrote for literary magazines. At the *Old Vic in London in 1937 he was a tactful Orlando to the Rosalind of the much older Edith *Evans. Next year he was Bolingbroke to the Richard ii of John *Gielgud. He became a celebrated film star. He played Macbeth in London and New York, 1947, and in the Old Vic's London season 1949–50 he was well received as Berowne in *Love's Labour's Lost* and as Hamlet, which he repeated at Elsinore. In the celebrated history cycle at Stratford in 1951 he was a capricious Richard ii and a Northumbrian Hotspur; he also played Prospero. At Stratford in 1953 he played Lear, Shylock, and a towering Antony to the Cleopatra of Peggy *Ashcroft; in 1958 he played Benedick and, at the age of 50, Hamlet—a performance acclaimed in Moscow. In 1963 he was Claudius in the inaugural production by the *National Theatre. By this time Redgrave, who was sometimes viewed as an intellectual actor, was suffering from Parkinson's disease. He has been the subject of a memoir by his son Corin and a therapeutic stage show by his daughter Lynn. *MJ*

Findlater, Richard, *Michael Redgrave. Actor* (1956)

Redgrave, Michael, *In my Mind's Eye* (1983)

Redgrave, Vanessa (b. 1937). The daughter of Michael Redgrave and Rachel Kempson, both actors, she made her name at Stratford-upon-Avon in 1961 when her young and vibrant Rosalind was acclaimed. She also played Katherine in *The Taming of the Shrew* and Imogen in *Cymbeline*. She went on to big parts in London and New York and is an internationally famous film star. She played Cleopatra under the direction of her husband Tony *Richardson in 1973; with Timothy Dalton as Antony in the West End in 1986; and again in London and Texas in 1995. In 2000 she played Prospero at the replica *Globe in London. *MJ*

Reed, Isaac (1742–1807), English editor. A retiring literary scholar, Reed helped Samuel *Johnson with *The Lives of the Poets* and edited other works including the *Biographica dramatica* (1782). He re-edited the Johnson–Steevens edition of Shakespeare and in 1803 published the 'first *variorum' edition of Shakespeare's works. *JM*

Vanessa Redgrave in the role which established her as a major actress, Rosalind, in Michael Elliott's RSC production of *As You Like It*, 1961.

Reformation. See RELIGION.

regal, a portable reed *organ with a raucous sound; some, known as 'bible regals', could be folded to look like a giant book. Indicated in Richard *Edwards's comedy *Damon and Pithias* (1564). *JB*

Regan, Lear's second daughter and the Duke of Cornwall's wife, is arguably more vicious than her elder sister Goneril, who poisons her, *The Tragedy of King Lear* 5.3 (*History* 24). *AB*

Rehan, Ada (1860–1916), Irish-born American actress whose forte, though she played Ophelia to Edwin *Booth's Hamlet (1873), was comedy. This was recognized by Augustin Daly, who made her the centrepiece of his Shakespearian revivals from Mistress Ford in 1886 onwards to Katherine (1887), Helena (1888), Rosalind (1889), Viola and Julia (1893), Beatrice (1896), Miranda (1897), and Portia (1898). As Daly's operations extended across the Atlantic Ada Rehan's performances were seen in London as well as New York. Rehan's most famous role was Katherine, though she paid for her effective, high-pitched entrance by having little in reserve for later climaxes. In contrast her Helena was unimpressive until the quarrel with Hermia, but as Rosalind, though she could not be cautioned for underplaying, she showed a delicacy and spontaneity which disarmed all but the sternest critics, amongst whom *Shaw insisted that 'Ada Rehan has yet created nothing but Ada Rehan.' *RF*

rehearsal. In London theatres of Shakespeare's time, which gave their performances in the afternoons, the morning was given over to rehearsals. Before meeting for a collective rehearsal each actor studied (that is, memorized) his *part, which was written out on a scroll giving only the lines spoken by a single character and the two or three cue words which end the preceding speech of another character. Snug in *A Midsummer Night's Dream* asks to be given the lion's part as soon as possible 'for I am slow of study' (1.2.62). Not until the first—sometimes the only—collective rehearsal would the actors find out what each other's characters were to say and do. *GE*

Reignier, Duke of Anjou. See RENÉ, DUKE OF ANJOU, KING OF NAPLES.

Reinhardt, Max (1873–1943), Austrian director and theatre manager. After early work as an actor, Reinhardt bought the Deutsches Theater in Berlin in 1906 and soon became internationally famous as a director of great innovation and power. His inclinations were to the spectacular and his productions of Shakespeare often were lavish, as with *A Midsummer Night's Dream* (Berlin, 1905, the first of twelve versions) which used real trees in the forest, and *The Tempest* (Berlin, 1915) which relied on a revolving stage to create the illusion of shifting locales. Even at his most spectacular, Reinhardt focused on psychological truth in acting. An eclectic artist, he was influenced by *Craig's designs and directed some of the first Shakespeare productions to use the modernist methods of simplification, symbol, and abstraction—as in *The Winter's Tale* (1904), *King Lear* (1908), *Hamlet* (1910), and an expressionist *Macbeth* (1916), usually on smaller stages in Berlin and Munich. He never lost the showman's touch, however, and was much sought after for his large-scale work in London and Europe. After the First World War he created the Grosses Schauspielehaus in Berlin and staged massive versions of the classics, including a modern-dress *Hamlet* in 1920. One of the founders of the Salzburg Festival, he became more active there and in Vienna in the 1920s. Reinhardt was a Jew; with the rise of Hitler his position in Berlin became impossible, so in 1933 he donated the Deutsches Theater to the nation and eventually moved to the USA, working on Broadway and in Hollywood. His film version of *A Midsummer Night's Dream* (1935), which now looks like high kitsch, nonetheless records some of Reinhardt's flair for Shakespeare, which at the beginning of the century had struck audiences as remarkable. *DK*

relics. See SHAKESPEARIANA.

religion. It is a tribute to the predominantly secular outlook of Shakespeare's works that they have survived so vigorously into an age in which religion, in the West at least, has to a large extent been relegated to the private sphere. In his own times, however, public affairs were dominated by the religious controversies which followed Henry VIII's quarrels with the papacy. During the Middle Ages, the Catholic Church of Rome had exercised hegemony over the religious life of Europe. But in the late 14th and 15th centuries the same social forces which inspired the Renaissance—the discovery and translation of ancient texts, printing with movable type, the spread of learning and decline of superstition, and the rise of nationalism—provoked a prolonged conflict over doctrine, ritual, and church governance known as the Reformation.

More than a century before Martin Luther drafted his 95 Theses (1517), an English sect (the Lollards) comprising followers of Oxford philosopher John Wyclif (*c*.1330–84) proposed a coherent doctrinal reform. Courtiers who accompanied Anne of Bohemia to England on her marriage to Richard II (1382) transmitted to Prague Lollard tracts which encouraged the first continental reformer, John Huss (*c*.1372–1415), and perhaps Luther himself. During the reign of Henry IV, Lollards were martyred under the Suppression of Heresy Act, *De haeretico comburendo* (1401), including Sir John *Oldcastle, who was burnt by Henry V (Shakespeare fictionalized the relationship between Oldcastle and the prince in *1* and *2 Henry IV*). Among other innovations, the Lollards rejected transubstantiation, the 13th-century dogma which held that words spoken by a priest could convert bread and wine into the Real Presence of the body and blood of Jesus Christ. Throughout the Reformation the nature of the Eucharist remained a focus of intense debate. The reformers accepted the *Bible as the sole authority on religion and a complete guide to salvation (*scriptura sola*), and demanded a reversion to the doctrine and ritual of the primitive Church (*ad fontes*). They held every baptized person a priest (Luther's 'priesthood of all believers') and, therefore, entitled to access to the Bible in vernacular translation. They believed each soul was predestined for salvation (election) or damnation (reprobation) before the creation of the world (cf. *Othello* 2.3.88–95), and that God's saving grace was a free gift (*sola gratia*) not conditional upon good works (*sola fide*). The reformers received baptism and communion as the only sacraments (rejecting penance, confirmation, marriage, extreme unction, and ordination). They dismissed as unscriptural Purgatory, the intercession of saints, kneeling to receive the Eucharist, pilgrimages, the adoration of icons, and the sale of indulgences. They demanded the dismantling of the hierarchical structure of the Church, and favoured the calling of ministers by each congregation and its elders. Against the immense wealth and influence of Rome—and the Pope's fearsome power of excommunication—the reformers advocated the 'divine right' of kings (Shakespeare interrogates this precept in *Richard II* and throughout the *Henry VI* plays). In 1555 the continental reformers established the principle *cuius regio, eius religio* (a monarch's right to define the religion of his subjects). The Vatican's efforts to suppress reform (the Counter-Reformation) fired political intrigue, warfare, and numerous martyrdoms recorded by John *Foxe in his *Acts and Monuments* (1563). In the aftermath of the Council of Trent (1545–63) reform suffused the Roman Church. A Catholic New Testament in English and the Gregorian reformed calendar appeared in 1582. As recently as 1999, the Roman Catholic and Lutheran churches signed a joint declaration on Luther's teaching on justification by faith alone (*sola gratia*).

In 1521 English Catholicism touched its high water mark when Henry VIII put his name to an anti-Lutheran polemic, the *Assertio septem sacramentorum*. The book included a defence of transubstantiation ('the altare sacrament') and earned the King and successors the papal honorific 'Defender of the Faith'. Henry remained a doctrinal conservative throughout his life; his overhaul of the English Church was a political event with only marginal theological nuances—a 'schism without heresy'. The challenge to Rome originated in Henry's pursuit of a divorce (1526–33) from Queen Catherine of Aragon, which Shakespeare examined in *All Is True* (*Henry VIII*). But Henry's campaign against papal supremacy in England gained impetus only after Thomas Cromwell turned the King's attention to expropriating the Church's wealth and income. Henry's depredations culminated in the dissolution of the monasteries during 1536–40 (Shakespeare glances at their 'ruined choirs' in Sonnet 73). When the Act for the Conditional Restraint of Annates (1532) threatened to deprive the papacy of the remission of one year's income by newly appointed incumbents, Clement VII acceded to Henry's nomination of Thomas Cranmer as Archbishop of Canterbury. Though Henry could hardly have foreseen it, the confirmation of Cranmer—who had won the King's favour by his support of the divorce—would prove decisive for the nation's theological reformation under Edward VI. The Act in Restraint of Appeals (1533) gave English ecclesiastical courts authority in 'testamentary' matters (including marriage and divorce) and allowed Cranmer to declare the King's marriage annulled; this legitimized Henry's bigamous marriage to Anne Boleyn (1532) and its illegitimate issue, *Elizabeth, while bastardizing Princess Mary (in Shakespeare's history plays and tragedies the legitimacy of royal heirs is a recurring theme). When Pope Paul III threatened excommunication unless Henry reverted to Catherine, the King extracted from his bishops an Abjuration of Papal Supremacy (1534), severing ecclesiastic ties with Rome. Concurrently, the Act of Supremacy declared Henry 'Supreme Head of the Church in England' (Shakespeare examines 'caesaropopism' in *Measure for Measure*, its Duke both prince and priest, or at least nominal friar). With their Church independent and their King wooing allies among Lutheran continental principalities, English reformers expected rapid and broad advances. But Henry's retrogressive Six Articles of 1536—the so-called 'whip of six strings'—revalidated auricular confession, private masses, vows of chastity, a celibate priesthood, and communion in one kind only, and made the denial of transubstantiation punishable by 'burning, without any abjuration'. Henry's death (1547) brought to the throne Edward VI (1537–53), 9-year-old son of Jane Seymour. Cranmer and the boy-king's protectors pressed for a reform on the continental model. The Edwardian Injunctions (1547) made English the language of the communion service, banned simony and the sale of benefices, ordered the destruction of shrines, and attacked 'superstitions' including pilgrimages, rosary beads, and guilds' private holy days. The Dissolution of Colleges Act suppressed thousands of chantries, and the Sacrament Act restored communion in both kinds. But the nature of the Eucharist continued in dispute. Edwardian reformers rejected both transubstantiation and 'consubstantiation', Luther's mystical belief that the bread and wine and the body and blood of Christ coexist in host and chalice after consecration. After years of temporizing, the Act of Uniformity (1552) promulgated a Second Edwardian Prayer Book (largely authored by Cranmer) which adopted the 'receptionist' view that the Eucharist was a memorial merely, and the communicant received Christ solely in the heart. On Edward's death (1553) the throne passed to Henry's daughter by Catherine, Catholic Mary Tudor. Her parliaments swiftly repealed the Edwardian and Henrican reform legislation and restored the religious status quo of 1529. But Mary and her advisers recognized a permanent Catholic restoration was dependent on the Queen (then 38 years old and unmarried) producing a viable heir. This necessity and Mary's zeal led to three catastrophic blunders which assured the ascendancy of English reform: Mary married Philip of Spain, prince of England's historic enemy; she permitted a revival of anti-Lollard statutes and an 'English Inquisition' which brought to the stake 300 persons including Archbishop Cranmer, and won for the Queen the sobriquet 'Bloody Mary'; finally, Mary restored the papal supremacy in England by compelling Parliament to kneel and receive absolution from Cardinal Reginald Pole (1554). These draconian acts painted reform in the colours of patriotism, moderation, and freedom, and drove many reformers into voluntary exile in Germany and Switzerland where their congregations assimilated the advanced ideas of continental Protestants. When Mary and her childhood sweetheart Pole died on 17 November 1558 the Catholic revival in England died with them. At news of Elizabeth's succession Marian exiles streamed back to England imbued with lofty (and radical) Calvinist ideas for reform. But Queen Elizabeth I advertised her predilection for religious compromise by prescribing both a sung Mass and Gospel readings in English at her coronation. The Queen's mingling of the old and new religions (the 'Elizabethan Settlement') perturbed reformers and conservatives alike. In 1559 Parliament repealed the Marian reversions, published an Act of Supremacy which abolished papal power and declared Elizabeth 'Supreme Governor' of the Church in England, and issued a new Act of Uniformity reimposing the Second Edwardian Prayer Book (with conservative modifications). The Queen also ordered a revision and expansion of the Edwardian Book of Homilies, and required the reading of excerpts every Sunday. Although Elizabeth subscribed to the 39 Articles (1563, rev. 1571), a series of concise statements of belief designed to resolve the principal doctrinal controversies, the evidence as to her personal faith is contradictory and inconclusive. Notably, her Prayer Book and Articles include a Eucharist formula which admits interpretation under both receptionism and the doctrine of Real Presence. In 1561 an order requiring churchmen to wear the traditional priestly garments ignited the Vestiarian Controversy; and the reformers' opposition—coupled with their personal austerity and moral exactitude—earned the pejorative *puritan* (a term which made its first recorded appearance in 1564). In *Twelfth Night* Shakespeare gibes at both the Puritans (2.3.135–6) and a sub-cult, the Brownists (3.2.30). Though generally united on doctrinal matters, the Puritan party was irreconcilably divided on the religious authority of the monarch and state. The 'episcopalian' wing (after *episcopus*, 'bishop') acknowledged monarchical discretion in sacred matters. The 'presbyterian' wing called for strict separation of Church and state and the eradication of the episcopacy, and wanted ministers to be at the call of individual congregations, with doctrinal matters subject to determination by a synod of elders (presbyters). (The latter faction triumphed in the Civil War of 1642–9 and an era of mutual toleration commenced only after the Restoration in 1660.) Throughout her reign Elizabeth vigorously defended her authority in religious matters. Archbishop John Whitgift's Ecclesiastical Commission examined suspected nonconformists under an oath *ex officio mero* which voided the protections against self-incrimination. In the ensuing Marprelate controversy, anonymous Puritan pamphleteers railed against the ceremony and venality of the episcopacy. In response, the conservatives enlisted the pens of Thomas *Nashe, John *Lyly, and perhaps others among Shakespeare's early London colleagues. With the death of Elizabeth (1603) and accession of *James VI and I, the Puritans anticipated thoroughgoing church reform. Although James's mother had been the Catholic Mary, Queen of Scots, the King was Protestant and his Scottish Church presbyterian. But miscalculations on both sides brought the King and Puritans into collision at the Hampton Court conference (1604). James rejected the Puritans' proposals for reform and proclaimed his support for episcopacy with the dictum 'No bishop, no king'. James also lectured his learned audience on the correlation between the apostolic succession and the divine right of kings—a dangerously obsolescent principle which led his Catholic-leaning son, *Charles I, to the block in 1649. James acceded to the Puritans' request for a new translation of the Bible, the 'Authorized Version' (1611), which depends heavily on William Tyndale's translation (1526). Rebuffed by James, some Puritans took ship for the New

World, settling the north-eastern region of what would become the *United States.

Shakespeare's personal opinions on all this have been the subject of much controversy. In the early 18th century, Richard Davies, chaplain of Corpus Christi College (Oxford), recorded on authority unknown that Shakespeare 'died a papist'. Like every English person of his time, Shakespeare descended from Catholic antecedents, and like many he numbered recusants among his extended family. His mother's cousin Edward Arden kept a priest disguised as his gardener; both men were arrested by Sir Thomas *Lucy and (perhaps wrongly) convicted of conspiring with Arden's erratic son-in-law John Sommerville to murder Queen Elizabeth. Arden was hanged at Tyburn (1583) and his head set up on London Bridge. Though the document is lost, scholars generally accept that Shakespeare's father John (d. 1601) signed the Catholic 'Last Will of the Soul' discovered in 1757 amid the rafters of the Henley Street house where William was born. In 1606, Shakespeare's daughter Susanna was cited on suspicion of recusancy, but the charge was dropped. Notwithstanding these instances, the tangible facts of Shakespeare's life—notably his baptism, marriage, and the language of his *will—imply he was born, lived, and died a conforming member of the Anglican Church. John Henry Cardinal Newman's declaration that Shakespeare 'was at heart a Catholic' (1873) reanimated curiosity about the playwright's religion. Recently, E. A. J. Honigmann and others have developed circumstantial evidence to support a hypothesis that young Shakespeare served as schoolmaster and participated in amateur theatricals in the household of the recusant de Hoghton family of Lancaster (under the name *Shakeshaft) during the period when the Jesuit martyr Fr. Edmund Campion visited the district (1580–1).

If William Shakespeare's spiritual life is mirrored in his work, then its salient characteristics are a refined knowledge of both the Genevan and Bishops' bibles (with particular affection for the Epistles of St Paul), and magnanimity toward the adherents of (almost) every religion which he depicts. When a pagan Lear movingly invokes his gods—'If you do love old men . . . if you yourselves are old' (2.2.362–5); when the Jew Shylock rebukes his despicable persecutors, 'Hath not a Jew eyes?' (3.1.52–3); when Cleopatra defiantly proclaims, 'I am again for Cydnus | To meet Mark Antony' (5.2.224–5)—the stark humanity of these unbaptized souls compels our sympathy and admiration. Unlike his dramatic contemporaries, Shakespeare even extends his grace to Catholicism. Wistfully, he glances at the ruined monasteries dotting the Tudor landscape in Sonnet 73 and in *Titus Andronicus* (5.1.21). He makes an abbess preside over the joyous conclusion of *The Comedy of Errors*, a play set in Ephesus, the city where Paul taught and Mary Magdalene was believed to have died. Although Friar Laurence's stratagem culminates in catastrophe for Juliet and Romeo, Shakespeare draws the Franciscan as a thoughtful, compassionate man. Toward Puritans, Shakespeare displays apparently less forbearance. But each of these instances may have a topical, rather than religious, inspiration. Puritanical Malvolio, target of anti-nonconformist humour (2.3.135–47) and cruel degradation in *Twelfth Night*, may be a caricature of the Oxford pedant Gabriel *Harvey, literary foe of Shakespeare's ne'er-do-well chum Tom Nashe. Angelo, surrogate ruler of 'stricture and firm abstinence' in *Measure for Measure*, may be Shakespeare's response to the Puritan elders of London whose hostility toward the theatres and brothels of the city's Southwark suburb was a continuing threat to the livelihood of the Globe sharers. In this cautionary tale, the draconian suppression of victimless sexual misconduct in the suburbs of Vienna produces evil consequences, and Angelo's Puritan-seeming asceticism (1.3.50–3, 1.4.56–60) is revealed as a visor for lasciviousness (2.4.163–4) and a history of faithlessness (3.1.215–32). By contrast, Shakespeare's portrait of the Lollard martyr Oldcastle is drawn with affection (Shakespeare altered the character's name to 'Falstaff' in deference to the martyr's heirs), and some 20th-century commentators have found meditations on the Reformation in *Hamlet*, with its allusions to Wittenberg (a centre of Lutheran learning) and its questions about Purgatory (1.5.9–22). The religious dimension of *Cymbeline*, too—a play set at the dawn of the Christian era, at the conclusion of which Cymbeline senses that 'The time of universal peace is near'—has also intrigued some modern commentators. In another late play, *All Is True* (*Henry VIII*), a mature Shakespeare and co-author John *Fletcher coolly dissect the Henrican reformation for the political event it was. But the playwright continues his remarkable even-handedness toward both old and new religions: Catholic Katherine is a woman of great dignity; reformer Thomas Cranmer is a man of conscience and humility; the Duke of Buckingham meets the headman with the dying words of William Tyndale on his lips (2.2.41–2); even Cardinal Wolsey experiences a purifying epiphany (3.2.429–58). Until new documentary evidence resolves the question of Shakespeare's personal religion we might best characterize his outlook as Christian, tolerant, humane. *SS*

Bray, Gerald (ed.), *Documents of the English Reformation* (1994)
Dickens, A. G., *The English Reformation* (1964)
Duffy, Eamon, *The Stripping of the Altars* (1992)
Honigmann, E. A. J., *Shakespeare: The 'Lost Years'* (1985)
Strype, John, *Ecclesiastical Memorials* (1822)
Strype, John, *Annals of the Reformation* (1824)

Renaissance Theatre Company. See BRANAGH, KENNETH.

René, Duke of Anjou, King of Naples. Defeated by Talbot at Orléans, *1 Henry VI* 2.1 (unhistorical), he consents to his daughter *Margaret's betrothal to Henry, 5.5. ('René' appears variously as 'Reignier', 'Reiner', 'Reynold', 'Reignard', and 'Ranard' in Shakespeare and *Holinshed.) *AB*

Renoldes, William (b. ?1556), soldier. Renoldes, an observant but unstable Londoner who thought that the Privy Council were using printed books to convey the Queen's secret love for him in code, indicates in a letter that Shakespeare's *Venus and Adonis* was in print by 21 September 1593. Later Renoldes maintained that in Ireland the Earl of *Southampton (Shakespeare's patron) would kiss, hug, and fondle a brother officer, Piers Edmondes. *PH*

repertory system. In the London theatres of Shakespeare's time, each playing company would present a different play every day, selecting from a repertory of between 20 and 40 plays (in a typical company of the 1590s) for which they owned the playbooks. The London audience's demand for new plays—largely attributable to the frequency with which the same people visited relatively few theatres—forced a successful young company such as the *Admiral's Men in the 1590s, who had relatively few revivable old plays, to add a new play to the repertory every two weeks. A new play which did badly on first performance might never be repeated, but a typical run would be about eight to twelve performances over four to six months. *GE*

Knutson, Roslyn Lander, *The Repertory of Shakespeare's Company 1594–1613* (1991)
Carson, Neil, *A Companion to Henslowe's Diary* (1988)

reported text. In their preface to the First Folio, Heminges and Condell assert that some of the earlier printed texts of Shakespeare's plays derived from 'stolen and surreptitious copies, maimed and deformed by the frauds and stealths of injurious impostors that exposed them'. The textual scholars associated with the New Bibliography, especially W. W. *Greg and A. W. Pollard, proposed that these 'stolen and surreptitious copies' were certain Shakespearian *quartos, pejoratively labelled 'bad quartos', that had no direct link to authorial manuscripts but were instead reconstructed from memory by an actor or a group of actors. Although it used to be supposed that a traitor actor would sell his reconstruction of a play to a pirate printer, a more likely scenario is that a company of actors playing in the provinces, having left the official playbooks back in London, might occasionally need to reconstruct a play from memory in order to perform it, and that this reconstructed text might eventually find its way to a printer.

Eight early quarto texts are widely viewed as memorial reconstructions, including the first editions of *The First Part of the Contention* (*2 Henry VI*) (1594), *Richard Duke of York* (*3 Henry VI*) (1595), *Romeo and Juliet* (1597), *Richard III* (1597), *Henry V* (1600), *The Merry Wives of Windsor* (1602), *Hamlet* (1603), and *Pericles* (1609). Editors are generally wary of the texts created through memorial reconstruction, but they sometimes make use of them as textual witnesses to early performances of Shakespeare's plays. In Q1 of *Hamlet*, for instance, the Ghost appears in Gertrude's closet '*in his night gown*' and the mad Ophelia enters '*playing on a lute, and her hair down singing*'. Such stage directions are often incorporated into edited texts.

The theory of 'memorial reconstruction' has been characterized as one of the triumphs of Shakespearian textual study in the 20th century, but it has recently come under fresh scrutiny. Paul Werstine has pointed out that since there is no external evidence to support the claim that the so-called 'bad quartos' represent versions of the plays reconstructed for touring, their seemingly privileged relation to early performance is entirely inferential. Recent scholarship does not reject memorial reconstruction as a viable explanation of textual origin, but it has radically narrowed the field. Laurie Maguire's extensive study of *Shakespearean Suspect Texts* (1996) concludes that a strong case for memorial reconstruction can be made with respect to *The Merry Wives of Windsor*, and a weaker case with respect to *Hamlet* and *Pericles*, but that *The First Part of the Contention* (*2 Henry VI*), *Richard Duke of York* (*3 Henry VI*), *Romeo and Juliet*, *Richard III*, and *Henry V* are definitely not memorial reconstructions. As ever in the surprisingly contentious field of textual criticism, however, these conclusions are not universally accepted. *ER*

Maguire, Laurie E., *Shakespearean Suspect Texts: The 'Bad' Quartos and their Contexts* (1996)
Pollard, A. W., *Shakespeare's Fight with the Pirates* (1920)
Werstine, Paul, 'Touring and the Construction of Shakespeare Textual Criticism', in Laurie E. Maguire and Thomas L. Berger (eds.), *Textual Formations and Reformations* (1998)

Restoration and eighteenth-century Shakespearian production. After the restoration of the monarchy in 1660 and the consequent reopening of the playhouses, theatre-going became a fashionable, social experience and the two companies granted royal patents competed to entertain and retain their audiences. Each included Shakespeare in its repertoire, not least because of the dearth of new plays. The King's Company led by Thomas *Killigrew acquired those plays that had been performed by the old King's Men before 1642, and the Duke's Company under Sir William *Davenant obtained exclusive rights to some of the remainder including *King Lear* and *The Tempest.* Both adapted the texts and the playing style to accommodate shifts in taste, stage technology, and audience expectation. The reputation of adaptations, once dismissed as risible, trivial aberrations, has risen in recent years and they are now regarded as integral to the stage survival of the bulk of the canon and significant to the development of Shakespeare's status as the national poet.

John *Dryden, acknowledging Davenant's help, explained the desire and intended effect of his symmetrical adaptation of *The Tempest* in 1667 through the creation of 'the Counterpart to Shakespeare's Plot, namely that of a Man who had never seen a Woman, that by this means those two characters of Innocence and Love might the more illustrate and commend each other'. His Prologue to the same work praised Shakespeare, justified the need to adapt his plays, and appealed for audience support:

As when a Tree's cut down the secret root
Lives underground, and thence new Branches shoot;
So, from old Shakespear's honour'd dust, this day
Springs up and buds a new reviving Play

. . . .

And he then writ, as people then believ'd.

. . . .

But, if for Shakespear we your grace implore,
We for our Theatre shall want it more.

Dryden's model became standard practice: the male lead, sometimes in role and occasionally, as in Bevill Higgons's prologue to George Granville's **The Jew of Venice* (an *adaptation of *The Merchant of Venice*, 1701), as the ghost of Shakespeare, delivered a prologue before each performance and the female lead spoke the epilogue. Nahum *Tate justified his own most famous adaptation, *The *History of King Lear* (1681), in another prologue:

If then this Heap of Flow'rs shall chance to wear
Fresh Beauty in the Order they now bear,
Ev'n this is Shakespear's Praise; each Rustick knows
'Mongst plenteous Flow'rs a Garland to Compose,
Which strung by his coarse Hand may fairer show,
But 'twas a Pow'r Divine first made 'em Grow.

Such speeches were intimate moments of communication in theatres that continued to reflect Elizabethan and Jacobean design, though descended from the indoor 'hall' theatres (such as the Blackfriars) rather than from the amphitheatres (such as the Globe). The earliest Restoration houses were adapted from real tennis courts, and featured a deep thrust stage with audience seated on three sides in pit, galleries, or boxes and with side entrances in close proximity to spectators. It was not until 1747 that *Garrick succeeded in banning the audience from access to the stage and behind the scenes. Actors performed in front of a *proscenium arch while at the back of the stage painted shutters, running in grooves, could be opened and closed to create *perspective sets, hitherto the preserve of court *masques. Stock scenes were reused and created a general sense of place rather than a specific setting.

The stage and auditorium were lighted, doubtless contributing to some of the excessive and flamboyant audience behaviour, and it was Garrick again, working with Philip de *Loutherbourg, who introduced sophisticated lighting effects, including pyrotechnics, and developed the use of stage machinery. Yet despite such simple staging, from the Restoration on, it was the visual experience that was emphasized whether in the singing and dancing episodes that were popular additions to *Davenant's *Macbeth* (1664), the 1674 operatic version of *The Tempest*, or the spectacle that was achieved through crowd scenes and lavish tableaux and processions. The 'Order of the Ovation' in the 1754 adaptation **Coriolanus*; *or, The Roman Matron* has 162 named parts, and the 'Additional Scene Representing the Funeral Procession to the Monument of the Capulets' was extensively puffed on the playbills of Garrick's adaptation of *Romeo and Juliet* (1748).

Many of these adaptations were significantly shorter than their originals, reduced to three acts with sub-plots removed, and were performed as part of double bills which offered variety to the audience and allowed actors to show off their range. At the *Covent Garden benefit for Thomas *Arne (17 April 1752) Mrs *Cibber appeared as *Desdemona, and then as Cinthia in her own play *The Oracle.* In 1753 at *Drury Lane Garrick's adaptations *Florizel and Perdita*, 'with proper Music, Songs, Dances and Decorations', and *Catharine and Petruchio* were performed together, both featuring Henry *Woodward and Richard Yates. Variety was also achieved through a rapidly changing repertoire and it was common for a production to play for no more than three consecutive nights. Mary *Robinson records playing ten Shakespearian roles during the winter season of 1777–8, including Ophelia, Perdita, Imogen, and Lady Macbeth, in a list of 22 parts that concludes '&c &c'.

Perhaps the most significant development of the period, indeed, was the introduction of actresses in 1660, marking the end of the transvestite tradition other than in comic roles such as the witches in Davenant's *Macbeth* and the Nurse in *Romeo and Juliet.* Elizabeth Howe has argued that the introduction of gratuitous scenes of sex, violence, and voyeurism in some adaptations—*Durfey's *Cymbeline* for example—and affecting speeches in others—*Cibber's *Richard III*—was the

The Tragedy of Hamlet

And ſo by continuance,and weakeneſſe of the braine
Into this frenſie, which now poſſeſſeth him:
And if this be not true, take this from this.
King Thinke you t'is ſo?
Cor. How? ſo my Lord, I would very faine know
That thing that I haue ſaide t'is ſo, poſitiuely,
And it hath fallen out otherwiſe.
Nay, if circumſtances leade me on,
Ile finde it out,if it were hid
As deepe as the centre of the earth.
King. how ſhould wee trie this ſame?
Cor. Mary my good lord thus,
The Princes walke is here in the galery,
There let *Ofelia*,walke vntill hee comes:
Your ſelfe and I will ſtand cloſe in the ſtudy,
There ſhall you heare the effect of all his hart,
And if it proue any otherwiſe then loue,
Then let my cenſure faile an other time.
King. ſee where hee comes poring vppon a booke.
Enter Hamlet.
Cor. Madame, will it pleaſe your grace
To leaue vs here?
Que. With all my hart. *exit.*
Cor. And here *Ofelia*, reade you on this booke,
And walke aloofe, the King ſhal be vnſeene.
Ham. To be,or not to be, I there's the point,
To Die, to ſleepe,is that all? I all:
No,to ſleepe,to dreame, I mary there it goes,
For in that dreame of death, when wee awake,
And borne before an euerlaſting Iudge,
From whence no paſſenger euer retur'nd,
The vndiſcouered country, at whoſe ſight
The happy ſmile,and the accurſed damn'd.
But for this,the ioyfull hope of this,
Whol'd beare the ſcornes and flattery of the world,
Scorned by the right rich,the rich curſſed of the poore?
The

Prince of Denmarke

The widow being oppreſſed,the orphan wrong'd,
The taſte of hunger, or a tirants raigne,
And thouſand more calamities beſides,
To grunt and ſweate vnder this weary life,
When that he may his full *Quietus* make,
With a bare bodkin, who would this indure,
But for a hope of ſomething after death?
Which puſles the braine, and doth confound the ſence,
Which makes vs rather beare thoſe euilles we haue,
Than flie to others that we know not of.
I that,O this conſcience makes cowardes of vs all,
Lady in thy orizons, be all my ſinnes remembred.
Ofel. My Lord, I haue ſought opportunitie,which now
I haue,to redeliuer to your worthy handes, a ſmall remembrance, ſuch tokens which I haue receiued of you.
Ham. Are you faire?
Ofel. My Lord.
Ham. Are you honeſt?
Ofel. What meanes my Lord?
Ham. That if you be faire and honeſt,
Your beauty ſhould admit no diſcourſe to your honeſty.
Ofel. My Lord, can beauty haue better priuiledge than with honeſty?
Ham. Yea mary may it; for Beauty may transforme
Honeſty, from what ſhe was into a bawd:
Then Honeſty can transforme Beauty:
This was ſometimes a Paradox,
But now the time giues it ſcope.
I neuer gaue you nothing.
Ofel. My Lord, you know right well you did,
And with them ſuch earneſt vowes of loue,
As would haue moou'd the ſtonieſt breaſt aliue,
But now too true I finde,
Rich giftes waxe poore, when giuers grow vnkinde.
Ham. I neuer loued you.
Ofel. You made me beleeue you did.
E Ham.

'To be or not to be', as it appears in the 1603 first quarto of *Hamlet*: this text is generally believed to have been supplied illicitly by an actor who had played Marcellus, Valtemand, and Lucianus, so that the scenes in which none of those characters appear, such as this one (3.1), are the least accurately rendered.

exploitative outcome of the innovation. Certainly actresses contributed to the social experience of theatre-going and while for some women (like Mary 'Perdita' Robinson and Dorothea *Jordan, a popular Viola, who both became royal mistresses) scandal remained associated with the profession, for others, particularly those who became involved in theatre management such as Anne *Bracegirdle and Elizabeth *Barry, the stage offered financial independence and social advancement.

Both men and women performed in what would now be regarded as a declamatory style, holding a pose with an appropriate gesture to deliver a speech and adopting an attitude and facial expression that reflected works on deportment and studies of physiognomy. (Something resembling this style of acting survived in *opera until the age of the close-up.) *Zoffany's portrait of David Ross as Hamlet (1757–67) shows the pose of an 18th-century gentleman gesturing asymmetrically with his feet planted at the approved 90-degree angle. As was customary in almost all Shakespeare of the period he is wearing contemporary dress—frock-coat, breeches, waistcoat, stock, and wig—and Hamlet's mental anguish is conveyed through a slight wrinkling of his left stocking. Contemporary fashion allowed women more extravagant outfits; Mary Robinson described her costume for her 1776 Drury Lane debut as Juliet: 'My dress was pale silver; my head was ornamented with white feathers, and my monumental suit, for the last scene, was white satin and completely plain; excepting that I wore a veil of the most transparent gauze, which fell quite to my feet from the back of my head, and a string of beads round my waist, to which was suspended a cross appropriately fashioned.' Garrick is credited with introducing a more naturalistic style of acting, yet it remained highly mannered, and his skill and reputation probably reflects a larger repertoire of attitudes that gave him greater variety as an actor. He exploited special effects, using a device to raise his hair when, as Hamlet, he encountered his father's ghost, and the dramatic start with which, as Richard III, he woke from his dream before the battle of Bosworth was one of the most popular moments on the 18th-century stage. It was the subject of a *Hogarth portrait, becoming a best-selling print, and it is undoubtedly such theatrical portraits that helped disseminate knowledge and popularity of Shakespearian productions, enhanced the reputation of actors in and out of role, and provide valuable evidence for the modern scholar. *CMSA*

Clark, Sandra (ed.), *Shakespeare Made Fit: Restoration Adaptations of Shakespeare* (1997)
Dobson, Michael, *The Making of the National Poet: Shakespeare, Adaptation and Authorship, 1660–1769* (1992)
Howe, Elizabeth, *The First English Actresses: Women and Drama 1660–1700* (1992)
Lennox-Boyd, Christopher, Shaw, Guy, and Halliwell, Sarah, *Theatre: The Age of Garrick: English Mezzotints from the Collection of the Hon. Christopher Lennox-Boyd* (1994)
Levy, M. J. (ed.), *The Memoirs of Mary Robinson* (1994)

retreat, a *trumpet signal for a military retreat, as in *1 Henry IV* 5.4.156. See FANFARE. *JB*

Return to the Forbidden Planet, a popular English musical (1981) by Bob Carlton, inspired by *The Tempest* and by the 1956 American sci-fi film **Forbidden Planet* (and heavily influenced by *The Rocky Horror Show*). Captain Tempest visits Planet D'Illyria, where he meets dastardly Doctor Prospero, his beautiful daughter Miranda, and the roller-skating robot Ariel. It was marketed for its 1999 revival as 'Shakespeare's rock and roll masterpiece', with songs by Jerry Lee Lewis, the Animals, the Beach Boys, Elvis Presley, and others. *TM*

Revels Office and accounts. The Office of the Revels, overseen by its Master, was formed to organize court entertainments at Christmas and Easter, but with the growth of the London theatre industry in the 1580s the players were increasingly able to manage their own productions and the office's role was changed to licensing and censoring. The accounts of the Revels Office illuminate court theatre but unfortunately are extant only for the periods 1571–89, 1604–5, and 1611–12. *GE*

'Revenge' is impersonated by Tamora, *Titus Andronicus* 5.2. *AB*

revenge tragedy. 'Revenge', Francis *Bacon explained in 1597, 'is a kind of wild justice, which the more man's nature runs to it, the more ought the law to weed it out.' Far from being synonymous with justice, revenge was regarded by Shakespeare's contemporaries as morally ambiguous and inherently tragic, as it implied a clash between the revenger's pursuit of personal justice and the legal system which had failed him.

The moral ambiguity of revenge is central to Thomas *Kyd's *The Spanish Tragedy* (*c.*1587?), the first and most influential English revenge tragedy. Kyd imitated *Senecan tragedy, a classical dramatic form characterized by bloody excesses, the appearance of a ghost demanding revenge, and the revenger's madness. Thereafter revenge tragedy flourished on the Elizabethan and the Jacobean stage. Shakespeare himself wrote two revenge tragedies, *Titus Andronicus* and *Hamlet*, although the revenge motif plays an important part in other plays, such as *Othello* and *The Tempest*. The moral ambiguity of revenge increases in Shakespeare. In *Titus Andronicus*, Tamora describes Titus' sacrificial murder of one of her sons as 'irreligious pity', as a 'barbaric' custom in 'civilized' Rome, which prompts revenge from both parties. In *Hamlet*, Shakespeare explores the theme of revenge even further, by focusing on the protagonist's delay in avenging his father's death and his resistance against action, violence, and blind retaliation. *SM*

Kerrigan, John, *Revenge Tragedy from Aeschylus to Armageddon* (1996)

revision, the practice of making small- or large-scale changes to a play during or after its composition by the original author(s) or after its composition by others. Revision includes alterations, additions, insertions, deletions, cuts, amendments, augmentations, and stop-press variants made in manuscript or printed copies of plays. Revision differs from *adaptation in that it does not involve overhauling a play (usually to modernize or regularize a text only to suit later taste, convention, or theatre conditions) but instead maintains the existing form, structure, and artistic vision of the original text.

In authorial revision, dramatists cut, add to, or otherwise alter their play either in the act of composition, that is, during the process of writing out their first draft, or *'foul papers', or sometime after composition due to external demands such as *censorship by the official censor, the *Master of the Revels, or theatre or acting company changes (such as a change of venue or personnel), or for their personal artistic reasons. A dramatist could make these later, post-foul paper revisions before the first performance while preparing a second draft, or 'fair copy', of the play, or during or after the first or subsequent performances, at which time the revisions were written into the company's licensed promptbook (known as the 'book') of the play.

Shakespeare made both small- and large-scale revisions in many of his plays, including *Romeo and Juliet*, *Love's Labour's Lost*, *Julius Caesar*, *The Merry Wives of Windsor*, *Troilus and Cressida*, *Richard II*, and numerous history plays such as *1* and *2 Henry IV*, at a variety of times for a variety of reasons. For example, the early printed texts of the first three plays mentioned above show *currente calamo* revisions, that is, second-thought changes in the act of composition, made in Shakespeare's foul papers or in the fair copies he made from them and before the plays' first performances. At some point after the first performances of the *Henry IV* plays he was forced by the censor to alter his original name for the character of the clownish knight from Sir John *Oldcastle to Sir John Falstaff because of complaints from Oldcastle's relatives. Shakespeare (or his acting company) also appears to have been censored into cutting the deposition scene, 3.3, in *Richard II* from the early printed quartos of the play, although it may not have been censored in performance.

Two pages from the Revels accounts for the Christmas season of 1604–5. Out of eleven performances by the King's Men, seven were of plays by Shakespeare (or 'Shaxberd')—*Othello* (*'The Moor of Venis'*), *The Merry Wives of Windsor*, *Measure for Measure*, *Love's Labour's Lost*, *Henry v*, and *The Merchant of Venice*, the last repeated at King James's own insistence.

Other authorial alterations were not due to censorship but to changes in time, space, or other conditions of performance. For example, after the death of Queen *Elizabeth in 1603, Shakespeare altered his allusions to that monarch in *The Merry Wives of Windsor* to suit her successor, King *James I, and music and other stage effects were added to plays when they moved from private to public or from public to private playhouses. When making required changes to update or revive an old play, Shakespeare also made other alterations for his own artistic reasons. Thus when revising these and other plays to suit some external demand, Shakespeare used the opportunity to review his work and to revise other parts of the plays, demonstrating that he considered the plays, although the official property of his acting company, as his own works in progress which he could reclaim and rewrite.

Shakespeare significantly rewrote at least *Hamlet*, *Othello*, and *King Lear* through small- and large-scale revision some years after their original composition in order to reshape these plays largely for his own artistic reasons. In revision he cut major speeches or entire scenes, including Hamlet's speech 'How all occasions do inform against me' in 4.4 in *Hamlet* and all of 4.3 in *King Lear*, as well as altering single words elsewhere (as in the speeches of Cordelia in *King Lear*, for example). These changes show a dramatist who is extremely concerned about maintaining the coherence and continuity of all of the formal elements of his plays, including plot, setting, and character, even to the most minute degree, when in the act of revising.

In non-authorial revision, dramatists, printers, and theatre company personnel such as scribes, promptbook keepers, and actors altered existing plays by other authors to suit changed performance or printing conditions, such as the expurgation of oaths after 1606. These revisions tended to be slight and seamless, as opposed to changes by adaptors who tended to overhaul an existing play into their own creation. Philip *Henslowe, who recorded his financial dealings with the Lord Admiral's Men, the chief rival to Shakespeare's acting company, the *Chamberlain's (later the King's) Men, paid professional dramatists such as Ben *Jonson, as well as hack or part-time writers, for their 'adicians' to and 'alteryngе' and 'mending' of existing plays for revival. Much of this type of work constituted minor revision rather than adaptation; Hamlet himself serves as a non-authorial reviser rather than an adaptor in *Hamlet* when he inserts some 'dozen or sixteen lines' (2.2.543) into a speech in 'The Mousetrap'. Non-authorial revisions were usually made to the company's existing promptbook, sometimes requiring the reviser or a scribe to make a new transcription of it. Revised plays had to be relicensed by the censor, but this requirement seems to have been ignored by most acting companies. Shakespeare may have begun his career by rewriting or adapting the plays of others, including his collaborators, but he appears to have made the bulk of the revisions to his own plays himself throughout his career, although revisers or adapters in the King's Men may have made other changes after his retirement or death.

Although none of Shakespeare's manuscripts survives, with the exception of a few pages of additions possibly in his hand in the collaborative manuscript of the play **Sir Thomas More*, we can supplement the evidence of the different early editions of his plays by studying the extant manuscripts of his contemporary dramatists which show overwhelming evidence of the types and patterns of authorial and/or non-authorial revision normal in the Shakespearian theatre. These include the manuscripts of Anthony *Munday's *John a Kent & John a Cumber*, Thomas *Heywood's *The Captives*, Thomas *Dekker's *The Welsh Ambassador*, Ben *Jonson's *The Gypsies Metamorphosed*, and Thomas *Middleton's *A Game at Chess*. These manuscripts show revisions and additions made interlinearly or marginally (in the left, right, top, or bottom margins), and/or in inserted sheets of paper. Cuts were frequently marked with a simple vertical line, often overlooked by later printers, in the left margin rather than with crossed-out passages within the text. In addition to internal evidence in manuscripts, dramatists commented on the extent of their authorial revision in their letters, memoirs, or prefaces to printed plays, demonstrating that it was a standard and acceptable practice for professional dramatists in this age to revise their plays.

Examination and collation of the early printed quarto and folio texts of Shakespeare's plays (some of which were printed from foul papers) show the same types and patterns of authorial revision as seen in the manuscripts of these dramatists, many of whom served as Shakespeare's colleagues throughout his career and as collaborators at the beginning or end of his career. Dramatists such as Shakespeare, Jonson, and Middleton worked within a *repertory system in which a play was performed occasionally and often subjected to revision for revival over a period of many years. Shakespeare and his colleagues clearly considered the later versions of their authorially revised plays not as improved or final but as alternative versions of their original texts; in fact they sometimes preferred early texts to later ones but considered all of them part of their creative output. This fact is amply demonstrated by Jonson's insistence on preserving the three variant texts of *The Gypsies Metamorphosed* and by Middleton's personal circulation of numerous, and variant, early and later texts of *A Game at Chess* without distinguishing amongst them. The revised plays of Shakespeare also reveal that later revised texts are not 'better' than but different from the originals and that no play which is still in the repertory can be considered to have a final form. These writers often objected to non-authorial revision and adaptation, preferring instead that the audience recognize the plays as they themselves wrote and rewrote them. As Hamlet instructs the actors in 3.2 in *Hamlet* in his defence of an author's text, 'Let those that play your clowns speak no more than is set down for them.' *GI*

Bentley, Gerald Eades, *The Profession of Dramatist in Shakespeare's Time, 1590–1642* (1971)
Foakes, R. A., and Rickert, R. T. (eds.), *Henslowe's Diary* (1961)
Greg, W. W., *The Shakespeare First Folio: Its Bibliographical and Textual History* (1955)
Honigmann, E. A. J., *The Stability of Shakespeare's Text* (1965)
Ioppolo, Grace, *Revising Shakespeare* (1991)
Taylor, Gary, and Warren, Michael, *The Division of the Kingdoms: Shakespeare's Two Texts of King Lear* (1986)

Reynaldo. **(1)** Polonius' servant, he is sent to spy on Laertes in Paris, *Hamlet* 2.1. **(2)** He is the Countess of Roussillon's steward in *All's Well That Ends Well* ('Rynaldo' or 'Rynardo' in the Folio, his name is sometimes spelled 'Rinaldo' in modern editions). *AB*

Reynolds, Frederick (1764–1841), prolific English minor playwright, who specialized in turning Shakespeare's comedies into *musicals, adapting, with the composer Henry *Bishop, *A Midsummer Night's Dream* (1816), *The Comedy of Errors* (1819), *Twelfth Night* (1820), *The Two Gentlemen of Verona* and *The Tempest* (1821), *The Merry Wives of Windsor* (1824), and *The Taming of the Shrew* (1828). These shows, 'with alterations, additions, songs, duets, glees, and chorusses', helped convince the English *Romantics that Shakespeare was too good for the stage. *MD*

Reynolds, William (1575–1632/3) a Stratford landowner to whom Shakespeare left 26*s.* 8*d.* to buy a mourning ring. *SW*

rhetoric, the art of persuasion in speech or writing. Cultivated in antiquity as an essential skill for those entitled to participate in public life, rhetoric was also codified into a long-lived body of theory, embodied notably in Aristotle's *Rhetoric* and later in Cicero's *De inventione* and Quintilian's *De institutione oratoria*. In this tradition, the art of making successful public speeches is often divided into five components: invention (finding the right arguments), disposition (orderly arrangement), style (appropriate language and turns of phrase), memorizing, and delivery (oratorical performance). Of these, 'style', which included the exploitation of figures of speech, came to be the most prominent. In the Middle Ages, rhetoric assumed an important place alongside logic and grammar in the basic *educational curriculum known as the *trivium*, and it provided the basis of poetics or literary theory, understood as a branch of eloquence. As an academic pursuit in the *grammar schools of the 16th century, rhetoric usually took the form of memorizing dozens of figures of speech as categorized in classical writings such as the pseudo-Ciceronian *Ad Herennium* or recent English adaptations such as *Puttenham's *Art of English Poesy* (1589).

It may be assumed, then, that Shakespeare and the educated section of his audience shared a highly codified knowledge of figurative language and of its persuasive uses. Rhetorical theory commonly distinguishes the major 'tropes' or figures of thought that extend the meanings of the words used (e.g. *metaphor, *simile, *metonymy, *irony, *paradox, *hyperbole, *prosopopoeia), from the lesser 'schemes' or figures of speech that exploit special arrangements of words (e.g. *anaphora, *antithesis, *anadiplosis, *chiasmus, *parison), and from figures of sound such as *onomatopoeia and *alliteration. Shakespeare's own conscious exploitation of the range of such devices is evident not only in set-piece examples of dramatic oratory such as John of Gaunt's speech on England (*Richard II* 2.1.31–68) or Mark Antony's funeral oration (*Julius Caesar* 3.2.74–245), but throughout his work. Awareness of the formal rhetorical tradition in which Shakespeare's figurative language is grounded may assist our understanding of the full resources of his *prose and verse style, and of its development: compare for example the rather rigid attachment to figures of repetition (anaphora, parison) in an early play such as *Richard III*, with the more flexibly metaphorical style of the later works. *CB*

Vickers, Brian, *In Defence of Rhetoric* (1988)
Vickers, Brian, 'Shakespeare's Use of Rhetoric', in K. Muir and S. Schoenbaum (eds.), *A New Companion to Shakespeare Studies* (1971)

rhyme, similarity of sound between syllables, usually at the ends of verse lines. The last stressed vowel in the line, with all sounds following it, usually comprises the rhyming element. If this be monosyllabic (e.g. def*ace*/pl*ace*—Sonnet 6), the rhyme is 'masculine'; if it has two syllables (e.g. vi*ewest*/ren*ewest*—Sonnet 3), it is 'feminine'. Rarer forms departing from 'full rhyme' include 'half-rhyme', in which the vowels do not match (d*umb*/t*omb*—Sonnet 101); 'eye rhyme', in which spellings match but sounds do not (*care*/*are*—Sonnet 112); and 'rime riche', in which the preceding consonants also match (*press*/ex*press*—Sonnet 140). *CB*

rhyme royal, a stanza form comprising seven iambic pentameters rhyming *ababbcc*. First used by *Chaucer in *Troilus and Criseyde* and other works, it was adopted by Shakespeare in *The Rape of Lucrece*. *CB*

Rice, John (*c.*1593–after 1630), actor (King's Men 1607–11, Lady Elizabeth's Men 1611–12/14, King's Men 1612/14–25). Rice was John *Heminges's apprentice and appeared with Richard *Burbage in a sea-pageant to honour *Henry's investiture as Prince of Wales in 1610;

this sea-pageant apparently provided the King's Men with costumes for Shakespeare's *The Tempest.* Rice disappears from the theatrical record after 1625 and John Heminges calls him a 'clerk' in his will of 1630, indicating that Rice had entered the priesthood. *GE*

Saenger, Michael Baird, 'The Costumes of Caliban and Ariel *qua* Sea-Nymph', *Notes and Queries*, 240 (1995)

Rich, Barnabe (?1540–1617), author and soldier. After fighting in the Low Countries and Ireland, Riche returned to England and, in 1581, published *Riche his Farewell to Military Profession.* Of all his writings, which include a number of pamphlets and a two-part romance, Riche was best known for this *Farewell*, a collection of eight prose stories including 'Of Apolonius and Silla'. This rendering of the familiar story of Silla's shipwreck, her disguise as a man, and the confusion with her twin brother was the primary source for *Twelfth Night.* Another story in the *Farewell* may have suggested the treatment of Malvolio's 'lunacy'. Further evidence of Shakespeare's familiarity with Riche's work may be found in *The Merry Wives of Windsor.* *JKS*

Rich, John (?1692–1761), manager, who inherited the patent of Lincoln's Inn Fields from his father Christopher, in 1714 and made the theatre the rival of *Drury Lane through its pantomime playing style. In 1732 he moved to the new theatre in *Covent Garden where the infamous Battle of the Romeos in 1750 was the most visible indication of his competition with *Garrick. *CMSA*

Richard II, (1367–1400) King of England (reigned 1377–99). See RICHARD II.

Richard II *(see opposite page)*

Richard III (1452–85), King of England (reigned 1483–5). He appears as crookback *Richard in *The First Part of the Contention* (*2 Henry VI*) and subsequently becomes Earl of *Gloucester in *Richard, Duke of York* (*3 Henry VI*) before enjoying his finest hour in *Richard III.* An entire association, the Richard III Society, is devoted to pointing out (with considerable justification) that he was innocent of most of the crimes which *Holinshed's chronicles and thence Shakespeare attribute to him. *AB*

Richard III *(see page 385)*

Richard, crookback. Later becoming Duke of Gloucester and then Richard III, he first appears in *The First Part of the Contention* (*2 Henry VI*). He kills Somerset at the battle of St Albans (5.2) (unhistorical: at the time Richard was 3). *AB*

Richard, Duke of Gloucester. See RICHARD, CROOKBACK; RICHARD DUKE OF YORK; RICHARD III.

Richard, Duke of York. **(1)** (1411–60). See 1 HENRY VI; THE FIRST PART OF THE CONTENTION; RICHARD DUKE OF YORK. **(2)** (1472–83). See EDWARD, PRINCE.

Richard Duke of York (3 Henry VI) *(see page 390)*

Richardes, Griffin. See GRIFFITH.

Richardson, Ian (b. 1934), British actor. Trained in Scotland, he played Hamlet at the Birmingham Rep and from 1960 until 1975 was a leading light at the *Royal Shakespeare Theatre, noted for his resilient verse-speaking and incisive characterization. His wide range included Oberon, Angelo, Iachimo, Coriolanus, and an acclaimed doubling of Richard II and Bolingbroke in alternation with Richard *Pasco. *MJ*

Richardson, Nicholas (fl. *c.*1614–25), fellow of Magdalen College, Oxford. In a sermon delivered at St Mary's church in 1620 and 1621, Richardson quoted *Romeo and Juliet* (2.1.221–6) to illustrate the theme of God's love for his saints even when they are 'hurt' by sin or adversity. *PH*

Richardson, Sir Ralph (1902–83), British actor. A magnetic, increasingly eccentric player, he had made his name at the *Birmingham Repertory Theatre and played a range of parts at the *Old Vic when Katharine Cornell invited him to play Mercutio to her Juliet in New York in 1935. He returned to the Vic under Tyrone *Guthrie where he triumphed as Bottom in *A Midsummer Night's Dream* and was Othello to Laurence *Olivier's suppressed homosexual Iago. After war service he co-directed with Olivier four fabled repertory seasons by the Old Vic Company in the West End: his great Shakespearian creation was Falstaff in both parts of *Henry IV.* By the time he led the Shakespeare Memorial Theatre at Stratford, however, in 1962, his verse-speaking had become so mannered that his Macbeth and Prospero seemed like sleepwalkers. For the Shakespeare quatercentary in 1964 he toured abroad as Bottom and Shylock, repeating the latter in the West End. Although he was Buckingham in Olivier's film *Richard III*, his old partner did not engage him at the *National Theatre. He never played the role that might have accommodated his hieratic late style, King Lear. *MJ*

Richardson, Samuel (1689–1761), English novelist. Richardson claimed Shakespearian tragedy as the model for his monumental novel *Clarissa* (1747–9), citing the original conclusion to *King Lear* as more truly religious than *Tate's then popular happy ending. In *Sir Charles Grandison* (1753–4) he guarantees the suitability of his heroine Harriet Byron by her liking for Shakespeare: her rival Clementina, taught *Hamlet* by Sir Charles, goes mad in the manner of Ophelia. *NJW*

Richardson, Tony (1928–91), British director. A pioneer of new drama and of British neo-realist cinema, he directed a visually exciting *Pericles* at Stratford in 1958, returning for the Memorial Theatre's 100th season to stage a busy, swirling *Othello* with Paul *Robeson. A brilliant *The Changeling* at the *Royal Court reclaimed that Jacobean masterpiece for the stage. Increasingly an international film-maker, he mounted in 1969 an innovative, unromantic *Hamlet* with Nicol *Williamson at the Roundhouse, London, and on Broadway as well as in 1973 an economical *Antony and Cleopatra* (starring his wife Vanessa *Redgrave) in a tent on London's Bankside. His last Shakespearian production was *As You Like It* (1979) in Los Angeles with Stockard Channing as Rosalind. *MJ*

Richardson, Tony, *Long Distance Runner: A Memoir* (1993)

Richardson, William (1743–1814), Scottish intellectual and professor at Glasgow University. Richardson published several very popular books on Shakespeare's characters which centre on the concept of a ruling passion. Characters examined include Macbeth, Hamlet, 'the Melancholy Jacques', Imogen, Richard III, King Lear, and Timon of Athens. *JM*

Richmond, Henry, Earl of. He becomes Henry VII after defeating Richard at *Bosworth in *Richard III.* Richmond calls Stanley his father-in-law (5.5.34), meaning stepfather, his mother's second husband. His mother was Margaret Beaufort, Countess of Richmond; his father Edmund Tudor, Earl of Richmond. *AB*

Rigg, Dame Diana (b. 1938), British actress. At the *Royal Shakespeare Company from 1959 she played many parts including Cordelia and Viola. At the *National Theatre her one Shakespearian role was Lady Macbeth. She played Cleopatra at *Chichester in 1985. *MJ*

Rinaldo. See REYNALDO.

Ristori, Adelaide (1822–1906), Italian actress who established an international reputation in a relatively small repertoire in which Shakespeare was represented by Lady Macbeth. Naturally gifted with an expressive face, a graceful figure, and a musical voice, Ristori studied her roles thoroughly and projected her psychological insights with great power. She first acted Lady Macbeth in an indifferent Italian translation in 1856; she performed the sleepwalking scene in English in 1873 and the entire role in English in 1882, when, though she was 'clear and distinct in utterance', it was—according to *Era*, 8 July 1882—her 'eloquence of gesture' that commanded most attention. *RF*

rival poet. Shakespeare's Sonnets 78–80 and 82–6, along perhaps with others, allude

(cont. on page 384)

Richard II

The most lyrical of Shakespeare's history plays, *Richard II* marks an enormous change from its predecessor in the genre, *Richard III*. It is written entirely in verse, as are *1 Henry VI*, *Richard Duke of York* (*3 Henry VI*), and *King John*, but neither these plays nor the three histories which continue the story of Bolingbroke's usurpation and its consequences (*1 and 2 Henry IV* and *Henry V*) match *Richard II*'s tragic plangency. In its heavy use of rhyme it is recognizably akin to *Romeo and Juliet* and *A Midsummer Night's Dream* (1595), and an invitation from Sir Edward Hoby to Sir Robert *Cecil dated 7 December 1595 to come to supper and see 'King Richard present himself to your view' has usually been identified as alluding to a private performance of *Richard II*, presumably then new. The dating of the play to 1595 is confirmed by its indebtedness to Samuel *Daniel's epic poem *The First Four Books of the Civil Wars*, entered in the *Stationers' Register in October 1594 but apparently only published in 1595.

Text: The play was entered in the Stationers' Register in 1597 and appeared in a quarto apparently set from Shakespeare's *foul papers in the same year. This text was reprinted twice in 1598, and a fourth quarto followed in 1608, this one, however, with 'new additions of the Parliament Scene, and the deposing of King Richard', passages omitted from the earlier editions. This fuller text was reprinted in 1615, and, annotated by reference to a promptbook, provided the basis for the text reproduced in the Folio in 1623. The Folio's text was itself reprinted as a quarto in 1634. Although deprived of oaths in compliance with the *Act to Restrain the Abuses of Players (1606), the Folio text is at some points superior to the quarto, particularly in its stage directions.

Sources: The large number of early editions, and the omission of the deposition scene, suggest a play, or at least a subject, of considerable topical interest: depicting the feasibility of dethroning a childless English monarch was clearly felt to be controversial during Elizabeth I's later years, and the episode depicting Richard's abdication was evidently a victim of political *censorship, probably removed in performance as well as in print until after the Queen's death. Sensitive as the play proved, however, Shakespeare's modifications to his historical material suggest, if anything, a toning-down of its potential for seditious application, though this did not deter the Earl of *Essex from having it revived as part of the preparations for his abortive attempted coup in 1601, any more than it mitigated Queen *Elizabeth's wrath, reported by *Lambarde, at the parallel this implied between her and King Richard. In particular, Shakespeare suppresses some of the justifications for Bolingbroke's usurpation: according to *Holinshed's *Chronicles*, the play's chief source, although Mowbray had not himself killed the Duke of Gloucester (but had merely allowed his murderers access to him), he had been directly ordered to do so by Richard. Shakespeare had read widely around his subject, not only in Daniel and Holinshed but in *The *Mirror for Magistrates*, and his depiction of John of Gaunt (the character most altered from Holinshed's version) owes something to an anonymous chronicle play about the earlier part of Richard's reign, *Thomas of Woodstock* (*c.*1592?), which may conceivably have had a now-lost sequel dramatizing the same events as Shakespeare's play. The most important dramatic precedent for *Richard II*, however, is *Marlowe's *Edward II* (*c.*1592), structurally similar in its depiction of an at once tyrannous and ineffectual English king who, achieving tragic pathos in defeat, is deposed, imprisoned, and murdered.

Synopsis: 1.1 Before King Richard II, Bolingbroke, the Duke of Hereford, accuses Thomas Mowbray, the Duke of Norfolk, of killing the Duke of Gloucester, which he denies: the two challenge one another, and Richard, unable to

Ian Richardson (left) as Bolingbroke and Richard Pasco as Richard in John Barton's celebrated RSC *Richard II*, 1973: presented in the deposition scene as mirror-images of each other, the two actors exchanged roles throughout the production.

command them to peace, concedes that they must fight a judicial combat. **1.2** Gloucester's widow rebukes her brother John of Gaunt, the Duke of Lancaster, for tamely accepting her husband's murder, praying that his son Bolingbroke may kill Mowbray, and bidding what she fears will be a last farewell. **1.3** After formal preliminaries, the judicial combat is stopped by Richard, who briefly consults his nobles before decreeing that both would-be combatants must be banished, Bolingbroke for ten years and Mowbray forever. After Mowbray's departure, however, the King shortens Bolingbroke's sentence to six years in exile, though Gaunt laments that he will certainly be dead before his son returns. Bolingbroke refuses Gaunt's attempts to console him. **1.4** Lord Aumerle brings Richard a mocking account of Bolingbroke's tearful departure: the King speaks scornfully of Bolingbroke's cultivation of popular opinion. One of his favourites, Green, urges Richard to put down a rebellion in Ireland, to which the King agrees. Another, Bushy, brings news that Gaunt is sick, and they leave to visit him, Richard hoping Gaunt will soon die so that his confiscated possessions may fund their Irish expedition.

2.1 With his brother the Duke of York, the dying Gaunt laments the King's extravagance and the fallen state of the country. When the King arrives with his followers Gaunt rebukes him with this and with the death of Gloucester before being carried off. Northumberland brings the news of Gaunt's death, upon which Richard, despite York's protests on behalf of Gaunt's heir Bolingbroke, seizes his entire estate. Left with Willoughby and Ross, Northumberland laments Richard's degeneracy, and announces that Bolingbroke is only awaiting Richard's departure for Ireland to land in the north with an army: all three hasten to join him.

2.2 The Queen is dismayed to hear of Bolingbroke's landing and of the nobles who have sided with him, as is York, regent in Richard's absence, whose loyalties are divided between Richard and Bolingbroke and who is further distressed by news of the Duchess of Gloucester's death. The King's favourites disperse to seek safety. 2.3 Near Berkeley Castle, Bolingbroke and Northumberland are joined by Northumberland's son Harry Percy, who brings news that Worcester has joined their cause, and by Ross and Willoughby. York accuses Bolingbroke of treasonously defying his sentence of banishment, but admits he has not sufficient force to arrest him: mollified by Bolingbroke's claim that he seeks only the due inheritance of his father's estate and title and to rid the court of parasites, he allows Bolingbroke's party to enter the castle. 2.4 To the dismay of Salisbury, the King's Welsh forces disperse, convinced Richard is dead.

3.1 Bolingbroke sends Bushy and Green to execution for denying him his inheritance and misleading the King. 3.2 Richard, back from Ireland, greets his native soil, urging it to repel Bolingbroke. Dismayed by Salisbury's news, he is rallied by Aumerle, but when Scrope brings word that Wiltshire, Bushy, and Green are all dead Richard sits on the ground and laments the mortality of kings. The Bishop of Carlisle urges him to fight, and Aumerle reminds him that York still has an army, but when Scrope reveals that York too has joined with Bolingbroke Richard despairs. 3.3 Bolingbroke and his supporters are outside Flint Castle: Richard appears on the walls, and Northumberland assures him that Bolingbroke wants only Gaunt's title and lands. Richard agrees to this demand, but in his lament at being forced to concede admits that he is utterly powerless and can himself ask only for a grave. Descending, he meets Bolingbroke, whose kneeling does not convince Richard of his fealty, and who at Richard's prompting agrees that they should leave for London. 3.4 The Queen learns that Richard's deposition is inevitable when she overhears a conversation between her gardeners.

4.1 In Parliament, Bolingbroke questions Bagot about the murder of Gloucester: Bagot accuses Aumerle, who denies the charge and challenges him. Fitzwalter and Harry Percy take Bagot's part, Surrey Aumerle's: Bolingbroke hopes to settle these arguments by recalling and trying Mowbray, but learns he has died. York arrives and announces that Richard has yielded his royal title to Bolingbroke. Bolingbroke is about to ascend the throne when the Bishop of Carlisle warns him that this usurpation can only lead to civil war: Northumberland arrests the Bishop for treason. Bolingbroke summons Richard so that he may abdicate in public: Richard does so, but in a performance that is both mocking and intended to excite pity, and he refuses to recite a list of the crimes which have justified his deposition. He accuses the assembled lords of treason and demands a mirror which, studying his reflection, he smashes, saying he has given away even his identity. After Bolingbroke sends Richard to the Tower and leaves, giving orders for his own coronation, Carlisle, the Abbot of Westminster, and Aumerle conspire together against him.

5.1 The Queen meets Richard on his way to the Tower: he bids her fly to France. Northumberland brings word that Richard is instead to be sent to Pomfret: Richard prophesies that in time Northumberland will turn against Bolingbroke. Richard and the Queen part. 5.2 York tells his Duchess of Bolingbroke's eager reception from the London crowds and their jeering at Richard. York finds that his son Aumerle is carrying a letter which reveals that he has plotted to assassinate Bolingbroke: despite his wife's pleas he hurries to betray this conspiracy to Bolingbroke, pursued by Aumerle and the Duchess. 5.3 Bolingbroke, now crowned as King Henry, longs for news of his dissolute son Harry. Aumerle arrives and, insisting on a private conference with the King, implores pardon. York arrives to warn of his son's treason, followed by his wife, who kneels with Aumerle to implore mercy: York in turn kneels to implore Bolingbroke not to spare his treacherous son, but Bolingbroke pardons Aumerle. 5.4 Sir Piers Exton is sure Bolingbroke wants him to kill Richard, and leaves for Pomfret. 5.5 Alone in his cell, Richard reflects on his past follies. A former groom has obtained permission to visit him, and tells how Bolingbroke rode Richard's favourite horse at his coronation. A keeper dismisses the groom: he has brought Richard's food but for once will not taste it before Richard eats. Exton arrives to kill Richard: Richard kills two of his helpers before dying, cursing Exton for killing a true king. Exton, preparing to carry the body to Bolingbroke, already regrets his deed. 5.6 King Henry hears of the defeat of various rebels against him, and pardons the Bishop of Carlisle. When Exton brings Richard's body he banishes him, vowing a pilgrimage to the Holy Land to expiate the crime of Richard's murder.

Artistic features: The play is remarkable among the histories for the carefully planned symmetry of its structure (by which, in effect, Richard and Bolingbroke exchange places) and for the formality, rhetorical and ceremonial, by which it evokes a lost medieval world. Many of its set-piece speeches, much anthologized, have become classics in their own right, most famously Gaunt's 'This royal throne of kings, this sceptred isle . . .' (2.1.40–68), and Richard's 'Let's talk of graves, of worms and epitaphs . . .' (3.2.141–73).

Critical history: The play was little valued by Enlightenment critics, who found it merely laboured and archaic, but the Romantics, particularly *Coleridge, were more in sympathy with its depiction of the eloquently helpless Richard. It appealed even more strongly to their 19th-century successors among the nostalgic *Pre-Raphaelite Brotherhood and the aesthetic movement, such as Walter *Pater, and in a famous essay ('At Stratford upon Avon', 1901) *Yeats wrote of his conviction that as a true poet Shakespeare of course preferred Richard II to the merely efficient Henry V. Modern criticism has explored the many analogies the play draws between royal power and the theatre, as its self-dramatizing King upstages his usurper, and has analysed the sacramental and ultimately sacrificial notion of kingship Richard espouses, often in relation to the late medieval doctrine of 'the king's two bodies'. Many commentators have also found in the play the first movement of a pattern of fall and redemption played out across the whole of Shakespeare's second tetralogy of histories.

Stage history: *Richard II* remained current after its notorious revival at the request of *Essex in 1601 (Augustine *Phillips's description of it under interrogation as 'an old play' thereafter may have been disingenuous): it was performed on board Captain *Keeling's ship HMS *Dragon* in 1607 and at the *Globe as late as 1631. Though archaic by the later 17th century, it was still controversial: when it was next revived, in Nahum *Tate's adaptation (1680), it was banned by the Crown after only two performances. Tate's attempt to avoid this prohibition by giving all the characters Italian names and retitling the play *The Sicilian Usurper* failed: he was especially chagrined by the ban, as his adaptation had been designed to turn Bolingbroke into a caricature of Charles II's populist political enemies and to make Richard a blameless martyr. The play was again rewritten in 1719, this time by Lewis *Theobald, who tried to make it fit contemporary tastes in pathos by supplying a love plot between Aumerle and Northumberland's daughter (both of whom die) and by developing the relationship between Richard and his Queen, who witnesses her husband's murder and remains onstage to speak an epilogue. This version at least avoided a ban, but soon disappeared from the repertory. Shakespeare's original was revived at Covent Garden in 1738, but after that had to wait until the 19th century before achieving anything like popularity. Edmund *Kean played Richard in 1815 (in a text adapted by Richard Wroughton), and the role was occasionally taken by *Macready, but the most successful production for many years was Charles *Kean's in 1857, staged with much medieval pomp which included an onstage presentation of Bolingbroke's procession into London with Richard in his wake, complete with large crowds of extras and real horses. After that, though William *Poel produced an experimental revival in 1899 (with Harley *Granville-Barker as Richard) and the play was taken up by Frank *Benson and Herbert Beerbohm *Tree in the years preceding the First World War, the play had to wait until the 1920s to achieve real prominence. George Hayes played Richard at the *Old Vic in 1924 (and again at Stratford thereafter), but the performance that really established the play was that of John *Gielgud, first at the Old Vic in 1929–30 (joined by Ralph *Richardson as Bolingbroke), then in the West End in 1937 (with Michael *Redgrave), and subsequently on international tours and on radio. The role was widely regarded as one of Gielgud's finest, and his lyrical delivery of the great speeches, preserved on sound *recordings, has influenced all the many Richards who have followed since the Second World War, among them Alec *Guinness, Michael Redgrave, Ian *McKellen, Alan *Howard, and, alternating the roles of Richard and Bolingbroke in John *Barton's celebrated RSC production of 1973, Richard *Pasco and Ian *Richardson. The play was also much revived, often with considerable supplementary spectacle, in post-war festivals in Italy, France, and Germany, including *Vilar's performance in the title role for the inaugural production of the Avignon Festival (1947). Two notable revivals since have further extended the play's possibilities. Deborah *Warner directed Fiona Shaw in the title role at the National Theatre in 1995, claiming this showy role for actresses, while Stephen Pimlott made a rare departure from the play's pageantry-dominated performance tradition by directing it in modern dress, with hints of both *Brecht and *Beckett, for the RSC in 2000, with Samuel West as Richard. *MD*

On the screen: The post-war popularity of the play was reflected by television versions screened by the BBC in 1950 and in the USA in 1954, but it was more substantially treated as two parts of the BBC series *An Age of Kings* (1960). A later BBC production (1970) starred Ian McKellen and Timothy West, and the BBC transmitted the play again in 1978, this time with Derek *Jacobi as King Richard and his great predecessor in the role, John Gielgud, as Gaunt. Deborah Warner's impressive National Theatre production was videotaped for television in 1996. *AD*

Recent major editions

Stanley Wells (New Penguin, 1969); Peter Ure (Arden 2nd series 1956); Andrew Gurr (New Cambridge, 1984)

Some representative criticism

Altick, R. D., 'Symphonic Imagery in *Richard II*', *Publications of the Modern Language Association*, 62 (1947)

Kantorowicz, Ernst H., in *The King's Two Bodies: A Study in Medieval Political Theology* (1957)

Rabkin, Norman, in *Shakespeare and the Common Understanding* (1967)

Rackin, Phyllis, *Stages of History: Shakespeare's English Chronicles* (1990)

Sanders, Wilbur, in *The Dramatist and the Received Idea* (1968)

Wilders, John, in *The Lost Garden: A View of Shakespeare's English and Roman History Plays* (1978)

cryptically to one or more other poets who strive to please the friend, either as patron or in a more intimately personal relationship. The rival wields 'a worthier pen' (Sonnet 79, l. 6) and is 'a better spirit' to whom the poet is 'inferior far' (Sonnet 80, ll. 2, 7). Sonnet 86 speaks of 'the proud full sail' of his 'great verse', and conjectures that 'his spirit' was 'by spirits taught to write | Above a mortal pitch'. He has an 'affable familiar ghost | Which nightly gulls him with intelligence'. And what really makes the poet (or Shakespeare) 'sick' is that the beloved's 'countenance filled up his line', depriving the Poet of 'matter'.

Commentators with a taste for proving the unprovable have brought forward evidence that virtually every poet of Shakespeare's time—and even of other times, such as Dante and Tasso—aroused Shakespeare's envy. Latching on to Shakespeare's apparent, if reluctant, admiration for the rival poet, some have proposed candidates who might deserve the compliment. So for example *Malone thought it might well be Edmund *Spenser. The characterization of the 'proud full sail' of the rival's 'great verse' has pointed others in the direction of writers of a grandiloquent style, especially *Marlowe (requiring an early dating of the Sonnets, since he died in 1593), and George *Chapman, translator of Homer. Others have used biographical

(cont. on page 393)

Richard III

The action of *Richard III* directly follows that of *Richard Duke of York* (*3 Henry VI*), written in 1591, and so may date from later that year to the temporary closure of the London theatres in June 1592. However, if the *Henry VI* plays were not composed in historical order, as some scholars believe, and Shakespeare wrote *1 Henry VI* after *The First Part of the Contention* (*2 Henry VI*) and *Richard Duke of York* but before *Richard III*, the latter was probably written after June 1592. *Titus Andronicus*, which shares features of neo-Senecan tragedy with *Richard III* and came before it, may also have been written after the *Henry VI* plays for performance outside London, which makes a date of 1592–3 for *Richard III* more likely. This time frame would explain the absence of any documentary evidence referring to the play before the *plague closed the theatres, a silence that seems telling in the view of its later manifest popularity. While it has a large number of roles, Elizabethan doubling practices allow it to be performed with a smaller cast than that required by the earlier *Henry VI* plays. A date of 1592–3 also supports the theory that publication of the anonymous *True Tragedy of Richard the Third* (1594)—a very different dramatization of events from Richard's reign—was intended to capitalize on the success of Shakespeare's play, which was subsequently listed in Francis *Meres's *Palladis Tamia* (1598).

Text: The play first appeared in a quarto edition in 1598 (known as Q1), after being entered in the Stationers' Register on 20 October. This was followed by five more editions derived successively from Q1, which most scholars believe was reconstructed from memory by players who originally performed it (probably the *Chamberlain's Men, Shakespeare's company, when they went on provincial tour in summer 1597 but left their promptbook in London). Another text of the play was published in the 1623 First Folio: this version is longer than Q1 and requires a larger cast and more onstage equipment. It is based on a scribal copy of Shakespeare's manuscript draft, but relies for certain details on one or more of the previously printed quarto texts. It also lacks a major passage found only in Q1, the so-called 'clock dialogue' (4.2.102–18). Thus, although the Folio version of the play is earlier overall and more rhetorically elaborate than the version preserved by Q1, it also contains elements which derive from Q1, as well as later agencies: for example, the Folio copy was censored to eliminate certain religious oaths, as required by the *Act to Restrain the Abuses of Players (1606), which sought to banish profanity from the stage. Some scholars have speculated that the Folio text may be Shakespeare's revision of the play first represented by Q1, but the opposite is more likely—that the play underlying Q1 probably represents a streamlined adaptation of the Folio text (the longest play in the canon other than *Hamlet*), better accommodated to actual conditions of stage performance.

Sources: *Richard III* synthesizes a diverse range of facts and contexts from historical, literary, and dramatic sources. The main documentary events derive from Edward *Halle's *Union of the Two Noble and Illustrious Families of Lancaster and York* (1548), and the compilation edited by Raphael *Holinshed, *Chronicles of England, Scotland, and Ireland* (2nd ed. 1587). In Halle, for example, Shakespeare found accounts of Richard's nightmare before Bosworth and the suggestion for his famous call for a horse (5.7.7). In Holinshed he read about the bleeding of Henry's corpse (1.2.55–6) and Richard's ominous pairing of 'Rougemont' and 'Richmond' (4.2.105–9). Both these chronicles incorporate an earlier source, Sir Thomas *More's *History of King Richard III*, which begins with Edward IV's death and ends with Buckingham's flight. More's account is biased against Richard to the point of

'That bottled spider, that foul bunch-backed toad' (*Richard III* 4.4.81). Anthony Sher in Bill Alexander's production, RSC, 1984: his Richard's likeness to a predatory arachnid was unforgettably enhanced by the black crutches on which he scuttled and swung across the stage.

making him mythically evil, but it also highlights his witty theatricalizing irony—traits that clearly attracted Shakespeare's interest. Richard's jaunty sangfroid and conspiratorial self-disclosure are also indebted to the dramatic traditions of the morality play Vice, and his Elizabethan heir, the Machiavel, who villainously parodies the pragmatic political philosophy of Niccolò *Machiavelli. The play was also influenced by the rhetorical conventions of *Senecan tragedy, particularly Lycus' wooing of Megara in *Hercules furens* for Richard's seduction of Lady Anne in 1.2, and *Troades* for the lamenting women in 4.4. Clarence's dream draws on *Spenser's *The Faerie Queene* (printed 1590), *Kyd's *The Spanish Tragedy*, and *The *Mirror for Magistrates* (1559 and later editions), the last a well-known series of politically moralizing tragedies of princes and other public figures.

Synopsis: **1.1** Richard, Duke of Gloucester, spurns the new opportunities for peace and leisure made possible by the triumph of his brother Edward IV and the House of York. Secretly he plots the downfall of those who stand between him and the throne. He turns Edward against his other elder brother George, Duke of Clarence, by libelling him with the suspicion of plotting to kill Edward, who imprisons him in the Tower. Richard meets Clarence on his way there, feigning sympathy. **1.2** Richard interrupts Lady Anne's mourning over the coffin of her father-in-law Henry VI, who was killed by Richard. Richard woos her, saying he killed Henry and her husband, Prince Edward, for the sake of her beauty, and that she must now charitably believe his motives were sincere. At first Anne scorns his claims, but ultimately, though still reluctantly, she yields. **1.3** Queen Elizabeth and her sons Dorset and Grey worry about Edward IV's illness and the prospect of Gloucester becoming protector over Prince Edward. Gloucester questions her family's loyalty to the Yorkists. Queen Margaret curses everyone with predictions of misfortune and death. Richard sends two murderers to dispatch Clarence. **1.4** Clarence recounts a nightmare in which he drowned after being inadvertently pushed overboard by Gloucester. He was then judged in the underworld for temporarily switching loyalties to the Lancastrians. After sleeping, he is awakened by the murderers, whom he tries but fails to talk out of killing him. The Second Murderer flees away remorsefully.

2.1 Edward reconciles the Queen and her family with the other lords, but the news of Clarence's death shatters this peace and grieves the King, who thought Clarence's death warrant had been cancelled. **2.2** The Duchess of York tries to conceal her grief for Clarence's death from his two children. Queen Elizabeth laments the death of Edward and fears for her children's safety. The lords prepare to bring Prince Edward from Ludlow to London. **2.3** Citizens fear the outbreak of factionalism while the Prince is still a child. **2.4** On hearing of Rivers's and Grey's imprisonment, Queen Elizabeth takes sanctuary with her young son the Duke of York, accompanied by the Duchess of York.

3.1 Prince Edward is welcomed to London by the lords and Mayor but misses his absent mother and brother. Against his better judgement, the Cardinal is persuaded to fetch the Duke of York out of sanctuary. The young princes reluctantly submit to Gloucester's advice to lodge temporarily in the Tower. Catesby is sent to find out Hastings's opinion about the idea of Gloucester becoming king. Gloucester promises Buckingham the earldom of Hereford for his support after he is crowned. **3.2** Lord Stanley's messenger reports to Buckingham his master's dreams of Gloucester's malevolence, but Buckingham dismisses his fears. Catesby reports the execution of Buckingham's enemies Rivers, Grey, and Vaughan that day at Pomfret, but Buckingham rejects his suggestion that Gloucester should become king. Stanley and Buckingham travel with Hastings to London. **3.3** Ratcliffe escorts Rivers, Grey, and Vaughan to execution. **3.4** The council gathers to plan the coronation. Richard accuses Hastings of keeping Mrs Shore who has bewitched his arm, and demands his execution. **3.5** Gloucester and Buckingham elaborate Hastings's alleged conspiracies to the Mayor to justify their summary execution of him to the populace. Buckingham rumours Edward's uncontrollable lust and his children's bastardy. **3.6** A scrivener observes that the indictment for Hastings's death was commissioned hours before he was accused of any crime, but nobody dares to speak openly about such state ruses. **3.7** The citizens refuse to believe Buckingham's stories about the princes' illegitimacy. The Mayor and citizens watch Gloucester's show of religious devotion with two bishops. Buckingham urges him to accept their faint request to become king, to which Richard consents after making a pretence of refusing.

4.1 Elizabeth is denied access to her sons in the Tower. Distressed at Lord Stanley's news of Richard's impending coronation, she sends Dorset overseas to join Richmond, while Lady Anne laments her misery as Richard's wife and future Queen. **4.2** Richard is enthroned. Buckingham hesitates to consent to killing the young princes and loses Richard's confidence. When he later agrees, claiming the earldom of Hereford as he was promised, Richard rebuffs him. Buckingham flees to Wales. Richard hires James Tyrrell to kill the princes. Tyrrell recounts the murderers' abhorrence of their deed, and reports the princes' deaths. Richard reveals Anne's death, Buckingham's revolt, and Ely's military alliance with Richmond. Rumours of Richmond's plans to marry Elizabeth of York spur Richard to woo her for himself. **4.4** The surviving women, led by Margaret, agonize their griefs and curse Richard. He asks the Queen to woo Princess Elizabeth on his behalf. She resists his threats and cajoling, ambiguously agreeing to write to him with her decision, which he interprets as submission. News arrives of Richmond's imminent invasion. Richard holds Stanley's son for assurance of his loyalty. Further reports of growing support for Richmond, Buckingham's capture, and Richmond's arrival at Milford Haven. **4.5** Stanley pledges to support

Richmond and relates the Queen's consent to her daughter's marriage to him.

5.1 Buckingham is led to execution, recalling how Margaret's curse has come true. 5.2 Richmond and his army march towards Leicester. 5.3 Richard pitches his tent in Bosworth field and prepares for battle next day. 5.4 Richmond encamps himself, sends word to Stanley, and plans for battle. 5.5 Richard retires and sleeps. Stanley promises Richmond aid covertly, to safeguard his son. Richmond prays and sleeps. The ghosts of Richard's victims—Prince Edward, Henry VI, Clarence, Rivers, Grey and Vaughan, Hastings, the two princes, Lady Anne, Buckingham—curse him in his sleep, while wishing Richmond victory. Richard starts awake, fearful and despairing; Richmond rises refreshed, and cheers his soldiers in an oration. 5.6 Richard plans his battle strategy, and rallies his army in an oration. 5.7 During the battle, Richard's horse is killed but he continues fighting. 5.8 Richmond defeats him in single combat. Stanley presents Richard's crown to Richmond, who proclaims a general pardon and looks forward to ending the country's civil wars by marrying Elizabeth and uniting the houses of Lancaster and York.

Artistic features: Although the play is dominated by Richard's *Marlovian vigour and his gleeful manipulation of *dramatic irony, it is notable, too, for the lyricism and formal rhetoric which characterize his victims, from Clarence's dream through the rival laments of the bereaved women.

Critical history: A number of allusions confirm the play's impact on Shakespeare's contemporaries and near-contemporaries (notably *Milton), and even during the long ascendancy of Colley *Cibber's stage adaptation Shakespeare's depiction of Richard was regularly cited as a startling example of the range and depth of his characterization. Dr *Johnson, however, felt that widespread praise for the play was undeserved: 'some parts are trifling, others shocking, and some improbable.' Along with Iago, though, Richard became a favourite with Romantic writers interested in creating their own Gothic, Satanic villains. Modern studies of the play have tended to divide between those which approach it as a self-contained tragedy focused on the titular character and those which see it as the final instalment of the larger historical drama played out across the *Henry VI* plays. One area of interest from the first perspective is the play's structural and rhetorical affinities with Greek and neo-Senecan tragedy, with Margaret, Elizabeth, and the Bosworth ghosts ritually invoking forces of nemesis and revenge, and Richmond acting as an agent of divine retribution. *Feminist critics have focused on the women's undeluded opposition to Richard—their collective agency, especially in 4.4, arguably transcending their individual moral positions. *Psychoanalytic theory has focused on the relationship between Richard's physical deformities and his deviant behaviour, initially disclosed in his two major soliloquies in *Richard Duke of York* (3.2, 5.6). *Freud argued that Richard exemplified the pathology of 'exceptional' persons who flaunt their physical limitations to excuse their antisocial desires, which serve as compensation: 'Nature has done me a grievous wrong in denying me the beauty of form which wins human love. Life owes me reparation for this, and I will see that I get it. I have a right to be an exception, to disregard the scruples by which others let themselves be held back. I may do wrong myself, since wrong has been done to me.' Richard's inner motives have also been discussed in terms of various sexual pathologies. Key scenes are his seduction of Lady Anne in 1.2 and proxy wooing of Elizabeth in 4.4. Historical scholarship has investigated Richard's Machiavellian dynamics of power, the dramatic origins of his theatrical flamboyance in the *morality play Vice, and the play's encoding of contemporary political debate over royal authority. The last of these crosses over to the second major critical perspective introduced by German Romantic critics such as A. W. *Schlegel, who interpreted *Richard III* as an evolutionary political epic stretching back through the preceding chronicle plays. In 1944 E. M. W. *Tillyard's *Shakespeare's History Plays* situated *Richard III* as the culmination of a national *commedia*: Richard is God's final scourge for the wrongful deposition of Richard II, which eventually led to the Wars of the Roses. Richmond's victory restores national order and redeems the country's political transgression. Since then, critics have moved away from Tillyard's providential reading, observing that the chronicles emphasize the practical benefits brought by Richmond's reconciliation of the warring houses of Lancaster and York as Henry VII. They also challenge Tillyard by highlighting elements of non-elite and popular culture (e.g. the citizens) that problematize claims for any single official ideology or traditional moral design.

Stage history: The play's initial popularity is attested by the number of early editions and the frequency of contemporary allusions and anecdotes, the most famous of which—in which Shakespeare pre-empts *Burbage at an assignation made by an eager female spectator of the play—is found in John *Manningham's diary, 1602. Beyond this apocryphal tale—an allegory about the rivalry between playwright and actor as to which is responsible for the role's seductive power—actual performance details from this period are rare. If the play dates from 1591–2, it was probably written for Lord Strange's Men, but if from 1592–3, then for Pembroke's Men (as the preceding reference to Burbage, their leading actor, suggests). In 1594 the play passed into the hands of the Chamberlain's Men, and then of their successors the King's Men, with Eliard *Swanston succeeding Burbage after 1624, including a performance at court on 16 November 1633. The play was revived after the Restoration without conspicuous success until Colley Cibber's melodramatic adaptation in 1700, only half of whose lines were by Shakespeare. Cibber cut Edward IV, Clarence, Margaret, and Hastings, but the simplified historical narrative appealed to actors and audiences, as *Garrick's performances from 1741 onwards confirmed. Edmund *Kean's intelligently expressive and emotionally intense interpretation was praised by *Byron in 1814. Charles *Macready tried briefly to revive Shakespeare's play in 1821, but Cibber continued to dominate until Henry *Irving's productions in 1877 and 1896–7. Yet these also severely cut and rearranged the text. Even after the staging of Shakespeare's original became commonplace, bits of Cibber ('Off with his head—so much for Buckingham') continued to be interpolated into performances of *Richard III*, including John *Barrymore's popular appearances in America in the 1920s, and Sir Laurence *Olivier's deliberately stagey film version. In Germany and Austria, however, strong interest in Shakespeare's histories stimulated integral and innovative performances from the mid-19th century, most notably by the Polish actor Bogumil Dawison at Dresden in the 1850s and 1860s. F. R. *Benson's *Richard III* appeared nearly every other season at Stratford-upon-Avon between 1894 and 1915, and was made into a *silent film in 1911 that today still conveys Benson's ruthless exuberance. Laurence Olivier followed Benson's example by transferring his celebrated 1944 *Old Vic performance to the screen in 1955. As with Olivier's other films, this expanded audiences for Shakespeare enormously, while also creating a permanently visible interpretation later actors have sometimes found oppressive. Ian *Holm successfully avoided comparisons with Olivier's 'limping panther' in Peter *Hall and John *Barton's three-part **Wars of the Roses* for the RSC in 1963–4, by making Richard's deformities more psychological than physical: reviewers described him as 'manic-depressive', 'schizophrenic', and 'psychopathic', while Dame Peggy *Ashcroft completed her triumphal performance as Margaret, now haggard and chilling. In 1984 the RSC's Antony *Sher recreated Richard as a 'bottled spider': a pair of crutches and a medieval gown with hanging sleeves gave the impression of six legs, as Sher scuttled rapidly about. Michael *Bogdanov and Michael *Pennington reverted to Barton's condensed cycle format for their eclectic and politicized production in 1986–9 for the *English Shakespeare Company, in which a strikingly bald and northern-accented Andrew Jarvis, initially in 1930s dress, finally appeared in a pinstriped suit before a computer screen. This production influenced Richard Eyre's 1990 National Theatre revival, in which Ian *McKellen caricatured Richard as a fascist dictator in a 1930s Britain; his performance became more flexible in Richard Loncraine's visually stylish 1996 film version. Al Pacino's 1996 film-documentary *Looking for Richard* conveys a credibly updated interpretation freed from Olivier's jokester-villainy, as does Ron Cook's largely unironic performance in Jane Howell's BBC *television production, first broadcast in 1983. In the United States and Canada, *Richard III* has remained very popular on stage. The Oregon Shakespeare Festival, to take just one example, has mounted successful productions every decade since the 1950s. Tyrone *Guthrie staged *Richard III* with Alec *Guinness to open the Ontario Stratford Festival in 1953, while Brian Bedford gleefully indulged audiences there in Robin Phillips's memorable 1977 production.

RWFM

On the screen: Two very different films were produced early in the 20th century, F. R. Benson's (1911) recording his stage production, while Frederick B. Warde acted the role in a highly spectacular American cinematic adaptation (1912) which included the arrival of a ship bringing the forces under the Earl of Richmond.

No significant sound version appeared until in 1955 Laurence Olivier directed his third Shakespeare film, taking the role of Richard himself. Many of his established team worked with him, notably William *Walton, whose music strikes a note of solemnity, reminding the viewer (as does an opening title) that Richard's ascent to the throne and reign are a mere episode in the history of the English Crown. Filmed in colour, the jaunty manipulations of Olivier's Richard amid the moral paralysis of the court have been seen as a counterpoise to both the triumph of the English in his *Henry V* (1944) and the dark, nostalgic brooding of *Hamlet* (1948). As part of its funding demanded, the film was broadcast on American television at the time of its release.

Olivier's film has overshadowed most of its successors: though Jane Howell's *Richard III* for BBC TV (1983) drew critical acclaim—as had her productions of the *Henry VI* plays—for finding inventive ways to use the medium, many found Ron Cook disappointingly lacking in camp as Richard. Richard Loncraine's *Richard III* (1996) imitates many of Olivier's procedures, notably an opening which introduces the cast during Edward's coronation festivities, though Loncraine preceded this with a violent episode owing more to the opening sequences of James Bond films. Ian McKellen's characterization has as much of Oswald Mosley in it as of Shakespeare's 'crookback' King, and the film is shot through with heavy irony. Memorably inventive is the use of familiar English locations to create a composite political world, ranging from power stations and derelict hotels to the Long Gallery of the Brighton Pavilion. It drew a divided critical reception, generally judged as clever rather than profound.

AD

Recent major editions

Antony Hammond (Arden 2nd series, 1981); Janis Lull (New Cambridge, 1999); John Jowett (Oxford, 2000)

Some representative criticism

Garber, Marjorie, 'Descanting on Deformity: *Richard III* and the Shape of History', in Heather Dubrow and Richard Strier (eds.), *The Historical Renaissance: New Essays on Tudor and Stuart Literature and Culture* (1988)

Loehlin, James N., ' "Top of the world, Ma": *Richard III* and Cinematic Convention', in Lynda E. Boose and Richard Burt (eds.), *Shakespeare the Movie* (1997)

Rackin, Phyllis, *Stages of History: Shakespeare's English Chronicles* (1990)

Rossiter, A. P., in *Angel with Horns and Other Shakespeare Lectures* (1961)

Sanders, Wilbur, *The Dramatist and the Received Idea: Studies in the Plays of Marlowe and Shakespeare* (1968)

Tillyard, E. M. W., in *Shakespeare's History Plays* (1946)

Richard Duke of York (3 Henry VI)

Shakespeare's darkest history play, detailing the worst civil chaos of the Wars of the Roses, was originally known and performed as *The True Tragedy of Richard Duke of York, with the Death of Good King Henry the Sixth, with the Whole Contention between the Two Houses Lancaster and York.* This title derives from the first text of the play, published in octavo (small-format book) in 1595. The alternative title is almost certainly editorial and comes from the better-known version of the play, longer by about 1,000 lines, published in the 1623 First *Folio. Like the titles of the other plays concerned with the events of Henry's reign, *3 Henry VI* was substituted when the Folio presented all the English histories in chronological order of their contents, even though Shakespeare did not compose the plays in this order.

Richard Duke of York was apparently written in 1591 as the continuation of *The First Part of the Contention*, which dates from 1590–1 and was published in 1594. It followed the publication of the second edition of *Holinshed's *Chronicles* (see below) in 1587, and probably *Spenser's *The Faerie Queene* (printed 1590). It must have been written before September 1592, when the playwright Robert *Greene parodied a line from *Richard Duke of York* (1.4.138) in an attack on Shakespeare in *Greene's Groatsworth of Wit*, referring to his 'Tiger's heart wrapped in a player's hide'. *Richard Duke of York* must also have been performed before an outbreak of the plague closed the theatres on 23 June. On 3 March in the same year the manager-owner of the Rose theatre, Philip *Henslowe, records a 'new' performance of 'Harry the VI' in his diary. This probably refers to *Part I*, which must have been performed by August 1592, when Thomas *Nashe admired it in *Piers Penniless his Supplication to the Devil.* This would leave the period between March and June for *Richard Duke of York* and *The First Part of the Contention* to have been written and performed. But this period has struck some, but not all, scholars as unrealistically brief, in which case Shakespeare must have written *Richard Duke of York* before *1 Henry VI.*

Text: The play was attributed to Shakespeare prior to the 1623 Folio by the title page of the unauthorized Pavier quarto of 1619 (Q3). Beginning in the late 18th century, however, Shakespeare's whole or part authorship began to be questioned. While the view that Shakespeare revised a play by Greene has been discounted, the Oxford editors leave open the possibility that certain scenes might not be wholly by Shakespeare. Some degree of collaboration in this or (more likely) the other *Henry VI* plays might explain Francis Meres's failure to mention them in *Palladis Tamia* (1598), which lists other—but not all—known Shakespeare plays. Other recent editors, however, believe Shakespeare was the sole author. *Richard Duke of York*'s poetic tone and dramatic structure are the most unified of the trilogy, and its action integrally looks forward to *Richard III.*

Publication of the octavo text (O) of *Richard Duke of York* in 1595 was probably covered by the *Stationers' Register entry for *The First Part of the Contention* on 12 March 1594. A second edition based on O was published in 1600 (Q2), as was the Pavier edition (Q3) in 1619. O's origins have been questioned since the 18th century. Edmond *Malone first argued that it was written by Greene and later revised by Shakespeare as the Folio version. Alternatively, Dr *Johnson and Edward *Capell speculated that O was a report of the Folio made from memory or shorthand. Building on this idea, Peter *Alexander demonstrated in 1929 that O was reconstructed from memory by actors (probably Pembroke's Men, named on O's title page). This remains the accepted explanation for O, notwithstanding corrective challenges to the universal applicability of memorial reporting. In 1928 Madeleine Doran suggested that O was also deliberately abridged for fewer players, though the most recent Oxford editor has shown that the personnel requirements of O and F are virtually identical. This edition revives Malone's idea that O is a first version of the play which Shakespeare revised and expanded in the Folio text.

The Folio text, which is generally clear, is based on Shakespeare's manuscript, since several missing, imprecise, or discretionary stage directions, and uncertainty over the historical figures represented by Montague, point to a draft in progress rather than a fair copy or finished state. Shakespeare's hand is also indicated by the names of several real contemporary actors, whom he had in mind to play characters in 1.2 and 3.1.

Sources: *Richard Duke of York*'s two documentary sources are Edward *Halle's *Union of the Two Noble and Illustrious Families of Lancaster and York* (1548), and the compilation edited by Raphael *Holinshed, *Chronicles of England, Scotland, and Ireland* (2nd edn. 1587). Halle is traditionally regarded as the dominant—and more ideologically conservative—influence, but recent scholarship has shifted the balance towards Holinshed. The Folio text sometimes stages Holinshed's version of events, whereas the octavo prefers Halle (e.g. 5.4–5). Sir Thomas *More's *History of King Richard III*, included by both chronicles, influences Gloucester's soliloquies (the one in 3.2 being the longest in the canon). Shakespeare alludes several times to *Gorboduc* (1561), as well as *The *Mirror for Magistrates*, **Kyd's The Spanish Tragedy*, and *Marlowe's *Tamburlaine*. The Folio's expanded version of Margaret's Tewkesbury oration in 5.4 draws on Arthur *Brooke's *The Tragical History of Romeus and Juliet* (1562). Shakespeare's portrayal of York's torment in 1.4 seems to allude to Passion scenes dramatized in various mystery cycles.

Synopsis: **1.1** The victorious Yorkists seize the throne and are confronted by Henry and his supporters. They dispute each other's title to the crown. Under threat, Henry agrees to disinherit his son Prince Edward in favour of York and his heirs on condition that York ceases the civil war and allows Henry to remain King for his lifetime. Margaret denounces Henry's decision and vows to defend her son's rights, marching against York. **1.2** York's sons Edward and Richard persuade him to break his oath and seize the crown immediately. **1.3** At the battle of Wakefield, Clifford pitilessly murders York's young son Rutland. **1.4** York is captured and derisively set on a molehill by Margaret and Clifford. He passionately deplores their torment before they kill him.

2.1 Edward and Richard learn of their father's death, while Warwick and Montague report a further Yorkist defeat. They rally to proclaim Edward Duke of York and future King. **2.2** Henry spurns Clifford's counsel for revenge. He dubs his son Prince Edward a knight. The Yorkists and Lancastrians exchange a violent parley. **2.3–4** At the battle of Towton, an exhausted Warwick is spurred to revenge his brother's death. A single combat between Clifford and Richard is broken off by Warwick's arrival. **2.5** Sent away from the battlefield by Margaret, Henry contrasts the fulfilling natural simplicity of the shepherd's life with the emotional stresses and empty ostentation of kingship. He laments the country's destruction by civil war, joined by a grieving son who has killed his father in battle, and a father who has killed his only son. Margaret, Prince Edward, and Exeter flee with Henry to Scotland. **2.6** Clifford faints and dies from his wounds, while the Yorkists verbally abuse his body. Edward heads to London to be crowned.

3.1 Returning secretly to England, Henry is captured and turned in by two gamekeepers. **3.2** Edward sexually blackmails Elizabeth, Lady Grey, a widow petitioning for repossession of her husband's lands. She insists upon marriage, to which he agrees. His choice of a commoner astonishes George, newly elevated Duke of Clarence, and Richard, Duke of Gloucester. Henry is reported captured and sent to the Tower. Alone on stage, Gloucester reveals his contempt for Edward and burning ambitions for the crown. Freed from ethical responsibility by his physical deformities, Gloucester turns to role-playing and Machiavellian policy to achieve his goals. **3.3** Margaret seeks the French King's aid. Warwick begins to negotiate the marriage of the King's sister Lady Bona to Edward. But letters arrive announcing Edward's marriage to Lady Grey, buoying Margaret and humiliating Warwick, who switches loyalties and vows to depose Edward.

4.1 Clarence, Gloucester, and others sneer at Edward's impolitic marriage. Clarence and Somerset leave Edward to join Warwick. **4.2–4** At night Warwick and Clarence surprise Edward in his camp-tent. Warwick uncrowns him and sends him under arrest to the Archbishop of York. **4.5** Queen Elizabeth laments Edward's capture and takes sanctuary to protect her unborn child. **4.6** Richard, Hastings, and Stanley rescue Edward while he is hunting and depart for Flanders to seek aid. **4.7** Henry is released from the Tower and appoints Warwick and Clarence joint protectors. Henry prophesies that the young Richmond—future Henry VII—will one day become king. **4.8** The Yorkists land in England ostensibly to claim Edward's dukedom at York. The Mayor is intimidated into granting them entry into the city, and Edward is proclaimed King. **4.9–10** Warwick and Clarence take leave of Henry, who is captured with Exeter by Edward and Gloucester and sent to the Tower.

5.1. The Yorkists confront Warwick at Coventry. Oxford, Montague, and Somerset arrive to support him, but Clarence switches sides back to his brothers. **5.1.** During the battle of Barnet, a fatally wounded Warwick dies after learning of Montague's death. **5.3.** Edward marches towards Tewkesbury to meet Margaret. **5.4** Margaret rallies her dispirited troops. **5.5** Edward defeats her and captures Prince Edward, who is impetuously killed by Edward, Gloucester, and Clarence.

Gloucester rushes away to the Tower. Margaret curses the others over her son's body. 5.6 Gloucester visits Henry, who intuits his son is dead and prophesies Gloucester's future slaughter by recalling the evil omens of his birth. Gloucester kills him but continues Henry's story of his destiny, vowing to kill his brothers and everyone else who stands in his way. 5.7 Edward relishes the fall of his enemies and, with Queen Elizabeth, delights in their new infant prince. Gloucester gives the child a Judas kiss. Edward banishes Queen Margaret to France, and announces Yorkist celebrations.

Critical history: *Richard Duke of York* has often been better appreciated on the stage than in academic criticism because much of its dramatic interest centres on intense battle scenes, which materialize its discursive themes of civil war's destruction of familial and social bonds. Nineteenth-century commentators, preoccupied with heroic character, had little use for Henry's pacifism and viewed Margaret simply as a she-wolf. But German Romantic critics situated the play in the wider context of Shakespeare's histories as part of a national epic. E. M. W. *Tillyard's influential *Shakespeare's History Plays* (1944) adopted this interpretation but emphasized the providential triumph of the Tudors, foreshadowed by Henry's prophecy over Richmond in 4.7. But Tillyard and others depressed critical interest in *Richard Duke of York* by claiming that Shakespeare was uninspired when writing it. The modern stage has dispelled this view, while revisionist critics have observed how little *Richard Duke of York* supports Tillyard's unifying vision of controlling providential order. More apparent is an early modern focus on the dangers of divided succession and dynastic factionalism, and the vision of an amoral universe of power-seeking individuals associated with the new philosophy of Niccolò *Machiavelli that explicitly inspires Gloucester. *Feminist critics have also learnt from stage performances, investigating the multiple social dimensions in Margaret's roles as militant mother upholding her son's rights against a disordered patriarchy.

Stage history: *Richard Duke of York* was probably first written for and performed by Lord Strange's Men, and then certainly staged by Pembroke's Men after they came into existence in May 1591. There is no further stage evidence until John *Crowne's Royalist adaptation, *The Misery of Civil-War* (1680, staged 1681), whose sensationalizing climax is the battle of Towton (2.2–6). From this point until the beginning of the 20th century, *Richard Duke of York* was performed in England only in inferior adaptations. Much of its final act and Gloucester's soliloquies were cannibalized by Colley *Cibber's hugely successful and long-lived *Tragical History of King Richard the Third* (1700). In Germany and Austria, however, strong interest in Shakespeare's histories among 19th-century critics stimulated many innovative productions. F. R. *Benson mounted *Richard Duke of York* at Stratford-upon-Avon in 1906, when all three *Henry vi* plays were first performed as a cycle (another idea borrowed from Germany). Benson's exuberant Gloucester was matched by his wife Constance's Margaret, played with 'unflagging force and spirit' despite heavy cuts. Sir Barry *Jackson and Douglas Seale's *Birmingham Repertory Theatre production in 1952 launched the play's modern stage life. Seale successfully alternated attention between still and lucid passages of formal verse, and energetic clashing armies. Barbara Jeffrey's fully humanized interpretation as Queen Margaret drew new attention to the role's tragic grandeur, as did Barbara *Jefford's when the production reappeared at the *Old Vic in 1957. Their moving performances were surpassed only by Dame Peggy *Ashcroft's 'revelation' in Peter *Hall and John *Barton's *Wars of the Roses* for the RSC in 1963–4. The condensed *Edward iv* began with Cade's rebellion and continued into *Richard Duke of York*. Barton also added hundreds of lines of Shakespearian pastiche to clarify personal motives and story-lines. *Richard Duke of York* was performed unadapted in Terry *Hands's well-received 1977 production of the whole trilogy. In 1986 Michael *Bogdanov and Michael *Pennington reverted to Barton's condensed format—minus his invented lines—for their eclectic 'post-Falklands' production, *The Wars of the Roses*, for the *English Shakespeare Company, which toured internationally between 1987 and 1989 (and is preserved on videotape). Adrian *Noble followed their abridgement in *The Plantagenets* in 1988, but with more traditional spectacle in the second play, 'House of York'. Katie Mitchell's stand-alone production at the RSC's Other Place in 1994, 'Henry vi: The Battle for the Throne', underlined the play's religious ritual and natural imagery to heighten its anti-war themes. In America, Pat Patton, recalling the experiences of Vietnam, chose Noble's 'House of York' for his stirring Oregon Shakespeare Festival production in 1992. Previous productions of *Richard Duke of York* at Ashland in 1955, 1966, and 1977 employed strong ensemble acting and Shakespeare's full script.

RWFM

On the screen: BBC TV broadcast the play as an episode in the series *An Age of Kings* (1960), but it appeared more memorably in 1965 when the BBC transmitted the RSC's *The Wars of the Roses* (1965). No mere recording of the stage production, the action was filmed by twelve cameras on an extended acting area. Inspired by *Brecht's self-conscious approach to theatricality, Jane Howell directed an equally playful and moving production for BBC television, first broadcast in 1983. Battle scenes were effectively varied in appearance, and speeches personalized by being spoken directly to the camera. *AD*

Recent major editions

Andrews S. Cairncross (Arden 2nd series, 1964); Michael Hattaway (New Cambridge, 1993); Randall Martin (Oxford, 2001)

Some representative criticism

Berry, Edward i., *Patterns of Decay: Shakespeare's Early Histories* (1975)

Brockbank, J. P., 'The Frame of Disorder: *Henry VI*', in John Russell Brown and Bernard Harris (eds.), *Early Shakespeare* (1961)

Jones, Emrys, *The Origins of Shakespeare* (1977)

Liebler, Naomi Conn, 'King of the Hill: Ritual and Play in the Shaping of *3 Henry VI*', in John W. Velz (ed.), *Shakespeare's Histories: A Quest for Form and Genre* (1996)

Potter, Lois, 'Recycling the Early Histories: "The Wars of the Roses" and "The Plantagenets" ', *Shakespeare Survey*, 43 (1991)

Rackin, Phyllis, *Stages of History: Shakespeare's English Chronicles* (1990)

Swander, Homer D., 'The Redisovery of *Henry VI*', *Shakespeare Quarterly*, 29 (1978)

evidence, arguing in circular fashion from their identification of other figures in the sequence; so for instance *Boaden, convinced that the Friend was Pembroke, proposed Samuel *Daniel on the grounds that he was brought up at the Pembrokes' home, Wilton House. And Sidney Lee's candidate, Barnabe *Barnes—one of the most despised of English versifiers—is dependent on a link with *Southampton. Robert Gittings, in his book *Shakespeare's Rival* (1960), proposed another member of the Southampton circle, Gervase *Markham, and Ben *Jonson has his supporters. *SW*

Schoenbaum, S., *Shakespeare's Lives* (1970, rev. edn. 1991)

Rivals, The. Sir William *Davenant's 1664 adaptation of *The Two Noble Kinsmen* shows a characteristically Restoration preference for *Fletcher's sections of the play, and compassionately supplies a happy ending, keeping its Arcite alive to marry Emilia and allowing the Jailer's Daughter to marry Palamon. *MD*

Raddadi, Mongi, *Davenant's Adaptations of Shakespeare* (1979)

Rivers, Earl. Lady Gray's brother, he flees with her after the capture of Edward IV, *Richard Duke of York* (*3 Henry VI*) 4.5. He becomes one of Richard's victims, *Richard III* 3.3, and his ghost appears at *Bosworth. He is based on Anthony Woodville, Baron Scales and 2nd Earl of Rivers, son of the Woodville of *1 Henry VI*. *AB*

Riverside Shakespeare. First issued in 1974, this edition of Shakespeare's works set a new standard for a well-illustrated, carefully edited, one-volume presentation of the collected works. Introductory sections deal with the historical background to Shakespeare, illustrated with colour plates, his language and style, the text, and the chronology and sources. The plays are printed roughly in the Folio order, comedies first, followed by histories, tragedies, and the late romances. The texts are carefully edited by G. Blakemore Evans, and each is followed by comprehensive textual notes. The poems are grouped after the plays, and appendices include an essay on stage history from 1660, documentary records relating to Shakespeare and his works, and a chronology of events and publications from 1552 to 1616, the year of Shakespeare's death.

Substantial critical introductions to the individual plays were supplied by a distinguished team, including Anne Barton and Frank Kermode. The edition immediately gained in importance when it was adopted as the basis for references in the *Harvard Concordance to Shakespeare*, compiled by Marvin Spevack (1973; see CONCORDANCES). A second edition of the Riverside, published in 1997, retains most features of the first edition, adding the texts of **Edward III* and *A Funeral Elegy, works of disputed authorship. The new edition also includes an incisive essay by Heather Dubrow on 20th-century criticism of Shakespeare. The introductions to individual works now seem rather dated, and the quirkiness of the textual editor's decision to retain some Elizabethan forms such as 'studient' for 'student' and 'inbark'd' for 'embarked' remains an irritant for many users. But the edition continues to be a strong contender in a crowded market, competing with the likes of the *Arden, *Bevington, *Norton, and *Oxford. *RAF*

Robert. See JOHN.

Roberts, James (fl. 1564–1608). London printer who published several of Shakespeare's plays in quarto. Roberts held the exclusive right to print playbills and appears to have had a close relationship with the Lord *Chamberlain's Men, for whom he may have made blocking entries in the Stationers' Register in order to prevent unauthorized publication of some of their plays. *ER*

Robeson, Paul (1898–1976), American actor. The son of a runaway slave, he became an all-American athlete, and a singer whose bass-baritone voice made him a household name. He played Othello in London in 1930 at the Savoy theatre, adjoining the hotel to which he had recently been refused admission. He first acted Othello in New York in 1943 at the age of 45; the production ran for 296 performances and then toured 46 North American cities. He was later ostracized for his political and racial views and had his passport withdrawn. Following a letter to *The Times* from J. Dover *Wilson, he returned to Britain, where in 1959 at Stratford-upon-Avon he played Othello with great dignity but without his old power. *MJ*

Robin, Falstaff's page in *The Merry Wives of Windsor*, is possibly the same person as the *Page in *2 Henry IV* and the *Boy in *Henry V*. *AB*

Robin Goodfellow, so-called in most stage directions and speech prefixes in *quarto and *Folio editions of *A Midsummer Night's Dream*, is a 'puck' (a generic name for a little devil, pixie or hobgoblin) and has often been called simply 'Puck'. He was a popular figure in 16th- and 17th-century folklore, though Shakespeare was the first to put him on stage. He acts as *Oberon's assistant in enchanting *Titania, *Bottom, and the lovers, and enjoys the confusion he causes when he accidentally enchants Lysander instead of Demetrius. (See also FAIRIES.)

In the 19th century it was a woman's part (sometimes a girl's—Ellen *Terry took the role aged 8), often hampered by attempts at rendering magic and flying through cumbersome machinery. In the 20th century the part has been played more often by men since *Granville-Barker's 1914 production (in which Puck was played by Donald Calthrop). A notable exception was Angela Laurier, the French contortionist, who took the part in Robert *Lepage's 1992 production. Male Pucks have tended to be more animalistic and malicious than their youthful, mischievous, female counterparts. Puck was dressed as a bird with claws in George *Devine's 1954 staging (alluding at once to *Ariel's disguise as a harpy and to Papageno in *Mozart's *The Magic Flute*), while in Elijah Moshinsky's 1981 BBC production Phil Daniels's more Calibanesque Puck wore an Elizabethan ruff but had wolfish fangs and lapped water from a pool. *AB*

Robinson, Mary 'Perdita' (1758–1800), English actress. She worked with *Garrick at Drury Lane from 1776 where success in *The Winter's Tale* and an affair with the Prince of Wales (later George IV) led to her sobriquet: His Highness was nicknamed 'Florizel'. Retiring from the stage when he abandoned her, she is best remembered as the subject of portraits by *Romney, Gainsborough, and Reynolds. *CMSA*

Robinson, Richard (*c*.1595–1648), actor (King's Men 1611–42). Apparently an accomplished female impersonator (mentioned in Jonson's *The Devil is an Ass* 2.8), Robinson was a sharer by 1619 and on 31 October 1622 he married Winifred Burbage, Richard *Burbage's widow. *GE*

ROBIN GOOD-FELLOW, HIS MAD PRANKES AND MERRY IESTS.

Full of honest Mirth, and is a fit Medicine for Melancholy.

Printed at *London* by *Thomas Cotes*, and are to bẽ sold by *Francis Grove*, at his shop on Snow-hill, neere the Sarazens-head. 1639.

Robin Goodfellow as priapic satyr: the title-page illustration to this 1639 jest-book reveals a great deal about the folkloric character Shakespeare harnessed as the agent of erotic mischief in *A Midsummer Night's Dream*.

Robson, Dame Flora (1902–84), British actress. A witty, versatile, and accomplished actress, Robson, never cut out for orthodox young heroines, played comparatively few Shakespearian roles but chose them well: they included Queen Katherine in Tyrone *Guthrie's *All Is True* (*Henry VIII*), 1933, Lady Macbeth (1933, repeated in New York in 1948), and a superb Paulina in Peter *Brook's *The Winter's Tale* (1951). *MD*

Roche, Walter (fl. 1569–82), a Lancashire man, fellow of Corpus Christi, Oxford (1559), rector of Droitwich (1569), master of the Stratford grammar school from Christmas 1569 to Michaelmas 1571. The young Shakespeare was probably taught by an usher in the same schoolroom. Roche was rector of *Clifford Chambers, close to Stratford, 1574–8. He witnessed deeds by John *Shakespeare in 1573 and 1575, and is recorded as living in Chapel Street in 1574 and 1582. *SW*

Rochfort Smith, Teena. See SMITH, TEENA ROCHFORT.

Roderigo, in love with Desdemona, is used in Iago's plots and eventually murdered by him, *Othello* 5.1.63. *AB*

Rogero. See RUGGIERO.

Rogers, Philip (fl. *c.*1600–?10), an apothecary and dealer in tobacco, pipes, and ale who was Shakespeare's neighbour in Stratford. Between March and May of 1604 he bought 20 bushels of malt for £1 19*s.* 10*d.* from members of Shakespeare's household, and on 25 June borrowed 2*s.* As he paid only 6*s.* of what was owed for the malt and the debt, Shakespeare sued him in the court of record at some unspecified date, employing William Tatherton as his solicitor. *SW*

Rolfe's Shakespeare. William J. Rolfe, formerly head of the High School in Cambridge, Massachusetts, edited Shakespeare's plays in separate volumes beginning in 1872. He aimed to present them in 'essentially the same way as Greek and Latin classics are edited for educational purposes', but he omitted lines he considered 'indelicate'. In conceiving an early version of what would now be called a 'school' edition, he also helped to foster the idea of Shakespeare as a 'classical' author. *RAF*

romance. The category of Shakespearian romance includes *Pericles*, *Cymbeline*, *The Winter's Tale*, and *The Tempest*. Despite similarities in chronology and concerns, *The Two Noble Kinsmen* is often excluded from this category, partly because of its collaborative authorship and partly because it has more in common with Fletcherian romance than with Shakespeare's 'canonical' romances. Edward *Dowden (1843–1913) first applied the term 'romance' to Shakespeare's late plays, which are alternatively referred to as *tragicomedies. Neither term, however, was used in the First Folio. The most prominent features of Shakespearian romance include sea journeys and shipwrecks, forced separations and improbable reunions, which were also prominent structural elements in earlier plays, such as *Twelfth Night* and *The Comedy of Errors*. The romances also share a recurrent concern with the father–daughter relationship, and complex staging, which was probably prompted by the fact that the King's Men started to use their indoor theatre at *Blackfriars in 1608.

Ben *Jonson anticipated later critics when he famously described *Pericles* as a 'mouldy tale'. Since then the romances have often been read as a celebration of the powers of the imagination, but also (from Lytton Strachey onwards) as a progressive decline from the artistic achievements of the mature tragedies. The almost undivided attention traditionally paid to the restorative quality of these plays' providential endings substantiated a familiar view according to which Shakespeare's *last plays represent a politically conservative attempt to legitimize Jacobean absolutism. Shakespeare's romances are now being reconsidered in relation to their specific historical context, including contemporary attitudes to *marriage and royal succession (*Pericles* and *The Winter's Tale*), the emergence of English *nationalism and Jacobean colonialist discourse (*Cymbeline* and *The Tempest*), the tension between homoerotic desire and patriarchy (*The Two Noble Kinsmen*), and ambivalent attitudes towards the Reformation (*All Is True* (*Henry VIII*)). *SM*

Edwards, Philip, *Shakespeare: A Writer's Progress* (1987)
Ryan, Kiernan, *Shakespeare: The Last Plays* (1999)

Romania. Shakespeare's plays first arrived in Romania in German translation, in the repertory of late 18th-century Viennese and Hungarian touring companies, and it was a German company which first staged a Shakespeare play in Romanian (*Othello*, Bucharest, 1816). During the revolutionary Romantic years which followed, however, translations were more often derived from French versions of the plays: such, for example, were the first Romanian translations of Shakespeare to be staged by Romanian companies, *The Merchant of Venice* (Moldavia, 1851) and *Romeo and Juliet* (Walachia, 1852). By the end of the century nearly all of Shakespeare's plays had been translated, increasingly from English editions (a tendency initiated, with *Macbeth*, 1864, and *Othello*, 1868, by P. P. Carp of the Junimea (Youth) group), and they exerted a growing influence on native literature. The greatest of Romanian poets, Mihai Eminescu (1850–89), engaged with Shakespeare throughout his career, and Shakespeare's influence is equally felt in the national, historical drama by which Romania expressed its aspirations towards independence from the Ottoman Empire. Romanian Shakespeare criticism begins at around the same time, in the work of the playwright I. L. Caragiale (author of a notable essay on Falstaff) and that of the pioneering Marxist Dobrogeanu-Gherea.

Since the inception of modern universities, Romanian Shakespeare criticism has been divided between the work of English literature specialists and the work of intellectuals more generally, the latter (such as George Calinescu, Tudor Vianu, and Ion Zamfirescu) often taking a more comparativist, pan-European perspective. In the 20th century, the plays were repeatedly translated by academics and poets alike, and staged with increasing frequency (with *Hamlet* a particular favourite in pre-war Bucharest, as discussed by the novelist Liviu Rebreanu). As elsewhere, the post-war period saw directors given increasing prominence (Ion Sava's 1946 *Macbeth*, influenced by the expressionist Yvan Goll, was a notable landmark), but under communism the pursuit of artistic individuality could be controversial: gifted directors such as Liviu *Ciulei, David Esrig, and Radu Penciulescu all defected to the West. Aptly, the collapse of Ceauçescu's regime in 1989 was heralded by a subversively topical *Hamlet*, directed by Alexandru Tocilescu, and since then a number of exiles have returned—Liviu Ciulei and Andrei Serban among them—to a vigorous Romanian Shakespearian theatre. *OB*

Beza, Marcu, *Shakespeare in Romania* (1931)
Stříbrný, Zdeněk, *Shakespeare and Eastern Europe* (2000)

Romano, Giulio. See GIULIO ROMANO.

Romanoff and Juliet, English play (1956) and film (1961), written, produced, and directed by Sir Peter Ustinov (b. 1921). Perhaps prompted by his Russian ancestry, Ustinov provides a Cold War comedy in which the children of the American and Russian ambassadors to 'Concordia' fall in love: it is a modernized version of the *Romeo and Juliet* story, without its tragic poetry. *TM*

Romanticism. The artistic movement that swept literary Europe across the end of the 18th century and the beginning of the 19th is conventionally thought of as a reaction against *neoclassicism, particularly in its French variants. Romantic texts, glorifying the imagination over the claims of literary form, commonly focus on an isolated individual consciousness, often engaged in transgressions against human and divine law, and often set against great natural landscapes.

In Britain, the Romantics' intense interest in Shakespeare was prompted by their apprehension of Shakespeare as a nature-taught outsider and a flouter of all inherited literary conventions, and, above all, as a poet of large sympathies and protean identity, the very reverse of the other figure that loomed largest in the English literary past, John *Milton. His romantic (and by now archaic) subject matter also seemed hospitable to poets who, on the one hand, were interested in depicting individual subjectivity and, on the other, wished to distinguish their work from the kinds of contemporary realism which had been adopted by the novel. He was accordingly taken as mentor by a number of poets, most notably *Keats, while his plays, especially *Hamlet*, *Macbeth*, and *The Tempest*, provided models for the *Gothic and Romantic fantasies of Horace Walpole, Mrs Radcliffe, Thomas *De Quincey, and Charles Maturin, to name only a few.

On the Continent, the spread of Romanticism was both a cause and a result of the *translation of the plays into other European languages: for many German and French readers, most familiar with the versions of *Tieck, *Schlegel, *Hugo, and others, Shakespeare remains an honorary Romantic writer. Encouraged by *Goethe, *Schiller took him as the governing spirit for his own national-historical plays. Shakespeare was also the spirit invoked to justify the period's investment, in Britain no less than abroad, in closet verse drama. Indeed, it is arguable that in this period Shakespeare's plays were more highly valued as poems than as theatrical scripts; the *Lambs' work is symptomatic of this, though it would be possible to identify the work of some contemporary actors, notably Edmund *Kean, as itself 'Romantic' in sensibility. One result of the period's decisive installation of Shakespeare at the centre of anglophone literary history was the growth of a substantial body of formidable European-wide criticism by the likes of *Coleridge, *Hazlitt, and Schlegel, which continues to exert a pervasive influence. *NJW*

Bate, Jonathan, *The Genius of Shakespeare* (1997)
Bate, Jonathan (ed.), *The Romantics on Shakespeare* (1992)

Rome is the scene of much of *Coriolanus* and *Julius Caesar*, some of *Antony and Cleopatra*, and nearly all of *Titus Andronicus*, collectively 'the Roman plays'. *The Rape of Lucrece* also has a Roman setting, while *Cymbeline* depicts the relations between Rome and ancient Britain. In the histories, 'Rome' is usually synonymous with the Catholic Church. *AB*

Romeo and Juliet *(see opposite page)*

Romney, George (1734–1802), English painter. He contributed to the *Shakespeare Gallery, where he displayed a depiction of *Lear in the Tempest*, 1798. The sincerity of Romney's aspirations to history painting cannot be doubted, but portraits constituted the majority of his output. Allegedly, Romney lacked sufficient patronage to develop his work on Shakespearian themes, but the artist was also noted for his lack of erudition by contemporaries, such as Lord Thurlow, who told the artist, 'before you paint Shakespeare, I advise you to read him'. Romney is frequently associated with Shakespeare through a series of portraits depicting Lady Emma Hamilton 'in character', such as *Lady Hamilton as Miranda* (now in the Philadelphia Museum of Art). Hamilton's likeness became a recurrent theme in Romney's *œuvre*, and appears in several works exhibited at the Shakespeare Gallery. The appearance of a Hamilton 'type' in Romney's depiction of *The Infant Shakespeare Attended by Nature and the Passions* was noted by the celebrated art historian Edgar Wind in 1930. *CT*

Ronsard, Pierre de (1524–85), French poet, perhaps the central figure in the *Pléiade movement. Ronsard was the author of almost 700 sonnets, some of them published in the collections *Amours* (1552) and *Œuvres* (1578). His influence may be detected in the imagery and themes of Shakespeare's sonnets and possibly in *Venus and Adonis*. *JKS*

Lever, J. W., 'Shakespeare's French Fruits', *Shakespeare Survey*, 6 (1953)

Rosalind. See As You Like It.

Rosaline. (1) She is doted on by Romeo before he meets Juliet: although on the guest-list for the Capulets' ball she does not appear in the play **(2)** One of the Princess of France's ladies, she is wooed by *Biron in *Love's Labour's Lost*. *AB*

Rosencrantz, with his companion Guildenstern, is asked by Claudius to find the cause of Hamlet's melancholy (2.2.271–95), but Hamlet mistrusts them and ultimately sends them to their deaths (5.2.13–63). *AB*

Rosencrantz and Guildenstern. See burlesques and travesties of Shakespeare's plays.

Rosencrantz and Guildenstern are Dead. See Stoppard, Sir Tom.

'Roses, their sharp spines being gone', sung by a boy at the beginning of *The Two Noble Kinsmen*; the original music is unknown. As a song for Theseus and Hippolyta's wedding, it has sometimes been transplanted into productions of *A Midsummer Night's Dream*. *JB*

Rose theatre. Philip *Henslowe, in partnership with one John Cholmley, built the first open-air amphitheatre playhouse on *Bankside, the Rose, in 1587. Excavation of the site has revealed that the Rose was an irregular fourteen-sided polygon approximately 74 feet (22 m) across and with a small, shallow, tapered stage which either fronted or formed a chord across three auditorium bays. This was considerably smaller than the *Swan and the *Globe which were later erected in the same district. Henslowe enlarged the Rose in 1592 but not by much and the main increase was in yard space. Prior to the Rose excavation it was generally assumed that Elizabethan theatrical amphitheatres were regular polygons and that their stages were rectangular and extended into the middle of the yard. In 1595 Henslowe paid for the installation of a 'throne in the heavens', presumably a device for lowering an actor to the stage from the stage cover. The layering of the foundations on the site indicates that the stage cover and its attendant stage posts were built no earlier than the alterations of 1592. A rainwater erosion line in the yard of the Rose, and Henslowe's payments to thatchers, indicate that the roof of the Rose was thatched.

Henslowe's accounts recording his income from the Rose name a great many plays, most of which are lost to us. Because a play might appear under more than one name, and more than one play might exist on the theme of, say, Henry v's life, identification of plays from Henslowe's records is not certain. However, Henslowe's 'tittus & ondronicus' was almost certainly Shakespeare's *Titus Andronicus*, and quite possibly 'harey the vj' was his *1 Henry vi*, indicating that these plays were performed at the Rose. Amongst other famous plays, Henslowe's record refers to Rose performances of *Marlowe's *Tamburlaine*, *The Jew of Malta*, and *Dr Faustus*, and of *Kyd's *The Spanish Tragedy*. Scott McMillin's analysis of the staging requirement of known Rose plays showed that if an 'enclosure' or 'discovery' were needed, the same play usually also called for playing 'aloft'. From this coincidence—both 'enclosure/discovery' and 'aloft' are needed, or neither is—McMillin concluded that a large stage booth served both functions which the permanent fixtures of the playhouse could not fulfil. Henslowe's attention focused on his new Fortune playhouse after 1600, and by 1606 the Rose had been pulled down. *GE*

Bowsher, Julian, and Blatherwick, Simon, 'The Structure of the Rose', in Franklin J. Hildy (ed.), *New Issues in the Reconstruction of Shakespeare's Theatre: Proceedings of the Conference Held at the University of Georgia, February 16–18, 1990* (1990)
McMillin, Scott, 'The Rose and The Swan', in John H. Astington (ed.), *The Development of Shakespeare's Theater* (1992)
Rutter, Carol Chillington (ed.), *Documents of the Rose Playhouse* (1984)

(cont. on page 402)

Romeo and Juliet

Shakespeare composed his definitive version of what is often called 'the greatest love story ever told' during the lyrical period of his career which also produced *Richard II* and *A Midsummer Night's Dream*, probably in the same year as these two plays, 1595. The play first appeared in print in 1597, in an unlicensed quarto edition apparently produced from a *reported text assembled by actors who had played Romeo and Paris. The title page proclaims that *Romeo and Juliet* has 'been often (with great applause) played publicly, by the Right Honourable Lord Hunsdon his servants': since Shakespeare's company was renamed the Lord Chamberlain's Men as of 17 March 1597, this edition must have gone to press before then. Furthermore, the work of producing it was interrupted by the seizure of its original printer's presses, an event which took place between 9 February and 27 March 1597, by which time the first four sheets had already been printed. Allowing time for the play's reportedly numerous performances and the compilation from memory of the manuscript, *Romeo and Juliet* could not very well have been written before late 1596. Its influence on *A Midsummer Night's Dream*, particularly visible in the changes Shakespeare made to his source for 'Pyramus and Thisbe', would place it just before that play. In any event the play cannot be earlier than 1593, since it shows the influence of English translations of two poems by Du Bartas only published in that year (in John Eliot's *Ortho-Epia Gallica*). The dating of *Romeo and Juliet* to 1595 is perhaps confirmed by the Nurse's remark that ''Tis since the earthquake now eleven years' (1.3.25), which may be a topical allusion to the earthquake which shook England in 1584.

Text: A second quarto, which calls the play *The Most Excellent and Lamentable Tragedy of Romeo and Juliet*, appeared in 1599, fuller and more reliable than the first: its variations in speech-prefixes, permissive stage directions, and accidental preservations of deleted false starts show that it was produced from Shakespeare's rough draft of the play, which its compositors, unfortunately, had trouble deciphering, sometimes resorting to the illicit first quarto for guidance. This edition was reprinted in 1609, 1623, and 1637, and a copy of the 1609 reprint served as the basis for the text published in the Folio in 1623, though some improvements to speech prefixes and stage directions suggest that this copy had been annotated by reference to a promptbook. Most recent editions of the play are based on the second quarto, but supplement it by reference both to the first quarto and to the Folio, particularly over details of staging.

Sources: Although it is undeniably more romantic to pretend that Shakespeare either made up the plot of *Romeo and Juliet* or transcribed it more or less directly from his own experience (as did the popular film *Shakespeare in Love*), the story of Verona's star-crossed couple had been popular throughout Europe for half a century before Shakespeare's dramatization. Tales of unfortunate aristocratic lovers proliferated in the Italian Renaissance: one early anticipation of the Romeo and Juliet story is that by Masuccio Salernitano, published in *Il novellino* (1474), but the first to use the names Romeo and Giulietta, and to set the tale in Verona against the backdrop of a feud between Montagues and Capulets, is Luigi da Porto's *Istoria novellamente ritrovata di due nobile amanti* (1535). This story was adapted by *Bandello, whose version appeared in *Le novelle di Bandello* (1560): his novella was translated into English in William *Painter's *Palace of*

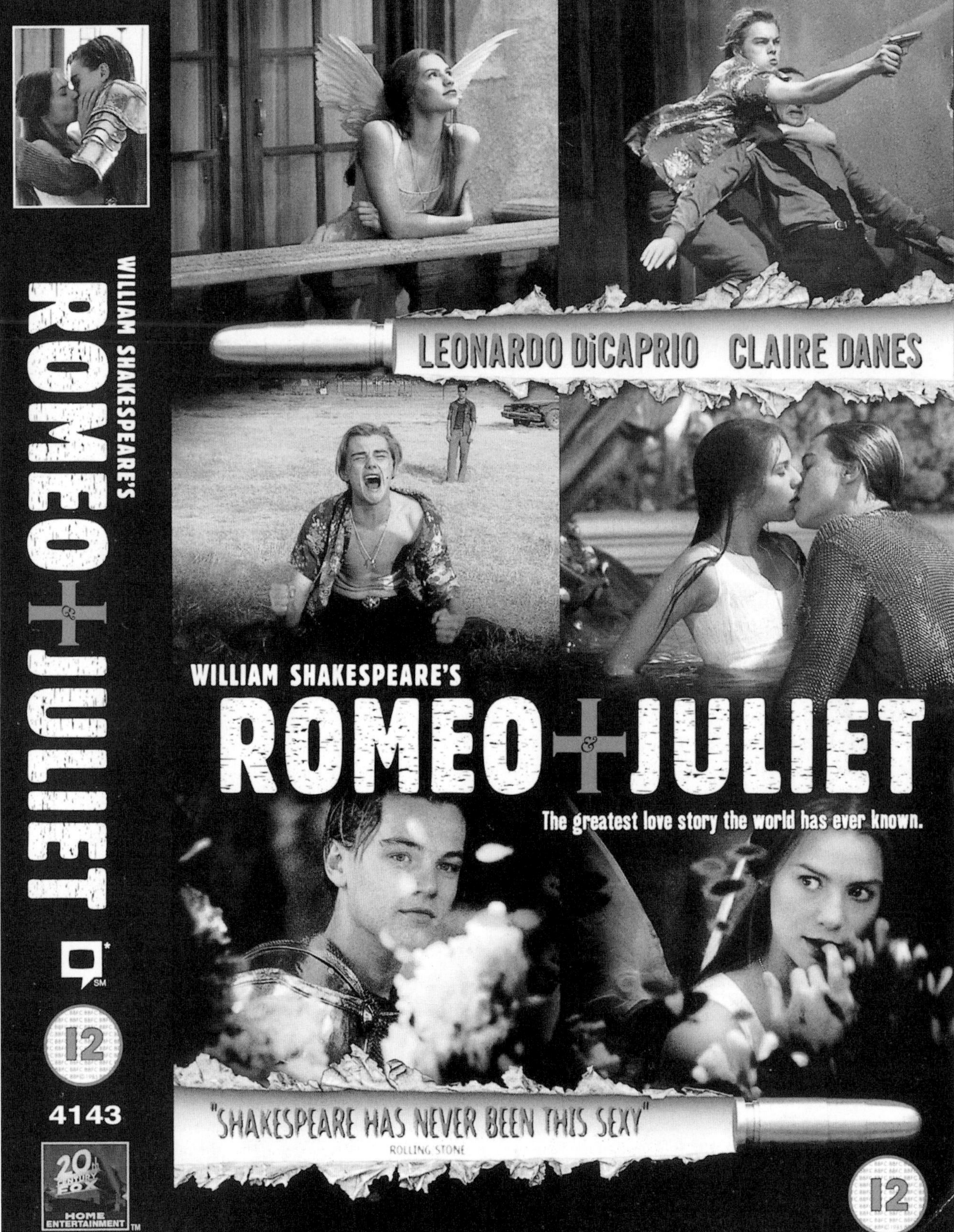

Packaging for the videotape of Baz Luhrmann's sensationally popular film *Romeo + Juliet* (1996): Shakespeare, allegedly, had never been this sexy.

Pleasure (1566–7), and was the source of a French version by Pierre Boaisteau, published in *Belleforest's *Histoires tragiques* (1559–82).

The French prose tale supplied the basis for Shakespeare's principal direct source, an English poem by Arthur *Brooke, *The Tragical History of Romeus and Juliet* (1562), which Shakespeare had already used when composing an earlier play with the same setting, *The Two Gentlemen of Verona.* (Brooke's preface refers to a now-lost English play on the same subject, but there is no evidence to suggest that Shakespeare knew this dramatic precedent.) Shakespeare follows Brooke's poem quite closely, retaining the emphasis on fate which Brooke had imitated from *Chaucer's *Troilus and Criseyde*, reusing some of Brooke's imagery, and denying the lovers the last interview in the tomb which they enjoy in most other versions of the story. Shakespeare, however, greatly develops some of the poem's minor characters—most spectacularly, Mercutio, the Nurse, and Tybalt—and fundamentally alters its perspective. Brooke's poem is mainly on the side of the lovers' parents, moralizing against 'dishonest desire' and disobedience: his Juliet, for example, is a 'wily wench' who takes pleasure in deceiving her mother into thinking she prefers Paris to Romeo, and the lovers' deaths are represented as righteous punishments for their own sins. As well as returning the story's principal sympathies to Romeo and Juliet, Shakespeare greatly compresses its action, to produce a fast-moving, tightly plotted play (punctuated by urgent references to the passage of time, and formally organized around the three successive interventions of the Prince at 1.1, 3.1, and 5.3) whose events take place over days rather than months. Within this controlled structure, Shakespeare produces some of his most exuberant poetry, for details of which he draws at times on other sources: these include Chaucer's *The Parliament of Fowls* for Mercutio's Queen Mab speech (1.4.53–94), a poem by Guillaume Du Bartas (1544–90) for the discussion of the nightingale and the lark in the 'aubade' scene (3.5.1–36), and *Daniel's *Complaint of Rosamond* (1592) for Romeo's description of Juliet's apparently dead body in the tomb (5.3.92–6).

Synopsis: Prologue: a Chorus outlines the story, requesting a patient hearing. **1.1** Servants of the Capulet family provoke a quarrel with their Montague counterparts, which, with the Capulet Tybalt's encouragement, develops into a full-scale brawl involving Capulet and Montague themselves, despite attempts by Benvolio, members of the Watch, and the wives of Capulet and Montague to restore order. The fighting is stilled by the arrival of the Prince, who threatens that if the feud breaks out once more Capulet and Montague will be executed. Left with Benvolio, Montague and his wife ask after their absent son Romeo, and employ Benvolio to investigate the cause of his solitary melancholy. Romeo reveals to Benvolio that he is suffering from unrequited love. **1.2** Capulet, bound to the peace, tells the Prince's kinsman Paris that if he can win his 13-year-old daughter Juliet's acceptance he may marry her. He invites Paris to a feast that night, and gives a list of the other intended guests to his servant Peter. Alone, Peter admits he cannot read, and when Romeo and Benvolio arrive he seeks their help. Learning of Capulet's feast, Benvolio hopes to cure Romeo's melancholy by taking him there and showing that his beloved Rosaline has no monopoly on beauty. **1.3** Capulet's wife, much interrupted by the digressive Nurse, tells Juliet of Paris's suit: they are called to the feast. **1.4** Romeo, Benvolio, and their friend Mercutio have masks and torches ready for their uninvited arrival at the Capulets' feast. Romeo has dreamed the occasion will be fatal to him, but Mercutio ridicules this notion, attributing dreams to the fairy Queen Mab. **1.5** During the dancing at the feast, Romeo is captivated by Juliet's beauty, renouncing his infatuation with Rosaline. Despite his mask he is recognized by Tybalt, whom Capulet has to restrain from challenging him. Romeo accosts Juliet and begs a kiss, subsequently learning her identity from the Nurse before he and his friends depart. Juliet similarly learns his.

2.0 The Chorus speaks of the mutual love of Romeo and Juliet, which they will pursue despite the dangers posed by their parents' enmity. **2.1** Returning from the feast, Romeo doubles back, concealing himself despite the mocking summons of Benvolio and Mercutio. Hidden, he sees Juliet emerge onto her balcony: when she sighs his name, wishing he were not a Montague, he reveals himself, and in the lyrical conversation which follows they exchange vows of love. Juliet promises to send by nine the following morning to Romeo, who is to arrange their marriage. **2.2** Friar Laurence is gathering medicinal herbs early the following morning when Romeo tells him of the night's events: at first chiding Romeo for so quickly abandoning his passion for Rosaline, he agrees to marry him to Juliet in the hopes of ending the feud between Montagues and Capulets. **2.3** Benvolio and Mercutio at last meet Romeo, and Mercutio banters with him against love. The Nurse arrives with Peter, and after much mockery from Mercutio is able to speak privately with Romeo: Juliet is to come to Laurence's cell that afternoon, and Romeo will send a rope-ladder by which she may later admit him at her window to consummate their secret marriage. **2.4** The Nurse teases an impatient Juliet before passing on Romeo's message. **2.5** Friar Laurence warns Romeo against immoderate love before Juliet arrives to be married.

3.1 Benvolio and Mercutio are accosted by Tybalt, who wishes to challenge Romeo: when Romeo arrives, however, he refuses to be provoked to fight, to the disgust of Mercutio, who draws his own sword. As Romeo tries to part the combatants, Mercutio is mortally wounded by Tybalt: incensed, Romeo fights and kills Tybalt before fleeing, aghast at what he has done. The Montagues and Capulets gather, with the Prince, Mercutio's kinsman, who, learning what has happened from Benvolio, sentences Romeo to immediate banishment. **3.2** Juliet's eager anticipation of her wedding night is cut short by the Nurse, who brings the news of Tybalt's death and Romeo's banishment: moved by her grief, the Nurse promises to find Romeo and bring him despite everything. 3.3 Friar Laurence brings Romeo, hidden at his cell, the news of his sentence, to his inconsolable despair. The Nurse arrives, and has to prevent Romeo from stabbing himself: the Friar reproaches Romeo for his frenzy, telling him to go to Juliet as arranged but leave for Mantua before the setting of the watch. 3.4 Capulet agrees with his wife and Paris that Juliet shall marry Paris the following Thursday. 3.5 Early the following morning Romeo reluctantly parts from Juliet, descending from her window. Her mother brings Juliet the news that, to dispel the sorrow they attribute to Tybalt's death, she is to marry Paris: Capulet arrives and, angry at Juliet's refusal, threatens to disown her unless she agrees to the match. After her parents' departure, the Nurse advises Juliet to marry Paris. Juliet feigns to agree, but resolves that unless Friar Laurence can help her she will kill herself.

4.1 Paris is with Friar Laurence when Juliet arrives: after his departure, the Friar advises Juliet that she should pretend to agree to the marriage, but that on its eve she should take a drug which he will give her, which will make her seem dead for 24 hours. She will be laid in the Capulets' tomb, where Romeo, summoned from Mantua by letter, can await her waking before taking her back with him. 4.2 The Capulets and the Nurse are making preparations for Juliet's wedding to Paris, to which she, returning, pretends to consent. Capulet brings forward its date to the following day. 4.3 Left alone in her chamber that night, Juliet, despite her apprehension at the prospect of awakening in the tomb, takes the Friar's potion. 4.4 The Capulets' busy preparations on the wedding morning are laid aside when the Nurse finds Juliet apparently dead: in the midst of their grief Friar Laurence takes charge of funeral arrangements. Hired musicians, no longer needed, jest with Peter.

5.1 In Mantua Romeo has dreamed he died but was awakened by Juliet when his servant Balthasar brings the news that Juliet is dead: intending to return to Verona and kill himself, Romeo buys poison from a needy apothecary. 5.2 Friar Laurence learns that his colleague Friar John has been prevented by plague quarantine restrictions from delivering his explanatory letter to Romeo: he hurries towards the Capulets' tomb. 5.3 Paris is strewing flowers at the tomb and reciting an epitaph for Juliet when Romeo arrives, sending an apprehensive Balthasar away: Paris attempts to arrest Romeo and is killed in the fight that ensues, asking, as he dies, to be laid with Juliet. Romeo opens the tomb and brings Paris's body inside. He speaks to the apparently dead Juliet, bidding her a last farewell, drinks the poison, kisses her, and dies. Friar Laurence arrives as Juliet begins to awaken: frightened by the approach of the watch, he attempts to persuade her to fly with him and enter a nunnery, but she will not leave. She finds that Romeo has taken poison, but there is none left for her: hearing the watch approaching, she takes his dagger and stabs herself. The Watch, finding the bodies, summon the Prince, the Capulets, and the Montagues (though Lady Montague has just died, in grief at her son's exile) and arrest Balthasar and Friar Laurence, who are able to explain the whole story to the assembled families. The Prince regards the deaths of Romeo, Juliet, Paris, and Mercutio as the families' punishments for their feud and his own for failing to quell it. Montague and Capulet shake hands, promising to build statues of the dead lovers.

Artistic features: *Romeo and Juliet* is, among much else, Shakespeare's greatest dramatic contribution to the boom in love sonnets which swept literary London in the late 1580s and early 1590s. The play teems with sonnets including its Chorus speeches and, most famously, the first dialogue between Romeo and Juliet, 1.5.92–106. Mercutio aptly observes of the enamoured Romeo that 'Now is he for the numbers that Petrarch flowed in' (2.3.36–7), and the play's entire plot brilliantly reanimates the clichéd Petrarchan *oxymoron whereby the adored mistress is referred to as a 'beloved enemy' (cf. 1.5.116–17, 137–40). Like a Petrarchan sonnet, too, the entire play changes in mood at a key turning point, resembling a romantic comedy during its ebullient early scenes but modulating decisively into tragedy with the death of Mercutio in 3.1.

Critical history: By now the impact of *Romeo and Juliet* extends across most artistic media (particularly *ballet, *opera, and *film) and across most of the world. It was sufficiently well thought of, in some circles at least, for an Oxford divine, Nicholas *Richardson, to quote it in a sermon in 1620, though it was sometimes criticized over the next two centuries for an over-indulgence in punning and rhyming. Because of the citizen status of its protagonists and the generic blending of its construction—its hospitality to the Nurse's comic garrulity and Mercutio's bawdy wordplay as well as to Romeo's sense of fate and the Prince's moralizing—the play was less acceptable than the other tragedies to *neoclassical tastes during the Restoration, but was decisively restored to critical favour thereafter. Although John *Dryden reported a tradition that Shakespeare had once remarked that he had been obliged to kill Mercutio in the third act 'lest he would have been killed by him', Dr *Johnson, who regarded *Romeo and Juliet* as one of Shakespeare's best plays, rejected this story, praising the death of Mercutio as an integral part of the play's structure. *Romantic writers and artists across the English-speaking world and continental Europe, from *Coleridge to *Berlioz, regarded the play as an unqualified presentation of an ideal love too good for the corrupt world. It was only later in the 19th century that some commentators began to express misgivings that the play was not sufficiently tragic, its conclusion produced too much by malign coincidence rather than character, and from the time of F. S. *Boas onwards various attempts were made to prove the lovers as properly blameworthy as they are in Brooke's poem. Others, meanwhile, insisted that the play's main theme was really the feud rather than the relationship between the innocent Romeo and Juliet. Since the later 20th century, critical writing about *Romeo and Juliet,* while still interested in the question of its genre, has concentrated more heavily on the play's notions of *sexuality, on its account of Veronese society and family structure, and on its language.

Stage history: Although the early quartos attest to the play's popularity in the theatres, no specific performances of *Romeo and Juliet* are recorded before the Restoration. When it reappeared in 1662, with *Betterton as Mercutio, both its style and its fusion of the comic and the tragic were hopelessly out of fashion ('It is a play of itself the worst that ever I heard in my life', opined *Pepys), and it was subsequently rewritten by Sir James Howard, who gave it a happy ending (though the tragic ending was performed on alternate nights). Howard's version, sadly, does not survive, but it had in any case been set aside by the time *Romeo and Juliet* was supplanted by Thomas Otway's successful adaptation *The History and Fall of *Caius Marius* (1679). Otway returned to the play's earlier sources to have his Juliet (Lavinia) awaken before Romeo (Young Marius) has finished dying of the poison, and a final dialogue between the lovers was retained when *Romeo and Juliet* returned to the stage in the 1740s, first as Theophilus *Cibber's heavily Otway-based *Romeo and Juliet: A Tragedy, Revised and Altered from Shakespeare* (acted at the Haymarket from 1744 onwards and printed in 1748) and then in David *Garrick's adaptation of 1748. Garrick's version was closer to the original, though he increased Juliet's age to 18 and eliminated much of what he dismissed as 'jingle and quibble', cutting puns, simplifying diction, and rewriting rhyme as blank verse (shortening even Romeo and Juliet's sonnet on meeting at the feast). In 1750 he further removed Romeo's initial crush on Rosaline and added an elaborate funeral procession for Juliet. In one of the most famous theatrical rivalries of all time, Garrick's Romeo at *Drury Lane competed with Spranger *Barry's at *Covent Garden for twelve successive nights in 1750 (ending only when Susannah *Cibber, Covent Garden's Juliet, fell ill), and the play was rarely out of the repertory of either theatre thereafter, acted more often than any other Shakespeare play during the remainder of the 18th century.

Garrick ceased to play Romeo in 1760, considering himself too old for the part, and the youth and naivety of the role deterred many subsequent actor-managers from attempting it at all, though the many actresses who made successful debuts as Juliet were rarely in any hurry to forsake the role, easily one of the longest and most attractive in Shakespearian tragedy. J. P. *Kemble and Sarah *Siddons gave up the parts after 1789, passing them on to Charles *Kemble and Dorothea *Jordan (later succeeded by Fanny *Kemble): Edmund *Kean failed as Romeo in 1815, and two of the most successful Romeos of the ensuing decades were women, Priscilla Horton (1834) and Charlotte *Cushman (1845–6, 1855), whose production was the first to abandon Garrick's added dialogue in the tomb. (Lydia Kelly had played the role in New York in 1829: the last major female Romeo was Fay Templeton in 1875.) Henry *Irving failed to convince opposite Ellen *Terry in a scenically elaborate production in 1882, which was better received when William Terriss and Mary *Anderson took over the leads during Irving's absence in America in 1884. (Terry later excelled as the Nurse.) Since then the play has remained immensely popular despite the continuing difficulties leading actors have experienced with the lyrical but comparatively unreflective leading role: *Gielgud, for example, was criticized for relying on his voice at the expense of his body when he played Romeo at 20 in 1924, but returned to it repeatedly, in 1929, for *Oxford University Dramatic Society in 1932 (with Peggy *Ashcroft, and Edith *Evans as the Nurse), and finally at the New Theatre in 1935, playing Mercutio to Laurence *Olivier's Romeo (again with Ashcroft and Evans). During this record-breaking production, Gielgud and Olivier exchanged roles, Olivier finally more comfortable as Mercutio, although he would play Romeo again (disastrously) in America in 1940. Juliet, however, has been a success for actresses including Claire *Bloom (1952, 1956), Dorothy *Tutin (1958), and Judi *Dench (in *Zeffirelli's production, 1960). Directors, meanwhile, have increasingly shied away from Romeo's traditional tights and short tunic to set the play in *modern dress (sometimes glibly translating the feud as a recognizable, topical equivalent), particularly since the success of **West Side Story*. *MD*

On the screen: *Romeo and Juliet* has been more filmed than any other Shakespeare play except *Hamlet*, and in more languages (seven, at the last count): the earliest film (1902) was followed by a number of other silents including one from Italy (1911), the first to use Veronese locations, which anticipated later films in delivering both impressive spectacle and athletic sword-fights. George Cukor's 1936 sound version included Leslie Howard (Romeo), Norma Shearer (Juliet), Basil Rathbone (Tybalt), and John *Barrymore (Mercutio) among the cast, on a lavishly constructed set. Renato Castellani's colourful film (1954) aimed at a neo-realist style at the expense of dramatic impact.

Franco Zeffirelli's *Romeo and Juliet* (1968) caught the fashionable waves of the 1960s and, championing the sincere innocence of the young amid inflexible parental attitudes, was immensely attractive to an adolescent viewing public. Zeffirelli used young inexperienced actors, Olivia Hussey (Juliet) and Leonard Whiting (Romeo), giving the action its visual youthfulness but losing poetic weight in the lines. Notwithstanding some gratuitous sentimentality, the screen is filled with colour, atmospheric contrasts, and passionate energy.

Alvin Rakoff's production for BBC TV (1978), a disappointing opening to the BBC/Time Life complete plays, set out to make the closeness of the Capulet family a dominant motif, thereby challenging the youth-centred priorities of Zeffirelli's. Forbidden by the series' commitment to full texts to sacrifice long speeches in the interests of dramatic pace, this production compensates for the inadequacy of the young performers in its leads by its detailed and sensitive exploration of family relationships, projecting an unusual sympathy for the older generation (notably Michael *Hordern's Capulet). As such it strives intelligently to use the medium to dramatize feeling rather than athletic action.

Baz Luhrmann's 1996 *William Shakespeare's Romeo+Juliet*, commercially the most successful of all films based on Shakespeare, is both disturbing and clever in juxtaposing the controlled manipulation of the world as the mass media deliver it with the confused but essentially sacrificial love of the teenage Romeo (Leonardo DiCaprio) and Juliet (Claire Danes). The film presents, with the speed and energy of MTV, images which reflect a postmodern American society and environment choked with the obsolescent and the discarded, including a good deal of religious kitsch. Encapsulating the dislocated action within the ephemerality of television news presentations highlights the confusion between a world in which order has disintegrated and one which is presented as managed. Although the play's script is heavily cut and sometimes almost inaudible over the film's pop music soundtrack, this is a witty and compelling attempt to translate the story into the terms of contemporary culture and the play into those of contemporary popular cinema. *AD*

Recent major editions

T. J. B. Spencer (New Penguin, 1967); Brian Gibbons (Arden 2nd series, 1980); G. Blakemore Evans (New Cambridge, 1984); Jill Levenson (Oxford, 2000)

Some representative criticism

Everett, Barbara, *Romeo and Juliet*: The Nurse's Story', *Critical Quarterly*, 14 (1972)

Hunter, G. K., 'Shakespeare's Earliest Tragedies: *Titus Andronicus* and *Romeo and Juliet*', *Shakespeare Survey*, 27 (1974)

Kahn, Coppélia, 'Coming of Age in Verona', *Modern Language Studies*, 8 (1977–8)

Levenson, Jill, *Plays in Performance: Romeo and Juliet* (1987)

Levin, Harry, 'Form and Formality in *Romeo and Juliet*', *Shakespeare Quarterly*, 11 (1960)

Porter, Joseph, *Shakespeare's Mercutio: His History and Drama* (1988)

Slater, Ann Pasternak, 'Petrarchanism Come True in *Romeo and Juliet*', in W. Habicht, D. J. Palmer, and R. Pringle (eds.), *Images of Shakespeare* (1988)

Ross, Lord. He is one of Bolingbroke's followers in *Richard II*. William de Ros was the 7th Baron Ros (d. 1414). *AB*

Ross (Rosse), Thane of. He bids farewell to Lady Macduff, *Macbeth* 4.2, and has to break the news to Macduff that she and her children have been murdered, 4.3. *AB*

Rossi, Ernesto (1827–96), Italian actor who spent most of his career touring the world with his own company in a repertoire which included several Shakespearian roles. In 1876 he appeared at Drury Lane—in Italian—as Hamlet, Lear, Macbeth, and Romeo. In Joseph Knight's opinion Rossi was 'great as an executant rather than an interpreter'; his concept of a character was unintelligible or alien or both, but it was redeemed by a brilliant display of technical proficiency. His experiment of playing Lear in Italian with the rest of the cast acting in English (New York 1881, London 1882) was not a success. *RF*

Carlson, Marvin, *The Shakespeare of the Italians* (1987)

Rossill. See Russell.

Rossini, Gioachino Antonio. See opera.

Rothe, Hans (1894–1977), German dramatist, whose translation of Shakespeare's complete plays (1922 ff., rev. 1963–4) into a modern idiom and with textual rearrangements, though effective on the stage, was controversial (and banned during the Third Reich). In *Shakespeare als Provokation* (1961) Rothe justified it on the basis of *disintegrationist theories. *WH*

Rotherham, Thomas. Archbishop of York in *Richard III*, his lines (in 2.4) are given to the Cardinal in the Oxford edition. He is based on Thomas Rotherham (or Rotheram, sometimes known as Thomas Scot) (1423–1500), created Archbishop of York in 1480. *AB*

Roubiliac, Louis François (1705–62), French sculptor. In 1758 he was commissioned by David *Garrick to execute a free-standing statue of Shakespeare for a 'Temple' dedicated to the poet and dramatist on Garrick's estate at Hampton, Middlesex. The completed statue is an example of Roubiliac's mature baroque workmanship, in which both gesture and dress are infused with motion, bestowing grandeur upon the subject. The statue was bequeathed to the British Museum by Garrick in 1779 and now stands in the entrance lobby to the *British Library. *CT*

round (dance). See roundel.

roundel, a round dance; a common formation in country dancing and *brawls. Shakespeare associates the round dance with *fairies (*A Midsummer Night's Dream* 2.1.140, 2.2.1, 3.1.101; *The Merry Wives of Windsor* 5.5.61) and *witches (*Macbeth* 1.3.30–2). *JB*

Roussillon, Dowager Countess of. She is Bertram's mother and Helen's guardian in *All's Well That Ends Well*. *AB*

Rowe, Nicholas (1674–1718), poet, playwright, and later Poet Laureate. The most successful dramatist of his age, Rowe was also the first editor of Shakespeare. His six-volume edition, published in 1709 by Jacob Tonson, was based largely on the 1685 Fourth *Folio. Rowe's edition focuses on issues related to performance of the plays rather than on textual problems. He modernized spelling and punctuation and divided the plays into acts and scenes which he numbered. His edition also regularized the entrances and exits of characters and attached a dramatis personae to each play for the first time. The edition included a preface, 'Some Account of the Life, &c of Mr. William Shakespeare', the first attempt at a biography of Shakespeare. Rowe later wrote *The Tragedy of Jane Shore* (1714), one of his most popular plays, 'in imitation of Shakespeare's style', a claim which his contemporaries ridiculed. *JM*

Rowington, a village some 12 miles (19 km) north of Stratford from which Shakespeare's family may have originated; 'More Shakespeares lived in Rowington in the sixteenth century than in any other Warwickshire parish' (Mark Eccles, *Shakespeare in Warwickshire*, 1961). *SW*

Rowley, Samuel (?1575–?1624), actor and dramatist with the Admiral's Men, possibly the brother of William, also a dramatist. Samuel revised Marlowe's *Doctor Faustus* (1601–2) and may have written the comic scenes. His most famous work, a history play about Henry VIII called *When You See Me, You Know Me*, was published in 1605 and reprinted in 1613. Shakespeare may have been inspired to 'correct' Rowley's view of Henry VIII (which took many liberties with chronicle history) through his own play, *All Is True*, first performed in 1613. Where Rowley's play featured much clowning, the prologue to *All Is True* warns the audience that it will not see 'a merry bawdy play'. Only a few details of Henry VIII's character suggest any further connection between the two plays. *JKS*

Rowley, William (*c*.1585–1626), comic actor and playwright. Rowley collaborated with many leading Jacobean playwrights, most notably Thomas *Middleton: he wrote the sub-plot for Middleton's masterpiece *The Changeling* (1653). *The *Birth of Merlin* (1622) was published as by Shakespeare and Rowley, and some think Rowley had a hand in Shakespeare's *Pericles.* *RM*

Rowse, A(lfred) L(eslie) (1903–97), Cornish historian, literary scholar, and autobiographer. Rowse's prodigious gifts are seen in a series of vivid historical and literary studies, many focusing upon the social, biographical, and personal aspects of Shakespeare's career, such as *William Shakespeare* (1963) and *Shakespeare's Southampton* (1965). In 1973 (in *Shakespeare's Sonnets* and *Shakespeare the Man*) he conjecturally (but dogmatically) identified Emilia Bassano-*Lanier as the *Dark Lady' of the Sonnets. Rowse was prolific, popularizing, and polemical; his blazon might well have figured a historian rampant above a venal, supine, and sentimental literary establishment. *TM*

Roxana title page. An engraved vignette on the title page of the second edition of William Alabaster's play *Roxana* (1632) shows a small, tapered stage backed by curtains and fronted by a rail. This has been thought a useful representation of an indoor playhouse, but the engraver, John Payne, is now known to have merely copied parts of other pictures and hence the engraving is of little direct value to theatre history. *GE*

Astington, John H., 'The Origins of the *Roxana* and *Messalina* Illustrations', *Shakespeare Survey*, 43 (1990)

Royal Shakespeare Company. What is now undoubtedly the most productive and significant Shakespeare theatre company in the world was created in 1961 by Peter (now Sir Peter) *Hall from the former *Shakespeare Memorial Theatre company in Stratford-upon-Avon. Hall's principal innovations were to acquire public (Arts Council) funding and a London base (the Aldwych theatre) for what had previously been only a Stratford summer festival company, thus allowing actors to be offered longer contracts and the company's work to be seen in the capital.

From that initial two-base, two-theatre operation, the RSC's pattern of work has developed into a complex enterprise involving many playing spaces and locations. In 1974 a studio theatre, the Other Place, opened in Stratford in a large shed that had formerly been a rehearsal room; initially largely for experimental productions, it soon became a central part of the company's work, presenting innovative interpretations of Shakespeare as well as productions of new plays; a transfer theatre in London, the Warehouse, soon followed. In 1982 the company moved into its purpose-built London home, the *Barbican theatre, with a main auditorium to take productions from the Royal Shakespeare Theatre and the Pit to take work from the Other Place. In 1986 a third theatre opened in Stratford, the Swan, created from what remained of the original 1879 Memorial Theatre after the fire of 1926, and offering a thrust-stage playing space in a 430-seat auditorium. No equivalent London transfer house yet exists for Swan productions, which are either scaled up to the Barbican main stage, or down to the Pit, or on occasions presented in other London theatres rented for the purpose. At the same time as its playing spaces have increased, the RSC has developed a policy of 'residencies' beyond Stratford and London. Since 1977 it has presented its entire Stratford season of work in three theatres in Newcastle-upon-Tyne, and since 1997 there has been a similar residency in Plymouth. A biennial residency in New York, offering part of the previous season's repertoire, has been developed since 1998. In addition to these regular repertoire residencies, many successful individual productions have been toured, nationally and internationally, following the repertoire seasons of which they were a part, and since the 1970s the company has sent out what have become annual regional tours, of Shakespeare and other work, to play locations without permanent theatres (and thus taking audience seating, as well as sets and costumes, with them). More recently, a series of large-scale single touring productions have been mounted, partly as vehicles for well-known actors to take on major Shakespeare roles on shorter contracts than commitment to a full Stratford/London repertoire season requires.

The length and range of that main repertoire season have varied over the years, with a major change in 1996 that reduced the Stratford season from ten months to seven and the London season from twelve to six, while adding the Plymouth residency. Typically the present main season will involve some 70 to 80 actors, most of them taking three roles and very few of them less than two, putting on ten or eleven productions in Stratford (four at the Royal Shakespeare Theatre, three or four at the Swan, three at the Other Place), of which about half will be Shakespeare, which then move to Newcastle, to London, to Plymouth, and perhaps finally to New York, the whole operation (from the start of rehearsals) lasting some eighteen to 20 months. Most productions are directed by freelance visiting directors, though beyond its artistic director the RSC has normally retained a small number of associate directors. Directors enjoy a high degree of autonomy, controlling their own production budgets and appointing their own designers, composers, lighting designers, fight directors, and any other specialists they may require; casting, however, normally requires some degree of collaboration with other directors, since a whole season of plays is being cast from the same company of actors.

Although a number of the RSC's distinguished former actors are listed as 'Associate Artists', this is an honorific title: there is no permanent company of the kind that one finds in some other European theatres, however much that may have been part of Hall's initial concept. Its longest contracts (for the Stratford/London season) are for eighteen months, and the fact that the beginning of one season overlaps by several months the end of its predecessor means that continuous employment with the company is impossible. Nevertheless, many actors return, often frequently, as do directors and designers, so that a loose, long-term continuity has developed. The RSC is the highest employer of actors in Britain and the fact that nearly all the sets, costumes, and properties for its large annual tally of productions are made in-house means that it also maintains a large staff of other theatre professionals.

The RSC is controlled by its artistic director who reports to a board of governors. Artistic directors since the creation of the company have been Peter Hall (1960–8), Trevor *Nunn (1968–78), Trevor Nunn and Terry *Hands (1978–86), Terry Hands (1986–91), and Adrian *Noble (1991–). Apart from its own box office (and it normally plays to something like 80% capacity in Stratford), the company is financed by a major annual grant from the Arts Council and, increasingly, from business sponsorship, whence it has achieved substantial recent funding agreements.

From a near 40-year history productions of major artistic significance are too numerous to list. They range from small-scale studio work such as Trevor Nunn's Other Place *Macbeth* in 1976, to epic main-stage productions of the history cycles, including Peter Hall's and John *Barton's seven-play version (the three parts of *Henry VI* reduced to two) in 1963–4 and the unprecedented 2000–1 enterprise of staging all eight plays of the two tetralogies across all the company's playing spaces, with two companies of actors and four directors. Beyond Shakespeare there have been major achievements with other Elizabethan and Jacobean playwrights (notably Ben *Jonson at the Swan), with Chekhov, with *Ibsen, with adaptations from other genres (such as *Nicholas Nickleby* and *Les Misérables*), and with new writing. But the company's ultimate commitment is to the exploration, and re-exploration, of Shakespeare; it enters the new millennium with plans for significant redevelopment of its Stratford playing spaces in continued pursuit of that central mission. *RLS*

Beauman, Sally, *The Royal Shakespeare Company: A History of Ten Decades* (1982)
Players of Shakespeare: Essays in Shakespearian Performance by Players with the Royal

Shakespeare Company, vol. i, ed. Philip Brockbank; vols. ii and iii, ed. Russell Jackson and Robert Smallwood; vol. iv, ed. Robert Smallwood (1985, 1988, 1993, 1998)

Royal Shakespeare Theatre, Stratford-upon-Avon, still sometimes known as the Shakespeare Memorial Theatre, the 1,300-seat proscenium-arch theatre (designed by Elisabeth Scott) which opened in 1932 (replacing the 1879 Memorial Theatre, gutted by fire in 1926), and which remains—despite perennial grumblings about acoustics and the gulf that separates the upper balcony from the stage—the home venue of the Royal Shakespeare Company. *MD*

RSC Collection and Gallery, Stratford-upon-Avon. A gallery containing portraits of celebrated performers and directors of Shakespearian drama, portraits of Shakespeare, and art depicting Shakespearian themes was opened in 1881. The collection was intended as the companion to the first *Shakespeare Memorial Theatre, opened in 1879: it survived the fire which gutted the theatre in 1926, and continues to flourish in its shell. The collection includes the celebrated *'Flower' portrait. *CT*

Rugby, John. He is Caius' servant in *The Merry Wives of Windsor*. *AB*

Ruggiero (Rogero). The second gentleman who has news of 'Nothing but bonfires' in *The Winter's Tale* is named Ruggiero, 5.2.21. *AB*

Rumour speaks the Induction to *2 Henry IV*. *AB*

Russell (Rossill) is one of *Oldcastle's companions in *1 Henry IV*. His name seems to have been changed to Peto at the same time as Oldcastle's name was changed to Falstaff, and Harvey's to Bardolph, probably for fear of offending the earls of Bedford, whose surname was Russell, and Sir William Harvey, who was about to marry the dowager Countess of Southampton. *AB*

Russell, Thomas (1570–1634), landowner. Shakespeare appointed him overseer of his *will, and left him £5. A prosperous man, he was the son of Sir Thomas, a Warwickshire member of Parliament, from whom he inherited property in the Stratford area; he studied at Queen's College, Oxford. He married as his second wife Anne Digges, widow of an eminent mathematician, one of whose sons, Leonard *Digges, was to write poems in praise of Shakespeare. *SW*

Hotson, L., *I, William Shakespeare do appoint Thomas Russell, esq.* (1937)

Russia and the former Soviet Union. Preceded by many other English writers, Shakespeare arrived late in Russia, giving little indication of the vast ocean of future commentary. His popularity and reputation in the Russian empire and its heir, the USSR, depended as much on politics and ideology as on literary fashion, and derived primarily from Shakespeare as tragedian. Often tamed, at times silenced, at others loudly appreciated, Shakespeare offers a window onto Russian culture and its love–hate relationship with the West.

Elizabeth I entertained numerous envoys from Ivan the Terrible, who, although still married to his seventh wife, pursued matrimonial, as well as commercial, alliances at the English court. Shakespeare's mockery of the Muscovites in *Love's Labour's Lost* may have glanced at Ivan's erratic and sometimes inept diplomacy. Practically minded, the Tsar and his immediate successors evinced little interest in English theatre or culture.

Alexander Sumarokov, the first translator of the 'inspired barbarian', is also notably the 'father' of Russian drama, suggesting a link between the creation of a native Russian theatre and interest in Shakespeare. Initiating a two-centuries-long tradition of working from French or German rather than English sources, Sumarokov followed P. A. de La Place, 'regularizing' and transforming *Hamlet* into moralistic discourses, and making Polonius the arch-villain who murders King Hamlet, and plots to kill Gertrude and marry Claudius to Ophelia (1748). The German-born and educated *Catherine II, a correspondent of Diderot and *Voltaire, adapted *The Merry Wives of Windsor*, in which Falstaff becomes 'Polkadov'—a Frenchified Russian entirely innocent of the rhetorical acrobatics of his Shakespearian ancestor—and remade *Timon of Athens* into the moralized *Spendthrift* (1786). Her support for Shakespeare did not extend to Nikolai Karamzin's *Julius Caesar* (1787), which she confiscated and banned; the play was not performed until 1897. Karamzin, Shakespeare's only champion in the 18th century, followed French dramatic practice and criticism but used 'the poet of nature' to argue for a break from their literary strictures. Particularly fond of Shakespeare's 'sweet melancholy' and of his knowledge of the human heart, Karamzin detested the comedies.

Although derivative in nature, 18th- and early 19th-century Russian periodicals were central to dissemination of knowledge about Shakespeare. The most frequently cited British journal was the *Spectator* (translated from the German, itself translated from the French) and, later, the *Edinburgh Review*. However, neither these periodicals nor the visit of an English company of actors (1772) dispelled still-widespread ignorance of Shakespeare. Thus, one translator hazarded that Hamlet or 'Othellon' was the name of a Latin writer.

The early 19th century, still taken with *neoclassicism and sentimentality, did not find Shakespeare congenial. Translations in this period included the work of Ivan Veliaminov (*Othello*, 1808) and Nikolai Gnedich (*King Lear*, 1838), both indebted to Jean-François Ducis, the most influential playwright in Russia. An admirer of the English 'Graveyard School', Stepan Viskovatov presented his versified Hamlet as a frequenter of tombs and ruins (1810). Although the first more-or-less faithful translation appeared in 1828 (Mikhail Vronchenko's *Hamlet*), the common practice of working from adaptations and translations prevailed, as indicated by the title page of Aleksander Rotchev's *Macbeth: A Tragedy of Shakespeare from the Works of Schiller* (1830).

The *Romantic movement and the growth of a native Russian theatre (1830s–1840s) mark a high period of Anglomania and the zenith of Shakespeare's popularity in tragedy. Nikolai Polevoi's *Hamlet* (1838) with Pavel Mochalov resulted in the first stage successes. Polevoi followed *Goethe's view of the Prince, changing and adding lines to make him appear weaker; hence his most famous line, 'Afraid, I am afraid of man!' Polevoi–Mochalov's emotional, melancholy Hamlet set the trend for subsequent Hamlets. *Othello* and *King Lear*, played as romantic melodramas, also entered the Russian repertoire; *Macbeth*, because of its regicide, was banned, while Shakespeare's comedies, in spite of the efforts of the great comic actor Mikhail Shchepkin, remained unappreciated.

Throughout the 1840s many more translations appeared, including Nikolai Ketcher's grand project, the complete plays in prose, sparking a continuing debate about prose/verse translations. The fashion for Shakespeare was manifested both in published excerpts from the criticism of *Pope, *Johnson, *Hazlitt, and Mrs *Jameson, and in the ardour of amateur companies. In 1847, at the strict theological seminar in St Petersburg, *Hamlet* was secretly performed at midnight in costumes constructed from notebooks. Touring companies took Shakespeare to the 'provinces', penetrating even Siberia. Serfs presented simplified versions of *Hamlet* for their masters, and the Prince entered popular speech as a coward in the phrase 'quaking Hamlet'.

The first poet to be deeply influenced by Shakespeare's style was Alexander *Pushkin (1799–1837). Impressed by his individualized characters, psychological insight, and the diversity of his dramatic invention, Pushkin referred to Shakespeare as Russia's 'father', yet also believed in a 'natural' Bard who wrote *Hamlet* without any dramatic theory. Pushkin's historical dramas, *Boris Godunov* in particular, for the first time infused Russian drama with a Shakespearian spirit. Other 19th-century writers influenced by Shakespeare or who drew on Shakespearian subject matter included Mikhail Lermontov, Nikolai Nekrasov, Alexander Ostrovsky, Afanasii Fet, and Nikolai Leskov.

'Enslaved by the drama of Shakespeare', the unrivalled 'tsar of poets', the influential literary critic Vissarion Belinsky (1812–48) frequently referred to Shakespeare in his essays, the most famous of which, on *Hamlet*, was inspired by Mochalov's performance. Echoing Goethe's Romantic interpretation and adulation, Belinsky's Bard 'understood heaven, earth, and hell' but was, nonetheless, an 'ignoramus', nescient of the meaning of his own plays. In the second half of the century, thanks especially to Ivan *Turgenev, Hamlet was transformed into an introspective, 'superfluous man'. Confirming his assertion that Shakespeare was 'engrafted' into Russian 'flesh and blood', Turgenev wrote prose tales on Shakespearian themes ('A Hamlet of Shchigrov District', 'The Diary of a Superfluous Man', 'A King Lear of the Steppes'). In his essay 'Hamlet and Don Quixote' (1860), he proposed that these characters embodied human nature's basic peculiarities: the first, a useless egoist; the second, an idealist. Although challenged by Ivan Goncharov, Turgenev's view held. In Dostoevsky, Hamlet is associated with 'rodent types', while in Chekhov 'hamletism' is a mere pose.

With the turn to realism, Shakespeare lost his prominence except for touring foreign actors. The black American Ira *Aldridge travelled widely throughout the empire. Later significant visitors included Ernesto *Rossi, Eleanore Duse, Sarah *Bernhardt, and Tommaso *Salvini.

Amid the 1860s–1870s' heated polemics between 'Slavophiles' and 'Westernizers', translations were compiled into the first collected works (Nikolai Nekrasov and Nikolai Gerbel). Shakespearian subjects began to animate music (M. A. Balakirev, Pyotr *Tchaikovsky) and visual art (I. Repnin, T. Shevchenko, I. N. Kramskii, M. Antokol'skii). The first staging of *The Taming of the Shrew* succeeded so well that it became a staple of the Russian comic repertoire. In the 1870s, Nikolai Storozhenko delivered the first university lectures on Shakespeare. *King Lear*, *The Tempest* and *The Winter's Tale* were reworked for children; the Russian Shakespeare Society (1873) and the first Shakespearian literary circles were founded (1875). By 1880, when Gerbel translated the Sonnets and narrative poems, all of Shakespeare was available. During this period of harsh censorship, interest in Shakespeare seriously declined but did not disappear, remaining even in odd places, such as Sunday school groups, and readings given to prisoners in Siberia. By the 1890s, in comparison with the modern Sardou, Shakespeare was dismissed by some as 'antique' and a 'fetish of scholars and lovers of the exotic'.

Political Shakespeare was not unknown, especially in the 'provinces'. In Ukraine, all performances and translations of Shakespeare into Ukrainian were banned by strict ukases (1863, 1876, 1881), thus turning Shakespeare into samizdat literature well before the Soviet period. At the turn of the century, after tumultuous applause greeted the assassination of Julius Caesar in a Russian production in Kiev, speakers in the Duma pressed for a repertoire which showed how to die for the Tsar, not how to kill him.

The most famous of Shakespeare's detractors was Leo *Tolstoy. His 'Shakespeare and the Drama' (1906), with its roots in Belinsky and Voltaire, reviled Shakespeare for the immorality of his tolerance; his inability to create characters; the uniformity and pomposity of his language; his scorn of the common people; and the arbitrariness of his plots.

At century's end, Alexander Lensky staged *The Tempest* and Konstantin *Stanislavsky, inspired by *Salvini, *Othello*. The most famous production, *Hamlet* (1912), was the result of Stanislavsky's respectful but difficult partnership with Gordon *Craig. Disappointed with its realistic incursions, and especially with the too-'Tolstoyan' Kachalov (Hamlet), Craig was also shocked that no one thought to consult an English text.

Although eclipsed during the First World War, revolutions, and civil war, Shakespeare's reputation was nonetheless well established before the creation of the USSR (1922). His characters and themes inspired writers as varied as Alexander Blok, Anna Akhmatova, Marina Tsvetaeva, Lesia Ukrainka, and Maxim Ryl's'kyi. However, throughout the 1920s, the place of the classics in the new Soviet order became much debated. When great Soviet playwrights failed to appear, Shakespeare was pressed into service. The absence of strict censorship coupled with a pluralism of artistic approaches created few, but nonetheless some of the most interesting, productions of the whole Soviet period. Among these is Les' (Oleksandr) Kurbas's *Macbeth* (1924, Kharkiv), an austere cubist-expressionist production with elements of Grand Guignol and pre-Brechtian alienation techniques.

As official control grew, so did the focus on class issues. The struggle between the declining aristocracy and rising bourgeoisie was found even in *As You Like It*, while (long before the view became a cliché of *new historicism) *The Tempest* was regarded as a blueprint for racial colonial domination. Low characters became spokesmen for the proletariat, and masses were indiscriminately added, including even to the tomb scene of *Romeo and Juliet*. Echoing Tolstoy, Vladimir Friche argued that Shakespeare's dislike of the common people meant that he was really the aristocratic Earl of *Rutland.

With Stalin's rise to power, academic theatres resumed their pre-revolutionary repertoire and methods. In 1934, the first All-Union Congress of Soviet Writers codified socialist realism as the basic method of Soviet literature and literary criticism, and ensured the continuity of an ethical-social approach to literature. Frequently referred to before and necessarily after 1934, *Marx and Engels, originators of the notion of Shakespeare as humanist and realist, became the touchstone of all Soviet criticism. Particular currency was given to Marx's analysis of capital in *Timon of Athens*, and to his letter to Ferdinand Lassalle (1859), urging him to 'Shakespearize', to individualize characters and provide them with a 'Falstaffian background'—a wide social panorama. Engels's preference for *The Merry Wives of Windsor*, 'worth a hundred German comedies', led to its special place in the Soviet repertoire.

No longer possible were productions such as Nikolai Akimov's zany *Hamlet* (music by Shostakovich, 1932), in which Ophelia was a drunken society girl and Hamlet a throne-grabber who pretends to be a ghost; or Sergei Radlov's moving *King Lear* (1934) at the State Jewish Theatre, starring Solomon Mikhoels. Unrelenting emphasis on realism created difficulties for an appreciation of some aspects of Shakespeare's work. *Après* Lytton Strachey, Alexander Smirnov attacked the 'feeble' romances, but otherwise argued that the humanist Shakespeare wrote classless, universal dramas.

Although marked by constant tension between communist ideology, imposed from above, and the actual interpretation of Shakespeare, many scholars and theatre artists kept a Russian Shakespeare alive, some through creative manipulation, others through capitulation. Aleksei Popov harnessed love to the progress of socialism (*The Taming of the Shrew*, 1938), while Sergei Radlov produced Stalin's favourite play, *Othello* (1935), in his preferred style: grandiose sets, folk songs, ballet-divertissements, and, at the centre, a hero who reminded Stalin of himself: rude of speech, an outsider, soldier, and erstwhile nomad.

On the eve of the Second World War, harsh criticism of the West reached a high pitch. Oleksandr Bilets'kyi attacked Freudian Shakespeare, while others (conveniently forgetting Friche) reprimanded anti-Stratfordian heretics. Stalin's offhand remark questioning the appropriateness of *Hamlet* at the Moscow Arts Theatre (1941) was enough to take it off the boards indefinitely. During the war, Shakespeare was, with some exceptions, squeezed out by nationalistic-propagandist Russian plays.

Some, like Boris *Pasternak, escaped into the spiritual sustenance of translation. Regarding Shakespeare as a 'child of nature', Pasternak approached translation like his forebears, as an 'original piece of dramatic writing'. His Hamlet, a self-sacrificing hero with little mockery, irony, or cynicism, speaks idiomatic, poetic Russian (1941). Introduced to the world by way of Grigori *Kozintsev's 1964 film, Pasternak's became the preferred stage version. His translation of two, and Samuil Marshak's complete, sonnets finally brought Shakespeare the poet to Russian attention and appreciation.

After the war, Stalin purged many Western sympathizers and mobilized writers to propagate ideas of Soviet supremacy. Shakespeare was tentatively offered as a friendly link between Russia and the West by the eminent and prolific scholar Mikhail Morozov, but virulent attacks on his 'primitive formalism' and his 'imitation' of Anglo-American methodology forced him into all-out attack on the West: although the Americans used Shakespeare as a 'subterfuge' to justify the 'subjugation of other people', the 'democratic' Shakespeare, finding his 'second fatherland' in the USSR, would awaken the masses from their sleep and liberate them from capitalism. Stalin's death (1953), however, initiated the 'Thaw' in literary policy and sparked *Hamlet* fever. The Prince, a 'titan of conscience', now became a 'brother-in-arms' in efforts to liquidate vestiges of Stalinism. Aleksandr Anikst and Israel Wertzman attacked the uncertain logic of violence and exposed the ordinariness of evil in the play. Alexander Parfenov argued that Shakespeare, a symbol of human culture, needed to be defended from the dictates of uncultured men in power. The state explicitly appropriated the Bard at the fourth centenary of his birth, permitting a plethora of books, articles, and festivities, and calling scholars and writers to the grand task of mastering the Shakespearian heritage and bringing it to the masses.

The late 1970s and 1980s drifted towards literary détente. Six issues were published of the Russian *Shakespeare Survey*, and all-Union festivals continued in Yerevan (Armenia). Emboldened, some directors probed danger zones. A rock version of *Romeo and Juliet* was produced outside Moscow, while at the small Taganka theatre in the city, Yuri Liubimov staged *Hamlet* in a metaphorical gulag starring poet/singer/songwriter Vladimir Vysots'kii.

What was possible in Moscow, however, was political in the satellite republics. The Georgian Mitsishvili's fears, voiced at the 1934 Congress, about the danger of minor literatures becoming only a pale copy of Russian proved—with few exceptions—to be prophetic. Despite the skill and efforts of such actors as the Georgian Veriko Andzhapardzhe or Akakyi Khorava, palsied banality descended on many of the republics' national theatres. Translated into 28 languages of the USSR, Shakespeare became a symbol of cross-cultural interests and a unifying—but also homogenizing—element of a vast Soviet readership: directives for the dominant style of production, translation, and interpretation came from Moscow. Still, the republics produced notable poets, who drew on Shakespearian themes, characters, and situations, taking inspiration and comfort from them. Thus, Lina Kostenko's 'only answer' to Soviet reality was 'to be!'

Appropriated by various sides of the ideological and aesthetic spectrum over the last 200 years, Shakespeare remains an inexhaustible, malleable source of creative activity, from theatre, opera, ballet, musical compositions, to poetic reinterpretation. Nor has the fall of the USSR altered that state of affairs. In the early 1990s, theatres in Kiev scurried to stage *Macbeth*, still one of the best glosses on the previous 70 years of the country's history. *IM*

Alekseev, M. P. (ed.), *Shekspir i russkaia kul'tura* (1965)
Makaryk, I. R., 'Soviet Views of Shakespeare's Comedies', *Shakespeare Studies*, 15 (1982)
Morozov, Mikhail M., *Shakespeare on the Soviet Stage*, trans. David Magarshack (1939: 1947)
Rowe, Eleanor, *Hamlet: A Window on Russia* (1976)

Rutland, Earl of. Third son of Richard Duke of York, he is slain by Clifford, *Richard Duke of York* (*3 Henry* VI) 1.3, despite the young man's pleading. He is based on Edmund, Earl of Rutland (1443–60). *AB*

Rutland, Francis Manners, 6th Earl of (1578–1632). See IMPRESA.

Rutland's Tutor. Unable to save his charge he is dragged away, *Richard Duke of York* (*3 Henry* VI) 1.3. *AB*

Rutland theory, a minor sub-heresy of the *Authorship Controversy which claims that Shakespeare's works were really composed by Roger Manners, 5th Earl of Rutland (d. 1612). The theory was first expounded by Peter Alvor in Germany in 1906, and attracted a few adherents on the Continent thereafter, but was most memorably developed by the American Claud W. Sykes in *Alias William Shakespeare?* (1947), in which Rutland is exposed as the real author by Sherlock Holmes. Less eccentric detectives have been deterred from this conclusion by the absence of evidence that Rutland composed anything whatsoever. *MD*

Rylance, Mark. See GLOBE RECONSTRUCTIONS.

Rylands, George (Dadie) (1902–99). Fellow of King's College, Cambridge. An advocate of clear verse speaking, he exerted an immense influence as teacher, actor, producer, and director with the university's *Marlowe Society, through which he brought *Love's Labour's Lost*, *Troilus and Cressida*, and the Henry VI plays to new prominence. He directed *Gielgud and *Ashcroft in *Hamlet* (1944), compiled the anthology *The Ages of Man*, and directed the first audio *recording of the entire canon. He inspired many leading theatre practitioners including John *Barton, Trevor *Nunn, Derek *Jacobi, and Ian *McKellen. *PME*

Rymer, Thomas (1641–1713), a historian and failed dramatist who wrote two treatises condemning English tragedy. In *A Short View of Tragedy* (1693), he famously attacks *Othello* as a 'bloody Farce', and suggests it should be retitled 'the Tragedy of the Handkerchief'. Rymer was subsequently vilified for his comments. *JM*

Rysbrack, John Michael (1694–1770), English sculptor of Dutch origin, who worked with *Scheemakers on the Temple of British Worthies at Stowe (which includes a bust of Shakespeare) in the 1730s. In 1758 he was commissioned by James West to produce an independent bust of Shakespeare: also called the 'Davenant' bust (now in Birmingham City Art Gallery), this much-reproduced piece of baroque statuary was executed in marble and depicts the subject in anachronistic Van Dyck dress. *CT*

sackbut, ancestor of the modern slide trombone, with less of a flared bell and a gentler sound. Often played in ensemble with *cornets. *JB*

Sadler, Hamnet (d. 1624) and **Judith** (d. 1614), friends of Shakespeare, probably the godparents of his twins, who bore the same names; the Sadlers, married before 1580, had fourteen children, seven of whom died young. They named a son William in 1597/8. Hamnet was a baker, with a shop at the corner of High Street and Sheep Street. He rebuilt it after it burned down in the fire of 1595, but had a succession of financial difficulties. His nephew Ralph (or Rafe) Smith was accused of misconduct with Susanna Hall (see SHAKESPEARE, SUSANNA), Shakespeare's daughter, in 1613. He sold his business and the lease of his house after his wife died in the following year. In 1616 he witnessed Shakespeare's *will, by which he received 26*s.* 8*d.* to buy a mourning ring. His name, Hamnet, also appears as Hamlet. *SW*

Sadler's Wells, theatre in Islington, north London. A wooden building for musical entertainment existed from 1683 close to the Wells which were the source of Mr Sadler's mineral waters. A stone theatre, erected in 1765, mounted spectacular and acrobatic shows; the great clown Joseph Grimaldi appeared in its pantomimes. For eighteen years from 1844 the actor-manager Samuel *Phelps presented 116 plays including (a record long unbroken) 31 of Shakespeare's. Less accomplished stock companies followed. Their history is recalled in Arthur Wing Pinero's sentimental comedy *Trelawney of 'The Wells'* (1898). The theatre, long in decline, was acquired by Lilian Baylis and rebuilt in 1931 as an outreach venture for the *Old Vic's seasons of Shakespeare, opera, and ballet. Her three Vic-Wells companies alternated between Islington and Lambeth—an awkward arrangement discontinued in 1937. After wartime exile on tour and in the West End, the drama company returned to the Old Vic. Sadler's Wells, totally remodelled with Lottery funds in 1998, became a receiving theatre for dance and opera. *MJ*

Arundell, Dennis, *The Story of Sadler's Wells, 1683–1977* (1978)

Sagarra, Josep Maria de (1894–1961), Catalan writer and translator of Shakespeare. He began his translations after the Spanish Civil War with the support of Barcelona patrons, and, with the surprising exception of *Hamlet*, managed to render 27 Shakespearian plays into his language. His are verse translations (in hendecasyllabic lines) and, despite stylistic limitations and the publication of the new Shakespearian versions by Salvador *Oliva, they have worn well. *ALP*

St Albans, Mayor of. See MAYOR OF ST ALBANS.

St Mary Overies. St Mary over the River is now known as the Cathedral Church of St Saviour and St Mary Overies, *Southwark. The original church was founded *c.*1106 although it is thought that it may have had a Saxon precursor. The cathedral church, parish church to *Bankside, contains monuments to (amongst others) John *Gower, John *Fletcher, Philip *Massinger, and Edmund *Shakespeare. *RSB*

Carlin, M., *Medieval Southwark* (1996)
Cherry, B., and Pevsner, N., *The Buildings of England. London 2: South* (1990)
Anon., *Southwark Cathedral* (1990)

Saint-Saëns, Camille. See OPERA.

Saintsbury, George (1845–1933), English schoolmaster, journalist, and academic. His comments on Shakespeare occur within the larger canvas of his *History of Elizabethan Literature* (1877), *A Short History of English Literature* (1898), and *A History of Criticism* (1900–4). *TM*

Salanio. See SALERIO.

Salarino. See SALERIO.

Salerio and **Solanio,** friends of Antonio and Bassanio in *The Merchant of Venice.* In early editions they are named Salanio and Salarino. *Capell and *Knight changed Salanio to Solanio to avoid confusion with Salarino in abbreviated *speech-prefixes. Salerio first appears as a new character in 3.2, who arrives with Lorenzo and reports on Antonio's losses, and his name may be a mistake for Salanio or Salarino. John Dover *Wilson suggested that the original characters were Salerio and Salanio (now Solanio), and that Salarino is a confusion of the two. *AB*

Salieri, Antonio. See OPERA.

Salisbury, Earl of. (1) The enemy of Suffolk and Cardinal Beaufort in *The First Part of the Contention* (*2 Henry VI*), and father of Warwick 'the Kingmaker', he becomes one of York's supporters. He is based on Richard Neville (1400–60), who was captured and put to death shortly after the battle of Wakefield (thus Warwick's assertion that his father 'came untimely to his death' by the house of York is erroneous, *Richard Duke of York* (*3 Henry VI*) 3.3.187). **(2)** He tries to prevent the dispersal of Richard's Welsh forces in *Richard II* 2.4. After Bolingbroke's rise to power he is beheaded (5.6.8). He is based on John de Montacute (Montague) (*c.*1350–1400), 3rd Earl of Salisbury. **(3)** He joins Louis the Dauphin after Arthur's death in *King John* but returns to John when he discovers the Dauphin's intended treachery. He is perhaps based on William de Longespée (d. 1226), illegitimate son of Henry II, who inherited the title of Earl of Salisbury

from his father-in-law. (4) He is one of the commanders at Agincourt (*Henry V* 4.3). In *1 Henry VI* he is slain by a cannon shot at Orléans, 1.6. He is based on Thomas de Montacute (Montague), 4th Earl of Salisbury, son of the Salisbury of *Richard II*, who died at Meung of wounds received at Tourelles. *AB*

Salom, Jaime (b. 1925), Spanish playwright and author of *El otro William* (*The Other William*, 1998), an anti-Stratfordian fantasy in which William Stanley, Earl of *Derby, appears as the real writer of Shakespeare's plays and Shakespeare is presented as an opportunist actor. In his introduction, Salom disapproves of the 'mysticism' of some varieties of *bardolatry, but offers no convincing argument to support his case, except the attribution of 'many scholars'. *ALP*

Salvini, Tommaso (1829–1915), Italian actor whose Othello and Hamlet at Vicenza in 1856 were landmarks in the performance of Shakespeare in Italy. Salvini pursued an international career for which his magnificent physique, expressive features, and vocal musicality made him supremely well suited and Shakespeare's plays provided a lingua franca. London first thrilled to his Othello in 1875 and marvelled as the veneer of the Moor's 'civilization' gave way to the groundswell of elemental, passionate jealousy. The admirers of his demonstrative and dismayed Macbeth were more numerous than those of his generous and glowing Hamlet, but it was on the basis of his Othello that he was judged—by *Modjeska—'the foremost tragedian of our times'. *RF*

Samson. See GREGORY.

Sand, George (Amandine-Aurore Lucille Dupin, Baronne Dudevant), (1804–76), French novelist. She diverted herself with a miniature theatre at Nohant where she kept open house for friends, writing plays which were seldom successful when produced. Her personal interest in theatre was seconded by an impressive output of dramatic criticism, often coloured by the political upheaval surrounding the 1848 revolution. In her celebrated 'Préface du théâtre' (1860), George Sand appealed to contemporary dramatists to break with the vogue for expensive but banal realistic theatrical productions, criticizing their writers for neglecting the public's thirst for poetic distraction: instead she championed the alternative world of dream and illusion celebrated in romantic comedies such as Shakespeare's *As You Like It.* Sand further extolled *Hamlet*, finding the tragic and unruly prince a perfect exemplar of the Romantic hero. *AC*

Sand, George, 'Préface du théâtre de George Sand', *La Presse* (8 Sept. 1860)

Sand, George, '*Hamlet*', in *L'Almanach du mois* (Feb. 1845)

Sands, Lord (Sir William Sands). In *All Is True* (*Henry VIII*) he is a guest at Wolsey's feast 1.4, and accompanies Buckingham to execution, 2.1. He is based on Sir William Sands (Sandys) (d. 1540). *AB*

Saturninus is the Emperor in *Titus Andronicus.* In the last scene after Titus kills Saturninus' wife Tamora, Saturninus kills Titus in revenge and is himself murdered by Lucius. *AB*

Saunder. See SIMPCOX, SIMON.

Sauny the Scot. See LACY, JOHN.

Savage, Thomas (*c.*1552–1611), a London goldsmith, born in Lancashire, who was granted, along with William Leveson, a half-interest in the ground lease of the Globe when Shakespeare and his colleagues bought it in 1599. His cousin was married to Sir Thomas Hesketh of Rufford, whom Alexander Houghton besought in his will to show kindness to William *Shakeshaft. *SW*

Savits, Jocza (1847–1915), Hungarian-born producer at the Bavarian Court Theatre, where in 1889 he founded the Munich Shakespeare Stage for non-decorative continuous performance. In his lengthy book *Shakespeare und die Bühne des Dramas* (Shakespeare and the Stage of Drama, 1917) he criticized lavish 19th-century performance styles. *WH*

Saxo Grammaticus (1150–?1200), Danish historian, author of the *Gesta Danorum* or *Historiae Daniae* (*c.*1185–1200), which includes the legend of Amleth, the origin of Shakespeare's *Hamlet.* Amleth's uncle Feng has killed Amleth's father and married his mother, a union that Saxo identifies as incestuous. The son puts on an antic disposition as he prepares for revenge and is sent to England but finally kills Feng to reign in Denmark himself. This story had circulated in manuscript and was well known in 1514 when it was translated into French by François de *Belleforest in his *Histoires tragiques*, the text Shakespeare used for *Hamlet.* The dramatist is unlikely to have known Saxo's work in the original. *JKS*

Gollancz, Israel, *The Sources of 'Hamlet'* (1926)

Saye, Lord. He pleads in vain for his life before Cade, *The First Part of the Contention* (*2 Henry VI*) 4.7. He is based on James Fiennes, Baron Say and Sele, Lord Treasurer 1449 (d. 1450). *AB*

Scales, Lord. He sends Matthew Gough to fight against Cade at Smithfield, *The First Part of the Contention* (*2 Henry VI*) 4.5. Thomas de Scales was the 7th Baron (*c.*1399–1460). Matthew Gough (Goche) was killed at London Bridge (rather than Smithfield, as in *The First Part of the Contention* 4.7). *AB*

Scandinavia. Shakespeare has figured prominently in Scandinavian literary and theatrical culture for the last 200 years, less as an object of *bardolatry than as stimulus and model or catalyst in the development of national drama and theatre and in the enrichment of the vernacular languages. More read than acted in the 19th century and more acted than read in the 20th, Shakespeare in Scandinavia is discussed here in terms of (1) reception and translation and (2) performance.

(1) Shakespeare arrived in Scandinavia, as in many other parts of Europe, with the precursors of the *Romantic movement. He was 'discovered' in the late 18th century and read together with Young's *Conjectures on Original Composition* (1759), Macpherson's *Ossian* (1762), and *Goethe's *Werther* (1774): as a wild, untutored, and melancholy genius. A fuller knowledge of Shakespeare's works was mediated by German scholarship, criticism, and translations, since English was not a language widely known or studied. *Oehlenschläger, who held that Shakespeare should be the model for every modern dramatist, had met the plays through *Tieck and passed on his enthusiasm partly through a translation of *A Midsummer Night's Dream* (1816) but mainly through his own dramatic works. The great *Schlegel–Tieck translation was to underlie, more or less directly, most Scandinavian 19th-century translations; and for many readers, such as Søren Kierkegaard (1813–55), it was *the* Shakespeare which they knew and cited. The Danish critic Georg *Brandes could claim in his monumental study *William Shakespeare* (1895–6) that Shakespeare had been 'reborn' in A. W. Schlegel. Still, the stage and the general reader needed texts in the vernacular. Shakespeare translations in Denmark, Norway, and Sweden have both reflected and affected the particular culture they serve. Four centuries of Danish hegemony, political and cultural, meant that, when at the end of the Napoleonic wars Norway was taken from Denmark and unwillingly attached to Sweden, the Danish and Norwegian languages were virtually identical. Nineteenth-century Norwegians read Danish translations. The earliest of these were in prose; Shakespearian verse was first attempted by Peter *Foersom, an actor and linguist with a passion to make Shakespeare alive to the Danish people. By 1825, when his translations (1807–18) of altogether ten plays had been augmented by P. F. Wulff, Denmark and Norway had a partial Shakespeare, heavily weighted towards tragedies and histories but both readable and actable. The next generation pressed for a *complete* Shakespeare to read, and eventually Edvard *Lembcke stepped in to revise and add to Foersom–Wulff and produce a *Collected Dramatic Works* (1861–73). With a smaller vocabulary than Foersom's, and a style of somewhat bland sameness across

the plays, Lembcke's would remain, for long and for lack of a better, the standard Danish Shakespeare. The more faithful translations (published 1887–1945) on which Valdemar Oesterberg worked over a lifetime turned out to be too abstruse for general readers, as for actors. Meanwhile, translations into Norwegian had become a reality, or rather two, as the country's language moved further away from Danish and itself split into two official languages. In *nynorsk* (New Norwegian), constructed out of regional dialects, poet-translators like Ivar Aasen and Arne Garborg struggled in the second half of the 19th century to recreate Shakespeare in a language with no literary tradition. The challenge was taken up by gifted writers: by the 1930s Henrik Rytter was able to publish 23 plays (1932–3); and, though there is still no *nynorsk* collected edition, Edvard Hoem has made excellent translations of individual plays. In the other, already literary, language (*bokmål*), the 1920s and 1930s saw a row of translations by different hands; in the late 1950s the poet André Bjerke began an impressive series of altogether eleven plays (1958–80); and the first collected edition of all 37 plays, gathering together various new and existing translations, including Bjerke's, appeared in the late 1990s. Translations into Swedish have followed a pattern of their own. In a culture that, throughout the 18th century and particularly in the reign of Gustav III (1771–92), had looked to France rather than Germany for literary models, there was more resistance to Shakespeare. In his defiant preface to the first Swedish translation of a Shakespeare play, a blank verse *Macbeth* (1813) modelled on *Schiller's version, E. G. *Geijer defends Shakespeare's 'taste' against strictures such as *Voltaire's. Though the Swedish Romantic poets often used a notional Shakespeare as a stick to beat their French-classical predecessors with, they did not translate him; and apart from a splendidly rhetorical translation of *Richard II* by J. H. Thomander (1825) there was little native precedent for Karl August *Hagberg, the anti-Romantic professor of aesthetics at Lund, who created the first complete Scandinavian Shakespeare translation (1847–51). Remarkably, he moulded Swedish to Shakespearian rhythms and locutions, even wordplay, and so produced a seminal masterpiece of national literature as well as a translation. It has also held the stage for more than 100 years, never really ousted by the novelist and poet Per *Hallström's complete but far less speakable translation (1922–31), nor by Åke Ohlmarks's (1962–9). As is everywhere common, new versions prepared for particular productions—such as Britt Hallqvists's responses to Ingmar *Bergman's demands for 'actable, sayable and above all understandable' texts—have tended not to survive their occasion.

(2) Looking back over 200 years of Shakespeare in Scandinavian theatre, the staging of his plays can be seen to have promoted both a sense of national identity—replacing performances of visiting foreign troupes, such as the 1792 German *Hamlet* in Copenhagen or the 1802 French *Othello* in Stockholm, with native acting in the mother tongue—and an interaction with international theatre, initially by imitation, like the 1860 Stockholm production of *A Midsummer Night's Dream* modelled in detail on Tieck's in Berlin (1843), but eventually by give and take, exemplified by *Bergman's 1986 *Hamlet* which was also brought to London. However, 200 years ago theatrical conditions were disparate: the capitals of both Sweden and Denmark had well-established 'royal' (or national) theatres, while Christiania (Oslo) was to have no professional theatre until 1827. Provincial theatre flourished in Denmark and Sweden: *Hamlet* was first performed in Swedish in Gothenburg (1787), while the Stockholm Royal Dramatic Theatre waited until 1819 for a Swedish (and much adapted) *Hamlet.* The first ever Shakespeare performance at the Copenhagen Royal Theatre was in 1813, when Foersom acted Hamlet in his own translation of that play. The Christiania theatre did not stage *Hamlet* until 1870; its first Shakespeare was *Macbeth* in 1844. When in 1852 the recently founded Norwegian Theatre in Bergen, still innocent of Shakespeare, sent its young stage-instructor Henrik *Ibsen to Copenhagen to study theatre practice, the repertoire of the Royal Theatre impressively included *Hamlet*, *King Lear*, *Romeo and Juliet*, and Sille *Beyer's adaptation of *As You Like It.* But the real energies of the mid-century Danish and Norwegian theatre were in indigenous 'Shakespearian' tragedy, and in Beyer's vaudeville reinventions of Shakespearian comedies. In 1861 Ibsen accused Norwegian audiences and critics of a conspiracy of pretence: a 'false' Shakespeare had become a cultural status symbol; and in his brief spell as artistic director of the Christiania theatre, 1865–7, Bjoernstjerne *Bjoernson initiated a tradition of 'genuine' Shakespeare. The Swedes had fared better: Hagberg's translations, both faithful and actable, stimulated an intensive Shakespeare culture in the 1850s and 1860s, beginning with an 1853 *Hamlet* and, under the direction of Ludvig Josephson, even reaching to a *Timon of Athens* in the 1860s. Increasingly aware of developments in European theatre, Scandinavian theatre around the turn of the century began to revise its ways with Shakespeare, away from elaborate painted scenery and panoramic spectacle. As actor-manager at the Royal Theatre in Copenhagen, Karl Mantzius (1860–1921) experimented with a 'Shakespeare-Bühne' in imitation of Jocza *Savits's in Munich; and a more sustained Danish Shakespeare renaissance came with Johannes Poulsen, who admired Max *Reinhardt. Between 1926 and 1937 he staged a series of sensational performances, including a *Tempest* with incidental music by *Sibelius. In Sweden Alf *Sjöberg was keenly receptive to impulses from abroad, not least Russia; during a long career at the Stockholm Royal Dramatic Theatre he directed altogether sixteen Shakespeare plays, from *1 Henry IV* (1935) to *Antony and Cleopatra* (1975). His passion for 'total theatre' shaped a Swedish Shakespeare tradition where movement, lighting, and music are as important as the text. Ingmar Bergman has both deepened and narrowed this, into a preoccupation with meta-theatre, as in his *Winter's Tale* (1994), and with psychosexual and familial relationships, as in his *King Lear* (1984). Often controversial, modern Scandinavian stage interpretations have also often been topical: Sjöberg made *Troilus and Cressida* (1967) reflect the war in Vietnam; *Macbeth* served in occupied Denmark, 1944, as an anti-Nazi play and in Stein Winge's 1999 Oslo production as an image of Kosovo. In all, the quantity and quality of theatrical activity, as of scholarship, indicate that being on the periphery of Europe and speaking minority languages is no bar to full membership of the Shakespearian community. *I-SE*

Fridén, A., *Macbeth in the Swedish Theatre 1838–1986* (1986)

Marker, F. J. and L. L., *The Scandinavian Theatre* (1975)

Smidt, K., 'The Discovery of Shakespeare in Scandinavia', in D. Delabastita and L. D'Hulst (eds.), *European Shakespeares* (1993)

Scarlatti, Domenico (1685–1757), Italian composer. His opera *Ambleto*, first performed in Rome in 1715, is based not on Shakespeare's play but on *Saxo Grammaticus' *Historia Daniae*, which (at one or two removes) was Shakespeare's principal source for *Hamlet.* The same libretto (by Apostolo Zeno and Pietro Giovanni Pariati) was also set by Giuseppe Carcani in 1742. *IBC*

Scarus. He stays loyal to Antony in *Antony and Cleopatra* and is promised a suit of gold armour by Cleopatra, 4.9.27. *AB*

scenery in the Elizabethan theatre. The pre-Restoration theatre used little or no scenery, the location of the action usually being denoted by dialogue. Philip *Henslowe's inventory of the Admiral's Men's equipment in 1598 listed a rock and a hell-mouth, as well as a 'city of Rome' which might have been a three-dimensional unit or else a cloth similar to 'the cloth of the Sun & Moon', together with a number of trees. Inigo *Jones introduced perspective scenery to the court masque and the first recorded dramatic use was for a performance under the auspices of Queen *Henrietta Maria of the French play *Artenice* at Somerset House in February 1626. *GE*

Scheemakers, Peter (1691–1781), Dutch sculptor. He completed in 1740 a marble statue of Shakespeare to a design by William Kent, commissioned by a committee including Alexander *Pope whose fund-raising activities included benefit performances of *Julius Caesar* and *Hamlet.* The work represents Shakespeare leaning on a plinth which is embellished with portraits of English monarchs in bas-relief. The image was lodged in Poets Corner, *Westminster abbey, and has been much reproduced (for many years a picture of it appeared on the £20 note): several copies exist, such as John Cheere's bronzed plaster version of 1749 (now in York Castle Museum), which formed part of a group including the poet Spenser. *CT*

Dobson, Michael, *The Making of the National Poet: Shakespeare, Adaptation and Authorship, 1660–1769* (1992)

Piper, David, *The Image of the Poet: British Poets and their Portraits* (1982)

Schiller, Friedrich (1759–1805), German poet and dramatist. His fascination for Shakespeare's great villains is reflected in some early plays (*Die Räuber*; The Robbers, 1781) and in his translation of *Macbeth* (1802) for the Weimar theatre. In critical writings he pleaded for the transformation of Shakespeare's 'naive' art into a more idealist, 'sentimentalist' mode that dominates in his later tragedies. *WH*

Schlegel, August Wilhelm (1767–1845), German Romantic author. In critical writings he emphasized the autonomous organism of Shakespeare's poetry, defining it as 'Romantic'. He is best known for his sensitive metrical translation of sixteen plays (1797), which, when completed under *Tieck's supervision (1832), became standard, although its Romantic stance now seems dated. *WH*

Schoenbaum, S(amuel) (1927–96), American academic and biographer, responsible for almost all of the most authoritative modern books on Shakespeare's life. *Shakespeare's Lives* (1970), a vivid history of attempts over 300 years to write Shakespeare's life, a monument of cultural as well as literary history, is probably the wittiest, best informed, and most acutely intelligent book about Shakespeare ever written. *William Shakespeare: A Documentary Life* (1975) reproduces facsimiles and commentaries upon (but not transcripts of) all extant original documents relevant to Shakespeare's life. *William Shakespeare: A Compact Documentary Life* (1977) digests much of this material into accessible narrative form. Schoenbaum also provides the commentary to *Shakespeare: The Globe and the World* (1977), the illustrated catalogue of an exhibition arranged by the *Folger Shakespeare Library; and his *William Shakespeare: Records and Images* (1981) supplements and completes an indispensable series of annotated illustrated reference collections. *TM*

scholarship has been described as 'systematic study, meant to retrieve, sustain, and advance the understanding of the past' (J. P. Brockbank). It may be distinguished from criticism as the discovery, assessment, and dissemination of factual information in the following broad areas: Shakespeare himself; the historical background to his life and works; their publication and performance; his reputation and place in society.

Scholarship in Shakespeare studies is international and collaborative, issuing in *journals such as *Shakespeare Survey, Shakespeare Studies, Shakespeare Quarterly, Shakespeare Jahrbuch,* and many others. However, in their respective fields, the great individual scholarly publications of all periods must include: *Heminges and *Condell's First *Folio (1623); Nicholas *Rowe's *Life* (prefaced to his edition of 1709); the repeatedly revised editions of George *Steevens (1766–93), Edward *Capell (1768), and Edmond *Malone (1790–1821), with their incorporation of many original documentary sources; those publications of the *Shakespeare Society (1840–53) uncontaminated by John Payne Collier's *forgeries; John Bartlett's *Concordance* (1894); E. K. *Chambers's *Elizabethan Stage* (1923) and *William Shakespeare: A Study of Facts and Problems* (1930); A. W. Pollard and G. R. Redgrave's *Short-Title Catalogue of English Books* (1926); W. W. *Greg's *Bibliography of the English Printed Drama* (1939–59) and *The Shakespeare First Folio* (1955); Geoffrey *Bullough's *Narrative and Dramatic Sources of* *Shakespeare (1957–75); Charlton Hinman's *Printing and Proofreading of the First Folio* (1963) and *Norton Facsimile: The First Folio of Shakespeare* (1968); Marvin Spevack's *Complete and Systematic Concordance to the Works of Shakespeare* (1968–75); Samuel *Schoenbaum's *Shakespeare's Lives* (1970) and *William Shakespeare: A Documentary Life* (1975); as well as the collective, cumulative scholarship of a continuing series of major modern editions published under the aegis of Methuen (Arden), Cambridge, and Oxford.

However, perhaps the most important scholarly resource for modern Shakespeare studies is a monument to the heroic age of Victorian scholarship, that indispensable reference work of language, *A New English Dictionary on Historical Principles,* now known as *The *Oxford English Dictionary.* For more than 50 years during its compilation and completion it was nurtured by citations from Shakespeare's works, some no doubt supplied by the learned American criminal lunatic Dr W. C. Minor; now, having achieved maturity in its many variant forms, it in turn is in a position to nourish the continuing scholarly investigation of Shakespeare. *TM*

Schoolmaster See GERALD.

School of Night, a phrase from *Love's Labour's Lost*—'Blacke is the badge of Hell, | The hue of dungions, and the Schoole of night' (4. 3. 252–3). 'Schoole' has often been considered a misprint of e.g. 'scowl', 'stole', 'style', 'soul', 'suit'. In 1903, however, Arthur Acheson proposed that it was the name of an atheistic coterie supposedly centring on Sir Walter *Ralegh. During the first half of the 20th century this theory influenced many interpretations of the play. *SW*

schools, Shakespeare in (British). Shakespeare's plays have been a presence in British schools since as early as 1728, when the Haymarket theatre advertised a production of *Julius Caesar* performed by 'the young Noblemen of the Westminster School'. Beyond the enduring tradition of the school play, Shakespeare has long been a cornerstone of the school syllabus, currently featuring at almost every level of British education.

For younger students (up to about 11 years old), school Shakespeare mainly comprises a study of Shakespeare's life and times. A 'Merrie England' approach directs students' acquaintance with Stratford and London. Work on pastimes, costume, the Globe, Queen Elizabeth I, constructs a benign picture of life in country, city, and court. Acting out scenes or short versions of plays has become increasingly popular, with teachers fashioning and directing scripts suitable to their students' abilities. Story and character dominate such versions. Fred Sedgwick shows that the stimulus of Shakespeare's language evokes writing of considerable quality from these younger students.

For older students, 'Life and Times' studies give way to the study of particular plays. In England, the study of Shakespeare is a compulsory element of the National Curriculum for 11–16-year-olds. At least two plays must be studied. Students are assessed at 14 on one play by a timed examination, and at 16 on another by coursework. For 14-year-olds, the choice of play is restricted to one of three prescribed by government decree (in 2001, these were *Macbeth, Twelfth Night, Henry V*). For 16-year-olds, teachers may choose any play for study, but the range selected is usually limited to a few of those most frequently performed.

Almost all 16–19-year-olds who opt to study English are required to gain detailed knowledge of at least one Shakespeare play as part of their course. A 'Life and Times' element returns with transformed emphasis and content. In A level examinations (for 17+-year-olds) students must, from 2001, answer 'context' questions on Shakespeare, showing their knowledge of the literary, social, and historical influences which helped shape his dramatic imagination. Here, the England of Elizabeth and James becomes recognizably that of modern scholarship: fractured, exploitative, conflictual. Examinations for these older students also increasingly require some knowledge of different critical and theoretical approaches to interpretation and staging.

In the last two decades of the 20th century, teaching methods and school editions underwent a sea change, much influenced by the research and development work of the Shakespeare and Schools project based at the University of Cambridge, and the Education Department of the *Folger Library in Washington, DC. Current classroom practice now acknowledges the plays as dramas for performance, rather than solely as literary texts for comprehension. In addition to acting out scenes or episodes, a wide range of active approaches is used, intended to involve every student in the class, rather than only the 'good speakers'.

At all ages, students' empathetic engagement and personal responses in interpretation are encouraged. For example, students imagine themselves as a character and express that character's feelings and thoughts provoked by the dilemma they face. Teachers attempt to balance this Bradley-like conception of characters as real persons with activities which emphasize the play as a dramatic, social, and historical construct. 'Directorial' tasks require students to seek, practically or in discussion or writing, how to stage scenes or episodes to greatest dramatic effect. Language activities aim at helping students understand Shakespeare's craftsmanship. Other assignments require students to relate aspects of the play to Shakespeare's or some later time, and to appreciate the changing nature of interpretation.

Visits to a stage production are seen as a priority by almost all teachers, but cost and distance place limits on students' experience of live theatre. Professional companies often provide education programmes for schools. In the UK the replica Globe (which has become a favoured site in the itinerary of school parties visiting London), the *Royal Shakespeare Company, the Royal *National Theatre, and many regional companies have flourishing education departments. All kinds of Shakespeare experiences are offered. Typically, on a school-based day workshop, up to 100 students spend a morning with actors in practical activities, and watch a production of around 90 minutes in the afternoon.

Videotapes are much used. Most younger students watch at least one 30-minute video of the **Animated Tales* twelve-play series (1992–4). For older students, teachers draw upon an extensive variety of video Shakespeare, including the BBC series of the canon (1978–85). Polanski's *Macbeth* (1971) has been the most frequently used version of that play. *Zeffirelli's once dominant *Romeo and Juliet* (1968) has yielded in classroom popularity to Baz Luhrmann's version (1996). Increasing use is made of interactive CDs and the huge variety of Shakespeare sites on the World Wide Web, but such resources lend themselves to individual, rather than group or whole-class, activity.

A school production of Shakespeare: Prince Charles as Macbeth, Gordonstoun, 1965.

Up to the 1990s, school editions took scholarly editions as their model, but abridged, expurgated, or avoided addressing 'unsuitable' passages (usually sexual). An explanatory impulse directed editors of these school editions. Glosses, notes, and scholarly essays combined with a didactic tone (and sometimes a parade of the editor's academic qualifications) to suggest that the implied reader was a passive student whose role was to absorb an authoritative and relatively unambiguous account of plot, character, themes, and language. Little or no acknowledgement was made of developments in Shakespearian scholarship from the 1970s.

The publication of the Cambridge School Shakespeare series (Cambridge University Press, 1991–) radically changed the nature of school editions. It uses the texts established for the New Cambridge series, and its editorial practices derive from the realities of school classrooms, the acceptance that Shakespeare's plays were written to be spoken and performed, and a commitment to reader-response theories which acknowledge that readers actively construct interpretation. It therefore provides a large number of individual, group, and whole-class activities to encourage physical and imaginative responses which aid understanding. Such activities also enable students to make informed judgements on the different ways in which, over time, the plays have been performed and critically considered. Throughout the 1990s a similar active pedagogy was adopted by other school editions. Extensive choice of 'active' editions is now available to teachers and students. *RG*

Gibson, Rex, *Teaching Shakespeare* (1998)

O'Brien, Peggy, *Shakespeare Set Free* (2 vols., 1993, 1994)

Sedgwick, Fred, *Shakespeare and the Young Writer* (1999)

Schröder, Friedrich Ludwig (1744–1816), German actor-manager. As theatre director in Hamburg (1771–80) he launched, in 1776, the first series of German Shakespeare productions, beginning with *Hamlet* and *Othello*, followed (1777–8) by *The Merchant of Venice, The Comedy of Errors, Measure for Measure, King Lear, Richard II, 1* and *2 Henry IV*, and *Macbeth*. Triumphant guest performances all over Germany confirmed his rank as promoter of a literature-oriented theatre. *WH*

Schubert, Franz (1797–1828), Austrian composer. He composed several non-theatrical songs, all dated 1826, of which 'Who is Sylvia' (from *The Two Gentlemen of Verona*) is best known. Some of his other music was adapted by Kurt Honolka to form the opera *Die Wunderinsel* (1958), based on *The Tempest*. *IBC*

Schücking, Levin Ludwig (1878–1964), German academic. His *Character Problems in Shakespeare's Plays* (1922) emphasizes the historically conventional nature (for example, in soliloquy or choric commentary) of many of Shakespeare's techniques of characterization. It represents, along with the work of Edgar Elmer Stoll (*Art and Artifice in Shakespeare*, 1935), a reaction against A. C. *Bradley's supposed obsession with psychological realism. *TM*

science, in modern usage, tends to imply a contrast with the humanities. Scientists carry out research according to scientific method in order to make new discoveries. The result is that the public gets an ever-changing picture of nature. All of this was quite different in Shakespeare's day.

In Shakespeare, 'science' can mean the understanding of politics and government (*Measure for Measure* 1.1.5), or of music and mathematics (*The Taming of the Shrew* 2.1.57). Sciences in general are a part of civilization: without them we become savages again (*Henry V* 5.2.58). The various fields of knowledge covered by the term differ in subject matter, but there is no suggestion that they differ in kind.

Nor is there any suggestion of a special experimental method to be used for making discoveries about the natural world. This is an idea that comes from *Bacon's *Novum organon*, published in 1620. Before that one did not create experiments: one reasoned about what could be observed. The reasoning went back to classical antiquity and gave a highly sophisticated world-picture. 'The huge firm earth' (*King John* 2.2.72) is a ball or globe in the centre of the universe. Everything heavy falls in towards it (e.g. *2 Henry IV* Induction 5, *The First Part of the Contention* (*2 Henry VI*) 3.2.410, *Richard II* 2.4.20, *Troilus and Cressida* 3.2.175). Fire, though, 'aspires' upwards or outwards (*Venus and Adonis* 149–50). Furthest away are 'the fixed stars of heaven' (*Richard II* 2.4.9). These are made of fire. Between their sphere and the earth is where the sun and planets move. 'Doubt thou the stars are fire,' says Hamlet, as if citing unquestionable fact, 'Doubt that the sun doth move, Doubt truth to be a liar, But never doubt I love' (*Hamlet* 2.2.116–19). The messenger in *Coriolanus* 5.4.46 is equally certain that 'the sun is fire'. As for us and our world, it consisted of the four elements, earth, air, fire, and water. Sir Toby Belch knew this (*Twelfth Night* 2.3.9), and so did Shakespeare in his own person (Sonnets 44–5). Indeed, expressed as the four humours, the four elements formed the basis of all medical theory (see MEDICINE).

The modern dispute, or alleged dispute, between science and *religion did not exist. There was, however, a kind of counterpart concerning the laws of nature. Were they, or were they not, unbreakable? 'We have our philosophical persons,' says Lafeu disapprovingly (*All's Well That Ends Well* 2.3.1–3), who make 'things supernatural and causeless' out to be 'modern and familiar' on the ground that 'miracles are past'. But the Archbishop of Canterbury (in *Henry V* 1.1.68–70) takes the other side, saying that since 'miracles are ceased' one must 'admit the means by which things are perfected'. There is a similar diversity of opinion on *astrology, some characters, like Ulysses, accepting it, others, like Hotspur, scorning it. But though the arguments on both sides are spirited and rational they show no awareness of the need for experimental proof or any knowledge of probability theory, so that they cannot be called scientific in our sense of the term. *MP*

Scofield, Paul (b. 1922), British actor. Early in his career at the Birmingham Repertory he played the Bastard in *King John* under the direction of the young Peter *Brook. At Stratford-upon-Avon 1946–8 he gave further imaginative performances under Brook as Mercutio, and as Don Armado in *Love's Labour's Lost*, and emerged as a charismatic star as Henry V, Troilus, and Hamlet. London beckoned; among his many West End roles were Richard II (directed by John *Gielgud) and Hamlet (by Brook) seen also in Moscow. In 1961 at Stratford, Ontario, he repeated Don Armado and played a much applauded Coriolanus. At Stratford-upon-Avon and on a world tour he was an intractable King Lear in the famous demystifying production by Brook, the basis for the later film (1971). Other parts were Timon of Athens and Macbeth at Stratford, Prospero at Leeds and in London, and Oberon at the *National Theatre. An intensely private man who is rumoured to have declined a knighthood, he was never inclined to direct plays or to manage companies. He won an Oscar for the film *A Man for All Seasons* (1966) and he appears in Kenneth *Branagh's film of *Henry V* and *Zeffirelli's film of *Hamlet*. *MJ*

Scot, Reginald (?1538–99), landed gentleman, MP, and author. His encyclopedic *Discovery of Witchcraft* (1584) refuted the power of *witches, alchemy, *astrology, and a great array of 'superstitions' and explained how some of these impressions were wrought. It is ironic that Scot's work of disabuse was plundered by Shakespeare and other dramatists so that they might create more 'realistic' or familiar *fairies, witches, and other apparitions. The representation of *Robin Goodfellow in *A Midsummer Night's Dream* may owe something to Scot's description. Hecate's song (now attributed to *Middleton) in *Macbeth* (4.1) also seems to derive from the *Discovery*. *JKS*

Scotland, in Shakespeare's day, was an independent country of perhaps 500,000 inhabitants. Like *Ireland, it was considered by many English commentators to be less civilized than England. Some Scottish intellectuals, such as George Buchanan, were, however, highly regarded throughout Europe and Scottish affairs were crucial on many occasions during Elizabeth's reign, most notably when the exiled Mary Stuart was executed in England (1587).

There has been speculation that Shakespeare may have visited Scotland in the company of the comedian Lawrence Fletcher, but the evidence is extremely tenuous. A clearer connection between Shakespeare and Scotland lies in the fact that in 1603 the Scottish King *James VI ascended the English throne, shortly thereafter bringing Shakespeare's company under his patronage, so that they became the King's Men. Scholars such as Alvin Kernan and Jonathan Goldberg have charted the way in which those Shakespeare plays written or revived after 1603 were inflected by James's concerns. The clearest instance of this is *Macbeth*, in which Shakespeare not only stages a crucial episode of Scottish history in a way which resonates with James's thinking, but also boldly opens the stage outward to incorporate the King within the play. In 4.1, the witches produce a 'show of eight kings' with Banquo following. This

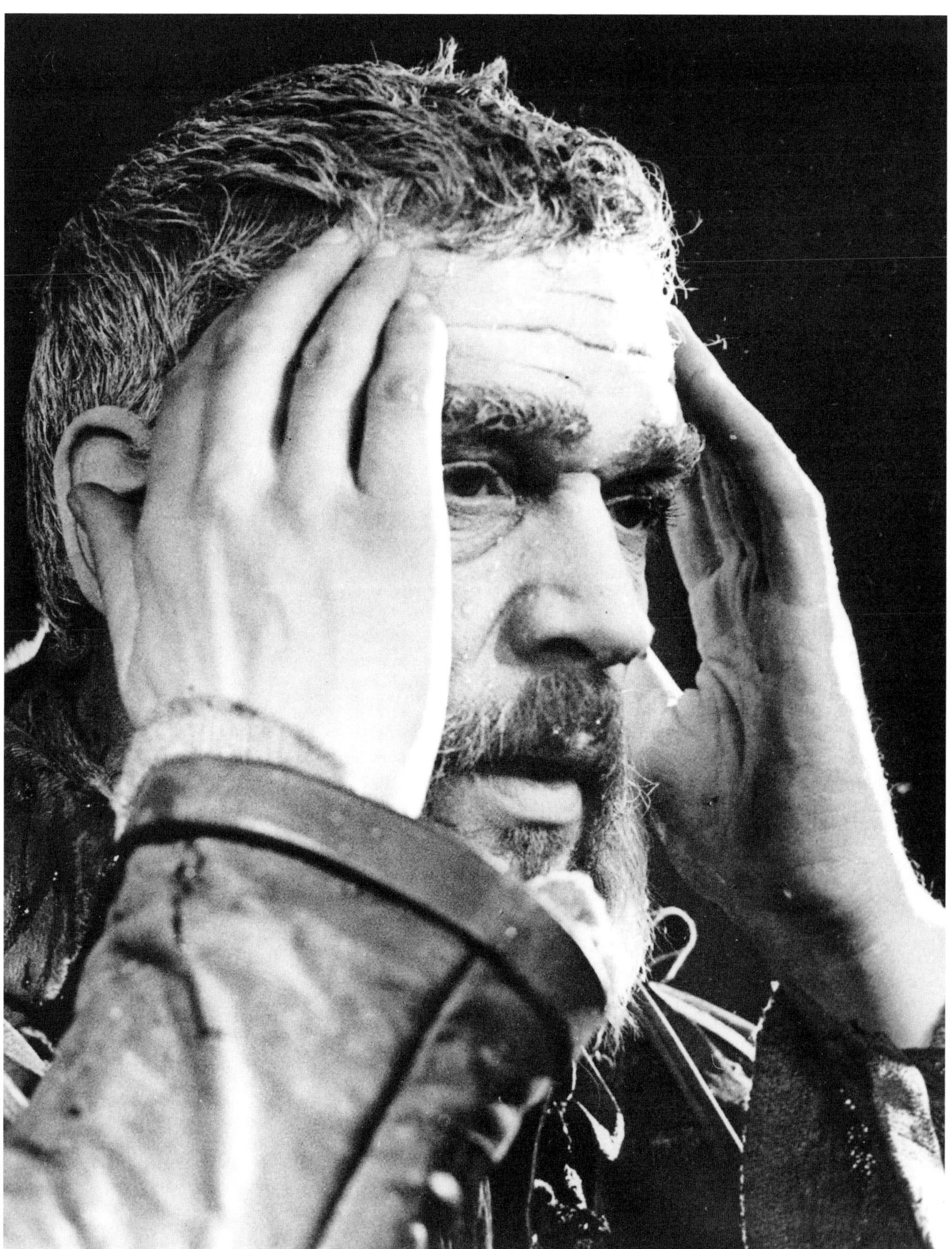

'O, let me not be mad, sweet heaven!' Paul Scofield as King Lear in Peter Brook's production, RSC, 1962.

represents the Scottish line of descent, traced by the Stuarts from Banquo. The eighth king 'bears a glass' (mirror), which, in the original court performance, would have been held up for James to see his own reflection, as the latest monarch of the Stuart line. The imagined harmonious relationship between England and Scotland presented in *Macbeth* echoes James's ambition of forging a single, united entity from his British kingdoms. The 'matter of Britain' is also rehearsed elsewhere in the Shakespeare canon, notably in *Lear* and *Cymbeline*, but also in some of the earlier plays, such as *Henry V*, where Henry's English army includes a representative Scot—Captain Jamy—in addition to an Irishman and Welshman.

A deep-seated anti-theatricalism within the Scottish Church meant that regular performances of Shakespeare were uncommon before the end of the 18th century. Nationalist sentiment may also have contributed to resistance to the English playwright: in 1756 an Edinburgh performance of John Home's pro-Scottish tragedy *Douglas* was greeted with an enthusiastic cry of 'Weel lads; what think you of Wully Shakespeare now?' By contrast with Scotland's relatively meagre theatrical tradition, the country boasts a long-standing tradition of Shakespeare publishing. As early as 1627 an edition of *Venus and Adonis* was published in Edinburgh. The first editions of the plays began to appear north of the border in 1752 and the first complete edition of the plays was published in Edinburgh in 1753. This text may have been edited by the Scottish scholar and churchman Hugh Blair, whose work was of central importance to the introduction of Shakespeare into the American educational system, as his *Lectures on Rhetoric and Belles-lettres*—which included extensive examples drawn from Shakespeare—proved to be an important textbook at many American universities. *Julius Caesar* has been translated into Scots Gallic by U. M. MacGilleamhoire (1911) and David Purves has produced a Scots version of *The Tragedie o Macbeth* (1992). *AM*

Scott, Sir Walter (1771–1832), Scottish poet and novelist. The series of historical novels produced by Scott from 1814 as 'The Author of *Waverley*' established him in contemporary opinion as 'the Shakespeare of novelists' (*Hazlitt famously dissenting). This was prompted by the sheer volume of his output, the extraordinary range of his characters (and their modes of speech), his interest in national history, and his teasingly obscure authorial persona as 'The Great Unknown'. Making extensive and pointed use of Shakespearian epigraph and allusion, the novels also frequently deploy the romance of the lost heir characteristic of the last plays. *NJW*

Scroop. See SCROPE.

Scrope (Scroop), Archbishop of York. See YORK, ARCHBISHOP OF.

Scrope (Scroop), Lord Henry, of Masham. Also known as Henry le Scrope, 3rd Baron Scrope of Masham (*c.*1376–1415). See CAMBRIDGE, RICHARD, EARL OF. *AB*

Scrope (Scroop), Richard le. See YORK, ARCHBISHOP OF.

Scrope (Scroop), Sir Stephen. He breaks bad news to Richard, *Richard II* 3.2. Stephen le Scrope was the 2nd Baron Scrope of Masham (d. 1408). *AB*

Sea and the Mirror, The. See AUDEN, W. H.

Sea Captain. See CAPTAINS.

Seacoal. George Seacoal is the name of the First Watchman, *Much Ado About Nothing* 3.3; Francis Seacoal is the scribe mentioned by Dogberry, 3.5.54. *AB*

Seale, Douglas (1913–99), British director. Originally an actor, he became director at the Birmingham Repertory Theatre. There between 1951 and 1953 he staged the three *Henry VI* plays first singly and then together. They were acclaimed at the Old Vic. Later at the Old Vic, at Stratford, and in North America he mounted actor-friendly versions of Shakespeare's plays. *MJ*

Sebastian. (1) He is mistaken for his cross-dressed twin sister in *Twelfth Night*. The parallel character in *Rich's 'Apolonius and Silla' is Silvio, and in *Bandello, Paolo. **(2)** He is Alonso's brother and Antonio's ally in *The Tempest*. *AB*

'Sebastian'. See JULIA.

Second Maiden's Tragedy, The (now also known as *The Lady's Tragedy*). Probably written by *Middleton, although occasionally attributed to *Chapman, this manuscript play was staged by the King's Men in 1611. It was unconvincingly attributed to Shakespeare in the later seventeenth century, an attribution which has found some minority support even in recent times. *SM*

See If You Like It. See COMEDY OF ERRORS, THE.

Segar, Sir William (d. 1633), who became Garter king-of-arms in 1603, wrote various military treatises including *The Book of Honour and Arms: Wherein is Discoursed the Causes of Quarrels and the Nature of Injuries* (1590). This book seems to have suggested some details of duelling practice in *Romeo and Juliet* and *Love's Labour's Lost*. *JKS*

Seleucus, Cleopatra's treasurer, tells Caesar she has reserved some of her treasure for herself, *Antony and Cleopatra* 5.2. *AB*

Sempronius. (1) Titus' kinsman, he appears *Titus Andronicus* 4.3 (mute). **(2)** He refuses to give Timon a loan, *Timon of Athens* 3.3. *AB*

senators, two Roman. They deliver the Emperor's commands, *Cymbeline* 3.7. *AB*

senators of Venice. They discuss the Turkish threat with the Duke of Venice, *Othello* 1.3. *AB*

Seneca, Lucius Annaeus (*c.*4 BC–AD 65), Roman philosopher and dramatist, tutor to Nero, who was forced to commit suicide for his alleged part in a conspiracy against the Emperor. Seneca immortalized his name as a Stoic through the famous dialogues *De providentia* and *De constantia sapientis*, and lengthier prose works such as *De clementia* and the *Epistulae morales*. Seneca was also the author of nine tragedies based on the works of Euripides and Sophocles including the *Hercules furens*, the *Troades*, *Medea*, and *Thyestes*. Where the Stoic philosophy dealt with the need for constancy in the face of human vicissitude and pain, the tragedies explored extremity in a sensationalist way, considering subjects such as adultery, incest, infanticide, and cannibalism, and the protagonist's violent response to adversity.

English Renaissance literature responded to both Senecas though it continued the 14th-century tradition of keeping them separate (Thomas *Lodge's *Works of Lucius Annaeus Seneca* (1614) did not contain any of Seneca's plays). The neo-Stoicism of 16th-century philosophers such as Justus Lipsius and Guillaume du Vair, and of writers such as *Montaigne, popularized Senecan epigrams about constancy and suicide. Shakespeare's plays are often indebted to Seneca's prose, for example *De beneficiis* in *Julius Caesar* and *De ira* in *The Tempest*. Yet the most important Senecan influence upon the English Renaissance stage was to come from the tragedies. The Roman was considered a paragon of tragic style. The terrible events that his plays dramatized were calls to *rhetoric, to the individual's utterance of a highly wrought, impassioned speech. This rhetoric was imitated in Elizabethan schools and began to make an impact on the stage. But it was not only Seneca's style that inspired Elizabethan dramatists but its content which seemed to meet with popular taste—the 'unnatural' scenes of incest and adultery, of murder and most importantly of revenge. In *The Spanish Tragedy*, Thomas *Kyd brought together a great number of Senecan motifs. The play begins with Revenge and a ghost in conversation. The action proceeds with the madness of Hieronimo, and the play-within-a-play that leads to murder and Hieronimo's self-mutilation. It also stresses the revenger's isolation from the world and the peripeteia of his actions which always lead to his own

Sir Walter Scott, who was nicknamed 'the Shakespeare of novelists' and did nothing to discourage this identification, aptly depicted 'on the occasion of his visit to Shakespeare's tomb in Holy Trinity Church, Stratford-upon-Avon on 8 April 1828' by the painter Sir William Allan, RA.

destruction. This English Seneca exerted an influence on Shakespearian tragedy from *Titus Andronicus* and *Richard III* through to *Hamlet* and *Macbeth*.

Whilst Shakespeare could not avoid the Senecanism of contemporary tragedy, there is evidence that he drew upon the Roman's tragedies more directly. Of the many translations available, Jasper Heywood's English *Troades*, *Thyestes*, and *Hercules furens* (1559–61) were significant as was the publication in 1581 of a collection of Seneca's plays, translated by various writers. The Roman was also frequently quoted in anthologies. Among the structural and thematic affinities between Senecan and Shakespearian tragedy, for example the banquet at which a parent unwittingly consumes his/her children (*Thyestes*/*Titus Andronicus*), or the successful wooing of a woman by the murderer of someone she loved (*Hercules furens*/*Richard III*), verbal echoes have been found to suggest that Shakespeare read at least some of Seneca in Latin. *JKS*

Braden, Gordon, *Renaissance Tragedy and the Senecan Tradition: Anger's Privilege* (1985)
Miles, Geoffrey, *Shakespeare and the Constant Romans* (1996)
Miola, Robert S., *Shakespeare and Classical Tragedy: The Influence of Seneca* (1992)

Senior, Duke. Rosalind's father, he is exiled by his brother Duke Frederick in *As You Like It*. *AB*

sennet, music associated with processions of dignitaries. The term usually signifies a more extended piece than a *flourish or a *tucket, and is seldom found outside a theatrical context. See *All Is True* (*Henry VIII*) 2.4., opening. *JB*

Servant of Cornwall. See CORNWALL, DUKE OF.

service. In Shakespeare's England, servants occupied a crucial economic role. Livery companies depended on apprentices, who trained for seven years to learn a craft. Households of the middling sorts employed male and female servants in a variety of duties. In larger, aristocratic establishments, servants, and their tasks, increased: such households would have boasted a steward (who supervised domestic conduct) and waiting-gentlewomen (who were taken on as ladies' companions).

Shakespeare deploys a range of servant types, often for comparative thematic purposes. Thus the contractual entanglements experienced by Gobbo, Shylock's manservant in *The Merchant of Venice*, have their counterpart in the network of obligations in which other characters participate. More usually, however, the dramatist finds in servants vehicles for debating notions of loyalty. The fidelity of Adam, the old servant in *As You Like It*, and the protests of the nameless servant who objects to Gloucester's blinding in *King Lear*, are put to work to question the values of appetitive and ego-driven societies.

Because of their implication in structures of authority, Shakespeare's servants are simultaneously constructed as questioning contemporary arrangements. Nowhere is this more apparent than in the representation of the maidservant. Margaret, Hero's attendant in *Much Ado About Nothing*, is permitted to criticize her mistress's idealistic romantic theories, while Emilia in *Othello* offers a similarly dispassionate reading of Desdemona's moral standards.

It is through the aristocratic household of *Twelfth Night*, perhaps, that Shakespeare's fullest investigation into service is conducted. The play revolves around a panoply of servant types—the gullible steward, the scheming maidservant, and the disguised page—and, via its social dislocations and derelictions in discipline, finds comic mileage in the unsettling spectacle of a total breakdown in domestic relations. *MTB*

Burnett, Mark Thornton, *Masters and Servants in English Renaissance Drama and Culture: Authority and Obedience* (1997)

Servilius, one of Timon's servants, unsuccessfully asks Lucius to loan Timon money, *Timon of Athens* 3.2. *AB*

sestet. See SONNET.

Setebos is a deity, or demon, worshipped by Sycorax in *The Tempest*. *AB*

Sexton. He presides over the examination of Conrad and Borachio, *Much Ado About Nothing* 4.2. *AB*

sexuality. The culture in which Shakespeare lived and worked can appear deeply contradictory when viewed from the perspective of modern notions of sexuality and sexual identity. On the one hand, a set of laws on the subject were in force which we would now associate with the most extreme Christian or Muslim fundamentalism. The ecclesiastical courts—commonly known as 'bawdy courts' because of their preoccupation with sexual offences—could enforce a wide range of public penances and other forfeits on those caught performing almost any sexual act outside *marriage (like those imposed on Shakespeare's fornicating son-in-law Thomas *Quiney), while sodomy was punishable by death under common law. On the other hand, the rate of illegitimate births was high (and illegitimate children were not necessarily viewed with disfavour: Shakespeare's bastards include the valiant Sir Richard Plantagenet of *King John* as well as the villainous Don John and Edmund); *prostitution was openly countenanced; and actual prosecutions for sodomy were very few. (Although Thersites derides Patroclus as a 'masculine whore', *Troilus and Cressida* as a whole does not seem to regard the possibility of a physical relationship between Achilles and his friend with any particular moral disfavour, any more than King *James troubled to conceal his intimate relationships with a succession of young male favourites.) Officially on the side of Angelo, Elizabethan society seems in practice to have been peopled by the likes of Lucio, and the subject of sexuality grows, if anything, still more complex when we turn to its manifestations in Shakespeare's theatre. The eroticization of the relation between performers and audience, and the organization in theatrical performance of the erotic desires, fantasies, and anxieties of all those who participate in the making of the theatrical event, makes the matter of Shakespearian sexuality a peculiarly fascinating and volatile one.

Recent critical discussions of sexuality in Shakespearian drama and poetry have broadly been divisible into two groups, aligned with the key influences on the history and theory of modern sexuality, *Freud and Foucault. Freudian accounts, understanding desire as a wayward, asocial drive that needs to be repressed or sublimated for the desiring subject to function as a stable member of society, were extremely influential in Shakespeare criticism for much of the 20th century, and have also played a profound role in shaping popular and theatrical understandings of the psychology of Shakespeare's characters. Such readings are, perhaps, most interesting when they trace how desire eludes or resists social constraints—*Measure for Measure*, not surprisingly, has often been read in these terms, as have the libidinal escapades of some of the early comedies. In contrast, studies of Shakespearian sexuality have recently been redirected by the work of Michel Foucault, whose *History of Sexuality* (especially vol. i, 1979) views sexuality not as an inchoate energy waiting to be moulded under social pressure, but as a historically and culturally specific organization of desire which is produced, in particular times and places, by disciplines of the body and the self. The most influential aspect of Foucault's work has been his decoupling of erotic acts from sexual identities, founding a claim (much contested by subsequent historians and literary scholars) that, until the late 19th century, people in Western European cultures did not experience their erotic desires as constitutive of a particular way of being in the world. In Shakespeare studies, this claim has stimulated far-reaching reconceptualizations of the dramatic representation of desire in the work of scholars like Valerie Traub and Jonathan Goldberg, and has also inspired counter-attacks, with Bruce Smith, for example, elaborating six Renaissance myths of male homoeroticism that effectively correspond to identity categories.

In different ways, both the Freudian and Foucauldian accounts seem pertinent to the acute and self-conscious sense expressed by Shakespeare's culture of the necessity to harness sexual energy in the service of the reproduction of society, in ways both literal and ideological. The Reformation's valorization of sexuality within marriage is relevant to this, and all the more so because it exists over against a vivid Shakespearian sense of desire as a transgressive, disruptive force, amoral, self-seeking, and unstable, potentially dangerous for both its subject and object (*A Midsummer Night's Dream*, *Twelfth Night*, *Measure for Measure*, the Sonnets). Unlike some of his contemporaries, however, Shakespeare rarely depicts marriage either as a site of sexual frustration and anxiety (outstanding exceptions being those late dramas that turn on male sexual panic, *Othello*, *Cymbeline*, and *The Winter's Tale*), or, more strikingly, as a locus of erotic pleasure and satisfaction. (Interestingly, it is the comedy in which Shakespeare most resembles his colleagues, *The Merry Wives of Windsor*, which provides the exception.)

Since the late 19th century, the spread of Freudian views about the centrality of sexuality to personal identity, the emergence of the recognized category of 'homosexuality', and the simultaneous rise of English studies and its institutionalization as an academic discipline have fostered a privileging of Shakespeare's writings as a site where the literary representation of homoerotic desire is charged with particular significance. The Sonnets have been at the heart of this process, not least because since the 1790s they have been thought to hold the key to Shakespeare's own sexuality; beyond the academic study of Shakespeare, key figures of queer culture like Oscar *Wilde and Derek Jarman have seized on the Sonnets, as well as many erotically charged moments in the plays, to enlist Shakespeare in gay culture. Such endeavours have been given new impetus by the impact, alongside earlier *feminist approaches, of lesbian and gay studies and queer theory in recent years. A focus on these issues crosses over several different critical approaches, ranging from traditional character-oriented criticism that makes a case for the homosexuality of Mercutio (*Romeo and Juliet*) or investigates the queerness of Shakespeare's Antonios (*The Merchant of Venice*, *The Tempest*), to studies of the sodomitical traces legible in the text of *Timon of Athens*. More recently, the scope of attention has been extended from same-sex desires and relationships to an investigation of Shakespearian bisexuality. In contrast, the formation of heterosexuality as such in Shakespearian drama has been subject to very little analysis, tending to be naturalized as 'love' or institutionalized under the rubric of marriage.

As the above examples suggest, male homoeroticism has been discussed far more extensively than desire between women (most often glanced at in discussions of Viola and Olivia in *Twelfth Night*, and of Emilia in *The Two Noble Kinsmen*), attesting both to the treatment of sexuality as an all-male spectacle on the transvestite stage, and to the gender separatist, male and female homosocial worlds in which the people of early modern Britain lived. This emphasis is a useful reminder that the subjective experience of sexuality cannot be detached either from constructions of gender, or from the social institutions in which both gender and sexuality are lived out. Yet the relation between gender and sexuality, libido and institution, remains complex. Plays, with their provisional trying on and discarding of identities, offer tremendous opportunities for the investigation of how provisional gender categories can be and how volatile the workings of erotic desire, and Shakespeare made the most of these opportunites throughout his career. *KC*

Goldberg, Jonathan, *Sodometries: Renaissance Texts, Modern Sexualities* (1992)
Orgel, Stephen, *Impersonations: The Performance of Gender in Shakespeare's England* (1996)
Smith, Bruce, *Homosexual Desire in Shakespeare's England: A Cultural Poetics* (1991)
Traub, Valerie, *Desire and Anxiety: Circulations of Sexuality in Shakespearean Drama* (1992)
Zimmerman, Susan, (ed.), *Erotic Politics: Desire on the Renaissance Stage* (1992)

Seyton (Seiton), Macbeth's attendant, announces the death of Lady Macbeth, 5.5.16. *AB*

Seyward. See SIWARD.

shadow, a term for the cover that shaded the apron stage of later open-air playhouses: see HEAVENS. *GE*

Shadow, Simon. He is one of Falstaff's recruits in *2 Henry IV* 3.2. *AB*

Shakeshaft, William. In his will of 1581, Alexander Houghton, a wealthy Catholic landowner of Lea Hall, Lancashire, left to his half-brother Thomas 'all my instruments belonging to musics, and all manner of play clothes, if he be minded to keep and do keep players; and if he will not keep and maintain players, then it is my mind and will that Sir Thomas Hesketh knight shall have the same instruments and play clothes, and I most heartily require the said Sir Thomas to be friendly unto Foke [i.e. Fulke] Gyllom and William Shakshafte, now dwelling with me, and either to take them unto his service, or else to help them to some good master.' In 1923 E. K. *Chambers noted the possibility that Shakeshaft was Shakespeare; the theme was developed by Oliver Baker in 1936 and later by Chambers himself and, most notably, by E. A. J. Honigmann (*Shakespeare: The 'Lost Years'*, 1985, rev. 1998). Spelling was fluid at this time, and Shakespeare's name appears in various forms, but there is no evidence that he or any member of his immediate family ever used this form of the name, whereas there were many other Shakeshafts in Lancashire. Shakespeare must have been back in the Stratford area well before his marriage in November 1582. Nevertheless, circumstantial evidence based on the link between John *Cottom and Stratford, the possibility that John *Shakespeare remained Catholic in later life, and the fact that the Houghtons and Hesketh were friendly with the family of the Earl of Derby, to whose acting company Shakespeare may have belonged early in his career, has fostered belief in the theory that Shakeshaft was Shakespeare. *SW*

Shakespeare, Anne (1571–9), younger sister of William, christened on 28 September 1571, buried on 4 April 1579, when her parents paid a special fee for 'the bell & paull' (i.e. pall, cloth carried or spread over the coffin). *SW*

Shakespeare, Edmund (1580–1607), Shakespeare's youngest brother, baptized 3 May 1580, who became an actor in London. His son, 'Edward sonne of Edward [*sic*] Shackspeere, Player: base-borne' was buried at St Giles, Cripplegate, on 12 August 1607; 'Edward' and 'Edmund' were often confused. The child may have been the 'Edward Shakesbye the sonne of Edward Shakesbye' baptized on 12 July at St Leonard's, Shoreditch, with a note that he came from Moorfields, the location of the Curtain theatre. 'Edmond Shakespeare a player' was buried at St Saviour's, Southwark, on 31 December of the same year, when someone—probably William—paid 20*s.* to have him 'buried in the Church with a forenoone knell of the great bell'. There would have been additional funeral expenses. Burial in the churchyard would have cost only 2*s.*, and a knell of the lesser bell, 1*s.* more. It was the winter of the Great Frost, and the Thames had frozen above London Bridge before Christmas. *SW*

Shakespeare, Gilbert (1566–1612), a younger brother of William whose name is found in the legal records in both London and Stratford, baptized on 13 October 1566. In 1597, while living in the parish of St Bride's, London, 'Gilbert Shackespere', a haberdasher, stood surety for William Sampson, a Stratford clockmaker; on 1 May 1602 he acted for William in taking delivery of the deed to land in Old Stratford; on 21 November 1609 he was one of several subjects of a bill of complaint, of which the details are unknown, instigated by Joan Bromley, a Stratford widow; and on 5 March 1610 he signed his name as witness to a lease in Stratford. The Stratford register records the burial on 3 February 1612 of 'Gilbert Shakspeare, adolescens', i.e. bachelor. *SW*

Shakespeare, Hamnet (Hamlet), (1585–96). Shakespeare's only son, christened with his twin sister Judith on 2 February 1585, buried at Stratford on 11 August 1596. He may have been named after Hamnet *Sadler. It has often been suggested that Constance's lament for Prince Arthur, in *King John*, beginning 'Grief fills the room up of my absent child' (3.4.93–105), reflects Shakespeare's grief, but Arthur is not dead, and the play's date is uncertain. *SW*

Shakespeare, Henry (d. 1596), brother of John, uncle of William; a farmer in *Snitterfield and *Ingon whose name recurs in many local records from 1570. He was imprisoned for debt in 1596, but at his death in December of the same year owned, according to one John Blythe, money and property 'amounting to great value'. His wife was named Margaret; two children, Lettice and James, were christened at Hampton Lucy in 1582 and 1585 respectively; James died in 1589. *SW*

Shakespeare, Joan (b. 1558; 1569–1646). Shakespeare had two sisters of this name. The first, her parents' first-born child, was christened on 15 September 1558 and died probably a year or two later. The second, christened on 15 April 1569, married a hatter, William Hart, before 1600. They had four children: William (1600–46—not the actor of the same name), Mary (1603–7), Thomas (1605–61), and Michael (1608–18). Joan's husband was buried on 17 April 1616, just a week before Shakespeare, who left Joan for life the western house in Henley Street—the *'Birthplace'—in which she was already living, along with £20 and all his wearing apparel. She died in 1646 and was buried on 4 November. Her son Thomas, who married in 1633, occupied the house after she died; and his son, also Thomas, became owner of it and the adjoining house by the will of Shakespeare's granddaughter Elizabeth *Hall. They remained in the family until 1806, when Thomas Court bought them. The family continued. John Shakespeare Hart (1753–1800), a chair-maker in Tewkesbury, is buried in the Abbey with a headstone which mistakenly calls him 'the sixth descendant from the poet Shakespeare', and his son William and grandson Thomas were buried in the Baptist burial-ground in Tewkesbury. *SW*

Shakespeare, John (before 1530–1601). Shakespeare's father, son of Richard, a householder in Stratford by 1552, was probably born before 1530. His business centred on animal skins: he trained as a glover and whittawer ('white tawer', i.e. a tanner, who treats animal skins with alum or lime), which required an apprenticeship of at least seven years. Glove-making flourished in the town, and at markets and fairs glovers had pride of place at the High Cross, the base of which can be seen at the Shakespeare Centre. John Shakespeare was also a wool-dealer and moneylender. His name occurs frequently in Stratford records; we have more mundane facts about him than about his famous son. This entry selects the more significant.

On 29 April 1552 he, with others, was fined for making a dunghill in Henley Street. In 1556 he bought a house and garden in the same street, and a house with a garden and croft (enclosed land) in the nearby Greenhill Street. By 1590, the only houses he owned in Stratford were two in Henley Street, now known jointly as Shakespeare's *Birthplace. He married Mary *Arden, probably in 1557 at Aston Cantlow; the church registers are lost. Their first child, *Joan, was born in September 1558.

John was one of Stratford's four constables in 1558 and 1559, and in 1559 and 1561 an affeeror—assessor of fines. Instead of signing his name to the court minutes he made his mark, a pair of glover's compasses. Having been brought up in the small village of Snitterfield he is likely to have received only a rudimentary *education, and seems not to have learned to write. He gradually rose on the Stratford town council, serving as one of the two chamberlains, who had charge of borough property and finances, from 1561 to 1563. A second daughter, Margaret, christened on 2 December 1562, was buried on 30 April 1563. William, the first son, followed in April 1564. Plague ravaged Stratford that summer; a council meeting attended by John in August was held in the chapel garden, to avoid infection. John and Mary's other children were Gilbert (1566), a second Joan (1569), Anne (1571), Richard (1574), and Edmund (1580).

On 4 July 1565 John was elected one of Stratford's fourteen aldermen; he became bailiff, the town's chief official, for a year from 1 October 1568. During his term of office professional players acted in Stratford for the first time—the Queen's Men and Worcester's Men, both in 1569. Around this time he was prosecuted for both usury and illegal wool-dealing; in 1570 he was accused of charging £20 interest on loans of £80 and £100 to John Musshem, apparently a business associate, and in 1572 of illegally buying £210 worth of wool. For one of the usury offences he was fined £2; the other cases ended inconclusively. Nevertheless, in 1571 he was elected chief alderman, serving as justice of the peace and as deputy to the new bailiff, Adrian Quiney. In the following January the two men were instructed to visit London on business connected with the borough's affairs. In 1575 John paid £40 for two houses in Stratford, with gardens and orchards.

This is his last known purchase of property, and at around this time his fortunes seem to have turned. Though he attended every council meeting for which records survive from 1568 to 1576, he is known to have attended only one thereafter (in 1582). In September 1586 he was replaced as alderman because he 'doth not come to the halls when they be warned nor hath not done of long time'. He had financial problems, and on 12 November 1578 raised cash by a transaction conveying 86 acres (35 ha) in *Wilmcote to Thomas Webbe and Humphrey Hooper (see Asbies); soon afterwards he borrowed £40 by mortgaging more of his wife's inheritance, a house and 56 acres (23 ha) in Wilmcote, to her sister's husband Edmund *Lambert, to whom he already owed money. On 15 October of the following year he and his wife sold a share in property at *Snitterfield. In 1580 he, along with 140 other men in England, was fined £40 for failing to find surety to keep the peace; why sureties were required is not known, and there is no record that his fine was paid. In 1582 he himself petitioned for sureties against four of his fellow townsmen (including the bailiff) 'for fear of death and mutilation of his limbs'.

From 1584 it is not always possible to distinguish William Shakespeare's father from a shoemaker from Warwick, also called John Shakespeare, who married a Stratford woman in that year and settled in Bridge Street; he too was often in debt. But it seems to be William's father who was named in two lists of Warwickshire recusants in 1592; the church commissioners reported of him and eight other Stratford men that they had failed to attend church 'for fear of process for debt'; he had not paid £7 plus damages owing since 1589. In 1599 he sued John Walford of Marlborough for a debt of £21.

By this time his fortunes seem to have been on the mend, perhaps because of William's prosperity. In 1596, when he was granted a coat of *arms and so officially became a gentleman, he was said to have 'lands and tenements of good wealth and substance', and to be worth £500. In 1599 he applied to impale his arms with those of his wife's family. He died in 1601 and was buried in Stratford on 8 September.

No secular will is known, but in 1757 (according to John *Jordan) a master bricklayer, Joseph Mosely, tiling the roof of the Henley Street house, found in the rafters a six-leaf manuscript lacking its opening now known as the Spiritual Last Will and Testament of John Shakespeare. In 1784 Jordan transcribed it, sending it six years later to Edmond *Malone along with an invented opening, and Malone printed it in his edition of Shakespeare. The manuscript is lost. This document claims to represent John Shakespeare's testament of Catholic faith. It is now known to derive from one composed, probably in the 1570s, by the saintly Cardinal Carlo Borromeo, which circulated widely among secret Catholics, partly as a result of the efforts of Jesuit priests such as Robert Parsons and Edmund Campion, who passed through the Midlands in the 1580s. The assumption is that around this time John Shakespeare acquired a copy of this formulaic document, filled his name in the blanks (or got someone else to do it for him), appended his signature or mark, and hid it (though the final paragraph asserts the writer's intention to carry the document continually about him, and to have it buried with him.) If genuine, it indicates that Shakespeare's father, born and brought up at a time when Catholicism was England's official religion, retained his faith after the Reformation, and thus that his son was brought up in a covertly Catholic household. *SW*

Eccles, Mark, *Shakespeare in Warwickshire* (1961)
Schoenbaum, S., *William Shakespeare: A Documentary Life* (1975, compact edn., 1977)

Shakespeare, Judith (1585–1662), Shakespeare's younger daughter, baptized with her twin *Hamnet on 2 February 1585, and possibly named after Judith *Sadler. At the age of 31, on 10 February 1616, she married Thomas *Quiney in Holy Trinity, Stratford. Having failed to obtain the special licence required for marriage during Lent, they were summoned to appear before the consistory court in Worcester cathedral. Quiney did not appear, and was excommunicated; it is not clear whether Judith suffered the same fate. The offence appears to have been a technicality, since Stratford clergymen solemnized three marriages in February. But a document discovered in 1964 suggests that the couple had special reasons to marry quickly. On 26 March 1616 Quiney was accused of 'incontinence' with Margaret Wheeler, who had been buried eleven days earlier with a child whose birth had probably caused her death. Quiney pleaded guilty, and was sentenced to perform public penance 'clothed in a sheet' for three Sundays in Stratford church. The sentence was commuted to acknowledgement of his crime wearing his own attire before the minister of Bishopton (close to Stratford) on his offering to pay 5*s.* to the poor of the parish. Discovery of the affair appears to have caused Shakespeare to make changes in his *will to safeguard Judith's interests; conceivably his death was hastened by these events.

In spite of its inauspicious start, the marriage was long-lasting. There were three sons, who all died young: Shakespeare (baptized in November 1616), at six months; Richard (baptized on 9 February, 1618), at 21, and Thomas (baptized on 23 January 1620), at 19. It seems a little odd that visitors to Stratford do not appear to have sought her out in her later years; around 1661 John *Ward made a note that he should visit her to find more about her father, but he left it too late; she was buried at Stratford, in a grave now unknown, on 9 February 1662. *SW*

Hanley, H. A., 'Shakespeare's Family in Stratford Records', *Times Literary Supplement* (21 May 1964)
Schoenbaum, S., *William Shakespeare: A Documentary Life* (1975, compact edn., 1977)

Shakespeare, Margaret (1562–3), sister of William, christened on 2 December 1562, buried on 30 April 1563. *SW*

Shakespeare, Richard (1574–1613), Shakespeare's younger brother, baptized on 11 March 1574, buried on 4 February 1612. No more is known of him. Another Richard Shakespeare, farmer of Snitterfield first heard of in 1529, who died in 1560 or 1561, was probably Shakespeare's grandfather. *SW*

Shakespeare, Susanna (Hall) (1583–1649), Shakespeare's elder daughter, baptized on 26 May 1583, six months after her parents' marriage. Legal documents from later in her life show that she learned to write. Nothing is heard of her until May 1606, when she was one of 21 Stratfordians reported to the ecclesiastical court for refusing to take Holy Communion at Easter. In the aftermath of the Gunpowder Plot the authorities were especially anxious to round up Catholic sympathizers. Initially she ignored the summons, but the case was later dismissed, indicating probably that in the meantime she, like other defendants, had fallen into line. On 5 June 1607 she married the strongly Protestant Dr John *Hall in Holy Trinity church. Her father gave her the very substantial gift of 107 acres (43 ha) of land in *Old Stratford as a marriage settlement, while probably retaining a life interest. It seems likely that the Halls started married life in the house in Old Town now known as *Hall's Croft, which may have been built for them. Their only child *Elizabeth was baptized on 21 February 1608. In 1613 their marriage was afflicted by scandal; in the consistory court held in Worcester cathedral, Susanna sued John *Lane for defamation after he had stated that she suffered from a venereal infection ('had the running of the reins', i.e. a discharge from the kidneys or loins, gonorrhea) adulterously contracted as the result of a liaison with Ralph Smith, a married hatter and haberdasher. She was represented by Robert Whatcott, later to witness her father's *will. Lane, a somewhat disreputable character, did not turn up to defend himself, and was excommunicated. Shakespeare's will appointed the Halls as his executors, and he left most of his property to Susanna. In 1625 she and her husband surrendered most of their share in the tithes to the corporation for £400. They moved into New Place, where she had lived as a child, soon after Shakespeare's death, and Susanna continued to live there with her daughter and son-in-law Thomas *Nash after John Hall died, in 1635. In 1637 she declared in court that a bailiff and his men, having failed to collect a judgement against Hall's estate, 'did break open the doors and study of the said house, and rashly did seize upon and take divers books, boxes, desks, moneys, bonds, bills, and other goods of great value'. Whether any of her father's property was seized, and whether she got it back, is not known. In 1643, Queen *Henrietta Maria stayed at New Place for two nights as she marched with a large body of troops from Newark, joining up with Prince Rupert and his army in Stratford on their way to meet *Charles I at Kineton, close to the site of the battle of Edgehill. After Nash died, in 1647, Susanna Hall and his widow successfully challenged his bequest of New Place and the *Blackfriars Gatehouse to his cousin Edward Nash.

Susanna Hall died on 11 July 1649 and was buried in Holy Trinity. Her gravestone, next to her husband's and close to those of her parents, bears an inscription describing her as 'wife to John Hall, gent., the daughter of William Shakespeare, gent.' The epitaph appears to attribute her 'wit' in part to her father, her piety entirely to her husband:

Witty above her sex, but that's not all,
Wise to salvation was good Mistress Hall.
Something of Shakespeare was in that, but this
Wholly of him with whom she's now in bliss.
Then, passenger, hast ne'er a tear
  To weep with her that wept with all?
That wept, yet set herself to cheer
  Them up with comforts cordial.
Her love shall live, her mercy spread,
When thou hast ne'er a tear to shed.

These lines, recorded by Dugdale, were erased in 1707 to make way for an epitaph on Richard Watts, 'committed to her grave in 1707', and restored in 1844. *SW*

Schoenbaum, S., *William, Shakespeare: A Documentary Life* (1975, compact edn., 1977)

Shakespeare, William (1564–1616), actor, playwright, poet, theatre administrator, and landowner; baptized, probably by John *Bretchgirdle, in Holy Trinity church, Stratford-upon-Avon, on Wednesday, 26 April 1564, the third child and first son of John *Shakespeare and his wife Mary (*Arden). His date of birth, traditionally celebrated on 23 April—St George's Day—is not known, but no more than a few days are likely to have elapsed between birth and baptism. The statement on his monument that he was 53 when he died on 23 April 1616 can only be understood to mean that he had started his 53rd year, i.e. had been born on or before 23 April 1564. *De Quincey suggested that his granddaughter Elizabeth Hall chose to be married on 22 April 1626 because this was his birthday, but this may reflect an anachronistic enthusiasm for anniversaries.

Shakespeare probably grew up in the Henley Street house known as the *Birthplace, with his younger sisters *Anne (d. 1579) and *Joan, and his younger brothers *Gilbert, *Richard, and

'Gulielmus filius Johannes Shakspere' [William son of John Shakespeare], the entry in the parish register of Holy Trinity church, Stratford-upon-Avon, recording Shakespeare's baptism, 26 April 1564.

the late-born *Edmund, who like him became an actor. Two sisters, *Joan and *Margaret, had died in infancy, and William was lucky to escape the plague, which hit the town a few months after he was born; in the second six months of 1564, at least 237 burials are recorded—something like one-eighth of the town's population.

Stratford had a splendid church, fine houses, a well-established *grammar school, and townsmen who were both educated and wealthy. It had regular links with London through carriers such as William Greenway (d. 1601), and throughout Shakespeare's boyhood and youth was frequently visited by leading companies of *actors. His father's position as bailiff in 1568, presiding over the burgesses and aldermen at meetings of the corporation, and undertaking other official duties such as presiding at fairs and markets and licensing travelling groups of actors to perform, would have carried privileges for his family. His sons are likely to have acquired the rudiments of their *education at a petty school, proceeding at the age of 6 or 7 to the King's New School, an established grammar school with a succession of well-qualified teachers, each assisted by an usher to help with the younger pupils. We have no lists of the school's pupils in Shakespeare's time, but his father's position would have qualified him to attend, and the school offered the kind of education in grammar, logic, and rhetoric that lies behind the plays and poems. A scene (4.1) in *The Merry Wives of Windsor* showing a master taking a pupil named William through his Latin grammar no doubt draws on memories of Shakespeare's own schooldays. Fellow pupils probably included Richard Field, who as a London printer was responsible for *Venus and Adonis* (1593), *The Rape of Lucrece* (1594), and *Love's Martyr* (see CHESTER, ROBERT) (1601). Shakespeare's education would have been furthered too by compulsory attendance with his family at church, where he would have become familiar with the *Bible, the Book of Common Prayer, and the Homilies. And though school hours were long and arduous, he would have found time for sports and pastimes in the surrounding countryside.

He is likely to have left school when he was about 15. What he did then has been the subject of much speculation. *Aubrey, in his random jottings about Shakespeare, stated that 'he had been in his younger years a schoolmaster in the country'. If true this might seem more likely to have been after rather than before his marriage, but some scholars have linked it with the hypothesis that he followed John *Cottom to Lancashire and is the William *Shakeshaft mentioned in the will of Alexander Houghton. If so, he was soon back home. He married Anne *Hathaway towards the end of 1582; a daughter, *Susanna, was baptized on 26 May of the following year, and twins, *Hamnet and *Judith, on 2 February 1585. Shakespeare must have been gainfully occupied during this time, but no one knows how. He may simply have helped his father with the family business. Presumably he started to write before joining a theatre company, but only a sonnet that seems to pun on the name 'Hathaway' has been assigned to his early years. The sole record of him during the so-called *'lost years' is a bare mention in a lawsuit involving his uncle by marriage, Edmund *Lambert, in 1587. It has been guessed that he joined the *Queen's Men when they visited Stratford in this year, but this distinguished company would have been unlikely to hire a novice. Still, Shakespeare's familiarity with plays in their later repertoire gives cause to suppose that he may at some point have been a member.

The first printed allusion, in Robert *Greene's *Groatsworth of Wit*, suggests that by 1592 he was well known on the theatrical scene. He had probably already written his earliest comedies and history plays (see CHRONOLOGY). During the plague years of 1593 and 1594 he seems to have thought of establishing himself as a non-dramatic poet; the Ovidian narrative poems, *Venus and Adonis* and *The Rape of Lucrece*, were published successively in 1593 and 1594, each with Shakespeare's dedication to the young Henry Wriothesley, 3rd Earl of *Southampton (1573–1624), who on this evidence, as well as that of later legend, may be regarded as Shakespeare's patron—though for how long and to what effect we cannot know. He has often been supposed to be the *'Fair Youth' of Shakespeare's Sonnets, most of which may well have been written round about 1593–6, though they may have been revised and reordered around 1602.

The earliest positive evidence of Shakespeare's affiliation with a particular theatre company comes on 15 March 1595, when he is named as joint payee of the Lord *Chamberlain's Men, formed a few months earlier for performances at court during the previous Christmas season. He was to remain with them for the rest of his working life, the only playwright of his time to enjoy so stable a relationship with a single company. We do not know the exact terms of his agreement with his colleagues, but he seems to have been expected to produce an average of around two plays a year, and to ring the changes among the dramatic kinds. Having demonstrated his versatility early in his career with the neo-Senecan tragedy of *Titus Andronicus*, the Plautine *Comedy of Errors*, and the tragical histories on the reigns of Henry VI and Richard III, he veered away from tragedy for a while during the late years of the century with more romantic comedies and with the comical histories of *Henry IV* and *Henry V*.

Inevitably Shakespeare had to base his professional life on London, and a number of legal records bear witness to his presence there (though as the name was not particularly uncommon we cannot be sure that all references are to the dramatist). In 1596, for example, one William Wayte petitioned for sureties of the peace against 'Willm Shakspere' and others; in November 1597 a William Shakespeare of Bishopsgate ward was listed as not having paid taxes due in February; on 1 October 1598 a man of the same name was named as a tax defaulter in the same ward, and in 1600 brought an action against one John *Clayton of Bedfordshire for a debt of £7. (This last record, usually ignored or dismissed, is as likely to refer to the dramatist as any of the others.) In a manuscript document of 16 May 1599 the newly built *Globe theatre is mentioned as being in the possession of William Shakespeare and others. The deposition made by William Shakespeare of Stratford-upon-Avon in the *Belott–Mountjoy case clearly shows that he was lodging with the Mountjoys in Silver Street in 1604.

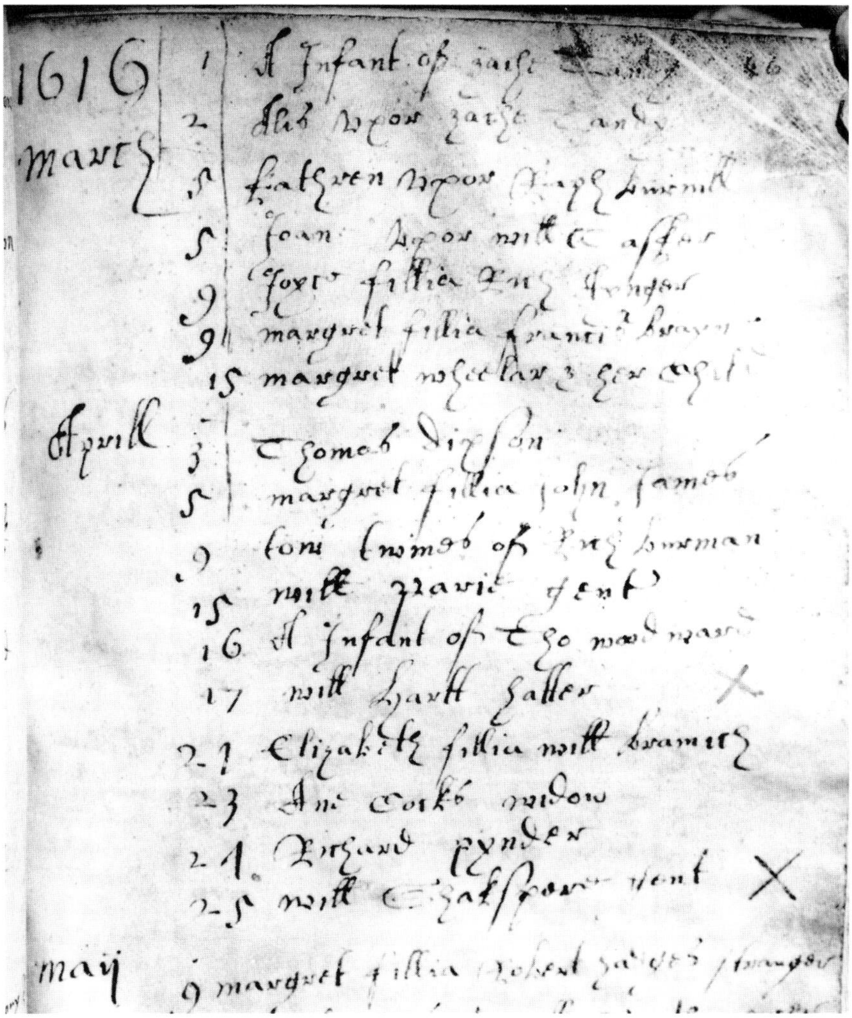

'Will Shakspeare gent' [gentleman], the entry in the parish register of Holy Trinity church, Stratford-upon-Avon, recording Shakespeare's burial, 25 April 1616.

Shakespeare's growing reputation as both poet and dramatist during the 1590s is witnessed by a variety of documentary evidence. He is mentioned as the author of *The Rape of Lucrece* in Henry Willobie's **Willobie his Avisa* in 1594 and, as 'Sweet Shakespeare', in William *Covell's *Polimanteia* in 1595. In 1598 his name appears for the first time on the title pages of any of his plays—the second quartos of *Richard II* and *Richard III* and the first (surviving) quarto of *Love's Labour's Lost*—and his narrative poems are praised by Richard *Barnfield in his *Poems in Divers Humours*. On 13 May 1602 an Inns of Court man, John *Manningham, confided to his journal a mildly scurrilous anecdote about Shakespeare and *Burbage, the leading actor of his company. In 1603 Shakespeare, along with other poets, is called upon—apparently in vain—to lament the death of Queen Elizabeth in Henry *Chettle's *A Mournful Ditty, entitled Elizabeth's Loss* and is named among 'The principal tragedians' in Ben *Jonson's *Sejanus*, just as in 1598 he had been named as one of the 'principal comedians' in Jonson's *Every Man in his Humour*. Apart from the list of actors in the First Folio, these are the only contemporary references to Shakespeare as actor, and it is usually assumed that he gave up acting around 1603. There is no contemporary record of which roles he played except a cryptic epigram by John *Davies referring to his playing 'some kingly parts in sport'; later gossip assigns to him Adam in *As You Like It* and the Ghost in *Hamlet*.

Shakespeare's succession of romantic comedies comes to an end probably around the close of the 16th century with *As You Like It* and, early in the 17th century, *Twelfth Night.* Subsequent essays in comic form are darker in tone. And in 1599, whether by personal inclination, professional necessity, or both, he had turned again to tragedy with *Julius Caesar*, followed before the death of Queen Elizabeth by *Hamlet* and *Othello.* Soon after the accession of James I, in 1603, his company of players came under James's patronage as the King's Men. He remained with them for the rest of his career, which saw the composition of the sequence of tragedies from *King Lear* to *Coriolanus*, the late romances, and, in collaboration with John Fletcher, **All Is True* (*Henry VIII*), *The *Two Noble Kinsmen*, and the lost **Cardenio.*

Along with references to Shakespeare in London go others relating to his family and to his home town. In August 1596 his only son died and was buried there. Shakespeare may have been in Stratford for the burial, but communications were slow; if the death was sudden and he was in London or on tour, he may have been unable to arrive in time. Two months later John Shakespeare was granted a coat of *arms, which gave him (and subsequently his son) the status of gentleman, though it was not until 1599 that John was permitted to impale his arms with those of the Arden family. In 1597 Shakespeare bought a substantial property, *New Place, said to have been the second largest house in Stratford. He was already very prosperous. There can be no doubt that he regarded New Place as home for him and his family. He is generally assumed to have spent almost all his working life away from Stratford, but he never seems to have established a real home in London, and it would not be surprising if he retreated to New Place as often as he could to work in peace as well as to see his family. His wife was to give birth to no more children, but since—to look no further—his elder daughter had only one child and his younger three, it seems gratuitous to use this fact to support the theory of a marital breakdown.

Though London was the centre of the theatrical profession, a succession of legal and other records indicates Shakespeare's continuing involvement with Stratford and its people. On 15 October 1598, for instance, Richard *Quiney, visiting London, wrote to him asking for a loan of the very considerable sum of £30; this is the only surviving item of Shakespeare's correspondence. In 1602 he consolidated his Stratford estates with the purchase, for £320, of land in *Old Stratford as well as buying a cottage in Chapel Lane. In 1605 he paid £440 for an interest in a lease of the Stratford tithes, which brought him £60 a year; in June 1607 Susanna married John Hall there; and there his first grandchild (and the only one he can have known), Elizabeth Hall, was born in 1608. His mother died there later that year.

From about 1609 Shakespeare's increasing involvement with Stratford along with the decrease in his output of plays suggests that he was withdrawing from his London responsibilities and spending more time at New Place. It is often said that he 'retired' to Stratford around this time, but he was only 45 years old in 1609, an age at which a healthy man was no more likely to 'retire' then than now. On the other hand, the increasingly introverted poetic style of his late work, especially in the plays written with *Fletcher, suggests a growing distaste for the demands of the popular theatre. He may have deliberately devoted himself to his family's business interests. If he was ill he was not totally disabled; he was in London for the Belott–Mountjoy suit in 1612, and in March 1613 bought the *Blackfriars Gatehouse. His younger brothers Gilbert and Richard died in Stratford in 1612 and 1613. In 1614 and 1615 he was involved in disputes relating to *enclosures of the land whose tithes he owned in the area. In February 1616 his second daughter Judith married Thomas Quiney, causing her father to make alterations to the draft of his *will, which he signed on 25 March. He died on 23 April, and was buried in a prominent position in Holy Trinity church.

No printed tributes marked the occasion, but memorial verses by William *Basse proposing that he be buried in Westminster abbey circulated widely in manuscript, and other verses printed in the First Folio may have been written years before they were published. Thomas Pavier embarked on an abortive collection of his plays in 1619, and the First *Folio of 1623, compiled by *Heminges and *Condell, both of whom, along with Richard Burbage, who died in 1619, are mentioned in his will, is his greatest memorial. A *monument which was commissioned presumably by members of his family, and was in position in Holy Trinity church by 1623, likens the Stratford landowner to Socrates and *Virgil; in the Folio, the memorial elegy by Jonson links this 'Star of Poets' with his home town as the 'Sweet Swan of Avon', and lines by Leonard *Digges speak of his 'Stratford monument'. The only two likenesses of Shakespeare with a strong claim to authenticity are the bust (by *Janssen) incorporated in the monument and the *Droeshout engraving. His widow died in 1623, the year in which the Folio collection of his plays appeared, and his last surviving descendant, Elizabeth Hall, who became Lady Bernard, in 1670.

Though we know more mundane facts about Shakespeare's life than about any other dramatist of his time except Ben Jonson, they reveal little of his personality. That lies buried deep beneath the surface of his writings. A dramatist's success is measured by the extent to which he removes himself from his plays, his 'nature | Subdued to what it works in, like the dyer's hand' (Sonnet 111). This makes it peculiarly difficult to arrive at an assured conception of Shakespeare as a person. Ben Jonson wrote that he 'loved the man', and did 'honour his memory (on this side idolatry) as much as any'. Other contemporaries—*Chettle, Heminges and Condell, Augustine Phillips—seem to have liked him; 'sweet' was a favourite epithet (though it may refer rather to his poetic style than to his personality); friends and colleagues left him money. But there is not much by way of personal testimony to go on.

Study of the records of his life creates the impression of an educated, well-read, and ambitious man who knew how to manage his business affairs and could pursue his financial interests astutely; who, while caring deeply for his family and his roots in Stratford, cared too for his career and was willing to make domestic sacrifices in order to pursue it, who took pleasure in his prosperity and the status it gave him, and who hoped to pass on something of what he had earned to his descendants. Absence of private utterances, with the possible but important exception of the Sonnets, suggests that, unlike the assertive and aggressive Ben Jonson, he kept himself to himself, a listener rather than a talker. That impression is supported by what *Keats was to call his 'negative capability'—the extraordinary capacity for empathy with a vast range of human beings revealed by the plays.

If we read the Sonnets as evidence of the inner man, we see beneath the controlled exterior a turbulent inner life, passions not easily mastered, self-knowledge wrested with difficulty and pain from the crucible of experience, an intense need to love and to be loved, a desire to idealize the beloved and to abase himself in the process, immense susceptibility to emotional pain, a demanding sexuality that led to adulterous relationships with one or more women, and possibly to male sexual relationships (in spite of the Sonnets' idealization of the 'fair friend'); a volatility of response that can veer rapidly from one extreme of emotion to its opposite; a belief in the power of the imagination along with an awareness of the fragility of illusion. We see this because of the shaping, expressive powers of art, because the man who has suffered this extremity of passion has also summoned up the self-control, the discipline to shape and contain it within the demanding verse structures of the sonnet form.

We might receive similar impressions from the plays alone. The ambition is there in the range and scope of the work, the determination to master all the dramatic kinds, the restless experimentation, the exploitation of the conventions of poetic drama in a manner that never quite loses sight of the need to entertain while constantly stretching the imaginative and intellectual responses of its audiences. The emotional turbulence is there in the frequent depiction of extreme states of mind, both comic and tragic. The sexuality, which can be both despicable and glorious, is omnipresent. So is the idealizing imagination that can transform man from a 'quintessence of dust' to 'the beauty of the world, the paragon of animals'. And all is projected by the deployment of a verbal and structural artistry that reflects the self-control and determination evident in the more practical aspects of the career. *SW*

Honan, Park, *Shakespeare: A Life* (1998)
Honigmann, E. A. J., *Shakespeare's Impact on his Contemporaries* (1992)
Schoenbaum, S., *William, Shakespeare: A Documentary Life* (1975, compact edition 1977)

Shakespeare and popular culture. See POPULAR CULTURE.

Shakespeare as a literary character. The celebrated selflessness with which Shakespeare absented himself from his own corpus, as well as frustrating orthodox biographers and stimulating the imaginations of the heretical (see AUTHORSHIP CONTROVERSY), has left a space which creative writers have been quick to fill in different ways since the later 17th century. Abstracting Shakespeare from his canon to appear in their own works (usually in the likeness of one of his own characters), dramatists, novelists, librettists, and screenwriters have produced what is by now an immense corpus of biographical fiction about Shakespeare, testifying no less vividly than literary criticism proper to changing notions of Shakespeare's authorship and its roles in the wider culture.

Shakespeare makes his first posthumous appearance on the stage to speak the prologue to John *Dryden's rewritten *Troilus and Cressida* in 1679: in this influential monologue, prefacing a play whose very existence shows how thoroughly Shakespeare's unadapted plays were themselves liable to seem archaic throwbacks to a dead-and-gone era, the author is depicted as a ghost. For Dryden Shakespeare is very much a version of Old Hamlet (just the role with which *Rowe's pioneering biography would identify him in 1709), an avenging spectre from less degenerate times. Although in some of the dead playwright's subsequent theatrical manifestations over the next half-century this phantom speaks prologues congratulating modern Britain on achievements which have surpassed those of Elizabethan England, he is more often engaged in lamenting the feebleness of his dramatic successors and the moral decay of his country. As adaptation went out of fashion during the 18th century, Shakespeare's ghost began to appear instead in poems demanding vindication at the hands of modern actors ('O save me from a dire impending fate, | Nor yield me up to Cibber and to Tate!', he begged *Garrick in the *London Magazine* for June 1750), and Shakespeare was still cast in the role of perturbed spirit when he made his first appearance in *fiction, this time decrying the immorality of the London tavern which bore his name in *Memoirs of the Shakespear's-Head in Covent-Garden. By the Ghost of Shakespear* (1755).

Shakespeare returned to flesh and blood only with the rise of historical fiction at the turn of the 19th century, as both playwrights and novelists grew at once more willing to reimagine the Elizabethan past in the likeness of the present and ever more convinced, in an age of personal biography, that the key to any poet's soul lay in his love life. The first play with Shakespeare as its protagonist, rescuing him from tragedy into romantic comedy, was Alexandre Duval's *Shakespeare amoureux*, acted in Paris in 1804, in which a curiously unmarried Shakespeare outwits a rival to marry the anachronistic actress who is rehearsing the role of Lady Anne in *Richard III*. Back in England, characteristically, writers were at first less interested in Shakespeare's sex life than in his social status: the *forgeries of William Henry Ireland in the 1790s had already included friendly letters from Queen Elizabeth to Shakespeare, and in Charles Somerset's *Shakspeare's Early Days* (premièred in 1829, with Charles *Kemble as Shakespeare) the young playwright, granted a vision of his future creations in a lavish dream-sequence, is cleared of a charge of deer-poaching and personally chosen as supreme English tragedian by the Queen herself.

Shakespeare had already been represented as Elizabeth's favourite writer in Walter *Scott's *Kenilworth* (1821), and Scott's imitators would continue to develop his romantic relationship with his sovereign: in Robert Folkstone Williams's *The Secret Passion* (1844), the finale of a trilogy (*Shakespeare and his Friends; or, 'The Golden Age' of Merry England*, 1838, *The Youth of Shakspeare*, 1839), the Queen 'would have had [Shakespeare] right willingly to have been her husband, had he not already a wife of his own'. Shakespeare's most impressive appearance as Bottom to Elizabeth's Titania, however, is in Ambroise Thomas's *opera *Le Songe d'une nuit d'été* (1850), in which the Queen becomes his Muse. Others were already using historical fiction to reassure their readers less of Shakespeare's quasi-royal status than of his domestic virtue, despite the problematic suggestions offered by his (increasingly studied) Sonnets: hence Emma Severn's *Anne Hathaway; or, Shakespeare in Love* (1845), and successors such as Sarah Sterling's *Shakespeare's Sweetheart* (1905) and William Saward's play *William Shakespeare* (1907), which adds Shakespeare's Romeo-like courtship of Anne to the plot of *Shakespeare's Early Days*.

The immense commercial success of the film *Shakespeare in Love* (co-scripted by Tom *Stoppard) at the end of the 20th century, which combines many motifs of these earlier works (along with a few more gleaned from Brahms and Simon's **No Bed for Bacon*, 1941), reveals how vigorously this tradition has survived despite modernism's professed disapproval for biography and the historical novel. Major contributors to Shakespeare's continuing afterlife as a character have included George Bernard *Shaw, Mark *Twain, Anthony *Burgess, Robert *Nye, Edward *Bond, and John *Mortimer, and the success in 2000 at Stratford, Ontario, of yet another play about Shakespeare's dealings with his Queen, Timothy Findley's *Elizabeth Rex*, suggests that the desire to imagine William Shakespeare in person, engaged in romance plots borrowed from his own writings, is as strong as ever at the dawn of the 21st century. *MD*

Franssen, Paul, and Hoenselaars, Ton (eds.), *The Author as Character* (1999)
O'Sullivan, Maurice, Jr. (ed.), *Shakespeare's Other Lives: Fictional Depictions of the Bard* (1997)
Schoenbaum, S., *Shakespeare's Lives* (1970)

Shakespeare as a surname. Over 80 spellings of the name are recorded by E. K. Chambers (*William Shakespeare*, 1930), including 'Shaxpere' in the marriage licence and 'Shaxberd' in the Revels account. Shakespeare uses variant forms in his surviving signatures, but the now standard spelling predominates, sometimes hyphenated, in printed documents including the dedications to the poems and the Folio. 'Shakespear', popular in the 18th century, was used by *Shaw; another spelling reformer, F. J. *Furnivall, preferred 'Shakspere'. *SW*

Shakespeare Association, founded by Sir Israel Gollancz in 1914 to promote knowledge of Shakespeare by meetings, lectures, and visits. Its publications include Shakespeare quarto facsimiles prepared by W. W. Greg, facsimiles of texts illustrating Shakespeare's England edited by G. B. Harrison (1931–8), and three volumes of *Shakespeare Survey* reviewing Shakespeare studies in Poland, France, and Serbia (1923–8). *SLB*

Shakespeare Association of America, founded in 1923, with Professor Ashley Thorndike as its president. It published the *Shakespeare Association Bulletin* from 1924, renamed **Shakespeare Quarterly* in 1950. In 1972 the association's name passed to a new organization, conceived by J. Leeds Barroll for the sponsorship of an annual meeting. The first SAA conference met in Washington, DC, in March 1973. Since the Boston meeting of 1988 the organization's annual conference has reached its climax at a social event known as the Malone Society Dance. *SLB*

Shakespeare Birthplace Trust is a registered charity incorporated by Act of Parliament

THEATRE, DONCASTER.

It is respectfully announced to the Public, that the extensive preparations for the above-named National Drama having been completed in the first style of Pictorial and Mechanical excellence,

This present Wednesday, Sept. 22, 1830.

Will be produced, for the first time here, with new Scenery, Machinery, and appropriate Costume, the Historical and Legendary National Drama of

Shakspeare's Early Days.

ORIGINAL MUSIC, composed, selected, and arranged by Mr. Aldridge, of the Theatre-Royal, Liverpool.—DECORATIONS by Messrs. Nelson, Dearlove, and Assistants.—MACHINERY by Mr. Breckell and Assistants.—DRESSES by Miss Smith and Assistants.

THE SCENERY BY MR. R. DONALDSON.

PREVIOUS TO THE DRAMA,

A New Shakspearean Overture, composed by Mr. Aldridge.

William Shakspeare (*From the Theatre Royal Norwich, his first appearance here.*)	Mr. RUMBALL
John Shakspeare (his father)	Mr. ANDREWS
Gilbert Shakspeare (his brother)	Mr. REDFORD
Lord Southampton	Mr. POWELL.
Earl of Leicester	Mr. SHAW
Sir Thomas Lucy, of Charlecote	Mr. STRICKLAND
Doctor Orthodox	Mr. KELLY
Robert Burbage	Mr. RAYMOND
Richard Tarleton	Mr. MELVILLE
Drawl (clerk to Sir Thomas Lucy)	Mr. SLAITER
Slyboots	Mr. YOUNG
Peter	Mr. JERROLD
Officer	Mr. NELSON
Citizens, &c.	
Queen Elizabeth	Miss PENLEY
Mary Shakspeare (mother of Wm. Shakspeare)	Mrs. MACNAMARA
Hostess of the Falcon Tavern	Mrs. STRICKLAND
Fairies.	
Oberon	Miss MAYOSS
Titania	Mrs. W. J. HAMMOND
Elves, Spirits, &c.	

In the course of the Drama, the following new Scenery, &c.

Outside of the HOUSE in which SHAKSPEARE WAS BORN, in Henley-street, Stratford.

DIORAMIC VIEW of Stratford-upon-Avon, the River, Church, &c.

SHAKSPEARE'S DRAMATIC VISION upon the Banks of the "SOFT FLOWING AVON,"

In which will be exhibited, in Peristrephic Progression, and Aereal Grouping, the principal Characters of Shakspeare's

POPULAR PLAYS.

1. TEMPEST.
Prospero—Caliban—Ariel—"Approach, Ariel, approach."

2. OTHELLO.
Othello & Iago—"I do not think but Desdemona's honest."

3. HENRY IV.
Falstaff and his Soldiers—"I'll not march through Coventry with them, that's flat."

4. HAMLET.
Hamlet and Ghost—"Lead on, I'll follow."

5. AS YOU LIKE IT.
Touchstone and Audrey—"Trip, Audrey, trip."

6. RICHARD III.
Tent Scene—"Give me another horse, bind up my wounds."

7. TAMING OF THE SHREW.
Catherine, Petruchio, and Grumio—"In faith I'll cuff thee if thou strik'st again."

8. KING LEAR.
Lear & Edgar—"Sir! I entertain you for one of my hundred."

9. HENRY VIII.
Queen Catherine & Wolsey—"Lord Cardinal, 'tis to you I speak."

10. JULIUS CÆSAR.
Antony mourning over Cæsar's body—"Oh! Pardon me thou bleeding piece of earth."

11. MERCHANT OF VENICE.
Shylock and Portia—"Is that the law."

12. ROMEO AND JULIET.
Romeo and Juliet—Capulet's Tomb—"She speaks, she lives, and we shall be happy."

13. MACBETH.
Macbeth and the Witches—"How now, ye secret, black, and midnight hags."

VIEW OF CHARLECOTE HALL, THE SEAT OF SIR THOMAS LUCY,

AND TRIAL OF SHAKSPEARE FOR DEER STEALING.

His Defence, and subsequent Lampoon upon his Persecutor.

Departure for London—Outside of the Globe Theatre, London, with the Rose and Bear Baiting Theatres in the distance.

PALACE OF QUEEN ELIZABETH.

COMPETITION OF POETS TO DECIDE THE CLAIMS OF TRAGEDY AND COMEDY.

THE PRIZE AWARDED TO SHAKSPEARE,

WHO TRIUMPHS OVER HIS RIVAL BY ELIZABETH'S DECREE.

AT THE END OF THE DRAMA,

A CHARACTERISTIC DANCE, by Mrs. NELSON.

After which, for the first time here, the new, and highly popular Interlude, entitled

POPPING THE QUESTION.

Mr. Primrose	Mr. STRICKLAND
Charles	Mr. MELVILLE
Ellen Murray	Miss STANFIELD
Bobbin	Miss ANGELL
Miss Biffin	Mrs. MACNAMARA
Miss Winterblossom	Mrs. STRICKLAND

After the Interlude, a SONG by Miss MAYOSS.

After which the laughable Farce of THE

IRISH VALET

A playbill for the first English play with Shakespeare as its protagonist, Charles Somerset's *Shakspeare's Early Days* (first performed in 1829). The synopsis of scenes makes it clear how much this play has in common with later specimens of this sub-genre such as *Shakespeare in Love*.

whose main objects are to promote the appreciation of Shakespeare's works, to maintain the five houses in or near Stratford-upon-Avon directly connected with Shakespeare and his family, and to provide a museum and library of books, manuscripts, and records of local interest with particular reference to Shakespeare. The trust's headquarters are at the Shakespeare Centre, adjacent to Shakespeare's Birthplace, in Stratford-upon-Avon. The trust came into existence after the purchase of Shakespeare's *Birthplace in 1847 in order to preserve it as a national monument and from the threat of physical removal offered by P. T. Barnum, a rival bidder at the public auction. It has since focused much of its resources on building conservation, acquiring the site of *New Place and the adjoining house of Thomas *Nash, the husband of Shakespeare's granddaughter, in 1862, *Anne Hathaway's Cottage in Shottery in 1892, the farm belonging to Shakespeare's mother's family in Wilmcote, now known as *Mary Arden's House, in 1968, and *Hall's Croft, the home of his daughter Susanna and her husband Dr John *Hall, in 1950 as well as other property in and around Stratford. The income from visitors to these historic houses supports and enhances the trust's collections and educational programmes. The museum artefacts, which include representations of Shakespeare and contemporary furniture and textiles, are displayed in the houses and in a permanent exhibition at the Shakespeare Centre. The trust's library, which early benefited from the donations and support of J. O. Halliwell-Phillipps, has acquired an outstanding collection of Shakespeare editions including all the folios and some quartos and representative works of the period. In 1964 it was enlarged by the deposit of the Royal Shakespeare Theatre's archives and library, a specialized collection of drama and performance material. The trust's Records Office has significant deposits relating to the life of Shakespeare and his family in Stratford, including the only surviving letter to the playwright, the papers of Shakespeare scholars and antiquarians, as well as Warwickshire family papers, and the records of the borough of Stratford-upon-Avon and its parish church. Under the guidance of Levi Fox, director 1945–89, and his successor Roger Pringle, the Trust has developed into an international centre for Shakespeare studies. It acts as the headquarters of the *International Shakespeare Association. *SLB*

Bearman, Robert, *Shakespeare in the Stratford Records* (1994)
Fox, Levi, *In Honour of Shakespeare: The History and Collections of the Shakespeare Birthplace Trust* (1972)
www.shakespeare.org.uk

Shakespeare Club of Stratford-upon-Avon was founded, as the Shakespearian Club, on 23 April 1824 and is the oldest Shakespeare society in existence. Under royal patronage from 1830 until its refounding in 1874, the Royal Shakespearean Club instituted the annual *birthday celebrations in Stratford and campaigned for the purchase of Shakespeare's *Birthplace for the nation in 1847. *SLB*

Shakespeare Gallery. A project to depict scenes from Shakespeare's plays, involving some of the foremost talents of 18th-century London's artistic community. The project was administered, although not originally conceived of, by John *Boydell. In November 1789 Boydell's print shop at Cheapside exhibited paintings inspired by Shakespearian drama to subscribers, an event which was to be accompanied by a plan to publish the plays in eight volumes, accompanied by engravings after the paintings at the gallery. Contributors included: James *Barry, Henry *Fuseli, Joshua Reynolds, Angelica Kauffman, James *Northcote, George *Romney, and Joseph *Wright of Derby. The purpose of the gallery, as professed by Boydell in the preface to the first catalogue was 'to advance the art towards maturity and establish an English School of Painting'. Negotiations with participating artists, however, were often beset with difficulties, produced by Boydell's unwillingness to accept paintings unlikely to sell prints. Joseph Wright of Derby's *Juliet in the Tomb*, for instance, was rejected on grounds of its scale. James Gillray, who was also unsuccessful in his applications for Boydell's patronage, produced, in June 1789, what became one of his most celebrated graphic satires, *Shakespeare Sacrificed—or the Offering to Avarice.* A critique of Boydell's anxiety to ensure the gallery's commercial success, the print also calls into question the seriousness of the gallery's aspiration to History Painting.

In the face of ongoing attacks from Gillray, press criticism, and shifts in public taste away from large-scale projects uniting history painting and literature, the gallery was sold by lottery, re-establishing its financial status. After attempts by Boydell to reacquire the gallery, it was auctioned by Mr Christie on 17 May 1805. *CT*

Shakespeare Institute, a postgraduate research centre located in Stratford-upon-Avon, part of the Department of English of the University of Birmingham. It is housed in Mason Croft, a mainly 18th-century house owned in the early part of this century by the novelist Marie Corelli. Founded in 1951 to support advanced study and research into the life and works of William Shakespeare and to provide materials for English teachers, overseas students, and the interested general public, the institute's wider aim was to enhance national prestige and international understanding. Its creation was part of an initiative after the Second World War to promote Shakespeare, Stratford-upon-Avon, and British culture, undertaken by the *British Council, the *Shakespeare Birthplace Trust, the *Shakespeare Memorial Theatre, and the university, which included the establishment of the International Shakespeare Conference which the institute has hosted from inception, an annual Shakespeare summer school, and **Shakespeare Survey.*

The Shakespeare Institute now offers taught programmes for the university's master's degree (since 1972) and postgraduate diploma (since 1989) and offers opportunities for postgraduate and postdoctoral research in an international community of students and scholars. Focusing on English literature 1550 to 1640 with an emphasis on the drama, its library is a working collection of over 50,000 items, including both primary and secondary materials, which from its foundation exploited the use of facsimiles in print, microform, photocopied, and, now, digitized formats. It is open to members of the University of Birmingham and to visitors on application.

The institute has had a series of distinguished scholars as directors and fellows, who include C. J. Sisson, R. A. Foakes, Philip Edwards, John Russell Brown, E. A. J. Honigmann, and Inga-Stina Ewbank. Allardyce *Nicoll, a theatre historian and its founder and first director (1951–61), aimed to create in Stratford a sort of Shakespeare university combining the resources of the theatre and the academy. In contrast his successor Terence Spencer (1961–78) saw the institute's future as a postgraduate centre for the Department of English and, in 1963, moved the institute's students and library to the university campus in Birmingham. Mason Croft meanwhile was developed as a centre for conferences and a programme of short courses for international university groups. Philip Brockbank, the institute's third director (1978–88), wishing to restore and promote a closer relationship with the theatre, worked successfully to return the institute to Stratford-upon-Avon. The library and students operated on a split site from 1988 to 1992 when the Birmingham building was finally vacated. Under the directorship of Stanley Wells (1988–98), who also held the university's first chair of Shakespeare studies, the institute's facilities were expanded by the addition of the Johnson Library in 1995, funded by substantial gifts from V. H. 'Johnnie' Johnson and friends and alumni of the institute, and, in 1998, by the Wells Room, named in his honour. Peter Holland became the Institute's fifth director in 1998.

From its earliest days the Shakespeare Institute acknowledged Dover *Wilson's description of Shakespeare's plays as 'libretti for stage performance' and placed Shakespeare in his theatrical context. Titles of all the most important British post-war editions of Shakespeare's works have been edited from the institute: the Penguin, the New Cambridge, the Oxford, and most recently the Electronic Arden. *SLB*

http://www.bham.ac.uk/english/shakespeare

Shakespeare Jahrbuch, German annual. Published since 1865, it is the oldest Shakespeare periodical still existing. Between 1964 and 1992, when the Cold War divided the Deutsche-Shakespeare Gesellschaft, separate issues were produced in East and West Germany. Its volumes contain critical articles, reviews, and documentation of Shakespeare performances in German. *WH*

Shakespeare Ladies' Club, a literary club organized in late 1736 under the leadership of Susanna, Countess of Shaftesbury, which, over two years, successfully pressed for the revival in the London theatres of Shakespeare's plays. Its members, sometimes called 'Shakespeare's Ladies', may have included writers Mary Cowper and Elizabeth Boyd. *SLB*

Shakespeare Memorial Theatre. Stratford's first permanent Shakespearian theatre, an offshoot of the *Shakespeare tercentenary of 1864, opened in 1879, with performances by a company led by Barry *Sullivan; Sullivan's best-loved successor here was Frank *Benson. It was destroyed by fire in 1926; its shell, long used as a rehearsal space, now houses the RSC's Swan theatre and the *RSC Collection and Gallery. Like the tercentenary itself, and indeed like its successor the *Royal Shakespeare Theatre, it was largely paid for by public subscription, heavily promoted and subsidized by Stratford's brewing dynasty the Flower family. *MD*

Shakespeare Newsletter was founded by Louis Marder in 1951 and edited and published by him for 41 years until 1991 when responsibility passed to the English Department at Iona College, New York. It presents news, reviews, and, most usefully, digests and abstracts of conference papers and seminars. *SLB*

Shakespeare on sound film. Sound films of Shakespeare were launched with the Hollywood Fairbanks/Pickford *The Taming of the Shrew* (1929), with its (probably apocryphal) credit ascribing 'additional dialogue' to Sam Taylor. Mary Pickford's wink at the point where she pledges obedience to Petruchio has been seen as a resounding statement on the 'rights of American women' (see Kenneth Rothwell's *A History of Shakespeare on Screen*, 1999).

The Max *Reinhardt/William Dieterle *A Midsummer Night's Dream* (1935) brought the German expressionistic style to a high point in filmed Shakespeare. Among the Hollywood cast were Mickey Rooney as Puck and James Cagney as Bottom. The directors set out to transpose the level of the play's audience engagement, tilting it towards Hollywood's dance and musical film genre. The fairies, more unnerving than appealing, anticipate Jan *Kott's view of the play as being suffused with darkness.

Paul Czinner's *As You Like It* (1936) featured Elisabeth Bergner and Laurence *Olivier as Rosalind and Orlando. Influenced by German cinematic style, it also incorporates traits of screwball comedy, its idealistic Orlando asserting himself against an unjust world echoing, suggests Rothwell, the despair of the great depression.

George Cukor's *Romeo and Juliet* (1936) featured Leslie Howard and Norma Shearer along with many British expatriates. Great expense was lavished on the film, with an immense reconstruction of Renaissance Verona as the set. If the Reinhardt *A Midsummer Night's Dream* had challenged the accepted cultural status of a Shakespeare comedy, Cukor's *Romeo and Juliet* tended towards veneration.

Shakespeare was not successful box-office material for cinema. Hollywood left Shakespeare well alone until the early 1950s with Joseph Mankiewicz's *Julius Caesar* (1953). With a convincing reconstruction set, it struck out in a refreshingly independent direction, incorporating the acting styles of James Mason, an established Hollywood film actor, as Brutus, John *Gielgud, the eminent British stage Shakespearian, as Cassius, and Marlon Brando, emerging from a more robust school of American method acting, as Mark Antony.

From the closing years of the Second World War the bright stars in the firmament of Shakespeare film were the Olivier trilogy *Henry V* (1944), *Hamlet* (1948), and *Richard III* (1955). Filled with colour, athletic action, and robust challenges to a confident and mocking enemy, *Henry V* was intended—and succeeded—as a morale-boosting venture. But in outliving the patriotic wave on which it was launched, it deserves recognition for the adventurous daring of its cinematography and the subtlety of its transitional devices. In transporting the language and action of Shakespeare's play into the cinematic arena, it never abandons its intrinsic theatricality.

With his monochrome *Hamlet* Olivier again made a film whose roots are firmly grounded in theatre. Its dark brooding tone matching the introspective loneliness of its hero makes it the antithesis of its 1944 predecessor. The long, elegiac camera movements with pained moments of concentration on detail make the lens into the eye of a narrator and effectively take us on the tragic journey which is *Hamlet.* Despite Olivier's disclaimer, the film is clearly underpinned with Freudian symbolism.

With *Richard III* Olivier returned to full chromatic film, setting the self-congratulatory villainy of Richard's dark personality against the solemn heraldic colours and music of the visuals and soundtrack. Olivier's performance remains intensely theatrical, ensuring through direct address that the cinema audience become accomplices. Olivier plays Richard as a consummate actor on a stage peopled with fools. With the exception of the battle—filmed on an incongruously arid Spanish plain—there is a fitting stagey feel about the sets.

In the year of the release of Olivier's *Hamlet,* Orson *Welles filmed *Macbeth.* Uneven in its dramatic effectiveness, its exploration of substance and form suggest that Welles had found a powerful cinematic language with which to articulate themes which underpin his view of the play.

In 1952 came Welles's *Othello.* The bravura style of its editing disrupts the dramatic flow of the play, but the interplay of light and darkness, sea and stone, high- and low-angle shots, suggest that the play is essentially about a fallen world.

In 1966 Welles's *Chimes at Midnight,* essentially a conflation of *1* and *2 Henry IV,* was released. It finds a fine balance between concentration on characters and integration of spatial detail to chart the painful severance of the friendship between the Prince and Falstaff. It captures, too, the nostalgia for an England of the past as young and old respond in their different ways to the new, coldly efficient order imposed by Bolingbroke.

If the trilogies of Olivier and Welles stand as the foundation upon which the growing edifice of Shakespearian film continues to rise, there emerged in the 1950s and early 1960s four films very different in their adaptive priorities. While Renato Castellani's neo-realistic *Romeo and Juliet* (1954) had little success in its own right, it anticipates *Zeffirelli's version in dramatizing the locations, so giving the streets and buildings of Verona a dramatic presence. Sergei Yutkevich's Russian *Othello* (1955) filled the screen with dramatically powerful and subtly colourful images. Akira *Kurosawa's 1957 *Kumonosu Djo* (*The Castle of the Spider's Web*) cut right across the lines of expectation in the West, presenting, with minimal dialogue, a version of *Macbeth* set in a feudal Japan dominated by regional war lords. Combining realism and Noh theatrical stylization, it captures in visual terms both the themes in Shakespeare's play and the emotions of the characters. Finally, the Russian director Grigori *Kozintsev directed *Hamlet* (1964), often considered the most profoundly satisfying of all Shakespeare films. Its deeply felt rightness emerges partly from the integration of elements—wood, iron, fire, water, stone—into the dramatization of its images, but mainly from the depth of dedicated intelligence and feeling with which Kozintsev engaged with the play. His book *Shakespeare, Time and Conscience* (1967) bears witness to this.

These three latter films were made in translation, which suggests that casting the play's ideas in a different language affords more freedom to recast the theatricality of the plays into cinematic drama.

The late 1960s and early 1970s brought to the screen five films of significance. Franco Zeffirelli's *The Taming of the Shrew* (1966) succeeded in transferring a Shakespeare comedy from the stage to the screen partly through the choice of actors, Elizabeth Taylor and Richard *Burton—known both for their other film roles and for the tempestuous nature of their marriage—and partly in the effective incorporation of older comic film devices such as the chase. Zeffirelli's *Romeo and Juliet* (1968) succeeded in a very different way. It aimed, by featuring young, inexperienced actors (Leonard Whiting and Olivia Hussey) and by stressing the generation gap between parents and children, to appeal to an adolescent film viewership. Tony *Richardson's *Hamlet* (1969) was the first major cinematic challenge to Olivier's 1948 film. It featured Nicol *Williamson as the Prince and was a remoulding of the Round House theatre production.

Roman Polanski's *Macbeth* (1971) attracted instant attention by the mixture of names among the credits. Financed by Playboy Productions with Kenneth *Tynan as its artistic adviser, the film pulled no punches in making blood imagery central to the visualization of the play. In the early 1970s two very different films of *King Lear* were released. For both filmmakers, the nature of the location was an essential cinematic dimension. Peter *Brook made his film (1971) amid the icy landscape of northern Denmark. Grigori Kozintsev found the barrenness he needed in the rocks of Kazantip. While Kozintsev's film, first shown in the West in 1972, brings out the frailty and yet the appealing nature of the King, Brook aimed to make a film which reduced the viewer's emotional involvement to a minimum.

No Shakespeare cinema film of any consequence was made during the rest of the 1970s, and it seemed that with the BBC project to film all the plays for television between 1978 and 1985, big-screen Shakespeare had had its day. Derek Jarman's *The Tempest* (1980) was the only cinema adaptation made between 1971 and 1989, when Kenneth *Branagh's *Henry V* was the forerunner of a new wave of films. It was followed by Franco Zeffirelli's *Hamlet* (1990), Peter Greenaway's *Prospero's Books* (1991), Christine Edzard's *As You Like It* (1992), Branagh's *Much Ado About Nothing* (1993), Oliver Parker's *Othello* (1995), Branagh's *Hamlet* (1996), Trevor *Nunn's *Twelfth Night* (1996), Adrian *Noble's *A Midsummer Night's Dream* (1996), Baz Luhrmann's *Romeo+Juliet* (1996), and Michael Hoffman's *A Midsummer Night's Dream* (1999).

Kenneth Branagh and Franco Zeffirelli became the trilogists of the 1990s, but where Olivier and Welles had to rely upon box-office returns, this unprecedented surge of films has been fuelled by the vigorous and profitable market for videos. It has meant that while the films have been ostensibly made for cinema exhibition, the overall predominance of close-up photography suggests that many of their images are framed for small-screen viewing. A mere three years after its release, few would find an opportunity to view Branagh's *Hamlet* crisply imaged on a cinema screen, let alone in its original 70 mm format. It has also meant that, in taking account of the predilections of a young, domestic viewership, the striving for instant appeal through both music and images has become increasingly important in recent Shakespeare films. *AD*

Boose, Lynda, and Burt, Richard, *Shakespeare: The Movie* (1997)
Buchman, Lorne M., *Still in Movement* (1991)
Davies, Anthony, *Filming Shakespeare's Plays* (1988)
Davies, Anthony, and Wells, Stanley (eds.), *Shakespeare and the Moving Image* (1994)
Jackson, Russell (ed.), *The Cambridge Companion to Shakespeare on Film* (2000)
Shaughnessy, Robert (ed.), *Shakespeare on Film* (1998)

Shakespeare Quarterly was founded by the *Shakespeare Association of America in 1950 as a successor to the *Shakespeare Association Bulletin* but since 1972 has been published by the *Folger Library. The *World Shakespeare Bibliography*, recording books, articles, book reviews, dissertations, theatrical productions, and theatre reviews, has appeared as a separate annual supplement since 1982. *SLB*

Shakespeare Recording Society. Between 1960 and 1968, the society had recordings made of 32 plays (excluding *Henry VI* and *Timon of Athens*). Howard O. Sackler directs leading Shakespearian actors in the G. B. Harrison edition, emphasizing the lyricism of the verse and making much use of the new stereo effects (Caedmon). See RECORDINGS. *JKC*

Shakespeare's grave. See GRAVE, SHAKESPEARE'S.

Shakespeare Society of China was founded in 1984. Its first decision was to sponsor a Shakespeare festival and to publish a series of annotated plays with bilingual notes. The society has published three issues of *Shakespeare Studies*, the only Chinese journal devoted to a non-Chinese man of letters. *HQX*

Shakespeare Studies, the title of two annual publications. **(1)** Issued by the Shakespeare Society of Japan since 1961, it covers articles by its members in English on Shakespeare and Elizabethan drama. **(2)** It is an international publication including essays, studies, and substantial book reviews, founded and edited by J. Leeds Barroll since 1965. *SLB*

Shakespeare Survey, founded by Allardyce Nicoll in 1948, is an annual publication, each volume having a theme, and includes as a standard feature 'The Year's Contributions to Shakespearian Study', reviewing new developments in critical and textual studies and Shakespeare's life, times, and stage. *Survey* also reprints selected papers from the International Shakespeare Conference. *SLB*

Shakespeare tercentenary of 1864. Though celebrated all over England and further afield, it was the occasion of intense rivalry between London and Stratford-upon-Avon. The London plans were riven by internal rivalries and resulted only in disparate performances and a tree-planting ceremony on Primrose Hill. In contrast Stratford, though it had its difficulties arising principally from actors' sense of their own importance, possessed the tremendous asset of Edward Fordham Flower, who pressed forward with an ambitious programme which included the construction of a special pavilion in which a banquet, a fancy dress ball, concerts, and performances of the plays took place. In Holy Trinity church on Sunday, 24 April, sermons were preached by Dr Richard Chenevix Trench, Archbishop of Dublin, and Dr Charles Wordsworth, Bishop of St Andrews and nephew of the poet, the import of which for the theatre was that its principal playwright was being embraced by the institution which had long been entrenched in its opposition to the stage.

The real significance of the Shakespeare tercentenary was that it confirmed Shakespeare's elevation to the status of national hero, though none at the time could have foreseen the patriotic role which his country would require him to play (in First World War propaganda) at the tercentenary of his death in 1916. *RF*

Foulkes, Richard, *The Shakespeare Tercentenary of 1864* (1984)

Shakespeare: The Animated Tales, versions of twelve Shakespeare plays, each lasting 30 minutes, with scripts adapted by Leon Garfield preserving Shakespeare's lines in abbreviated form and using a variety of animation techniques. Made in Moscow in collaboration between the Welsh television company S4C and the Russian State Animation Studio, the films were first shown in 1992. *SW*

Shakespeare Wallah, 1965 black-and-white film, produced and directed by Ismail Merchant and James Ivory, who have since become internationally famous for sumptuous versions of literary classics. A real-life Shakespeare troupe, led by Geoffrey Kendal and his family, tour India, with the company disrupted by romance, creating a metadramatic docu-fiction. *TM*

Shakespeare Yearbook. Published annually since 1990, it has an interdisciplinary approach to Shakespeare studies, concentrating especially on articles addressing comparative literary issues and the reception of Shakespeare in specific countries. Later volumes are devoted to special themes, e.g. *Shakespeare and Opera, Shakespeare in Japan.* *SLB*

Shakespeariana. Strictly, the term means anything relating to Shakespeare—in 19th-century usage, generally essays and monographs on Shakespearian topics—but in current parlance it generally implies artefacts, either connected with Shakespeare or depicting him. These may be divided into three sometimes overlapping categories: relics, souvenirs, and objects of (sometimes easy) virtu. **(1)**. Relics. As the desire for tangible contact with the Author grew across the 18th and 19th centuries, pilgrims to Stratford were shown, and sometimes offered for sale, ever-larger collections of objects said to have been owned or used by Shakespeare, including his alleged pencil case, gloves, brooch, favourite shovel-board, numerous chairs, and a 'gold tissue toilet cover or table cover' said to have been given to him by 'his friend and admirer Queen Elizabeth'. The greatest source of relics, however, as of early souvenirs, was the *mulberry tree supposed to have been planted by Shakespeare in his garden at *New Place. The multiplication of these relics in the great age of nascent *bardolatry parallels that of spurious *portraits, and reached its apogee with the *forgeries of W. H. Ireland: with the rise of modern historical scholarship, supremely exemplified by Ireland's nemesis Edmond *Malone, the production of relics largely gave place to the manufacture of souvenirs. **(2)**. Souvenirs. Among Shakespeariana, objects sold to commemorate a pilgrimage to Stratford or to some Shakespeare-related event or festival elsewhere. Prior to 1769, Shakespearian pilgrims generally carved themselves a piece of the mulberry tree or a hunk of one of the poet's alleged pieces of furniture, but from the *Jubilee onwards such activities were gradually replaced by the purchase of commercially manufactured souvenirs, from mulberry-wood snuff boxes to engravings of the *Birthplace. The standard souvenir of modern times has been the picture postcard, but most mass-produced media have been deployed sooner or later around Stratford: one of the earliest surviving coloured prints for a 3-D stereoscopic viewer depicts *Anne Hathaway's Cottage. **(3)**. Objects of virtu. Ornaments, bibelots, *ceramics, tea towels, and so on depicting Shakespeare, his characters, views of Stratford, and the like have similarly multiplied since the 18th century, often placing the National Poet into reassuringly domestic contexts (as, for example, the decoration on a teapot): early examples include a porcelain scent bottle modelled on *Scheemakers's statue of Shakespeare (*c*.1750), and more recent specialized variants would include mouse-mats, screen-savers, and the T-shirt designed by Kasumi to commemorate the Shakespeare Association of America's 1998 conference at Cleveland, Ohio (home of the Rock'n'Roll Hall of Fame), which conflates Bill Shakespeare with Bill Haley. Anyone doubting the status of bardolatry as a world religion need only visit the gift shops at Anne Hathaway's Cottage or the *Folger Shakespeare Library for reassurance. One of the largest collections of Shakespeariana extant belongs to Louis Marder, former editor of *Shakespeare Newsletter*: smaller ones can be seen in the dining rooms of many Stratford bed and breakfast establishments. *MD*

Bristol, Michael, *Big Time Shakespeare* (1996)
Schoenbaum, S., *Shakespeare's Lives* (1970, rev. edn. 1991)

'Shall I die', a love poem (headed 'A Song' in the Oxford edition) of nine ten-line stanzas ascribed to 'William Shakespeare' in a manuscript collection of poems probably assembled in the late 1630s, now in the *Bodleian Library. This is the only contemporary clue to its authorship. Another, unattributed version survives in a manuscript at Yale. Written in a verse form not found elsewhere in the period but resembling lines spoken by *Robin Goodfellow in *A Midsummer Night's Dream* (3.2.36–46), it has a demanding rhyme-scheme which creates the impression of a virtuoso exercise. It exhibits numerous parallels with plays of Shakespeare dating from around 1593–5. Its existence was no secret, but when Gary Taylor, working on the poems for the *Oxford edition of 1986, drew attention to it in 1985 it became the centre of a vast amount of media attention. Many scholars have attacked its ascription to Shakespeare, often erroneously stating that this was made by the Oxford editors rather than the transcriber of the Bodleian manuscript, which also includes, and ascribes to Shakespeare, the *'Epitaph on Elias James'. Given the fact that a number of works were falsely ascribed to Shakespeare during his lifetime and later, the attribution cannot be regarded as certain; but the compiler of a manuscript had less to gain by a false attribution than a publisher. *SW*

Shallow, Robert. He is a country justice who supplies Falstaff with recruits, *2 Henry IV* 3.2, and lends him 'a thousand pound', 5.4.72. In *The Merry Wives of Windsor* he is angry with Falstaff, 1.1; and intends Anne Page for his cousin Slender. *AB*

Shank, John (*c*.1580–1636), actor (Pembroke's Men some time within 1597–1600, Queen's Men some time within 1597–1603, Prince's Men 1610–1612, Palatine's Men (Palsgrave's Men) from 1613, King's Men by 1619 until 1631). In the Sharers Papers dispute of 1635 (initiated by his purchase of Globe and Blackfriars shares from William, son of John *Heminges), Shanks described himself to the Lord Chamberlain as an old man who 'served your noble father, and after that the late Queene Elizabeth, then King James, and now his royal majesty'. Shank was named in the Prince's Men's patent of 1610, the Palatine's Men's patent of 1613, and the King's Men's patent of 1619, and in the 1623 Shakespeare Folio actor list. Contemporary allusions indicate that Shank was a comedian. *GE*

shared lines, verse lines shared or split between two or more speakers, a frequent device for composing fast-paced dramatic dialogue. See SHORT LINES. *GTW*

sharer, one of the core members of a playing company, required to put up capital to purchase costumes and playbooks and receiving in return a proportionate share of the profits after playhouse rent and hired men's wages had been paid. Most sharers—like Shakespeare—were leading actors in the company. *GE*

Sharpham, Edward (1576–1608), dramatist. For the Blackfriars boys Sharpham wrote *The Fleer* and *Cupid's Whirligig*, both published in 1607 and showing echoes of Shakespeare. *The Fleer* contains the line 'Faith, like Thisbe in the play, 'a has almost killed himself with the scabbard', alluding to stage business from early performances of Shakespeare's *A Midsummer Night's Dream* (Flute-as-Thisbe stabbing himself with Pyramus' scabbard instead of his sword) which survived into 20th-century productions. *GE*

Shaw, George Bernard (1856–1950), Irish playwright and critic. 'Shakespeare is a far taller man than I am,' wrote Bernard Shaw, 'but I stand on his shoulders.' The theatre criticism of GBS in the *Saturday Review* between 1895 and 1898 shows his deep love and knowledge of Shakespeare's plays which 'began when I was a small boy'. Yet these reviews are crammed with attacks on the 'poor foolish old Swan'. In one notorious piece he wrote: 'With the single exception of *Homer, there is no eminent writer, not even Sir Walter *Scott, who I can despise so entirely as I despise Shakespear when I measure my mind against his.' These reviews, and much that he wrote in the prefaces to his own plays, were a form of artistic electioneering in which Shaw attacked the sentimental *bardolatry of Henry *Irving and other leading actor-managers who, while worshipping Shakespeare, diminished his work. What especially bothered Shaw was that their revivals of Shakespeare occupied the space in the theatrical repertory which he wanted for the Shavian theatre of ideas that would, Shaw hoped, begin to do for the British stage what Ibsen and *Strindberg had done in *Scandinavia.

In his correspondence with Ellen *Terry, who was finding difficulty in learning her lines as Imogen in *Cymbeline*, Shaw struck a note of tender indignation against the bard ('what a DAMNED fool Shakespear was!') for giving the actress to whom he was addressing his love letters such unnecessary trouble. 'If I were you I should cut the part so as to leave the paragon out and the woman in.' His 'Intelligent Actress's Guide to Cymbeline' led some 40 years later to Shaw's hilarious work of deconstruction entitled *Cymbeline Refinished* (1936), a rewriting of the last act which retains 89 lines of Shakespeare's, but none of them spoken by Imogen, whom he converts into the New Woman he believed Ellen Terry might have been had he been able to lure her away from Irving's *Lyceum.

Shaw's work is full of Shakespearian references and associations, from *O'Flaherty, V.C.* (1915), which discovers Shakespeare to have been born in Cork, to *The Dark Lady of the Sonnets* (1910), in which Shakespeare is revealed as an arch-plagiarist whose most famous lines are first uttered by everyone else including Queen *Elizabeth. In his last play, *Shakes versus Shav* (1949), a work for puppets written in his 93rd year, Shaw points to the influence of *King Lear* on his own *Heartbreak House* (1916–17). 'Nothing', he wrote in this final preface, 'can extinguish my interest in Shakespear.' *MH*

Shaw, July (1571–1629), witness to Shakespeare's *will, a Stratford wool merchant and maltster who from 1597 lived close to *New Place. He rose in status and prosperity, acquiring additional property and serving as churchwarden, burgess, and chamberlain; elected alderman in 1613, he was bailiff in 1616, by which time he had the rank of gentleman, and served again in 1627–8. *SW*

Sheep-Shearing, The. See WINTER'S TALE, THE

Shelton, Thomas. See CERVANTES SAAVEDRA, MIGUEL DE.

Shepherd. The father of Joan la Pucelle is denied by her, *1 Henry VI* 5.6. *AB*

Shepherd, Old. Father of the Clown in *The Winter's Tale*, he finds the abandoned baby Perdita and brings her up as his daughter. *AB*

Shepherd, Young. See CLOWNS.

Sher, Sir Antony (b. 1949), South African/British actor, artist, and novelist. Sher joined the Royal Shakespeare Company in 1982. His remarkable Richard *III* in Bill Alexander's 1985 production scuttled around on crutches, like a giant spider (see page 386). Other notable roles include the Fool (*King Lear*, 1982–3), Shylock (1988), Leontes (1998), and Macbeth (1999). *BR*

Sher, Anthony, *The Year of the King* (1985)

Sheridan, Thomas (1719–88), Anglo-Irish actor, educationalist, and father of Richard Brinsley Sheridan. He was born in Dublin and moved to Drury Lane after a successful appearance as Richard III at Smock Alley in 1743. He played Hamlet and was regarded by Charles Churchill (author of *The Rosciad*) as second only to *Garrick as a tragedian. He took the lead in his own adaptation, *Coriolanus; or, The Roman Matron* (Covent Garden, 1754) but left the stage after failed management in Dublin and worked on elocution and education reform. *CMSA*

Sheriff. He whispers to Essex, *King John* 1.1.43. *AB*

Shipmaster. See MASTER OF A SHIP.

Shipwreck, The, a spectacular puppet version of *The Tempest*, based largely on *Davenant and *Dryden's adaptation, performed 'at the Patagonian Theatre on Exeter-'Change' in 1780. The play multiplies Prospero's problems by introducing 'several witches' as his enemies (missing links between Sycorax and *Macbeth*'s Weird Sisters), but retains its customary happy ending. *MD*

Shore, Jane. The mistress of Edward IV, she is said to have become the mistress of Hastings and Lord Gray, successively. She does not appear in *Richard III*, but Richard accuses her of witchcraft, and condemns Hastings as her 'protector', 3.4. *AB*

Short, Peter. See PRINTING AND PUBLISHING.

shorthand. Note-taking by individuals in the playhouse for personal use was a frequent practice, acknowledged and accepted by the players, but attempts to take down an entire play using early systems of shorthand were frowned upon. The dramatist Thomas *Heywood complained that his plays were 'corrupt and mangled, (copied only by the ear)' and blamed the poor textual quality of one play on shorthand: 'some by Stenography, drew the plot: put it in print: (scarce one word true).' It has been suggested that the Q1 text of *King Lear* derives from a shorthand report, perhaps compiled by an audience member after attending repeated performances. *ER*

Davidson, Adele, 'Shakespeare and Stenography Reconsidered', *Analytical and Enumerative Bibliography*, NS 6 (1992)

Duthie, G. I., *Elizabethan Shorthand and the First Quarto of 'King Lear'* (1949)

short lines, iambic lines of less than the standard ten syllables (tetrameter, trimeter, or dimeter). These may **(1)** appear within a speech of mostly regular lines, usually for variety, but sometimes with expressive effect:

> And a most instant tetter bark'd about,
> Most lazar-like, with vile and loathsome crust,
> All my smooth body.
> (*Hamlet* 1.5.71–3)

Or they may **(2)** end a speech with a pithy final phrase and/or **(3)** link one speech with another (see SHARED LINES). The Macbeths do both here:

> I had most need of blessing, and 'Amen'
> Stuck in my throat.
> These deeds must not be thought.
> (*Macbeth* 2.2.30–31)

Finally, **(4)** they may be evidence of some omission, error, or mislineation in the text.

Shakespeare's poems are almost entirely written in full pentameter lines. The only notable exceptions are the trochaic tetrameters of 'The *Phoenix and Turtle' and the iambic tetrameters of Sonnet 145. *GTW*

Shrewsbury is the county town of Shropshire. Henry IV defeated the Percys and their allies 3 miles (5 km) north-east of the town in 1403 (*1 Henry IV*, Act 5). *AB*

Shylock. See MERCHANT OF VENICE, THE.

Shylock; or, The Merchant of Venice Preserved. See BURLESQUES AND TRAVESTIES OF SHAKESPEARE'S PLAYS.

Sibelius, Jan (1865–1957), Finnish composer. Sibelius composed incidental music for two Shakespeare plays: *Twelfth Night* (Op. 60), which was staged in Helsinki in 1909, and *The Tempest* (Op. 109), first performed in Copenhagen in 1926. The music for the latter was published for concert use as an overture and two orchestral suites. *IBC*

Sicilia, the Latin name for Sicily, is Leontes' kingdom, and the scene of *The Winter's Tale* 1, 2, 3.1 and 3.2, and 5. *AB*

Sicinius Velutus. See BRUTUS, JUNIUS.

Siddons, Sarah (1755–1831), great English tragic actress. She was the eldest of twelve children, daughter of provincial manager Roger Kemble and actress Sarah Ward. All surviving siblings had stage careers, most famously her brothers John and Charles. Her first known role was as Ariel with her father's company in Coventry in

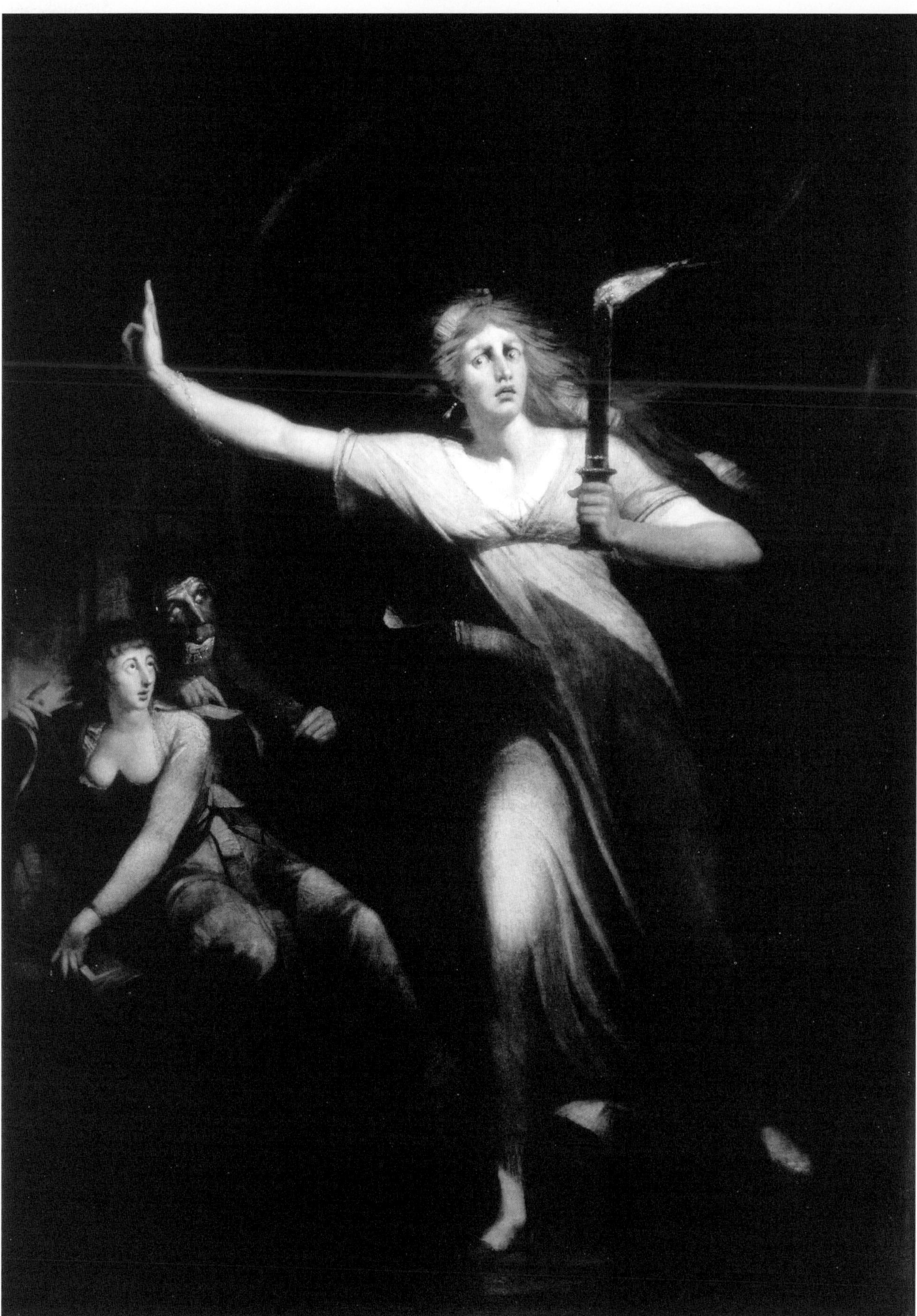

Sarah Siddons, possibly the greatest Lady Macbeth of all, in the sleepwalking scene: mezzotint after Henry Fuseli, 1783.

1776, and, well suited in her youth to breeches parts, other early roles included Rosalind and Hamlet. She made her London debut for *Garrick as Portia in 1775, weeks after the birth of her second child, but was not a success and her contract was not renewed. Returning to the provinces, she played seasons at Liverpool and Bristol and most successfully at Bath where in 1779 she gave her first performance as Lady Macbeth, the role in which she was to achieve her greatest fame.

In 1782 she returned to *Drury Lane (now headed by R. B. Sheridan) and was an immediate success as Isabella in *The Fatal Marriage*, engendering an emotional response that was to characterize her relationships with her audiences. The following year she played her first London Shakespeare as Isabella in *Measure for Measure* and then Constance to her brother John's King John. She was later to play Desdemona to his Othello, Ophelia to his Hamlet, Imogen to his Posthumus, Cordelia to his Lear, Katherine to his Petruchio, and Cleopatra to his Antony. When Kemble took over the management of Drury Lane in 1788, Siddons's performances as Queen Katherine and Volumnia—a grand figure in grand productions—contributed to the success of his *Henry VIII* and *Coriolanus*. Her Lady Macbeth, first seen in London in 1779, was repeated for the opening of the new Drury Lane in 1794, and again for the new Covent Garden in 1809. Her performance in the sleepwalking scene drew the greatest acclaim and at her final performance, in June 1812, the play was concluded at this point.

A handsome actress and a star, Siddons inspired great affection and respect. Touring throughout her career, she had a national reputation, drawing crowds in Dublin and Edinburgh as well as English cities. The effect which *Hazlitt described—'She raised the tragedy to the skies ... it was something above nature. We can conceive of nothing grander'—is evident in the many portraits, by Opie, Gainsborough, Lawrence, *Fuseli, and Hoppner among others, which capture her nobility.

CMSA

Highfill, Philip H., Burnim, Kalman A., and Langhans, Edward A. (eds.), *A Biographical Dictionary of Actors, Actresses, Musicians, Dancers, Managers, and Other Stage Personnel in London, 1660–1800*, vol. XIV (1991)

Sidney, Sir Philip (1554–86), poet and courtier, patron and soldier. Sidney was celebrated by his contemporaries as an ideal embodiment of Renaissance humanism. He also embodied many of the frustrations of the Elizabethan courtier, dependent upon the Queen's favour for political advancement, upon wealthy relatives for financial advancement, and upon his Petrarchan mistress for other favours. In his writing, Sidney celebrates poetry's power to move and instruct, whilst he chafes against the necessity of taking up a pen rather than a sword. Not the least frustrating aspect of Sidney's biography was his own early and unnecessary death at the battle of Zutphen during the *Dutch wars.

None of Sidney's work was published in his lifetime though it may have circulated in manuscript. The romance *Arcadia*, published in 1590, the sonnet sequence *Astrophil and Stella* (1591 and 1598), and *An Apology for Poetry* (1595) had a powerful influence upon English Renaissance literature. The publication of *Astrophil* possibly inspired the vogue for sonnet cycles in the 1590s. Moreover, although the *Apology* attacked English drama for disregarding the unities of time and place, and ignoring decorum by mingling clowns and kings, Sidney's works were to inspire English dramatists, in particular that despiser of all unities, Shakespeare. *Arcadia* is the primary source for the Gloucester sub-plot in *King Lear*. The blind king of Paphlagonia has rejected his loyal son. He puts himself in the hands of his other bastard son, who deposes the King and causes him to be blinded and cast out. The King's subsequent desire to throw himself from a rock is also Gloucester's chosen method of suicide. Other possible *Arcadian* influences are found in *The Winter's Tale*, *Twelfth Night*, *Hamlet*, and *Pericles*. That Shakespeare was familiar with Sidney's *Astrophil and Stella* is attested to by *Romeo and Juliet*, particularly the echoes of Sonnet 85 in Romeo's final speech in the Capulet tomb.

JKS

Thaler, A., *Shakespeare and Sir Philip Sidney: The Influence of 'The Defense of Poesy'* (1947)

'Sigh no more, ladies'. Sung by Balthasar in *Much Ado About Nothing* 2.3.61. A setting (MS) by Thomas Ford (d. 1648) for three voices, with slight differences to the text in the first verse, and two additional verses, might possibly be an arrangement of the original song from the play. The large number of more recent settings include those by *Arne, Balfe, Coates, Moeran, Quilter, J. C. Smith, Warlock, and *Vaughan Williams.

JB

signatures, Shakespeare's. Six Shakespeare signatures are generally regarded as authentic: one on his deposition in the *Belott–Mountjoy suit, one on the conveyance and one on the mortgage deed of the *Blackfriars Gatehouse, and three on his *will. Copies of *Ovid's *Metamorphoses* (1602) in the Bodleian Library, *Florio's translation of *Montaigne (1603) in the *British Library, and Lambarde's *Archaionomia* (1568) in the *Folger Library bear signatures whose authenticity has had strong support. There are many known *forgeries, including around 80 by Samuel Ireland.

SW

Schoenbaum, S., *William Shakespeare: Records and Images* (1981).

Signet Shakespeare (1963). First put together, with a general introduction by Sylvan Barnet, for publication by Harcourt Brace in 1963, this attractive one-volume American edition, reissued in 1972, presented the plays in chronological order. Ideas about the order in which the plays were written have changed considerably in recent years, and it is instructive to compare the chronology assumed in this edition with that of the *Oxford edition (1986, followed by the *Norton, 1997). The Signet, for example, began with *The Comedy of Errors* and *1 Henry VI*, while the earliest plays in the Oxford are *The Two Gentlemen of Verona* and *The Taming of the Shrew*. The Signet text was attractively presented in double columns, and each play had an introduction by a different scholar or critic, among them W. H. *Auden, who provided a characteristic preamble to the Sonnets. The edition was eclipsed by the *Riverside (1974), which had more lavish illustrations, including some in colour, and a more elaborate apparatus.

RAF

Silence, a country justice, is Shallow's friend in *2 Henry IV*.

AB

silent films. A short scene featuring Beerbohm *Tree acting the death moments of King John (1899) is now preserved as the first Shakespeare film, after which the centre of interest moved to France with a film of the duel scene from Sarah *Bernhardt's *Hamlet* (1900), and a *Hamlet* (1907) and *Julius Caesar* (1907) from Georges Méliès. In Italy, the combination of spectacle and theatricality evident in grand *opera influenced the filming of Shakespearian drama, the Roman and Italian Renaissance plays arousing the most lively interest. Versions of *Julius Caesar* were filmed in 1908, 1910, and 1914, and Enrico Guazzoni directed *Marcantonio e Cleopatra* in 1913.

Cinema in England had more of a struggle to be recognized as an art. There emerged a tendency—which persisted until quite recently—to put famous stage actors before the camera and to base films upon stage productions. A classic instance is the *Hamlet* (1913) which featured Sir Johnston *Forbes-Robertson with the entire Drury Lane theatre cast transferred to a film set at Lulworth Cove.

A number of early silent films emerged from America. In 1916 D. W. Griffith brought Beerbohm Tree to Hollywood for a *Macbeth* and in the same year the American actor Frederick B. Warde was filmed as Lear in Edwin Thanhouser's *King Lear*, which incorporates influences from Griffith's *Birth of a Nation* as

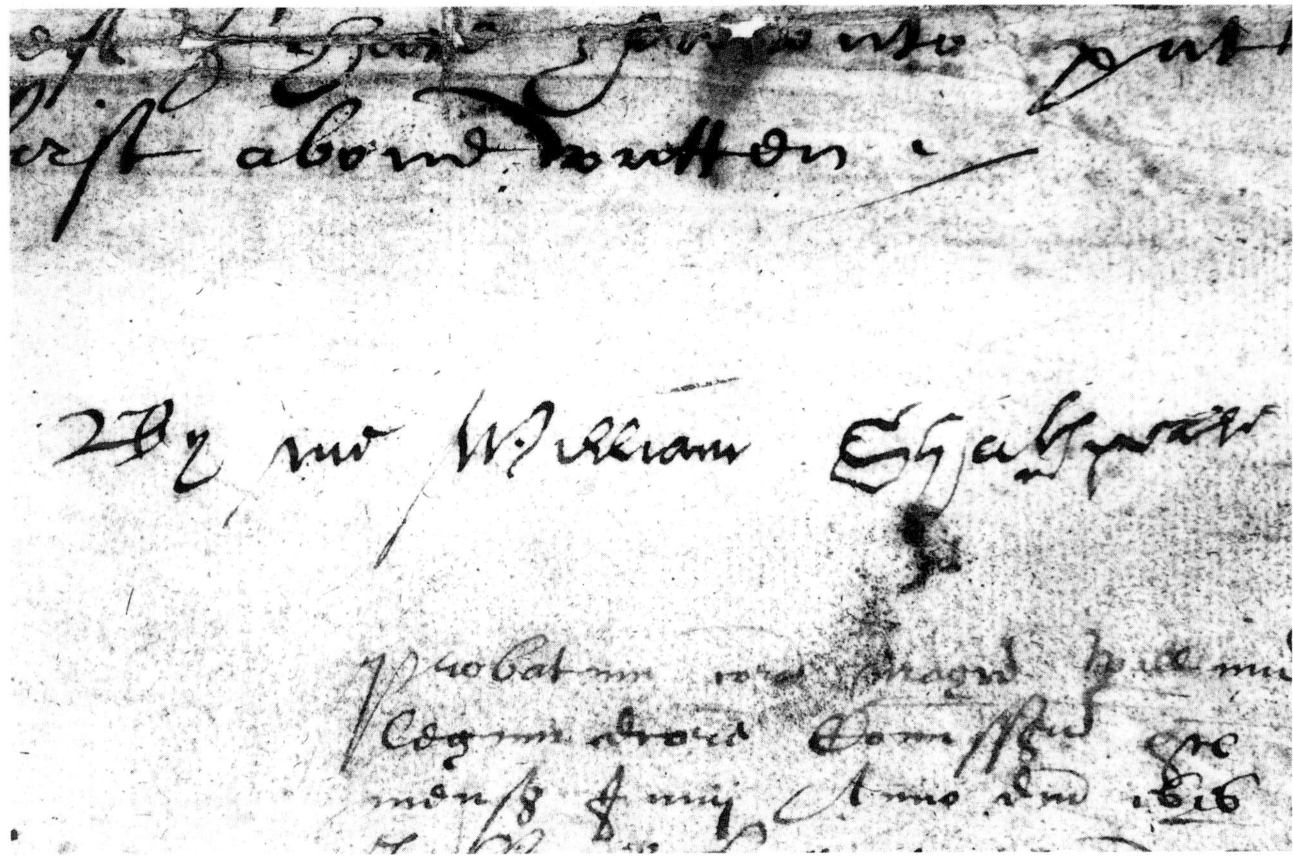

'By me William Shakspeare': the (shaky?) signature from the last sheet of Shakespeare's will, 25 March 1616.

well as transitional devices originally conceived by Méliès. While American Shakespeare films were beginning to discover an essentially cinematic idiom, there remained a reluctance to sever the links between film, theatre, and the literary text.

The most enduring silent Shakespeare films emerged from Germany. Svend Gade's *Hamlet* (1920) with Asta Nielsen in the title role explores gender theory with Hamlet a woman in love with Horatio. It is arguably the first Shakespeare film which appropriates a play to explore psychological theory extrinsic to the play. Its immense studio interiors coupled with its detailed concentration also make it innovatively filmic. The 1922 *Othello* directed by Dimitri Buchowetzki with Emil Jannings in the title role and Werner *Krauss as Iago is an early adaptation of Shakespeare to the German style of expressionistic theatre. Such silent films remain of historical interest, though mainly now for the ways in which they anticipate the quest for an appropriate cinematic language for Shakespeare subsequently pursued in the talkies. (See SHAKESPEARE ON SOUND FILM) *AD*

Ball, Robert Hamilton, *Shakespeare on Silent Film* (1968)
Jackson, Russell (ed.), *The Cambridge Companion to Shakespeare on Film* (2000)
McKernan, Luke, and Terris, Olwen (eds.), *Walking Shadows: Shakespeare in the National Film and Television Archive* (1994)

Silius. See VENTIDIUS.

Silvia, the Duke of Milan's daughter, is in love with Valentine in *The Two Gentlemen of Verona.* *AB*

Silvius, a shepherd in *As You Like It,* is unrequitedly in love with Phoebe. Montanus is the parallel character in *Lodge's *Rosalynde.* *AB*

simile, a common figure of speech that makes an explicit comparison between two things or actions, as in Jaques' image of a boy 'creeping like snail | Unwillingly to school' (*As You Like It* 2.7.146–7). *CB*

Simmes, Valentine. See PRINTING AND PUBLISHING.

Simonides, King. The King of Pentapolis, after seeming angry with Pericles, eagerly assents to his marriage with his daughter Thaisa, *Pericles* 9. *AB*

Simpcox, Simon. Supposedly miraculously cured of blindness, Gloucester exposes him as a fraud, abetted by his wife, *The First Part of the Contention* (*2 Henry VI*) 2.1. His forename is Saunder in many editions, though he names himself both Simon and Saunder in the scene. *AB*

Simpcox's Wife. See SIMPCOX, SIMON.

Simple, Peter. He is Slender's servant in *The Merry Wives of Windsor.* *AB*

Simpson, Richard (1820–76), English scholar and sometime cleric. Simpson was the first to ascribe part of **Sir Thomas More* to Shakespeare (*Notes and Queries,* 1871); and one of the first to discuss both politics (in *The Politics of Shakspere's Historical Plays,* 1874) and, with Henry G. Bowden, Shakespeare's possible Catholicism (in *The Religion of Shakspere,* 1899). *TM*

Simrock, Karl (1802–76), German scholar, poet, and translator. He began his Germanic studies with a collection of Shakespeare's popular sources (1831), but is best known for his translations of medieval poetry (including *Beowulf*). He also translated fifteen Shakespeare plays, mainly for F. Dingelstedt's collective German edition (1867–9). *WH*

Sincler (Sinclo), John (fl. 1592–1604), actor (Pembroke's Men 1592–3, Chamberlain's King's Men 1598–1604). Sincler is named in the plot of *2 Seven Deadly Sins* (performed before 1594, possibly by Strange's Men), the 1623 Folio texts of *Richard Duke of York* (*3 Henry VI*) and *The Taming of the Shrew*, and in the 1600 quarto of *2 Henry IV*, and appears as himself in the Induction to *Marston's *The Malcontent*. His absence from company lists indicates that he was a hired man, not a sharer, and allusions to his appearance suggest that he was particularly thin. *GE*

Sinden, Sir Donald (b. 1923), British actor. A man of warmth and ebullience, he has played everything from television sitcom to King Lear. Having appeared in supporting parts at Stratford-upon-Avon, he was featured in 23 British films, 1952–60. His fruitful connection with the *Royal Shakespeare Company began in 1963 with a virile Richard Plantagenet in the cycle *The Wars of the Roses*; he returned to play Malvolio, Henry VIII, Benedick, and a glowering, Kaiser-like King Lear. Sadly he was never cast as Macbeth. His rich, resonant voice is much imitated by comedians, but, although occasionally in comedy he goes over the top (as in Benedick's soliloquies), he is a much finer artist than his detractors recognize. He played Polonius to the young Stephen Dillane's Hamlet for Peter *Hall in 1994. A scholar of theatre history, he has published two volumes of autobiography, *A Touch of the Memoirs* and *Laughter in the Second Act*. *MJ*

sinkapace. See CINQUEPACE.

Sir Clyomon and Clamides, an anonymous play, first performed in 1570 but not published until 1599, which Shakespeare may have remembered from his childhood and had recourse to in the composition of *As You Like It*. The play features a shepherd, Corin, who gives employment to a princess, escaped from the court in male disguise. Unlike Shakespeare's Corin, this shepherd relates in bawdy dialect the amorous exploits of the country wenches, suggesting a practical attitude towards the business of sheep-rearing and of courtship. Thus, *Sir Clyomon* may have contributed to the more realistic and earthy aspects of pastoralism in *As You Like It*. *JKS*

Sir John Oldcastle Part 1. Attributed to Shakespeare on the title page of the 1600 quarto, but written by *Drayton, *Munday, Richard Hathaway, and Robert Wilson. The authors were prompted to vindicate this Protestant martyr after the irreverent treatment he had received in *1 Henry IV*: it is highly ironic that this play should ever have been attributed to Shakespeare, who was compelled to rename *Oldcastle Sir John Falstaff in subsequent plays. *SM*

Sir Thomas More. In the British Library is an undated dramatic manuscript, in several hands, catalogued as BL, MS Harleian 7368, and bearing the title 'The Booke [i.e. playscript] of Sir Thomas Moore'. The general consensus among the many scholars who have studied this document since the 19th century is that the story behind it runs roughly as follows. In the early to mid-1590s Anthony *Munday, assisted by Henry *Chettle, composed an episodic play about the rise and fall of Thomas More, and submitted a fair copy of it (largely in Munday's hand) to the *Master of the Revels, Sir Edmund *Tilney. Tilney refused to approve it for performance as it stood, partly on the grounds that its depictions of rioting against foreign immigrants made it potentially inflammatory at a time when such disturbances were breaking out again, and he annotated the manuscript to demand revisions which would have involved losing as much as half of the play. Some time later—probably soon after the death of Queen Elizabeth (1603), which would have made some of the play's depiction of her father Henry VIII's court less sensitive—a number of additions were made to the script, though they do not meet Tilney's objections (the play was never acted, revised or unrevised). The additions are in several different hands, among them 'Hand B' (Thomas *Heywood?), 'Hand E' (Thomas *Dekker), and 'Hand D', which bears a close resemblance both to the handwriting of Shakespeare's attested *signatures and to the habits of *spelling and of *handwriting implied by printed editions of his works.

It is now generally agreed that Shakespeare wrote the section of the manuscript known as Addition II.D, which is the only specimen we have of writing for the stage in his own hand, and probably Addition III, though this has been copied by a scribe ('Hand C'). Addition II.D is a scene some 164 lines long, in which More single-handedly quells the xenophobic 'Ill May Day' riot of 1517, and was probably based on a comparable scene in Munday and Chettle's first draft: III is a 21-line soliloquy in which More reflects on his promotion to Lord Chancellor. Shakespeare does not seem even to have read Munday and Chettle's drama in its entirety, and consequently those editions of his complete works which accept the two additions as his (such as the *Riverside and the *Oxford) print only Shakespeare's small contribution to the play rather than the whole text.

The manuscript of II.D is of immense interest for the light it can shed on Shakespeare's working practices: if nothing else, its messy appearance, with deletions, false starts, and every appearance of speedy composition, both confirms the account *Heminges and *Condell supply in the *Folio of Shakespeare's facility and calls into question their assertion that they scarce found 'a blot in his papers'. Beyond the question of its palaeography and authorship, the Ill May Day scene, close in imagery and thematic concerns to other work from Shakespeare's early Jacobean period, provides one of Shakespeare's most sustained attacks on bigotry, and though *Sir Thomas More* has little real stage history as such, More's speech to the crowd has featured powerfully in Shakespearian *recitations and one-man shows, notably that of Sir Ian *McKellen, who played More in a Nottingham production of 1964. *MD*

Hamilton, Charles, *In Search of Shakespeare* (1985)
Howard-Hill, T. H. (ed.), *'Sir Thomas More': The Play and the Problem* (1989)
Sisson, C. J. (ed.), *Sir Thomas More* (1954)
Wells, Stanley, and Taylor, Gary, *Shakespeare: A Textual Companion* (1987)

Sisson, C. J. (1885–1966), English scholar. C. J. Sisson brought to bear his 'long familiarity with Elizabethan handwriting' (Preface) on the text of Shakespeare by incorporating many new readings and restoring a light punctuation in his scholarly one-volume edition (*Complete Works*, 1954). He explained his innovations in *New Readings in Shakespeare* (1956), which are often ingenious and worth considering, but many of them have not won general acceptance. *RAF*

Siward (Seyward in *Folio editions), the Earl of Northumberland, leads the attack on Macbeth, *Macbeth* 5. *AB*

Siward, Young. Son of Siward, he is killed by Macbeth, *Macbeth* 5.7. *AB*

Sjöberg, Alf (1903–80), Swedish stage and screen director. At the Royal Dramatic Theatre in Stockholm he directed sixteen Shakespeare plays between 1935 and 1974, developing a Swedish tradition of visually exciting and often politically topical Shakespeare. *I-SE*

Marker, F. J. and L.-L., *The Scandinavian Theatre* (1975)

slavery. See TRAVEL, TRADE, AND COLONIALISM.

Slender, Master Abraham. He is the dim-witted cousin of Shallow, in love with Anne Page in *The Merry Wives of Windsor*. *AB*

Sly, Christopher. He is a drunken tinker, persuaded by a lord that he is a deranged nobleman in the Induction of *The Taming of the Shrew*. *AB*

Sly, William (*c.*1573–1608), actor (*Chamberlain's-King's Men by 1598 until 1608). Sly is named in the roles of Porrex in 'Sloth' and a lord in 'Lechery' in the *plot of *2 Seven Deadly Sins* (performed before 1594, possibly by Strange's Men). By 1597 he was with the Chamberlain's Men and received, with John *Heminges, payment for court performances. His name appears in the actor lists for *Jonson's *Every Man out of his Humour*, *Every Man in his Humour*, *Sejanus*, and *Volpone* in Jonson's 1616 all marry god forbid that

moo nay certainly you ar

for to the king god hath his offyc lent
of dread of Iustyce, power and Comaund
hath bid him rule, and willd you to obay
and to add ampler maiestie to this
he ~~god~~ hath not le only lent the king his figure
his throne ~~and~~ sword, but gyven him his owne name
calls him a god on earth, what do you then
rysing gainst him that god himsealf enstalls
but ryse gainst god, what do you to your sowles
in doing this o desperat ~~ar~~ as you are.
wash your foule mynds with teares and those same hands
that you lyke rebells lyft against the peace
lift vp for peace, and your vnreuerent knees
~~that~~ make them your feet to kneele to be forgyven
~~is safer warrs, then euer you can make~~
~~whose discipline is ryot; why euen your warrs hurly~~
~~cannot proceed but by obedienc~~ what rebell captaine
as mutynies ar incident, by his name
can still the rout who will obay ~~th~~ a traytor
or howe can well that proclamation sounde
when ther is no adicion but a rebell
to quallyfy a rebell, youle put downe straingers
kill them cutt their throts possesse their howses
and leade the matie of lawe in liom
to slipp him lyke a hound; ~~sayeng~~ say nowe the king
as he is clement, yf thoffendor moorne
shoold so much com to short of your great trespas
as but to banysh you, whether woold you go.
what Country by the nature of your error
shoold gyve you harber go you to ffraunc or flanders
to any Iarman province, ~~to~~ spane or portigall
nay any where ~~why you~~ that not adheres to Ingland
why you must needs be straingers, woold you be pleasd
to find a nation of such barbarous temper
that breaking out in hiddious violence
woold not afoord you, an abode on earth
whett their detested knyves against your throtes
spurne you lyke doggs, and lyke as yf that god
owed not nor made not you, nor that the elamentes
wer not all appropriat to ~~ther~~ your Comforts.
but charterd vnto them, what woold you thinck
to be thus vsd, this is the straingers case
and this your momtanish inhumanyty

all fayth a saies trewe letts ~~vs~~ do as we may be doon by

~~all~~ Linco weele be ruld by you master moor yf youle stand our
freind to procure our pardon

moor Submyt you to theise noble gentlemen
entreate their mediation to the kinge
gyve vp yoursealf to forme obay the maiestrate
and thers no doubt, but mercy may be found
yf you so seek it

From addition IID of *Sir Thomas More* (c.1603?), one of the passages most convincingly attributed to Shakespeare: here the humane More quells a riot against foreign refugees. Shakespeare's distinctive 'p' (see HANDWRITING) is visible in the word 'peace', which occurs twice shortly before the cancelled lines.

Folio, in the actor list in the Shakespeare *Folio of 1623, and in the King's Men patent of 1603. Sly also appears as himself in the Induction to *Marston's *The Malcontent.* Although not an original housekeeper of the *Globe he acquired a share in it after Augustine *Phillips died in 1605 and just before his own death he became a housekeeper of the *Blackfriars. *GE*

Smetana, Bedřich (1824–84), Czech composer. For the Shakespeare tercentenary celebrations in Prague in 1864 Smetana composed a *Festival March* and also conducted *Berlioz's *Roméo et Juliette.* Three years later he composed some fanfares for the second act of a production of *Richard III* in Prague; his tone poem *Richard III* (composed in 1857–8) was performed before the start of the performance. *IBC*

Smethwick, John. See FOLIOS.

Smidt, Kristian (b. 1916), Norwegian Shakespeare scholar. He has made distinguished contributions to international scholarship in the areas of textual studies (particularly on *Richard III*, 1969, 1970) and of genre criticism (with four books on *Unconformities in Shakespearian drama*, 1982–93), and has also written on problems of Shakespeare translation. *I-SE*

Smith, Dame Maggie (b. 1934), British actress. An outstanding player, especially in high comedy, she became in 1962 a founder member of the *National Theatre under Laurence *Olivier, to whose Othello she played Desdemona on stage and on film. She also played Beatrice to the Benedick of her then husband Robert *Stephens. Feeling cheated of Rosalind—a part she seemed born to play—when the National staged its all-male *As You Like It*, she moved to the Festival Theatre, Stratford, Ontario, where her Cleopatra, Titania, Lady Macbeth, and Rosalind were acclaimed. She was Duchess of York in the Richard Loncraine/Ian *McKellen film of *Richard III* (1996). *MJ*

Smith, Teena (Mary Lilian) Rochfort (1861–83), English scholar. The poet Robert Browning wrote to the founder of the New Shakespeare Society, Frederick *Furnivall, referring to the recently deceased Teena as 'your sweet lost intimate'. Ann Thompson (*Shakespeare Quarterly*, summer 1998) describes how Teena, burning letters in 1883, fatally set fire to herself. Her brief career is a cautionary Victorian tale, fortunately unthinkable in modern post-feminist academia, of an ardent young female scholar undertaking 'the most complex presentation of the texts of *Hamlet* ever attempted' (an edition of four parallel texts), encouraged if not exploited by the infatuated enthusiasm of an older married male mentor. *TM*

Smith the Weaver. See WEAVER, SMITH THE.

Smock Alley. In the 17th and 18th centuries, Smock Alley, Dublin, was a key location for Shakespearian performance: the theatre's copy of the Third *Folio (1663) survives, in which fourteen of the plays are marked up for performance. Managed from 1745 to 1758 by Thomas *Sheridan, the theatre followed the trends set by comparable London establishments. It closed in 1788. *MTB*

Snare. See FANG.

Snitterfield, a village some 3 miles (5 km) north of Stratford where Shakespeare's paternal grandfather Richard *Shakespeare owned a house and farmed land owned by Robert Arden, Shakespeare's maternal grandfather. John *Shakespeare lived there before moving to Stratford in 1551. William Shakespeare's aunt Margaret Webbe, last surviving sister of Mary *Arden, was buried there in 1614. *SW*

Snout, Tom. He is a tinker in *A Midsummer Night's Dream*, given the parts of Pyramus' father (see 1.2.59) and the 'Wall' (5.1) in the interlude. (In *quarto editions the latter part was given to *Flute.) *AB*

Snug is a joiner who is given the part of the 'Lion' in the interlude of *A Midsummer Night's Dream.* *AB*

Société Française Shakespeare, founded in 1977 as the national French Shakespeare society, affiliated to the *International Shakespeare Association. Its members are academics and students or amateurs. From the first it established close links with the world of theatre, and the aim of its members is to promote the knowledge and appreciation of Shakespeare in France. Two conferences are held each year in November and February: the first is dedicated to the Shakespearian work on the national syllabus of competitive examinations for the recruitment of secondary-school teachers, and the second focuses on a theme agreed two years beforehand. Proceedings of both conferences are published annually. *J-MM*

Soest portrait. This half-length oil painting, executed at some time after 1656 by the Dutch artist Gerard Soest (1600–81), may conceivably be based on the *Chandos portrait: it now hangs in the Shakespeare Centre in Stratford. Its presentation of a comparatively refined-looking, soulful, uncorpulent Shakespeare pleased 18th-century bardolaters, but it has no authority as a likeness. *CT*

Solanio. See SALERIO.

Soldier who has killed his father. In *Richard Duke of York* (*3 Henry VI*) he laments his tragedy before King Henry, 2.5, followed by a second soldier who has killed his son. *AB*

Soldier who has killed his son. See SOLDIER WHO HAS KILLED HIS FATHER. *AB*

soliloquy, a dramatic speech uttered by a single character, usually alone on the stage, either as a confidential disclosure to the audience or in private but audible self-communion. This kind of speech may reveal motives that are hidden from the other characters, as with Richard of Gloucester (e.g. *Richard III* 1.1.1–41); or unfold a character's inner tensions and doubts, as in Shakespeare's most admired soliloquies—those of Brutus, Hamlet, and Macbeth. The device may also serve comic purposes, as in Malvolio's soliloquies (e.g. *Twelfth Night* 3.4.63–82). *CB*

Solinus, Duke of Ephesus. He condemns Egeon to death if he cannot pay a ransom of 100 marks, *The Comedy of Errors* 1.1. *AB*

Somerset, Duke of. **(1)** Edmund Beaufort (d. 1455), the 2nd Duke of Somerset, continues the feud of his elder brother (see (3) below) against the Duke of York in *The First Part of the Contention* (*2 Henry VI*); is made regent of France, 1.3.215 (but has to report France lost, 3.1.85); willingly goes to prison to avert York's attack, 4.8, but when York finds him at liberty, 5.1, it precipitates the Wars of the Roses. He is killed by crookback Richard at St Albans (5.2). **(2)** The Duke of Somerset in *Richard Duke of York* (*3 Henry VI*) appears to be a composite of the brothers Henry and Edmund Beaufort, the 3rd and 4th dukes of Somerset, respectively. He defects with Clarence in protest against Edward's marriage (4.1.121)—Henry Beaufort (d. 1464) also deserted Edward, to rejoin the Lancastrians, whom he had supported initially. The Somerset of Act 5, however, seems always to have been a Lancastrian, like Edmund Beaufort (d. 1471). **(3)** The 1st Duke of Somerset, John Beaufort (1404–44), nephew of Cardinal Beaufort and the Duke of Exeter, and grandfather of Henry VII, tries to keep the peace between Gloucester and the Bishop of Winchester (who becomes Cardinal Beaufort), but quarrels with Richard Plantagenet (later called the Duke of York), inviting those who side with him to pluck a red rose, *1 Henry VI* 2.4.31–3, in the Temple Garden scene. *AB*

Somerville reports the approach of Clarence's troops to Warwick, *Richard Duke of York* (*3 Henry VI*) 5.1. He is called Summerfield in the quarto, Somervile in *Folio editions, and was first called Sir John Somerville by *Capell. *AB*

songs in the plays range from snatches of popular *ballads to lyrics several stanzas long. The First *Folio edition indicates text to be

The Soest portrait of Shakespeare, executed by Gerard Soest (1600–81), pleased the playwright's 18th-century admirers (including Sir Joshua Reynolds, who painted this meticulous copy), but has no authority as a likeness.

sung through indentation and italic typeface, though apparently not with absolute consistency.

Since there is no music in the early editions of the plays and no scores survive that can be associated with particular productions in Shakespeare's lifetime, it is impossible to state categorically that any setting from the period would have been used in the first production of the play. Some songs survive with words and music together in manuscripts of Shakespeare's time or earlier, although words rarely match the play-texts exactly (e.g. the *Willow song). Others, published considerably later in the mid-17th century, have been attributed to composers such as Robert *Johnson, who were active at the time of the original productions.

More details of tunes and settings are given under the heading for each song; see also 'BALLAD', 'BROADSIDE BALLAD', and 'MUSIC IN THE PLAYS'. *JB*

Seng, Peter J., *The Vocal Songs in the Plays of Shakespeare* (1967)
Sternfeld, Frederick W. (ed.), *Songs from Shakespeare's Tragedies* (1964)

sonnet, a short lyric poem, usually of fourteen rhyming lines which in English are of ten syllables (in French twelve, in Italian eleven). The two principal patterns of the sonnet's rhyme-scheme are (i) the Italian or *Petrarchan form, in which the first eight lines (the octave) are distinguished from the last six (the sestet) by rhyme, by a pause, and by a 'turn' in the direction of the poem's thought, the standard rhyme-scheme being *abbaabba, cdecde*, often varied to *abbaabba, cdcdcd*; and (ii) the English or Shakespearian form, established by Surrey, comprising three quatrains and a final couplet rhyming *ababcdcdcdefef, gg*, or, in *Spenser's preferred variant, *ababbabccdcd, ee*. *CB*

Sonnets *(see page 438)*

Sonnets to Sundry Notes of Music. A second, or supplementary title page in *The *Passionate Pilgrim* provides this heading for the last six poems in the volume. There is no clear reason for the division. *SW*

Son who has killed his father. see SOLDIER WHO HAS KILLED HIS FATHER.

soothsayers. (1) A soothsayer warns Caesar to 'Beware the ides of March', *Julius Caesar* 1.2 and 3.1. **(2)** A soothsayer 'reads' the hands of Charmian and Iras, *Antony and Cleopatra* 1.2, and warns Antony away from Octavius Caesar, 2.3. **(3)** In *Cymbeline* 5.6.434, a soothsayer named Philharmonus interprets his own vision 4.2.348–54, and Posthumus' 'label', 5.6. *AB*

Sophocles. See GREEK DRAMA.

Sothern, Edward Hugh (1859–1933), English-born American actor who followed his Hamlet (New York, 1900) with Romeo (1904, opposite his future wife Julia *Marlowe), Benedick, Petruchio, and Malvolio; and later (1909–10)—less successfully—Antony and Macbeth. Regarded as America's leading Shakespearian actor, Sothern was also well received in London (1907). *RF*

soundings (of trumpets). At outdoor playhouses a trumpet was sounded three times to indicate that a performance was about to begin. The figure standing in the hut of the *Swan in de Witt's drawing might be a trumpeter, although his instrument lacks the distinctive bell-mouth. The more refined indoor hall playhouses did not use this device. *GE*

sources. Speculation about the influences upon Shakespeare began during his lifetime. In those critical responses to Shakespeare's work that survive, he is identified as a disciple of *Ovid, as a modern-day *Plautus and *Seneca, as the author of Italian-style comedies. However, Shakespeare's attempts to locate himself within a literary tradition were not always met with such approbation. In *Greene's Groatsworth of Wit* (published in 1592), Robert *Greene accused the poet of stealing the words of his fellow dramatists. Shakespeare is portrayed as an 'upstart crow, beautified with our feathers, that with his tiger's heart wrapped in a player's hide, supposes he is as well able to bombast out a blank verse as the best of you'. Greene accuses Shakespeare of presumption in borrowing the lines of a university-educated dramatist, perhaps himself. The image of the tiger's heart comes from *Richard Duke of York* (*3 Henry VI*), a play that Shakespeare may have written in collaboration with Greene or have based on one of Greene's earlier works. Whatever their relationship, the older dramatist identifies Shakespeare as one whose writing is not pure invention (as later critics would claim) but dependent upon the inventiveness of others, dressed in borrowed plumes. Nevertheless, it is also significant to a study of Shakespeare's sources that Greene lays his charge of plagiarism by plagiarizing Shakespeare. Both dramatists were working in a culture of continual imitation, quotation, and *allusion. Prose romances were rewritten as plays, old plays were rewritten as new, classical texts were translated, adapted, and plundered for moral sententiae, apothegms, and imagery. Greene's own first extant play, *Alphonsus, King of Aragon*, was deeply indebted to *Marlowe's *Tamburlaine*.

Assumptions about Shakespeare's reading have invariably depended upon a culture's attitude towards imitation and originality. In 1630, *Milton published a poem praising Shakespeare as an imaginative genius, 'fancy's child', apparently unencumbered by any literary debts. Ten years later, a dedicatory epistle by Leonard *Digges was posthumously published in an edition of Shakespeare's *Poems*, commending the poet for *not* borrowing from Greek, Latin, or English writers: 'Nor begs he from each witty friend a scene | To piece his acts with. All that he doth write | Is pure his own.' As Greene could have testified, this was blatantly untrue, but did not prevent the *Romantic conception of Shakespeare as an artless genius whose work was pure inspiration. When critics did acknowledge Shakespeare's debt to his sources, it was often to his detriment. In *Shakespear Illustrated* (1753–4), Charlotte *Lennox complained that in almost every case the original source was superior to Shakespeare's adaptation and deplored his 'lack of invention' that he should have to rely on these works at all.

In the 21st century, attitudes towards Shakespeare's borrowing are very different. Scholarship has embraced a large number of sources for Shakespeare. There are works to which he returned again and again, perhaps part of his own library. These include Sir Thomas North's translation of *Plutarch's *Lives of the Noble Grecians and Romans*, *Holinshed's *Chronicles*, Ovid's *Metamorphoses* in Latin and in Golding's translation, and the Geneva *Bible. An edition of *Chaucer's works, *Florio's translation of *Montaigne's *Essais*, and a collection of Senecan tragedies were probably also part of Shakespeare's collection. Apart from these, the dramatist drew upon a variety of other sources. Shakespeare clearly learnt and borrowed a great deal from his contemporaries, from *Lyly's comedies and Marlowe's plays and poetry, from Greene's romances, *Lodge's *Rosalynde*, and a number of anonymous plays. He also knew well *Sidney's *Arcadia*, *Spenser's *Faerie Queene*, and the sonnets of Spenser, *Sidney, and *Daniel. Collections of Italian romances such as *Boccaccio's *Decameron*, *Cinthio's *Hecatommithi*, and *Bandello's *Novelle* (the latter reproduced in *Belleforest's *Histoires tragiques*) provided many of the plots for Shakespeare's plays. Classical literature, other than that of Ovid and Seneca, is represented in the canon by reference to *Virgil, Plautus, *Terence, *Apuleius, *Lucan, and *Lucian. Other historians to whom Shakespeare was indebted include Edward *Halle, Jean *Froissart, John *Foxe, Richard *Grafton, and William *Warner. *The *Mirror for Magistrates* was another important historical source. Among didactic writings, Shakespeare seems to have known *Castiglione's *The Courtier*, *Elyot's *The Book of the Governor*, and various tracts including Samuel *Harsnett's *Declaration of Egregious Popish Impostures* and William *Strachey's *True Reportary of the Wrack and Redemption of Sir Thomas Gates*.

The number of potential sources for Shakespeare continues to grow, partly through the discovery of further relevant texts, partly

(cont. on page 441)

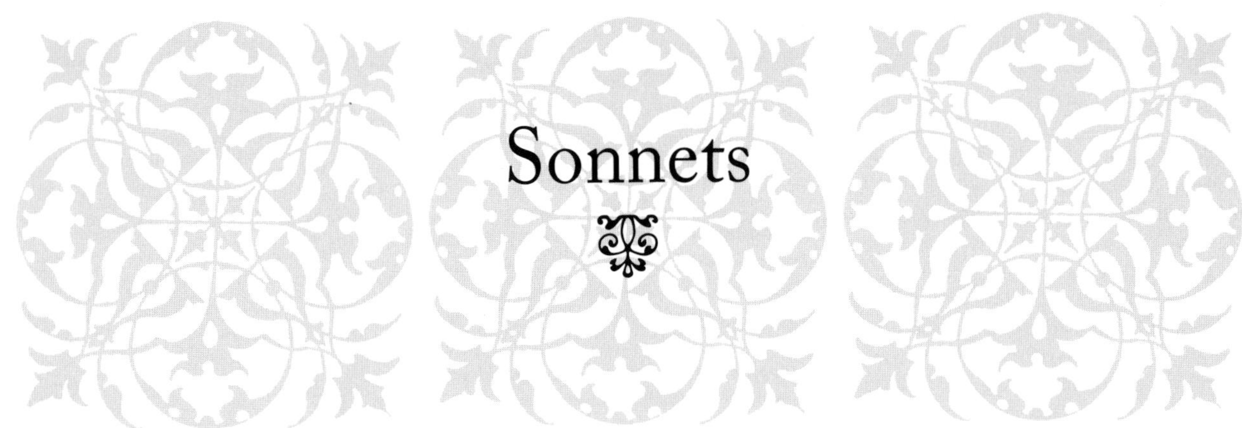

Sonnets

Despite his contemporaries' preference for *Venus and Adonis* and *The Rape of Lucrece*, the Sonnets have long been regarded as Shakespeare's most important and distinctive contributions to *lyric poetry, as well as the most profoundly enigmatic works in the canon. In certain select circles Shakespeare already had a reputation as a sonneteer by 1598, when Francis *Meres wrote of 'his sugared sonnets among his private friends', but although two of his sonnets reached print the following year (in *The *Passionate Pilgrim*) his whole sequence only appeared in 1609, with *A *Lover's Complaint* as its coda. (A *Stationers' Register entry of 1600 for a book called *Amours* by I.D., 'with certain other sonnets by W.S.', could conceivably refer to some of Shakespeare's sonnets, but the issue is clouded by the existence of another sonneteering W.S., William Smith, who had published a sequence of his own in 1596.) The title page of the 1609 quarto is dominated by Shakespeare's surname, and implies that the sonnets of this by-now celebrated dramatist and narrative poet have long been eagerly desired by the reading public: it offers 'SHAKE-SPEARES SONNETS. Never before Imprinted.'

Although the subsequent history of the Sonnets suggests that this book failed at first to excite as its printer clearly hoped it would, its implication that these poems had been awaiting publication for some time by 1609 is borne out by their style. It is probable that Shakespeare had begun writing sonnets some fifteen years before this quarto appeared, in the mid-1590s, during the boom in the form that extended from the posthumous publication of Sir Philip *Sidney's *Astrophil and Stella* in 1591 through Samuel *Daniel's *Delia* (1592), Michael *Drayton's *Idea's Mirror* (1594), and Edmund *Spenser's *Amoretti* (1595), among many other English sonnet sequences. Suggestively, Shakespeare's sonnets share rare vocabulary with *Love's Labour's Lost* (a play which includes no fewer than seven sonnets in its text), *A Midsummer Night's Dream*, and *Richard II*, all of them composed around 1594–5. But Shakespeare was still writing in this form after Meres's report of the existence of some of his sonnets in manuscript: Sonnet 107, for example, appears to allude to the death of Queen Elizabeth in early 1603 ('The mortal moon hath her eclipse endured'). Variants between the 1609 texts of Sonnets 2 and 106 and versions transcribed in 17th-century manuscripts, and between the 1609 texts of 138 and 144 and the versions published in *The Passionate Pilgrim*, suggest that Shakespeare revised some of the earlier-composed poems when organizing his collected sonnets into the sequence published in 1609. The positioning of *A Lover's Complaint* as the tailpiece to the sequence—itself convincingly dated to around 1603–4—suggests that Shakespeare finished assembling the collection at around that time.

TEXT: The 1609 text of the Sonnets, published by Thomas Thorpe, is on the whole a good one, though its punctuation is demonstrably not authorial (two recognizably different compositors display quite different preferences) and an unusual recurrent misprint of 'their' for 'thy', found nowhere else in the canon, suggests that the edition was printed from a manuscript not in Shakespeare's own handwriting. *Shakespeare's Sonnets*, however, was Shakespeare's least reprinted quarto: its contents reappeared only in 1640, in John Benson's pirated volume *Poems: Written by W. Shakespeare, Gent.*, which includes most of the sonnets along with *A Lover's Complaint*, 'The *Phoenix and Turtle', *The Passionate Pilgrim*, and various non-Shakespearian poems by the likes of Ben *Jonson and John *Milton. Benson reordered the sonnets and gave them titles, running some of them together, and, anticipating subsequent anxieties about their content, he made verbal changes to make some refer to a woman rather than a man.

The question hanging over the belated 1609 quarto of *Shakespeare's Sonnets* has always been whether it too, like Benson's opportunistic reprint, was unauthorized, a question hardly simplified by its notoriously baffling dedication to *'Mr W.H.':

TO.THE.ONLY.BEGETTER.OF.
THESE.ENSUING.SONNETS.
MR.W.H. ALL.HAPPINESS.
AND.THAT.ETERNITY.
PROMISED.
BY.
OUR.EVER-LIVING.POET.
WISHETH.
THE.WELL-WISHING.
ADVENTURER.IN.
SETTING.
FORTH.
T.T.

'T.T.' is presumably the printer Thomas Thorpe, but beyond that no wholly convincing explanation of what this dedication is supposed to imply—or any clue as to whether Thorpe transcribed it from the manuscript or composed it himself—has ever been found. Does 'begetter', for example, mean the person who inspired the poems, or the person who wrote them, or the person who obtained the manuscript? Like so much else about the Sonnets, this dedication has provoked endless biographical speculation, and it is admittedly different in kind from the authorial dedications Shakespeare supplied when he published *Venus and Adonis* and *The Rape of Lucrece*. However, the view that the publication of the Sonnets was Thorpe's own unauthorized 'adventure' has usually been based on the questionable assumption that the poems themselves are so compromisingly autobiographical that Shakespeare must have actively sought to prevent their being made public, and while this view certainly invests the appearance of the 1609 quarto with ample drama (exemplified by the relevant episode of John *Mortimer's biographical novel *Will Shakespeare*, which imagines the poet smashing the type of a projected second edition after his wife has complained about the first) it is a very difficult one to substantiate. Given Thorpe's otherwise untarnished reputation and the lack of any evidence that Shakespeare took offence at the appearance of this book (compared to his reported displeasure over *The Passionate Pilgrim*), it seems reasonable to assume that the publication was legitimate.

Sources: Beyond their general debt to the entire European tradition of the sonnet back to *Petrarch, Shakespeare's Sonnets are among his least obviously derivative or allusive works. In form, however, they are specifically indebted to the sonnet's chief English importers, Sir Thomas Wyatt (1503–42) and Henry Howard, Earl of Surrey (1515–47), who had generally translated their Italian originals not only into English but into a different shape of sonnet, replacing the Petrarchan division of the sonnet's fourteen lines into sense-units of eight and six (the octave and the sestet, often rhymed *abbacddc efgefg*) into the simpler 'English' (and subsequently 'Shakespearian') pattern of three quatrains and a couplet (usually rhymed *abab cdcd efef gg*). This form of sonnet had been employed by other English sonneteers between Wyatt's time and Shakespeare's, but rarely as exclusively. Some specific literary borrowings can be traced: Shakespeare's first few sonnets echo a specimen from Erasmus' widely known treatise *De conscribendis epistolis*, a model letter advising a young man to marry, and his last two are variations on an anacreontic epigram from *The Greek Anthology*, while in between different commentators have detected thematic and sometimes verbal debts to *Ovid, Sidney, Spenser, *Marlowe, and Henry Constable (whose *Diana*, 1594, assuming it pre-dates Shakespeare's poem, anticipates Sonnet 99, 'The forward violet thus did I chide'). However, Shakespeare, in common with his most successful fellow sonneteers, seems for most of the sequence to be writing without specific literary models, a fact which, coupled with the poems' very few references to mythology, has contributed to the willingness of many readers to treat the sequence as unmediated autobiography. Indeed Shakespeare is strikingly original in the uses to which he puts the sonnet form: instead of wooing a chaste mistress on the grounds that she ought to be producing beautiful children, the first group of sonnets attempts instead to persuade a beautiful young man to marry on the same grounds, and when the sonnets do turn their attentions to a female addressee they do so with a contemptuous bitterness unequalled by any previous anti-Petrarchan writer. Although Richard *Barnfield's *Cynthia* (1595) includes 20 homoerotic sonnets addressed to a boy, no other English sonnet sequence of its time is as preoccupied as Shakespeare's with an intense relationship between two men.

Synopsis: The first seventeen sonnets, the most uniform group in the sequence, are addressed to the *'Fair Youth', urging him to marry and beget an heir. Down to Sonnet 126, the poems which ensue appear to chart a developing relationship with this man, who the poet promises will be rendered immortal by his verses (verses which neglect, however, to specify his name); different sonnets celebrate the mutuality of their love, or lament the young man's mortality, or regret temporary separations. Others suggest events within this relationship: 41 and 42 seem to record that the young man has been seduced by the poet's mistress, 78–86 express jealousy over his relationship with a *'rival poet', 87–90 lament that the friend has forgotten the poet, 91–6 suggest a friendship renewed despite doubts as to the friend's constancy, and 117–20 apologize for a lapse in the poet's own fidelity.

Sonnet 126, 'O thou my lovely boy'—unusually, a poem in six rhymed couplets rather than a sonnet proper—marks a turning point: the last poem addressed to the young man, it offers a final warning to him of his inescapable mortality. The next sonnets, 127–52, are known as the *'Dark Lady' group, addressed to or concerned with an unfashionably dark-haired, dark-eyed, and dark-complexioned mistress. For the most part, these poems reproach her: she is a tyrant, black in deeds as well as in looks (131), and an adultress (152); she has seduced the poet's friend (133–4); the poet is foolish to love anyone so obviously unworthy (137, 147–52) and is clearly deceiving himself (138), asking her in one sonnet to confess her infidelity (139) and in the next to say she loves him even though this is not true (140). The poet, aware of the delusions of lust but unable to avoid its trap (129), woos his mistress regardless with a series of sexual puns on the name 'Will' (135–6, 143); he is torn between 'a man right fair' and 'a woman coloured ill', suspecting they are lovers (144).

Among this latter group of sonnets, however, are two which seem incongruous. Sonnet 145 (unusually, in octosyllabics), with its apparent pun on 'Hathaway' (' "I hate" from hate away she threw, | And saved my life, saying "not you" '), may date from Shakespeare's courtship in the early 1580s, while Sonnet 146 is more conventionally Christian than the rest of the sequence, resolving to cherish the soul rather than the mortal body. The whole sequence ends with 153 and 154, two sonnets allegorizing the poet's love by means of fables about Cupid. In the 1609 quarto it is then followed by *A Lover's Complaint.*

Artistic features: To read Shakespeare's sequence in the hopes of decoding an implied story, keen though some of these poems seem to be to encourage this strategy, is inevitably to do violence to the lyric compression and self-enclosure of the individual sonnets which compose it, and to the rich variety of tone and technique they achieve despite or rather through the formal limitations of their strict fourteen-line structure. Perhaps the most characteristic feature of Shakespeare's Sonnets is their fine poise between the idea developed over the three quatrains and its qualification or repudiation in the final couplet: it is impossible to decide, for example, whether in Sonnet 30, 'When to the sessions of sweet silent thought', the concluding assertion that 'all losses are restored' by the thought of the friend constitutes a triumphant repudiation of the three quatrains' preceding evocation of life's inevitable costs or a poignantly unconvincing defiance.

Critical history: Although some of the Sonnets were transcribed in manuscript collections during the early 17th century (particularly Sonnet 2), Benson's pirated, doctored edition offered their only 17th-century reprint: out of date by the time of their publication, Shakespeare's Sonnets were in his own age his least popular poems. Most 18th-century editions were based on Benson, and while the sonnet form was itself out of fashion Shakespeare's experiments with it were felt to be particularly embarrassing. George Chalmers, writing in 1796, refused to accept that 'Shakespeare, a husband, a father, a moral man, addressed a hundred and twenty, nay, a hundred and twenty-six *Amorous* Sonnets to a *male* object!', and claimed that the Young Man poems, advocating marriage and procreation, were really addressed to the Queen ('Elizabeth was often considered as a man,' he insisted). It was Edmond *Malone who first singled out the Sonnets as reliable (and uncompromising) clues to Shakespeare's inner life, a development which coincided with the revaluation of the sonnet form among the Romantic poets: *Wordsworth, indeed, revised his low opinion of the sequence to produce his influential sonnet 'Scorn not the sonnet' in 1827, claiming that 'with this key | Shakespeare unlocked his heart.' The bulk of 19th-century comment on the Sonnets, though, is preoccupied with their alleged biographical content at the expense of their artistry, seeking to identify the originals for the Fair Youth, the Dark Lady, and Mr W.H. rather than to explicate the poetry *per se.* The first attempt to make unambiguous confessional sense of Shakespeare's sequence by putting the poems into a different order was made by Charles *Knight in 1841, and many more followed. Nineteenth-century discussions of the young man sequence extend from *Coleridge's attempt to excuse the Sonnets' apparent homoeroticism to Oscar *Wilde's celebration of it (in his story 'The Portrait of Mr W.H.' and at his notorious trial in 1895, an event which effectively 'outed' Shakespeare and paved the way for the Sonnets' subsequent presence in gay subculture). Only with the rise of modernism in the early 20th century—with its delight in complexity, irony, and ambiguity—did the Sonnets at last appear to belong in the mainstream of English poetry, valued and emulated by exponents of the art from Robert Graves to *Auden, and cherished, in particular, by the academic *new critics of the mid-century and their structuralist successors. Outstanding and influential readings include *Empson's account of Sonnet 94, Roman Jakobson and Lawrence Jones's meticulous dissection of Sonnet 129, and the work of Stephen Booth and Helen Vendler. While much criticism remains preoccupied with the question of whether these poems can be read as confessional and whether they constitute evidence about Shakespeare's own *sexuality (with Sonnet 20 a particular bone of contention), the Sonnets are now more widely enjoyed than ever as triumphs of Shakespeare's art as well as potential glimpses of Shakespeare's life. *MD*

Recent major editions

John Kerrigan (New Penguin, 1986); Katharine Duncan-Jones (Arden 3rd series 1998); Stephen Booth (Berkeley, 1977)

Some representative criticism

Booth, Stephen, *An Essay on Shakespeare's Sonnets* (1969)
Empson, William, in *Seven Types of Ambiguity* (1930)
Fineman, Joel, *Shakespeare's Perjured Eye* (1986)
Jakobson, Roman, and Jones, Lawrence, *Shakespeare's Verbal Art in th'Expence of Spirit* (1970)
Krieger, Murray, *A Window to Criticism: Shakespeare's Sonnets and Modern Poetics* (1964)
Mahood, M. M., *Shakespeare's Wordplay* (1957)
Vendler, Helen, *The Art of Shakespeare's Sonnets* (1999)

through our increased understanding of the accessibility of texts. Shakespeare is now generally credited with the ability to read Latin and French, probably Italian and perhaps a little Spanish. There remains no evidence that he knew Greek. Moreover, verbal echoes have suggested that Shakespeare may have known a source in the Italian or Spanish original as well as in the English translation. Where materials not published or not available in English at the right time might once have been discounted as sources, it is now often argued that Shakespeare read foreign editions, or that an English translation existed but is now lost, or that he had recourse to a manuscript copy. A further expansion in the field of potential sources has been recently brought about by changing attitudes towards what constitutes an influence. Critics are now highly sensitive to context, to the literary traditions, the contemporary ideas, the political and historic events that might have impinged upon the author's work. Essential to this interest in Shakespeare's borrowings is an understanding of imitation in the terms of Early Modern England.

The deliberate imitation of classical models was a central part of the English *grammar-school *education. Pupils would learn passages of classical texts by heart and use them as the basis for their own compositions. It was thought that only thus could the young writer achieve an elevated style of his own. In the *Discoveries*, Ben *Jonson describes how the writer must 'convert the substance, or Riches of an other Poet, to his own use . . . Not, to imitate servilely . . . but, to draw forth out of the best, and choicest flowers, with the Bee, and turn all into Honey.' It was not necessarily a question of borrowing a particular phrase or image to recall its meaning in another text and thus to draw a parallel, but rather of adapting the image for one's own purposes. To borrow from a great classical source could carry prestige, depending upon the skill with which the artist had incorporated the allusion into his own work.

The reading habits of the English Renaissance were largely shaped by this practice of *imitatio*. In the essay 'On the Education of Children', Montaigne laments the fact that he never seems to engage deeply with anything he reads but flits from passage to passage, borrowing here and there, without any profound grasp of the whole. He assigns this to a weakness in his intellect but it was a reading habit shared by many of his contemporaries. People wrote down particular phrases or quotations in commonplace books or did their reading of Seneca, Plato, and others from anthologies, filled with the choicest epigrams. Indeed, one of the problems of tracing literary allusions is the myriad sources from which they might have come. Moreover, the importance of memorialization at this time means that we should expect a great number of unconscious echoes and associations to appear in 16th- and 17th-century literature.

Shakespeare is sometimes very candid about his reading. He has a copy of Ovid's *Metamorphoses* taken onto the stage in *Titus Andronicus*. In *Pericles*, *Gower appears as Chorus to introduce and oversee the play. Chaucer too is invoked at the beginning of *The Two Noble Kinsmen*. Elsewhere in the canon there are tributes to Marlowe, Plautus, Seneca, and *Petrarch. But Shakespeare is also typical in the number of works he refers to without any obvious acknowledgement, in his reference to different versions of the same text, and in the pleasure he obviously took in reading analogically. In particular, he seems to have relished the creative fusion of disparate materials into one dramatic form, so that *King Lear* is a meld of Arcadian romance, chronicle history, tragicomedy, anti-Catholic polemic, and contemporary news.

Before considering how Shakespeare adapted his sources, it is worth noting that, at least in comparison with Jonson, Shakespeare was unusually dependent upon his reading. Geoffrey *Bullough's *Narrative and Dramatic Sources of Shakespeare* runs to eight volumes. The sources accumulated for Jonson could be contained in one. The distinction is not reflective of educational background. Though neither attended university, Jonson was a famous autodidact whose classical learning (including his knowledge of Greek) easily outstripped Shakespeare's. The distinction lies in the fact that Jonson invented the majority of his plots whilst Shakespeare borrowed his from elsewhere, sometimes from what Jonson called 'mouldy tales'. Only the plots of *A Midsummer Night's Dream*, *Love's Labour's Lost*, *The Merry Wives of Windsor*, and *The Tempest* seem to have been conceived by Shakespeare. Perhaps Shakespeare's imagination did not easily lend itself to plotting, requiring him to be constantly in search of new material and also requiring him to recycle plots.

But how did Shakespeare adapt his sources? Contraction is one of his most common habits. The action of Arthur *Brooke's *The Tragical History of Romeus and Juliet* and of Chaucer's *Troilus and Criseyde* takes place over a series of months. Shakespeare encompasses the same action in a matter of days. This is partly a dramatic effect but it also influences our interpretation of the action, making us feel more sympathetic to the star-crossed lovers, and perhaps less warm towards the perfidious Cressida. In Holinshed's account, Macbeth ruled over Scotland for ten years very successfully before the murder of the former King was finally avenged. Shakespeare omits the happy reign for reasons of expediency and to darken the character of Macbeth.

Of the *additions* Shakespeare makes to his sources, one of the most characteristic is the inclusion of a comedy sub-plot in which a clown will play a prominent role. This method is apparent in the *Henry IV* plays where the minor roles of Ned Poins, Gadshill, and Oldcastle in the **Famous Victories of Henry V* are considerably expanded. The appearance of a clown in the tragedies (an offence against classical decorum) is particularly significant in *King Lear*, though *Hamlet* includes a lament for the lost clown, Yorick, and even *Macbeth* has its Porter. This innovation is related to Shakespeare's frequent disregard for the genre of his source. The anonymous play *The True Chronicle History of *King Leir* was already a fusion of pastoral, comedy, tragedy, and history when Shakespeare took it over. Shakespeare reinforced the tragic element so that, against all expectations created by the anonymous play and other sources, in *King Lear* the battle is lost and both Cordelia and Lear die at the end. He would also turn tragedy to comedy. At the end of Greene's romance *Pandosto: The Triumph of Time*, the Hermione character is dead and the King's incestuous desire for his daughter leads him to commit suicide. In *The Winter's Tale*, Hermione is restored to her husband and her daughter, thus preventing the development of the incest plot, allowing the play to end happily.

As far as characterization is concerned, Shakespeare tends to alter his sources to make character more psychologically consistent with plot. The action appears to proceed from, rather than being imposed upon, the protagonists. Shakespeare also makes his characters more 'realistic' by suggesting complex inner lives for them, expressed through soliloquy, through other characters' speculations about them, and through dramatic metaphors such as Othello's fragmented speech and unconsciousness. Sometimes, rather than providing motivations, Shakespeare strips them away. In Cinthio's story, the Iago figure sets out to destroy Disdemona after she spurns his love. In Greene's *Pandosto*, the King has good reason to suspect his wife's fidelity. Shakespeare also expands the roles played by women in his sources, keeping Queen Margaret alive long after her historical counterpart was dead so that she could appear in all three *Henry VI* plays and *Richard III*.

We might also perceive in Shakespeare's alterations a desire to complicate the action, not merely by adding a sub-plot as he does in *The Comedy of Errors* where the initial confusion of Plautus' *Menaechmi* is doubled, but by exploring some of the complex ethical and intellectual issues the action throws up. The clear moral framework of Shakespeare's sources often tends to dissolve under the tension he places upon it. The audience is asked to judge between the king who asserts divine right and the nobility who accuse him of crimes against the state; the brother who wants life at any price and the sister who will not sacrifice her immortal soul; the imperatives of revenge and mercy. These dilemmas are often more easily resolved, if they exist at all, in Shakespeare's sources.

Shakespearian criticism has come a long way: from Leonard Digges's insistence that Shakespeare's work was 'pure his own', to an appreciation of the dramatist's creativity and invention in adapting his sources. As Jonathan Bate expresses it in *The Genius of Shakespeare*, 'The range and extent of Shakespeare's indebtedness is a badge of his genius, not a blemish upon it.' *JKS*

Bate, Jonathan, *The Genius of Shakespeare* (1997)

Bullough, Geoffrey, *Narrative and Dramatic Sources of Shakespeare* (8 vols., 1957–75)

Southampton, Henry Wriothesley, 3rd Earl of (1573–1624), Shakespeare's patron from 1593, and the dedicatee of *Venus and Adonis* (1593) and *The Rape of Lucrece* (1594), the latter a poem which no doubt appealed to Southampton's interest in republican thought.

Southampton was also the patron of Thomas *Nashe and John *Florio, sometime tutor in Southampton's household, a connection which may have allowed Shakespeare to learn the Italian necessary for researching the plots of plays including *The Merchant of Venice* and *Measure for Measure.* A keen frequenter of the playhouses, Southampton is recorded by the professional letter-writer Rowland Whyte in 1600 passing 'away the time in London merely in going to plays every day' in the company of Roger Manners, Earl of Rutland.

Southampton is one of the main contenders for the *'Fair Youth' of Shakespeare's Sonnets: Southamptonites, such as T. W. *Baldwin, argue that his initials 'H.W.' are reversed to 'W.H.' in the printer's dedication, and that the epithet 'Mr', inappropriate for one of Southampton's rank, is a sign of intimacy. They find added evidence for Southampton as 'W.H.' in the 'golden tresses' that the Sonnets celebrate: Southampton was notoriously vain, wearing his auburn hair long, below his shoulders. Southampton was also the patron of the youthful writer Barnabe *Barnes, often identified as the *rival poet of Sonnets 80 and 86.

Like the other main candidate for 'W.H.', Mr William Herbert, Southampton was initially reluctant to marry (a subject broached in the first seventeen sonnets). In 1590, when Burghley (see Cecil, Robert) suggested a union between Southampton, then aged 17, and his granddaughter Elizabeth Vere, daughter of the 17th Earl of Oxford, Southampton declined the offer. He later fell for the charms of Elizabeth *Vernon, one of *Elizabeth I's ladies-in-waiting, whom he married in 1595 after she became pregnant. Their clandestine marriage infuriated Elizabeth, who imprisoned them both for a short spell in the *Fleet.

Soon after his arrival at court in 1590, Southampton became closely allied with Elizabeth's favourite Robert Devereux, Earl of *Essex, sharing his enthusiasm for Sidneian Protestant knighthood. The association proved dangerous. Southampton was persuaded to join Essex's doomed insurrection in 1601. On Thursday, 5 February, Southampton sent 40*s.* to Shakespeare's company at the *Globe, requesting them to revive *Richard II*, which the conspirators hoped would stir the London crowds to rebellion through its depiction of a successful usurpation. The plan, and Essex's coup, failed. Essex was executed; Southampton was imprisoned for life and stripped of his titles.

Southampton was released from prison on the accession of *James I in 1603. His titles were restored, and he was rehabilitated into political life, becoming a member of the East India and Somers Island Companies, and of the Virginia Company's Council. Southampton's involvement with the Virginia Company may have given Shakespeare access to manuscript accounts of the wreck of the *Sea-Adventure* off Bermuda in 1609, an incident that helped inspire *The Tempest.* *CS*

Southern Africa. The history of Shakespeare in Southern Africa provides an object lesson for the argument that Shakespeare is always a political matter. As elsewhere, Shakespeare was introduced by missionaries and colonists and remained consistently important to settler communities, particularly those of British extraction. Nathaniel James Merriman, in a series of lectures delivered at Grahamstown halfway through the 19th century, recommended Shakespeare as exemplar of 'mankind', a sentiment echoed by the last prime minister of the Cape, John x. Merriman, in 1916 at the celebrations on the tercentenary of Shakespeare's death. Lovedale Seminary, founded by the Glasgow Missionary Society in 1841, was in the 1920s teaching plays such as *The Merchant of Venice, Macbeth, Julius Caesar,* and *The Tempest.* Both during the segregation and apartheid periods and after, Shakespeare has featured in secondary and tertiary education. The kind of Shakespeare taught for much of the 20th century has been strongly influenced by the teachings of Mathew *Arnold, the work of A. C. *Bradley, versions of *New Criticism, and the *Scrutiny* critics. As the inevitability of the demise of apartheid became clear the Shakespeare's Schools Text Project, created by the chairman's fund of Anglo-American Corporation in 1987, declared its intention, in a transitional and post-apartheid society, of promoting the survival of the teaching of Shakespeare at all South African secondary schools. Contributions to Shakespeare scholarship in the first half of the 20th century include F. C. Kolbe's *Shakespeare's Way: A Psychological Study* (1930), a study of key motifs in the texts. Geoffrey Durrant, Christina van Heyningen, Colin Gardner, and Derek Marsh (who emigrated to Australia) applied traditional South African approaches during the 1950s and beyond. By contrast, Wulf Sachs's *Black Hamlet* (1937) offers in some respects a more adventurous approach. Sachs, a training psychoanalyst from Lithuania, attempts, in a discussion of the life of John Chavafambira, to explore the intersections between psychoanalysis, *Hamlet* as version of the universal condition, and the colonial/racial situation.

Performance of Shakespeare was also supported by settler communities in the 19th century. Early recorded productions of Shakespeare in Southern Africa include a performance of *Hamlet* by soldiers of the garrison at Port Elizabeth in 1799. In 1829 the first civilian theatre company was formed in Cape Town to provide, over the years, a number of Shakespeare productions for the homesick colonial populace. *Othello* was a much performed play during the 19th century—in what appear to be uniformly racist interpretations—whilst by contrast segregationist and apartheid South Africa in the 20th century avoided it. During the 20th century, productions of Shakespeare, whether in white schools, universities, or by local professional companies, have been mostly tied to current matriculation set plays; a more recent performance of *Julius Caesar* with black actors and a black director hardly challenged a long tradition of uninspired productions for captive audiences, providing profits for theatre practitioners but no new admirers for Shakespeare. Against this trend, Welcome Msomi's Zulu appropriation of *Macbeth,* called *Umabatha,* first performed in the early 1970s and subsequently abroad including a run at London's Aldwych theatre and more recently at the *Globe, engaged in part with an evocation of Zulu nationalism, although the conditions of its production and marketing have been criticized. Janet *Suzman's Market Theatre production of *Othello* with John Kani in the title role during the late 1980s was a much-fêted attack upon racist and misogynist phobias, especially around interracial love.

In 1904 Beerbohm *Tree's production of *The Tempest* elicited a response from W. T. Stead, reading it in the context of King Lobengula and the Matebele uprising. Despite the use of Shakespeare within colonial, segregationist, and apartheid institutions, Shakespeare in the 20th century attracted the interest of an impressive list of black writers, politicians, activists, and thinkers in ways that evidence varying degrees of affiliation, appropriation, or active resistance. His plays have been frequently translated, most

Henry Wriothesley, 3rd Earl of Southampton, by Nicholas Hilliard, certainly Shakespeare's patron and possibly the 'Fair Youth' or 'Young Man' of the Sonnets.

famously by Solomon T. Plaatje, who translated six plays into Sechuana only two of which, his version of *The Comedy of Errors, Diphoshoso-Phoso* (1930), and *Julius Caesar* (1937), survive. Other plays have also been translated into Sechuana, Xhosa, and Afrikaans. Plaatje, who contributed to Israel *Gollancz's tercentenary collection *A Book of Homage to Shakespeare*, is also author of *Native Life in South Africa*, which offered a powerful argument against the anti-black land policies of the government of his day, as well as a founder member of what was to become the African National Congress. Recently his translations of Shakespeare have been viewed as appropriations designed to empower Sechuana culture rather than to promote Shakespeare. Z. K. Matthews, who wrote *Freedom for my People*, records the positive impact upon him of the study of Shakespeare at school in 1915–16. In the 1950s, Lewis Nkosi notes that knowledge of Shakespeare became for black students, as well as a status symbol, a means of affiliation with the erstwhile colonial centre—then perceived as more enlightened than apartheid South Africa. Ndabaningi Sithole of Zimbabwe in 1959 argued that a knowledge of Shakespeare contributed to African Nationalism. Others who have drawn on Shakespeare include Can Themba, Es'kia Mphahlele, Peter Abrahams, Bloke Modisane, the assassinated head of the South African Communist Party Chris Hani, and the present South African President Thabo Mbeki.

In the last two decades debate over the historical and present or future use of Shakespeare has intensified. In 1987 Martin Orkin, prompting an outcry from traditionalist South African Shakespearians, maintained that Shakespeare had been used within cultural and educational institutions in ways that complemented apartheid, and has argued then and on other occasions for appropriation of the text in struggles against reactionary or neo-colonial usages of it. David Johnson, almost a decade later, positions Shakespeare as always part of colonial conspiracy and use of him as always evidence of false consciousness. By contrast, the traditionalists, as apartheid seemed finally to be reaching its nadir, established in the 1980s the Shakespeare Society of Southern Africa, the activities of which remain determinedly Arnoldian and unrepentantly bardolatrous in inclination. More interrogative enquiry occurred at the conference entitled 'Shakespeare—Postcoloniality—Johannesburg 1996' which, held in Johannesburg, attracted an unprecedented number of international scholars not only from the West but from Asian, Middle Eastern, Australasian, as well as Southern African countries and which resulted in the appearance of the volume *Postcolonial Shakespeares*. As the 20th century draws to its close, constituencies advocating a focus on local literatures argue for the abandonment of Shakespeare, described by some as already 'dust in the townships', university courses on Shakespeare dwindle noticeably, and little or no research is being undertaken. On the other hand his work continues to be admired, although mainly by South Africans of European descent. It is still performed on stage fairly regularly although, as earlier, mostly in tandem with current school curricula, where, again, its presence so far has been maintained. *MO*

Johnson, David, *Shakespeare and South Africa* (1996)
Johnson, Lemuel A., *Shakespeare in Africa (and Other Venues): Import and the Appropriation of Culture* (1998)
Nixon, Rob, 'Appropriations of *The Tempest*', *Critical Inquiry*, 13/3 (1987)
Orkin, Martin, *Shakespeare against Apartheid* (1987)
Orkin, Martin, *Drama and the South African State* (1991)
Quince, Rohan, *Shakespeare in South Africa: Stage Productions during the Apartheid Era* (1999)

Southwark, the London borough south of the Thames which includes the *Bankside district. *RSB*

Southwell, John. See HUME, SIR JOHN.

souvenirs. See SHAKESPEARIANA.

Soyinka, Wole (b. 1934), Nigerian playwright, poet, novelist, and political activist. Soyinka's plays combine influences from his own Yoruba culture, Shakespeare, and the Greeks. Soyinka studied Shakespeare with G. Wilson *Knight at Leeds (Knight's *Golden Labyrinth* acknowledges a Soyinka essay on *Lear*), and Soyinka's theatre of ceremony, festival, and ritual frequently echoes Shakespeare: *Macbeth* in *A Dance of the Forests* (1963); the chronicle plays in *Kongi's Harvest* (1967); *Antony* in *Death and the King's Horseman* (1975). A 1983 paper (*Shakespeare Survey*, 36) confirms this eclecticism. *TM*

Spain. Despite the enmity between Spain and Shakespeare's England—reflected very lightly in the caricature of Don Armado in *Love's Labour's Lost*—Spain had taken Shakespeare to its heart by the mid-19th century. The works of Shakespeare were already held in some private libraries in Spain from the 17th century, though it took them some time to come to public notice. The first play to be translated and staged was *Hamlet* (in 1772), but the translation, by Ramón de la *Cruz, was based on J. F. Ducis's neoclassical French version.

The next Shakespearian play to be translated, now from the English, was also *Hamlet* (in 1798). It was a prose translation by Leandro Fernández de *Moratín, who added an introduction, a biography of Shakespeare, and extensive critical notes. Despite his mixed feelings towards Shakespeare, it was Moratín who at the time most contributed to making him known in Spain. His translation was not used in the theatre, where, until well into the first half of the 19th century, Shakespearian performances were based on Ducis's versions and later on various theatrical adaptations. The most popular play on the Spanish stage in this period was *Othello* (*Hamlet* and *Macbeth* failed), which was also the subject of parodies and *zarzuelas* (a type of Spanish operetta).

The first criticism independent of translations was the *Estudio crítico sobre las tragedias de Shakespeare* (1829), by Manuel *Herrera Bustamante. After this, the reception of Shakespeare in 19th-century Spain was conditioned, perhaps impaired, by the pre-existence of Spanish classical drama, and comparison with Calderón was at the centre of such studies as the *Discurso sobre Shakespeare y Calderón* (1849) by Juan Federico Muntadas and *Shakespeare y Calderón* (1881, the centenary of Calderón) by Aureliano Pereira.

Spain has contributed to offering an image of Shakespeare as a 'man of the theatre' by turning him into a stage character in various plays from the 19th century on. First there was *Shakespeare enamorado*, staged in 1828, a translation of Alexandre Duval's *Shakespeare amoureux*. Then Enrique Zumel's play *Guillermo Shakespeare*, produced and published in 1853, which was based on Clemence Robert's French novel about the playwright. The most remarkable was *Un drama nuevo* (A New Drama) (1867), by Manuel *Tamayo y Baus, widely staged in Spain and abroad, and well received in the USA. A contemporary example of this tendency is *El otro William* by Jaime *Salom, produced and published in 1998.

Later in the 19th century various Italian companies playing in Madrid and Barcelona contributed to the popularization of Shakespeare's plays and encouraged Spanish companies and impresarios to put on new Shakespearian productions. This Italian influence may have stimulated new translations, among them two new series which attempted a closer rendering of the originals than ever before. The translators, Jaime *Clark and Guillermo *Macpherson, both of British origin, living in Spain, provided verse translations from the English. Clark only lived to translate ten plays (*Obras de Shakespeare*, 5 vols., 1872–6?), but Macpherson managed to translate 23 (*Dramas de Shakespeare*, 8 vols., 1873).

The example of Clark and Macpherson did not go far, as new prose translations did not cease to appear. Thus the publication of Shakespeare's complete works in the prose translations of Luis *Astrana Marín in 1929 almost outshone Clark's and Macpherson's versions and possibly discouraged verse renderings for several decades. In 1967 José María *Valverde provided new prose translations of the complete plays, but regretted not having enough time to produce them in verse.

This tendency has been countered by two new series of translations by university teachers of English, both grounded on a more solid philological foundation than previous attempts. The team-translations of the *'Instituto Shakespeare' of Valencia University, supervised by Manuel Ángel *Conejero, which started to appear in 1979, use free verse to render Shakespeare's blank verse and aim at being above all theatrical translations. Those by Ángel-Luis *Pujante, of Murcia University, begun in 1986, are also in free verse and seek a balance between three fidelities: to Shakespeare's language, to the dramatic nature of the plays, and to the language of the reader. This interest in Shakespeare is also present in other departments of English at Spanish universities, which have produced works of criticism and scholarship, particularly Seville (Rafael Portillo), Málaga (Pilar Hidalgo and José Ramón Díaz), Barcelona (Pilar Zozaya), Alicante (José Manuel González), and Madrid (Cándido Pérez Gállego and Josephine Bregazzi).

Shakespeare has also been widely translated into the other vernacular languages of Spain from the beginning of the 20th century, particularly into Catalan. The most outstanding of the Catalan translators was Josep Maria de *Sagarra, who, starting in the 1940s, translated 27 plays into Catalan hendecasyllabic lines. However, the new translations by Salvador *Oliva in free verse, begun in the 1980s, have gained much ground. Shakespeare's works were also systematically translated into Basque by Bedita Larrakoetxea and published in the 1970s. No complete translation of Shakespeare into Galician has been produced so far, the various versions being either individual attempts or providing the scripts for stage performance in that language.

As to Spanish Shakespearian productions in the 20th century, they tend to be haphazard and to depend, in the first half of the century, on factors like the pre-eminence of the theatre director, the influence of the cinema, and the loss of influence of the audiences, and, in the second half, on the inconsistencies of subsidized art. Plays widely and frequently translated like *Hamlet* have not been staged in proportion to their popularity among readers, and vice versa (e.g. *The Taming of the Shrew* before the Civil War), the exception being *A Midsummer Night's Dream* in the last three decades. At the end of the century Shakespeare is the most staged playwright in Spain, even more than Calderón, Lope, and Tirso put together, but there is a tendency to stick to well-known plays rather than to try others seldom or never staged.

ALP

González Fernández de Sevilla, Jośe Manuel (ed.), *Shakespeare en España: crítica, traducciones y representaciones* (1993)

Martínez, Eduardo Juliá, *Shakespeare en España: traducciones, imitaciones e influencia de las obras de Shakespeare en la literatura española* (1918)

Par, Alfonso, *Representaciones shakespearianas en España* (2 vols., 1936, 1940)

Portillo, Rafael, and Gómez-Lara, Manuel J., 'Shakespeare in the New Spain; or, What You Will', in Michael Hattaway et al. (eds.), *Shakespeare in the New Europe* (1994)

Pujante, Ángel-Luis, 'Spanish and European Shakespeares: Some Considerations', in F. Toda Iglesia et al. (eds.), *Actas del XXI Congreso Internacional AEDEAN* (1999)

Thomas, Sir Henry, 'Shakespeare in Spain', *Proceedings of the British Academy*, 35 (1949)

Speaight, Robert (1904–76), British actor and author. Having been Falstaff in *2 Henry IV* while an undergraduate at Oxford, he played Osric and the First Player to the Hamlet of John *Barrymore at the Haymarket and Edmund in *King Lear* at the Old Vic, both in 1931. Next year he returned to the Vic as King John, Malvolio, Cassius, and Hamlet. He created Becket in T. S. Eliot's *Murder in the Cathedral* at Canterbury in 1935 and repeated this performance in Britain and abroad over 1,000 times. He was also Christ in the BBC's radio cycle *The Man Born to be King* in 1941. With his mellifluous voice he became identified with the revival of poetic drama and religious plays. He wrote copiously—often biographies of Catholic thinkers and artists. Among his books which touch on Shakespeare are *William Poel and the Elizabethan Revival*, *Nature in Shakespearean Tragedy*, *Shakespeare on the Stage: An Illustrated History*, and his memoirs *The Property Basket.* For more than ten years he contributed reviews of British productions to *Shakespeare Quarterly.* *MJ*

speech-prefixes. In the early printed texts of Shakespeare's plays, speeches are introduced by a prefix or heading in which the character's name or title appears, usually in a brief or abbreviated form, in a contrasting typeface (usually italic) and slightly indented from the left margin of the text column. An individual character may be assigned a variety of different speech-prefixes. In Q2 *Romeo and Juliet*, Lady Capulet's speech-prefixes include *Capulet's Wife*, *Wife*, *Old Lady*, *Lady*, and *Mother.* This variation may result from authorial inconsistency, but it is also possible that compositors changed speech-prefixes on their own initiative when their supply of certain letters of italic type ran short. Shakespeare's attitude toward speech-prefixes may be inferred from the **Sir Thomas More* manuscript in which he three times wrote simply '*other*' as a speech-prefix, leaving the matter of providing the names of the specific characters to a theatrical scribe. *ER*

Speed is Valentine's 'clownish servant' in *The Two Gentlemen of Verona.* *AB*

Speed, John (?1552–1629), historian and cartographer, brought up as a tailor by his father. Fulke *Greville's patronage gave Speed the wherewithal to devote himself to history and maps. He compiled a series of 54 maps of England and Wales by John Norden and Christopher Saxton, published in 1611 as *The Theatre of the Empire of Great Britain* with a description accompanying each map. The work helped compound the emergent concept of the English empire and, through the pictures of the 'wild Irish man', provided a reminder of the so-called barbarous people at its fringes—an image that is often reproduced in commentaries on Caliban in editions of *The Tempest*, probably performed in the same year as Speed's *Theatre* was produced.

Speed's *Theatre* was accompanied by his *History of Great Britain* (1611), covering the period from the Roman conquest to the reign of *James I, and a source for those scenes in the Fletcher–Shakespeare collaboration *All Is True* (*Henry VIII*) probably written by John *Fletcher. *CS*

spelling. The spelling of most current editions of Shakespeare's plays is a modernized form of that of their earliest editions, which was the *compositor's rather than the author's and displayed much irregularity. From the very beginning of printing in England compositors had failed to adopt a standard spelling, a situation which concerned scholars like Sir John Cheke (1514–57) and John Hart (*c.*1510–1574), who suggested a reform of spelling based on phonetic principles. They were opposed by Richard *Mulcaster (*c.*1530–1611) who argued for an agreed form of non-phonetic regularization; most of his recommendations were eventually accepted, a standard being reached about 1650. The spelling reform controversy provided Shakespeare with a target for satire. For example, in *Love's Labour's Lost*, he ridicules the schoolmaster Holofernes, who criticizes the affected courtier Armado for not pronouncing *b* in *debt* and *doubt*, although, in fact, these words were derived from French *dette* and *doute* in the Middle Ages, and not directly from Latin *debitum* and *dubitum* as Holofernes assumed. Other spellings where incorrect views prevailed about the origin of a word include such a form as *spight* modelled incorrectly on *delight* and *night.* *VS*

Wells, Stanley, *Modernizing Shakespeare's Spelling* (1979)

Spencer, Gabriel (1576–98), actor (Pembroke's Men 1597, Admiral's Men 1598), killed by Ben *Jonson on 22 September 1598. Spencer was probably the 'Gabriel' whose name appears in the 1623 Folio text of *Richard Duke of York* (*3 Henry VI*) 1.2. *GE*

Spenser, Edmund (*c*.1552–99), poet. Spenser spent most of his life in Ireland following his appointment in 1580 as secretary to Lord Grey of Wilton, the Lord Deputy of Ireland. Only after Tyrone's rebellion of 1598 destroyed his home did Spenser return to England. His reputation for poetry did not prevent him from dying in poverty there.

After graduating from Cambridge, Spenser published his first major work, *The Shepheardes Calendar*, a series of twelve pastoral eclogues (1579). He subsequently wrote in various genres: elegy (*Astrophel*), the sonnet sequence (*Amoretti*), the pastoral (*Colin Clout's Come Home Again*), the 'Epithalamion', and 'Prothalamion', all published in 1595 except for the last named in 1596. But the work which occupied him for the whole of his life (and which he would never complete) was his epic poem *The Faerie Queene*. In 1590, Spenser returned from Ireland to present the first three books of this work to Queen Elizabeth, who expressed her gratification at its idealization of herself by awarding the poet a pension. All six books were published in 1596, and an edition including the Mutabilitie Cantos in 1609. Drawing upon classical and Italian epic, chronicle history and pastoral, Spenser produced a unique English epic which celebrated the nation's historical and cultural past and present. Shakespeare's debt to *The Faerie Queene* varies in kind. He took hints for the Hero/Claudio plot of *Much Ado About Nothing* and details about Lear and Cymbeline from book 2. But particular images from Spenser's poetry, in the *Faerie Queene* and elsewhere, are to be found scattered throughout Shakespeare's work. *JKS*

Potts, A. F., *Shakespeare and 'The Faerie Queene'* (1958)

Watkins, W. B. C., *Shakespeare and Spenser* (1950)

Spielmann, Marion Harry (1858–1949), English iconographer. Following James Boaden's 1824 study, Spielmann's *Portraits of Shakespeare* (1906–7) is the most important investigation of the provenance and authority of, among many later versions, the *Janssen monument, *Droeshout, and *Chandos representations of Shakespeare. His own portrait collection was sold to America in 1937. *TM*

split lines, see SHARED LINES.

spondee, a metrical unit ('foot') consisting of two successive stressed syllables; in English a device of metrical variation, not the basis for whole lines. 'Then in the blazon of | sweet beau- | ty's best' (Sonnet 106.5). *CB/GTW*

Sprague, Arthur Colby (1895–1991), American academic. A pioneering practitioner of research and criticism in the stage history of Shakespeare's plays. Publications include: *Shakespeare and the Actors* (1944), with vivid accounts of Mrs *Siddons, Edmund *Kean, and Edwin *Booth; *Shakespearian Players and Performances* (1953); and *Shakespeare's Histories: Plays for the Stage* (1964). *TM*

Spurgeon, Caroline (1869–1941), English academic. Her *Shakespeare's Imagery and What it Tells Us* (1935) indexes all Shakespeare's images, revealing the significance of *imagery drawn preponderantly from a single field—sickness in *Hamlet*, or garments in *Macbeth*. Her approach, though mainly enumerative, nevertheless stimulated a new school of language-centred criticism. *TM*

squinting line, also called 'amphibious section' or 'common section', a short line (such as 'Be it so', below) that may equally well be heard as completing the previous short line or as itself completed by the next short line. The ambiguity may be heard in the theatre but is difficult to represent in a printed text: *GTW*

> BRUTUS. After my speech is ended.
> ANTONY. Be it so:
> I do desire no more.
> (*Julius Caesar* 3.1.251–2)

Stafford, Edward. See BUCKINGHAM, DUKE OF.

Stafford, Henry. See BUCKINGHAM, DUKE OF.

Stafford, Humphrey. See BUCKINGHAM, DUKE OF.

Stafford, Sir Humphrey. He helps Buckingham arrest the Duchess of Gloucester and her associates (1.4), and is killed with his brother in attempting to quell the Cade rebellion in *The First Part of the Contention* (*2 Henry VI*) (4.3). He should not be confused with Buckingham in the same play, also called Humphrey Stafford. *AB*

Stafford, Lord. See PEMBROKE, EARL OF.

Stafford's Brother. See STAFFORD, SIR HUMPHREY.

stage decoration, Elizabethan. Elizabethan public places were always brightly decorated and that playhouses were no exception is indicated by John Stockwood's sermon at Paul's Cross of 1578 which refers to the Theatre as 'the gorgeous playing palace', by Thomas White's sermon at Paul's Cross of 1577 calling the Theatre and *Curtain 'sumptuous theatre houses', and Philip *Stubbes's reference to the *Theatre and Curtain as 'Venus' palaces'. We must discount anti-theatrical exaggeration, but the contract for the Fortune (based on the *Globe) called for 'carved proportions called satyrs' and De Witt's drawing of the *Swan—which looks somewhat bare—is accompanied by a description of fake-marble painting of the wooden posts. It seems that brightly painted wood carvings covered the bare walls inside a playhouse.

During a riot at the Swan in 1602 the audience attacked 'the hangings [and] curtains' and there must have been a cloth against the back wall of the stage for Richard *Tarlton to amuse audiences by poking his head through it, for Volpone to peep over, and for Polonius and Claudius to hide behind. It seems likely that the hangings were embroidered or painted in keeping with the general brightness of the playhouses, although in the anonymous *A Warning for Fair Women* Tragedy says, 'The stage is hung with black and I perceive | The auditors prepared for tragedy,' and in *Dekker's *Northward Ho!* 4.1 Bellamont anticipates 'the stage hung all with black velvet' for his tragedy. *GE*

stage directions. Indications of entrances and exits along with calls for specific action, gesture, and special effects are placed apart from the text of the dialogue and set in a contrasting typefont (usually italic) in the quartos and folios of Shakespeare's plays. Although it was once assumed that stage directions originated with the bookkeeper, recent studies of extant dramatic manuscripts have established that stage directions are more likely to be authorial than to be additions by playhouse personnel. Shakespeare's most famous direction for stage action is no doubt '*Exit pursued by a bear*' in *The Winter's Tale*. *ER*

stage doors. Most theatres of Shakespeare's time had two stage doors, in some cases flanking a larger central opening which could be used for ceremonial entrances and exits. If no central opening existed, a 'discovery' (for example Ferdinand and Miranda 'at chess' in Shakespeare's *The Tempest* 5.1.173) might have been effected within the space behind a large stage door. Given the rapid turnover of plays and the short rehearsal periods, it is likely that a predetermined convention rather than an ad hoc decision told an actor which door to use for each entrance and exit. *GE*

stage furniture. Most plays of Shakespeare's time can be performed with little more than the actors and their costumes. Beds are occasionally called for and the most useful piece of furniture would have been a multi-purpose stage booth (rather like an old-fashioned four-poster bed) which could, with minor alterations, also serve as the monarch's dais of state (containing a *throne), a discovery space, a pulpit, a tomb, or to provide a playing space above the stage level. *GE*

The 'permissive' stage directions on this page from the second, 'good' quarto of *Hamlet*, 1604—*'Enter King, and two or three'* and *'Enter Rosencraus and all the rest'*—resemble pre-production suggestions from the playwright rather than stipulations from a theatrical bookkeeper. This text is thought to have been printed from Shakespeare's own manuscript.

Ham. The body is with the King, but the King is not with the body. The King is a thing.

Guyl. A thing my Lord.

Ham. Of nothing, bring me to him. *Exeunt.*

Enter King, and two or three.

King. I haue sent to seeke him, and to find the body.
How dangerous is it that this man goes loose,
Yet must not we put the strong Law on him,
Hee's lou'd of the distracted multitude,
VVho like not in their iudgement, but theyr eyes,
And where tis so, th'offenders scourge is wayed
But neuer the offence: to beare all smooth and euen,
This suddaine sending him away must seeme
Deliberate pause, diseases desperat growne,
By desperat applyance are relieu'd
Or not at all.

Enter Rosencraus and all the rest.

King. How now, what hath befalne?

Ros. Where the dead body is bestowd my Lord
VVe cannot get from him.

King. But where is hee?

Ros. Without my lord, guarded to know your pleasure.

King. Bring him before vs.

Ros. How, bring in the Lord. *They enter.*

King. Now *Hamlet*, where's *Polonius*?

Ham. At supper.

King. At supper, where.

Ham. Not where he eates, but where a is eaten, a certaine conuacation of politique wormes are een at him: your worme is your onely Emperour for dyet, we fat all creatures els to fat vs, and wee fat our selues for maggots, your fat King and your leane begger is but variable seruice, two dishes but to one table, that's the end.

King. Alas, alas.

Ham. A man may fish with the worme that hath eate of a King, & eate of the fish that hath fedde of that worme.

King. *King.* VVhat doost thou meane by this?

Ham. Nothing but to shew you how a King may goe a progresse

stage-keeper, the hired man responsible for sweeping the stage and attaching the playbills to posts near the playhouse, and occasionally called upon for small non-speaking roles in the performance. *GE*

Stanislavsky (Alekseev), Konstantin Sergeevich (1863–1938), Russian actor-director, closely associated with *Chekhov, whose 'system' of acting—designed to balance the actor's inner experience of his role with its precise vocal and physical expression—remains influential throughout Western theatre.

Stanislavsky's work with Shakespeare started in *Much Ado About Nothing* (1896, as Benedick), *Othello* (1896, as the Moor), *Twelfth Night* (1897), and *Julius Caesar* (1903, as Brutus), all produced at the Moscow Society of Art and Literature. At its successor, the famous Moscow Arts Theatre, Stanislavsky staged *The Merchant of Venice* in 1898: controversially, he refused to treat it as Shylock's tragedy and gave the usurer a strong Jewish accent. He revived *Twelfth Night* in 1899, and staged it again in 1917, but the centrepiece of his encounter with Shakespeare was *Hamlet* (1911), co-directed with Gordon *Craig. The production tested the universality of Stanislavsky's realism-oriented acting system, and proved that it could not easily be applied to Shakespeare's poetic text. At the same time Stanislavsky, uncomfortable with tragedy, tried to turn *Hamlet* into a mystery play, with Hamlet a Christ-like figure and Fortinbras an archangel. His career-long grappling with Shakespeare ended in anticlimax when the *Othello* he planned while recovering from a stroke in Nice in 1930 opened and failed in Moscow without his knowledge.

Konstantin Stanislavsky as Benedick, Moscow, 1897.

Stanislavsky's system was debased almost into a psychological therapy in the 1940s and 1950s by the Actors Studio in New York, whose neglect of vocal technique made their 'method-acting' graduates a positive liability in Shakespeare: but it has been adapted successfully by Shakespearian actors around the world, ever since Stanislavsky's writings first appeared in the 1920s. *AO*

Stanislavsky, Konstantin, *Stanislavsky on the Art of the Stage*, trans. and introd. David Magarshack (1950)

Stanley, George. See STANLEY, LORD, EARL OF DERBY.

Stanley, Sir John. He is to take the disgraced Duchess of Gloucester to the Isle of Man, *The First Part of the Contention* (*2 Henry VI*) 2.4. *AB*

Stanley, Lord, Earl of Derby. He professes loyalty to Richard in *Richard III*, but Richard distrusts him and keeps Stanley's son George (Richmond's half-brother) as a hostage. At *Bosworth Stanley refuses to lend military support to Richard (5.6.73) and crowns Richmond Henry VII after his victory. Called Derby by Shakespeare, Thomas Stanley (*c.*1435–1504) was only created Earl of Derby by Henry VII. *AB*

Stanley, Sir Thomas (d. ?1576), uncle of Ferdinando Stanley, Lord Strange, buried at Tong in Shropshire. E. A. J. Honigmann argues that Shakespeare was commissioned to write an epitaph between 1600 and 1603, well after Sir Thomas's death and that of his wife Margaret Vernon, buried with him in 1596. *CS*

Stanley, Sir William. He helps Edward IV escape, *Richard Duke of York* (*3 Henry VI*) 4.6 (mute). *AB*

Starveling, Robin. He is a tailor, given the part of Thisbe's mother in the interlude of *A Midsummer Night's Dream* 1.2.56, and 'Moonshine' in the performance itself, 5.1. *AB*

Stationers' Company and Register. The Stationers' Company of London, a trade guild chartered in 1557, served as the organization that ordered trade practices of printers, publishers, booksellers, and bookbinders. Among the early articles by which the stationers regulated themselves was an ordinance enabling a printer to secure his right to a work (an early form of *copyright) by recording the title with his name in a register book. What stationers called *'copy' belonged to the member concerned once he or she had 'entered' it in this volume. Once entered, a copy could be 'assigned' to other members in a variety of ways: it could be sold, exchanged, mortgaged, or even subdivided into shares. The entries of Shakespearian texts in the Stationers' Register chronicle the publishing fortunes of his poems, individual plays, and the four *folios from the 1590s to the Restoration. *ER*

statuary. Following the spate of public, free-standing statues of Shakespeare produced during the 18th century by sculptors such as *Scheemakers and *Rysbrack, Shakespeare statuary began to be mass-produced on a scale appropriate to the domestic interior. Numerous statuettes of varying quality were produced in England during the 19th century, including those by Edward William Wynn (1811–85). Public *monuments to Shakespeare erected in the 19th century and since (such as the statues in Central Park, New York, and Lincoln Park, Chicago) have in general imitated Scheemakers's much-reproduced statue quite closely: even the *Gower memorial in Stratford modifies its general design only by showing a seated Shakespeare and adding likenesses of four of his characters. *CT*

Steevens, George (1736–1800), English Shakespearian editor and commentator. Steevens produced a groundbreaking old-spelling reprint of *quarto texts entitled *Twenty of the Plays of Shakespeare* (1766), the great variorum expansions of Samuel *Johnson's 1765 edition (1773, 1778), and (in retaliation to Edmond *Malone) a new fifteen-volume variorum (1793). *MLW*

Groom, Nick, 'Introduction' to *The Johnson–Steevens Edition of the Plays of William Shakespeare* (12 vols., 1995), vol. i.
Sherbo, Arthur, *The Achievement of George Steevens* (1990)

Stefano (Stephano). **(1)** He is one of Portia's servants in *The Merchant of Venice*, and appears as a messenger, 5.1. **(2)** *The Tempest.* See Trinculo. *AB*

Stein, Peter (b. 1937), German theatre director. Stein's approach at the Berlin Schaubühne theatre (1970–85) was characterized by prolonged collective research into the social and political context of any play, leading to a two-evening spectacular pageant-exhibition-recreation of the Elizabethan era in *Shakespeare's Memory* (1976). This was in preparation for his 1977 multiple-stage production, with real trees and a pool, of *As You Like It* in a film studio on the outskirts of Berlin. Stein has also memorably staged Ibsen, Gorky, and O'Neill, as well as opera, including Verdi's *Otello* (Welsh National Opera, 1986) and *Falstaff* (WNO, 1988). *Julius Caesar* (1992) was presented at the Salzburg summer festival, where he had become theatre director; his final co-production there in 1997 was *Othello* (directed by Sam Mendes for the Royal *National Theatre) at the Perner-Insel theatre in Hallein. *TM*

Stephens, Sir Robert (1931–95), British actor. Recruited from the *Royal Court to Laurence *Olivier's National Theatre from its inception, he played Benedick to the Beatrice of his then wife Maggie *Smith as well as Jaques in *As You Like It.* Notorious later for drinking and hell-raising, he made a glorious comeback at Stratford as a vulnerable Falstaff (1991) and as a moving, frail King Lear (1993). *MJ*

Sterne, Laurence (1713–68), Anglo-Irish cleric and novelist. Sterne's chosen literary persona Mr Yorick—witty, humorous, volatile, much possessed with death, memory, time, and melancholia—owes as much to Prince Hamlet as to his jester. He governs *Tristram Shandy* (1760–7) and *A Sentimental Journey* (1768) (both crammed with digressions on *Hamlet*), and, scandalously, Sterne's sermons, published as *The Sermons of Mr Yorick* (1760). Appropriately, Sterne's own skull was exhumed by grave-robbers (and recognized by an acquaintance, at an anatomy lecture). *NJW*

Stewart, Patrick (b. 1940), British actor. The balding Yorkshireman has won worldwide iconic status as Captain Picard in the television series *Star Trek: The Next Generation.* Earlier from 1966 he was a stalwart of the *Royal Shakespeare Company, where his roles included Touchstone, Hector, King John, Cassius, Enobarbus, Titus Andronicus, Shylock, and Leontes. In 1998 in Washington, DC, he played a white Othello with black Americans as the Venetians and Cypriots. *MJ*

stichomythia, dramatic dialogue in which two characters rapidly exchange single lines partly echoing one another's previous utterances, as in *Richard III* 4.4.274–98. *CB*

Stoll, Elmer Edgar (1874–1959), American professor and critic, best known in Shakespeare studies for his vigorous, at times cantankerous essays (written over the period 1914–44) critical of Romantic Shakespeare criticism, especially that of A. C. *Bradley. In the spirit of early 20th-century professionalism Stoll believed that interpretative problems in Shakespeare studies could be solved through knowledge of Elizabethan stage techniques and assumptions. For example, he thought that soliloquies were always reliable and that in general, as he put it, in drama things *must* be as they seem. Consequently, Stoll believed *Coleridge and Bradley, with their philosophical interests, were overly subtle complicators of what he thought of as Shakespeare's essentially simple art. Similarly, he was scornful of the *modernist criticism of *Empson, Brooks, and other *New Critics, and he criticized American historical critics like Lily Campbell for being too specialized and downplaying Elizabethan theatrics in favour of antiquarianism. *HG*

Stopes, Charlotte Carmichael (1841–1929), Scottish scholar, member of the New Shakspere Society. Her research into local associations is objective rather than fanciful (although occasionally inaccurate). Books include *Shakespeare's Warwickshire Contemporaries* (1897, rev. 1907) and *Shakespeare's Family* (1901). *Shakespeare's Environment* (1914) reproduces her findings on John *Shakespeare's accumulating debts and obligations. *TM*

Stoppard, Sir Tom (b. 1937), Czech-born British playwright. Stoppard's habitual witty and inventive appropriation of classic literature (Shakespeare, Byron, Wilde, Joyce) is a mixture of challenge, confrontation, parody, and tribute. *Rosencrantz and Guildenstern are Dead* (1966; film 1990) places two of *Hamlet*'s supernumeraries centre stage, puzzling in Beckettian fashion about both the nature of the action and the meaning of the universe. *Dogg's Hamlet, Cahoot's Macbeth* (1979) offers two separate but linked plays, each incorporating truncated versions of the respective Shakespeare texts, the second reflecting Stoppard's continuing preoccupation with oppressive censorship in the former Czechoslovakia. Stoppard's contribution to the 1998 film *Shakespeare in Love* (on which he is co-credited as scriptwriter alongside the American Marc Norman) is assumed to be the script's exhilarating wit and the exuberant combination of comedy and romance it achieves by its sly recycling of the structure of *Romeo and Juliet.* *TM*

Stow, John (1525–1605), historian. His *Survey of London* (1598, 1603, later expanded by *Munday) is still a valuable resource for Shakespearian scholars, describing many aspects of *London's built environment and its cultural activities. He is buried in the church of St Andrew Undershaft, Leadenhall Street, where there is a memorial to him. *RSB*

Kingsford, C. L. (ed.), *A Survey of London by John Stowe* (2 vols., 1908)
Wheatley, H. B. (ed.), *John Stow: The Survey of London* (1987)

Roger Jackson — Entred for his Copie under the handes of Mr Bill warden A booke called A daylie exercise of Pietie devided into 4 parts vizt. Confession of Sinnes Thanksgiving Prayers Obsecration written in latine by John Gerard and translated into English provided he bringe further authority before it be printed — vjd

12° Feb. 1629 — wth mr Dor ffeatlyes hand to this booke of mr Jacksons.

Mr Blounte Isaak Jaggard — Entred for their Copie under the handes of Mr Doctor Worrall and Mr Cole warden Mr William Shakspeers Comedyes Histories & Tragedyes soe manie of the said Copies as are not formerly entred to other men. vizt. — vijs

Comedyes.
The Tempest
The two gentlemen of Verona
Measure for Measure
The Comedy of Errors
As you like it
All's well that ends well
Twelfe night
The winters tale

Histories
The thirde parte of Henry ye sixt
Henry the eight

Tragedies.
Coriolanus
Timon of Athens
Julius Caesar
Mackbeth
Anthonie & Cleopatra
Cymbeline

11° Novembris

Nath: Newburie — Entred for his Copie under the handes of Mr Dor ffeatlie and Mr Cole warden A booke called, A sweet posie for gods saints to smell on conteyninge manie sweete and choise flowers — vjd

Nath: Butter — Entred for his Copie under the handes of Mr Cottington and Mr Cole warden A booke called The Wonderfull resignation of Mustapha and the advancinge of Amurath a yonger brother of the lattie deposed Osman — vjd

14° Novembris

Mr Jackson — Entred for his Copie under the handes of Mr Dor Pierce and Mr Hall warden A booke called An exposition upon the ten Comandemts by Mr Peter Barker minister at Storesame in Dorsetshire — vjd

Gwyneth Paltrow as Lady Viola and Joseph Fiennes as Shakespeare in John Madden's film *Shakespeare in Love*, scripted by Tom Stoppard and Marc Norman, 1998.

Strachey, William (fl. 1588–1620), secretary to Sir Thomas Gates and Lord De La Warr at the English colony at Jamestown. Strachey travelled to Virginia on the *Sea-Adventure* in 1609 when it was wrecked off the coast of Bermuda. Among the accounts of this incident, Strachey's *A True Reportary of the Wrack and Redemption of Sir Thomas Gates, Knight* is the one Shakespeare seems to have relied on most in writing *The Tempest.* Written as a private letter, the *Reportary* was not published until its inclusion in Samuel Purchas's *Pilgrims* (1625) but Shakespeare's connections with the Virginia Company make it likely he read the manuscript. He may also have known Strachey. *JKS*

Frey, Charles, *The Tempest* and the New World', *Shakespeare Quarterly*, 30 (1979)

strain, a section of a song or dance-based instrumental piece (see *Twelfth Night* 1.1.4); often repeated with *divisions. *JB*

strangers, one called Hostilius, discuss Timon's fortunes, *Timon of Athens* 3.2. *AB*

The entry in the Stationers' Register for the hitherto unpublished plays printed in the First Folio, 8 November 1623.

Stratford Festival Theatre, Ontario. See CANADA; GUTHRIE, SIR TYRONE.

Stratford-upon-Avon is the Warwickshire town where William Shakespeare was born, brought up, and educated, where he later bought property, and where he died and was buried. The population of Shakespeare's Stratford can only be roughly estimated, but in 1600 was certainly no more than 2,500 and was probably less. It was, however, growing around this time—from a figure perhaps as low as 1,600 in 1550—due mainly to a drift from the countryside to the town. Its topography was, and still is, based on a grid pattern of streets laid out when Stratford was founded, as a 'new' town, around 1200. The focal point was the present-day Wood Street/Bridge Street axis, along the line of the main road through the town. Much of this had originally been left as open space as a site for the town's market, but by Shakespeare's time, large sections had been filled in, including a row of buildings up the centre of Bridge Street. At the west end of Wood Street, then near the edge of the town, was another open space, which still survives, where the cattle market was held. Branching off from Bridge Street to the north-west was a busy thoroughfare, Henley Street, where Shakespeare's father, John, set himself up as a glove-maker in the 1550s (in the house now preserved as Shakespeare's *Birthplace); again on an important route out of town. High Street, to the south of the main road, was a main shopping area. Beyond that, in Sheep Street and Chapel Street, the atmosphere was quieter, and minor streets, like Ely Street, Scholars Lane, and Waterside, were, for the most part, either undeveloped or lined with barns. The parish church stood (and still stands) somewhat apart from the town, marking the site of the original village. This had been left undisturbed when the new town had been laid out alongside it, but by Shakespeare's day had dwindled to a few large houses occupied by town gentry.

In Shakespeare's time, the state of the roads meant that travel at more than walking pace, even for those fortunate to own a horse and cart, was rarely possible. Most country-dwellers wishing to exchange their farm produce for items they could not make for themselves depended almost entirely on towns within a radius of 5 miles (8 km) or so. As a result, places like Stratford, with populations which now seem very small, had fairs and a weekly market and a whole range of shops and small businesses.

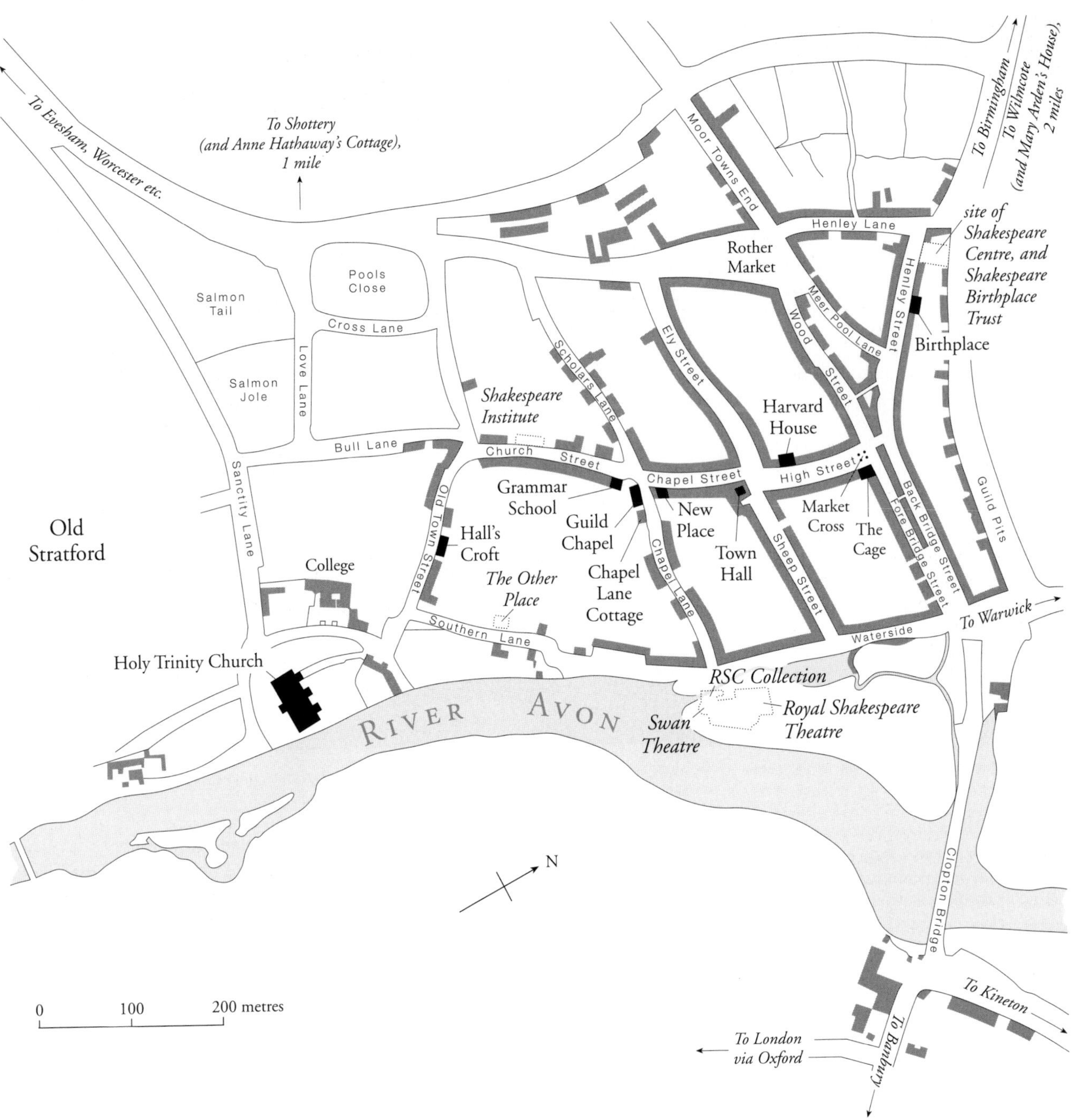

To Evesham, Worcester etc.
To Shottery
(and Anne Hathaway's Cottage),
1 mile
To Birmingham
To Wilmcote
(and Mary Arden's House),
2 miles
Moor Towns End
Henley Lane
Rother
Market
site of
Shakespeare
Centre, and
Shakespeare
Birthplace
Trust
Pools
Close
Salmon
Tail
Cross Lane
Love Lane
Salmon
Jole
Scholars Lane
Ely Street
Wood Street
Meer Pool Lane
Henley Street
Birthplace
Shakespeare
Institute
Harvard
House
Bull Lane
Church Street
Chapel Street
High Street
Sanctity Lane
Grammar
School
Guild
Chapel
New
Place
Market
Cross
The
Cage
Old
Stratford
Old Town Street
Hall's
Croft
Chapel Lane
Town
Hall
Sheep Street
Back Bridge Street
Fore Bridge Street
Guild Pits
College
The Other
Place
Chapel
Lane
Cottage
Southern Lane
Waterside
To Warwick
Holy Trinity Church
RSC Collection
River Avon
Swan
Theatre
Royal Shakespeare
Theatre
N
Clopton Bridge
0
100
200 metres
To Kineton
To London
via Oxford
To Banbury

Stratford-upon-Avon: based on the earliest reliable map (by Samuel Winter, 1768)

Some dealt in food but there were also tailors, shoemakers, glove-makers (including Shakespeare's father), wheelwrights, carpenters, blacksmiths, tinsmiths, and many more. Others, like vintners, mercers, and drapers, dealt in goods brought into the town from more distant parts. On Thursday, market day, the town was exceptionally busy. Some of the streets were named after the particular market held in them, Sheep Street, for example, and Rother Street (after the Old English word for cattle), or Corn Street (now Chapel Street) and Swine Street (now Ely Street). Shakespeare's grandfathers, Richard Shakespeare and Robert Arden, from the nearby villages of Snitterfield and *Wilmcote, would have been typical of the many country-dwellers making their way to Stratford on market day.

Stratford was particularly well placed to serve as a market centre, at an important crossing of the River Avon where several routes converged. The Avon also marked a division between contrasting regions, the open Feldon to the south, largely given over to the growing of crops, and the more wooded area, the Arden, to the north, where cattle farming was more common. Stratford's market was thus an obvious place for the exchange of the different types of produce from these two regions. In the 1490s, a wealthy Stratford townsman, Hugh *Clopton, had made sure the routes to the south remained passable throughout the year by paying for the construction of the fine stone bridge that still spans the river.

'One of the chiefest towns in England for malt-making . . .': Stratford's brewing company, Flower & Sons, influential patrons of the town's Shakespearian theatres since the 19th century, have long celebrated their association with the playwright on their beer-mats.

Stratford was famous for its malting—the roasting and grinding of grain, usually barley, for use in brewing. This was best carried out as near as possible to where the crops grew, as untreated grain was bulky and expensive to transport. The cereal-growing areas to the south of Stratford were particularly productive, hence the growth of the industry in the town: in one contemporary document Stratford is cited as 'one of the chiefest towns in England for malt-making'.

In 1553, Stratford was granted a charter of incorporation. This created a form of town council (the corporation), made up of aldermen and chief burgesses, headed by a high bailiff. They were given various properties in the town formerly belonging to the Guild of the Holy Cross. This was a medieval religious foundation which, until the Reformation, had also provided a school for the sons of its members and almshouses for the sick and infirm. These responsibilities passed, with the guild property, to the new corporation. In this way the corporation came to administer the *grammar school, where Shakespeare is believed to have received his *education. The corporation was not elected: its first aldermen were named in the charter, and they were given the job of nominating the chief burgesses. New members were chosen in the same way as and when vacancies occurred. Its membership came quickly to be made up of the principal tradesmen in the town, including Shakespeare's father, who was nominated to join the corporation in 1557, rising to serve as high bailiff in the year 1568/9.

Like most other towns at the time, Stratford was beset by religious division. At one extreme were those who clung to the old Catholic faith and who were fined for it (including, it is believed, Shakespeare's father). They also risked accusations of treason whenever a national conspiracy was uncovered. At the other extreme were the Puritan reformers who wished to do away with bishops altogether and who saw the church courts as a means of carrying the Reformation into every aspect of people's lives. The majority, however, preferred to avoid taking up these conflicting positions. It is true that, in order to make its Protestant position clear, the Stratford Corporation ordered the defacement of the images in the *Guild Chapel in 1564. Moreover, in 1602 and 1612, it passed by-laws to restrict the activities of travelling players, and in 1605, much anti-Catholic fervour erupted when it was discovered that one of the *Gunpowder Plotters had been living at nearby Clopton House. On the other hand, the demands of Puritan extremists, who sought to use the law to regulate private morals, eventually proved too much for the corporation, leading, in the 1620s and 1630s, to a serious quarrel with the vicar.

Concentrations of people in towns presented problems. Water supplies, mainly wells and streams, could become contaminated, and the lack of a proper system to remove human and animal waste was a particularly acute problem at a time when livestock markets were held in the street and cattle slaughtered on the spot. The corporation did what it could to tackle these problems: 'muckhills' were set up in locations where they were least likely to cause offence, and fines imposed on those who failed to use them: Shakespeare's father was one of these, fined in 1552 for making a muckheap near his house in Henley Street instead of using the authorized one at the out-of-town end of the street. Butchers were ordered not to throw their 'garbages' out into the street, but to carry them out of the town to 'some convenient place', and pigs left by their owners to roam the streets were impounded. Nevertheless, outbreaks of disease were common, with particularly serious results for children. In the 1560s, the decade when Shakespeare was born, only one in three children was likely to survive into adulthood. Shakespeare's own son Hamnet died at the age of 11. Adults were also at risk from epidemics. The year 1558 was one of high mortality, with influenza apparently the cause. Far more devastating was an outbreak of bubonic plague in

1564, the year of Shakespeare's birth, which carried away around 15 per cent of the population. An epidemic of a different type struck in 1597, second only in severity to that in the plague year. Its precise nature is unknown but it was linked to the disastrous weather conditions of the period 1594–7, when heavy summer rains destroyed the harvests, leaving the poor malnourished and prone to infectious disease.

This shortage of food in the 1590s led to serious riots in many large towns and protests in smaller ones, including Stratford. One measure the authorities took was to try to restrict the activities of the maltsters, who were thought to be wasting what little grain there was in the production of beer rather than bread. Others were simply accused of hoarding grain and malt in an attempt to profit out of steeply rising prices. In Stratford, this resulted in the 'Noate of corn and malt' of 1597, featuring Shakespeare's name, and those of some 74 other leading townsmen, some of whom clearly possessed more grain than they needed to feed their families. Serious *fires in 1594 and 1595 made this bad situation worse. At a time when fire-fighting equipment was virtually non-existent and buildings constructed of timber and thatch, town fires were a constant hazard. However, to suffer two in successive years, destroying at least 120 houses (perhaps as much as a quarter of the housing stock), at a time when the town was already experiencing general hardship, was particularly serious. The outbreak was blamed on shoddy backland development which had grown up to house the migrant poor who had drifted into the town. In petitions to the government, the corporation talked of 700 paupers in the town, at least a third of the population. This is reflected in the soaring death rate in 1596 and 1597, and in the regulations brought in by the corporation in an effort to deal with the problem of the poor. Vagrants were denied entry to the town, and newcomers driven out. Townspeople sheltering 'strangers and inmates' were fined and 'tippling houses' more closely regulated. There was another serious epidemic in 1608, probably smallpox, a fire in 1614, and in 1616, the year of Shakespeare's death, a further outbreak of disease, probably typhus, the 'new fever' which Shakespeare's son-in-law, Dr John *Hall, noted in his casebook the following year. On the other hand, there is no evidence that the town went into serious economic decline. Many of Stratford's fine timber-framed buildings, including the richly decorated Harvard House in High Street, date from immediately after the fires of 1594/5, telling evidence of the wealth of the town's leading tradesmen.

RB

Dyer, Alan, 'Crisis and Resolution: Government and Society in Stratford, 1540–1640', in Robert Bearman (ed.), *The History of an English Borough: Stratford-upon-Avon 1196–1996* (1997)

Hughes, Ann, 'Building a Godly Town: Religious and Cultural Divisions in Stratford-upon-Avon, 1560–1640', in Robert Bearman (ed.), *The History of an English Borough: Stratford-upon-Avon 1196–1996* (1997)

Jones, Jeanne E., *Family Life in Shakespeare's England: Stratford-upon-Avon 1570–1630* (1996)

Martin, J. M., 'A Warwickshire Town in Adversity: Stratford-upon-Avon in the Sixteenth and Seventeenth Centuries', *Midland History*, 7 (1982)

Stratford-upon-Avon, Elizabethan, and the theatre. In 1569 John *Shakespeare, the playwright's father, as bailiff of Stratford, approved payments of 9*s.* to the Queen's players and 12*d.* to the Earl of Worcester's players for official performances in the guildhall. These are the earliest recorded performances by professional players in the town. From then onwards many theatre companies visited the town—more, no doubt, than are recorded. Leicester's Men played there in 1573, Warwick's Men in 1574–5 and 1576, Worcester's Men in 1576 and 1577, Leicester's and Worcester's again in 1576–7, Strange's in 1579, Essex's also probably in August 1579, Derby's in 1580, Worcester's again in 1581–2, Berkeley's and Chandos's in 1582–3, and Oxford's, Worcester's, and Essex's in 1585–6. In 1586–7 five companies appeared: the Queen's, Essex's, Leicester's, Stafford's and another (unnamed). Clearly the young Shakespeare had ample opportunity to see plays and to encounter actors. When the Queen's Men arrived in 1587, one of their number, William Knell, had just been killed, in Thame, Oxfordshire. His widow was to marry John *Heminges. It has been conjectured that Shakespeare took Knell's place. In 1583, the Stratford officials contributed to a performance given at Whitsuntide by local amateurs and organized by one Davy Jones, who had married Elizabeth, daughter of Adrian Quiney, in 1577; after her death two years later, he married Frances Hathaway. Perhaps Shakespeare took part; he may even have written the script.

In 1602 it was ordered 'that there shall be no plays or enterlewdes played in the Chamber, the guild halle, nor in any parte of any howse or Courte from hensforward'. This presumably reflects a trend towards Puritanism. When the King's Men visited Stratford for the first time in 1622 they were given money but refused permission to play. *SW*

Eccles, Mark, *Shakespeare in Warwickshire* (1961)

Strato. Brutus asks three followers—Clitus (sometimes spelled 'Clytus'), Dardanius, and Volumnius—to help him commit suicide when faced with defeat at Philippi. They each refuse in turn, but Strato agrees, holding his sword for him to run on to it, *Julius Caesar* 5.5.49. The account of Brutus' death broadly follows that of *Plutarch. *AB*

Strauss, Richard (1864–1949), German composer. He composed incidental music for a performance of *Romeo and Juliet* (Munich, 1887) and published, as part of Op. 67, three *Lieder der Ophelia* (1918). His tone poem *Macbeth* (1886–8), while reflecting some incidents from the play, is essentially a psychological study. *IBC*

Street, Peter (1553–1609), carpenter-builder of the *Globe and *Fortune playhouses. Street completed his apprenticeship in 1577 and may have helped build the *Theatre in 1576; detailed knowledge of its construction would have been useful when he transformed it into the Globe in 1599. *GE*

Edmond, Mary, 'Peter Street, 1553–1609: Builder of Playhouses', *Shakespeare Survey*, 45 (1993)

Strehler, Giorgio (1921–97), Italian director, founder of the Piccolo Teatro in Milan, and a major figure in world theatre. His first productions of Shakespeare occurred in 1948 but after contact with *Brecht he recognized the political potential in the texts. *Coriolanus* in 1957 used epic theatre methods to underline its contemporary relevance; the *Henry VI* plays, staged over two nights as *Il gioco dei potenti* (The Game of the Mighty, 1965), openly drew upon speeches from other plays to illustrate Jan *Kott's theory of the histories as an endless cycle of bloodshed; *King Lear* (1972) presented Lear and Gloucester as old men taunted like animals in a circus. His greatest production of Shakespeare was *The Tempest* (1978), which used baroque scenography to equate Prospero's magic with the controlled artifice of the theatre itself. Throughout his career Strehler relied on the actor Tino Carraro for major Shakespeare roles. *DK*

Strindberg, August (1849–1912), Swedish playwright. Influenced by Hagberg's 1847 translation and *Brandes's 1896 biographical study, he came to regard Shakespeare as 'my teacher'. Strindberg only ever saw four plays in performance, but regarded *Hamlet* as 'a revelation, and a milestone in my gloomy life'. His five *Open Letters to the Intimate Theatre* (1908–9, collected 1919) also refer to Shakespeare's tragedies and histories, which inspired his own cycle of plays on Swedish history. The plot and situation of his misogynistic masterpiece *The Father* (1887)—the destruction of a military man by paranoid sexual jealousy—irresistibly suggest *Othello*. *TM*

strip-cartoon Shakespeare. 'The Cartoon Shakespeare', presenting the text of popular plays inset within a series of illustrations of the

The closet scene from *Hamlet*, as seen in Stephen Grant and Tom Mandrake's 'Classics Illustrated' strip-cartoon edition, 1990.

LEAVE WRINGING OF YOUR HANDS. PEACE! SIT YOU DOWN AND LET ME WRING YOUR HEART.
FOR SO I SHALL IF IT BE MADE OF PENETRABLE STUFF, IF DAMNED CUSTOM HAVE NOT BRAZED IT SO THAT IT IS PROOF AND BULWARK AGAINST SENSE.
WHAT HAVE I DONE THAT THOU DAR'ST WAG THY TONGUE IN NOISE SO RUDE AGAINST ME?
THOU WRETCHED, RASH, INTRUDING FOOL, FAREWELL! I TOOK THEE FOR THY BETTER.
TAKE THY FORTUNE. THOU FIND'ST TO BE TOO BUSY IS SOME DANGER.
O, SUCH A DEED AS FROM THE BODY OF CONTRACTION PLUCKS THE VERY SOUL, AND SWEET RELIGION MAKES A RHAPSODY OF WORDS!
O, SHAME! WHERE IS THY BLUSH? REBELLIOUS HELL, IF THOU CANST MUTINY IN A MATRON'S BONES..
TO FLAMING BEAUTY LET VIRTUE BE AS WAX AND MELT IN HER OWN FIRE.
PROCLAIM NO SHAME WHEN THE COMPULSIVE ARDOR GIVES THE CHARGE, SINCE FROST ITSELF AS ACTIVELY DOTH BURN, AND REASON PANDERS WILL.
O HAMLET, SPEAK NO MORE! THOU TURN'ST MY EYES INTO MY VERY SOUL...
NAY! BUT TO LIVE IN THE RANK SWEAT OF AN ENSEAMED BED, STEWED IN CORRUPTION, HONEYING AND MAKING LOVE OVER THE NASTY STY!
THESE WORDS LIKE DAGGERS ENTER IN MINE EARS. NO MORE, SWEET HAMLET!
A MURDERER AND A VILLAIN!
A SLAVE THAT IS NOT TWENTIETH PART THE TITHE OF YOUR PRECEDENT LORD. A VICE OF KINGS.
A CUTPURSE OF THE EMPIRE AND THE RULE THAT..
FROM THE SHELF A PRECIOUS DIADEM STOLE.. AND PUT IT.. IN HIS POCKET..
NO MORE!
A KING OF SHREDS AND PATCHES! SAVE ME AND HOVER O'ER ME WITH YOUR WINGS, YOU HEAVENLY GUARDS!

action, was launched in 1982. Several artists with different styles contributed, creating their own vision of the settings. John H. Howard, for instance, who illustrated *Twelfth Night* (1985), chose to show a modern setting, with telephones and a Feste who plays the saxophone. By contrast, 'Von' represents the characters of *Macbeth* as ancient Britons. 'Von' also worked on *A Midsummer Night's Dream* for a rival series (1985), setting this play in ancient Athens. Other efforts at presenting Shakespeare to teenagers in the guise of a comic-book include the American 'Classics Illustrated' series. *RAF*

structuralism and poststructuralism are related interdisciplinary theories of signification which made themselves felt in Shakespeare criticism after about 1980. Structuralism had begun around 1910 in the linguistic theories of Ferdinand de Saussure and continued in Central Europe and the Soviet Union, but it only became an important intellectual force in the West in the 1950s and 1960s in France through the structuralist anthropology of Claude Lévi-Strauss, who thought culture and myth could be described, like Saussure's 'language', as a system of binary opposites. Structuralism reached the USA and UK primarily in the 1970s as an interdisciplinary movement with an important branch in literary studies, but it was largely subsumed by what came to be called poststructuralism in the 1980s.

Structuralism was an important influence in English and American literary theory from the 1970s onwards, but Shakespeare studies at first seemed to resist this development in favour of its traditional methods. Pioneering structuralist or semiotic works in Shakespeare studies were written in the 1970s by Terence Hawkes and Howard Felperin, and important work at that time was done in Italy, notably by Alessandro Serpiero, but the impact of this work on the larger field was limited.

Poststructuralism developed in several countries in the 1970s and 1980s as a critique that shared structuralism's idea of a world constructed through language but which broke with some of its other crucial tenets. The key initial figure developing this critique was French philosopher Jacques Derrida, who was especially critical of the structuralist idea of binary opposites. As Derrida's influence developed, Jacques Lacan and Michel Foucault, who had for a time been interpreted as 'structuralists', were relabelled as poststructuralists when it was recognized that their writings anticipated many of Derrida's ideas about language as open-ended and anti-systematic.

The influence of poststructuralism seemed to overtake Shakespeare studies suddenly after 1980 when, according to E. A. J. Honigmann ('The New Shakespeare', *New York Review of Books*, 35/5 (31 Mar. 1988)), the face of Shakespeare studies changed 'more suddenly than ever before'. The year 1985 in particular saw the publication of three influential critical anthologies marking the new influence of poststructuralism: Patricia Parker and Geoffrey Hartmann (eds.), *Shakespeare and the Question of Theory*; Jonathan Dollimore and Alan Sinfield (eds.), *Political Shakespeare: New Essays in Cultural Materialism*; and John Drakakis (ed.), *Alternative Shakespeares*. Parker and Hartmann featured specifically Derridean criticism of Shakespeare, notably the work of the leading Shakespearian deconstructionist Howard Felperin, whose book *Beyond Deconstruction* (also 1985) dealt centrally with Shakespeare. Terry Eagleton contributed a short but provocative instance of politicized deconstruction in his 1986 *William Shakespeare*. But the major line of poststructuralist criticism in Shakespeare studies (few used the label 'structuralist' after Derrida's critique became popular) was of the 'contextualist' variety modelled on the work of Michel Foucault and the related social theory of *feminists, *Marxists, and postcolonialists which became known as *new historicism, *cultural materialism, and poststructuralist feminism, so that, while 'traditional' criticism continued in Shakespeare studies after the changeover, much of the new work in the field has been broadly poststructuralist in its premisses and methods, especially recent feminism, psychoanalysis, new historicism, and cultural materialism. *HG*

Stubbes, Philip (*c.*1555–*c.*1610), pamphleteer. Educated at both Oxford and Cambridge, Stubbes published the popular tract *A Crystal Glass for Christian Women* (1591), and a virulent assault on the stage, *The Anatomy of Abuses* (1583), which condemns plays as incitements 'to idleness, unthriftiness, whoredom, wantonness, drunkenness, and what not'. *RM*

Students, The. See LOVE'S LABOUR'S LOST.

Sturley (Strelly), Abraham (d. 1614), a Worcester man who, after graduating from Cambridge, served Sir Thomas *Lucy at Charlecote and moved to Stratford around 1580. He was bailiff in 1596, and on 24 January 1598 wrote to his friend and townsman Richard *Quiney, who was in London on town affairs, that Shakespeare was interested in buying 'some odd yardland'—about 30 acres (12 ha)—'or other at Shottery'. He wished Quiney to encourage Shakespeare to invest in Stratford tithes, which he did only in 1605. On 4 November of the same year, Sturley replied sceptically to a letter from Quiney 'which imported ... that our countryman Master William Shakespeare [M^r^ Wm. Shak.] would procure us money, which I will like of as I shall hear when, and where, and how', while encouraging Quiney to do all he could to bring it about. This appears to respond to news about Quiney's letter to Shakespeare of 25 October. *SW*

Suffolk, Duke of. (1) William de la Pole, 1st Duke of Suffolk. See SUFFOLK, EARL OF. (2) Based on Charles Brandon (d. 1545, created Duke of Suffolk 1514), in *All Is True* (*Henry VIII*), he plays a part in the downfall of Wolsey (3.2) and the arraignment of Cranmer (5.2); acts as High Steward at the coronation of Anne Boleyn (4.1); and is present at the christening of Princess Elizabeth (5.4). *AB*

Suffolk, Earl of. In *1 Henry VI* he picks a red (Lancastrian) rose in the Temple Garden scene (2.4.37). At Angiers he captures Margaret of Anjou, arranges her marriage to Henry VI, and woos her for himself (5.5). In *The First Part of the Contention* (*2 Henry VI*), now the Duke of Suffolk and the lover of Margaret (there is no historical evidence for the latter), he secures the disgrace of the Duchess of Gloucester, and the murder of the Duke of Gloucester, for which he is banished (3.2.299–301). He is killed by Walter Whitmore (4.1.140). William de la Pole was the 4th Earl and 1st Duke of Suffolk (1396–1450). *AB*

Sullivan, Sir Arthur (1842–1900), English composer. He composed incidental music for productions of *The Tempest* (Leipzig, 1861), *The Merchant of Venice* (Manchester, 1871), *The Merry Wives of Windsor* (London, 1874), *Henry VIII* (Manchester, 1877), and *Macbeth* (London, 1888). He also set a number of Shakespeare lyrics as solo songs or madrigals. *IBC*

Sullivan, Barry (1821–91), actor, born in England, but of Irish parentage. He made his London debut as Hamlet in 1852, when he was commended for his slender figure, graceful attitudes, and absence of claptrap. Amongst the Shakespearian roles which Sullivan subsequently added to his repertoire, in a career which took him to America, Canada, and Australia, were Jaques, Faulconbridge, Macbeth, Benedick, and Richard III. By 1879 when he played Hamlet and Benedick at the opening of the *Shakespeare Memorial Theatre in Stratford-upon-Avon, his girth and acting style had broadened to excess, but admirers such as *Shaw preferred to remember him in his heyday, to his rivals as 'Hyperion to a satyr'. *RF*

Summerfield. See SOMERVILLE.

Surrey, Duke of. He challenges Fitzwalter, *Richard II* 4.1. *AB*

Surrey, Earl of. (1) In *Richard III* he is put in command of the vanguard at *Bosworth with Norfolk, his father (5.6.26). In *Folio editions he has a short speaking part at the beginning of 5.3. In *All Is True* (*Henry VIII*), now called the Duke of Norfolk, he plays a part in the downfall of Wolsey. Thomas Howard (1443–1524) was the 2nd Duke of Norfolk, made Earl of Surrey 1483, and the grandfather of Anne Boleyn. **(2)** He is eager to take revenge on Wolsey for his father-in-law Buckingham's fate in *All Is True*. Thomas Howard (1473–1554), Earl of Surrey and 3rd Duke of Norfolk, was the eldest son of Surrey (1). He was the father of the poet Henry Howard, Earl of Surrey. **(3)** He calls on the insomniac King with Warwick, *2 Henry IV* 3.1 (mute). *AB*

Surveyor, Buckingham's. He gives evidence against Buckingham, *All Is True* (*Henry VIII*) 1.2. He is based on *Holinshed's account of Charles Knyvet (Knevet). *AB*

Sutton Cop Hill (cophill; cop-hill, in folios and quartos), or Sutton Coldfield, is a town in Warwickshire. Sir John sends his recruits there, *1 Henry IV* 4.2.3. *AB*

Suzman, Janet (b. 1939), actress and director. Born into a South African family vigorously opposed to apartheid, she acted with intelligence and glamour at the *Royal Shakespeare Theatre at Stratford where between 1963 and 1973 her parts included Katharina the Shrew, Rosalind, and (outstandingly) Cleopatra. In 1988 in Johannesburg she directed a politically resonant *Othello* with the Bantu actor John Kani which was televised in Britain. *MJ*

Suzuki, Tadashi (b. 1939), Japanese director. A leading figure in the 1960s avant-garde theatre in Japan, Suzuki later became an internationally influential director mainly with his method of training actors. He has directed classical Western plays, transposing them to a Japanese setting, and often worked with Noh and Kyogen actors. His major Shakespearian production is *King Lear* (1989), which unfolds itself as a fantasy of an old Japanese living in a hospital. *TK*

Swanston, Eliard (d. 1651), actor (Lady Elizabeth's Men 1622, King's Men 1624–42). Swanston played a number of roles for the King's Men including the lead in Shakespeare's *Othello* and *Richard III* in the 1630s. A housekeeper (one of the initiators of the Sharers Papers dispute) at the Globe and the Blackfriars, Swanston unusually (for an actor) took the parliamentary side in the Civil War. *GE*

Aernout van Buchel's copy of the drawing of the Swan playhouse made by his friend Johannes de Witt while visiting England, *c.*1596. This is the only reliable drawing we have of the inside of an open-air playhouse of Shakespeare's time.

Swan theatre. The Swan was built in 1595 by Francis Langley in the Bankside district of south London and it was clearly intended to compete with the nearby Rose owned by Philip *Henslowe. In 1596 a Dutch humanist scholar, Johannes de Witt, visited the Swan and drew a picture of it which his friend and fellow classicist Aernout van Buchel copied; this copy is extant. De Witt's sketch is the only surviving interior view of an open-air playhouse of the period and it shows a virtually round amphitheatre of somewhere between 16 and 24 sides with a stage projecting into the yard surmounted by a stage cover supported on two pillars. External views of the Swan also appear in a number of pictures of London, including a 1627 map of the Paris Garden Manor which appears to show the Swan having a single exterior staircase. None of the external views of the Swan is a reliable guide to its dimensions, but the Hope playhouse contract specified that it should be 'of such large compass, form, wideness, and height as the Plaihouse called the Swan'. *Hollar's sketch of the second Globe shows the Hope to be about 100 feet (30 m) across, and we may assume the Swan was about the same.

De Witt described the Swan as the largest of the London playhouses of its day and wrote that it was made out of an aggregate of flint stones ('ex coacervato lapide pyrritide'), a detail we must doubt given the construction practices of the day. The large wooden columns supporting the stage cover were painted like marble so cleverly as 'to deceive the most inquiring eye', and perhaps the external rendering too was deceptive. The described marbling, the circular shape, and the use of classical columns with ornate bases and capitals put the Swan in a neoclassical, *Palladian tradition of design emerging at the end of the 16th century despite the apparent Tudor bareness of the sketch.

The Swan was closed in 1597 when Pembroke's Men played *The Isle of Dogs* (now lost) by Thomas *Nashe and Ben *Jonson, which was highly critical of the government and which landed the dramatists in jail. By 1602 it appears to have been operating again: the hoaxer Richard Vennar circulated a playbill describing an entertainment called *England's Joy*, 'to be Played at the Swan this 6 of November, 1602'. Having received the takings Vennar tried to flee without providing a performance and the expectant audience 'when they saw themselves deluded, revenged themselves upon the hangings, curtains, chairs, stools, walls' of the playhouse. Langley died in 1601 and the Paris Garden estate was sold to Hugh Browker. The Swan had a revival of theatrical activity between 1611 and 1615, as shown by the receipts of the estate's overseers and also the allusion in Middleton and *Dekker's *The Roaring Girl* (1611) to a 'new play i' the Swan'. The only extant play known to have been performed at the Swan is Thomas Middleton's *A Chaste Maid in Cheapside* (1613), presumably during the 1611–15 revival of activity. After 1620 the Swan was occasionally used for prize-fighting, and in 1632 Nicholas Goodman described it as 'now fallen in decay, and like a dying *swan*, hanging down her head, seemed to sing her own dirge'. Herbert Berry discovered that in 1634 the Swan was used by the commissioners of the Court of Requests as a venue for taking evidence in a lawsuit concerning the Globe, and such men 'would not take official evidence in a hovel' so presumably the building had been restored to some of its former elegance. *GE*

Swan theatre, Stratford-upon-Avon. See ROYAL SHAKESPEARE COMPANY.

Sweden. See SCANDINAVIA.

Swinburne, Algernon Charles (1837–1909), English poet. Swinburne's passionate admiration for Shakespeare began at 6 with a bowdlerized copy. He contrived to end his own eulogistic *Study of Shakespeare* (1880) on the exalted name of Imogen; while an appendix burlesques the 'incomparable blackguard' F. J. *Furnivall and his New Shakspere Society. *TM*

Switzerland. Thomas *Platter, a Basle traveller, was the first to describe a performance of *Julius Caesar* in *London (1599). Zurich played a crucial role in establishing Shakespeare's poetic (rather than theatrical) genius in the German-speaking world. Johann Jakob Bodmer (1698–1783) defended Shakespeare against German neoclassicist critics. A correspondent of his, Simon Grynäus, produced the first blank verse translation into German (of *Romeo and Juliet*) in 1758, and the first collected translations, by Christoph Martin *Wieland and Johann Joachim *Eschenburg, appeared there (1762–6, 1775–82 respectively). The painter Johann Heinrich Füssli (*Fuseli in England) (1741–1825) received early Shakespearian inspiration in his home town. Ulrich Bräker (1735–98), a farmer from Toggenburg in eastern Switzerland, produced a sophisticated document of Shakespearomania. Swiss writers have repeatedly adapted Shakespeare, e.g. Gottfried Keller in his *novella* 'Romeo und Julia auf dem Dorfe' (1856), and Friedrich Dürrenmatt in his play *König Johann* (1968). *BE*

Bircher, Martin, and Straumann, Heinrich, *Shakespeare und die deutsche Schweiz bis zum Beginn des 19. Jahrhunderts* (Shakespeare and German-Speaking Switzerland to the Beginning of the 19th Century) (1971)

Bräker, Ulrich, *A Few Words about William Shakespeare's Plays* (*Etwas über William Shakespeares Schauspiele*), trans. Derek Bowman (1979)

Stadler, Edmund (ed.), *Shakespeare und die Schweiz* (Shakespeare and Switzerland) (1964)

Sycorax, Caliban's mother, a witch, dies long before the action of *The Tempest* begins. In the *Dryden/Davenant version of the play the name is given to Caliban's sister. *AB*

syllabic variation. See ANAPTYXIS; SYNAERESIS; SYNCOPE.

synaeresis, the fusing or elision of adjacent vowel sounds within a word: *violent.* But Shakespeare, like other poets, often treats such combinations differently in the same or neighbouring lines: 'As *fi* | *re* drives | out *fire,* | so pity pity' (*Julius Caesar* 3.1.171). *GTW*

syncope (syncopation), the fusing of syllables in polysyllabic words, frequently evident, as the metre shows, in words like *natural, general,* and even *el'quence, in'cent, count'feit, vag'bond.* All these suggest a speedy delivery of lines on the Renaissance English stage. *GTW*

synecdoche, a figure of speech, related to *metonymy, in which some thing or person is referred to by naming only some part thereof, as when York addresses Bolingbroke's 'banished and forbidden legs' (*Richard II* 2.3.89). *CB*

tabor, a double-headed drum with gut snares on one or both heads, associated with dance when played together with the three-holed *pipe by one person (see *The Winter's Tale* 4.4.183). *JB*

Tailor. In *The Taming of the Shrew* 4.3 he brings a gown for Katherine which Petruccio rejects. *AB*

Taine, Hippolyte (1821–93), French historian and critic. Taine's rationalist objections to the passionate and absurd excesses of Shakespeare, particularly in language and style, owe something to *Voltaire; but he ends by acknowledging Shakespeare's prodigious, if extravagant and frenzied, genius (see *A History of English Literature*, 1865). *TM*

'Take, O take those lips away', sung by a boy in *Measure for Measure* 4.1.1. A setting by John *Wilson, published in 1652, may date back to an early revival of the play. Later settings include those by Alcock, Chilcot, Galliard, Giordani, Jackson, Weldon (18th century); *Bishop, Chausson, Macfarren, Parry, Pearsall (19th century); and van Dieren, Quilter, Rubbra, Warlock, *Vaughan Williams (20th century). *JB*

Talbot, Lord. Commander of the English forces in France, he is reported as having been made prisoner, *1 Henry VI* 1.1.145. He returns from captivity, 1.6, and enjoys great military success until killed with his son *John Talbot at Bordeaux, 4.7. Also called John (*c.*1388–1453), the real 6th Baron Talbot, 1st Earl of Shrewsbury, died with his son at Castillon 22 years after *Joan la Pucelle was executed. *AB*

Talbot, Young. See John Talbot.

Tamayo y Baus, Manuel (1829–98), one of the most significant Spanish playwrights of the 19th century. His play *Un drama nuevo* (A New Drama, 1867) is set in Elizabethan England, and the protagonists are Shakespeare's company of actors. It is the third and most important 19th-century Spanish play in which Shakespeare is a stage character. It contains a hero who is jealous on stage and in real life, and an Iago-figure who feeds his jealousy. It was performed in English as *Yorick* and *Yorick's Love.* There is also a published English translation: *A New Drama: A Tragedy in Three Acts from the Spanish*, trans. John Driscoll Fitz-Gerald and Thacher Howland Guild (1915). The play was made into a film in Spain in 1946 by Juan de Orduña. *ALP*

Tamer Tamed, The See Fletcher, John; Taming of the Shrew, The.

Taming of a Shrew, The, an anonymous play, entered in the Stationers' Register in 1594 and first printed in the same year, whose precise relation to Shakespeare's longer and more sophisticated *The Taming of the Shrew* has long puzzled scholars. Efforts to date it or track its performance history are complicated by the existence of Shakespeare's play, which on stylistic grounds must have been written before *The Taming of a Shrew* was published: *Henslowe's 'Diary', for example, records a performance of 'the Tamynge of A Shrowe' at Newington Butts on 11 June 1594 (by either the Admiral's Men or the *Chamberlain's Men or both), which could be either play. *The Taming of a Shrew* has a similar main plot and sub-plot to *The Taming of the Shrew,* though some characters have different names—Ferando (Petruccio) tames Kate, while her sister Philema (Bianca) is won by Aurelius (Lucentio). More strikingly, it has a similar frame-narrative, only here it is completed. Christopher Sly, duped into thinking himself a lord, watches the whole of the inset play, interrupting it from time to time with ribald and impertinent comments, and afterwards is taken back, drunkenly asleep, to the refuse heap where he was found, where he wakes up and decides that the whole experience must have been a dream—an instructive one, however, since he means to employ Ferando's methods on his own wife. This final phase of the Christopher Sly Induction has often been transplanted from *The Taming of a Shrew* into productions of Shakespeare's *The Taming of the Shrew,* which at some stage in its existence probably offered a similar closure.

Most of the possible hypotheses about the connections between this play and *The Taming of the Shrew* have been argued at some point: some scholars have seen it as a source, some a first draft, some a garbled reported text, some a botched plagiarism, some an alternative version of a common lost source. What is certain is that *The Taming of a Shrew* is a highly derivative play—some passages are taken almost verbatim from *Marlowe—and the balance of probability, supported by early allusions to passages found only in *The Taming of the Shrew*—suggests that it borrows from Shakespeare rather than vice versa. *MD*

Craig, Hardin, '*The Shrew* and *A Shrew*', in *Elizabethan Studies in Honor of George F. Reynolds* (1945)

Lancashire, Anne, and Levenson, Jill, 'Anonymous Plays', in Terence P. Logan and Denzell S. Smith (eds.), *The Predecessors of Shakespeare: A Survey and Bibliography of Recent Studies in English Renaissance Drama* (1973)

Wells, Stanley, and Taylor, Gary, 'No Shrew, A Shrew, and The Shrew: Internal Revision in *The Taming of the Shrew*', in B. Fabian and K. Tetzeli von Rosador (eds.), *Shakespeare: Text, Language Criticism* (1987)

Taming of the Shrew, The *(see page 460)*

Tamora, Queen of the Goths, vainly pleads for the life of her son Alarbus, *Titus Andronicus* 1.1;

(cont. on page 463)

The Taming of the Shrew

The most enduringly popular of the early comedies, if also the most potentially offensive, *The Taming of the Shrew* has sometimes been regarded as Shakespeare's first play—partly on the sentimental grounds that its Induction's allusions to Warwickshire reflect the homesickness of a Stratford man newly arrived in London. Although the sophistication of its dramatic structure and scenic technique compared to those of *The Two Gentlemen of Verona* make this placing in the *chronology unlikely, the play does belong to the very first phase of Shakespeare's writing career: while evidence as to its date is complicated by the existence of a similar play, *The *Taming of a Shrew*, published anonymously in 1594, it seems certain that *The Taming of the Shrew* was already extant by 1592, when passages without any equivalent in *A Shrew* were echoed in another anonymous play, *A Knack to Know a Knave*. In 1593 Shakespeare's play was remembered again, this time by the poet Antony Chute, whose poem *Beauty Dishonoured* includes the line 'He calls his Kate, and she must come and kiss him.' *The Taming of the Shrew* requires a similar size of cast to *The First Part of the Contention* (*2 Henry* VI) and *Richard Duke of York* (*3 Henry* VI), and shares rare vocabulary with both plays: it is likely that it was composed at around the same time as Shakespeare's earliest histories, *c.*1590–1.

Text: Although *The Taming of a Shrew* appeared in quarto in 1594, 1596, and 1607, *The Taming of the Shrew* was not printed until the publication of the Folio in 1623. Its text is among the most puzzling in the canon: for one thing it lacks a completion to the frame-narrative of Christopher Sly, which disappears after 1.1 (though one possible ending is preserved by *The Taming of a Shrew*, which is probably a garbled plagiarism of Shakespeare's play). In incidentals the Folio text is a mess, and an inconsistent mess at that: some speech-prefixes preserve the names of actors rather than characters ('Sinclo' (see Sincler, John) for one of the players, 'Nick' for a messenger in 3.1), consistent with a text derived from *foul papers, while some speech-prefix errors suggest a scribe who has been misled by authorial use of an abbreviated alias to designate a character currently in disguise. Some passages suggest the Folio text derives from foul papers, in which Shakespeare's process of initial composition is still visible (4.4, for example, suggests indecision as to whether the location is outside Baptista's house or outside Tranio's lodging), others—notably 'Sinclo's' reference to 'Soto', apparently an interpolated allusion to John *Fletcher's *Women Pleased* (*c.*1620?)—suggest a manuscript which has been altered for a late Jacobean revival, perhaps in conjunction with Fletcher's sequel *The Woman's Prize; or, The Tamer Tamed*. This last hypothesis, however, is itself rendered problematic by the fact that the Folio text has not been expurgated to comply with the *Act to Restrain the Abuses of Players. It seems impossible to decide whether the Folio text derives from foul papers or from a transcript which has undergone some theatrical adaptation: some of its inconsistencies have been explained by the hypothesis that Shakespeare may have been working with a collaborator, but this theory has not been generally accepted.

Sources: *The Taming of the Shrew* has an impeccably literary sub-plot—the Bianca–Lucentio story is derived from George *Gascoigne's pioneering prose comedy *Supposes* (1566), itself a translation of *Ariosto's *I suppositi* (1509)—but its main plot belongs more to folklore than to high culture. Although countless *ballads depict a husband disciplining an unruly wife (among them *A Merry Jest of a Shrewd and Cursed Wife*, 1550), most of these are far more brutal than Shakespeare's play (in *A Merry Jest*, for example, the shrew is beaten up and wrapped in the skin of a dead horse), and none is close enough in detail to the Petruccio–Kate story to be cited as a specific source, though the play clearly belongs in the same general tradition. Some commentators, however, have detected the influence of a relatively humane colloquy by the Dutch humanist Erasmus (*c.*1466–1536), translated in 1557 as 'A Merry Dialogue, Declaring the Properties of Shrewd Shrews and Honest Wives'. The Induction, too, detailing the adventure of a peasant duped into believing himself a lord, derives from a story widespread through folklore and told in various earlier ballads, and Shakespeare does not seem to have had any single precedent in mind as he composed his own Warwickshire variant on the theme.

Synopsis: Induction 1 Christopher Sly, a beggarly tinker, falls asleep after being ejected from a tavern for breaking glasses, and is found by a lord out hunting, who instructs his men to take Sly to his house, put him to bed, and persuade him when he wakes that he is its lord, who has been suffering from delusions. The Lord welcomes a troupe of players, and gives order that his page Bartholomew shall be dressed for the role of Sly's lady. **Induction 2** As instructed, the servingmen tell Sly he is a lord who has been mentally ill for fifteen years, to the grief of his lady: accepting the story, Sly is eager to resume conjugal relations with the cross-dressed Bartholomew, but is put off, and instead agrees to watch the players perform a comedy.

1.1 Lucentio, arriving in Padua to study, falls in love with Bianca when he sees her with her father Baptista, her elder sister Katherine, and two rivals for her love, Gremio and Hortensio. Baptista declares that Bianca may be courted only after the angry and disdainful Katherine is married, and that meanwhile Bianca will be tutored at home. Hortensio and Gremio agree that they must find some man willing to marry Katherine. Lucentio, overhearing all this, hits upon a strategy with his servant Tranio: he will gain access to Bianca by disguising himself as a schoolmaster while Tranio, seconded by his other servant Biondello, fills the role of Lucentio. They exchange clothes. (Above, Sly is apparently bored by the play.) **1.2** Petruccio, arriving from Verona with his servant Grumio, calls on his friend Hortensio, and, learning of Katherine's dowry, agrees to woo her despite her reported shrewishness: he also agrees to recommend a disguised Hortensio to Baptista as Bianca's music teacher. Gremio arrives with the disguised Lucentio, whom he will present to Baptista as a tutor for Bianca: he agrees with Hortensio to co-sponsor Petruccio's wooing of Katherine. Tranio arrives, disguised as Lucentio, and announces his own intention of courting Bianca: he too agrees to fund Petruccio's suit, and Petruccio and the rivals repair to a tavern.

2.1 Katherine has tied Bianca's hands, and is interrogating her about her suitors when Baptista arrives, separates them, and sends them indoors. The company arrive from the tavern: Petruccio offers himself as a suitor for Katherine (confirming that her dowry is 20,000 crowns and half of Baptista's land in reversion) and presents Hortensio, disguised as Licio, as a

50 KATHARINE AND PETRUCHIO.

To offer war, where they should kneel for peace :
Or seek for rule, supremacy, and sway,
Where bound to love, to honour, and obey !

CURTAIN FALLS.

LONDON:
WILLOUGHBY & CO., PRINTERS, 109, GOSWELL STREET.

George Cruikshank's concluding image of Kate, from an 1838 illustrated edition of Garrick's adaptation *Katharine and Petruchio*, at once celebrates her taming and acknowledges the violence by which it is accomplished.

music master. Gremio offers Lucentio, disguised as Cambio, as a tutor: both supposed teachers are accepted and sent to the two women, though Hortensio soon returns, after Katherine has broken his head with a lute, and is sent to Bianca instead. At Petruccio's insistence he is left alone and Katherine sent to him: in the wrangling conversation which follows Petruccio affects to disregard the contempt she displays, declares that he was born to tame her, and tells the returning Baptista that she has agreed to marry him the following Sunday. Despite Katherine's protests Baptista agrees, and Petruccio leaves to prepare for the wedding. Gremio and the disguised Tranio now attempt to outbid one another for Bianca's hand, Tranio promising all Lucentio's father Vincentio's wealth, an offer Baptista accepts on condition that Vincentio confirms it. Tranio realizes he will need to produce a surrogate Vincentio.

3.1 Hortensio and Lucentio, furious rivals, each declare their identities and purposes to Bianca under cover of teaching her: she seems to favour Lucentio, and Hortensio is disgusted at the idea that she might welcome the courtship of a mere tutor. 3.2 After keeping his bride and the company waiting, Petruccio arrives for his wedding in grossly tattered and absurd clothes. 3.3 Gremio tells Lucentio and Tranio of Petruccio's rough and swaggering behaviour during the marriage service: when the company arrive from the church, Petruccio refuses even to stay for the wedding breakfast, despite Katherine's protests, and takes her away immediately.

4.1 Grumio, arriving at Petruccio's country house to prepare his master's welcome, tells the servant Curtis of the foul and uncomfortable journey Katherine has suffered. When Petruccio and Katherine arrive, Petruccio abuses the servants, rejects the food they bring, and insists that Katherine goes to bed hungry: alone, he explains that his strategy is to break her spirit by depriving her of food and sleep, always pretending that he is doing so for her own good, and he asks whether anyone in the audience knows of a better way of taming a shrew. 4.2 Hortensio leads Tranio where he may see the mutual courting of Bianca and Lucentio: Tranio feigns shock and abandons his pretended suit, while Hortensio, forswearing Bianca, leaves to court a wealthy widow he means to marry instead, intending to call on Petruccio on the way. Lucentio, Bianca, and Tranio agree on their strategy for obtaining Baptista's consent by producing a false Vincentio to assure a marriage portion. Tranio persuades a passing Mantuan pedant that he is in mortal danger in Padua because of fictitious hostilities between the two city-states, and must disguise himself for safety: he explains that the Pedant can easily pass for Vincentio if he only goes through some formalities about a marriage settlement, in which Tranio will brief him. 4.3 At Petruccio's house Grumio loyally refuses to let Katherine have any food, and assists Petruccio, watched by Hortensio, in rejecting the new cap and gown ordered from a haberdasher and a tailor for Katherine to wear on her bridal visit to her father. Petruccio insists the clothes are not good enough, abuses the tradesmen, and tells Katherine they will go only when she shows complete obedience. 4.4 Tranio presents the Pedant, dressed as Vincentio, to Baptista, and they agree to sign the marriage settlement between Lucentio and Bianca at Tranio's lodgings over supper. 4.5 Biondello, on Tranio's instructions, advises Lucentio to marry Bianca privately while her father is busy over the pretended marriage settlements. 4.6 On their way to Baptista's house, Petruccio makes Katherine humour him by calling the sun the moon, and when they meet the real Vincentio he at first makes her greet him as if he were a young girl. Learning Vincentio's identity, Petruccio congratulates him on his son's marriage to Bianca, news which is confirmed by Hortensio before he leaves to woo the Widow.

5.1 Lucentio and Bianca hasten from his lodging towards their surreptitious wedding. Petruccio and Katherine arrive, bringing Vincentio, who knocks and is answered by the Pedant. The Pedant insists that he is Vincentio, supported by Biondello, who denies having ever seen the real Vincentio before (and is beaten by him), and when Tranio arrives in Lucentio's clothes, Vincentio becomes convinced that his son has been murdered by his servants. Baptista is trying to have Vincentio taken to prison as an impostor when the newly-wed Lucentio and Bianca arrive (at which Tranio, Biondello, and the Pedant flee), and Lucentio confesses all. Petruccio agrees to follow them all and see how the affair turns out on condition that Katherine kisses him in the street: she does so. 5.2 The entire reconciled cast are assembled at Lucentio's banquet, celebrating his wedding to Bianca and Hortensio's to the Widow; after the three brides leave the chamber, each husband bets 20 crowns that his wife will return most obediently when summoned. Bianca and the Widow refuse to come, but Katherine comes immediately, and at Petruccio's bidding fetches the other two wives, throws off her hat, and preaches a long homily on wifely obedience, thereby winning him the wager. A delighted Baptista adds another 20,000 crowns to Petruccio's winnings. (In *The Taming of a Shrew*, Sly, now asleep, is put back into his own clothes and returned to where the Lord found him: awakened at dawn by a tapster, he says he has had a wonderful dream, and since he now knows how to tame a shrew has no fear of returning home to his wife.)

Artistic features: *The Taming of the Shrew* is the first of Shakespeare's comedies to hint at his power to pursue a serious idea across a whole range of comic plots and situations, taking up the notions of identity and persuasion initiated by the Induction (which has already modelled the production of an 'ideal' wife through the transformation of Bartholomew), and developing them through each of the intrigues of the play proper.

Critical history: Long dismissed as a simple-minded, robust farce (*Johnson's verdict, though he was impressed by Shakespeare's interlinking of the two main plots, was merely that the play was 'very popular and diverting'), *The Taming of the Shrew* has been taken ever more seriously since the early 20th century, and not only because that period has seen the emergence of modern *feminism. As with its stage history, the play has divided interpreters between those who wish to excuse or celebrate Petruccio's behaviour towards Kate and those who wish to condemn it—essentially, between those who regard the 'taming' as a benign piece of psychic or social therapy inflicted in the cause of mutual love, and those who see it as simply an expression of the naked power of Elizabethan men over Elizabethan women. Many commentators have related Katherine's speech on *marriage to wider Elizabethan doctrines of authority and social subordination (notably E. M. W. *Tillyard in *The Elizabethan World Picture*, 1943), but opinion on the play remains profoundly divided as to whether her submission is to be accepted and welcomed at face value or whether the play suggests it is to be viewed with scepticism, irony, or even revulsion.

Stage history: Partly because of this very controversy over how we are to take Petruccio's triumph, the play has been inspiring adaptations and spin-offs ever since *The Taming of a Shrew*: around 1611, for example, *Fletcher produced a sequel (in which the characters have all miraculously become English), *The Woman's Prize; or, The Tamer Tamed*, in which Petruccio's second wife Maria proves much less tractable than the now-dead Kate. Although Shakespeare's original was performed at court in the 1630s and in the early 1660s, *The Taming of the Shrew* was rewritten by John *Lacy in 1667 as *Sauny the Scot*, a largely prose version of the play, anglicized to match *The Woman's Prize*, and dominated by Lacy's performance as the caricatured Scottish servant Sauny (Grumio, 'Sander' in *A Shrew*). Despite two topical rewritings of the Induction (both as *The *Cobbler of Preston*, 1716) and a 1735 ballad opera (*A *Cure for a Scold*), this was the version that held the stage until the mid-18th century, when it was supplanted by David *Garrick's three-act afterpiece **Catharine and Petruchio* (1754). Garrick's version, eliminating the Bianca plot and insisting that Petruchio loves Catharine all along and only feigns his various tactical brutalities, was not finally replaced until after Augustin *Daly's production of the original in 1887–8, with Ada *Rehan as Kate, though the original had been revived twice in the 1840s, by Benjamin Webster in 1844 (in a precociously quasi-Elizabethan staging by J. R. *Planché) and by Samuel *Phelps in 1856. The play has enjoyed frequent revivals ever since, with great Kates including Violet *Vanbrugh, Laurence *Olivier (his debut, in a school production, 1922), Edith *Evans, Barbara *Jefford, and Vanessa *Redgrave (at Stratford in 1961, and in London 25 years later). Since feminism's second wave in the 1970s, the tradition of playing Petruccio and Kate as a couple who fall happily in love in between their less happy lines has often given place to more critical productions, which have sometimes overcompensated by rendering Petruccio more brutal: Charles *Marowitz's 1973 adaptation *The Shrew* has Petruchio (as the role was then known) sodomizing Kate onstage, and in Michael *Bogdanov's 1978 RSC production Jonathan Pryce, a loutish, set-demolishing Sly, burst into the play-within-the-play as Petruchio on a phallic motorbike. He was finally slightly abashed, however, by Paola Dionisotti's submission speech, which many successive actresses have sought to reclaim as an act of perverse defiance. *MD*

On the screen: The earliest film (1908) is of historical interest in being the work of D. W. Griffith. Five silent versions followed before Sam Taylor's adaptation (1929), the first Shakespeare film to have a soundtrack with English dialogue. Two television productions followed, one for BBC TV (1939) by Dallas Bower and George Schaefer's American production (1956) with Maurice Evans as Petruchio. *Zeffirelli's film (1966) filled the screen with colour and captivatingly robust action, with Elizabeth Taylor as Kate and Richard *Burton as a powerful, swaggering, though unsubtle Petruchio. Jonathan *Miller's production for BBC TV (1980), criticized for failing to give Kate sufficient dramatic weight in her own right, tackled the play along surprisingly unorthodox lines, casting John Cleese as a Puritan Petruchio. *AD*

Recent major editions

Ann Thompson (New Cambridge, 1984); H. J. Oliver (Oxford, 1982); Brian Morris (Arden 2nd series, 1981); G. R. Hibbard (New Penguin, 1968)

Some representative criticism

French, Marilyn, in *Shakespeare's Division of Experience* (1982)

Nevo, Ruth, in *Comic Transformations in Shakespeare* (1980)

Rose, Mary Beth, in *The Expense of Spirit: Love and Marriage in English Renaissance Drama* (1980)

Rutter, Carol (ed.), *Clamorous Voices: Shakespeare's Women Today* (1985)

Seronsy, C. C., ' "Supposes" as a Unifying Theme in *The Taming of the Shrew*', *Shakespeare Quarterly*, 14 (1963)

---

she becomes Saturninus' Empress while remaining Aaron's mistress; she is able to avenge her son before falling victim to terrible revenge herself. *AB*

Tarlton, Richard (d. 1588), actor (Sussex's Men 1578, Queen's Men 1583–8), jester, and writer. The earliest record of Tarlton is as author of a ballad in 1570 and by the end of the 1570s he was also being alluded to as an actor. In 1585 he wrote *The Seven Deadly Sins* for the Queen's Men which Gabriel Harvey claimed that Thomas *Nashe plagiarized for his *Piers Penniless* (1592). Dozens of allusions to Tarlton's comic improvisations survive in Elizabethan verse and prose and a collection of his so-called 'jests' was published in the late 1590s, although the earliest surviving edition is from 1611. This jest-book gives a sense of his clowning talents (which included fencing, verse improvisation, and playing instruments) and some biographical detail: he performed his clowning at inns and at court, he was Protestant, he ran an inn and an 'ordinary' (eatery), and he had facial deformities considered comic. The woodcut of Tarlton printed with his jest-book was copied from a Flemish model and is no more than a general guide to his appearance, and John Scottowe's copy of this woodcut cramps Tarlton's body to fit it into a prescribed space on the page, introducing deformities which cannot be presumed in the man. One of Tarlton's trademarks was to thrust his head through a curtain at the back of a stage and peer at the audience before the performance, and he was famous too for his *jigs performed after a theatrical performance. *GE*

Wiles, David, *Shakespeare's Clown: Actor and Text in the Elizabethan Playhouse* (1987)

Tarquin. See Rape of Lucrece, The.

Tate, Nahum (1652–1715), poet and playwright. Reviled by early 20th-century critics for daring to adapt Shakespeare, and successfully at that, Tate was in his own time a highly respected writer, made Poet Laureate in 1692: his achievements include the libretto for Purcell's *Dido and Aeneas* (1689) and collaborations with John *Dryden on *The Second Part of Absalom and Achitophel* (1682) and with Nicholas Brady on the *New Version of the Psalms* (1696). Born in Ireland and educated at Trinity College, Dublin, Tate had settled in London by his mid-twenties, and was soon writing plays, many based on pre-Restoration originals (including *Jonson's *Eastward Ho* and *The Devil is an Ass* and *Webster's *The White Devil*). Of his three adaptations of Shakespeare, his topical *Richard II* (1680) was banned and *The *Ingratitude of a Commonwealth* (a gory version of *Coriolanus*, 1681) was never popular, but *The *History of King Lear* (complete with happy ending, 1681) held the stage, with some progressive alterations, for a century and a half. Despite this success, however, Tate died in hiding from his creditors. *MD*

Taurus commands Caesar's land force at Actium, *Antony and Cleopatra* 3.8 and 3.10. *AB*

Tawyer, William (d. 1625), musician and actor (King's Men by 1624). Tawyer was apprenticed to John *Heminges and appears in a stage direction in the 1623 Folio text of *A Midsummer Night's Dream* 5.1 and in a list of King's Men musicians protected from arrest by Henry *Herbert in 1624. *GE*

Taylor, John (1580–1653), the 'water poet'. Raised in Gloucester and apprenticed to a London waterman, Taylor was pressed into the navy, but he eventually became a waterman again. In his versified *The Price of Hempseed* (1620), he cites Shakespeare among thirteen English poets who, through paper's medium, live 'immortally'. *PH*

Taylor, Joseph (*c.*1586–1652), actor (York's Men 1610, Lady Elizabeth's Men 1611–16, Charles's Men 1616–19, King's Men 1619–42). Taylor enters the theatrical record with his unauthorized transfer from York's Men to Lady Elizabeth's Men in 1610–11 and had established himself sufficiently to replace Richard *Burbage as the leading King's Man on the latter's death in March 1619. In his *Roscius Anglicanus* (1708) John Downes claimed that Thomas *Betterton's performance as Hamlet was derived, via William *Davenant, from 'Mr. Taylor of the *Black-Fryars* Company' who was 'instructed by the Author Mr. Shakespear'. Downes's reference to the playhouse might suggest the Blackfriars Boys (1600–8) rather than the King's Men, in which case Shakespeare instructed the adolescent Taylor in something other than Hamlet. Certainly by the time Taylor joined the King's Men in 1619—between their patent of 27 March, from which he is absent, and their livery warrant of 19 May where he appears—Shakespeare and Burbage were dead. Taylor appears in the 1623 Folio list of players, and he played Ferdinand in Webster's *The Duchess of Malfi*, Hamlet, Iago, Truewit in Jonson's *Epicoene*, and Face in Jonson's *The Alchemist*. After John Heminges's death in 1630 Taylor became a housekeeper of the Globe and the Blackfriars and he and John Lowin took over as joint managers of the King's Men. *GE*

Tchaikovsky, Pyotr (Ilyich) (1840–93), Russian composer. He composed orchestral works based on *The Tempest* (1873) and *Hamlet* (1888), but is best known for his fantasy overture *Romeo and Juliet* (1869, rev. 1870, 1880), which was first choreographed as a ballet in 1937. He also composed incidental music for *Hamlet* (1891) and considered writing *operas based on *Othello* and *Romeo and Juliet*; for the latter there survives an uncompleted duet. *IBC*

Tearsheet, Doll. Falstaff's mistress, she appears in *2 Henry IV* 2.4, and is arrested, 5.4. *AB*

television. Televised Shakespeare has been performance history's disdained foster-child. Whether broadcast live as in the earliest years or filmed for television from original scripts, cut from big-screen versions or filmed from a stage production, it has rarely achieved the status of large-screen *film (itself something of a stepchild). The reasons are simple: television Shakespeare may be interrupted by commercials, shaped to fit a specific time-slot (particularly in the USA), prepared on the cheap without the production values of big-time film, and the victim of small image size, fuzzy contrast, shallow depth of field, and other defects of low-resolution output. In spite of these shortcomings, Shakespeare on television has had a notable past and promises to be even more significant in the HDTV and DVD future. More than any other form, TV has brought Shakespeare to the millions. No one has made a film of *All's Well That Ends Well*, but there have

Jonathan Miller directing John Cleese as Petruccio in the BBC TV *The Taming of the Shrew*, 1980.

been four TV versions, three extant. No excellent film of *Antony and Cleopatra* exists, but Trevor *Nunn's 1974 adaptation of his RSC production, with Janet *Suzman, Richard Johnson, and Patrick *Stewart, stands out as a splendid performance in any medium. To understand the potential of TV, one must look at its strongest, not its weakest, productions.

The BBC broadcast the first full-length Shakespeare in the infancy of television, before the Second World War: *Julius Caesar* in modern dress, enhanced by newsreel film footage (1938). The BBC broadened its achievement with ambitious series, such as *An Age of Kings—Richard II*; *1* and *2 Henry IV*; *Henry V*; *1*, *2*, and *3 Henry VI*; and *Richard III*—over a period of fifteen weeks in 1960. These broadcasts proved that a generous budget, seasoned cast, and intelligent production choices could yield impressive results in made-for-television Shakespeare. The BBC also demonstrated that television could respect the language and the setting of a fine stage production, adapting *The Wars of the Roses*—the *Royal Shakespeare Company's productions of the *Henry VI* plays and *Richard III*—into three television productions.

Like these two series of history plays, the best received of the 36 BBC Shakespeare plays, broadcast 1978–85, were those rarely seen on stage or film, such as, from the first season, *All Is True* (*Henry VIII*). The spare and symbolic sets and action of the *Henry VI* plays (1982–3) and *Titus Andronicus* (1984–5), directed brilliantly by Jane Howell, confirm that television can accommodate diverse scenic styles, from her austere vision to the lushly realistic *All's Well That Ends Well* (1981) directed by Elijah Moshinsky. *Hamlet* (1981) and *Macbeth* (1982) are also creditable thanks to Derek *Jacobi's and Nicol *Williamson's inventive performances in the eponymous roles rather than to production choices. But the series, even at its worst, repays study, with many bright moments.

In the *United States, the leading sponsor of early Shakespeare on television was the Hallmark Greeting Card Company, whose Hallmark Hall of Fame productions broadcast *Hamlet* live in 1953, starring Maurice *Evans, directed by George Schaefer. The pair had produced their 'GI' *Hamlet* during the Second World War for service personnel overseas; meant for a mass audience, it served as a template for their TV production. The best of the eight Hallmark productions is probably *The Tempest* (1960), which avoids the problematic side of the play and focuses on pastel delight, with Lee Remick as Miranda, Evans as a kindly but magisterial Prospero, and Richard *Burton as Caliban. NBC-TV had broadcast Hallmark's first *Macbeth*, with Evans and Judith *Anderson, in colour, but few people had colour sets in 1954. By 1960, when the same principals (Evans, Anderson, Schaefer) made *Macbeth* again, it was filmed in colour on location, meant for cinema release as well as for broadcast. One misses the scary immediacy of live performance—a stagehand makes an unscheduled appearance in the 1953 *Hamlet*. A second *Hamlet*—filmed in 1970, with Richard Chamberlain as Hamlet, Richard Johnson as Claudius, and directed by Peter Wood—marked the end of Hallmark Shakespeare productions. Chamberlain's was the first Hamlet that Kenneth *Branagh saw, and one can recognize in his design for his 1996 film some hints of Peter Roden's television setting, featuring a large hall dominated by a grand stairway. Hallmark, of course, was not the only American sponsor: Kenneth Rothwell reports that, between 1949 and 1979, 'nearly fifty televised Shakespeare programs appeared in the United States' (1999).

Some films fatten their budgets from television connections (the Olivier *Richard III*, simultaneously released in cinemas and broadcast in 1956, is a case in point, as is Adrian *Noble's Channel 4 Films screen adaptation of his RSC *A Midsummer Night's Dream*, 1996–7). And feature films are now routinely made available on video after their theatrical runs. Celebrated individual productions have been produced specifically for television and these too are released on video. In Britain Granada TV produced *King Lear*, starring Laurence *Olivier, directed by Michael Elliott (1983), affording viewers an excellent opportunity to see Olivier in a full-length production when a stage performance would have overtaxed him. The prehistoric setting, the King's gentleness at first with Cordelia, played with tender rectitude by Anna Calder-Marshall, and the chillingly beautiful Diana *Rigg as Regan, make this a fascinating addition to the *Lear* collection. Ragnar Lyth's *Hamlet* (1984), for Swedish television, is a visually striking low-budget adaptation, unfortunately not yet available on video. Straight-to-video productions need not be listed in detail here (see Rothwell, 'Electronic Shakespeare'). A commendable example, however, is the first and best of the Bard Series, the 1979 *Merry Wives of Windsor*, produced by R. Thad Taylor and recorded on the stage of the Los Angeles Globe theatre.

Live staged Shakespeare sometimes appears on TV. The PBS Television broadcast of William Ball's sprightly American Conservatory Theatre of San Francisco *Taming of the Shrew* (1976) releases the play's antic energy. Another more serious *Shrew*, filmed with audience in view at the Stratford, Ontario, Shakespeare Festival (1981), uses the Sly frame to good advantage. *Kiss me, Petruchio* (1981), a glimpse of a performance, stars Raul Julia and Meryl Streep as Petruchio and Kate and as themselves backstage during a performance of *The Taming of the Shrew* in the Park (the *New York Shakespeare Festival, 1978). This documentary improves upon the full production, extracting the gold and leaving the dross behind. Multiple video versions of plays like *The Taming of the Shrew* allow viewers to compare choices as no other medium can.

Often producers separate the filming of a play from its editing rather than edit on the spot in the control room. That distance from its stage origin can make for a disappointing translation. But for those who did not have the opportunity to see a stage production or who seek to recall details, video is a blessing. *Hamlet* with Richard Burton, directed by John *Gielgud, recorded on film during performance (1964) for two cinema screenings but eventually made available on video, captures the musicality and variety of Burton's delivery. Michael *Bogdanov and Michael *Pennington caught with multiple cameras during performance at least some of the energy of their postmodern, seven-part, *English Shakespeare Company *Wars of the Roses* (*Richard II* to *Richard III*, 1989–90).

Most stage-to-screen productions do not risk filming a stage performance but instead shoot it in a studio, without an audience. Ian *McKellen and Judi *Dench appear in Trevor Nunn's powerful version of *Macbeth*, staged at the Other Place, Stratford-upon-Avon (1976); adapted for Thames Television (1979), it was shot on a sound set. Kevin Kline reconceived for television his 1990 performance, as actor and director, of Hamlet at the New York Public Theater. These suggest stage while taking advantage of studio technology.

Televised Shakespeare has led to its integration into general consciousness. A 1998 episode of the American series *Mystery Science Theatre 3000* showcases Peter Wirth's *Hamlet*, starring Maximilian Schell. While the black and white production unfolds with its dubbed-in English, the serial's characters, a human and two robotic friends, make snide remarks. Imagine that! A 40-year-old German *Hamlet* for television making an almost full-length appearance (80 minutes of the original 127) on a sci-fi show for kids. Shakespeare appears everywhere on TV (accounting for perhaps 0.01% of allusions); and with Shakespeare more available on video, a mass audience may recognize such allusions whether on *The Simpsons* or *Star Trek*. (See also POPULAR CULTURE.)

Any generalization about the medium can be overturned by contrary examples, but a few suggest themselves: TV is an intimate medium, on both sides of the tube. Actors in dialogue are apt to be close together; they can whisper; their expressions in close-up drive the drama. The audience is close, alone or with a few others, at ease, requiring energy from the screen to focus its attention. Directed by the actors and the *mise-en-scène*, the audience will pay careful attention to the language. On the other hand, viewing large scenes on news programmes (the movement of armies, New Year's Eve fireworks) readies audiences for at least occasional panoramas. Though TV partakes of aspects of film, stage, and *radio, televised Shakespeare is not exactly like Shakespeare in any other medium, and its possibilities are enormous. *BK*

Bulman, J. C., and Coursen, H. R. (eds.), *Shakespeare on Television: An Anthology of Essays and Reviews* (1988)
Kliman, Bernice W., 'Setting in Television Productions', in *Hamlet: Film, Television, and Audio Performance* (1988)
Rothwell, Kenneth S., 'Electronic Shakespeare: From Television to the Web', in *A History of Shakespeare on Screen: A Century of Film and Television* (1999)
Rothwell, Kenneth S., and Melzer, Annabelle Henkin, *Shakespeare on Screen: An International Filmography and Videography* (1990)
Shakespeare on Film Newsletter, ed. Bernice W. Kliman and Kenneth S. Rothwell (1976–92), incorporated since 1992 in the *Shakespeare Bulletin*

'Tell me, where is Fancy bred?', sung by a member of Portia's train in *The Merchant of Venice* 3.2.63. The original music is unknown. *JB*

Tempest, The *(see page 470)*

Temple Grafton, one of the 'Shakespeare villages', 5 miles (8 km) west of Stratford. On her marriage, Anne *Hathaway was described as being 'of Temple Grafton'. A conjectured explanation is that the marriage took place there. If so it is likely to have been performed by the vicar John Frith, described in a Puritan survey of 1576 as 'an old priest and unsound in religion' (implying that he was a Catholic), who 'can neither preach nor read well', and whose 'chiefest trade is to cure hawks that are hurt or diseased, for which purpose many do usually repair to him'. *SW*

Temple Shakespeare, a pocket hardback edition for the general reader edited by Israel Gollancz with minimal prefaces and glossaries between 1894 and 1896. The later *New Temple edition preserves the pocket format, but is in other respects quite different. *RAF*

Tennyson, Alfred Tennyson, Baron (known as Alfred, Lord Tennyson) (1809–92), English Poet Laureate. Tennyson, like most eminent literary Victorians, was steeped in Shakespeare from childhood, through reading rather than the stage, although he saw Fanny *Kemble perform at Christmas in 1829 and discussed *Hamlet* with Henry *Irving after a Lyceum performance in March 1874. He even thought to emulate Shakespeare with *Queen Mary: A Drama* (1874; abridged and performed 18 April 1876). Among his poems, 'Mariana' (from *Poems, Chiefly Lyrical,* 1830) is inspired by *Measure for Measure*; a satirical poem addressed to Bulwer Lytton, *The New Timon, and the Poets,* appeared in *Punch* (28 February 1846); the intense elegiac emotion expressed for Arthur Henry Hallam in *In Memoriam* (1850) is sometimes compared to the Sonnets; and the introspective inactivity of the hero of *Maud* (1855) is often identified with Hamlet. On his deathbed Tennyson called out for Shakespeare, and he was buried with a copy of *Cymbeline* in his hand. *TM*

Terence (?190–?159 BC), Roman comic dramatist, brought to Rome from Carthage as a slave but later freed for his literary talents. Like *Plautus, he adapted the Greek New Comedy, specifically the plays of Menander, to produce six plays based on the same stock characters and intrigue plots. Terence's style and plotting were studied in 16th-century grammar schools, where he was also attributed with the invention of the five-act structure. Shakespeare's debt to the Roman may include echoes from his plays *Andrian* and *The Eunuch*, in *The Taming of the Shrew, Love's Labour's Lost,* and *Much Ado About Nothing.* *JKS*

Miola, Robert S., *Shakespeare and Classical Comedy: The Influence of Plautus and Terence* (1992)
Salingar, Leo, *Shakespeare and the Traditions of Comedy* (1974)

Terry, Dame Ellen (1847–1928), English actress, who made her debut under the exacting tutelage of Charles and Ellen *Kean at the Princess's theatre, where (between 1854 and 1859) she played the Duke of York (*Richard III*), Mamillius, Puck, Prince Arthur, and Fleance, attracting the attention of Lewis Carroll. In her early teens Terry alternated engagements in London and Bath/Bristol, where she was admired as Titania and Desdemona.

Although her marriage in 1864 to the artist G. F. Watts deprived the stage of her talents for several years, she was not entirely lost to Shakespeare; her husband's several portraits of her included one as Ophelia. Ellen Terry's ravishing beauty (in particular her golden hair) made her—in W. Graham Robertson's words—'par excellence the Painter's actress', but more significantly it also made her the visual embodiment of ideal femininity during the apogee of stage pictorialism.

In 1875, one year after returning to the stage, she appeared as Portia—'so fresh and charming . . . so fair and gentle . . . it is the very poetry of acting' wrote Clement Scott—in the Bancrofts' scenically innovative revival of *The Merchant of Venice* with designs by the architect E. W. Godwin, who was the father of her two—illegitimate—children. In 1878 Ellen Terry became Henry *Irving's leading lady at the Lyceum where, beginning with Ophelia (1878) and ending with Volumnia (1901), she also played Portia, Lady Anne, Beatrice, Juliet, Viola, Lady Macbeth, Queen Katherine, Cordelia, and Imogen. As the main quality which Ellen Terry brought to these roles, in addition to her beauty, grace, and charm, was a seemingly artless naturalness and spontaneity, her success tended to be in ratio to the congruence between her and the part. Thus Lady Macbeth and Queen Katherine were mistakes, but Henry *James, who had been totally unsusceptible to the charms of Terry's Portia, wrote of her Imogen (1896), 'no part she has played in late years is so much of the exact fit of her particular gifts'. At the Lyceum the display of Ellen Terry's gifts was never the determining factor: that was Irving's role. Thus as Ophelia and Lady Macbeth she had to defer in costume and interpretation (respectively) to Irving's Hamlet and Macbeth, and she never played Rosalind, to whom she was ideally suited.

After her long partnership with Irving ended, Ellen Terry pursued her career elsewhere. In 1902 she appeared as Mistress Page with Beerbohm *Tree and in 1903 she gave a reprise as Beatrice in her son Edward Gordon *Craig's production of *Much Ado* at the Imperial theatre. Increasingly subject to poor sight and failing memory, Ellen Terry devoted herself to her Shakespeare lectures, which she gave in Britain, America, and Australia 1910–21. These form the basis of her *Four Lectures on Shakespeare,* published posthumously in 1932. Ellen Terry died at her home in Smallhythe (Kent), which is now the property of the National Trust and houses the extensive archive which is an indispensable resource for biographers not only of Ellen Terry but also of her daughter Edy Craig. *RF*

Auerbach, Nina, *Ellen Terry: Player in her Time* (1987)
Craig, Edith, and St John, Christopher (eds.), *Ellen Terry's Memoirs* (1933)
Manvell, Roger, *Ellen Terry: A Biography* (1968)

Tetralogy, First, a term for Shakespeare's first four English history plays—*1 Henry VI, The First Part of the Contention* (*2 Henry VI*), *Richard Duke of York* (*3 Henry VI*), and *Richard III*—when they are discussed as a multi-part narrative and/or performed as a cycle. Though composed first, chronologically they follow the reigns of Richard II, Henry IV, and Henry V dramatized in the Second Tetralogy. *RWFM*

Tetralogy, Second, a term for *Richard II, 1* and *2 Henry IV,* and *Henry V* when they are discussed as a group or performed as a cycle: see also HENRIAD. *MD*

tetrameter, a verse line of four feet, used by Shakespeare principally **(1)** as an occasional variation from *pentameter, **(2)** as the basic metre of *songs ('Take, O, take those lips away' (*Measure for Measure* 4.1.1 ff.)), **(3)** for the rhymed and songlike speeches of special kinds of characters: the *fairies sometimes in *A*

John Singer Sargent's celebrated portrait of Ellen Terry as Lady Macbeth, 1889: the dress she wore in the role, still preserved at her house in Kent, is embroidered with the wing-cases of beetles.

Midsummer Night's Dream, the witches in *Macbeth*, or lovers who are would-be poets (*Love's Labour's Lost* 4.3.99–118). *GTW*

textual criticism. A. E. Housman famously defined textual criticism as 'the science of discovering errors in texts, and the art of removing them'. The traditional goal of textual criticism is to reconstruct the process by which a text was transmitted to an existing document and to restore that text to its original form. Shakespearian textual critics are primarily interested in the nature of the lost manuscripts that served as printers' copy for the early *quartos and *folios.

The principles of modern textual criticism are articulated in W. W. *Greg's 'The Rationale of Copy-Text' (1950). Greg argues that an editor may best approximate an author's finally intended text by adopting as 'copy text' the printed text closest to the author's manuscript and then emending that copy text with any later variants judged to be authorial based upon an understanding of how the error occurred in the transmission of the text.

In the case of *Hamlet*, analysis of textual features in the second quarto (1604/5) suggests that it was set into type from Shakespeare's *foul papers. This hypothesis would explain a number of readings in the Q2 text—such as the spelling 'Gertrad'—as instances in which the compositor misread Shakespeare's *handwriting, in the known examples of which the letter *a* and the letter *u* are often indistinguishable. In the Folio text of the play, which appears to derive from a theatrical playbook, Hamlet's mother is named 'Gertrude'. Since Q2 represents the text closest to the author's manuscript it might be chosen as the copy text for a critical edition. But an exercise in textual criticism reveals compelling reasons for believing that the name that Shakespeare intended and the name that was spoken onstage was 'Gertrude' and therefore provides an editor with a rationale for emending the quarto text by reference to the Folio variant. *ER*

Greg, W. W., 'The Rationale of Copy-Text', *Studies in Bibliography*, 3 (1950–1)
Housman, A. E., 'The Application of Thought to Textual Criticism', *Proceedings of the Classical Association*, 18 (1921)

Thaisa, daughter of King Simonides, marries Pericles. She is thought to have died giving birth to Marina, *Pericles* 11, but survives to be reunited with her family, 22. *AB*

Char. Oh *Cleopatra*, thou art taken Queene.
Cleo. Quicke,quicke,good hands.
Pro. Hold worthy Lady,hold:
Doe not your ſelfe ſuch wrong,who are in this
Releeu'd, but not betraid.
Cleo. What of death too that rids our dogs of languiſh
Pro. *Cleopatra*, do not abuſe my Maſters bounty, by
Th'vndoing of your ſelfe: Let the World ſee
His Nobleneſſe well acted, which your death
Will neuer let come forth.
Cleo. Where art thou Death?

out a mind, the Faries Coach-makers: & in this ſtate ſhe
gallops night by night,through Louers braines: and then
they dreame of Loue.On Courtiers knees,that dreame on
Curſies ſtrait: ore Lawyers fingers, who ſtrait dreamt on
Fees, ore Ladies lips, who ſtrait on kiſſes dreame, which
oft athe angry Mab with bliſters plagues, becauſe their
breath with Sweet meats tainted are. Sometime ſhe gallops ore a Courtiers noſe, & then dreames he of ſmelling
out a ſute: & ſomtime comes ſhe with Tith pigs tale,tick-
ling a Parſons noſe as a lies aſleepe, then he dreames of
another Benefice. Sometime ſhe driueth ore a Souldiers

A textual crux in *Antony and Cleopatra* (5.2.41): does the Folio text say 'languish' or 'anguish'? What some editors read as an 'l', others see as an accidental 'inked space', comparable to the one between 'strait' and 'dreamt' on the fourth line of this passage from the same edition's *Romeo and Juliet*.

Thaliart (Thaliard) is Antiochus' henchman in *Pericles* 1 and 3. *AB*

Theatre, the first substantial purpose-built London playhouse in England since Roman times, built in 1576 by James *Burbage in the Shoreditch district just north-east of the City and hence beyond the jurisdiction of the anti-theatrical Puritan city fathers. Although the *Red Lion was earlier (built 1567), the Theatre appears to have been considerably more substantial than its predecessor and indeed its timbers survived in the form of the *Globe until the fire of 1613. The only contemporary picture of the Theatre is the sketch belonging to Abram Booth now in the University of Utrecht library. This shows an apparently round open-air structure with a superstructural hut like that at the *Swan, but artistic distortion of proportion (especially height) limits this picture's usefulness concerning the Theatre's size. The presence of the superstructural hut does not prove that the Theatre had a stage cover and posts similar to those of the Swan since this might be merely the top of a 'turret' like that at the Red Lion. Patrons could apparently stand in the yard around the stage and either stand or sit in the galleries which enclosed the yard.

When it was built the Theatre was available to any playing company to use and the precise occupancy is largely untraceable before the settlement of 1594 which licensed the *Chamberlain's Men to use the Theatre and the Admiral's Men to use the Rose. Shakespeare's plays written in the latter half of the 1590s, *Love's Labour's Lost, Richard II, Romeo and Juliet, A Midsummer Night's Dream, King John, The Merchant of Venice, 1* and *2 Henry IV*, and *Much Ado About Nothing*, would have been written for the Theatre. The nearby *Curtain playhouse was described as an 'esore' to the Theatre in 1585, which suggests an obscure financial connection which might have involved the Chamberlain's Men playing at the Curtain. The lease on the site expired in 1597, and when negotiations for its renewal stalled and the Blackfriars project was thwarted the Burbages engaged the master carpenter Peter *Street to dismantle the building and to re-erect the timbers as the Globe on a new site south of the river. *GE*

Berry, Herbert, 'Aspects of the Design and Use of the First Public Playhouse', in Herbert Berry (ed.), *The First Public Playhouse: The Theatre in Shoreditch 1576–1598* (1979)

Lusardi, James P., 'The Pictured Playhouse: Reading the Utrecht Engraving of Shakespeare's London', *Shakespeare Quarterly*, 44 (1993)

Theatre Museum, London, the national museum of the performing arts in the UK. It houses permanent displays and special exhibitions from its own collections of costumes, designs, paintings, photographs, and other memorabilia of the British stage—inevitably, heavily featuring Shakespeare—and makes available its book and archive collections for consultation. *SLB*

http://theatremuseum.vam.ac.uk

theatres, Elizabethan and Jacobean. The Romans built amphitheatres in Britain during their occupation, but we know of no purpose-built theatres erected between their departure and the construction of the open-air galleries and stage of the *Red Lion in Stepney in 1567. More substantial than the Red Lion were James *Burbage's *Theatre in *Shoreditch built in 1576 and Henry Lanham's nearby *Curtain built in 1577, both of which echoed the circular shape of the Roman amphitheatres. Also in 1576 Richard Farrant began to use the Upper Frater of the *Blackfriars Dominican monastery as a playhouse and some time in the 1570s the Paul's playhouse opened. The first playhouse south of the river was probably the one at Newington Butts, about which almost nothing is known, but in 1587 Philip *Henslowe built his open-air *Rose theatre on *Bankside and this was joined by its neighbours the *Swan (1595) and the *Globe (1599). There had long been an animal-baiting ring in the south bank area known as Paris Garden, but the theory that open-air playhouses developed out of the tradition of placing a touring company's portable stage and booth inside a baiting ring is unproven. In truth we do not know where the open-air circular playhouse design came from, other than imitation of the Roman style. In 1599–1600 Henslowe built a new open-air playhouse, the Fortune, north of the river, but broke with tradition in making the gallery ranges in the form of a square.

Until 1608, when the King's Men regained the Blackfriars, the indoor theatres were used exclusively by companies of child actors and the open-air playhouses dominated the adult industry. It was customary at the indoor playhouses to divide the performance into five acts and for short musical interludes to fill the intervals, and this practice spread to the outdoor playhouses with the King's Men's acquisition of the Blackfriars. The terminology 'public' and 'private' theatre for the open-air and indoor theatres respectively is misleading as both kinds were open to the public, although the considerably higher cost of entrance to the indoor theatres kept out all but the middle and upper classes. In 1616 Christopher *Beeston built the indoor Cockpit theatre in Drury Lane which competed directly with the Blackfriars for the elite market, and a number of new theatres followed before the Civil War. All the theatres were closed by order of Parliament in 1642 as war became inevitable and those which were still structurally sound were converted into dwellings or their timbers stripped for reuse elsewhere. *GE*

Foakes, R. A., *Illustrations of the English Stage 1580–1642* (1985)

Pro. Spirits, which by mine Art
I haue from their confines call'd to enact
My present fancies.
Fer. Let me liue here euer,
So rare a wondred Father, and a wiſe
Makes this place Paradiſe.
Pro. Sweet now, ſilence:
Iuno and *Ceres* whiſper ſeriouſly,
There's ſomething elſe to doe: huſh, and be mute
Or elſe our ſpell is mar'd.

A famous textual crux in *The Tempest* (4.1.123): 'wise' or 'wife'? Is the crucial letter a worn 'f', a long 's', or a long 's' mistakenly substituting for an 'f'? (Cf. the specimens of 's' and 'f' in 'present fancies' at the end of Prospero's previous speech.) The differing forensic verdicts of successive textual critics have inevitably been influenced by their critical understanding of the line's context and purport.

'Then they for sudden joy did weep', a misquoted mid-16th-century ballad, sung by the Fool in *The Tragedy of King Lear* 1.4.156. F. W. Sternfeld's *Songs from Shakespeare's Tragedies* (1964) gives a tune from an early 17th-century source. *JB*

Theobald, Lewis (1688–1744), English Shakespearian editor. In his *Shakespeare Restored* (1726), which was a response to the inadequacies of Alexander *Pope's edition, and in his own edition of *The Works of Shakespeare* (1733), Theobald was the first to bring to Shakespeare methods previously developed and employed in classical and biblical editing and commentary. Rejecting Pope's free and aesthetic approach to the Shakespearian text, Theobald insisted that, at points of apparent corruption, the editor must resort in the first place to collation of 'the older Copies', and avoid imposing alterations on the basis of a modern taste. At the same time he argued that, where surviving texts were apparently irrecoverably corrupt, the editor must resort to a responsible and essentially interpretative process of conjectural textual *emendation founded upon '*Reason* or *Authorities*'. For such an editorial task Theobald was well qualified by his critical intelligence, professional familiarity with the theatre, acquaintance with secretary hand, and above all by his exceptionally extensive reading in the drama and other writings of Shakespeare's time. Alexander Pope, stung by the demolition of his own editorial work in *Shakespeare Restored*, and lacking and despising Theobald's knowledge of 'all such reading as was never read', constructed in his first *Dunciad* (1728) a distorted but influential picture of Theobald as a dull and pedantic verbal critic. Nevertheless, Theobald's edition was reprinted seven times in its own century, and his textual and interpretative judgements have been drawn on by many later editors, including virtually all his 18th-century successors. *MLW*

Jarvis, Simon, *Scholars and Gentlemen: Shakespearian Textual Criticism and Representations of Scholarly Labour, 1725–1765* (1995)
Jones, Richard Foster, *Lewis Theobald: His Contribution to English Scholarship* (1919)
Seary, Peter, *Lewis Theobald and the Editing of Shakespeare* (1990)
Walsh, Marcus, *Shakespeare, Milton and Eighteenth-Century Literary Editing* (1997)

'There dwelt a man in Babylon', the opening of a mid-16th-century *broadside, 'The Ballad of Constant Susanna', quoted or sung by Sir Toby in *Twelfth Night* 2.3.75. The tune is 'Would not good King Solomon', also known as 'Guerre guerre gay'. *JB*

Thersites inveighs against his fellow Greeks throughout *Troilus and Cressida*. A cowardly figure with a small part in *Homer's *Iliad*, he does not appear in medieval romances. *AB*

Theseus advises Hermia to obey her father Egeus in *A Midsummer Night's Dream* 1.1. He and his followers find the sleeping lovers in the wood, 4.1, and he announces that their weddings will be celebrated with his own to Hippolyta. In *The Two Noble Kinsmen* he postpones his wedding to Hippolyta in order to make war on Creon at the three queens' request: he imprisons Palamon and Arcite, and eventually decrees the terms on which they will conclude their rivalry: after a formal combat, the winner will marry Emilia; the loser will be executed. He is a legendary Greek hero, best known for defeating the Minotaur and seducing a long series of women. *AB*

'They bore him barefaced on the bier', sung by Ophelia in *Hamlet* 4.5.165, often to the tune 'Walsingham'; see 'How should I your true love know'. *JB*

Thidias is Caesar's messenger to Cleopatra: Antony orders him to be whipped for kissing her hand, *Antony and Cleopatra* 3.13. He is called Thyreus by *Plutarch (*Theobald and many later editors have followed this spelling). *AB*

Thirlby, Styan (?1686–1753), English theologian and critic, whose annotated copy of *Pope's edition of Shakespeare (1723–5), together with a list of emendations and a commentary, were used by *Theobald when preparing his edition. Thirlby's notes were consulted again by Dr *Johnson when he was preparing his own edition: he borrowed them from Edward Walpole, to whom Thirlby had bequeathed his library. *CMSA*

'Thisbe'. See FLUTE, FRANCIS.

Thomas, Ambroise. See OPERA; SHAKESPEARE AS A CHARACTER.

Thomas, Friar. See FRIAR THOMAS.

Thomas, Lord Cromwell. Derived from *Foxe's *Book of Martyrs*, this anonymous play is tentatively attributed to Wentworth Smith. The ascription to Shakespeare is not sustainable, despite the initials 'W.S.' printed on the 1602 and 1613 quartos. *SM*

Thomas of Woodstock, an anonymous play, unpublished during Shakespeare's lifetime though perhaps written *c.*1592–5, which influenced *Richard II*. *Woodstock* was also known as *The First Part of the Reign of King Richard the Second* and Shakespeare's play has been proposed as Part 2. This theory is based on the fact that Shakespeare omitted some of the obvious events of Richard's reign or referred only briefly to them, in particular the blank charters and the murder of Gloucester, as if confident that they were already known to his audience. But the latter would not have needed to know *Woodstock* to have filled in these gaps and the two-part play theory is further problematized

(cont. on page 474)

The Tempest

Printed as the first play in the Folio, *The Tempest* has always enjoyed a special prominence in the Shakespeare canon. Its first recorded performance took place at James I's court on 1 November 1611, and it cannot have been much more than a year old then. *The Tempest* is indebted to three texts unavailable before the autumn of 1610, namely William *Strachey's *True Reportary of the Wrack and Redemption of Sir Thomas Gates* (completed in Virginia in July 1610, and circulated in manuscript before its eventual publication in 1625), Sylvester *Jourdan's *Discovery of the Bermudas* (printed in 1610, with a dedication dated 13 October), and the Council of Virginia's *True Declaration of the Estate of the Colony in Virginia* (entered in the Stationers' Register in November 1610 and printed before the end of the year). An apparently irresistible urge to identify Prospero with Shakespeare (visible since the 1660s) has led many commentators to think of *The Tempest* as the playwright's personal farewell to the stage, and while this view seems both sentimental and slightly inaccurate (since Shakespeare was yet to co-write *Cardenio*, *All Is True* (*Henry VIII*), and *The Two Noble Kinsmen* with *Fletcher), this probably was his last unassisted work for the theatre, completed in 1611. Its position in the Folio may reflect his colleagues' recognition of this fact.

Text: The Folio provides the only authoritative text of the play: it was prepared with care, apparently from a literary transcript by the scribe Ralph *Crane. The text's unusually detailed stage directions were probably elaborated by Crane for the benefit of readers from briefer indications in his copy, but they may well reflect his accurate recollections of seeing the play staged. *The Tempest* calls for an unusual quantity of *music, and the words of its *songs are preserved in a number of 17th-century manuscripts. These all seem to derive from the Folio text, but some may supplement it by accurately recording where breaks came between verses and refrains.

Sources: The three texts from late 1610 which lie behind this play supplied Shakespeare with the story of a much-discussed shipwreck in the West Indies. The *Sea-Adventure*, flagship of a nine-strong flotilla taking 500 colonists from Plymouth to Virginia, struck the coast of Bermuda in a storm on 29 July 1609 and was presumed lost, but in May 1610 the bulk of its crew and passengers reached Jamestown, having wintered on Bermuda and built themselves pinnaces. The accounts Shakespeare read, which gave hints for details in the play such as the St Elmo's fire with which *Ariel adorns the storm (1.2.197–204), represent the preservation of the survivors as the work of Providence (just as Gonzalo regards the outcome of the play's story, 5.1.204–16). It may be significant to the play's depictions of authority and subordination that these texts are almost as interested in the suppression of potential mutiny as they are in the unfamiliar climate and natural history of Bermuda, and it is probably relevant to the play that before their landing there the mariners had regarded the island as a haunt of evil spirits.

Beyond these local sources, the play is indebted to Shakespeare's other reading about *travel, trade, and colonialism, notably in Robert Eden's *History of Travel* (1577), from which he derived the name of Sycorax's god Setebos, and in *Montaigne's essay 'Of the Cannibals', the source for Gonzalo's vision of an ideal commonwealth (2.1.149–74). *Caliban's name may be related to 'Carib' as well as to 'Cannibal', suggesting that Shakespeare had read early accounts of *Caribbean native cultures. Other important debts are to *Ovid's *Metamorphoses*, from which Shakespeare took Prospero's farewell to his magic (5.1.33–57) almost verbatim (tellingly, from a speech by the sorceress Medea), and to *Virgil's *Aeneid*, particularly its depiction of Aeneas' dealings with Dido, Queen of Carthage, whom Shakespeare remembered often during this play about a ship wrecked between Tunis and Italy. The main plot of the play, though—unusually, largely told in retrospect, the play neoclassically confining itself to showing the last few hours of the story in a single location—is Shakespeare's own.

Synopsis: **1.1** Alonso, King of Naples, his son Ferdinand, their ally Antonio, Duke of Milan, and a number of courtiers are returning to Italy from Alonso's daughter's wedding to the King of Tunis when their ship is driven aground in a violent storm, the sailors struggling in vain to preserve it between the interruptions of their aristocratic passengers. All are convinced they are about to drown. **1.2** After the storm, Prospero reassures his daughter Miranda that no one has perished in the shipwreck, which he caused and controlled by magic. For the first time he tells her of how, twelve years earlier, they came to this island. The rightful Duke of Milan, Prospero was usurped by his brother Antonio, who, governing the state while Prospero studied magic, promised that Milan would pay tribute to Naples in return for Alonso's military backing for his coup. Prospero and the 3-year-old Miranda were set adrift far out to sea in a small boat provisioned and supplied with Prospero's books only at the insistence of a humane Neapolitan courtier, Gonzalo. Since then Prospero has brought Miranda up on the island where they came ashore, in ignorance of his royalty, but now his enemies have been brought to the island and their future depends on the next few hours. While Miranda falls into a magically induced sleep, Prospero summons his spirit Ariel, who describes how he executed the storm and how he has left the mariners and passengers, the former asleep on the safely harboured ship, Ferdinand alone, and the rest dispersed around the island. When Ariel reminds Prospero of his promise to free him from his labours, the enchanter reminds him of his twelve-year confinement in a pine at the hands of the banished Algerian witch Sycorax (now dead, though survived by her son Caliban), and threatens to renew such an imprisonment if Ariel complains again. Promising to free him after two days, Prospero commands Ariel to reappear as a sea-nymph, visible only to him. Miranda awakens and Prospero summons their slave Caliban, who curses them, remembering their kinder treatment when they first came to the island, which he insists is rightfully his. He has been enslaved since an attempt to rape Miranda, which he unrepentantly remembers. Prospero sends him to fetch fuel, threatening him with torments. After Caliban's departure, the invisible Ariel leads Ferdinand to them with the song 'Come unto these yellow sands', confirming the Prince's belief that his father has drowned with another, 'Full fathom five thy father lies'. Ferdinand and Miranda fall in love instantly, and he proposes to her: this is just as Prospero has planned, but he feigns displeasure, offering to imprison Ferdinand, who is magically paralysed when he attempts to draw his sword.

2.1 Elsewhere on the island, Gonzalo tries to comfort Alonso, who is convinced Ferdinand has drowned: Antonio and Alonso's brother Sebastian, however, ridicule Gonzalo and reproach Alonso for marrying his daughter to an African. Gonzalo, further mocked by Antonio and Sebastian, speaks of the utopian community he imagines establishing on the island. The invisible Ariel plays music and all sleep except Antonio and Sebastian: Antonio persuades Sebastian he should seize the opportunity to make himself King of Naples by violence, and they both draw swords to kill Alonso and Gonzalo. Ariel, however, rouses Gonzalo with a song, 'While you here do snoring lie', and the whole party awakens, obliging the two would-be assassins to pretend they have drawn because alarmed by a noise as of lions. **2.2** Caliban, seeing the jester Trinculo, thinks he is one of Prospero's tormenting spirits, and lies hiding under his gaberdine: Trinculo, finding him, at first thinks him a monstrous fish whom he wishes he could exhibit lucratively at English fairs, but decides he must be a thunder-struck native. When it begins to rain, he too takes shelter under the gaberdine. Alonso's drunken butler Stefano, drinking sack preserved from the wreck and singing, thinks the gaberdine is a four-legged monster, then a two-headed one too, before he realizes the truth and is reunited with Trinculo. Caliban, given some of Stefano's sack, thinks him a god, swears allegiance to him, and sings in joy of his deliverance from Prospero's slavery.

3.1 Concealed, Prospero watches with approval as Ferdinand, enslaved and bearing logs for him, speaks with Miranda and the two vow to marry. **3.2** Increasingly drunk, Caliban begins to fall out with Trinculo, a quarrel exacerbated by Ariel, who invisibly simulates Trinculo's voice and contradicts Caliban as he speaks of Prospero. Caliban proposes that Stefano should murder Prospero during his afternoon nap and marry Miranda, a scheme to which he and Trinculo agree. They sing a catch, the tune of which Ariel invisibly plays on a tabor and pipe. Caliban reassures the Italians that the island is full of harmless magical sounds. **3.3** Alonso and his hungry fellows are astonished when spirits lay out a banquet before them, inviting them to dine. As Prospero watches invisibly from above, Alonso, Antonio, and Sebastian are about to eat when Ariel appears in the shape of a harpy, makes the banquet disappear, and speaks of the three's sinfulness, reminding them of the banishment of Prospero. Prospero congratulates Ariel on his performance. Alonso, convinced Ferdinand has died in punishment for his own role in Antonio's usurpation, is stricken with guilt.

4.1 Prospero, explaining that Ferdinand's servitude was only a test of his love, blesses his engagement to Miranda, though he warns the Prince severely against premarital sex. To celebrate the occasion, Prospero's spirits perform a masque in which Iris, at Juno's behest, summons Ceres (played by Ariel) to help bless the couple, in the welcome absence of Venus and Cupid. During a dance of nymphs and reapers, however, Prospero remembers Caliban's plot, and hastily terminates the unfinished masque, apologizing to

Ferdinand for his distraction but pointing out that all the world is as mortal and fragile as was the spirits' performance. After the couple have gone, Ariel tells Prospero how he has led Caliban, Stefano, and Trinculo through thorns and a filthy pool on their way to seek him: at Prospero's bidding he hangs out fancy clothing, and while Stefano and Trinculo are distracted by the task of stealing it—to Caliban's impatience—Prospero and Ariel drive the three of them away to more torment with spirits in the shapes of hunting dogs.

5.1 Prospero, in his magic robes, listens to Ariel's compassionate description of the sufferings of Alonso and his party (imprisoned by magic on Prospero's instructions), and resolves that since they are penitent he will not pursue vengeance against them. While Ariel goes to release them, he draws a circle with his staff, remembering the magnificent achievements of his magic powers but vowing to renounce them. Alonso and his followers are led into the circle by Ariel, still charmed, and Prospero speaks to them. Ariel sings 'Where the bee sucks', a song of his imminent freedom, as he dresses Prospero in his former clothes as Duke of Milan. Alonso, Gonzalo, and the others recover their wits and are astonished to be greeted by Prospero. Prospero forgives Antonio, but demands the restoration of his dukedom, pointing out privately that he knows of the earlier assassination attempt against Alonso. When Alonso speaks in grief about the presumed death of Ferdinand, Prospero says he too lost a child in the recent storm, and draws a curtain to reveal Miranda and Ferdinand playing chess together. Alonso and Ferdinand are happily reunited. Miranda is astonished at the beauty of mankind, and Alonso and Gonzalo bless her engagement to Ferdinand. Ariel brings the Master and Boatswain, who are amazed to report that the ship and crew are perfectly intact. Ariel then brings Caliban, Stefano, and Trinculo, whose conspiracy Prospero describes. Caliban, admitting he was foolish to believe his drunken companions gods, is sent to tidy Prospero's cell while his former confederates return their stolen clothing. Prospero promises he will tell his whole story before they set sail for Italy the following morning, and assures Ariel that he will be free as soon as he has provided a wind which will enable them to catch up with the rest of Alonso's fleet. Alone, Prospero speaks an epilogue, in rhyme, saying that now that he has no magic powers he needs the audience's indulgent applause to free him.

Artistic features: As even the above synopsis may suggest, *The Tempest* works less as a straightforward narrative than as a series of rich but profoundly enigmatic images, often arranged in symmetrical patterns: the parallel servitudes of Caliban and Ariel, Caliban and Ferdinand; the paired younger brothers Antonio and Sebastian; Prospero's magical control of the sea and of the spectacle; Ariel's performances as sea-nymph, as harpy, and as Ceres. As such it is closer to lyric, as well as more crammed with lyrics, than any other Shakespeare play, a haunting sea-poem in which celebration over what can be restored and sorrow over what must be lost are inextricably intertwined.

Critical history: The mysterious qualities of *The Tempest*—the sense that the play reveals only glimpses of its purposes, quite apart from dramatizing only a few hours of its characters' lives—have given it a richer afterlife in drama, literature, and the other arts than almost any other Shakespeare play, as subsequent writers and artists have sought to explain, supplement, and extend it. Versions of Prospero the master illusionist have haunted the theatre (F. G. Waldron composed the first of several sequels, *The Virgin Queen*, in 1796) and, especially, film (allusions to *The Tempest* have, for example, become almost *de rigueur* in science fiction, from the 1956 outer-space version **Forbidden Planet* onwards). The play's interpreters in other media include *Hogarth, *Fuseli (who based his drawings of Prospero on portraits of Leonardo da Vinci), Iris *Murdoch, Aimé *Césaire (anti-colonialist author of *Une tempête*), and W. H. *Auden, and very nearly included *Mozart.

From the Restoration onwards the play was regarded as a display of imaginative liberties not possible (or permissible) for lesser writers: *Dryden, for example, cited both Caliban and Ariel as specimens of Shakespeare's abilities to go beyond nature. His critical observations on the play, though, are perhaps less revealing as comments on it than the adaptation he co-wrote with *Davenant in 1667, *The Tempest; or, The Enchanted Island.* Davenant, according to Dryden, 'found that somewhat might be added to the design of Shakespeare . . . and therefore to put the last hand to it, he designed the counterpart to Shakespeare's plot, namely that of a man who had never seen a woman'. In the adaptation, which elaborates on the symmetries of Shakespeare's original, Prospero is also responsible for a naive male ward, Hippolito, doomed to die if he ever meets a woman, and Miranda has a sister, Dorinda: in a coyly Edenic scene Dorinda and Hippolito do meet, despite Prospero's prohibitions, and when Hippolito (uninstructed in the monogamous codes of civil society) finds himself just as enthusiastic about Miranda as he is about her sister he is killed in a duel by Ferdinand. Meanwhile Caliban, too, has a sister (confusingly, called Sycorax) whom he pairs off with Trinculo (though she is just as keen on Stefano), and the rival attempts by the mutineers to claim the island by marriage displace their attempted coup against Prospero. Prospero's role, meanwhile, is greatly reduced: he never renounces his magic, which is in the event exceeded by that of Ariel, who is able to provide a magic cure to revive the dead Hippolito and permit a happy ending. Davenant and Dryden make *The Tempest* more orderly, and a good deal lighter, but their invention of the Hippolito plot makes fully visible the fears of sexuality, women, and death which seem to trouble Prospero in the original.

The identification of Prospero with *The Tempest*'s author is already visible in the prologue to Davenant and Dryden's adaptation, and it became a commonplace of 18th-century poetry and prose about Shakespeare (made fully explicit by Thomas Campbell in 1838), which generally regarded the Duke of Milan as a figure of serene wisdom. The 19th century in general maintained this view, seeing the play as an autumnal work about a magician who comes to terms with the renunciation of his powers and the marriage of his only child: according to Victor *Hugo, for whom *The Tempest* was a powerfully mythic text which completed the Bible, this 'last creation of Shakespeare' has 'the solemn tone of a testament' and offers 'the supreme denouement, dreamed by Shakespeare, for the bloody drama of Genesis. It is the expiation of the primordial crime.' Even Hugo, though, had some misgivings about Prospero (calling him 'the master of Nature and the despot of destiny'), and in time the univocally pro-Prospero reading of the play came under pressure, especially from commentators who found Caliban as potentially sympathetic as his master. The play had already come to function for some as an allegory about slavery and colonialism by the 1840s, when the Brough brothers' *burlesque *The Enchanted Isle* depicted Caliban as a black abolitionist who sings the 'Marseillaise', and Charlotte Barnes hybridized the play (in *The Forest Princess*, 1844) with the story of Pocahontas. During the 20th century this view would be developed by many anti-colonial writers, particularly Octave Mannoni in *East Africa, and would become a commonplace of *cultural materialist and *new historicist criticism from the 1970s onwards. The extent to which the play, though set in the Mediterranean, is in any sense 'about' the New World (and a colonial enterprise which in Shakespeare's time barely existed) has been a contentious question throughout the post-war period (not coincidentally, a period when Shakespeare studies have been increasingly dominated by North American critics). Discussions of the play in recent years have often been dominated by the question of Shakespeare's level of approval for Prospero and the related question of the nature, black or white, of his magic.

Stage history: After its court performance in November 1611, *The Tempest* was again played for the royal family in 1613 during the celebrations of Princess *Elizabeth's wedding. No further performances of the original are recorded until the mid-18th century: from 1667 the play was displaced by Davenant and Dryden's adaptation (supplied with further *operatic embellishments in 1674, including a masque of Neptune and a girlfriend for Ariel), which became the most popular show of its time (popular enough, for example, to be wickedly parodied by Thomas *Duffett). Regularly revived at Christmas, its cast including an actress as Hippolito, a middle-aged comedian as Sycorax, and Ariel as the perfect good fairy, this play is one of the ancestors of English pantomime. David *Garrick experimented with his own drastically shortened *The Tempest: An Opera* (1756), but after its failure he instead revived a conservatively abridged text of Shakespeare's original. To 18th-century audiences, however, Shakespeare's play lacked 'business', and the Dryden–Davenant version returned, first as the puppet play *The *Shipwreck* (1780). John Philip *Kemble (a righteously authoritarian Prospero) restored Hippolito and Dorinda to the stage proper in 1789, though he gradually included more of Shakespeare's text over the next decade. Frederick *Reynolds's musical version in 1821 was again based on the Dryden–Davenant adaptation, and it was not until 1838 that the original play (though supplemented with lavish special effects) was again restored, by W. C. *Macready. Spectacle characterized subsequent revivals by Charles *Kean (1857), whose production employed 140 stagehands, Samuel *Phelps (1871), and Beerbohm *Tree, whose 1904 production centred on Caliban, played by himself, who was left alone to watch the Italians' ship departing in a wistful final tableau.

In the 20th century the play was revived more frequently, with major Prosperos including Robert *Atkins (1915) and, especially, John *Gielgud, who played Ferdinand in 1926 but had already graduated to a Dantesque Prospero at the *Old Vic in 1930 (with Ralph *Richardson as Caliban). Gielgud repeated the role in 1940, in 1957 (for Peter *Brook at Stratford), and in 1973 (for Peter *Hall at the National), and his intellectual, mellifluous, exquisitely spoken rendering of the part (particularly its rhetorical set pieces) has been immensely influential (and, through sound *recordings and the film *Prospero's Books*, is likely to remain so). Even within Gielgud's performances as Prospero, however, there was an increasing sense that the Duke of Milan could no longer be played as a benign, Father Christmas-like magus: Brook's production stressed Prospero's obsessive brooding, while Hall had Gielgud present him as puritanically vengeful, successfully acting out his plan but not with meditative detachment. These directions have been pursued by others, too: Derek *Jacobi was a young and passionate Prospero in 1983, John *Wood an unpredictably irritable one in Nicholas Hytner's production of 1988, Alec McCowen a frail, patronizing showman finally spat upon by Simon Russell Beale's freed Ariel in Sam Mendes's production of 1993. At the same time the play has continued to inspire theatrical adaptations and variations, among them Philip Osment's *This Island's Mine* (Gay Sweatshop, 1987–8). The further opening up of the play's text to contemporary questions of gender and power visible in recent criticism has continued to expand the theatrical possibilities of this haunting, conflicted, and mysterious play. *MD*

On the screen: Dallas Bower's BBC TV production (1939) with Peggy *Ashcroft as Miranda was one of the last Shakespeare broadcasts before the BBC closed its television service for the length of the war. The American Hallmark television series produced a memorable *The Tempest* (1960) with Maurice *Evans (Prospero), Lee Remick (Miranda), and Richard *Burton (Caliban). Michael *Hordern's Prospero for BBC TV (1979) was judged dignified but undisturbing, whereas Derek Jarman's *The Tempest* (1980) aroused fierce critical response since it resonates with an underlying agenda which seeks to subvert heterosexual orthodoxy. Jarman presents a dark view of the relationships in the play, Heathcote Williams's Prospero crushing Caliban's fingers underfoot and Toyah Willcox's Miranda displacing innocent winsomeness with brazen and compulsive sexuality. The priorities in this

film are more readily understood when viewed in the context of the whole Jarman *œuvre*. Peter Greenaway's *Prospero's Books* (1991), using highly sophisticated technology, bases a rewriting of the play's action on the books that Gonzalo packs to accompany Prospero in his exile, John Gielgud taking on the multiple personality of Shakespeare, Greenaway, and Prospero, so that the film is essentially about the process of writing, filming, and experiencing simultaneously. The last of the books is Shakespeare's First Folio with blank pages waiting for Shakespeare's *The Tempest* to cover them. *AD*

RECENT MAJOR EDITIONS

Stephen Orgel (Oxford, 1987); Frank Kermode (Arden 2nd series, 1954); Virginia Vaughan (Arden 3rd series, 1999); Anne Barton (New Penguin, 1968)

SOME REPRESENTATIVE CRITICISM

Berger, Harry, 'Miraculous Harp: A Reading of Shakespeare's *Tempest*', *Shakespeare Studies*, 15 (1969)

Cartelli, Thomas, 'Prospero in Africa', in Jean Howard and Marion O'Connor (eds.), *Shakespeare Reproduced* (1987)

Greenblatt, Stephen, 'Learning to Curse', in Fredi Chiapelli (ed.), *First Images of America* (1976)

Hulme, Peter, and Sherman, William H. (eds.), *'The Tempest' and its Travels* (2000)

Mannoni, Octave, *Psychologie de la colonisation* (1950; trans. as *Prospero and Caliban*, 1956)

Maus, Katharine Eisaman, 'Arcadia Lost: Politics and Revision in the Restoration *Tempest*', *Renaissance Drama*, NS13 (1982)

Morse, Ruth, 'Monsters, Magicians, Movies: *The Tempest* and the Final Frontier', *Shakespeare Survey*, 53 (2000)

Peterson, Douglas, in *Time, Tide and Tempest* (1973)

Shakespeare Survey, 43 (*'The Tempest' and after*) (1991)

Sundelsohn, David, in *Shakespeare's Restorations of the Father* (1983)

Vaughan, Alden and Virginia Mason, *Caliban: A Cultural History* (1990)

---

by the considerable overlap between the plays and their differences in tone and emphasis. Bolingbroke does not appear at all in *Woodstock* and the representation of Richard is far less sympathetic than that of Shakespeare. Nevertheless, the portrayal of Gloucester as a man of honesty, loyalty, and integrity, in defiance of *Holinshed's *Chronicles*, is common to both and may have been a source for Gaunt. It is in 2.1, where Gaunt describes Richard's abuses of England, that the verbal correspondences between the two plays are clustered. *JKS*

Thorndike, Dame Sybil (1882–1976), English actress. Brought up in a high Anglican clergyhouse, she spent three years in North America playing out of doors on a far-flung tour of pastoral plays with Ben *Greet. Back in England she worked in pioneering modern drama, marrying Lewis Casson. During the First World War years, as a member of the first regular Shakespearian company at the Old Vic, she played many of Shakespeare's women and (men being at the front) Lear's Fool and Prince Hal. She was admired as a tragedienne, playing in Gilbert Murray's translations from the Greek and Shaw's *St Joan* but also Queen Katherine in *All Is True* (*Henry VIII*), Volumnia to Laurence *Olivier's Coriolanus, and Constance in *King John*. Early in the Second World War she toured Welsh mining villages as Lady Macbeth, and in the famous *Old Vic seasons at the New Theatre she was Queen Margaret to Olivier's Richard III and Mistress Quickly to Ralph *Richardson's Falstaff. A passionate Christian Socialist and a pacifist, she was made a Companion of Honour and, when her ashes were interred in Westminster Abbey, John *Gielgud described her as the most greatly loved English actress since Ellen Terry. *MJ*

Sprigge, Elizabeth, *Sybil Thorndike Casson* (1971)

Thorpe, Thomas. See MR W. H.; PRINTING AND PUBLISHING; SONNETS.

three-man songs, simple songs for three voices (see *The Winter's Tale* 4.3.41). Also known as 'free-men's songs'. *JB*

'Three merry men be we', a snatch of song quoted in many 17th-century plays and lyrics, including by Sir Toby in *Twelfth Night* 2.3.73. *JB*

throne (state). The official chair of a monarch was set on a raised dais under a canopy and the combined property, or either of its components, could be called a throne or state. An ordinary chair placed within a multi-purpose stage booth was the simplest way to represent the state. In 1595 Philip *Henslowe paid carpenters for 'making the throne in the heavens' at the Rose and in the prologue to *Every Man in his Humour* *Jonson mocked plays in which a 'creaking throne comes down' from above the stage, but in these cases 'throne' means simply 'chair used for descents' rather than the monarchical state which would have been carried or pushed onto the stage. *GE*

Throne of Blood. See KUROSAWA, AKIRA.

Thump, Peter. See HORNER, THOMAS.

Thurio is one of Valentine's rivals for Silvia in *The Two Gentlemen of Verona.* *AB*

Thyreus. See THIDIAS.

Tieck, Ludwig (1773–1853), German Romantic author. He translated anonymous Elizabethan plays, many of which he ascribed to Shakespeare (*Alt-Englisches Theater*, 1811; *Shakespeares Vorschule*, 1923–9), but his projected 'Book on Shakespeare' remained fragmentary. Tieck supervised his daughter Dorothea's and W. von Baudissin's completion of A. W. *Schlegel's translation ('Schlegel–Tieck' Shakespeare, 1825–33). In novellas he dealt with Shakespeare's life and theatre (*Dichterleben*, 1826; *Der junge Tischlermeister*, 1836). He staged an exemplary *Midsummer Night's Dream* in Berlin (1843). *WH*

Tillyard, E(ustace) M(andeville) W(etenhall) (1889–1962), English academic, long one of the most widely consulted of modern critics. *Shakespeare's Last Plays* (1938), *Shakespeare's History Plays* (1944), and *Shakespeare's Problem Plays* (1950) all argue for a pattern of organic relations and development between plays often considered discretely. His *The Elizabethan World Picture* (1943), once the almost canonical account of commonly held Elizabethan beliefs about man's place in the universe, has recently come under fierce attack, particularly by *cultural materialists, for disguising the scepticism, tension, and equivocation underlying conventional orthodoxy. Its dogmatic stance may be questionable, but its usefulness in transmitting esoteric ideas persists. *TM*

Tilney, Sir Edmund. See CENSORSHIP; MASTER OF THE REVELS; SIR THOMAS MORE.

Timandra. See PHRYNIA.

Time is a personification who acts as 'Chorus', *The Winter's Tale* 4.1, to explain the passing of sixteen years. *AB*

Timon of Athens *(see opposite page)*

Tippett, Sir Michael (1905–98), English composer. Tippett's first major opera, *The Midsummer Marriage* (1955), though clearly influenced by *A Midsummer Night's Dream* in mood and theme, uses none of Shakespeare's text. *The Knot Garden* (1970), however, draws

(cont. on page 477)

Timon of Athens

This bitter, schematic fable of bankruptcy and misanthropy—which enjoys the dubious distinction of being perhaps the least popular play in the Shakespeare canon—shares many concerns, and a good deal of rare vocabulary, with *King Lear*, and was probably written shortly before it, in 1604–5. It may have been influenced by an anonymous academic play, *Timon* (acted at one of the Inns of Court *c.*1602), and by the depiction of Timon found in William *Painter's *Palace of Pleasure* (1566), a work on which Shakespeare drew for the plot of *All's Well That Ends Well* (1604–5). However, there is no external evidence to help date the play, which went unmentioned in any extant document until its appearance in the First Folio in 1623.

Text: It is quite possible that *Timon of Athens* would have been omitted from the Folio had its compilers not experienced last-minute difficulties in obtaining *Troilus and Cressida*: Charlton *Hinman's study of the Folio's printing showed that this play occupies space originally intended for *Troilus and Cressida*. The reasons for the play's near-exclusion are not known, but they may relate to its status as a collaboration. The Folio text is a highly unusual one, full of loose ends of plot (notably the virtually irrelevant episode in which Alcibiades pleads in vain on behalf of a soldier guilty of manslaughter, 3.6), and anomalies in its lineation and in its use of pronouns. Although some commentators have preferred to think of it as an 'unfinished' work by Shakespeare alone, many editors since Charles *Knight in the 1830s have regarded it as a collaborative work, and it is now widely accepted that about a third of the play was composed by the young Thomas *Middleton. Careful independent studies of language, oaths, spelling, rare vocabulary, and other forensic details have identified Middleton's share as 1.2, all of Act 3 except Timon's devastating appearance at his mock-feast in 3.7, and the dialogue between Timon and Flavius at the end of 4.3. It is clear from the Folio text that the play was set from foul papers, with each playwright's share written in his own hand and betraying quite different habits with incidentals.

Sources: The principal source for *Timon of Athens* is a digression in *Plutarch's life of Mark Antony, from which the play takes Timon's epitaph almost verbatim. Shakespeare and Middleton must also have known *Lucian's dialogue *Timon misanthropus* (either directly or indirectly, perhaps through the anonymous *Timon* play), which supplies Timon's discovery of gold during his self-imposed exile in the woods and its consequences.

Synopsis: **1.1** Outside the rich Timon's house a jeweller, a merchant, a mercer, a poet, and a painter cluster in hopes of his patronage, and he is visited by senators; the Poet, discussing all this with the Painter, has composed an allegory warning Timon that Fortune is fickle. Timon, arriving, speaks courteously to all his suitors, pays his friend Ventidius' debt to free him from prison, and gives his servant Lucilius money to enable him to marry an old Athenian's daughter. He accepts the offerings of the Poet, the Painter, and the Jeweller, and welcomes Alcibiades, 20 of his fellow knights, and even the snarling philosopher Apemantus, who rails at his fellow guests as parasites. **1.2** At Timon's great banquet Apemantus continues to satirize the flatterers around him, who shower Timon with gifts but receive larger ones in return. A masque of Amazons is performed. Flavius, Timon's steward, knows his coffers are almost exhausted.

2.1 A senator is calculating the sums Timon owes, and hurriedly sends his factor Caphis to call in his own debts before Timon is bankrupt. **2.2** Flavius is besieged by Timon's creditors, on whom Apemantus vents his satirical wit while Flavius is finally able to convince Timon that he has given away his entire estate. Timon confidently sends servants to three of his friends, Lucius, Lucullus, and Sempronius, in order to borrow money from them. Flavius reports that the senators have already declined to make such a loan, but

Timon sends him to borrow from Ventidius, who has recently inherited a fortune.

3.1 Lucullus at first assumes Timon's servant has come to bring him another gift, but when he learns he has come for money he attempts to bribe him to tell Timon he has not seen him. The servant throws back the bribe and curses him. 3.2 Lucius, hearing from three strangers of Lucullus' conduct, is indignant on Timon's behalf, but when he is himself asked for money he makes elaborate excuses: the strangers reflect on his hypocrisy. 3.3 Sempronius, too, refuses to lend Timon money, affecting to be too offended at not having been asked first. 3.4 Timon's house is besieged by his creditors' servants: eventually he himself emerges and rants at them. 3.5 The furious Timon tells an uncomprehending Flavius to invite Lucius, Lucullus, and Sempronius to dinner once more. 3.6 Alcibiades pleads with the senators for the life of one of his soldiers, who has committed manslaughter, and grows so angry at their refusal that they banish him: he vows to rally his troops and attack Athens in revenge. 3.7 Timon's friends, convinced his apparent bankruptcy must have been a test of their loyalty, gather eagerly for the feast. Covered dishes are brought in: Timon recites a satirical grace before their lids are lifted, revealing only stones in lukewarm water. He rants at his guests and beats them, vowing eternal misanthropy.

4.1 Outside Athens Timon curses the city, tearing off his clothes to live in the woods as a beast. 4.2 Flavius bids a poignant farewell to his fellow servants, sharing his remaining money with them: he sets off loyally to find and assist Timon. 4.3 Timon, still cursing mankind, digs for roots but finds gold. When Alcibiades arrives with two courtesans, Phrynia and Timandra, Timon gives them gold, to encourage the women to infect the world with venereal diseases and to help Alcibiades destroy Athens and then himself. After their departure, Apemantus arrives, and in a long philosophical dialogue points out that Timon's extreme misanthropy is merely the inverse of his former pride. After Timon finally drives Apemantus away, three thieves arrive, to whom Timon gives gold in order to sponsor their profession, but his sermon and his money in fact convert them to a love of peace. When Flavius arrives, however, Timon is moved by his fidelity, though he nonetheless insists that he stay away in future.

5.1 The Poet and the Painter also come in the hopes of obtaining gold from Timon: he drives them away with blows and curses. 5.2 Flavius brings two senators to Timon's cave, who beg him to return to Athens in honour and lead their defence against Alcibiades, but he professes indifference to his country's fate and suggests that to avoid death at Alcibiades' hands the citizens should all hang themselves. He says he has been writing his epitaph, and means to be buried between high and low tides on the beach. 5.3 The news of Timon's refusal to help Athens reaches the city. 5.4 A soldier, seeking Timon, finds only a gravestone: unable to read its inscription, he takes an impression of it for Alcibiades to interpret. 5.5 The senators surrender to Alcibiades, who promises to kill only his own enemies and those of Timon. The Soldier brings the news of Timon's death and seaside burial, and Alcibiades reads the misanthropic poem he composed as his epitaph. Though he knows Timon would scorn his grief, Alcibiades mourns Timon, and enters Athens with promises of peace.

ARTISTIC FEATURES: Constructed more as a series of emblems than as a narrative, and falling sharply into two very distinct halves—the first three acts depicting Timon's fall from grace, the last two his invective and death outside Athens—*Timon of Athens* is more remarkable for its poetry than for its drama, in this, perhaps, resembling the late romances. Timon's final vision of the tide washing his grave (5.4.99–108) certainly suggests a near-religious perspective beyond the reach of an ordinary play—let alone one so cynical about human motivation as this otherwise appears to be.

CRITICAL HISTORY: Although Samuel *Johnson valued the play for its clear moral lesson against trusting in false friends, most commentators have found its remorseless insistence on this point crude, and even Johnson felt the play was deficient in structure. *Coleridge, influentially, considered it an 'after vibration' of *King Lear*, 'a *Lear* of the satirical drama, a *Lear* of ordinary life'. *Hazlitt was unusual in his unqualified enthusiasm for the play, which he valued for its unrelenting earnestness, but generally the play has been valued for individual passages rather than as a whole: Karl *Marx, for example, was deeply affected by Timon's moralizing against gold (4.3.25–45), initiating a reading of the play's vision of capitalist economics later developed by Kenneth *Muir. Much discussion of the play has been devoted to explaining its perceived incompetence: around the turn of the 20th century, it became fashionable to attribute the melancholy of the 'problem plays' and tragedies to a personal crisis above which Shakespeare finally rose to produce the romances, and Frank Harris's view that Timon's ranting vents Shakespeare's own 'scream of suffering' (developed in *Shakespeare the Man*, 1909) was even echoed by E. K. *Chambers, who decided that Shakespeare must have suffered a nervous breakdown while drafting the play and never completed it thereafter. More recent criticism has returned to the play's relations to the other works within the canon, whether the problem comedies, the romances (towards which Timon's sea-poetry seems to reach), or *Coriolanus* (whose hero's military campaign against his own city is prefigured by that of Alcibiades, while his proud refusal of a reciprocal social contract is anticipated by Timon's absolutist generosity and absolutist misanthropy). The play's most enthusiastic modern champion was G. Wilson *Knight, who regarded it as one of Shakespeare's supreme achievements, and was given to performing Timon's speech of self-exile (4.1) in public lectures, complete with the removal of his clothes.

STAGE HISTORY: No productions of *Timon of Athens* are recorded before the première of Thomas Shadwell's adaptation, *The History of Timon of Athens, the Man-Hater*, in 1678. Shadwell shared the view of the Folio text adopted by many modern critics, declaring in a preface that 'it has the inimitable hand of Shakespear in it, which never made more masterly strokes than this. Yet I can truly say, I have made it into a play.' Shadwell's main contribution, filling a deficiency perceived by many readers since, was to add a love plot, extending the play's opposition between loyal servants and false friends by supplying Timon with a loyal mistress, Evandra, and an affected, mercenary fiancée, Melissa. With Thomas *Betterton as Timon and masque music composed by *Purcell, this adaptation established itself in the repertory, frequently revived down to 1745. It was succeeded by another adaptation in 1771, by Richard Cumberland, who deprived Timon of his rival girlfriends (times had changed) and instead provided a virtuous daughter Evanthe, whose amorous complications with Alcibiades and Lucius fill out the plot. Spranger *Barry played Timon in a grand Drury Lane production staged by *Garrick, but it lasted for only eleven performances. A subsequent reworking of Shadwell's adaptation by Thomas *Hull (1786) achieved only one. In 1816 George Lamb attempted to restore Shakespeare's text, though he left some of Cumberland's changes to the ending and cut Alcibiades' mistresses: the result was an all-male *Timon of Athens*, which succeeded thanks to Edmund *Kean's terrifying passion in the title role. Sporadic 19th-century revivals followed: Samuel *Phelps was successful as Timon (1851, 1856), and Frank *Benson rearranged the play into three acts for a Stratford revival in 1892. Since then, however, it has only occasionally been produced, and has rarely been fully convincing: Nugent *Monck's 1935 production is remembered chiefly for its incidental music by a 21-year-old Benjamin *Britten, Barry *Jackson's post-war modern-dress production of 1947 for the bomb crater that was the set for the second half. Ralph *Richardson and Paul *Scofield, however, each found an other-worldly quality in the title role, and in 1999 Michael *Pennington played Timon sensitively in Gregory Doran's RSC production. *MD*

On the screen: The only screen version on record is Jonathan Miller's BBC TV production, 1981. The cast included Jonathan Pryce as Timon (who delivered his last speech in a disconcerting upside-down close-up), Norman Rodway, Sebastian Shaw, and Diana Dors. *AD*

Recent major editions

H. J. Oliver (Arden 2nd series, 1963); Gary Taylor, in *The Complete Oxford Middleton* (2001); G. R. Hibbard (New Penguin, 1970)

Some representative criticism

Empson, William, 'Timon's Dog', in *The Structure of Complex Words* (1951)

Goldberg, Jonathan, in *Sodometries: Renaissance Texts, Modern Sexualities* (1992)

Jackson, MacDonald P., *Studies in Attribution: Middleton and Shakespeare* (1979)

Knight, G. Wilson, in *The Wheel of Fire* (1930, 1949)

Muir, Kenneth, '*Timon of Athens* and the Cash Nexus', *Modern Quarterly Miscellany*, 1 (1947)

Soellner, Rolf, *Timon of Athens* (1949)

heavily on *The Tempest*: it includes quotations from his *Songs from Ariel*, written for a production of *The Tempest* at the Old Vic in May 1962. *IBC*

tireman, the wardrobe-keeper in a playhouse, responsible for the acquisition and orderly (moth-free) storage of the costumes and for repairs and alterations. Like other non-performing hired men, the tireman could be called upon for small roles. *GE*

tiring house. Any place concealed from the audience could be used as the actors' dressing (or 'tiring') place, but in the purpose-built playhouses the back wall of the stage (or *frons scenae*), pierced by the stage doors, was also the front wall of the tiring house. As well as a changing room, the tiring house was a storage space for the properties, the costumes, and presumably the playbooks. In de Witt's drawing of the *Swan the tiring house is labelled 'mimorum aedes' (actors' house) and its roof forms the floor of the balcony over the stage which could be used for playing 'above'. *GE*

Titania, the queen of the *fairies in *A Midsummer Night's Dream*, refuses to give up a changeling boy she has adopted to Oberon. When asleep, he drugs her so that she will fall madly in love with the first person she sees. This is Bottom, who has an ass's head (also by fairy magic): she takes him to her bower. After obtaining the changeling from her, Oberon takes pity and removes the enchantment. Now disgusted by Bottom, she is reconciled to Oberon.

Before the Second World War, actresses who played Titania usually aimed at an ethereal, queenly elegance and beauty. In the last half of the 20th century, however, her sexual desires have come under investigation, notably by Jan *Kott who argued that 'The slender, tender and lyrical Titania longs for animal love. . . . Sleep frees her from inhibitions. The monstrous ass is being raped by the poetic Titania, while she still keeps on chattering about flowers' (*Shakespeare our Contemporary*, 1963). This interpretation influenced Peter *Brook's groundbreaking 1970 production, which started what has almost become a modern stage convention of 'doubling' the actors who play Titania and Oberon with Hippolyta and Theseus, so that sexual issues in the mortal world are seen to be reflected in the dreamlike fairy world. *AB*

Titinius is sent on a mission by Cassius at Philippi, *Julius Caesar* 5.3. Cassius despairs and kills himself when he thinks Titinius has been slain. Titinius kills himself with Cassius' sword. *AB*

title pages were affixed to early Shakespearian *quartos to identify their contents and were often tacked on walls to advertise them. These title pages generally provide the title of the play, the name of the dramatist, and the printer's *device and *imprint. They also frequently give the name of the acting company and the theatre ('his Majesty's Servants, at the Globe on the Bankside') or details of the play's performance history ('As it was presented before her Highness this last Christmas'), the text's claims to authority ('according to the true and perfect copy'), its publication history ('Newly imprinted and enlarged'), and even a capsule summary ('With the extreme cruelty of Shylock the Jew towards the said Merchant, in cutting a just pound of his flesh: and the obtaining of *Portia* by the choice of three chests'). *ER*

Titus Andronicus *(see page 478)*

Titus Lartius. See Lartius, Titus.

Titus' Servant. See Hortensius' Servant.

tobacco, made from the dried leaves of the south American plant *nicotiana tabacum*, was first introduced to England in the 1560s.

William Harrison wrote in 1573, 'In these days the taking-in of the smoke of the Indian herb called Tobacco, by an instrument formed like a little ladle, whereby it passes from the

(cont. on page 481)

Titus Andronicus

Shakespeare's earliest and most notoriously violent tragedy, sensationally popular in his lifetime but only restored to critical favour in the late 20th century, may have had its first run of performances interrupted by plague. *Henslowe's 'Diary' reports that a play called 'titus & ondronicus' was performed by Sussex's Men at the *Rose theatre on 24 January 1594. The play was entered in the *Stationers' Register on 6 February 1594, only a few days after the Rose theatre was closed down following an outbreak of *plague. Recent editors disagree on the exact date of composition. Verbal parallels in *The *Troublesome Reign of King John*, published in 1591, and *A Knack to Know a Knave*, performed on 10 June 1592, along with the listing of three different acting companies on the *title page of the 1594 *quarto, suggest composition around 1590–1. Both internal and external evidence in favour of this early date is, however, easily confuted. The verbal parallels might derive from another play called *Titus and Vespacia*, which Henslowe recorded as being performed at the Rose on 11 April 1592. Besides, the listing of the three acting companies on the title page of the 1594 quarto might not be meant to be interpreted as a chronology of the play's stage history, as actors from Lord Strange's and *Pembroke's Men were employed by Sussex's Men during the brief 1593–4 winter season. Editors who argue in favour of an earlier date of composition tend to credit an old theory according to which the authorship of *Titus Andronicus* is collaborative and George *Peele is Shakespeare's most likely collaborator. Conversely, editors who believe that this tragedy was written between late 1593 and early 1594 believe it to be entirely Shakespearian.

Text: The first quarto edition of *Titus Andronicus* was published in 1594, followed by two reprints in 1600 and 1611. Q1 was typeset from Shakespeare's foul papers, as suggested by the lack of essential *stage directions, the irregularity of the *speech-prefixes, and occasional false starts and second thoughts. The second and the third quartos emended obvious compositorial mistakes and introduced new ones, which were then inherited by the 1623 *Folio edition, set from an annotated copy of Q3.

The main alterations introduced into the 1623 edition, including more extensive stage directions, *act division, normalized speech-prefixes, and a whole new scene, the so-called fly-killing scene in Act 3, clearly derive from a *promptbook. Although most editors choose Q1 as their copy text, because of its direct link to the author's holograph, most of the *Folio variants are added to it, as they reflect original staging practices and conventions.

The fortunate discovery of the only extant copy of Q1 in Sweden in 1904 allowed 20th-century editors to realize that the ending as it appears in Q2 and the later editions was a compositorial mistake. The *compositor of Q2 must have attempted to replace the missing lines from the last two pages in his copy of Q1, which had been accidentally damaged.

Sources: *Titus Andronicus* has no direct sources. The play has often been connected to a narrative which, although surviving only in an 18th-century chapbook, was believed to derive from a much earlier version of the Titus story which Shakespeare dramatized. This theory has recently been discredited in favour of an alternative hypothesis according to which Shakespeare modelled the character of Lavinia on *Ovid's Philomel (*Metamorphoses*, book 6). It is however generally agreed that instead of borrowing from specific sources, Shakespeare turned to popular dramatic precedents, such as *Kyd's adaptation of Senecan *revenge tragedy, and other Elizabethan tragedies of blood.

SYNOPSIS: 1.1 Saturninus and Bassianus, the sons of the late Emperor of Rome, claim the right to succeed their father, but Marcus Andronicus, a tribune of the people, offers the crown to his brother Titus, as a reward for his victorious military campaigns against the Goths. The issue of the succession is temporarily postponed while Titus, who has lost 21 of his 25 sons in the recent wars, grants his eldest son Lucius permission to give proper burial to his brothers and appease their souls by sacrificing the eldest son of Tamora, the Queen of the Goths. Tamora and her two surviving sons, Chiron and Demetrius, plan to avenge his death. When offered the crown, Titus declines it and bestows it on Saturninus, who asks and obtains the hand of his daughter Lavinia. Bassianus, who is already engaged to Lavinia, reclaims his betrothed with the help of Titus' sons. Enraged by their disobedience, Titus kills his youngest son Mutius. Instead of helping Titus rescue Lavinia, Saturninus turns his back on his benefactor and obtains Tamora's consent to marry him. Betrayed by his sons and his Emperor, Titus finally agrees to give Mutius an honourable burial. Tamora, the new Empress, persuades Saturninus to put up with the Andronici, who have the support of the people of Rome, and wait patiently for the day when they can safely 'massacre them all'. Aaron, Tamora's black servant and lover, settles a dispute between Chiron and Demetrius over Lavinia, by suggesting that they should both rape her in the woods.

2.1 Titus organizes a royal hunt to celebrate the Emperor's wedding. 2.2 Aaron and Tamora meet in the woods and Aaron discloses his plans to have Lavinia raped and Bassianus killed. Tamora tells her sons that Bassianus and Lavinia have been threatening to take her life. Prompted by Tamora, Chiron and Demetrius kill Bassianus and rape Lavinia. Aaron lures Titus' sons Quintus and Martius into the pit where Chiron and Demetrius have thrown Bassianus' body and forges a letter in order to blame Titus' sons for Bassianus' murder. 2.3 Marcus stumbles upon Lavinia, who has been raped and mutilated.

3.1. Titus pleads for his sons' lives in vain and Lucius is banished for attempting to set them free. Lavinia is brought before Titus and the sight of her mangled body triggers Titus' maddened despair, which is only momentarily relieved by Aaron's offer to release his sons in exchange for Titus' right hand. Lucius and Marcus step in and offer to sacrifice their own right hand in order to spare Titus. Titus pretends to accept their offer but then asks Aaron to cut off his hand, while Lucius and Marcus are looking for an axe offstage. After Titus' selfless sacrifice, Marcus urges him not to give way to despair, but Marcus himself gives in to it, when a messenger returns Titus his mutilated hand and the severed heads of his two sons. The climax of Titus' distress is marked by a sublime, heart-rending bout of hysterical laughter. Titus' laughter ushers in the second movement of the tragedy, which is entirely devoted to Titus' attempts to avenge himself on his enemies. Lucius is sent to the Goths to seek their help. 3.2 Titus' lament is interrupted when Marcus kills a fly. Titus is outraged by Marcus' cruelty and is ready to disown him for causing pain to the fly and its relations. Marcus humours Titus' madness by pointing out that he killed the fly because it was as black as Aaron. Titus is pacified but then admits that the whole episode is absurd.

4.1 Lavinia manages to disclose the identity of her attackers by pointing to the Philomel story in a copy of Ovid's *Metamorphoses* and by drawing their names on the sand. The Andronici vow to carry out their revenge against Tamora and her associates. 4.2 Titus sends Chiron and Demetrius a bundle of weapons as a gift. The latter fail to decipher the real meaning of the Horatian maxim which Titus attaches to the gift. Aaron, however, realizes that Chiron and Demetrius have been detected. A nurse enters bearing Tamora and Aaron's baby. Because of its dark complexion, Tamora wants Aaron to dispatch it. Aaron however praises the beauty of the baby's dark skin, and plans to have it raised by a Goth and have the Goth's own newly born baby raised as the Emperor's son. 4.3 Titus indulges his maddened sorrow and shoots arrows bearing his pleas for justice into the sky. The Clown is sent to the Emperor with one of Titus' messages and is executed as a result. 4.4 The Goths led by Lucius are marching towards Rome. Tamora reassures Saturninus and explains how she will get Titus to agree to summon his son Lucius to Rome and arrange a parley with him.

5.1 Aaron is captured by Lucius and boasts about his evil deeds; he is unrepentant and unabashed by the prospect of death. 5.2 Tamora disguises herself as Revenge and visits Titus accompanied by her two sons, who are themselves disguised as her ministers, Murder and Rape. Tamora believes Titus to be mad as a result of his sorrows, but Titus sees through her disguise. He pretends to comply with Tamora's request and summons his son Lucius to his house, but he also offers to arrange for a banquet to entertain his guests. As soon as Tamora leaves, Titus kills her sons and bakes a pasty for the banquet with their blood and bones. 5.3 In the final scene, Titus welcomes his guests. After asking Saturninus' advice on what a father should do when his daughter has been violated, he slays Lavinia. When asked who raped Lavinia, Titus reveals the ingredients of the pasty which the Emperor and Empress have just fed on. Titus then stabs Tamora and is killed by the Emperor. Lucius finally slays the Emperor and, after reflecting on the lessons to be learned from such bloody excesses, he is unanimously elected as the new Emperor of Rome.

ARTISTIC FEATURES: *Titus Andronicus* is a sophisticated revenge tragedy, where the binary oppositions of good and evil, Roman and Goth, civilization and barbarism are systematically questioned. The aftermath of the unrelenting deconstruction of Roman values leaves Titus stranded in a nightmare world, where Lavinia's body becomes his new 'map of woe' and her speechless complaint a new alphabet. The first act of *Titus Andronicus*, which was often attributed to George *Peele because of the un-Shakespearian quality of its dramatic diction, is now regarded as one of Shakespeare's most daring experiments with contemporary stage conventions. Particularly impressive is Shakespeare's use of the upper stage as the Senate House in Act 1, as a result of which those in power constantly overlook the powerless and the opposing parties confronting each other on the main stage. Similarly versatile is the use of the *trapdoor leading to the cellar underneath the main stage, which after serving as the entrance to the tomb of the Andronici in Act 1 becomes the 'subtle pit' in Act 2.

CRITICAL HISTORY: The question of authorship has dominated the critical history of *Titus Andronicus* well into the 20th century. Although Francis *Meres included *Titus Andronicus* in the list of Shakespeare's plays in his *Palladis Tamia* (1598), his attribution was repeatedly contested. In 1687, Edward Ravenscroft claimed that 'some anciently conversant with the stage' told him that Shakespeare 'gave some master-touches to one or two of the principal parts or characters' in a play written by a 'private author'. Ravenscroft described the play as a 'most incorrect and undigested piece ... rather a heap of rubbish than a structure'. It is however likely that his views were at least partly prompted by a wish to justify his 1678 adaptation, called *Titus Andronicus; or, The Rape of Lavinia*, which is even more gruesome than the original. *Gildon perpetuated Ravenscroft's views by expressing his dislike for the play and by arguing that *Titus Andronicus* is 'none of Shakespeare's plays'. Most of the 18th-century editors of Shakespeare followed suit. *Capell however advanced the hypothesis of an early date of composition and accounted for Shakespeare's indulgent representation of violence on stage by relating the play to the popularity enjoyed by the 'blood tragedies' written in the late 1580s and early 1590s. In 1785 *Malone ascribed the play to Marlowe, Shakespeare's main rival at the beginning of his career. Only towards the middle of the 20th century did critics start to overlook the vexed question of authorship in order to establish the intrinsic qualities of the play itself. Peter *Brook's cornerstone production at Stratford in 1955 triggered off an unprecedented number of critical articles, although hardly any full-length study of the play appeared before the 1980s. The play is currently very popular thanks to the advent of critical and cultural theories and the greater attention devoted to issues of gender, *sexuality, and race. Critics now tend to regard *Titus Andronicus* as at very least an interesting precursor of the mature tragedies.

STAGE HISTORY: The Henry *Peacham drawing, representing key moments from Acts 1 and 5, is the only surviving illustration of the contemporary staging, if not of an actual performance, of a Shakespearian play. *Titus Andronicus* was very popular on the Elizabethan stage and was revived unaltered after the Restoration, as John Downes reports in his *Roscius Anglicanus* (1708). Ravenscroft adapted *Titus Andronicus* in 1678 and his version enjoyed a successful revival in 1720, thanks to James *Quin's virtuoso performance as Aaron. Aaron remained the leading role in the only major 19th-century revival, when the black American actor Ira *Aldridge played him in a heavily adapted version of the original, which turns Shakespeare's villain into a noble and dignified character.

Robert *Atkins was the first 20th-century director to restore Shakespeare's original to the stage in his 1923 production at the *Old Vic. Members of Atkins's audience fainted as a result of his attempt to stage the Shakespearian original as faithfully as possible. In his memorable 1955 production at Stratford-upon-Avon, starring Laurence *Olivier as Titus, Vivien *Leigh as Lavinia, and Anthony *Quayle as Aaron, Peter Brook opted for a stylized rendition of violence, which lent an almost mythical dimension to both characters and action. In her shockingly realistic 1985 production at the Swan in Stratford-upon-Avon, Deborah *Warner reversed the tendency towards stylization initiated by Brook in the 1950s. Warner's Lavinia, played by Sonia Ritter, was horribly disfigured and Brian Cox's wilful and senile Titus was also remarkable for his psychological verisimilitude. *SM*

ON THE SCREEN: Jane Howell directed the imaginative BBC TV production, with Trevor Peacock in the title role (1985). By making Young Lucius the observer of the action, she raised the question of how horrific acts of violence affect child witnesses. In this her production was imitated by Julie Taymor's impressive and eclectic Hollywood film (2000), with Anthony Hopkins as Titus. *AD*

RECENT MAJOR EDITIONS

E. M. Waith (Oxford, 1984); J. Bate (Arden 3rd series, 1995); J. Berthoud with S. Massai (New Penguin 2001)

SOME REPRESENTATIVE CRITICISM

Dessen, A. C., *'Titus Andronicus': Shakespeare in Performance* (1989)

James, H., 'Cultural Disintegration in *Titus Andronicus*: Mutilating Titus, Virgil and Rome', in James Redmond (ed.), *Themes in Drama* (1991)

Kolin, P. C. *'Titus Andronicus': Critical Essays* (1995).

Waith, E. M. W., 'The Metamorphosis of Violence in *Titus Andronicus*', *Shakespeare Survey*, 10 (1957) mouth into the head and stomach, is greatly taken-up and used in England.'

Sir Walter *Ralegh is credited with popularizing the smoking of tobacco at the English court, and it is enthusiastically recommended in his protégé Edmund *Spenser's *The Faerie Queene*. References to tobacco, and depictions of smoking (generally, using clay pipes), occur in the writings of several playwrights, including Ben *Jonson ('He does take this same filthy roguish tobacco, the finest, and cleanliest!', *Every Man in his Humour* 1.4): *Middleton and *Dekker's *The Roaring Girl* even puts a tobacconist's shop on the stage. The Shakespeare canon, however, is strictly a non-smoking area: there are no occurrences of the word 'tobacco' in Shakespeare's works, nor appropriate usages of the allied terms 'smoke', 'smoking', or 'pipe'.

Numerous late 16th-century woodcuts and paintings portray pipe-smoking, but the widespread use of tobacco had many opponents, the first important English book against it being *Opinions of the Late and Best Physicians Concerning Tobacco* (1595). The most notable anti-tobacconist was King *James who, in *A Counterblast to Tobacco* (1604), called smoking 'a custom loathsome to the eye, hateful to the nose, harmful to the brain, dangerous to the lungs and in the black stinking fume thereof, nearest resembling the horrible Stygian smoke of the pit that is bottomless'.

In 1614 the Star Chamber imposed a tax on tobacco and in 1619 the Privy Council forbade its planting in England, to safeguard the monopoly of the Virginia colonists. *MM*

Tolstoy, Count Leo (Lev) Nikolayevich (1828–1910), Russian novelist, frequently compared to Shakespeare for his universality, invention of character, steadiness of vision, breadth of life represented, and devotion to truth. Yet Tolstoy is probably the most implacable dissenter to Shakespeare's reputation in modern times, complaining (in *Shakespeare and the Drama*, 1904) of his unnaturalness, implausibility, cheap theatricality, aristocratic sympathies, moral indifference, and hyperbolic language—preferring, for example, the source play *King Leir* to Shakespeare's. G. Wilson *Knight's *Shakespeare and Tolstoy* (1934) considers the objections, while George Orwell's essay 'Lear, Tolstoy, and the Fool' (1947) argues for a degree of identification on Tolstoy's part. It is ironic that Tolstoy's own final flight with his daughter Alexandra (Sasha) and death in a stationmaster's cottage in Astopovo resemble nothing more than the tragic fate of Lear and Cordelia. *TM*

'Tomorrow is Saint Valentine's day', sung by Ophelia in *Hamlet* 4.5.47. As with *'How should I your true love know', a tune traditionally sung at Drury Lane in the late 18th century ('The Soldier's Life') can be traced back to Shakespeare's time, but in this case without any link between lyrics and tune title. *JB*

Tooley, Nicholas (?1582/3–1623), actor (King's Men by 1605 to 1623). If Edmond's identification is correct, Tooley was a wealthy Anglo-Flemish orphan whose Warwickshire relatives Shakespeare would have known from childhood. In his will Tooley thanked Cuthbert *Burbage's wife for her 'motherly care' of him. Augustine *Phillips in his will called Tooley his 'fellow', which indicates that Tooley was by then a sharer in the King's Men. A surviving annotated cast list indicates that Tooley played Ananias in Jonson's *The Alchemist* and Corvino in Jonson's *Volpone*. The 1619 King's Men patent names Tooley after *Heminges, Burbage, Condell, and *Lowin and the 1623 Folio, published after his death, names him as principal actor. *GE*

Edmond, Mary, 'Yeomen, Citizens, Gentlemen and Players: The Burbages and their Connections', in R. B. Parker and S. P. Zitner (eds.), *Elizabethan Theater: Essays in Honor of S. Schoenbaum* (1996)

Topsell, Edward (1572–*c*.1625), cleric and writer on natural history. He compiled *The History of Four-Footed Beasts* (1607) and *The History of Serpents* (1608). These exhaustive accounts of prevailing zoological traditions provide much of the beast lore found in Shakespeare's plays, along with illustrations of *monsters, half-man, half-beast, akin to Caliban's description in *The Tempest*. *CS*

'To shallow rivers, to whose falls', sung by Sir Hugh Evans in *The Merry Wives of Windsor* 3.1.16, misquoting part of *Marlowe's song 'Come live with me and be my love'; the lyrics have been wrongly attributed to Shakespeare because of their inclusion in *The *Passionate Pilgrim*. The original tune survives, and was used for several *broadside ballads. *JB*

Tottel, Richard (d. 1594), author of an anthology of poetry called *Songs and Sonnets* popularly known as *Tottel's Miscellany*, published in 1557. It included work by *Chaucer, Wyatt, and Surrey and was obviously familiar to Shakespeare. The Gravedigger's song in *Hamlet* derives from a poem in the *Miscellany*, and Slender refers to it as the 'Book of Songs and Sonnets' in *The Merry Wives of Windsor* (1.1.181–2). *JKS*

Touchstone is a court jester who follows Rosalind and Celia to the forest of *Ardenne in *As You Like It*. *AB*

tragedy. The rise of modernity coincided with the enthusiastic rediscovery of the classics and a renewed interest in tragedy, the most theorized and admired dramatic form since Aristotle identified its main structural features in his *Poetics*. *Seneca was the most widely imitated model among early English playwrights, after the example set by Thomas Sackville and Thomas Norton's *Gorboduc* (1565) and Thomas *Kyd's *The Spanish Tragedy* (1592). Imitation of classical models was however never slavish or pedantic. In his *Apology for Poetry*, the classicist Sir Philip *Sidney praised *Gorboduc* for 'climbing the heights of Seneca's style', but regretted the interference of native influences which spoil the formal purity of the original. The main influences Sidney had in mind are the English *morality play and the *de casibus* tradition, a typically medieval form best exemplified by the tragic narrative accounts of the fall of illustrious men collected in *The *Mirror for Magistrates*, one of the most popular sources of tragic plots used by Shakespeare and his contemporaries.

Shakespeare was affected by both the classic and the native traditions, but he consistently departed from received conventions and aimed for a more sophisticated realism by 'suit[ing] the action to the word, the word to the action' (*Hamlet* 3.2.17–18). Shakespeare notoriously disregarded the Aristotelian doctrine of the three unities of time, space, and action. He also put more emphasis on character than on fate by reducing the omnipresent gods of classical tragedy to significant but relatively rare manifestations of the supernatural, such as the *ghost in *Hamlet* or the *witches in *Macbeth*. The gods are invoked but they remain silent. Unlike classical tragedy, Shakespearian tragedy often denies its audience cathartic relief. In Shakespeare's tragedies, recognition is not necessarily followed by redemption. *Johnson famously claimed to find Cordelia's death at the end of *King Lear* unbearable and to prefer the happy ending devised by Nahum *Tate for its 1681 adaptation.

Shakespeare departed as radically from the *de casibus* tradition as from his classical models. Far from exemplifying the medieval notion of the 'Wheel of Fortune', which denies human agency, Shakespeare's tragedies suggest that catastrophe ultimately proceeds from his characters' actions. Psychological realism is therefore heightened at the expense of tragic irony. The result of Shakespeare's highly experimental use of earlier dramatic conventions is a corpus of tragedies as diverse as *Titus Andronicus* and *Romeo and Juliet* or *Hamlet* and *Coriolanus*, or as innovative as *Othello*, a domestic tragedy featuring the first black tragic hero in English dramatic literature.

Shakespeare's mature tragedies are often interpreted as the dramatist's response to the political unrest and ideological uncertainties which characterized the last years of *Elizabeth I's reign and the period following *James I's accession to the throne of England. The radical quality of Shakespeare's tragic imagination is particularly evident in *King Lear*, where the King's painful and gradual realization of his fallibility and frailty represents a clear challenge to the basic tenets of absolutism and the doctrine of the divine right of kings, as expounded by James I in *Basilikon Doron* (pub. 1599). *SM*

Dollimore, J., *Radical Tragedy* (1984)
Miola, R., *Shakespeare and Classical Tragedy* (1992)

Tragedy of King Lear, The. See KING LEAR.

***Tragical History of King Richard III,* The.** See RICHARD III.

tragicomedy is a Renaissance invention. Aristotle never mentioned it in his *Poetics* and Cicero expressed his disapproval of any 'mixed-mood' dramatic form in his famous maxim '*turpe comicum in tragedia et turpe tragicum in comedia*' (the comic is abhorrent in tragedy and the tragic is abhorrent in comedy).

*Cinthio (1504–73) and Giovanni Battista Guarini (1538–1612) first theorized tragicomedy in connection with the pastoral tradition. Some English dramatists retained the pastoral setting: see, for example, *Fletcher's *The Faithful Shepherdess* (1609–10), Samuel *Daniel's *Hymen's Triumph* (1615), or Ben *Jonson's *Sad Shepherd* (1629). Others, however, concentrated on the double structure of tragicomedy, which often stretches the plot to the limits of verisimilitude by hinging on a sudden change of fortune which leads to the comic resolution of a potentially tragic situation.

Despite adverse criticism, such as *Sidney's, who dismissed 'mongrel tragicomedy' as a corruption of the formal purity of the classical forms, Shakespeare 'flirted' with both forms of tragicomedy. In *The Winter's Tale*, the comic resolution of a potentially tragic situation takes place against the backdrop of pastoral Bohemia. In *Measure for Measure*, on the other hand, Shakespeare retains the double structure of tragicomedy but dispenses with the pastoral setting. *SM*

McMullan, G., and Hope, J., *The Politics of Tragicomedy* (1992)

Tranio, Lucentio's servant in *The Taming of the Shrew*, takes on his master's identity at his request (see 1.1.196–215). *AB*

transcripts. Shakespeare's original *'foul paper' manuscripts would probably have been transcribed, either by the playwright or by a professional scribe, to provide a 'fair copy' of the play for use in the playhouse. Other manuscript copies may also have been in circulation. The publisher Humphrey *Moseley speaks of the seemingly common practice of plays being 'transcribed' by the actors for their 'private friends'. *ER*

translation, the rendering of Shakespeare texts into another language, is inalienably part of the process whereby Shakespeare has been, and is being, received in non-English-speaking countries. Hence Shakespeare translation has not only **(1)** linguistic but also **(2)** theatrical and cultural—even political—aspects. As translations multiply throughout the world, each language offers its own resistance or adaptability to Shakespeare's ways with his native language; and each country, as part of its cultural programme, has its own history of Shakespeare translation. Within that context, each individual translator becomes an interpreter of Shakespearian texts, with results which vary from faithful imitation to radical *adaptation.

1. Shakespeare explored and exploited to the full the potentials of the English language of his time, coining new words and bending grammar and syntax to serve his poetic and dramatic ends. This exacerbates the problems already inherent in any interlingual translation of literary texts: how, Victor *Hugo asked, do you translate 'unsex me here' (*Macbeth* 1.5.40), or 'we have kissed away | Kingdoms and provinces' (*Antony and Cleopatra* 3.10.7–8)? English is a hybrid language, and the effects Shakespeare gains from combining and contrasting words of Germanic and of Romance origin—as in Macbeth's feeling that the blood on his hands will 'The multitudinous seas incarnadine, | Making the green one red' (2.2.60–1)—resist reproduction in the more homogeneous European languages. The further the language system is from that of English, the greater the challenge: how do you translate Hamlet's most famous soliloquy into Japanese, a language which has no verbal equivalent of 'To be'? Whatever the target language, the translator faces formidable problems in attempting to do justice to Shakespeare's associative imagination which compacts *metaphor with metaphor, packs many different meanings into a word or phrase, and excels in puns and other forms of wordplay. How, if he aims for fidelity, does the translator of the plays or the poems avoid explicating that which in the original is implicit or suggested? Add to this the fact that Shakespeare's lines were written by an actor and to be spoken and acted, their sounds and rhythms crucial to the dramatic experience but more or less difficult to reproduce in another language, and it is all the more remarkable that language has not proved a barrier to the spread of Shakespeare, whether read or performed. The journal which was founded by Toshikazu Oyama in the early 1970s as *Shakespeare Translation*, and devoted its early issues to language problems such as those outlined above, significantly changed its title in the mid-1980s to *Shakespeare Worldwide.*

2. Worldwide now, Shakespeare translation first began in earnest in 18th-century Europe. Since then, as Shakespeare texts have been mediated through the particular poetics and politics of various cultures, translations have found their place on a sliding scale between faithfulness and adaptation. Across the European continent, Shakespeare was 'discovered' through translations into the two culturally dominant languages, French and German, and well into the 19th century was often translated from these, at second hand. In Poland the earliest translations were from the German prose adaptations by *Schröder who, to make Shakespeare acceptable in the German theatre, had cut and restructured *Hamlet* from political tragedy to domestic intrigue with a happy ending for the Prince. Early Russian translations were based on French neoclassical versions, including those of Ducis who, though he knew no English, was the author of acting versions in rhyming alexandrines which brought Shakespeare to the Parisian stage as well as to other parts of Europe. By the early 19th century a gap was perceived between (adapted) Shakespeare as theatre and ('genuine') Shakespeare as literature, famously articulated by *Goethe who came to believe *Hamlet* stageable only in adaptations like Schröder's and that Shakespeare was a dramatist only for the inner eye of the reader. Meanwhile the German *Sturm und Drang* movement had initiated the worship of Shakespeare as a natural genius whose works were the supreme antidote to the values of *neoclassicism with its restrictive aesthetics and social hierarchies. On the one hand, this promoted faithful renderings of the original texts, culminating in the great translation of all the plays of Shakespeare which was begun by *Schlegel in 1797 and completed under the supervision of *Tieck in 1833, and which itself became a model and part-source—Shakespeare 'reborn'—for a number of other European translations. On the other, it made Shakespeare translation the prime site of the struggle between French neoclassicism and German *Romanticism for cultural hegemony in Europe. In the 20th century the Schlegel–Tieck translation was to be anathematized as lumpy, monumental, and philistine by *Brecht, who made his own translation and stage adaptation of *Coriolanus*—one example, among countless others, of translation as ideologically motivated rewriting of Shakespeare. For, while in many countries mid-19th-century translations became canonized as part of the national literary heritage, Shakespeare translation as a phenomenon has never solidified: new translations have both formed and been formed by the ideological concerns and theatrical tastes of new generations. Transplanted Shakespeare was functional in the evolution of *Arab drama, and in 1901 the director of Tanyus Abduh's Ducis-inspired version of *Hamlet* also drew on indigenous tradition, making the Prince sing a soliloquy. In modern Japan, directors like *Ninagawa and *Suzuki have tapped the energies underlying theatrical traditions of Noh and Kabuki to make Shakespeare texts seem both contemporary and

international. Even when not thus mediated, translated texts have proved capable of carrying new significance as needed: culturally prestigious on the surface and politically subversive underneath. Newly independent African states have found *Julius Caesar* strangely contemporary. Altogether, the history of Shakespeare translation supports Ben *Jonson's verdict, 'not of an age, but for all time', in that it shows Shakespeare's texts not to be so closely bound within the limits of one language and culture that translation becomes radically impossible. *I-SE*

Delabastita, D., and D'hulst, L. (eds.), *European Shakespeares* (1993)

Shakespeare Survey, 48: *Shakespeare and Cultural Exchange* (1995)

Shakespeare Translation/Shakespeare Worldwide (Tokyo, 1974–)

trapdoors. Access to the understage 'hell' was provided by a trapdoor set in the floor of the stage, probably near the centre. Hellish characters ascended and descended through this trapdoor, most easily by provision of a ladder placed underneath the hole, although the technology for a mechanical elevator platform was available. Left open, the trapdoor could also make a useful grave such as that needed for Ophelia's burial in Shakespeare's *Hamlet* 5.1. *GE*

travel, trade, and colonialism. Travel tales of voyages constituted one of the largest categories of popular reading of Shakespeare's period. To Richard *Hakluyt's *Principal Navigations* (1 vol., 1589; 3 vols., 1599–1603), with its title page announcing the intention of celebrating the 'navigations, voyages, traffiques and discoveries of the English nation', can be added those by William Biddulph (1609), John Cartwright (1611), Anthony Sherley (1613), and William Lithgow (1614) to the Orient, North Africa, and Asia, and by Sir John Hawkins (1569), Thomas Hariot (1588), Walter *Ralegh (1596), and John Smith (1608) to the New World. Works by the Frenchman Cartier (1580), the merchant of Venice Cesare Federici (1588), and the Dutchman Jan Huyghen van Linschoten (1598) were available in translation.

Shakespeare's plays abound with references to travel literature. The tale related by Othello is a superb encapsulation of many of the key elements of the genre, including 'Of being taken by the insolent foe | And sold to slavery, of my redemption thence, | And portance in my traveller's history . . . and of the cannibals that each other eat, | The Anthropopaghi, and men whose heads | Do grow beneath their shoulders' (*Othello* 1.3.136–44). The prediction made by the host of the Garter Inn that Falstaff will 'speak like an Anthropophaginian unto thee' (*The Merry Wives of Windsor* 4.5.8) can be traced back to the dubious but much-read travel accounts by the 14th-century Sir John Mandeville, still treated as authoritative well into the 16th century, while the story told by the First Witch about the woman whose 'husband's to Aleppo gone, master o'the Tiger' (*Macbeth* 1.3.6) might well refer to public awareness of the tribulations of the sailors on a vessel of that name that had sailed for Aleppo in December 1604 and had returned in June 1606.

Tales are also discounted. At the sight of strange shapes bringing in a banquet, Sebastian observes that he will from now on believe in unicorns as well as that there is in Arabia a tree in which a phoenix reigns—to which Antonio, the usurping Duke of Naples, responds: 'Travellers ne'er did lie, | Though fools at home condemn 'em' (*The Tempest* 3.3.26–7): itself, perhaps, an echo of the saying later collected in Camden's *Remains* (1614): 'Old men and travellers may lie by authority.'

The majority of references to voyages highlight the benefits, notably the economic. Egeon tells the Duke of Ephesus that 'Our wealth increased | By prosperous voyages I often made' (*The Comedy of Errors* 1.1.39–40); Titania refuses to hand over the changeling boy to Oberon because the child's dead mother would sometimes return to her with goods 'As from a voyage, rich with merchandise' (*A Midsummer Night's Dream* 2.1.134). Panthino criticizes his master because he lets his son stay at home while 'other men of slender reputation | Put forth their sons to seek preferment' by sending them 'to discover islands far away' (*The Two Gentlemen of Verona* 1.3.6–9). When Falstaff woos both Mistress Page and Mistress Ford he is candid about his objectives: 'I will be cheaters to them both, and they shall be exchequers to me. They shall be my East and West Indies, and I will trade to them both' (*The Merry Wives of Windsor* 1.4.62–5).

References to trade should be read in the context of the emergence, in England, of arguments in favour of mercantilism and for a break with the times of Drake, Frobisher, Hawkins, Ralegh, and others, several of whom were keener on shipping slaves to New World colonies of other European nations than in trading. Profit, for them, was in plunder and in privateering—often at the patriotic expense of other Europeans.

That central difference thus calls into question the validity of speculations concerning the playwright's views on colonialism. England, in Shakespeare's lifetime, was not a colonial power. More importantly, there was no desire, at that time, to embark on such a project. Even though Grenville had (1574) proposed that South America be colonized, England had only one colony—Bermuda (1609) in the West Indies. Attempts on the North American mainland at Roanoke (1587) had failed and the settlement at Virginia (1607) did not begin to take root until 1612. While the Levant Company had a presence in Constantinople and in cities such as Aleppo, and the English East India Company in Agra, the ambassadors sent to the Ottoman, Persian, and Mughal rulers went there not as dispossessors but as supplicants begging for permission for the right to trade—often in contest with other Europeans.

The plays mirror that imperative of being able to discriminate: not only between persons—'Which is the merchant here, and which the Jew?' (*The Merchant of Venice* 4.1.172)—but also between categories (Amazons; pagans; cannibals; savages; etc.) and geographical spaces (Africa; the Orient; India; the New World; the Antipodes). It is more likely that the origins of the stories about these categories are in the Greek and Roman classics (themselves infused with Arabic elements) rather than directly traceable to the travel accounts.

References to Africa illustrate the reliance on antecedent classical sources. Egypt is known because of the Nile, the pyramids, and serpents. Then there are the 'black Ethiopes'—a favourite image for making comparisons between women: Sylvia's fairness 'Shows Julia but a swarthy Ethiope' (*The Two Gentlemen of Verona* 2.6.26); the sonnet written by Dumaine: 'Thou for whom great Jove would swear | Juno but an Ethiop were' (*Love's Labour's Lost* 4.3.115–16). But if Rosalind's charge that she is being defied 'Like Turk to Christian. Women's gentle brain | Could not drop forth such giant-rude invention, | Such Ethiop words, blacker in their effect | Than in their countenance' (*As You Like It* 4.3.34–7) is the often-cited view, then recall that Thaisa describes to King Simonides 'A knight of Sparta . . . | And the device he bears upon his shield | Is a black Ethiop reaching at the sun' (*Pericles* 6.18–20).

The distinctions, as well as the consequences which follow, are clearest with regard to the Indies. The 'dead Indian' the English will pay tenfold to see yet 'will not give a doit to relieve a lame beggar' (*The Tempest* 2.2.30–3) and Othello's 'base Indian' who 'threw a pearl away | Richer than all his tribe' (*Othello* 5.2.356–7) are probably from the New World. Their subcontinental counterpart is seen as much more dangerous: the image of 'the rude and savage man of Ind | At the first op'ning of the gorgeous east, | Bows . . . his vassal head and, strucken blind, | Kisses the base ground with obedient breast' (*Love's Labour's Lost* 4.3.223). Still, against cultural and religious difference is ranged the tangible wealth of 'metal of India' (*Twelfth Night* 2.5.12) that makes trade worthwhile: Troilus casts himself in the role of 'merchant' who will negotiate with Pandarus in order to succeed with Cressida, whose 'bed is India; there she lies, a pearl' (*Troilus and Cres-*

sida 1.1.103, 100). Finally, not only can the Duke of Norfolk claim that, in their triumphant splendour at the Field of the Cloth of Gold, the English had 'Made Britain India'; there is also the observation that, having married Anne Boleyn, 'Our King has all the Indies in his arms' (*All Is True* (*Henry VIII*) 1.1.21, 4.1.45).

Then there are the differences between Indians and Turks. Turks are the common enemy of Christians. The Bishop of Carlisle reminds that 'banished Norfolk fought | For Jesu Christ in glorious Christian field, | Streaming the ensign of the Christian cross | Against black pagans, Turks, and Saracens' (*Richard II* 4.1.83–6). Henry hopes that the son born from his marriage with Catherine will 'compound a boy, half-French, half-English, that shall go to Constantinople and take the Turk by the beard' (*Henry V* 5.2.205–7). Indeed he can already, as the newly crowned King at the end of *2 Henry IV*, confidently forget how his father had acquired the crown by observing: 'This is the English not the Turkish court; | Not Amurath [Murad] an Amurath succeeds | But Harry Harry' (5.2.47–9). While Turks, in Shakespeare's texts, are never once referred to by the epithet of 'the terrible Turk' that will later become common, there is at least one reference to a predecessor view, that of the Turk as liar. Iago defends his lie to his wife Emilia: 'Nay, it is true, or else I am a Turk' (*Othello* 2.1.116).

All in all, it is the complexity of the differences that matter. The Christian Duke of Venice can, when it suits him, require a 'gentle answer' from that alien Other, Shylock the Jew. Such behaviour is not to be expected 'From stubborn Turks and Tartars never trained | To offices of tender courtesy' (*The Merchant of Venice* 4.1.31–2). It is fascinatingly fitting, then, that it is a differently placed Other, that in-between figure the *Moor, without whose military skill Venice would be in peril, who can ask the brawlers Iago and Cassio: 'Are we turned Turks, and to ourselves do that | Which heaven hath forbid the Ottomites? | For Christian shame, put by this barbarous brawl' (*Othello* 2.3.163–5). *KP*

Canny, Nicholas (ed.), *The Origins of Empire: British Overseas Enterprise to the Close of the Seventeenth Century* (1998)

Fuler, Mary C., *Voyages in Print: English Travel in America, 1576–1624* (1995)

Gillies, John, *Shakespeare and the Geography of Difference* (1997)

Knapp, Jeffrey, *An Empire Nowhere: England, America and Literature from 'Utopia' to 'The Tempest'* (1992)

Loomba, Ania, 'Shakespeare and Cultural Difference', in Terence Hawkes (ed.), *Alternative Shakespeares 2* (1996)

travellers are robbed by Sir John and his companions, *1 Henry IV* 2.2. *AB*

Travers gives Northumberland the first news of his son Hotspur's death, *2 Henry IV* 1.1.34–48. *AB*

Trebonius is one of the conspirators in *Julius Caesar*, based on Caius Trebonius, consul in 45 BC. *AB*

Tree, Sir Herbert Beerbohm (1853–1917), English actor-manager, in whose early career Shakespeare barely featured, but whose sixteen sumptuous Shakespearian revivals were the centrepiece of his management at Her/His Majesty's theatre (1897–1915).

Tree defended his principles of Shakespearian production in 'The Living Shakespeare: A Defence of Modern Taste' (in *Thoughts and After-Thoughts*, 1913): historically accurate spectacular theatre achieved with all the resources and care lavished on modern plays. Thus Tree engaged antiquarians, Academicians (Alma-Tadema), scenic artists (Joseph Harker), pageant masters (L. N. Parker), and crowd-commandants (Louis Calvert) to achieve some of the most spectacular revivals of Shakespeare ever. Though vulnerable amongst so much 'scenic embellishment', Tree upheld the importance of 'all-round casts' and in productions such as *Julius Caesar* (1898), with himself as Mark Antony, Louis Calvert as Casca, Lewis Waller as Brutus, and Frank McLeay as Cassius, he achieved an effective synthesis of all the theatre arts. Elsewhere he erred—far—on the side of excess. The interpolation of 'The Signing of Magna Carta' in *King John* (1899) was not without precedent and could be forgiven; Shylock's extended—room by room—search of his house for his missing daughter and Malvolio's entourage of four miniature, aping Malvolios could not be.

For Tree public taste was the ultimate arbiter and he pointed to the long runs and huge attendances (*Julius Caesar* 240,000, *King John* 170,000, and *A Midsummer Night's Dream* 220,000 in London alone). Not that Tree was indifferent to the higher claims upon him as a leader of his profession; he undertook tours of Germany (1907) and America (1915–16) and in 1905 inaugurated his annual Shakespeare Festival in which six plays were performed in six days, including productions by *Benson and *Poel. A brief excerpt of Tree's *King John*, the first Shakespeare film, is included in *Silent Shakespeare* (BFI, 1999). The Tree archive at the University of Bristol is a major resource. *RF*

tribunes, Roman. They receive orders from Rome, *Cymbeline* 3.7. *AB*

trimeter, a verse line of three feet, used by Shakespeare as an occasional variation from pentameter, or occasionally in songs or the bad verse of lovesick characters (*Hamlet* 2.2.116–19). *GTW*

Trinculo is Alonso's jester in *The Tempest*. He and Stefano (Alonso's butler) are separated from the rest of the royal party when they are shipwrecked. They become drunk and plot against Prospero with Caliban. *AB*

trochee, a metrical unit ('foot') comprising one stressed syllable followed by one unstressed syllable. Shakespeare's trochaic verse appears in many dramatic songs and in 'The Phoenix and Turtle', e.g. 'Hearts remote yet not asunder'. Trochees are often used as a variation in iambic verse, especially in the first foot or after a mid-line break in syntax: 'Spūr thĕm | to youthful work, | rēin thĕm | from ruth' (*Troilus and Cressida* 5.3.48). *CB/GTW*

Troilus and Cressida *(see opposite page)*

Troublesome Reign of King John, The, a chronicle play, published anonymously, in two parts, in 1591. The original title pages give some idea of how closely Shakespeare followed this drama when composing his own *King John*, promising 'the discovery of King Richard Cœur-de-Lion's base son (vulgarly called the Bastard Falconbridge)' and 'the death of Arthur Plantagenet, the landing at Lewes, and the poisoning of King John at Swinstead Abbey'. Confusion as to the relation between this drama and Shakespeare's began early: the two parts of *The Troublesome Reign* were published together in a 1611 edition which credits them to 'W. Sh.', and a 1622 reprint spells this attribution out, claiming the plays were 'Written by W. Shakespeare'. Some early editors, including *Pope, accepted this attribution, regarding *The Troublesome Reign* as a first draft of *King John*, but it is now more usually attributed to George *Peele. E. A. J. Honigmann's view that *The Troublesome Reign* is in fact an imitation of Shakespeare's play has met with little support.

The Troublesome Reign of King John is first and foremost an anti-Catholic play. Although Shakespeare follows much of its structure he omits, for example, a comic scene in which the Bastard, looting a monastery, finds a nun hiding there, and he makes John's death appear to have far less to do with his anticipation of the Reformation. In *The Troublesome Reign* the monk who kills John has a soliloquy explaining his motives (vengeance for the ransacked monasteries), the poisoning takes place on stage (the monk dies too, having been obliged to taste from the fatal wassail cup first), and the Bastard subsequently kills the abbot who granted the monk absolution for his intended crime. Shakespeare's toning down of all this may have something to do with the later date of his own *King John*—*The Troublesome Reign* probably dates from the time of the Spanish Armada invasion scare of 1588, when anti-Catholic feeling ran especially high—but the difference between

(cont. on page 488)

Troilus and Cressida

Shakespeare's tragicomedy of an aimless love in the midst of a futile war may be the last play he wrote before the death of Queen Elizabeth. It was entered in the Stationers' Register in February 1603, and must have been written after 1598, when one of its sources, George *Chapman's *Seven Books of the Iliads of Homer*, was published: its armed Prologue is probably an allusion to Ben *Jonson's *Poetaster*, acted in 1601, and since metrical tests place it after *Hamlet* and *Twelfth Night* but before *Measure for Measure* and *Othello* its likeliest date of composition is 1602.

Text: This ambiguous play has a thoroughly ambiguous textual history. Despite its 1603 entry in the *Stationers' Register, the play appeared in *quarto only in 1609, in an edition (set from Shakespeare's *foul papers) which exists in two contradictory states: one promises on its title page that it prints *Troilus and Cressida* 'As it was acted by the King's Majesty's servants at the Globe', while the other not only omits this claim but adds an epistle to the reader which instead states that the play has never been acted at all ('you have here a new play, never staled with the stage, never clapper-clawed with the palms of the vulgar'). This circumstance has led to a profusion of hypotheses about the play's early history, including the theory that it was written for private performance, perhaps at one of the Inns of Court, and a conjecture that performance was forbidden because Shakespeare's portrait of Achilles was perceived as a reflection on the Earl of *Essex. It is always possible, however, that whoever wrote the 1609 epistle to the reader had merely been misinformed about a play acted seven years earlier, or was deliberately lying in the hopes of selling a play which had been acted at the Globe but had not been popular. The circumstances in which the play reappeared in the *Folio are no less striking: the play was to be reprinted from the quarto, but was apparently withdrawn due to difficulties in securing the copyright (and its intended place in the volume was filled by *Timon of Athens*). However, at the last minute (too late for it to be listed on the Folio's contents page) clearance was obtained for *Troilus and Cressida*, and so was a theatrical manuscript of the play, and it was squeezed into the volume, its text set from a copy of the quarto annotated by reference to this promptbook. The very existence of such a manuscript shows that the play had been acted, by 1623 at least, though the more than 500 substantive changes between quarto and Folio texts suggest that at some time Shakespeare had a number of second thoughts, including the addition of a prologue and the deletion of Pandarus' epilogue (reproduced from the quarto, though apparently marked for omission). Although the quarto calls it the 'History' or 'Famous History' of Troilus and Cressida, and its prefatory epistle describes it as a witty comedy, the Folio prints it among the tragedies: commentators have been puzzling over how to understand the play's tone and genre ever since.

Sources: Shakespeare's chief source for the love plot was *Chaucer's masterpiece *Troilus and Criseyde*, his reading of it perhaps coloured by Robert Henryson's sequel *The Testament of Cresseid*, in which Cressida, deserted by Diomedes, becomes a leprous beggar (mistakenly attributed to Chaucer in Thynne's 1532 edition of his collected works). The play's depiction of the Trojan War freely blends and modifies elements from a number of different accounts: George Chapman's translation *Seven Books of the Iliads of *Homer* (from which Shakespeare drew the character of Thersites, though not his actions); William Caxton's *Recuyell of the Histories of Troy* (1475) and John Lydgate's *Troy Book* (*c.*1412–20), both derived from a common Italian original (these supplied material for most of the play's battle scenes and the debate in Troy, among much else); and *Ovid's *Metamorphoses* (from which Shakespeare derived his opposition between the intelligent Ulysses and the 'blockish' Ajax, adding this dimension of Ajax's character to what is already a compound of two quite different figures in Lydgate, the ill-spoken Oyleus Ajax and the pride-hating Thelamonyous Ajax). Beyond these major sources, Ulysses' speech on degree (1.3.74–137) draws on Sir

Thomas *Elyot's *The Governor* (1531), and details of Shakespeare's depiction of the truce (and Hector's view of his fellow Trojan princes as unfit for moral philosophy, 2.2.162–6) show the influence of Robert *Greene's *Euphues his Censure to Philautus* (1587).

SYNOPSIS: An armed prologue explains that the play begins in the middle of the Trojan War, briefly recounting its cause, Paris's theft of Menelaus' wife Helen. 1.1 In Troy, Troilus is impatient with the slow progress of the dilatory and petulant Pandarus, who is supposed to be wooing his niece Cressida on Troilus' behalf: at first languishing in love-sickness, Troilus eventually goes with Aeneas to join the fighting outside the city walls. 1.2 Pandarus speaks at length of Troilus' virtues to Cressida, though she feigns indifference: together they watch the Trojan warriors filing back into the city, Pandarus eagerly pointing out Troilus. After Pandarus leaves, Cressida admits in soliloquy that she already loves Troilus but is holding off to increase his sense of her value. 1.3 In the Greek camp Agamemnon, Nestor, Ulysses, Diomedes, and Menelaus discuss the failure of morale which has prevented them from achieving victory despite seven years besieging Troy: Ulysses diagnoses that the Greek army has lost its sense of hierarchy, imitating Achilles, who remains in his tent with Patroclus making sarcastic jokes at the leadership's expense. Aeneas brings a message from Troy: Hector challenges any Grecian willing to vouch for his mistress's worth to single combat, a challenge clearly intended for their pre-eminent warrior Achilles. Ulysses convinces Nestor they should rig a lottery to ensure that Ajax fights Hector rather than Achilles, partly so that morale may not be further damaged by the possible defeat of their best fighter, but partly to humble Achilles' pride.

2.1 The illiterate Ajax beats Thersites for refusing to read him a proclamation about Hector's challenge: Achilles and Patroclus intervene, enjoying Thersites' satirical ranting against Ajax until he turns on them. Achilles affects indifference about Hector's challenge. 2.2 In Troy King Priam and his sons Hector, Troilus, Paris, and Helenus debate the ethics of keeping Helen: Hector argues that she is not worth the casualties the war has already caused, but Troilus insists that they should remain constant to their original purpose. Their sister Cassandra arrives, prophesying the destruction of Troy unless Helen is restored to the Greeks. Troilus, however, is unmoved, and Paris wishes to keep his abducted partner. Hector, though unpersuaded by their arguments, concedes that he too means to maintain the quarrel for the sake of Troy's prestige, and tells them of the challenge he has sent the Greeks. 2.3 Thersites, still furious at his beating from Ajax, amuses Achilles and Patroclus with his railing. When the other Greek commanders arrive, with Ajax, Achilles withdraws into his tent and refuses to speak with them: meanwhile the commanders flatter Ajax, who grows increasingly proud, to their concealed amusement.

3.1 Pandarus calls privately on Paris, at home at Helen's insistence, to ask him to excuse Troilus' impending absence from supper: Paris guesses Troilus has an assignation with Cressida. Helen insists that Pandarus should sing a song, and he does, 'Love, love, nothing but love'. Helen and Paris go to help unarm Hector after his day's combat. 3.2 Troilus waits in the orchard while Pandarus fetches Cressida, giddy with anticipation: Pandarus embarrassingly brings the couple together, encouraging their kisses. Before Pandarus takes them indoors to a bedchamber, each of the three makes a promise: Troilus that faithful lovers shall in future be called 'as true as Troilus', Cressida that if she be false to him faithless women shall be called 'as false as Cressid', and Pandarus that all goers-between shall be called 'panders' after him. 3.3 In the Greek camp Cressida's father, the defector Calchas, requests that Cressida should be brought from Troy in exchange for a Trojan prisoner, Antenor: Agamemnon agrees. The Greek lords process past Achilles' tent, pretending not to be interested in him: after their departure Ulysses lectures Achilles about humanity's disregard for past achievements compared to its enthusiasm for present deeds, however trifling by comparison, and reveals that the commanders know that the reason he has been refusing to fight is a liaison with one of Priam's daughters, Polyxena. After Ulysses leaves his arguments are seconded by Patroclus: a troubled Achilles sends Thersites to request that Hector should be invited to visit his tent after his combat with Ajax.

4.1 Early in the morning Diomedes arrives in Troy to fetch Cressida and is conducted towards her lodging by Aeneas and Paris. 4.2 Troilus and Cressida, tenderly parting, are interrupted first by a coyly mocking Pandarus and then by the arrival of Aeneas, who privately tells Troilus that Cressida must go to the Greeks. 4.3 Pandarus tells a distraught Cressida the news. 4.4 Troilus is sent to fetch Cressida. 4.5 Troilus and Cressida say their private farewells in haste and distress, Troilus upsetting Cressida further by telling her to be true; they exchange tokens, a glove and a sleeve, before Diomedes arrives with Paris and Aeneas. Diomedes offends Troilus by offering to be Cressida's protector as the party sets out for the city gate. 4.6 The Greek lords await Hector's arrival to fight with Ajax: when Diomedes brings Cressida, they each try to kiss her in turn, though she refuses Menelaus and also Ulysses, who after her departure accuses her of sluttishness. The Trojan party, including Troilus, arrives. 4.7 Hector breaks off his combat with Ajax on the grounds that they are cousins. He is formally introduced to each of the Greek leaders: Achilles insolently says he is considering where he will mortally wound Hector, and promises to fight with him the following day. Agreeing that their truce will last until then, all leave for Agamemnon's tent except Troilus and Ulysses: Troilus asks Ulysses to take him later to Calchas' tent.

5.1 Achilles reads a letter from Polyxena forbidding him to fight the following day while Thersites accuses Patroclus of being Achilles' catamite. After supper Hector is brought to Achilles' tent by the Grecian lords: Ulysses and Troilus follow Diomedes towards Calchas' tent, and Thersites in turn, anticipating mischief, follows them. 5.2 Concealed with Ulysses,

Troilus watches in horror as Cressida flirts uneasily with an insistent Diomedes, to whom she eventually gives the sleeve Troilus gave her: after Diomedes leaves she speaks in dismay at her own inconstancy. Unseen, Thersites comments cynically on the whole interview. After Cressida departs, Troilus rages, unable at first to accept the truth of what he has seen, and vows to kill Diomedes in the next day's battle. **5.3** The following morning Andromache, joined by Cassandra and later Priam, begs her husband Hector not to fight, convinced he will be killed: he himself tries to persuade Troilus to stay in Troy, but both men leave for the battle, Troilus after tearing up a love letter from Cressida delivered by the ailing Pandarus. **5.4–9** In the battle, punctuated by Thersites' commentary, Troilus fights Diomedes: Nestor sends the body of the slain Patroclus to Achilles: and Achilles at last rejoins the fighting, determined to kill Hector. After Troilus drives back both Ajax and Diomedes at once, Achilles and Hector duel: Hector bests Achilles, who leaves. Hector pursues and kills a splendidly armed Greek while Achilles instructs his Myrmidon troops to surround and kill Hector. Thersites' enjoyment of a duel between Paris and Menelaus is interrupted by Margareton, a bastard son of Priam, whom he flees. As it grows dark, Hector unarms, alone: Achilles has his Myrmidons kill him, and they leave to tie Hector's body behind Achilles' horse and drag it around the battlefield. **5.10** The Greeks, learning Achilles has killed Hector, are convinced their ultimate victory is inevitable. **5.11** Troilus brings Paris, Aeneas, and others the news of Hector's death, consoled only by thoughts of vengeance. (In the quarto he is then accosted by Pandarus, whom he shuns, and Pandarus speaks an epilogue, lamenting how bawds are reviled by their post-coital customers: he anticipates his own imminent death from venereal diseases, which he proposes to bequeath to the audience.)

Artistic features: *Troilus and Cressida* has an unusually arcane and learned vocabulary (some of it legal), and a penchant for set-piece displays of rhetoric, which have sometimes been adduced in support of the theory that it was written for the Inns of Court. The play's scepticism about all forms of chivalric idealism, most obviously expressed by the cynical Thersites (who reduces the epic of Troy and the love of Troilus and Cressida to 'wars and lechery'), has led some to see it as merely a satirical, anti-heroic burlesque, but Shakespeare's compassion for his characters—most obviously the lovers, who for all their failings are given one of the most moving valediction scenes in the canon—remains as evident as always.

Critical history: Although Ulysses' speeches on degree, and on the need for perseverance ('Time hath, my lord, | A wallet at his back . . .', 3.3.139–84), were often anthologized among Shakespeare's beauties (and are still sometimes quoted, misleadingly, as unmediated expressions of Shakespeare's own views), the play as a whole was generally regarded with baffled dislike until the middle of the 20th century. *Dryden, prefacing his 1679 adaptation, laments that Shakespeare's style is 'so pestered with figurative expressions that it is as affected as it is obscure', and his equal objections to the play's characterization and plotting are made clear by his alterations to them: his Troilus resists Cressida's removal to the Greek camp, and his misunderstood Cressida (though she humours Diomedes) is faithful to him throughout, eventually killing herself to prove it. Dr *Johnson had little sympathy for either Cressida or Pandarus, whom he thought 'detested and contemned' by all readers, and his views were echoed by 19th-century commentators horrified by the play's cynicism and sexual indelicacy: as late as 1924 Agnes Mure Mackenzie (in *The Women in Shakespeare's Plays*) could describe *Troilus and Cressida* as 'the work of a man whose soul is poisoned with filth'. Mackenzie is one of several early 20th-century critics (among them *Chambers and Frank *Harris) who attempted to explain the play, like *Timon of Athens* and the other *'problem plays', as the morbid symptom of a personal crisis, while others tried to excuse it as Shakespeare's contribution to the ill-natured *'War of the Theatres'. By the 1930s, however, these approaches were already giving place to a very different estimate of the play's artistic success. In the era of high *modernism the play's difficulty, intellectuality, and frank, Donne-like concern with sexuality made it a favourite with academic critics, among them George Wilson *Knight and Una Ellis-Fermor, and its depiction of a pointless but apparently unstoppable war helped preserve its position in the academic canon through the era of Vietnam. Its reflections on time and the mutability of personal identity have been much studied, while *feminist criticism has been particularly interested in Cressida, a heroine who seems to transact her own personal life outside the normative categories of 'maid, widow, or wife'.

Stage history: No records survive of pre-Restoration performances, and though Shakespeare's original may have been revived at *Smock Alley in Dublin in the 1670s, in England the play would only be seen in Dryden's tidy version (performed with reasonable frequency between 1679 and 1734) before the 20th century. Even Dryden's version was most praised for its new scenes, notably a quarrel and reconciliation between Troilus and Hector and a rhetorical confrontation between Troilus and Diomedes. The original was first revived in Munich in 1898 (played, by an all-male cast, as a blackly comic skit on Homer) and other German productions followed. The play was at last revived semi-professionally, to an unconvinced London audience, in 1907, and a similar venture by William *Poel in 1912–13 is remembered only for the young Edith *Evans's coquettish Cressida. The *Marlowe Society produced the play in Cambridge in 1922, where its perspective on war was received sympathetically by the First World War veterans in its audience, but the first fully professional English production, at the *Old Vic the following year, was a critical failure. More successful, however, was a modern-dress revival at the Westminster theatre in 1938, and since the Second World War the play has been revived frequently, becoming something of a directors' favourite. Tyrone *Guthrie's 1956 Old Vic production was

the first of many to costume the play on the eve of the First World War, with cavalry sabres about to give place to machine guns: a notable successor in this respect was the 1985 RSC production, with Juliet Stevenson as a sympathetic Cressida more betrayed by Anton Lesser's Troilus than vice versa. Dorothy *Tutin had played the role far more flirtatiously in Peter *Hall and John *Barton's legendary 1960 version at Stratford, with Max Adrian as Pandarus and Denholm Elliott as Troilus: other important revivals include Sam Mendes's RSC production of 1991, with Amanda Root as Cressida, Ralph Fiennes as a neurotically insecure Troilus, and Simon Russell Beale as the most wonderfully repulsive Thersites in living memory. *MD*

On the screen: It is a sign of the play's return to favour since the Second World War that three television adaptations have been made, the first in 1954, a National Youth Theatre production (1966), and Jonathan Miller's classically dressed BBC TV production (1981). *AD*

Recent major editions

Kenneth Muir (Oxford, 1984); Kenneth Palmer (Arden 2nd series, 1982); David Bevington (Arden 3rd series, 1998)

Some representative criticism:

Bayley, John, 'Time and the Trojans', *Essays in Criticism*, 25 (1975)

Dollimore, Jonathan, in *Radical Tragedy* (1984)

Ellis-Fermor, Una, in *The Frontiers of Drama* (1945)

Knight, G. Wilson, in *The Wheel of Fire* (1949)

McAlindon, T., 'Language, Style and Meaning in *Troilus and Cressida*', *Publications of the Modern Language Association*, 84 (1969)

Thompson, Ann, in *Shakespeare's Chaucer: A Study in Literary Origins* (1978)

---

the two plays has encouraged speculation about Shakespeare's own *religion. *MD*

Jones, Emrys, in *The Origin of Shakespeare* (1977)

Smallwood, Robert, in his New Penguin edition of *King John* (1974)

True Tragedy of Richard III, The, an anonymous play, probably performed first in 1591, of which only the debased printed text of 1594 remains. That Shakespeare knew the *True Tragedy* is apparent from a single line in *Hamlet*, 'The croaking raven doth bellow for revenge' (3.2.241–2), a paraphrase of two lines from the play. That Shakespeare borrowed from the *True Tragedy* when writing *Richard III* is less apparent. Nevertheless, there are similarities between the two plays in, for example, their use of chronicle history. Both diverge from their sources in comparable ways. Moreover, some of the surprising omissions in *Richard III* might be explained by Shakespeare's familiarity with the *True Tragedy*. The downfall of Jane Shore and the murder of the princes are major events in the chronicles and in the *True Tragedy* that barely feature in Shakespeare's play. Perhaps the dramatist was unwilling to repeat material recently enacted in the *True Tragedy*. Another link between the two plays might be their Senecanism, in particular their use of ghosts. The *True Tragedy* begins with the ghost of Clarence calling for revenge and ends with ghosts who accuse Richard in a dream before the battle of Bosworth. Nevertheless, this kind of revenge structure was very popular at the time and the *Mirror for Magistrates* also features Clarence's ghost. The evidence for a direct connection between the plays remains unconvincing. *JKS*

True Tragedy of Richard Duke of York and the Good King Henry the Sixth, The. See Richard Duke of York.

trumpet. The word is used as a stage direction to indicate various kinds of *fanfare or signal. The instrument itself is associated with royalty or high rank in a ceremonial context, and with cavalry in a military context (*drums indicate infantry). Trumpets were also played in the *soundings. *JB*

Trundell, John. See printing and publishing.

Tsubouchi, Shoyo (1859–1935), Japanese writer. The pioneer of the modern theatre movement in Japan, whose real name was Yuzo Tsubouchi, studied at the University of Tokyo. In many ways he represented the contradictory nature of the so-called modernization of Japan, because while he advocated modern realism in literature he was at the same time irresistibly attracted to traditional Japanese theatre, especially Kabuki and Bunraku. In 1906 he established the Literary Society in order to train actors intelligent enough to cope with European drama, and the society produced Shakespeare as well as other Western playwrights before it was disbanded in 1913. Tsubouchi eventually translated the complete canon of Shakespeare. His translations retain a strong flavour of Kabuki, and while they are highly regarded for their literary merit, they are hardly used for stage productions any more as they sound rather archaic. He was an influential critic and novelist as well as a playwright in his own right, and many of his plays are still performed regularly, especially by Kabuki actors. He served for many years as a professor of English at Waseda University in Tokyo, which has a theatre museum named after him. *TK*

Tubal, a Jew, brings Shylock mixed news, *The Merchant of Venice* 3.1. *AB*

tucket, a stage direction indicating a *trumpet call associated with an individual of high rank, as in *The Merchant of Venice* 5.1.122. An extended musical example is the opening to Monteverdi's *L'Orfeo* (1607), in effect a tucket for his patrons, the Gonzagas. *JB*

Tudor Shakespeare. *The Complete Works*, ed. Peter *Alexander (London: Collins, 1951), offered a simple, compact collection of the plays and poems, excluding *The Two Noble Kinsmen* and other works since attributed to Shakespeare. The editor provided a brief general introduction, a plain text in double columns per page, and a glossary at the end. The edition established at once a deserved reputation for good textual scholarship. Its modest size, weight, and price ensured that it became very popular, and was widely used by students and teachers. By the time of its twelfth reprint in 1966, Collins's boasted 'clear type' had worn here and there rather badly, and some features, such as the retention of scene locations introduced in the 18th century, seemed old-fashioned. It was reissued in 1994 with additional brief introductory material by Germaine Greer, Anthony *Burgess, and Alex Yearling, and prefaces to individual plays contributed by faculty at Glasgow University, where Peter Alexander taught. *RAF*

Turgenev, Ivan (1818–83), Russian novelist and critic. His 'Hamlet of the Schigrovsky District' (1849, in *A Sportsman's Sketches*) offers a provincial version of the 'superfluous man'. *Don Quixote and Hamlet* (1860) contrasts two prevailing Russian character types: the one of ideals, faith, and conviction; the other sceptical, rational, and ironic. *TM*

Turks. See travel, trade and colonialism.

Turner, William. (1) (d. 1568), physician, author of an ever-expanding *Herbal*, published in parts from 1551 to 1568, which records botanical knowledge displayed in plays such as *The Tragedy of King Lear* and *Love's Labour's*

Dorothy Tutin as Cressida, with Max Adrian as Pandarus, in the John Barton–Peter Hall *Troilus and Cressida*, RSC, 1960: one reviewer described her as 'a rippling wisp of carnality that is almost unbearably alluring'.

Lost. **(2)** (fl. 1613), author of *A Dish of Lenten Stuff* (1613), in which he contrasts the playhouses north of the Thames (the purveyors of bawdy *jigs) with the romantic comedies provided by the *Bankside theatres. *CS*

Tutin, Dame Dorothy (b. 1931), British actress. Tiny and husky-voiced, she had already acted several of Shakespeare's young women when in 1953 she enjoyed a great London success as the vulnerable young girl in Graham Greene's *The Living Room.* She went on to Stratford where from 1958 she played, often under Peter *Hall's direction, romantic heroines: Viola, Juliet, Ophelia, Portia, Rosalind—and a sultry Cressida. In 1977 as Cleopatra for Prospect Productions she seemed miscast. Her later Shakespearian parts were Lady Macbeth at the *Old Vic and Queen Katherine in *Henry VIII* at *Chichester. *MJ*

Tutor, Rutland's. See RUTLAND'S TUTOR.

Twain, Mark (Samuel Langhorne Clemens) (1835–1910), American writer, journalist, and lecturer. Twain specifically exploits Shakespeare in pieces such as his fragmentary *burlesque of *Hamlet* (1881), in which a travelling booksalesman, Basil Stockmar, attempts to present the Ghost with a sample copy; his pornographic pseudo-diary of a court cup-bearer *1601; or, Conversation, as it Was by the Social Fireside, in the Time of the Tudors* (1882), including a character called 'Master Shakspur'; and *Is Shakespeare Dead?* (1909), a reflection upon art and immortality, driven by uncertainty that either Shakespeare or *Bacon could ever have produced the works. Twain read Shakespeare's plays in preparation for *The Prince and the Pauper* (1881), and *The Adventures of Huckleberry Finn* (1884) contains incidents and characters deliberately reminiscent of *Romeo and Juliet, Hamlet,* and *King Lear.* *TM*

Twelfth Night; or, What You Will *(see opposite page)*

twentieth-century Shakespearian production. Though Shakespeare's fame had grown steadily since about 1750, in the 20th century he became the dominant writer for the stage for much of the world. Performance of his plays vastly increased in frequency and varied in style, intention, and reception. Two issues seem paramount for a summary account: the replacement of the star actor by the director as the chief aesthetic force, and alterations to the architecture of the theatre and the design of the stage under the influence of *modernism.

1900–45 The century began with the historicist mode triumphant in Britain and elsewhere. Despite the work of William *Poel, who sought to recover the Elizabethan theatrical condition of the plays, and the complaints made by *Shaw and others against the over-literal Shakespeare of Henry *Irving and Beerbohm *Tree, the common method of Victorian production continued well past 1900. The plays were interpreted as historical stories, and were illustrated with lavish costumes, settings, and striking ceremonies with large numbers of supernumerary actors, all of which forced severe cutting and rearrangement of the texts. The actor-manager ruled the company and took centre stage, often disregarding the value of smaller roles. Audiences delighted in the display of the star as well as in material stage display, and Shakespeare's work—with its opportunities for grandiloquent playing, its classic status, and its exotic locales—seemed well suited to such spectacular expression. The challenges to this mode appeared early in the century through the work of the newly defined stage director, were affected by calls for aesthetic and social renovation from European modernism, and applied to Shakespeare first through the work of Edward Gordon *Craig. Though he directed few productions, Craig's designs and theoretical writings from 1903 forward proposed a Shakespeare uncluttered by realism; instead of localized settings the stage would convey ideas and impressions through abstract means.

Max *Reinhardt in Berlin was the Shakespeare director first affected. His spectacular, realist productions of plays like *A Midsummer Night's Dream* (1905 on) and *The Tempest* (1915) were balanced by smaller-scale versions of *The Winter's Tale* (1906) and *King Lear* (1908) that were Craigian in their visual approach. Reinhardt's work, widely admired in Europe, was seen by Harley *Granville-Barker, who took some of its profit back to London in three famous productions at the Savoy theatre, the first major examples of modernist Shakespeare in Britain. *The Winter's Tale* and *Twelfth Night* in 1912 used simplified and abstract settings, a modified stage arrangement influenced by Poel, bright frontal lighting, nearly complete texts, and sought speed in the verse and the flow of scenes. *A Midsummer Night's Dream* (1914) pushed Barker's methods even further; the fairies were fantastic creatures all in gold who looked like gods or fetishes from India and moved with choreographed swiftness.

Though Barker and Craig both retired from directing after the war, modernist productions gained force in Central and Eastern Europe under their influence, often using political interpretations of the plays to comment on contemporary events, with directors such as Leopold Jessner in Berlin, Leon Schiller in Warsaw, or Jirí Frejka in Prague. Shakespeare in Britain tended to be much more conservative; indeed there was a notable return to the older mode with stars such as John *Gielgud, Laurence *Olivier, and Ralph *Richardson often directing their own productions between the wars like Victorian actor-managers. Nonetheless the influence of the director continued to be felt, as witnessed by the success of inventive artists like Tyrone *Guthrie and Theodore *Komisarjevsky who relied on the institutional theatres of the *Old Vic and the *Shakespeare Memorial Theatre in Stratford to insulate their work from the hit-or-flop acerbity of the commercial theatre. The regional repertory theatres, which had spread throughout Britain after the war, were often adventurous. Barry *Jackson of the Birmingham Rep brought the first modern-dress Shakespeare to London (*Hamlet* in 1925), while Terence *Gray of the Cambridge Festival Theatre copied continental avant-garde methods in an expressionist *Richard III* of 1928. In New York a pattern of commercial production similar to London's was spiced by the modernist work of the designer Robert Edmond Jones (for the actor John *Barrymore in the 1920s), while the exotic and modern-dress experiments of Orson *Welles (a 'voodoo' *Macbeth* and an anti-fascist *Julius Caesar*, 1936–7) brought cinematic devices to the stage, preparing the way for the Shakespeare films Welles and Olivier would make shortly thereafter.

1945–80 The two major developments after the Second World War were also institutional in nature and demonstrated the ascendancy of the director. The first was the creation of the Stratford Shakespearian Festival in a small town in Ontario in *Canada, far removed from the traditional centres of Shakespeare activity. Here in 1953 Guthrie designed a stage with a fixed background in mock 16th-century style, and placed it in the middle of a large tent with a semicircular seating arrangement. (A permanent theatre was built in 1956.) The idea, indebted to Poel, was to recapture the spirit of the Elizabethan theatre by architectural means, though the audience configuration owed more to the ancient theatre at Epidaurus than to the Globe. Guthrie developed a fluid form of playing that centred the actor on a relatively bare platform, with spectators as visible collaborators in a non-illusionist environment. His achievements were widely admired and the basic shape of theatre was copied through the 1960s and 1970s. Summer festivals dedicated in whole or part to Shakespeare sprang up swiftly, particularly coast-to-coast in the USA, often using open stages (like the *New York Shakespeare Festival and the Ashland Shakespeare Festival in Oregon).

The second major development took place in the original Stratford. Following some remarkable productions by the young Peter *Brook after the war (including a revelatory *Titus Andronicus* with Olivier in 1955), another young man, Peter *Hall, was invited to manage the Shakespeare Memorial Theatre in 1960. Hall quickly transformed it into the *Royal Shakespeare Company, a theatre ensemble along European lines with a semi-permanent

(cont. on page 494)

Twelfth Night; or, What You Will

One of Shakespeare's best-loved comedies, encompassing a formidable range of moods and dramatic styles, *Twelfth Night* is first mentioned in the diary of a law student, John *Manningham, who saw it performed in the hall of Middle Temple on 2 February 1602. The play was probably at most a few months old at the time, as a number of details in the text suggest. Maria mentions 'the new map with the augmentation of the Indies' (3.2.74–5), usually identified as one first published in Richard *Hakluyt's *Voyages* in 1599; 2.3 quotes from a number of songs first published in 1600 (in Robert *Jones's *First Book of Songs and Airs*); while Feste's view that the phrase 'out of my element' is 'overworn' (3.1.57–8) alludes to a running joke against the expression in Thomas *Dekker's *Satiromastix*, premièred by Shakespeare's company in 1601. The *Chamberlain's Men performed an unnamed play on Twelfth Night in 1601 before Elizabeth's court and her guest of honour Don Virginio Orsino, Duke of Bracciano: despite Leslie *Hotson's strenuous arguments, this is unlikely to have been *Twelfth Night*, though Shakespeare's choice of the name Orsino for the play's duke when he wrote his play later in 1601 may have been influenced by recollections of the occasion.

Text: The play was first printed in the *Folio in 1623, in a good text derived from a literary transcript of the play prepared by a scribe (possibly especially for this purpose). The view that the text shows signs of post-performance revision is no longer widely accepted.

Sources: Two or even three of the play's sources were recognized very early: Manningham commented that the play was 'much like the *Comedy of Errors* or *Menaechmi* in Plautus, but most like ... that in Italian called *Inganni*'. The resemblances between *Twelfth Night* and *Plautus' *Menaechmi*, the source for Shakespeare's earlier play about identical *twins, are clear (*The Comedy of Errors* similarly sets its comedy of mistaken identity within a poignant framework of separation and reunion), though its debts to an Italian play are more complicated. By *Inganni*, Manningham meant the anonymous *Gl'ingannati* (The Deceived, 1531), which indeed provided the ultimate source for the relationships between the characters whom Shakespeare rechristened Orsino, Olivia, Viola, and Sebastian. Shakespeare, however, probably knew *Gl'ingannati* only at second or third hand, via prose versions in *Bandello's *Novelle* (1554) and *Belleforest's *Histoires tragiques* (1571) which were themselves adapted by Barnabe *Rich in 'Apollonius and Silla', the second story in his *Farewell to Military Profession* (1581). The sub-plot of the gulled steward, however, has no such literary source, and attempts to identify Malvolio as a hostile portrait of a particular Elizabethan courtier have been uniformly unconvincing.

Synopsis: **1.1** Orsino, duke of *Illyria, listens to music as he languishes for the love of Countess Olivia: when Valentine reports that Olivia refuses his suit, vowing to mourn her dead brother for seven years, he comforts himself with the reflection that a woman capable of such emotion for a mere brother will in due course love passionately. **1.2** Viola, washed up in Illyria after a shipwreck in which she fears her twin brother Sebastian has perished, learns from the ship's Captain of Olivia's vow and Orsino's suit: with his help she intends to disguise herself as a eunuch and enter Orsino's service. **1.3** At Olivia's house her dissolute uncle Sir Toby Belch detains the rich but foolish Sir Andrew Aguecheek, another hopeful suitor to Olivia: Sir Andrew's ineptitude is demonstrated by his incompetent repartee with the witty servant Maria. **1.4** Viola, disguised as 'Cesario', has become such a favourite of Orsino that he sends her to court Olivia on his behalf, an errand she accepts reluctantly, confessing in an aside that she herself loves Orsino. **1.5** The clown Feste has incurred Olivia's displeasure by a long absence, but contrives to regain her favour by riddling that she is more foolish than he for mourning that her brother is in Heaven. Her steward Malvolio, however, remains Feste's adversary, and is gently rebuked by Olivia for his ungenerosity of spirit. Olivia sends Feste to look after Sir Toby, who is already drunk. Viola, after refusing to be put off by a baffled Malvolio, is eventually admitted to Maria and Olivia: besting Maria's wit, she secures a private interview with Olivia, whom she rebukes for her pride, though she acknowledges her beauty. Olivia dismisses Orsino's suit but grows increasingly interested in 'Cesario', who she hopes will come again: after Viola leaves, she sends Malvolio after her with a ring she claims was left as an unwanted gift from Orsino.

2.1 Sebastian tells his devoted friend Antonio of Viola, whom he believes to have drowned. Antonio, though he has mortal enemies at Orsino's court, decides to follow Sebastian there. 2.2 Malvolio gives Viola the ring Olivia claimed she had left as a present. Alone, Viola realizes that Olivia has fallen in love with Cesario, and wonders how this complicated situation will resolve itself. 2.3 After midnight, Sir Toby and Sir Andrew have Feste sing a song, 'O mistress mine', and join him in singing catches: Maria warns them they are too loud, and Malvolio arrives to rebuke them for disturbing the household, threatening Sir Toby that Olivia's displeasure may result in his banishment from it. Sir Toby is affronted at this check from a mere servant, and, after Malvolio leaves, Maria, with his eager encouragement, plots revenge: she will forge a letter from Olivia to trick the steward into thinking his mistress is in love with him. 2.4 Orsino speaks of love with Viola: they listen to Feste sing 'Come away, come away death'. Defending women against the charge of being less constant than men, Viola speaks of her own feelings and predicament under cover of describing a sister who pined away through concealing her love. Orsino sends her again to woo Olivia. 2.5 Sir Toby, Sir Andrew, Maria, and another servant, Fabian, hide in the garden and watch Malvolio approach the forged letter Maria has placed in his path. Malvolio is already imagining becoming Count through marriage to Olivia and lecturing Sir Toby when he finds it. Despite the letter's obscure anagram of 'M.O.A.I.' and its refusal actually to name either its addressee or its feigned author, its purport is clear: a confession of love from Olivia in which she urges Malvolio to spurn Sir Toby, smile, and wear yellow stockings, cross-gartered. Malvolio, completely taken in, is overjoyed, and hastens to comply. Maria hurries her confederates towards Olivia to watch for Malvolio's transformation.

3.1 Viola, also on her way to Olivia, meets Feste, who wittily begs money: she also meets Sir Toby and Sir Andrew, who is impressed with the courtliness with which Viola greets Olivia. When they are alone, Olivia confesses her love: when Viola says she can only pity her, Olivia feigns that she might yet love Orsino, in the hopes of inducing Viola to come again on his behalf. 3.2 Sir Andrew, about to leave on the grounds that Olivia obviously prefers Cesario to himself, is persuaded by Sir Toby and Fabian that Olivia is deliberately offering him a chance of proving his valour, and he leaves to write a challenge to Cesario. Maria fetches the others to see Malvolio, who has already changed his stockings. 3.3 Antonio, in danger because of his former participation in a sea-fight in which he helped to plunder Orsino's galleys, gives the sightseeing Sebastian his purse, arranging to meet him discreetly at an inn later. 3.4 Olivia has sent after Viola once more, but is distracted from her own affairs by the appearance of the cross-gartered Malvolio, whose smiling quotations from the forged letter convince his mistress he has lost his wits. After she leaves to see Viola, Sir Toby, Fabian, and Maria speak to Malvolio as if they believe he is possessed: he leaves, still confident of Olivia's love. Sir Andrew has written an incompetent and cowardly challenge for Cesario, which Sir Toby resolves not to deliver, preferring to challenge Cesario in person. Olivia and Viola enter, Viola once more asking Olivia to bestow her love on Orsino rather than on herself: after Olivia's departure, Sir Toby tells Viola that Sir Andrew means to duel with her, convincing Viola of his implacable and expert rage. Sir Toby then persuades Sir Andrew that Viola is equally furious and deadly: their mutually terrified sword-fight, however, is interrupted by the arrival of Antonio, who mistakes Viola for Sebastian. Antonio is about to fight with Sir Toby when officers arrive to arrest the newcomer: he asks Viola for the return of his purse, and is shocked when she denies receiving it, leaving heartbroken for prison. Viola begins to hope her brother may still be alive. Sir Andrew, now convinced of Viola's cowardice, follows her to renew his challenge.

4.1 Sebastian meets Feste, who is offended not to be recognized by him: Sir Andrew arrives and strikes Sebastian, who is quick to avenge the blow, and finds himself at drawn swords with Sir Toby when Olivia arrives and similarly takes Sebastian for Cesario. Sebastian is at once puzzled and delighted by her tender attention, and departs with her. 4.2 Malvolio, presumed mad, is locked up in darkness: Feste pretends to be Sir Topas, a curate sent to examine his alleged demonic possession, but eventually agrees to bring Malvolio ink, paper, and a light that he may write to Olivia. 4.3 Sebastian, though still bewildered, is delighted by Olivia's love, and agrees to go with her and a priest to be married.

5.1 Feste refuses to let Fabian see the letter he has promised to give Olivia from Malvolio, and begs money from Orsino, who arrives with Viola and other attendants. Antonio is brought before them: Orsino remembers his valour despite regarding him as a pirate, but counters his renewed accusations of falsehood against Viola by witnessing that Viola has been at his court for the last three months rather than in Antonio's company as he alleges. This discussion is cut short by the arrival of Olivia. Orsino says he knows his rightful place in her heart has been usurped by Cesario, whom he threatens to kill: when Viola promises she loves Orsino above all else, and means to leave with him come what may, Olivia produces the priest, who bears witness that Cesario and Olivia are married. Sir Andrew arrives, followed by Sir Toby, who has been wounded in a fight they have provoked with Sebastian: they are shocked to find Viola there. Sebastian now arrives, to apologize to his newly married wife for hurting her kinsman: as the onlookers marvel at seeing him and Viola at once, he is at first overjoyed to see Antonio again before he sees his disguised sister. The twins tentatively question one another to confirm each other's identities: Viola explains that if her male clothes hinder his recognition, she can reclaim her own from the Sea Captain. It becomes clear how Olivia has come to marry Sebastian after falling in love with Cesario, and Orsino realizes that Viola, disguised, has often confessed that she loves him. The Sea Captain who has her clothes, however, has been arrested at Malvolio's suit, so Malvolio is summoned: meanwhile Fabian reads Olivia his evidently sane letter (replacing Feste, who insists on reading it in too mad a voice). Orsino agrees to marry Viola in a double celebration at Olivia's house. Malvolio arrives and confronts Olivia with the letter he found in the garden: she explains that it is forged, and Fabian and Feste confess their trick (Fabian revealing that Sir Toby has married Maria as a reward for her wit, Feste saying he took part in order to avenge Malvolio's criticism of his fooling). Malvolio leaves, vowing revenge on them all. Orsino sends after him, in order that Viola's female clothes can be retrieved for her wedding: meanwhile he will continue to call her Cesario. Feste is left alone to sing a song as an epilogue, 'When that I was and a little tiny boy'.

Artistic features: Rich in songs—provided for Robert *Armin, the original Feste, who had replaced the less intellectual and melodious fool Will *Kempe in 1599—and peopled by characters who are given to reflecting eloquently but passively on their imprisonment within their own and one another's fantasies, *Twelfth Night* is the most lyrical of the mature comedies. At the close of its at once atrociously cruel and exquisitely funny sub-plot, one of Shakespeare's most Jonsonian, even the puritanical Malvolio rises to the dignity of blank verse.

Critical history: Although apparently highly regarded in Shakespeare's time and thereafter—Leonard *Digges's dedicatory verse in Benson's 1640 edition of Shakespeare's poems includes the couplet 'The Cockpit galleries, boxes, all are full | To hear Malvolio, that cross-gartered gull'—the play fell from favour for 80 years after the Restoration, its Italianate intrigues and fancies dismissed as unrealistic. As late as 1765 Dr *Johnson, who called the play 'elegant and easy, and in some of the lighter scenes exquisitely humorous', objected that the winding-up of the main plot 'wants credibility and fails to produce the proper instruction required in the drama, as it exhibits no true picture of life'. The play was valued more highly by *Romantic critics such as *Schlegel, who singled out the importance of both music and the concept of 'fancy' to the play in his *Course of Lectures on Dramatic Literature* (1809–11), while *Hazlitt considered it 'one of the most delightful of Shakespeare's comedies . . . perhaps too good-natured for comedy'. In the 19th century Viola, the most acceptably bashful and passive of Shakespeare's comic heroines, was a favourite of moralist critics, and her imaginary youth is described with particular enthusiasm in Mary Cowden *Clarke's *The Girlhood of Shakespeare's Heroines* (1850–1). In academic criticism she has often been upstaged, however, by two other characters. Charles *Lamb was one of the first commentators to speak in favour of Malvolio, and Lamb's contemporaries also singled out another figure often seen as providing the play's keynote, Feste, later the subject of an important essay by A. C. *Bradley. Twentieth-century criticism has treated both of these characters ever more seriously, as perceptions of the play's happy comedy have increasingly given place to a sense of its social tensions and sexual undercurrents: recent discussions have related it to the *'problem plays' as often as to what might otherwise seem its more natural companion piece, *As You Like It.* Malvolio has been viewed as a comic antagonist whose potentially tragic dignity approaches that of Shylock: Feste has been identified as a detached, ironic commentator on the play whose freelance status and penchant for puns mirror the elusiveness of language and desire themselves. Since the Second World War *Twelfth Night* has provided fertile ground for anthropologically inclined critics who have pursued its title's allusion to seasonal rituals of misrule and inversion, and its intrigues have been equally attractive to *Marxists interested in the social cross-dressing of Malvolio and to *feminists and queer theorists interested in the gender cross-dressing of Viola and the hints of homoeroticism which inform her relations with Orsino and Olivia, not to mention Antonio's adoration of Sebastian.

Stage history: A similar trajectory—from unfashionably whimsical trifle to happy romantic comedy to bittersweet drama of social and sexual identity—informs *Twelfth Night*'s post-Restoration stage history. The play was evidently popular down to the Civil War, as Digges's poem suggests: a court performance is recorded in 1622 as 'Malvolio' (a title by which *Charles I would also call the play, in a note on the contents page of his copy of the Folio). Doubtless remembering the play's earlier success in court circles, *Davenant revived it in the early 1660s, the role of Viola now transformed by the arrival of professional actresses into a breeches part, but the play was laid aside after 1669, when *Pepys, who had earlier dismissed it as 'but a silly play', described it as 'one of the weakest plays that ever I saw on the stage'. The extent to which its lyricism had gone out of fashion is vividly suggested by a short-lived, largely prose adaptation, *Love Betrayed; or, The Agreeable Disappointment* (1703), which, as its author William Burnaby candidly admitted in a preface, rejected most of Shakespeare's poetry and much of his plotting entirely: 'Part of the tale of this play, I took from Shakespeare, and about fifty of his lines.' The original was restored, however, in 1741, performed at Drury Lane by the company who revived *The Merchant of Venice* and *As You Like It* during the same season: Charles *Macklin was Malvolio, Hannah *Pritchard played Viola, and Kitty *Clive Olivia. Since then, the play's popularity has never waned, with the role of

Malvolio attracting star actors and actor-managers from Richard Yates through Samuel *Phelps, Henry *Irving, and Beerbohm *Tree down to Donald *Wolfit, Laurence *Olivier, and Donald *Sinden. Viola has been an equally important role for actresses (her soliloquy in 2.2, 'I left no ring with her. What means this lady?', has long been the most familiar of audition pieces), offering in the 18th and 19th centuries an irresistible combination of professed modesty with the titillation provided by male costume's display of her figure. Dorothea *Jordan was a sensation in the 1790s, and Leigh *Hunt's account of the part is dominated by his attention to Ann Maria Tree's limbs: 'It is impossible not to be struck . . . with a leg like this. It is fit for a statue: still fitter for where it is.' Equally appealing successors in the part included Charlotte *Cushman, Ada *Rehan, and Ellen *Terry. Increasing decorative elaboration in the 19th century led to frequent transpositions of scenes, a tendency which culminated in Beerbohm Tree's 1901 production, where most of the scenes in Olivia's garden had to be run consecutively, as its set's real grass and fountains could not be changed during the performance. The way forward, however, was more accurately pointed by Harley *Granville-Barker's revival at the Savoy in 1912: its styling was influenced by William *Poel's experiments with neo-Elizabethan open stages, its Malvolio, Henry Ainley, was heartbreakingly overwrought in the prison scene, and its Feste, Hayden Coffin, was the most melancholy for many years. Since then the play's ever more frequent productions have, in general, become progressively more autumnal: major revivals have included Tyrone *Guthrie's (1937, with Olivier as Sir Toby, Alec *Guinness as Sir Andrew, and Jessica Tandy confusingly doubling Viola and Sebastian), John *Gielgud's (1955, with Olivier as Malvolio and Vivien *Leigh as Viola), and John *Barton's delicately Elizabethan RSC production of 1969 (with Judi *Dench as Viola). Two memorable productions of the 1980s instructively paralleled contemporary trends in criticism: Ariane *Mnouchkine staged an exotic, ambiguous Illyria in her Théâtre du Soleil production of 1982, while *Cheek by Jowl's 1985 touring production stressed the play's homoeroticism, eventually pairing off Feste with Antonio. *MD*

On the screen: The earliest film of *Twelfth Night* was a silent version made in America in 1910. No fewer than five television versions have been made for the BBC, culminating in the 1980 production with Alec McCowen as Malvolio and Felicity Kendal as Viola. An American TV production (1957) with Maurice *Evans, Denholm Elliott, and Max Adrian was well received. Especially memorable was John Dexter's production for British commercial television (1970) with Alec Guinness (Malvolio), Tommy Steele (Feste), Ralph *Richardson (Sir Toby Belch), and Joan Plowright (Viola). A brooding production directed by Judi *Dench for Kenneth *Branagh's Renaissance Theatre Company, with music by Paul McCartney, is also preserved on videotape, directed by Paul Kafno (1990). Only two cinema films provide a full treatment of the play. The 1955 Russian film directed by Yakow Fried balances boisterous comedy with subtle characterization, and Trevor *Nunn's *Twelfth Night* (1996), filmed in Cornwall, stresses visually the play's recurrent sea imagery. Nunn's strong cast—including Nigel Hawthorne as Malvolio, Imogen Stubbs as Viola, and Ben *Kingsley as Feste—capture both the play's poignancy and its fun. *AD*

Recent major editions

Roger Warren and Stanley Wells (Oxford, 1994); Elizabeth Story Donno (New Cambridge, 1985); J. M. Lothian and T. W. Craik (Arden 2nd series, 1975)

Some representative criticism

Barber, C. L., in *Shakespeare's Festive Comedy* (1959)

Booth, Stephen, '*Twelfth Night*, 1.1: Malvolio as Audience', in Paul Erickson and Coppélia Kahn (eds.), *Shakespeare's 'Rough Magic': Essays in Honour of C. L. Barber* (1985)

Bradley, A. C., 'Feste the Jester', in Israel Gollancz (ed.), *A Book of Homage to Shakespeare* (1916)

Callaghan, Dympna, in *Shakespeare without Women* (2000)

Greenblatt, Stephen, in *Shakespearean Negotiations* (1988)

Hotson, Leslie, *The First Night of 'Twelfth Night'* (1954)

Jardine, Lisa, in *Reading Shakespeare Historically* (1996)

Leggatt, Alexander, in *Shakespeare's Comedies of Love* (1974)

Orgel, Stephen, in *Impersonations* (1996)

Salingar, L. G., 'The Design of *Twelfth Night*', *Shakespeare Quarterly*, 9 (1958)

---

company of actors, directors, and designers. He also acquired the Aldwych theatre as a London base and set about gaining the public funding that permitted rapid expansion. The new order made it possible to develop a social attitude to Shakespeare's work, to keep productions in the repertory for extended periods, bring them to London, and tour them regularly. The company's international visibility rose dramatically, most notably with Brook's *King Lear* in 1962 and Hall's *The *Wars of the Roses* (1963–4), a seven-part adaptation of the history plays which established a company style: excellent verse-speaking combined with a rough and even brutal form of physical playing. Under the artistic directorships of Trevor *Nunn and Terry *Hands in the 1970s, the RSC lost some of its socially engaged posture but consolidated itself as a major international theatre, especially with grand ventures like Nunn's staging of the Roman plays in 1972 and Hands's almost-uncut *Henry VI* (1977). Some of the most powerful productions of this time were directed by John *Barton (*Troilus and Cressida* of 1968, *Richard II* of 1973), or by Nunn in a chamber venue called the Other Place that sat about 140 (*Macbeth*, 1976).

The influence of Jan *Kott's *Shakespeare our Contemporary* was behind much of the RSC's best work in the period and was heavily felt in Europe, while Brecht was followed from the late 1950s by directors like Roger *Planchon in Lyon and Giorgio *Strehler in Milan, who made socialist commentary out of Shakespeare. Strehler was one of the most consistently inventive of interpreters, his work culminating in a remarkable *Tempest* in 1978. In the Soviet Union and in the Eastern Bloc Shakespeare grew in official importance, though after 1968 approved productions frequently vied with 'dissident' ones—often indebted to Kott—that tended to use Shakespeare's texts as coded messages about regimes that could not be criticized openly. Yuri Lyubimov's *Hamlet* (Moscow, 1971) is representative of the same trend in the Soviet Union,

Laurence Olivier and Vivien Leigh as the Macbeths in Glen Byam Shaw's production, Shakespeare Memorial Theatre, 1955.

a production in which a travelling curtain, like the forces of history, swept all before it into the grave.

1980–2000 Around the end of the 1970s, as the Cold War receded and new concerns occupied artists internationally, Shakespeare performance became more varied and less predictable. Directors in the period retained most of their power, though often it was modulated by the growing importance of designers for productions that returned to the spectacular mode. In a male-dominated profession women directors like Ariane *Mnouchkine in France, Deborah *Warner in England, and Karin Beier in Germany brought new ideas and approaches, while actors like Alan *Howard and Helen *Mirren established international reputations through Shakespeare. The RSC remained important but no longer held the dominant artistic position as Shakespeare spread around the globe in a mélange of fashions. Productions at Stratford by Michael *Bogdanov, however (e.g. *The Taming of the Shrew* in 1978 and *Romeo and Juliet* in 1986), were consistently stimulating and often attracted young audiences. With the actor Michael *Pennington, Bogdanov went on to found the *English Shakespeare Company as a touring organization, and their marathon rendition of the history plays, *The Wars of the Roses* (1987–8), was an exciting experiment that used post-modern strategies of crossing time periods. Warner's work with the RSC and the *National Theatre was particularly gripping, from powerful versions of *Titus Andronicus* and *King Lear* (1987 and 1990, with Brian Cox acting in both) to *Richard II* (1995) with Fiona Shaw playing the King in a gender-neutral manner.

One of the continuing troubles of the RSC lay in its theatres. London operations were transferred in 1982 to the *Barbican Arts Centre, an uninviting building with a main house even more unsuited for Shakespeare than the large theatre in Stratford. A smaller space with an open plan, the Swan (1986) has been a godsend at Stratford; this and the remodelled Other Place were sites for much of the company's most valuable work. Some mainstream British productions suffered from a connection to 'heritage' made during the Thatcher–Major years, a movement that stressed the high art or ancestral merit in Shakespeare and was in opposition to the contemporary values ascribed to the plays in the earlier post-war period. A battle for the ownership of the national dramatist was taking place and spread beyond the academy onto the pages of the popular press, with members of the royal family entering the fray. Theatres, suffering declining subsidies in the same period, were often forced to rely on an appeal to cultural tourism to fill their seats. This was most apparent in the construction of 'Shakespeare's Globe' in London, a project begun by the American actor Sam Wanamaker in the 1970s and completed in 1997 after his death. Controversy has surrounded both the cultural intent of the project and its claim to architectural authenticity, though few deny the powerful effect of watching a play while standing in the yard of the open-roofed space. The productions staged there in the summers have yet to reach first-class status but have returned audiences to a central role in Shakespeare performance.

Shakespeare became in these years dramatic currency for much of the world. The long German tradition of innovative performance continued; older directors like Peter *Zadek and Peter *Stein were still active in the 1990s, while younger ones brought unexpected ideas for a post-Cold War world, like Karin Beier's 'Euro-Shakespeare'—a rendition of *A Midsummer Night's Dream* (1995) that used fourteen actors from nine countries, all speaking their native languages. Some Paris performances relied upon the intercultural method of crossing Shakespeare with Kabuki or Kathakali (Mnouchkine's history plays, 1981–4), or seeing *The Tempest* through Indian and African styles (Brook, 1990), while Daniel Mesguich showed a series of plays influenced by the cultural theories of Derrida and Lacan. The Québécois director Robert *Lepage, in productions in English and French (and sometimes in both), added to the growing interest of seeing Shakespeare's work as related to colonial formations and globalized or postcolonial circumstances. In Tokyo the remarkable direction of Yukio *Ninagawa combined Japanese traditional ideas with Western styles (*Macbeth* and *The Tempest* in the 1980s, *A Midsummer Night's Dream* and *Hamlet* in the 1990s, all touring to the UK), and Hideki Noda transposed the plays into modern Japanese environments (his 1990 *Much Ado About Nothing*, for example, was set in the world of sumo wrestling). After the disruptions of the Cultural Revolution even *China staged Shakespeare festivals in the period. If all the world had not yet been conquered by a 400-year-old dead white male dramatist, much of it found Shakespeare's work rich enough to appropriate again and again. *DK*

Beauman, Sally, *The Royal Shakespeare Company* (1982)
Berry, Ralph, *On Directing Shakespeare* (1989)
Holland, Peter, *English Shakespeares* (1997)
Hortmann, Wilhelm, *Shakespeare on the German Stage* (1998)
Kennedy, Dennis (ed.), *Foreign Shakespeare* (1993)
Kennedy, Dennis, *Looking at Shakespeare* (1993)
Speaight, Robert, *Shakespeare on the Stage* (1973)

Twine, Laurence (fl. 1564–76), prelate and translator. Twine's romance *The Pattern of Painful Adventures* is one of the sources for Shakespeare's *Pericles*. Twine took his story of a wandering protagonist called Apollonius of Tyre, a riddle concerning incest, and an innocent girl in a brothel from a Latin collection of stories called *Gesta Romanorum*. The *Pattern* may have been published as early as 1576 but also appeared in editions of 1594 and 1607. It was probably the latter that Shakespeare read and that he drew upon for Marina's scenes. *JKS*

twins feature prominently in two of Shakespeare's plays, *The Comedy of Errors* (which complicates its source play, *Plautus' *The Menaechmi*, by adding a second pair of identical brothers, the Dromios, as servants to Antipholus of Syracuse and Antipholus of Ephesus respectively) and *Twelfth Night* (which depends on the biologically impossible resemblance between Viola and her brother Sebastian: in nature identical twins are always of the same sex). Many have been tempted to find autobiographical resonances in these scenes, particularly in the latter play, since Shakespeare was himself the father of Hamnet and Judith, born 26 May 1583 (see Shakespeare, Hamnet; Shakespeare, Judith). Hamnet had died in August 1596: *Twelfth Night* (1601) perhaps poignantly entertains the notion that a dead twin brother might remain alive in the likeness of his surviving sister ('I my brother know | Yet living in my glass', observes the disguised Viola, 3.4.371–2). *MD*

Two Gentlemen of Verona, The *(see opposite page)*

Two Noble Kinsmen, The *(see page 500)*

Tybalt is the hot-tempered nephew of Capulet's wife. He kills Mercutio and is himself killed by Romeo, *Romeo and Juliet* 3.1. *AB*

Tyler, Richard (1566–1636), friend, probably schoolmate, of Shakespeare, who left him a ring in the first draft of his will. He was replaced by Hamnet *Sadler, possibly because in the meantime he had been accused of misappropriating funds raised for victims of the great Stratford *fire. He had a son called William, and two of his daughters bear the same names as Shakespeare's, but Tyler's wife, too, was Susanna. He signed a deed of 1617/18 relating to the transfer of the *Blackfriars Gatehouse. *SW*

Tyler, Thomas (1826–1902), English scholar, a founding member of the New Shakespeare Society (1873). On 13 June 1884 (and later on 11 October 1889) he was the first to propose, against some resistance, Mary Fitton, the Queen's maid of honour, as the *'Dark Lady' of the Sonnets (see his edition, 1890). *TM*

Tymandra. See Phrynia.

(cont. on page 503)

The Two Gentlemen of Verona

This perennially fresh and pleasantly fallible comedy may be Shakespeare's first work for the professional stage, probably composed around 1590. The first of the six Shakespearian comedies mentioned by Francis *Meres's *Palladis Tamia* in 1598, its dramatic technique suggests inexperience, and its tone is far closer to that of the courtly comedies of the 1580s (such as *Lyly's *Midas*, 1588–9, which at one point it echoes) than is that of any other Shakespearian comedy. Certain scholars have placed *The Two Gentlemen of Verona* in the mid-1590s, sometimes on the grounds that its debts to Arthur *Brooke's poem *Romeus and Juliet* suggest a date closer to that of the infinitely more accomplished *Romeo and Juliet*, but allusions in *Richard Duke of York* (*3 Henry VI*) show that Shakespeare already knew Brooke's poem much earlier. While others have evolved theories of piecemeal revision that would date certain passages as late as 1598, no modern scholar has placed the bulk of its composition any later than 1594, and recent studies have tended to place it earlier in the canon rather than later.

Text: The play is printed as the second play in the First *Folio, 1623: there is no evidence of any earlier attempt to publish it. The Folio text, which is for the most part a reliable one (though unusually short), seems to derive from a transcript by the scribe Ralph *Crane: it displays characteristic features of his work such as the listing at the head of each scene of all the characters who will appear in it, and the omission of all stage directions except exits. Various inconsistencies may suggest that Crane was transcribing Shakespeare's own *foul papers, an authorial draft which retained a high proportion of loose ends, but the text's consistency with *speech-prefixes (unusual even for Crane) may suggest that he was working from a fair copy prepared for theatrical use, in which case its brevity may result from abridgement for some specific performance. The small amount of profanity in *The Two Gentlemen of Verona* as it stands, which distinguishes it sharply from the other early comedies, supports this latter possibility, suggesting that the play had been expurgated for a revival since the *Act to Restrain Abuses of Players, 1606.

Sources: Jorge de *Montemayor's prose romance *La Diana enamorada* (1559) provided the outline of the Proteus and Julia plot, perhaps in Bartholomew Yonge's translation (1582, printed 1598), but more probably via the lost play **Felix and Philiomena* (performed at court in 1585). A parallel to the Proteus–Valentine–Silvia situation is found in the story of Titus and Gisippus in *Boccaccio's *Decameron*, retold in Sir Thomas *Elyot's *The Governor* (1531), which Shakespeare may echo in his last scene. Other details are drawn from *Ovid, from *Lyly's *Sapho and Phao* (1584), and from Brooke's *Romeus and Juliet* (1562): some of the play's minor confusions as to whether the action is taking place in Verona, Mantua, or Milan may result from Shakespeare's alternation between different sources. Only the Lance and Crab scenes seem entirely original.

Synopsis: **1.1** Valentine parts from his friend Proteus, whom he mocks for being in love with Julia, in order to travel to Milan. His servant Speed, who has just delivered a love letter to Julia for Proteus to no apparent effect, follows him. **1.2** Julia receives Proteus' letter from her maid Lucetta, who speaks in his favour: she appears to be angry, and tears the letter up, but cannot subsequently resist the temptation to reassemble such pieces as she can. **1.3** Proteus' father resolves to give Proteus the same opportunities Valentine is enjoying by sending him, too, to the Milanese court: surprised while reading his first love letter from Julia, Proteus, in part as a result of feigning that the letter is from Valentine, is compelled to agree to this course of action.

2.1 In Milan, Valentine has fallen in love with Silvia. She has commissioned Valentine to write a letter for her to 'one she loves', and when she inspects what he has written he cannot understand what she means by telling him to keep it; Speed has to explain that Valentine is himself the object of her love. **2.2** Exchanging rings with vows of mutual fidelity, Proteus and Julia part. **2.3** Proteus' servant Lance and his dog Crab are also off to Milan: deploring the dry-eyed callousness of his dog, Lance comically re-enacts his lachrymose parting from his family. **2.4** Valentine bickers with his rival for Silvia's love, Thurio, until her father the Duke announces the imminent arrival of Proteus. Valentine presents his friend to Silvia, and, when Silvia and Thurio have departed, reveals his plan to elope with her, in which he enlists Proteus as an accomplice. Left alone, Proteus confesses that he has himself fallen in love with Silvia. **2.5** Speed welcomes Lance to Milan, and they joke about their masters' loves. **2.6** Proteus decides to reveal Valentine's planned elopement to the Duke, so as to ensure Valentine's banishment and leave only the dim-witted Thurio as a rival. **2.7** The lovelorn Julia instructs Lucetta to provide her with a male disguise in which she can safely follow Proteus to Milan.

3.1 Proteus betrays the imminent elopement of Silvia with Valentine to the Duke, who finds Valentine already equipped with the rope ladder by which he means to effect it. The Duke immediately banishes Valentine, who receives hypocritical comfort from Proteus. Lance detains Speed for a pragmatic discussion about a milkmaid whom he is proposing to marry. **3.2** Ostensibly only at the Duke's insistence and in the interests of Thurio, whose suit the Duke favours, Proteus agrees to slander Valentine to Silvia, and to help Thurio woo her with poetry and music.

4.1 Valentine and Speed are ambushed by outlaws, who, impressed by Valentine's eloquence, offer him the choice of being killed or becoming their leader: he chooses the latter. **4.2** Proteus reflects on his falsehood, and the reproaches with which Silvia has so far repaid his courtship, before Thurio arrives with musicians, who perform the song *'Who is Silvia? What is she?' beneath her window. Meanwhile, conducted by her host, Julia has arrived, disguised as a page, and she watches both the serenade and, after Thurio's departure, Proteus' continuing attempts to woo Silvia. **4.3** Silvia enlists the help of Sir Eglamour to follow Valentine into exile. **4.4** Lance laments the misbehaviour of Crab, whom he has offered as a gift to Silvia in place of a lapdog from Proteus which he has lost, describing how he has often been forced to assume responsibility for Crab's unhygienic misdemeanours. Proteus arrives with the disguised Julia, whom, as 'Sebastian', he unwittingly takes into his employment as a worthier messenger than Lance has been: he entrusts her with the very ring she herself gave him at parting as a gift for Silvia. Horrified at her situation, Julia nonetheless goes to perform this errand, though Silvia refuses the ring: the two women fall into conversation about the supposedly absent Julia, whom Silvia pities.

5.1 Sir Eglamour and Silvia fly from Milan and towards the forest. **5.2** The Duke brings the news of their flight to Proteus, Thurio, and Julia, who each agree to follow him in his pursuit of them. **5.3** In the forest, three outlaws have captured Silvia while others chase the fleeing Sir Eglamour. **5.4** Valentine reflects on the suitability of the forest as a setting for his solitary yearning for Silvia: hearing the sounds of a struggle, he hides, and sees Proteus, still followed by the disguised Julia, arrive with Silvia, whom he has rescued from the outlaws. Both Julia and Valentine watch in dismay as Proteus courts the resolute Silvia with increasing aggression until he actually attempts rape, at which Valentine confronts him with his treachery. On Proteus' repentance, Valentine accepts him once more as a friend, and abruptly resigns Silvia to him. At this Julia faints, and when her identity is discovered a yet more penitent Proteus disavows his preference for Silvia. Valentine joins their hands. The outlaws arrive with the Duke and Thurio as captives, and when the cowardly Thurio, threatened by Valentine, renounces his own claim on Silvia, she is bestowed by the Duke on Valentine. Valentine successfully requests the Duke to repeal the outlaws' banishment along with his own, and with the double marriage of Valentine and Silvia, Proteus and Julia in prospect, all set off back towards Milan.

Artistic features: The play shows a reliance on soliloquy, asides, and duologues unique in the canon: one of the reasons the famous serenade scene, 4.2, stands out so vividly is that it is one of the play's only fully successful scenes involving more than three characters at a time. The play shows unusual carelessness (the Duke is sometimes referred to as 'the Emperor', and Shakespeare often appears to forget that his two Veronese gentlemen are not at home at his court in Milan), but its verse, though sometimes lame, can rise to moments of genuine and unexpected lyricism (as in Proteus' advice to Thurio, 3.2.72–86), and the supple comic prose of Lance's monologues has rarely been excelled.

Critical history: Neglected for two centuries after Shakespeare's death (with Upton refusing to believe it was authentically Shakespearian, and *Johnson's praise confined to individual passages at the expense of its structure), the play has frequently suffered from being read solely as an unsuccessful anticipation of the later comedies, particularly *Twelfth Night*, and discussions of *The Two Gentlemen of Verona* in its own right are still comparatively rare. Along with the other early comedies, it has often been dismissed as apprentice work, and most commentators have found Valentine's attempt to give away Silvia to the man who has just tried to rape her profoundly objectionable. Much modern writing about the play has concentrated on attempting to explain this gesture, whether in terms of Renaissance views on the relative claims of friendship, love, and gratitude, or in terms of the literary conventions of courtly romance. It is noticeable that the play has been consistently more highly regarded on the Continent than in Britain, with G. G. *Gervinus among its few 19th-century advocates (drawing attention, in *Shakespeare*, 1849–50, to its sophisticated use of parallelism, a subject taken up a century later in an important essay by Harold F. Brooks). H. B. Charlton, in his influential account of

Shakespearian comedy (1938), claimed that the play was an artistic failure, its aspirations towards romance producing only ludicrous bathos, and while subsequent critics (such as Alexander Leggatt) have been less inclined to regard all an audience's laughs at the central characters' expense as unintended by Shakespeare, the notion that certain figures in the play (notably Julia) are fatally out of drawing with the play's Lylyan genre remains a prevalent one in recent discussions.

Stage history: The Folio's text may suggest that the play was still in use by Shakespeare's company as late as 1606, but since the Renaissance it has been one of his least successful plays in the theatre: in England only *Love's Labour's Lost* was slower to be revived as Shakespeare's comedies increased in status and popularity down the 18th century. The earliest recorded performances of *The Two Gentlemen of Verona* did not take place until 1762, at *Drury Lane, in a version adapted by the minor playwright Benjamin Victor, who tried to lighten the last act by adding new material for Lance, Crab, and Speed and removing Valentine's renunciation of Silvia to Proteus (a cut often repeated over the ensuing years as the romantic celebration of male friendship over love grew ever less usual in the culture at large). The play was revived briefly at *Covent Garden in 1784, and by J. P. *Kemble in 1790 and 1808, but its only really popular British production before the mid-20th century was in 1821, when Frederick *Reynolds initiated a recurrent strand in its stage history by drastically adapting it as a *musical.

In common with subsequent 19th-century productions, this version idealized Valentine, who is presented as a figure of perfect chivalry in the only well-known painting derived from this play, the *Pre-Raphaelite Holman Hunt's *Valentine Rescuing Silvia from Proteus* (later renamed *The Two Gentlemen of Verona*), 1851. The play was a failure successively for William Charles *Macready (1841), Charles *Kean (1846 in New York, 1848 in London), Samuel *Phelps (1857), Osmond Tearle (Stratford, 1890), Augustin *Daly (1895, with Ada *Rehan as Julia), and Harley *Granville-Barker (1904), and while William *Poel's 'Elizabethan' production at His Majesty's theatre (1910) attracted some attention, sporadic revivals in Stratford and London during the inter-war years still failed to establish the play in the British public's imagination. In theatrical circles the play even acquired the derisive nickname 'The Walking Gentlemen' ('walking gentleman' is stock-company slang for a wholly undistinguished minor male role). The play was more popular with French and German audiences (Theodore Fontane, seeing Phelps's revival, had clamoured for a Berlin production as early as 1857), enjoying a major production at the Odéon in 1902, and proving immensely popular in Weimar Germany in Hans *Rothe's free translation (1933): it has held the stage in Europe since the Second World War in productions such as that of Gundalf Gründgen (Düsseldorf, 1948).

The play's post-war fortunes in the English-speaking theatre have been more mixed. At Regent's Park in 1949 it was heavily abridged by Robert *Atkins to share a bill with *The Comedy of Errors*, but within ten years came two far more lavish, and highly successful, productions at the *Old Vic, one (by Denis Carey, transferring to London from Bristol) in the style of a Renaissance masque (1952, with John *Neville as Valentine), and one (by Michael Langham, 1957) in a Regency setting (with Barbara *Jefford as Julia). Both added a great deal of incidental music. Attempts to supplement the appeal of music and decor by resort to post-Freudian psychology have generally been unsuccessful: Robin Phillips's incipiently camp 1970 production for the RSC (which set the play in an adolescent, beach-oriented world reminiscent of body-building advertisements) pleased few, and John *Barton's harshly satiric abbreviation of 1981 (on a double bill with an equally truncated *Titus Andronicus*) few more. The most successful English-language productions of the play have continued to be musical adaptations, notably Joseph Papp's 1971 revival in New York, and David Thacker's 1994 RSC production at the Swan, given a 1930s setting and supplied with additional songs from the works of Cole *Porter and his contemporaries. For directors such as these the poor esteem in which the play has generally been held, licensing inventive stage-business and making the play's naive charm always come as something of a pleasant surprise, seems to have been positively liberating. *MD*

On the screen: *The Two Gentlemen of Verona* has yet to tempt Hollywood, though various glimpses of it appear in the popular *Shakespeare in Love* (1998). The one extant full-length production on video is the BBC TV version, 1978, which cast convincingly young but disappointingly inept performers in the leads but boasted a strong Lance in Tony Haygarth. *AD*

Recent major editions

Clifford Leech (Arden 2nd series, 1969); Kurt Schlueter (New Cambridge, 1990)

Some representative criticism

Brooks, Harold F., 'Two Clowns in a Comedy (to Say Nothing of the Dog): Speed, Launce (and Crab) in *The Two Gentlemen of Verona*', *Essays and Studies* (1963)

Charlton, H. B., in *Shakespearian Comedy* (1938)

Dobson, Michael, 'A Dog at All Things: The Transformation of the Onstage Canine, 1550–1850', *Performance Research International*, 5/2 (2000)

Hamilton, A. C., in *The Early Shakespeare* (1967)

Leggatt, Alexander, in *Shakespeare's Comedy of Love* (1974)

Schlueter, June (ed.), *The Two Gentlemen of Verona: Critical Essays* (1996)

Tillyard, E. M. W., in *Shakespeare's Early Comedies* (1965)

Wells, Stanley, 'The Failure of *The Two Gentlemen of Verona*', *Shakespeare Jahrbuch*, 94 (1963)

The Two Noble Kinsmen

This bitter-sweet tragicomedy of love and death, co-written with John *Fletcher, includes what was almost certainly Shakespeare's last writing for the stage. Excluded from the *Folio, presumably because of its collaborative authorship, the play was not published until 1634: both the *Stationers' Register entry and the quarto's title page attribute it to 'William Shakespeare and John Fletcher'. The play borrows its *morris dance (3.5) from Francis *Beaumont's *Masque of the Inner Temple and Gray's Inn* (February 1613), while its prologue's reference to 'our losses' almost certainly alludes to the burning down of the *Globe (June 1613). Probably composed during 1613–14, *The Two Noble Kinsmen* may well have been the first play to appear at the rebuilt Globe on its opening in 1614: certainly two sarcastic allusions to 'Palamon' in Ben *Jonson's *Bartholomew Fair* (premièred in October 1614) suggest that Jonson expected this play to be fresh in his spectators' minds.

Text: The 1634 quarto provides the only substantive text of *The Two Noble Kinsmen*, and its various inconsistencies—including variant spellings, such as 'Perithous' and 'Pirithous', 'Ialor' and 'Iaylor'—suggest that it was set from *foul papers in the hands of both playwrights, though these had probably been annotated with reference to later performances (some stage directions, for example, accidentally mention the actors Curtis Greville and Thomas Tuckfield, who were both members of the King's Company only between 1625 and mid-1626). The general scholarly consensus, based on variant spellings in the text and, especially, considerations of style, metre, and vocabulary, is that Shakespeare wrote Act 1, 2.1, 3.1–2, and most of Act 5 (excluding 5.4), and Fletcher the rest (including the Prologue and Epilogue). Although both playwrights presumably agreed on the overall structure of the play, it appears from minor discrepancies between their respective shares that they wrote independently of one another, Shakespeare concentrating on the Theseus frame-narrative and the establishment and closure of the Palamon–Arcite plot, Fletcher on the intervening rivalry between Palamon and Arcite and the sub-plot of the Jailer's Daughter.

Sources: The play is primarily a dramatization of Geoffrey *Chaucer's Knight's Tale, the first and one of the most highly regarded of *The Canterbury Tales*: this well-known work had already been dramatized at least twice, once by Richard Edwards as *Palaemon and Arcyte* (performed before Queen Elizabeth at Christ Church, Oxford, in 1566, but never printed) and once as another lost play with the same title, acted in 1594. Surviving eyewitness accounts of Edwards's play suggest that Shakespeare and Fletcher may have remembered it at some points (their Palamon, for example, recalls at 5.6.44–5 that he has said Venus is false: in fact he has not done so, though his counterpart in Edwards's play did). Shakespeare and Fletcher may also have known Chaucer's source, *Boccaccio's *Teseida* (in which Arcite's horse falls backwards onto him, as in the play, rather than pitching him off forwards as in Chaucer). Their chief alterations to Chaucer are the addition of the three queens and their interruption to Theseus' wedding procession (itself influenced by Shakespeare's earlier treatment of Theseus' wedding preparations in *A Midsummer Night's Dream*), the stipulation that the loser of the Palamon–Arcite duel must die, and the added sub-plot of the Jailer's Daughter. This sub-plot itself recalls earlier motifs in the Shakespeare canon: most obviously her madness recalls Ophelia and Desdemona's remembered maid Barbara, but her position as lovestruck helper of her father's prisoner (and her obsession with storms at sea) also recalls Miranda's role in *The Tempest* 3.1.

Synopsis: A prologue, comparing new plays to maidenhoods, boasts that this one derives from Chaucer and ought to please. 1.1 Preceded by a boy who sings an epithalamium, 'Roses, their sharp spines being gone', Theseus and his bride Hippolyta pass towards their wedding, accompanied by Theseus' comrade Pirithous and sister Emilia: they are stopped, however, by three mourning queens, whose husbands, killed fighting against the evil Creon of Thebes, have been denied burial. Their kneeling plea that Theseus should postpone his wedding until he has defeated Creon is seconded by Hippolyta and Emilia, and Theseus complies. 1.2 In Thebes, the inseparable cousins Palamon and Arcite, though anxious about the vicious state of their uncle Creon's regime, prepare to fight against Theseus. 1.3 Pirithous parts from Hippolyta and Emilia in order to rejoin Theseus. The women discuss the rival claims of same-sex friendship and love, Emilia tenderly remembering her dead friend Flavina. 1.4 The three queens bless Theseus for defeating Creon. Seeing the wounded and unconscious Palamon and Arcite, who have fought nobly, he orders they should be tended but kept prisoner. 1.5 The three queens process towards the separate funerals of their husbands to the dirge 'Urns and odours, bring away', and bid one another a solemn farewell.

2.1 A wooer talks with the Jailer about his projected marriage to the Jailer's Daughter, who speaks enthusiastically about the prisoners Palamon and Arcite. 2.2 Palamon and Arcite are consoling one another for their lost liberty with promises of eternal friendship when Palamon sees Emilia from the window, gathering flowers with her woman in the garden beneath. He falls in love with her, as does Arcite, and the two immediately quarrel as rivals for her. The Jailer takes Arcite away, released by Theseus but banished to Thebes, and takes Palamon to a cell with no view of the garden. 2.3 Arcite resolves to disguise himself so that he may remain near Emilia: learning from some countrymen of a sporting contest before Theseus, he decides to compete in it. 2.4 The Jailer's Daughter, in love with Palamon, decides to arrange his escape in the hope of earning his love. 2.5 The disguised Arcite is victor in the wrestling before Theseus, and Pirithous makes him master of horse to Emilia. 2.6 The Jailer's Daughter has freed Palamon and is about to run away from her father's house to meet him in the woods with food and a file to remove his manacles.

3.1 Arcite, who has followed Theseus, Emilia, and their party into the woods on their May morning hunt, is reflecting on how Palamon would envy him his position when Palamon, overhearing him, emerges from a bush. They agree that Arcite will fetch food and a file, and duel with Palamon when he has recovered his strength. 3.2 Sleepless and hungry, the Jailer's Daughter has failed to find Palamon, who she imagines has been eaten by wolves: full of self-reproach, she is beginning to lose her wits. 3.3 Arcite brings Palamon food: as he eats, the rivals reminisce about each other's past loves. 3.4 The Jailer's Daughter, mad, imagines a shipwreck. 3.5 Gerald the schoolmaster is rehearsing five countrymen, five countrywomen, and a taborer in the morris dance they are to

Imogen Stubbs as the Jailer's Daughter in Barry Kyle's production of *The Two Noble Kinsmen*, which opened the RSC's new Swan theatre in Stratford, 1986.

perform before Theseus when they realize they are a woman short: however, they recruit the mad Jailer's Daughter, and when Theseus and his party arrive they perform their elaborate dance, prefaced by Gerald's rhyming oration, as planned. 3.6 Arcite brings Palamon sword and armour: they arm each other carefully, but their duel is interrupted by the arrival of Theseus, Hippolyta, Emilia, and Pirithous. Learning of their identities and purposes, Theseus sentences both to death, but they are reprieved at the suit of Hippolyta and Emilia. However, they refuse Emilia's offer of peaceable banishment, refusing to renounce their quarrel over her, and when Emilia will not choose between them Theseus finally agrees that their mortal duel must resume. In a month's time each is to return with three knights: the winner of the contest will marry Emilia, the loser will be executed along with his three seconds.

4.1 The Jailer is relieved to learn that Palamon has cleared him of treason by explaining that it was his daughter who let him out of prison, but the Wooer brings the news of the Jailer's Daughter's madness, narrating how he found her wandering and singing and had to rescue her from drowning in a lake. She arrives herself with the Jailer's Brother, full of mad tales of Palamon's potency, and imagines sailing a ship to find Palamon in the woods: they do what they can to humour her. 4.2 Emilia, studying portraits of Arcite and of Palamon, is still unable to prefer one to the other. Theseus and Pirithous speak admiringly of the knights with whom the two rivals have returned to fight for Emilia. 4.3 A doctor, summoned by the Jailer and the Wooer, interviews the Jailer's Daughter, and prescribes that the Wooer should pretend to be Palamon.

5.1 Palamon and Arcite, accompanied by their seconds, bid a solemn farewell. Arcite prays at the altar of Mars for success in the combat, and is encouraged by a sound of thunder and arms. 5.2 Palamon prays at the altar of Venus for success in his quest for Emilia, and is encouraged by music and fluttering doves. 5.3 Emilia prays at the altar of Diana that if she is not to remain a maid she should be won by the contender who loves her best or has the truest title to her. A rose falls from the tree on the altar. 5.4 Despite the Jailer's misgivings, the Wooer, impersonating Palamon, takes the Doctor's advice to lead the Jailer's Daughter away to bed. 5.5 Emilia cannot bear to watch the combat, but hears its progress by offstage shouts and the reports of a servant: Palamon almost wins, but is defeated by Arcite. The victorious Arcite is presented to her by Theseus, who speaks regretfully of the doomed Palamon's valour. 5.6 Palamon and his three knights are about to be executed: Palamon bequeathes the Jailer his money as a wedding portion for his daughter. Pirithous arrives just in time to halt the execution, reporting that in the midst of his triumphal entry into Athens Arcite has been fatally injured, his horse rearing up and falling backwards onto him. Theseus, Hippolyta, and Emilia return, with the dying Arcite carried in a chair. Arcite bequeathes Emilia to Palamon. Theseus reflects on the ambiguous justice with which the gods have fulfilled their omens, and on humanity's restless impatience with what it has in favour of desire for what it lacks. An epilogue wonders anxiously how the audience have liked the play, assuring them it was intended only to please.

Artistic features: Shakespeare's sections of the play share their densely figured, knotty syntax and imagery with his other late romances, and display a similar interest in spectacularly rendered ritual. The play's stagecraft suggests it was composed with the *Blackfriars theatre in mind, and as a large-cast play with a classical-cum-medieval setting which makes extensive use of music it has much in common with other plays in the King's Company's Jacobean repertoire, not only *Pericles* but Thomas *Heywood's *The Golden Age*, *The Silver Age*, and *The Brazen Age*.

Critical history: Although some 19th-century critics accepted the quarto's attribution, *The Two Noble Kinsmen* was generally accepted into the Shakespeare canon only in the 20th century, and much critical writing about it continues to be preoccupied with the question of its authorship. Its restoration to the Shakespeare corpus, however, coincided with *modernism's high valuation for the complexities of Shakespeare's later style and with the ritual elements of drama. It coincided, too, with a *Freudian interest in the representation of *sexuality, and in recent years the Jailer's Daughter's 'green-sickness' and the controversial therapy applied to it have attracted a good deal of attention, as has the juxtaposition between the kinsmen's homosocial rivalry and the near-lesbianism of Emilia's passionate championing of female friendship.

Stage history: The play reappeared after the Restoration as *Davenant's cheerful adaptation *The *Rivals* (1664), its action transferred to a harmless Arcadia in which Celania (the Jailer's Daughter) marries Philander (Palamon) and Arcite survives to marry Heraclia (Emilia). This version influenced two later 18th-century rewritings, the much darker *Palamon and Arcite; or, The Two Noble Kinsmen* by Richard Cumberland (1779), and a musical, *Midsummer Night's Dream*-like version by F. G. Waldron, *Love and Madness; or, The Two Noble Kinsmen* (1795). The play was not revived professionally again until an *Old Vic production in 1928, designed to suggest a pretty homage to a Chaucerian Merry England. Despite many student productions it then disappeared from the professional stage until a more symbolic, morris-dance-free revival at the *Open Air Theatre in Regent's Park in 1974. Since then *The Two Noble Kinsmen* has been successfully revived at, among other venues, the Los Angeles Globe Playhouse (1979), the Edinburgh Festival (in a highly sexualized all-male production by the Cherub Theatre, 1979), the Centre Dramatique de Courneuve (also 1979), the Oregon Shakespeare Festival (1994), and the reconstructed *Globe (2000), but its most celebrated modern production remains Barry Kyle's, which opened the RSC's Swan auditorium in 1986. The main plot was given a stylized, samurai look, the rituals were impressive, and as the Jailer's Daughter Imogen Stubbs morris-danced away with the entire show, as

performers in that challenging but wonderfully showy role often do. The play has yet to be filmed. *MD*

Recent major editions

E. M. Waith (Oxford, 1989); G. R. Proudfoot (Regents Renaissance Drama series, 1970); N. Bawcutt (New Penguin, 1977); Lois Potter (Arden 3rd series, 1997)

Some representative criticism

Bertram, Paul, *Shakespeare and 'The Two Noble Kinsmen'* (1965)

Bruster, Douglas, 'The Jailer's Daughter and the Politics of Madwomen's Language', *Shakespeare Quarterly*, 46 (1995)

Foakes, R. A., 'Tragicomedy and Comic Form', in A. R. Braunmuller and J. C. Bulman (eds.), *Comedy from Shakespeare to Sheridan* (1986)

Frey, C. H. (ed.), *Shakespeare, Fletcher and 'The Two Noble Kinsmen'* (1989)

McMullan, Gordon, and Hope, Jonathan (eds.), *The Politics of Tragicomedy: Shakespeare and After* (1992)

Magnusson, Lynne, 'The Collapse of Shakespeare's High Style in *The Two Noble Kinsmen*', *English Studies in Canada*, 13 (1987)

Thompson, Ann, in *Shakespeare's Chaucer: A Study of Literary Origins* (1978)

Tynan, Kenneth (1927–80), British journalist and man of the theatre. A stage-struck, self-publicizing wit and dandy, he descended on London from Oxford and quickly dislodged the incumbent drama critic on the *Observer*. In *He that Plays the King* (1950) and subsequent books he vividly conjured up in print Shakespearian performances and productions. As literary manager in the early days of the *National Theatre he influenced the choice of plays and directors by the founder Laurence *Olivier, whose biography he aspired to write. *MJ*

Tyrrel, Sir James. Ordered by Richard to kill the princes in the Tower, *Richard III* 4.2, he suborns Dighton and Forrest to commit the murders. Guilty or not, the real Tyrrel died in 1502. *AB*

Tyrwhitt, Thomas (1730–86), a scholar and critic whose *Observations and Conjectures upon Some Passages of Shakespeare* (1766) was largely concerned with textual emendation. Other observations contributed to *Steevens's 1778 edition of Shakespeare and *Malone's Supplement of 1780. He was the first to draw attention to the list of Shakespeare's plays in *Meres's *Palladis Tamia* and to Robert *Greene's reference to Shakespeare on stage. *CMSA*

Ulrici, Hermann (1806–84), German academic. *Shakespeares dramatische Kunst* (1839; *Shakespeare's Dramatic Art*, 1876) is an attempt, leading later to the work of Edward *Dowden, to trace the growth and development of Shakespeare's dramatic art. He accepts James Boaden's 1837 identification of *'Mr W.H.' as William Herbert, 3rd Earl of *Pembroke.

TM

Ulysses is one of the Greek commanders in *Troilus and Cressida*, based on the character of the same name from *Homeric legend. *AB*

Underhill, William (1555–97), recusant. He inherited *New Place in 1570 and sold it to Shakespeare in 1597. His son Fulke was executed at Warwick in 1598–9 for poisoning him. His second son Hercules (b. 1581) confirmed Shakespeare's ownership of New Place. *SW*

'Under the greenwood tree', sung by Amiens in *As You Like It* 2.5.1. The earliest surviving setting is by Thomas *Arne (1741). Among many 20th-century settings are those by Coates, Gurney, Howells, Jacob, Moeran, Parry, and Quilter. The 'greenwood song' had been a genre in English verse long before Shakespeare; examples survive from the late Middle Ages. *JB*

Underwood, John (*c.*1588–1624), actor (Blackfriars Boys 1601–8, King's Men 1608–24). Underwood first appears in the Blackfriars Boys cast lists for *Jonson's *Cynthia's Revels* and *Poetaster* and he was one of the 'boys growing up to be men' (the others were William *Ostler and Nathan *Field) who joined the King's Men when the Blackfriars reverted to the Burbages in 1608. Underwood's name occurs in 22 King's Men's cast lists (including the 1623 Folio), although his only known roles are as Delio in *Webster's *The Duchess of Malfi*, Dapper in Jonson's *The Alchemist*, and Bonario in Jonson's *Volpone*. His will indicates that he owned shares in the *Curtain, *Globe, and *Blackfriars playhouses. *GE*

United States of America. There is no record of any performance of Shakespeare's work in the early American colonies—understandably, given their Puritan leanings—nor do his works appear to have been widely read in North America during this period. In 1752 a production of *Richard III* was mounted in New York by Thomas Kean and Walter Murray, probably the first full-scale production of any play by Shakespeare to be performed in what eventually became the United States of America. Shakespeare's works were well known to the founding fathers. George Washington owned a one-volume edition of Shakespeare's works, though he makes no significant reference to any of the plays in his extensive writings and personal papers. He also regularly attended the theatre and undoubtedly saw a number of Shakespeare's plays performed (including the *Davenant–Dryden adaptation of *The Tempest*, performed in Philadelphia during the 1784 discussions of the constitution). John *Adams quoted extensively from Shakespeare's works, often in a context of political reflection on the institutions of government. In the *Discourses on Davila* (1790–1) he used passages from *Troilus and Cressida* to support arguments for class distinctions based on true merit within the social structure of the new American democracy. Abigail Adams attended plays with her husband, and frequently quoted from Shakespeare's works in her private correspondence. There are numerous quotations from Shakespeare in the commonplace books of Thomas Jefferson, who thought the plays valuable as moral instruction. In 1786 Adams and Jefferson made a visit to Shakespeare's *birthplace in *Stratford-upon-Avon. In a diary entry for that day, Adams laments the apparent indifference of Stratford residents to the historical importance and the originality of Shakespeare's achievement.

The great theorist of Shakespeare's originality is Ralph Waldo *Emerson, who provides a fully elaborated account of the poet in *Representative Men* (1850). Emerson maintains that 'the great Shakespeare' was unknown to the men and women of Elizabethan England. The originality of his work is a 'discovery' of modern culture. Although he acknowledges that other countries have a certain capacity for appreciating the bard—he nominates Shakespeare the 'father of German literature' through translations by *Wieland and *Schlegel—Emerson maintains that the 'wisdom of life' revealed in Shakespeare's work can be most powerfully felt in the United States: 'He wrote the text of modern life; the text of manners: he drew the man of England and Europe; the father of the man in America.' Shakespeare's works are a powerful medium of tuition for the autonomous or self-governing citizen of democracy. For this reason Shakespeare and America have a strong elective affinity, for it is in America, according to Emerson, that the social aims of individuality and self-reliance will be most fully realized.

Emerson's idealization of Shakespeare was not universally accepted by his contemporaries, including his occasional tenant Henry David Thoreau, who admired the 'wildness' he found in *Hamlet*, but in general felt that America had no genuine need for the bookishness of European literature, Shakespeare included. Walt Whitman, though he respected Shakespeare's talents as a poet, felt the works were 'poisonous to the idea of the pride and dignity of the common people, the life-blood of democracy'. Mark *Twain had a much more radically sceptical view of Shakespeare's writings, especially vis-à-vis their relationship to their author. In one of his last books, *Is Shakespeare Dead?*

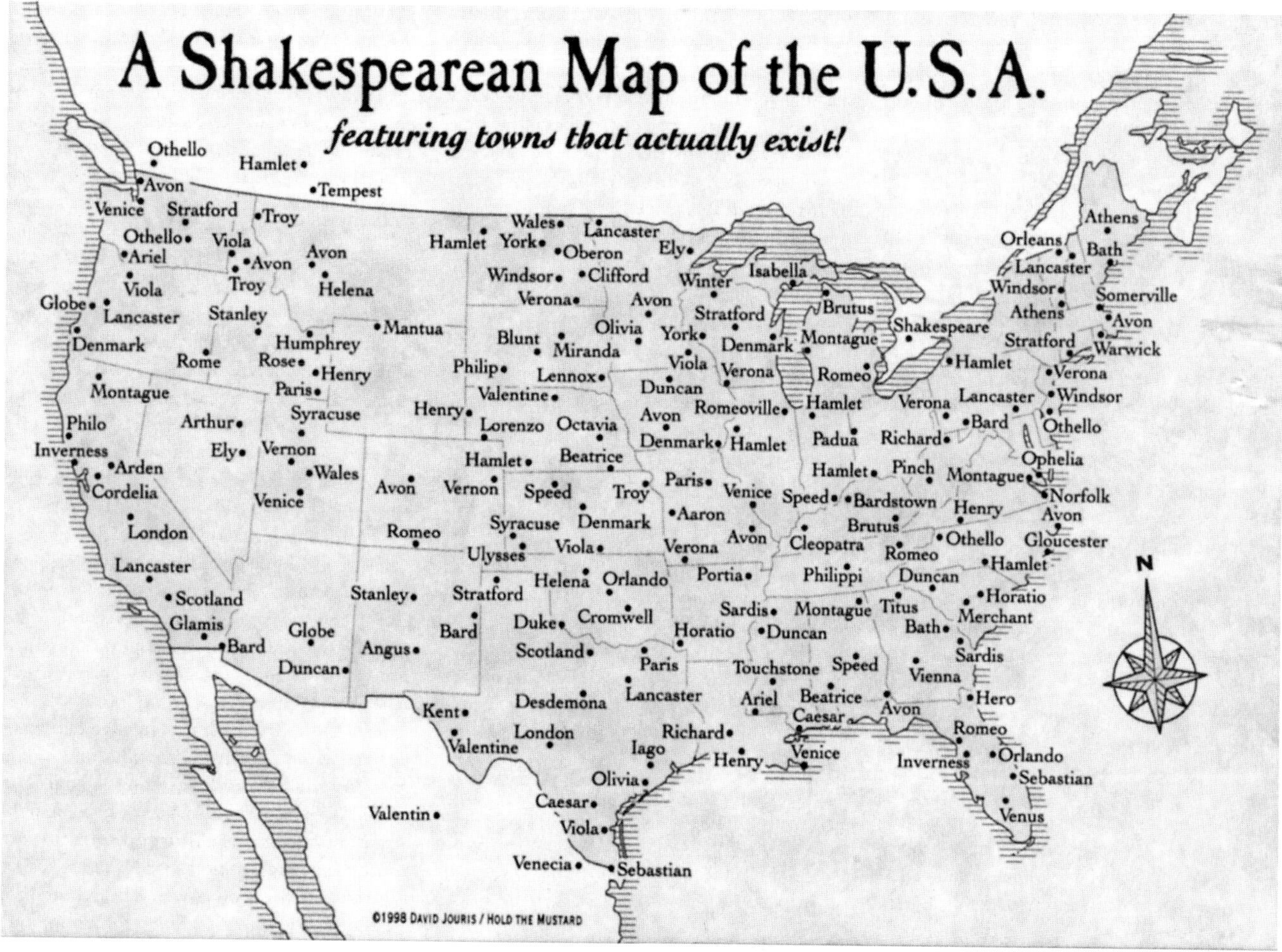

This 1998 novelty postcard, which assumes a thorough familiarity with the Shakespeare canon, attests to the continuing presence of Shakespeare in American popular culture.

(1909), he maintains that William Shakespeare is not in fact the author of the works that bear his name. Twain originally became interested in the question of Shakespeare's authorship with the publication of Delia *Bacon's *Philosophy of the Plays of Shakspere Unfolded* in 1857. This interest was fuelled by the publication of works such as Nathaniel Holmes's *Authorship of the Plays Attributed to Shakespeare* (1866) and Ignatius Donnelly's *The Great Cryptogram* (1888). Twain's own scepticism about Shakespeare's authorship was prompted by his observation that the technical discourse of seamanship and other trades in the plays was unconvincing. He found evidence, however, of expert handling of the vocabulary of the law courts. The real Shakespeare, therefore, must have been a lawyer. William Shakespeare of Stratford is a 'false claimant' who could not have been the author of 'Shakespeare's' works.

Twain's brilliant pastiche of quotations from *Hamlet* and *Macbeth* in *Huckleberry Finn* (1885) suggests the various ways Shakespearian drama was democratized in the United States during the 19th century through its close and familiar engagement with American popular cultural forms. Audiences who preferred their Shakespeare 'straight' could enjoy the work of touring companies, both English and home-grown, that performed the plays in cities and towns from east to west during the 19th century. Edwin *Booth, son of the British actor Junius Brutus *Booth, managed the Winter Garden theatre in New York where many of Shakespeare's plays were performed. Edwin's brother John Wilkes Booth, Lincoln's assassin, was himself a well-known actor of Shakespearian roles. The first of the great American-born actor-managers was Edwin *Forrest, who was especially popular for his renditions of Othello and King Lear. But Shakespeare was also performed by many itinerant companies on the American frontier, where the plays were often combined with circus acts and other forms of popular entertainment. There is also a large body of Shakespeare parody, *burlesque, *adaptation, and other derivative forms extant from this period. At times the plays were extensively adapted with a view to making them more immediately topical. Public tensions between traditional and more populist approaches to Shakespearian performance eventually broke out in a bloody riot in May 1849 at the Astor Place Opera House in New York City. The provocation for this incident arose from antagonism between the American actor Edwin Forrest and his British rival William Charles *Macready. Macready was disliked for his affiliation with the wealthier and more privileged theatre-goers. He was driven from the stage by a crowd of working men who supported Forrest, both for his acting style and for his strongly nativist approach to Shakespearian drama.

Discussion of Shakespeare's plays frequently took place in organized clubs. *Shakespeariana* (1883–93) was a magazine created in response to the burgeoning American interest in Shakespeare. Its content ranged from debate over textual cruces to the latest developments in *Baconian theory, and it took a particular interest in Shakespeare clubs. In 1888, the magazine published a list of about 100 Shakespeare societies unearthed by the editorial department. The smallest, 'the club of two', carried on its proceedings entirely by correspondence. One of the most prestigious, the Shakespeare Society of *New York, had a library which comprised 2,000–3,000 volumes. Through these clubs, members acquired speaking, organization, and leadership skills that enabled them to develop and express their ideas in a public forum. Shakespeare societies cultivated self-reliance in forming opinions along with behaviours promoting civil group interaction. Willingness to consider alternative positions and to develop effective means of resolving conflicts were elements critical to the successful function of the public sphere. Engagement with the works of Shakespeare proved particularly useful to this end. Because of the dramatic nature of the material, members were often encouraged to assume roles during club readings, a practice that helped to enrich empathetic identification with alien viewpoints. Shakespeare societies were both gender-specific and mixed, and generally had between twelve and 30 members. They were instrumental in training women for public life in an atmosphere of public debate which, in the first half of the 19th century at least, consisted primarily of boisterous, white, male voices. Although clubs diffiered in areas of interest and levels of sophistication, proceedings were generally characterized quite seriously as 'work'. The Philadelphia Shakespeare society, formed in 1851 by four young lawyers, was initially more of a lark than a serious endeavour. 'Chance or fancy at the meeting' determined the play to be read, according to founding member Garrick Mallery. By the sixth year the membership had swelled to fifteen and at the meetings there was 'an infinity of good eating and drinking, but an infinitesimal amount of Shaksper, discussed. Indeed, on one occasion, the Society was disgraced by the omission to read or even quote a single line of the Poet.' By the following year, however, a more systematic study had begun, including plans for a library. When Horace Howard *Furness joined in 1860, members had agreed to prepare papers for each meeting.

Horace Howard Furness and his associates in the Philadelphia Shakespeare Society worked from the *Variorum edition of 1821, supplemented by an extensive reference library of commentary and philological scholarship. In order to eliminate this cumbersome physical apparatus Furness conceived the idea of a *new Variorum edition, the first volume of which was published in 1871. Furness was later instrumental in founding the first English department at the University of Pennsylvania. His extensive personal collection of early editions and other Shakespeariana forms the basis for the Furness collection at that university. An even more ambitious collection of rare books and manuscripts was assembled at around the same time by Henry Clay Folger, President of the Standard Oil Company. Folger's initial interest in Shakespeare was stimulated by a lecture given by Ralph Waldo Emerson at Amherst College, when Folger was an undergraduate. Folger's wife Emily Clara Jordan studied English literature at Vassar College and wrote her Master's thesis on Shakespeare's First Folio. Together the Folgers built up a massive collection of early *quartos, along with some 80 copies of the First *Folio. The site for the *Folger Library was chosen carefully so that the study of Shakespeare would dovetail neatly with existing American institutions. The library was built along the extension of a line joining the Lincoln Memorial, the Washington Monument, the US Capitol, the Library of Congress, and the Supreme Court. The Folger Library is now one of the world's major institutional and archival resources for the study of Shakespeare's plays.

Important 19th-century editions of Shakespeare were compiled by Henry *Hudson (1880–1), Richard Grant White (1857–66), and Joseph Crosby. E. E. Willoughby completed his *Printing of the First Folio* in 1932. Since its opening in 1932, the Folger Collection has been used by American editors of Shakespeare, most notably Charlton *Hinman, who began the laborious work of collating the various extant copies of the First Folio. Other important American editors of Shakespeare's works have included J. G. *McManaway, Fredson *Bowers, W. A. Neilson (1906), George Lyman *Kittredge (1936), Hardin Craig (1951), and David *Bevington (1973). American scholars such as Hardin Craig, Alfred *Harbage, and Louis B. Wright pioneered the critical exegesis of Shakespeare's plays read in their historical context. A number of gifted women scholars, including Lily Bess Campbell, Madeleine Doran, and Rosalie Colie, contributed significantly to this research programme. From about 1980 a major renovation of historical scholarship has developed, taking its inspiration from the work of Stephen Greenblatt. The vernacular tradition of Shakespeare criticism that traces its origins back to the work of Ralph Waldo Emerson continues in the voluminous writings on Shakespeare by Harold Bloom.

Shakespeare continues to figure prominently in American mass culture at the beginning of the 21st century. Max *Reinhardt's film version of *A Midsummer Night's Dream* (1935) established Shakespeare's commercial and artistic viability in mass media. In the late summer of 1938, the CBS and NBC networks produced competing cycles of Shakespearian works for the *radio. CBS used a number of contemporary film stars, such as Humphrey Bogart (Hotspur) and Edward G. Robinson (Petruchio), while NBC leaned almost exclusively on the then-fading talent of John *Barrymore. Orson *Welles, who played Sir Toby Belch for CBS, also produced, directed, and starred in notable film versions of *Macbeth* (1948) and *Othello* (1952). American film-makers have also adapted Shakespeare's works extensively by grouping large, recognizable fragments of works by Shakespeare into new, often contrasting, stories. Welles's *Chimes at Midnight* (1965) is a comprehensive reworking of Shakespeare's Lancastrian tetralogy told from the point of view of Falstaffi. There is a large group of works in which the production of one or more plays by Shakespeare provides the background for a story about the 'real life' of one or more actors. These works are often preoccupied with the interpenetration of artistic representation and ordinary reality. In George Cukor's *A Double Life* (1947), Ronald Colman appears as an actor whose performance in *Othello* provokes him to murder his own wife. Pastiche has become increasingly important in contemporary films such as Gus Van Sant's *My Own Private Idaho* (1991), which includes extensive quotation and paraphrase of the two parts of Shakespeare's *Henry IV*. *Looking for Richard* (1996) is filmed as a 'documentary' that follows the effiorts of a group of well-known American actors, led by Al Pacino, to make a film version of *Richard III*. Part of the point of this film is to demonstrate the effectiveness of American speech rhythms and intonation in speaking Shakespearian blank verse.

Cole *Porter's *Kiss Me Kate* (1951), and Jerome Robbins's and Leonard Bernstein's **West Side Story* (1957) are durable favourites as *musicals on the stage, as well as in their cinematic iterations. Shakespeare's familiarity is perhaps most vividly apparent in *Shakespearean Spinach*, a 1940 animated cartoon version of *Romeo and Juliet* with Popeye and Olive Oyl in the lead roles. *A Witch's Tangled Hare*, a 1959 Warner Brothers cartoon, offiers Bugs Bunny and Witch Hazel in a pastiche of selections from *Macbeth, Romeo and Juliet*, and *Hamlet*. Shakespearian parody has been featured in episodes of *Happy Days, Gilligan's Island, The Andy Griffith Show*, and *Moonlighting*. In the early 1950s comic-book (see STRIP-CARTOON SHAKESPEARE) versions of *Hamlet, Macbeth, Romeo and Juliet*, and *A Midsummer Night's Dream* were published by Classics Illustrated (a series later revived). Each of these condensed texts concludes with the following suggestion: 'Now that you have read the Classics Illustrated edition, don't miss the added enjoyment of reading the original, obtainable at your school or public library.' The contemporary vitality of Shakespeare's role in American *popular culture is perhaps most dramatically manifested in a series of comic-books 'suggested for mature readers' by the British author Neil Gaiman, published by DC comics. In this series, Shakespeare's genius as a poet is closely tied to his ordinariness as a man. His art records the various fragments of his own day-to-day experience, ranging from his feelings for his daughter Judith to his encounter in a local inn with two drunken sailors. These and similar incidents provide materials for *The Tempest*. In *The Sandman* comics, the story of

Shakespeare's life is articulated as a modern myth of self-realization. According to this highly American, democratic vision, Shakespeare's genius is nothing more than the ability to feel more keenly and to record one's own experience more vividly than other people do. *MB*

Bristol, Michael, *Shakespeare's America/America's Shakespeare* (1990)
Cartelli, Thomas, *Repositioning Shakespeare: National Formations, Postcolonial Appropriations* (1999)
Dunn, Esther Cloudman, *Shakespeare in America* (1939)
Gayley, Charles Mills, *Shakespeare and the Founders of Liberty in America* (1917)
Kuhl, E.P., 'Shakespeare and the Founders of America: *The Tempest*', *Philological Quarterly*, 41 (1962)
Levine, Lawrence, *Highbrow/Lowbrow: The Emergence of Cultural Hierarchy in America* (1988)
Rawlings, Peter (ed.), *Americans on Shakespeare, 1776–1914* (1999)
Thaler, Alwin, *Shakespeare and Democracy* (1941)

university performances. Dramatic performance and rhetoric were taught at Oxford and Cambridge as part of a classical humanist *education and from the mid-16th century plays in English were performed by the academic amateurs alongside plays in Latin. By the early 17th century the London theatre industry's effect was being felt. The *Parnassus plays written between 1598 and 1602 and performed at St John's College, Cambridge, made direct reference to the *Chamberlain's Men, Shakespeare, and *Jonson, and *The Tragedy of Caesar and Pompey*, 'Privately acted by the Students of Trinity Colledge in Oxford' according to the 1607 title page, was clearly influenced by the professional theatre's output. The universities could also be ahead of the industry: in 1605 *James I was entertained at Christ Church, Oxford, by Latin plays performed on a stage designed by Inigo *Jones using Sebastiano Serlio's principles of perspective foreshortening, a precursor of post-Restoration staging. *GE*

Boas, Frederick S., *University Drama in the Tudor Age* (1914)

'University Wits', a group of university-educated playwrights who are often credited with transforming English drama in the 1580s from the form it had taken for much of the 16th century—the didactic allegorical *interlude, written in monotonous, metrically clumsy verse—into the richly various forms it assumed in the 1590s, full of action and versatile poetry. This is not, perhaps, quite fair to the earlier English drama, which is sometimes clever and entertaining—nor to the many writers of the 1580s who did not attend university, such as Thomas *Kyd—but there is no denying the extraordinary theatrical metamorphosis that took place between 1580 and 1590, nor the University Wits' involvement in it. They were Thomas *Lodge, John *Lyly, and George *Peele from Oxford, and Robert *Greene, Christopher *Marlowe, and Thomas *Nashe from Cambridge. One striking thing about these writers is the sheer diversity of their achievements: with the exception of Marlowe and Peele, they all wrote prose as well as poetry and plays, and their influence on Shakespeare and his contemporaries was equally powerful in all three literary modes. Their learning, their ambition, and the pleasure they took in displaying their skills are evident in nearly everything they wrote. *RM*

'Upon the King', a four-line poem printed, anonymously and without title, beneath the engraving of King *James I on the frontispiece of the King's *Works*, edited by James Mountague, Bishop of Winchester, and published in 1616. It is ascribed to Shakespeare in two early manuscripts now in the *Folger Library. *SW*

ur-*Hamlet*, the name given to a play now lost, of unknown authorship, which may have been the main source for Shakespeare's *Hamlet*. The earliest reference to such a play is found in Thomas *Nashe's preface to *Menaphon* by Robert *Greene (1589) wherein he condemns those writers who plunder *Seneca for 'whole *Hamlets*—I should say handfuls—of tragicall speeches'. In 1594 a play called *Hamlet*, apparently old, was performed at Newington Butts. It may have been this play that Thomas *Lodge saw, inspiring the comparison in *Wit's Misery and the World's Madness* (1596) between a devil and 'the ghost, which cried so miserably at the Theatre, "Hamlet, revenge" '. The most likely author of the ur-*Hamlet* is *Kyd, whose name is punningly associated with the play in Nashe's preface. This would also explain the similarities between *The Spanish Tragedy* and *Hamlet*. Something about the nature of the ur-*Hamlet* may be glimpsed in the differences between the first and second quartos of Shakespeare's tragedy. Q1 (1603), probably a memorial reconstruction, gives Gertrude a greater part in the action and refers to Hamlet actually landing on English soil. In producing his text of Shakespeare's play, the author might have deliberately or accidentally borrowed these features from the ur-*Hamlet*. *JKS*

'Urns and odours, bring away', sung by an unspecified person or persons at the entrance of the three queens, with attendants, in *The Two Noble Kinsmen* 1.5.1. The original music is unknown. *JB*

Ursula is one of Hero's waiting-gentlewomen in *Much Ado About Nothing*. *AB*

Urswick, Christopher. See CHRISTOPHER, SIR.

vagrancy was not a problem peculiar to Elizabethan England: Acts of Parliament forbidding the movement of beggars from one place to another date from 1388. But the situation was exacerbated by the suppression, in the 1530s and 1540s, of those religious houses which had hitherto provided poor relief. The resultant increase in the number of beggars led to a series of measures confirming the illegality of vagrancy and seeking to make individual parishes responsible for their own poor, culminating in the great Poor Law of 1601 which defined exactly how this responsibility should be established. This did little, however, to solve the problem and the seeking out, arrest, and removal of vagrants to their parish of 'legal' settlement remained a preoccupation of parish and borough officials for many years; hence Dogberry's instruction to the watch to 'comprehend all vagrom men' (*Much Ado About Nothing* 3.3.32). *RB*

Tate, W. E., *The Parish Chest* (3rd edn. 1983)

Valentine. **(1)** He is in love with Silvia in *The Two Gentlemen of Verona*, but has to contend with his rivals Proteus and Thurio. **(2)** One of Titus' kinsmen, he helps restrain Chiron and Demetrius, *Titus Andronicus* 5.3. **(3)** He is one of Orsino's attendants in Act 1 of *Twelfth Night*. *AB*

Valeria brings news of the war to Volumnia and Virgilia, *Coriolanus* 1.3; joins in welcoming Coriolanus, 2.1; and accompanies the other women to the Volscian camp, 5.3. *AB*

Valerius, a Theban, tells Palamon and Arcite of Theseus' campaign against Thebes, *The Two Noble Kinsmen* 1.2. *AB*

Valerius, Publius. He is mentioned in the Argument of *The Rape of Lucrece*. *AB*

Valk, Frederick (1901–56), German actor. Born in Hamburg of Portuguese-Jewish extraction, he became leading man of the German-speaking theatre in Prague, where he played many of Shakespeare's protagonists. An actor of great emotional and physical power, he arrived in 1939 as a refugee in England, where on account of his guttural accent he was allowed to play only two of his Shakespearian roles—the outsiders Shylock and Othello. In 1955 he was invited to play Shylock at Stratford, Ontario, by Tyrone *Guthrie, who always regretted Valk never played Lear in Britain. He died suddenly at 55 shortly after playing his last Othello in Toronto. *MJ*

Valk, Diana, *Shylock for a Summer* (1958)

Valtemand (Voltimand) and Cornelius are sent with a message from Claudius to Norway, *Hamlet* 1.2.41, and bring a reply, 2.2.60–80. *AB*

Valverde, José María (1926–96). Spanish professor, poet, and translator of Shakespeare. He translated all the plays in prose (1967), but, unlike Luis *Astrana, he used natural, straightforward contemporary Spanish. He confessed that his were failed translations, as he should have rendered Shakespeare in verse, but did not have the time to do so. *ALP*

Vanbrugh, Violet (1867–1942), British actress. In 1892 she understudied Ellen *Terry and played Anne Boleyn in Henry *Irving's production of *All Is True* (*Henry VIII*) in which she later acted Queen Katherine with Beerbohm *Tree. Other strong parts were Lady Macbeth, and Mistress Ford in *The Merry Wives of Windsor*, often with her sister Dame Irene Vanbrugh as Mistress Page. Like their brother Sir Kenneth Barnes, principal of the Royal Academy of Dramatic Art for 46 years, they greatly advanced the status of the acting profession. *MJ*

Variorum Shakespeare. The idea of a variorum edition that would include a full range of information about Shakespeare, his stage, as well as texts annotated with the 'corrections and illustrations of various commentators' (title page, 1803, 1813, 1821) grew out of the work of Dr *Johnson, George *Steevens, and Edmond *Malone. Dr Johnson's edition of Shakespeare appeared in 1765 and provided a basis for the more scholarly edition by Steevens in 1773. This edition was reissued in ten volumes in 1773, and again in 1778–80, and 1785. A fourth edition, expanded to fifteen volumes, appeared in 1793, and this was followed in 1803 by a fifth edition in 21 volumes, revised and augmented by Isaac *Reed. This edition, which incorporated Malone's final researches on the English stage and on the chronology of Shakespeare's plays, is generally regarded as the first Variorum edition. Steevens disliked Shakespeare's poems, and omitted them from editions under his sway, so that they do not appear in 1803 or in the reprint of this edition in 1813. The first full Variorum edition therefore is that of 1821, also in 21 volumes, sometimes called the Boswell–Malone edition, because James Boswell, the son of Dr Johnson's biographer, oversaw it and relied on the superior text of Malone's edition of 1790. The first volume contains prefaces from earlier editions, commendatory verses, and an essay on metre; the second, a life of Shakespeare and Malone's reconsideration of the chronology of the plays; and the third presents an extended version of Malone's history of the English stage. In the remaining volumes, the works are heavily annotated on the page, and for the first time dated in an order close to that now generally accepted. This edition provided a basis for later scholarly editions of Shakespeare, and for *Furness's *New Variorum, begun in 1871. *RAF*

Varrius. **(1)** He is greeted by Duke Vincentio, *Measure for Measure* 4.5, and is present, 5.1 (mute part). **(2)** He delivers news to Pompey, *Antony and Cleopatra* 2.1. *AB*

Varro. **(1)** See VARRO'S SERVANT. **(2)** See VARRUS.

Varro's Servant and **Isidore's Servant** appear in *Timon of Athens* 2.2 to collect their masters' debts from Timon. Two of Varro's servants also try to claim debts, 3.4 (one of them is addressed by the name Varro). *AB*

Varrus (Varro) and **Claudio** are attendants who sleep as the ghost of Caesar appears to Brutus, *Julius Caesar* 4.2. *AB*

Vaughan, Sir Thomas. He is executed with Rivers and Gray, *Richard III* 3.3, and his ghost appears to Richard at *Bosworth, 5.5. *AB*

Vaughan Williams, Ralph (1872–1958), English composer. Vaughan Williams's interest in placing his work in an English musical tradition traced particularly to the 16th century encouraged a lifelong engagement with Shakespeare. He set lyrics from the plays throughout his career (some, such as *'Orpheus with his lute', 1901, 1925, more than once), composed incidental music for *Richard II* and *1 Henry IV* (1913), and dared to take on *Verdi by writing his own operatic treatment of *The Merry Wives of Windsor*, *Sir John in Love* (1924–8). Appropriately, one of his last film scores was for *The England of Elizabeth* (1955). *IBC*

Vaux. **(1)** He brings Margaret the news that Cardinal Beaufort is dying, *The First Part of the Contention (2 Henry VI)* 3.2.372–82. **(2)** Sir Nicholas Vaux is put in charge of Buckingham before his execution, *All Is True (Henry VIII)* 2.1. *AB*

Venice, in Shakespeare's day the pre-eminent city in Italy for commerce, arts, and politics, is the setting for much of *The Merchant of Venice* and Act 1 of *Othello*. *AB*

Venice, Duke of. **(1)** He presides over the court in *The Merchant of Venice* 4.1. **(2)** He presides over the senators who send Othello to Cyprus and acquits him of bewitching Desdemona, *Othello* 1.3. *AB*

ventage, the finger hole of a wind instrument (see *Hamlet* 3.2.345). *JB*

Ventidius **(1)** He is very grateful for Timon's generosity, *Timon of Athens* 1.2, but refuses to help him later in the play. **(2)** He rejects Silius' suggestion that he should continue his campaign in Parthia after defeating Pacorus, *Antony and Cleopatra* 3.1 (based on *Plutarch's account of Publius Ventidius Bassus). *AB*

Venus and Adonis *(see page 510)*

Verbruggen, Susannah (1667–1703), leading actress with *Betterton's company. She was a comedienne and breeches role specialist. Her first husband, the actor William Mountfort, was murdered. Her second husband, John Verbruggen, played Cassius to Betterton's Brutus in 1707. *CMSA*

Verdi, Giuseppe (1813–1901), Italian composer. Verdi composed three Shakespearian operas, *Macbeth* (1847), *Otello* (1887), and *Falstaff* (1893), of which the last two are widely regarded as among the finest Shakespearian operas ever written. Verdi was attracted by the strong emotions and sense of drama in Shakespeare's plays, with which he became acquainted through French and Italian verse and prose translations rather than through the stage. As early as 1843 he toyed with the idea of setting *King Lear*, but the Teatro La Fenice in Venice, for which he was to compose the opera, lacked the first-rate bass or baritone that Verdi would have required, and the idea was shelved.

Macbeth, Verdi's first Shakespearian work, marks a departure in Verdi's approach to opera. It was unusual at the time to set such a dark, tense subject with no love interest. Verdi was intensely involved in all aspects of the opera's production. He worked closely with the librettist Francesco Maria Piave (some lines were added by Andrea Maffei), supervised the rigorous rehearsals, and paid much attention to such matters as the historical accuracy of the settings, the lighting, and the actions of the singers. The opera is in four acts and presents a concentrated version of Shakespeare's play. It received its première at the Teatro della Pergola, Florence, on 14 March 1847, with Marianna Barbieri-Nini as the powerful Lady Macbeth, supported by Felice Varesi in the somewhat weaker role of Macbeth. The opera was an instant success. Many years later, at the request of Léon Escudier, Verdi revised the work for the Théâtre Lyrique, Paris (translated by Charles Nuitter and Alexandre Beaumont), where it was performed on 21 April 1865. The revisions include Lady Macbeth's chilling aria 'La luce langue'. The Paris performance was a failure, although this is the version generally staged today. The murderers' chorus in the second act was parodied by Arthur *Sullivan in *The Pirates of Penzance*.

In 1850 Verdi again contemplated a *King Lear* opera. Despite a completed libretto by Antonio Somma a few years later (he had first worked on it with Salvatore Cammarano, who died in 1852) the project faltered once more. Verdi returned to it periodically for the rest of his life, but was unable to realize it as an opera. Around this time he was also offered a *Hamlet* libretto by Giulio Carcano and invited to compose a *Tempest* opera, both of which he declined.

Verdi's final two masterpieces, *Otello* and *Falstaff*, were the result of inspired collaborations with the librettist Arrigo Boito. *Otello*, which received its première at La Scala, Milan, on 5 February 1887, with Victor Maurel as Iago, Francesco Tamagno as Otello, and Romilda Pantaleone as Desdemona, was Verdi's first new opera for fifteen years. It was a long time in preparation: the idea was first suggested in 1879 but most of the composing took place between 1884 and 1886. Boito reduced Shakespeare's play from over 3,000 lines to 800, omitting the opening scene but otherwise following the original closely. Verdi's response to the text was noticeably more Germanic than his previous works, with few set pieces, more use of through-composed techniques and leitmotifs, and a greater sensitivity to the text, resulting in a more complete fusion of music and drama than before. The opera was a resounding success, and is regarded today by some as Verdi's most perfect opera. For the Paris première at the Théâtre de l'Opéra in 1894 Verdi added a *ballet scene to the third act, though this is rarely played today.

In *Falstaff* Verdi continued his move away from great singable tunes and rousing choruses to a more intricate, endless flow of music with virtuosic orchestral tone-colouring and almost symphonic development of musical material; the opera ends with a magnificent comic fugue. With Victor Maurel in the title role, *Falstaff* was first performed at La Scala on 9 February 1893 to the inevitable rapturous reception, though its musical style later puzzled its listeners. Based on *The Merry Wives of Windsor*, but also including material from both parts of *Henry IV*, it was the 80-year-old Verdi's first comic opera for over 50 years. Unlike previous works, this opera was written not to a commission but simply out of fascination with the character of Falstaff. Verdi revised the opera extensively in March 1893 and January 1894 before its French première. *IBC*

Vere, John de. See OXFORD, EARL OF.

Verges is the headborough (petty constable) who apprehends and interrogates Borachio and Conrad with Dogberry in *Much Ado About Nothing*. *AB*

Vernon. **(1)** See BASSET. **(2)** Sir Richard Vernon is one of the rebels in *1 Henry IV*, condemned to death after the battle of Shrewsbury, 5.5. *AB*

Vernon, Elizabeth (fl. 1595), one of *Elizabeth I's ladies-in-waiting, and the mistress of Henry Wriothesley, Earl of *Southampton. He married her in 1595, after she became pregnant, a covert marriage which angered Elizabeth, and earned them both a brief spell of imprisonment in the Fleet. Those who identify Southampton as the *Fair Youth of the Sonnets have sometimes considered Shakespeare's poetic advice in

(cont. on page 512)

Venus and Adonis

This exuberant erotic poem, at once funny and compassionate, was Shakespeare's most popular published work in his own time, running through at least ten editions between its first appearance in 1593 and its author's death in 1616, with another six published by 1636. It remains one of the few major works in world literature to depict the passionate pursuit of a male object by a female subject. Shakespeare's auspicious debut in print may owe its existence to the outbreak of *plague that closed the London theatres for nearly two years in July 1592, during which the young playwright apparently turned to an alternative career, as a poet, and to an alternative source of income, a patron. Shakespeare's dedication of *Venus and Adonis* to Henry Wriothesley, Earl of *Southampton, calls it the 'first heir of my invention', implicitly contrasting this legitimate venture into verse on a classical subject with Shakespeare's 'illegitimate' earlier work for the stage: as a bid for literary respectability, the poem's composition in 1592–3 may in part have been spurred by the attack Robert *Greene had made on the 'upstart crow . . . Shake-scene' in *Greene's Groatsworth of Wit* (1592).

Text: The 1593 first quarto of *Venus and Adonis* was so popular that it survives in only one copy, now in the *Bodleian Library: all the rest were presumably read to death. It was entered in the *Stationers' Register on 18 April, and a letter from the deranged William *Renoldes (who construed its publication as a love letter to him from Queen Elizabeth) shows that it was on bookstalls by 21 September. It was printed by Richard Field (printer, too, of its successor, *The Rape of Lucrece*), who was born in Stratford only two years before Shakespeare and may have been at school with him. (Innogen's passing reference to 'Richard du Champ' in *Cymbeline*—the name she invents for her dead 'master' at 4.2.379—may be a private joke between them). Field did his job well, apparently working from Shakespeare's own manuscript: unusually, Shakespeare may even have corrected the proofs, making this one of the most reliable of all his printed texts.

Sources: The story of Venus and Adonis is told in book 10 of *Ovid's *Metamorphoses*, which Shakespeare consulted both in the original Latin and in Arthur Golding's English translation (1565–7). Shakespeare greatly elaborates on Ovid's account (a mere 75 lines long compared to the 1,194 of Shakespeare's poem), and as well as supplying rhetorical expansion and additional detail (such as the incident in which Adonis' stallion frustrates his escape attempt by running off with a mare) he fundamentally alters its drama. In the original, Venus' passion for the mortal Adonis (inadvertently caused by Cupid, as the narrator Orpheus explains) is reciprocated, and they hunt together (though Venus advises her lover to pursue only fairly harmless animals, telling a cautionary tale which Shakespeare omits): she leaves for Cyprus, but returns after Adonis has been mortally wounded, metamorphosing him into an anemone. Shakespeare transforms the story by making Adonis into a reluctant and prudish adolescent, who appears to join the boar-hunt primarily as an excuse to avoid a renewal of Venus' undesired assaults. Shakespeare's solicitous goddess, powerless to overcome his reluctance, stays nearby to wait anxiously for Adonis, and his metamorphosis is also outside her agency: she is left to pick a flower which spontaneously springs up where his miraculously melted body lay, placing an eternal curse on love as she makes her at once heartbroken and petulant departure towards Cyprus.

Shakespeare's alterations to his material are influenced in part by other stories in Ovid (principally those of Salmacis and Hermaphroditus, and Echo and Narcissus, the latter cited by Venus at l. 161), and in part by a growing fashion for the Ovidian 'erotic epyllion' (miniature epic on an amorous theme) which had begun with the publication of Thomas

*Lodge's *Scilla's Metamorphosis* in 1589 (written in the same six-line stanzaic form Shakespeare adopts here, rhyming *ababcc*). This vogue would find its most famous expression in *Marlowe's *Hero and Leander*, not published until 1598 but composed at around the same time as *Venus and Adonis* (shortly before Marlowe's murder in May 1593). Shakespeare's poem shares with these other examples of its genre the combination of passionate and sensual subject matter with a wry and urbane narrative voice.

SYNOPSIS: A Latin motto, from Ovid's *Amores* (1.15), declares Shakespeare's poetic ambition: in Marlowe's translation it runs 'Let base-conceited wits admire vile things, | Fair Phoebus lead me to the Muses' springs.' A dedication to the Earl of Southampton promises 'some graver labour' if these 'unpolished lines' prove acceptable.

As young Adonis, who prefers hunting to love, is going hunting in the afternoon, Venus hurries to accost him (ll. 1–6). Imploring a kiss, Venus pulls Adonis from his horse, which she tethers to a tree, and pushes him to the ground, silencing his protests with kisses (ll. 7–48). Despite Adonis' objections to her immodest behaviour, Venus will not let him go, kissing him hungrily: eventually she promises to release him if he will give her one kiss in return (ll. 49–90). This he promises, but in the event refuses to provide (ll. 49–90). Venus makes a long and eloquent wooing speech, using all the arguments she can muster, including the accusation that Adonis is too proud of his own beauty (like Narcissus), which he ought to transmit to posterity through procreation (ll. 91–174). Unmoved, Adonis complains that he is getting sunburned and wishes to leave (ll. 175–86). Venus rails petulantly at his indifference (ll. 187–216). Temporarily overcome by tears, Venus is unable to speak further, and when she renews her amorous pleading Adonis merely smiles scornfully, his dimples making him more beautiful than ever (ll. 217–52).

Adonis breaks away and makes for his horse, but a young mare emerges from a nearby copse and Adonis' stallion (which is lovingly described, ll. 289–300) breaks his reins and eagerly joins her. Ignoring Adonis' attempts to recapture the stallion, the two horses run away into the wood (ll. 253–324). Adonis sits sullenly: Venus approaches again, takes his hand and renews her suit, urging him to follow his horse's example (ll. 325–408). Adonis insists that her wooing is futile and misplaced, since he is unripe for love (ll. 409–26). Undeterred, Venus continues to plead, but seeing Adonis is about to reproach her again she faints. Alarmed, Adonis attempts to revive her, eventually resorting to kisses (ll. 427–80). Venus, reviving, speaks of her joy (ll. 481–522). Adonis, however, still points out that he is too young for love, and that it is growing late, but he promises and gives a farewell kiss (ll. 523–40). Inflamed with desire, Venus renews her kissing, though Adonis refuses to meet her again the following day, saying he will be hunting the boar. She pulls him down on top of her, but to no avail (ll. 541–612).

Venus warns Adonis against the perils of boar-hunting, urging him instead to hunt only hares, foxes, or deer (ll. 613–713). Venus renews her pleading for love, explaining that the night is dark to reproach Adonis' coldness and encourage prodigality (ll. 715–68). Adonis refuses Venus, accusing her of miscalling lust by the name of love, and at last makes his escape (ll. 769–816).

Alone, Venus wanders lost in the dark: noticing how her moans echo, she spends the night extemporizing an echoing song about the sorrows of love (ll. 829–40). At daybreak she hurries to a myrtle grove and listens for the sounds of Adonis' hunt (ll. 817–70). The anxious Venus can hear that a boar-hunt is in progress, and hears that the hounds are afraid: to her horror she sees the boar, its mouth stained with blood (ll. 871–912). Finding a series of wounded dogs, she fears Adonis must have been killed, and exclaims against death (ll. 913–54). Weeping, she hears the huntsmen again and, convinced Adonis is alive, reproaches herself for being so fearful (ll. 955–1026).

Venus is stunned to find Adonis killed by the boar (ll. 1027–68). She speaks an elegy for Adonis, imagining that the boar (which has killed him by sinking its tusks into his groin) was only kissing him as she would have liked to, and falls weeping on his body (ll. 1069–122). Venus looks into Adonis' dead eyes (ll. 1123–34). She prophesies that since her beloved Adonis is dead love will hereafter always be attended with sorrows, which she enumerates (ll. 1135–64).

Adonis' body has melted away and a purple flower has sprung in its place, which Venus vows to cherish in her breast (ll. 1165–88). Venus returns to Cyprus in her dove-drawn chariot, intending to mourn in seclusion (ll. 1189–94).

ARTISTIC FEATURES: The poem's set-piece displays of rhetoric alternate with vivid, sensual evocations of a mythological world whose freshness matches that of Ovid's original, a world which exists purely to provide the appropriate setting for Venus' attempted seduction and whose every detail can reflect her desires and her experience (from the behaviour of Adonis' horse to the vulnerable snail to which her consciousness' stunned temporary retreat is likened on finding his body, ll. 1033–44).

CRITICAL HISTORY: The immense success of *Venus and Adonis* in its time is attested not only by its profusion of editions but by a number of contemporary comments: by *Meres in 1598 ('the sweet witty soul of Ovid lives in mellifluous and honey-tongued Shakespeare, witness his *Venus and Adonis*'), by *Barnfield in the same year, by *Weever in 1599, and by Gabriel *Harvey in 1600 ('the younger sort takes much delight in Shakespeare's *Venus and Adonis*'). The poem is cited repeatedly and with particular enthusiasm in the *Parnassus plays ('I'll worship sweet Master Shakespeare, and to know him will lay his *Venus and Adonis* under my pillow'), and to judge from quotations within other contemporary plays, passages from it became part of the common lexicon of attempted seduction: it is even specifically mentioned by some disapproving moralists. After the last reprint of the quarto in 1675, however, the poem fell from favour (along with *The Rape of Lucrece* and the Sonnets), and it was left out

of most 18th-century editions of Shakespeare. Although *Malone guardedly remarked in 1780 that it was not 'so entirely devoid of poetical merit as it has been represented' it was not until the Romantic period that *Venus and Adonis* inspired any renewed enthusiasm, notably from *Coleridge and *Keats (though *Hazlitt, in common with many others, still found it repellently artificial). Both its subject matter and its delight in rhetorical display alienated many Victorians, and it is only in the self-consciously 'liberated' post-war period that *Venus and Adonis* has generated a significant critical literature, much of it, however, determined to explain or even excuse the poem by placing it in its original literary context. *MD*

RECENT MAJOR EDITIONS

In Hyder Rollins, *The Poems* (New Variorum, 1938); *The Poems*, ed. F. T. Prince (Arden 2nd series 1960); *The Narrative Poems*, ed. Maurice Evans (Penguin, 1989); *The Poems*, ed. John Roe (New Cambridge, 1992)

SOME REPRESENTATIVE CRITICISM

Bradbrook, M. C., in *Shakespeare and Elizabethan Poetry* (1951)
Coleridge, Samuel Taylor, in *Biographia literaria* (1817)
Hulse, Clark, *Metamorphic Verse: The Elizabethan Minor Epic* (1981)
Keach, William, *Elizabethan Erotic Narratives* (1977)
Smith, Peter J., 'A "Consummation Devoutly to be Wished": The Erotics of Narration in *Venus and Adonis*', *Shakespeare Survey*, 53 (2000)

---

favour of procreation as a contributory factor. *SW*

Verona, in northern Italy, is the scene of some of *The Two Gentlemen of Verona* and nearly all of *Romeo and Juliet.* Petruccio in *The Taming of the Shrew* is a gentleman of Verona. *AB*

Verona, Prince of. See ESCALUS, PRINCE OF VERONA.

Versification. See METRE.

Vestris, Madame Elizabeth (1797–1856), English actress, dancer, singer, and manageress, who made her stage debut—in opera—with her first husband (Armand Vestris) in 1815. Her early successes were in 'breeches' parts (she excelled as Macheath) in which her renowned legs were displayed to advantage. In 1824 she appeared as Rosalind and Mistress Ford at Drury Lane, but it was not until she and her second husband Charles Mathews assumed the management of Covent Garden in 1839 that Shakespeare figured prominently in her career.

Their first choice was *Love's Labour's Lost,* not performed since Shakespeare's time and, though there were cuts (little regretted in the comic scenes) and transpositions, it was by the standards of the day remarkably faithful to Shakespeare's text. Madame Vestris was well suited to Rosaline, but the correct and gorgeous costumes and the imaginative stage arrangements—in both of which *Planché had a hand—attracted most attention and praise.

For *A Midsummer Night's Dream* (1840) Planché prepared the acting version—nothing but Shakespeare—the historically accurate (Athenian) costumes, furnishings, and architecture and created—through the artistry of Thomas Grieve—a spell-binding finale. Few, least of all *Macready, would have expected Vestris to distinguish herself as a producer of Shakespeare, but she did so with influential effect. *RF*

Vienna is the scene of *Measure for Measure.* Hamlet tells us that 'The Mousetrap' is 'the image of a murder done in Vienna' (*Hamlet* 3.2.227). *AB*

Vigny, Alfred de (1797–1863), French poet and dramatist. Vigny translated *Othello,* adapted *The Merchant of Venice,* and turned toward Shakespeare for inspiration in composing his own historical drama *La Maréchale d'Ancre.* Here Shakespeare's histories were adopted as a model by a Romantic determined to place subjects from French national history onto the French stage. Presented at the *Comédie-Française in 1840, *La Maréchale d'Ancre* introduced audacious innovations into French theatre, unabashedly presenting the supernatural and using an unclassically complicated plot. Although Vigny's pioneering spirit was a source of motivation for many playwrights of his time, his elaborate post-Shakespearian stage compositions drew disapproval from dramatic critics who found them too unwieldy for the French stage. In later life, he withdrew to what Sainte-Beuve famously called his *tour d'ivoire* (ivory tower). *AC*

Partridge, Eric, *The French Romantics' Knowledge of English Literature (1820–48)* (1924)

Vilar, Jean (1912–71), French actor and director. He founded the Avignon Festival (1947) and was first manager of the Théâtre National Populaire (1951), where he promoted a demanding art, after *Copeau, for vast audiences. He opened the Avignon Festival in the title role for *Richard II*'s French première (1947), and played Macbeth in 1953. *ISG*

Vincentio (1) He is the father of Lucentio in *The Taming of the Shrew.* **(2)** Vincentio, the Duke of Vienna in *Measure for Measure,* having resigned his power to Angelo, poses as 'Friar Lodowick' to observe ensuing events incognito. *AB*

viol, a bowed instrument in three main sizes held on the lap or between the legs, with six strings tuned similarly to the *lute, popular for domestic music-making in consort and with a fine surviving repertoire by *Byrd and others. In Italian called the viola da gamba, hence Sir Andrew Aguecheek's 'viol-de-gamboys' in *Twelfth Night* 1.3.23. *JB*

Viola. See TWELFTH NIGHT.

Violenta, a friend of Widow Capilet, appears but does not speak in some editions of *All's Well That Ends Well* 3.5. *AB*

violin. In Shakespeare's time the violin had a lower status than now; it was played mainly by professionals for dance. See FIDDLER; REBEC. *JB*

Virgil (Publius Vergilius Maro) (70–19 BC) was the most famous Latin poet. He wrote *pastoral verse (*Eclogues* and *Georgics*) before embarking on his masterpiece, the *Aeneid,* a grand epic about the foundation of Rome and its culmination in the imperial *pax Augusta.* The poem was profoundly influenced by *Homer's two epics. Shakespeare frequently echoes the first six books of the *Aeneid,* as in the painting of the siege of Troy in *The Rape of Lucrece* (*Aeneid* 1.456–93); and he boldly rewrites *Aeneid* 6.456–76 when in *Antony and Cleopatra* Antony refers to Dido and her Aeneas wanting troops to match his and Cleopatra's. *RW*

Baldwin, T. W., *William Shakespere's Small Latine & Lesse Greeke,* ii (1944)
Bono, Barbara, *Literary Transvaluation from Vergilian Epic to Shakespearian Tragicomedy* (1984)
Gransden, K. W., *Virgil: The Aeneid* (1990)
Griffin, Jasper, *Virgil* (1986)
Martindale, Charles (ed.), *The Cambridge Companion to Virgil* (1997)

Virgilia, Coriolanus' wife, accompanies the other women to the Voscian camp to appeal to him, *Coriolanus* 5.3. *AB*

virginal(s), in Shakespeare's time, the generic term for plucked string keyboard instruments, as 'harpsichord' is now; later it came to refer more specifically to the smaller rectangular-shaped instrument. 'Virginalling' (*The Winter's*

A reluctant Sir John is concealed in the buck-basket in Verdi's final masterpiece *Falstaff* (1893–4), based on *The Merry Wives of Windsor*. Gabriella Tucci as Mistress Ford, Regina Resnik as Mistress Quickly, Rosalind Elias as Mistress Page, and Anselmo Colzani as Falstaff, Metropolitan Opera, New York, 1964.

Tale 1.2.127) refers to the finger action in playing. *JB*

Visconti, Luchino (1906–76), Italian film and theatre director. His Shakespeare productions included *As You Like It* in Rome in 1948, designed in surrealist style by Salvador Dali, and a lavish *Troilus and Cressida* in the Boboli Gardens in Florence in 1949, designed by Franco *Zeffirelli. *DK*

Vitez, Antoine (1930–90), French actor, translator (from Russian and Greek), director (Théâtre d'Ivry, 1972–81, Théâtre National de Chaillot, 1981–8, *Comédie-Française, 1988–90), drama teacher (Lecocq school of mime, Conservatoire National de Paris, 1968–81, and in the schools of drama he ran at Ivry and Chaillot), and theorist. He reappraised the musicality of the classical French *alexandrine and the use of sober sets. In his six-hour *Hamlet* (1982, Lepoutre's translation), a passionate Claudius was Hamlet's age, the unspecified costumes recalled *Craig and *Copeau, and the white setting offered a broken perspective full of dark corners. *ISG*

vocabulary. A salient feature of 16th- and 17th-century English was the dramatic expansion of vocabulary which occurred in Shakespeare's lifetime. It was manifested largely in two ways; first by the incorporation into English of words borrowed from foreign languages and secondly, by the creation, often by poets and dramatists, of numerous neologisms. This extraordinary increase in vocabulary provided Shakespeare with several artistic possibilities. Latinate diction, for example, enabled him to create a 'grand style' (as it was termed by rhetoricians) to characterize the language of royalty and the nobility, as exemplified in the speech of Ulysses. Its excessive use, on the other hand, enabled Shakespeare to satirize the speech of affected courtiers like Osric and Armado; while its misuse, when the speaker mistook either form or meaning, was derided, somewhat unkindly, in the speech of working men and women. The alternative source of lexical expansion was the creation of neologisms by various means such as by the addition of affixes to existing words, the use of a word in a different grammatical function, as in 'to lip a wanton' where a noun functions as a verb, and compounding two or more words to create new ones. *VS*

volta, la, an energetic turning dance derived from the *cinquepace, disapproved of by some because the man had to hold the woman more closely than usual, in order to help her execute a high jump in each measure. References in *Henry V* 3.5.33 and *Troilus and Cressida* 4.5.87 imply that it was a fashionable accomplishment *c.*1600. *JB*

Voltaire (François Marie Arouet) (1694–1778), French writer and philosopher. Voltaire epitomizes the academic attitude of the great majority of French playwrights and translators who hoped to make Shakespeare accessible to the French public by adapting his works to classical taste. Like most French authors,

Voltaire takes a Pygmalion approach to the English playwright by breathing the spirit of the 'grand siècle' into the Renaissance model. Voltaire's popularity as an Enlightenment playwright was partially due to the influence of Shakespearian drama. *Julius Caesar*, *Hamlet*, and *Othello* served as blueprints for Voltaire's most famous tragedies: *La Mort de César* (1743), *Zaïre* (1732), and *Sémiramis* (1748).

These three historical tragedies display the French taste for simplicity and respect for classical decorum, thus diverging greatly from the original Shakespearian model. The revolutionary objective of Voltaire's dramatic project, founded on the tenets of historical realism, scarcely escaped the academic limitations of his age which necessitated radical changes in Shakespeare's works, thus resulting in audacious expurgative measures and plagiarism. This rationalist reflex, typical of French authors and translators, highlights the attempt to submit Shakespeare's plays to the antiquated taste of their forefathers.

In order to break free from the French tradition Voltaire looked to foreign theatre for inspiration. It was during his exile in London that he first tasted the stimulating effects of exotic local colour. The contrast of Christian and Islamic customs in *Zaïre*, of Babylonian traditions in *Sémiramis*, and the evocation of historical events such as the overthrow of the Roman Republic under Caesar in *La Mort de César* all testify to his desire to adapt themes from national history for the French stage.

Julius Caesar, which Voltaire reworked in alexandrines under the title of *La Mort de César* (1743), amplifies the patriotic and republican spirit of the Roman Emperor. In this way Voltaire paid tribute to the moral and philosophical overtones of the Enlightenment thinkers. In the end, the 18th-century playwright and propagandist proved to be an inveterate defender of French theatrical traditions. Although he looked to Shakespeare for inspiration that would enable him to master monumental historical stage scenes, he remained, in fact, acutely attentive to the 'bienséances', thus diluting the powerful effects of theatrical realism by suppressing historical scenes of bloodshed, eliminating sub-plots such as love intrigues, and virtually suppressing feminine roles. In his later writings Voltaire considers the Shakespearian theatre, with its unclassical hospitality to onstage deaths, 'barbaric', and despite his various attempts to emulate Shakespeare he came to personify a hostile French classicism to generations of patriotic English bardolaters. *AC*

Draper, F. W. M. *The Rise and Fall of the French Romantic Drama* (1923)

Voltaire, 'Introduction a *Semiramis*', in *Œuvres complètes* (1828)

Voltaire, 'Lettres sur la tragédie' (18), in *Lettres philosophiques* (1988)

Voltimand. See VALTEMAND.

Volumnia exults in her son's military prowess and encourages his political ambitions, advising him to conceal his disdain for the plebians (*Coriolanus* 3.2) in order to become consul. After Coriolanus' banishment and his defection to the Volsces, she leads his wife Virgilia, son Martius, and friend Valeria to intercede for the Romans, successfully appealing to his personal loyalties.

In the mid-18th century, a version of Shakespeare's play, incorporating revisions made some years earlier by James Thomson and entitled *Coriolanus; or, The Roman Matron*, was produced by Thomas *Sheridan, its title signifying the prominence accorded to the role of Coriolanus' mother. Volumnia remains one of the few major roles for older women in Shakespeare: great interpreters have included Edith *Evans, Irene *Worth, Barbara *Jefford, and Judi *Dench. Though in the 20th century a greater interest in the class politics of the play tended to diminish her importance, an increased awareness of gender issues emphasized her part in creating Coriolanus' destructive and self-destructive masculinity. She sees him as her product—'Thy valiantness was mine, thou suck'st it from me' (3.2.129)—but, as Janet Adelman has influentially argued in her psychoanalytic reading of the play, having 'fed' his fantasies of omnipotence and uncompromising independence, it is she who asks him to give them up at the end of the play, resulting in his death. *AB*

Adelman, Janet, ' "Anger's my Meat": Feeding, Dependency, and Aggression in *Coriolanus*', in Murray M. Schwartz and Coppélia Kahn (eds.), *Representing Shakespeare: New Psychoanalytic Essays* (1980)

Volumnius. See STRATO.

Vortigern and Rowena. See FORGERY.

Voss, Johann Heinrich (1751–1826), German poet, translator of *Homer (1781). His metrical translation of Shakespeare's complete plays (1818–29), undertaken in collaboration with his sons Heinrich and Abraham Voss, kept closer to the peculiarities of the original than that of A. W. *Schlegel, with which it competed. *WH*

Wagner, Richard. See OPERA.

Wales. Though Frederick J. Harries contended that Shakespeare was of Welsh descent, musing on the possibility that 'the Celtic strain in [his] blood may be held to account for the sporadic appearance of genius in an unremarkable middle-class family' (*Shakespeare and the Welsh*, 1919), and W. J. Hughes proposed that the *'lost years' were spent in Brecon (*Wales and the Welsh in English Literature*, 1924), Shakespeare's presence in Wales should not be understood literally, but rather analysed in the context of English–Welsh cultural interactions, particularly in relation to performance and education. Shakespeare's histories display considerable interest in the assimilation of Wales to the interests of the London-based Tudor nation-state, most obviously in their depiction of Glyndŵr in *1 Henry IV*, a process in which the plays have continued to participate. Shakespeare has been one of the instruments of English cultural influence in Wales, particularly insofar as the teaching of his plays is implicated in the high prestige with which the Welsh have traditionally endowed an English education. Thus despite the bilingualism of Welsh society, there has been little call for Shakespeare to be translated into Welsh, although fragmentary MS translations of *Macbeth* and *Hamlet* exist, as well as a complete version by Ioan Pedr of *1 Henry IV*, made for the Bangor Eisteddfod Genedlaethol (national arts festival) of 1874.

Since the visit of the Prince's Men to Hereford in 1609, travelling companies of English players, with plays by Shakespeare and his contemporaries—or extracts from them—in their repertoire, have been regular visitors to Wales, as well as to the border towns like Hereford and Ludlow that made an important contribution to Welsh cultural life. In the latter part of the 18th century, the Welsh gentry that formed the mainstay of the touring companies' audiences eagerly embraced the fashion for private theatricals: the outstanding exponent was Sir Watkin Williams Wynn, who built a costly small theatre at his estate at Wynnstay, in north-east Wales. Eleven of Shakespeare's plays were performed there, including *Cymbeline* and *The Merry Wives of Windsor*, works which have a certain Welsh interest. Once fixed commercial theatres were established at towns such as Brecon and Cardiff, Shakespeare was as much of a popular staple there as in other British provincial cultural centres: the oldest extant bill from such a theatre advertises a production of another play with crucial Welsh aspects, *1 Henry IV*, at Holyhead in 1787.

Since then, the centrality of Shakespeare to the literary curriculum in Welsh as much as English *schools has underwritten his cultural presence in Wales and helped to ensure regular performances of his plays at regional repertory theatres such as Theatr Clwyd in Mold, while more experimental companies like Swansea-based Volcano have fashioned a distinctive Welsh vision of the Shakespearian canon, in performances based on the Sonnets and *Macbeth*. *KC*

Walker, Henry (d. 1616), a musician of London, born in Herefordshire, who sold Shakespeare the *Blackfriars Gatehouse in 1613. *SW*

Walker, William (1608–80), son of Henry Walker, a Stratford alderman. Shakespeare stood godfather to him on 16 October 1608 and left him 20*s*. in gold. He became bailiff of Stratford in 1649. *SW*

Walkley, Thomas. See PRINTING AND PUBLISHING.

'Wall'. See SNOUT, TOM.

Wallace, Charles William (1865–1932), American academic. He and his wife made important documentary discoveries about shareholdings at the Globe and Blackfriars theatres (*Keysar v. Burbage*, 1610; *Ostler v. Heminges*, 1615; *Witter v. Heminges and Condell*, 1619). In 1909, among *Belott v. Mountjoy* papers, he discovered a deposition signed by Shakespeare. *TM*

Walley, Henry. See PRINTING AND PUBLISHING.

Walton, Sir William (1902–83), English composer. A youthful setting of 'Tell me, where is Fancy bred?' (*The Merchant of Venice*) dates from 1916, and he apparently also set 'Where the bee sucks' (*The Tempest*), though this is no longer extant. However, Walton is most remembered for his splendid scores for films starring Laurence *Olivier. The first of these was *As You Like It* (1936), from which was published separately *'Under the Greenwood Tree'. The later Shakespearian film scores, all directed and produced by Olivier, were *Henry V* (1943–4), *Hamlet* (1947), and *Richard III* (1955). Walton also composed incidental music for a production of *Macbeth* (first performed at the Opera House, Manchester, on 16 January 1942). His opera *Troilus and Cressida* (1954, and later revisions) is based on *Chaucer rather than Shakespeare. *IBC*

war. England was at war for more than half of Shakespeare's adult life: Queen *Elizabeth I's foreign policy could not avert conflict with Spain, and there were also early colonial wars in *Ireland. Both of these contributed to England's economic difficulties in the period, but they had relatively little direct effect on the life of the country: though threatened with invasion by four Spanish Armadas between 1588 and 1601, the country was never actually occupied by a hostile foreign power, and battles fought on English soil were part of the medieval past dramatized in the history plays and *King Lear*.

In late 16th-century England, to go to war was to travel overseas.

There was no standing army at this time: every able-bodied Englishman between the ages of 16 and 60 was liable for conscription. Attitudes to this opportunity were divided. Many did not wish to go (for the chances of returning alive and uninjured were not good), and in practice some local justices of the peace would offer recruiting officers, as Justice Shallow does in *2 Henry IV*, a pool of men selected with a view to clearing the district of its least desirable residents. Yet for a society whose noblemen played at battle in the annual jousting contests on the Queen's accession day, warfare was also a focus of national pride and chivalric mythology. Shakespeare typically evokes both sides of the question: there is patriotism in the treatment of the French campaigns of *1 Henry VI* and *Henry V*, but the plays also never lose sight of the bloody, destructive realities of battle. *MW*

Hale, John R., *The Art of War and Renaissance England* (1961)
Jorgensen, Paul A., *Shakespeare's Military World* (1956)
Somogyi, Nicholas de, *Shakespeare's Theatre of War* (1998)

Warburton, William (1698–1779), Bishop of Gloucester, theologian, controversial writer, and Shakespearian editor. The learned and brilliant Warburton was not best qualified as a Shakespearian scholar, and his eight-volume edition of the dramatic works (1747) has been notorious as an example of obtuseness in interpretation and wilfulness in textual conjecture. *MLW*

Jarvis, Simon, *Scholars and Gentlemen: Shakespearian Textual Criticism and Representations of Scholarly Labour, 1725–1765* (1995)

Ward, Dame Genevieve (1838–1922), American-born actress who, when voice problems forced her to abandon her career as an opera singer, became letter-perfect in fourteen stage roles, five of them Shakespeare, within six months. In her debut as Lady Macbeth at the Theatre Royal, Manchester, in 1873 she displayed the—operatic—qualities of powerful voice, expressive features, and graceful gestures which were to thrill audiences the world over. High points included Lady Macbeth in French (Paris, 1877) and the Queen in *Cymbeline* with *Irving (1896), who restored Queen Margaret (*Richard III*, 1896) for her, a role which she repeated with *Benson, for whom she also played Volumnia, and Martin Harvey. In 1921 she was made DBE, the first actress to receive the honour. *RF*

Ward, John (1629–81), vicar of Stratford, 1662–81, formerly a medical student. His voluminous notebooks record information and anecdotes about Shakespeare. Writing around 1661–3 he expressed his sense, probably because interest in Shakespeare was growing, that he should learn more about him and his works: 'Remember to peruse Shakespeare's plays and be versed in them, that I may not be ignorant in that matter.' He noted, 'I have heard that Mr Shakespeare was a natural wit, without any art at all; he frequented the plays all his younger time, but in his elder days lived at Stratford, and supplied the stage with two plays every year, and for that had an allowance so large that he spent at the rate of £1,000 a year, as I have heard.' And he is the source of the story of Shakespeare's death: 'Shakespeare, Drayton, and Ben Jonson had a merry meeting and, it seems, drank too hard, for Shakespeare died of a fever there contracted.' Drayton was a frequent visitor to *Clifford Chambers, near Stratford, but there is no evidence that Jonson was ever in the neighbourhood.

Ward also made a note that he should 'see Mrs Quiney'—presumably Shakespeare's daughter Judith, widow of *Thomas. She might well have passed on invaluable information about her father, but the meeting seems not to have taken place; she died early in 1662 aged 77. *SW*

Warner, David (b. 1941), British actor. He made an impact as a tall, gangling, saintly Henry VI in the cycle *The *Wars of the Roses* at the *Royal Shakespeare Theatre in 1962 (televised 1965). His Richard II was less impressive, but in Peter *Hall's *Hamlet* (1965), a production which emphasized generational conflict, his Prince, trailing a college scarf, seemed to embody the student disaffection and alienation of the 1960s. *MJ*

Warner, Deborah (b. 1959), British director. Having trained as an actress, she founded in 1980 Kick Theatre for which she mounted in tiny spaces four plays by Shakespeare. In 1987 she staged an extraordinary *Titus Andronicus*, poised on a knife edge between horror and farce, at the Swan theatre, Stratford, later mounting a vivid *King John* at The Other Place. At the *National she staged *King Lear* with Brian Cox, her Titus, on the big Lyttelton stage; more challengingly she directed her frequent collaborator Fiona Shaw as Richard II in the smaller Cottesloe. *MJ*

Warner, William (*c.*1558–1609), historian and translator. Warner produced the first English translation of Plautus' *Menaechmi*, one of the sources of *The Comedy of Errors*. Unpublished until 1595, the translation was written for the perusal of Warner's private friends. Since Warner's patron was Henry Carey, Lord *Hunsdon, the Lord Chamberlain and patron of Shakespeare's company, it is possible that Shakespeare saw the manuscript, though the verbal correspondences are few. Warner was also the author of *Albion's England*, a popular verse chronicle that dealt with the origins of the English nation. When he published this work in 1584 it consisted of four volumes. This number had risen to sixteen through a process of continual revision and expansion by the time of its republication in 1606. Here, Shakespeare could have found the legends of Lear and Macbeth. The account of Lear is brief, describing Gonoril's attempt on the King's life but omitting any reference to Cordelia's fate. The Macbeth narrative focuses on Fleance and the foundation of the Stuart line but also refers to the prophecy of 'Weird-Elves' and the murder of Banquo. In this narrative, Warner may well have been influenced by Shakespeare. *JKS*

'War of the Theatres'. Between 1599 and 1602 three playwrights directed personal satire at each other in their plays: *Jonson in his *Every Man out of his Humour*, *Marston in his *Histrio-mastix*, *Jack Drum* and *What You Will*, and *Dekker and Marston in their *Satiromastix*. This poets' quarrel (or 'poetomachia') may be symptomatic of conflict between the open-air playhouses (occupied by adult actors) and indoor playhouses (occupied by *children's companies) which is also reflected in Rosencrantz's reference to the 'little eyases' (child actors) who 'berattle the common stages' (*Hamlet* 2.2.343). However, the entire 'war' may simply have been a publicity-seeking fabrication and the 'little eyases' passage written later than 1602. *GE*

Knutson, Roslyn L., 'Falconer to the Little Eyases: A New Date and Commercial Agenda for the "little Eyases" Passage in *Hamlet*', *Shakespeare Quarterly*, 46 (1995)
Small, Roscoe Addison, *The Stage-Quarrel between Ben Jonson and the So-Called Poetasters* (1899)

Wars of the Roses (1964). See BARTON, JOHN; HALL, PETER; ASHCROFT, PEGGY; SINDEN, DONALD; ROYAL SHAKESPEARE COMPANY. (1986). See ENGLISH SHAKESPEARE COMPANY; BOGDANOV, MICHAEL; PENNINGTON, MICHAEL.

Wart, Thomas. He is one of Falstaff's recruits, *2 Henry IV* 3.2. *AB*

Warton, Joseph (1722–1800), English critic and poet. He opposed the literary concept of 'correctness', praising Shakespeare's 'warblings wild' over Addison's 'coldly correct' poetry ('The Enthusiast'). Warton wrote a variety of critical essays including commentaries on Shakespeare for Samuel *Johnson's periodical the *Adventurer* and a lengthy study of the works of Pope. *JM*

Warwick, Earl of. (1) In *2 Henry IV* he comforts King Henry (3.1) and defends the character of Prince Harry (4.3). Henry erroneously calls him Neville, 3.1.61, but the character is based on Richard Beauchamp, Earl of Warwick 1382–

1439. (Neville, the Earl of Warwick who appears in *The First Part of the Contention* (*2 Henry VI*) and *Richard Duke of York* (*3 Henry VI*), inherited Beauchamp's title of Earl of Warwick by marrying his daughter Anne.) In *Henry V*, though present as part of the English army in 4.7 and 5.2, he speaks only one line, 4.8.20. In *1 Henry VI* he plucks a white rose (2.4.36), helps Plantagenet to recover his title of Duke of York (3.1), and condemns Joan la Pucelle (5.6). **(2)** In *The First Part of the Contention* he quarrels with Suffolk (1.3 and more seriously 3.2) and Old Lord Clifford (5.1). He joins the Yorkists with his father (2.2) and helps to win the first battle of St Albans (5.2–3). In *Richard Duke of York* he continues to support York, and has York's son crowned Edward IV, but when he discovers the latter has married Lady Gray he captures him (4.3) and returns the crown to Henry VI. He is mortally wounded at Barnet (5.2). He is based on Richard Neville (1428–71), son-in-law of the preceding Warwick, son of the Salisbury of *The First Part of the Contention*, and maternal grandfather of Clarence's son (Warwick (3)). After his death he was known as 'the Kingmaker'. **(3)** See CLARENCE'S SON. *AB*

Wayte, William. See GARDINER, WILLIAM.

weak ending, the use of an unstressed syllable at the end of a line where a stressed syllable should be found; thus as the tenth syllable of an iambic pentameter. *CB*

Weaver, Smith the. Cade's sarcastic follower appears in *The First Part of the Contention* (*2 Henry VI*) 4.2 and 4.7. *AB*

Webster, John (*c.*1579–1634), dramatist. The son of a coachmaker, he probably went to the *Merchant Taylors' School, then to the Inns of Court. He worked for several companies, including the King's Men and the Children of Paul's—for whom he composed two satirical comedies, *Westward Ho* (1607) and *Northward Ho* (1607), in collaboration with Thomas *Dekker. He also wrote an intriguing tragicomedy, *The Devil's Law-Case* (*c.*1619), and prose essays: in 1615 he added 32 new Characters to Sir Thomas Overbury's Theophrastic collection, *New and Choice Characters of Several Authors*. But Webster is best known for writing two of the greatest Jacobean tragedies, *The White Devil* (1612) and *The Duchess of Malfi* (1613). These are astonishingly bleak investigations into the corrupt system of 'courtly reward and punishment' which both sustains and devastates the European aristocracy. Central to the tragedies are two character types: the cynical gentleman-servant, closely related to the hero of John *Marston's tragicomedy *The Malcontent* (1604), who comments on and participates in the murderous plots of his aristocratic masters; and the woman of 'great spirit', who fights to establish her independence against all the social and physical constraints imposed on her by patriarchal custom. These plays are among the most powerful poetic representations of entrapment and resistance in early modern literature. *RM*

Bradbrook, M. C., *John Webster: Citizen and Dramatist* (1980)
Luckyj, Christina, *A Winter's Snake: Dramatic Form in the Tragedies of John Webster* (1989)

Webster, Margaret (1905–72), British director. Born into a theatrical dynasty about which she wrote in *The Same Only Different* (1969), she acted at the *Old Vic in London but found her true vocation in the 1930s when she directed Maurice *Evans as Richard II and Hamlet in New York. In 1943 she was acclaimed for her direction of Paul *Robeson, the first black American to play Othello in New York. Much later as a liberal she found it hard to get work in the States and undertook guest productions at the Old Vic and Stratford. Her straightforward directorial approach is summed up in her *Shakespeare without Tears* (1942). *MJ*

'Wedding is great Juno's crown', sung by Hymen in *As You Like It* 5.4.139; the original music is unknown. *JB*

Weelkes, Thomas (1576–1623), composer noted for his fine church music and madrigals. His career was at times turbulent, including dismissal from Chichester cathedral for drunkenness and profanity in 1617. *JB*

Weever, John (1586–1632), poet. Born in Lancashire and educated at Queens' College, Cambridge, Weever neatly imitated the form of a Shakespearian sonnet in 'Ad Gulielmum Shakespear', printed in his *Epigrams* (1599). Perhaps he had seen unpublished Shakespeare sonnets, or had noticed the interpolated sonnets in *Romeo and Juliet* (1597). *PH*

Welcombe, a small village about a mile and a half (2.4 km) from Stratford. In 1605 Shakespeare paid £440 for the tithes on land here and nearby. He became involved in the controversial plans to subject the land to *enclosure in 1614. *SW*

Welcombe enclosure. In 1614 procedures were instigated to *enclose land at *Welcombe in which Shakespeare had an interest as a tithe-holder, and possibly also as a copyholder. He and Thomas *Greene were to be compensated for loss. Stratford's corporation opposed the scheme. A number of Greene's notes about it have survived. Shakespeare's attitude is unclear. He may have favoured it, as is suggested in Edward *Bond's play *Bingo* (1973). *SW*

Welles, Orson (1915–85), American actor and director. A precocious star performer and director at the Mercury theatre in pre-war New York, he produced an influential modern-dress, anti-fascist *Julius Caesar* when he was only 22. Among the many uncompleted projects of his post-*Citizen Kane* years were three Shakespeare films. *Macbeth* (1948), scorned by Shakespeare lovers, attracted excited and enthusiastic critical comment from cineastes, especially in France. His *Othello* (made in fits and starts on a shoestring budget) was released in 1952, followed by a restored version in 1993. *Chimes at Midnight* (1966), adapted from the *Henry IV* plays, was appropriately released in some countries under the name of the character Welles played, as *Falstaff*. Although it arguably distorts the priorities in the *Henry IV* plays, it is considered not only Welles's Shakespearian masterpiece, but one of the most powerful Shakespeare films. *AD*

Wesker, Arnold (b. 1932), English playwright. His *Birth of Shylock and Death of Zero Mostel* (1997) chronicles the failed 1977 Broadway production of his play *Shylock* (originally *The Merchant*, 1976). Wesker, reacting against Laurence *Olivier's mannered interpretation of Shakespeare's character, presents an alternative Shylock: intelligent, compassionate, and deeply moral. *TM*

West Africa. Shakespeare is said to have first reached African waters on board a ship, anchored off Sierra Leone in 1607, where performances of *Hamlet* and *Richard II* were given. As was the case in *East Africa, missionary and colonial activity from the 19th century on ensured the presence of Shakespeare in various educational and cultural practices. The Church Missionary Society established the Grammar School for Boys in Freetown, Sierre Leone, in 1849; Lemuel Johnson, who attended the school in the 20th century, recalls studying *Macbeth*, *The Merchant of Venice*, *Julius Caesar*, *1 Henry IV*, *Henry V*, and *King Lear*. Dependence on Cambridge University School and Higher School Certificate requirements during the colonial period and beyond ensured the continuing influence of Shakespeare. E. T. Johnson translated *Julius Caesar* into Yoruba in the 1930s and G. E. Hood of Achimota College, Accra, records performances at his school of *Twelfth Night* in the 1930s. Performances of Shakespeare in West Africa include a screen adaptation of *Hamlet*, shot in Ghana and shown at a Commonwealth Arts Festival, and, during the colonial period, visits by performers of Shakespeare arranged by the British Council. In 1954 Molly Mahood delivered her Inaugural Lecture at the University of Ibadan. Both she and Eldred Jones (Fourah Bay College, University of Sierra Leone) have made significant contributions to Shakespeare studies, Jones contributing as well to the study of local literatures. Michael Echeruo (Nigeria) and Lemuel Johnson (Sierra Leone), who have also worked on Shakespeare, now work in the United States.

In an essay that has since become a 'classic' of cultural anthropology, Laura Bohannan gives an account of her attempt to impart *Hamlet* to the Tiv; the essay provides an example of the misrecognitions that may occur for all the participants in any cultural encounter or clash. However, in comparison with East, Central, and *Southern Africa, the reception of Shakespeare in West African countries appears markedly less interrogative of the problematics of a colonial Shakespeare. Hints of potentially complex views of the Shakespeare text are to be found in Ben Okri's response in 1987 in the journal *West Africa* to an RSC production of *Othello* with Ben *Kingsley in the title role as well as in Lemuel Johnson's recent work and in his appropriation in the 1970s of the figure of Caliban, relocated in Freetown and presented as victim of neocolonialism. Even so, as late as the early 1990s Shakespeare was still a compulsory text at secondary level in Sierra Leone, prompting Handel Kashope Wright to wonder, rather belatedly in comparison with the debate in other parts of Africa, why this continues at the expense of local literatures.

As in other parts of Africa, the reception of Shakespeare has involved politicians and cultural activists as well as writers. James Kwegyir Aggrey, who left the Gold Coast for the United States, cited Shakespeare as an important influence; a pamphlet in 1952 salutes Kwame Nkrumah by means of Shakespeare allusion; and in 1960 Nigeria's Chief Awolowo insisted that 'some of the mighty lines of Shakespeare must have influenced my outlook on life'. The specific influence of Shakespeare on a number of West African writers has also been remarked upon. Wole *Soyinka read English under George Wilson *Knight and the influence of Shakespeare on his work has been noted, especially that of *A Midsummer Night's Dream* as well as of *Macbeth* on *A Dance in the Forests*. Soyinka himself has noted that between 1899 and 1950 some sixteen plays of Shakespeare had been translated or adapted by *Arab poets and dramatists. The Nigerian playwright John Pepper Clark argues for the example of Shakespeare as model, taking up the instance of Caliban to advocate a variety of registers within African writing. Shakespeare's influence has been detected too in the work of other Nigerians including the Onitsha Market Pamphleteers. *MO*

***West Side Story*,** Broadway musical (1957) and Hollywood film (1961), with the story of *Romeo and Juliet* transposed to fit young immigrant groups on New York's waterfront. Invigorating adaptation (Arthur Laurents), choreography (Jerome Robbins), and songs (Leonard Bernstein and Stephen Sondheim) make this the most successful modern *adaptation of Shakespeare. *TM*

Westminster. The burial place of Edward the Confessor, there may have been a church on the site of Westminster Abbey as early as the late 8th century. The abbey became a centre for royal ceremonial from the 13th century and emphasis on the abbey led to Westminster Hall, built by William II in 1097/9, becoming the centre of royal administration: as such it features crucially in Shakespeare's histories, notably the *Henry IV* plays. The abbey became the resting place of poets as well as monarchs after *Spenser was buried near *Chaucer in 1599: Ben *Jonson, who would himself be added to what has become known as 'Poets' Corner' in due course, comments on Shakespeare's burial in Stratford instead of in the abbey in his dedicatory poem to the First *Folio. Shakespeare received an honorary *monument in the abbey in 1741, a statue by *Scheemakers funded by public subscription. *RSB*

Inwood, S., *A History of London* (1998)

Westminster, Abbot of. He plots against Bolingbroke with Aumerle and the Bishop of Carlisle at the end of Act 4 of *Richard II*. His death is announced, 5.6.19–21. *AB*

Westmorland (Westmoreland), Earl of (1) As one of King Henry's supporters he is angry when Henry makes York his heir, *Richard Duke of York* (*3 Henry VI*) 1.1. Historically, Ralph Neville (d. 1484), the 2nd Earl of Westmorland, supported neither Henry nor York. **(2)** In *1 Henry IV* he leads the King's forces against the rebels (see 3.2.171, 4.1.88–9, 5.4, and 5.5.36–9) and in *2 Henry IV* he is Prince John's right-hand man against the rebels. In *Henry V* he accompanies King Harry at Agincourt (unhistorical). He was the grandfather of the preceding Westmorland and was also called Ralph Neville (1364–1425), the 1st Earl of Westmorland. *AB*

'What shall he have that killed the deer?', sung by the two Lords in *As You Like It* 4.2.10. A round published by John Hilton (1652) may possibly be a version of the original music. *JB*

Whately (Whateley), Anne, the name of Shakespeare's bride according to his marriage licence (see Hathaway, Anne). Though almost certainly the result of clerical error, it has stimulated fantasies. In *The Man Shakespeare* (1909), Frank *Harris (of whom Oscar *Wilde wrote in a letter of 1899 that he was 'upstairs, thinking about Shakespeare at the top of his voice') supposed that Shakespeare was persuaded to jilt a woman of this name in favour of Anne Hathaway; Ivor Brown and Anthony *Burgess are among those who followed suit. *SW*

'When Arthur first in court', the opening of a *broadside ballad sung by Falstaff in *2 Henry IV* 2.4.32. The tune is 'Flying fame'. *JB*

'When daffodils begin to peer', sung by Autolycus in *The Winter's Tale* 4.3.1. The original music is unknown; an anonymous tune was published by Joseph Ritson (1783), and a setting attributed to William Boyce (long after his death) was brought out by William Linley (1816); 20th-century settings include those by Ireland, Quilter, and Warlock. *JB*

'When daisies pied', sung by Spring at the end of *Love's Labour's Lost*, and followed by Winter singing 'When icicles hang by the wall'. The earliest surviving music for the two songs is by Richard *Leveridge (*c.*1725); this was followed in the mid-18th century by the more familiar *Arne versions. Twentieth-century settings include those by Finzi, Moeran (both songs), Stravinsky, Warlock ('When daisies pied'), Quilter, and *Vaughan Williams ('When icicles hang by the wall'). *JB*

'When griping grief the heart doth wound'. See Edwards, Richard.

'When icicles hang by the wall'. See 'When daisies pied'.

'When that I was and a little tiny boy', sung by Feste at the end of *Twelfth Night*; the original music is unknown. The tune traditionally used comes from a setting composed by the singer Joseph Vernon, published *c.*1772. It is possible that Vernon arranged a melody already familiar for the song. More recent settings include those by Dankworth, Korngold, Quilter, Schumann, Sibelius, and Stanford. *JB*

'Where is the life that late I led?', fragment of a lost ballad, sung by Petruccio in *The Taming of the Shrew* 4.1.126, and quoted by Pistol in *2 Henry IV* 5.3.139; it formed the basis for a song in Cole *Porter's *Kiss Me Kate*. The original music is unknown. *JB*

'Where the bee sucks', sung by Ariel in *The Tempest* 5.1.88. The setting by Robert *Johnson may well have been used in an early production during Shakespeare's life (see 'Full fathom five'), although it is not now as familiar as *Arne's version from the mid-18th century. There is a later 17th-century setting by Humfrey; 20th-century composers include Arnold, Martin, Moeran, Quilter, *Tippett. *JB*

Whetstone, George (?1544–?1587), author, adventurer, and soldier who fought at the battle of Zutphen at which *Sidney was killed. Whetstone's works include *The Rock of Regard*, published in 1576, consisting of 68 pieces of prose and verse, many drawn from Italian *novelle*. Among these tales is 'Cressid's Complaint', Whetstone's contribution to the growing condemnation of Cressida in the 16th century, which offered her story as a fable warning against wantonness. However, Whetstone's most popular work was the two-part play

Promos and Cassandra, published in 1578 though never acted. The play is based on a story in *Cinthio's *Hecatommithi* about a woman who is offered the choice of losing her virginity to the magistrate who has condemned her brother to death, thereby saving him, or letting her brother die. Whetstone returned to this story in 1582 when he adapted it into a *novella*, in the *Heptameron of Civil Discourses* (reprinted as *Aurelia* in 1593). Shakespeare certainly drew upon the tragicomedy *Promos and Cassandra* for *Measure for Measure*. He may also have had recourse to Whetstone's prose version. *JKS*

'While you here do snoring lie', sung by Ariel in *The Tempest* 2.1.302; the earliest surviving setting is by *Arne, from the mid-18th century. *JB*

White, William. See PRINTING AND PUBLISHING.

Whitefriars theatre. See CHILDREN'S COMPANIES; FIELD, NATHAN.

Whitehall, formerly a property known as York Place and in the ownership of the Archbishop of York until the Henrician dissolution: after Wolsey's fall the land went to the King, with the name later applying to the whole street (see *All Is True* (*Henry VIII*) 4.1.94–101). Whitehall became the main royal residence until 1698 and is the location of Inigo *Jones's Banqueting House, built 1619–25 for the performance of *masques: a wooden hall on the same site had already been an important venue for court theatrical performances. *RSB*

Inwood, S., *A History of London* (1998)

Whiter, Walter (1758–1832), English philologist. His *Specimen of a Commentary on Shakespeare* (1794) is regarded as a precursor of 20th-century *'imagery' criticism. Influenced by John Locke's psychological doctrine of the association of ideas, Whiter demonstrated several such recurrent clusters—for example, *flatterers*, *dogs*, and *sweetmeats*—in Shakespeare's language. *TM*

Whitmore, Walter. He is Suffolk's murderer, *The First Part of the Contention* (*2 Henry VI*) 4.1. *AB*

Whittington, Thomas, a shepherd employed by Anne *Hathaway's parents. In his will dated 25 March 1601 he left 'unto the poore people of Stratford 40[s]. that is in the hand of Anne Shaxspere, wyf unto M[r] Willyam Shaxspere, and is due debt unto me, beyng payd to myne Executor by the sayd Wyllyam Shaxspere or his assigns'. Anne's brothers also owed him money; probably his employers acted as his bankers. *SW*

'Who is Silvia?', song in *The Two Gentlemen of Verona* 4.2.38; the singer is not identified specifically. Many commentators agree on Proteus, although some have assumed the performer to be one or more of the musicians present during the scene. The original music is unknown; the earliest to survive is by *Leveridge (1727), but the best-known setting is *Schubert's 'An Sylvia' (1826). More recent composers include Coates, Dankworth, Finzi, German, Howells, Quilter, Rubbra. *JB*

'Whoop, do me no harm, good man', a *ballad tune title quoted by the Old Shepherd's servant in *The Winter's Tale* 4.4.199. *JB*

widows. (1) A widow marries Hortensio, appearing in *The Taming of the Shrew* 5.2. **(2)** Widow Capilet (Capulet), is the keeper of the hostel of St Francis in *Florence. She and her daughter Diana assist Helen with her marital problems in *All's Well That Ends Well*. *AB*

Wieland, Christoph Martin (1733–1813), German poet. His prose translation of 22 plays (1766–7) first acquainted the German reading public with Shakespeare's work. For *A Midsummer Night's Dream* he used verse; it also inspired his poem *Oberon* (1780). *WH*

Wilde, Oscar (Fingal O'Flahertie Wills) (1854–1900), Irish playwright and author. Wilde's *Portrait of Mr W.H.* (1889), in which 'homoerotic fantasy successfully masquerades as fiction and criticism' (*Schoenbaum), identifies the 'onlie begetter' of the Sonnets as William or Willie Hughes, a boy-actor playing women's parts, a first name which is certainly punned on in Sonnets 135–6, 143, and a last which may be in Sonnet 20, 'A man in hew all *Hews* in his controwling'. The fiction's use of a hanging portrait of *Mr W.H. seems almost analogous to Wilde's other corrupted portrait, that of *Dorian Gray* (1891). Wilde's citation of Shakespeare's Sonnets during his notorious trial in 1895 had a permanent impact on popular views of Shakespeare's *sexuality. *TM*

Wilkins, George (fl. 1603–8), playwright. Little is known about Wilkins's life. Among other things, he wrote a popular domestic tragedy based on a real murder case, *The Miseries of Enforced Marriage*, performed by Shakespeare's company, which went through four editions between 1607 and 1637. He also wrote a piece of prose fiction, *The Painful Adventures of Pericles Prince of Tyre* (1608). This steals passages from a version of the story by Laurence *Twine, written in the 1570s and reprinted in 1607. Twine's narrative is a source of Shakespeare's *Pericles*, and Wilkins's fiction also incorporates passages from the play. Many scholars, including the editors of the Oxford Shakespeare (1986), contend that Wilkins co-wrote *Pericles* with Shakespeare, and that some of the passages he quotes in *The Painful Adventures* may be more accurately recorded there than in the corrupt first edition of the play (1609). *RM*

will, Shakespeare's. Shakespeare seems to have drafted his will in January 1616, shortly before his daughter Judith was to be married. The final draft (no fair copy survives) is dated 25 March 1616. From time to time it is claimed to be in his own hand, but Mark Eccles, who worked extensively and intensively on the Stratford records, is one of many scholars who believe it to have been drafted and written by the lawyer Francis *Collins (d. 1617), who had drawn up the indentures for Shakespeare's purchase of tithes in 1605, since 'the handwriting matches exactly his handwriting in the Council Book'. Others dispute this, arguing that it was drawn up by a clerk employed by Collins. It is a formal document, obviously phrased by a lawyer; but it clearly reflects Shakespeare's considered, and reconsidered, intentions. The first sheet, recopied from an earlier draft, is dated 'Januarij', which has been corrected to 'Martij'. This page is mostly concerned with Judith *Shakespeare, and the recopying was probably necessitated by changes following her marriage to Thomas *Quiney and the scandal of his liaison with the unfortunate Margaret Wheeler.

The second and third sheets are not recopied but contain a number of changes and additions. Each sheet bears Shakespeare's *signature, that on the last page preceded by the words 'By me'. They are in a different hand from the will, but D. Thomas, in *Shakespeare in the Public Records* (1985), claimed that even these were written by a clerk.

The will opens with a formulaic declaration of faith. Shakespeare's principal bequests are as follows:

1. To his daughter Judith, £100 as a marriage portion and £50 more on condition that she surrender to her sister Susanna her rights in a cottage in *Chapel Lane; the interest on another £150 was to go to her or, if she had died, to her children three years after the date of the will, and she would continue to receive the interest for as long as she was married. Her husband could claim the £150 only if he settled lands of equal value on her. She was also to have her father's silver-and-gilt bowl.

2. To his sister *Joan (Hart), £20, all his wearing apparel, and the house in which she was living in Henley Street for as long as she lived, at an annual rent of 12*d.*

3. To Joan's three sons, £5 each.

4. To his granddaughter Elizabeth *Hall (then 8 years old), all his plate except the bowl left to Judith.

5. To the poor of Stratford, £10.

6. To Thomas *Combe, his sword.

7. To Thomas *Russell, £5.

8. To Francis Collins, £13 6*s.* 8*d.*

9. To Hamnet *Sadler, 26*s.* 8*d.* to buy a ring (replacing what had apparently been a similar bequest to Richard *Tyler the elder).

10. To William Reynolds, 26*s.* 8*d.* to buy a ring.

11. To his 7-year-old godson William *Walker, 20*s.* in gold.

12. To Anthony *Nash, John *Nash, and to his 'fellows' John *Heminges, Richard *Burbage, and Henry *Condell, 26*s.* 8*d.* to buy them rings.

13. To his daughter Susanna (Hall), *New Place, two houses in Henley Street, all his 'barnes stables Orchardes gardens landes tenementes & hereditamentes' in the Stratford area along with the *Blackfriars Gatehouse, all in entail to Susanna and her heirs male, his daughter Judith and her heirs male, and 'for default of such issue' to his 'Right heires'.

14. To his wife his 'second best bed with the furniture' (this is an added bequest).

15. To John and Susanna Hall, all his remaining property.

The Halls were the executors, and Thomas Russell and Francis Collins the overseers. Five witnesses signed the will: Francis Collins, July Shaw, John Robinson, Hamnet Sadler, and Robert Whatcott.

The will is preserved in the Public Record Office, London. Its existence was known by October 1737, when George Vertue noted that a copy was also owned by Shakespeare Hart, owner of the *Birthplace and a descendant of Shakespeare's sister Joan. It seems to have been first printed in the posthumous third edition (1752) of *Theobald's edition. It has been the subject of endless interpretation and speculation, especially in relation to the bequest to Anne of the second-best bed and to the absence of reference to books and papers, which are likely however to have been listed in an inventory which has not survived. They probably passed to John *Hall, whose will lists a 'Study of Bookes' bequeathed to Thomas Nash. It may also be noted that the will does not mention Shakespeare's patron of his younger days, the Earl of *Southampton, his 'cousin' Thomas *Greene, his alleged bastard William *Davenant, or any member of his wife's family, although Anne's brother Bartholomew lived in Shottery with his wife and four children. *SW*

Schoenbaum, S., *William Shakespeare: A Documentary Life* (1975, compact edn. 1977)

William, Touchstone's rival for Audrey, is warned off by him, *As You Like It* 5.1. *AB*

William, Lord Hastings. See HASTINGS, LORD.

Williams, Clifford (b. 1926), British director. A former actor with a special interest in mime, he joined the *Royal Shakespeare Company at Stratford in 1963 where he directed a brilliantly farcical *Comedy of Errors*, which was frequently revived. He staged a controversial all-male *As You Like It* at the *National Theatre in 1967 and has also directed abroad. *MJ*

Williams, Harcourt (1880–1957), actor and director. Having gone on the stage at 17 he had experience with Ellen *Terry and Beerbohm *Tree and played Macbeth at the Birmingham Repertory in 1915. His influential contribution to the staging of Shakespeare came when he was unexpectedly engaged as a director of productions at the *Old Vic. He was determined to break away from the slow deliberation of the Shakespeare voice and to give speed and pace to his productions, along the lines recommended by *Granville-Barker in his *Prefaces.* He engaged promising actors like John *Gielgud, Donald *Wolfit, and Peggy *Ashcroft and, within the financial limits imposed by Lilian *Baylis, greatly improved the visual design. He continued acting into old age and can be seen as the King of France in *Olivier's film of *Henry v.* *MJ*

Williams, John (d. ?1634), unsuccessful theatrical entrepreneur and possibly a musician. Together with John Cotton and Thomas Dixon, John Williams was granted a licence to built an amphitheatre for 'martial exercises, and extraordinary shows', but King *James wrote to the Privy Council revoking this licence on 29 September 1620. On 28 September 1626 another attempt by Cotton and Williams to build an amphitheatre was blocked. This John Williams might have been the musician to the King buried in St Peter's, Paul's Wharf, in 1634. *GE*

Williams, Michael. (1) A soldier at Agincourt, he falls victim to King Harry's practical joke, *Henry v* 4.1, 4.7, and 4.8. **(2)** The versatile and accomplished *RSC actor of the same name (1935–2001), ingeniously cast in the role in Kenneth *Branagh's film (1989). *AB*

Williams, Raymond. See CULTURAL MATERIALISM.

Williamson, Nicol (b. 1938), Scottish actor and director. Noted for playing self-destructive anti-heroes, Williamson shocked audiences in 1969 by playing Hamlet as, in his words, 'a frightening man, an unpleasant man'. In 1982, he directed and starred in an exceedingly dark *Macbeth* for the Circle in the Square theatre, New York. *BR*

Willobie his Avisa, a poem by Henry Willobie (b. *c.*1575) printed in 1594. Commendatory verses include the first literary reference to Shakespeare by name:

> Yet Tarquin plucked his glistering grape,
> And Shakespeare paints poor Lucrece' rape.

The deliberately enigmatic poem tells how Avisa, an innkeeper's wife, rejected many suitors, including 'Henry Willobego', who confided his love to 'his familiar friend, W.S.', recently recovered from a similar passion. W.S. 'in viewing afar off the course of this loving comedy . . . determined to see whether it would sort to a happier end for this new actor than it did for the old player'. Willobie was related by marriage to Shakespeare's friend Thomas *Russell. Shakespeare may be 'W.S.' *SW*

Willoughby, Lord. He is one of Bolingbroke's supporters in *Richard II*, based on William de Willoughby, 5th Baron Willoughby de Eresby (d. 1409). *AB*

Willow song, sung by Desdemona in *Othello* 4.3.38. Not included in the quarto text (1622), it is one of many additions made to the *Folio edition (1623). Desdemona says that the song is 'an old thing', and it survives in various manuscript versions from the period, with additional stanzas and textual variants, as well as two different melodies. Later composers include Humfrey (17th century); Giordani, Hook (18th century); and Coleridge-Taylor, *Parry, Sullivan, *Vaughan Williams (late 19th and early 20th century). *JB*

'Will you buy any tape', sung by Autolycus in *The Winter's Tale* 4.4.313. The original music is unknown; the first four lines fit the tune of *'Jog on', sung previously by Autolycus. *JB*

Wilmcote is a village about two and a half miles (4 km) from Stratford, home of Shakespeare's mother Mary *Arden, and location of *Mary Arden's House. There her father owned the estate known as *Asbies which he willed to her in 1556. *SW*

Wilmot, James. See BACONIAN THEORY.

Wilson, John (1595–1674), composer and lutenist. Settings of Shakespeare songs appear in his publications. Some of these are now attributed to Robert *Johnson (e.g. *'Full fathom five'). There has also been confusion with an actor and singer named as Jacke Wilson in a stage direction (First Folio) for *Much Ado About Nothing*, shortly before *'Sigh no more, ladies'. *JB*

Wilson, John Dover (1881–1969), English academic, editor, and critic. His vast learning, liberal sensibility, and critical vigour were widely diffused in the volumes of the New *Cambridge edition of Shakespeare, which he edited (with Sir Arthur *Quiller-Couch and others) 1921–66. His 1936 edition of *Hamlet*, its text based on the then unfashionable second quarto of 1604/5, was prepared for and justified in *The Manuscript of Shakespeare's 'Hamlet'* (1934), as were its 'Elizabethan' interpretations of the play (particularly respecting the Ghost and the dumb show) in *What Happens in 'Hamlet'* (1935). His characteristic combination of insight and enthusiasm are equally apparent in: *The Essential Shakespeare* (1932), 'a biographical adventure'; *The Fortunes of Falstaff* (1953); and *Shakespeare's Happy Comedies* (1969). An edition by A. L. *Rowse of *Shakespeare's Sonnets* (1963), in which Rowse claimed that only a 'true historian' could solve the relevant biographical problems, provoked a vigorous polemic in which Dover Wilson's urbane introduction for the New Cambridge *Sonnets* was separately printed with a predictably provocative subtitle *An Introduction for Historians and Others* (1963), just in time for the quatercentenary celebrations. His vivid and varied compilation of Elizabethan prose, *Life in Shakespeare's England* (in print since 1911), has remained a popular student companion. *TM*

Winchester, Bishop of. (1) See Beaufort, Cardinal. **(2)** See Gardiner.

Winchester House, or Palace, was built by Henry of Blois, Bishop of Winchester and brother of King Stephen, in the mid-12th century. It was the London home of the bishops and the seat of their jurisdiction over the *Liberty of the *Clink. The west wall and its rose window still stand. *RSB*

Carlin, M., *Medieval Southwark* (1996)

Wincot. In *The Taming of the Shrew*, Christopher Sly mentions 'Marian Hacket, the fat alewife of Wincot' (Induction 2, 20). This could be an alternative name for *Wilmcote, or for Willicote or Little Wilmcote, other small villages close to Stratford. *SW*

Windsor, or the countryside nearby, is the scene of *The Merry Wives of Windsor*, and is mentioned in *1* and *2 Henry IV* and *1 Henry VI*. *AB*

***Winter's Tale*, The** *(see page 522)*

Wise, Andrew. See printing and publishing.

witchcraft. 'Witch' is a term so slippery that whole law-books were devoted to defining it. Very generally, for most ordinary English people in Shakespeare's day, a witch was someone with the power of doing harm, either through her own body or will, or through the use of magic, but for learned demonologists a witch was a person who had exchanged his or her soul for the power to summon the devil to do harm on his or her behalf. The second definition gradually displaced the first during the reigns of first Elizabeth and then James, but this made little impact on popular belief. What did make a growing impact was scepticism: beginning with Reginald *Scot's *Discovery of Witchcraft* (1584) and continuing with Samuel *Harsnett's *Declaration of Egregious Popish Impostures* (1603), elite disbelief in witchcraft gathered pace until even *James I was unmasking pretended demoniacs rather than endorsing their fantasies. Witch prosecutions declined under James, having peaked during the years of the Armada panic, and declined still more sharply under *Charles, who sent his own personal physician to prove that a group of women condemned in Lancashire in 1633 were innocent.

It was for this sceptical audience that Shakespeare produced *Macbeth* (and for which *Middleton supplied its later Hecate passages), responding to a vogue for witch plays created by Ben *Jonson's *Masque of Queens*: it includes many more witches than its sources, but uses almost entirely sceptical materials as its sources, principally Scot. Like Scot, the play displays what it takes to be popular witch-beliefs to an audience that has parted company with them. (Similarly, demoniac possession in *King Lear* is based on Harsnett, and is here explicitly fraudulent.) *Macbeth* in its Folio form contains transplanted material from Middleton's grossly comical *The Witch*, which may be more closely related to the Overbury poisoning scandal than to popular witch beliefs, about which neither he nor Shakespeare may have had any knowledge independent of Scot. By contrast, witchcraft in *The First Part of the Contention* (*2 Henry VI*) is explicity related to Catholicism and treason against England in the person of Joan la Pucelle, who when declared to be a witch appears to owe more to the witches in book 3 of *Spenser's *The Faerie Queene* than to anything that might be found in the countryside. In *Richard III*, by contrast, Richard's accusations of witchcraft against his political enemies are the paranoid fictions of an unstable tyrant, while in *The Merry Wives of Windsor* the 'witch' of Brainford does not exist: she is simply Falstaff in disguise. This play, in which Mistress *Quickly makes a splendidly sceptical queen or quean of the *fairies, is a sophisticated comic riposte to what its author took to be popular credulity, and in it one sees the Shakespeare who befriended Ben Jonson, the arch-sceptic. In this play Mistress Quickly and Anne Page owe a little to the clever, matchmaking, cunning-woman of *Lyly's *Mother Bombie*, a character later revived by *Heywood in his *Wise Woman of Hogsden*. It is ironic, therefore, that most people's ideas about early modern witchcraft are based at least in part on the words of a man who profoundly disbelieved in what he wrote. Though Shakespeare's Weird Sisters were eventually triumphant, they were in their time at variance with the use of witches as characters in domestic tragicomedies such as *The Witches of Lancashire* and *The Witch of Edmonton*, which sought explicitly to defuse what they took to be popular superstition by mockery and biting satire. *DP*

Briggs, Robin, *Witches and Neighbours* (1996)
Purkiss, Diane, *The Witch in History* (1996)
Roper, Lyndal, *Oedipus and the Devil* (1994)
Willis, Deborah, *Malevolent Nurture* (1996)

witches, three. They meet again to make equivocal predictions with disastrous consequences, *Macbeth* 1.1 ff. *AB*

***Wits, The*, title page.** *The Wits* (1662) is a collection of 'drolls' or comic episodes from popular plays adapted for independent performance, and it has a title-page engraving (probably by John Chantry) showing seven figures together on a stage, including Sir John Falstaff and a Hostess (originally from Shakespeare's *1 Henry IV*), and a 'Changling', presumably Antonio from Middleton and Rowley's play *The Changeling*. A second, enlarged, edition of *The Wits*, printed in 1672–3 with a coarse copy of the original title-page engraving, contains Francis Kirkman's preface which associates the drolls with Robert *Cox and the Red Bull playhouse, but the engraving is of little theatrical interest, being derived from non-theatrical sources. (See page 118.) *GE*

Astington, John H., '*The Wits* Illustration, 1662', *Theatre Notebook*, 47 (1993)

Witter, John (fl. *c*.1600–20), a Londoner who married the actor Augustine *Phillips's widow in 1606. By remarrying she forfeited her husband's share in the *Globe, but five years later John *Heminges, who had succeeded her as executor, leased it back to the couple. When the Globe burned down they were unable to meet their share of the cost of rebuilding, so their rights passed back to Heminges, who gave half of them to *Condell. In April 1619 Witter, who had abandoned his now-dead wife, sued Heminges and Condell. The court case, which Witter lost, provides important information about the company's organization. *SW*

Wallace, C. W., 'Shakespeare and his London Associates . . .', *Nebraska University Studies*, 10 (1910)

Woffington, Margaret (Peg) (?1717–1760), actor, singer, and dancer, probably born in Dublin where her successful career began as a child performer with the gymnast Signora Violante. She progressed to a singing and dancing Dorinda in *The Tempest; or, The Enchanted Island* and Ophelia, and achieved huge popularity in breeches roles, most famously as Sir Harry Wildair in *The Constant Couple*. She triumphed as Cordelia at *Covent Garden in 1740 and quickly became a fashionable beauty and wit, painted by *Hogarth, Hudson, and *Zoffany. She was not considered to have a great voice but had a broad Shakespearian repertoire including Rosalind, Adriana, and Nerissa at *Drury Lane from 1741. In 1742 she performed in Dublin with *Garrick (with whom she had an affair) playing Cordelia to his Lear and Lady Anne to his Richard III. She played Viola in the 1745 Drury Lane revival of *Twelfth Night*. In much demand as a leading lady she also played Desdemona to *Quin's

(cont. on page 525)

The Winter's Tale

Although it clearly belongs among the late romances—with its artful structure and almost insolent mastery of complex narrative and characterization—*The Winter's Tale* is difficult to date with precision. A dance of satyrs in Act 4 (4.4.340–1) seems to be borrowed from Ben *Jonson's *Masque of Oberon*, acted at court on 1 January 1611, but its irrelevance there and the awkwardness with which it is introduced by the surrounding dialogue suggests that this may be a late interpolation, indicating that the play was written before Jonson's masque rather than after it. In any event *The Winter's Tale* had been completed by May 1611, when Simon *Forman saw it at the Globe: his journal entry describing the performance supplies the only reliable external evidence for the play's date of composition. Internal evidence is more ambiguous. Autolycus' grisly account of the torments allegedly in store for the Clown (4.4.784–92) derives from the same material in *Boccaccio that Shakespeare uses in *Cymbeline*: this suggests that the two plays are close in date but cannot reveal which was written first. A number of minor debts to *Plutarch, however (principally characters' names), suggest that *The Winter's Tale* may be the closer in date of the two to *Antony and Cleopatra* and *Coriolanus*, and most stylistic tests place it closer to Shakespeare's sections of *Pericles* (1607) than is *Cymbeline*. It was probably composed just before *Cymbeline*, in 1609–10.

Text: The play first appeared in the *Folio in 1623, as the last of the comedies: the copy for it seems to have arrived late (in December 1622 at the earliest), when the next section of the book was already in production. The text's idiosyncrasies of spelling, its paucity of stage directions, its heavy punctuation, and its habit of listing all the characters who are to appear in a scene at its opening indicate that it was set from a transcript prepared by the scribe Ralph *Crane, though Crane's customary willingness to intervene in the interests of tidiness make it difficult to deduce the nature of the copy he was transcribing. If the satyr dance in Act 4 is indeed a late interpolation Crane was probably transcribing a promptbook.

Sources: *The Winter's Tale* is primarily a dramatization of Robert *Greene's prose romance *Pandosto* (subtitled *The Triumph of Time*, and also known as 'The History of Dorastus and Fawnia'), which had first appeared in 1588 and had gone through five editions before Shakespeare composed *The Winter's Tale*. Shakespeare had probably known this work for some time: in any case he was not working from its most recent edition, printed in 1607, since this text alters the wording of the oracle's declaration, and the play here follows the earlier editions verbatim. Shakespeare changes the principals' names (Pandosto becomes Leontes, Bellaria becomes Hermione; Egistus becomes Polixenes; Dorastus and Fawnia become Florizel and Perdita), exchanges the places of *Bohemia and Sicilia (though even in Greene Bohemia is miraculously provided with a coast), and drastically alters the story's tragic ending. The statue scene is entirely Shakespeare's invention (though it draws in part on the story of Pygmalion and Galatea, told in *Ovid's *Metamorphoses*): in *Pandosto*, Bellaria is genuinely and finally dead after the trial scene, and when years later Fawnia is brought to Pandosto's court he falls in love with her. After learning of her identity, he commits suicide. The play has no other major sources, though it derives incidental details from a number of texts (besides Plutarch and Boccaccio). Polixenes' defence of art (4.4.89–97) borrows from a similar passage in *Puttenham's *Art of English Poesy* (1589), while Shakespeare's knowledge of *Giulio Romano (5.2.96) probably derives, whether at first or second hand, from Giorgio Vasari's *Vite de' piu eccellenti* *pittori, scultori, e architettori* (1550). The scene of the mother's statue in Paulina's gallery may have been influenced, too, by *James I's commissioning of painted memorial sculptures of his predecessor *Elizabeth I (completed in 1607) and of his mother Mary Stuart (completed before 1612), both in *Westminster Abbey.

Synopsis: **1.1** Camillo, a courtier to Leontes, King of Sicilia, exchanges courtesies with Archidamus, who is visiting in the train of Leontes' childhood friend Polixenes, King of Bohemia. They speak enthusiastically of Leontes' young son Mamillius. **1.2** Polixenes has been in Sicilia nine months, and plans to embark for Bohemia the following day. Leontes implores him to stay another week, and when his pregnant Queen Hermione adds her own entreaties Polixenes finally relents. Leontes becomes convinced that Polixenes and Hermione are conducting an affair: he talks aside with Mamillius, watching them together. After Polixenes and Hermione have gone and Mamillius has been dismissed, Leontes calls Camillo and tells him of his conviction about Hermione: overruling Camillo's insistence that the Queen is innocent, he commands him to poison Polixenes. Alone, Camillo reflects in horror on his situation, and when Polixenes arrives he tells him everything and agrees to help him make his escape.

2.1 Mamillius is about to tell his mother a horror story suitable for winter when Leontes arrives with a courtier, Antigonus: Polixenes' reported flight with Camillo seems to confirm all his suspicions. Dismissing Mamillius, he accuses Hermione of being pregnant by Polixenes, and despite her protestations of innocence has her taken to prison. When his courtiers take her part, he tells them he has sent Cleomenes and Dion to consult Apollo's oracle at Delphi for confirmation of Hermione's guilt. **2.2** Antigonus' wife Paulina calls at the prison and learns from Hermione's attendant Emilia that she has given birth to a daughter: reassuring the Jailer that the child is not included in the warrant against Hermione, Paulina proposes to show the baby to Leontes in the hope of restoring him to sanity. **2.3** A sleepless Leontes learns further of Mamillius' illness since the imprisonment of his mother. Paulina confronts him with his child, hoping to persuade him of its legitimacy by its resemblance to him: refusing to believe her, he finally has her dismissed, and then commands her husband Antigonus to take the baby and abandon it in some wilderness beyond his country's borders. When news arrives that the messengers are on their way from the oracle, preparations are instigated for Hermione's trial.

3.1 Cleomenes and Dion reflect with satisfaction on their experiences at Apollo's oracle. **3.2** Before Leontes, Hermione is formally accused of treasonous adultery with Polixenes: she eloquently denies the charge, and refers her innocence to the oracle. Cleomenes and Dion swear they have faithfully brought the oracle's written declaration, sealed and unread. Unsealed, the scroll declares that Hermione is innocent and her daughter truly begotten, and adds that 'the King shall live without an heir if that which is lost be not found'. Leontes at first refuses to believe this, but after a messenger brings the news that Mamillius has died, on which Hermione collapses and is taken away by Paulina and her attendants, he accepts the truth of the oracle. He is already repenting when Paulina returns and tells him Hermione too has died: welcoming her bitter reproaches, he promises to mourn his dead wife and son perpetually. **3.3** Antigonus has dreamed of Hermione's ghost, who told him to call the baby Perdita and leave it in Bohemia, prophesying that Antigonus would never see Paulina again. Believing the child must really be Polixenes', he has been brought to the Bohemian coast by ship, and as the weather worsens he leaves Perdita there, with a scroll explaining her name and identity and a box containing gold. He is chased away by a bear. An old shepherd arrives and finds the child: he is joined by his son, the Clown, who recounts seeing the bear eating Antigonus and his ship being wrecked in the storm with all hands. They open the box and set off home with Perdita, the Clown proposing to bury the remains of Antigonus on his way.

4.1 The figure of Time speaks a chorus, explaining that the play now skips sixteen years, during which Leontes grieves in seclusion, and will resume in Bohemia, where Perdita has grown up as a shepherdess. **4.2** Polixenes persuades Camillo to postpone his longed-for return to Sicilia in order to help him investigate his truant son Florizel's reported passion for a beautiful shepherdess: they will disguise themselves and visit her father's cottage. **4.3** Autolycus, a courtier-turned-pedlar-cum-confidence trickster, sings 'When daffodils begin to peer': when the Clown arrives, on his way to buy ingredients for the sheep-shearing feast over which his supposed sister Perdita is to preside, Autolycus pretends to have been beaten and robbed, and picks his pocket. Singing 'Jog on, jog on, the footpath way', Autolycus sets off for the sheep-shearing in quest of further prey. **4.4** Florizel, disguised as the rustic 'Doricles', congratulates Perdita on the robes she is wearing as Queen of the Feast, and reassures her of his honourable determination to marry her despite their difference in rank. The Old Shepherd brings the occasion's guests, among them the Clown, the countrywomen Mopsa and Dorcas, and the disguised Polixenes and Camillo: Perdita distributes flowers among them, disagreeing courteously with Polixenes as she does so about the ethics of artificially cross-breeding cultivated flowers. The young people dance, and a servant brings news of the approach of a pedlar, who is admitted. The Clown does not recognize Autolycus as the thief who robbed him earlier, and after Autolycus advertises his wares with the song 'Lawn as white as driven snow' the Clown is squabbled over by Mopsa and Dorcas, who have both been hoping for love tokens from him. Autolycus sells them improbable ballads and sings a song in a trio with Mopsa and Dorcas, 'Get you hence, for I must go': after their departure he further proclaims his wares with the song 'Will you buy any tape'. Dancers arrive and perform a dance of twelve satyrs. Polixenes, meanwhile, has been speaking with the Old Shepherd, who thoroughly approves of 'Doricles' ' courtship of Perdita, and when he and Camillo ask Florizel about it the Prince, refusing to explain why his father should not be told of the matter, invites them to witness his engagement to Perdita. Polixenes furiously reveals his identity and accuses his son of betraying the throne, condemning the Old Shepherd to death for treason (but then withdrawing the sentence) and threatening Perdita with torture if she ever sees Florizel again: he storms off alone. The grieved Old Shepherd reproaches Florizel and Perdita for concealing the Prince's identity from him, and leaves convinced he is undone. Perdita believes her romance with Florizel is now over, but the Prince insists that his father's displeasure has not affected his determination to marry her. Camillo persuades them to run away to Sicilia, where they may marry and live until Polixenes is reconciled to the match. Florizel disguises himself by exchanging clothes with Autolycus, who has sold all his wares, and he and Perdita hurry away. Camillo, however, means privately to inform Polixenes of the couple's escape, and to return to Sicilia with him when he pursues them. Autolycus, left alone, is delighted with the money he has received for agreeing to wear a better suit of clothes, and when the dismayed Old Shepherd and the Clown arrive, hoping to present the proofs of Perdita's true identity to Polixenes in order to escape punishment for treason, he impersonates a courtier and accepts a bribe for his supposed assistance. Deciding to assist his former master Florizel, Autolycus leads them not to Polixenes but towards the ship on which Florizel and Perdita are embarking for Sicilia.

5.1 Cleomenes and Dion wish that after his years of penitent mourning Leontes would remarry and beget an heir, but Paulina reminds him of Hermione's virtues and the King agrees to marry only by her direction. When Florizel and Perdita arrive, giving out that they are already married, Leontes welcomes them eagerly, struck with Florizel's resemblance to his father and with Perdita's beauty: but when news arrives that Polixenes and Camillo have arrived in pursuit, Florizel admits that he and Perdita are not married and that she is not, as he earlier claimed, a princess. Leontes undertakes to try to reconcile Polixenes to their marriage. 5.2 Autolycus hears from three gentlemen of the extraordinary emotional scene that has taken place when the Old Shepherd opened the box with which he found Perdita, revealing her true identity to Leontes, Polixenes, Florizel, and Perdita. The royal party have now gone to Paulina's house to see a wonderfully lifelike statue, by Giulio Romano, of the dead Hermione. Autolycus is patronized and forgiven by the Clown and the Old Shepherd, newly elevated to the gentry for their part in the Princess's upbringing and restoration. 5.3 Paulina draws a curtain to reveal Hermione's statue: a moved Leontes is particularly impressed that the sculptor, as Paulina explains, has aged the likeness to show Hermione as she would look were she still alive. Perdita kneels before her mother's image. Camillo and Polixenes urge Leontes to abandon his sorrows, but he insists he would rather stay staring at the statue. Paulina tells Leontes that she could if he wished make the statue move and speak, without recourse to black magic. With his encouragement, and to the sound of music, she calls the statue from its pedestal. Taking its warm hand, Leontes realizes that this is indeed Hermione. She embraces him and greets her long-lost daughter, explaining that she has kept herself alive because the oracle's pronouncement gave her hope of seeing her child again. Leontes matches Paulina with Camillo, and asks pardon from Polixenes and Hermione for his former suspicions.

ARTISTIC FEATURES: The play is perhaps most remarkable for its almost programmatic movement through the tragedy of Acts 1 to 3 to the pastoral comedy of Act 4 (pivoting on the immortal stage direction, 'Exit, pursued by a bear', at once catastrophic and farcical) and finally into the tentative, fragile *tragicomedy of Act 5, its final scene at once wholly implausible and irresistibly moving.

CRITICAL HISTORY: Though the play was popular before the Civil War, this calculated mix of genres has made it controversial ever since: *Dryden dismissed it in 1672 (along with *Measure for Measure* and *Love's Labour's Lost*) as 'grounded on impossibilities, or at least, so meanly written, that the comedy neither caused your mirth, nor the serious part your concernment'. Ben *Jonson had already ridiculed Shakespeare's depiction of a Bohemian coast in conversation with Drummond of Hawthornden in 1619 (though the idea of a sea coast of Bohemia seems to have been a proverbial joke before the play was written, incorporated as a knowing gesture, like the play's title, Mamillius' interrupted story, or Autolycus' impossible ballads, towards the play's fairy-tale basis). Such deviations from plausibility—whether with regard to its geography, its only partly explained sixteen-year concealment of Hermione, or its depiction of Leontes' unprovoked jealousy—provoked further objections over the course of the 18th and 19th centuries, most virulently from Charlotte *Lennox, who thought the statue scene 'a low . . . contrivance'. Though the play still had its admirers (among them Victor *Hugo and Thomas Campbell) it only came into its own in mainstream criticism during the 20th century, partly as a result of *modernism's enthusiasms for verbal difficulty (with which this play abounds) and for the links between drama and seasonal ritual (which the play's highly conscious movement from winter to summer, tragedy to comedy, carefully underlines). Among the romances, it has attracted more attention than *Cymbeline*, though less than the perennially popular and controversial *The Tempest*: in recent criticism *The Winter's Tale* has figured importantly in discussions of Shakespeare's handling of genre, his thinking about art and artifice, his depictions of *marriage and the family, and his understanding (and manipulation) of wonder.

STAGE HISTORY: When Simon Forman saw the play at the Globe in May 1611 he was struck by its plot (if not by the statue scene, which he does not mention) and especially by Autolycus ('the rogue that came in all tattered like colt-pixie . . . Beware of trusting feigned beggars or fawning fellows').

Whatever features of the play pleased contemporaries, it was well liked at court, where it was acted in November 1611, during the celebrations of Princess *Elizabeth's wedding over Christmas 1612–13, in 1618, possibly 1619, in 1624, and in 1634. After this, however, it fell from favour (though it may have formed the basis of a *droll called **Dorastus and Fawnia*), and when it was revived in the 18th century it generally appeared only in truncated pieces. The play was performed whole, briefly, at both the semi-legal *Goodman's Fields theatre and at *Covent Garden during the 'Shakespeare boom' of 1741, but thereafter was usually reduced to its pastoral scenes, with more or less of the fifth act grafted hastily on as an ending: Macnamara Morgan produced the first such adaption of the second half of the play as *The Sheep-Shearing; or, Florizel and Perdita* (1754), which excludes Leontes and has the Old Shepherd turn out to be Antigonus after all. He was successfully emulated by David *Garrick, whose popular afterpiece *Florizel and Perdita: A Dramatic Pastoral* (1756) restores both Leontes and much of the ending: the Sicilian King is washed up in Bohemia after a shipwreck, where he helps Florizel and Perdita, and the statue scene is conducted by an expatriated Paulina. Attempts to reclaim the whole play (by Charles Marsh, whose 1756 adaptation was never acted, and by Thomas *Hull in 1771) were less popular, and it was only restored by *Kemble in 1802 (who still used Garrick's ending until 1811).

The play was little revived in the 19th century, though *Macready, *Phelps, and (briefly) *Irving all experimented with the role of Leontes: two conspicuous productions, however, were those of Charles *Kean and Mary *Anderson. Kean adopted *Hanmer's long-discredited emendation of 'Bohemia' to 'Bithynia', setting this most historically eclectic of plays in a consistent ancient Greek period, his 1856 production decorated by meticulous reference to artefacts in the British Museum. This revival was vividly and meticulously *burlesqued by the Brough brothers' *Perdita; or, The Royal Milkmaid* (1856). In 1887 Mary Anderson drew notice by doubling Hermione and Perdita (a distracting trick which would be repeated by Judi *Dench in Trevor *Nunn's production of 1969). Ellen *Terry played Hermione in Beerbohm *Tree's condensed three-act production of 1906: *Granville-Barker's attempt to restore a full text in 1912 was a critical failure. It would still be hard to name a stage production that had been genuinely popular rather than not discreditable, or that had done equal justice to the play's elements of tragedy and of comedy, though Peter *Brook's production of 1951, with John *Gielgud as Leontes, impressed many critics, as did Declan Donellan and Nick Ormerod's production for the Russian Maly company in 1999. Notable performers as Leontes have included Patrick *Stewart (icily obsessive, 1983), Jeremy Irons (relapsing into infantile insecurity, 1986), and Antony *Sher (pathologically jealous as if for medical reasons, 1998). *MD*

On the screen: The earliest film recorded is a ten-minute American silent version (1910), followed by Italian (1913) and German films (1914). A now-scarce film of *The Winter's Tale* was made in 1960, with Laurence Harvey as Leontes, and there was a BBC TV production two years later, but Jane Howell's production (1980) for the BBC series remains its most satisfactory screen incarnation: for its time it was adventurous in its use of the medium, with stylized settings and considerable use of close-up asides to camera. *AD*

Recent major editions

Stephen Orgel (Oxford, 1996); J. H. P. Pafford (Arden, 1963); Ernest Schanzer (New Penguin, 1969)

Some representative criticism

Barber, C. L., in *Shakespeare's Festive Comedy* (1959)

Bartholomeusz, Dennis, '*The Winter's Tale' on the Stage in England and America, 1611–1976* (1982)

Belsey, Catherine, in *Shakespeare and the Loss of Eden* (1999)

Bishop, T. G., in *Shakespeare and the Theatre of Wonder* (1996)

Bristol, Michael, 'In Search of the Bear', *Shakespeare Quarterly*, 42 (1991)

Cavell, Stanley, in *Disowning Knowledge* (1987)

Coghill, Nevill, 'Six Points of Stage-craft in *The Winter's Tale*', *Shakespeare Survey*, 11 (1958)

Morse, William R., 'Metacriticism and Materiality: The Case of Shakespeare's *The Winter's Tale*, *English Literary History*, 58 (1991)

Wilson, Harold S., 'Nature and Art in *The Winter's Tale*', *Shakespeare Association Bulletin*, 18 (1943)

Othello and Lady Macbeth to his Macbeth (Covent Garden, 1748–9), Queen Elizabeth to Thomas *Sheridan's Richard III (Dublin, 1752), and the Queen to *Barry's Hamlet (Covent Garden, 1757). *CMSA*

Wolfit, Sir Donald (1902–68), the last of the actor-managers. Coming from yeoman stock, he learned his craft in the provinces. At the *Old Vic in 1929–30 he played Tybalt, Lorenzo, Cassio, Touchstone, Macduff, and a strong Claudius. From 1936 he acted a dozen roles during two summer seasons at the Memorial Theatre at Stratford, including Hamlet. In the autumn of 1937 he decided to become an actor-manager. Thereafter for fourteen seasons (with appearances in London and abroad) he toured provincial towns. There was a different play most nights; and the supporting actors were seldom well rehearsed. Wolfit, with his tireless voice and Elizabethan gusto, was always centre stage as Hamlet, Macbeth, Shylock, Petruchio, Richard III, Malvolio, Jonson's Volpone, and *Massinger's Sir Giles Overreach. He was reckoned the greatest Lear of his time. But for him many Britons would never have seen Shakespeare staged. In 1955 Tyrone *Guthrie invited him to the *Old Vic, but after a towering success in *Marlowe's *Tamburlaine the Great*, Wolfit quarrelled with the management. Ronald Harwood evoked him and a vanished era in *The Dresser*, successful as both a play and a film. *MJ*

Harwood, Ronald, *Sir Donald Wolfit CBE: His Life and Work in the Unfashionable Theatre* (1971)

Wolsey, Cardinal. Thomas Wolsey (*c.*1475–1530) helps secure the execution of Buckingham and the divorce of Katherine, but opposes King Henry's marriage to Anne Boleyn before

Sir Donald Wolfit in his greatest role, King Lear, as photographed by Angus McBean.

meeting his downfall in *All Is True* (*Henry VIII*) 3.2. *AB*

Woman's Prize, The; or, The Tamer Tamed. See FLETCHER, JOHN; TAMING OF THE SHREW, THE.

Wood, Anthony à (1632–95), a notoriously ill-tempered antiquary whose collection *Athenae Oxonienses* included anecdotal material about Sir William *Davenant contributed by John *Aubrey. *CMSA*

Wood, John (b. 1930), British actor. Having acted at Oxford from 1954 and with the *Old Vic he came into his own with his idiosyncratic, intelligent playing of varied parts at the *Royal Shakespeare Company; his Brutus (1973), Don Armado (1990), Prospero (1988), and King Lear (1990) were critically acclaimed. He has also excelled in plays by Tom *Stoppard. *MJ*

Woodville, Lieutenant of the Tower of London who refuses Gloucester entry to the Tower, *1 Henry VI* 1.4 (based on Richard Woodville (Widvill), father of Rivers and Lady Gray). *AB*

Woodward, Henry (1717–77), English actor. He began his stage career as a child actor, became a dancer and mime at *Covent Garden, and from 1738 was the most famous Harlequin and comic at *Drury Lane, playing Mercutio, Touchstone, Lucio, Polonius, and a combative Petruchio to Kitty *Clive's Catharine in *Garrick's adaptation. He returned to London after unsuccessful management in Dublin and made his final appearance as Stephano in 1777. *CMSA*

Wooer. Under the Doctor's instructions he has sex with the Jailer's Daughter in *The Two Noble Kinsmen* to cure her of her madness. *AB*

Woolf, (Adeline) Virginia (1882–1941), English novelist and critic. Woolf's influential essay in *feminist criticism *A Room of one's Own* (1929) speculates on the obstacles that might have confronted Shakespeare's sister had she been as talented as the Bard. More comically her mock-historical novel *Orlando* (1928) draws on *As You Like It*, depicting an immortal Elizabethan courtier and admirer of Shakespeare who, Ganymede-like, becomes a woman. *NJW*

Woolfenden, Guy (b. 1937), English composer. He joined the *Royal Shakespeare Company in Stratford-upon-Avon in 1961 and was its principal composer from 1963 until 1998. In this role he composed over 150 scores, including music for all of Shakespeare's plays. His setting of *The Comedy of Errors* (1976, dir. Trevor *Nunn) won two major awards. *IBC*

Woolshop. See MAIDENHEAD INN.

Worcester, Earl of. Brother of Northumberland, and Hotspur's uncle, his rebellion is eventually defeated, and he is executed, *1 Henry IV* 5.5.14 (based on Thomas Percy (*c.*1344–1403)). *AB*

Worcester's Men. See STRATFORD-UPON-AVON, ELIZABETHAN, AND THE THEATRE.

Wordsworth, William (1770–1850), English poet. No less than his verse drama *The Borderers* (1796–7), Wordsworth's great autobiographical poem *The Prelude* (1805/1850) resonates with echoes of *Hamlet*, *Macbeth*, and *Othello*, here associated both with Wordsworth's childhood guilts and with his adult anxieties about the ambition, usurpation, and regicide enacted by the French Revolution. In 'Scorn not the sonnet' (1827) Wordsworth influentially cited the Sonnets as themselves autobiographical, claiming that 'with this key | Shakespeare unlocked his heart'. *NJW*

World Shakespeare Congress. See INTERNATIONAL SHAKESPEARE ASSOCIATION.

Worth, Irene (b. 1916), American actress. Born in Nebraska, she trained with the English elocutionist Elsie Fogerty. Her distinguished career as a Shakespearian began with the *Old Vic Company in 1951. At the first Shakespeare Festival at Stratford, Ontario, under Tyrone *Guthrie in 1953 she appeared as Helena in *All's Well That Ends Well* and Queen Margaret in *Richard III*, returning in 1959 to star as Rosalind. She was a leading presence in the Royal Shakespeare Company from 1962, playing challenging modern parts as well as Goneril in Peter *Brook's revelatory *King Lear*, a part she repeated in his film. She played Gertrude in *Hamlet* at Greenwich (1974) and Volumnia in *Coriolanus* at the *National (1984), a part she has also played for BBC television. *MJ*

Wotton, Sir Henry (1568–1639), diplomat. In a letter of 2 July 1613 to Sir Edmund Bacon, Wotton described how the Globe theatre burned down on 29 June 1613 during a performance of *All Is True* (*Henry VIII*), then a 'new play'. Wotton may mean that the play was then relatively new; it could have had two or three earlier stagings. A young London merchant named Henry Bluett, writing on 4 July to his uncle Mr Richard Weeks, of Somersetshire, also referred to *All Is True* as 'new', but added that 'it had been acted not passing 2 or 3 times before'. *PH*

Wright, James (1643–1713), antiquary and author of the anonymous *Historia histrionica: An Historical Account of the English Stage* (1699). Written as a dialogue between Lovewit and an old cavalier, it is a useful source of information on early 17th-century plays, players, and playhouses and includes references to *Hamlet* and *Othello*. *CMSA*

Wright of Derby, Joseph (1734–97), English painter. Wright's contribution to the *Shakespeare Gallery was plagued by his problematic relationship with John *Boydell. The painter had acquired fame through his paintings of modern subjects, which depicted polite and informed members of the community of taste engaged in activities that reflected or contributed to advances in science, learning, and art. Wright's conception of painting was, arguably, too grand for Boydell's purposes. The artist's *Prospero in his Cell with Ferdinand and Miranda*, completed in 1789, was criticized for its treatment of figures, particularly that of Ferdinand, who, as one critic stated, was 'not sufficiently historical or practical for the rest of the picture'. Wright evidently failed to assign sufficient importance to narrative in his works for the Shakespeare Gallery. Boydell turned down two paintings by Wright: the first, *The Winter's Tale* (now lost), depicted an over-dominant coastal landscape; the second, *Juliet in the Tomb* (now lost), was shown, instead, at the Royal Academy exhibition of 1790. *CT*

Wright, W(illiam) Aldis (1836–1914), English academic and editor, with W. G. Clark and J. Glover, of the first *Cambridge edition of Shakespeare (9 vols., 1863–6). Its textual apparatus included variant readings from all early and some later editions. Its one-volume version, the *Globe* (1864), created a reference standard for almost a century. *TM*

Wroxall is a small village about 12 miles (19 km) north of Stratford and close to Rowington, where Shakespeare's ancestors may have come from. The name Shakespeare was common in the neighbourhood during the 16th century. Wroxall had a priory where an Isabel Shakespeare was prioress in 1501 and a Jane Shakespeare subprioress in 1525. *SW*

X, Malcolm. See JAMES I THEORY.

Yale Elizabethan Club, a literary and social club for Yale University undergraduates, founded in 1911 with the support of Alexander Smith Cochran, who donated the nucleus of a library of Tudor and Stuart literary texts, including the entire collection of Shakespeare folios, *quartos, and *apocryphal plays formerly owned by Alfred Huth. *SLB*

Yale Shakespeare. This American pocket edition of the individual works started to appear in 1918, and a revised series was issued beginning in 1954. It was advanced for its time in featuring texts based where possible on the early quartos, and in adding no stage or scene divisions not in the original texts. It also preserved original lineation and punctuation as far as was practicable in a modernized edition. *RAF*

yard, the uncovered space around the stage at the open-air Renaissance playhouses. Spectators who stood in the yard paid the least to enter (usually 1 penny) and, at the cost of tired legs, had the best view. If rain started during a performance those in the yard were probably allowed to enter the galleries for the usual additional penny. Puns on the yard's occupants and their intelligence are common, ranging from the mild 'understanders' to Hamlet's *'groundlings' (3.2.11) which, as well as referring to the fact that they stand on the ground, may intentionally liken them to the ground-feeding fish of the same name which have large mouths and small bodies. *GE*

Yates, Dame Frances Amelia (1899–1981), English academic, author of a long series of learned studies of the English and European Renaissance, particularly in areas of secret, occult, and recondite knowledge, such as *The Occult Philosophy in the Elizabethan Age* (1979). Other works throw new light on the intellectual and philosophical background to Shakespeare's plays, including theories of the Elizabethan stage: *New Light on the Globe Theater* (1966); *The Art of Memory* (1966); *The Theatre of the World* (1969); *Astraea* (1975); and *Shakespeare's Last Plays* (1975). *TM*

Yates, Mary Ann (1728–87), English actress. She first acted at *Drury Lane with *Garrick in 1753 and subsequently played many Shakespearian heroines including Portia, Rosalind, Viola, Imogen, and Cleopatra, and Julia to her comedian husband's Lance in Benjamin Victor's adaptation of *The Two Gentlemen of Verona* (1762). Famed for her dignified playing, she was painted as the Tragic Muse by *Romney, and as Volumnia for *Bell's Shakespeare. *CMSA*

Yeats, William Butler (1865–1939), Irish poet and playwright, 'the voice of Irish cultural consciousness coming to maturity' (Roy Foster). The most obvious immediate influences on Yeats's poetry are Blake, Maeterlinck, and the French symbolists; and on his plays the Noh tradition of Japan. But his attempt, with Lady Gregory and others, to establish an Irish Literary (later National) Theatre in Dublin, 1899, with Irish plays on Irish subjects, seems to reproduce something of Shakespeare's patriotic creation of a similar English national identity through the use of native history, legend, and folklore. Yeats's painter father read to him from boyhood, including Shakespeare, and he learned 'to set certain passages in Shakespeare above all else in literature'. In his own essays on a literature beyond realism (a literature of symbolism, myth, and allegory), Yeats frequently takes Shakespeare as illustration and touchstone, as in 'At Stratford-on-Avon' (1901), where Yeats refers to what he calls 'Shakespeare's myth': 'a wise man who was blind from very wisdom, and an empty man who thrust him from his place, and saw all that could be seen from very emptiness'. Yeats's earlier poems frequently echo Shakespearian phraseology, as well as receiving from the tragedies a series of fatalistic gestures in the face of heroic death; later poems of rage and madness in old age (much information about which comes from unpublished letters to his close woman friend Mrs Olivia Shakespear) certainly conjure images reminiscent of King Lear and the Fool. *TM*

Yonge, Bartholomew. See MONTEMAYOR, JORGE DE.

Yorick is the name of the late King of Denmark's long-deceased jester, whose skull Hamlet picks up, *Hamlet* 5.1.179. His much-quoted line on doing so, 'Alas, poor Yorick . . .' (5.1.180), has made this the most famous posthumous bit-part in world literature: one bardolater (André Tchaikowsky, a distinguished composer and pianist) even bequeathed his own skull to the RSC in the hopes of playing it after death. *AB*

York, Archbishop of. **(1)** *Richard III*. See CARDINAL; ROTHERHAM, THOMAS. **(2)** In *1 Henry IV* he joins Northumberland's rebellion, but in *2 Henry IV* he is tricked by Prince John into dismissing his forces (4.1) and executed (based on Richard le Scrope (*c.*1350–1405)). *AB*

York, Duchess of. **(1)** Cicely Neville (1415–95) grieves for her sons Clarence and Edward IV (*Richard III* 2.2), but curses her other son King Richard 4.4.184–96. **(2)** She pleads for the life of her son Aumerle first with her husband York, *Richard II* 5.2, and then with King Henry, 5.3 (unhistorical). *AB*

York, Duke of. **(1)** For Richard Plantagenet (1411–60), 3rd Duke of York, see HENRY VI PART I; THE FIRST PART OF THE CONTENTION; RICHARD DUKE OF YORK. **(2)** See EDWARD, EARL OF MARCH. **(3)** Edward Plantagenet (1373–1415), elder brother of Richard, Earl of Cambridge, and uncle to the Duke of York of the *Henry VI* plays, appears under the name of Duke of Aumerle in *Richard II*. As Duke of York in *Henry V* he is given the honour of leading the vanguard at Agincourt (4.3.130–2) but dies on the field (4.6.3–8). **(4)** Edmund de Langley (1341–1402) is depicted as an old man who finds his responsibilities as regent in *Richard II* burdensome. His support for Richard dwindles and it is he who announces his abdication and first hails Bolingbroke as King Henry (4.1.98–103). Despite the protestations of his wife the Duchess of York, he denounces his son Aumerle to King Henry, 5.3. **(5)** for Richard (1472–83), see EDWARD, PRINCE. *AB*

York, Mayor of. See MAYOR OF YORK.

Yorkshire Tragedy, A, a tragedy based on real-life murders committed in Yorkshire in 1605, which was included (among other *apocryphal works) in the Third *Folio, probably because Pavier and *Jaggard had published it as Shakespeare's in 1608 and 1619. It is now attributed to Thomas *Middleton. *SM*

Young, Charles Mayne (1777–1856), English actor, less majestical than J. P. *Kemble, less passionate than Edmund *Kean, who made an impressive London debut as Hamlet (1807). Equally accomplished in comedy and tragedy, he played Falstaff, Cassius, Iago, and Macbeth. *RF*

Young Cato. See CATO, YOUNG.

Young Lucius. See LUCIUS, YOUNG.

Young Siward. See SIWARD, YOUNG.

Your Own Thing (1968), American rock *musical based on *Twelfth Night*; book by Donald Driver; music and lyrics by Hal Hester, and lyrics by Hal Hester and Danny Apolinar. This curious specimen of psychedelic kitsch includes twelve numbers, some, such as 'Coming Away, Death', directly from songs in the play. *TM*

'You spotted snakes', the lullaby sung by the fairies in *A Midsummer Night's Dream* 2.2.9. The original music is unknown; the only well-known setting is *Mendelssohn's 'Bunte Schlangen' (1843), from his incidental music to the play. *JB*

Zadek, Peter (b. 1926), German director. From 1933 to 1958, Zadek lived in England, where he studied Shakespeare at Oxford and directed extensively. Returning to Germany, he joined with designer Wilfried Minks to develop the Bremen style of theatre. Untraditional, anti-intellectual, and deliberately shocking, Zadek's productions emphasize non-verbal communication over speech, a priority exemplified by his visceral production of *Measure for Measure* (1967). Although Jewish himself, Zadek directed *The Merchant of Venice* (1973) with Hans Mahnke as an extremely unsympathetic Shylock. His famous 'clown show' *King Lear* (1974) was developed through improvisation and intensive ensemble work, a technique he also used for *Othello* (1976) and *Hamlet* (1977). His later *Hamlet*, with Angela Winkler in the title role, was highly acclaimed at the Edinburgh Festival in 2000. *BR*

Zeffirelli, Franco (b. 1923), prolific Italian theatre and film director. Zeffirelli directed a visually stylish *Romeo and Juliet* at the Old Vic in 1960 (with Judi *Dench as Juliet), and his subsequent film version (1968), in which he used young actors and employed a rapid-paced cinematographic style for the fight sequences, was an immediate box-office success. Less widely admired, but no less effective as accessible Shakespeare, was his *The Taming of the Shrew* (1966), with Richard *Burton and Elizabeth Taylor. His equally mainstream *Hamlet* (1990), with Mel Gibson, attracted interest and generally favourable response rather than acclaim. *AD*

Zhu Shenghao (1912–44), a major Chinese translator of Shakespeare, who began his *translation in 1935. Although poverty-stricken and constantly haunted by illness, Zhu managed to render 31 plays before his death: 27 of them were published in 1947. His translation was used as the basis for *The Complete Works* published in 1978 in Beijing. *HQX*

Zoffany, Johann (1735–1810), German painter. Zoffany painted numerous portraits of David *Garrick and his contemporaries. Garrick appeared almost annually in Zoffany's submissions to exhibitions held by the Society of Artists between 1762 and 1766. These portraits, depicting Garrick 'in character', were central to the actor's self-styling as a stage hero. Later portraits such as *Mr and Mrs Garrick before the Temple of Shakespeare*, 1763 (depicting the couple at their estate in Hampton, Middlesex), characterize the actor as a gentleman of taste and refinement. As upwardly mobile as Garrick, Zoffany went on to win several commissions from the royal family. Many of Zoffany's 'stage' portraits from productions of Shakespeare were engraved and entered mass circulation: these include *Garrick and Mrs Pritchard in Macbeth* (made into a mezzotint, 1776) and *Mr Powell as Posthumus* (mezzotint, 1770). *CT*

Zuccaro, Federico (1543–1609), Italian painter. Zuccaro was active in England in 1573–4, where he painted *Elizabeth and a number of her courtiers: the fact that Shakespeare was a child at the time did not deter certain 19th-century critics from identifying one of Zuccaro's English portraits as a likeness of the playwright. *CT*

The British Isles and France in the English Histories and Macbeth

English Histories

1. Agincourt, battle of, 1415 (*Henry v* 4)
2. Angers (*King John* 2.1)
3. Barnet, battle of, 1471 (*Richard Duke of York* (*3 Henry vi*) 5.1–3)
4. Berkeley (*Richard ii* 2.2.119, 2.3)
5. Bordeaux (*1 Henry vi* 4.2, 4.5, 4.6, 4.7)
6. Bosworth, battle of, 1485 (*Richard iii* 5.3–7)
7. Bramham Moor, battle of, 1408 (reported *2 Henry iv* 4.4.97–9)
8. Brecon (Brecknock) (*Richard iii* 4.2.124–5)
9. Bridgnorth (*1 Henry iv* 3.2.175–8)
10. Bristol Castle (*Richard ii* 2.2.135–40, 2.3.162–6, 3.1, 3.2.137–8)
11. Calais (Thomas of Woodstock, Duke of Gloucester, put to death there; Mowbray accused of the crime and of embezzlement *Richard ii* 1.1.87–141; Henry v embarks for England after Agincourt, *Henry v* 4.8.125–6, 5.0.6–7; Henry vi embarks from there *1 Henry vi* 4.1.169–73; Warwick governs *Richard Duke of York* (*3 Henry vi*) 1.1.239)
12. Chertsey (*Richard iii* 1.2.29, 202, 213)
13. Ci'cester (Cirencester) (*Richard ii* 5.6.1–4)
14. Coventry (*Richard ii* 1.1.196–9, 1.2.44–6, 56, 1.3; *Richard Duke of York* (*3 Henry vi*) 4.9.32, 5.1; *1 Henry iv* 4.2)
15. Doncaster (mentioned *1 Henry iv* 5.1.41–71)
16. Dover (*King John* 5.1.30–1; *1 Henry vi* 5.1.49–50; see also *King Lear* 8 (3.1), 13 (3.6), 14 (3.7), 15 (4.1), 20 (4.5))
17. Dunsmore (*Richard Duke of York* (*3 Henry vi*) 5.1.1–3)
18. Dunstable (*All Is True* (*Henry viii*) 4.1.24–38)
19. Flint Castle (*Richard ii* 3.3)
20. Gads Hill (Gadshill) (*1 Henry iv* 1.2.123–31, 2.2–3)
21. Gisors (reported lost *1 Henry vi* 1.1.57–61)
22. Gualtres Forest (*2 Henry iv* 4.1–2)
23. Guyenne (reported lost *1 Henry vi* 1.1.57–61)
14\. Hames Castle (*3 Henry vi* 5.5.1–4)
24\. Harfleur (besieged by Henry v, 1415 *Henry v* 3.0–3)
25\. Harlechly (Harlech or 'Barkloughly') Castle (*Richard ii* 3.2)
26\. Ha'rfordwest (Haverford West) (*Richard iii* 4.5.6–7)
27\. Holmedon (Homildon Hill), battle of, 1402 (*1 Henry iv* 1.1.49–75)
28\. Kenilworth Castle (*The First Part of the Contention* (*2 Henry vi*) 4.4.38–44)
29\. Lincoln Washes (*King John* 5.6.40–3)
30\. Lynn (King's Lynn) (*Richard Duke of York* (*3 Henry vi*) 4.6.20–2)
31\. Maine (claimed for Arthur *King John* 1.1.11; lost, with Anjou, to England *1 Henry vi* 4.3.45–6; claimed by René *1 Henry vi* 5.5.107–125.3; duly ceded to René *The First Part of the Contention* (*2 Henry vi*) 1.1.48–59, 4.1.86, 4.2.158–9, 4.7.64)
32\. Milford (Haven) (Richmond lands there *Richard iii* 4.4.463–5; see also *Cymbeline* 3.2.43–5 et seq., 3.4.27–8, 142–5, 3.5, 3.6, 4.2)
33\. Monmouth (birthplace of Henry v *Henry v* 4.7.11–51)
34\. Mortimer's Cross, battle of, 1461 (traditionally the site of the portent of three suns depicted in *Richard Duke of York* (*3 Henry vi*) 2.1)
35\. Northampton (*Richard Duke of York* (*3 Henry vi*) 4.9.15; *Richard iii* 2.4.1)
36\. Orléans (*1 Henry vi* 1.2)
37\. Paris (reported lost *1 Henry vi* 1.1.61; Henry vi crowned there *1 Henry vi* 3.8, 4.1; reported lost again *The First Part of the Contention* (*2 Henry vi*) 1.1.215)
38\. Pleshey (*Richard ii* 1.2.66, 2.2.120)
39\. Poitiers/Poitou (*King John* 1.1.11, 2.1.28–9; reported lost *1 Henry vi* 1.1.61, 4.3.45–6)
40\. Pomfret (Pontefract) Castle (*Richard ii* 5.1.51–2, 5.5)
41\. Ravenspurgh (*Richard ii* 2.1.298, 2.2.49–51, 2.3.8–12; *1 Henry iv* 1.3.245, 3.2.93–6, 4.3.79; *Richard Duke of York* (*3 Henry vi*) 5.8.7–9)
42\. Rheims (reported lost *1 Henry vi* 1.1.60–1)
43\. Rouen (*1 Henry vi* 1.1.60–1, 3.2–7)
44\. Ruge-mont Castle (Exeter) (*Richard iii* 4.2.105–9)
45\. Saint Albans (1st battle of, 1455 *The First Part of the Contention* (*2 Henry vi*) 5.1–5; 2nd battle of 1461 *Richard Duke of York* (*3 Henry vi*) 1.111–136)
46\. Saint Edmunsberry or bury (Bury St Edmunds) (*King John* 5.2–5; *The First Part of the Contention* (*2 Henry vi*) 2.4.71–2, 3.1, 3.2)
47\. Salisbury (*Richard iii* 4.4.3802; *All Is True* (*Henry viii*) 1.2.194–9)
48\. Sandal Castle (Wakefield)(*Richard Duke of York* (*3 Henry vi*) 1.2)
49\. Scotland (*Richard Duke of York* (*3 Henry vi*) 3.3.23–9; *Richard iii* 3.7.15–22; *1 Henry* vi 1.3.255–62)
50\. Severn, River (*1 Henry iv* 1.3.92–111, 3.1.61–4, 69–76)
51\. Shrewsbury, battle of, 1403 (*1 Henry iv* 5)
52\. Somme, River (*Henry v* 3.5)
53\. Southampton (Henry v embarks for France *Henry v* 2.0, 2.2)
54\. Swineshead (Swinsted) (*King John* 5.3, 5.7)
55\. Tewkesbury, battle of, 1471 (*Richard Duke of York* (*3 Henry vi*) 5.3.18–19, 5.4–5; remembered *Richard iii* 1.2.225–8)
56\. Touraine (claimed *King John* 2.1.151–3)
57\. Tours (lost *1 Henry vi* 4.3.45–6; wedding ceremony remembered *The First Part of the Contention* (*2 Henry vi*) 1.1.1–16, 1.3.53–7)
58\. Towton, battle of, 1461 (*Richard Duke of York* (*3 Henry vi*) 2.2–6)
59\. Trent, River (*1 Henry iv* 3.1.69–136)
60\. Troyes (historically, setting of the negotiations depicted in *Henry v* 5.2)
48\. Wakefield, battle of, 1460 (*Richard Duke of York* (*3 Henry vi*) 1.3–4)
61\. Wales (mentioned many times; scene of *Richard ii* 2.4 and see Flint, Harlechly: see also Milford Haven *1 Henry* iv 3.1)
62\. Wye, River (*1 Henry iv* 3.1.61–4; *Henry v* 4.7.21–51)
63\. York (mentioned many times; scene of *The First Part of the Contention* (*2 Henry vi*) 1.3; *Richard Duke of York* (*3 Henry vi*) 2.2, 4.8)

Macbeth

64\. Birnam Wood (4.1.106–10, 5.2, 5.3, 5.5, 5.4, 5.10)
65\. Colmekill (Iona) (2.4.34–6)
66\. Dunsinane Castle (4.1.106–10, 5.3, 5.4, 5.5–11)
67\. Glamis Castle (traditionally the scene of Duncan's murder, though the play places it at Inverness) (1.5–2.3)
68\. Saint Colum's inch (Inchcolm Island) (1.2.60–2)
69\. Inverness (1.4.42–3, 1.5–2.3)

70\. Stratford-upon-Avon

The royal family in Shakespeare's English Histories

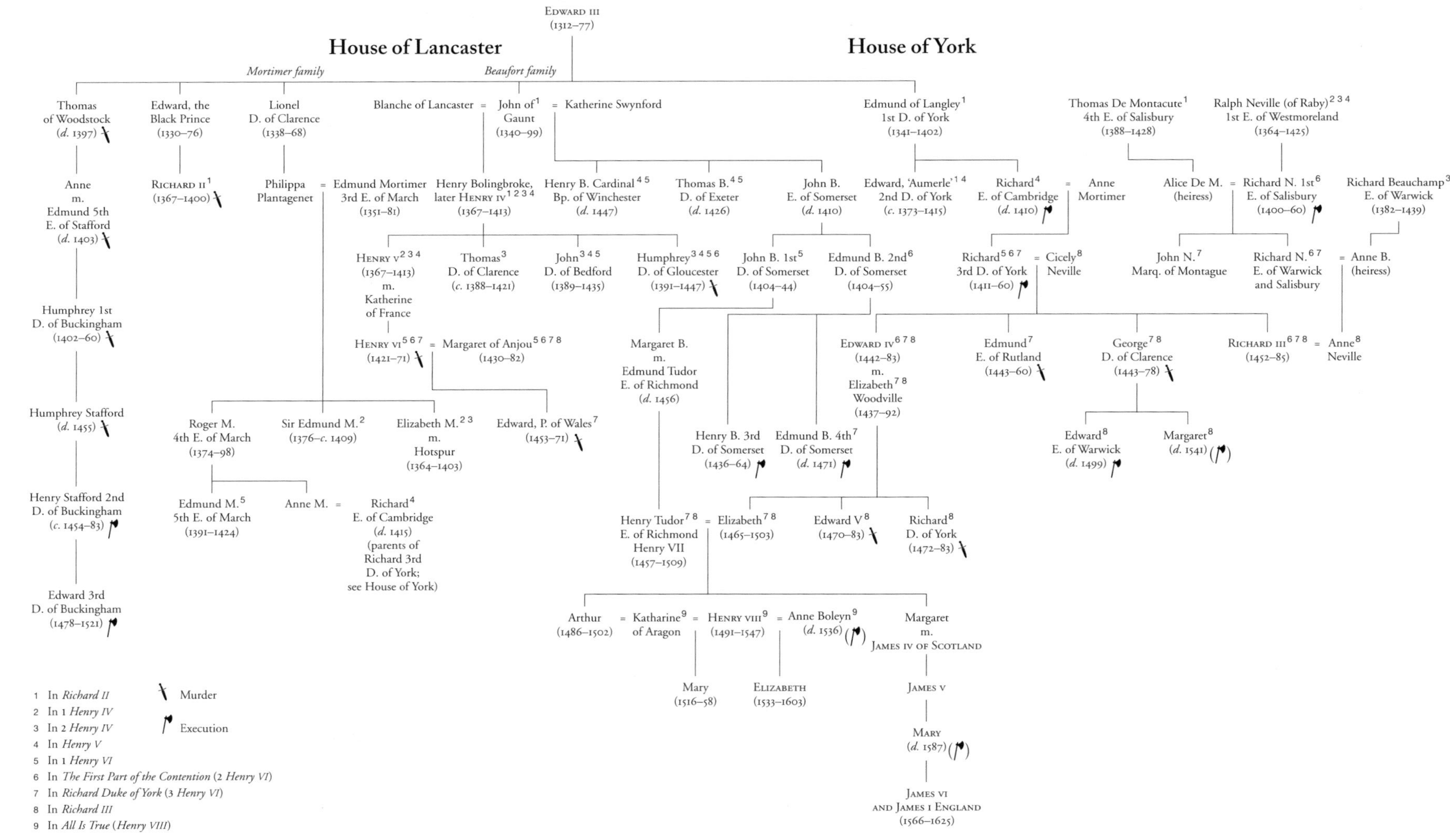

Shakespeare's life, works, and reception: a partial chronology, 1564–1999

The conjectural dates of composition supplied here for the plays are based on the 'Canon and Chronology' section in *William Shakespeare: A Textual Companion*, by Stanley Wells and Gary Taylor, with John Jowett and William Montgomery (1987), where more detailed information and discussion may be found.

1564 26 Apr.: Shakespeare baptized in Stratford-upon-Avon

1582 28 Nov.: marriage licence issued for William Shakespeare and Anne Hathaway

1583 26 May: baptism of Susanna, their daughter

1585 2 Feb.: baptism of Hamnet and Judith, their twin son and daughter

*c.*1590 *The Two Gentlemen of Verona*

*c.*1591 *The Taming of the Shrew*; *The First Part of the Contention* (*2 Henry VI*); *Richard Duke of York* (*3 Henry VI*)

1592 Robert Greene refers to Shakespeare as an 'upstart crow'. *1 Henry VI*; *Titus Andronicus*

*c.*1593 *Richard III*

1593 publication of *Venus and Adonis*

1594 *Comedy of Errors*; publication of *The Rape of Lucrece*

*c.*1594–5 *Love's Labour's Lost*

1595 *Richard II*; *Romeo and Juliet*; *A Midsummer Night's Dream*

1595 15 Mar.: Shakespeare named as joint payee of the Lord Chamberlain's Men, founded in 1594

1596 *King John*

1596 11 Aug.: burial of Hamnet Shakespeare in Stratford-upon-Avon

1596 Oct.: draft of the grants of arms to John Shakespeare

1596–7 *The Merchant of Venice*; *1 Henry IV*

1597 4 May: Shakespeare buys New Place, Stratford-upon-Avon

*c.*1597–8 *The Merry Wives of Windsor*; *2 Henry IV*

1598 Shakespeare listed as one of the 'principal comedians' in Jonson's *Every Man in his Humour. Much Ado About Nothing.* Mention of Shakespeare in Francis Meres's *Palladis Tamia*

*c.*1598–9 *Henry V*

1599 building of the Globe: *Julius Caesar*

*c.*1599–1600 *As You Like It*

---

*c.*1600–1 *Hamlet*; *Twelfth Night*

1601 8 Sept.: burial of John Shakespeare in Stratford-upon-Avon

*c.*1602 *Troilus and Cressida*

1602 2 Feb.: John Manningham notes performance of *Twelfth Night* at the Middle Temple

1602 1 May: Shakespeare pays £320 for land in Old Stratford

1603 *Measure for Measure.* Shakespeare named among the 'principal tragedians' in Jonson's *Sejanus*

1603 May: Shakespeare named in documents conferring the title of King's Men on their company

*c.*1603–4 composition of *A Lover's Complaint*; *Sir Thomas More*

1604 *Othello*

1604–5 *All's Well That Ends Well*

1605 24 July: Shakespeare pays £440 for an interest on the tithes in Stratford. *Timon of Athens*

1605–6 *King Lear*

1606 *Macbeth*; *Antony and Cleopatra*

1607 *Pericles*

1607 5 June: Susanna Shakespeare marries John Hall

1608 the King's Men take over the indoor Blackfriars theatre. *Coriolanus*

1608 9 Sept.: burial of Shakespeare's mother in Stratford

1609 publication of the *Sonnets* (composed *c.*1593–1603). *The Winter's Tale*

1610 *Cymbeline*

1611 *The Tempest*

1612 Shakespeare testifies in the Belott–Mountjoy case

1613 Globe burns down during a performance of *All Is True* (*Henry VIII*)

1613 10 Mar.: Shakespeare buys the Blackfriars Gatehouse

1613–14 *The Two Noble Kinsmen*

1614 Sept.: Shakespeare involved in enclosure disputes in Stratford

1616 10 Feb.: Judith Shakespeare marries Thomas Quiney

1616 25 Mar.: Shakespeare's will drawn up in Stratford

1616 25 Apr.: Shakespeare buried in Stratford (the monument records that he died on 23 Apr.)

1623 8 Aug.: burial of Anne Shakespeare in Stratford

1623 publication of the First Folio

1632 publication of the Second Folio

1642 (start of Civil War) A parliamentary edict temporarily forbids performance of plays: the Globe closed down

1644 15 Apr.: the Globe demolished

1649 16 July: burial of Susanna Hall in Stratford

1660 Charles II restored to the throne in May. He grants warrants for two playing companies and theatres in August. The first actress appears on the English stage, possibly as Desdemona

1662 Judith, Shakespeare's last surviving child, dies

1663 Third Folio published

1664 second edition of the 1663 Folio of Shakespeare's plays published with seven plays not collected before

1664 Margaret Cavendish writes the first critical prose essay on Shakespeare

1670 Shakespeare's only grandchild dies

1681 Nahum Tate's *King Lear* first performed

1685 Fourth Folio published

1688 (Glorious Revolution)

1709 Jacob Tonson publishes Nicholas Rowe's edition of *The Works of Mr. William Shakespeare*, including a biographical preface; lists of dramatis personae given for the first time

1709 Betterton plays Hamlet for the last time (first time in 1660)

1711 Thomas Johnson begins issuing pocket-size editions of the plays

1725 Alexander Pope's edition of Shakespeare's plays published

1733 Theobald's edition of Shakespeare's plays published

1733 Voltaire writes the first French translation of Shakespeare's work (the 'To be or not to be' soliloquy)

1736 'Shakespeare Ladies Club' established in London

1741 in a boom season on the London stage Charles Macklin plays Shylock and Garrick makes his debut

1741 Shakespeare first translated into German (C. W. von Borck's *Julius Caesar*)

1745 (Second Jacobite rising)

1747 Warburton's edition of Shakespeare's plays published

1747 David Garrick takes over Drury Lane Theatre

1750 Colley Cibber's (1699) adaptation of *Richard III* opens in New York City

1751 William Hawkins, professor of poetry at Oxford, begins lectures in Latin on 'Shakesperio'

1752 William Dodd's anthology *The Beauties of Shakespear* published

1753 Charlotte Lennox publishes her three-volume *Shakespear Illustrated*: the first full-length book on Shakespeare by an American-born critic and the first collection and analysis of Shakespeare's sources, with an introduction by Samuel Johnson

1756 the first known Italian translation of a Shakespeare play (*Julius Caesar*) published by Domenico Valentini

1758 Roubiliac's statue of Shakespeare, commissioned by Garrick, is placed in his 'Temple'

1761 *The Tempest* and *King Lear* are the first Shakespeare plays to be printed in North America (New York City)

1765 Johnson's edition of Shakespeare's plays published

1769 Elizabeth Montagu's *Essay on the Writings and Genius of Shakespeare* published

1769 Garrick mounts his 'Shakespeare Jubilee' at Stratford-upon-Avon; the tourist industry at Stratford begins

1772 the first Spanish translation of Shakespeare is staged (*Hamlet* by Ramón de la Cruz, based on a French version)

1774 William Richardson, professor of humanity at Glasgow University, publishes *A Philosophical Analysis and Illustration of Some of Shakespeare's Remarkable Characters*

1776 (Declaration of Independence) Pierre Le Tourneur begins publishing the first complete French translation of Shakespeare's plays

1777 Maurice Morgann publishes *An Essay on the Dramatic Character of Sir John Falstaff*

1778 Malone publishes the first conjectural chronology of Shakespeare's works, based partly on numerical assessments of style

1780 Malone publishes the first critical edition of Shakespeare's sonnets

1785 Eusebio Luzzi's *Romeo and Juliet* (Venice) and Charles le Picq's *Macbeth* (London) are the earliest complete ballets based on Shakespeare's work

1787 *Hamlet* first performed in Swedish in Gothenburg

1789 (French Revolution) Alderman John Boydell presents his exhibition of specially commissioned paintings of scenes from Shakespeare's plays

1790 Malone publishes his edition of *The Plays and Poems of William Shakespeare*, including the poems (which become an integral part of the Shakespeare canon) and a chronology.

1797 A. W. von Schlegel publishes his translation of sixteen plays into German, finished by Ludwig Tieck and others in 1832

1800 a playbill for *Henry IV* at Robert Sidaway's theatre is the earliest known evidence for performance of Shakespeare in Australia

1807 Henrietta Maria Bowdler anonymously publishes a collection of 20 plays in *The Family Shakespeare*, credited to her brother Thomas Bowdler in the second edition of 1818 (true attribution discovered in 1966)

1807 Mary Lamb publishes *Tales from Shakespear*, 20 prose stories based on the plays, six of which were written by her brother Charles Lamb; Mary Lamb's contribution was not acknowledged until 1838

1815 (Battle of Waterloo)

1816 Rossini composes the opera *Otello*.

1823 Stendhal's *Racine et Shakespeare* published, expanded 1825

1825 Peter Foersom's Danish translations of ten of Shakespeare's plays (1807–18) are augmented by P. F. Wulff. Edvard Lembcke later adds to the Foersom–Wulff translation to produce a *Collected Dramatic Works* (1861–73).

1825 America's first theatre riot begins when Edmund Kean refuses to perform *Richard III*

1826 Mendelssohn composes an orchestral overture to *A Midsummer Night's Dream*

1828 Mikhail Vronchenko's *Hamlet* is the first attempt at a faithful translation of a Shakespeare play into Russian

1837 (accession of Victoria)

1839 Berlioz's choral symphony *Roméo et Juliette* performed in Paris

1843 Mendelssohn composes incidental music for Ludwig Tieck's production of *A Midsummer Night's Dream*, including the 'Wedding March'

1844–7 Julian Verplanck's New York edition of Shakespeare's plays published

1847–93 Verdi composes operas based on *Macbeth* (1847), *Othello* (1887), and *Falstaff* (1893)

1848 (year of revolutions in Europe) Anasztáz Tomori finances the translation of Shakespeare's works into Hungarian, co-ordinated by János Arany

1849 31 people are shot dead at the 'Astor Place Riot' after a performance of Macready's *Macbeth*, New York City

1851 Philadelphia Shakespeare Society established

1852 *Bhanumati Chittavilasa*, a Bengali version of *The Merchant of Venice*, is one of the earliest Indian adaptations of any foreign play

1855 Iakovos Polylas's prose version of *The Tempest* is the earliest known translation of Shakespeare into Greek

1857 Delia Bacon publishes *The Philosophy of the Plays of Shakspere Unfolded*, arguing that his plays had been written by Francis Bacon

1862 Berlioz composes his last work inspired by Shakespeare, *Béatrice et Bénédict*, a comic opera

1863–6 'Cambridge Shakespeare' first published, edited by William George Clark, John Glover, and William Aldis Wright; they number the lines within each scene to facilitate reference for the first time

1864 Deutsche Shakespeare-Gesellschaft founded in Weimar and begins publishing *Shakespeare Jahrbuch* in 1865

1864 Globe edition of Shakespeare's works published (it continued to be reprinted until 1978)

1865 (end of American Civil War)

1868 Ambroise Thomas composes a tragic opera based on *Hamlet*

1868 Birmingham Shakespeare Library opens
1868 earliest known performance of Shakespeare in Bulgaria takes place (an amateur performance of *Romeo and Juliet*)
1871 Horace Howard Furness begins to publish the first series of variorum editions of individual plays
1873 Russian Shakespeare Society founded
1874 Frederick James Furnivall establishes the New Shakspere Society; first volume of *The New Shakspere Society's Transactions* published
1874 earliest known Hebrew translation of a Shakespeare play published by Isaac Edward Salkinson (*Romeo and Juliet*)
1874 Ioan Pedr translates *1 Henry IV* into Welsh
1875–7 complete works translated into Polish
1879 Shakespeare Memorial Theatre opens on 23 April
1880 A. S. Kok publishes the first complete Dutch translation of Shakespeare's works
1881 William Poel's production based on the 1603 *Hamlet* staged
1886 first Yiddish translation of Shakespeare published (*Julius Caesar*)
1894 John Bartlett publishes the *New and Complete Concordance of the Dramatic Works and Poems of Shakespeare*
1899 Sarah Bernhardt plays Hamlet
1899 Beerbohm Tree performing the dying moments of King John is the earliest preserved film of Shakespeare being acted

---

1904 A. C. Bradley's *Shakespearean Tragedy* published
1906 a musical Arab version of *Romeo and Juliet* is produced by the Egyptian actor and producer Cheik Salama El Higazy
1911 *Julius Caesar* translated into Scots Gallic by U. M. MacGilleamhoire
1913 Sigmund Freud publishes an essay on 'The Theme of the Three Caskets', pioneering psychoanalytic readings
1914 (start of First World War)
1922 Liang Shiqui begins his translation of Shakespeare into Chinese (completed and published in Taiwan, 1967)
1923 the first full production of *Troilus and Cressida* staged since the 17th century
1923 Barry Jackson's Birmingham Repertory Theatre produce *Cymbeline* in modern dress
1929 Douglas Fairbanks and Mary Pickford appear in a version of *The Taming of the Shrew*: the first Shakespeare film with sound
1930 *The Merchant of Venice* staged in Shanghai: the earliest known performance of Shakespeare in China
1932 new Shakespeare Memorial Theatre (now Royal Shakespeare Theatre) opens in Stratford
1934 René-Louis Piachaud's production of *Coriolan* leads to riots in Paris
1935 Bolshoi theatre (Moscow) commissions Sergei Prokofiev's ballet score to *Romeo and Juliet* (rejected by the Bolshoi and first staged in Czechoslovakia in 1938)
1935 Max Reinhardt's film of *A Midsummer Night's Dream* appears
1937 in Orson Welles's production of *Julius Caesar* at the Mercury Theatre in New York City, Caesar's supporters wear the brown shirts of Mussolini's supporters
1939 (start of Second World War)
1944 Laurence Olivier's film of *Henry V* produced; his film of *Hamlet* comes out in 1948
1949 Bertolt Brecht helps to form the Berliner Ensemble
1951 Cole Porter's musical *Kiss Me Kate* opens, based on *The Taming of the Shrew*
1951 Shakespeare Institute founded by Allardyce Nicoll
1953 (coronation of Queen Elizabeth II) Tyrone Guthrie founds the Stratford Festival, Ontario
1954 Joseph Papp founds the New York Shakespeare Festival
1957 Jerome Robbins and Leonard Bernstein's musical *West Side Story* (based on *Romeo and Juliet*) opens in New York
1960 Royal Shakespeare Company founded under artistic directorship of Peter Hall
1963 Shakespeare Society of Korea established
1964 Grigori Kozintsev's film of *Hamlet* produced; his film of *King Lear* comes out in 1969
1965 Cultural Revolution bans all translation, production, and criticism of Shakespeare in China
1965 Orson Welles's film *Chimes at Midnight* produced
1970 Peter Brook's production of *A Midsummer Night's Dream* performed by the RSC
1976 Edward Bond's *Bingo* performed by the RSC
1979 BBC begins its series of productions of Shakespeare's plays for television
1984 the Shakespeare Society of China founded
1986 Beijing-Shanghai Shakespeare festival in April stages 28 different productions of Shakespeare's plays
1986 Oxford Shakespeare published
1986 Swan Theatre opens at Stratford
1989 Rose Theatre excavated
1989 Kenneth Branagh's film of *Henry V* released
1990 (resignation of Margaret Thatcher)
1993 an annual international Shakespeare Festival is established in Gdansk
1993 Shakespeare Society of the Low Countries founded
1996 Shakespeare's Globe (a conjectural reconstruction of the original theatre) opens in London
1997 the first Australian Shakespeare Festival held at Bowral
1999 the film *Shakespeare in Love* wins 7 Oscars at the Academy Awards

Further reading

The sheer volume and diversity of writing about Shakespeare defies all attempts at compiling a representative short reading list. The following is intended primarily to supplement the bibliographies appended to entries in the body of this Companion by pointing to a few accessible, introductory studies for the general reader, and by indicating some standard reference works from which to obtain further suggestions.

General introductory overviews

The increasing specialization and professionalization of the academic world has led, regrettably, to the virtual extinction of up-to-the-minute books describing and interpreting Shakespeare's oeuvre for a non-student readership. Among the small crop published during the 1990s, Harold Bloom's best-selling *Shakespeare: The Invention of the Human* (1998), every bit as hyperbolic and bardolatrous as its title implies, cannot be recommended, and Maynard Mack's *Everybody's Shakespeare* (1993), largely confined to the tragedies, seems a little dated. The most attractive exceptions to this trend are Jonathan Bate's patchy but highly readable *The Genius of Shakespeare* (1997), which is particularly good on the development of Shakespeare's reputation, and Stanley Wells' *Shakespeare: the Poet and his Plays* (1997, a revision of *Shakespeare: A Dramatic Life*, 1994). Another lively general survey of Shakespeare's output reached print rather belatedly at the dawn of the twenty-first century, namely W. H. *Auden's introductory course on Shakespeare, given in New York in 1946–7, and published as *Lectures on Shakespeare*, ed. Arthur Kirsch (2000).

Journals and reference works

The major Shakespearian periodicals are described elsewhere under *journals and in their own individual entries. The three most important are the German **Shakespeare Jahrbuch* (1864–), the British **Shakespeare Survey* (annual, 1948–), and the American **Shakespeare Quarterly* (1950–): the latter produces the annual *World Shakespeare Bibliography*, now also available as an immense and ever-growing set of CD-Roms. Further electronic resources for the study of Shakespeare, including Shakespearian websites, are described under *electronic media. The ease and sophistication with which catalogues of books and journals can now be stored on computers is beginning to make even the most reliable of printed bibliographies—such as Stanley Wells' *Shakespeare: A Bibliographical Guide* (1990)—look in danger of obsolescence, but the printed catalogue of the *Birmingham Shakespeare Library remains a valuable resource, and that of the *Folger Shakespeare Library, at the time of going to press, had not been wholly replaced by its online catalogue at *http://www.folger.edu*. Other important Shakespearian holdings which can be readily searched via computer include those of the *British Library (at *http://www.bl.ac.uk*) and those of the immense Widener Library at Harvard (at *http://www.hollisweb.harvard.edu*).

Useful general reference works on Shakespeare include *The Cambridge Companion to Shakespeare*, edited by Margreta de Grazia and Stanley Wells (2001), which supplies up-to-the-minute essays on important topics within the academic study of Shakespeare. It is in general more immediately readable than David Scott Kastan's *A Companion to Shakespeare* (1999), which is principally aimed at North American postgraduate students. Less oriented towards the university market, and still valuable despite having been in some areas overtaken by fresh research and changing intellectual priorities, are two comprehensive encyclopaedias, F. E. *Halliday's *A Shakespeare Companion* (last revised in 1964) and Oscar Campbell and Edward Quinn's much larger *A Shakespeare Encyclopaedia* (1966). Both, however, are now out of print, and the former has been in part replaced by Stanley Wells' less compendious but much prettier *Shakespeare: An Illustrated Dictionary* (1978, revised 1985, and revised again, with fewer illustrations but considerable updating, as *The Oxford Dictionary of Shakespeare*, 1998).

Shakespeare's life

Further reading on this subject can be found after the entries on *biographies, on William *Shakespeare, on *education and on *Stratford-upon-Avon: those with a taste for the pathological may also want to consult some of the titles listed under *Authorship Controversy. On all of these topics the work of Samuel *Schoenbaum is especially recommended, notably *William Shakespeare: A Compact Documentary Life* (1977): the most reliable biography since is Park Honan's *Shakespeare: A Life* (1999).

Criticism on the plays and poems

The short lists of representative critical reading appended to the entries on each of Shakespeare's works in this Companion are necessarily highly selective. Outside the bibliographies cited above, the best place to start looking for a wider range of criticism on any given Shakespearian text is usually in the introduction to a good single-work edition of it, in a series such as the *Oxford, the *Arden, or the *New Cambridge. Major trends in Shakespeare criticism since his own time are described in the entry on *critical history, and in the separate entries cross-referenced from it. A helpful anthology of the first two centuries of Shakespeare's critical reception is provided by Brian Vickers' six-volume *Shakespeare: the Critical Heritage, 1623–1801* (1974–81); the crucial three decades which followed are admirably cherry-picked in Jonathan Bate's *The Romantics on Shakespeare* (1992). A very useful and attractive survey of the last hundred years' contributions to the understanding of Shakespeare's works is provided by Michael Taylor's *Shakespeare Criticism in the Twentieth Century* (2001).

Shakespeare's language

Further reading on this subject can be found listed after the entry on *English. Standard reference works include Marvin Spevack's *The Harvard Concordance to Shakespeare* (1973) and C. T. Onions' much-reprinted *A Shakespeare Glossary* (1911); a good starting-point is provided by N. F. Blake's *Shakespeare's Language: An Introduction* (1983). Other accessible studies include M. M. Mahood, *Shakespeare's Wordplay* (1957); R. A. Lanham, *The Motives of Eloquence* (1976); and Marion Trousdale, *Shakespeare and the Rhetoricians* (1982).

Shakespeare's literary context

As the entries on *sources and on *education suggest, the most important reference books on Shakespeare's reading remain T. W. Baldwin's *Shakespeare's Smalle Latine and Lesse Greeke* (2 vols, 1947) and Geoffrey *Bullough's *Narrative and Dramatic Sources of Shakespeare* (8 vols, 1957–75). Other important studies in this field include Emrys Jones' *The Origins of Shakespeare* (1976), Robert S. Miola's two books on Shakespeare's debts to ancient drama (*Shakespeare and Classical Comedy* and *Shakespeare and Classical Tragedy*, 1992) and his wider-ranging *Shakespeare's Reading* (2000), Steven Marx's *Shakespeare and the Bible* (2000), and Kenneth Muir's *The Sources of Shakespeare's Plays* (1975). On Shakespeare's literary relations with his dramatic contemporaries, particularly readable discussions include James Shapiro's *Rival Playwrights: Marlowe, Jonson, Shakespeare* (1991) and Martin Wiggins' *Shakespeare and the Drama of his Time* (2000). A useful introduction to the whole period is provided by chapters 2 to 4 of *The Oxford Illustrated History of English Literature*, edited by Pat Rogers (1987); chapter 3, by Philip Edwards, provides a good short introduction to Shakespeare's achievement and its place in the context of Renaissance drama as a whole.

Shakespeare's theatrical context

For further works discussing the theatrical world within which Shakespeare worked, see particularly the reading lists appended to the entries on Elizabethan *acting, on the *acting profession, on the *Chamberlain's/King's Men, on Elizabethan and Jacobean *theatres, on Philip *Henslowe, and on *censorship. Standard works in this field include G. E. Bentley's *The Jacobean and Caroline Stage* (7 vols, 1966), E. K.*Chambers' *The Elizabethan Stage* (4 vols, 1923), and, more recently, Andrew Gurr's *The Shakespearian Stage* (3rd edition, 1992) and Andrew Gurr and Mariko Ichikawa's *Staging in Shakespeare's Theatres* (2000): Gurr's work incorporates, among much else, the findings from the partial excavations of the *Rose and *Globe theatres carried out in the late 1980s and early 1990s. Surviving visual evidence about the Shakespearian theatre is usefully collected in R. A. Foakes, ed., *Illustrations of the English Stage, 1580–1642* (1985).

Shakespeare's times

As with literary criticism, the writing of history, too, has become increasingly professionalized over the last few decades, and up-to-date introductions to Shakespeare's period and its culture aimed at the non-specialist are comparatively few. W. R. Elton's *Shakespeare's World: Renaissance Intellectual Contexts* (1970) is still useful, as are Julia Briggs' *This Stage-Play World* (1983, revised 1997) and Keith Thomas's *Religion and the Decline of Magic* (1971). A useful reference work combining perspectives on the English Renaissance with information on the writing of the period is Michael Hattaway's *A Companion to English Renaissance Literature and Culture* (2000). For further suggestions, see the reading lists appended to the entries listed under 'Historical, social and cultural context' in the Thematic listing of entries.

The transmission of Shakespeare's texts

On this topic, see particularly the reading lists appended to the entries on *editing, on *printing and publishing, on *folios, and on *quartos. An excellent introduction to the subject is provided in the *Oxford edition of Shakespeare's works (edited by Stanley Wells and Gary Taylor, 1986), and it is handled in greater depth and detail by Stanley Wells et al, *William Shakespeare: A Textual Companion* (1987).

Shakespeare on stage and screen

Many of the most important works on the performance of Shakespeare since his own time are listed after the entries on *Restoration and eighteenth-century Shakespearian production, *nineteenth-century Shakespearian production, *twentieth-century Shakespearian production, *Shakespeare on sound film, *silent films, and *television. An attractive introduction to the history of Shakespeare's interpretation and reinterpretation in the theatre is provided by Jonathan Bate and Russell Jackson, eds., *Shakespeare: An Illustrated Stage History* (1996), while the most up-to-date authoritative surveys of the interpretation of Shakespeare in the cinema are offered by Ken Rothwell's *A History of Shakespeare on Screen* (1999) and Russell Jackson, ed., *The Cambridge Companion to Shakespeare on Film*

(2000). One particularly appealing and original perspective on the whole question of the stagecraft of Shakespeare's plays and the ways in which it has been realized is offered by M. M. Mahood's *Playing Bit Parts in Shakespeare* (1998, a revision of *Bit Parts in Shakespeare's Plays*, 1992).

Shakespeare and the other arts

On Shakespeare's posthumous involvement in art-forms outside poetry and the theatre, see especially the reading lists appended to the entries on *ballet, *dance, *fiction, *painting, *music, *opera, and *songs in the plays. The most comprehensive reference work on Shakespeare in music is *A Shakespeare Music Catalogue*, edited by Bryan Gooch and David Thatcher (5 vols, 1991), while the most wide-ranging general book on Shakespeare in the visual arts remains W. Moelwyn Merchant's *Shakespeare and the Artist* (1959). The catalogues of the art collection at the Folger and of the *RSC Collection and Gallery at Stratford are important resources in this field.

Shakespeare around the globe

See the reading lists appended to entries on individual countries and regions and, especially, the entry on *translation. A worthwhile collection of recent essays on Shakespeare's participation in cultures beyond the British Isles is provided by John Joughlin, ed., *Shakespeare and National Culture* (1997); see also Michael Hattaway, Boika Sokolova, and Derek Roper, eds., *Shakespeare in the New Europe* (1994), and Ania Loomba and Martin Orkin, eds., *Postcolonial Shakespeares* (1998).

MD

Picture acknowledgements

The publishers wish to thank the following who have kindly given permission to reproduce illustrations as identified by the page numbers. While every effort has been made to secure permissions, we may have failed in a few cases to trace the copyright holder. We apologise for any apparent negligence.

4 Ford Motor Company
14 Shakespeare Centre Library, Stratford-upon-Avon
18 Oldham Art Gallery, Lancashire/Bridgeman Art Library, London
22 The Folger Shakespeare Library, Washington, D.C.
23 The Folger Shakespeare Library, Washington, D.C.
24 © Nobby Clark
32 The Folger Shakespeare Library, Washington, D.C.
36 SCR Photo Library
38 The Folger Shakespeare Library, Washington, D.C.
39 The Folger Shakespeare Library, Washington, D.C.
42 From the RSC Collection with the permission of the Governors of the Royal Shakespeare Theatre
43 Mary Evans Picture Library
44 Shakespeare Centre Library, Stratford-upon-Avon
47 © Woodmansterne Limited, Watford
49 © Tate Gallery, London 2001
56 Shakespeare Centre Library, Stratford-upon-Avon (photo: David Farrell)
57 By permission of the Trustees of Dulwich Picture Gallery
59 The British Library (2304b.17)
63 The Folger Shakespeare Library, Washington, D.C.
65 © Stratford Shakespeare Festival Foundation of Canada (photo: Robert C. Ragsdale)
67 The Folger Shakespeare Library, Washington, D.C.
69 Oxford University Press
73 By courtesy of the National Portrait Gallery, London
75 © John Haynes
81 Beinecke Rare Book and Manuscript Library, Yale University
94 From the RSC Collection with the permission of the Governors of the Royal Shakespeare Theatre
100 The Folger Shakespeare Library, Washington, D.C.
109 © John Haynes/Royal National Theatre Archive
111 Shakespeare Centre Library, Stratford-upon-Avon
117 The Folger Shakespeare Library, Washington, D.C.
118 The Folger Shakespeare Library, Washington, D.C.
126 By courtesy of the National Portrait Gallery, London
131 By courtesy of the National Portrait Gallery, London
132 © The Board of Trustees of the Victoria & Albert Museum, London
134 The National Gallery of Scotland
136 Shakespeare Centre Library, Stratford-upon-Avon
144 From the RSC Collection with the permission of the Governors of the Royal Shakespeare Theatre
146 The Folger Shakespeare Library, Washington, D.C.
147 From Bowles & Carver, *Old English Cuts and Illustrations for Artists and Craftspeople* (Dover Publications, Inc., New York 1970)
150 © The British Museum, London
152 Agnès Varda/Agence Enguérand, Paris
157 Mary Evans Picture Library
165 Hulton Getty
169 © Woodmansterne Limited, Watford
170 Shakespeare Centre Library, Stratford-upon-Avon
171 © The Board of Trustees of the Victoria & Albert Museum, London
178 Shakespeare Centre Library, Stratford-upon-Avon
189 BFI Films: Stills, Posters and Designs
203 Hulton Getty
206 Reproduced by kind permission of the Winn Family and the National Trust
209 From *Shakespeare's England: An Account of the Life and Manners of his Age*, edited by Sidney Lee, 1916, Clarendon Press, Oxford
212 Shakespeare Centre Library, Stratford-upon-Avon
216 Hulton Getty
221 By courtesy of the National Portrait Gallery, London
222 Royal Commission on Historical Monuments (Neg. No. BB64/444)
226 By courtesy of the National Portrait Gallery, London
234 The Illustrated London News Picture Library
235 © The British Museum, London
236 © The Board of Trustees of the Victoria & Albert Museum, London
238 The Bodleian Library, University of Oxford
243 Shakespeare Centre Library, Stratford-upon-Avon (photo: Angus McBean)
254 Shakespeare Centre Library, Stratford-upon-Avon (photo: Angus McBean)
257 © Guildhall Library
260 Marquess of Bath, Longleat House, Warminster, Wiltshire
276 The Kobal Collection
278 Shakespeare Centre Library, Stratford-upon-Avon
282 Shakespeare Centre Library, Stratford-upon-Avon
301 © Gamma/Michèle Laurent/Frank Spooner Pictures
317 The British Library (MS Portland Loan 29/246, p.18)
325 BFI Films: Stills, Posters and Designs
326 © Anne Kirchbach/Bayerische Staatsoper, Munich
340 The Folger Shakespeare Library, Washington, D.C.
354 © Tate Gallery, London 2001
355 By permission of the Houghton Library, Harvard University
362 Henry E. Huntington Library and Art Gallery, San Marino, California
363 Elizabethan Club of Yale University
371 Shakespeare Centre Library, Stratford-upon-Avon (photo: Angus McBean)
376 The British Library (C34 l.16 D4v-E)
378 © Public Record Office (AO 3/908/13)
382 Shakespeare Centre Library, Stratford-upon-Avon (photo: Joe Cocks Studio Collection)
386 Shakespeare Centre Library, Stratford-upon-Avon (photo: Reg Wilson)
394 The British Library (C57 b.55)
398 The Moviestore Collection
411 PA News Photo Library
413 Shakespeare Centre Library, Stratford-upon-Avon
415 Shakespeare Centre Library, Stratford-upon-Avon
420 Shakespeare Centre Library, Stratford-upon-Avon
421 Shakespeare Centre Library, Stratford-upon-Avon
430 Louvre, Paris/Peter Willi/Bridgeman Art Library, London
432 © Public Record Office
434 British Library (MS Harl.7368 f.9)
436 From the RSC Collection with the permission of the Governors of the Royal Shakespeare Theatre
443 By kind permission of His Grace the Duke of Buccleugh and Queensberry, K.T.
447 Elizabethan Club of Yale University
448 Novosti c/o SCR photo Library
450 Worshipful Company of Stationers
451 The Kobal Collection
453 Whitbread Beer Company
455 Copyright © 1990 by The Berkley Publishing Group and First Publishing Inc. All rights reserved.
457 From *Shakespeare's England: An Account of the Life and Manners of his Age*, edited by Sidney Lee, 1916, Clarendon Press, Oxford
464 © BBC
467 © Tate Gallery, London 2001
468 The Folger Shakespeare Library, Washington, D.C.
468 The Folger Shakespeare Library, Washington, D.C.
469 The Folger Shakespeare Library, Washington, D.C.
489 Shakespeare Centre Library, Stratford-upon-Avon (photo: Angus McBean)
495 Shakespeare Centre Library, Stratford-upon-Avon (photo: Angus McBean)
501 © Donald Cooper/Photo*stage*
505 © 1998 David Jouris/Hold the Mustard Productions
513 Metropolitan Opera Archives, New York
526 © The Board of Trustees of the Victoria & Albert Museum, London